THE

ANTE-NICENE FATHERS

TRANSLATIONS OF

The Writings of the Fathers down to A.D. 325

THE REV. ALEXANDER ROBERTS, D.D.,

AND

JAMES DONALDSON, LL.D.,

EDITORS

AMERICAN REPRINT OF THE EDINBURGH EDITION

REVISED AND CHRONOLOGICALLY ARRANGED, WITH BRIEF PREFACES AND
OCCASIONAL NOTES

BY

A. CLEVELAND COXE, D.D.

VOLUME VIII

*THE TWELVE PATRIARCHS, EXCERPTS AND EPISTLES, THE CLEMENTINA, APOCRYPHA, DECRETALS,
MEMOIRS OF EDESSA AND SYRIAC DOCUMENTS, REMAINS OF THE FIRST AGES.*

AUTHORIZED EDITION

T&T CLARK
EDINBURGH

WM. B. EERDMANS PUBLISHING COMPANY
GRAND RAPIDS, MICHIGAN

British Library Cataloguing in Publication Data

Ante-Nicene Fathers.
1. Fathers of the church
I. Robertson, Alexander   II. Donaldson, James
230'.13   BR60.A62

T&T Clark ISBN 0 567 09381 6

Eerdmans ISBN 0-8028-8094-0

Reprinted 1995

FATHERS OF THE THIRD AND FOURTH CENTURIES

THE TWELVE PATRIARCHS, EXCERPTS AND EPISTLES, THE CLEMENTINA, APOCRYPHA,
DECRETALS, MEMOIRS OF EDESSA AND SYRIAC DOCUMENTS,
REMAINS OF THE FIRST AGES

AMERICAN EDITION

CHRONOLOGICALLY ARRANGED, WITH NOTES, PREFACES, AND ELUCIDATIONS,

BY

A. CLEVELAND COXE, D.D.

Τὰ ἀρχαῖα ἔθη κρατείτω.
THE NICENE COUNCIL.

INTRODUCTORY NOTICE

THIS volume completes the American series, according to our agreement. But it will be found to afford much material over and above what was promised, and the editorial labour it has exacted has been much greater than might at first be suspected. The Bibliography with which the work is supplemented, and which is the original work of Dr. Riddle, has been necessarily thrown into the Index by the overgrowth of this volume in original matter.

The Apocryphal works of the Edinburgh collection have been here brought together, and "Fragments" have been sifted, and arranged on a plan strictly practical. To my valued collaborator Dr. Riddle I have committed a task which demanded a specialist of his eminent qualifications. He has had, almost exclusively, the task of editing the *Pseudo-Clementina* and the *Apocryphal New Testament.* To myself I assigned the *Twelve Patriarchs* and *Excerpts,* the *Edessene Memoirs and other Syriac Fragments,* the *False Decretals,* and the *Remains of the First Ages.* I have reserved this retrospect of historic truth and testimony to complete the volume. As in music the tune ends on the note with which it began, so, after the greater part of the volume had been surrendered to forgery and fiction (valuable, indeed, for purposes of comparison and reference, but otherwise unworthy of a place among primitive witnesses), I felt it refreshing to return to genuine writings and to authentic histories. The pages of Melito and others will restore something of the flavour of the Apostolic Fathers to our taste, and the student will not close his review of the *Ante-Nicene Fathers* with last impressions derived only from their fraudulent imitators and corrupters.

The editor-in-chief renews his grateful acknowledgments to those who have aided him in his undertaking, with whose honoured names the reader is already acquainted. Nor can he omit an expression of thanks to the reverend brother [1] to whom the hard work of the Indexes has been chiefly committed. It would be equally unjust not to mention his obligations to the meritorious press which has produced these pages with a general accuracy not easily ensured under difficulties such as have been inseparable from this undertaking.[2] The support which has been liberally afforded to the enterprise by Christians of divers names and communions ought not to be recognised by words of mere recognition : it is a token of their common interest in a common origin, and a sign, perhaps, of a longing for that precious unity and brotherhood which was the glory of the martyr ages, for which all should unite in praise to God. To the Christian press a grateful tribute is due from the editor and his publishers alike ; more especially as it has encouraged, so generally, the production of another series, of which the first volume has already appeared, and which will familiarize the minds and hearts of thousands with the living thought and burning piety of those great doctors of the post-Nicene period, to whom the world owes such immense obligations, but who have been so largely unknown to millions even of educated men, except as bright and shining names.

It is a cheering token, that, while the superficial popular mind may even be disposed to regard

---

[1] The Rev. C. W. Hayes, M.A., of Westfield, N.Y.   [2] The Boston Press of Rand Avery Company.

this collection as a mere museum of fossils, having little or no connection with anything that interests our age, there is a twofold movement towards a fresh investigation of the past, which it seems providentially designed to meet. Thus, among Christians there is a general appetite for the study of primitive antiquity, stimulated by the decadence of the Papacy, and by the agitations concerning the theology of the future which have arisen in Reformed communions; while, on the other hand, scientific thought has pushed inquiry as to the sources of the world's enlightenment, and has found them just here, — in the school of Alexandria, and in the Christian writers of the first three centuries. " It is instructive," says a forcible thinker,[1] and a disciple of Darwin and Huxley, " to note how closely Athanasius approaches the confines of modern scientific thought." And again he says : " The intellectual atmosphere of Alexandria for two centuries before and three centuries after the time of Christ was *more modern* than anything that followed, down to the days of Bacon and Descartes."

It would be unmanly in the editor to speak of the difficulties and hindrances through which he has been forced to push on his work, while engaged in other and very sacred duties. The conditions which alone could justify the publishers in the venture were quite inconsistent with such an editorial performance as might satisfy his own ideas of what should be done with such materials. Four years instead of two, he felt, should be bestowed on such a work; and he thought that two years might suffice only in case a number of collaborators could be secured for simultaneous employment. When it was found that such a plan was impracticable, and that the idea must be abandoned if not undertaken and carried forward as it has been, then the writer most reluctantly assumed his great responsibility in the fear of God, and in dependence on His loving-kindness and tender mercy. Of the result, he can only say that " he has done what he could " in the circumstances. He is rewarded by the consciousness that at least he has enabled many an American divine and scholar to avail himself of the labours of the Edinburgh translators, and to feel what is due to them, when, but for this publication, he must have remained in ignorance of what their erudition has achieved and contributed to Christian learning in the English tongue.

And how sweet and invigorating has been his task, as page after page of these treasures of antiquity has passed under his hand and eye ! With unfailing appetite he has risen before daylight to his work; and far into the night he has extended it, with ever fresh interest and delight. Obliged very often to read his proofs, or prepare his notes, at least in their first draught, while journeying by land or by water, he has generally found in such employments, not additional fatigue, but a real comfort and resource, a balance to other cares, and a sweet preparation and invigoration for other labours. Oh, how much he owes, under God, to these " guides, philosophers, and friends," — these Fathers of old time, — and to " their Father and our Father, their God and our God " ! What love is due from all who love Christ, for the words they have spoken, and the deeds they have done, to assure us that the Everlasting Word is He to whom alone we can go for the words of life eternal !

A. C. C.

---

[1] John Fiske, *The Idea of God*, Boston, 1886, pp. 73, 86.

CONTENTS OF VOLUME VIII

THE TESTAMENTS OF THE TWELVE PATRIARCHS

[TRANSLATED BY THE REV. ROBERT SINKER, M.A., TRINITY COLLEGE, CAMBRIDGE.]

INTRODUCTORY NOTICE

to

THE TESTAMENTS OF THE TWELVE PATRIARCHS

THIS very curious fragment of antiquity deserves a few words in anticipation of the translator's valuable preface. Grabe's *Spicilegium* is there referred to; but it may be well also to consult his citations, in elucidation, of Bull's *Defensio Fidei Nicænæ*,[1] where he treats the work with respect. My most valued authority, however, on this subject, is Lardner,[2] who gives a very full account of the work with his usual candor and learning. He seems to treat the matter with a needless profusion of space and consideration; yet in a much later volume of his great treatise he recurs to the subject[3] with expressions of satisfaction that he had dealt with it so largely before.

Cave placed the composition of the *Testaments* about A.D. 192, but concedes a much earlier origin to the first portion of the work. Origen quotes from it, and Tertullian is supposed to have borrowed from it one of his expositions, as will be noted in its place. Lardner clears it from charges of Ebionitism,[4] but thinks the author was so far in accord with that heresy as to use expressions savouring of "Unitarianism." Of this charge he is not justly susceptible, it appears to me: quite otherwise. If we can imagine Trypho coming to the light after his kindly parting with Justin,[5] I can conceive of such a man as the author of this work. He is a Christian awakening to the real purport of the Old-Testament Scriptures, and anxious to lead rather than drive his brethren after the flesh to the discovery of Him "concerning whom Moses in the law and the prophets did write:" not a "Judaizing Christian," as Cave imagined, but the reverse, — a Christianizing Jew. Now, I must think that such a writer would weave into his plan many accepted traditions of the Jews and many Rabbinical expositions of the sacred writers. He was doubtless acquainted with that remarkable passage in the Revelation in which the patriarchs are so honourably named,[6] and with that corresponding passage which seems to unite the twelve patriarchs with the twelve apostles.[7] St. Paul's claim for the twelve tribes before Agrippa[8] would naturally impress itself on such a mind. Whether the product of such a character with such a disposition would naturally be such an affectionate and filial attempt as this to identify the religion of the Crucified with the faith of the Jewish fathers,[9] may be judged of by my reader.

---

[1] Vol. v. p. 176, ed. 1827.

[2] *Credib.*, vol. ii. pp. 345-364.

[3] Vol. vi. p. 384.

[4] The honour done to St. Paul is enough to settle any suspicion of this sort.

[5] See vol. i. p. 270, note 2, this series.

[6] Rev. vii. 4. Dan is excepted.

[7] Rev. iv. 4. See vol. vii. p. 348, this series.

[8] Acts xxvi. 7.

[9] See *The Christ of Jewish History* in Stanley Leathes' *Bampton Lectures*, p. 51, ed. New York, 1874; also Westcott, *Introduction to Study of the Gospels*, 3d ed., London, Macmillans, 1867. Note, on the *Book of Henoch*, pp. 69, 93-101; on the *Book of Jubilees*, p. 109. He puts this book into the first century, later than Henoch, earlier than the *Twelve Patriarchs*. Consult this work on the Alexandrian Fathers, on inspiration of Scripture, etc.; and note the Jewish doctrine of the Messiah, pp. 86, 143, 151, also the apocryphal traditions of words of our Lord, p. 428.

It appears to me an ill-advised romance; not more a "pious fraud" than several fictions which have attracted attention in our own times, based on the traditions of the Hebrews. The legends of the "Wandering Jew" have grown out of corresponding instincts among Christians. To me they appear like the profane "Passion-plays" lately revived among Christians, — a most unwarrantable form of teaching even truth. But as to the work itself, seeing it exists, I must acknowledge that it seems to me a valuable relic of antiquity, and an interesting specimen of the feelings and convictions of those believers over whom St. James presided in Jerusalem: [1] "Israelites indeed," but "zealous of the law." They were now convinced that Abraham and Isaac and Jacob, with Moses and all the prophets, looked for the Messiah who had appeared in Jesus of Nazareth. The author of this book was anxious to show that the twelve patriarchs were twelve believers in the Paschal Lamb, and that they died in Christian penitence and faith.

He, then, who will read or study the following waif of the olden time, as I have done, will not find it unprofitable reading. It really supplies a key to some difficulties in the Scripture narrative. It suggests what are at least plausible counterparts of what is written. "To the pure all things are pure;" and I see nothing that need defile in any of the details which expose the sins, and magnify the penitence, of the patriarchs. In fact, Lardner's objection to one of the sections in the beautiful narrative of Joseph strikes me as extraordinary. It is the story of a heroic conflict with temptation, the like of which was doubtless not uncommon in the days of early Christians living among heathens; [2] and I think it was possibly written to inspire a Joseph-like chastity in Christian youth. "I do not suppose," says Lardner, "that the virtue of any of these ancient Hebrews was complete according to the Christian rule." I am amazed at this; I have always supposed the example of Joseph the more glorious because he flourished as the flower of chastity in a gross and carnal age. Who so pure as he save John the Baptist, that morning star that shone so near the Sun of Righteousness in the transient beauty of his "heliacal rising"? Surely Joseph was a type of Christ in this as in other particulars, and our author merely enables us to understand the "fiery darts" which he was wont to hurl back at the tempter. I own (reluctantly, because I dislike this form of teaching) that for me the superlative ode of the dying Jacob receives a reflected lustre from this curious book, especially in the splendid eulogy with which the old patriarch blesses his beloved Joseph. "The author," says Lardner, "in an indirect manner . . . bears a large testimony to the Christian religion, to the facts, principles, and books of the New Testament. He speaks of the nativity of Christ, the meekness and unblameableness of His life, His crucifixion at the instigation of the Jewish priests, the wonderful concomitants of His death, His resurrection, and ascension. He represents the character of the Messiah as God and man: the Most High God with men, eating and drinking with them; the Son of God; the Saviour of the world, of the Gentiles and Israel; as Eternal High Priest and King. He likewise speaks of the effusion of the Holy Spirit upon the Messiah, attended with a voice from heaven; His unrighteous treatment by the Jews; their desolations and the destruction of the Temple upon that account; the call of the Gentiles; the illuminating them generally with new light; the effusion of the Spirit upon believers, but especially, and in a more abundant measure, upon the Gentiles. . . . There are allusions to the Gospels of St. Matthew, St. Luke and St. John, the Acts of the Apostles, and of the Epistles to Ephesians, First Thessalonians, First Timothy, Hebrews, and First St. John, also to the Revelation. So far as consistent with the assumed character of his work, the author declares the canonical authority of the Acts of the Apostles and the Epistles of St. Paul." Of which of the minor writers among the Ante-Nicene Fathers can so much be said?

Regarded as a sort of Jewish surrender to Justin's argument with Trypho, this book is interesting, and represents, no doubt, the convictions of thousands of Jewish converts of the first age. It is, in short, worthy of more attention than it has yet received.

---

[1] Acts xxi. 18-26. To my mind a most touching history, in which it is hard to say whether St. Paul or St. James is exhibited in the more charming light. It suggests the absolute harmony of their Epistles.

[2] Vol. i. Elucid. II. p. 57, this series.

Here follows Mr. Sinker's valuable INTRODUCTORY NOTICE : —

THE apocryphal work known as the *Testaments of the Twelve Patriarchs* professes to be, as its name implies, the utterances of the dying patriarchs, the sons of Jacob. In these they give some account of their lives, embodying particulars not found in the scriptural account, and build thereupon various moral precepts for the guidance of their descendants. The book partakes also of the nature of an Apocalypse : the patriarchs see in the future their children doing wickedly, stained with the sins of every nation ; and thus they foretell the troubles impending on their race. Still at last God will put an end to their woe, and comfort is found in the promise of a Messiah.

There can be little or no doubt that the author was a Jew, who, having been converted to Christianity, sought to win over his countrymen to the same faith, and thus employed the names of the patriarchs as a vehicle for conveying instruction to their descendants, as winning by this means for his teaching at any rate a *prima facie* welcome in the eyes of the Jewish people.

It does not seem hard to settle approximately the limits of time within which the book was probably written. It cannot be placed very late in the second century, seeing that it is almost certainly quoted by Tertullian,[1] and that Origen[2] cites the *Testaments* by name, apparently indeed holding it in considerable respect. We can, however, approximate much more nearly than this ; for the allusions to the destruction of Jerusalem assign to the *Testaments* a date subsequent to that event. This will harmonize perfectly with what is the natural inference from several passages, — namely, that the Gentiles now were a majority in the Church, — as well as with the presence of the many formulæ to express the incarnation, and with the apparent collection of the books of the New Testament into a volume.[3]

On the other hand, important evidence as to the posterior limit of the date of writing may be derived from the language used with reference to the priesthood. Christ is both High Priest and King, and His former office is higher than the latter, and to Him the old priesthood must resign its rights. Now such language as this would be almost meaningless after Hadrian's destruction of Jerusalem consequent on the revolt of Bar-Cochba (A.D. 135), after which all power of Judaism for acting directly upon Christianity ceased ; and, indeed, on the hypothesis of a later date, we should doubtless find allusions to the revolt and its suppression. On the above grounds, we infer that the writing of the *Testaments* is to be placed in a period ranging from late in the first century to the revolt of Bar-Cochba ; closer than this it is perhaps not safe to draw our limits.[4]

The language in which the *Testaments* were written was no doubt the Hellenistic Greek in which we now possess them ; presenting as they do none of the peculiar marks which characterize a version. Whether there were a Hebrew work on which the present was modelled — a supposition by no means improbable in itself — we cannot tell, nor is it a matter of much importance. The phenomena of the book itself may be cited in support of this conclusion : for instance, the use of the word διαθήκη in its ordinary classical meaning of " testament," not " covenant " as in Hellenistic Greek, for which former meaning there would be no strictly equivalent word in Hebrew ; the numerous instances of paronomasia, such as ἀθετεῖν, νουθετεῖν,[5] ἀφαίρεσις, ἀναίρεσις,[6] λιμός, λοιμός,[6] ἐν τάξει, ἄτακτον,[7] τάξις, ἀταξία ;[8] the frequent use of the genitive absolute, and of the verb μέλλειν ; the use of various expressions pertaining to the Greek philosophy, as διάθεσις, αἴσθησις, φύσις, τέλος.

It seems doubtful how far we can attempt with safety to determine accurately the religious standpoint of the writer beyond the obvious fact of his Jewish origin, though some have attempted

---

[1] *Adv. Marcionem*, v. 1 ; *Scorpiace*, 13 ; cf. *Benj.* 11.
[2] *Hom. in Josuam*, xv. 6 ; cf. *Reub.* 2, 3.
[3] *Benj.* 11.
[4] [Compare Westcott, *Introduction to Study of the Gospels*, p. 132, ed. Boston, 1862.]
[5] *Benj.* 4.
[6] *Judah* 23.
[7] *Naph.* 2.
[8] *Naph.* 3.

to show that he was a Nazarene, and others a Jewish Christian of Pauline tendencies. We shall therefore content ourselves with referring those who seek for more specific information on this point to the works mentioned below.

To refer now briefly to the external history of our document, we meet with nothing definite, after its citation by Origen, for many centuries: there are possible allusions in Jerome[1] and in Procopius Gazæus;[2] there is also a mention of πατριάρχαι in the *Synopsis Sacræ Scripturæ* found among the writings of Athanasius, as well as in the *Stichometria* of Nicephorus of Constantinople, on which it is probably based. Again, in the Canons of the Council of Rome (494 A.D.) under Gelasius, and of the Council of Bracara (563 A.D.), are possible references, though it is far from improbable that in some of the foregoing passages the reference may be to a writing τῶν τριῶν Πατριαρχῶν alluded to in the *Apostolic Constitutions*,[3] or is even of somewhat loose application.

After this a blank ensues until the middle of the thirteenth century, when it was brought to the knowledge of Western Europe by Robert Grosseteste, Bishop of Lincoln, the earliest of the great English reformers.[4] We cite here the account of the matter given by Matthew Paris, although of course we need not accept all the opinions of the old chronicler respecting the document in question: "At this same time, Robert, Bishop of Lincoln, a man most deeply versed in Latin and Greek, accurately translated the *Testaments of the XII. Patriarchs* from Greek into Latin. These had been for a long time unknown and hidden through the jealousy of the Jews, on account of the prophecies of the Saviour contained in them. The Greeks, however, the most unwearied investigators of all writings, were the first to come to a knowledge of this document, and translated it from Hebrew into Greek, and have kept it to themselves till our times. And neither in the time of the blessed Jerome nor of any other holy interpreter could the Christians gain an acquaintance with it, through the malice of the ancient Jews. This glorious treatise, then, the aforesaid bishop (with the help of Master Nicolaus, a Greek, and a clerk of the Abbey of St. Alban's) translated fully and clearly, and word for word, from Greek into Latin, to the strengthening of the Christian faith, and to the greater confusion of the Jews."[5]

Again, after speaking of the death of "Master John de Basingstokes, Archdeacon of Leicester," a man of very great learning in Latin and Greek, he proceeds:[6] "This Master John had mentioned to Robert, Bishop of Lincoln, that when he was studying at Athens he had seen and heard from learned Greek doctors certain things unknown to the Latins. Among these he found the *Testaments of the XII. Patriarchs*, that is to say, of the sons of Jacob. Now it is plain that these really form part of the sacred volume, but have been long hidden through the jealousy of the Jews, on account of the evident prophecies about Christ which are clearly seen in them. Consequently this same bishop sent into Greece; and when he obtained them, he translated them from Greek into Latin, as well as certain other things."

After this it would seem as though the same fate still pursued our document, for the entire Greek text was not printed until the eve of the eighteenth century, when it was published for the first time by Grabe, whose edition has been several times reprinted.[7]

Four Greek MSS. of the *Testaments* are known to exist:—

1. The MS. Ff. i. 24 in the University Library of Cambridge, to which it was given by Archbishop Parker, whose autograph it bears on its first page. It is a quarto on parchment, of 261 leaves (in which the *Testaments* occupy ff. 203*a*–261*b*), double columns, 20 lines in a column, handwriting of the tenth century. It is furnished with accents and breathings, and a fairly full punctuation. There are very strong grounds for believing that it was this MS. that Grosseteste's

---

[1] *Adv. Vigilantium*, c. 6.
[2] *Comm. in Genesin*, c. 38.
[3] vi. 16. [See vol. vii. p. 457, this series.]
[4] [Of whom see Lightfoot, *Apostolic Fathers*, Part II. vol. i. p. 77, ed. London, 1885.]
[5] *Historia Anglorum*, A.D. 1242, p. 801, ed. London, 1571.
[6] *Op. cit.* A.D. 1252, p. 1112.
[7] *Vide infra.*

version was made, exhibiting as it does a very large amount of curious verbal coincidence with it.[1] The text of this MS. has been that given in the various editions mentioned below.

2. The MS. Barocci 133 in the Bodleian Library at Oxford, where it came with the rest of the Barocci collection from Venice, and was presented to the University by its Chancellor, the Earl of Pembroke. It is a quarto volume; and except a leaf or two of parchment, containing writing of an older period, consists of a number of treatises on paper, apparently by several different hands, in the writing of the latter part of the fourteenth century. The *Testaments* occupy ff. 179a–203b. The amount of difference between this MS. and the preceding is considerable, and is sufficient to show that it has had no direct communication with the latter. A large number of omissions occur in it, in some instances amounting to entire chapters. The variations of this MS. are given more or less fully in the various editions.

3. A MS. in the Vatican Library at Rome, not yet edited. It is said to be a small quarto on paper, written in a very distinct hand, though unfortunately some leaves are damaged. It bears a subscription with the date 1235. I owe my knowledge of this MS. to an article by Dr. Vorstman in the *Godgeleerde Bijdragen* for 1866, p. 953 sqq.

4. A MS. discovered by Tischendorf in the island of Patmos, of which no details have yet been published.[2]

The entire Greek text of the *Testaments* was first printed by Grabe in his *Spicilegium Patrum et Hæreticorum*, Oxford, 1698, professedly from the Cambridge MS., but in reality from some very inaccurate transcript of it, very possibly from one made by Abednego Seller, also in the Cambridge University Library, Oo. vi. 92. Grabe also gave a few of the variations of the Oxford MS. Fabricius, in his *Codex Pseudepigraphus Veteris Testamenti*,[3] gives little more than a reprint from Grabe. In the second edition of the latter (1714) the true text has been restored in several passages; but in many places Grosseteste's Latin version, which witnessed to the true reading, was altered to suit Grabe's incorrect text. Fabricius' second edition (1722) is perhaps, on the whole, less accurate than his first. Since then the text and notes, as given in Grabe's second edition, have been reprinted, with but few additions, by Gallandi, in his *Bibliotheca Veterum Patrum*, vol. i. p. 193 sqq., Venice, 1765, and in Migne's *Patrologia Græca*, vol. ii., Paris, 1857. The text of the Cambridge MS., with a full statement of the variations of the Oxford MS., has recently been edited directly from the MSS. by myself, Cambridge, 1869; from this edition the present translation has been made.

The MSS. of Grosseteste's Latin version are numerous, there being no less than twelve in Cambridge alone; and it has been frequently printed, both with the editions of the Greek text and independently.[4]

Besides the Latin version, the *Testaments* have also been translated into several European languages, in all cases apparently from the Latin. The English translation made by Arthur Golding was first printed by John Daye in Aldersgate in 1581, and has since been frequently reproduced; the British Museum, which does not possess all the editions, having no less than eleven.[5]

The author of the French translation[6] appears to believe, as the English translator had done, that we have here really the last words of the sons of Jacob. A German translation has also several times been published,[7] and a German translation in MS. is to be found in the British Museum.[8] We may further mention a Dutch translation (Antwerp, 1570), a Danish translation

---

[1] See, e.g., the curious reading in *Levi* 18, καὶ στήσει, where the Latin MSS. are unanimous in giving *stare faciet;* also the mistake of 'Ιακώβ for 'Ρουβήμ in *Issachar* 1.

[2] See Tischendorf, *Aus dem heiligen Lande*, p. 341.

[3] Hamburgh, 1713.

[4] e.g., 1483; Hagenau, 1532; Paris, 1549; and often.

[5] This English translation having been made from the Latin, the printed editions of which swarm with inaccuracies (Grosseteste's Latin version itself being a most exact translation), I have been able to make much less use of it than I could have desired. It has, however, been compared throughout.

[6] Monsieur Macé, Chefecier, curé de Saint Opportune, Paris, 1713.

[7] e.g., Vienna, 1544; Strasburg, 1596; Hamburgh, 1637.

[8] MSS. Harl., 1252.

(1601), and a MS. Icelandic translation of the eighteenth century in the British Museum, add. MSS 11,068.

For further information on the subject of the *Testaments*, reference may be made, in addition to works already mentioned, to the following : — Nitzsch, *Commentatio Critica de Testamentis XII. Patriarcharum, libro V. T. Pseudepigrapho* (Wittenberg, 1810) ; Ritschl, *Die Entstehung der altkatholischen Kirche* (Bonn, 1850 ; ed. 2, 1857), p. 171 sqq.; Vorstman, *Disquisitio de Testamentorum XII. Patriarcharum origine et pretio* (Rotterdam, 1857) ; Kayser in Reuss and Cunitz's *Beiträge zu den theol. Wissenschaften* for 1851, pp. 107–140 ; Lücke, *Einleitung in die Offenbarung des Joh.*, vol. i. p. 334 sqq., ed. 2. R. S.

TRINITY COLLEGE, CAMBRIDGE.
February 21, 1871.

THE TESTAMENTS OF THE TWELVE PATRI-ARCHS

I. — THE TESTAMENT OF REUBEN CONCERNING THOUGHTS

1. THE copy of the Testament of Reuben, what things he charged his sons before he died in the hundred and twenty-fifth year of his life. When he was sick two years after the death of Joseph, his sons and his sons' sons were gathered together to visit him. And he said to them, My children, I am dying, and go the way of my fathers. And when he saw there Judah and Gad and Asher, his brethren, he said to them, Raise me up, my brethren, that I may tell to my brethren and to my children what things I have hidden in my heart, for from henceforth my strength faileth me. And he arose and kissed them, and said, weeping: Hear, my brethren, give ear to Reuben your father, what things I command you. And, behold, I call to witness against you this day the God of heaven, that ye walk not in the ignorance of youth and fornication wherein I ran greedily, and I defiled the bed of Jacob my father. For I tell you that He smote me with a sore plague in my loins for seven months; and had not Jacob our father prayed for me to the Lord, surely the Lord would have destroyed me. For I was thirty years old when I did this evil in the sight of the Lord, and for seven months I was sick even unto death; and I repented for seven years in the set purpose of my soul before the Lord. Wine and strong drink I drank not, and flesh entered not into my mouth, and I tasted not pleasant food,[1] mourning over my sin, for it was great. And it shall not so be done in Israel.

2. And now hear me, my children, what things I saw in my repentance concerning the seven spirits of error. Seven spirits are given against man from Beliar, and they are chief of the works of youth; and seven spirits are given to him at his creation, that in them should be done every work of man.[2] The first (1) spirit is of life, with which man's whole being is created. The second (2) spirit is of sight, with which ariseth desire. The third (3) spirit is of hearing, with which cometh teaching. The fourth (4) spirit is of smelling, with which taste is given to draw air and breath. The fifth (5) spirit is of speech, with which cometh knowledge. The sixth (6) spirit is of taste, with which cometh the eating of meats and drinks; and by them strength is produced, for in food is the foundation of strength. The seventh (7) spirit is of begetting and sexual intercourse, with which through love of pleasure sin also entereth in: wherefore it is the last in order of creation, and the first of youth, because it is filled with ignorance, which leadeth the young as a blind man to a pit, and as cattle to a precipice.

3. Besides all these, there is an eighth (8) spirit of sleep, with which is created entrancement of man's nature, and the image of death. With these spirits are mingled the spirits of error. The first (1), the spirit of fornication, dwelleth in the nature and in the senses; the second (2) spirit of insatiateness in the belly; the third (3) spirit of fighting in the liver and the gall. The fourth (4) is the spirit of fawning and trickery, that through over-officiousness a man may be fair in seeming. The fifth (5) is the spirit of arrogance, that a man may be stirred up and become high-minded. The sixth (6) is the spirit of lying, in perdition and in jealousy to feign words, and to conceal[3] words from kindred and friends. The seventh (7) is the spirit of injustice, with which are theft and pilferings, that a man may work the desire of his heart; for injustice worketh together with the other spirits by means of craft. Besides all these, the spirit of sleep, the eighth (8) spirit, is conjoined with error and fantasy. And so perisheth every young man, darkening his mind from the truth, and not understanding the law of God, nor obeying the

---

[1] There seems a reminiscence here of the words of Dan. x. 3, LXX. [For proofs of penitence, see p. 11, note 3, *infra.*
[2] For this use of πνεύματα as applied to the senses, we may cite Plutarch (*De placitis philosophorum*, iv. 21), who, speaking with reference to the Stoic philosophy, says, ἡ μὲν ὅρασίς ἐστι πνεῦμα διατεῖνον ἀπὸ τοῦ ἡγεμονικοῦ μέχρις ὀφθαλμῶν.

[3] This clause is only found in Cd. Oxon.; it seems demanded by the following ἀπό.

admonitions of his fathers, as befell me also in my youth.

And now, children, love the truth, and it shall preserve you. I counsel you, hear ye Reuben your father. Pay no heed to the sight of a woman, nor yet associate privately with a female under the authority of a husband, nor meddle with affairs of womankind. For had I not seen Bilhah bathing in a covered place, I had not fallen into this great iniquity.[1] For my mind, dwelling on the woman's nakedness, suffered me not to sleep until I had done the abominable deed. For while Jacob our father was absent with Isaac his father, when we were in Gader, near to Ephratha in Bethlehem, Bilhah was drunk, and lay asleep uncovered in her chamber; and when I went in and beheld her nakedness, I wrought that impiety, and leaving her sleeping I departed. And forthwith an angel of God revealed to my father Jacob concerning my impiety, and he came and mourned over me, and touched her no more.[2]

4. Pay no heed, therefore, to the beauty of women, and muse not upon their doings; but walk in singleness of heart in the fear of the Lord, and be labouring in works, and roaming in study and among your flocks, until the Lord give to you a wife whom He will, that ye suffer not as I did. Until my father's death I had not boldness to look stedfastly into the face of Jacob, or to speak to any of my brethren, because of my reproach; and even until now my conscience afflicteth me by reason of my sin. And my father comforted me; for he prayed for me unto the Lord, that the anger of the Lord might pass away from me, even as the Lord showed me. From henceforth, then, I was protected, and I sinned not. Therefore, my children, observe all things whatsoever I command you, and ye shall not sin. For fornication is the destruction of the soul, separating it from God, and bringing it near to idols, because it deceiveth the mind and understanding, and bringeth down young men into hell before their time. For many hath fornication destroyed; because, though a man be old or noble, it maketh him a reproach and a laughing-stock with Beliar and the sons of men. For in that Joseph kept himself from every woman, and purged his thoughts from all fornication, he found favour before the Lord and men. For the Egyptian woman did many things unto him, and called for magicians, and offered him love potions, and the purpose of his soul admitted no evil desire. Therefore the God of my fathers delivered him from every visible and hidden death. For if fornication overcome not the mind, neither shall Beliar overcome you.

5. Hurtful are women, my children; because, since they have no power or strength over the man, they act subtilly through outward guise how they may draw him to themselves; and whom they cannot overcome by strength, him they overcome by craft. For moreover the angel of God told me concerning them, and taught me that women are overcome by the spirit of fornication more than men, and they devise in their heart against men; and by means of their adornment they deceive first their minds, and instil the poison by the glance of their eye, and then they take them captive by their doings, for a woman cannot overcome a man by force.

Therefore flee fornication, my children, and command your wives and your daughters that they adorn not their heads and their faces; because every woman who acteth deceitfully in these things hath been reserved to everlasting punishment. For thus they allured the Watchers[3] before the flood; and as these continually beheld them, they fell into desire each of the other, and they conceived the act in their mind, and changed themselves into the shape of men, and appeared to them in their congress with their husbands; and the women, having in their minds desire toward their apparitions, gave birth to giants, for the Watchers appeared to them as reaching even unto heaven.[4]

6. Beware, therefore, of fornication; and if you wish to be pure in your mind, guard your senses against every woman. And command them likewise not to company with men, that they also be pure in their mind. For constant meetings, even though the ungodly deed be not wrought, are to them an irremediable disease, and to us an everlasting reproach of Beliar; for fornication hath neither understanding nor godliness in itself, and all jealousy dwelleth in the desire thereof. Therefore ye will be jealous against the sons of Levi, and will seek to be exalted over them; but ye shall not be able, for God will work their avenging, and ye shall die by an evil death. For to Levi the Lord gave the sovereignty, and to Judah,[5] and to me also with them,[6] and to Dan and Joseph, that we should be for rulers. Therefore I command you to hearken to Levi, because he shall know the law of the Lord, and shall give ordinances for judgment and sacrifice for all Israel until the com-

---

[1] Cf. Gen. xxxv. 22. The Gader mentioned below is the Edar of ver. 21, the Hebrew ע being reproduced, as often, by γ.

[2] [This section is censured by Lardner as unsuitable to dying admonitions. He forgets Oriental simplicity.]

[3] This name, occurring once again in the *Testaments* (*Naph.* 3), is one frequently found applied to the angels as the custodians of the world and of men. Thus, in the Chaldee of Daniel (iv. 10, 14, 20: 13, 17, 23, Eng. Ver.), we find the expression עִיר, which Aquila and Symmachus render ἐγρήγορος. The corresponding Ethiopic term is of frequent occurrence in the book of Enoch, not only of the fallen angels (e.g., x. 9, 15, xvi. 1, etc.), but of the good (xii. 2, 3, etc., ed. Dillmann). See also Gesenius, *Thesaurus, s.v.* עִיר.

[4] [Gen. vi. 4; Revised margin, 1 Cor. xi. 10; Jude 6, 7.]

[5] [See Lardner on this root idea of our author, vol. ii. p. 353; but he is wrong as to Levi and Mary. Also *Joseph*, sec. 19, note 2, *infra*.]

[6] The reading of Cd. Oxon., μετ' αὐτόν, is doubtless to be preferred.

pletion of the times of Christ, the High Priest whom the Lord hath declared. I adjure you by the God of heaven to work truth each one with his neighbour; and draw ye near to Levi in humbleness of heart, that ye may receive a blessing from his mouth. For he shall bless Israel; and *specially* Judah, because him hath the Lord chosen to rule over all the peoples. And worship we his Seed, because He shall die for us in wars visible and invisible, and shall be among you an everlasting king.

7. And Reuben died after that he had given command to his sons; and they placed him in a coffin until they bore him up from Egypt, and buried him in Hebron in the double [1] cave where his fathers were.

---

[1] i.e., Machpelah, which in Hebrew means double, and is so rendered by the LXX., e.g., Gen. xxiii. 9.

II. — THE TESTAMENT OF SIMEON CONCERNING ENVY.

1. THE copy of the words of Simeon, what things he spake to his sons before he died, in the hundred and twentieth year of his life, in the year in which Joseph died. For they came to visit him when he was sick, and he strengthened himself and sat up and kissed them, and said to them : —

2. Hear, O my children, hear Simeon your father, what things I have in my heart. I was born of Jacob my father, his second son; and my mother Leah called me Simeon, because the Lord heard her prayer.[1] I became strong exceedingly; I shrank from no deed, nor was I afraid of anything. For my heart was hard, and my mind was unmoveable, and my bowels unfeeling : because valour also has been given from the Most High to men in soul and in body. And at that time I was jealous of Joseph because our father loved him;[2] and I set my mind against him to destroy him, because the prince of deceit sent forth the spirit of jealousy and blinded my mind, that I regarded him not as a brother, and spared not Jacob my father. But his God and the God of his fathers sent forth His angel, and delivered him out of my hands. For when I went into Shechem to bring ointment for the flocks, and Reuben to Dotham, where were our necessaries and all our stores, Judah our brother sold him to the Ishmaelites. And when Reuben came he was grieved, for he wished to have restored him safe to his father.[3] But I was wroth against Judah in that he let him go away alive, and for five months I continued wrathful against him; but God restrained me, and withheld from me all working of my hands, for my right hand was half withered for seven days. And I knew, my children, that because of Joseph this hap-

pened to me, and I repented and wept; and I besought the Lord that He would restore my hand unto me, and that I might be kept from all pollution and envy, and from all folly. For I knew that I had devised an evil deed before the Lord and Jacob my father, on account of Joseph my brother, in that I envied him.

3. And now, children, take heed of the spirit of deceit and of envy. For envy ruleth over the whole mind of a man, and suffereth him neither to eat, nor to drink, nor to do any good thing : it ever suggesteth to him to destroy him that he envieth; and he that is envied ever flourisheth, but he that envieth fades away. Two years of days I afflicted my soul with fasting in the fear of the Lord, and I learnt that deliverance from envy cometh by the fear of God. If a man flee to the Lord, the evil spirit runneth away from him, and his mind becometh easy. And henceforward he sympathizeth with him whom he envied, and condemneth not those who love him, and so ceaseth from his envy.

4. And my father asked concerning me, because he saw that I was sad; and I said, I am pained in my liver. For I mourned more than they all, because I was guilty of the selling of Joseph. And when we went down into Egypt, and he bound me as a spy, I knew that I was suffering justly, and I grieved not. Now Joseph was a good man, and had the Spirit of God within him : compassionate and pitiful, he bore not malice against me; nay, he loved me even as the rest of his brothers. Take heed, therefore, my children, of all jealousy and envy, and walk in singleness of soul and with good heart, keeping in mind the brother of your father, that God may give to you also grace and glory, and blessing upon your heads, even as ye saw in him. All his days he reproached us not concerning this thing, but loved us as his own soul, and beyond his own sons; and he glorified us, and gave riches, and cattle, and fruits freely to us all. Do ye then also, my beloved children, love each one his brother with a good heart, and remove

---

[1] Gen. xxix. 33.
[2] That Simeon was prominent in the hostility to Joseph, is perhaps implied by his detention in Egypt as a surety for the return of the others; and Jewish tradition generally accords with this view. Cf. the Targum of the Pseudo-Jonathan on Gen. xxxvii. 19: "Simeon and Levi, who were brothers in counsel, said one to another, Let us kill him." Also this same Targum on Gen. xlii. 24: "And he took from them Simeon, who had counselled to kill him." Cf. also *Breshith Rabba*, § 91.
[3] [Gen. xxxvii. 22, 29, xlii. 22.]

from you the spirit of envy, for this maketh savage the soul and destroyeth the body; it turneth his purposes into anger and war, and stirreth up unto blood, and leadeth the mind into frenzy, and suffereth not prudence to act in men: moreover, it taketh away sleep, and causeth tumult to the soul and trembling to the body. For even in sleep some malicious jealousy, deluding him, gnaweth at his soul, and with wicked spirits disturbeth it, and causeth the body to be troubled, and the mind to awake from sleep in confusion; and as though having a wicked and poisonous spirit, so appeareth it to men.

5. Therefore was Joseph fair in appearance, and goodly to look upon, because there dwelt not in him any wickedness; for in trouble of the spirit the face declareth it. And now, my children, make your hearts good before the Lord, and your ways straight before men, and ye shall find grace before God and men. And take heed not to commit fornication, for fornication is mother of all evils, separating from God, and bringing near to Beliar. For I have seen it inscribed in the writing of Enoch [1] that your sons shall with you be corrupted in fornication, and shall do wrong against Levi with the sword. But they shall not prevail against Levi, for he shall wage the war of the Lord, and shall conquer all your hosts; and there shall be a few divided in Levi and Judah, and there shall be none [2] of you for sovereignty, even as also my father Jacob prophesied in his blessings.

6. Behold, I have foretold you all things, that I may be clear from the sin of your souls. Now, if ye remove from you your envy, and all your stiffneckedness, as a rose shall my bones flourish in Israel, and as a lily my flesh in Jacob, and my odour shall be as the odour of Libanus; and as cedars shall holy ones be multiplied from me for ever, and their branches shall stretch afar off. Then shall perish the seed of Canaan, and a remnant shall not be to Amalek, and all the Cappadocians [3] shall perish, and all the Hittites [4]

shall be utterly destroyed. Then shall fail the land of Ham, and every people shall perish. Then shall all the earth rest from trouble, and all the world under heaven from war. Then shall Shem be glorified, because the Lord God, the Mighty One of Israel, shall appear upon earth as man,[5] and saved by Him Adam.[6] Then shall all the spirits of deceit be given to be trampled under foot, and men shall rule over the wicked spirits. Then will I arise in joy, and will bless the Most High because of His marvellous works, because God hath taken a body and eaten with men and saved men.

7. And now, my children, obey Levi, and in Judah shall ye be redeemed: [7] and be not lifted up against these two tribes, for from them shall arise to you the salvation of God. For the Lord shall raise up from Levi as it were a Priest,[8] and from Judah as it were a King, God and man.[5] So shall He save all the Gentiles and the race of Israel. Therefore I command you all things, in order that ye also may command your children, that they may observe them throughout their generations.

8. And Simeon made an end of commanding his sons, and slept with his fathers, being an hundred and twenty years old. And they laid him in a coffin of incorruptible wood, to take up his bones to Hebron. And they carried them up in a war of the Egyptians secretly: for the bones of Joseph the Egyptians guarded in the treasure-house of the palace; for the sorcerers told them that at the departure of the bones of Joseph there should be throughout the whole of Egypt darkness and gloom, and an exceeding great plague to the Egyptians, so that even with a lamp a man should not recognise his brother.

9. And the sons of Simeon bewailed their father according to the law of mourning, and they were in Egypt until the day of their departure from Egypt by the hand of Moses.

---

[1] [See *Speaker's Com.*, N.T., vol. iv. p. 387, ed. Scribners.]
[2] The Cam. MS. seems wrongly to omit the negative here. The reference is doubtless to Gen. xlix. 7.
[3] The reference seems to be to the Philistines. Cf. Deut. ii. 23, Amos ix. 7, where the LXX. reads Καππαδοκία.
[4] [For modern views of these, see *Encyc. Brit.*, s. v. "Hittites."]

[5] [Two of the many passages that leave no room for Lardner's imaginary "Unitarianism" in this author.]
[6] The construction here is awkward of the participles after ὅτι: possibly a clause may have dropped out after Ἀδάμ.
[7] [See p. 10, note 5, *supra*.]
[8] [John the Baptist. His greatness is declared by Christ Himself.]

III. — THE TESTAMENT OF LEVI CONCERNING THE PRIESTHOOD AND ARROGANCE.

1. THE copy of the words of Levi, what things he appointed to his sons, according to all that they should do, and what things should befall them until the day of judgment. He was in sound health when he called them to him,

for it had been shown to him that he should die. And when they were gathered together he said to them: —

2. I Levi was conceived in Haran and born there, and after that I came with my father to

Shechem. And I was young, about twenty years of age, when with Simeon I wrought the vengeance on Hamor for our sister Dinah. And when we were feeding our flocks in Abel-Maul, a spirit of understanding of the Lord came upon me,[1] and I saw all men corrupting their way, and that unrighteousness had built to itself walls, and iniquity sat upon towers; and I grieved for the race of men, and I prayed to the Lord that I might be saved. Then there fell upon me a sleep, and I beheld a high mountain: this is the mountain of Aspis[2] in Abel-Maul. And behold, the heavens were opened, and an angel of God said to me, Levi, enter. And I entered from the first heaven into the second, and I saw there water hanging between the one and the other. And I saw a third heaven far brighter than those two, for there was in it a height without bounds. And I said to the angel, Wherefore is this? And the angel said to me, Marvel not at these, for thou shalt see four other heavens brighter than these, and without comparison, when thou shalt have ascended thither: because thou shalt stand near the Lord, and shalt be His minister, and shalt declare His mysteries to men, and shalt proclaim concerning Him who shall redeem Israel;[3] and by thee and Judah shall the Lord appear among men, saving in them every race of men; and of the portion of the Lord shall be thy life, and He shall be thy field and vineyard, fruits, gold, silver.

3. Hear, then, concerning the seven[4] heavens. The lowest is for this cause more gloomy, in that it is near all the iniquities of men. The second hath fire, snow, ice, ready for the day of the ordinance of the Lord, in the righteous judgment of God: in it are all the spirits of the retributions for vengeance on the wicked. In the third are the hosts of the armies which are ordained for the day of judgment, to work vengeance on the spirits of deceit and of Beliar. And the heavens up to the fourth above these are holy, for in the highest of all dwelleth the Great Glory, in the holy of holies, far above all holiness. In the heaven next to it are the angels of the presence of the Lord, who minister and make propitiation to the Lord for all the ignorances of the righteous; and they offer to the Lord a reasonable sweet-smelling savour, and a bloodless offering. And in the heaven below this are the angels who bear the answers to the angels of the presence of the Lord. And in the heaven next to this are thrones, dominions, in which hymns are ever offered to God. Therefore, whenever the Lord looketh upon us, all of us are shaken; yea, the heavens and the earth, and the abysses, are shaken at the presence of His majesty; but the sons of men, regarding not these things, sin, and provoke the Most High.

4. Now, therefore, know that the Lord will execute judgment upon the sons of men; because when the rocks are rent,[5] and the sun quenched, and the waters dried up, and the fire trembling, and all creation troubled, and the invisible spirits melting away, and the grave[6] spoiled in the suffering of the Most High,[7] men unbelieving will abide in their iniquity, therefore with punishment shall they be judged. Therefore the Most High hath heard thy prayer, to separate thee from iniquity, and that thou shouldest become to Him a son, and a servant, and a minister of His presence. A shining light of knowledge shalt thou shine in Jacob, and as the sun shalt thou be to all the seed of Israel. And a blessing shall be given to thee, and to all thy seed, until the Lord shall visit all the heathen in the tender mercies of His Son, even for ever. Nevertheless thy sons shall lay hands upon Him to crucify Him; and therefore have counsel and understanding been given thee, that thou mightest instruct thy sons concerning Him, because he that blesseth Him shall be blessed, but they that curse Him shall perish.

5. And the angel opened to me the gates of heaven, and I saw the holy temple, and the Most High upon a throne of glory. And He said to me, Levi, I have given thee the blessings of the priesthood until that I shall come and sojourn in the midst of Israel. Then the angel brought me to the earth, and gave me a shield and a sword, and said, Work vengeance on Shechem because of Dinah, and I will be with thee, because the Lord hath sent me. And I destroyed at that time the sons of Hamor, as it is written in the heavenly tablets.[8] And I said to Him, I pray Thee, O Lord, tell me Thy name, that I may call upon Thee in a day of tribulation. And He said, I am the angel who intercedeth for the race of Israel, that He smite them not utterly, because every evil spirit attacketh it. And after these things I was as it were awaked, and blessed the Most High, and the angel that intercedeth for the race of Israel, and for all the righteous.[9]

---

[1] [Isa. xi. 2.]
[2] See below, c. 6.
[3] Cf. Luke xxiv. 21.
[4] For the Jewish idea of seven heavens, cf. Clement of Alexandria, *Strom.*, iv. 7; and Wetstein's note on 2 Cor. xii. 2; [also vol. vii. note 11, this series; and vol. ii. note 7, p. 438, this series].

[5] [Matt. xxvii. 51–53.]
[6] [Hades, rather.]
[7] [ἐπὶ τῷ πάθει τοῦ Ὑψίσ-ου. Compare Tatian, vol. ii. p. 71, this series.]
[8] This document, the idea of which is that of a book containing what is fore-ordained in heaven as to the course of the future, is one often appealed to in Apocalyptic literature, when some oracular declaration of weighty import is needed. Thus, in the Book of Enoch, the angel Uriel tells Enoch that the tablets contain all wisdom, the dying Enoch tells his children that the tablets are the source of all understanding, etc. (see, e.g., cc. 81. 1; 93. 2; 106. 19, ed. Dillmann). In the Book of Jubilees, again, it is said that inscribed on the tablets are, e.g., the punishment of the angels who sinned with mortal women, the plan of the division of weeks, the name of Abraham as the friend of God, etc. (cc. 5, 6, 19). See also *Test. Asher*, 2, 7, *infra*.
[9] [Gen. xlviii. 16. The Jehovah-Angel.]

6. And when I came to my father I found a brazen shield;[1] wherefore also the name of the mountain is Aspis, which is near Gebal, on the right side of Abila; and I kept these words in my heart. I took counsel with my father, and with Reuben my brother, that he should bid the sons of Hamor that they should be circumcised; for I was jealous because of the abomination which they had wrought in Israel. And I slew Shechem at the first, and Simeon slew Hamor. And after this our brethren came and smote the city with the edge of the sword; and our father heard it and was wroth, and he was grieved in that they had received the circumcision, and after that had been put to death, and in his blessings he dealt otherwise *with us*. For we sinned because we had done this thing against his will, and he was sick upon that day. But I knew that the sentence of God was for evil upon Shechem; for they sought to do to Sarah as they did to Dinah our sister, and the Lord hindered them. And so they persecuted Abraham our father when he was a stranger, and they harried his flocks when they were multiplied upon him; and Jeblae his servant, born in his house, they shamefully handled. And thus they did to all strangers, taking away their wives by force, and the men themselves driving into exile. But the wrath of the Lord came suddenly upon them to the uttermost.[2]

7. And I said to my father, Be not angry, sir, because by thee will the Lord bring to nought the Canaanites, and will give their land to thee, and to thy seed after thee. For from this day forward shall Shechem be called a city of them that are without understanding; for as a man mocketh at a fool, so did we mock them, because they wrought folly in Israel to defile our sister. And we took our sister from thence, and departed, and came to Bethel.

8. And there I saw a thing again even as the former, after we had passed seventy days. And I saw seven men in white raiment saying to me, Arise, put on the robe of the priesthood, and the crown of righteousness, and the breastplate of understanding, and the garment of truth, and the diadem of faith, and the tiara of miracle, and the ephod of prophecy.[3] And each one of them bearing each of these things put them on me, and said, From henceforth become a priest of the Lord, thou and thy seed for ever. And

the first anointed me with holy oil, and gave to me the rod of judgment. The second washed me with pure water, and fed me with bread and wine, the most holy things,[4] and clad me with a holy and glorious robe. The third clothed me with a linen vestment like to an ephod. The fourth put round me a girdle like unto purple. The fifth gave to me a branch of rich olive. The sixth placed a crown on my head. The seventh placed on my head a diadem of priesthood, and filled my hands with incense, so that I served as a priest to the Lord. And they said to me, Levi, thy seed shall be divided into three branches,[5] for a sign of the glory of the Lord who is to come; and first shall he be that hath been faithful; no portion shall be greater than his. The second shall be in the priesthood. The third — a new name shall be called over Him, because He shall arise as King from Judah, and shall establish a new priesthood, after the fashion of the Gentiles, to all the Gentiles.[6] And His appearing shall be unutterable, as of an exalted[7] prophet of the seed of Abraham our father. Every desirable thing in Israel shall be for thee and for thy seed, and everything fair to look upon shall ye eat, and the table of the Lord shall thy seed apportion, and some of them shall be high priests, and judges, and scribes; for by their mouth shall the holy place be guarded. And when I awoke, I understood that this thing was like unto the former. And I hid this also in my heart, and told it not to any man upon the earth.

9. And after two days I and Judah went up to Isaac after[8] our father; and the father of my father blessed me according to all the words of the visions which I had seen: and he would not come with us to Bethel. And when we came to Bethel, my father Jacob saw in a vision concerning me, that I should be to them for a priest unto the Lord; and he rose up early in the morning, and paid tithes of all to the Lord through me. And we came to Hebron to dwell there, and Isaac called me continually to put me in remembrance of the law of the Lord, even as the angel of God showed to me. And he taught me the law of the priesthood, of sacrifices, whole burnt-offerings, first-fruits, free-will offerings, thank-offerings. And each day he was instructing me, and was busied for me before the Lord. And he said to me, Take heed, my child, of the spirit of fornication; for this shall

---

[1] ἀσπίς. The Latin version gives the other meaning to ἀσπίς here, of asp or viper. The epithet χαλκῆν, however, renders "shield" much more probable, as there seems nothing in the context pointing to the "brazen serpent."

[2] A quotation from 1 Thess. ii. 16, where the context also is similar to the present. [See Lardner's refutation of the learned Grabe on this quotation, vol. ii. p. 359.]

[3] With the whole of this passage we may compare the description of the vestments of Aaron. See especially Ex. xxix. 5, 6 (LXX.). The πέταλον is the translation of צִיץ, the plate of gold on the forehead of the high priest over the mitre. The λογίον, or λογεῖον, is the breastplate, with the Urim and Thummim. For the ποδήρης, see Ex. xxviii. 27 (LXX.).

[4] On the possible reference here to the elements of the Eucharist, see Grabe's note, *Spicilegium, in loc.*

[5] Nitzsch (p. 19, n. 37) explains this division into three ἀρχαί, as referring to the three orders of the Christian priesthood. This, however, seems improbable. Cf. Kayser, p. 119; Vorstman, p. 41. It is far more probable that the reference is to Moses, Aaron, and Christ. Thus with πιστεύσας we may compare Num. xii. 7. For this use of ἀρχή, cf. Gen. ii. 10. [Isa. lxvi. 21.]

[6] [Rom. xvi 15, 16, 17, Greek. Compare Heb. v. 1.]

[7] Or, if we follow the reading of Cd. Oxon., "Prophet of the Most High."

[8] Or rather, with Cd. Oxon., "with our father."

continue, and shall by thy seed pollute the holy things. Take therefore to thyself, while yet thou art young, a wife, not having blemish, nor yet polluted, nor of the race of the Philistines or Gentiles. And before entering into the holy place, bathe ;[1] and when thou offerest the sacrifice, wash ; and again when thou finishest the sacrifice, wash. Of twelve trees ever having leaves, offer up *the fruits* to the Lord, as also Abraham taught me ; and of every clean beast and clean bird offer a sacrifice to the Lord, and of every firstling and of wine offer first-fruits ; and every sacrifice thou shalt salt with salt.[2]

10. Now, therefore, observe whatsoever I command you, children ; for whatsoever things I have heard from my fathers I have made known to you. I am clear from all your ungodliness and transgression which ye will do in the end of the ages against the Saviour of the world, acting ungodly, deceiving Israel, and raising up against it great evils from the Lord.[3] And ye will deal lawlessly with Israel, so that Jerusalem shall not endure your wickedness ; but the veil of the temple shall be rent, so as not to cover your shame. And ye shall be scattered as captives among the heathen, and shall be for a reproach and for a curse, and for a trampling under foot. For the house which the Lord shall choose shall be called Jerusalem, as is contained in the book of Enoch the righteous.[4]

11. Therefore, when I took a wife I was twenty-eight years old, and her name was Melcha. And she conceived and bare a son, and she called his name Gersham, for we were sojourners in our land : for Gersham is interpreted sojourning. And I saw concerning him that he would not be in the first rank. And Kohath was born in my thirty-fifth year, towards the east. And I saw in a vision that he was standing on high in the midst of all the congregation. Therefore I called his name Kohath, which meaneth, beginning of majesty and instruction. And thirdly, she bare to me Merari, in the fortieth year of my life ; and since his mother bare him with difficulty, she called him Merari, which meaneth my bitterness, because he also died. And Jochebed was born in my sixty-fourth year, in Egypt, for I was renowned then in the midst of my brethren.

12. And Gersham took a wife, and she bare to him Lomni and Semei. And the sons of Kohath, Ambram, Isaar, Chebro, and Ozel. And

the sons of Merari, Mooli and Homusi. And in my ninety-fourth year Ambram took Jochebed my daughter to him to wife, for they were born in one day, he and my daughter. Eight years old was I when I went into the land of Canaan, and eighteen years when I slew Shechem, and at nineteen years I became priest, and at twenty-eight years I took a wife, and at forty years I went into Egypt. And behold, ye are my children, my children even *of* a third generation. In my hundred and eighteenth year Joseph died.

13. And now, my children, I command you that ye fear our Lord with your whole heart, and walk in simplicity according to all His[5] law. And do ye also teach your children learning, that they may have understanding in all their life, reading unceasingly the law of God ; for every one who shall know the law of God shall be honoured, and shall not be a stranger wheresoever he goeth. Yea, many friends shall he gain more than his forefathers ; and many men shall desire to serve him, and to hear the law from his mouth. Work righteousness, my children, upon the earth, that ye may find *treasure* in the heavens, and sow good things in your souls, that ye may find them in your life. For if ye sow evil things, ye shall reap all trouble and affliction. Get wisdom in the fear of God with diligence ; for though there shall be a leading into captivity, and cities be destroyed, and lands and gold and silver and every possession shall perish, the wisdom of the wise none can take away, save the blindness of ungodliness and the palsy of sin : for even among his enemies shall it be to him glorious, and in a strange country a home, and in the midst of foes shall it be found a friend. If a man teach these things and do them, he shall be enthroned with kings, as was also Joseph our brother.

14. And now, my children, I have learnt from the writing of Enoch that at the last ye will deal ungodly, laying your hands upon the Lord in all malice ; and your brethren shall be ashamed because of you, and to all the Gentiles shall it become a mocking. For our father Israel shall be pure from the ungodliness of the chief priests who shall lay their hands upon the Saviour of the world. Pure is the heaven above the earth, and ye are the lights of the heaven as the sun and the moon. What shall all the Gentiles do if ye be darkened in ungodliness? So shall ye bring a curse upon our race for whom came the light of the world, which was given among you for the lighting up of every man.[6] Him will ye desire to slay, teaching commandments contrary to the ordinances of God. The offerings of the Lord will ye rob, and from His portion will ye steal ; and before ye sacrifice to the Lord, ye will take the choicest parts, in despitefulness eating them

---

[1] We constantly find Peter, in the *Clementine Homilies* and *Recognitions*, combining with the Agapæ the practice of bathing. Cf., e.g., *Recog.*, iv. 3, v. 36.
[2] Cf. *Hom.*, xiv. 1. [Lev. ii. 13; Mark ix. 49.]
[3] [Annas and Caiaphas. John xix. 11.]
[4] This document is frequently quoted in the *Testaments:* cf. *Sim.* 5; *Levi* 14, 16; *Judah* 18; *Dan* 5; *Naph.* 4; *Benj.* 9. Most of these citations, however, are not to be found in the work as it has come down to us. We must therefore either assume the reference to some other books of Enoch not now extant, or rather perhaps that they are general appeals to the spirit of the book, regarded as a great fount of prophecy.

[5] Read αὐτοῦ with Cd. Oxon.
[6] [John i. 4–9, viii. 12, ix. 5, etc.]

with harlots. Amid excesses[1] will ye teach the commandments of the Lord, the women that have husbands will ye pollute, and the virgins of Jerusalem will ye defile; and with harlots and adulteresses will ye be joined. The daughters of the Gentiles will ye take for wives, purifying them with an unlawful purification; and your union shall be like unto Sodom and Gomorrah in ungodliness. And ye will be puffed up because of the priesthood lifting yourselves up against men. And not only so, but being puffed up also against the commands of God, ye will scoff at the holy things, mocking in despitefulness.

15. Therefore the temple which the Lord shall choose shall be desolate in uncleanness, and ye shall be captives throughout all nations, and ye shall be an abomination among them, and ye shall receive reproach and everlasting shame from the righteous judgment of God; and all who see you shall flee from you. And were it not for Abraham, Isaac, and Jacob our fathers, not one from my seed should be left upon the earth.

16. And now I have learnt in the book of Enoch that for seventy weeks will ye go astray, and will profane the priesthood, and pollute the sacrifices, and corrupt the law, and set at nought the words of the prophets. In perverseness ye will persecute righteous men, and hate the godly; the words of the faithful will ye abhor, and the man who reneweth the law in the power of the Most High will ye call a deceiver;[2] and at last, as ye suppose, ye will slay Him, not understanding His resurrection, wickedly taking upon your own heads the innocent blood.[3] Because of Him shall your holy places be desolate, polluted even to the ground, and ye shall have no place that is clean; but ye shall be among the Gentiles a curse and a dispersion, until He shall again look upon you, and in pity shall take you to Himself through faith and water.[4]

17. And because ye have heard concerning the seventy weeks, hear also concerning the priesthood; for in each jubilee there shall be a priesthood. In the first jubilee, the first who is anointed into the priesthood shall be great, and shall speak to God as to a Father; and his priesthood shall be filled with the fear of the Lord, and in the day of his gladness shall he arise for the salvation of the world. In the second jubilee, he that is anointed shall be conceived in the sorrow of beloved ones; and his priesthood shall be honoured, and shall be glorified among all. And the third priest shall be held fast in sorrow; and the fourth shall be in grief, because unrighteousness shall be laid upon him exceedingly, and all Israel shall hate each one his neighbour. The fifth shall be held fast in darkness, likewise also the sixth and the seventh. And in the seventh there shall be such pollution as I am not able to express, before the Lord and men, for they shall know it who do these things. Therefore shall they be in captivity and for a prey, and their land and their substance shall be destroyed. And in the fifth week they shall return into their desolate country, and shall renew the house of the Lord. And in the seventh week shall come the priests, worshippers of idols, contentious, lovers of money, proud, lawless, lascivious, abusers of children and beasts.

18. And after their punishment shall have come from the Lord, then will the Lord raise up to the priesthood a new Priest, to whom all the words of the Lord shall be revealed; and He shall execute a judgment of truth upon the earth,[5] in the fulness of days. And His star shall arise in heaven,[6] as a king shedding forth the light of knowledge in the sunshine of day, and He shall be magnified in the world until His ascension. He shall shine forth as the sun in the earth, and shall drive away all darkness from the world under heaven, and there shall be peace in all the earth. The heavens shall rejoice in His days, and the earth shall be glad, and the clouds shall be joyful, and the knowledge of the Lord shall be poured forth upon the earth, as the water of seas; and the angels of the glory of the presence of the Lord shall be glad in Him. The heavens shall be opened, and from the temple of glory shall the sanctification come upon Him with the Father's voice, as from Abraham the father of Isaac. And the glory of the Most High shall be uttered over Him, and the spirit of understanding and of sanctification shall rest upon Him in the water. He shall give the majesty of the Lord to His sons in truth for evermore; and there shall none succeed Him for all generations, even for ever.[7] And in His priesthood shall all sin come to an end, and the lawless shall rest from evil, and the just shall rest in Him. And He shall open the gates of paradise, and shall remove[8] the threatening sword against Adam; and He shall give to His saints to eat from the tree of life,[9] and the spirit of holiness shall be on them. And Beliar shall be bound by Him, and He shall give power to His children to tread

---

[1] The word πλεονεξία, like the English "excess," has not unfrequently special reference to sins of sensuality. Cf. 1 Cor. v. 11, Eph. iv. 19, v. 3, 5, Col. iii. 5, 1 Thess. iv. 6, the context in all of which passages points strongly to this conclusion. See Suicer's *Thesaurus*, *s.v.*

[2] Cf. Matt. xxvii. 63, where ἐκεῖνος ὁ πλάνος is said of our Lord.

[3] [Matt. xxvii. 25.]

[4] [John iii. 5; Isa. xii. 3; 1 Pet. iii. 20.]

[5] [Jer. xxxiii. 15.]

[6] [Matt. ii. 2. Constant references to the Gospels proofs of text.]

[7] An additional clause occurs here in Cd. Oxon., which generally has a tendency to omit; the copyist of Cd. Cam. having possibly looked on to the same initial words in the next clause: "And in His priesthood shall the Gentiles be multiplied in knowledge on the earth, and shall be enlightened through the grace of the Lord; but Israel shall be minished in ignorance, and be darkened in sorrow."

[8] The reading of Cd. Oxon. here, ἀποστήσει, is to be preferred to Cd. Cam., στήσει. Grosseteste's Latin version, in all probability made from the latter, has *stare faciet*. [See p. 7, note 1, *supra*.]

[9] [Rev. ii. 7.]

upon the evil spirits.[1] And the Lord shall rejoice in His children, and the Lord shall be well pleased in His beloved for ever. Then shall Abraham and Isaac and Jacob be joyful, and I will be glad, and all the saints shall put on gladness.

19. And now, my children, ye have heard all; choose therefore for yourselves either the darkness or the light, either the law of the Lord or the works of Beliar. And we answered our father,

saying, Before the Lord will we walk according to His law. And our father said, The Lord is witness, and His angels are witnesses, and I am witness, and ye are witnesses, concerning the word of your mouth. And we said, We are witnesses. And thus Levi ceased giving charge to his sons; and he stretched out his feet, and was gathered to his fathers, after he had lived a hundred and thirty-seven years. And they laid him in a coffin, and afterwards they buried him in Hebron, by the side of Abraham, and Isaac, and Jacob.

---

[1] [Luke x. 18, 19.]

IV.—THE TESTAMENT OF JUDAH CONCERNING FORTITUDE, AND LOVE OF MONEY, AND FORNICATION.

1. THE copy of the words of Judah, what things he spake to his sons before he died. They gathered themselves together, and came to him, and he said to them: I was the fourth son born to my father, and my mother called me Judah, saying, I give thanks to the Lord, because He hath given to me even a fourth son.[1] I was swift and active in my youth, and obedient to my father in everything. And I honoured my mother and my mother's sister. And it came to pass, when I became a man, that my father Jacob prayed over me, saying, Thou shalt be a king, and prosperous in all things.

2. And the Lord showed me favour in all my works both in the field and at home. When I saw that I could run with the hind, then I caught it, and prepared meat for my father. I seized upon the roes in the chase, and all that was in the plains I outran. A wild mare I outran, and I caught it and tamed it; and I slew a lion, and plucked a kid out of its mouth. I took a bear by its paw, and rolled it over a cliff; and if any beast turned upon me, I rent it like a dog. I encountered the wild boar, and overtaking it in the chase, I tore it. A leopard in Hebron leaped upon the dog, and I caught it by the tail, and flung it from me, and it was dashed to pieces in the coasts of Gaza. A wild ox feeding in the field I seized by the horns; and whirling it round and stunning it, I cast it from me, and slew it.

3. And when the two kings of the Canaanites came in warlike array against our flocks, and much people with them, I by myself rushed upon King Sur and seized him; and I beat him upon the legs, and dragged him down, and so I slew him. And the other king, Taphue,[2] I slew as he sat

upon his horse, and so I scattered all the people. Achor the king, a man of giant stature, hurling darts before and behind as he sat on horseback, I slew; for I hurled a stone of sixty pounds weight, and cast it upon his horse, and killed him. And I fought with Achor for two hours, and I killed him; and I clave his shield into two parts, and I chopped off his feet. And as I stripped off his breastplate, behold, eight men his companions began to fight with me. I wound round therefore my garment in my hand; and I slang stones at them, and killed four of them, and the rest fled. And Jacob my father slew Beelisa, king of all the kings, a giant in strength, twelve cubits high; and fear fell upon them, and they ceased from making war with us. Therefore my father had no care in the wars when I was among my brethren. For he saw in a vision concerning me, that an angel of might followed me everywhere, that I should not be overcome.

4. And in the south there befell us a greater war than that in Shechem; and I joined in battle array with my brethren, and pursued a thousand men, and slew of them two hundred men and four kings. And I went up against them upon the wall, and two other kings I slew; and so we freed Hebron, and took all the captives of the kings.

5. On the next day we departed to Areta,[3] a city strong and walled and inaccessible, threatening us with death. Therefore I and Gad approached on the east side of the city, and Reuben and Levi on the west and south. And they that were upon the wall, thinking that we were alone, charged down upon us; and so our brethren secretly climbed up the wall on both sides by ladders, and entered into the city, while the men knew it not. And we took it with the edge of the sword; and those who had taken

---

[1] Gen. xxix. 35. [The name = Praise. So Gen. xlix. 3.]
[2] In c. 5 we find this name, with a slight variety of spelling, as that of a place over which this king may have ruled. It is doubtless equivalent to the Hebrew Tappuah, a name of several cities mentioned in the Old Testament. See Josh. xv. 34, xvi. 8, xvii. 8, 1 Chron. ii. 43. Cf. Thapha, *Jubilees*, 34.

[3] Cd. Oxon. reads ἑτέραν; but cf. Aresa, *Jubilees*, 34.

refuge in the tower, — we set fire to the tower, and took both it and them. And as we were departing the men of Thaffu set upon our captives, and we took it with our sons, and fought with them even to Thaffu; and we slew them, and burnt their city, and spoiled all the things that were therein.

6. And when I was at the waters of Chuzeba,[1] the men of Jobel came against us to battle, and we fought with them; and their allies from Selom[2] we slew, and we allowed them no means of escaping, and of coming against us. And the men of Machir[3] came upon us on the fifth day, to carry away our captives; and we attacked them, and overcame them in fierce battle: for they were a host and mighty in themselves, and we slew them before they had gone up the ascent of the hill. And when we came to their city, their women rolled upon us stones from the brow of the hill on which the city stood. And I and Simeon hid ourselves behind the town, and seized upon the heights, and utterly destroyed the whole city.

7. And the next day it was told us that the cities[4] of the two kings with a great host were coming against us. I therefore and Dan feigned ourselves to be Amorites, and went as allies into their city. And in the depth of night our brethren came, and we opened to them the gates; and we destroyed all the men and their substance, and we took for a prey all that was theirs, and their three walls we cast down. And we drew near to Thamna,[5] where was all the refuge of the hostile kings. Then having received hurt I was wroth, and charged upon them to the brow of the hill; and they slang at me with stones and darts; and had not Dan my brother aided me, they would have been able to slay me. We came upon them therefore with wrath, and they all fled; and passing by another way, they besought my father, and he made peace with them, and we did to them no hurt, but made a truce with them, and restored to them all the captives. And I built Thamna, and my father built Rhambael.[6] I was twenty years old when this war befell, and the Canaanites feared me and my brethren.

8. Moreover, I had much cattle, and I had for

the chief of my herdsmen Iran[7] the Adullamite. And when I went to him I saw Barsan, king of Adullam, and he made us a feast; and he entreated me, and gave me his daughter Bathshua to wife. She bare me Er, and Onan, and Shelah; and the two of them the Lord smote that they died childless: for Shelah lived, and his children are ye.

9. Eighteen years we abode at peace, our father and we, with his brother Esau, and his sons with us, after that we came from Mesopotamia, from Laban. And when eighteen years were fulfilled, in the fortieth year of my life, Esau, the brother of my father, came upon us with much people and strong; and he fell by the bow of Jacob, and was taken up dead in Mount Seir: even as he went above Iramna[8] was he slain. And we pursued after the sons of Esau. Now they had a city with walls of iron and gates of brass; and we could not enter into it, and we encamped around, and besieged them. And when they opened not to us after twenty days, I set up a ladder in the sight of all, and with my shield upon my head I climbed up, assailed with stones of three talents' weight; and I climbed up, and slew four who were mighty among them. And the next day Reuben and Gad entered in and slew sixty others. Then they asked from us terms of peace; and being aware of our father's purpose, we received them as tributaries. And they gave us two hundred cors of wheat, five hundred baths of oil, fifteen hundred measures of wine, until we went down into Egypt.

10 After these things, my son Er took to wife Tamar, from Mesopotamia, a daughter of Aram.[9] Now Er was wicked, and he doubted concerning Tamar, because she was not of the land of Canaan. And on the third day an angel of the Lord smote him in the night, and he had not known her, according to the evil craftiness of his mother, for he did not wish to have children from her. In the days of the wedding-feast I espoused Onan to her; and he also in wickedness knew her not, though he lived with her a year. And when I threatened him, he lay with her,[10] . . . according to the command of his mother, and he also died in his wickedness. And I wished to give Shelah also to her, but my wife Bathshua suffered it not; for she bore a spite against Tamar, because she was not of the daughters of Canaan, as she herself was.

11. And I knew that the race of Canaan was wicked, but the thoughts of youth blinded my heart. And when I saw her pouring out wine,

---

[1] Cf. c. 12: also Chezib (Gen. xxxviii. 5), Chozeba (1 Chron. iv. 22), and Achzib (Josh. xv. 44; Mic. i 14), all of which are probably different names for the same place, and all connected with Judah.

[2] Cf. Selo, *Jubilees*, *l.c.*

[3] Cf. 1 Chron. xi. 36. [Here the translator supplies a note of doubt, — an interrogation-point.]

[4] Cd. Oxon. reads Γαας πόλις βασιλέων. Cf. Josh. xxiv. 30; Judg. ii. 9; 2 Sam. xxiii. 30. Cf. also "Gaiz," *Jubilees*, *l.c.*

[5] The Timnah of the Old Testament, which name is, however, borne by several places. Most probably it is the Timnah near Bethshemesh, on the north frontier of Judah, in the neighbourhood, that is, of many of the other localities mentioned in the *Testaments*. This may be the same as the Timnathah on the Danite frontier (Josh. xix. 43), and with the Timnathah where Samson's wife dwelt (Judg. xiv. 1 sqq.). The geographical position of Timnah-serah is against the allusion being it here. Cf., however, *Jubilees*, c. 34, where *Thamnathares* is one of the hostile towns.

[6] Cf. Robel, *Jubilees*, *l.c.*

[7] Cf. Gen. xxxviii. 1.

[8] Cd. Oxon. ἐν Ἀνονιράμ, probably *per incuriam scribæ*, for ἐπάνω Ἱράμ.

[9] This seems to arise from the wish to disconnect Israel as far as possible from non-Shemite associations. Cf. the Targum of Onkelos on Gen. xxxviii. 6. "Judah took a wife for Er, his first-born, *a daughter of the great Shem*, whose name was Tamar."

[10] διέφθειρε δὲ τὸ σπέρμα ἐπὶ τὴν γῆν.

in the drunkenness of wine was I deceived, and I fell before her. And while I was away, she went and took for Shelah a wife from the land of Caanan. And when I knew what she had done, I cursed her in the anguish of my soul, and she also died in the wickedness of her sons.

12. And after these things, while Tamar was a widow, she heard after two years that I was going up to shear my sheep; then she decked herself in bridal array, and sat over against the city by the gate. For it is a law of the Amorites, that she who is about to marry sit in fornication seven days by the gate.[1] I therefore, being drunk at the waters of Chozeb, recognised her not by reason of wine; and her beauty deceived me, through the fashion of her adorning. And I turned aside to her, and said, I would enter in to thee. And she said to me, What wilt thou give me? And I gave her my staff, and my girdle, and my royal crown; and I lay with her, and she conceived. I then, not knowing what she had done, wished to slay her; but she privily sent my pledges, and put me to shame. And when I called her, I heard also the secret words which I spoke when lying with her in my drunkenness; and I could not slay her, because it was from the Lord. For I said, Lest haply she did it in subtlety, and received the pledge from another woman: but I came near her no more till my death, because I had done this abomination in all Israel. Moreover, they who were in the city said that there was no bride in the city, because she came from another place, and sat for awhile in the gate, and she thought that no one knew that I had gone in to her.[2] And after this we came into Egypt to Joseph, because of the famine. Forty and six years old was I, and seventy and three years lived I there.

13. And now, my children, in what things soever I command you hearken to your father, and keep all my sayings to perform the ordinances of the Lord, and to obey the command of the Lord God. And walk not after your lusts, nor in the thoughts of your imaginations in the haughtiness of your heart; and glory not in the works of the strength of youth, for this also is evil in the eyes of the Lord. For since I also gloried that in wars the face of no woman of goodly form ever deceived me, and upbraided Reuben my brother concerning Bilhah, the wife of my father, the spirits of jealousy and of fornication arrayed themselves within me, until I fell before Bathshua the Canaanite, and Tamar who was espoused to my sons. And I said to my father-in-law, I will counsel with my father, and so will I take thy daughter. And he showed me a boundless store

of gold in his daughter's behalf, for he was a king. And he decked her with gold and pearls, and caused her to pour out wine for us at the feast in womanly beauty. And the wine led my eyes astray, and pleasure blinded my heart; and I loved her, and I fell, and transgressed the commandment of the Lord and the commandment of my fathers, and I took her to wife. And the Lord rewarded me according to the thought of my heart, insomuch that I had no joy in her children.

14. And now, my children, be not drunk with wine; for wine turneth the mind away from the truth, and kindleth in it the passion of lust, and leadeth the eyes into error. For the spirit of fornication hath wine as a minister to give pleasures to the mind; for these two take away the power from a man. For if a man drink wine to drunkenness, he disturbeth his mind with filthy thoughts to fornication, and exciteth his body to carnal union; and if the cause of the desire be present, he worketh the sin, and is not ashamed. Such is wine, my children; for he who is drunken reverenceth no man. For, lo, it made me also to err, so that I was not ashamed of the multitude in the city, because before the eyes of all I turned aside unto Tamar, and I worked a great sin, and I uncovered the covering of the shame of my sons. After that I drank wine I reverenced not the commandment of God, and I took a woman of Canaan to wife. Wherefore, my children, he who drinketh wine needeth discretion; and herein is discretion in drinking wine, that a man should drink as long as he keepeth decency; but if he go beyond this bound, the spirit of deceit attacketh his mind and worketh his will; and it maketh the drunkard to talk filthily, and to transgress and not to be ashamed, but even to exult in his dishonour, accounting himself to do well.

15. He that committeth fornication, and [3] uncovereth his nakedness, hath become the servant of fornication, and escapeth not [4] from the power thereof, even as I also was uncovered. For I gave my staff, that is, the stay of my tribe; and my girdle, that is, my power; and my diadem, that is, the glory of my kingdom. Then I repented for these things, and took no wine or flesh until my old age, nor did I behold any joy. And the angel of God showed me that for ever do women bear rule over king and beggar alike; and from the king they take away his glory, and from the valiant man his strength, and from the beggar even that little which is the stay of his poverty.

---

[1] [*Herod.* i., cap. 199; Baruch vi. 43.]
[2] [To this section Lardner objects. But compare Gen. xxxviii. 12.]

[3] Cd. Oxon. here reads the additional clause, ζημιούμενος οὐκ αἰσθάνεται καὶ ἄδοξον οὐκ αἰσχύνεται. Κἂν γάρ τις βασιλεύσῃ, πορνεύων, — perhaps omitted from Cd. Cant. through the homœoteleuton.
[4] Cd. Oxon. omits the negative. The βασίλεια will then be that from which the man falls by his sin.

16. Observe therefore, my children, moderation in wine; for there are in it four evil spirits — of (1) lust, of (2) wrath, of (3) riot, of (4) filthy lucre. If ye drink wine in gladness, with shamefacedness, with the fear of God, ye shall live. For if ye drink not with shamefacedness, and the fear of God departeth from you, then cometh drunkenness, and shamelessness stealeth in. But [1] *even* if ye drink not at all, take heed lest ye sin in words of outrage, and fighting, and slander, and transgression of the commandments of God; so shall ye perish before your time. Moreover, wine revealeth the mysteries of God and men to aliens, even as I also revealed the commandments of God and the mysteries of Jacob my father to the Canaanitish Bathshua, to whom God forbade to declare them. And wine also is a cause of war and confusion.

17. I charge you, therefore, my children, not to love money, nor to gaze upon the beauty of women; because for the sake of money and beauty I was led astray to Bathshua the Canaanite. For I know that because of these two things shall ye who are my race fall into wickedness; for even wise men among my sons shall they mar, and shall cause the kingdom of Judah to be diminished, which the Lord gave me because of my obedience to my father.[2] For I never disobeyed a word of Jacob my father, for all things whatsoever he commanded I did. And Abraham, the father of my father, blessed me that I should be king in Israel, and Isaac further blessed me in like manner. And I know that from me shall the kingdom be established.

18. For I have read also in the books of Enoch the righteous what evils ye shall do in the last days. Take heed, therefore, my children, of fornication and the love of money; hearken to Judah your father, for these things do withdraw you from the law of God, and blind the understanding of the soul, and teach arrogance, and suffer not a man to have compassion upon his neighbour: they rob his soul of all goodness, and bind him in toils and troubles, and take away his sleep and devour his flesh, and hinder the sacrifices of God; and he remembereth not blessing, and he hearkeneth not to a prophet when he speaketh, and is vexed at the word of godliness. For one who serveth two passions contrary to the commandments of God cannot obey God, because they have blinded his soul, and he walketh in the day-time as in the night.

19. My children, the love of money leadeth to idols; because, when led astray through money, men make mention of those who are no gods, and it causeth him who hath it to fall into madness. For the sake of money I lost my children, and but for the repentance of my flesh, and the humbling of my soul, and the prayers of Jacob my father, I should have died childless. But the God of my fathers, who is pitiful and merciful, pardoned me, because I did it in ignorance.[3] For the prince of deceit blinded me, and I was ignorant as a man and as flesh, being corrupted in sins; and I learnt my own weakness while thinking myself unconquerable.[4]

20. [5] Learn therefore, my children, that two spirits wait upon man — the spirit of truth and the spirit of error; and in the midst is the spirit of the understanding of the mind, to which it belongeth to turn whithersoever it will. And the works of truth and the works of error are written upon the breast of men, and each one of them the Lord knoweth. And there is no time at which the works of men can be hid from Him; for on the bones of his breast hath he been written down before the Lord. And the spirit of truth testifieth all things, and accuseth all; and he who sinneth is burnt up by his own heart, and cannot raise his face unto the Judge.

21. And now, my children, love Levi, that ye may abide, and exalt not yourselves against him, lest ye be utterly destroyed. For to me the Lord gave the kingdom, and to him the priesthood, and He set the kingdom beneath the priesthood. To me He gave the things upon the earth; to him the things in the heavens. As the heaven is higher than the earth, so is the priesthood of God higher than the kingdom upon the earth. For the Lord chose him above thee, to draw near to Him, and to eat of His table and first-fruits, even the choice things of the sons of Israel, and thou shalt be to them as a sea. For as, on the sea, just and unjust are tossed about, some taken into captivity while others are enriched, so also shall every race of men be in thee, some are in jeopardy and taken captive, and others shall grow rich by means of plunder. For they who rule will be as great sea-monsters, swallowing up men like fishes: free sons and daughters do they enslave; houses, lands, flocks, money, will they plunder; and with the flesh of many will they wrongfully feed the ravens and the cranes; and they will go on further in evil, advancing on still in covetousness. And there shall be false prophets like tempests, and they shall persecute all righteous men.

22. And the Lord shall bring upon them divisions one against another, and there shall be continual wars in Israel; and among men of other race shall my kingdom be brought to an end, until the salvation of Israel shall come, until the appearing of the God of righteousness, that

---

[1] Cd. Oxon. reads τί δὲ λέγω; μηδ' ὅλως πίνετε, which seems much more suitable to the context.
[2] [1 Kings xi. 1, and ver. 11.]

[3] [Num. xv. 25 and Acts iii. 17.]
[4] [See cap. 13, p. 19, *supra*.]
[5] Cd. Oxon. omits the whole of this chapter.

Jacob and all the Gentiles may rest in peace.[1] And he shall guard the might of my kingdom for ever : for the Lord sware to me with an oath that the kingdom should never fail from me, and from my seed for all days, even for ever.

23. Now I have much grief, my children, because of your lewdness, and witchcrafts, and idolatries, which ye will work against the kingdom, following them that have familiar spirits ; ye[2] will make your daughters singing girls[3] and harlots for divinations and demons of error, and ye will be mingled in the pollutions of the Gentiles : for which things' sake the Lord shall bring upon you famine and pestilence, death and the sword, avenging siege, and dogs for the rending in pieces of enemies, and revilings of friends, destruction and blighting of eyes, children slaughtered, wives carried off, possessions plundered, temple of God in flames, your land desolated, your own selves enslaved among the Gentiles, and they shall make some of you eunuchs for their wives ; and whenever ye will return to the Lord with humility of heart, repenting and walking in all the commandments of God, then will the Lord visit you in mercy and in love, bringing you from out of the bondage of your enemies.

24. And after these things shall a Star arise to you from Jacob in peace, and a Man shall rise from my seed, like the Sun of righteousness, walking with the sons of men[4] in meekness and righteousness, and no sin shall be found in Him. And the heavens shall be opened above Him, to shed forth the blessing of the Spirit from the Holy Father ; and He shall shed forth a spirit of grace upon you, and ye shall be unto Him sons in truth, and ye shall walk in His commandments, the first and the last. This is the Branch of God Most High, and this the Well-spring unto life for all flesh. [5] Then shall the sceptre of my kingdom shine forth, and from your root shall arise a stem ; and in it shall arise a rod of righteousness to the Gentiles, to judge and to save all that call upon the Lord.

25. And after these things shall Abraham and Isaac and Jacob arise unto life, and I and my brethren will be chiefs, even your sceptre in Israel : Levi first, I the second, Joseph third, Benjamin fourth, Simeon fifth, Issachar sixth, and so all in order. And the Lord blessed Levi ; the Angel of the Presence, me ; the powers of glory,[6] Simeon ; the heaven, Reuben ; the earth, Issachar ; the sea, Zebulun ; the mountains, Joseph ; the tabernacle, Benjamin ; the lights of heaven, Dan ; the fatness of earth, Naphtali ; the sun, Gad ; the olive, Asher : and there shall be one people of the Lord, and one tongue ; and there shall no more be a spirit of deceit of Beliar, for he shall be cast into the fire for ever. And they who have died in grief shall arise in joy, and they who have lived in poverty for the Lord's sake shall be made rich, and they who have been in want shall be filled, and they who have been weak shall be made strong, and they who have been put to death for the Lord's sake shall awake in life.[7] And the harts of Jacob shall run in joyfulness, and the eagles of Israel shall fly in gladness ; but the ungodly shall lament, and sinners shall weep, and all the people shall glorify the Lord for ever.

26. Observe, therefore, my children, all the law of the Lord, for there is hope for all them who follow His way aright. And he said to them : I die before your eyes this day, a hundred and nineteen years old. Let no one bury me in costly apparel, nor tear open my bowels,[8] for this shall they who are kings do : and carry me up to Hebron with you. And Judah, when he had said these things, fell asleep ; and his sons did according to all whatsoever he commanded them, and they buried him in Hebron with his fathers.

---

[1] [Rom. xi. 26.]
[2] The reading of Cd. Oxon. is doubtless to be preferred, which joins κληδοσι και δαιμοσι πλανης to what precedes.
[3] [Eccles. ii. 8; Ecclus. ix. 4.]
[4] [Prov. viii. 31.]
[5] Cd. Oxon. omits from here to end of c. 25.

[6] [Eph. iii. 10.]
[7] [2 Macc. vii. 9-36 and Heb. xi. 35.]
[8] i.e., for the purpose of embalmment.

V. — THE TESTAMENT OF ISSACHAR CONCERNING SIMPLICITY.

1. THE record of the words of Issachar. He called his sons, and said to them : Hearken, my children, to Issachar your father ; give ear to my words, ye who are beloved of the Lord. I was the fifth son born to Jacob, even the hire of the mandrakes.[1] For Reuben[2] brought in mandrakes from the field, and Rachel met him and took them. And Reuben wept, and at his voice Leah my mother came forth. Now these mandrakes were sweet-smelling apples which the land of Aram produced on high ground below a ravine of water. And Rachel said, I will not give them to thee, for they shall be to me instead of children. Now there were two apples ; and Leah said, Let it suffice thee that thou hast taken the husband of my virginity : wilt thou also take these? And she said, Behold, let Jacob be to thee this night instead of the mandrakes of thy

---

[1] See Gen. xxx. 14 sqq.
[2] The Cam. MS. reads Ἰακώβ by an obvious error.

son. And Leah said to her, Boast not, and vaunt not thyself; for Jacob is mine, and I am the wife of his youth. But Rachel said, How so? for to me was he first espoused, and for my sake he served our father fourteen years. What shall I do to thee, because the craft and the subtlety of men are increased, and craft prospereth upon the earth? And were it not so, thou wouldest not now see the face of Jacob. For thou art not his wife, but in craft wert taken to him in my stead. And my father deceived me, and removed me on that night, and suffered me not to see him; for had I been there, it had not happened thus. And Rachel said, Take one mandrake, and for the other thou shalt hire him from me for one night. And Jacob knew Leah, and she conceived and bare me, and on account of the hire [1] I was called Issachar.

2. Then appeared to Jacob an angel of the Lord, saying, Two children shall Rachel bear; for she hath refused company with her husband, and hath chosen continency. And had not Leah my mother given up the two apples for the sake of his company, she would have borne eight sons; and for this thing she bare six, and Rachel two: because on account of the mandrakes the Lord visited her. For He knew that for the sake of children she wished to company with Jacob, and not for lust of pleasure. [2] For she went further, and on the morrow too gave up Jacob that she might receive also the other mandrake. Therefore the Lord hearkened to Rachel because of the mandrakes: for though she desired them, she ate them not, but brought them to the priest of the Most High who was at that time, and offered them up in the house of the Lord.

3. When, therefore, I grew up, my children, I walked in uprightness of heart, and I became a husbandman for my parents and my brethren, and I brought in fruits from the field according to their season; and my father blessed me, for he saw that I walked in simplicity. And I was not a busybody in my doings, nor malicious and slanderous against my neighbour. I never spoke against any one, nor did I censure the life of any man, but walked in the simplicity of my eyes. Therefore when I was thirty years old I took to myself a wife, for my labour wore away my strength, and I never thought upon pleasure with women; but through my labour my sleep sufficed me, and my father always rejoiced in my simplicity. For on whatever I laboured I offered first to the Lord, by the hands of the priests, of all my produce and all first-fruits; then to my father, and then took for myself. And the Lord increased twofold His benefits in my hands; and Jacob also knew that God aided my simplicity, for on every poor man and every one in distress

I bestowed the good things of the earth in simplicity of heart.

4. And now hearken to me, my children, and walk in simplicity of heart, for I have seen in it all that is well-pleasing to the Lord. The simple coveteth not gold, defraudeth not his neighbour, longeth not after manifold dainties, delighteth not in varied apparel, doth not picture to himself to live a long life, but only waiteth for the will of God, and the spirits of error have no power against him. For he cannot allow within his mind a thought of female beauty, that he should not pollute his mind in corruption. No envy can enter into his thoughts, no jealousy melteth away his soul, nor doth he brood over gain with insatiate desire; for he walketh in uprightness of life, and beholdeth all things in simplicity, not admitting in his eyes malice from the error of the world, lest he should see the perversion of any of the commandments of the Lord.

5. Keep therefore the law of God, my children, and get simplicity, and walk in guilelessness, not prying over-curiously into the commands of God and the business of your neighbour; but love the Lord and your neighbour, have compassion on the poor and weak. Bow down your back unto husbandry, and labour in tillage of the ground in all manner of husbandry, offering gifts unto the Lord with thanksgiving; for with the first-fruits of the earth did the Lord bless me, even as He blessed all the saints from Abel even until now. For no other portion is given to thee than of the fatness of the earth, whose fruits are raised by toil; for our father Jacob blessed me with blessings of the earth and of first-fruits. And Levi and Judah were glorified by the Lord among the sons of Jacob; for the Lord made choice of them, and to the one He gave the priesthood, to the other the kingdom. Them therefore obey, and walk in the simplicity of your father; for unto Gad hath it been given to destroy the temptations that are coming upon Israel.

6. I know, my children, that in the last times your sons will forsake simplicity, and will cleave unto avarice, and leaving guilelessness will draw near to malice, and forsaking the commandments of the Lord will cleave unto Beliar, and leaving husbandry will follow after their wicked devices, and shall be dispersed among the Gentiles, and shall serve their enemies. And do you therefore command these things to your children, that if they sin they may the more quickly return to the Lord; for He is merciful, and will deliver them even to bring them back into their land.

7. I am a hundred and twenty-two years old, and I know not against myself a sin unto death. Except my wife, I have not known any woman. I never committed fornication in the haughtiness of my eyes; I drank not wine, to be led astray thereby; I coveted not any desirable thing that

---

[1] *Sachar.*
[2] [Tobit viii. 7, 8.]

was my neighbour's; guile never entered in my heart; a lie never passed through my lips; if any man grieved, I wept with him, and I shared my bread with the poor. I never ate alone; I moved no landmark; in all my days I wrought godliness and truth. I loved the Lord with all my strength; likewise also did I love every man even as my own children. So ye also do these things, my children, and every spirit of Beliar shall flee from you, and no deed of malicious men shall rule over you; and every wild beast shall ye sub-

due, having with yourselves the God of heaven walking with men in simplicity of heart.

And he commanded them that they should carry him up to Hebron, and bury him there in the cave with his fathers. And he stretched out his feet and died, the fifth son of Jacob, in a good old age; and with every limb sound, and with strength unabated, he slept the eternal sleep.[1]

---

[1] [See *Dan*, note 12, p. 26, *infra.* " Eternal " = " long."]

VI. — THE TESTAMENT OF ZEBULUN CONCERNING COMPASSION AND MERCY.

1. THE record of Zebulun, which he enjoined his children in the hundred [1] and fourteenth year of his life, thirty-two years after the death of Joseph. And he said to them: Hearken to me, sons of Zebulun, attend to the words of your father. I am Zebulun, a good gift [2] to my parents. For when I was born our father was increased very exceedingly, both in flocks and herds, when with the streaked rods he had his portion. I know not, my children, that in all my days I have sinned, save only in thought. Nor do I remember that I have done any iniquity, except the sin of ignorance which I committed against Joseph; for I screened my brethren, not telling to my father what had been done. And I wept sore in secret, for I feared my brethren, because they had all agreed together, that if any one should declare the secret, he should be slain with the sword. But when they wished to kill him, I adjured them much with tears not to be guilty of this iniquity.

2. For Simeon and Gad came against Joseph to kill him. And Joseph fell upon his face, and said unto them, Pity me, my brethren, have compassion upon the bowels of Jacob our father: lay not upon me your hands to shed innocent blood, for I have not sinned against you; yea, if I have sinned, with chastening chastise me, but lay not upon me your hand, for the sake of Jacob our father. And as he spoke these words, I pitied him and began to weep, and my heart melted within me, and all the substance of my bowels was loosened within my soul. And Joseph also wept, and I too wept with him; and my heart throbbed fast, and the joints of my body

trembled, and I was not able to stand. And when he saw me weeping with him, and them coming against him to slay him, he fled behind me, beseeching them. And Reuben rose and said, My brethren, let us not slay him, but let us cast him into one of these dry pits which our fathers digged and found no water. For for this cause the Lord forbade that water should rise up in them, in order that Joseph might be preserved; and the Lord appointed it so, until they sold him to the Ishmaelites.

3. For in the price of Joseph, my children, I had no share; but Simeon and Gad and six other of our brethren took the price of Joseph, and bought sandals [3] for themselves, their wives, and their children, saying, We will not eat of it, for it is the price of our brother's blood, but will tread it down under foot, because he said that he was king over us, and so let us see what his dreams mean. Therefore is it written in the writing of the law of Enoch, that whosoever will not raise up seed to his brother, his sandal shall be unloosed, and they shall spit into his face.[4] And the brethren of Joseph wished not that their brother should live, and the Lord loosed unto them the sandal of Joseph. For when they came into Egypt they were unloosed by the servants of Joseph before the gate, and so made obeisance to Joseph after the fashion of Pharaoh. And not only did they make obeisance to him, but were spit upon also, falling down before him forthwith, and so they were put to shame before the Egyptians; for after this the Egyptians heard all the evils which we had done to Joseph.

4. After these things they brought forth food; for I through two days and two nights tasted nothing, through pity for Joseph. And Judah ate not with them, but watched the pit; for he feared lest Simeon and Gad should run back and slay him. And when they saw that I also ate not,

---

[1] The Ox. MS. reads 150, and refers the event to two years after Joseph's death. The text of the Cam. MS. gives an impossible result here, as it would make Zebulun twenty-eight years younger than Joseph, who died at the age of 110. According to the Ox. MS., Reuben (cf. c. 1) and Zebulun would die in the same year, the former at 125, the latter 150. A comparison of *Test. Reub.*, c. 1, shows the most probable solution to be to give the numerals, ριδ´, β´.

[2] The derivation of Zebulun seems to be from זְבֻל, a collateral form of זבד, to give. Hence Leah plays on the double meaning of the former verb, Gen. xxx. 20.

[3] Cf. the Targum Ps. Jon. on Gen. xxxvii. 28.
[4] [Deut. xxv. 7, 8, 9. See Lardner on the *animus* of these quotations from Enoch, as it strikes him, vol. ii. p. 350.]

they set me to watch him until he was sold. And he remained in the pit three days and three nights, and so was sold famishing. And when Reuben heard that while he was away Joseph had been sold, he rent his clothes about him, and mourned, saying, How shall I look in the face of Jacob my father? And he took the money, and ran after the merchants, and found no one; for they had left the main road, and journeyed hastily through rugged byways.[1] And Reuben ate no food on that day. Dan therefore came to him, and said, Weep not, neither grieve; for I have found what we can say to our father Jacob. Let us slay a kid of the goats, and dip in it the coat of Joseph; and we will say, Look, if this is the coat of thy son: for they stripped off from Joseph the coat of our father when they were about to sell him, and put upon him an old garment of a slave. Now Simeon had the coat, and would not give it up, wishing to rend it with his sword; for he was angry that Joseph lived, and that he had not slain him. Then we all rose up together against him, and said, If thou give it not up, we will say that thou alone didst this wickedness in Israel; and so he gave it up, and they did even as Dan had said.

5. And now, my children, I bid you to keep the commands of the Lord, and to show mercy upon your neighbour, and to have compassion towards all, not towards men only, but also towards beasts. For for this thing's sake the Lord blessed me; and when all my brethren were sick I escaped without sickness, for the Lord knoweth the purposes of each. Have therefore compassion in your hearts, my children, because even as a man doeth to his neighbour, even so also will the Lord do to him. For the sons of my brethren were sickening, were dying on account of Joseph, because they showed not mercy in their hearts; but my sons were preserved without sickness, as ye know. And when I was in Canaan, by the sea-coast, I caught spoil of fish for Jacob my father; and when many were choked in the sea, I abode unhurt.

6. I was the first who made a boat to sail upon the sea, for the Lord gave me understanding and wisdom therein; and I let down a rudder behind it, and I stretched a sail on an upright mast in the midst; and sailing therein along the shores, I caught fish for the house of my father until we went into Egypt; and through compassion, I gave of my fish to every stranger. And if any man were a stranger, or sick, or aged, I boiled the fish and dressed them well, and offered them to all men as every man had need, bringing them together and having compassion upon them. Wherefore also the Lord granted me to take much fish: for he that imparteth unto his neigh-

bour, receiveth manifold more from the Lord. For five years I caught fish, and gave thereof to every man whom I saw, and brought sufficient for all the house of my father. In the summer I caught fish, and in the winter I kept sheep with my brethren.

7. Now I will declare unto you what I did. I saw a man in distress and nakedness in wintertime, and had compassion upon him, and stole away[2] a garment secretly from my house, and gave it to him who was in distress. Do you therefore, my children, from that which God bestoweth upon you, show compassion and mercy impartially to all men, and give to every man with a good heart. And if ye have not at the time wherewith to give to him that asketh you, have compassion for him in bowels of mercy. I know that my hand found not at the time wherewith to give to him that asked me, and I walked with him weeping for more than seven furlongs, and my bowels yearned towards him unto compassion.

8. Have therefore yourselves also, my children, compassion towards every man with mercy, that the Lord also may have compassion upon you, and have mercy upon you; because also in the last days God sendeth His compassion on the earth, and wheresoever He findeth bowels of mercy, He dwelleth in him. For how much compassion a man hath upon his neighbours, so much also hath the Lord upon him. For when we went down into Egypt, Joseph bore no malice against us, and when he saw me he was filled with compassion. And looking towards him, do ye also, my children, approve yourselves without malice, and love one another; and reckon not each one the evil of his brother, for this breaketh unity, and divideth all kindred, and troubleth the soul: for he who beareth malice hath not bowels of mercy.

9. Mark the waters, that they flow together, and sweep along stones, trees, sand; but if they are divided into many streams, the earth sucketh them up, and they become of no account. So also shall ye be if ye be divided. Divide not yourselves into two heads, for everything which the Lord made hath but one head; He gave two shoulders, hands, feet, but all the members are subject unto the one head. I have learnt by the writing of my fathers, that in the last days ye will depart from the Lord, and be divided in Israel, and ye will follow two kings, and will work every abomination, and every idol will ye worship, and your enemies shall lead you captive, and ye shall dwell among the nations with all infirmities and tribulations and anguish of soul. And after these things ye will remember the Lord, and will repent, and He will lead you back; for He is

---

[1] Cam. MS. διὰ τραγλοκολπητῶν; Ox. MS. διὰ τρωγλοδυτῶν.   [2] [" Finis *non* determinat probitatem actus."]

merciful and full of compassion, not imputing evil to the sons of men, because they are flesh, and the spirits of error deceive them in all their doings. And after these things shall the Lord Himself arise to you,[1] the Light of righteousness, and healing[2] and compassion shall be upon His wings. He shall redeem all captivity of the sons of men from Beliar, and every spirit of error shall be trodden down. And He shall bring back all the nations to zeal for Him, and ye shall see God in the fashion of a man[3] whom the Lord shall choose, Jerusalem is His name. And again with the wickedness of your words will ye provoke Him to anger, and ye shall be cast away, even unto the time of consummation.

---

[1] Mal. iv. 2.
[2] The Ox. ms. reads: "And ye shall return from your land, and ye shall see the Lord in Jerusalem for His name's sake." [Heb. vii. 2. At least, SALEM is His name.]
[3] [Another of those unequivocal passages which refute Lardner's charge of "Unitarianism" in this book.]

10. And now, my children, grieve not that I am dying, nor be troubled in that I am passing away from you. For I shall arise once more in the midst of you, as a ruler in the midst of his sons; and I will rejoice in the midst of my tribe, as many as have kept the law of the Lord, and the commandments of Zebulun their father.[4] But upon the ungodly shall the Lord bring everlasting fire, and will destroy them throughout all generations. I am hastening away unto my rest, as did my fathers; but do ye fear the Lord your God with all your strength all the days of your life. And when he had said these things he fell calmly asleep, and his sons laid him in a coffin; and afterwards they carried him up to Hebron, and buried him with his fathers.

---

[4] [Ezek. xlviii. 26, 27. An important example of Hebrew exposition of this prophet.]

VII.—THE TESTAMENT OF DAN CONCERNING ANGER AND LYING.

1. THE record of the words of Dan, which he spake to his sons in his last days. In the hundred and twenty-fifth year of his life he called together his family, and said: Hearken to my words, ye sons of Dan; give heed to the words of the mouth of your father. I have proved in my heart, and in my whole life, that truth with just dealing is good and well-pleasing to God, and that lying and anger are evil, because they teach man all wickedness. I confess this day to you, my children, that in my heart I rejoiced concerning the death of Joseph, a true and good man; and I rejoiced at the selling of Joseph, because his father loved him more than us. For the spirit of jealousy and of vainglory said to me, Thou also art his son. And one of the spirits of Beliar wrought with me, saying, Take this sword, and with it slay Joseph; so shall thy father love thee when he is slain. This is the spirit of anger that counselled me, that even as a leopard devoureth a kid, so should I devour Joseph. But the God of Jacob our father gave him not over into my hands that I should find him alone, nor suffered me to work this iniquity, that two tribes should be destroyed in Israel.[1]

2. And now, my children, I am dying, and I tell you of a truth, that unless ye keep yourselves from the spirit of lying and of anger, and love truth and long-suffering, ye shall perish. There is blindness in anger, my children, and no wrathful man regardeth any person with truth: for though it be a father or a mother, he behaveth towards

---

[1] [The tribes of Ephraim and Manasseh.]

them as enemies; though it be a brother, he knoweth him not; though it be a prophet of the Lord, he disobeyeth him; though a righteous man, he regardeth him not; a friend he doth not acknowledge. For the spirit of anger encompasseth him with the nets of deceit, and blindeth his natural eyes, and through lying darkeneth his mind, and giveth him a sight of his own making. And wherewith encompasseth he his eyes? In hatred of heart; and he giveth him a heart of his own against his brother unto envy.

3. My children, mischievous is anger, for it becometh as a soul to the soul itself; and the body of the angry man it maketh its own, and over his soul it getteth the mastery, and it bestoweth upon the body its own power, that it may work all iniquity; and whenever the soul doeth aught, it justifieth what has been done, since it seeth not. Therefore he who is wrathful, if he be a mighty man, hath a treble might in his anger; one by the might and aid of his servants, and a second by his wrath, whereby he persuadeth and overcometh in injustice: and having a third of the nature of his own body, and of his own self working the evil. And though the wrathful man be weak, yet hath he a might twofold of that which is by nature; for wrath ever aideth such in mischief. This spirit goeth always with lying at the right hand of Satan, that his works may be wrought with cruelty and lying.

4. Understand ye therefore the might of wrath, that it is vain. For it first of all stingeth him in word: then by deeds it strengtheneth

him who is angry, and with bitter punishments disturbeth his mind, and so stirreth up with great wrath his soul. Therefore, when any one speaketh against you, be not [1] ye moved unto anger. And if any man praiseth you as good, be not lifted up nor elated, either to the feeling or showing of pleasure.[2] For first it pleaseth the hearing, and so stirreth up the understanding to understand the grounds for anger; and then, being wrathful, he thinketh that he is justly angry. If ye fall into any loss or ruin, my children, be not troubled; for this very spirit maketh men desire that which hath perished, in order that they may be inflamed by the desire. If ye suffer loss willingly, be not vexed, for from vexation he raiseth up wrath with lying. And wrath with lying is a twofold mischief;[3] and they speak one with another that they may disturb the mind; and when the soul is continually disturbed, the Lord departeth from it, and Beliar ruleth over it.

5. Observe, therefore, my children, the commandments of the Lord, and keep His law; and depart from wrath, and hate lying, that the Lord may dwell among you, and Beliar may flee from you. Speak truth each one with his neighbour, so shall ye not fall into lust and confusion; but ye shall be in peace, having the God of peace, so [4] shall no war prevail over you. Love the Lord through all your life, and one another with a true heart. For I know that in the last days ye will depart from the Lord, and will provoke Levi unto anger, and will fight against Judah; but ye shall not prevail against them. For an angel of the Lord shall guide them both; for by them shall Israel stand. And whensoever ye depart from the Lord, ye will walk in all evil, working the abominations of the Gentiles, going [5] astray with women of them that are ungodly; and the spirits of error shall work in you with all malice. For I have read in the book of Enoch the righteous, that your prince is Satan, and that all the spirits of fornication and pride shall be subject unto Levi, to lay a snare for the sons of Levi, to cause them to sin before the Lord. And my sons will draw near unto Levi, and sin with them in all things; and the sons of Judah will be covetous, plundering other men's goods like lions. Therefore shall ye be led away with them in captivity, and there shall ye receive all the plagues of Egypt, and all the malice of the Gentiles: and so, when ye return to the Lord, ye shall obtain mercy, and He shall bring you into His sanctuary, calling peace upon you; and there shall arise unto you from the tribe of Judah and of Levi the salvation of the

Lord;[6] and He shall make war against Beliar, and He shall give the vengeance of victory to our coasts. And the captivity shall He take from Beliar, even the souls of the saints, and shall turn disobedient hearts unto the Lord, and shall give to them who call upon Him everlasting peace; and the saints shall rest in Eden, and the righteous shall rejoice in the new Jerusalem, which shall be unto the glory of God for ever and ever. And no longer shall Jerusalem endure desolation, nor Israel be led captive; for the Lord shall be in the midst of her, dwelling among men,[7] even the Holy One of Israel reigning over them [8] in humility and in poverty;[9] and he who believeth on Him shall reign in truth in the heavens.

6. And now, my children, fear the Lord, and take heed unto yourselves of Satan and his spirits; and draw near unto God, and to the Angel [10] that intercedeth for you, for He is a Mediator between God and man for the peace of Israel. He shall stand up against the kingdom of the enemy; therefore is the enemy eager to destroy all that call upon the Lord. For he knoweth that in the day on which Israel shall believe,[11] the kingdom of the enemy shall be brought to an end; and the very angel of peace shall strengthen Israel, that it fall not into the extremity of evil. And it shall be in the time of the iniquity of Israel, that the Lord will depart from them, and will go after him that doeth His will, for unto none of His angels shall it be as unto him. And His name shall be in every place of Israel, and among the Gentiles — Saviour. Keep therefore yourselves, my children, from every evil work, and cast away wrath and all lying, and love truth and long-suffering; and the things which ye have heard from your father, do ye also impart to your children, that the Father of the Gentiles may receive you: for He is true and long-suffering, meek and lowly, and teacheth by His works the law of God. Depart, therefore, from all unrighteousness, and cleave unto the righteousness of the law of the Lord: and bury me near my fathers.

7. And when he had said these things he kissed them, and slept the long sleep.[12] And his sons buried him, and after that they carried up his bones to the side of Abraham, and Isaac, and Jacob. Nevertheless, as Dan had prophesied unto them that they should forget the law of their God, and should be alienated from the land of their inheritance, and from the race of Israel, and from their kindred, so also it came to pass.

---

1 The reading of the Ox. MS., μὴ κινεῖσθε, is to be taken.
2 Cam. MS. εἰς εἰδέαν; Ox. MS. εἰς ἀηδίαν.
3 Read κακόν.
4 The Ox. MS. omits from here to τοῖς ἔθνεσι Σωτήρ in c. 6.
5 Ἐκ τ ρεύοντες may be an error for ἐκπορνεύοντες, which Grabe wrongly gives as the reading of the Cam. MS.

6 [The root idea, p. 18, notes 5, 6, *supra*.]
7 Rev. xxi. 3.]
8 [Here is the Chiliasm of Barnabas, vol. i. p. 146.]
9 [That is, not with the glory of His throne above.]
10 Cf. Dorner, *Doctrine of the Person of Christ*, Introd., p. 15, Eng. transl.
11 [Rom. xi. 15.]
12 [See *Zebulun* 10, p. 25, *supra*.]

VIII. — THE TESTAMENT OF NAPHTALI CONCERNING NATURAL GOODNESS.

1. THE record of the testament of Naphtali, what things he ordained at the time of his death in the hundred and thirty-second year of his life. When his sons were gathered together in the seventh month, the fourth day of the month, he, being yet in good health, made them a feast and good cheer. And after he was awake in the morning, he said to them, I am dying; and they believed him not. And he blessed the Lord, and affirmed that after yesterday's feast he should die. He began then to say to his sons: Hear, my children; ye sons of Naphtali, hear the words of your father. I was born from Bilhah; and because Rachel dealt craftily, and gave Bilhah in place of herself to Jacob, and she bore me upon Rachel's lap, therefore was I called Naphtali.[1] And Rachel loved me because I was born upon her lap; and when I was of young and tender form, she was wont to kiss me, and say, Would that I might see a brother of thine from my own womb, like unto thee! whence also Joseph was like unto me in all things, according to the prayers of Rachel. Now my mother was Bilhah, daughter of Rotheus the brother of Deborah, Rebecca's nurse, and she was born on one and the self-same day with Rachel. And Rotheus was of the family of Abraham, a Chaldean, fearing God, free-born and noble; and he was taken captive, and was bought by Laban; and he gave him Aena his handmaid to wife, and she bore a daughter, and called her Zilpah, after the name of the village in which he had been taken captive. And next she bore Bilhah, saying, My daughter is eager after what is new, for immediately that she was born she was eager for the breast.

2. And since I was swift on my feet like a deer, my father Jacob appointed me for all errands and messages, and as a deer[2] did he give me his blessing. For as the potter knoweth the vessel, what it containeth, and bringeth clay thereto, so also doth the Lord make the body in accordance with the spirit, and according to the capacity of the body doth He implant the spirit, and the one is not deficient from the other by a third part of a hair; for by weight, and measure, and rule is every creature of the Most High.[3] And as the potter knoweth the use of each vessel, whereto it sufficeth, so also doth the Lord know the body, how far it is capable for goodness, and when it beginneth in evil; for there is no created thing and no thought which the Lord knoweth not, for He created every man

after His own image. As man's strength, so also is his work; and as his mind, so also is his work; and as his purpose, so also is his doing; as his heart, so also is his mouth; as his eye, so also is his sleep; as his soul, so also is his word, either in the law of the Lord or in the law of Beliar. And as there is a division between light and darkness, between seeing and hearing, so also is there a division between man and man, and between woman and woman; neither is it to be said that there is any superiority in anything, either of the face or of other like things.[4] For God made all things good in their order, the five senses in the head, and He joineth on the neck to the head, the hair also for comeliness, the heart moreover for understanding, the belly for the dividing of the stomach, the calamus[5] for health, the liver for wrath, the gall for bitterness, the spleen for laughter, the reins for craftiness, the loins for power, the ribs for containing, the back for strength, and so forth. So then, my children, be ye orderly unto good things in the fear of God, and do nothing disorderly in scorn or out of its due season. For if thou bid the eye to hear, it cannot; so neither in darkness can ye do the works of light.

3. Be ye not therefore eager to corrupt your doings through excess, or with empty words to deceive your souls; because if ye keep silence in purity of heart, ye shall be able to hold fast the will of God, and to cast away the will of the devil. Sun and moon and stars change not their order; so also ye shall not change the law of God in the disorderliness of your doings. Nations went astray, and forsook the Lord, and changed their order, and followed stones and stocks, following after spirits of error. But ye shall not be so, my children, recognising in the firmament, in the earth, and in the sea, and in all created things, the Lord who made them all, that ye become not as Sodom, which changed the order of its nature. In like manner also the Watchers[6] changed the order of their nature, whom also the Lord cursed at the flood, and for their sakes made desolate the earth, that it should be uninhabited and fruitless.

4. These things I say, my children, for I have read in the holy writing of Enoch that ye yourselves also will depart from the Lord, walking according to all wickedness of the Gentiles, and

---

[1] Gen. xxx. 8. Josephus, *Ant.*, i. 19. 7.
[2] Gen. xlix. 21.
[3] [Wis. xi. 20; Ecclus. xlii. 7.]

[4] The Greek text here is obviously corrupt, and doubtless one or two words are wanting. The reading of the Cam. MS. is, οὐκ ἔστιν εἰπεῖν ὅτι ἐν τῷ ἑνὶ τοῖς προσώποις ἢ τῶν ὁμοίων. In the Ox. MS. the passage is wanting.
[5] It seems very doubtful what is meant by κάλαμος here. I have thought it best, therefore, to leave the matter open. The Ox. MS punctuates στομάχου κάλ.
[6] Cf. *Reuben* 5 [note 3, p. 10, *supra*].

ye will do according to all the iniquity of Sodom. And the Lord will bring captivity upon you, and there shall ye serve your enemies, and ye shall be covered with all affliction and tribulation, until the Lord shall have consumed you all. And after that ye shall have been diminished and made few, ye will return and acknowledge the Lord your God ; and He will bring you back into your own land, according to His abundant mercy. And it shall be, after that they shall come into the land of their fathers, they will again forget the Lord and deal wickedly ; and the Lord shall scatter them upon the face of all the earth, until the compassion of the Lord shall come, a Man working righteousness and showing mercy unto all them that are afar off, and them that are near.

5. For in the fortieth year of my life, I saw *in a vision* that the sun and the moon were standing still on the Mount of Olives, at the east of Jerusalem. And behold Isaac, the father of my father, saith to us, Run and lay hold of them, each one according to his strength ; and he that seizeth them, his shall be the sun and the moon. And we all of us ran together, and Levi laid hold of the sun, and Judah outstripped the others and seized the moon, and they were both of them lifted up with them. And when Levi became as a sun, a certain young man gave to him twelve branches of palm ; and Judah was bright as the moon, and under his feet were twelve rays. And Levi and Judah ran, and laid hold each of the other. And, lo, a bull upon the earth, having two great horns, and an eagle's wings upon his back ; and we wished to seize him, but could not. For Joseph outstripped us, and took him, and ascended up with him on high. And I saw, for I was there, and behold a holy writing appeared to us, saying : Assyrians, Medes, Persians, Elamites, Gelachæans, Chaldeans, Syrians, shall possess in captivity the twelve tribes of Israel.

6. And again, after seven months, I saw our father Jacob standing by the sea of Jamnia, and we his sons were with him. And, behold, there came a ship sailing by, full of dried flesh, without sailors or pilot ; and there was written upon the ship, Jacob. And our father saith to us, Let us embark on our ship. And when we had gone on board, there arose a vehement storm, and a tempest of mighty wind ; and our father, who was holding the helm, flew away from us. And we, being tost with the tempest, were borne along over the sea ; and the ship was filled with water and beaten about with a mighty wave, so that it was well-nigh broken in pieces. And Joseph fled away upon a little boat, and we all were divided upon twelve boards, and Levi and Judah were together. We therefore all were scattered even unto afar off. Then Levi, girt about with sackcloth, prayed for us all unto the

Lord. And when the storm ceased, immediately the ship reached the land, as though in peace. And, lo, Jacob our father came, and we rejoiced with one accord.

7. These two dreams I told to my father ; and he said to me, These things must be fulfilled in their season, after that Israel hath endured many things. Then my father saith unto me, I believe that Joseph liveth, for I see always that the Lord numbereth him with you. And he said, weeping, Thou livest, Joseph, my child, and I behold thee not, and thou seest not Jacob that begat thee. And he caused us also to weep at these words of his, and I burned in my heart to declare that he had been sold, but I feared my brethren.

8. Behold, my children, I have shown unto you the last times, that all shall come to pass in Israel. Do ye also therefore charge your children that they be united to Levi and to Judah. For through Judah shall salvation arise unto Israel, and in Him shall Jacob be blessed. For through his tribe shall God be seen dwelling among men on the earth, to save the race of Israel, and He shall gather together the righteous from the Gentiles. If ye work that which is good, my children, both men and angels will bless you ; and God will be glorified through you among the Gentiles, and the devil will flee from you, and the wild beasts will fear you, and the angels will cleave to you. For as if a man rear up a child well, he hath a kindly remembrance thereof ; so also for a good work there is a good remembrance with God. But him who doeth not that which is good, men and angels shall curse, and God will be dishonoured among the heathen through him, and the devil maketh him his own as his peculiar instrument, and every wild beast shall master him, and the Lord will hate him. For the commandments of the law are twofold, and through prudence must they be fulfilled. For there is a season for a man to embrace his wife, and a season to abstain therefrom [1] for his prayer. So then there are two commandments ; and unless they be done in due order, they bring about sin. So also is it with the other commandments. Be ye therefore wise in God, and prudent, understanding the order of the commandments, and the laws of every work, that the Lord may love you.

9. And when he had charged them with many such words, he exhorted them that they should remove his bones to Hebron, and should bury him with his fathers. And when he had eaten and drunken with a merry heart, he covered his face and died. And his sons did according to all things whatsoever Naphtali their father had charged them.

---

1 [Eccles. iii. 5; 1 Cor. vii. 5.]

IX. — THE TESTAMENT OF GAD CONCERNING HATRED.

1. THE record of the testament of Gad, what things he spake unto his sons, in the hundred and twenty-seventh year of his life, saying : I was the seventh son born to Jacob, and I was valiant in keeping the flocks. I guarded at night the flock ; and whenever the lion came, or wolf, or leopard, or bear, or any wild beast against the fold, I pursued it, and with my hand seizing its foot, and whirling it round, I stunned it, and hurled it over two furlongs, and so killed it. Now Joseph was feeding the flock with us for about thirty days, and being tender, he fell sick by reason of the heat. And he returned to Hebron to his father, who made him lie down near him, because he loved him. And Joseph told our father that the sons of Zilpah and Bilhah were slaying the best of the beasts,[1] and devouring them without the knowledge of Judah and Reuben. For he saw that I delivered a lamb out of the mouth of the bear, and I put the bear to death ; and the lamb I slew, being grieved concerning it that it could not live, and we ate it, and he told our father. And I was wroth with Joseph for that thing until the day that he was sold into Egypt. And the spirit of hatred was in me, and I wished not either to see Joseph or to hear him. And he rebuked us to our faces for having eaten of the flock without Judah. And whatsoever things he told our father, he believed him.

2. I confess now my sin, my children, that oftentimes I wished to kill him, because I hated him to the death, and there were in no wise in me bowels of mercy towards him. Moreover, I hated him yet more because of his dreams ; and I would have devoured him out of the land of the living, even as a calf devoureth the grass from the earth. Therefore I and Judah sold him to the Ishmaelites for thirty[2] pieces of gold, and ten of them we hid, and showed the twenty to our brethren : and so through my covetousness I was fully bent on his destruction. And the God of my fathers delivered him from my hands, that I should not work iniquity in Israel.

3. And now, my children, hearken to the words of truth to work righteousness, and all the law of the Most High, and not go astray through the spirit of hatred, for it is evil in all the doings of men. Whatsoever a man doeth, that doth the hater abhor : though he worketh the law of the Lord, he praiseth him not ; though he feareth the Lord, and taketh pleasure in that which is righteous, he loveth him not : he dispraiseth the truth, he envieth him that ordereth his way aright, he delighteth in evil-speaking, he loveth arrogance, for hatred hath blinded his soul ; even as I also looked on Joseph.

4. Take heed therefore, my children, of hatred ; for it worketh iniquity against the Lord Himself : for it will not hear the words of His commandments concerning the loving of one's neighbour, and it sinneth against God. For if a brother stumble, immediately it wisheth to proclaim it to all men, and is urgent that he should be judged for it, and be punished and slain. And if it be a servant, it accuseth him to his master, and with all affliction it deviseth against him, if it be possible to slay him. For hatred worketh in envy, and it ever sickeneth with envy against them that prosper in well-doing, when it seeth or heareth thereof. For as love would even restore to life the dead, and would call back them that are condemned to die, so hatred would slay the living, and those that have offended in a small matter it would not suffer to live. For the spirit of hatred worketh together with Satan through hastiness[3] of spirit in all things unto men's death ; but the spirit of love worketh together with the law of God in long-suffering unto the salvation of men.[4]

5. Hatred is evil, because it continually abideth with lying, speaking against the truth ; and it maketh small things to be great, and giveth heed to darkness as to light, and calleth the sweet bitter, and teacheth slander, and war, and violence, and every excess of evil ; and it filleth the heart with devilish poison. And these things I say to you from experience, my children, that ye may flee hatred, and cleave to the love of the Lord. Righteousness casteth out hatred, humility destroyeth hatred. For he that is just and humble is ashamed to do wrong, being reproved not of another, but of his own heart, because the Lord vieweth his intent : he speaketh not against any man, because the fear of the Most High overcometh hatred. For, fearing lest he should offend the Lord, he will not do any wrong to any man, no, not even in thought. These things I learnt at last, after that I had repented concerning Joseph. For true repentance after a godly sort destroyeth unbelief, and driveth away the darkness, and enlighteneth the eyes, and giveth knowledge to the soul, and guideth the mind to salvation ; and those things which it hath not learnt from man, it knoweth through repentance. For God

---

[1] Cf. Targum Ps. Jon. of Gen. xxxvii. 2.
[2] The narrative of Genesis (xxxvii. 28) gives twenty pieces of silver; the LXX. twenty pieces of gold, with which latter agrees Josephus' μνῶν εἴκοσιν (Antiq., ii. 3. 3). [It is worthy of note that Judas took a meaner price for the "Son of Joseph."]

[3] For this unusual use of ὀλιγοψυχία, cf. Prov. xiv. 29, LXX. where there is the same contrast with μακροθυμία.
[4] [This passage is cited by Lardner as conspicuously fine.]

brought upon me a disease of the heart; and had not the prayers of Jacob my father intervened, it had hardly failed that my spirit had departed. For by what things a man transgresseth, by the same also is he punished.[1] For in that my heart was set mercilessly against Joseph, in my heart too I suffered mercilessly, and was judged for eleven months, for so long a time as I had been envious against Joseph until he was sold.

6. And now, my children, love ye each one his brother, and put away hatred from your hearts, loving one another in deed, and in word, and in thought of the soul. For in the presence of our father I spake peaceably with Joseph; and when I had gone out, the spirit of hatred darkened my mind, and moved my soul to slay him. [2] Love ye therefore one another from your hearts; and if a man sin against thee, tell him of it gently, and drive out the poison of hatred, and foster not guile in thy soul. And if he confess and repent, forgive him; and if he deny it, strive not with him, lest he swear, and thou sin doubly. Let not a stranger hear your secrets amid your striving, lest he hate and become thy enemy, and work great sin against thee; for ofttimes he will talk guilefully[3] with thee, or evilly overreach thee, taking his poison from himself. Therefore, if he deny it, and is convicted and put to shame, and is silenced, do not tempt him on. For he who denieth repenteth, so that he no more doeth wrong against thee; yea also, he will honour thee, and fear thee, and be at peace with thee. But if he be shameless, and abideth in his wrongdoing, even then forgive him from the heart, and give the vengeance to God.

7. If a man prospereth more than you, be not grieved, but pray also for him, that he may have perfect prosperity. For perchance it is expedient for you thus; and if he be further exalted, be not envious, remembering that all flesh shall die: and offer praise to God, who giveth things good and profitable to all men. Seek out the judgments of the Lord, and so shall thy mind rest and be at peace. And though a man become rich by evil means, even as Esau the brother of my father, be not jealous; but wait for the end of the Lord. For either He taketh His benefits away from the wicked, or leaveth them still to the repentant, or to the unrepentant reserveth punishment for ever. For the poor man who is free from envy, giving thanks to the Lord in all things, is rich among all men, because he hath not evil jealousy of men. Put away, therefore, hatred from your souls, and love one another with uprightness of heart.

8. And do ye also tell these things to your children, that they honour Judah and Levi, for from them shall the Lord raise up a Saviour to Israel.[4] For I know that at the last your children shall depart from them, and shall walk in all wickedness, and mischief, and corruption before the Lord. And when he had rested for a little while, he said again to them, My children, obey your father, and bury me near to my fathers. And he drew up his feet, and fell asleep in peace. And after five years they carried him up, and laid him in Hebron with his fathers.

---

[1] [Wis. xi. 16.]
[2] The Ox. MS. omits from here to the last clause of c. 7.
[3] For δολωφωνῆσαι, the reading of the Cam. MS. here, Grabe conjectured δολοφονῆσει. Probably δολοφωνῆσει is to be preferred.

[4] [The Virgin was the daughter of Judah, but had kinship with Levi. Luke i. 36. Compare Jer. xxxiii. 20-22.]

X. — THE TESTAMENT OF ASHER CONCERNING TWO FACES OF VICE AND VIRTUE.

1. The record of the testament of Asher, what things he spake to his sons in the hundred and twentieth year of his life. While he was still in health, he said to them: Hearken, ye children of Asher, to your father, and I will declare to you all that is right in the sight of God. Two ways[1] hath God given to the sons of men, and two minds, and two doings, and two places, and two ends. Therefore all things are by twos, one corresponding to the other. There are two ways of good and evil, with which are the two minds in our breasts distinguishing them. Therefore if the soul take pleasure in good, all its actions are in righteousness; and though it sin, it straightway repenteth. For, having his mind set upon righteousness, and casting away maliciousness, he straightway overthroweth the evil, and uprooteth the sin. But if his mind turn aside in evil, all his doings are in maliciousness, and he driveth away the good, and taketh unto him the evil, and is ruled by Beliar; and even though he work what is good, he perverteth it in evil. For whenever he beginneth as though to do good, bringeth the end of his doing to work evil, seeing that the treasure of the devil is filled with the poison of an evil spirit.

2. There is then, he saith, a soul which speaketh the good for the sake of the evil, and the end of the doing leadeth to mischief.[2] There is a man who showeth no compassion upon him

---

[1] [See the *Duæ Viæ*, vol. vii., p. 377, this series.]

[2] [This section is commended by Dr. Lardner.]

who serveth his turn in evil; and this thing hath two aspects, but the whole is evil. And there is a man that loveth him that worketh evil; he likewise dwelleth in evil, because he chooseth even to die in an evil cause for his sake: and concerning this it is clear that it hath two aspects, but the whole is an evil work. And though there is love, it is but wickedness concealing the evil, even as it beareth a name that seemeth good, but the end of the doing tendeth unto evil. Another stealeth, worketh unjustly, plundereth, defraudeth, and withal pitieth the poor: this, too, hath a twofold aspect, but the whole is evil. Defrauding his neighbour he provoketh God, and sweareth falsely against the Most High, and yet pitieth the poor: the Lord who commandeth the law he setteth at nought and provoketh, and refresheth the poor; he defileth the soul, and maketh gay the body; he killeth many, and he pitieth a few: and this, too, hath a twofold aspect. Another committeth adultery and fornication, and abstaineth from meats; yet in his fasting he worketh evil, and by his power and his wealth perverteth many, and out of his excessive wickedness worketh the commandments: this, too, hath a twofold aspect, but the whole is evil. Such men are as swine or hares;[1] for they are half clean, but in very deed are unclean. For God in the Heavenly[2] Tablets hath thus declared.

3. Do not ye therefore, my children, wear two faces like unto them, of goodness and of wickedness; but cleave unto goodness only, for in goodness doth God rest, and men desire it. From wickedness flee away, destroying the devil by your good works; for they that are double-faced serve not God, but their own lusts, so that they may please Beliar and men like unto themselves.

4. For good men, even they that are single of face, though they be thought by them that are double-faced to err, are just before God. For many in killing the wicked do two works, an evil by a good; but the whole is good, because he hath uprooted and destroyed that which is evil. One man hateth him that showeth mercy, and doeth wrong to the adulterer and the thief: this, too, is double-faced, but the whole work is good, because he followeth the Lord's example, in that he receiveth not that which seemeth good with that which is really bad.[3] Another desireth not to see good days with them that riot, lest he defile his mouth and pollute his soul: this, too, is double-faced, but the whole is good, for such men are like to stags and to hinds, because in a wild condition they seem to be unclean, but they are altogether clean; because they walk in a zeal for God, and abstain from what God also hateth and forbiddeth by His commandments, and they ward off the evil from the good.

5. Ye see therefore, my children, how that there are two in all things, one against the other, and the one is hidden by the other.[4] Death succeedeth to life, dishonour to glory, night to day, and darkness to light; and all things are under the day, and just things under life: wherefore also everlasting life awaiteth death. Nor may it be said that truth is a lie, nor right wrong; for all truth is under the light, even as all things are under God. All these things I proved in my life, and I wandered not from the truth of the Lord, and I searched out the commandments of the Most High, walking with singleness of face according to all my strength unto that which is good.

6. Take heed therefore ye also, my children, to the commandments of the Lord, following the truth with singleness of face, for they that are double-faced receive twofold punishment. Hate the spirits of error, which strive against men. Keep the law of the Lord, and give not heed unto evil as unto good; but look unto the thing that is good indeed, and keep it in all commandments of the Lord, having your conversation unto Him, and resting in Him: for the ends at which men aim do show their righteousness, and know the angels of the Lord from the angels of Satan. For if the soul depart troubled, it is tormented by the evil spirit which also it served in lusts and evil works; but if quietly and with joy it hath known the angel of peace, it shall comfort him in life.

7. Become not, my children, as Sodom, which knew not the angels of the Lord, and perished for ever. For I know that ye will sin, and ye shall be delivered into the hands of your enemies, and your land shall be made desolate, and ye shall be scattered unto the four corners of the earth. And ye shall be set at nought in the Dispersion as useless water, until the Most High shall visit the earth; and He shall come as man, with men eating and drinking, and in peace breaking the head of the dragon through water. He shall save Israel and all nations, God speaking in the person of man. Therefore tell ye these things to your children, that they disobey Him not. For I have read in the Heavenly Tablets that in very deed ye will disobey Him, and act ungodly against Him, not giving heed to the law of God, but to the commandments of men. Therefore shall ye be scattered as Gad and as Dan my brethren, who shall know not their own lands, tribe, and tongue. But the Lord will gather you together in faith through

---

[1] Cf. Lev. xi. 5, 7. [Vol. ii. p. 555, note 6.]
[2] Cf. *Levi* 5. [P. 13, note 8, *supra*.]
[3] [Matt. v. 45. This seems contradictory.]

[4] The Ox. MS. adds, ἐν τῇ εὐφροσύνῃ ἢ μέθη, ἐν τῷ γέλωτι τὸ πένθος, ἐν τῷ γάμῳ ἢ ἀκρασία. [Ecclus. xlii. 24.]

the hope of His tender mercy, for the sake of Abraham, and Isaac, and Jacob.[1]

8. And when he had said these things unto them, he charged them, saying: Bury me in Hebron. And he fell into a peaceful sleep, and died; and after this his sons did as he had charged them, and they carried him up and buried him with his fathers.

---

[1] [The Hebrew triad, father, son, and proceeding.]

XI. — THE TESTAMENT OF JOSEPH CONCERNING SOBRIETY.

1. THE record of the testament of Joseph. When he was about to die he called his sons and his brethren together, and said to them: My children and brethren, hearken to Joseph the beloved of Israel; give ear, my sons, unto your father. I have seen in my life envy and death, and I wandered not in the truth of the Lord. These my brethren hated me, and the Lord loved me: they wished to slay me, and the God of my fathers guarded me: they let me down into a pit, and the Most High brought me up again: I was sold for a slave, and the Lord made me free: I was taken into captivity, and His strong hand succoured me: I was kept in hunger, and the Lord Himself nourished me: I was alone, and God comforted me: I was sick, and the Most High visited me: I was in prison, and the Saviour showed favour unto me; in bonds, and He released me; amid slanders, and He pleaded my cause; amid bitter words of the Egyptians, and He rescued me; amid envy and guile, and He exalted me.

2. And thus Potiphar[1] the chief cook[2] of Pharaoh entrusted to me his house, and I struggled against a shameless woman, urging me to transgress with her; but the God of Israel my father guarded me from the burning flame. I was cast into prison, I was beaten, I was mocked; and the Lord granted me to find pity in the sight of the keeper of the prison. For He will in no wise forsake them that fear Him, neither in darkness, nor in bonds, nor in tribulations, nor in necessities. For not as man is God ashamed, nor as the son of man is He afraid, nor as one that is earth-born is He weak, or can He be thrust aside; but in all places is He at hand, and in divers ways doth He comfort, departing for a little to try the purpose of the soul. In ten temptations He showed me approved, and in all of them I endured; for endurance is a mighty charm, and patience giveth many good things.

3. How often did the Egyptian threaten me with death! How often did she give me over to punishment, and then call me back, and threaten me when I would not company with her! And she said to me, Thou shalt be lord of me, and all that is mine, if thou wilt give thyself unto me, and thou shalt be as our master. Therefore I remembered the words of the fathers of my father Jacob, and I entered into my chamber[3] and prayed unto the Lord; and I fasted in those seven years, and I appeared to my master as one living delicately, for they that fast for God's sake receive beauty of face.[4] And if one gave me wine, I drank it not; and I fasted for three days, and took my food and gave it to the poor and sick. And I sought the Lord early, and wept for the Egyptian woman of Memphis, for very unceasingly did she trouble me, and at night she came to me under the pretence of visiting me; and at first, because she had no male child, she feigned to count me as a son. And I prayed unto the Lord, and she bare a male child; therefore for a time she embraced me as a son, and I knew it not. Last of all, she sought to draw me into fornication. And when I perceived it, I sorrowed even unto death; and when she had gone out I came to myself, and I lamented for her many days, because I saw her guile and her deceit. And I declared unto her the words of the Most High, if haply she would turn from her evil lust.

4. How often has she fawned upon me with words as a holy man, with guile in her talk, praising my chastity before her husband, while desiring to destroy me when we were alone. She lauded me openly as chaste, and in secret she said unto me, Fear not my husband; for he is persuaded concerning thy chastity, so that even should one tell him concerning us he would in no wise believe. For all these things I lay upon the ground in sackcloth, and I besought God that the Lord would deliver me from the Egyptian. And when she prevailed nothing, she came again to me under the plea of instruction, that she might know the word of the Lord. And she said unto me, If thou willest that I should leave my idols, be persuaded by me, and I will persuade my husband to depart from his idols, and we will walk in the law of thy Lord. And I said unto

---

[1] The Greek spelling here is Φωτιμάρ, in the later chapters Πετεφρίς (Πεντεφρῆς, Cd. Oxon.). The former is more like the Hebrew, the latter really the LXX. spelling, Πετεφρῆς. We may perhaps see herein a trace of a double authorship in the *Test. Joseph.*

[2] Cf. Gen. xxxix. 1, LXX., and Josephus (*Antiq.*, ii. 4. 1), who calls Potiphar μαγειρων ὁ βασιλεύς. The view of the Eng. ver. is most probably correct, though we find טבח used in the sense of cook in 1 Sam. ix. 23.

[3] [Matt. vi. 6. He veils the quotation by a fiction, as to authorship, to support the plan of his work.]

[4] [Dan. i. 15.]

her, The Lord willeth not that those who reverence Him should be in uncleanness, nor doth He take pleasure in them that commit adultery. And she held her peace, longing to accomplish her evil desire. And I gave myself yet more to fasting and prayer, that the Lord should deliver me from her.

5. And again at another time she said unto me, If thou wilt not commit adultery, I will kill my husband, and so will I lawfully take thee to be my husband. I therefore, when I heard this, rent my garment, and said, Woman, reverence the Lord, and do not this evil deed, lest thou be utterly destroyed; for I will declare thy ungodly thought unto all men. She therefore, being afraid, besought that I would declare to no one her wickedness. And she departed, soothing me with gifts, and sending to me every delight of the sons of men.

6. And she sendeth to me food sprinkled with enchantments. And when the eunuch who brought it came, I looked up and beheld a terrible man giving me with the dish a sword, and I perceived that her scheme was for the deception of my soul. And when he had gone out I wept, nor did I taste that or any other of her food. So then after one day she came to me and observed the food, and said unto me, What is this, that thou hast not eaten of the food? And I said unto her, It is because thou filledst it with death; and how saidst thou, I come not near to idols, but to the Lord alone? Now therefore know that the God of my father hath revealed unto me by an angel thy wickedness, and I have kept it to convict thee, if haply thou mayest see it and repent. But that thou mayest learn that the wickedness of the ungodly hath no power over them that reverence God in chastity, I took it and ate it before her, saying, The God of my fathers and the Angel of Abraham shall be with me. And she fell upon her face at my feet, and wept; and I raised her up and admonished her, and she promised to do this iniquity no more.

7. But because her heart was set upon me to commit lewdness, she sighed, and her countenance fell. And when her husband saw her, he said unto her, Why is thy countenance fallen? And she said, I have a pain at my heart, and the groanings of my spirit do oppress me; and so he comforted her who was not sick. Then she rushed in to me while her husband was yet without, and said unto me, I will hang myself, or cast myself into a well or over a cliff, if thou wilt not consent unto me. And when I saw the spirit of Beliar was troubling her, I prayed unto the Lord, and said unto her, Why art thou troubled and disturbed, blinded in sins? Remember that if thou killest thyself, Sethon, the concubine of thy husband, thy rival, will beat thy children, and will destroy thy memorial from off the earth.

And she said unto me, Lo then thou lovest me; this alone is sufficient for me, that thou carest for my life and my children: I have expectation that I shall enjoy my desire. And she knew not that because of my God ·I spake thus, and not because of her. For if a man hath fallen before the passion of a wicked desire, then by that hath he become enslaved, even as also was she. And if he hear any good thing with regard to the passion whereby he is vanquished, he receiveth it unto his wicked desire.

8. I declare unto you, my children, that it was about the sixth hour when she departed from me; and I knelt before the Lord all that day, and continued all the night; and about dawn I rose up weeping, and praying for a release from the Egyptian. At last, then, she laid hold of my garments, forcibly dragging me to have connection with her. When, therefore, I saw that in her madness she was forcibly holding my garments, I fled away naked. And she falsely accused me to her husband, and the Egyptian cast me into the prison in his house; and on the morrow, having scourged me, the Egyptian[1] sent me into the prison in his house. When, therefore, I was in fetters, the Egyptian woman fell sick from her vexation, and listened to me how I sang praises unto the Lord while I was in the abode of darkness, and with glad voice rejoiced and glorified my God only because by a pretext I had been rid of the Egyptian woman.

9. How often hath she sent unto me, saying, Consent to fulfil my desire, and I will release thee from thy bonds, and I will free thee from the darkness! And not even in thoughts did I incline unto her. For God loveth him who in a den of darkness fasteth with chastity, rather than him who in secret chambers liveth delicately without restraint. And whosoever liveth in chastity, and desireth also glory, and if the Most High knoweth that it is expedient for him, He bestoweth this also upon him, even as upon me. How often, though she were sick, did she come down to me at unlooked-for times, and listened to my voice as I prayed! And when I heard her groanings I held my peace. For when I was in her house she was wont to bare her arms, and breasts, and legs, that I might fall before her; for she was very beautiful, splendidly adorned for my deception. And the Lord guarded me from her devices.[2]

10. Ye see therefore, my children, how great things patience worketh, and prayer with fasting. And if ye therefore follow after sobriety and purity in patience and humility of heart, the Lord will dwell among you, because He loveth sobriety.

---

1 This repetition of a clause seems like the slip of a copyist. The Ox. MS. reads, εἰς τὴν εἱρκτὴν τοῦ Φαραώ.
2 [To this section Lardner takes exception, as unbecoming to the gravity of Joseph.]

And wheresoever the Most High dwelleth, even though a man fall into envy, or slavery, or slander, the Lord who dwelleth in him, for his sobriety's sake not only delivereth him from evil, but also exalteth and glorifieth him, even as me. For in every way the man is guarded, whether in deed, or in word, or in thought. My brethren know how my father loved me, and I was not exalted in my heart; although I was a child, I had the fear of God in my thoughts. For I knew that all things should pass away, and I kept myself within bounds, and I honoured my brethren; and through fear of them I held my peace when I was sold, and revealed not my family to the Ishmaelites, that I was the son of Jacob, a great man and a mighty.

11. Do ye also, therefore, have the fear of God in your works, and honour your brethren. For every one who worketh the law of the Lord shall be loved by Him. And when I came to the Indocolpitæ with the Ishmaelites, they asked me, and I said that I was a slave from their house, that I might not put my brethren to shame. And the eldest of them said unto me, Thou art not a slave, for even thy appearance doth make it manifest concerning thee. And he threatened me even unto death. But I said that I was their slave. Now when we came into Egypt, they strove concerning me, which of them should buy me and take me. Therefore it seemed good to all that I should remain in Egypt with a merchant of their trade, until they should return bringing merchandise. And the Lord gave me favour in the eyes of the merchant, and he entrusted unto me his house. And the Lord blessed him by my means, and increased him in silver and gold, and I was with him three months and five days.

12. About that time the Memphian wife of Potiphar passed by with great pomp, and cast her eyes upon me, because her eunuchs told her concerning me. And she told her husband concerning the merchant, that he had become rich by means of a young Hebrew, saying, And they say that men have indeed stolen him out of the land of Canaan. Now therefore execute judgment with him, and take away the youth to be thy steward; so shall the God of the Hebrews bless thee, for grace from heaven is upon him.

13. And Potiphar was persuaded by her words, and commanded the merchant to be brought, and said unto him, What is this that I hear, that thou stealest souls out of the land of the Hebrews, and sellest them for slaves? The merchant therefore fell upon his face, and besought him, saying, I beseech thee, my lord, I know not what thou sayest. And he said, Whence then is thy Hebrew servant? And he said, The Ishmaelites entrusted him to me until they should return. And he believed him not, but commanded him to be stripped and beaten. And when he persisted, Potiphar said, Let the youth be brought. And when I was brought in, I did obeisance to the chief of the eunuchs — for he was third in rank with Pharaoh, being chief of all the eunuchs, and having wives and children and concubines. And he took me apart from him, and said unto me, Art thou a slave or free? And I said, A slave. And he said unto me, Whose slave art thou? And I said unto him, The Ishmaelites'. And again he said unto me, How becamest thou their slave? And I said, They bought me out of the land of Canaan. And he believed me not, and said, Thou liest: and he commanded me to be stripped and beaten.

14. Now the Memphian woman was looking through a window while I was being beaten, and she sent unto her husband, saying, Thy judgment is unjust; for thou dost even punish a free man who hath been stolen, as though he were a transgressor. And when I gave no other answer though I was beaten, he commanded that we should be kept in guard, until, said he, the owners of the boy shall come. And his wife said unto him, Wherefore dost thou detain in captivity this noble child, who ought rather to be set at liberty, and wait upon thee? For she wished to see me in desire of sin, and I was ignorant concerning all these things. Then said he to his wife, It is not the custom of the Egyptians to take away that which belongeth to others before proof is given. This he said concerning the merchant, and concerning me, that I must be imprisoned.

15. Now, after four and twenty days came the Ishmaelites; and having heard that Jacob my father was mourning because of me, they said unto me, How is it that thou saidst that thou wert a slave? and lo, we have learnt that thou art the son of a mighty man in the land of Canaan, and thy father grieveth for thee in sackcloth. And again I would have wept, but I restrained myself, that I should not put my brethren to shame. And I said, I know not, I am a slave. Then they take counsel to sell me, that I should not be found in their hands. For they feared Jacob, lest he should work upon them a deadly vengeance. For it had been heard that he was mighty with the Lord and with men. Then said the merchant unto them, Release me from the judgment of Potiphar. They therefore came and asked for me, saying, He was bought by us with money. And he sent us away.

16. Now the Memphian woman pointed me out to her husband, that he should buy me; for I hear, said she, that they are selling him. And she sent a eunuch to the Ishmaelites, and asked them to sell me; and since he was not willing to traffic with them, he returned. So when the

eunuch had made trial of them, he made known to his mistress that they asked a large price for their slave. And she sent another eunuch, saying, Even though they demand two minæ of gold, take heed not to spare the gold ; only buy the boy, and bring him hither. And he gave them eighty pieces of gold for me, and told his mistress that a hundred had been given for me. And when I saw it I held my peace, that the eunuch should not be punished.

17. Ye see, my children, what great things I endured that I should not put my brethren to shame. Do ye also love one another, and with long-suffering hide ye one another's faults. For God delighteth in the unity of brethren, and in the purpose of a heart approved unto love. And when my brethren came into Egypt, and learnt that I returned their money unto them, and upbraided them not, yea, that I even comforted them, and after the death of Jacob I loved them more abundantly, and all things whatsoever he commanded I did very abundantly, then they marvelled. For I suffered them not to be afflicted even unto the smallest matter ; and all that was in my hand I gave unto them. Their children were my children, and my children were as their servants ; their life was my life, and all their suffering was my suffering, and all their sickness was my infirmity. My land was their land, my counsel their counsel, and I exalted not myself among them in arrogance because of my worldly glory, but I was among them as one of the least.

18. If ye also therefore walk in the commandments of the Lord, my children, He will exalt you there, and will bless you with good things for ever and ever. And if any one seeketh to do evil unto you, do ye by well-doing pray for him, and ye shall be redeemed of the Lord from all evil. For, behold, ye see that through long-suffering I took unto wife even the daughter of my [1] master. And a hundred talents of gold were given me with her ; for the Lord made them to serve me. And He gave me also beauty as a flower above the beautiful ones of Israel ; and He preserved me unto old age in strength

and in beauty, because I was like in all things to Jacob.

19. Hear ye also, my children, the visions which I saw. There were twelve deer feeding, and the nine were divided and scattered in the land, likewise also the three. And I saw that from Judah was born a virgin wearing a linen [2] garment, and from her went forth a Lamb, without spot, and on His left hand there was as it were a lion ; and all the beasts rushed against Him, and the lamb overcame them, and destroyed them, and trod them under foot. And because of Him the angels rejoiced, and men, and all the earth. And these things shall take place in their season, in the last days. Do ye therefore, my children, observe the commandments of the Lord, and honour Judah and Levi ; for from them shall arise unto you the Lamb of God, by grace saving all the Gentiles and Israel. For His kingdom is an everlasting kingdom, which shall not be shaken ; but my kingdom among you shall come to an end as a watcher's [3] hammock, which after the summer will not appear.

20. I know that after my death the Egyptians will afflict you, but God will undertake your cause, and will bring you into that which He promised to your fathers. But carry ye up my bones with you ; [4] for when my bones are taken up, the Lord will be with you in light, and Beliar shall be in darkness with the Egyptians. And carry ye up Zilpah your mother, and lay her near Bilhah, by the hippodrome, by the side of Rachel.[5] And when he had said these things, he stretched out his feet, and slept the long sleep. And all Israel bewailed him, and all Egypt, with a great lamentation. For he felt even for the Egyptians even as his own members, and showed them kindness, aiding them in every work, and counsel, and matter.

---

[1] Another account is given in the *Targ. Ps. Jon.* of Gen. xli. 45, "And he gave him to wife Asenath, whom Dinah bare to Shechem: and the wife of Potipherah prince of Tanes brought up."

[2] This wearing of a linen garment would seem to imply a connection with the priestly tribe. St. Luke (i. 36) indeed calls the Virgin the kinswoman of Elisabeth. On this tendency to associate the old sacerdotal tribe with the new royalty of Messiah, cf., e.g., *Protevangel. Jacobi*, cc. 6, 7, 9; Augustine. *contra Faustum*, xxiii. 4; Epiphanius, *Hær.*, lxxviii. 13. [See *Reuben*, sec. 6, p. 10, *supra*.]

[3] Isa. i. 8, xxiv. 20.

[4] Cf. *Test. Simeon* 8, and *Jubilees* 46. The account of Joseph's burial in the *Targ. Ps. Jon.* on Gen. l. 26 is: "And Joseph died, a hundred and ten years old; and they embalmed him, and placed him in a coffin, and sank him in the middle of the Nile of Egypt."

[5] Cf. Gen. xlviii. 7, LXX.

XII. — THE TESTAMENT OF BENJAMIN CONCERNING A PURE MIND.

1. THE record of the words of Benjamin, which he set forth to his sons, after he had lived a hundred and twenty years. And he kissed them, and said : As Isaac was born to Abraham in his hundredth year, so also was I to Jacob. Now since Rachel died in giving me birth, I had no milk ; therefore I was suckled by Bilhah her handmaid. For Rachel remained barren for twelve years after that she had borne Joseph : and she prayed the Lord with fasting twelve days, and she conceived and bare me. For our father loved Rachel dearly, and prayed that he

might see two sons born from her : therefore was
I called the son of days, which is Benjamin.¹

2. When therefore I went into Egypt, and
Joseph my brother recognised me, he said unto
me, What did they tell my father in that they
sold me? And I said unto him, They dabbled
thy coat with blood and sent it, and said, Look
if this is the coat of thy son. And he said to
me, Even so, brother ; for when the Ishmaelites
took me, one of them stripped off my coat, and
gave me a girdle, and scourged me, and bade
me run. And as he went away to hide my garment, a lion met him, and slew him ; and so his
fellows were afraid, and sold me to their companions.

3. Do ye also therefore, my children, love the
Lord God of heaven, and keep His commandments, and be followers of the good and holy
man Joseph ; and let your mind be unto good,
even as ye know me. He that hath his mind
good seeth all things rightly. Fear ye the Lord,
and love your neighbour ; and even though the
spirits of Beliar allure you into all troublous
wickedness, yet shall no troublous wickedness
have dominion over you, even as it had not over
Joseph my brother. How many men wished to
slay him, and God shielded him ! For he that
feareth God and loveth his neighbour cannot be
smitten by Beliar's spirit of the air, being shielded
by the fear of God ; nor can he be ruled over by
the device of men or of beasts, for he is aided
by the love of the Lord which he hath towards
his neighbour. For he even besought our father
Jacob that he would pray for our brethren, that
the Lord would not impute to them the evil
that they devised concerning Joseph. And thus
Jacob cried out, My child Joseph, thou hast prevailed over the bowels of thy father Jacob. And
he embraced him, and kissed him for two hours,
saying, In thee shall be fulfilled the prophecy of
heaven concerning the Lamb of God, even the
Saviour of the world, that spotless shall He be
delivered up for transgressors, and sinless² shall
He be put to death for ungodly men in the blood
of the covenant, for the salvation³ of the Gentiles
and of Israel, and shall destroy Beliar, and them
that serve him.

4. Know ye, my children, the end of the good
man ? Be followers of his compassion in a good
mind, that ye also may wear crowns of glory.
The good man hath not a dark eye ; for he
showeth mercy to all men, even though they be
sinners, even though they devise evil concerning

him. So he that doeth good overcometh the
evil, being shielded by Him that is good ; and
he loveth the righteous as his own soul. If any
one is glorified, he envieth him not ; if any one
is enriched, he is not jealous ; if any one is valiant, he praiseth him ; he trusteth and laudeth
him that is sober-minded ; he showeth mercy to
the poor ; he is kindly disposed toward the
weak ; he singeth the praises of God ; as for him
who hath the fear of God, he protecteth him as
with a shield ; him that loveth God he aideth ;
him that rejecteth the Most High he admon-
isheth and turneth back ; and him that hath the
grace of a good spirit, he loveth even as his own
soul.

5. If ye have a good mind, my children, then
will both wicked men be at peace with you, and
the profligate will reverence you and turn unto
good ; and the covetous shall not only cease from
their inordinate desire, but shall even give the
fruits of their covetousness to them that are afflicted. If ye do well, even the unclean spirits
shall flee from you ; yea, the very beasts shall flee
from you in dread. For where the reverence for
good works is present unto the mind, darkness
fleeth away from him. For if any one is injurious to a holy man, he repenteth ; for the holy
man showeth pity on his reviler, and holdeth his
peace. And if any one betray a righteous soul,
and the righteous man, though praying, be humbled for a little while, yet not long after he
appeareth far more glorious, even as was Joseph
my brother.

6. The mind of the good man is not in the
power of the deceit of the spirit of Beliar, for
the angel of peace guideth his soul. He gazeth
not passionately on corruptible things, nor gath-
ereth together riches unto desire of pleasure ;
he delighteth not in pleasure, he hurteth not his
neighbour, he pampereth not himself with food,
he erreth not in the pride of his eyes, for the
Lord is his portion. The good mind admitteth
not the glory and dishonour of men, neither
knoweth it any guile or lie, fighting or reviling ;
for the Lord dwelleth in him and lighteth up his
soul, and he rejoiceth towards all men at every
time. The good mind hath not two tongues, of
blessing and of cursing, of insult and of honour,
of sorrow and of joy, of quietness and of trouble, of hypocrisy and of truth, of poverty and of
wealth ; but it hath one disposition, pure and un-
corrupt, concerning all men. It hath no double
sight,⁴ nor double hearing ; for in everything
which he doeth, or speaketh, or seeth, he
knoweth that the Lord watcheth his soul, and
he cleanseth his mind that he be not condemned
by God and men. But of Beliar every work is
twofold, and hath no singleness.

---

¹ The ordinary theory as to the meaning of Benjamin is comparatively late, and seems doubtful. The *Targum Jerushalmi* (on
Gen. xxxv. 18), and the *Breshith Rabba*, § 82, make Benjamin and
Benoni synonymous. Cf. Josephus, *Antiq.*, i. 21. 3; Cyril, *Glaph.
in Gen.*, lib. iv. With the view mentioned in the text, cf. Arethas on
Rev. vii. 8 (Cramer's *Catena*, viii. 289).
² This would seem to be the earliest instance of the application of
the word ἀναμάρτητος to our Lord.
³ [How could any Christian more fully testify to the Nicene
Faith? So the *Gloria in Excelsis*.]

⁴ [Matt. vi. 22; Luke xi. 34.]

7. Flee ye therefore, my children, the evil-doing of Beliar; for it giveth a sword to them that obeyeth, and the sword is the mother of seven evils. First the mind conceiveth through Beliar, and first there is envy; secondly, desperation; thirdly, tribulation; fourthly, captivity; fifthly, neediness; sixthly, trouble; seventhly, desolation. Therefore also Cain is delivered over to seven vengeances by God, for in every hundred years the Lord brought one plague upon him. Two hundred years he suffered, and in the nine hundredth year he was brought to desolation at the flood, for Abel his righteous brother's sake. In seven[1] hundred years was Cain judged, and Lamech in seventy times seven; because for ever those who are likened unto Cain in envy unto hatred of brethren shall be judged with the same punishment.

8. Do ye also therefore, my children, flee ill-doing, envy, and hatred of brethren, and cleave to goodness and love. He that hath a pure mind in love, looketh not after a woman unto fornication; for he hath no defilement in his heart, because the Spirit of God resteth in him. For as the sun is not defiled by shining over dung and mire, but rather drieth up both and driveth away the ill smell; so also the pure mind, constrained among the defilements of the earth, rather edifieth, and itself suffereth no defilement.

9. Now I suppose, from the words of the righteous Enoch, that there will be also evil-doings among you: for ye will commit fornication with the fornication of Sodom, and shall perish all save a few, and will multiply inordinate lusts with women; and the kingdom of the Lord shall not be among you, for forthwith He will take it away. Nevertheless the temple of God shall be built in your portion, and shall be glorious among you. For He shall take it, and the twelve tribes shall be gathered together there, and all the Gentiles, until the Most High shall send forth His salvation in the visitation of His only-begotten one. And He shall enter into the front[2] of the temple, and there shall the Lord be treated with outrage, and He shall be lifted up upon a tree. And the veil of the temple shall be rent, and the Spirit of God shall descend upon the Gentiles as fire poured forth. And He shall arise from the grave, and shall ascend from earth into heaven: and I know how lowly He shall be upon the earth, and how glorious in the heaven.

10. Now when Joseph was in Egypt, I longed to see his visage and the form of his countenance; and through the prayers of Jacob my father I saw him, while awake in the daytime, in his full and perfect shape. Know ye therefore, my children, that I am dying. Work therefore truth

and righteousness each one with his neighbour, and judgment unto faithful doing, and keep the law of the Lord and His commandments; for these things do I teach you instead of all inheritance. Do ye also therefore give them to your children for an everlasting possession; for so did both Abraham, and Isaac, and Jacob. All these things they gave us for an inheritance, saying, Keep the commandments of God until the Lord shall reveal His salvation to all nations. Then shall ye see Enoch, Noah, and Shem, and Abraham, and Isaac, and Jacob, arising on the right hand in gladness. Then shall we also arise, each one over our tribe, worshipping the King of heaven, who appeared upon the earth in the form of a man of humility. And as many as believed on Him on the earth shall rejoice with Him;[3] and then shall all men arise, some unto glory and some unto shame. And the Lord shall judge Israel first, even for the wrong they did unto Him; for when He appeared as a deliverer, God in the flesh, they believed Him not. And then shall He judge all the Gentiles, as many as believed Him not when He appeared upon earth. And He shall reprove Israel among the chosen ones of the Gentiles, even as He reproved Esau among the Midianites, who deceived their brethren, so that they fell into fornication and idolatry; and they were alienated from God, and became as they that were no children in the portion of them that fear the Lord. But if ye walk in holiness in the presence of the Lord, ye shall dwell in hope again in me, and all Israel shall be gathered unto the Lord.

11. And I shall no longer be called a ravening wolf[4] on account of your ravages, but a worker of the Lord, distributing food to them that work what is good. And one[5] shall rise up from my seed in the latter times, beloved of the Lord, hearing upon the earth His voice, enlightening with new knowledge all the Gentiles, bursting in upon Israel for salvation with the light of knowledge, and tearing it away from it like a wolf, and giving it to the synagogue of the Gentiles. And until the consummation of the ages shall he be in the synagogues of the Gentiles, and among their rulers, as a strain of music in the mouth of all;[6] and he shall be inscribed in the holy books, both his work and his word, and he shall be a chosen one of God for ever; and because of him my father Jacob instructed me, saying, He shall fill up that which lacketh of thy tribe.

---

[1] For ἑπτακοσίοις ἔτεσιν the Ox. MS. reads simply ἑπτά.
[2] This would seem to be the meaning of πρῶτος ναός.

[3] [Rev. xx. 5, 6. See p. 25, note 4, supra.]
[4] Gen. xlix. 27. This passage, referring to St. Paul (who was of the tribe of Benjamin, Rom. xi. 1, Phil. iii. 5), is quoted by Tertullian, Adversus Marcionem, v. 1. [See vol. iii. p. 430, this series.]
[5] Compare Scorpiace, cap. 13 [with reference to Gen. xxv. 34 and xxvii. 25, vol. iii. p. 646, this series. Lardner adds Origen, Hom. in Ezech., iv. tom. iii. p. 731; Theodoret, in Gen. Quæst., cx. tom. i. p. 77; and Augustine, Serm., 279 (and passim), tom. v. ed. Benedict.].
[6] [" Mel in ore, melos in aure, melodia in corde."—St. Bernard.]

12. And when he finished his words, he said: I charge you, my children, carry up my bones out of Egypt, and bury me at Hebron, near my fathers. So Benjamin died a hundred and twenty-five years old, in a good old age, and they placed him in a coffin. And in the ninety-first year of the departure of the children of Israel from Egypt, they and their brethren brought up the bones of their fathers secretly in a place which is called Canaan; and they buried them in Hebron, by the feet of their fathers. And they returned from the land of Canaan, and dwelt in Egypt until the day of their departing from the land of Egypt.

NOTE BY THE AMERICAN EDITOR.

I HAD prepared annotations for these pages which I find will require more space than this overloaded volume can afford. Let me indicate some sources of information which the student may find convenient. Thus, in Liddon's *Bampton Lecture* (4th ed., London, 1869), consult p. 71 for remarks on Philo and Alexandrian Jews; see also p. 91. Concerning the "Book of Enoch," pp. 7 and 302; see Westcott, *Study of the Gospels* (London, 1867), p. 109, a reference to the *Book of Jubilees*, and its lack of reference to Messiah. See Jewish doctrine of the Messiah, pp. 86, 143, 151; the "Book of Henoch," pp. 69, 93, 101; apocryphal words of Jews, p. 428. He places the "Book of Henoch" earlier than the "Book of Jubilees," and the "Twelve Patriarchs" after that. Compare Westcott's *Historic Faith* (London, 1883), a quotation from Goldwin Smith, on "the blood of Christ," note 8, p. 237.

I cannot forbear to note, among useful suggestions in these *Testaments*, that (on p. 11) of the share of Simeon in the persecution of Joseph. It explains the real purpose of Joseph in selecting Simeon as the hostage to be left in Egypt (Gen. xlii. 21–24.) Joseph heard the mutual reproaches of his brothers, and foresaw that Simeon would be made to suffer as most guilty: so he was withdrawn. Again, a like anxiety (Gen. xlv. 2) appears when Simeon was sent back with them to his father. Other suggestions may be noted as substantially illustrating the sacred narrative.

EXCERPTS OF THEODOTUS

OR

SELECTIONS FROM THE PROPHETIC SCRIPTURES

[TRANSLATED BY THE REV. WILLIAM WILSON, M.A.]

INTRODUCTORY NOTICE

TO

EXCERPTS OF THEODOTUS; OR, SELECTIONS FROM THE PROPHETIC SCRIPTURES.

WE may thank Mr. Wilson, the translator, for separating this collection, absolutely, from the works of Clement of Alexandria, to which it has been made an appendix.   The reference to "our Pantænus" gives the only colour for such a collocation with so great a name.   It is the work of a Montanist, perhaps, who may have had some relations with the Alexandrian school; but it is hard to say precisely who, of three or four named Theodotus (all heretics), may have made the compilation, more especially because disjointed and contradictory fragments seem mixed up in it as it is commonly edited.   Dupin (perhaps too readily copying Valesius) appears to think Clement may have been the compiler, but that, like the *Hypotyposes*, the work was the product of days when he was imperfectly educated in Christian truth.   It seems to me more reasonable to conclude that these excerpts, and what goes by the name of *Fragments from the Hypotyposes*, are alike corrupt or forged documents, for which Clement's name has been borrowed, to give them some credit; and I can desire no better authority for this opinion than that of Jeremiah Jones, with the arguments to be found in his learned work on the *Canon.*[1]

The wretched performance, therefore, is valuable chiefly as illustrating certain heresies of the second century; but, incidentally, it is of considerable importance as confirming the orthodox writers in those books and doctrines to which it bears witness in coincidence with them.

I regret that the Edinburgh editors give us not a line of information as to their estimate of these extracts, or concerning authorship and like matters of interest and natural curiosity.

---

[1] Vol. i. pp. 371-376.   These *Selections* are often quoted as "Eclogues."

EXCERPTS OF THEODOTUS [1]

OR

SELECTIONS FROM THE PROPHETIC SCRIPTURES [2]

I. THOSE around Sedrach, Misak, and Abednago in the furnace of fire, say as they praise God, "Bless, ye heavens, the Lord; praise and exalt Him for ever;" then, "Bless, ye angels, the Lord;" then, "Bless the Lord, all ye waters that are above heaven." So the Scriptures assign the heavens and the waters to the class of pure powers [3] as is shown in Genesis. Suitably, then, inasmuch as "power" is used with a variety of meaning, Daniel adds, "Let every power bless the Lord;" then, further, "Bless the Lord, sun and moon;" and, "Bless the Lord, ye stars of heaven. Bless the Lord, all ye that worship *Him;* praise and confess the God of gods, for His mercy is for ever." It is written in Daniel, on the occasion of the three children praising in the furnace.

II. "Blessed art Thou, who lookest on the abysses as Thou sittest on the cherubim," says Daniel, in agreement with Enoch, [4] who said, "And I saw all sorts of matter." For the abyss, which is in its essence boundless, is bounded by the power of God. These material essences then, from which the separate genera and their species are produced, are called abysses; since you would not call the water alone the abyss, although matter is allegorically called water, the abyss.

III. "In the beginning God made the heaven and the earth," [5] both terrestrial and celestial things. And that this is true, the Lord said to Osee, "Go, take to thyself a wife of fornication, and children of fornication: because the land committing fornication, shall commit fornication, *departing* from the Lord." [6] For it is not the element *of earth* that he speaks of, but those that dwell in the element, those who have an earthly disposition.

IV. And that the Son is the beginning [7] *or head*, Hosea teaches clearly: "And it shall be, that in the place in which it was said to them, Ye are not my people, they shall be called the children of the living God: and the children of Judah and the children of Israel shall be gathered to the same place, and they shall place over them one head, [8] and they shall come up out of the land; for great is the day of Jezreel." [9] For whom one believes, him He chooses. But one believes the Son, who is the head; wherefore also he said in addition: "But I will have mercy on the sons of Judah, and will save them by the Lord their God." [10] Now the Saviour who saves is the Son of God. He is then the head. [7]

V. The Spirit by Osee says, "I am your Instructor;" [11] "Blow ye [12] the trumpet upon the hills of the Lord; sound upon the high places." [13] And is not baptism itself, which is the sign of regeneration, an escape from matter, by the teaching of the Saviour, a great impetuous stream, ever rushing on and bearing us along? The Lord accordingly, leading us out of disorder, illumines us by bringing us into the light, which is shadowless and is material no longer.

VI. This river and sea of matter two prophets [14] cut asunder and divided by the power of the Lord, the matter being bounded, through both divisions of the water. Famous leaders both, by whom the signs were believed, they complied with the will of God, so that the righteous man may proceed from matter, having journeyed through it first. On the one of these commanders also was imposed the name of our Saviour. [15]

---

[1] [I have prefixed this title, which Mr. Wilson has omitted, possibly because these extracts are themselves somewhat abridged.]

[2] [For all the confusions about Theodotus and the divers persons so called, see Lardner, *Credib.*, viii. 572-579. These are the extracts commonly called the *Eclogues* or *Excerpts of Theodotus;* but they do not contain certain passages, which may have been interpolations.]

[3] Spirits.

[4] [See vol. vi., this series, note 9, p. 147.]

[5] Gen. i. 1.

[6] Hos. i. 2.

[7] ἀρχή.

[8] ἀρχήν.

[9] Hos. i. 10, 11.

[10] Hos. i. 7.

[11] Hos. v. 2.

[12] "Blow ye the cornet in Gibeah, and the trumpet in Ramah."—A. V.

[13] Hos. v. 8.

[14] Moses who divided the sea, and Joshua who divided the Jordan.

[15] Joshua = Jesus.

VII. Now, regeneration is by water and spirit, as was all creation: "For the Spirit of God moved on the abyss."[1] And for this reason the Saviour was baptized, though not Himself needing[2] to be so, in order that He might consecrate the whole water for those who were being regenerated. Thus it is not the body only, but the soul, that we cleanse. It is accordingly a sign of the sanctifying of our invisible part, and of the straining off from the new and spiritual creation of the unclean spirits that have got mixed up with the soul.

VIII. "The water above the heaven." Since baptism is performed by water and the Spirit as a protection against the twofold fire, — that which lays hold of what is visible, and that which lays hold of what is invisible; and of necessity, there being an immaterial element of water and a material, is it a protection against the twofold[3] fire. And the earthly water cleanses the body; but the heavenly water, by reason of its being immaterial and invisible, is an emblem of the Holy Spirit, who is the purifier of what is invisible, as the water of the Spirit, as the other of the body.

IX. God, out of goodness, hath mingled fear with goodness. For what is beneficial for each one, that He also supplies, as a physician to a sick man, as a father to his insubordinate child: "For he that spareth his rod hateth his son."[4] And the Lord and His apostles walked in the midst of fear and labours. When, then, the affliction is sent in the person of a righteous man,[5] it is either from the Lord rebuking him for a sin committed before, or guarding him on account of the future, or not preventing by the exercise of His power an assault from without,[6] — for some good end to him and to those near, for the sake of example.

X. Now those that dwell in a corrupt body, like those who sail in an old ship, do not lie on their back, but are ever praying, stretching their hands to God.

XI. The ancients were exceedingly distressed, unless they had always some suffering in the body. For they were afraid, that if they received not in this world the punishment of the sins which, in numbers through ignorance, accompany those that are in the flesh, they would in the other world suffer the penalty all at once. So that they preferred curative treatment here. What is to be dreaded is, then, not external disease, but sins, for which disease *comes*, and disease of the

soul, not of the body: "For all flesh is grass,"[7] and corporeal and external good things are temporary; "but the things which are unseen are eternal."[8]

XII. As to knowledge, some elements of it we already possess; others, by what we do possess, we firmly hope *to attain*. For neither have we attained all, nor do we lack all. But we have received, as it were, an earnest of the eternal blessings, and of the ancestral riches. The provisions for the Lord's way are the Lord's beatitudes. For He said: "Seek," and anxiously seek, "the kingdom of God, and all these things shall be added to you: for the Father knoweth what things ye have need of."[9] .Thus He limits not only our occupations, but our cares. For He says: "Ye cannot, by taking thought, add aught to your stature."[10] For God knows well what it is good for us to have and what to want. He wishes, therefore, that we, emptying ourselves of worldly cares, should be filled with that which is directed towards God. "For we groan, desiring to be clothed upon with that which is incorruptible, before putting off corruption." For when faith is shed abroad, unbelief is nonplussed. Similarly also with knowledge and righteousness. We must therefore not only empty the soul, but fill it with God. For no longer is there evil in it, since that has been made to cease; nor yet is there good, since it has not yet received good. But what is neither good nor evil is nothing. "For to the swept and empty house return,"[11] if none of the blessings of salvation has been put in, the unclean spirit that dwelt there before, taking with him seven other unclean spirits. Wherefore, after emptying the soul of what is evil, we must fill with the good God that which is His chosen dwelling-place. For when the empty rooms are filled, then follows the seal, that the sanctuary may be guarded for God.

XIII. "By two and three witnesses every word is established."[12] By Father, and Son, and Holy Spirit, by whose witness and help the prescribed commandments ought to be kept.[13]

XIV. Fasting, according to the signification of the word, is abstinence from food. Now food makes us neither more righteous nor less. But mystically it shows that, as life is maintained in individuals by sustenance, and want of sustenance is the token of death; so also ought we to fast from worldly things, that we may die to the world, and after that, by partaking of divine sustenance, live to God. Especially does fasting

---

[1] Gen. i. 2.
[2] [In a quotation which Jones makes from the *Excerpts* (not found here) the reverse is shamelessly asserted. *Canon,* vol. i. p. 375.]
[3] διπλόης — substantive.
[4] Prov. xiii. 24.
[5] ὅταν οὖν πιστοῦ σώματος ᾖ.
[6] The sense is hazy, but about as clear as that to be obtained by substituting conjecturally for προσβολὴν (assault), πρὸς βολήν, or ἐπιβολήν, or ἐπιβουλήν.

[7] Isa. xl. 6.
[8] 2 Cor. iv. 18.
[9] Matt. vi. 33, 32.
[10] Matt. vi 27; Luke xii. 25.
[11] Matt. xii. 44.
[12] Deut. xvii. 6.
[13] [This looks as if the text of the *three witnesses* had been in this compiler's copy of St. John's First Epistle. See vol. iii. Elucid. III. p. 631. St. Augustine also seems to me to sustain the African text in the *De Civit.*, lib. v. cap. xi. p. 154, ed. Migne.]

empty the soul of matter, and make it, along with the body, pure and light for the divine words. Worldly food is, then, the former life and sins; but the divine food is faith, hope, love, patience, knowledge, peace, temperance. For " blessed are they that hunger and thirst after" God's "righteousness; for they shall be filled."[1] The soul, but not the body, it is which is susceptible of this craving.

xv. The Saviour showed to the believing apostles prayer to be stronger than faith in the case of a demoniac, whom they could not cleanse, when He said, Such things are accomplished by prayer. He who has believed has obtained forgiveness of sins from the Lord; but he who has attained knowledge, inasmuch as he no longer sins, obtains from himself the forgiveness of the rest.

xvi. For as cures, and prophecies, and signs are performed by the agency of men, God working in them, so also is Gnostic teaching. For God shows His power through men. And the prophecy rightly says, " I will send to them a man who will save them."[2] Accordingly He sends forth at one time prophets, at another apostles, to be saviours of men. Thus God does good by the agency of men. For it is not that God can do some things, and cannot do others: He is never powerless in anything. No more are some things done with, and some things against His will; and some things by Him, and some things by another. But He even brought us into being by means of men, and trained us by means of men.

xvii. God made us, having previously no existence. For if we had a previous existence, we must have known where we were, and how and why we came hither. But if we had no pre-existence, then God is the sole author of our creation. As, then, He made us who had no existence; so also, now that we are made, He saves us by His own grace, if we show ourselves worthy and susceptible; if not, He[3] will let us pass to our proper end. For He is Lord both of the living and the dead.

xviii. But see the power of God, not only in the case of men, in bringing to existence out of non-existence, and making them when brought into being grow up according to the progress of the time of life, but also in saving those who believe, in a way suitable to each individual. And now He changes both hours, and times, and fruits, and elements. For this is the one God, who has measured both the beginning and the end of events suitably to each one.

xix. Advancing from faith and fear to knowledge, man knows how to say Lord, Lord; but not as His slave, he has learned to say, Our Father.[4] Having set free the spirit of bondage, which produces fear, and advanced by love to adoption, he now reverences from love Him whom he feared before. For he no longer abstains from what he ought to abstain from out of fear, but out of love clings to the commandments. " The Spirit itself," it is said, " beareth witness when we cry, Abba,[4] Father."[5]

xx. Now the Lord with His precious blood redeems us, freeing us from our old bitter masters, that is, our sins, on account of which the spiritual *powers* of wickedness ruled over us. Accordingly He leads us into the liberty of the Father, — sons that are co-heirs and friends. " For," says the Lord, " they that do the will of my Father are my brethren and fellow-heirs."[6] " Call no man, therefore, father to yourselves on earth."[7] For it is masters that are on earth. But in heaven is the Father, of whom is the whole family, both in heaven and on earth.[8] For love rules willing *hearts*, but fear the unwilling. One kind of fear is base; but the other, leading us as a pedagogue to good, brings us to Christ, and is saving.

xxi. Now if one has a conception of God, it by no means corresponds with His worthiness. For what can the worthiness of God be? But let him, as far as is possible, conceive of a great and incomprehensible and most beautiful light; inaccessible, comprehending all good power, all comely virtue; caring for all, compassionate, passionless, good; knowing all things, foreknowing all things, pure, sweet, shining, stainless.

xxii. Since the movement of the soul is self-originated, the grace of God demands from it what the soul possesses, willingness as its contribution to salvation. For the soul wishes to be its own good; which the Lord, *however*, gives it. For it is not devoid of sensation so as to be carried along like a body. Having is the result of taking, and taking of willing and desiring; and keeping hold of what one has received, of the exercise of care and of ability. Wherefore God has endowed the soul with free choice, that He may show it its duty, and that it choosing, may receive and retain.

xxiii. As through the body the Lord spake and healed, so also formerly by the prophets, and now by the apostles and teachers. For the Church is the minister of the Lord's power. Thence He then assumed humanity,[9] that by it He might

---

[1] Matt. v. 6.
[2] Isa. xix. 20.
[3] The reading is, εἰ μὴ παρήσει πρὸς τὸ οἰκεῖον τέλος; and the Latin translator renders, "si non segnes simus ad finem proprium." It seems better, with Sylburgius, to take εἰ μὴ as equivalent to εἰ δὲ μὴ, and to put a comma after μὴ, so as to render as above.

[4] [A happy reference to the Lord's Prayer as connected with St. Paul's reference to the Abba; and it is worth while to compare the use of this word with the prayer as used in the synagogue. Vol. v. Elucid. III. p. 559, this series.]
[5] Rom. viii. 15; Gal. iv. 6.
[6] Matt. xii. 50.
[7] Matt. xxiii. 9.
[8] Eph. iii. 15.
[9] ἄνθρωπον.

minister to the Father's will. And at all times, the God who loves humanity [1] invests Himself with man for the salvation of men, — in former times with the prophets, and now with the Church. For it is fitting that like should minister to like, in order to a like salvation.

XXIV. For we are of the earth. . . . Cæsar is the prince, for the time being, whose earthly image is the old man, to which he has returned. To him, then, we are to render the earthly things, which we bore in the image of the earthly, and the things of God to God. For each one of the passions is on us as a letter, and stamp, and sign. Now the Lord marks us with another stamp, and with other names and letters, faith instead of unbelief, and so forth. Thus we are translated from what is material to what is spiritual, " having borne the image of the heavenly." [2]

XXV. John says : " I indeed baptize you with water, but there cometh after me He that baptizeth with the Spirit and fire." [3] But He baptized no one with fire. But some, as Heraclius says, marked with fire the ears of those who were sealed ; understanding so the apostolic saying, " For His fan is in His hand, to purge His floor : and He will gather the wheat into the garner ; but the chaff He will burn with fire unquenchable." [4] There is joined, then, the expression " by fire " to that " by the Spirit ; " since He separates the wheat from the chaff, that is, from the material husk, by the Spirit ; and the chaff is separated, being fanned by the wind : [5] so also the Spirit possesses a power of separating material forces. Since, then, some things are produced from what is unproduced and indestructible, — that is, the germs of life,— the wheat also is stored, and the material part, as long as it is conjoined with the superior part, remains ; when separated from it, it is destroyed ; for it had its existence in another thing. This separating element, then, is the Spirit, and the destroying element is the fire : and material fire is to be understood. But since that which is saved is like wheat, and that which grows in the soul like chaff, and the one is incorporeal, and that which is separated is material ; to the incorporeal He opposes spirit, which is rarefied and pure — almost more so than mind ; and to the material *He opposes* fire, not as being evil or bad, but as strong and capable of cleansing away evil. For fire is conceived as a good force and powerful, destructive of what is baser, and conservative of what is better. Wherefore this fire is by the prophets called wise.

XXVI. Thus also, then, when God is called " a consuming fire," it is because a name and sign,

not of wickedness, but of power, is to be selected. For as fire is the most potent of the elements, and masters all things ; so also God is all-powerful and almighty, who is able to hold, to create, to make, to nourish, to make grow, to save, having power of body and soul. As, then, fire is superior to the elements, so is the Almighty Ruler to gods, and powers, and principalities. The power of fire is twofold : one power conduces to the production and maturing of fruits and of animals, of which the sun is the image ; and the other to consumption and destruction, as terrestrial fire. When, then, God is called a consuming fire, *He is called* a mighty and resistless power, to which nothing is impossible, but which is able to destroy.

Respecting such a power, also, the Saviour says, " I came to send fire upon the earth," [6] indicating a power to purify what is holy, but destructive, as they say, of what is material ; and, as we should say, disciplinary. Now fear pertains to fire, and diffusion to light.

XXVII. Now the more ancient men [7] did not write, as they neither wished to encroach on the time devoted to attention bestowed on what they handed down, in the way of teaching, by the additional attention bestowed on writing, nor spent the time for considering what was to be said on writing. And, perhaps convinced that the function of composition and the department of teaching did not belong to the same cast of mind, they gave way to those who had a natural turn for it. For in the case of a speaker, the stream of speech flows unchecked and impetuous, and you may catch it up hastily. But that which is always tested by readers, meeting with strict [8] examination, is thought worthy of the utmost pains, and is, so to speak, the written confirmation of *oral* instruction, and of the voice so wafted along to posterity by written composition. For that which was committed in trust to the elders, speaking in writing, uses the writer's help to hand itself down to those who are to read it. As, then, the magnet, repelling other matter, attracts iron alone by reason of affinity ; so also books, though many read them, attract those alone who are capable of comprehending them. For the word of truth is to some " foolishness," [9] and to others a " stumbling-block ; " [9] but to a few " wisdom." [9] So also is the power of God found to be. But far from the Gnostic be envy. For it is for this reason also that he asks whether it be worse to give to the unworthy, or not commit to the worthy ; and runs the risk, from his abundant love of communicating, not

---

[1] φιλάνθρωπος.
[2] 1 Cor. xv. 49.
[3] Matt. iii. 11.
[4] Matt. iii. 12.
[5] Or spirit — πνεύματος.

[6] Luke xii. 49.
[7] πρεσβύτεροι.
[8] It seems better, with Sylb., to read ἀκριβοῦς, qualifying ἐξετάσεως (as above), than ἀκριβῶς, adv. qualifying βασανιζόμενον, tested.
[9] 1 Cor. i. 18.

only to every one who is qualified, but sometimes also to one unworthy, who asks importunately; not on account of his entreaty (for he loves not glory), but on account of the persistency of the petitioner who bends his mind towards faith with copious entreaty.

XXVIII. There are those calling themselves Gnostics who are envious of those in their own house more than strangers. And, as the sea is open to all, but one swims, another sails, and a third catches fish; and as the land is common, but one walks, another ploughs, another hunts, — somebody else searches the mines, and another builds a house : so also, when the Scripture is read, one is helped to faith, another to morality, and a third is freed from superstition by the knowledge of things. The athlete, who knows the Olympic stadium, strips for training, contends, and becomes victor, tripping up his antagonists who contend against his scientific method, and fighting out the contest. For scientific knowledge [1] is necessary both for the training of the soul and for gravity of conduct; making the faithful more active and keen observers of things. For as there is no believing without elementary instruction, so neither is there comprehension without science. [1]

XXIX. For what is useful and necessary to salvation, such as *the knowledge of* the Father, and Son, and Holy Spirit, and also of our own soul, are wholly requisite; and it is at once beneficial and necessary to attain to the scientific account of them. And to those who have assumed the lead in doing good, much experience is advantageous; so that none of the things which appear to be known necessarily and eruditely by others may escape their notice. The exposition, too, of heterodox teaching affords another exercise of the inquiring soul, and keeps the disciple from being seduced from the truth, by his having already had practice beforehand in sounding all round on warlike instruments of music. [2]

XXX. The life of the Gnostic rule, (as they say that Crete was barren of deadly animals,) is pure from every evil deed, and thought, and word; not only hating no one, but beyond envy and hatred, and all evil-speaking and slander.

XXXI. In length of days, it is not on account of his having lived long that the man is to be regarded happy, to whose lot it has also fallen, through his having lived, to be worthy of living for ever. He has pained no one, except in instructing by the word the wounded in heart, as it were by a salutary honey, which is at once sweet and pungent. So that, above all, the Gnostic preserves the decorous along with that which is in accordance with reason. For passion

being cut away and stript off from the whole soul, he henceforth consorts and lives with what is noblest, which has now become pure, and emancipated to adoption.

XXXII. Pythagoras thought that he who gave things their names, ought to be regarded not only the most intelligent, but the oldest of the wise men. We must, then, search the Scriptures accurately, since they are admitted to be expressed in parables, and from the names hunt out the thoughts which the Holy Spirit, propounding respecting things, teaches by imprinting His mind, so to speak, on the expressions; that the names used with various meanings, being made the subject of accurate investigation, may be explained, and that that which is hidden under many integuments may, being handled and learned, come to light and gleam forth. For so also lead turns white as you rub it; white lead being produced from black. So also scientific knowledge (gnosis), shedding its light and brightness on things, shows itself to be in truth the divine wisdom, the pure light, which illumines the men whose eyeball is clear, unto the sure vision and comprehension of truth.

XXXIII. Lighting, then, our torch [3] at the source of that light, by the passionate desire which has it for its object, and striving as much as possible to be assimilated to it, we become men [4] full of light, [5] Israelites indeed. For He called those friends and brethren who by desire and pursuit aimed after likeness to the Divinity.

XXXIV. Pure places and meadows have received voices and visions of holy phantasms. [6] But every man who has been perfectly purified, shall be thought worthy of divine teaching and of power.

XXXV. Now I know that the mysteries of science (gnosis) are a laughing-stock to many, especially when not patched up with sophistical figurative language. And the few are at first startled at them; as when light is suddenly brought into a convivial party in the dark. Subsequently, on getting used and accustomed, and trained to reasoning, as if gladdened and exulting for delight, they *praise* the Lord. . . . For as pleasure has for its essence release from pain; so also has knowledge the removal of ignorance. For as those that most asleep think they are most awake, being under the power of dreamvisions very vivid and fixed; so those that are most ignorant think that they know most. But blessed are they who rouse themselves from this sleep and derangement, and raise their eyes to the light and the truth.

XXXVI. It is, therefore, equally requisite for him who wishes to have a pupil who is docile,

---

[1] γνῶσις.
[2] [It is not to be doubted that much sound Alexandrian teaching is here mixed up with folly.]

[3] [Compare Tatian's use of a like figure, vol. ii. note 2, p. 67, this series.]
[4] φῶτες.
[5] φωτός.
[6] [A Montanist token.]

and has blended faith with aspiration, to exercise himself and constantly to study by himself, investigating the truth of his speculations; and when he thinks himself right, to descend to questions regarding things contiguous. For the young birds make attempts to fly in the nest, exercising their wings.

XXXVII. For Gnostic virtue everywhere makes man good, and meek, and harmless,[1] and painless, and blessed, and ready to associate in the best way with all that is divine, in the best way with men, at once a contemplative and active divine image, and turns him into a lover of what is good by love. For what is good,[2] as there it is contemplated and comprehended by wisdom, is here by self-control and righteousness carried into effect through faith: practising in the flesh an angelic ministry; hallowing the soul in the body, as in a place clear and stainless.

XXXVIII. Against Tatian,[3] who says that the words, "Let there be light,"[4] are supplicatory. If, then, He is supplicating the supreme God, how does He say, "I am God, and beside me there is none else?"[5] We have said that there are punishments for blasphemies, for nonsense, for outrageous expressions; which are punished and chastised by reason.

XXXIX. And he said, too, that on account of their hair and finery, women are punished by the Power that is set over these matters; which also gave to Samson strength in his hair; which punishes the women who allure to fornication through the adornment of their hair.

XL. As by the effluence of good, people are made good, in like manner are they made bad. Good is the judgment of God, and the discrimination of the believing from the unbelieving, and the judgment beforehand, so as not to fall into greater judgment — this judgment being correction.

XLI. Scripture says that infants which are exposed are delivered to a guardian angel, and that by him they are trained and reared. "And they shall be," it says, "as the faithful in this world of a hundred years of age." Wherefore also Peter, in the Revelation,[6] says: "And a flash of fire, leaping from those infants, and striking the eyes of the women." For the just shines forth as a spark in a reed, and will judge the nations.[7]

XLII. "With the holy Thou wilt be holy."[8] "According to thy praise is thy name glorified;"

God being glorified through our knowledge, and through the inheritance. Thus also it is said, "The Lord liveth," and "The Lord hath risen."[9]

XLIII. "A people whom I knew not hath served me;"[10] — by covenant I knew them not, alien sons, who desired what pertained to another.

XLIV. "Magnifying the salvations of His king."[11] All the faithful are called kings, brought to royalty through inheritance.

XLV. Long-suffering is sweetness above honey; not because it is long-suffering, but in consequence of the fruit of long-suffering. Since, then, the man of self-control is devoid of passion, inasmuch as he restrains the passions, not without toil; but when habit is formed, he is no longer a man of self-control, the man having come under the influence of one habit and of the Holy Spirit.

XLVI. The passions that are in the soul are called spirits, — not spirits of power, since in that case the man under the influence of passion would be a legion of demons; but *they are so called* in consequence of the impulse they communicate. For the soul itself, through modifications, taking on this and that other sort of qualities of wickedness, is said to receive spirits.

XLVII. The Word does not bid us renounce property;[12] but to manage property without inordinate affection; and on anything happening, not to be vexed or grieved; and not to desire to acquire. Divine Providence bids keep away from possession accompanied with passion, and from all inordinate affection, and *from this* turns back those still remaining[13] in the flesh.

XLVIII. For instance, Peter says in the Apocalypse,[14] that abortive infants shall share the better fate;[15] that these are committed to a guardian angel, so that, on receiving knowledge, they may obtain the better abode, having had the same experiences which they would have had had they been in the body. But the others shall obtain salvation merely, as being injured and pitied, and remain without punishment, receiving this reward.

XLIX. The milk of women, flowing from the breasts and thickening, says Peter in the Apocalypse,[16] will produce minute beasts, that prey on flesh, and running back into them will consume them: teaching that punishments arise for sins. He says that they are produced from sins; as it was for their sins that the people were sold. And for their want of faith in Christ, as the apostle says, they were bitten by serpents.

[1] For ἀβλαβές in the text, we must, translating thus, read ἀβλαβῆ. If we translate, as we may, "Gnostic virtue is a thing everywhere good, and meek," etc., no change is required in the reading.
[2] τὸ καλὸν.
[3] [From some lost work of his]
[4] Gen. i. 3.
[5] Isa. xlv. 6.
[6] [On these quotations see Lardner, *Credib.*, ii. 256, and Jones, *Canon*, vol. i. p. 373.]
[7] Wisd. iii. 7.
[8] Ps. xviii. 26.

[9] Luke xxiv. 34.
[10] Ps. xviii. 43.
[11] Ps. xviii. 50.
[12] κτήσεως, instead of κτίσεως, as in the text, and κτῆσιν for κτίσιν in the next clause.
[13] Ἀναστρέφει ἐπὶ μόνους τοὺς ἐν σαρκί. For which, as slightly preferable, Sylburg. proposes ἔτι μένοντας ἐν σαρκί, as above.
[14] [See note 6, p. 48, *supra*.]
[15] Adopting the reading μοίρας, instead of that in the text, πείρας.
[16] [See note 6, p. 48, *supra*.]

L. An ancient said that the embryo is a living thing; for that the soul entering into the womb after it has been by cleansing prepared for conception, and introduced by one of the angels who preside over generation, and who knows the time for conception, moves the woman to intercourse; and that, on the seed being deposited, the spirit, which is in the seed, is, so to speak, appropriated, and is thus assumed into conjunction in the process of formation. He cited as a proof to all, how, when the angels give glad tidings to the barren, they introduce souls before conception. And in the Gospel "the babe leapt"[1] as a living thing. And the barren are barren for this reason, that the soul, which unites for the deposit of the seed, is not introduced so as to secure conception and generation.

LI. "The heavens declare the glory of God."[2] The heavens are taken in various meanings, both those defined by space and revolution, and those by covenant, — the immediate operation of the first-created angels. For the covenants caused a more especial appearance of angels, — that[3] in the case of Adam, that in the case of Noah, that in the case of Abraham, that in the case of Moses. For, moved by the Lord, the first-created angels exercised their influence on the angels attached to the prophets, considering the covenants the glory of God. Furthermore, the things done on earth by angels were done by the first-created angels to the glory of God.

LII. It is the Lord that is principally denominated the Heavens, and then the First-created; and after these also the holy men before the Law, as the patriarchs, and Moses, and the prophets; then also the apostles. "And the firmament showeth His handiwork." He applies the term "firmament"[4] to God, the passionless and immoveable, as also elsewhere the same David says, "I will love Thee, O Lord, my strength[4] and my refuge."[5] Accordingly, the firmament itself shows forth the work of His hands, — that is, shows and manifests the work of His angels. For He shows forth and manifests those whom He hath made.

LIII. "Day unto day uttereth speech." As the heavens have various meanings, so also has day. Now speech is the Lord; and He is also frequently called day. "And night unto night showeth forth knowledge." The devil knew that the Lord was to come. But he did not believe that He was God; wherefore also he tempted Him, in order to know if He were powerful. It is said, "he left[6] Him, and departed from Him for a season;" that is, he postponed the discovery till the resurrection. For he knew that He who was to rise was the Lord. Likewise also the demons; since also they suspected that Solomon was the Lord, and they knew that he was not so, on his sinning. "Night to night." All the demons knew that He who rose after the passion was the Lord. And already Enoch[7] had said, that the angels who transgressed taught men astronomy and divination, and the rest of the arts.

LIV. "There are no speeches or words whose voices are not heard," neither of days nor nights. "Their sound is gone forth unto all the earth." He has transferred the discourse to the saints alone, whom he calls both heavens and days.

LV. The stars, spiritual bodies, that have communications with the angels set over them, and are governed by them, are not the cause of the production of things, but are signs of what is taking place, and will take place, and have taken place in the case of atmospheric changes, of fruitfulness and barrenness, of pestilence and fevers, and in the case of men. The stars do not in the least degree exert influences, but indicate what is, and will be, and has been.

LVI. "And in the sun hath He set His tabernacle." There is a transposition here. For it is of the second coming that the discourse is. So, then, we must read what is transposed in its due sequence: "And he, as a bridegroom issuing from his chamber, will rejoice as a giant to run his way. From heaven's end is his going forth; and there is no one who shall hide himself from his heat;" and then, "He hath set His tabernacle in the sun."

Some say that He deposited the Lord's body in the sun, as Hermogenes. And "His tabernacle," some say, is His body, others the Church of the faithful.

Our Pantænus[8] used to say, that prophecy utters its expressions indefinitely for the most part, and uses the present for the future, and again the present for the past. Which is also seen here.[9] For "He hath set" is put both for the past and the future. For the future, because, on the completion of this period, which is to run according to its present[10] constitution, the Lord will come to restore the righteous, the faithful, in whom He rests, as in a tent, to one and the same unity; for all are one body, of the same race, and have chosen the same faith and righteousness. But some as head, some as eyes, some as ears, some as hands, some as breasts, some as feet, shall be set, resplendent, in the sun. "Shine forth as the sun,"[11] or in the sun; since an angel

---

[1] Luke i. 43.
[2] Ps. xix. 1. [Here follow notes on successive verses, some not unworthy of an orthodox Father.]
[3] i.e., the covenant.
[4] στερέωμα.
[5] Ps. xviii. 1.
[6] For ἐὰν, which is the reading of the text, Sylburgius' suggestion of εἴα or εἴασε has been adopted.

[7] [See note 9, p. 3, supra.]
[8] [No doubt he may have said this.]
[9] Or rather, as Sylb. points out, this is a case of the past used for the present, etc.
[10] παρουσίαν, κατάστασιν, the reading of the text, is, as Sylburg. remarks, plainly corrupt; παροῦσαν, as above, is the most obvious correction.
[11] Matt. xiii. 43.

high in command is in the sun. For he is appointed for rule over days ; as the moon is for ruling over night.[1] Now angels are called days. Along with the angels in[2] the sun, it is said, they shall have assigned to them one abode, to be for some time and in some respects the sun, as it were the head of the body which is one. And, besides, they also are the rulers of the days, as that angel in the sun, for the greater purpose for which he before them[3] migrated to the same place. And again destined to ascend progressively, they reach the first abode, in accordance with the past " He hath set : " so that the first-created angels shall no longer, according to providence, exercise a definite ministry, but may be in repose, and devoted to the contemplation of God alone ; while those next to them shall be promoted to the post which they have left ; and so those beneath them similarly.

LVII. There are then, according to the apostle, those on the summit,[4] the first-created. And they are thrones, although Powers, being the first-created, inasmuch as God rests in them, as also in those who believe. For each one, according to his own stage of advancement, possesses the knowledge of God in a way special to himself ; and in this knowledge God reposes, those who possess knowledge being made immortal by knowledge. And is not " He set His tabernacle in the sun " to be understood thus ? God " set in the sun," that is, in the God who is beside Him, as in the Gospel, Eli, Eli,[5] instead of my God, my God. And what is " above all rule, and authority, and power, and every name that is named," are those from among men that are made perfect as angels and archangels, *so as to rise* to the nature of the angels first-created. For those who are changed from men to angels are instructed for a thousand years by the angels after they are brought to perfection. Then those who have taught are translated to archangelic authority ; and those who have learned instruct those again who from men are changed to angels. Thus afterwards, in the prescribed periods, they are brought to the proper angelic state of the body.

LVIII. " The law of God is perfect, converting souls."[6] The Saviour Himself is called Law and Word, as Peter in " the Preaching," and the prophet : " Out of Zion shall go forth the Law, and the Word of the Lord from Jerusalem." [7]

LIX. " The testimony of the Lord is sure, making children wise." The covenant of the Lord is true, making wise children ; those free from evil, both the apostles, and then also us. Besides, the testimony of the Lord, according to which He rose again after His passion, having been verified by fact, led the Church to confirmation in faith.

LX. " The fear of the Lord is pure, enduring for ever." He says that those who have been turned from fear to faith and righteousness endure for ever.

" The judgments of the Lord are true," — sure, and incapable of being overturned ; and giving rewards according to what is right, bringing the righteous to the unity of the faith. For this is shown in the words, " justified for the same." [8] " Such desires [9] are above gold and precious stone."

LXI. " For also Thy servant keeps them." Not that David alone is called servant ; but the whole people saved is called the servant of God, in virtue of obedience to the command.

LXII. " Cleanse me from my secret *faults ;* " — thoughts contrary to right reason — defects. For He calls this foreign to the righteous man.

LXIII. " If they have not dominion over me, then shall I be innocent." If those who persecute me as they did the Lord, do not have dominion over me, I shall not be innocent. For no one becomes a martyr unless he is persecuted ; nor appears righteous, unless, being wronged, he takes no revenge ; nor forbearing . . .

---

[1] Gen. i. 18.
[2] μεθ' here clearly should be καθ' or ἐφ'.
[3] If we may venture to change αὐτοῦ into αὐτῶν.
[4] Ἐν τῇ ἀκρῇ ἀποκαταστάσει. The last word yields no suitable sense, and conjecture as to the right reading is vain ; and we have left it untranslated. The Latin translator renders " qui in summa arce collocati sunt."
[5] Ἥλιος is (with marvellous ignorance of the Hebrew tongue, as Combefisius notices) here identified with Eli, אֵלִי.

[6] Ps. xix. 8.
[7] Isa. ii. 3.
[8] Ps. xix. 12, Septuagint.
[9] αἱ τοιαῦται ἐπιθυμίαι, for which the Septuagint has ἐπιθυμητά as in A. V.

TWO EPISTLES CONCERNING VIRGINITY

ATTRIBUTED TO CLEMENT OF ROME.

[TRANSLATED BY THE REV. B. P. PRATTEN.]

INTRODUCTORY NOTICE

TO

TWO EPISTLES CONCERNING VIRGINITY

BY PROFESSOR M. B. RIDDLE, D.D.

AMONG the "Pseudo-Clementina" the *Two Epistles concerning Virginity* must properly be placed. The evidence against the genuineness seems conclusive; yet, with the exception of the homily usually styled the *Second Epistle of Clement*,[1] no spurious writings attributed to the great Roman Father can be assigned an earlier date than these two letters. Uhlhorn, in view of the reference to the *sub-introductæ*, thinks they were written shortly before the time of Cyprian;[2] and this seems very probable. Jerome was acquainted with the writings (*Ad Jovinum*, i. 12), and possibly Epiphanius (*Hær.*, xxx. 15). Hence we may safely allow an early date. Yet these evidences of age tell against the genuineness.

1. Early works of this character would not have disappeared from notice to such an extent, had they been authenticated as writings of Clement. Supporting, as they do, the ascetic tendency prevalent in the Western Church at and after the date when they are first noticed by Christian writers, they would have been carefully preserved and frequently cited, had they been genuine. The name of the great Roman Father would have been so weighty, that the advocates of celibacy would have kept the documents in greater prominence. The silence of Eusebius respecting the letters is an important fact in this discussion.

2. A second argument against the genuineness is derived from the ascetic tone itself. Such pronounced statements are not, we must firmly hold, to be found in the Christian literature of the sub-apostolic age. This historical argument is further sustained by other indications in the epistles. They point to a stage of ecclesiastical development which belongs to a much later period than that of Clement.

3. The use of Scripture in these letters seems to be conclusive against the Clementine authorship. A comparison with the citations in the genuine Epistle of Clement shows that these writings make much greater use of the Pauline (particularly the Pastoral) Epistles; that the Old Testament is less frequently cited, and that the mode of handling proof-texts is that of a later age.

4. The judgment of the most candid patristic scholars is against the genuineness. Of Protestants, Wetstein stands alone in supporting the Clementine authorship; and his position is readily explained by the fact that he discovered the Syriac version which restored the writings to modern scholars (see below). The genuineness is defended by Villecourt and Beelen (see below), also by Möhler, Champagny, and Brück. But such experts as Mansi, Hefele, Alzog, and Funk, among Roman Catholics, unite with Protestant scholars in assigning a later date, and consequently in denying the Clementine authorship.

---

[1] See vol. vii. pp. 509–523.

[2] Against this class Cyprian stoutly contended. Comp. Cyprian, *Ante-Nicene Fathers*, vol. v. pp. 357, 358, 587–592.

TRANSLATOR'S INTRODUCTORY NOTICE.

WHILE the great mass of early Christian literature bearing the name of Clement of Rome is undoubtedly spurious, the case is somewhat different with regard to the two following epistles. Not only have Roman Catholic writers maintained their genuineness with great ingenuity and learning, but Wetstein, who first edited them, argued powerfully for their being received as the authentic productions of Clement; and even Neander has admitted that they may possibly have been written by that friend and fellow-labourer of the apostles.

Their literary history in modern times is somewhat curious. Wetstein unexpectedly discovered them appended to a copy of the Syriac Peschito version of the New Testament furnished to him by Sir James Porter, then British ambassador at Constantinople. He soon afterwards (1752) published them in Syriac, accompanied by a Latin version of his own, with Prolegomena, in which he upheld their genuineness. This speedily called forth two works, one by Lardner (1753), and a second by Venema (1754), in both of which their authenticity was disputed. To these writings Wetstein himself, and, after his death, Gallandius, published rejoinders; but the question remained as far from positive settlement as ever, and continues *sub judice* even at the present day.

It is generally admitted (and, of course, *asserted* by those that maintain their truly Clementine origin) that Greek was the original language of these epistles. Many have argued that they contain plain references to the *sub-introductæ* spoken of in the literature of the third century, and that therefore they were probably composed in the Oriental Church about that period.

These epistles have been very carefully edited in recent times by the Roman Catholic scholars Villecourt (1853) and Beelen (1856). Both have argued strenuously for the genuineness of the letters, but it may be doubted if they have succeeded in repelling all the objections of Lardner and Venema. Beelen's work is a highly scholarly production, and his Prolegomena are marked by great fulness and perspicuity.

A German translation of these epistles was published by Zingerle (1821). They are now for the first time translated into the English language.

The translation is made from the text of Beelen.

The division into chapters is due to Wetstein.

TWO EPISTLES CONCERNING VIRGINITY

THE FIRST EPISTLE OF THE BLESSED CLEMENT, THE DISCIPLE OF PETER THE APOSTLE.

CHAP. I. — THE SALUTATION.

To all those who love and cherish their life *which is* in Christ through God the Father, and obey the truth of God in hope of eternal life; to those who bear affection towards their brethren and towards their neighbours in the love of God; to the blessed *brother* virgins,[1] who devote themselves to preserve virginity "for the sake of the kingdom of heaven;"[2] and to the holy *sister* virgins: the peace which is in God.[3]

CHAP. II. — FOR TRUE VIRGINITY PERFECT VIRTUE IS NECESSARY.

Of all virgins of either sex who have truly resolved to preserve virginity for the sake of the kingdom of heaven — of each and every one of them it is required that he be worthy of the kingdom of heaven in every thing. For not by eloquence[4] or renown,[5] or by station[6] and descent, or by beauty or strength, or by length of life,[7] is the kingdom of heaven obtained; but it is obtained by the power of faith, when a man exhibits the works of faith. For whosoever is truly righteous, his works testify concerning his faith, that he is truly a believer, with a faith which is great, a faith which is perfect, a faith which is in God, a faith which shines in good works, that the Father of all may be glorified through Christ. Now, those who are truly virgins for the sake of God give heed to Him who hath said, " Let not righteousness and faith fail thee; bind them on thy neck, and thou shalt find favour for thyself; and devise thou good things before God and before men."[8] "The paths," therefore, " of the righteous shine as the light, and the light of them advances until the day is perfect."[9] For the beams of their light illumine the whole creation even now by good works, as those who are truly " the light of the world,"[10] giving light to " those who sit in darkness,"[11] that they may arise and go forth from the darkness by the light of the good works of the fear of God, " that they may see our good works, and glorify our Father who is in heaven."[12] For it is required of the man of God, that in all his words and works he be perfect, and that in his life he be adorned with all exemplary and well-ordered behaviour,[13] and do all his deeds in righteousness, as a man of God.

CHAP. III. — TRUE VIRGINS PROVE THEMSELVES SUCH BY SELF-DENIAL, AS DOES THE TRUE BELIEVER BY GOOD WORKS.

For virgins are a beautiful pattern to believers, and to those who shall believe. The name alone, indeed, without works, does not introduce into the kingdom of heaven; but, if a man be truly a believer, such an one can be saved. For, if a person be only called a believer in name, whilst he is not such in works, he cannot possibly be a believer. " Let no one," therefore, " lead you astray with the empty words of error."[14] For, merely because a person is called a virgin, if he be destitute of works excellent and comely, and suitable to virginity, he cannot possibly be saved. For our Lord called such virginity as that " foolish," as He said in the Gospel;[15] and because it had neither oil nor light, it was left outside of the kingdom of heaven, and was shut out from the joy of the bridegroom, and was reckoned with His enemies. For such persons as these " have the appearance only of the fear of God, but the power of it they deny."[16] For they " think with themselves that they are something, whilst they are nothing, and are deceived. But let every one constantly try[17] his works,"[18] and know himself; for empty worship does he offer, whosoever he be that makes profession of virginity and

---

[1] In later Greek παρθένος was used of both sexes (*comp.* Rev. xiv. 4). The Syriac original employs both a masculine and a feminine form. This will not always be indicated in the following translation.
[2] Matt. xix. 12.
[3] Or " to the holy virgins who are in God: peace." So Zingerle, and probably Wetstein.
[4] Zing., not so well, takes this to mean, " by the confession of the mouth " (durch das mündliche Bekenntniss), comparing Matt. vii. 21.
[5] *Lit.* " by word or by name."
[6] The Greek word σχῆμα, here adopted in the Syriac, is sometimes thus used. — BEELEN.
[7] *Lit.* " much time."
[8] Prov. iii. 3, 4 (LXX.).
[9] *Lit.* " fixed." Prov. iv. 18.

[10] Matt. v. 14.
[11] Isa. ix. 2; Matt. iv. 16.
[12] Matt. v. 16; 1 Pet. ii. 12.
[13] Probably referring to 1 Cor. xiv. 40.— BEELEN.
[14] Eph. v. 6.
[15] Matt. xxv. 2.
[16] 2 Tim. iii. 5.
[17] *Lit.* " let every one be trying."
[18] Gal. vi. 3, 4.

sanctity, " and denies its power." For virginity of such a kind is impure, and disowned by all good works. For " every tree whatsoever is known from its fruits." [1] " See that thou understand [2] what I say : God will give thee understanding." [3] For whosoever engages before God to preserve sanctity must be girded with all the holy power of God. And, if with true fear [4] he crucify his body, he for the sake of the fear of God excuses himself from that word *in* which *the Scripture* [5] has said : " Be fruitful, and multiply," [6] and *shuns* all the display, and care, and sensuality, [7] and fascination of this world, and its revelries and its drunkenness, and all its luxury and ease, and withdraws from the entire life of [8] this world, and from its snares, and nets, and hindrances ; and, whilst thou walkest [9] upon the earth, be zealous that thy work and thy business be in heaven.

CHAP. IV. — CONTINUATION OF THE REMARKS ON SELF-DENIAL ; OBJECT AND REWARD OF TRUE VIRGINS.

For he who covets for himself these things *so great and excellent*, withdraws and severs himself on this account from all the world, that he may go *and* live a life divine and heavenly, like the holy angels, in work pure and holy, and " in the holiness [10] of the Spirit of God," [11] and that he may serve God Almighty through Jesus Christ for the sake of the kingdom of heaven. On this account he severs himself from all the appetites of the body. And not only does he excuse himself from this *command*, " Be fruitful, and multiply," but he longs for the " hope promised " and prepared " and laid up in heaven " [12] by God, who has declared with His mouth, and He does not lie, that it is " better than sons and daughters," [13] and that He will give to virgins a notable place in the house of God, which is *something* " better than sons and daughters," and better than *the place of* those who have passed a wedded life in sanctity, and whose " bed has not been defiled." [14] For God will give to virgins the kingdom of heaven, as to the holy angels, by reason of this great and noble profession.

CHAP. V. — THE IRKSOMENESS AND THE ENEMIES OF VIRGINITY.

Thou desirest, then, to be a virgin ? Knowest thou what hardship and irksomeness there is in true virginity — that which stands constantly at all seasons before God, and does not withdraw *from His service*, and " is anxious how it may please its Lord with a holy body, and with *its* spirit ? " [15] Knowest thou what great glory pertains to virginity, and is it for this that thou dost *set thyself to* practise it ? Dost thou really know and understand what it is thou art eager to do ? Art thou acquainted with the noble task of holy virginity ? Dost thou know how, like a man, to enter " lawfully " upon [16] this contest and " strive," [17] that, in the might of the Holy Spirit, [18] thou choosest this for thyself, that thou mayest be crowned with a crown of light, and that they may lead thee about in *triumph* through " the Jerusalem above " ? [19] If so be, then, that thou longest for all these things, conquer the body ; conquer the appetites of the flesh ; conquer the world in the Spirit of God ; conquer these vain things of time, which pass away and grow old, and decay, and come to an end ; conquer the dragon ; [20] conquer the lion ; [21] conquer the serpent ; [22] conquer Satan ; — through Jesus Christ, who doth strengthen thee by the hearing of His words and the divine Eucharist. [23] " Take up thy cross and follow " [24] Him who makes thee clean, Jesus Christ thy Lord. Strive to run straight forward and boldly, not with fear, but with courage, relying on the promise of thy Lord, that thou shalt obtain the victor-crown [25] of thy " calling on high " [26] through Jesus Christ. For whosoever walks perfect in faith, and not fearing, doth in very deed receive the crown of virginity, which is great in its toil and great in its reward. Dost thou understand and know how honourable a thing is sanctity ? [27] Dost thou understand how great and exalted and excellent is the glory of virginity ? [28]

CHAP. VI. — DIVINITY OF VIRGINITY.

The womb of a holy virgin [29] carried our Lord Jesus Christ, the Son of God ; and the body

---

[1] Matt. xii. 33. [More probably Luke vi. 44. — R.]
[2] Or " consider." There is no play on words in the passage quoted (2 Tim. ii. 7), nor perhaps was this intended in the Syriac.
[3] 2 Tim. ii. 7.
[4] *Lit.* " true in fear *of God*." The reading is probably faulty. — BEELEN
[5] The ellipsis is usually to be thus filled up in these epistles. [In similar cases which follow, italics will not be used. — R.]
[6] Gen. i. 28.
[7] Or " the sensual pleasures."
[8] Or " from all intercourse with."
[9] Either something is here omitted by the transcriber, or Clement has varied the form of expression.— BEELEN.
[10] " Sanctification." — BEELEN. [So A. V. The R. V. correctly renders ἁγιασμός, " sanctification," in every instance. — R.]
[11] 2 Thess. ii. 13.
[12] Col. i. 5.
[13] Isa. lvi. 4, 5.
[14] Heb. xiii. 4.

[15] 1 Cor. vii. 34.
[16] *Lit.* " descend to."
[17] 2 Tim. ii. 5.
[18] The words, " in the might of the Holy Spirit," appear to obscure the sense. — BEELEN.
[19] Gal. iv. 26.
[20] Rev. xii. 7.
[21] 1 Pet. v. 8.
[22] 2 Cor. xi. 3.
[23] *Lit.* " the Eucharist of the Godhead." [This is an evidence of later date than the sub-apostolic age. — R.]
[24] Matt. xvi. 24.
[25] *Lit.* " crown of victory."
[26] Phil. iii. 14.
[27] i.e., continency. [The use of the terms " sanctity," " holy," etc., in the limited sense of " continency," " chaste," etc., is strong evidence of the later origin. — R.]
[28] The last two sentences properly belong to chap. vi.
[29] Or " the Holy Virgin."

which our Lord wore, and in which He carried on the conflict in this world, He put on from a holy virgin. From this, therefore, understand the greatness and dignity of virginity. Dost thou wish to be a Christian? Imitate Christ in every thing. John, the ambassador, he who came before our Lord, he "than whom there was not a greater among those born of women,"[1] the holy messenger of our Lord, was a virgin. Imitate, therefore, the ambassador of our Lord, and be his follower[2] in every thing. *That* John, again, who "reclined on the bosom of our Lord, and whom He greatly loved,"[3] — he, too, was a holy person.[4] For it was not without reason that our Lord loved him. Paul, also, and Barnabas, and Timothy, with all the others, "whose names are written in the book of life,"[5] — these, I say, all cherished and loved sanctity,[6] and ran in the contest, and finished their course without blemish, as imitators of Christ, and as sons of the living God. Moreover, also, Elijah and Elisha, and many other holy men, we find to have lived a holy[7] and spotless life. If, therefore, thou desirest to be like these, imitate them with all thy power. For the Scripture has said, "The elders who are among you, honour; and, seeing their manner of life and conduct, imitate their faith."[8] And again it saith, "Imitate me, my brethren, as I *imitate* Christ."[9]

CHAP. VII. — THE TRUE VIRGIN.

Those, therefore, who imitate Christ, imitate Him earnestly. For those who have "put on Christ"[10] in truth, express His likeness in their thoughts, and in their whole life, and in all their behaviour: in word, and in deeds, and in patience, and in fortitude, and in knowledge, and in chastity, and in long-suffering, and in a pure heart, and in faith, and in hope, and in full and perfect love towards God. No virgin, therefore, unless they be in everything as Christ, and as those "who are Christs,"[11] can be saved. For every virgin who is in God is holy in her body and in her spirit, and is constant in the service of her Lord, not turning away from it any whither, but waiting upon Him always in purity and holiness in the Spirit of God, being "solicitous how she may please her Lord,"[12] *by living* purely and without stain, and solicitous to be pleasing before Him in every thing. She who is such does not withdraw from our Lord, but in spirit is *ever* with her Lord: as it is written, "Be ye holy, as I am holy, saith the Lord."[13]

CHAP. VIII. — VIRGINS, BY THE LAYING ASIDE OF ALL CARNAL AFFECTION, ARE IMITATORS OF GOD.

For, if a man be only in name called holy, he is not holy; but he must be holy in everything: in his body and in his spirit. And those who are virgins rejoice at all times in becoming like God and His Christ, and are imitators of them. For in those that are such there is not "the mind[14] of the flesh." In those who are truly believers, and "in whom the Spirit of Christ dwells"[15] — in them "the mind of the flesh" cannot be: which is fornication, uncleanness, wantonness; idolatry,[16] sorcery; enmity, jealousy, rivalry, wrath, disputes, dissensions, ill-will; drunkenness, revelry; buffoonery, foolish talking, boisterous laughter; backbiting, insinuations; bitterness, rage; clamour, abuse, insolence of speech; malice, inventing of evil, falsehood; talkativeness,[17] babbling;[18] threatenings, gnashing of teeth, readiness to accuse,[19] jarring,[20] disdainings, blows; perversions *of the right*,[21] laxness *in judgment;* haughtiness, arrogance, ostentation, pompousness, *boasting* of family, of beauty, of position, of wealth, of an arm of flesh;[22] quarrelsomeness, injustice,[23] eagerness for victory; hatred, anger, envy, perfidy, retaliation;[24] debauchery, gluttony, "overreaching (which is idolatry),"[25] "the love of money (which is the root of all evils);"[26] love of display, vainglory, love of rule, assumption, pride (which is called death, and which "God fights against").[27] Every man with whom are these and such like things — every such man is of the flesh. For, "he that is born of the flesh is flesh; and he that is of the earth speaketh of the earth,"[28] and his thoughts are of the earth. And "the mind of the flesh is enmity towards God. For it does not submit itself to the law of God; for it cannot *do so*,"[29] because it is in the flesh, "in which dwells no good,"[30] because the Spirit of God is

---

[1] Matt. xi. 11.
[2] *Lit.* "lover," or "friend."
[3] John xxi. 20.
[4] i.e., a virgin.
[5] Phil. iv. 3.
[6] i.e., virginity.
[7] i.e., celibate, or chaste.
[8] Heb. xiii. 7.
[9] 1 Cor. xi. 1.
[10] Rom. xiii. 14.
[11] Gal. v. 24.
[12] 1 Cor. vii. 32.

[13] 1 Pet. i. 15 (*cf.* Lev. xi. 44).
[14] Rom. viii. 6 (φρόνημα).
[15] Rom. viii. 9.
[16] *Lit.* "the worship of idols." The single word ‎ܟ̈ܘܡܪܐ, sometimes used to express "idolatry" (as in *Eph. Syr.*, opp. tom. i. p. 116), is not found in these epistles.
[17] *Lit.* "much talking."
[18] *Lit.* "empty words."
[19] The word thus rendered is not in the lexicons, but is well illustrated by Isa. xxix. 21 (" that *make* a man an offender "), where the Hiphil of חטא is used, corresponding to the Aphel of the same root, from which the present word is derived.
[20] The word is used in the Peschito of 1 Tim. vi. 5, to express διαπαρατριβαὶ ("incessant quarrellings," *Alf.*); [R. V., "wranglings."— R.].
[21] *Ex. Conject.* Beelen. The word is not in the lexicons.
[22] Or "power."
[23] *Lit.* "folly;" but so used in 2 Cor. xii. 13.
[24] Or "returning of evils."
[25] Col. iii. 5.
[26] 1 Tim. vi. 10.
[27] 1 Pet. v. 5; Jas. iv. 6.
[28] John iii. 6, 31.
[29] Rom. viii. 7.
[30] Rom. vii. 18.

not in it. For this cause justly does the Scripture say regarding such a generation as this : " My Spirit shall not dwell in men for ever, because they are flesh." [1] " Whosoever, therefore, has not the Spirit of God in him, is none of His : " [2] as it is written, " The Spirit of God departed from Saul, and an evil spirit troubled him, which was sent upon him from God." [3]

CHAP. IX. — CONTINUATION OF THE SUBJECT OF MORTIFICATION ; DIGNITY OF PERSONS CONSECRATED TO GOD.

He in whomsoever the Spirit of God is, is in accord with the will of the Spirit of God ; and, because he is in accord with the Spirit of God, therefore does he mortify the deeds of the body and live unto God, " treading down and subjugating the body and keeping it under ; so that, while preaching to others," he may be a beautiful example and pattern to believers, and may spend his life in works which are worthy of the Holy Spirit, so that he may " not be cast away," [4] but may be approved before God and before men. For in " the man who is of God," [5] with him *I say* there is nothing of the mind of the flesh ; and especially in virgins *of either sex ;* but the fruits of all of them are " the fruits of the Spirit " [6] and of life, and they are truly the city of God, and the houses and temples in which God abides and dwells, and among which He walks, as in the holy city of heaven. For in this " do ye appear to the world as lights, in that ye give heed to the Word of life," [7] and thus ye are in truth the praise, and the boast, and the crown of rejoicing, and the delight of good servants in our Lord Jesus Christ. For all who see you will " acknowledge that ye are the seed which the Lord hath blessed ; " [8] in very deed a seed honourable and holy, and " a priestly kingdom, a holy people, the people of the inheritance," [9] the heirs of the promises of God ; *of* things which do not decay, nor wither ; of " that which eye hath not seen, and ear hath not heard, and which hath not come up into the heart of man ; of that which God hath prepared for those who love Him and keep His commandments." [10]

CHAP. X. — DENUNCIATION OF DANGEROUS AND SCANDALOUS ASSOCIATION WITH MAIDENS.

Now, we are persuaded of you, my brethren, that your thoughts are occupied about those things which are requisite for your salvation. [11] But we speak thus [12] in consequence of the evil rumours and reports concerning shameless men, who, under pretext of the fear of God, have their dwelling with maidens, and *so* expose themselves to danger, and walk with them along the road and in solitary places [13] alone — a course which is full of dangers, and full of stumbling-blocks and snares and pitfalls ; nor is it in any respect right for Christians and those who fear God so to conduct themselves. Others, too, eat and drink with them at entertainments *allowing themselves* in loose behaviour and much uncleanness — such as ought not to be among believers, and especially among those who have chosen for themselves *a life of* holiness. [14] Others, again, meet together for vain and trifling conversation and merriment, and that they may speak evil of one another ; and they hunt up tales against one another, and are idle : persons with whom we do not allow you even to eat bread. Then, others gad about among the houses of virgin brethren or sisters, on pretence of visiting them, or reading the Scriptures *to them*, or exorcising them. Forasmuch as they are idle and do no work, they pry into those things which ought not to be inquired into, and by means of plausible words make merchandise of the name of Christ. *These are* men from whom the divine apostle kept aloof, because of the multitude of their evil *deeds ;* as it is written : " Thorns sprout in the hands of the idle ; " [15] and, " The ways of the idle are full of thorns." [16]

CHAP. XI. — PERNICIOUSNESS OF IDLENESS ; WARNING AGAINST THE EMPTY LONGING TO BE TEACHERS ; ADVICE ABOUT TEACHING AND THE USE OF DIVINE GIFTS.

Such are the ways of all those who do not work, but go hunting for tales, and think to themselves that this is profitable and right. [17] For such persons are like those idle and prating widows " who go wandering about [18] among houses " [19] with their prating, and hunt for idle tales, and carry them from house to house with much exaggeration, without fear of God. And besides all this, barefaced men as they are, [20] under pretence of teaching, they set forth a variety of doctrines. And would that they taught the doctrines of truth ! But it is this which is *so* disquieting, that they understand not what they mean, and assert that which is not *true :* because they wish to be teachers, and to display themselves as skil-

---

1 Gen. vi. 3. [This is an example of the vicious method of interpretation, not yet extirpated, which carries Paul's distinctive use of the term " flesh " back to the Pentateuch, where no ethical sense is necessarily implied. — R.]
2 Rom. vii. 9. [The Apostle speaks of " the Spirit of *Christ*."—R.]
3 1 Sam. xvi. 14.
4 1 Cor. ix. 27.
5 1 Tim. vi. 11.
6 Gal. v. 22.
7 Phil. ii. 15, 16.
8 Isa. lxi. 9.
9 1 Pet. ii. 9.
10 1 Cor. ii. 9.

11 Or " life."
12 The words which follow, " concerning those things which we speak," appear not to be genuine. — BEELEN.
13 Beelen supposes a ἐν διὰ δυοῖν: " along the lonely road."
14 i.e., virginity.
15 Prov. xxvi. 9.
16 Prov. xv. 19 (LXX.).
17 *Lit.* " profit and righteousness."
18 *Lit.* " go about and wander."
19 1 Tim. v. 13.
20 *Lit.* " in their barefacedness."

ful in speaking; because they traffic in iniquity in the name of Christ — which it is not right for the servants of God *to do*. And they hearken not to that which the Scripture has said : " Let not many be teachers among you, my brethren, and be not all of you prophets." [1] For " he who does not transgress in word is a perfect man, able to keep down and subjugate his whole body." [2] And, " If a man speak, let him speak in the words [3] of God." [4] And, " If there is in thee understanding, give an answer to thy brother ; but if not, put thy hand on thy mouth." [5] For, " at one time *it is proper* to keep silence, and at another time to speak." [6] And again it says : " When a man speaks in season, it is honourable [7] to him." [8] And again it says : " Let your speech be seasoned with grace. For it is required of a man to know how to give an answer to every one in season." [9] For " he that utters whatsoever comes to his mouth, that man produces strife ; and he that utters a superfluity of words increases vexation ; and he that is hasty with his lips falls into evil. For because of the unruliness of the tongue cometh anger ; but the perfect man keeps watch over his tongue, and loves his soul's life." [10] For these are they " who by good words and fair speeches lead astray the hearts of the simple, and, while offering them blessings, lead them astray." [11] Let us, therefore, fear the judgment which awaits teachers. For a severe judgment will those teachers receive " who teach, but do not," [12] and those who take *upon them* the name of Christ falsely, and say : We teach the truth, and *yet* go wandering about idly, and exalt themselves, and make their boast " in the mind of the flesh." [13] These, moreover, are like " the blind man who leads the blind man, and they both fall into the ditch." [14] And they will receive judgment, because in their talkativeness and their frivolous teaching they teach natural [15] wisdom, and the " frivolous error of the plausible words of the wisdom of men," [16] " according to the will of the prince of the dominion of the air, and of the spirit which works in those men who will not obey, according to the training of this world, and not according to the doctrine of Christ." [17] But if thou hast received " the word of knowledge, or

the word of instruction, or of prophecy," [18] blessed be God, " who helps every man without grudging — that God who gives to every man and does not upbraid *him*." [19] With the gift, therefore, which thou hast received from our Lord, serve *thy* spiritual brethren, the prophets who know that the words which thou speakest are *those* of our Lord ; and declare the gift which thou hast received in the Church for the edification of the brethren in Christ (for good and excellent are those things which help the men of God), if so be that they are truly with thee. [20]

CHAP. XII. — RULES FOR VISITS, EXORCISMS, AND HOW PEOPLE ARE TO ASSIST THE SICK, AND TO WALK IN ALL THINGS WITHOUT OFFENCE.

Moreover, also, this is comely and useful, that a man " visit orphans and widows," [21] and especially those poor persons who have many children. These things are, without controversy, required of the servants of God, and comely and suitable for them. This also, again, is suitable and right and comely for those who are brethren in Christ, that they should visit those who are harassed by evil spirits, and pray and pronounce adjurations [22] over them, intelligently, *offering* such prayer as is acceptable before God ; not with a multitude of fine words, [23] well prepared and arranged, so that they may appear to men eloquent and of a good memory. *Such men* are " like a sounding pipe, or a tinkling cymbal ; " [24] and they bring no help to those over whom they make their adjurations ; but they speak with terrible words, and affright people, but do not act with true faith, according to the teaching of our Lord, who hath said : " This kind goeth not out but by fasting and prayer," [25] offered unceasingly and with earnest mind. And let them holily ask and beg of God, with cheerfulness and all circumspection and purity, without hatred and without malice. In this way let us approach a brother or a sister who is sick, and visit them in a way that is right, without guile, and without covetousness, and without noise, and without talkativeness, and without such behaviour as is alien from the fear of God, and without haughtiness, but with the meek and lowly spirit of Christ. Let them, therefore, with fasting and with prayer make their adjurations, and not with the elegant and well-arranged and fitly-ordered words of learning, but as men who have received the gift of healing from God, confidently, to the glory of

[1] 1 Cor. xii. 29. [But compare Jas. iii. 1: " Be not many teachers" (R.V.), which precedes the next citation. — R.]
[2] Jas. iii. 2.
[3] *Lit.* " speech."
[4] 1 Pet. iv. 11.
[5] Ecclus. v. 14.
[6] Eccl. iii. 7.
[7] *Lit.* " beautiful."
[8] Prov. xxv. 11.
[9] *Lit.* " in his place." Col. iv. 6.
[10] *Lit.* " his soul for life." Prov. xviii. 6, xiii. 3, xxi. 23.
[11] Rom. xvi. 17-19.
[12] Matt. xxiii. 3.
[13] Col. ii. 18.
[14] Matt. xv. 14.
[15] As 1 Cor. xv. 44 (ψυχικός). — See Jas. iii. 15 [also 1 Cor. ii. 13, 14. — R.].
[16] See Col. ii. 8.
[17] Eph. ii. 2; Col. ii. 8.

[18] 1 Cor. xii. 8-10.
[19] Jas i. 5.
[20] An obscure clause, which Beelen supposes to be due to the misapprehension of the Syrian translator. Perhaps the difficulty will be met if we read " gifts," as do Wets. and Zing., by a change in the pointing.
[21] Jas. i. 27.
[22] Or " exorcisms."
[23] *Lit.* " elegant and numerous words."
[24] 1 Cor. xiii. 1.
[25] Matt. xvii. 21. [Or Mark ix. 29; the verse in Matthew is of doubtful genuineness. — R.]

God. By[1] your fastings and prayers and perpetual watching, together with your other good works, mortify the works of the flesh by the power of the Holy Spirit. He who acts thus "is a temple of the Holy Spirit of God."[2] Let this man cast out demons, and God will help him. For it is good that a man help those that are sick. Our Lord hath said: "Cast out demons," at the same time *commanding* many other acts of healing; and, "Freely ye have received, freely give."[3] For such persons as these a goodly recompense is *laid up* by God, because they serve their brethren with the gifts which have been given them by the Lord. This is also comely and helpful to the servants of God, because they act according to the injunctions of our Lord, who hath said: "I was sick, and ye visited Me, and so on."[4] And this is comely and right and just, that we visit our neighbours for the sake of God with all seemliness of manner and purity of behaviour; as the Apostle hath said: "Who is sick, and I am not sick? who is offended, and I am not offended?"[5] But all these things are spoken in reference to the love with which a man should love his neighbour. And in these things let us occupy ourselves,[6] without giving offence, and let us not do anything with partiality or for the shaming of others, but let us love the poor as the servants of God, and especially let us visit them. For this is comely before God and before men, that we should remember the poor, and be lovers of the brethren and of strangers, for the sake of God and for the sake of those who believe in God, as we have learnt from the law and from the prophets, and from our Lord Jesus Christ, concerning the love of the brotherhood and the love of strangers: for ye know the words which have been spoken concerning the love of the brotherhood and the love of strangers;[7] powerfully are the words spoken to all those who do them.

CHAP. XIII. — WHAT PRIESTS SHOULD BE AND SHOULD NOT BE.

Beloved brethren! that a man should build up and establish the brethren on the faith in one

God, this also is manifest and well-known. This too, again, is comely, that a man should not be envious of his neighbour. And moreover, again, it is suitable and comely that all those who work the works of the Lord should work the works of the Lord in the fear of God. Thus is it required of them to conduct themselves. That "the harvest is great, but the workmen are few," this also is well-known and manifest. Let us, therefore, "ask of the Lord of the harvest" that He would send forth workmen into the harvest;[8] such workmen as "shall skilfully dispense the word of truth;" workmen "who shall not be ashamed;"[9] faithful workmen; workmen who shall be "the light of the world;"[10] workmen who "work not for the food that perisheth, but for that food which abideth unto life eternal;"[11] workmen who shall be such as the apostles; workmen who imitate the Father, and the Son, and the Holy Spirit; who are concerned for the salvation of men; not "hireling"[12] workmen; not workmen to whom the fear of God and righteousness appear to be gain; not workmen who "serve their belly;" not workmen who "with fair speeches and pleasant words mislead the hearts of the innocent;"[13] not workmen who imitate the children of light, while they are not light but darkness — "men whose end is destruction;"[14] not workmen who practise iniquity and wickedness and fraud; not "crafty workmen;"[15] not workmen "drunken" and "faithless;"[16] nor workmen who traffic in Christ;[17] not misleaders; not "lovers of money; not malevolent."[18]

Let us, therefore, contemplate and imitate the faithful who have conducted themselves well in the Lord, as is becoming and suitable to our calling and profession. Thus let us do service before God in justice and righteousness, and without blemish, "occupying ourselves with things good and comely before God *and* also before men."[19] For this is comely, that God be glorified in us in all things.

Here endeth the first Epistle of Clement.

---

[1] Or "in."
[2] 1 Cor. vi. 19.
[3] Matt. x. 8.
[4] *Lit.* "and things similar to these," Matt. xxv. 36.
[5] 2 Cor. xi. 29.
[6] *Lit.* "let us be."
[7] Beelen here omits, as spurious, the words, "because this same thing is pleasant and agreeable to you: because ye are all taught of God."

[8] Matt. ix. 37, 38.
[9] *Lit.* "without shame," 2 Tim. ii. 15.
[10] Matt. v. 14.
[11] John vi. 27.
[12] John x. 12, 13.
[13] Rom. xvi. 18.
[14] Phil. iii. 19.
[15] 2 Cor. xi. 13.
[16] See Matt. xxiv. 45-51.
[17] [Comp. the term χριστέμπορος, "Christ-monger," "Christ-trafficker," in *Teaching*, chap. xii. 5, vol. vii. p. 381. — R.]
[18] 1 Tim. iii. 3; Tit. i. 7.
[19] Rom. xii. 17.

THE SECOND EPISTLE OF THE SAME CLEMENT.

CHAP. I. — HE DESCRIBES THE CIRCUMSPECTNESS OF HIS INTERCOURSE WITH THE OTHER SEX, AND TELLS HOW IN HIS JOURNEYS HE ACTS AT PLACES WHERE THERE ARE BRETHREN ONLY.

I WOULD, moreover, have you know, my brethren, of what sort is our conduct in Christ, as well as that of all our brethren, in the *various* places in which we are. And if so be that you approve it, do ye also conduct yourselves in like manner in the Lord. Now we, if God help us, conduct ourselves thus : with maidens we do not dwell, nor have we anything in common with them ; with maidens we do not eat, nor drink ; and, where a maiden sleeps, we do not sleep ; neither do women wash our feet, nor anoint us ; and on no account do we sleep where a maiden sleeps who is unmarried or has taken the vow : [1] even though she be in some other place *if she be* alone, we do not pass the night there.[2] Moreover, if it chance that the time *for rest* overtake us in a place, whether in the country, or in a village, or in a town, or in a hamlet,[3] or wheresoever we happen to be, and there are found brethren in that place, we turn in to one who is a brother, and call together there all the brethren, and speak to them words of encouragement and exhortation.[4] And those among us who are gifted in speaking will speak such words as are earnest, and serious, and chaste, in the fear of God, and *exhort them* to please God in everything, and abound and go forward in good works, and " be free from [5] anxious care in everything," [6] as is fit and right for the people of God.

CHAP. II. — HIS BEHAVIOUR IN PLACES WHERE THERE WERE CHRISTIANS OF BOTH SEXES.

And if, moreover, it chance that we are distant from our homes and from our neighbours, and the day decline and the eventide overtake us, and the brethren press us, through love of the brotherhood and by reason of their affection for strangers, to stay with them, so that we may watch with them, and they may hear the holy word of God and do *it*, and be fed with the words of the Lord, so that they may be mindful of them, and they set before us bread and water and that which God provides, and we be willing and consent to stay through the night with them ; if there be there a holy man,[7] with him

we turn in and lodge, and that same brother will provide and prepare whatever is necessary for us ; and he himself waits upon us, and he himself washes our feet for us and anoints us with ointment, and he himself gets ready a bed for us, that we may sleep in reliance on God. All these things will that consecrated brother, who is in the place in which we tarry, do in his own person. He will himself serve the brethren, and each one of the brethren who are in the same place will join with him in rendering all those services [8] which are requisite for the brethren. But with us may no female, whether young maiden or married woman, be there at that time ; [9] nor she that is aged,[10] nor she that has taken the vow ; not even a maid-servant, whether Christian or heathen ; but there shall only be men with men. And, if we see it to be requisite to stand and pray for the sake of the women, and to speak words of exhortation and edification, we call *together* the brethren and all the holy sisters and maidens, *and* likewise all the other women who are there, *inviting them* with all modesty and becoming behaviour to come and feast on the truth.[11] And those among us who are skilled in speaking speak to them, and exhort them in those words which God has given us. And then we pray, and salute [12] one another, the men the men. But the women and the maidens will wrap their hands in their garments ; *and* we also, with circumspection and with all purity, our eyes looking upwards, shall wrap our right hand in our garments ; and then they will come and give us the salutation on our right hand wrapped in our garments. Then we go where God permits us.

CHAP. III. — RULES FOR THE CONDUCT OF CELIBATE BRETHREN IN PLACES WHERE THERE ARE ONLY MARRIED CHRISTIANS.

And if again we chance to come into a place where there is no consecrated brother, but all are married, all those who are there will receive the brother who comes to them, and minister to him, and care for his wants [13] in everything, assiduously, with good-will. And the brother shall be ministered to by them in the way that is suit-

---

[1] *Lit.* " or *is* a daughter of the covenant."
[2] Beelen's rendering, " we do not even pass the night," seems not to be favoured either by the arrangement or the context.
[3] *Lit.* " dwelling-place."
[4] Or " consolation." So παράκλησις in the N. T. has both senses.
[5] *Lit.* " without."
[6] Phil. iv. 6.
[7] i.e., one who has taken the vow of celibacy.

[8] *Lit.* " will with him minister all those things."
[9] [The minuteness of all these precepts is of itself suspicious. The " simplicity " of the earlier age had evidently passed when these prohibitions were penned. — R.]
[10] ܟܣܝܐ, Beelen's conjecture for ܟܣܝܐ, " rich." Zingerle proposes ܟܣܝܐ, " about *to be married*."
[11] *Lit.* " come to the delight of the truth."
[12] *Lit.* " ask of the peace of."
[13] *Lit.* " for that which is his ; " or " for what *belongs to him*."

able. And the brother will say to the married persons who are in that place : We holy men do not eat or drink with women, nor are we waited on by women or by maidens, nor do women wash our feet for us, nor do women anoint us, nor do women prepare our bed for us, nor do we sleep where women sleep, so that we may be without reproach in everything, lest any one should be offended or stumble at us. And, whilst we observe all these things, "we are without offence to every man."[1] As persons, therefore, "who know the fear of the Lord, we persuade men, and to God we are made manifest."[2]

CHAP. IV. — CONDUCT OF THE HOLY MAN WHERE THERE ARE WOMEN ONLY.

But if we chance to come into a place where there are no *Christian* men, but all the believers are women and maidens,[3] and they press us to pass the night there in that place, we call them all together to some suitable place,[4] and ask them how they do ; and according to that which we learn from them, and what we see to be their state of mind, we address them in a suitable manner, as men fearing God. And when they have all assembled and come *together*, and we see that they are in peace,[5] we address to them words of exhortation in the fear of God, and read the Scripture to them, with purity and in the concise[6] and weighty words of the fear of God. We do everything as for their edification. And as to those who are married, we speak to them in the Lord in a manner suited to them. And if, moreover, the day decline and the eventide draw on, we select, in order to pass the night there, a woman who is aged and the most exemplary[7] of them all ; and we speak to her to give us a place all to ourselves, where no woman enters, nor maiden. And this old woman herself will bring us a lamp, and whatever is requisite for us she will herself bring us. From love to the brethren, she will bring whatever is requisite for the service of stranger brethren. And she herself, when the time for sleep is come, will depart and go to her house in peace.

CHAP. V. — WHERE THERE IS ONLY ONE WOMAN, THE FATHER DOES NOT MAKE A STAY ; HOW CAREFULLY STUMBLING-BLOCKS MUST BE AVOIDED.

But if, moreover, we chance upon a place, and find there one believing woman only, and no other person be there but she only, we do not stop there, nor pray there, nor read the Scrip-

tures there, but we flee as from before the face of a serpent, and as from before the face of sin. Not that we disdain the believing woman — far be it from us to be so minded towards our brethren in Christ ! — but, because she is alone, we are afraid lest any one should make insinuations against us in words of falsehood. For the hearts of men are firmly set[8] on evil. And, that we may not give a pretext to those who desire to get a pretext against us and to speak evil of us, and that we may not be a stumbling-block to any one, on this account we cut off the pretext of those who desire to get a pretext against us ; on this account we must be "on our guard that we be to no one a stumbling-block, neither to the Jews, nor to the Gentiles, nor yet to the Church of God ; and we must not seek that which is profitable to ourselves only, but that which is for the profit of many, so that they may be saved."[9] For this does not profit us, that another stumble because of us. Let us, therefore, be studiously on our guard at all times, that we do not smite our brethren and give them to drink of a disquieting conscience through our being to them a stumbling-block. For "if for the sake of meat our brother be made sad, or shocked, or made weak, or caused to stumble, we are not walking in the love of God. For the sake of meat thou causest him to perish for whose sake Christ died."[10] For, *in* "thus sinning against your brethren and wounding their sickly consciences, ye sin against Christ Himself. For, if for the sake of meat my brother is made to stumble," let us *who are* believers say, "Never will we eat flesh, that we may not make our brother to stumble."[11] These things, moreover, does ever one who truly loves God, who truly takes up his cross, and puts on Christ, and loves his neighbour ; the man who watches over himself that he be not a stumbling-block to any one, that no one be caused to stumble because of him and die because he is constantly with maidens and lives in the same house with them — a thing which is not right — to the overthrow of those who see and hear. Evil conduct like this is fraught with stumbling and peril, and *is* akin[12] to death. But blessed is that man who is circumspect and fearful in everything for the sake of purity !

CHAP. VI. — HOW CHRISTIANS SHOULD BEHAVE THEMSELVES AMONG HEATHENS.

If, moreover, it chance that we go to a place in which there are no Christians, and it be im-

---

[1] 2 Cor. vi. 3.
[2] 2 Cor. v. 11.
[3] *Lit.* "all of them are believing women and maidens."
[4] *Lit.* "some place on the right side." The Syrian translator has probably mistaken the meaning of εἰς ἕνα τόπον δεξιόν, where δεξιόν may be compared with *dexter* in Hor., *Sat.*, ii. 1, 18. — BEELEN.
[5] Probably meaning, "when we have inquired of their welfare."
[6] *Lit.* "compressed."
[7] *Lit.* "chaste," or "modest."

[8] Or "are set and fixed."
[9] 1 Cor. x. 32, 33.
[10] Rom. xiv. 15. [The Apostle's noble and consistent counsel to the "strong" brethren at Rome is in sharp contrast with the use here made of it. Only one of the "weak" brethren could have written this epistle. — R.]
[11] 1 Cor. viii. 12, 13.
[12] *Lit.* "near."

portant for us to stay there a few days, let us be "wise as serpents, and harmless as doves;"[1] and let us "not be as the foolish, but as the wise,"[2] in all the *self*-restraint of the fear of God, that God may be glorified in everything through our Lord Jesus Christ, through our chaste and holy behaviour. For, "whether we eat, or drink, or do anything else, let us do it as for the glory of God."[3] Let "all those who see us acknowledge that we are a blessed seed,"[4] "sons of the living God,"[5] in everything — in all *our* words, in shamefastness, in purity, in humility, forasmuch as we do not copy the heathen in anything, nor are *as* believers like *other* men, but in everything are estranged from the wicked. And we "do not cast that which is holy before dogs, nor pearls before swine;"[6] but with all possible *self*-restraint, and with all discretion, and with all fear of God, and with earnestness of mind we praise God. For we do not minister where heathens are drinking and blaspheming in their feasts with words of impurity, because of their wickedness.[7] Therefore do we not sing *psalms* to the heathens, nor do we read to them the Scriptures, that we may not be like *common* singers, either those who play on the lyre,[8] or those who sing with the voice, or *like* soothsayers, as many are, who follow these practices and do these things, that they may sate themselves with a paltry mouthful of bread, and who, for the sake of a sorry cup of wine, go *about* "singing the songs of the Lord in the strange land"[9] of the heathen, and doing what is not right. Do not so, my brethren; we beseech you, my brethren, let not these deeds be done among you; but put away those who choose thus to behave themselves with infamy and disgrace. It is not proper, my brethren, that these things should be so. But we beseech you, brethren in righteousness, that these things be so *done* with you as with us, as for a pattern of believers, and of those who shall believe. Let us be of the flock of Christ, in all righteousness, and in all holy and unblemished conduct, behaving ourselves with uprightness and sanctity, as is right for believers, and observing those things which are praiseworthy, and pure, and holy, and honourable, and noble; and do ye promote[10] all those things which are profitable. For ye are "our joy, and our crown," and our hope, and our life, "if so be that ye stand in the Lord."[11] So be it![12]

[1] Matt. x. 16.
[2] Eph. v. 15.
[3] 1 Cor. x. 31.
[4] Isa. lxi. 9.
[5] Phil. ii. 15.
[6] Matt. vii. 6.
[7] Beelen joins " because of their wickedness " with the words that follow.
[8] Or " cithara."
[9] Ps. cxxxvii. 4.
[10] Or " set on foot."
[11] Phil. iv. 1.
[12] Or " Amen."

CHAP. VII. — USES OF CONSIDERING ADMONITORY EXAMPLES, AS WELL AS INSTRUCTIVE PATTERNS.

Let us consider, therefore, my brethren, and see how all the righteous fathers conducted themselves during the whole time of their sojourn in *this* life, and let us search and examine from the law *down* to the New Testament. For this is both becoming and profitable, that we should know how many men there have been, and who *they were*, that have perished through women; and who and how many have been the women that have perished through men, by reason of the constancy with which they have associated with one another. And further, also, for the same reason, I will show how many have been the men, and who *they were*, that lived all their lifetime, and continued even to the close, with one another in *the performance of* chaste works without blemish. And it is manifest and well-known that this is so.[13]

CHAP. VIII. — JOSEPH AND POTIPHAR'S WIFE; OF WHAT KIND LOVE TO FEMALES OUGHT TO BE.

There is Joseph, faithful, and intelligent, and wise, and who feared God in everything. Did not a woman conceive an excessive passion for the beauty of this chaste and upright man? And, when he would not yield and consent to gratify her passionate desire,[14] she cast the righteous man into every kind of distress and torment, to within a little of death,[15] by *bearing* false witness. But God delivered him from all the evils that came upon him through *this* wretched woman. Ye see, my brethren, what distresses the constant sight of the person of the Egyptian woman brought upon the righteous man. Therefore, let us not be constantly with women, nor with maidens. For this is not profitable for those who truly wish to "gird up their loins."[16] For it is required that we love the sisters in all purity and chasteness, and with all curbing of thought, in the fear of God, not associating constantly with them, nor finding access to them at every hour.

CHAP. IX. — SAMSON'S ADMONITORY FALL.

Hast thou not heard concerning Samson the Nazarite, "with whom was the Spirit of God,"[17] the man of great strength? This man, who was a Nazarite, and consecrated to God, and who was *gifted* with strength and might, a woman brought to ruin with *her* wretched body, and with *her* vile passion. Art thou, perchance, such a man as he? Know thyself, and know the measure of

[13] Wetstein and Zingerle join on this sentence to the next, by a change of the construction.
[14] *Lit.* " her passion and her desire."
[15] *Lit.* " even to death."
[16] Luke xii. 35.
[17] Judges xiii. 25.

thy strength.[1] "The married woman catcheth precious souls."[2] Therefore, we do not allow any man whatsoever to sit with a married woman; much less to live in the same house with a maiden who has taken the vow, or to sleep where she sleeps, or to be constantly with her. For this is to be hated and abominated by those who fear God.

CHAP. X. — DAVID'S SIN, SO ADMONITORY TO US WEAK MEN.

Does not the case of David instruct thee, whom God "found a man after His heart,"[3] one faithful, faultless, pious, true? This same man saw the beauty of a woman — I mean of Bathsheba — when he saw her as she was cleansing herself and washing unclothed. This woman the holy man saw, and was thoroughly[4] captivated with desire by the sight of her.[5] See, then, what evils he committed because of a woman, and *how* this righteous man sinned, and gave command that the husband of this woman should be killed in battle. Ye have seen what wicked schemes he laid and executed, and *how*, because of his passion for a woman, he perpetrated a murder — *he*, David, who was called "the anointed of the Lord."[6] Be admonished, O man : for, if such men as these have been brought to ruin through women, what is *thy* righteousness, or what art thou among the holy, that thou consortest with women and with maidens day and night, with much silliness, without fear of God? Not *thus*, my brethren, not thus let us conduct ourselves ; but let us be mindful of that word which is spoken concerning a woman : "Her hands lay snares, and her heart spreadeth nets ; but the just shall escape from her, whilst the wicked falleth into her hands."[7] Therefore let us, who are consecrated,[8] be careful not to live in the same house with females who have taken the vow. For such conduct as this is not becoming nor right for the servants of God.

CHAP. XI. — ADMONITORY HISTORY OF THE INCESTUOUS CHILDREN OF DAVID.

Hast thou not read concerning Amnon and Tamar, the children of David? This Amnon conceived a passion for his sister, and humbled her, and did not spare her, because he longed for her with a shameful passion ; and he proved wicked and profligate because of his constant intercourse with her, without the fear of God, and he "wrought uncleanness in Israel."[9]

Therefore, it is not proper for us, nor right for us, to associate with sisters, *indulging* in laughter and looseness ; but *we ought to behave towards them* with all chasteness and purity, and in the fear of the Lord.

CHAP. XII. — SOLOMON'S INFATUATION THROUGH WOMEN.

Hast thou not read the history of Solomon, the son of David, the man to whom God gave wisdom, and knowledge, and largeness of mind,[10] and riches, and much glory, beyond all men? Yet this same man, through women, came to ruin,[11] and departed from the Lord.

CHAP. XIII. — THE HISTORY OF SUSANNA TEACHES CIRCUMSPECTION WITH THE EYES AND IN SOCIETY.

Hast thou not read, and dost thou not know, concerning those elders who were in the days of Susanna, who, because they were constantly with women, and looking upon the beauty which was another's,[12] fell into the depths of wantonness, and were not able to keep themselves in a chaste mind,[13] but were overcome by a depraved disposition, and came suddenly[14] upon the blessed Susanna to corrupt her. But she did not consent to their foul passion, but cried unto God, and God saved her out of the hands of the bad old men. Does it not, therefore, behove us to tremble and be afraid, forasmuch as these old men, judges and elders of the people of God, fell from their dignity because of a woman? For they did not keep in mind that which is said : "Look thou not on the beauty which is another's ;" and, "The beauty of woman has destroyed many ;"[15] and "With a married woman do not sit ;"[16] and that, again, *in* which it says : "Is there any one that puts fire in his bosom, and does not burn his clothes ;"[17] or, "Does a man walk on fire, and his feet are not scorched? So whosoever goeth in to another man's wife is not pure from evil, and whosoever comes near to her shall not escape."[18] And again it says : "Thou shalt not long after the beauty a woman, lest she take thee captive with her eyelids ;"[19] and, "Thou shalt not look upon a maiden, lest thou perish through desire of her ;"[20] and, "With a woman that sings beautifully thou shalt not constantly be ;"[21] and, "Let him that thinketh he standeth take heed lest he fall."[22]

---

[1] *Lit.* "know thy measure."
[2] Prov. vi. 26.
[3] 1 Sam. xvi. 13; Ps. lxxxix. 20, seqq.; Acts xiii. 22.
[4] *Lit.* "verily."
[5] "By the pleasure *derived* from the sight of her." — BEELEN.
[6] Ps. xviii. 50; 2 Sam. xix. 21.
[7] Eccl. vii. 26.
[8] *Lit.* "holy."
[9] Gen. xxxiv. 7.

[10] *Lit.* "heart."
[11] Or "perished."
[12] Susanna having a husband, Joachim.
[13] *Lit.* "a mind of chasteness."
[14] *Lit.* "rose."
[15] Ecclus. ix. 8, 9.
[16] Ecclus. ix. 12.
[17] Prov. vi. 27.
[18] Prov. vi. 28, 29.
[19] Prov. vi. 25.
[20] Ecclus. ix. 5.
[21] Ecclus. ix. 4.
[22] 1 Cor. x. 12.

CHAP. XIV. — EXAMPLES OF CIRCUMSPECT BEHAVIOUR FROM THE OLD TESTAMENT.

But see what it says also concerning *those* holy men, the prophets, and concerning the apostles of our Lord. Let us see whether any one of *these* holy men was constantly with maidens, or with young married women, or with such widows as the divine apostle declines to receive. Let us consider, in the fear of God, the manner of life of *these* holy men. Lo! we find it written concerning Moses and Aaron, that they acted and lived in the company of [1] men, who *themselves also* followed a course of conduct like theirs. And thus *did* Joshua also, the son of Nun. Woman was there none with them; but they by themselves used holily to minister before God, men with men. And not only so; but they taught the people, that, whensoever the host moved, every tribe should move on apart, and the women with the women apart, and that they should go into the rear behind the host, and the men also apart by their tribes. And, according to the command of the Lord, so did they set out, like a wise people, that there might be no disorder on account of the women when the host moved. With beautiful and well-ordered arrangements did they march without stumbling. For lo! the Scriptures bear testimony to my words: "When the children of Israel had crossed over the Sea of Suth, Moses and the children of Israel sang the praises of the Lord, and said: We will praise the Lord, because He is exceedingly to be praised." [2] And, after that Moses had finished [3] singing praises, then Miriam, the sister of Moses and Aaron, took a timbrel in her hands, and all the women went out after her, and sang praises with her, women with women apart, and men with men apart. Then again, we find that Elisha and Gehazi and the sons of the prophets lived together in the fear of God, and that they had no females living with them. Micah *too*, and all the prophets likewise, we find to have lived in this manner in the fear of the Lord.

CHAP. XV. — THE EXAMPLE OF JESUS; HOW WE MAY ALLOW OURSELVES TO BE SERVED BY WOMEN.

And, not to extend our discourse to *too* great length, what shall we say concerning our Lord Jesus Christ? Our Lord Himself was constantly with His twelve disciples when He had come *forth* to the world. And not only so; but also, when He was sending them out, He sent them out two and two together, men with men; but women were not sent with them, and neither in the highway nor in the house did they associate with women or with maidens: and thus they pleased God in every-thing. Also, when our Lord Jesus Christ Himself was talking with the woman of Samaria by the well alone, "His disciples came" and found Him talking with her, "and wondered that Jesus was standing and talking with a woman." [4] Is He not a rule, such as may not be set aside, an example, and a pattern to all the tribes of men? And not only so; but also, when our Lord was risen from the place of the dead, and Mary came to the place of sepulture, she ran and fell at the feet of our Lord and worshipped Him, and would have taken hold of Him. But He said to her: "Touch Me not; for I am not yet ascended to My Father." [5] Is it not, then, matter for astonishment, that, while our Lord did not allow Mary, the blessed woman, to touch His feet, yet *thou* livest with them, and art waited on by women and maidens, and sleepest where they sleep, and women wash thy feet for thee, and anoint thee! Alas for this culpable state of mind! Alas for this state of mind which is destitute of fear! Alas for this affrontery and folly which is without fear of God! Dost thou not judge thine own self? Dost thou not examine thine own self? Dost thou not know thine own self and the measure of thy strength? These things, moreover, are trustworthy, and these things are true and right; and these are rules immutable for those who behave themselves uprightly in our Lord. Many holy women, again, ministered to holy men of their substance, as the Shunammite woman ministered to Elisha; but she did not live with him, but the prophet lived in a house apart. And, when her son died, she wanted to throw herself at the feet of the prophet; but his attendant would not allow her, but restrained her. But Elisha said to his servant: "Let her alone, because her soul is distressed." [6] From these things, then, we ought to understand their manner of life. To Jesus Christ our Lord women ministered of their substance; but they did not live with him; but chastely, and holily, and unblameably they behaved before the Lord, and finished their course, and received the crown in [7] our Lord God Almighty.

CHAP. XVI. — EXHORTATION TO UNION AND TO OBEDIENCE; CONCLUSION.

Therefore, we beseech you, our brethren in our Lord, that these things be observed with you, as with us, and that we may be of the same mind, that we may be one in you and ye may be one in us, and that in everything we may be *of* one soul and one heart in our Lord. Whosoever knoweth the Lord heareth us; and every one

---

[1] *Lit.* "their conduct and living was with."
[2] Exod. xv. 1.
[3] *Lit.* "ceased from."

[4] John iv. 27.
[5] John xx. 17.
[6] 2 Kings iv. 27.
[7] Beelen suggests the reading "from," or to render the present text "by."

who is not of God heareth not us. He who desires truly to keep sanctity heareth us; and the virgin who truly desires to keep virginity heareth us; but she who does not truly desire to keep virginity doth not hear us. Finally, farewell in our Lord, and rejoice in the Lord, all ye saints Peace and joy be with you from God the Father through Jesus Christ our Lord. So be it.

Here endeth the Second Epistle of Clement, the disciple of Peter. His prayer be with us! So be it.

PSEUDO-CLEMENTINE LITERATURE

INTRODUCTORY NOTICE

TO THE

PSEUDO-CLEMENTINE LITERATURE

By PROFESSOR M. B. RIDDLE, D.D.

THE name "Pseudo-Clementine Literature" (or, more briefly, "Clementina") is applied to a series of writings, closely resembling each other, purporting to emanate from the great Roman Father. But, as Dr. Schaff remarks, in this literature he is evidently confounded with "Flavius Clement, kinsman of the Emperor Domitian." [1] These writings are three in number: (1) the *Recognitions*, of which only the Latin translation of Rufinus has been preserved; [2] (2) the *Homilies*, twenty in number, of which a complete collection has been known since 1853; (3) the *Epitome*, "an uninteresting extract from the *Homilies*, to which are added extracts from the letter of Clement to James, from the *Martyrium* of Clement by Simeon Metaphrastes, etc." [3] Other writings may be classed with these; but they are of the same general character, except that most of them show the influence of a later age, adapting the material more closely to the orthodox doctrine.

The *Recognitions* and the *Homilies* appear in the pages which follow. The former are given a prior position, as in the Edinburgh series. It probably cannot be proven that these represent the earlier form of this theological romance; but the *Homilies*, "in any case, present the more doctrinally developed and historically important form of the other treatises, which are essentially similar." [4] They are therefore with propriety placed after the *Recognitions*, which do not seem to have been based upon them, but upon some earlier document. [5]

The critical discussion of the *Clementina* has been keen, but has not reached its end. It necessarily involves other questions, about which there is still great difference of opinion. A few results seem to be established: —

(1) The entire literature is of Jewish-Christian, or Ebionitic, origin. The position accorded to "James, the Lord's brother," in all the writings, is a clear indication of this; so is the silence respecting the Apostle Paul. The doctrinal statements, "though not perfectly homogeneous" (Uhlhorn), are Judaistic, even when mixed with Gnostic speculation of heathen origin. This tendency is, perhaps, not so clearly marked in the *Recognitions* as in the *Homilies;* but both partake largely of the same general character. More particularly, the literature has been connected with the Ebionite sect called the Elkesaites; and some regard the *Homilies* as containing a further development of their system. [6] This is not definitely established, but finds some

---

[1] *History of the Christian Church*, vol. ii. p. 436, new edition.
[2] See the Introductory Note of the Edinburgh translator.
[3] Uhlhorn, article *Clementines*, Schaff-Herzog, i. p. 497. A second *Epitome* has been published by Dressel; see Introductory Notice to *Homilies*.
[4] Lechler, *Apostolic and Post-Apostolic Times*, ii. p. 268, Edinburgh translation, 1886, from 3d edition.
[5] Uhlhorn; see *infra*.
[6] Comp. Uhlhorn, p. 392; Schaff, *History*, ii. p. 436; Lechler, ii. p. 288. See Schaff-Herzog, i. art. *Elkesaites*.

support in the resemblance between the baptismal forms, as given by Hippolytus in the case of the Elkesaites,[1] and those indicated in the *Recognitions* and *Homilies*, especially the latter.[2]

(2) The entire literature belongs to the class of fictitious writing "with a purpose." The Germans properly term the *Homilies* a "Tendenz-Romance." The many "lives of Christ" written in our day to insinuate some other view of our Lord's person than that given in the canonical Gospels, furnish abundant examples of the class. The Tübingen school, finding here a real specimen of the influence of party feeling upon quasi-historical literature, naturally pressed the *Clementina* in support of their theory of the origin of the Gospels.

(3) The discussion leaves it quite probable, though not yet certain, that all the works are "independent elaborations — perhaps at first hand, perhaps at second or third — of some older tract not now extant."[3] Some of the opinions held respecting the relations of the two principal works are given by the Edinburgh translator in his Introductory Notice. It is only necessary here to indicate the progress of the modern discussion. Neander, as early as 1818, gave some prominence to the doctrinal view of the *Homilies*. He was followed by Baur, who found in these writings, as indicated above, support for his theory of the origin of historical Christianity. It is to be noted, however, that the heterogeneous mixture of Ebionism and Gnosticism in the doctrinal views proved perplexing to the leader of the Tübingen school. Schliemann[4] took ground against Baur, collecting much material, and carefully investigating the question. Both authors gave the priority to the *Homilies*. While Baur went too far in one direction, Schliemann, perhaps, failed to recognise fully the basis of truth in the position of the former. The next important step in the discussion was made by Hilgenfeld,[5] whose views are briefly given in the Notice which follows. Hilgenfeld assigned the priority to the *Recognitions*, though he traced all the literature to an earlier work. Uhlhorn[6] at first attempted to prove that the *Recognitions* were a revision of the *Homilies*. Further contributions were made by Lehmann[7] and Lipsius.[8] The former discovered in the *Recognitions* two distinct parts by different authors (i.–iii., iv.–ix.), tracing all the literature to the *Kerygma* of Peter. The latter finds the basis of the whole in the *Acta Petri*, which show a strong anti-Pauline tendency.

Influenced by these investigations, Uhlhorn modified his views. Lechler,[9] while not positive in his convictions, makes the following prudent statement : "An older work lies at the basis both of the *Homilies* and *Recognitions*, bearing the title, *Kerygmen des Petrus*.[10] To this document sometimes the *Homilies*, sometimes the *Recognitions*, correspond more faithfully ; its historical contents are more correctly seen from the *Recognitions*, its doctrinal contents from the *Homilies*." Other views, some of them quite fanciful, have been presented.

The prevalent opinion necessarily leaves us in ignorance of the authors of this literature. The date of composition, or editing, cannot be definitely fixed. In their present form the several works may be as old as the first half of the third century, and the common basis may be placed in the latter half of the second century.

How far the anti-Pauline tendency is carried, is a matter of dispute. Baur and many others think Simon is meant to represent Paul ;[11] but this is difficult to believe, though we must admit

---

[1] See Hippolytus, *Refutation of all Heresies*, book ix. 8-12, *Ante-Nicene Fathers*, vol. v. pp. 131-134. The forms occur in chap. 10, pp. 132, 133.

[2] See *Recognitions*, i. 45-48: *Homilies*, Epistle of Peter to James, 4, Homily XIV. 1.

[3] This is the last opinion of Uhlhorn (Herzog, *Real-Encykl.*, 1877, art. *Clementinen;* comp. Schaff-Herzog, i. p. 498). This author had previously defended the priority of the *Homilies* (*Die Homilien und Rekognitionen des Clemens Romanus*, Göttingen, 1854; comp. Herzog, edition of 1854, art. *Clementinen*).

[4] *Die Clementinen nebst den verwandten Schriften, und der Ebionitismus*, Hamburg, 1844.

[5] *Die Clementinischen Rekognitionen und Homilien, nach ihrem Ursprung und Inhalt dargestellt*, Jena, 1848.

[6] See *supra*, note 3. Uhlhorn found the nucleus of the literature in *Homilies*, xvi.-xix.

[7] *Die Clementinischen Schriften*, Gotha, 1869.

[8] *Die Quellen der römischen Petrussage*, Kiel, 1872.

[9] *Apostolic and Post-Apostolic Times*, vol. ii. p. 270.

[10] So Hilgenfeld, Lehmann, Uhlhorn.

[11] See especially *Homilies*, xvii. 19. Here there is "probably only an incidental sneer at Paul" (Schaff, *History*, ii. p. 438).

the disposition to ignore the Apostle to the Gentiles. As to the literary merit of these productions the reader must judge.

For convenience in comparison of the two works, the following table has been prepared, based on the order of the *Recognitions*. The correspondences are not exact, and the reader is referred to the footnotes for fuller details. This table gives a general view of the arrangement of the two narratives : —

RECOGNITIONS.	HOMILIES.	RECOGNITIONS.	HOMILIES.
I.	I., II.	VI.	XI.
II., III.	III.	VII.	XII., XIII.
——	IV.–VII.	VIII., IX.	XIV., XV.
IV.	VIII., IX.	——	XVI.–XIX.
V.	X., XV.	X.	XX.

INTRODUCTORY NOTICE TO THE RECOGNITIONS OF CLEMENT

[BY THE TRANSLATOR, REV. THOMAS SMITH, D.D.]

THE *Recognitions of Clement* is a kind of philosophical and theological romance. The writer of the work seems to have had no intention of presenting his statements as facts; but, choosing the disciples of Christ and their followers as his principal characters, he has put into their mouths the most important of his beliefs, and woven the whole together by a thread of fictitious narrative.

The *Recognitions* is one of a series; the other members of which that have come down to us are the *Clementine Homilies* and two *Epitomes*.[1]

The authorship, the date, and the doctrinal character of these books have been subjects of keen discussion in modern times. Especial prominence has been given to them by the Tübingen school. Hilgenfeld says: "There is scarcely a single writing which is of so great importance for the history of Christianity in its first stage, and which has already given such brilliant disclosures at the hands of the most renowned critics in regard to the earliest history of the Christian Church, as the writings ascribed to the Roman Clement, the *Recognitions* and *Homilies*."[2] The importance thus attached to these strange and curious documents by one school of theologians, has compelled men of all shades of belief to investigate the subject; but after all their investigations, a great variety of opinion still prevails on almost every point connected with these books.

We leave our readers to judge for themselves in regard to the doctrinal statements, and confine ourselves to a notice of some of the opinions in regard to the authorship and date of the *Recognitions*.[3]

The first question that suggests itself in regard to the *Recognitions* is, whether the *Recognitions* or the *Homilies* are the earliest form of the book, and what relation do they bear to each other? Some maintain that they are both the productions of the same author, and that the one is a later and altered edition of the other; and they find some confirmation of this in the preface of Rufinus. Others think that both books are expansions of another work which formed the basis. And others maintain that the one book is a *rifacimento* of the other by a different hand. Of this third party, some, like Cave, Whiston, Rosenmüller, Staüdlin, Hilgenfeld, and many others, believe that the *Recognitions* was the earliest[4] of the two forms; while others, as Clericus, Möhler, Lücke, Schliemann, and Uhlhorn, give priority to the *Clementines*. Hilgenfeld supposes that the original writing was the Κήρυγμα Πέτρου, which still remains in the work; that besides this there are three parts, — one directed against Basilides, the second the *Travels of Peter* (περίοδοι), and the third the *Recognitions*. There are also, he believes, many interpolated passages of a much later date than any of these parts.[5]

---

[1] [See *supra*, p. 69, and Introductory Notice to *Homilies*. — R.]

[2] *Die Clementinischen Rekognitionen und Homilien, nach ihrem Ursprung und Inhalt dargestellt*, von Dr. Adolf Hilgenfeld, Jena, 1848, p. 1. [Despite the morbid taste of this school for heretical writings, and the now proven incorrectness of the "tendency-theory," due credit must be given to Baur and his followers for awakening a better critical discernment among the students of ecclesiastical history. Hilgenfeld's judgments, in the higher and lower criticism also, are frequently very incorrect; but he has done much to further a correct estimate of the *Clementina*. See Introductory Notice, *supra*. — R.]

[3] [The title, which varies in different manuscripts, is derived from the "narrating, in the last books, of the re-union of the scattered members of the Clementine family, who all at last find themselves together in Christianity, and are baptized by Peter" (Schaff, *History*). — R.]

[4] See Schliemann, *Die Clementinen*, Hamburg, 1844, p. 295.

[5] [See a brief account of the discussion *supra*, p. 70. — R.]

No conclusion has been reached in regard to the author. Some have believed that it is a genuine work of Clement. Whiston maintained that it was written by some of his hearers and companions. Others have attributed the work to Bardesanes. But most acknowledge that there is no possibility of discovering who was the author.

Various opinions exist as to the date of the book. It has been attributed to the first, second, third, and fourth centuries, and some have assigned even a later date. If we were to base our arguments on the work as it stands, the date assigned would be somewhere in the first half of the third century. A passage from the *Recognitions* is quoted by Origen [1] in his *Commentary on Genesis*, written in 231 ; and mention is made in the work of the extension of the Roman franchise to all nations under the dominion of Rome,—an event which took place in the region of Caracalla, A.D. 211. The *Recognitions* also contains a large extract from the work *De Fato*, ascribed to Bardesanes, but really written by a scholar of his. Some have thought that Bardesanes or his scholar borrowed from the *Recognitions ;* but more recently the opinion has prevailed, that the passage was not originally in the *Recognitions*, but was inserted in the *Recognitions* towards the middle of the third century, or even later. [2]

Those who believe the work made up of various documents assign various dates to these documents. Hilgenfeld, for instance, believes that the Κήρυγμα Πέτρου was written before the time of Trajan, and the *Travels of Peter* about the time of his reign.

Nothing is known of the place in which the *Recognitions* was written. Some, as Schliemann, have supposed Rome, some Asia Minor, and recently Uhlhorn has tried to trace it to Eastern Syria. [3]

The Greek of the *Recognitions* is lost. The work has come down to us in the form of a translation by Rufinus of Aquileia (*d.* 410 A.D.). In his letter to Gaudentius, Rufinus states that he omitted some portions difficult of comprehension, but that in regard to the other parts he had translated with care, and an endeavour to be exact even in rendering the phraseology.

The best editions of the *Recognitions* are those by Cotelerius, often reprinted, and by Gersdorf, Lipsiæ, 1838 ; but the text is not in a satisfactory condition.

---

[1] *Philocalia*, cap. 22.

[2] See Merx, *Bardesanes von Edessa*, Halle, 1863, p. 113.

[3] *Die Homilien und Rekognitionen des Clemens Romanus, nach ihrem Ursprung und Inhalt dargestellt*, von Gerhard Uhlhorn, Göttingen, 1854, p. 429. [Schaff thinks " the *Homilies* probably originated in East Syria, the *Recognitions* in Rome." But Rufinus gives no intimation of the Roman origin of the Greek work he translated. Still, the apparently more orthodox character of the *Recognitions* suggests an editor from the Western Church. — R.]

RECOGNITIONS OF CLEMENT

RUFINUS, PRESBYTER OF AQUILEIA; HIS PREFACE TO CLEMENT'S BOOK OF RECOGNITIONS.

TO BISHOP GAUDENTIUS.

To thee, indeed, O Gaudentius, thou choice glory of our doctors, belongs such vigour of mind, yea, such grace of the Spirit, that whatever you say even in the course of your daily preaching, whatever you deliver in the church, ought to be preserved in books, and handed down to posterity for their instruction. But we, whom slenderness of wit renders less ready, and now old age renders slow and inactive, though after many delays, yet at length present to you the work which once the virgin Sylvia of venerable memory enjoined upon us, that we should render Clement into our language, and you afterwards by hereditary right demanded of us; and thus we contribute to the use and profit of our people, no small spoil, as I think, taken from the libraries of the Greeks, so that we may feed with foreign nourishment those whom we cannot with our own. For foreign things usually seem both more pleasant, and sometimes also more profitable. In short, almost everything is foreign that brings healing to our bodies, that opposes diseases, and neutralizes poisons. For Judæa sends us *Lacryma balsami*, Crete *Coma dictamni*, Arabia her flower of spices, India reaps her crop of spikenard; which, although they reach us in a somewhat more broken condition than when they leave their native fields, yet retain entire the sweetness of their odour and their healing virtue. Receive therefore, my soul,[1] Clement returning to you; receive him now in a Roman dress. And wonder not if haply the florid countenance of eloquence appear less in him than usual. It matters not, provided the sense tastes the same. Therefore we transport foreign merchandise into our country with much labour. And I know not with how grateful countenances my countrymen welcome me, bringing to them the rich spoils of Greece, and unlocking hidden treasures of wisdom with the key of our language. But may God grant your prayers, that no unlucky eye nor any livid aspect may meet us, lest, by an extreme kind of prodigy, while those from whom he is

taken do not envy, yet those upon whom he is bestowed should repine. Truly it is right to point out the plan of our translation to you, who have read these works also in Greek, lest haply in some parts you may think the order of translation not kept. I suppose you are aware that there are two editions in Greek of this work of Clement, — the Ἀναγνώσεις, that is, *Recognitions;* and that there are two collections of books, differing in some points, but in many *containing* the same narrative. In short, the last part of this work, in which is the relation concerning the transformation of Simon, is contained in one of the collections, but is not at all in the other.[2] There are also in both collections some dissertations concerning the Unbegotten God and the Begotten, and on some other subjects, which, to say nothing more, are beyond our comprehension.[3] These, therefore, as being beyond our powers, I have chosen to reserve for others, rather than to produce in an imperfect state. But in the rest, we have given our endeavour, so far as we could, not to vary either from the sentiments or even from the language and modes of expression; and this, although it renders the style of the narrative less ornate, yet it makes it more faithful. The epistle in which the same Clement, writing to James the Lord's brother, informs him of the death of Peter, and that he had left him his successor in his chair and teaching, and in which also the whole subject of church order is treated, I have not prefixed to this work, both because it is of later date, and because I have already translated and published it.[4] But I do

---

[1] Var. readings: "magnanimous one," "my lord," "my friend."

[2] [The reference is probably to the transformation of the father of Clement into the appearance of Simon Magus. This is narrated in both the *Recognitions* (book x. 53, etc.) and in the *Homilies* (xx. 12, etc.), though the latter book closes without any statement of the restoration. It would seem unlikely, then, that Rufinus refers to the *Homilies* as the "other" collection. The recovery of the closing portion of that work has given us its account of the transformation. — R.]

[3] [How far Rufinus has omitted portions which occured in Greek cannot be known. It is quite probable that the apparent heresy of some passages, rather than their incomprehensibility, led him to omit them. This may be urged in favour of the priority of the *Homilies*, but is not conclusive. — R.]

[4] [There is no good reason for doubting that Rufinus refers to the extant epistle prefixed to the *Homilies*, and forming, with "the Epistle of Peter to James," which precedes it, a preface and fictitious authentication of that collection. — R.]

not think it out of place to explain here what in that letter will perhaps seem to some to be inconsistent. For some ask, Since Linus and Cletus were bishops in the city of Rome before this Clement, how could Clement himself, writing to James, say that the chair of teaching was handed over to him by Peter?[1] Now of this we have heard this explanation, that Linus and Cletus were indeed bishops in the city of Rome before Clement, but during the lifetime of Peter: that is, that they undertook the care of the episcopate, and that he fulfilled the office of apostleship; as is found also to have been the case at Cæsarea, where, when he himself was present, he yet had Zacchæus, ordained by himself, as bishop. And in this way both statements will appear to be true, both that these bishops are reckoned before Clement, and yet that Clement received the teacher's seat on the death of Peter. But now let us see how Clement, writing to James the Lord's brother, begins his narrative.

[1] [The language of Rufinus confirms that of Irenæus, Eusebius, and Jerome, as to the episcopal succession at Rome (assuming that Cletus and Anacletus, named by Irenæus, is identical with Cletus). For other variations, see Church Histories and Encyclopædias (under *Clemens Romanus*). The current opinion at Rome in the beginning of the fifth century is evident from this passage. Comp. *Ante-Nicene Fathers*, vol. i. pp. 1, 2. — R.]

RECOGNITIONS OF CLEMENT

BOOK I.

CHAP. I. — CLEMENT'S EARLY HISTORY ; DOUBTS.

I CLEMENT, who was born in the city of Rome,[1] was from my earliest age a lover of chastity ; while the bent of my mind held me bound as with chains of anxiety and sorrow. For a thought that was in me — whence originating, I cannot tell — constantly led me to think of my condition of mortality, and to discuss such questions as these : ' Whether there be for me any life after death, or whether I am to be wholly annihilated : whether I did not exist before I was born, and whether there shall be no remembrance of this life after death, and so the boundlessness of time shall consign all things to oblivion and silence ; so that not only we shall cease to be, but there shall be no remembrance that we have ever been. This also I revolved in my mind : when the world was made, or what was before it was made, or whether it has existed from eternity. For it seemed certain, that if it had been made, it must be doomed to dissolution ; and if it be dissolved, what is to be afterwards? — unless, perhaps, all things shall be buried in oblivion and silence, or something shall be, which the mind of man cannot now conceive.

CHAP. II. — HIS DISTRESS.

While I was continually revolving in my mind these and such like questions, suggested I know not how, I was pining away wonderfully through excess of grief ; and, what was worse, if at any time I thought to cast aside such cares, as being of little use, the waves of anxiety rose all the higher upon me. For I had in me that most excellent companion, who would not suffer me to rest — the desire of immortality : for, as the subsequent issue showed, and the grace of Almighty God directed, this bent of mind led me to the quest of truth, and the acknowledgment of the true light ; and hence it came to pass, that ere long I pitied those whom formerly in my ignorance I believed to be happy.

---

[1] [The first six chapters closely resemble the corresponding chapters of Homily I. The variations are no greater than might readily appear in a version. — R.]

CHAP. III. — HIS DISSATISFACTION WITH THE SCHOOLS OF THE PHILOSOPHERS.

Having therefore such a bent of mind from my earliest years, the desire of learning something led me to frequent the schools of the philosophers. There I saw that nought else was done, save that doctrines were asserted and controverted without end, contests were waged, and the arts of syllogisms and the subtleties of conclusions were discussed. If at any time the doctrine of the immortality of the soul prevailed, I was thankful ; if at any time it was impugned, I went away sorrowful. Still, neither doctrine had the power of truth over my heart. This only I understood, that opinions and definitions of things were accounted true or false, not in accordance with their nature and the truth of the arguments, but in proportion to the talents of those who supported them. And I was all the more tortured in the bottom of my heart, because I was neither able to lay hold of any of those things which were spoken as firmly established, nor was I able to lay aside the desire of inquiry ; but the more I endeavoured to neglect and despise them, so much the more eagerly, as I have said, did a desire of this sort, creeping in upon me secretly as with a kind of pleasure, take possession of my heart and mind.

CHAP. IV. — HIS INCREASING DISQUIET.

Being therefore straitened in the discovery of things, I said to myself, Why do we labour in vain, since the end of things is manifest? For if after death I shall be no more, my present torture is useless ; but if there is to be for me a life after death, let us keep for that life the excitements that belong to it, lest perhaps some sadder things befall me than those which I now suffer, unless I shall have lived piously and soberly ; and, according to the opinions of some of the philosophers, I be consigned to the stream of dark-rolling Phlegethon, or to Tartarus, like Sisyphus and Tityus, and to eternal punishment in the infernal regions, like Ixion and Tantalus. And again I would answer to myself : But these things are fables; or if it be so, since the matter is in doubt, it is better to live piously. But again I would ponder with myself, How should I restrain myself from the lust of sin, while uncertain as to the reward of righteousness? — and all the more when I have no certainty what righteousness is, or what is pleasing to God; and when I cannot ascertain whether the soul be immortal, and be such that it has anything to hope for; nor do I know what the future is certainly to be. Yet still I cannot rest from thoughts of this sort.

CHAP. V. — HIS DESIGN TO TEST THE IMMORTALITY OF THE SOUL.

What, then, shall I do? This shall I do. I shall proceed to Egypt, and there I shall cultivate the friendship of the hierophants or prophets, who preside at the shrines. Then I shall win over a magician by money, and entreat him, by what they call the necromantic art, to bring me a soul from the infernal regions, as if I were desirous of consulting it about some business. But this shall be my consultation, whether the soul be immortal. Now, the proof that the soul is immortal will be put past doubt, not from what it says, or from what I hear, but from what I see: for seeing it with my eyes, I shall ever after hold the surest conviction of its immortality; and no fallacy of words or uncertainty of hearing shall ever be able to disturb the persuasion produced by sight. However, I related this project to a certain philosopher with whom I was intimate, who counselled me not to venture upon it; " for," said he, " if the soul should not obey the call of the magician, you henceforth will live more hopelessly, as thinking that there is nothing after death, and also as having tried things unlawful. If, however, you seem to see anything, what religion or what piety can arise to you from things unlawful and impious? For they say that transactions of this sort are hateful to the Divinity, and that God sets Himself in opposition to those who trouble souls after their release from the body." When I heard this, I was indeed staggered in my purpose; yet I could not in any way either lay aside my longing, or cast off the distressing thought.

CHAP. VI. — HEARS OF CHRIST.

Not to make a long story of it, whilst I was tossed upon these billows of my thought, a certain report, which took its rise in the regions of the East in the reign of Tiberius Cæsar, gradually reached us; and gaining strength as it passed through every place, like some good message sent from God, it was filling the whole world, and suffered not the divine will to be concealed in silence. For it was spread over all places,

announcing that there was a certain person in Judæa, who, beginning in the spring-time,[1] was preaching the kingdom of God to the Jews, and saying that those should receive it who should observe the ordinances of His commandments and His doctrine. And that His speech might be believed to be worthy of credit, and full of the Divinity, He was said to perform many mighty works, and wonderful signs and prodigies by His mere word; so that, as one having power from God, He made the deaf to hear, and the blind to see, and the lame to stand erect, and expelled every infirmity and all demons from men; yea, that He even raised dead persons who were brought to Him; that He cured lepers also, looking at them from a distance; and that there was absolutely nothing which seemed impossible to Him. These and such like things were confirmed in process of time, not now by frequent rumours, but by the plain statements of persons coming from those quarters; and day by day the truth of the matter was further disclosed.

CHAP. VII. — ARRIVAL OF BARNABAS AT ROME.

At length meetings began to be held in various places in the city, and this subject to be discussed in conversation, and to be a matter of wonder who this might be who had appeared, and what message He had brought from God to men; until, about the same year, a certain man, standing in a most crowded place in the city, made proclamation to the people, saying: " Hear me, O ye citizens of Rome. The Son of God is now in the regions of Judæa, promising eternal life to every one who will hear Him, but upon condition that he shall regulate his actions according to the will of Him by whom He hath been sent, even of God the Father. Wherefore turn ye from evil things to good, from things temporal to things eternal. Acknowledge that there is one God, ruler of heaven and earth, in whose righteous sight ye unrighteous inhabit His world. But if ye be converted, and act according to His will, then, coming to the world to come, and being made immortal, ye shall enjoy His unspeakable blessings and rewards."[2] Now, the man who spoke these things to the people was from the regions of the East, by nation a Hebrew, by name Barnabas, who said that he himself was one of His disciples, and that he was sent for this end, that he should declare these things to those who would hear them.[3] When I heard these things, I began, with the rest of the

---

[1] V. R. in the time of Tiberius Cæsar.
[2] [In Homily I. a warning of future punishment is added. — R.]
[3] [The narrative in the *Homilies* is fuller; the preacher at Rome is not named: Clement attempts to go to Judæa, is driven to Alexandria, and meets Barnabas there: the occurrences here given in chaps. 8-11 are placed in Alexandria, whence Clement goes, after the departure of Barnabas, to Cæsarea, where he meets Peter (comp. chap. 12). — R.]

multitude, to follow him, and to hear what he had to say. Truly I perceived that there was nothing of dialectic artifice in the man, but that he expounded with simplicity, and without any craft of speech, such things as he had heard from the Son of God, or had seen. For he did not confirm his assertions by the force of arguments, but produced, from the people who stood round about him, many witnesses of the sayings and marvels which he related.

CHAP. VIII.—HIS PREACHING.

Now, inasmuch as the people began to assent willingly to the things which were sincerely spoken, and to embrace his simple discourse, those who thought themselves learned or philosophic began to laugh at the man, and to flout him, and to throw out for him the grappling-hooks of syllogisms, like strong arms. But he, unterrified, regarding their subtleties as mere ravings, did not even judge them worthy of an answer, but boldly pursued the subject which he had set before him. At length, some one having proposed this question to him as he was speaking, Why a gnat has been so formed, that though it is a small creature, and has six feet, yet it has got wings in addition; whereas an elephant, though it is an immense animal, and has no wings, yet has only four feet; he, paying no attention to the question, went on with his discourse, which had been interrupted by the unseasonable challenge, only adding this admonition at every interruption : " We have it in charge to declare to you the words and the wondrous works of Him who hath sent us, and to confirm the truth of what we speak, not by artfully devised arguments, but by witnesses produced from amongst yourselves. For I recognise many standing in the midst of you whom I remember to have heard along with us the things which we have heard, and to have seen what we have seen. But be it in your option to receive or to spurn the tidings which we bring to you. For we cannot keep back what we know to be for your advantage, because, if we be silent, woe is to us ; but to you, if you receive not what we speak, destruction. I could indeed very easily answer your foolish challenges, if you asked for the sake of learning truth, — I mean as to the difference of a gnat and an elephant ; but now it were absurd to speak to you of these creatures, when the very Creator and Framer of all things is unknown by you."

CHAP. IX.—CLEMENT'S INTERPOSITION ON BEHALF OF BARNABAS.

When he had thus spoken, all, as with one consent, with rude voice raised a shout of derision, to put him to shame, and to silence him,

crying out that he was a barbarian and a madman. When I saw matters going on in this way, being filled, I know not whence, with a certain zeal, and inflamed with religious enthusiasm, I could not keep silence, but cried out with all boldness, " Most righteously does Almighty God hide His will from you, whom He foresaw to be unworthy of the knowledge of Himself, as is manifest to those who are really wise, from what you are now doing. For when you see that preachers of the will of God have come amongst you, because their speech makes no show of knowledge of the grammatical art, but in simple and unpolished language they set before you the divine commands, so that all who hear may be able to follow and to understand the things that are spoken, you deride the ministers and messengers of your salvation, not knowing that it is the condemnation of you who think yourselves skilful and eloquent, that rustic and barbarous men have the knowledge of the truth ; whereas, when it has come to you, it is not even received as a guest, while, if your intemperance and lust did not oppose, it ought to have been a citizen and a native. Thus you are convicted of not being friends of truth and philosophers, but followers of boasting and vain speakers. Ye think that truth dwells not in simple, but in ingenious and subtle words, and produce countless thousands of words which are not to be rated at the worth of one word. What, then, do ye think will become of you, all ye crowd of Greeks, if there is to be, as he says, a judgment of God? But now give over laughing at this man to your own destruction, and let any one of you who pleases answer me ; for, indeed, by your barking you annoy the ears even of those who desire to be saved, and by your clamour you turn aside to the fall of infidelity the minds that are prepared for faith. What pardon can there be for you who deride and do violence to the messenger of the truth when he offers to you the knowledge of God? whereas, even if he brought you nothing of truth, yet, even for the kindness of his intentions towards you, you ought to receive with gratitude and welcome."

CHAP. X.—INTERCOURSE WITH BARNABAS.

While I was urging these and similar arguments, a great excitement was stirred up amongst the bystanders, some being moved with pity as towards a stranger, and approving my speech as in accordance with that feeling ; others, petulant and stolid, rousing the anger of their undisciplined minds as much against me as against Barnabas. But as the day was declining to evening, I laid hold of Barnabas by the right hand, and led him away, although reluctantly, to my house ; and there I made him remain, lest perchance any one of the rude rabble should lay hands upon him. While we were thus placed in contact for a few days, I gladly heard him discoursing the word of truth; yet he hastened his departure, saying that he must by all means celebrate at Judæa a festal day of his religion which was approaching, and that there he should remain in future with his countrymen and his brethren, evidently indicating that he was horrified at the wrong that had been done to him.

CHAP. XI. — DEPARTURE OF BARNABAS.

At length I said to him, "Only expound to me the doctrine of that man who you say has appeared, and I will arrange your sayings in my language, and will preach the kingdom and righteousness of Almighty God; and after that, if you wish it, I shall even sail along with you, for I am extremely desirous to see Judæa, and perhaps I shall remain with you always." To this he answered, "If indeed you wish to see our country, and to learn those things which you desire, set sail with me even now; or, if there be anything that detains you now, I shall leave with you directions to my dwelling, so that when you please to come you may easily find me; for to-morrow I shall set out on my journey." When I saw him determined, I went down with him to the harbour, and carefully took from him the directions which he gave me to find his dwelling. I told him that, but for the necessity of getting some money which was due to me, I should not at all delay, but that I should speedily follow him. Having told him this, I commended him to the kindness of those who had charge of the ship, and returned sad; for I was possessed of the memory of the intercourse which I had had with an excellent guest and a choice friend.

CHAP. XII. — CLEMENT'S ARRIVAL AT CÆSAREA, AND INTRODUCTION TO PETER.

Having then stopped for a few days, and having in some measure finished the business of collecting what was owing to me (for I neglected many things through my desire of hastening, that I might not be hindered from my purpose), I set sail direct for Judæa, and after fifteen days landed at Cæsarea Stratonis, which is the largest city in Palestine.[1] When I had landed, and was seeking for an inn, I learned from the conversation of the people, that one Peter, a most approved disciple of Him who appeared in Judæa, and showed many signs and miracles divinely performed among men, was going to hold a discussion of words and questions the next day with one Simon, a Samaritan. Having heard this, I asked to be shown his lodging; and having found

it, and standing before the door, I informed the doorkeeper who I was, and whence I came; and, behold, Barnabas coming out, as soon as he saw me rushed into my arms, weeping for joy, and, seizing me by the hand, led me in to Peter. Having pointed him out to me at a distance. "This," said he, "is Peter, of whom I spoke, to you as the greatest in the wisdom of God, and to whom also I have spoken constantly of you. Enter, therefore, as one well known to him. For he is well acquainted with all the good that is in thee, and has carefully made himself aware of your religious purpose, whence also he is greatly desirous to see you. Therefore I present you to him to-day as a great gift." At the same time, presenting me, he said, "This, O Peter, is Clement."

CHAP. XIII. — HIS CORDIAL RECEPTION BY PETER.

But Peter most kindly, when he heard my name, immediately ran to me and kissed me. Then, having made me sit down, he said, "Thou didst well to receive as thy guest Barnabas, preacher of the truth, nothing fearing the rage of the insane people. Thou shalt be blessed. For as you have deemed an ambassador of the truth worthy of all honour, so the truth herself shall receive thee a wanderer and a stranger, and shall enroll thee a citizen of her own city; and then there shall be great joy to thee, because, imparting a small favour, thou shalt be written heir of eternal blessings. Now, therefore, do not trouble yourself to explain your mind to me; for Barnabas has with faithful speech informed me of all things about you and your dispositions, almost daily and without ceasing, recalling the memory of your good qualities. And to point out to you shortly, as to a friend already of one mind with us, what is your best course; if there is nothing to hinder you, come along with us, and hear the word of the truth, which we are going to speak in every place until we come even to the city of Rome; and now, if you wish anything, speak."

CHAP. XIV. — HIS ACCOUNT OF HIMSELF.

Having detailed to him what purpose I had conceived from the beginning, and how I had been distracted with vain inquiries, and all those things which at first I intimated to thee, my lord James, so that I need not repeat the same things now, I willingly agreed to travel with him; "for that," said I, "is just what I was most eagerly desirous of. But first I should wish the scheme of truth to be expounded to me, that I may know whether the soul is mortal or immortal; and if immortal, whether it shall be brought into judgment for those things which it does here. Further, I desire to know what that righteousness

---

[1] [The two accounts of the meeting with Peter at Cæsarea are closely parallel. — R.]

is, which is pleasing to God; then, further, whether the world was created, and why it was created, and whether it is to be dissolved, and whether it is to be renovated and made better, or whether after this there shall be no world at all; and, not to mention everything, I should wish to be told what is the case with respect to these and such like things." To this Peter answered, "I shall briefly impart to you the knowledge of these things, O Clement: therefore listen.

CHAP. XV. — PETER'S FIRST INSTRUCTION: CAUSES OF IGNORANCE.

"The will and counsel of God has for many reasons been concealed from men; first, indeed, through bad instruction, wicked associations, evil habits, unprofitable conversation, and unrighteous presumptions. On account of all these, I say, first error, then contempt, then infidelity and malice, covetousness also, and vain boasting, and other such like evils, have filled the whole house of this world, like some enormous smoke, and preventing those who dwell in it from seeing its Founder aright, and from perceiving what things are pleasing to Him. What, then, is fitting for those who are within, excepting with a cry brought forth from their inmost hearts to invoke His aid, who alone is not shut up in the smoke-filled house, that He would approach and open the door of the house, so that the smoke may be dissipated which is within, and the light of the sun which shines without may be admitted.

CHAP. XVI. — INSTRUCTION CONTINUED: THE TRUE PROPHET.

"He, therefore, whose aid is needed for the house filled with the darkness of ignorance and the smoke of vices, is He, we say, who is called the true Prophet, who alone can enlighten the souls of men, so that with their eyes they may plainly see the way of safety. For otherwise it is impossible to get knowledge of divine and eternal things, unless one learns of that true Prophet; because, as you yourself stated a little ago, the belief of things, and the opinions of causes, are estimated in proportion to the talents of their advocates: hence, also, one and the same cause is now thought just, now unjust; and what now seemed true, anon becomes false on the assertion of another. For this reason, the credit of religion and piety demanded the presence of the true Prophet, that He Himself might tell us respecting each particular, how the truth stands, and might teach us how we are to believe concerning each.[1] And therefore, before all else, the credentials of the prophet himself must be examined with all care; and when you have once ascer-

tained that he is a prophet, it behoves you thenceforth to believe him in everything, and not further to discuss the particulars which he teaches, but to hold the things which he speaks as certain and sacred; which things, although they seem to be received by faith, yet are believed on the ground of the probation previously instituted. For when once at the outset the truth of the prophet is established on examination, the rest is to be heard and held on the ground of the faith by which it is already established that he is a teacher of truth. And as it is certain that all things which pertain to divine knowledge ought to be held according to the rule of truth, so it is beyond doubt that from none but Himself alone can it be known what is true."

CHAP. XVII. — PETER REQUESTS HIM TO BE HIS ATTENDANT.

Having thus spoken, he set forth to me so openly and so clearly who that Prophet was, and how He might be found, that I seemed to have before my eyes, and to handle with my hand, the proofs which he produced concerning the prophetic truth; and I was struck with intense astonishment, how no one sees, though placed before his eyes, those things which all are seeking for. Whence, by his command, reducing into order what he had spoken to me, I compiled a book concerning the true Prophet, and sent it to you from Cæsarea by his command. For he said that he had received a command from you to send you every year an account of his sayings and doings.[2] Meantime, at the beginning of his discourse which he delivered to me the first day, when he had instructed me very fully concerning the true Prophet, and very many things besides, he added also this: "See," said he, "for the future, and be present at the discussions which whenever any necessity arises, I shall hold with those who contradict; against whom, when I dispute, even if I shall seem to be worsted, I shall not be afraid of your being led to doubt of those things which I have stated to you; because, even if I shall seem to be beaten, yet those things shall not therefore seem to be uncertain which the true Prophet has delivered to us. Yet I hope that we shall not be overcome in disputations either, if only our hearers are reasonable, and friends of truth, who can discern the force and bearing of words, and recognise what discourse comes from the sophistical art, not containing truth, but an image of truth; and what that is, which, uttered simply and without craft, depends for all its power not on show and ornament, but on truth and reason."

---

[1] [This discourse is given somewhat more fully here than in the *Homilies*. — R.]

[2] [Comp. Homily I. 20, where there is a curious inconsistency. Both accounts seem to insert this to tally with the fictitious relation to James, and both may be used to support the theory of a common documentary basis. — R.]

CHAP. XVIII. — HIS PROFITING BY PETER'S INSTRUC-
TION.

To this I answered: "I give thanks to God
Almighty, because I have been instructed as I
wished and desired. At all events, you may
depend upon me so far, that I can never come
to doubt of those things which I have learned of
you; so that even if you yourself should at any
time wish to transfer my faith from the true
Prophet, you should not be able, because I have
drunk in with all my heart what you have spoken.
And that you may not think that I am promising
you a great thing when I say that I cannot be
moved away from this faith, it is with me a certainty, that whoever has received this account of
the true Prophet, can never afterwards so much
as doubt of its truth. And therefore I am confident with respect to this heaven-taught doctrine,
in which all the art of malice is overborne. For
in opposition to *this* prophecy neither any art can
stand, nor the subtleties of sophisms and syllo-
gism; but every one who hears of the true
Prophet must of necessity long immediately for
the truth itself, nor will he afterwards, under pretext of seeking the truth, endure diverse errors.
Wherefore, O my lord Peter, be not further anxious about me, as if I were one who does not
know what he has received, and how great a gift
has been conferred on him. Be assured that you
have conferred a favour on one who knows and
understands its value: nor can I be easily deceived on that account, because I seem to have
gotten quickly what I long desired; for it may
be that one who desires gets quickly, while
another does not even slowly attain the things
which he desires."

CHAP. XIX. — PETER'S SATISFACTION.

Then Peter, when he heard me speak thus,
said: "I give thanks to my God, both for your
salvation and for my own peace; for I am greatly delighted to see that you have understood
what is the greatness of the prophetic virtue,
and because, as you say, not even I myself, if I
should wish it (which God forbid!), should be
able to turn you away to another faith. Now
henceforth begin to be with us, and to-morrow
be present at our discussions, for I am to have
a contest with Simon the magician." When he
had thus spoken, he retired to take food along
with his friends; but he ordered me to eat by
myself;[1] and after the meal, when he had sung
praise to God and given thanks, he rendered to
me an account of this proceeding, and added,
"May the Lord grant to thee to be made like to
us in all things, that, receiving baptism, thou

mayest be able to meet with us at the same
table." Having thus spoken, he ordered me to
go to rest, for by this time both fatigue and the
time of the day called to sleep.

CHAP. XX. — POSTPONEMENT OF DISCUSSION WITH
SIMON MAGUS.

Early next morning Zacchæus[2] came in to us,
and after salutation, said to Peter: "Simon puts
off the discussion till the eleventh day of the
present month, which is seven days hence, for
he says that then he will have more leisure for
the contest. But to me it seems that his putting
off is also advantageous to us, so that more may
come together, who may be either hearers or
judges of our disputation. However, if it seem
proper to you, let us occupy the interval in discussing among ourselves the things which, we
suppose, may come into the controversy; so that
each of us, knowing what things are to be proposed, and what answers are to be given, may
consider with himself if they are all right, or if
an adversary shall be able to find anything to object, or to set aside the things which we bring
against him. But if the things which are to be
spoken by us are manifestly impregnable on
every side, we shall have confidence in entering
upon the examination. And indeed, this is my
opinion, that first of all it ought to be inquired
what is the origin of all things, or what is the
immediate[3] thing which may be called the cause
of all things which are: then, with respect to
all things that exist, whether they have been
made, and by whom, through whom, and for
whom; whether they have received their subsistence from one, or from two, or from many;
and whether they have been taken and fashioned
from none *previously* subsisting, or from some:
then, whether there is any virtue in the highest
things, or in the lower; whether there is anything which is better than all, or anything that is
inferior to all; whether there are any motions,
or none; whether those things which are seen
were always, and shall be always; whether they
have come into existence without a creator,
and shall pass away without a destroyer. If, I
say, the discussion begin with these things, I
think that the things which shall be inquired into,
being discussed with diligent examination, will
be easily ascertained. And when these are ascertained, the knowledge of those that follow
will be easily found. I have stated my opinion;
be pleased to intimate what you think of the
matter.[4]

---

[1] [In the *Homilies* this is not expressed, but implied. The whole
passage suggests a separatism quite contrary to Pauline precept.
Compare the more detailed statement of separatism in book ii. 70, 72,
vii. 29; Homily XIII. 4. — R.]

[2] [Identified in the *Homilies* with the publican of Jericho. Fifteen others are named in Homily II. 1; some of them are introduced
in *Recognitions*, ii. 1. — R.]

[3] Here we follow a marginal reading.

[4] [This chapter has no direct parallel in the *Homilies*. While
there is a general resemblance in the remainder of book i. to Homily
II., much of the matter is peculiar, or at least introduced in a connection different from that of the *Homilies*. — R.]

CHAP. XXI. — ADVANTAGE OF THE DELAY.

To this Peter answered : " Tell Simon in the meantime to do as he pleases, and to rest assured that, Divine Providence granting, he shall always find us ready." Then Zacchæus went out to intimate to Simon what he had been told. But Peter, looking at us, and perceiving that I was saddened by the putting off of the contest, said : " He who believes that the world is administered by the providence of the Most High God, ought not, O Clement, my friend, to take it amiss, in whatever way particular things happen, being assured that the righteousness of God guides to a favourable and fitting issue even those things which seem superfluous or contrary in any business, and especially towards those who worship Him more intimately ; and therefore he who is assured of these things, as I have said, if anything occur contrary to his expectation, he knows how to drive away grief from his mind on that account, holding it unquestionable in his better judgment, that, by the government of the good God, even what seems contrary may be turned to good. Wherefore, O Clement, even now let not this delay of the magician Simon sadden you : for I believe that it has been done by the providence of God, for your advantage ; that I may be able, in this interval of seven days, to expound to you the method of our faith without any distraction, and the order continuously, according to the tradition of the true Prophet, who alone knows the past as it was, the present as it is, and the future as it shall be : which things were indeed plainly spoken *by Him*, but are not plainly written ; so much so, that when they are read, they cannot be understood without an expounder, on account of the sin which has grown up with men, as I said before. Therefore I shall explain all things to you, that in those things which are written you may clearly perceive what is the mind of the Lawgiver."

CHAP. XXII. — REPETITION OF INSTRUCTIONS.

When he had said this, he began to expound to me point by point of those chapters of the law which seemed to be in question, from the beginning of the creation even to that point of time at which I came to him at Cæsarea, telling me that the delay of Simon had contributed to my learning all things in order. " At other times," said he, " we shall discourse more fully on individual points of which we have now spoken shortly, according as the occasion of our conversation shall bring them before us ; so that, according to my promise, you may gain a full and perfect knowledge of all. Since, then, by this delay we have to-day on our hands, I wish to repeat to you again what has been spoken, that it may be the better recalled to your memory." Then he began in this way to refresh my recollection of what he had said : " Do you remember, O friend Clement, the account I gave you of the eternal age, that knows no end ? " Then said I, " Never, O Peter, shall I retain anything, if I can lose or forget that."

CHAP. XXIII. — REPETITION CONTINUED.

Then Peter, having heard my answer with pleasure, said : " I congratulate you because you have answered thus, not because you speak of these things easily, but because you profess that you remember them ; for the most sublime truths are best honoured by means of silence. Yet, for the credit of those things which you remember concerning things not to be spoken,[1] tell me what you retain of those things which we spoke of in the second place, which can easily be spoken out, that, perceiving your tenacity of memory, I may the more readily point out to you, and freely open, the things of which I wish to speak." Then I, when I perceived that he rejoiced in the good memory of his hearers, said : " Not only am I mindful of your definition, but also of that preface which was prefixed to the definition ; and of almost all things that you have expounded, I retain the sense complete, though not all the words ; because the things that you have spoken have been made, as it were, native to my soul, and inborn. For you have held out a most sweet cup to me in my excessive thirst. And that you may not suppose that I am occupying you with words, being unmindful of things, I shall now call to mind the things which were spoken, in which the order of your discussion greatly helps me ; for the way in which the things that you said followed by consequence upon one another, and were arranged in a balanced manner, makes them easily recalled to memory by the lines of their order. For the order of sayings is useful for remembering them : for when you begin to follow them point by point in succession, when anything is wanting, immediately the sense seeks for it ; and when it has found it, retains it, or at all events, if it cannot discover it, there will be no reluctance to ask it of the master. But not to delay in granting what you demand of me, I shall shortly rehearse what you delivered to me concerning the definition of truth.

CHAP. XXIV. — REPETITION CONTINUED.

" There always was, there is now, and there ever shall be, that by which the first Will be-

---

[1] That is, that I may be sure that you remember these things.

gotten from eternity consists; and from the first Will *proceeds* a second Will. After these came the world; and from the world came time : from this, the multitude of men; from the multitude the election of the beloved, from whose oneness of mind the peaceful kingdom of God is constructed. But the rest, which ought to follow these, you promised to tell me at another time. After this, when you had explained about the creation of the world, you intimated the decree of God, "which He, of His own good pleasure, announced in the presence of all the first angels," and which He ordained as an eternal law to all; and how He established two kingdoms, — I mean that of the present time and that of the future, — and appointed times to each, and decreed that a day of judgment should be expected, which He determined, in which a severance is to be made of things and of souls : so that the wicked indeed shall be consigned to eternal fire for their sins; but those who have lived according to the will of God the Creator, having received a blessing for their good works, effulgent with brightest light, introduced into an eternal abode, and abiding in incorruption, shall receive eternal gifts of ineffable blessings."

CHAP. XXV. — REPETITION CONTINUED.

While I was going on thus, Peter, enraptured with joy, and anxious for me as if I had been his son, lest perhaps I should fail in recollection of the rest, and be put to shame on account of those who were present, said : "It is enough, O Clement; for you have stated these things more clearly than I myself explained them." Then said I, "Liberal learning has conferred upon me the power of orderly narration, and of stating those things clearly for which there is occasion. And if we use learning in asserting the errors of antiquity, we ruin ourselves by gracefulness and smoothness of speech; but if we apply learning and grace of speech to the assertion of the truth, I think that not a little advantage is thereby gained. Be that as it may, my lord Peter, you can but imagine with what thankfulness I am transported for all the rest of your instruction indeed, but especially for the statement of that doctrine which you gave : There is one God, whose work the world is, and who, because He is in all respects righteous, shall render to every one according to his deeds. And after that you added : For the assertion of this dogma countless thousands of words will be brought forward; but in those to whom is granted knowledge of the true Prophet, all this forest of words is cut down. And on this account, since you have delivered to me a discourse concerning the true Prophet, you have

strengthened me with all confidence of your assertions." And then, having perceived that the sum of all religion and piety consists in this, I immediately replied : "You have proceeded most excellently, O Peter : wherefore, in future, expound unhesitatingly, as to one who already knows what are the foundations of faith and piety, the traditions of the true Prophet, who alone, as has been clearly proved, is to be believed. But that exposition which requires assertions and arguments, reserve for the unbelievers, to whom you have not yet judged it proper to commit the indubitable faith of prophetic grace." When I had said this, I added : "You promised that you would give at the proper time two things : first this exposition, at once simple and entirely free from error; and then an exposition of each individual point as it may be evolved in the course of the various questions which shall be raised. And after this you expounded the sequence of things in order from the beginning of the world, even to the present time; and if you please, I can repeat the whole from memory."

CHAP. XXVI. — FRIENDSHIP OF GOD ; HOW SECURED.

To this Peter answered : "I am exceedingly delighted, O Clement, that I commit my words to so safe a heart; for to be mindful of the things that are spoken is an indication of having in readiness the faith of works. But he from whom the wicked demon steals away the words of salvation, and snatches them away from his memory, cannot be saved, even though he wish it; for he loses the way by which life is reached. Wherefore let us the rather repeat what has been spoken, and confirm it in your heart, that is, in what manner or by whom the world was made, that we may proceed to the friendship of the Creator. But His friendship is secured by living well, and by obeying His will; which will is the law of all that live. We shall therefore unfold these things briefly to you, in order that they may be the more surely remembered.

CHAP. XXVII. — ACCOUNT OF THE CREATION.

"In the beginning,[1] when God had made the heaven and the earth,[2] as one house, the shadow

---

[1] [Hilgenfeld regards chaps. 27-72 as part of the Jewish-Christian document called *Kerygma Petri*, of which an outline is given in book iii. 75. This he thinks was of Roman origin. Certainly these chapters bear many marks of an earlier origin than most of the pseudo-Clementine literature. Much of the matter is not found elsewhere in this literature : the tone of the discourse is much superior; the instruction, represented as given to Clement, is quite well adapted to his needs as a heathen inquirer; the views presented are not so extravagant as much that occurs in the *Homilies;* the attempt to adjust the statements to the New-Testament narrative is skilfully made, and there is not lacking a great *vraisemblance.* It may not be improper to add, that the impressions first given in regard to this passage were made upon the writer of this note quite independently of Hilgenfeld's theory; some of them committed to writing without a thought of maintaining that theory. — R.]

[2] Gen. i. 1.

which was cast by the mundane bodies involved in darkness those things which were enclosed in it. But when the will of God had introduced light, that darkness which had been caused by the shadows of bodies was straightway dispelled : then at length light is appointed for the day, darkness for the night. And now the water which was within the world, in the middle space of that first heaven and earth, congealed as if with frost, and solid as crystal, is distended, and the middle spaces of the heaven and earth are separated as by a firmament of this sort ; and that firmament the Creator called heaven, so called by the name of that previously made : and so He divided into two portions that fabric of the universe, although it was but one house. The reason of the division was this, that the upper portion might afford a dwelling-place to angels, and the lower to men. After this, the place of the sea and the chaos which had been made received that portion of the water which remained below, by order of the eternal Will ; and these flowing down to the sunk and hollow places, the dry land appeared ; and the gatherings of the waters were made seas. And after this the earth, which had appeared, produced various species of herbs and shrubs. It gave forth fountains also, and rivers, not only in the plains, but on the mountains. And so all things were prepared, that men who were to dwell in it might have it in their power to use all these things according to their will, that is, either for good or evil.

CHAP. XXVIII. — ACCOUNT OF THE CREATION CONTINUED.

" After this He adorns that visible heaven with stars. He places in it also the sun and the moon, that the day might enjoy the light of the one, the night that of the other ; and that at the same time they might be for an indication of things past, present, and future. For they were made for signs of seasons and of days, which, although they are seen indeed by all, are understood only by the learned and intelligent. And when, after this, He had ordered living creatures to be produced from the earth and the waters, He made Paradise, which also He named a place of delights. But after all these things He made man, on whose account He had prepared all things, whose internal species [1] is older, and for whose sake all things that are were made, given up to his service, and assigned to the uses of his habitation.

CHAP. XXIX. — THE GIANTS : THE FLOOD.

" All things therefore being completed which are in heaven, and in earth, and in the waters,

and the human race also having multiplied, in the eighth generation, righteous men, who had lived the life of angels, being allured by the beauty of women, fell into promiscuous and illicit connections with these ; [2] and thenceforth acting in all things without discretion, and disorderly, they changed the state of human affairs and the divinely prescribed order of life, so that either by persuasion or force they compelled all men to sin against God their Creator. In the ninth generation are born the giants, so called from of old,[3] not dragon-footed, as the fables of the Greeks relate, but men of immense bodies, whose bones, of enormous size, are still shown in some places for confirmation. But against these the righteous providence of God brought a flood upon the world, that the earth might be purified from their pollution, and every place might be turned into a sea by the destruction of the wicked. Yet there was then found one righteous man, by name Noah, who, being delivered in an ark with his three sons and their wives, became the colonizer of the world after the subsiding of the waters, with those animals and seeds which he had shut up with him.

CHAP. XXX. — NOAH'S SONS.

" In the twelfth generation, when God had blessed men, and they had begun to multiply,[4] they received a commandment that they should not taste blood, for on account of this also the deluge had been sent. In the thirteenth generation, when the second of Noah's three sons had done an injury to his father, and had been cursed by him, he brought the condition of slavery upon his posterity. His elder brother meantime obtained the lot of a dwelling-place in the middle region of the world, in which is the country of Judæa ; the younger obtained the eastern quarter, and he the western. In the fourteenth generation one of the cursed progeny first erected an altar to demons, for the purpose of magical arts, and offered there bloody sacrifices. In the fifteenth generation, for the first time, men set up an idol and worshipped it. Until that time the Hebrew language, which had been given by God to men, bore sole sway. In the sixteenth generation the sons of men migrated from the east, and, coming to the lands that had been assigned to their fathers, each one marked the place of his own allotment by his own name. In the seventeenth generation Nimrod I. reigned in Babylonia, and built a city, and thence mi-

---

[1] That is, his soul, according to the doctrine of the pre-existence of souls.

[2] Gen. vi. 2. [Compare with this chapter Homily VIII. 12-17, where there are many more fanciful details. — R.]

[3] The writer here translates the words of the Septuagint, οἱ γίγαντες οἱ ἀπ' αἰῶνος οἱ ἄνθρωποι οἱ ὀνομαστοί, illi qui a seculo nominantur. We have given the translation of our authorized version. It is likely, however, that the writer believed the name to imply that they lived to a great age, as is maintained by Diodorus quoted by Suicer on the word, or he may have traced the word to γῆ.

[4] Gen. ix. 1.

grated to the Persians, and taught them to worship fire.[1]

CHAP. XXXI. — WORLD AFTER THE FLOOD.

"In the eighteenth generation walled cities were built, armies were organized and armed, judges and laws were sanctioned, temples were built, and the princes of nations were adored as gods. In the nineteenth generation the descendants of him who had been cursed after the flood, going beyond their proper bounds which they had obtained by lot in the western regions, drove into the eastern lands those who had obtained the middle portion of the world, and pursued them as far as Persia, while themselves violently took possession of the country from which they expelled them. In the twentieth generation a son for the first time died before his father,[2] on account of an incestuous crime.

CHAP. XXXII. — ABRAHAM.

"In the twenty-first generation there was a certain wise man, of the race of those who were expelled, of the family of Noah's eldest son, by name Abraham, from whom our Hebrew nation is derived.[3] When the whole world was again overspread with errors, and when for the hideousness of its crimes destruction was ready for it, this time not by water, but fire, and when already the scourge was hanging over the whole earth, beginning with Sodom, this man, by reason of his friendship with God, who was well pleased with him, obtained from God that the whole world should not equally perish. From the first this same man, being an astrologer, was able, from the account and order of the stars, to recognise the Creator, while all others were in error, and understood that all things are regulated by His providence. Whence also an angel,[4] standing by him in a vision, instructed him more fully concerning those things which he was beginning to perceive. He showed him also what belonged to his race and posterity, and promised him that those districts should be restored rather than given to them.

CHAP. XXXIII. — ABRAHAM: HIS POSTERITY.

"Therefore Abraham, when he was desirous to learn the causes of things, and was intently pondering upon what had been told him, the true Prophet appeared to him, who alone knows the hearts and purpose of men, and disclosed to him all things which he desired. He taught him the knowledge of the Divinity; intimated

the origin of the world, and likewise its end; showed him the immortality of the soul, and the manner of life which was pleasing to God; declared also the resurrection of the dead, the future judgment, the reward of the good, the punishment of the evil, — all to be regulated by righteous judgment: and having given him all this information plainly and sufficiently, He departed again to the invisible abodes. But while Abraham was still in ignorance, as we said to you before, two sons were born to him, of whom the one was called Ismael, and the other Heliesdros. From the one are descended the barbarous nations, from the other the people of the Persians, some of whom have adopted the manner of living and the institutions of their neighbours, the Brachmans. Others settled in Arabia, of whose posterity some also have spread into Egypt. From them some of the Indians and of the Egyptians have learned to be circumcised, and to be of purer observance than others, although in process of time most of them have turned to impiety what was the proof and sign of purity.

CHAP. XXXIV. — THE ISRAELITES IN EGYPT.

"Nevertheless, as he had got these two sons during the time while he still lived in ignorance of things, having received the knowledge of God, he asked of the Righteous One that he might merit to have offspring by Sarah, who was his lawful wife, though she was barren. She obtained a son, whom he named Isaac, from whom came Jacob, and from him the twelve patriarchs, and from these twelve seventy-two. These, when famine befell, came into Egypt with all their family; and in the course of four hundred years, being multiplied by the blessing and promise of God, they were afflicted by the Egyptians. And when they were afflicted the true Prophet appeared to Moses,[5] and struck the Egyptians with ten plagues, when they refused to let the Hebrew people depart from them, and return to their native land; and he brought the people of God out of Egypt. But those of the Egyptians who survived the plagues, being infected with the animosity of their king, pursued after the Hebrews. And when they had overtaken them at the sea-shore, and thought to destroy and exterminate them all, Moses, pouring out prayer to God, divided the sea into two parts, so that the water was held on the right hand and on the left as if it had been frozen, and the people of God passed as over a dry road; but the Egyptians who were pursuing them, rashly entering, were drowned. For when the last of the Hebrews came out, the last of the Egyptians went down into the sea; and straight-

---

[1] [With this chapter compare Homily IX. 3–7. — R.]
[2] Gen. xi. 28.
[3] [This orderly and consistent explanation of the Old-Testament economy (chaps. 32–39) is peculiar to the *Recognitions.* — R.]
[4] Gen xv., xxii.

[5] Exod. iii.

way the waters of the sea, which by his command were held bound as with frost, were loosed by his command who had bound them, and recovering their natural freedom, inflicted punishment on the wicked nation.

CHAP. XXXV. — THE EXODUS.

"After this, Moses, by the command of God, whose providence is over all, led out the people of the Hebrews into the wilderness; and, leaving the shortest road which leads from Egypt to Judæa, he led the people through long windings of the wilderness, that, by the discipline of forty years, the novelty of a changed manner of life might root out the evils which had clung to them by a long-continued familiarity with the customs of the Egyptians. Meantime they came to Mount Sinai, and thence the law was given to them with voices and sights from heaven, written in ten precepts, of which the first and greatest was that they should worship God Himself alone, and not make to themselves any appearance or form [1] to worship. But when Moses had gone up to the mount, and was staying there forty days, the people, although they had seen Egypt struck with the ten plagues, and the sea parted and passed over by them on foot, manna also given to them from heaven for bread, and drink supplied to them out of the rock that followed [2] them, which kind of food was turned into whatever taste any one desired; and although, being placed under the torrid region of heaven, they were shaded by a cloud in the day-time, that they might not be scorched by the heat, and by night were enlightened by a pillar of fire, lest the horror of darkness should be added to the wasteness of the wilderness; — those very people, I say, when Moses stayed in the mount, made and worshipped a golden calf's head, after the fashion of Apis, whom they had seen worshipped in Egypt; and after so many and so great marvels which they had seen, were unable to cleanse and wash out from themselves the defilements of old habit. On this account, leaving the short road which leads from Egypt to Judæa, Moses conducted them by an immense circuit of the desert, if haply he might be able, as we mentioned before, to shake off the evils of old habit by the change of a new education.

CHAP. XXXVI. — ALLOWANCE OF SACRIFICE FOR A TIME.

"When meantime Moses, that faithful and wise steward, perceived that the vice of sacrificing to idols had been deeply ingrained into the people from their association with the Egyptians, and that the root of this evil could not be ex-

tracted from them, he allowed them indeed to sacrifice, but permitted it to be done only to God, that by any means he might cut off one half of the deeply ingrained evil, leaving the other half to be corrected by another, and at a future time; by Him, namely, concerning whom he said himself, 'A prophet shall the Lord your God raise unto you, whom ye shall hear even as myself, according to all things which He shall say to you. Whosoever shall not hear that prophet, his soul shall be cut off from his people.' [3]

CHAP. XXXVII. — THE HOLY PLACE.

"In addition to these things, he also appointed a place in which alone it should be lawful to them to sacrifice to God. [4] And all this was arranged with this view, that when the fitting time should come, and they should learn by means of the Prophet that God desires mercy and not sacrifice, [5] they might see Him who should teach them that the place chosen of God, in which it was suitable that victims should be offered to God, is his Wisdom; and that on the other hand they might hear that this place, which seemed chosen for a time, often harassed as it had been by hostile invasions and plunderings, was at last to be wholly destroyed. [6] And in order to impress this upon them, even before the coming of the true Prophet, who was to reject at once the sacrifices and the place, it was often plundered by enemies and burnt with fire, and the people carried into captivity among foreign nations, and then brought back when they betook themselves to the mercy of God; that by these things they might be taught that a people who offer sacrifices are driven away and delivered up into the hands of the enemy, but they who do mercy and righteousness are without sacrifices freed from captivity, and restored to their native land. But it fell out that very few understood this; for the greater number, though they could perceive and observe these things, yet were held by the irrational opinion of the vulgar: for right opinion with liberty is the prerogative of a few.

CHAP. XXXVIII. — SINS OF THE ISRAELITES.

"Moses, [7] then, having arranged these things, and having set over the people one Ausès to bring them to the land of their fathers, himself by the command of the living God went up to a certain mountain, and there died. Yet such was the manner of his death, that till this day no one has found his burial-place. When, therefore, the people reached their fathers' land, by the providence of God, at their first onset the

---

[1] That is, picture or statue.
[2] Comp. 1 Cor. x. 4.

[3] Deut. xvii. 15; Acts iii. 22, 23.
[4] Deut. xii. 11; 2 Chron. vii. 12.
[5] Hos. vi. 6; Matt. ix. 13, xii. 7.
[6] Matt. xxiv. 2; Luke xix. 44.
[7] Deut. xxxi.-xxxiv.

inhabitants of wicked races are routed, and they enter upon their paternal inheritance, which was distributed among them by lot. For some time thereafter they were ruled not by kings, but judges, and remained in a somewhat peaceful condition. But when they sought for themselves tyrants rather than kings, then also with regal ambition they erected a temple in the place which had been appointed to them for prayer ; and thus, through a succession of wicked kings, the people fell away to greater and still greater impiety.

CHAP. XXXIX. — BAPTISM INSTITUTED IN PLACE OF SACRIFICES.

" But when the time began to draw near that what was wanting in the Mosaic institutions should be supplied, as we have said, and that the Prophet should appear, of whom he had foretold that He should warn them by the mercy of God to cease from sacrificing ; lest haply they might suppose that on the cessation of sacrifice there was no remission of sins for them, He instituted baptism by water amongst them, in which they might be absolved from all their sins on the invocation of His name, and for the future, following a perfect life, might abide in immortality, being purified not by the blood of beasts, but by the purification of the Wisdom of God. Subsequently also an evident proof of this great mystery is supplied *in the fact*, that every one who, believing in this Prophet who had been foretold by Moses, is baptized in His name, shall be kept unhurt from the destruction of war which impends over the unbelieving nation, and the place itself ; but that those who do not believe shall be made exiles from their place and kingdom, that even against their will they may understand and obey the will of God.

CHAP. XL. — ADVENT OF THE TRUE PROPHET.

" These things therefore having been fore-arranged, He who was expected comes, bringing signs and miracles as His credentials by which He should be made manifest. But not even so did the people believe, though they had been trained during so many ages to the belief of these things. And not only did they not believe, but they added blasphemy to unbelief, saying that He was a gluttonous man and a belly-slave, and that He was actuated by a demon,[1] even He who had come for their salvation. To such an extent does wickedness prevail by the agency of evil ones ; so that, but for the Wisdom of God assisting those who love the truth, almost all would have been involved in impious delusion. Therefore He chose us twelve,[2] the first who believed in Him, whom He named apostles ; and

afterwards other seventy-two most approved disciples,[3] that, at least in this way recognising the pattern of Moses,[4] the multitude might believe that this is He of whom Moses foretold, the Prophet that was to come.[5]

CHAP. XLI. — REJECTION OF THE TRUE PROPHET.

" But some one perhaps may say that it is possible for any one to imitate a number ; but what shall we say of the signs and miracles which He wrought ? For Moses had wrought miracles and cures in Egypt. He also of whom he foretold that He should rise up a prophet like unto himself, though He cured every sickness and infirmity among the people, wrought innumerable miracles, and preached eternal life, was hurried by wicked men to the cross ; which deed was, however, by His power turned to good. In short, while He was suffering, all the world suffered with Him ; for the sun was darkened, the mountains were torn asunder, the graves were opened, the veil of the temple was rent,[6] as in lamentation for the destruction impending over the place. And yet, though all the world was moved, they themselves are not even now moved to the consideration of these so great things.

CHAP. XLII. — CALL OF THE GENTILES.

" But inasmuch as it was necessary that the Gentiles should be called into the room of those who remained unbelieving,[7] so that the number might be filled up which had been shown to Abraham,[8] the preaching of the blessed kingdom of God is sent into all the world. On this account worldly spirits are disturbed, who always oppose those who are in quest of liberty, and who make use of the engines of error to destroy God's building ; while those who press on to the glory of safety and liberty, being rendered braver by their resistance to these spirits, and by the toil of great struggles against them, attain the crown of safety not without the palm of victory. Meantime, when He had suffered, and darkness had overwhelmed the world from the sixth even to the ninth hour,[9] as soon as the sun shone out again, and things were returned to their usual course, even wicked men returned to themselves and their former practices, their fear having abated. For some of them, watching the place with all care, when they could not prevent His rising again, said that He was a magician ; others pretended that he was stolen away.[10]

---

[1] Matt. ix.; John vii.
[2] Matt. x.

[3] Luke x.
[4] Num. xi. 16.
[5] Deut. xviii. 15.
[6] Matt. xxvii. 45, 51, 52.
[7] [Chaps. 42, 43, show little of the Ebionitic tendency, except in the attempt to reduce the difference between Jews and Christians to the single point of belief in the Messiahship of Jesus. — R.].
[8] Gen. xv.; Acts xiii.
[9] Matt. xxvii. 45.
[10] Matt. xxviii. 13.

CHAP. XLIII. — SUCCESS OF THE GOSPEL.

"Nevertheless, the truth everywhere prevailed ; for, in proof that these things were done by divine power, we who had been very few became in the course of a few days, by the help of God, far more than they. So that the priests at one time were afraid, lest haply, by the providence of God, to their confusion, the whole of the people should come over to our faith. Therefore they often sent to us, and asked us to discourse to them concerning Jesus, whether He were the Prophet whom Moses foretold, who is the eternal Christ.[1] For on this point only does there seem to be any difference between us who believe in Jesus, and the unbelieving Jews. But while they often made such requests to us, and we sought for a fitting opportunity, a week of years was completed from the passion of the Lord, the Church of the Lord which was constituted in Jerusalem was most plentifully multiplied and grew, being governed with most righteous ordinances by James, who was ordained bishop in it by the Lord.

CHAP. XLIV. — CHALLENGE BY CAIAPHAS.

"But when we twelve apostles, on the day of the passover, had come together with an immense multitude, and entered into the church of the brethren, each one of us, at the request of James,[2] stated briefly, in the hearing of the people, what we had done in every place.[3] While this was going on, Caiaphas, the high priest, sent priests to us, and asked us to come to him, that either we should prove to him that Jesus is the eternal Christ, or he to us that He is not, and that so all the people should agree upon the one faith or the other ; and this he frequently entreated us to do. But we often put it off, always seeking for a more convenient time."

Then I, Clement, answered to this : "I think that this very question, whether He is the Christ, is of great importance for the establishment of the faith ; otherwise the high priest would not so frequently ask that he might either learn or teach concerning the Christ."

Then Peter : "You have answered rightly, O Clement ; for as no one can see without eyes, nor hear without ears, nor smell without nostrils, nor taste without a tongue, nor handle anything without hands, so it is impossible, without the true Prophet, to know what is pleasing to God."

And I answered : "I have already learned from your instruction that this true prophet is

the Christ ; but I should wish to learn what *the Christ* means, or why He is so called, that a matter of so great importance may not be vague and uncertain to me."

CHAP. XLV. — THE TRUE PROPHET : WHY CALLED THE CHRIST.

Then Peter began to instruct me in this manner : [4] "When God had made the world, as Lord of the universe, He appointed chiefs over the several creatures, over the trees even, and the mountains, and the fountains, and the rivers, and all things which He had made, as we have told you ; for it were too long to mention them one by one. He set, therefore, an angel as chief over the angels, a spirit over the spirits, a star over the stars, a demon over the demons, a bird over the birds, a beast over the beasts, a serpent over the serpents, a fish over the fishes, a man over men, who is Christ Jesus. But He is called *Christ* by a certain excellent rite of religion ; for as there are certain names common to kings, as Arsaces among the Persians, Cæsar among the Romans, Pharaoh among the Egyptians, so among the Jews a king is called *Christ*. And the reason of this appellation is this : Although indeed He was the Son of God, and the beginning of all things, He became man ; Him first God anointed with oil which was taken from the wood of the tree of life : from that anointing therefore He is called *Christ*. Thence, moreover, He Himself also, according to the appointment of His Father, anoints with similar oil every one of the pious when they come to His kingdom, for their refreshment after their labours, as having got over the difficulties of the way ; so that their light may shine, and being filled with the Holy Spirit, they may be endowed with immortality.[5] But it occurs to me that I have sufficiently explained to you the whole nature of that branch from which that ointment is taken.

CHAP. XLVI. — ANOINTING.

"But now also I shall, by a very short representation, recall you to the recollection of all these things. In the present life, Aaron, the first high priest,[6] was anointed with a composition of chrism, which was made after the pattern of that spiritual ointment of which we have spoken before. He was prince of the people, and as a king received first-fruits and tribute from the people, man by man ; and having undertaken the office

---

[1] John xii. 34.
[2] [Evidently "the Lord's brother." Comp. chap. 68. — R.]
[3] [This account of occurrences in Jerusalem (chaps. 45–70) is probably meant to supplement Acts v. and viii. The date tallies with the stoning of Stephen, to which there is no allusion. The whole bears abundant marks of "manipulation" of the New-Testament record. — R.]

[4] [The discourse of chaps. 45–52 is interesting from its christological consistency. The doctrine, while showing Ebionitic origin, is closer to the Catholic view than that of the *Homilies*. — R.]
[5] [The references to oil in chaps. 45–48, particularly the connection of anointing with baptism, have been regarded, since the discovery of the full text of Hippolytus, as showing traces of relationship to the system of the Elkesaites. See Introductory Notice. In the forms given by Hippolytus (see *Ante-Nicene Fathers*, v. pp. 132, 133) the oil is represented as one of "seven witnesses" to be adjured by the subject of baptism. — R.]
[6] Exod. xxix. ; Lev. viii.

of judging the people, he judged of things clean and things unclean. But if any one else was anointed with the same ointment, as deriving virtue from it, he became either king, or prophet, or priest. If, then, this temporal grace, compounded by men, had such efficacy, consider now how potent was that ointment extracted by God from a branch of the tree of life, when that which was made by men could confer so excellent dignities among men. For what in the present age is more glorious than a prophet, more illustrious than a priest, more exalted than a king?"

CHAP. XLVII. — ADAM ANOINTED A PROPHET.

To this, I replied : "I remember, Peter, that you told me of the first man that he was a prophet ; but you did not say that he was anointed. If then there be no prophet without anointing, how could the first man be a prophet, since he was not anointed?" Then Peter, smiling, said : "If the first man prophesied, it is certain that he was also anointed. For although he who has recorded the law in his pages is silent as to his anointing, yet he has evidently left us to understand these things. For as, if he had said that he was anointed, it would not be doubted that he was also a prophet, although it were not written in the law ; so, since it is certain that he was a prophet, it is in like manner certain that he was also anointed, because without anointing he could not be a prophet. But you should rather have said, If the chrism was compounded by Aaron, by the perfumer's art, how could the first man be anointed before Aaron's time, the arts of composition not yet having been discovered?" Then I answered, "Do not misunderstand me, Peter ; for I do not speak of that compounded ointment and temporal oil, but of that simple and eternal *ointment*, which you told me was made by God, after whose likeness you say that that other was compounded by men."

CHAP. XLVIII. — THE TRUE PROPHET, A PRIEST.

Then Peter answered, with an appearance of indignation : "What ! do you suppose, Clement, that all of us can know all things before the time? But not to be drawn aside now from our proposed discourse, we shall at another time, when your progress is more manifest, explain these things more distinctly.

"Then, however, a priest or a prophet, being anointed with the compounded ointment, putting fire to the altar of God, was held illustrious in all the world. But after Aaron, who was a priest, another is taken out of the waters. I do not speak of Moses, but of Him who, in the waters of baptism, was called by God His Son.[1] For it is Jesus who has put out, by the grace of baptism, that fire which the priest kindled for sins ; for, from the time when He appeared, the chrism has ceased, by which the priesthood or the prophetic or the kingly office was conferred.

CHAP. XLIX. — TWO COMINGS OF CHRIST.

"His coming, therefore, was predicted by Moses, who delivered the law of God to men ; but by another also before him, as I have already informed you. He therefore intimated that He should come, humble indeed in His first coming, but glorious in His second. And the first, indeed, has been already accomplished ; since He has come and taught, and He, the Judge of all, has been judged and slain. But at His second coming He shall come to judge, and shall indeed condemn the wicked, but shall take the pious into a share and association with Himself in His kingdom. Now the faith of His second coming depends upon His first. For the prophets — especially Jacob and Moses — spoke of the first, but some also of the second. But the excellency of prophecy is chiefly shown in this, that the prophets spoke not of things to come, according to the sequence of things ; otherwise they might seem merely as wise men to have conjectured what the sequence of things pointed out.

CHAP L. — HIS REJECTION BY THE JEWS.

"But what I say is this : It was to be expected that Christ should be received by the Jews, to whom He came, and that they should believe on Him who was expected for the salvation of the people, according to the traditions of the fathers ; but that the Gentiles should be averse to Him, since neither promise nor announcement concerning Him had been made to them, and indeed He had never been made known to them even by name. Yet the prophets, contrary to the order and sequence of things, said that He should be the expectation of the Gentiles, and not of the Jews.[2] And so it happened. For when He came, He was not at all acknowledged by those who seemed to expect Him, in consequence of the tradition of their ancestors ; whereas those who had heard nothing at all of Him, both believe that He has come, and hope that He is to come. And thus in all things prophecy appears faithful, which said that He was the expectation of the Gentiles. The Jews, therefore, have erred concerning the first coming of the Lord ; and on this point only there is disagreement betwixt us and them. For they themselves know and expect that Christ shall come ; but that He has come already in humility — even He who is called Jesus — they do not know. And this is a great confirmation of His coming, that all do not believe on Him.

---

[1] Matt. iii. 17.

[2] Gen. xlix. 10.

CHAP. LI. — THE ONLY SAVIOUR.

"Him, therefore, has God appointed in the end of the world; because it was impossible that the evils of men could be removed by any other, provided that the nature of the human race were to remain entire, i.e., the liberty of the will being preserved. This condition, therefore, being preserved inviolate, He came to invite to His kingdom all righteous ones, and those who have been desirous to please Him. For these He has prepared unspeakable good things, and the heavenly city Jerusalem, which shall shine above the brightness of the sun, for the habitation of the saints. But the unrighteous, and the wicked, and those who have despised God, and have devoted the life given them to diverse wickednesses, and have given to the practice of evil the time which was given them for the work of righteousness, He shall hand over to fitting and condign vengeance. But the rest of the things which shall then be done, it is neither in the power of angels nor of men to tell or to describe. This only it is enough for us to know, that God shall confer upon the good an eternal possession of good things."

CHAP. LII. — THE SAINTS BEFORE CHRIST'S COMING.

When he had thus spoken, I answered: "If those shall enjoy the kingdom of Christ, whom His coming shall find righteous, shall then those be wholly deprived of the kingdom who have died before His coming?" Then Peter says: "You compel me, O Clement, to touch upon things that are unspeakable. But so far as it is allowed to declare them, I shall not shrink from doing so. Know then that Christ, who was from the beginning, and always, was ever present with the pious, though secretly, through all their generations; especially with those who waited for Him, to whom He frequently appeared. But the time was not yet that there should be a resurrection of the bodies that were dissolved; but this seemed rather to be their reward from God, that whoever should be found righteous, should remain longer in the body; or, at least, as is clearly related in the writings of the law concerning a certain righteous man, that God translated him.[1] In like manner others were dealt with, who pleased His will, that, being translated to Paradise, they should be kept for the kingdom. But as to those who have not been able completely to fulfil the rule of righteousness, but have had some remnants of evil in their flesh, their bodies are indeed dissolved, but their souls are kept in good and blessed abodes, that at the resurrection of the dead, when they shall recover their own bodies, purified even by the dissolu-

tion, they may obtain an eternal inheritance in proportion to their good deeds. And therefore blessed are all those who shall attain to the kingdom of Christ; for not only shall they escape the pains of hell, but shall also remain incorruptible, and shall be the first to see God the Father, and shall obtain the rank of honour among the first in the presence of God.

CHAP. LIII. — ANIMOSITY OF THE JEWS.

"Wherefore there is not the least doubt concerning Christ; and all the unbelieving Jews are stirred up with boundless rage against us, fearing lest haply He against whom they have sinned should be He. And their fear grows all the greater, because they know that, as soon as they fixed Him on the cross, the whole world showed sympathy with Him; and that His body, although they guarded it with strict care, could nowhere be found; and that innumerable multitudes are attaching themselves to His faith. Whence they, together with the high priest Caiaphas, were compelled to send to us again and again, that an inquiry might be instituted concerning the truth of His name. And when they were constantly entreating that they might either learn or teach concerning Jesus, whether He were the Christ, it seemed good to us to go up into the temple, and in the presence of all the people to bear witness concerning Him, and at the same time to charge the Jews with many foolish things which they were doing. For the people was now divided into many parties, ever since the days of John the Baptist.

CHAP. LIV. — JEWISH SECTS.

"For when the rising of Christ was at hand for the abolition of sacrifices, and for the bestowal of the grace of baptism, the enemy, understanding from the predictions that the time was at hand, wrought various schisms among the people, that, if haply it might be possible to abolish the former sin,[2] the latter fault might be incorrigible. The first schism, therefore, was that of those who were called Sadducees, which took their rise almost in the time of John. These, as more righteous than others, began to separate themselves from the assembly of the people, and to deny the resurrection of the dead,[3] and to assert that by an argument of infidelity, saying that it was unworthy that God should be worshipped, as it were, under the promise of a reward. The first author of this opinion was Dositheus; [4] the second was Simon. Another schism is that of the Samaritans; for

---

[1] Gen. v. 24.

[2] That is, the sin of sacrifice.
[3] Matt. xxii. 23.
[4] [Comp. book ii. 8-11 and Homily II. 24. The writer here confuses the later Dositheus with an earlier teacher, whose disciple Zadok was the founder of the sect of the Sadducees. — R.]

they deny the resurrection of the dead, and assert that God is not to be worshipped in Jerusalem, but on Mount Gerizim. They indeed rightly, from the predictions of Moses, expect the one true Prophet; but by the wickedness of Dositheus they were hindered from believing that Jesus is He whom they were expecting. The scribes also, and Pharisees, are led away into another schism; but these, being baptized by John, and holding the word of truth received from the tradition of Moses as the key of the kingdom of heaven, have hid it from the hearing of the people.[1] Yea, some even of the disciples of John, who seemed to be great ones, have separated themselves from the people, and proclaimed their own master as the Christ. But all these schisms have been prepared, that by means of them the faith of Christ and baptism might be hindered.

CHAP. LV. — PUBLIC DISCUSSION.

" However, as we were proceeding to say, when the high priest had often sent priests to ask us that we might discourse with one another concerning Jesus; when it seemed a fit opportunity, and it pleased all the Church, we went up to the temple, and, standing on the steps together with our faithful brethren, the people kept perfect silence; and first the high priest began to exhort the people that they should hear patiently and quietly, and at the same time witness and judge of those things that were to be spoken. Then, in the next place, exalting with many praises the rite of sacrifice which had been bestowed by God upon the human race for the remission of sins, he found fault with the baptism of our Jesus, as having been recently brought in in opposition to the sacrifices. But Matthew,[2] meeting his propositions, showed clearly, that whosoever shall not obtain the baptism of Jesus shall not only be deprived of the kingdom of heaven, but shall not be without peril at the resurrection of the dead, even though he be fortified by the prerogative of a good life and an upright disposition. Having made these and such like statements, Matthew stopped.

CHAP. LVI. — SADDUCEES REFUTED.

" But the party of the Sadducees, who deny the resurrection of the dead, were in a rage, so that one of them cried out from amongst the people, saying that those greatly err who think that the dead ever arise. In opposition to him, Andrew, my brother, answering, declared that it is not an error, but the surest matter of faith,

that the dead rise, in accordance with the teaching of Him of whom Moses foretold that He should come the true Prophet. ' Or if,' says he, ' you do not think that this is He whom Moses foretold, let this first be inquired into, so that when this is clearly proved to be He, there may be no further doubt concerning the things which He taught.' These, and many such like things, Andrew proclaimed, and then stopped.

CHAP. LVII. — SAMARITAN REFUTED.

" But a certain Samaritan, speaking against the people and against God, and asserting that neither are the dead to rise, nor is that worship of God to be maintained which is in Jerusalem, but that Mount Gerizim is to be reverenced, added also this in opposition to us, that our Jesus was not He whom Moses foretold as a Prophet to come into the world. Against him, and another who supported him in what he said, James and John, the sons of Zebedee, strove vigorously; and although they had a command not to enter into their cities,[3] nor to bring the word of preaching to them, yet, lest their discourse, unless it were confuted, should hurt the faith of others, they replied so prudently and so powerfully, that they put them to perpetual silence. For James made an oration concerning the resurrection of the dead, with the approbation of all the people; while John showed that if they would abandon the error of Mount Gerizim, they should consequently acknowledge that Jesus was indeed He who, according to the prophecy of Moses, was expected to come; since, indeed, as Moses wrought signs and miracles, so also did Jesus. And there is no doubt but that the likeness of the signs proves Him to be that prophet of whom he said that He should come, ' like himself.' Having declared these things, and more to the same effect, they ceased.

CHAP. LVIII. — SCRIBES REFUTED.

" And, behold, one of the scribes, shouting out from the midst of the people, says: ' The signs and miracles which your Jesus wrought, he wrought not as a prophet, but as a magician.' Him Philip eagerly encounters, showing that by this argument he accused Moses also. For when Moses wrought signs and miracles in Egypt, in like manner as Jesus also did in Judæa, it cannot be doubted that what was said of Jesus might as well be said of Moses. Having made these and such like protestations, Philip was silent.

CHAP. LIX. — PHARISEES REFUTED.

" Then a certain Pharisee, hearing this, chid Philip because he put Jesus on a level with Mo-

---

[1] Luke xi. 52.
[2] [Here we encounter that favourite notion of apocryphal writers, that each Apostle must be represented as contributing his portion to the statement and defence of the faith. — R.]

[3] Matt. x. 5.

ses. To whom Bartholomew, answering, boldly declared that we do not only say that Jesus was equal to Moses, but that He was greater than he, because Moses was indeed a prophet, as Jesus was also, but that Moses was not the Christ, as Jesus was, and therefore He is doubtless greater who is both a prophet and the Christ, than he who is only a prophet. After following out this train of argument, he stopped. After him James the son of Alphæus gave an address to the people, with the view of showing that we are not to believe on Jesus on the ground that the prophets foretold concerning Him, but rather that we are to believe the prophets, that they were really prophets, because the Christ bears testimony to them; for it is the presence and coming of Christ that show that they are truly prophets: for testimony must be borne by the superior to his inferiors, not by the inferiors to their superior. After these and many similar statements, James also was silent. After him Lebbæus began vehemently to charge it upon the people that they did not believe in Jesus, who had done them so much good by teaching them the things that are of God, by comforting the afflicted, healing the sick, relieving the poor; yet for all these benefits their return had been hatred and death. When he had declared these and many more such things to the people, he ceased.

CHAP. LX. — DISCIPLES OF JOHN REFUTED.

"And, behold, one of the disciples of John asserted that John was the Christ, and not Jesus, inasmuch as Jesus Himself declared that John was greater than all men and all prophets.[1] 'If, then,' said he, 'he be greater than all, he must be held to be greater than Moses, and than Jesus himself. But if he be the greatest of all, then must he be the Christ.' To this Simon the Canaanite, answering, asserted that John was indeed greater than all the prophets, and all who are born of women, yet that he is not greater than the Son of man. Accordingly Jesus is also the Christ, whereas John is only a prophet: and there is as much difference between him and Jesus, as between the forerunner and Him whose forerunner he is; or as between Him who gives the law, and him who keeps the law. Having made these and similar statements, the Canaanite also was silent. After him Barnabas,[2] who also is called Matthias, who was substituted as an apostle in the place of Judas, began to exhort the people that they should not regard Jesus with hatred, nor speak evil of Him. For it were far more proper, even for one who might be in ignorance or in doubt concerning Jesus, to love than to hate Him. For God has affixed a reward to love, a penalty to hatred. 'For the very fact,' said he, 'that He assumed a Jewish body, and was born among the Jews, how has not this incited us all to love Him?' When he had spoken this, and more to the same effect, he stopped.

CHAP. LXI. — CAIAPHAS ANSWERED.

"Then Caiaphas attempted to impugn the doctrine of Jesus, saying that He spoke vain things, for He said that the poor are blessed;[3] and promised earthly rewards; and placed the chief gift in an earthly inheritance; and promised that those who maintain righteousness shall be satisfied with meat and drink; and many things of this sort He is charged with teaching. Thomas, in reply, proves that his accusation is frivolous; showing that the prophets, in whom Caiaphas believes, taught these things much more, and did not show in what manner these things are to be, or how they are to be understood; whereas Jesus pointed out how they are to be taken. And when he had spoken these things, and others of like kind, Thomas also held his peace.

CHAP. LXII. — FOOLISHNESS OF PREACHING.

"Therefore Caiaphas, again looking at me, and sometimes in the way of warning and sometimes in that of accusation, said that I ought for the future to refrain from preaching Christ Jesus, lest I should do it to my own destruction, and lest, being deceived myself, I should also deceive others. Then, moreover, he charged me with presumption, because, though I was unlearned, a fisherman, and a rustic, I dared to assume the office of a teacher. As he spoke these things, and many more of like kind, I said in reply, that I incurred less danger, if, as he said, this Jesus were not the Christ, because I received Him as a teacher of the law; but that he was in terrible danger if this be the very Christ, as assuredly He is: for I believe in Him who has appeared; but for whom else, who has never appeared, does he reserve his faith? But if I, an unlearned and uneducated man, as you say, a fisherman and a rustic, have more understanding than wise elders, this, said I, ought the more to strike terror into you. For if I disputed with any learning, and won over you wise and learned men, it would appear that I had acquired this power by long learning, and not by the grace of divine power; but now, when, as I have said, we unskilled men convince and overcome you wise men, who that has any sense does not perceive that this is not a work of human subtlety, but of divine will and gift?

---

[1] Matt. xi. 9, 11.
[2] We should doubtless read "Barsabas."

[3] Matt. v. 3; Luke vi. 20.

CHAP. LXIII. — APPEAL TO THE JEWS.

"Thus we argued and bore witness; and we who were unlearned men and fishermen, taught the priests concerning the one only God of heaven; the Sadducees, concerning the resurrection of the dead; the Samaritans, concerning the sacredness of Jerusalem (not that we entered into their cities, but disputed with them in public); the scribes and Pharisees, concerning the kingdom of heaven; the disciples of John, that they should not suffer John to be a stumbling-block to them; and all the people, that Jesus is the eternal Christ. At last, however, I warned them, that before we should go forth to the Gentiles, to preach to them the knowledge of God the Father, they should themselves be reconciled to God, receiving His Son; for I showed them that in no way else could they be saved, unless through the grace of the Holy Spirit they hasted to be washed with the baptism of threefold invocation, and received the Eucharist of Christ the Lord, whom alone they ought to believe concerning those things which He taught, that so they might merit to attain eternal salvation; but that otherwise it was utterly impossible for them to be reconciled to God, even if they should kindle a thousand altars and a thousand high altars to Him.

CHAP. LXIV. — TEMPLE TO BE DESTROYED.

" ' For we,' said I, 'have ascertained beyond doubt that God is much rather displeased with the sacrifices which you offer, the time of sacrifices having now passed away; and because ye will not acknowledge that the time for offering victims is now past, therefore the temple shall be destroyed, and the abomination of desolation [1] shall stand in the holy place; and then the Gospel shall be preached to the Gentiles for a testimony against you, that your unbelief may be judged by their faith. For the whole world at different times suffers under divers maladies, either spreading generally over all, or affecting specially. Therefore it needs a physician to visit it for its salvation. We therefore bear witness to you, and declare to you what has been hidden from every one of you. It is for you to consider what is for your advantage.'

CHAP. LXV. — TUMULT STILLED BY GAMALIEL.

"When I had thus spoken, the whole multitude of the priests were in a rage, because I had foretold to them the overthrow of the temple. Which when Gamaliel, a chief of the people, saw — who was secretly our brother in the faith, but by our advice remained among them — because they were greatly enraged and moved with intense fury against us, he stood up, and said,[2] ' Be quiet for a little, O men of Israel, for ye do not perceive the trial which hangs over you. Wherefore refrain from these men; and if what they are engaged in be of human counsel, it will soon come to an end; but if it be from God, why will you sin without cause, and prevail nothing? For who can overpower the will of God? Now therefore, since the day is declining towards evening, I shall myself dispute with these men to-morrow, in this same place, in your hearing, so that I may openly oppose and clearly confute every error.' By this speech of his their fury was to some extent checked, especially in the hope that next day we should be publicly convicted of error; and so he dismissed the people peacefully.

CHAP. LXVI. — DISCUSSION RESUMED.

"Now when we had come to our James, while we detailed to him all that had been said and done, we supped, and remained with him, spending the whole night in supplication to Almighty God, that the discourse of the approaching disputation might show the unquestionable truth of our faith. Therefore, on the following day, James the bishop went up to the temple with us, and with the whole church. There we found a great multitude, who had been waiting for us from the middle of the night. Therefore we took our stand in the same place as before, in order that, standing on an elevation, we might be seen by all the people. Then, when profound silence was obtained, Gamaliel, who, as we have said, was of our faith, but who by a dispensation remained amongst them, that if at any time they should attempt anything unjust or wicked against us, he might either check them by skilfully adopted counsel, or might warn us, that we might either be on our guard or might turn it aside; — he therefore, as if acting against us, first of all looking to James the bishop, addressed him in this manner: —

CHAP. LXVII. — SPEECH OF GAMALIEL.

" ' If I, Gamaliel, deem it no reproach either to my learning or to my old age to learn something from babes and unlearned ones, if haply there be anything which it is for profit or for safety to acquire (for he who lives reasonably knows that nothing is more precious than the soul), ought not this to be the object of love and desire to all, to learn what they do not know, and to teach what they have learned? For it is most certain that neither friendship, nor kindred, nor lofty power, ought to be more precious to men than truth. Therefore you, O brethren, if ye know anything more, shrink not from laying it

---

[1] Dan. ix. 27; Matt. xxiv. 15.

[2] Acts v. 35-39.

before the people of God who are present, and also before your brethren; while the whole people shall willingly and in perfect quietness hear what you say. For why should not the people do this, when they see even me equally with themselves willing to learn from you, if haply God has revealed something further to you? But if you in anything are deficient, be not ye ashamed in like manner to be taught by us, that God may fill up whatever is wanting on either side. But if any fear now agitates you on account of some of our people whose minds are prejudiced against you, and if through fear of their violence you dare not openly speak your sentiments, in order that I may deliver you from this fear, I openly swear to you by Almighty God, who liveth for ever, that I will suffer no one to lay hands upon you. Since, then, you have all this people witnesses of this my oath, and you hold the covenant of our sacrament as a fitting pledge, let each one of you, without any hesitation, declare what he has learned; and let us, brethren, listen eagerly and in silence.'

CHAP. LXVIII. — THE RULE OF FAITH.

"These sayings of Gamaliel did not much please Caiaphas; and holding him in suspicion, as it seemed, he began to insinuate himself cunningly into the discussions: for, smiling at what Gamaliel had said, the chief of the priests asked of James, the chief of the bishops,[1] that the discourse concerning Christ should not be drawn but from the Scriptures; 'that we may know,' said he, 'whether Jesus be the very Christ or no.' Then said James, 'We must first inquire from what Scriptures we are especially to derive our discussion.' Then he, with difficulty, at length overcome by reason, answered, that it must be derived from the law; and afterwards he made mention also of the prophets.

CHAP. LXIX. — TWO COMINGS OF CHRIST.

"To him our James began to show, that whatsoever things the prophets say they have taken from the law, and what they have spoken is in accordance with the law. He also made some statements respecting the books of the Kings, in what way, and when, and by whom they were written, and how they ought to be used. And when he had discussed most fully concerning the law, and had, by a most clear exposition, brought into light whatever things are in it concerning Christ, he showed by most abundant proofs that Jesus is the Christ, and that in Him are fulfilled all the prophecies which related to His humble advent. For he showed that two advents of Him are foretold: one in humiliation, which

He has accomplished; the other in glory, which is hoped for to be accomplished, when He shall come to give the kingdom to those who believe in Him, and who observe all things which He has commanded. And when he had plainly taught the people concerning these things, he added this also: That unless a man be baptized in water, in the name of the threefold blessedness, as the true Prophet taught, he can neither receive remission of sins nor enter into the kingdom of heaven; and he declared that this is the prescription of the unbegotten God. To which he added this also: 'Do not think that we speak of two unbegotten Gods, or that one is divided into two, or that the same is made male and female. But we speak of the only-begotten Son of God, not sprung from another source, but ineffably self-originated; and in like manner we speak of the Paraclete.'[2] But when he had spoken some things also concerning baptism, through seven successive days he persuaded all the people and the high priest that they should hasten straightway to receive baptism.

CHAP. LXX. — TUMULT RAISED BY SAUL.

"And when matters were at that point that they should come and be baptized, some one of our enemies,[3] entering the temple with a few men, began to cry out, and to say, 'What mean ye, O men of Israel? Why are you so easily hurried on? Why are ye led headlong by most miserable men, who are deceived by Simon, a magician?' While he was thus speaking, and adding more to the same effect, and while James the bishop was refuting him, he began to excite the people and to raise a tumult, so that the people might not be able to hear what was said. Therefore he began to drive all into confusion with shouting, and to undo what had been arranged with much labour, and at the same time to reproach the priests, and to enrage them with revilings and abuse, and, like a madman, to excite every one to murder, saying, 'What do ye? Why do ye hesitate? Oh, sluggish and inert, why do we not lay hands upon them, and pull all these fellows to pieces?' When he had said this, he first, seizing a strong brand from the altar, set the example of smiting. Then others also, seeing him, were carried away with like madness. Then ensued a tumult on either side, of the beating and the beaten. Much blood is shed; there is a confused flight, in the midst of which that enemy attacked James, and threw him headlong from the top of the steps; and supposing him to be dead, he cared not to inflict further violence upon him.

---

[1] [This title is consistent with the position accorded to James the Lord's brother in the entire pseudo-Clementine literature. — R.]

[2] [This sentence seems to have been framed to accord with the Catholic doctrine. — R.]

[3] A marginal note in one of the manuscripts states that this enemy was Saul. [This is confirmed by chap. 71. — R.]

CHAP. LXXI. — FLIGHT TO JERICHO.

" But our friends lifted him up, for they were both more numerous and more powerful than the others ; but, from their fear of God, they rather suffered themselves to be killed by an inferior force, than they would kill others. But when the evening came the priests shut up the temple, and we returned to the house of James, and spent the night there in prayer. Then before daylight we went down to Jericho, to the number of 5000 men. Then after three days one of the brethren came to us from Gamaliel, whom we mentioned before, bringing to us secret tidings that that enemy had received a commission from Caiaphas, the chief priest, that he should arrest all who believed in Jesus, and should go to Damascus with his letters, and that there also, employing the help of the unbelievers, he should make havoc among the faithful ; and that he was hastening to Damascus chiefly on this account, because he believed that Peter had fled thither.[1] And about thirty days thereafter he stopped on his way while passing through Jericho going to Damascus. At that time we were absent, having gone out to the sepulchres of two brethren which were whitened of themselves every year, by which miracle the fury of many against us was restrained, because they saw that our brethren were had in remembrance before God.

CHAP. LXXII. — PETER SENT TO CÆSAREA.

" While, therefore, we abode in Jericho, and gave ourselves to prayer and fasting, James the bishop sent for me, and sent me here to Cæsarea, saying that Zacchæus had written to him from Cæsarea, that one Simon, a Samaritan magician, was subverting many of our people, asserting that he was one *Stans*,[2] — that is, in other words, the Christ, and the great power of the high God, which is superior to the Creator of the world ; at the same time that he showed many miracles, and made some doubt, and others fall away to him. He informed me of all things that had been ascertained respecting this man from those who had formerly been either his associates or his disciples, and had afterwards been converted to Zacchæus. ' Many therefore there are, O Peter,' said James, ' for whose safety's sake it behoves you to go and to refute the magician, and to teach the word of truth. Therefore make no delay ; nor let it grieve you that you set out alone, knowing that God by Jesus will go with you, and will help you, and that soon, by His grace, you will have many associates and sympathizers. Now be

sure that you send me in writing every year an account of your sayings and doings, and especially at the end of every seven years.' With these expressions he dismissed me, and in six days I arrived at Cæsarea.[3]

CHAP. LXXIII. — WELCOMED BY ZACCHÆUS.

" When I entered the city, our most beloved brother Zacchæus met me ; and embracing me, brought me to this lodging, in which he himself stayed, inquiring of me concerning each of the brethren, especially concerning our honourable brother James. And when I told him that he was still lame on one foot, on his immediately asking the cause of this, I related to him all that I have now detailed to you, how we had been called by the priests and Caiaphas the high priest to the temple, and how James the archbishop, standing on the top of the steps, had for seven successive days shown the whole people from the Scriptures of the Lord that Jesus is the Christ ; and how, when all were acquiescing that they should be baptized by him in the name of Jesus, an enemy did all those things which I have already mentioned, and which I need not repeat.

CHAP. LXXIV. — SIMON MAGUS CHALLENGES PETER.

" When Zacchæus had heard these things, he told me in return of the doings of Simon ; and in the meantime Simon himself — how he heard of my arrival I do not know — sent a message to me, saying, ' Let us dispute to-morrow in the hearing of the people.' To which I answered, ' Be it so, as it pleaseth you.' And this promise of mine was known over the whole city, so that even you, who arrived on that very day, learned that I was to hold a discussion with Simon on the following day, and having found out my abode, according to the directions which you had received from Barnabas, came to me. But I so rejoiced at your coming, that my mind, moved I know not how, hastened to expound all things quickly to you, yet especially that which is the main point in our faith, concerning the true Prophet, which alone, I doubt not, is a sufficient foundation for the whole of our doctrine. Then, in the next place, I unfolded to you the more secret meaning of the written law, through its several heads, which there was occasion to unfold ; neither did I conceal from you the good things of the traditions. But what remains, beginning from to-morrow, you shall hear from day to day in connection with the questions which will be raised in the discussion with Simon,

---

[1] Acts xxii. 5. [There is an evident attempt to cast a slur upon the Apostle Paul, but the suppression of the name is significant. — R.]
[2] [Comp. book ii. 7 and Homily II. 22, 24. — R.]

[3] [The visit of Peter to Cæsarea narrated in Acts x. was for a very different purpose. It is probable that the author of the *Recognitions* connected the persecution by Saul and the sorceries of Simon because of the similar juxtaposition in Acts viii. — R.]

until by God's favour we reach that city of Rome to which we believe that our journey is to be directed."

I then declared that I owed him all thanks for what he had told me, and promised that I would most readily do all that he commanded. Then, having taken food, he ordered me to rest, and he also betook himself to rest.

BOOK II.

CHAP. I. — POWER OF HABIT.

WHEN the day dawned which had been fixed for the discussion with Simon, Peter, rising at the first cock-crowing, aroused us also: for we were sleeping in the same apartment, thirteen of us in all; [1] of whom, next to Peter, Zacchæus was first, then Sophonius, Joseph and Michæas, Eliesdrus, Phineas, Lazarus, and Elisæus: after these I (Clement) and Nicodemus; then Niceta and Aquila, who had formerly been disciples of Simon, and were converted to the faith of Christ under the teaching of Zacchæus. Of the women there was no one present. As the evening light [2] was still lasting, we all sat down; and Peter, seeing that we were awake, and that we were giving attention to him, having saluted us, immediately began to speak, as follows: —

"I confess, brethren, that I wonder at the power of human nature, which I see to be fit and suited to every call upon it. This, however, it occurs to me to say of what I have found by experience, that when the middle of the night is passed, I awake of my own accord, and sleep does not come to me again. This happens to me for this reason, that I have formed the habit of recalling to memory the words of my Lord, which I heard from Himself; and for the longing I have towards them, I constrain my mind and my thoughts to be roused, that, awaking to them, and recalling and arranging them one by one, I may retain them in my memory. From this, therefore, whilst I desire to cherish the sayings of the Lord with all delight in my heart, the habit of waking has come upon me, even if there be nothing that I wish to think of. Thus, in some unaccountable way, when any custom is established, the old custom is changed, provided indeed you do not force it above measure, but as far as the measure of nature admits. For it is not possible to be altogether without sleep; otherwise night would not have been made for rest."

CHAP. II. — CURTAILMENT OF SLEEP.

Then I, when I heard this, said: "You have very well said, O Peter; for one custom is superseded by another. For when I was at sea, I was at first distressed, and all my system was disordered, so that I felt as if I had been beaten, and could not bear the tossing and tumult of the sea; but after a few days, when I had got accustomed to it, I began to bear it tolerably, so that I was glad to take food immediately in the morning along with the sailors, whereas before it was not my custom to eat anything before the seventh hour. Now, therefore, simply from the custom which I then acquired, hunger reminds me about that time at which I used to eat with the sailors; which, however, I hope to get rid of, when once another custom shall have been formed. I believe, therefore, that you also have acquired the habit of wakefulness, as you state; and you have wished at a fitting time to explain this to us, that we also may not grudge to throw off and dispense with some portion of our sleep, that we may be able to take in the precepts of the living doctrine. For when the food is digested, and the mind is under the influence of the silence of night, those things which are seasonably taught abide in it."

CHAP. III. — NEED OF CAUTION.

Then Peter, being pleased to hear that I understood the purport of his preface, that he had delivered it for our advantage; and commending me, doubtless for the purpose of encouraging and stimulating me, began to deliver the following discourse: [3] "It seems to me to be seasonable and necessary to have some discussion relating to those things that are near at hand; that is, concerning Simon. For I should wish to know of what character and of what conduct he is. Wherefore, if any one of you has any knowledge of him, let him not fail to inform me; for it is of consequence to know these things beforehand. For if we have it in charge,

---

[1] [With this list compare that in iii. 68, where four others are added (or substituted), and some importance given to the number twelve. See also Homily II. 1. The variety and correspondence point to the use of a common basis. — R.]

[2] That is, the lamp which had been lighted in the evening.

[3] [In the *Homilies* the discourse before the discussion with Simon is much fuller. — R.]

that when we enter into a city we should first learn who in it is worthy,[1] that we may eat with him, how much more is it proper for us to ascertain who or what sort of man he is to whom the words of immortality are to be committed ! For we ought to be careful, yea, extremely careful, that we cast not our pearls before swine.[2]

CHAP. IV. — PRUDENCE IN DEALING WITH OPPONENTS.

" But for other reasons also it is of importance that I should have some knowledge of this man. For if I know that in those things concerning which it cannot be doubted that they are good, he is faultless and irreproachable, — that is to say, if he is sober, merciful, upright, gentle, and humane, which no one doubts to be good qualities, — then it will seem to be fitting, that upon him who possesses these good virtues, that which is lacking of faith and knowledge should be conferred ; and so his life, which is in other respects worthy of approbation, should be amended in those points in which it shall appear to be imperfect. But if he remains wrapped up and polluted in those sins which are manifestly such, it does not become me to speak to him at all of the more secret and sacred things of divine knowledge, but rather to protest and confront him, that he cease from sin, and cleanse his actions from vice. But if he insinuate himself, and lead us on to speak what he, while he acts improperly, ought not to hear, it will be our part to parry him cautiously. For not to answer him at all does not seem proper, for the sake of the hearers, lest haply they may think that we decline the contest through want of ability to answer him, and so their faith may be injured through their misunderstanding of our purpose."

CHAP. V. — SIMON MAGUS, A FORMIDABLE ANTAGONIST.

When Peter had thus spoken to us, Niceta asks permission to say something to him ;[3] and Peter having granted permission, he says : " With your pardon, I beseech you, my lord Peter, to hear me, who am very anxious for thee, and who am afraid lest, in the contest which you have in hand with Simon, you should seem to be overmatched. For it very frequently happens that he who defends the truth does not gain the victory, since the hearers are either prejudiced, or have no great interest in the better cause. But over and above all this, Simon himself is a most vehement orator, trained in the dialectic art, and in the meshes of syllo-

gisms ; and what is worse than all, he is greatly skilled in the magic art. And therefore I fear, lest haply, being so strongly fortified on every side, he shall be thought to be defending the truth, whilst he is alleging falsehoods, in the presence of those who do not know him. For neither should we ourselves have been able to escape from him, and to be converted to the Lord, had it not been that, while we were his assistants, and the sharers of his errors, we had ascertained that he was a deceiver and a magician."

CHAP. VI. — SIMON MAGUS : HIS WICKEDNESS.

When Niceta had thus spoken, Aquila also, asking that he might be permitted to speak, proceeded in manner following : " Receive, I entreat thee, most excellent Peter, the assurance of my love towards thee ; for indeed I also am extremely anxious on thy account. And do not blame us in this, for indeed to be concerned for any one cometh of affection ; whereas to be indifferent is no less than hatred. But I call God to witness that I feel for thee, not as knowing thee to be weaker in debate, — for indeed I was never present at any dispute in which thou wert engaged, — but because I well know the impieties of this man, I think of thy reputation, and at the same time the souls of the hearers, and above all, the interests of the truth itself. For this magician is vehement towards all things that he wishes, and wicked above measure. For in all things we know him well, since from boyhood we have been assistants and ministers of his wickedness ; and had not the love of God rescued us from him, we should even now be engaged in the same evil deeds with him. But a certain inborn love towards God rendered his wickedness hateful to us, and the worship of God attractive to us. Whence I think also that it was the work of Divine Providence, that we, being first made his associates, should take knowledge in what manner or by what art he effects the prodigies which he seems to work. For who is there that would not be astonished at the wonderful things which he does? Who would not think that he was a god come down from heaven for the salvation of men? For myself, I confess, if I had not known him intimately, and had taken part in his doings, I would easily have been carried away with him. Whence it was no great thing for us to be separated from his society, knowing as we did that he depends upon magic arts and wicked devices. But if thou also thyself wish to know all about him — who, what, and whence he is, and how he contrives what he does — then listen.

CHAP. VII. — SIMON MAGUS : HIS HISTORY.

" This Simon's father was Antonius, and his mother Rachel. By nation he is a Samaritan, from a village of the Gettones ; by profession a magi-

---

[1] Matt. x. 11.
[2] Matt. vii. 6.
[3] [The statements of Niceta and Aquila are introduced in the *Homilies* before the postponement of the discussion with Simon. There is a remarkable variety in the minor details respecting Simon as given in the two narratives. — R.]

cian, yet exceedingly well trained in the Greek literature; desirous of glory, and boasting above all the human race, so that he wishes himself to be believed to be an exalted power, which is above God the Creator, and to be thought to be the Christ, and to be called the *Standing One*. And he uses this name as implying that he can never be dissolved, asserting that his flesh is so compacted by the power of his divinity, that it can endure to eternity. Hence, therefore, he is called the *Standing One*, as though he cannot fall by any corruption.

CHAP. VIII. — SIMON MAGUS: HIS HISTORY.

" For after that John the Baptist was killed, as you yourself also know, when Dositheus had broached his heresy,[1] with thirty other chief disciples, and one woman, who was called *Luna*[2] — whence also these thirty appear to have been appointed with reference to the number of the days, according to the course of the moon — this Simon, ambitious of evil glory, as we have said, goes to Dositheus, and pretending friendship, entreats him, that if any one of those thirty should die, he should straightway substitute him in room of the dead: for it was contrary to their rule either to exceed the fixed number, or to admit any one who was unknown, or not yet proved; whence also the rest, desiring to become worthy of the place and number, are eager in every way to please, according to the institutions of their sect, each one of those who aspire after admittance into the number, hoping that he may be deemed worthy to be put into the place of the deceased, when, as we have said, any one dies. Therefore Dositheus, being greatly urged by this man, introduced Simon when a vacancy occurred among the number.

CHAP. IX. — SIMON MAGUS: HIS PROFESSION.

" But not long after he fell in love with that woman whom they call Luna; and he confided all things to us as his friends: how he was a magician, and how he loved Luna, and how, being desirous of glory, he was unwilling to enjoy her ingloriously, but that he was waiting patiently till he could enjoy her honourably; yet so if we also would conspire with him towards the accomplishment of his desires. And he promised that, as a reward of this service, he would cause us to be invested with the highest honours, and we should be believed by men to be gods; ' Only, however, on condition,' says he, 'that you confer the chief place upon me, Simon, who by magic

art am able to show many signs and prodigies, by means of which either my glory or our sect may be established. For I am able to render myself invisible to those who wish to lay hold of me, and again to be visible when I am willing to be seen.[3] If I wish to flee, I can dig through the mountains, and pass through rocks as if they were clay. If I should throw myself headlong from a lofty mountain, I should be borne unhurt to the earth, as if I were held up; when bound, I can loose myself, and bind those who had bound me; being shut up in prison, I can make the barriers open of their own accord; I can render statues animated, so that those who see suppose that they are men. I can make new trees suddenly spring up, and produce sprouts at once. I can throw myself into the fire, and not be burnt; I can change my countenance, so that I cannot be recognised; but I can show people that I have two faces. I shall change myself into a sheep or a goat; I shall make a beard to grow upon little boys; I shall ascend by flight into the air; I shall exhibit abundance of gold, and shall make and unmake kings. I shall be worshipped as God; I shall have divine honours publicly assigned to me, so that an image of me shall be set up, and I shall be worshipped and adored as God. And what need of more words? Whatever I wish, that I shall be able to do. For already I have achieved many things by way of experiment. In short,' says he, ' once when my mother Rachel ordered me to go to the field to reap, and I saw a sickle lying, I ordered it to go and reap; and it reaped ten times more than the others. Lately, I produced many new sprouts from the earth, and made them bear leaves and produce fruit in a moment; and the nearest mountain I successfully bored through.'

CHAP. X. — SIMON MAGUS: HIS DECEPTION.

" But when he spoke thus of the production of sprouts and the perforation of the mountain, I was confounded on this account, because he wished to deceive even us, in whom he seemed to place confidence; for we knew that those things had been from the days of our fathers, which he represented as having been done by himself lately. We then, although we heard these atrocities from him, and worse than these, yet we followed up his crimes, and suffered others to be deceived by him, telling also many lies on his behalf; and this before he did any of the things which he had promised, so that while as yet he had done nothing, he was by some thought to be God.

---

[1] [Comp. i. 54. In Homily II. 23 Simon is said to be a follower of John the Baptist, one of the thirty chief men; so Dositheus. Here Dositheus is represented as the head of a separate sect; so in i. 54. — R.]

[2] [Called " Helena" in the *Homilies*, and identified apparently with Helen, the cause of the Trojan War. — R.]

[3] [The statements made in the *Recognitions* respecting the claims of Simon are more extravagant and blasphemous than those occurring in the *Homilies*. Comp. the latter, ii, 26–32. — R.]

CHAP. XI. — SIMON MAGUS, AT THE HEAD OF THE SECT OF DOSITHEUS.

"Meantime, at the outset, as soon as he was reckoned among the thirty disciples of Dositheus, he began to depreciate Dositheus himself, saying that he did not teach purely or perfectly, and that this was the result not of ill intention, but of ignorance. But Dositheus, when he perceived that Simon was depreciating him, fearing lest his reputation among men might be obscured (for he himself was supposed to be the *Standing One*), moved with rage, when they met as usual at the school, seized a rod, and began to beat Simon; but suddenly the rod seemed to pass through his body, as if it had been smoke. On which Dositheus, being astonished, says to him, 'Tell me if thou art the *Standing One*, that I may adore thee.' And when Simon answered that he was, then Dositheus, perceiving that he himself was not the Standing One, fell down and worshipped him, and gave up his own place as chief to Simon, ordering all the rank of thirty men to obey him; himself taking the inferior place which Simon formerly occupied. Not long after this he died.

CHAP. XII. — SIMON MAGUS AND LUNA.

"Therefore, after the death of Dositheus, Simon took Luna to himself; and with her he still goes about, as you see, deceiving multitudes, and asserting that he himself is a certain power which is above God the Creator, while Luna, who is with him, has been brought down from the higher heavens, and that she is Wisdom, the mother of all things, for whom, says he, the Greeks and barbarians contending, were able in some measure to see an image of her; but of herself, as she is, as the dweller with the first and only God, they were wholly ignorant. Propounding these and other things of the same sort, he has deceived many. But I ought also to state this, which I remember that I myself saw. Once, when this Luna of his was in a certain tower, a great multitude had assembled to see her, and were standing around the tower on all sides; but she was seen by all the people to lean forward, and to look out through all the windows of that tower.[2] Many other wonderful things he did and does; so that men, being astonished at them, think that he himself is the great God.

CHAP. XIII. — SIMON MAGUS: SECRET OF HIS MAGIC.

"Now when Niceta and I once asked him to explain to us how these things could be effected by magic art, and what was the nature of that

___
[1] The meaning seems to be, that she was seen at all the windows at once. — TR.

thing, Simon began thus to explain it to us as his associates. 'I have,' said he, 'made the soul of a boy, unsullied and violently slain, and invoked by unutterable adjurations, to assist me; and by it all is done that I command.' 'But,' said I, 'is it possible for a soul to do these things?' He answered: 'I would have you know this, that the soul of man holds the next place after God, when once it is set free from the darkness of his body. And immediately it acquires prescience: wherefore it is invoked for necromancy.' Then I answered: 'Why, then, do not the souls of persons who are slain take vengeance on their slayers?' 'Do you not remember,' said he, 'that I told you, that when it goes out of the body it acquires knowledge of the future?' 'I remember,' said I. 'Well, then,' said he, 'as soon as it goes out of the body, it immediately knows that there is a judgment to come, and that every one shall suffer punishment for those evils that he hath done; and therefore they are unwilling to take vengeance on their slayers, because they themselves are enduring torments for their own evil deeds which they had done here, and they know that severer punishments await them in the judgment. Moreover, they are not permitted by the angels who preside over them to go out, or to do anything.' 'Then,' I replied, 'if the angels do not permit them to come hither, or to do what they please, how can the souls obey the magician who invokes them?' 'It is not,' said he, 'that they grant indulgence to the souls that are willing to come; but when the presiding angels are adjured by one greater than themselves, they have the excuse of our violence who adjure them, to permit the souls which we invoke to go out: for they do not sin who suffer violence, but we who impose necessity upon them.' Thereupon Niceta, not able longer to refrain, hastily answered, as indeed I also was about to do, only I wished first to get information from him on several points; but, as I said, Niceta, anticipating me, said: 'And do you not fear the day of judgment, who do violence to angels, and invoke souls, and deceive men, and bargain for divine honour to yourself from men? And how do you persuade us that there shall be no judgment, as some of the Jews confess, and that souls are not immortal, as many suppose, though you see them with your very eyes, and receive from them assurance of the divine judgment?'

CHAP. XIV. — SIMON MAGUS, PROFESSES TO BE GOD.

"At those sayings of his Simon grew pale; but after a little, recollecting himself, he thus answered: 'Do not think that I am a man of your race. I am neither magician, nor lover of Luna, nor son of Antonius. For before my mother Rachel and he came together, she, still a virgin, conceived me, while it was in my power to be either small or great, and to appear as a man among men.[1] Therefore I have chosen you first as my friends, for the purpose of trying you, that I may place you first in my heavenly and unspeakable places when I shall have proved you. Therefore I have pretended to be a man, that I might more clearly ascertain if you cherish entire affection towards me.' But when I heard that, judging him indeed to be a wretch, yet wondering at his impudence; and blushing for him, and at the same time fearing lest he should attempt some evil against us, I beckoned to Niceta to feign for a little along with me, and said to him: 'Be not angry with us, corruptible men, O thou incorruptible God, but rather accept our affection, and our mind willing to know who God is; for we did not till now know who thou art, nor did we perceive that thou art he whom we were seeking.'

CHAP. XV. — SIMON MAGUS, PROFESSED TO HAVE MADE A BOY OF AIR.

" As we spoke these and such like words with looks suited to the occasion, this most vain fellow believed that we were deceived ; and being thereby the more elated, he added also this : ' I shall now be propitious to you, for the affection which you bear towards me as God ; for you loved me while you did not know me, and were seeking me in ignorance. But I would not have you doubt that this is truly to be God, when one is able to become small or great as he pleases ; for I am able to appear to man in whatever manner I please. Now, then, I shall begin to unfold to you what is true. Once on a time, I, by my power, turning air into water, and water again into blood, and solidifying it into flesh, formed a new human creature — a boy — and produced a much nobler work than God the Creator. For He created a man from the earth, but I from air — a far more difficult matter ; and again I unmade him and restored him to air, but not until I had placed his picture and image in my bedchamber, as a proof and memorial of my work.' Then we understood that he spake concernnig that boy, whose soul, after he had been slain by violence, he made use of for those services which he required.

CHAP. XVI. — SIMON MAGUS : HOPELESSNESS OF HIS CASE.

But Peter, hearing these things, said with tears :[2] "Greatly do I wonder at the infinite patience of God, and, on the other hand, at the audacity of human rashness in some. For what further reason can be found to persuade Simon that God judges the unrighteous, since he persuades himself that he employs the obedience of souls for the service of his crimes ? But, in truth, he is deluded by demons. Yet, although he is sure by these very things that souls are immortal, and are judged for the deeds which they have done, and although he thinks that he really sees those things which we believe by faith ; though, as I said, he is deluded by demons, yet he thinks that he sees the very substance of the soul. How shall such a man, I say, be brought to confess either that he acts wickedly while he occupies such an evil position, or that he is to be judged for those things which he hath done, who, knowing the judgment of God, despises it, and shows himself an enemy to God, and dares commit such horrid things ? Wherefore it is certain, my brethren, that some oppose the truth and religion of God, not because it appears to them that reason can by no means stand with faith, but because they are either involved in excess of wickedness, or prevented by their own evils, or elated by the swelling of their heart, so that they do not even believe those things which they think that they see with their own eyes.

CHAP. XVII. — MEN ENEMIES TO GOD.

" But, inasmuch as inborn affection towards God the Creator seemed to suffice for salvation to those who loved Him, the enemy studies to pervert this affection in men, and to render them hostile and ungrateful to their Creator. For I call heaven and earth to witness, that if God permitted the enemy to rage as much as he desires, all men should have perished long ere now ; but for His mercy's sake God doth not suffer him. But if men would turn their affection towards God, all would doubtless be saved, even if for some faults they might seem to be corrected for righteousness But now the most of men have been made enemies of God, whose hearts the wicked one has entered, and has turned aside towards himself the affection which God the Creator had implanted in them, that they might have it towards Him. But of the rest, who seemed for a time to be watchful, the enemy, appearing in a phantasy of glory and splendour, and promising them certain great and mighty things, has caused their mind and heart to wander away from God ; yet it is for some just reason that he is permitted to accomplish these things."

---

[1] [This parody of the miraculous conception is not found in the Homilies. — R.]
[2] [In Homily II. 37-53 the discourse of Peter is quite different, and far less worthy. In Homily III. 1-28 a similar discourse is given, just before the discussion with Simon, abounding in statements that suggest erroneous views of Scripture, and indicate a Gnostic origin. — R.]

CHAP. XVIII. — RESPONSIBILITY OF MEN.

"To this Aquila answered: "How, then, are men in fault, if the wicked one, transforming himself into the brightness of light,[1] promises to men greater things than the Creator Himself does?" Then Peter answered: "I think," says he, "that nothing is more unjust than this; and now listen while I tell you how unjust it is. If your son, whom you have trained and nourished with all care, and brought to man's estate, should be ungrateful to you, and should leave you and go to another, whom perhaps he may have seen to be richer, and should show to him the honour which he owed to you, and, through hope of greater profit, should deny his birth, and refuse you your paternal rights, would this seem to you right or wicked?" Then Aquila answered: "It is manifest to all that it would be wicked." Then Peter said: "If you say that this would be wicked among men, how much more so is it in the case of God, who, above all men, is worthy of honour from men; whose benefits we not only enjoy, but by whose means and power it is that we began to be when we were not, and whom, if we please, we shall obtain from Him to be for ever in blessedness! In order, therefore, that the unfaithful may be distinguished from the faithful, and the pious from the impious, it has been permitted to the wicked one to use those arts by which the affections of every one towards the true Father may be proved. But if there were in truth some strange God, were it right to leave our own God, who created us, and who is our Father and our Maker, and to pass over to another?" "God forbid!" said Aquila. Then said Peter: "How, then, shall we say that the wicked one is the cause of our sin, when this is done by permission of God, that those may be proved and condemned in the day of judgment, who, allured by greater promises, have abandoned their duty towards their true Father and Creator; while those who have kept the faith and the love of their own Father, even with poverty, if so it has befallen, and with tribulation, may enjoy heavenly gifts and immortal dignities in His kingdom? But we shall expound these things more carefully at another time. Meantime I desire to know what Simon did after this."

CHAP. XIX. — DISPUTATION BEGUN.

And Niceta answered: "When he perceived that we had found him out, having spoken to one another concerning his crimes, we left him, and came to Zacchæus, telling him those same things which we have now told to you. But he,

receiving us most kindly, and instructing us concerning the faith of our Lord Jesus Christ, enrolled us in the number of the faithful." When Niceta had done speaking, Zacchæus, who had gone out a little before, entered, saying, "It is time, O Peter, that you proceed to the disputation; for a great crowd, collected in the court of the house, is awaiting you, in the midst of whom stands Simon, supported by many attendants." Then Peter, when he heard this, ordering me to withdraw for the sake of prayer (for I had not yet been washed from the sins which I had committed in ignorance), said to the rest, "Brethren, let us pray that God, for His unspeakable mercy through His Christ, would help me going out on behalf of the salvation of men who have been created by Him." Having said this, and having prayed, he went forth to the court of the house, in which a great multitude of people were assembled; and when he saw them all looking intently on him in profound silence, and Simon the magician standing in the midst of them like a standard-bearer, he began in manner following.[2]

---

[1] 2 Cor. xi. 14.

[2] [Three discussions with Simon Magus are detailed in the pseudo-Clementine literature, — one in the *Recognitions*, ii. 20–iii. 48; *two* in the *Homilies*, iii. 30–58 and xvi.–xix. The differences between these are quite remarkable.

I. *External Differences.* — That in the *Recognitions* is assigned to Cæsarea, and is represented as lasting three days, details of each day's discussion being given. The earlier one in the *Homilies* is given the same place and time, but it is very brief. The details of the first day alone are mentioned; and it resembles that in the *Recognitions* less than does the later one. This is represented as taking place at Laodicea, and as occupying four days. The account is the longest of the three. In its historical setting this discussion has no parallel in the *Recognitions*. Faustus, the father of Clement, is made the umpire; and this discussion before him takes the place of the discussions with him which occupy so large a part of *Recognitions*, viii.–x.

II. *Internal Differences.* — Of course, there are many thoughts common to the discussions; but the treatment is so varied as to form one of the most perplexing points in the literary problem. All are somewhat irregular in arrangement, hence an analysis is difficult.

The discussion in the *Recognitions* seems to be more ethical and philosophical than those in the *Homilies*; the latter contain more theosophical views. Both of them emphasize the falsehoods of Scripture, and abound more in sophistries and verbal sword-play. In the *Recognitions*, against Simon's polytheism and theory of an unknowable God, Peter opposes the righteousness of God, emphasizing the freedom of the will, discussing the existence and origin of evil, reverting to the righteousness of God as proving the immortality of the soul. The defeat of Simon is narrated in a peculiar way.

The Cæsarean discussion in the *Homilies* is very briefly narrated. After the preliminary parley, Simon attacks the God of the Scriptures, attributing defects to Him. Peter's reply, while explaining many passages correctly, is largely taken up with a statement of the view of the Scriptures peculiar to the *Homilies*. This is really the weapon with which Simon is defeated. The discussion, therefore, presents few points of resemblance to that in the *Recognitions*.

The Laodicean discussion in the *Homilies*, covering four days, is of a higher character than the preceding. It is not strictly parallel to that in the *Recognitions*. The opening argument is concerning polytheism. To Peter's monotheism Simon opposes the contradictions of Scripture: these Peter explains, including some christological statements which lead to a declaration of the nature, name, and character of God. On the second day, after some personal discussion, Simon asserts that Christ's teaching differs from that of Peter; the argument reverts to the shape and figure of God. The evidence of the senses is urged against fancied revelations, which are attributed to demons. On the third day the question of God the Framer of the world is introduced, and His moral character. Peter explains the nature of revelation, with some sharp personal thrusts at Simon, but soon reverts to the usual explanation of Scripture.

On the fourth day the existence of the evil one becomes the prominent topic; the existence of sin is pressed; and the discussion closes with a justification of the inequalities of human life, and an expression of judgment against Simon by Faustus.

Throughout these portions footnotes have been added, to indicate the correspondences of thought in the several accounts. — R.]

CHAP. XX. — THE KINGDOM OF GOD AND HIS RIGHTEOUSNESS.

" Peace be to all of you who are prepared to give your right hands to truth : [1] for whosoever are obedient to it seem indeed themselves to confer some favour upon God ; whereas they do themselves obtain from Him the gift of His greatest bounty, walking in His paths of righteousness. Wherefore the first duty of all is to inquire into the righteousness of God and His kingdom ; [2] His righteousness, that we may be taught to act rightly ; His kingdom, that we may know what is the reward appointed for labour and patience ; in which kingdom there is indeed a bestowal of eternal good things upon the good, but upon those who have acted contrary to the will of God, a worthy infliction of penalties in proportion to the doings of every one. It becomes you, therefore, whilst you are here, — that is, whilst you are in the present life, — to ascertain the will of God, while there is opportunity also of doing it. For if any one, before he amends his doings, wishes to investigate concerning things which he cannot discover, such investigation will be foolish and ineffectual. For the time is short, and the judgment of God shall be occupied with deeds, not questions. Therefore before all things let us inquire into this, what or in what manner we must act that we may merit to obtain eternal life.

CHAP. XXI. — RIGHTEOUSNESS THE WAY TO THE KINGDOM.

" For if we occupy the short time of this life with vain and useless questions, we shall without doubt go into the presence of God empty and void of good works, when, as I have said, our works shall be brought into judgment. For everything has its own time and place. This is the place, this the time of works ; the world to come, that of recompenses. That we may not therefore be entangled, by changing the order of places and times, let us inquire, in the first place, what is the righteousness of God ; so that, like persons going to set out on a journey, we may be filled with good works as with abundant provision, so that we may be able to come to the kingdom of God, as to a very great city. For to those who think aright, God is manifest even by the operations of the world which He hath made, using the evidence of His creation ; [3] and therefore, since there ought to be no doubt about God, we have now to inquire only about His righteousness and His kingdom. But if our mind suggest to us to make any inquiry concerning secret and hidden things before we inquire into the works of righteousness, we ought to render to ourselves a reason, because if acting well we shall merit to obtain salvation : then, going to God chaste and clean, we shall be filled with the Holy Spirit, and shall know all things that are secret and hidden, without any cavilling of questions ; whereas now, even if any one should spend the whole of his life in inquiring into these things, he not only shall not be able to find them, but shall involve himself in greater errors, because he did not first enter through the way of righteousness, and strive to reach the haven of life.

CHAP. XXII. — RIGHTEOUSNESS ; WHAT IT IS.

" And therefore I advise that His righteousness be first inquired into, that, pursuing our journey through it, and placed in the way of truth, we may be able to find the true Prophet, running not with swiftness of foot, but with goodness of works, and that, enjoying His guidance, we may be under no danger of mistaking the way. For if under His guidance we shall merit to enter that city to which we desire to come, all things concerning which we now inquire we shall see with our eyes, being made, as it were, heirs of all things. Understand, therefore, that the way is this course of our life ; the travellers are those who do good works ; the gate is the true Prophet, of whom we speak ; the city is the kingdom in which dwells the Almighty Father, whom only those can see who are of pure heart.[4] Let us not then think the labour of this journey hard, because at the end of it there shall be rest. For the true Prophet Himself also from the beginning of the world, through the course of time, hastens to rest. For He is present with us at all times ; and if at any time it is necessary, He appears and corrects us, that He may bring to eternal life those who obey Him. Therefore this is my judgment, as also it is the pleasure of the true Prophet, that inquiry should first be made concerning righteousness, by those especially who profess that they know God. If therefore any one has anything to propose which he thinks better, let him speak ; and when he has spoken, let him hear, but with patience and quietness : for in order to this at the first, by way of salutation, I prayed for peace to you all."

CHAP. XXIII. — SIMON REFUSES PEACE.

To this Simon answered : [5] " We have no need of your peace ; for if there be peace and con-

---

[1] [This opening sentence occurs in the *Homilies*, but in other parts the discourses differ. This is far more dignified and consistent than that in the *Homilies*, which at once introduces a claim to authority as messenger of the Prophet. — R.]

[2] Matt. vi. 33.

[3] Rom. i. 20.

[4] Matt. v. 8.

[5] [In Homily III. 38, 39, Simon is represented as at once attacking the Apostle and his monotheism ; the arguments are, in the main, those given in chap. 39 of this book. Chaps. 23–36 are without a direct parallel in the *Homilies*. — R.]

cord, we shall not be able to make any advance towards the discovery of truth. For robbers and debauchees have peace among themselves, and every wickedness agrees with itself; and if we have met with this view, that for the sake of peace we should give assent to all that is said, we shall confer no benefit upon the hearers; but, on the contrary, we shall impose upon them, and shall depart friends. Wherefore, do not invoke peace, but rather battle, which is the mother of peace; and if you can, exterminate errors. And do not seek for friendship obtained by unfair admissions; for this I would have you know, above all, that when two fight with each other, then there will be peace when one has been defeated and has fallen. And therefore fight as best you can, and do not expect peace without war, which is impossible; or if it can be attained, show us how."

CHAP. XXIV. — PETER'S EXPLANATION.

To this Peter answered: "Hear with all attention, O men, what we say. Let us suppose that this world is a great plain, and that from two states, whose kings are at variance with each other, two generals were sent to fight: and suppose the general of the good king gave this counsel, that both armies should without bloodshed submit to the authority of the better king, whereby all should be safe without danger; but that the opposite general should say, No, but we must fight; that not he who is worthy, but he who is stronger, may reign, with those who shall escape; — which, I ask you, would you rather choose? I doubt not but that you would give your hands to the better king, with the safety of all. And I do not now wish, as Simon says that I do, that assent should be given, for the sake of peace, to those things that are spoken amiss; but that truth be sought for with quietness and order.

CHAP. XXV. — PRINCIPLES ON WHICH THE DISCUSSION SHOULD BE CONDUCTED.

"For some, in the contest of disputations, when they perceive that their error is confuted, immediately begin, for the sake of making good their retreat, to create a disturbance, and to stir up strifes, that it may not be manifest to all that they are defeated; and therefore I frequently entreat that the investigation of the matter in dispute may be conducted with all patience and quietness, so that if perchance anything seem to be not rightly spoken, it may be allowed to go back over it, and explain it more distinctly. For sometimes a thing may be spoken in one way and heard in another, while it is either advanced too obscurely, or not attended to with sufficient care; and on this account I desire that our con-

versation should be conducted patiently, so that neither should the one snatch it away from the other, nor should the unseasonable speech of one contradicting interrupt the speech of the other; and that we should not cherish the desire of finding fault, but that we should be allowed, as I have said, to go over again what has not been clearly enough spoken, that by fairest examination the knowledge of the truth may become clearer. For we ought to know, that if any one is conquered by the truth, it is not he that is conquered, but the ignorance which is in him, which is the worst of all demons; so that he who can drive it out receives the palm of salvation. For it is our purpose to benefit the hearers, not that we may conquer badly, but that we may be well conquered for the acknowledgment of the truth. For if our speech be actuated by the desire of seeking the truth, even although we shall speak anything imperfectly through human frailty, God in His unspeakable goodness will fill up secretly in the understandings of the hearers those things that are lacking. For He is righteous; and according to the purpose of every one, He enables some to find easily what they seek, while to others He renders even that obscure which is before their eyes. Since, then, the way of God is the way of peace, let us with peace seek the things which are God's. If any one has anything to advance in answer to this, let him do so; but if there is no one who wishes to answer, I shall begin to speak, and I myself shall bring forward what another may object to me, and shall refute it."

CHAP. XXVI. — SIMON'S INTERRUPTION.

When therefore Peter had begun to continue his discourse, Simon, interrupting his speech, said: "Why do you hasten to speak whatever you please? I understand your tricks. You wish to bring forward those matters whose explanation you have well studied, that you may appear to the ignorant crowd to be speaking well; but I shall not allow you this subterfuge. Now therefore, since you promise, as a brave man, to answer to all that any one chooses to bring forward, be pleased to answer me in the first place." Then Peter said: "I am ready, only provided that our discussion may be with peace." Then Simon said: "Do not you see, O simpleton, that in pleading for peace you act in opposition to your Master, and that what you propose is not suitable to him who promises that he will overthrow ignorance? Or, if you are right in asking peace from the audience, then your Master was wrong in saying, 'I have not come to send peace on earth, but a sword.'[1] For either you say well, and he not well; or else, if your Master

---

[1] Matt. x. 34.

said well, then you not at all well: for you do not understand that your statement is contrary to his, whose disciple you profess yourself to be."

CHAP. XXVII. — QUESTIONS AND ANSWERS.

Then Peter: "Neither He who sent me did amiss in sending a sword upon the earth, nor do I act contrary to Him in asking peace of the hearers. But you both unskilfully and rashly find fault with what you do not understand: for you have heard that the Master came not to send peace on earth; but that He also said, 'Blessed are the peace-makers, for they shall be called the very sons of God,'[1] you have not heard. Wherefore my sentiments are not different from those of the Master when I recommend peace, to the keepers of which He assigned blessedness." Then Simon said: "In your desire to answer for your Master, O Peter, you have brought a much more serious charge against him, if he himself came not to make peace, yet enjoined upon others to keep it. Where, then, is the consistency of that other saying of his, 'It is enough for the disciple that he be as his master?'"[2]

CHAP. XXVIII. — CONSISTENCY OF CHRIST'S TEACHING.

To this Peter answered: "Our Master, who was the true Prophet, and ever mindful of Himself, neither contradicted Himself, nor enjoined upon us anything different from what Himself practised. For whereas He said, 'I am not come to send peace on earth, but a sword; and henceforth you shall see father separated from son, son from father, husband from wife and wife from husband, mother from daughter and daughter from mother, brother from brother, father-in-law from daughter-in-law, friend from friend,' all these contain the doctrine of peace; and I will tell you how. At the beginning of His preaching, as wishing to invite and lead all to salvation, and induce them to bear patiently labours and trials, He blessed the poor, and promised that they should obtain the kingdom of heaven for their endurance of poverty, in order that under the influence of such a hope they might bear with equanimity the weight of poverty, despising covetousness; for covetousness is one, and the greatest, of most pernicious sins. But He promised also that the hungry and the thirsty should be satisfied with the eternal blessings of righteousness, in order that they might bear poverty patiently, and not be led by it to undertake any unrighteous work. In like manner, also, He said that the pure in heart

are blessed, and that thereby they should see God, in order that every one desiring so great a good might keep himself from evil and polluted thoughts.

CHAP. XXIX. — PEACE AND STRIFE.

"Thus, therefore, our Master, inviting His disciples to patience, impressed upon them that the blessing of peace was also to be preserved with the labour of patience. But, on the other hand, He mourned over those who lived in riches and luxury, who bestowed nothing upon the poor; proving that they must render an account, because they did not pity their neighbours, even when they were in poverty, whom they ought to love as themselves. And by such sayings as these He brought some indeed to obey Him, but others He rendered hostile. The believers therefore, and the obedient, He charges to have peace among themselves, and says to them, 'Blessed are the peacemakers, for they shall be called the very sons of God.'[3] But to those who not only did not believe, but set themselves in opposition to His doctrine, He proclaims the war of the word and of confutation, and says that 'henceforth ye shall see son separated from father, and husband from wife, and daughter from mother, and brother from brother, and daughter-in-law from mother-in-law, and a man's foes shall be they of his own house.'[4] For in every house, when there begins to be a difference betwixt believer and unbeliever, there is necessarily a contest: the unbelievers, on the one hand, fighting against the faith; and the believers, on the other, confuting the old error and the vices of sins in them.

CHAP. XXX. — PEACE TO THE SONS OF PEACE.

"In like manner, also, during the last period of His teaching, He wages war against the scribes and Pharisees, charging them with evil deeds and unsound doctrine, and with hiding the key of knowledge which they had handed down to them from Moses, by which the gate of the heavenly kingdom might be opened.[5] But when our Master sent us forth to preach, He commanded us, that into whatsoever city or house we should enter, we should say, 'Peace be to this house.' 'And if,' said He, 'a son of peace be there, your peace shall come upon him; but if there be not, your peace shall return to you.' Also that, going out from that house or city, we should shake off upon them the very dust which adhered to our feet. 'But it shall be more tolerable for the land of Sodom and Gomorrah in the day of judgment than for that city or house.'[6] This indeed He

---

[1] Matt. v. 9.
[2] Matt. x. 25.

[3] Matt. v. 9.
[4] Matt. x. 35, 36: Luke xii. 53.
[5] Matt. xxiii.; Luke xi.
[6] Matt. x. 12-15; Luke x. 5, 6.

commanded to be done at length, if first the word of truth be preached in the city or house, whereby they who receive the faith of the truth may become sons of peace and sons of God; and those who will not receive it may be convicted as enemies of peace and of God.

CHAP. XXXI. — PEACE AND WAR.

"Thus, therefore, we, observing the commands of our Master, first offer peace to our hearers, that the way of salvation may be known without any tumult. But if any one do not receive the words of peace, nor acquiesce in the truth, we know how to direct against him the war of the word, and to rebuke him sharply by confuting his ignorance and charging home upon him his sins. Therefore of necessity we offer peace, that if any one is a son of peace, our peace may come upon him; but from him who makes himself an enemy of peace, our peace shall return to ourselves. We do not therefore, as you say, propose peace by agreement with the wicked, for indeed we should straightway have given you the right hand; but only in order that, through our discussing quietly and patiently, it might be more easily ascertained by the hearers which is the true speech. But if you differ and disagree with yourself, how shall you stand? He must of necessity fall who is divided in himself; 'for every kingdom divided against itself shall not stand.'[1] If you have aught to say to this, say on."

CHAP. XXXII. — SIMON'S CHALLENGE.

Then said Simon: "I am astonished at your folly. For you so propound the words of your Master, as if it were held to be certain concerning him that he is a prophet; while I can very easily prove that he often contradicted himself. In short, I shall refute you from those words which you have yourself brought forward. For you say, that he said that every kingdom or every city divided in itself shall not stand; and elsewhere you say, that he said that he would send a sword, that he might separate those who are in one house, so that son shall be divided from father, daughter from mother, brother from brother; so that if there be five in one house, three shall be divided against two, and two against three.[2] If, then, everything that is divided falls, he who makes divisions furnishes causes of falling; and if he is such, assuredly he is wicked. Answer this if you can."

CHAP. XXXIII. — AUTHORITY.

Then Peter: "Do not rashly take exception, O Simon, against the things which you do not understand. In the first place, I shall answer your assertion, that I set forth the words of my Master, and from them resolve matters about which there is still doubt. Our Lord, when He sent us apostles to preach, enjoined us to teach all nations[3] the things which were committed to us. We cannot therefore speak those things as they were spoken by Himself. For our commission is not to *speak*, but to *teach* those things, and from them to show how every one of them rests upon truth. Nor, again, are we permitted to speak anything of our own. For we are sent; and of necessity he who is sent delivers the message as he has been ordered, and sets forth the will of the sender. For if I should speak anything different from what He who sent me enjoined me, I should be a false apostle, not saying what I am commanded to say, but what seems good to myself. Whoever does this, evidently wishes to show himself to be better than he is by whom he is sent, and without doubt is a traitor. If, on the contrary, he keeps by the things that he is commanded, and brings forward most clear assertions of them, it will appear that he is accomplishing the work of an apostle; and it is by striving to fulfil this that I displease you. Blame me not, therefore, because I bring forward the words of Him who sent me. But if there is aught in them that is not fairly spoken, you have liberty to confute me; but this can in no wise be done, for He is a prophet, and cannot be contrary to Himself. But if you do not think that He is a prophet, let this be first inquired into."

CHAP. XXXIV. — ORDER OF PROOF.

Then said Simon: "I have no need to learn this from you, but how these things agree with one another. For if he shall be shown to be inconsistent, he shall be proved at the same time not to be a prophet." Then says Peter: "But if I first show Him to be a prophet, it will follow that what seems to be inconsistency is not such. For no one can be proved to be a prophet merely by consistency, because it is possible for many to attain this; but if consistency does not make a prophet, much more inconsistency does not. Because, therefore, there are many things which to some seem inconsistent, which yet have consistency in them on a more profound investigation; as also other things which seem to have consistency, but which, being more carefully discussed, are found to be inconsistent; for this reason I do not think there is any better way to judge of these things than to ascertain in the first instance whether He be a prophet who has spoken those things which appear to be inconsistent. For it is evident that, if He be found a

---

[1] Matt. xii. 25.
[2] Luke xii. 51-53.

[3] Matt. xxviii. 19, 20.

prophet, those things which seem to be contradictory must have consistency, but are misunderstood. Concerning these things, therefore, proofs will be properly demanded. For we apostles are sent to expound the sayings and affirm the judgments of Him who has sent us; but we are not commissioned to say anything of our own, but to unfold the truth, as I have said, of His words."

CHAP. XXXV. — HOW ERROR CANNOT STAND WITH TRUTH.

Then Simon said : " Instruct us, therefore, how it can be consistent that he who causes divisions, which divisions cause those who are divided to fall, can either seem to be good, or to have come for the salvation of men." Then Peter said : " I will tell you how our Master said that every kingdom and every house divided against itself cannot stand; and whereas He Himself did this, see how it makes for salvation. By the word of truth He certainly divides the kingdom of the world, which is founded in error, and every house in it, that error may fall, and truth may reign. But if it happen to any house, that error, being introduced by any one, divides the truth, then, where error has gained a footing, it is certain that truth cannot stand." Then Simon said : " But it is uncertain whether your master divides error or truth." Then Peter : " That belongs to another question ; but if you are agreed that everything which is divided falls, it remains that I show, if only you will hear in peace, that our Jesus has divided and dispelled error by teaching truth."

CHAP. XXXVI. — ALTERCATION.

Then said Simon : " Do not repeat again and again your talk of peace, but expound briefly what it is that you think or believe." Peter answered : " Why are you afraid of hearing frequently of peace? or do you not know that peace is the perfection of law? For wars and disputes spring from sins ; and where there is no sin, there is peace of soul ; but where there is peace, truth is found in disputations, righteousness in works." Then Simon : " You seem to me not to be able to profess what you think." Then Peter : " I shall speak, but according to my own judgment, not under constraint of your tricks. For I desire that what is salutary and profitable be brought to the knowledge of all ; and therefore I shall not delay to state it as briefly as possible. There is one God ; and He is the creator of the world, a righteous judge, rendering to every one at some time or other according to his deeds.[1] But now for the asser-

tion of these things I know that countless thousands of words can be called forth."

CHAP. XXXVII. — SIMON'S SUBTLETY.

Then Simon said : " I admire, indeed, the quickness of your wit, yet I do not embrace the error of your faith. For you have wisely foreseen that you may be contradicted ; and you have even politely confessed, that for the assertion of these things countless thousands of words will be called forth, for no one agrees with the profession of your faith. In short, as to there being one God, and the world being His work, who can receive this doctrine? Neither, I think, any one of the Pagans, even if he be an unlearned man, and certainly no one of the philosophers ; but not even the rudest and most wretched of the Jews, nor I myself, who am well acquainted with their law." Then Peter said : " Put aside the opinions of those who are not here, and tell us face to face what is your own." Then Simon said : " I can state what I really think ; but this consideration makes me reluctant to do so, that if I say what is neither acceptable to you, nor seems right to this unskilled rabble, you indeed, as confounded, will straightway shut your ears, that they may not be polluted with blasphemy, forsooth, and will take to flight because you cannot find an answer ; while the unreasoning populace will assent to you, and embrace you as one teaching those things which are commonly received among them ; and will curse me, as professing things new and unheard of, and instilling my error into the minds of others."

CHAP. XXXVIII. — SIMON'S CREED.

Then Peter : " Are not you making use of long preambles, as you accused us of doing, because you have no truth to bring forward? or if you have, begin without circumlocution, if you have so much confidence. And if, indeed, what you say be displeasing to any one of the hearers, he will withdraw ; and those who remain shall be compelled by your assertion to approve what is true. Begin, therefore, to expound what seemeth to you to be right." Then Simon said : " I say that there are many gods ; but that there is one incomprehensible and unknown to all, and that He is the God of all these gods." Then Peter answered : " This God whom you assert to be incomprehensible and unknown to all, can you prove His existence from the Scriptures of the Jews,[2] which are held to be of authority, or from some others of which we are all ignorant,

---

[1] [The discussion in the *Homilies* is represented as virtually beginning with this statement of the Apostle: comp. Homily III. 37. The arguments here, however, are given with greater detail. — R.]

[2] [In both the *Recognitions* and the *Homilies* the contest turns upon the monotheistic teaching of the Old Testament and the supreme Deity of Jehovah. This is rightly regarded as an evidence of Ebionitic origin. But Gnostic elements enter again and again. — R.]

or from the Greek authors, or from your own writings? Certainly you are at liberty to speak from whatever writings you please, yet so that you first show that they are prophetic; for so their authority will be held without question."

CHAP. XXXIX. — ARGUMENT FOR POLYTHEISM.

Then Simon said : " I shall make use of assertions from the law of the Jews only. For it is manifest to all who take interest in religion, that this law is of universal authority, yet that every one receives the understanding of this law according to his own judgment. For it has so been written by Him who created the world, that the faith of things is made to depend upon it. Whence, whether any one wishes to bring forward truth, or any one to bring forward falsehood, no assertion will be received without this law. Inasmuch, therefore, as my knowledge is most fully in accordance with the law, I rightly declared that there are many gods, of whom one is more eminent than the rest, and incomprehensible, even He who is God of gods. But that there are many gods, the law itself informs me. For, in the first place, *it says this in the passage* where one in the figure of a serpent speaks to Eve, the first woman, ' On the day ye eat of the tree of the knowledge of good and evil, ye shall be as gods,' [1] that is, as those who made man; and after they have tasted of the tree, God Himself testifies, saying to the rest of the gods, ' Behold, Adam is become as one of us ; ' [2] thus, therefore, it is manifest that there were many gods engaged in the making of man. Also, whereas at the first God said to the other gods, ' Let us make man after our image and likeness ; ' [3] also His saying, ' Let us drive him out ; ' [2] and again, ' Come, let us go down, and confound their language ; ' [4] all these things indicate that there are many gods. But this also is written, ' Thou shalt not curse the gods, nor curse the chief of thy people ; ' [5] and again this writing, ' God alone led them, and there was no strange god with them,' [6] shows that there are many gods. There are also many other testimonies which might be adduced from the law, not only obscure, but plain, by which it is taught that there are many gods. [7] One of these was chosen by lot, that he might be the god of the Jews. But it is not of him that I speak, but of that God who is also his God, whom even the Jews themselves did not know. For he is not their God, but the God of those who know him."

CHAP. XL. — PETER'S ANSWER.

When Peter had heard this, he answered: " Fear nothing, Simon : for, behold, we have neither shut our ears, nor fled ; but we answer with words of truth to those things which you have spoken falsely, asserting this first, that there is one God, even the God of the Jews, who is the only God, the Creator of heaven and earth, who is also the God of all those whom you call gods. If, then, I shall show you that none is superior to Him, but that He Himself is above all, you will confess that your error is above all." [8] Then Simon said : " Why, indeed, though I should be unwilling to confess it, would not the hearers who stand by charge me with unwillingness to profess the things that are true ? "

CHAP. XLI. — THE ANSWER, CONTINUED.

" Listen, then," says Peter, " that you may know, first of all, that even if there are many gods, as you say, they are subject to the God of the Jews, to whom no one is equal, than whom no one can be greater ; for it is written that the prophet Moses thus spoke to the Jews : ' The Lord your God is the God of gods, and the Lord of lords, the great God.' [9] Thus, although there are many that are called gods, yet He who is the God of the Jews is alone called the God of gods. For not every one that is called God is necessarily God. Indeed, even Moses is called a god to Pharaoh, [10] and it is certain that he was a man ; and judges were called gods, and it is evident that they were mortal. The idols also of the Gentiles are called gods, and we all know that they are not ; but this has been inflicted as a punishment on the wicked, that because they would not acknowledge the true God, they should regard as God whatever form or image should occur to them. Because they refused to receive the knowledge of the One who, as I said, is God of all, therefore it is permitted to them to have as gods those who can do nothing for their worshippers. For what can either dead images or living creatures confer upon men, since the power of all things is with One ?

CHAP. XLII. — GUARDIAN ANGELS.

" Therefore the name *God* is applied in three ways : [11] either because he to whom it is given is truly God, or because he is the servant of him who is truly ; and for the honour of the sender, that his authority may be full, he that is sent is

[1] Gen. iii. 5.
[2] Gen. iii. 22.
[3] Gen i. 26.
[4] Gen. xi. 7.
[5] Exod. xxii. 28.
[6] Deut. xxxii. 12.
[7] [Compare Homily XVI. 6. — R.]

[8] [The reply of Peter here is of a higher character than that given in the *Homilies* (see iii. 40, etc.). Indeed, the report of the entire discussion in the *Recognitions* shows a superior conception of the Apostle. — R.]
[9] Deut. x. 17.
[10] Exod. vii. 1.
[11] [This remarkable chapter is peculiar to the *Recognitions*. The angelology seems to be Ebionitic, rather than Gnostic. — R.]

called by the name of him who sends, as is often done in respect of angels : for when they appear to a man, if he is a wise and intelligent man, he asks the name of him who appears to him, that he may acknowledge at once the honour of the sent, and the authority of the sender. For every nation has an angel, to whom God has committed the government of that nation ; and when one of these appears, although he be thought and called God by those over whom he presides, yet, being asked, he does not give such testimony to himself. For the Most High God, who alone holds the power of all things, has divided all the nations of the earth into seventy-two parts, and over these He hath appointed angels as princes. But to the one among the archangels who is greatest, was committed the government of those who, before all others, received the worship and knowledge of the Most High God. But holy men also, as we have said, are made gods to the wicked, as having received the power of life and death over them, as we mentioned above with respect to Moses and the judges. Wherefore it is also written concerning them, 'Thou shalt not curse the gods, and thou shalt not curse the prince of thy people.'[1] Thus the princes of the several nations are called gods. But Christ is God of princes, who is Judge of all. Therefore neither angels, nor men, nor any creature, can be truly gods, forasmuch as they are placed under authority, being created and changeable : angels, for they were not, and are ; men, for they are mortal ; and every creature, for it is capable of dissolution, if only He dissolve it who made it. And therefore He alone is the true God, who not only Himself lives, but also bestows life upon others, which He can also take away when it pleaseth Him.

CHAP. XLIII. — NO GOD BUT JEHOVAH.

"Wherefore the Scripture exclaims, in name of the God of the Jews, saying, ' Behold, behold, seeing that I am God, and there is none else besides me, I will kill, and I will make alive ; I will smite, and I will heal ; and there is none who can deliver out of my hands.'[2] See therefore how, by some ineffable virtue, the Scripture, opposing the future errors of those who should affirm that either in heaven or on earth there is any other god besides Him who is the God of the Jews, decides thus : ' The Lord your God is one God, in heaven above, and in the earth beneath ; and besides Him there is none else.'[3] How, then, hast thou dared to say that there is any other God besides Him who is the God of the Jews ? And again the Scripture says, ' Be-

hold, to the Lord thy God belong the heaven, and the heaven of heavens, the earth, and all things that are in them : nevertheless I have chosen your fathers, that I might love them, and you after them.'[4] Thus that judgment is supported by the Scripture on every side, that He who created the world is the true and only God.

CHAP. XLIV. — THE SERPENT, THE AUTHOR OF POLYTHEISM.

"But even if there be others, as we have said, who are called gods, they are under the power of the God of the Jews ; for thus saith the Scripture to the Jews, ' The Lord our God, He is God of gods, and Lord of lords.'[5] Him alone the Scripture also commands to be worshipped, saying, ' Thou shalt worship the Lord thy God, and Him only shalt thou serve ;'[6] and, ' Hear, O Israel : the Lord thy God is one God.'[7] Yea, also the saints, filled with the Spirit of God, and bedewed with the drops of His mercy, cried out, saying, ' Who is like unto Thee among the gods? O Lord, who is like unto Thee?'[8] And again, ' Who is God, but the Lord ; and who is God, but our Lord?'[9] Therefore Moses, when he saw that the people were advancing, by degrees initiated them in the understanding of the monarchy and the faith of one God, as he says in the following words : ' Thou shalt not make mention of the names of other gods ;'[10] doubtless remembering with what penalty the serpent was visited, which had first named *gods*.[11] For it is condemned to feed upon dust, and is judged worthy of such food, for this cause, that it first of all introduced the name of *gods* into the world. But if you also wish to introduce many gods, see that you partake not the serpent's doom.

CHAP. XLV. — POLYTHEISM INEXCUSABLE.

"For be sure of this, that you shall not have us participators in this attempt ; nor will we suffer ourselves to be deceived by you. For it will not serve us for an excuse in the judgment, if we say that you deceived us ; because neither could it excuse the first woman, that she had unhappily believed the serpent ; but she was condemned to death, because she believed badly. For this cause therefore, Moses, also commending the faith of one God to the people, says, ' Take heed to thyself, that thou be not seduced from the Lord thy God.'[12] Observe that he

---

[1] Exod. xxii. 28.
[2] Deut. xxxii. 39.
[3] Deut. iv. 39.
[4] Deut. x. 14, 15.
[5] Deut. x. 17.
[6] Deut. vi. 13, x. 20.
[7] Deut. vi. 4.
[8] Ps. lxxxvi. 8, lxxi. 19.
[9] Ps. xviii. 31.
[10] Josh. xxiii. 7, in Sept.
[11] Gen. iii. [The same thought occurs in Homily X. 10, 11. — R.]
[12] Deut. viii. 11.

makes use of the same word which the first woman also made use of in excusing herself, saying that she was seduced ; but it profited her nothing. But over and above all this, even if some true prophet should arise, who should perform signs and miracles, but should wish to persuade us to worship other gods besides the God of the Jews, we should never be able to believe him. For so the divine law has taught us, handing down a secret injunction more purely by means of tradition, for thus it saith : ' If there arise among you a prophet, or one dreaming a dream, and give you signs or wonders, and these signs or wonders come to pass, and he say to you, Let us go and worship strange gods, whom ye know not ; ye shall not hear the words of that prophet, nor the dream of that dreamer, because proving he hath proved you, that he may see if ye love the Lord your God.' [1]

CHAP. XLVI. — CHRIST ACKNOWLEDGED THE GOD OF THE JEWS.

" Wherefore also our Lord, who wrought signs and wonders, preached the God of the Jews ; and therefore we are right in believing what He preached. But as for you, even if you were really a prophet, and performed signs and wonders, as you promise to do, if you were to announce other gods besides Him who is the true God, it would be manifest that you were raised up as a trial to the people of God ; and therefore you can by no means be believed. For He alone is the true God, who is the God of the Jews ; and for this reason our Lord Jesus Christ did not teach them that they must inquire after God, for Him they knew well already, but that they must seek His kingdom and righteousness,[2] which the scribes and Pharisees, having received the key of knowledge, had not shut in, but shut out.[3] For if they had been ignorant of the true God, surely He would never have left the knowledge of this thing, which was the chief of all, and blamed them for small and little things, as for enlarging their fringes, and claiming the uppermost rooms in feasts, and praying standing in the highways, and such like things ; which assuredly, in comparison of this great charge, ignorance of God, seem to be small and insignificant matters."

CHAP. XLVII. — SIMON'S CAVIL.

To this Simon replied : [4] " From the words of your master I shall refute you, because even he introduces to all men a certain God who was unknown. For although both Adam knew the God who was his creator, and the maker of the world ; and Enoch knew him, inasmuch as he was translated by him ; and Noah, since he was ordered by him to construct the ark ; and although Abraham, and Isaac, and Jacob, and Moses, and all, even every people and all nations, know the maker of the world, and confess him to be a God, yet your Jesus, who appeared long after the patriarchs, says : ' No one knows the Son, but the Father ; neither knoweth any one the Father, but the Son, and he to whom the Son has been pleased to reveal Him.' [5] Thus, therefore, even your Jesus confesses that there is another God, incomprehensible and unknown to all.

CHAP. XLVIII. — PETER'S ANSWER.

Then Peter says : " You do not perceive that you are making statements in opposition to yourself. For if our Jesus also knows Him whom ye call the unknown God, then He is not known by you alone. Yea, if our Jesus knows Him, then Moses also, who prophesied that Jesus should come, assuredly could not himself be ignorant of Him. For he was a prophet ; and he who prophesied of the Son doubtless knew the Father. For if it is in the option of the Son to reveal the Father to whom He will, then the Son, who has been with the Father from the beginning, and through all generations, as He revealed the Father to Moses, so also to the other prophets ; but if this be so, it is evident that the Father has not been unknown to any of them. But how could the Father be revealed to you, who do not believe in the Son, since the Father is known to none except him to whom the Son is pleased to reveal Him ? But the Son reveals the Father to those who honour the Son as they honour the Father." [6]

CHAP. XLIX. — THE SUPREME LIGHT.

Then Simon said : " Remember that you said that God has a son, which is doing Him wrong ; for how can He have a son, unless He is subject to passions, like men or animals ? But on these points there is not time now to show your profound folly, for I hasten to make a statement concerning the immensity of the supreme light ; and so now listen. My opinion is, that there is a certain power of immense and ineffable light, whose greatness may be held to be incomprehensible, of which power even the maker of the world is ignorant, and Moses the lawgiver, and Jesus your master." [7]

---

[1] Deut. xiii. 1–3.
[2] Matt. vi. 33.
[3] Luke xi. 52.
[4] [Compare Homily XVII. 4. — R.]

[5] Matt. xi. 27. [Comp. Luke x. 22. This objection is given in Homilies XVII. 4, XVIII. 4. — R.]
[6] John v. 23.
[7] [This chapter presents the topic which is made the main point in a subsequent discussion with Simon ; see Homily XVIII. — R.]

CHAP. L. — SIMON'S PRESUMPTION.

Then Peter:[1] "Does it not seem to you to be madness, that any one should take upon himself to assert that there is another God than the God of all; and should say that he supposes there is a certain power, and should presume to affirm this to others, before he himself is sure of what he says? Is any one so rash as to believe your words, of which he sees that you are yourself doubtful, and to admit that there is a certain power unknown to God the Creator, and to Moses, and the prophets, and the law, and even to Jesus our Master, which power is so good, that it will not make itself known to any but to one only, and that one such an one as thou! Then, further, if that is a new power, why does it not confer upon us some new sense, in addition to those five which we possess, that by that new sense, bestowed upon us by it, we may be able to receive and understand itself, which is new? Or if it cannot bestow such a sense upon us, how has it bestowed it upon you? Or if it has revealed itself to you, why not also to us? But if you of yourself understand things which not even the prophets were able to perceive or understand, come, tell us what each one of us is thinking now; for if there is such a spirit in you that you know those things which are above the heavens, which are unknown to all, and incomprehensible by all, much more easily do you know the thoughts of men upon the earth. But if you cannot know the thoughts of us who are standing here, how can you say that you know those things which, you assert, are known to none?

CHAP. LI. — THE SIXTH SENSE.

"But believe me, that you could never know what light is unless you had received both vision and understanding from light itself; so also in other things. Hence, having received understanding, you are framing in imagination something greater and more sublime, as if dreaming, but deriving all your hints from those five senses, to whose Giver you are unthankful. But be sure of this, that until you find some new sense which is beyond those five which we all enjoy, you cannot assert the existence of a new God." Then Simon answered: "Since all things that exist are in accordance with those five senses, that power which is more excellent than all cannot add anything new." Then Peter said: "It is false; for there is also a sixth sense, namely that of foreknowledge: for those five senses are capable of knowledge, but the sixth is that of foreknowledge; and this the prophets possessed. How, then, can you know a God who is unknown

to all, who do not know the prophetic sense, which is that of prescience?" Then Simon began to say: "This power of which I speak, incomprehensible and more excellent than all, ay, even than that God who made the world, neither any of the angels has known, nor of the demons, nor of the Jews, nay, nor any creature which subsists by means of God the creator. How, then, could that creator's law teach me that which the creator himself did not know, since neither did the law itself know it, that it might teach it?"

CHAP. LII. — REDUCTIO AD ABSURDUM.

Then Peter said: "I wonder how you have been able to learn more from the law than the law was able to know or to teach; and how you say that you adduce proofs from the law of those things which you are pleased to assert, when you declare that neither the law, nor He who gave the law — that is, the Creator of the world — knows those things of which you speak! But this also I wonder at, how you, who alone know these things, should be standing here now with us all, circumscribed by the limits of this small court." Then Simon, seeing Peter and all the people laughing, said: "Do you laugh, Peter, while so great and lofty matters are under discussion?" Then said Peter: "Be not enraged, Simon, for we are doing no more than keeping our promise: for we are neither shutting our ears, as you said, nor did we take to flight as soon as we heard you propound your unutterable things; but we have not even stirred from the place. For indeed you do not even propound things that have any resemblance to truth, which might to a certain extent frighten us. Yet, at all events, disclose to us the meaning of this saying, how from the law you have learned of a God whom the law itself does not know, and of whom He who gave the law is ignorant." Then Simon said: "If you have done laughing, I shall prove it by clear assertions." Then Peter said: "Assuredly I shall give over, that I may learn from you how you have learned from the law what neither the law nor the God of the law Himself knows."

CHAP. LIII. — SIMON'S BLASPHEMY.

Then says Simon: "Listen: it is manifest to all, and ascertained in a manner of which no account can be given,[2] that there is one God, who is better than all, from whom all that is took its beginning; whence also of necessity all things that are after him are subject to him, as the chief

[2] We render by a periphrasis the expression *ineffabili quadam ratione compertum.* The meaning seems to be, that the belief of the existence and unity of God is not the result of reasoning, but of intuition or instinct.

and most excellent of all. When, therefore, I had ascertained that the God who created the world, according to what the law teaches, is in many respects weak, whereas weakness is utterly incompatible with a perfect God, and I saw that he is not perfect, I necessarily concluded that there is another God who is perfect.[1] For this God, as I have said, according to what the writing of the law teaches, is shown to be weak in many things. In the first place, because the man whom he formed was not able to remain such as he had intended him to be ; and because he cannot be good who gave a law to the first man, that he should eat of all the trees of paradise, but that he should not touch the tree of knowledge ; and if he should eat of it, he should die. For why should he forbid him to eat, and to know what is good and what evil, that, knowing, he might shun the evil and choose the good? But this he did not permit ; and because he did eat in violation of the commandment, and discovered what is good, and learned for the sake of honour to cover his nakedness (for he perceived it to be unseemly to stand naked before his Creator), he condemns to death him who had learned to do honour to God, and curses the serpent who had shown him these things. But truly, if man was to be injured by this means, why did he place the cause of injury in paradise at all? But if that which he placed in paradise was good, it is not the part of one that is good to restrain another from good.

CHAP. LIV. — HOW SIMON LEARNED FROM THE LAW WHAT THE LAW DOES NOT TEACH.

"Thus, then, since he who made man and the world is, according to what the law relates, imperfect, we are given to understand, without doubt, that there is another who is perfect. For it is of necessity that there be one most excellent of all, on whose account also every creature keeps its rank. Whence also I, knowing that it is every way necessary that there be some one more benignant and more powerful than that imperfect God who gave the law, understanding what is perfect from comparison of the imperfect, understood even from the Scripture that God who is not mentioned there. And in this way I was able, O Peter, to learn from the law that the law did not know. But even if the law had not given indications from which it might be gathered that the God who made the world is imperfect, it was still possible for me to infer from those evils which are done in this world, and are not corrected, either that its creator is powerless, if he cannot correct

what is done amiss ; or else, if he does not wish to remove the evils, that he is himself evil ; but if he neither can nor will, that he is neither powerful nor good. And from this it cannot but be concluded that there is another God more excellent and more powerful than all. If you have aught to say to this, say on."

CHAP. LV. — SIMON'S OBJECTIONS TURNED AGAINST HIMSELF.

Peter answered : "O Simon, they are wont to conceive such absurdities against God who do not read the law with the instruction of masters, but account themselves teachers, and think that they can understand the law, though he has not explained it to them who has learned of the Master.[2] Nevertheless now, that we also may seem to follow the book of the law according to your apprehension of it ; inasmuch as you say that the creator of the world is shown to be both impotent and evil, how is it that you do not see that that power of yours, which you say is superior to all, falls and lies under the very same charges? For the very same thing may be said of it, that it is either powerless, since it does not correct those things which here are done amiss ; or if it can and will not, it is evil ; or if it neither can nor will, then it is both impotent and imperfect. Whence that new power of yours is not only found liable to a similar charge, but even to a worse one, if, in addition to all these things, it is believed to be, when it is not. For He who created the world, His existence is manifest by His very operation in creating the world, as you yourself also confess. But this power which you say that you alone know, affords no indication of itself, by which we might perceive, at least, that it is, and subsists.

CHAP. LVI. — NO GOD ABOVE THE CREATOR.

"What kind of conduct, then, would it be that we should forsake God, in whose world we live and enjoy all things necessary for life, and follow I know not whom, from whom we not only obtain no good, but cannot even know that he exists? Nor truly does he exist. For whether you call him light, and brighter than that light which we see, you borrow that very name from the Creator of the world ; or whether you say that he is a substance above all, you derive from Him the idea with enlargement of speech.[3] Whether you make mention of mind, or goodness, or life, or whatever else, you borrow the words from Him. Since, then, you have nothing new con-

---

[1] [The argument of Simon here differs from that represented in Homilies XVII., XVIII. There Simon asserts that the Framer of the world is not the highest God, because He is not both just and good. Comp. also book iii. 37, 38. — R.]

[2] [The attitude of the Apostle Peter toward the Old Testament is differently represented in the Homilies, where false views are admitted to exist in the Scriptures. Comp. Homilies II. 38, 40, 41, 51, III. 4, 5, etc. — R.]
[3] That is, you take the idea of substance from the God of the Jews, and only enlarge it by the addition of the words above all.

cerning that power you speak of, not only as regards understanding, but even in respect of naming him, how do you introduce a new God, for whom you cannot even find a new name? For not only is the Creator of the world called a Power, but even the ministers of His glory, and all the heavenly host. Do you not then think it better that we should follow our Creator God, as a Father who trains us and endows us as He knows how? But if, as you say, there be some God more benignant than all, it is certain that he will not be angry with us; or if he be angry, he is evil. For if our God is angry and punishes, He is not evil, but righteous, for He corrects and amends His own sons. But he who has no concern with us, if he shall punish us, how should he be good? Inflicting punishments upon us because we have not been drawn by vain imaginations to forsake our own Father and follow him, how can you assert that he is so good, when he cannot be regarded as even just?"

CHAP. LVII. — SIMON'S INCONSISTENCY.

Then Simon: "Do you so far err, Peter, as not to know that our souls were made by that good God, the most excellent of all, but they have been brought down as captives into this world?" To this Peter answered: "Then he is not unknown by all, as you said a little while ago; and yet how did the good God permit his souls to be taken captive, if he be a power over all?" Then Simon said: "He sent God the creator to make the world; and he, when he had made it, gave out that himself was God." Then Peter said: "Then he is not, as you said, unknown to Him who made the world; nor are souls ignorant of him, if indeed they were stolen away from him. To whom, then, can he be unknown, if both the Creator of the world know him, as having been sent by him; and all souls know him, as having been violently withdrawn from him? Then, further, I wish you would tell us whether he who sent the creator of the world did not know that he would not keep faith? For if he did not know it, then he was not prescient; while if he foreknew it, and suffered it, he is himself guilty of this deed, since he did not prevent it; but if he could not, then he is not omnipotent. But if, knowing it as good, he did not prohibit it, he is found to be better, who presumed to do that which he who sent him did not know to be good."

CHAP. LVIII. — SIMON'S GOD UNJUST.

Then Simon said: "He receives those who will come to him, and does them good." Peter answered: "But there is nothing new in this; for He whom you acknowledge to be the Creator of the world also does so." Then Simon:

"But the good God bestows salvation if he is only acknowledged; but the creator of the world demands also that the law be fulfilled." Then said Peter: "He saves adulterers and men-slayers, if they know him; but good, and sober, and merciful persons, if they do not know him, in consequence of their having no information concerning him, he does not save! Great and good truly is he whom you proclaim, who is not so much the saviour of the evil, as he is one who shows no mercy to the good." Then Simon: "It is truly very difficult for man to know him, as long as he is in the flesh; for blacker than all darkness, and heavier than all clay, is this body with which the soul is surrounded." Then says Peter: "That good God of yours demands things which are difficult; but He who is truly God seeks easier things. Let him then, since he is so good, leave us with our Father and Creator; and when once we depart from the body, and leave that darkness that you speak of, we shall more easily know Him; and then the soul shall better understand that God is its Creator, and shall remain with Him, and shall no more be harassed with diverse imaginations; nor shall wish to betake itself to another power, which is known to none but Simon only, and which is of such goodness that no one can come to it, unless he be first guilty of impiety towards his own father! I know not how this power can be called either good or just, which no one can please except by acting impiously towards him by whom he was made!"

CHAP. LIX. — THE CREATOR OUR FATHER.

Then Simon: "It is not impious for the sake of greater profit and advantage to flee to him who is of richer glory." Then Peter: "If, as you say, it is not impious to flee to a stranger, it is at all events much more pious to remain with our own father, even if he be poor. But if you do not think it impious to leave our father, and flee to another, as being better than he; and you do not believe that our Creator will take this amiss; much more the good God will not be angry, because, when we were strangers to him, we have not fled to him, but have remained with our own Creator. Yea, I think he will rather commend us the more for this, that we have kept faith with God our Creator; for he will consider that, if we had been his creatures, we should never have been seduced by the allurements of any other to forsake him. For if any one, allured by richer promises, shall leave his own father and betake himself to a stranger, it may be that he will leave him in his turn, and go to another who shall promise him greater things, and this the rather because he is not his son, since he could leave even him who by nature was his father." Then Simon said: "But what if souls are from him, and do not know him, and he is truly their father?"

CHAP. LX. — THE CREATOR THE SUPREME GOD.

Then Peter said : " You represent him as weak enough. For if, as you say, he is more powerful than all, it can never be believed the weaker wrenched the spoils from the stronger.[1] Or if God the Creator was able by violence to bring down souls into this world, how can it be that, when they are separated from the body and freed from the bonds of captivity, the good God shall call them to the sufferance of punishment, on the ground that they, either through his remissness or weakness, were dragged away to this place, and were involved in the body, as in the darkness of ignorance? You seem to me not to know what a father and a God is : but I could tell you both whence souls are, and when and how they were made ; but it is not permitted to me now to disclose these things to you, who are in such error in respect of the knowledge of God." Then said Simon : "A time will come when you shall be sorry that you did not understand me speaking of the ineffable power." Then said Peter : " Give us then, as I have often said, as being yourself a new God, or as having yourself come down from him, some new sense, by means of which we may know that new God of whom you speak ; for those five senses, which God our Creator has given us, keep faith to their own Creator, and do not perceive that there is any other God, for so their nature necessitates them."

CHAP. LXI. — IMAGINATION.

To this Simon answered : " Apply your mind to those things which I am going to say, and cause it, walking in peaceable paths, to attain to those things which I shall demonstrate. Listen now, therefore. Did you never in thought reach forth your mind into regions or islands situated far away, and remain so fixed in them, that you could not even see the people that were before you, or know where yourself were sitting, by reason of the delightfulness of those things on which you were gazing?" And Peter said : "It is true, Simon, this has often occurred to me." Then Simon said : "In this way now reach forth your sense into heaven, yea above the heaven, and behold that there must be some place beyond the world, or outside the world, in which there is neither heaven nor earth, and where no shadow of these things produces darkness ; and consequently, since there are neither bodies in it, nor darkness occasioned by bodies, there must of necessity be immense light ; and consider of what sort that light must be, which is never succeeded by darkness. For if the light of this sun

fills this whole world, how great do you suppose that bodiless and infinite light to be? So great, doubtless, that this light of the sun would seem to be darkness and not light, in comparison."

CHAP. LXII. — PETER'S EXPERIENCE OF IMAGINATION.

When Simon thus spoke, Peter answered :[2] " Now listen patiently concerning both these matters, that is, concerning the example of stretching out the senses, and concerning the immensity of light. I know that I myself, O Simon, have sometimes in thought extended my sense, as you say, into regions and islands situated afar off, and have seen them with my mind not less than if it had been with my eyes. When I was at Capernaum, occupied in the taking of fishes, and sat upon a rock, holding in my hand a hook attached to a line, and fitted for deceiving the fishes, *I was so absorbed* that I did not feel a fish adhering to it while my mind eagerly ran through my beloved Jerusalem, to which I had frequently gone up, waking, for the sake of offerings and prayers. But I was accustomed also to admire this Cæsarea, hearing of it from others, and to long to see it ; and I seemed to myself to see it, although I had never been in it ; and I thought of it what was suitable to be thought of a great city, its gates, walls, baths, streets, lanes, markets, and the like, in accordance with what I had seen in other cities ; and to such an extent was I delighted with the intentness of such inspection, that, as you said, I neither saw one who was present and standing by me, nor knew where myself was sitting." Then said Simon : " Now you say well."

CHAP. LXIII. — PETER'S REVERIE.

Then Peter : " In short, when I did not perceive, through the occupation of my mind, that I had caught a very large fish which was attached to the hook, and that although it was dragging the hook-line from my hand, my brother Andrew, who was sitting by me, seeing me in a reverie and almost ready to fall, thrusting his elbow into my side as if he would awaken me from sleep, said : ' Do you not see, Peter, what a large fish you have caught? Are you out of your senses, that you are thus in a stupor of astonishment? Tell me, What is the matter with you?' But I was angry with him for a little, because he had withdrawn me from the delight of those things which I was contemplating ; then I answered that I was not suffering from any malady, but that I was mentally gazing on the beloved Jerusalem, and at the same time on Cæsarea ; and

---

[1] Luke xi. 22.

[2] [This story (chaps. 62–65) is peculiar to the *Recognitions*. In Homily XVII. 14–19 there is an argument against the trustworthiness of supernatural visions, which is supposed to be anti-Pauline in its aim. — R.]

that, while I was indeed with him in the body, in my mind I was wholly carried away thither. But he, I know not whence inspired, uttered a hidden and secret word of truth.

CHAP. LXIV. — ANDREW'S REBUKE.

"'Give over,' says he, 'O Peter. What is it that you are doing? For those who are beginning to be possessed with a demon, or to be disturbed in their minds, begin in this way. They are first carried away by fancies to some pleasant and delightful things, then they are poured out in vain and fond motions towards things which have no existence. Now this happens from a certain disease of mind, by reason of which they see not the things which are, but long to bring to their sight those which are not. But thus it happens also to those who are suffering phrenzy, and seem to themselves to see many images, because their soul, being torn and withdrawn from its place by excess of cold or of heat, suffers a failure of its natural service. But those also who are in distress through thirst, when they fall asleep, seem to themselves to see rivers and fountains, and to drink; but this befalls them through being distressed by the dryness of the unmoistened body. Wherefore it is certain that this occurs through some ailment either of the soul or body.'

CHAP. LXV. — FALLACY OF IMAGINATION.

"In short, that you may receive the faith of the matter; concerning Jerusalem, which I had often seen, I told my brother what places and what gatherings of people I had seemed to myself to see. But also concerning Cæsarea, which I had never seen, I nevertheless contended that it was such as I had conceived it in my mind and thought. But when I came hither, and saw nothing at all like to those things which I had seen in phantasy, I blamed myself, and observed distinctly, that I had assigned to it gates, and walls, and buildings from others which I had seen, taking the likeness in reality from others. Nor indeed can any one imagine anything new, and of which no form has ever existed. For even if any one should fashion from his imagination bulls with five heads, he only forms them with five heads out of those which he has seen with one head. And you therefore, now, if truly you seem to yourself to perceive anything with your thought, and to look above the heavens, there is no doubt but that you imagine them from those things which you see, placed as you are upon the earth. But if you think that there is easy access for your mind above the heavens, and that you are able to conceive the things that are there, and to apprehend knowledge of that immense light, I think that for him who can

comprehend these things, it were easier to throw his sense, which knows how to ascend thither, into the heart and breast of some one of us who stand by, and to tell what thoughts he is cherishing in his breast. If therefore you can declare the thoughts of the heart of any one of us, who is not pre-engaged in your favour, we shall perhaps be able to believe you, that you are able to know those things that are above the heavens, although these are much loftier."

CHAP. LXVI. — EXISTENCE AND CONCEPTION.

To this Simon replied:[1] "O thou who hast woven a web of many frivolities, listen now. It is impossible that anything which comes into a man's thoughts should not also subsist in truth and reality. For things that do not subsist, have no appearances;[2] but things that have no appearances, cannot present themselves to our thoughts." Then said Peter: "If everything that can come into our thoughts has a subsistence, then, with respect to that place of immensity which you say is outside the world, if one thinks in his heart that it is light, and another that it is darkness, how can one and the same place be both light and darkness, according to their different thoughts concerning it?" Then said Simon: "Let pass for the present what I have said; and tell us what you suppose to be above the heavens."

CHAP. LXVII. — THE LAW TEACHES OF IMMENSITY.

Then said Peter: "If you believed concerning the true fountain of light, I could instruct you what and of what sort is that which is immense, and should render, not a vain fancy, but a consistent and necessary account of the truth, and should make use, not of sophistical assertions, but testimonies of the law and nature, that you might know that the law especially contains what we ought to believe in regard to immensity. But if the doctrine of immensity is not unknown to the law, then assuredly nought else can be unknown to it; and therefore it is a false supposition of yours, that there is anything of which the law is not cognisant. Much more shall nothing be unknown to Him who gave the law. Yet I cannot speak anything to you of immensity and of those things which are without limit, unless first you either accept our account of those heavens which are bounded by a certain limit, or else propound your own account of them. But if you cannot understand concerning those which are comprehended within fixed boundaries, much more can you neither know nor learn anything concerning those which are without limit."

---

[1] [The remaining chapters of this book have no exact parallel in the *Homilies.* — R.]
[2] That is, have no visible or sensible *species*, according to the Platonic theory of perception.

CHAP. LXVIII. — THE VISIBLE AND THE INVISIBLE HEAVEN.

To this Simon answered : " It seems to me to be better to believe simply that God is, and that that heaven which we see is the only heaven in the whole universe." But Peter said : " Not so ; but it is proper to confess one God who truly is ; but that there are heavens, which were made by Him, as also the law says, of which one is the higher, in which also is contained the visible firmament ; and that that higher heaven is perpetual and eternal, with those who dwell in it ; but that this visible heaven is to be dissolved and to pass away at the end of the world, in order that that heaven which is older and higher may appear after the judgment to the holy and the worthy." To this Simon answered : " That these things are so, as you say, may appear to those who believe them ; but to him who seeks for reasons of these things, it is impossible that they can be produced from the law, and especially concerning the immensity of light."

CHAP. LXIX. — FAITH AND REASON.

Then Peter : " Do not think that we say that these things are only to be received by faith, but also that they are to be asserted by reason. For indeed it is not safe to commit these things to bare faith without reason, since assuredly truth cannot be without reason. And therefore he who has received these things fortified by reason, can never lose them ; whereas he who receives them without proofs, by an assent to a simple statement of them, can neither keep them safely, nor is certain if they are true ; because he who easily believes, also easily yields. But he who has sought reason for those things which he has believed and received, as though bound by chains of reason itself, can never be torn away or separated from those things which he hath believed. And therefore, according as any one is more anxious in demanding a reason, by so much will he be the firmer in preserving his faith."

CHAP. LXX. — ADJOURNMENT.

To this Simon replied : " It is a great thing which you promise, that the eternity of boundless light can be shown from the law." And when Peter said, " I shall show it whenever you please," Simon answered : " Since now it is a late hour, I shall stand by you and oppose you to-morrow ; and if you can prove that this world was created, and that souls are immortal, you shall have me to assist you in your preaching." When he had said thus, he departed, and was followed by a third part of all the people who had come with him, who were about one thousand men. But the rest with bended knees prostrated themselves before Peter ; and he, invoking upon them the name of God, cured some who had demons, healed others who were sick, and so dismissed the people rejoicing, commanding them to come early the next day. But Peter, when the crowds had withdrawn, commanded the table to be spread on the ground, in the open air, in the court where the disputation had been held, and sat down together with those eleven ; but I dined reclining with some others who also had made a beginning of hearing the word of God, and were greatly beloved.

CHAP. LXXI. — SEPARATION FROM THE UNCLEAN.

But Peter, most benignantly regarding me, lest haply that separation might cause me sorrow, says to me : " It is not from pride, O Clement, that I do not eat with those who have not yet been purified ; but I fear lest perhaps I should injure myself, and do no good to them.[1] For this I would have you know for certain, that every one who has at any time worshipped idols, and has adored those whom the pagans call gods, or has eaten of the things sacrificed to them, is not without an unclean spirit ; for he has become a guest of demons, and has been partaker with that demon of which he has formed the image in his mind, either through fear or love.[2] And by these means he is not free from an unclean spirit, and therefore needs the purification of baptism, that the unclean spirit may go out of him, which has made its abode in the inmost affections of his soul, and what is worse, gives no indication that it lurks within, for fear it should be exposed and expelled.

CHAP. LXXII. — THE REMEDY.

" For these unclean spirits love to dwell in the bodies of men, that they may fulfil their own desires by their service, and, inclining the motions of their souls to those things which they themselves desire, may compel them to obey their own lusts, that they may become wholly vessels of demons.[3] One of whom is this Simon, who is seized with such disease, and cannot now be healed, because he is sick in his will and purpose. Nor does the demon dwell in him against his will ; and therefore, if any one would drive it out of him, since it is inseparable from himself, and, so to speak, has now become his very soul, he should seem rather to kill him, and to incur the guilt of manslaughter. Let no one of you therefore be saddened at being separated from eating with us, for every one ought to observe that it is for just so long a time as he

---

[1] [Comp. book i. 19, vii. 29; Homilies I. 22, XIII. 4. — R.]
[2] 1 Cor x. 20.
[3] [On the demonology of this work see book iv. 15-19; comp, Homily IX. 8-22. — R.]

pleases. For he who wishes soon to be baptized is separated but for a little time, but he for a longer who wishes to be baptized later. Every one therefore has it in his own power to demand a shorter or a longer time for his repentance; and therefore it lies with you, when you wish it, to come to our table; and not with us, who are not permitted to take food with any one who has not been baptized. It is rather you, therefore, who hinder us from eating with you, if you interpose delays in the way of your purification, and defer your baptism." Having said thus, and having blessed, he took food. And afterwards, when he had given thanks to God, he went into the house and went to bed; and we all did the like, for it was now night.

BOOK III.[1]

CHAP. I. — PEARLS BEFORE SWINE.

Meantime Peter, rising at the crowing of the cock, and wishing to rouse us, found us awake, the evening light still burning; and when, according to custom, he had saluted us, and we had all sat down, he thus began. " Nothing is more difficult, my brethren, than to reason concerning the truth in the presence of a mixed multitude of people. For that which is may not be spoken to all as it is, on account of those who hear wickedly and treacherously; yet it is not proper to deceive, on account of those who desire to hear the truth sincerely. What, then, shall he do who has to address a mixed multitude? Shall he conceal what is true? How, then, shall he instruct those who are worthy? But if he set forth pure truth to those who do not desire to obtain salvation, he does injury to Him by whom he has been sent, and from whom he has received commandment not to throw the pearls of His words before swine and dogs,[2] who, striving against them with arguments and sophisms, roll them in the mud of carnal understanding, and by their barkings and base answers break and weary the preachers of God's word. Wherefore I also, for the most part, by using a certain circumlocution, endeavour to avoid publishing the chief knowledge concerning the Supreme Divinity to unworthy ears." Then, beginning from the Father, and the Son, and the Holy Spirit, he briefly and plainly expounded to us, so that all of us hearing him wondered that men have forsaken the truth, and have turned themselves to vanity.

CHAP. XII.[3] — SECOND DAY'S DISCUSSION.

But when the day had dawned, some one came in and said: " There is a very great multitude waiting in the court, and in the midst of them stands Simon, endeavouring to preoccupy the ears of the people with most wicked persuasions." Then Peter, immediately going out, stood in the place where he had disputed the day before, and all the people turning to him with joy, gave heed to him. But when Simon perceived that the people rejoiced at the sight of Peter, and were moved to love him, he said in confusion: " I wonder at the folly of men, who call me a magician, and love Peter; whereas, having knowledge of me of old, they ought to love me rather. And therefore from this sign those who have sense may understand that Peter may rather seem to be the magician, since affection is not borne to me, to whom it is almost due from acquaintance, but is abundantly expended upon him, to whom it is not due by any familiarity."[4]

CHAP. XIII. — SIMON A SEDUCER.

While Simon was talking on in this style, Peter, having saluted the people in his usual way, thus answered: " O Simon, his own conscience is sufficient for every one to confute him; but if you wonder at this, that those who are acquainted with you not only do not love you but even hate you, learn the reason from me. Since you are a seducer, you profess to proclaim the truth; and on this account you had many friends who had a desire to learn the truth. But when they saw in you things contrary to what you professed, they being, as I said, lovers of truth, began not only not to love you, but even to hate you. But yet they did not immediately forsake you, because you still promised that you could show them what is true. As long, therefore, as no one was present who could show them, they bore with you; but since the hope of better instruction has dawned upon them, they despise you, and seek to know what they understand to be better. And you indeed, acting by nefarious arts, thought at first that you should escape detection. But

---

[1] [The larger part of book iii. has no direct parallel in the *Homilies*, though, of course, many of the views presented are given in the latter under different circumstances. — R.]

[2] Matt. vii. 6.

[3] Chaps. ii.-xii. are wanting in the MSS. of best authority; and it seems to us indisputable that they form no part of the original work. For this reason, and because we have found them utterly untranslatable, we have omitted them.

[4] [Comp. Homily XVII. 2 for a similar accusation made by Simon. — R.]

you are detected. For you are driven into a corner, and, contrary to your expectation, you are made notorious, not only as being ignorant of the truth, but as being unwilling to hear it from those who know it. For if you had been willing to hear, that saying would have been exemplified in you, of Him who said that ' there is nothing hidden which shall not be known, nor covered which shall not be disclosed.' " [1]

CHAP. XIV. — SIMON CLAIMS THE FULFILMENT OF PETER'S PROMISE.

While Peter spoke these words, and others to the same effect, Simon answered : " I will not have you detain me with long speeches, Peter ; I claim from you what you promised yesterday. You then said that you could show that the law teaches concerning the immensity of the eternal light, and that there are only two heavens, and these created, and that the higher is the abode of that light, in which the ineffable Father dwells alone for ever ; but that after the pattern of that heaven is made this visible heaven, which you asserted is to pass away. You said, therefore, that the Father of all is one, because there cannot be two infinites ; else neither of them would be infinite, because in that in which the one subsists, he makes a limit of the subsistence of the other. Since then you not only promised this, but are able to show it from the law, leave off other matters and set about this." Then Peter said : " If I were asked to speak of these things only on your account, who come only for the purpose of contradicting, you should never hear a single discourse from me ; but seeing it is necessary that the husbandman, wishing to sow good ground, should sow some seeds, either in stony places, or places that are to be trodden of men, or in places filled with brambles and briers (as our Master also set forth, indicating by these the diversities of the purposes of several souls),[2] I shall not delay."

CHAP. XV. — SIMON'S ARROGANCE.

Then said Simon : " You seem to me to be angry ; but if it be so, it is not necessary to enter into the conflict." Then Peter : " I see that you perceive that you are to be convicted, and you wish politely to escape from the contest ; for what have you seen to have made me angry against you, a man desiring to deceive so great a multitude, and when you have nothing to say, pretending moderation, who also command, forsooth, by your authority that the controversy shall be conducted as you please, and not as order demands ? " Then Simon : " I shall enforce myself to bear patiently your unskilfulness, that I may show that you indeed wish to seduce the

people, but that I teach the truth. But now I refrain from a discussion concerning that boundless light. Answer me, therefore, what I ask of you. Since God, as you say, made all things, whence comes evil ? " [3] Then said Peter : " To put questions in this way is not the part of an opponent, but of a learner. If therefore you wish to learn, confess it ; and I shall first teach you how you ought to learn, and when you have learned to listen, then straightway I shall begin to teach you. But if you do not wish to learn, as though you knew all things, I shall first set forth the faith which I preach, and do you also set forth what you think to be true ; and when the profession of each of us has been disclosed, let our hearers judge whose discourse is supported by truth." To this Simon answered : " This is a good joke : behold a fellow who offers to teach me ! Nevertheless I shall suffer you, and bear with your ignorance and your arrogance. I confess, then, I do wish to learn ; let us see how you can teach me."

CHAP. XVI. — EXISTENCE OF EVIL.

Then Peter said : " If you truly wish to learn, then first learn this, how unskilfully you have framed your question ; for you say, Since. God has created all things, whence is evil ? But before you asked this, three sorts of questions should have had the precedence : *First*, Whether there be evil ? *Secondly*, What evil is ? *Thirdly*, To whom it is, and whence ? " To this Simon answered : " Oh thou most unskilful and unlearned, is there any man who does not confess that there is evil in this life ? Whence I also, thinking that you had even the common sense of all men, asked, whence evil is ; not as wishing to learn, since I know all things, least of all from you, who know nothing, but that I might show you to be ignorant of all things. And that you may not suppose that it is because I am angry that I speak somewhat sternly, know that I am moved with compassion for those who are present, whom you are attempting to deceive." Then Peter said : " The more wicked are you, if you can do such wrong, not being angry ; but smoke must rise where there is fire. Nevertheless I shall tell you, lest I should seem to take you up with words, so as not to answer to those things which you have spoken disorderly. You say that all confess the existence of evil, which is verily false ; for, first of all, the whole Hebrew nation deny its existence."

CHAP. XVII. — NOT ADMITTED BY ALL.

Then Simon, interrupting his discourse, said : " They do rightly who say that there is no evil."

---

[1] Matt. x. 26.
[2] Luke viii. 5. [Comp. Matt. xiii. 3, etc.; Mark iv. 3, etc. — R.]
[3] [In Homily XIX. the discussion with Simon is respecting the existence of the evil one. Here the treatment is apparently of a higher philosophical character. — R.]

Then Peter answered : "We do not propose to speak of this now, but only to state the fact that the existence of evil is not universally admitted. But the second question that you should have asked is, What is evil? — a substance, an accident, or an act? And many other things of the same sort. And after that, towards what, or how it is, or to whom it is evil, — whether to God, or to angels, or to men, to the righteous or the wicked, to all or to some, to one's self or to no one? And then you should inquire, Whence it is? — whether from God, or from nothing; whether it has always been, or has had its beginning in time ; whether it is useful or useless? and many other things which a proposition of this sort demands." To this Simon answered : " Pardon me ; I was in error concerning the first question ; but suppose that I now ask first, whether evil is or not? "

CHAP. XVIII. — MANNER OF CONDUCTING THE DISCUSSION.

Then Peter said : " In what way do you put the question ; as wishing to learn, or to teach, or for the sake of raising the question? If indeed as wishing to learn, I have something to teach you first, that coming by consequence and the right order of doctrine, you may understand from yourself what evil is. But if you put the question as an instructor, I have no need to be taught by you, for I have a Master from whom I have learned all things. But if you ask merely for the sake of raising a question and disputing, let each of us first set forth his opinion, and so let the matter be debated. For it is not reasonable that you should ask as one wishing to learn, and contradict as one teaching, so that after my answer it should be in your discretion to say whether I have spoken well or ill. Wherefore you cannot stand in the place of a gainsayer and be judge of what we say. And therefore, as I said, if a discussion is to be held, let each of us state his sentiments ; and while we are placed in conflict, these religious hearers will be just judges."

CHAP. XIX. — DESIRE OF INSTRUCTION.

Then Simon said : " Does it not seem to you to be absurd that an unskilled people should sit in judgment upon our sayings?" Then Peter : "It is not so ; for what perhaps is less clear to one, can be investigated by many, for oftentimes even a popular rumour has the aspect of a prophecy. But in addition to all this, all these people stand here constrained by the love of God, and by a desire to know the truth, and therefore all these are to be regarded as one, by reason of their affection being one and the same towards the truth ; as, on the other hand, two

are many and diverse, if they disagree with each other. But if you wish to receive an indication how all these people who stand before us are as one man, consider from their very silence and quietness how with all patience, as you see, they do honour to the truth of God, even before they learn it, for they have not yet learned the greater observance which they owe to it. Wherefore I hope, through the mercy of God, that He will accept the religious purpose of their mind towards Him, and will give the palm of victory to him who preaches the truth, that He may make manifest to them the herald of truth."

CHAP. XX. — COMMON PRINCIPLES.

Then Simon : "On what subject do you wish the discussion to be held? Tell me, that I also may define what I think, and so the inquiry may begin." And Peter answered : " If, indeed, you will do as I think right, I would have it done according to the precept of my Master, who first of all commanded the Hebrew nation, whom He knew to have knowledge of God, and that it is He who made the world, not that they should inquire about Him whom they knew, but that, knowing Him, they should investigate His will and His righteousness ; because it is placed in men's power that, searching into these things, they may find, and do, and observe those things concerning which they are to be judged. Therefore He commanded us to inquire, not whence evil cometh, as you asked just now, but to seek the righteousness of the good God, and His kingdom ; and all these things, says He, shall be added to you."[1] Then Simon said : " Since these things are commanded to Hebrews, as having a right knowledge of God, and being of opinion that every one has it in his power to do those things concerning which he is to be judged, — but my opinion differs from theirs, — where do you wish me to begin? "

CHAP. XXI. — FREEDOM OF THE WILL.

Then said Peter : "I advise that the first inquiry be, whether it be in our power to know whence we are to be judged." But Simon said : "Not so ; but concerning God, about whom all who are present are desirous to hear." Then Peter : "You admit, then, that something is in the power of the will : only confess this, if it is so, and let us inquire, as you say, concerning God." To this Simon answered : " By no means " Then Peter said : " If, then, nothing is in our power, it is useless for us to inquire anything concerning God, since it is not in the power of those who seek to find ; hence I said well, that this should be the first inquiry, whether

---

[1] Matt. vi. 33.

anything is in the power of the will."[1] Then said Simon: "We cannot even understand this that you say, if there is anything in the power of the will." But Peter, seeing that he was turning to contention, and, through fear of being overcome, was confounding all things as being in general uncertain, answered: "How then do you know that it is not in the power of man to know anything, since this very thing at least you know?"

CHAP. XXII. — RESPONSIBILITY.

Then Simon said: "I know not whether I know even this; for every one, according as it is decreed to him by fate, either does, or understands, or suffers." Then Peter said: "See, my brethren, into what absurdities Simon has fallen, who before my coming was teaching that men have it in their power to be wise and to do what they will, but now, driven into a corner by the force of my arguments, he denies that man has any power either of perceiving or of acting; and yet he presumes to profess himself to be a teacher! But tell me how then God judges according to truth every one for his doings, if men have it not in their own power to do anything? If this opinion be held, all things are torn up by the roots; vain will be the desire of following after goodness; yea, even in vain do the judges of the world administer laws and punish those who do amiss, for they had it not in their power not to sin; vain also will be the laws of nations which assign penalties to evil deeds. Miserable also will those be who laboriously keep righteousness; but blessed those who, living in pleasure, exercise tyranny, living in luxury and wickedness. According to this, therefore, there can be neither righteousness, nor goodness, nor any virtue, nor, as you would have it, any God. But, O Simon, I know why you have spoken thus: truly because you wished to avoid inquiry, lest you should be openly confuted; and therefore you say that it is not in the power of man to perceive or to discern anything. But if this had really been your opinion, you would not surely, before my coming, have professed yourself before the people to be a teacher. I say, therefore, that man is under his own control." Then said Simon: "What is the meaning of being under his own control? Tell us." To this Peter: "If nothing can be learned, why do you wish to hear?" And Simon said: "You have nothing to answer to this."

CHAP. XXIII. — ORIGIN OF EVIL.

Then said Peter: "I shall speak, not as under compulsion from you, but at the request of the hearers. The power of choice is the sense of the soul, possessing a quality by which it can be inclined towards what acts it wills." Then Simon, applauding Peter for what he had spoken, said: "Truly you have expounded it magnificently and incomparably, for it is my duty to bear testimony to your speaking well. Now if you will explain to me this which I now ask you, in all things else I shall submit to you. What I wish to learn, then, is this: if what God wishes to be, is; and what He does not wish to be, is not. Answer me this." Then Peter: "If you do not know that you are asking an absurd and incompetent question, I shall pardon you and explain; but if you are aware that you are asking inconsequently, you do not well." Then Simon said: "I swear by the Supreme Divinity, whatsoever that may be, which judges and punishes those who sin, that I know not what I have said inconsequently, or what absurdity there is in my words, that is, in those that I have just uttered."

CHAP. XXIV. — GOD THE AUTHOR OF GOOD, NOT OF EVIL.

To this Peter answered: "Since, then, you confess that you are ignorant, now learn. Your question demanded our deliverance on two matters that are contrary to one another. For every motion is divided into two parts, so that a certain part is moved by necessity, and another by will; and those things which are moved by necessity are always in motion, those which are moved by will, not always. For example, the sun's motion is performed by necessity to complete its appointed circuit, and every state and service of heaven depends upon necessary motions. But man directs the voluntary motions of his own actions. And thus there are some things which have been created for this end, that in their services they should be subject to necessity, and should be unable to do aught else than what has been assigned to them; and when they have accomplished this service, the Creator of all things, who thus arranged them according to His will, preserves them. But there are other things, in which there is a power of will, and which have a free choice of doing what they will. These, as I have said, do not remain always in that order in which they were created; but according as their will leads them, and the judgment of their mind inclines them, they effect either good or evil; and therefore He hath proposed rewards to those who do well, and penalties to those who do evil.[2]

CHAP. XXV. — "WHO HATH RESISTED HIS WILL?"

"You say, therefore, if God wishes anything to be, it is; and if He do not wish it, it is not.

---

[1] [Comp. Homilies XI. 8, XIX. 15. But in the *Recognitions* this topic is more frequently treated. See chap. 26, and elsewhere. — R.]

[2] [Comp. Homily XIX. 12. The argument here is far more philosophical. — R.]

But if I were to answer that what He wishes is, and what He wishes not is not, you would say that then He wishes the evil things to be which are done in the world, since everything that He wishes is, and everything that He wishes not is not. But if I had answered that it is not so that what God wishes is, and what He wishes not is not, then you would retort upon me that God must then be powerless, if He cannot do what He wills; and you would be all the more petulant, as thinking that you had got a victory, though you had said nothing to the point. Therefore you are ignorant, O Simon, yea very ignorant, how the will of God acts in each individual case. For some things, as we have said, He has so willed to be, that they cannot be otherwise than as they are ordained by Him; and to these He has assigned neither rewards nor punishments; but those which He has willed to be so that they have it in their power to do what they will, He has assigned to them according to their actions and their wills, to earn either rewards or punishments. Since, therefore, as I have informed you, all things that are moved are divided into two parts, according to the distinction that I formerly stated, everything that God wills is, and everything that He wills not is not."

CHAP. XXVI. — NO GOODNESS WITHOUT LIBERTY.

To this Simon answered: " Was not He able to make us all such that we should be good, and that we should not have it in our power to be otherwise?" Peter answered: " This also is an absurd question. For if He had made us of an unchangeable nature and incapable of being moved away from good, we should not be really good, because we could not be aught else; and it would not be of our purpose that we were good; and what we did would not be ours, but of the necessity of our nature.[1] But how can that be called good which is not done of purpose? And on this account the world required long periods, until the number of souls which were predestined to fill it should be completed, and then that visible heaven should be folded up like a scroll, and that which is higher should appear, and the souls of the blessed, being restored to their bodies, should be ushered into light; but the souls of the wicked, for their impure actions being surrounded with fiery spirit, should be plunged into the abyss of unquenchable fire, to endure punishments through eternity. Now that these things are so, the true Prophet. has testified to us; concerning whom, if you wish to know that He is a prophet, I shall instruct you by innumerable declarations. For of those things which were spoken by Him, even now

everything that He said is being fulfilled; and those things which He spoke with respect to the future are believed to be about to be fulfilled, for faith is given to the future from those things which have already come to pass."

CHAP. XXVII. — THE VISIBLE HEAVEN: WHY MADE.

But Simon, perceiving that Peter was clearly assigning a reason from the head of prophecy, from which the whole question is settled, declined that the discourse should take this turn; and thus answered: " Give me an answer to the questions that I put, and tell me, if that visible heaven is, as you say, to be dissolved, why was it made at first?" Peter answered: " It was made for the sake of this present life of men, that there might be some sort of interposition and separation, lest any unworthy one might see the habitation of the celestials and the abode of God Himself, which are prepared in order to be seen by those only who are of pure heart.[2] But now, that is in the time of the conflict, it has pleased Him that those things be invisible, which are destined as a reward to the conquerers." Then Simon said: " If the Creator is good, and the world is good, how shall He who is good ever destroy that which is good? But if He shall destroy that which is good, how shall He Himself be thought to be good? But if He shall dissolve and destroy it as evil, how shall He not appear to be evil, who has made that which is evil?"

CHAP. XXVIII. — WHY TO BE DISSOLVED.

To this Peter replied: " Since we have promised not to run away from your blasphemies, we endure them patiently, for you shall yourself render an account for the things that you speak. Listen now, therefore. If indeed that heaven which is visible and transient had been made for its own sake, there would have been some reason in what you say, that it ought not to be dissolved. But if it was made not for its own sake, but for the sake of something else, it must of necessity be dissolved, that that for which it seems to have been made may appear. As I might say, by way of illustration, however fairly and carefully the shell of the egg may seem to have been formed, it is yet necessary that it be broken and opened, that the chick may issue from it, and that may appear for which the form of the whole egg seems to have been moulded. So also, therefore, it is necessary that the condition of this world pass away, that that sublimer condition of the heavenly kingdom may shine forth."

---

[1] [Comp. Homily XIX. 15. — R.]

[2] Matt. v. 8.

CHAP. XXIX. — CORRUPTIBLE AND TEMPORARY THINGS MADE BY THE INCORRUPTIBLE AND ETERNAL.

Then Simon : "It does not seem to me that the heaven, which has been made by God, can be dissolved. For things made by the Eternal One are eternal, while things made by a corruptible one are temporary and decaying." Then Peter : "It is not so. Indeed corruptible and temporary things of all sorts are made by mortal creatures ; but the Eternal does not always make things corruptible, nor always incorruptible ; but according to the will of God the Creator, so will be the things which He creates. For the power of God is not subject to law, but His will is law to His creatures." Then Simon answered : "I call you back to the first question. You said now that God is visible to no one ; but when that heaven shall be dissolved, and that superior condition of the heavenly kingdom shall shine forth, then those who are pure in heart[1] shall see God ; which statement is contrary to the law, for there it is written that God said, 'None shall see my face and live.'"[2]

CHAP. XXX. — HOW THE PURE IN HEART SEE GOD.

Then Peter answered : "To those who do not read the law according to the tradition of Moses, my speech appears to be contrary to it ; but I will show you how it is not contradictory. God is seen by the mind, not by the body ; by the spirit, not by the flesh. Whence also angels, who are spirits, see God ; and therefore men, as long as they are men, cannot see Him. But after the resurrection of the dead, when they shall have been made like the angels,[3] they shall be able to see God. And thus my statement is not contrary to the law ; neither is that which our Master said, 'Blessed are they of a pure heart, for they shall see God.'[1] For He showed that a time shall come in which of men shall be made angels, who in the spirit of their mind shall see God." After these and many similar sayings, Simon began to assert with many oaths, saying : "Concerning one thing only render me a reason, whether the soul is immortal, and I shall submit to your will in all things. But let it be to-morrow, for to-day it is late." When therefore Peter began to speak, Simon went out, and with him a very few of his associates ; and that for shame. But all the rest, turning to Peter, on bended knees prostrated themselves before him ; and some of those who were afflicted with diverse sicknesses, or invaded by demons, were healed by the prayer of Peter, and departed rejoicing, as having obtained at once the doctrine of the

true God, and also His mercy. When therefore the crowds had withdrawn, and only we his attendants remained with him, we sat down on couches placed on the ground, each one recognising his accustomed place, and having taken food, and given thanks to God, we went to sleep.

CHAP. XXXI. — DILIGENCE IN STUDY.

But on the following day, Peter, as usual, rising before dawn, found us already awake and ready to listen ; and thus began : "I entreat you, my brethren and fellow-servants, that if any of you is not able to wake, he should not torment himself through respect to my presence, because sudden change is difficult ; but if for a long time one gradually accustoms himself, that will not be distressing which comes of use. For we had not all the same training ; although in course of time we shall be able to be moulded into one habit, for they say that custom holds the place of a second nature. But I call God to witness that I am not offended, if any one is not able to wake ; but rather by this, if, when any one sleeps all through the night, he does not in the course of the day fulfil that which he omitted in the night. For it is necessary to give heed intently and unceasingly to the study of doctrine, that our mind may be filled with the thought of God only ; because in the mind which is filled with the thought of God, no place will be given to the wicked one."

CHAP. XXXII. — PETER'S PRIVATE INSTRUCTION.

When Peter spoke thus to us, every one of us eagerly assured him, that ere now we were awake, being satisfied with short sleep, but that we were afraid to arouse him, because it did not become the disciples to command the master ; "and yet even this, O Peter, we had almost ventured to take upon ourselves, because our hearts, agitated with longing for your words, drove sleep wholly from our eyes. But again our affection towards you opposed it, and did not suffer us violently to rouse you." Then Peter said : "Since therefore you assert that you are willingly awake through desire of hearing, I wish to repeat to you more carefully, and to explain in their order, the things that were spoken yesterday without arrangement. And this I propose to do throughout these daily disputations, that by night, when privacy of time and place is afforded, I shall unfold in correct order, and by a straight line of explanation, anything that in the controversy has not been stated with sufficient fulness." And then he began to point out to us how the yesterday's discussion ought to have been conducted, and how it could not be so conducted on account of the contentiousness or the unskilfulness of his opponent ; and how therefore he only made use of assertion,

[1] Matt. v. 8.
[2] Ex. xxxiii. 20.
[3] Matt. xxii. 30.

and only overthrew what was said by his adversary, but did not expound his own doctrines either completely or distinctly. Then repeating the several matters to us, he discussed them in regular order and with full reason.

CHAP. XXXIII. — LEARNERS AND CAVILLERS.

But when the day began to be light, after prayer he went out to the crowds and stood in his accustomed place, for the discussion; and seeing Simon standing in the middle of the crowd, he saluted the people in his usual way, and said to them: "I confess that I am grieved with respect to some men, who come to us in this way that they may learn something, but when we begin to teach them, they profess that they themselves are masters, and while indeed they ask questions as ignorant persons, they contradict as knowing ones. But perhaps some one will say, that he who puts a question, puts it indeed in order that he may learn, but when that which he hears does not seem to him to be right, it is necessary that he should answer, and that seems to be contradiction which is not contradiction, but further inquiry.

CHAP. XXXIV. — AGAINST ORDER IS AGAINST REASON.

"Let such a one then hear this: The teaching of all doctrine has a certain order, and there are some things which must be delivered first, others in the second place, and others in the third, and so all in their order; and if these things be delivered in their order, they become plain; but if they be brought forward out of order, they will seem to be spoken against reason. And therefore order is to be observed above all things, if we seek for the purpose of finding what we seek. For he who enters rightly upon the road, will observe the second place in due order, and from the second will more easily find the third; and the further he proceeds, so much the more will the way of knowledge become open to him, even until he arrive at the city of truth, whither he is bound, and which he desires to reach. But he who is unskilful, and knows not the way of inquiry, — as a traveller in a foreign country, ignorant and wandering, if he will not employ a native of the country as a guide, — undoubtedly when he has strayed from the way of truth, shall remain outside the gates of life, and so, involved in the darkness of black night, shall walk through the paths of perdition. Inasmuch therefore, as, if those things which are to be sought, be sought in an orderly manner, they can most easily be found, but the unskilful man is ignorant of the order of inquiry, it is right that the ignorant man should yield to the knowing one, and first learn the order of inquiry, that so at length he may find the method of asking and answering.

CHAP. XXXV. — LEARNING BEFORE TEACHING.

To this Simon replied: "Then truth is not the property of all, but of those only who know the art of disputation, which is absurd; for it cannot be, since He is equally the God of all, that all should not be equally able to know His will." Then Peter: "All were made equal by Him, and to all He has given equally to be receptive of truth. But that none of those who are born, are born with education, but education is subsequent to birth, no one can doubt. Since, therefore, the birth of men holds equity in this respect, that all are equally capable of receiving discipline, the difference is not in nature, but in education. Who does not know that the things which any one learns, he was ignorant of before he learned them?" Then Simon said: "You say truly." Then Peter said: "If then in those arts which are in common use, one first learns and then teaches, how much more ought those who profess to be the educators of souls, first to learn, and so to teach, that they may not expose themselves to ridicule, if they promise to afford knowledge to others, when they themselves are unskilful?" Then Simon: "This is true in respect of those arts which are in common use; but in the word of knowledge, as soon as any one has heard, he has learned."

CHAP. XXXVI. — SELF-EVIDENCE OF THE TRUTH.

Then said Peter: "If indeed one hear in an orderly and regular manner, he is able to know what is true; but he who refuses to submit to the rule of a reformed life and a pure conversation, which truly is the proper result of knowledge of the truth, will not confess that he knows what he does know. For this is exactly what we see in the case of some who, abandoning the trades which they learned in their youth, betake themselves to other performances, and by way of excusing their own sloth, begin to find fault with the trade as unprofitable." Then Simon: "Ought all who hear to believe that whatever they hear is true?" Then Peter: "Whoever hears an orderly statement of the truth, cannot by any means gainsay it, but knows that what is spoken is true, provided he also willingly submit to the rules of life. But those who, when they hear, are unwilling to betake themselves to good works, are prevented by the desire of doing evil from acquiescing in those things which they judge to be right. Hence it is manifest that it is in the power of the hearers to choose which of the two they prefer. But if all who hear were to obey, it would be rather a necessity of nature, leading all in one way. For as no one can be persuaded to become shorter or taller, because the force of nature does not permit it; so also, if either all were converted to the truth by a word, or all were not converted, it would be the force of nature which compelled all in the one case, and none at all in the other, to be converted."

CHAP. XXXVII. — GOD RIGHTEOUS AS WELL AS GOOD.

Then said Simon : "Inform us, therefore, what he who desires to know the truth must first learn." Then Peter : "Before all things it must be inquired what it is possible for man to find out. For of necessity the judgment of God turns upon this, if a man was able to do good and did it not. And therefore men must inquire whether they have it in their power by seeking to find what is good, and to do it when they have found it ; for this is that for which they are to be judged. But more than this there is no occasion for any one but a prophet to know ; for what is the need for men to know how the world was made? This, indeed, would be necessary to be learned if we had to enter upon a similar construction. But now it is sufficient for us, in order to the worship of God, to know that He made the world ; but how He made it is no subject of inquiry for us, because, as I have said, it is not incumbent upon us to acquire the knowledge of that art, as though we were about to make something similar. But neither are we to be judged for this, why we have not learned how the world was made, but only for that, if we be without knowledge of its Creator. For we shall know that the Creator of the world is the righteous and good God, if we seek Him in the paths of righteousness. For if we only know regarding Him that He is good, such knowledge is not sufficient for salvation. For in the present life not only the worthy, but also the unworthy, enjoy His goodness and His benefits. But if we believe Him to be not only good, but also righteous, and if, according to what we believe concerning God, we observe righteousness in the whole course of our life, we shall enjoy His goodness for ever. In a word, to the Hebrews, whose opinion concerning God was that He is only good, our Master said that they should seek also His righteousness ;[1] that is, that they should know that He is good indeed in this present time, that all may live in His goodness, but that He shall be righteous at the day of judgment, to bestow eternal rewards upon the worthy, from which the unworthy shall be excluded.

CHAP. XXXVIII. — GOD'S JUSTICE SHOWN AT THE DAY OF JUDGMENT.

Then Simon : "How can one and the same being be both good and righteous?"[2] Peter answered : "Because without righteousness, goodness would be unrighteousness ; for it is the part of a good God to bestow His sunshine and rain equally on the just and the unjust ;[3] but this would seem to be unjust, if He treated the good and the bad always with equal fortune, and were it not that He does it for the sake of the fruits, which all may equally enjoy who are born in this world. But as the rain given by God equally nourishes the corn and the tares, but at the time of harvest the crops are gathered into the barn, but the chaff or the tares are burnt in the fire,[4] so in the day of judgment, when the righteous shall be introduced into the kingdom of heaven, and the unrighteous shall be cast out, then also the justice of God shall be shown. For if He remained for ever alike to the evil and the good, this would not only not be good, but even unrighteous and unjust ; that the righteous and the unrighteous should be held by Him in one order of desert."

CHAP. XXXIX. — IMMORTALITY OF THE SOUL.

Then said Simon : "The one point on which I should wish to be satisfied is, whether the soul is immortal ; for I cannot take up the burden of righteousness unless I know first concerning the immortality of the soul ; for indeed if it is not immortal, the profession of your preaching cannot stand." Then said Peter : "Let us first inquire whether God is just ; for if this were ascertained, the perfect order of religion would straightway be established." Then Simon : "With all your boasting of your knowledge of the order of discussion, you seem to me now to have answered contrary to order ; for when I ask you to show whether the soul is immortal, you say that we must first inquire whether God is just." Then said Peter : "That is perfectly right and regular." Simon : "I should wish to learn how."

CHAP. XL. — PROVED BY THE SUCCESS OF THE WICKED IN THIS LIFE.

"Listen, then," said Peter : "Some men who are blasphemers against God, and who spend their whole life in injustice and pleasure, die in their own bed and obtain honourable burial ; while others who worship God, and maintain their life frugally with all honesty and sobriety, die in deserted places for their observance of righteousness, so that they are not even thought worthy of burial. Where, then, is the justice of God, if there be no immortal soul to suffer punishment in the future for impious deeds, or enjoy rewards for piety and rectitude?" Then Simon said : "It is this indeed that makes me

---

[1] Matt. vi. 33.
[2] [Comp. Homilies XVII. 4, etc., XVIII. 1. The objection is of Gnostic origin. — R.]

[3] Matt. v. 45.
[4] Matt. iii. 12.

incredulous, because many well-doers perish miserably, and again many evil-doers finish long lives in happiness." [1]

CHAP. XLI. — CAVILS OF SIMON.

Then said Peter: " This very thing which draws you into incredulity, affords to us a certain conviction that there shall be a judgment. For since it is certain that God is just, it is a necessary consequence that there is another world, in which every one receiving according to his deserts, shall prove the justice of God. But if all men were now receiving according to their deserts, we should truly seem to be deceivers when we say that there is a judgment to come ; and therefore this very fact, that in the present life a return is not made to every one according to his deeds, affords, to those who know that God is just, an indubitable proof that there shall be a judgment." Then said Simon : " Why, then, am I not persuaded of it ? " Peter : " Because you have not heard the true Prophet saying, ' Seek first His righteousness, and all these things shall be added to you.' " [2] Then said Simon : " Pardon me if I am unwilling to seek righteousness, before I know if the soul is immortal." Then Peter : " You also pardon me this one thing, because I cannot do otherwise than the Prophet of truth has instructed me." Then said Simon : " It is certain that you cannot assert that the soul is immortal, and therefore you cavil, knowing that if it be proved to be mortal, the whole profession of that religion which you are attempting to propagate will be plucked up by the roots. And therefore, indeed, I commend your prudence, while I do not approve your persuasiveness ; for you persuade many to embrace your religion, and to submit to the restraint of pleasure, in hope of future good things ; to whom it happens that they lose the enjoyment of things present, and are deceived with hopes of things future. For as soon as they die, their soul shall at the same time be extinguished."

CHAP. XLII. — " FULL OF ALL SUBTLETY AND ALL MISCHIEF."

But Peter, when he heard him speak thus, grinding his teeth, and rubbing his forehead with his hand, and sighing with profound grief, said : [3] " Armed with the cunning of the old serpent, you stand forth to deceive souls ; and therefore, as the serpent is more subtile than any other beast, you profess that you are a teacher from the beginning. And again, like the serpent you wished to introduce many gods ;

but now, being confuted in that, you assert that there is no God at all. For by occasion of I know not what unknown God, you denied that the Creator of the world is God, but asserted that He is either an evil being, or that He has many equals, or, as we have said, that He is not God at all. And when you had been overcome in this position, you now assert that the soul is mortal, so that men may not live righteously and uprightly in hope of things to come. For if there be no hope for the future, why should not mercy be given up, and men indulge in luxury and pleasures, from which it is manifest that all unrighteousness springs ? And while you introduce so impious a doctrine into the miserable life of men, you call yourself pious, and me impious, because, under the hope of future good things, I will not suffer men to take up arms and fight against one another, plunder and subvert everything, and attempt whatsoever lust may dictate. And what will be the condition of that life which you would introduce, that men will attack and be attacked, be enraged and disturbed, and live always in fear ? For those who do evil to others must expect like evil to themselves. Do you see that you are a leader of disturbance and not of peace, of iniquity and not of equity ? But I feigned anger, not because I could not prove that the soul is immortal, but because I pity the souls which you are endeavouring to deceive. I shall speak, therefore, but not as compelled by you ; for I know how I should speak ; and you will be the only one who wants not so much persuasion as admonition on this subject. But those who are really ignorant of this, I shall instruct as is suitable."

CHAP. XLIII. — SIMON'S SUBTERFUGES.

Then says Simon : " If you are angry, I shall neither ask you any questions, nor do I wish to hear you." Then Peter : " If you are now seeking a pretext for escaping, you have full liberty, and need not use any special pretext. For all have heard you speaking all amiss, and have perceived that you can prove nothing, but that you only asked questions for the sake of contradiction ; which any one can do. For what difficulty is there in replying, after the clearest proofs have been adduced, ' You have said nothing to the purpose ? ' But that you may know that I am able to prove to you in a single sentence that the soul is immortal, I shall ask you with respect to a point which all know ; answer me, and I shall prove to you in one sentence that it is immortal." Then Simon, who had thought that he had got, from the anger of Peter, a pretext for departing, stopped on account of the remarkable promise that was

---

[1] [Comp. Homily XIX. 23. — R.]
[2] Matt. vi. 33.
[3] [The concluding portion of this discussion (chaps. 42-48) is peculiar alike in its argument and its colloquies. — R.]

made to him, and said: "Ask me then, and I shall answer you what all know, that I may hear in a single sentence, as you have promised, how the soul is immortal."

CHAP. XLIV. — SIGHT OR HEARING?

Then Peter: "I shall speak so that it may be proved to you before all the rest. Answer me, therefore, which of the two can better persuade an incredulous man, seeing or hearing?" Then Simon said: "Seeing." Then Peter: "Why then do you wish to learn from me by words, what is proved to you by the thing itself and by sight?" Then Simon: "I know not what you mean." Then Peter: "If you do not know, go now to your house, and entering the inner bed-chamber you will see an image placed, containing the figure of a murdered boy clothed in purple; ask him, and he will inform you either by hearing or seeing. For what need is there to hear from him if the soul is immortal, when you see it standing before you? For if it were not in being, it assuredly could not be seen. But if you know not what image I speak of, let us straightway go to your house, with ten other men, of those who are here present."[1]

CHAP. XLV. — A HOME-THRUST.

But Simon hearing this, and being smitten by his conscience, changed colour and became bloodless; for he was afraid, if he denied it, that his house would be searched, or that Peter in his indignation would betray him more openly, and so all would learn what he was. Thus he answered: "I beseech thee, Peter, by that good God who is in thee, to overcome the wickedness that is in me. Receive me to repentance, and you shall have me as an assistant in your preaching. For now I have learned in very deed that you are a prophet of the true God, and therefore you alone know the secret and hidden things of men."[2] Then said Peter: "You see, brethren, Simon seeking repentance; in a little while you shall see him returning again to his infidelity. For, thinking that I am a prophet, forasmuch as I have disclosed his wickedness, which he supposed to be secret and hidden, he has promised that he will repent. But it is not lawful for me to lie, nor must I deceive, whether this infidel be saved or not saved. For I call heaven and earth to witness, that I spoke not by a prophetic spirit what I said, and what I intimated, as far as was possible, to the listening crowds; but I learned from some who once were his associates in his works, but have now been converted to our faith, what things he did

in secret. Therefore I spoke what I knew, not what I foreknew."

CHAP. XLVI. — SIMON'S RAGE.

But when Simon heard this, he assailed Peter with curses and reproaches, saying: "Oh most wicked and most deceitful of men, to whom fortune, not truth, hath given the victory. But I sought repentance not for defect of knowledge, but in order that you, thinking that by repentance I should become your disciple, might entrust to me all the secrets of your profession, and so at length, knowing them all, I might confute you. But as you cunningly understood for what reason I had pretended penitence, and acquiesced as if you did not understand my stratagem, that you might first expose me in presence of the people as unskilful, then foreseeing that being thus exposed to the people, I must of necessity be indignant, and confess that I was not truly penitent, you anticipated me, that you might say that I should, after my penitence, again return to my infidelity, that you might seem to have conquered on all sides, both if I continued in the penitence which I had professed, and if I did not continue; and so you should be believed to be wise, because you had foreseen these things, while I should seem to be deceived, because I did not foresee your trick. But you foreseeing mine, have used subtlety and circumvented me. But, as I said, your victory is the result of fortune, not of truth: yet I know why I did not foresee this; because I stood by you and spoke with you in my goodness, and bore patiently with you. But now I shall show you the power of my divinity, so that you shall quickly fall down and worship me.

CHAP. XLVII. — SIMON'S VAUNT.

"I am the first power, who am always, and without beginning.[3] But having entered the womb of Rachel, I was born of her as a man, that I might be visible to men. I have flown through the air; I have been mixed with fire, and been made one body with it; I have made statues to move; I have animated lifeless things; I have made stones bread; I have flown from mountain to mountain; I have moved from place to place, upheld by angels' hands, and have lighted on the earth. Not only have I done these things; but even now I am able to do them, that by facts I may prove to all, that I am the Son of God, enduring to eternity, and that I can make those who believe on me endure in like manner for ever. But your words are all vain; nor can you perform any real works *such as I have now mentioned*,

---

[1] [Comp. book ii. 15 and Homily II. 26. — R.]
[2] [Evidently parodied from Acts viii. 18–24. This incident is peculiar to the *Recognitions*. — R.]

[3] [Compare with this chapter book ii. 9, 14; Homily II. 32. — R.]

as he also who sent you is a magician, who yet could not deliver himself from the suffering of the cross."

CHAP. XLVIII. — ATTEMPTS TO CREATE A DISTURBANCE.

To this speech of Simon, Peter answered: "Do not meddle with the things that belong to others; for that you are a magician, you have confessed and made manifest by the very deeds that you have done; but our Master, who is the Son of God and of man, is manifestly good; and that he is truly the Son of God has been told, and shall be told to those to whom it is fitting. But if you will not confess that you are a magician, let us go, with all this multitude, to your house, and then it will be evident who is a magician." While Peter was speaking thus, Simon began to assail him with blasphemies and curses, that he might make a riot, and excite all so that he could not be refuted, and that Peter, withdrawing on account of his blasphemy, might seem to be overcome. But he stood fast, and began to charge him more vehemently.

CHAP. XLIX. — SIMON'S RETREAT.

Then the people in indignation cast Simon from the court, and drove him forth from the gate of the house; and only one person followed him when he was driven out.[1] Then silence being obtained, Peter began to address the people in this manner: "You ought, brethren, to bear with wicked men patiently; knowing that although God could cut them off, yet He suffers them to remain even till the day appointed, in which judgment shall pass upon all. Why then should not we bear with those whom God suffers? Why should not we bear with fortitude the wrongs that they do to us, when He who is almighty does not take vengeance on them, that both His own goodness and the impiety of the wicked may be known? But if the wicked one had not found Simon to be his minister, he would doubtless have found another: for it is of necessity that in this life offences come, 'but woe to that man by whom they come;'[2] and therefore Simon is rather to be mourned over, because he has become a choice vessel for the wicked one, which undoubtedly would not have happened had he not received power over him for his former sins. For why should I further say that he once believed in our Jesus, and was persuaded that souls are immortal?[3] Although in this he is deluded by demons, yet he has persuaded himself that he has the soul of a murdered boy ministering to

him in whatever he pleases to employ it in; in which truly, as I have said, he is deluded by demons, and therefore I spoke to him according to his own ideas: for he has learned from the Jews, that judgment and vengeance are to be brought forth against those who set themselves against the true faith, and do not repent. But there are men to whom, as being perfect in crimes, the wicked one appears, that he may deceive them, so that they may never be turned to repentance.

CHAP. L. — PETER'S BENEDICTION.

"You therefore who are turned to the Lord by repentance, bend to Him your knees." When he had said this, all the multitude bent their knees to God; and Peter, looking towards heaven, prayed for them with tears that God, for His goodness, would deign to receive those betaking themselves to Him. And after he had prayed, and had instructed them to meet early, the next day, he dismissed the multitude. Then according to custom, having taken food, we went to sleep.

CHAP. LI. — PETER'S ACCESSIBILITY.

Peter, therefore, rising at the usual hour of the night, found us waking; and when, saluting us, in his usual manner, he had taken his seat, first of all Niceta said: "If you will permit me, my lord Peter, I have something to ask of you." Then Peter said: "I permit not only you, but all, and not only now, but always, that every one confess what moves him, and the part in his mind that is pained, in order that he may obtain healing. For things which are covered with silence, and are not made known to us, are cured with difficulty, like maladies of long standing; and therefore, since the medicine of seasonable and necessary discourse cannot easily be applied to those who keep silence, every one ought to declare in what respect his mind is feeble through ignorance. But to him who keeps silence, it belongs to God alone to give a remedy. We indeed also can do it, but by the lapse of a long time. For it is necessary that the discourse of doctrine, proceeding in order from the beginning, and meeting each single question, should disclose all things, and resolve and reach to all things, even to that which every one requires in his mind; but that, as I have said, can only be done in the course of a long time. Now, then, ask what you please."

CHAP. LII. — FALSE SIGNS AND MIRACLES.

Then Niceta said: "I give you abundant thanks, O most clement Peter; but this is what I desire to learn, how Simon, who is the enemy

---

[1] [This account of the close of the discussion is peculiar to the *Recognitions.* — R.]
[2] Matt. xviii. 7.
[3] Acts viii. 13.

of God, is able to do such and so great things? For indeed he told no lie in his declaration of what he has done." To this the blessed Peter thus answered : "God, who is one and true, has resolved to prepare good and faithful friends for His first begotten ; but knowing that none can be good, unless they have in their power that perception by which they may become good, that they may be of their own intent what they choose to be, — and otherwise they could not be truly good, if they were kept in goodness not by purpose, but by necessity, — has given to every one the power of his own will, that he may be what he wishes to be. And again, fore-seeing that that power of will would make some choose good things and others evil, and so that the human race would necessarily be divided into two classes, He has permitted each class to choose both a place and a king, whom they would. For the good King rejoices in the good, and the wicked one in the evil. And although I have expounded those things more fully to you, O Clement, in that treatise in which I dis-coursed on predestination and the end, yet it is fitting that I should now make clear to Niceta also, as he asks me, what is the reason that Simon, whose thoughts are against God, is able to do so great marvels.

CHAP. LIII. — SELF-LOVE THE FOUNDATION OF GOODNESS.

"First of all, then, he is evil, in the judgment of God, who will not inquire what is advanta-geous to himself. For how can any one love another, if he does not love himself? Or to whom will that man not be an enemy, who cannot be a friend to himself? In order, therefore, that there might be a distinction between those who choose good and those who choose evil, God has concealed that which is profitable to men, i.e., the possession of the kingdom of heaven, and has laid it up and hidden it as a secret treas-ure, so that no one can easily attain it by his own power or knowledge. Yet He has brought the report of it, under various names and opinions, through successive generations, to the hearing of all : so that whosoever should be lovers of good, hearing it, might inquire and discover what is profitable and salutary to them ; but that they should ask it, not from themselves, but from Him who has hidden it, and should pray that access and the way of knowledge might be given to them : which way is opened to those only who love it above all the good things of this world ; and on no other condition can any one even un-derstand it, however wise he may seem ; but that those who neglect to inquire what is profitable and salutary to themselves, as self-haters and self-enemies, should be deprived of its good things, as lovers of evil things.

CHAP. LIV. — GOD TO BE SUPREMELY LOVED.

"It behoves, therefore, the good to love that *way* above all things, that is, above riches, glory, rest, parents, relatives, friends, and everything in the world. But he who perfectly loves this pos-session of the kingdom of heaven, will un-doubtedly cast away all practice of evil habit, negligence, sloth, malice, anger, and such like. For if you prefer any of these to it, as loving the vices of your own lust more than God, you shall not attain to the possession of the heavenly kingdom ; for truly it is foolish to love anything more than God. For whether they be parents, they die ; or relatives, they do not continue ; or friends, they change. But God alone is eternal, and abideth unchangeable. He, therefore, who will not seek after that which is profitable to himself, is evil, to such an extent that his wick-edness exceeds the very prince of impiety. For he abuses the goodness of God to the purpose of his own wickedness, and pleases himself ; but the other neglects the good things of his own salvation, that by his own destruction he may please the evil one.

CHAP. LV. — TEN COMMANDMENTS CORRESPONDING TO THE PLAGUES OF EGYPT.

"On account of those, therefore, who by neglect of their own salvation please the evil one, and those who by study of their own profit seek to please the good One, ten things have been prescribed as a test to this present age, according to the number of the ten plagues which were brought upon Egypt. For when Moses, according to the commandment of God, demanded of Pharaoh that he should let the people go, and in token of his heavenly commis-sion showed signs, his rod being thrown upon the ground was turned into a serpent.[1] And when Pharaoh could not by these means be brought to consent, as having freedom of will, again the magicians seemed to do similar signs, by permission of God, that the purpose of the king might be proved from the freedom of his will, whether he would rather believe the signs wrought by Moses, who was sent by God, or those which the magicians rather seemed to work than actually wrought. For truly he ought to have understood from their very name that they were not workers of truth, because they were not called messengers of God, but magi-cians, as the tradition also intimates. More-over, they seemed to maintain the contest up to a certain point, and afterwards they confessed of themselves, and yielded to their superior.[2] Therefore the last plague is inflicted,[3] the de-

---

[1] Ex. vii., viii.
[2] Ex. viii. 19.
[3] Ex. xii.

struction of the first-born, and then Moses is commanded to consecrate the people by the sprinkling of blood; and so, gifts being presented, with much entreaty he is asked to depart with the people.

CHAP. LVI. — SIMON RESISTED PETER, AS THE MAGICIANS MOSES.

"In a similar transaction I see that I am even now engaged. For as then, when Moses exhorted the king to believe God, the magicians opposed him by a pretended exhibition of similar signs, and so kept back the unbelievers from salvation; so also now, when I have come forth to teach all nations to believe in the true God, Simon the magician resists me, acting in opposition to me, as they also did in opposition to Moses; in order that whosoever they be from among the nations that do not use sound judgment, they may be made manifest; but that those may be saved who rightly distinguish signs from signs." While Peter thus spoke, Niceta answered: "I beseech you that you would permit me to state whatever occurs to my mind." Then Peter, being delighted with the eagerness of his disciples, said: "Speak what you will."

CHAP. LVII. — MIRACLES OF THE MAGICIANS.

Then said Niceta: "In what respect did the Egyptians sin in not believing Moses, since the magicians wrought like signs, even although they were done rather in appearance than in truth? For if I had been there then, should I not have thought, from the fact that the magicians did like things to those which Moses did, either that Moses was a magician, or that the magicians wrought their signs by divine commission? For I should not have thought it likely that the same things could be effected by magicians, even in appearance, which he who was sent by God performed. And now, in what respect do they sin who believe Simon, since they see him do so great marvels? Or is it not marvellous to fly through the air, to be so mixed with fire as to become one body with it, to make statues walk, brazen dogs bark, and other such like things, which assuredly are sufficiently wonderful to those who know not how to distinguish? Yea, he has also been seen to make bread of stones. But if he sins who believes those who do signs, how shall it appear that he also does not sin who has believed our Lord for His signs and works of power?"

CHAP. LVIII. — TRUTH VEILED WITH LOVE.

Then said Peter: "I take it well that you bring the truth to the rule, and do not suffer hindrances of faith to lurk in your soul. For thus you can easily obtain the remedy. Do you remember that I said, that the worst of all things is when any one neglects to learn what is for his good?" Niceta answered: "I remember." Then Peter: "And again, that God has veiled His truth, that He may disclose it to those who faithfully follow Him?" "Neither," said Niceta, "have I forgotten this." Then said Peter: "What think you then? That God has buried His truth deep in the earth, and has heaped mountains upon it, that it may be found by those only who are able to dig down into the depths? It is not so; but as He has surrounded the mountains and the earth with the expanse of heaven, so hath He veiled the truth with the curtain of His own love, that he alone may be able to reach it, who has first knocked at the gate of divine love.

CHAP. LIX. — GOOD AND EVIL IN PAIRS.

"For, as I was beginning to say,[1] God has appointed for this world certain pairs; and he who comes first of the pairs is of evil, he who comes second, of good. And in this is given to every man an occasion of right judgment, whether he is simple or prudent. For if he is simple, and believes him who comes first, though moved thereto by signs and prodigies, he must of necessity, for the same reason, believe him who comes second; for he will be persuaded by signs and prodigies, as he was before. When he believes this second one, he will learn from him that he ought not to believe the first, who comes of evil; and so the error of the former is corrected by the emendation of the latter. But if he will not receive the second, because he has believed the first, he will deservedly be condemned as unjust; for unjust it is, that when he believed the first on account of his signs, he will not believe the second, though he bring the same, or even greater signs. But if he has not believed the first, it follows that he may be moved to believe the second. For his mind has not become so completely inactive but that it may be roused by the redoubling of marvels. But if he is prudent, he can make distinction of the signs. And if indeed he has believed in the first, he will be moved to the second by the increase in the miracles, and by comparison he will apprehend which are better; although clear tests *of miracles* are recognised by all learned men, as we have shown in the regular order of our discussion. But if any one, as being whole and not needing a physician, is not moved to the first, he will be drawn to the second by the very continuance of the thing, and will make a distinction of signs and marvels after this fashion; — he who is of

---

[1] [The substance of chaps. 59, 60, occurs in Homily II. 33, 34, just before the postponement of the discussion with Simon. — R.]

the evil one, the signs that he works do good to no one ; but those which the good man worketh are profitable to men.

CHAP. LX. — USELESSNESS OF PRETENDED MIRACLES.

" For tell me, I pray you, what is the use of showing statues walking, dogs of brass or stone barking, mountains dancing, of flying through the air, and such like things, which you say that Simon did ? But those *signs* which are of the good One, are directed to the advantage of men, as are those which were done by our Lord, who gave sight to the blind and hearing to the deaf, raised up the feeble and the lame, drove away sicknesses and demons, raised the dead, and did other like things, as you see also that I do. Those signs, therefore, which make for the benefit of men, and confer some good upon them, the wicked one cannot do, excepting only at the end of the world. For then it shall be permitted him to mix up with his signs some good ones, as the expelling of demons or the healing of diseases ; by this means going beyond his bounds, and being divided against himself, and fighting against himself, he shall be destroyed. And therefore the Lord has foretold, that in the last times there shall be such temptation, that, if it be possible, the very elect shall be deceived ; that is to say, that by the marks of signs being confused, even those must be disturbed who seem to be expert in discovering spirits and distinguishing miracles.

CHAP. LXI. — TEN PAIRS.

" The ten pairs [1] of which we have spoken have therefore been assigned to this world from the beginning of time. Cain and Abel were one pair. The second was the giants and Noah ; the third, Pharaoh and Abraham ; the fourth, the Philistines and Isaac ; the fifth, Esau and Jacob ; the sixth, the magicians and Moses the lawgiver ; the seventh, the tempter and the Son of man ; the eighth, Simon and I, Peter ; the ninth, all nations, and he who shall be sent to sow the word among the nations ; the tenth, Antichrist and Christ. Concerning these pairs we shall give you fuller information at another time." When Peter spoke thus, Aquila said : " Truly there is need of constant teaching, that one may learn what is true about everything."

CHAP. LXII. — THE CHRISTIAN LIFE.

But Peter said : " Who is he that is earnest toward instruction, and that studiously inquires into every particular, except him who loves his own soul to salvation, and renounces all the affairs of this world, that he may have leisure to attend to the word of God only ? Such is he whom alone the true Prophet deems wise, even he who sells all that he has and buys the one true pearl,[2] who understands what is the difference between temporal things and eternal, small and great, men and God. For he understands what is the eternal hope in presence of the true and good God. But who is he that loves God, save him who knows His wisdom ? And how can any one obtain knowledge of God's wisdom, unless he be constant in hearing His word ? Whence it comes, that he conceives a love for Him, and venerates Him with worthy honour, pouring out hymns and prayers to Him, and most pleasantly resting in these, accounteth it his greatest damage if at any time he speak or do aught else even for a moment of time ; because, in reality, the soul which is filled with the love of God can neither look upon anything except what pertains to God, nor, by reason of love of Him, can be satisfied with meditating upon those things which it knows to be pleasing to Him. But those who have not conceived affection for Him, nor bear His love lighted up in their mind, are as it were placed in darkness and cannot see light ; and therefore, even before they begin to learn anything of God, they immediately faint as though worn out by labour ; and filled with weariness, they are straightway hurried by their own peculiar habits to those words with which they are pleased. For it is wearisome and annoying to such persons to hear anything about God ; and that for the reason I have stated, because their mind has received no sweetness of divine love."

CHAP. LXIII. — A DESERTER FROM SIMON'S CAMP.

While Peter was thus speaking, the day dawned ; and, behold, one of the disciples of Simon came, crying out : [3] " I beseech thee, O Peter, receive me, a wretch, who have been deceived by Simon the magician, to whom I gave heed as to a heavenly God, by reason of those miracles which I saw him perform. But when I heard your discourses, I began to think him a man, and indeed a wicked man ; nevertheless, when he went out from this I alone followed him, for I had not yet clearly perceived his impieties. But when he saw me following him, he called me blessed, and led me to his house ; and about the middle of the night he said to me, ' I shall make you better than all men, if you will remain with me even till the end.' When I had promised him this, he demanded of me an oath of perseverance ; and having got this, he placed upon my shoulders some of his polluted and accursed secret things, that I might carry them, and or-

---

[2] Matt. xiii. 46.
[3] [This incident is narrated only in the *Recognitions.* — R.]

dered me to follow him. But when we came to the sea, he went aboard a boat which happened to be there, and took from my neck what he had ordered me to carry. And as he came out a little after, bringing nothing with him, he must have thrown it into the sea. Then he asked me to go with him, saying that he was going to Rome, and that there he would please the people so much, that he should be reckoned a god, and publicly gifted with divine honours. 'Then,' said he, 'if you wish to return hither, I shall send you back, loaded with all riches, and upheld by various services.' When I heard this, and saw nothing in him in accordance with this profession, but perceived that he was a magician and a deceiver, I answered : 'Pardon me, I pray you ; for I have a pain in my feet, and therefore I am not able to leave Cæsarea. Besides, I have a wife and little children, whom I cannot leave by any means.' When he heard this, he charged me with sloth, and set out towards Dora, saying, 'You will be sorry, when you hear what glory I shall get in the city of Rome.' And after this he set out for Rome, as he said ; but I hastily returned hither, entreating you to receive me to penitence, because I have been deceived by him."

CHAP. LXIV. — DECLARATION OF SIMON'S WICKED-NESS.

When he who had returned from Simon had thus spoken, Peter ordered him to sit down in the court. And he himself going forth, and seeing immense crowds, far more than on the previous days, stood in his usual place ; and pointing out him who had come, began to discourse as follows : "This man whom I point out to you, brethren, has just come to me, telling me of the wicked practices of Simon, and how he has thrown the implements of his wickedness into the sea, not induced to do so by repentance, but being afraid lest, being detected, he should be subjected to the public laws. And he asked this man, as he tells me, to remain with him, promising him immense gifts ; and when he could not persuade him to do so, he left him, reproaching him for sluggishness, and set out for Rome." When Peter had intimated this to the crowd, the man himself who had returned from Simon stood up, and began to state to the people everything relating to Simon's crimes. And when they were shocked by the things which they heard that Simon had done by his magical acts, Peter said :[1]

CHAP. LXV. — PETER RESOLVES TO FOLLOW SIMON.

"Be not, my brethren, distressed by those things that have been done, but give heed to the future : for what is passed is ended ; but the things which threaten are dangerous to those who shall fall in with them. For offences shall never be wanting in this world,[2] so long as the enemy is permitted to act according to his will ; in order that the prudent and those who understood his wiles may be conquerors in the contests which he raises against them ; but that those who neglect to learn the things that pertain to the salvation of their souls, may be taken by him with merited deceptions. Since, therefore, as you have heard, Simon has gone forth to preoccupy the ears of the Gentiles who are called to salvation, it is necessary that I also follow upon his track, so that whatever disputations he raises may be corrected by us. But inasmuch as it is right that greater anxiety should be felt concerning you who are already received within the walls of life, — for if that which has been actually acquired perish, a positive loss is sustained ; while with respect to that which has not yet been acquired, if it can be got, there is so much gain ; but if not, the only loss is that there is no gain ; — in order, therefore, that you may be more and more confirmed in the truth, and the nations who are called to salvation may in no way be prevented by the wickedness of Simon, I have thought good to ordain Zacchæus as pastor over you,[3] and to remain with you myself for three months ; and so to go to the Gentiles, lest through our delaying longer, and the crimes of Simon stalking in every direction, they should become incurable."

CHAP. LXVI. — ZACCHÆUS MADE BISHOP OF CÆSA-REA ; PRESBYTERS AND DEACONS ORDAINED.

At this announcement all the people wept, hearing that he was going to leave them ; and Peter, sympathizing with them, himself also shed tears ; and looking up to heaven, he said : "To Thee, O God, who hast made heaven and earth, and all things that are in them, we pour out the prayer of supplication, that Thou wouldest comfort those who have recourse to Thee in their tribulation. For by reason of the affection that they have towards Thee, they do love me who have declared to them Thy truth. Wherefore guard them with the right hand of Thy compassion ; for neither Zacchæus nor any other man can be a sufficient guardian to them." When he had said this, and more to the same effect, he laid his hands upon Zacchæus, and prayed that he might blamelessly discharge the duty of his bishopric. Then he ordained twelve presbyters and four deacons, and said : "I have

---

[1] [With the remainder of the book compare Homily III. 58–73. The resemblance is general rather than particular. — R.]

[2] Matt. xviii. 7, Luke xvii. 1.

[3] [In the *Homilies* full details are given respecting the choice of Zacchæus (who is identified with the publican in Luke xix.), his unwillingness to serve; precepts are also added concerning Church officers. — R.]

ordained you this Zacchæus as a bishop, knowing that he has the fear of God, and is expert in the Scriptures. You ought therefore to honour him as holding the place of Christ, obeying him for your salvation, and knowing that whatever honour and whatever injury is done to him, redounds to Christ, and from Christ to God. Hear him therefore with all attention, and receive from him the doctrine of the faith; and from the presbyters the monitions of life; and from the deacons the order of discipline. Have a religious care of widows; vigorously assist orphans; take pity on the poor; teach the young modesty; — and in a word, sustain one another as circumstances shall demand; worship God, who created heaven and earth; believe in Christ; love one another; be compassionate to all; and fulfil charity not only in word, but in act and deed."

CHAP. LXVII. — INVITATION TO BAPTISM.

When he had given them these and such like precepts, he made proclamation to the people, saying: "Since I have resolved to stay three months with you, if any one desires it, let him be baptized; that, stripped of his former evils, he may for the future, in consequence of his own conduct, become heir of heavenly blessings, as a reward for his good actions. Whosoever will, then, let him come to Zacchæus and give his name to him, and let him hear from him the mysteries of the kingdom of heaven. Let him attend to frequent fastings, and approve himself in all things, that at the end of these three months he may be baptized on the day of the festival. But every one of you shall be baptized in ever flowing waters, the name of the Trine Beatitude being invoked over him; he being first anointed with oil sanctified by prayer, that so at length, being consecrated by these things, he may attain a perception of holy things." [1]

CHAP. LXVIII. — TWELVE SENT BEFORE HIM.

And when he had spoken at length on the subject of baptism, he dismissed the crowd, and betook himself to his usual place of abode; and there, while the twelve stood around him (viz. Zacchæus and Sophonias, Joseph and Michæus, Eleazar and Phineas, Lazarus and Eliseus, I Clement and Nicodemus, Niceta and Aquila), he addressed us to the following effect: "Let us, my brethren, consider what is right; for it is our duty to bring some help to the nations, which are called to salvation. You have yourselves heard that Simon has set out, wishing to anticipate our journey. Him we should have followed step by step, that wheresoever he tries

to subvert any, we might immediately confute him. But since it appears to me to be unjust to forsake those who have been already converted to God, and to bestow our care upon those who are still afar off, I think it right that I should remain three months with those in this city who have been turned to the faith, and should strengthen them; and yet that we should not neglect those who are still far off, lest haply, if they be long infected with the power of pernicious doctrine, it be more difficult to recover them. Therefore I wish (only, however, if you also think it right), that for Zacchæus, whom we have now ordained bishop, Benjamin the son of Saba be substituted; and for Clement (whom I have resolved to have always by me, because, coming from the Gentiles, he has a great desire to hear the word of God) there be substituted Ananias the son of Safra; and for Niceta and Aquila, who have been but lately converted to the faith of Christ, Rubelus the brother of Zacchæus, and Zacharias the builder. I wish, therefore, to complete the number of twelve by substituting these four for the other four, that Simon may feel that I in them am always with him." [2]

CHAP. LXIX. — ARRANGEMENTS APPROVED BY ALL THE BRETHREN.

Having therefore separated me, Clement, and Niceta and Aquila, he said to those twelve: "I wish you the day after to-morrow to proceed to the Gentiles, and to follow in the footsteps of Simon, that you may inform me of all his proceedings. You will also inquire diligently the sentiments of every one, and announce to them that I shall come to them without delay; and, in short, in all places instruct the Gentiles to expect my coming." When he had spoken these things, and others to the same effect, he said: "You also, my brethren, if you have anything to say to these things, say on, lest haply it be not right which seems good to me alone." Then all, with one voice applauding him, said: "We ask you rather to arrange everything according to your own judgment, and to order what seems good to yourself; for this we think to be the perfect work of piety, if we fulfil what you command."

CHAP. LXX. — DEPARTURE OF THE TWELVE.

Therefore, on the day appointed, when they had ranged themselves before Peter, they said: "Do not think, O Peter, that it is a small grief to us that we are to be deprived of the privilege of hearing you for three months; but since it is

---

[1] This may be translated, "that he may partake of holy things." Cotelerius supposes the words "holy things" to mean the body and blood of Christ.

[2] [Compare with this chapter the lists in book ii 1 and in Homily II. 1. The special significance attached to the number twelve is peculiar to this passage. — R.]

good for us to do what you order, we shall most readily obey. We shall always retain in our hearts the remembrance of your face; and so we set out actively, as you have commanded us." Then he, having poured out a prayer to the Lord for them, dismissed them. And when those twelve who had been sent forward had gone, Peter entered, according to custom, and stood in the place of disputation. And a multitude of people had come together, even a larger number than usual; and all with tears gazed upon him, by reason of what they had heard from him the day before, that he was about to go forth on account of Simon. Then, seeing them weeping, he himself also was similarly affected, although he endeavoured to conceal and to restrain his tears. But the trembling of his voice, and the interruption of his discourse, betrayed that he was distressed by similar emotion.

CHAP. LXXI. — PETER PREPARES THE CÆSAREANS FOR HIS DEPARTURE.

However, rubbing his forehead with his hand, he said: "Be of good courage, my brethren, and comfort your sorrowful hearts by means of counsel, referring all things to God, whose will alone is to be fulfilled and to be preferred in all things. For let us suppose for a moment, that by reason of the affection that we have towards you, we should act against His will, and remain with you, is He not able, by sending death upon me, to appoint to me a longer separation from you? And therefore it is better for us to carry out this shorter separation with His will, as those to whom it is prescribed to obey God in all things. Hence you also ought to obey Him with like submission, inasmuch as you love me from no other reason than on account of your love of Him. As friends of God, therefore, acquiesce in His will; but also judge yourselves what is right. Would it not have seemed wicked, if, when Simon was deceiving you, I had been detained by the brethren in Jerusalem, and had not come to you, and that although you had Zacchæus among you, a good and eloquent man? So now also consider that it would be wicked, if, when Simon has gone forth to assail the Gentiles, who are wholly without a defender, I should be detained by you, and should not follow him. Wherefore let us see to it, that we do not, by an unreasonable affection, accomplish the will of the wicked one.

CHAP. LXXII. — MORE THAN TEN THOUSAND BAPTIZED.

"Meantime I shall remain with you three months, as I promised. Be ye constant in hearing the word; and at the end of that time, if any are able and willing to follow us, they may

do so, if duty will admit of it. And when I say *if duty will admit*, I mean that no one by his departure must sadden any one who ought not to be saddened, as by leaving parents who ought not to be left, or a faithful wife, or any other person to whom he is bound to afford comfort for God's sake." Meantime, disputing and teaching day by day, he filled up the time appointed with the labour of teaching; and when the festival day arrived, upwards of ten thousand were baptized.

CHAP. LXXIII. — TIDINGS OF SIMON.

But in those days a letter was received from the brethren who had gone before, in which were detailed the crimes of Simon, how going from city to city he was deceiving multitudes, and everywhere maligning Peter, so that, when he should come, no one might afford him a hearing. For he asserted that Peter was a magician, a godless man, injurious, cunning, ignorant, and professing impossible things. "For," says he, "he asserts that the dead shall rise again, which is impossible. But if any one attempts to confute him, he is cut off by secret snares by him, through means of his attendants. Wherefore, I also," says he, "when I had vanquished him and triumphed over him, fled for fear of his snares, lest he should destroy me by incantations, or compass my death by plots." They intimated also that he mainly stayed at Tripolis.[1]

CHAP. LXXIV. — FAREWELL TO CÆSAREA.

Peter therefore ordered the letter to be read to the people; and after the reading of it, he addressed them and gave them full instructions about everything, but especially that they should obey Zacchæus, whom he had ordained bishop over them. Also he commended the presbyters and the deacons to the people, and not less the people to them. And then, announcing that he should spend the winter at Tripolis, he said: "I commend you to the grace of God, being about to depart to-morrow, with God's will. But during the whole three months which he spent at Cæsarea, for the sake of instruction, whatever he discoursed of in the presence of the people in the day-time, he explained more fully and perfectly in the night, in private to us, as more faithful and completely approved by him. And at the same time he commanded me, because he understood that I carefully stored in my memory what I heard, to commit to writing whatever seemed worthy of record, and to send it to you, my lord James, as also I did, in obedience to his command.

---

[1] [In Homily III. 58 Simon is represented as doing great miracles at Tyre. Peter follows him there, but finds that he has gone. The long discussions with him are assigned to Laodicea. See *Homilies*, xvi., etc. — R.]

CHAP. LXXV. — CONTENTS OF CLEMENT'S DE-
SPATCHES TO JAMES.

The first book,[1] therefore, of those that I formerly sent to you, contains an account of the
true Prophet, and of the peculiarity of the understanding of the law, according to what the
tradition of Moses teacheth. The second contains an account of the beginning, and whether
there be one beginning or many, and that the
law of the Hebrews knows what immensity is.
The third, concerning God, and those things
that have been ordained by Him. The fourth,
that though there are many that are called gods,
there is but one true God, according to the testimonies of the Scriptures. The fifth, that there
are two heavens, one of which is that visible
firmament which shall pass away, but the other
is eternal and invisible. The sixth, concerning
good and evil; and that all things are subjected
to good by the Father; and why, and how, and
whence evil is, and that it co-operates with good,
but not with a good purpose; and what are the
signs of good, and what those of evil; and what
is the difference between duality and conjunction. The seventh, what are the things which
the twelve apostles treated of in the presence
of the people in the temple. The eighth, con-

cerning the words of the Lord which seem to
be contradictory, but are not; and what is the
explanation of them. The ninth, that the law
which has been given by God is righteous and
perfect, and that it alone can make pure. The
tenth, concerning the carnal birth of men, and
concerning the generation which is by baptism;
and what is the succession of carnal seed in
man; and what is the account of his soul, and
how the freedom of the will is in it, which, seeing it is not unbegotten, but made, could not be
immoveable from good. Concerning these several subjects, therefore, whatever Peter discoursed
at Cæsarea, according to his command, as I have
said, I have sent you written in ten volumes.[2]
But on the next day, as had been determined,
we set out from Cæsarea with some faithful men,
who had resolved to accompany Peter.

---

[1] Cotelerius remarks that these ten books previously sent to James
(if they ever existed) ought to be distinguished from the ten books of
the *Recognitions*, which were addressed to the same James, but
written after those now mentioned.

[2] [This chapter furnishes some positive evidence that the *Recognitions* are based upon an earlier work. The topics here named do
not correspond with those of the *Homilies*, except in the most general way. Hence this passage does not favour the theory that the
author of the *Recognitions* had the *Homilies* before him when he
wrote. Even in xvi.-xix. of the later work, which Uhlhorn regarded as the nucleus of the entire literature, the resemblances are
slight. As already intimated (see Introductory Notice, p. 71), Uhlhorn has abandoned this theory.

On the other hand, the chapter bears marks of being the conclusion to a complete document. It can therefore be urged, in support of the new view of Lehmann (*Die Clementinischen Schriften*,
Gotha, 1869), that the *Recognitions* are made up of two parts (books
i.-iii., iv.-x.) by two different authors, both parts being based on
earlier documents. This chapter is regarded by Hilgenfeld as containing a general outline of the *Kerygma Petri*, a Jewish-Christian
document of Roman origin. In i. 27-72 he finds a remnant of this
document incorporated in the *Recognitions*. — R.]

BOOK IV.

CHAP. I. — HALT AT DORA.

HAVING set out from Cæsarea on the way to
Tripolis, we made our first stoppage at a small
town called Dora, because it was not far distant;
and almost all those who had believed through
the preaching of Peter could scarcely bear to be
separated from him, but walked along with us,
again and again gazing upon him, again and
again embracing him, again and again conversing with him, until we came to the inn. On the
following day we came to Ptolemais, where we
stayed ten days; and when a considerable number had received the word of God, we signified
to some of them who seemed particularly atten-
tive, and wished to detain us longer for the sake
of instruction, that they might, if so disposed,
follow us to Tripolis. We acted in the same
way at Tyre, and Sidon, and Berytus, and announced to those who desired to hear further
discourses, that we were to spend the winter at

Tripolis.[1] Therefore, as all those who were anxious followed Peter from each city, we were a
great multitude of elect ones when we entered
into Tripolis. On our arrival, the brethren who
had been sent before met us before the gates of
the city; and taking us under their charge, conducted us to the various lodgings which they
had prepared. Then there arose a commotion

---

[1] [In books iv.-vi. the scene is laid at Tripolis. The same city
is the locality to which Homilies VIII.-XI. are assigned. The intervening portion (Homilies IV.-VII.) gives the details of the journey
here alluded to, telling of various discourses at Tyre. Some of the
matter of these discourses occurs in the *Recognitions*, but under different circumstances. The heathen disputants are not the same.

The parallelisms of the portions assigned to Tripolis are as follows:
book iv. has its counterpart in Homily VIII. and in much of Homily
IX.; book v. has a parallel in Homily X. and in parts of XI.;
book vi. in its general outline resembles Homily XI.

The discourses of the Apostle as given in the *Recognitions*
are more orderly and logical than those in the *Homilies*. The views
presented differ somewhat, in accordance with the general character
of the two works. Much of the matter in the *Recognitions* occurs in
a different order in the *Homilies*, but the internal evidence seems to
point to the priority of the former. Both might be different manipu-
lations of a common documentary source, but that theory is not
necessarily applicable to these portions of the literature. — R.]

in the city, and a great assemblage of persons desirous to see Peter.[1]

CHAP. II. — RECEPTION IN THE HOUSE OF MARO.

And when we had come to the house of Maro, in which preparation had been made for Peter, he turned to the crowd, and told them that he would address them the day after to-morrow. Therefore the brethren who had been sent before assigned lodgings to all who had come with us. Then, when Peter had entered into the house of Maro, and was asked to partake of food, he answered that he would by no means do so, until he had ascertained whether all those that had accompanied him were provided with lodgings. Then he learned from the brethren who had been sent before, that the citizens had received them not only hospitably, but with all kindness, by reason of their love towards Peter; so much so, that several were disappointed because there were no guests for them; for that all had made such preparations, that even if many more had come, there would still have been a deficiency of guests for the hosts, not of hosts for the guests.

CHAP. III. — SIMON'S FLIGHT.

Thereupon Peter was greatly delighted, and praised the brethren, and blessed them, and requested them to remain with him. Then, when he had bathed in the sea, and had taken food, he went to sleep in the evening; and rising, as usual, at cock-crow, while the evening light was still burning, he found us all awake. Now there were in all sixteen of us, viz. Peter and I, Clement, Niceta and Aquila, and those twelve who had preceded us.[2] Saluting us, then, as was his wont, Peter said: "Since we are not taken up with others to-day, let us be taken up with ourselves. I shall tell you what took place at Cæsarea after your departure, and you shall tell us of the doings of Simon here." And while the conversation was going on on these subjects, at daybreak some of the members of the family came in and told Peter that Simon, when he heard of Peter's arrival, departed in the night, on the way to Syria. They also stated that the crowds thought that the day which he had said was to intervene was a very long time for their affection, and that they were standing in impatience before the gate, conversing among themselves about those things which they wished to hear, and that they hoped that they should by all means see him before the time appointed; and that as the day became lighter the multitudes were increasing, and that they were trusting confidently, whatever they might be presuming upon, that they should hear a discourse from him.

"Now then," said they, "instruct us to tell them what seems good to you; for it is absurd that so great a multitude should have come together, and should depart with sadness, through no answer being returned to them. For they will not consider that it is they that have not waited for the appointed day, but rather they will think that you are slighting them."

CHAP. IV. — THE HARVEST PLENTEOUS.

Then Peter, filled with admiration, said:[3] "You see, brethren, how every word of the Lord spoken prophetically is fulfilled. For I remember that He said, 'The harvest indeed is plenteous, but the labourers are few; ask therefore the Lord of the harvest, that He would send out labourers into His harvest.'[4] Behold, therefore, the things which are foretold in a mystery are fulfilled. But whereas He said also, 'Many shall come from the east and the west, from the north and the south, and shall recline in the bosom of Abraham, and Isaac, and Jacob;'[5] this also is, as you see, in like manner fulfilled. Wherefore I entreat you, my fellow-servants and helpers, that you would learn diligently the order of preaching, and the ways of absolutions, that ye may be able to save the souls of men, which by the secret power of God acknowledge whom they ought to love, even before they are taught. For you see that these men, like good servants, long for him whom they expect to announce to them the coming of their Lord, that they may be able to fulfil His will when they have learned it. The desire, therefore, of hearing the word of God, and inquiring into His will, they have from God; and this is the beginning of the gift of God, which is given to the Gentiles, that by this they may be able to receive the doctrine of truth.

CHAP. V. — MOSES AND CHRIST.

"For so also it was given to the people of the Hebrews from the beginning, that they should love Moses, and believe his word; whence also it is written: 'The people believed God, and Moses His servant.'[6] What, therefore, was of peculiar gift from God toward the nation of the Hebrews, we see now to be given also to those who are called from among the Gentiles to the faith. But the method of works is put into the power and will of every one, and this is their own; but to have an affection towards a teacher of truth, this is a gift of the heavenly Father. But salvation is in this, that you do His will of whom you have conceived a love and affection through the gift of God; lest that saying of His

---

[1] ["Maroones," Homily VIII. 1. — R.]
[2] [Comp. Homily VIII. 3. — R.]

[3] [With chaps. 4–11 compare Homily VIII. 4–11. The correspondence is quite close. — R.]
[4] Matt. ix. 37, 38.
[5] Luke xiii. 29; Matt. viii. 11.
[6] Ex. xiv. 31.

be addressed to you which He spoke, 'Why call ye me Lord, Lord, and do not what I say?'[1] It is therefore the peculiar gift bestowed by God upon the Hebrews, that they believe Moses; and the peculiar gift bestowed upon the Gentiles is that they love Jesus. For this also the Master intimated, when He said, 'I will confess to Thee, O Father, Lord of heaven and earth, because Thou hast concealed these things from the wise and prudent, and hast revealed them to babes.'[2] By which it is certainly declared, that the people of the Hebrews, who were instructed out of the law, did not know Him; but the people of the Gentiles have acknowledged Jesus, and venerate Him; on which account also they shall be saved, not only acknowledging Him, but also doing His will. But he who is of the Gentiles, and who has it of God to believe Moses, ought also to have it of his own purpose to love Jesus also. And again, the Hebrew, who has it of God to believe Moses, ought to have it also of his own purpose to believe in Jesus; so that each of them, having in himself something of the divine gift, and something of his own exertion, may be perfect by both. For concerning such an one our Lord spoke, as of a rich man, 'Who brings forth from his treasures things new and old.'[3]

CHAP. VI. — A CONGREGATION.

"But enough has been said of these things; for time presses, and the religious devotion of the people invites us to address them." And when he had thus spoken, he asked where there was a suitable place for discussion. And Maro said: "I have a very spacious hall[4] which can hold more than five hundred men, and there is also a garden within the house; or if it please you to be in some public place, all would prefer it, for there is nobody who does not desire at least to see your face." Then Peter said: "Show me the hall, or the garden." And when he had seen the hall, he went in to see the garden also; and suddenly the whole multitude, as if some one had called them, rushed into the house, and thence broke through into the garden, where Peter was already standing, selecting a fit place for discussion.

CHAP. VII. — THE SICK HEALED.

But when he saw that the crowds had, like the waters of a great river, poured over the narrow passage, he mounted upon a pillar which happened to stand near the wall of the garden, and first saluted the people in a religious manner. But some of those who were present, and who had been for a long time distressed by demons,

threw themselves on the ground, while the unclean spirits entreated that they might be allowed but for one day to remain in the bodies that they had taken possession of. But Peter rebuked them, and commanded them to depart; and they went out without delay. After these, others who had been afflicted with long-standing sicknesses asked Peter that they might receive healing; and he promised that he would entreat the Lord for them as soon as his discourse of instruction was completed. But as soon as he promised, they were freed from their sicknesses;[5] and he ordered them to sit down apart, with those who had been freed from the demons, as after the fatigue of labour. Meantime, while this was going on, a vast multitude assembled, attracted not only by the desire of hearing Peter, but also by the report of the cures which had been accomplished. But Peter, beckoning with his hand to the people to be still, and settling the crowds in tranquillity, began to address them as follows: —

CHAP. VIII. — PROVIDENCE VINDICATED.

"It seems to me necessary, at the outset of a discourse concerning the true worship of God, first of all to instruct those who have not as yet acquired any knowledge of the subject, that throughout the divine providence must be maintained to be without blame, by which the world is ruled and governed. Moreover, the reason of the present undertaking, and the occasion offered by those whom the power of God has healed, suggest this subject for a beginning, viz. to show that for good reason very many persons are possessed of demons, that so the justice of God may appear. For ignorance will be found to be the mother of almost all evils. But now let us come to the reason.

CHAP. IX. — STATE OF INNOCENCE A STATE OF ENJOYMENT.

"When God had made man after His own image and likeness, He grafted into His work a certain breathing and odour of His divinity, that so men, being made partakers of His Only-begotten, might through Him be also friends of God and sons of adoption. Whence also He Himself, as the true Prophet, knowing with what actions the Father is pleased, instructed them in what way they might obtain that privilege. At that time, therefore, there was among men only one worship of God — a pure mind and an uncorrupted spirit. And for this reason every creature kept an inviolable covenant with the human race. For by reason of their reverence of the Creator, no sickness, or bodily disorder, or corruption of food, had power over them;

---

[1] Luke vi. 46.
[2] Matt. xi. 25.　[Luke x. 21; comp. Homily XVIII. 15-17. — R.]
[3] Matt. xiii. 52.
[4] Ædes, in the singular, probably a temple.

[5] [In Homilies VIII. 8, 24, IX. 24, the healing takes place after the discourses. — R.]

whence it came to pass, that a life of a thousand years did not fall into the frailty of old age.

CHAP. X. — SIN THE CAUSE OF SUFFERING.

"But when men, leading a life void of distress, began to think that the continuance of good things was granted them not by the divine bounty, but by the chance of things, and to accept as a debt of nature, not as a gift of God's goodness, their enjoyment without any exertion of the delights of the divine complaisance, — men, being led by these things into contrary and impious thoughts, came at last, at the instigation of idleness, to think that the life of gods was theirs by nature, without any labours or merits on their part. Hence they go from bad to worse, to believe that neither is the world governed by the providence of God, nor is there any place for virtues, since they knew that they themselves possessed the fulness of ease and delights, without the assignment of any works previously, and without any labours were treated as the friends of God.

CHAP. XI. — SUFFERING SALUTARY.

"By the most righteous judgment of God, therefore, labours and afflictions are assigned as a remedy to men languishing in the vanity of such thoughts. And when labour and tribulations came upon them, they were excluded from the place of delights and amenity. Also the earth began to produce nothing to them without labour; and then men's thoughts being turned in them, they were warned to seek the aid of their Creator, and by prayers and vows to ask for the divine protection. And thus it came to pass, that the worship of God, which they had neglected by reason of their prosperity, they recovered through their adversity; and their thoughts towards God, which indulgence had perverted, affliction corrected. So therefore the divine providence, seeing that this was more profitable to man, removed from them the ways of benignity and abundance, as being hurtful, and introduced the way of vexation and tribulation.[1]

CHAP. XII. — TRANSLATION OF ENOCH.

"But[2] that He might show that these things were done on account of the ungrateful, He translated to immortality a certain one of the first race of men, because He saw that he was not unmindful of His grace, and because he hoped to call on the name of God;[3] while the rest, who were so ungrateful that they could not be amended and corrected even by labours and tribulations, were condemned to a terrible death. Yet amongst them also He found a certain one, who was righteous with his house,[4] whom He preserved, having enjoined him to build an ark, in which he and those who were commanded to go with him might escape, when all things should be destroyed by a deluge: in order that, the wicked being cut off by the overflow of waters, the world might receive a purification; and he who had been preserved for the continuance of the race, being purified by water, might anew repair the world.

CHAP. XIII. — ORIGIN OF IDOLATRY.

"But when all these things were done, men turned again to impiety;[5] and on this account a law was given by God to instruct them in the manner of living. But in process of time, the worship of God and righteousness were corrupted by the unbelieving and the wicked, as we shall show more fully by and by. Moreover, perverse and erratic religions were introduced, to which the greater part of men gave themselves up, by occasion of holidays and solemnities, instituting drinkings and banquets, following pipes, and flutes, and harps, and diverse kinds of musical instruments, and indulging themselves in all kinds of drunkenness and luxury. Hence every kind of error took rise; hence they invented groves and altars, fillets and victims, and after drunkenness they were agitated as if with mad emotions. By this means power was given to the demons to enter into minds of this sort, so that they seemed to lead insane dances and to rave like Bacchanalians; hence were invented the gnashing of teeth, and bellowing from the depth of their bowels; hence a terrible countenance and a fierce aspect in men, so that he whom drunkenness had subverted and a demon had instigated, was believed by the deceived and the erring to be filled with the Deity.

CHAP. XIV. — GOD BOTH GOOD AND RIGHTEOUS.

"Hence, since so many false and erratic religions have been introduced into the world,[6] we have been sent, as good merchants, bringing unto you the worship of the true God, handed down from the fathers, and preserved; as the seeds of which we scatter these words amongst you, and place it in your choice to choose what seems to you to be right. For if you receive those things which we bring you, you shall not

---

[1] [In Homily VIII. 12–16 there is inserted a curious account of the fall of man and angels, and of a race of giants. — R.]
[2] [Chap. 12 has no exact parallel in the *Homilies*, but Homily VIII. 17 resembles it. — R.]
[3] There seems to be here a mixing up of the translation of *Enoch* with the statement that in the days of *Enos* men began to call on the name of the Lord; Gen. iv. 26.

[4] Gen. vi. 9.
[5] [There is a similar chapter in Homily IX. 7, but in a discourse on the following day. — R.]
[6] [With chaps. 14–22 compare Homily IX. 8–18. The general outline is the same, and the resemblances quite close in the larger part of both passages. — R.]

only be able yourselves to escape the incursions of the demon, but also to drive them away from others; and at the same time you shall obtain the rewards of eternal good things. But those who shall refuse to receive those things which are spoken by us, shall be subject in the present life to diverse demons and disorders of sicknesses, and their souls after their departure from the body shall be tormented for ever. For God is not only good, but also just; for if He were always good, and never just to render to every one according to his deeds, goodness would be found to be injustice. For it were injustice if the impious and the pious were treated by Him alike.

CHAP. XV. — HOW DEMONS GET POWER OVER MEN.

"Therefore demons, as we have just said, when once they have been able, by means of opportunities afforded them, to convey themselves through base and evil actions into the bodies of men, if they remain in them a long time through their own negligence, because they do not seek after what is profitable to their souls, they necessarily compel them for the future to fulfil the desires of the demons who dwell in them. But what is worst of all, at the end of the world, when that demon shall be consigned to eternal fire, of necessity the soul also which obeyed him, shall with him be tortured in eternal fires, together with its body which it hath polluted.

CHAP. XVI. — WHY THEY WISH TO POSSESS MEN.

"Now that the demons are desirous of occupying the bodies of men, this is the reason. They are spirits having their purpose turned to wickedness. Therefore by immoderate eating and drinking, and lust, they urge men on to sin, but only those who entertain the purpose of sinning, who, while they seem simply desirous of satisfying the necessary cravings of nature, give opportunity to the demons to enter into them, because through excess they do not maintain moderation. For as long as the measure of nature is kept, and legitimate moderation is preserved, the mercy of God does not give them liberty to enter into men. But when either the mind falls into impiety, or the body is filled with immoderate meat or drink, then, as if invited by the will and purpose of those who thus neglect themselves, they receive power as against those who have broken the law imposed by God.

CHAP. XVII. — THE GOSPEL GIVES POWER OVER DEMONS.

"You see, then, how important is the acknowledgment of God, and the observance of the divine religion, which not only protects those who believe from the assaults of the demon, but also gives them command over those who rule over others. And therefore it is necessary for you, who are of the Gentiles, to betake yourselves to God, and to keep yourselves from all uncleanness, that the demons may be expelled, and God may dwell in you. And at the same time, by prayers, commit yourselves to God, and call for His aid against the impudence of the demons; for 'whatever things ye ask, believing, ye shall receive.'[1] But even the demons themselves, in proportion as they see faith grow in a man, in that proportion they depart from him, residing only in that part in which something of infidelity still remains; but from those who believe with full faith, they depart without any delay. For when a soul has come to the faith of God, it obtains the virtue of heavenly water, by which it extinguishes the demon like a spark of fire.

CHAP. XVIII. — THIS POWER IN PROPORTION TO FAITH.

"There is therefore a measure of faith, which, if it be perfect, drives the demon perfectly from the soul; but if it has any defect, something on the part of the demon still remains in the portion of infidelity; and it is the greatest difficulty for the soul to understand when or how, whether fully or less fully, the demon has been expelled from it. For if he remains in any quarter, when he gets an opportunity, he suggests thoughts to men's hearts; and they, not knowing whence they come, believe the suggestions of the demons, as if they were the perceptions of their own souls. Thus they suggest to some to follow pleasure by occasion of bodily necessity; they excuse the passionateness of others by excess of gall; they colour over the madness of others by the vehemence of melancholy; and even extenuate the folly of some as the result of abundance of phlegm. But even if this were so, still none of these could be hurtful to the body, except from the excess of meats and drinks; because, when these are taken in excessive quantities, their abundance, which the natural warmth is not sufficient to digest, curdles into a sort of poison, and it, flowing through the bowels and all the veins like a common sewer, renders the motions of the body unhealthy and base. Wherefore moderation is to be attained in all things, that neither may place be given to demons, nor the soul, being possessed by them, be delivered along with them to be tormented in eternal fires.

CHAP. XIX. — DEMONS INCITE TO IDOLATRY.

"There is also another error of the demons, which they suggest to the senses of men, that

[1] Matt. xxi. 22.

they should think that those things which they suffer, they suffer from such as are called gods, in order that thereby, offering sacrifices and gifts, as if to propitiate them, they may strengthen the worship of false religion, and avoid us who are interested in their salvation, that they may be freed from error; but this they do, as I have said, not knowing that these thing are suggested to them by demons, for fear they should be saved. It is therefore in the power of every one, since man has been made possessed of free-will, whether he shall hear us to life, or the demons to destruction. Also to some, the demons, appearing visibly under various figures, sometimes throw out threats, sometimes promise relief from sufferings, that they may instil into those whom they deceive the opinion of their being gods, and that it may not be known that they are demons. But they are not concealed from us, who know the mysteries of the creation, and for what reason it is permitted to the demons to do those things in the present world; how it is allowed them to transform themselves into what figures they please, and to suggest evil thoughts, and to convey themselves, by means of meats and of drink consecrated to them, into the minds or bodies of those who partake of it, and to concoct vain dreams to further the worship of some idol.

CHAP. XX. — FOLLY OF IDOLATRY.

"And yet who can be found so senseless as to be persuaded to worship an idol, whether it be made of gold or of any other metal? To whom is it not manifest that the metal is just that which the artificer pleased? How then can the divinity be thought to be in that which would not be at all unless the artificer had pleased? Or how can they hope that future things should be declared to them by that in which there is no perception of present things? For although they should divine something, they should not straightway be held to be gods; for divination is one thing, divinity is another. For the Pythons also seem to divine, yet they are not gods; and, in short, they are driven out of men by Christians. And how can that be God which is put to flight by a man? But perhaps you will say, What as to their effecting cures, and their showing how one can be cured? On this principle, physicians ought also to be worshipped as gods, for they cure many; and in proportion as any one is more skilful, the more he will cure.

CHAP. XXI. — HEATHEN ORACLES.

"Whence it is evident that they, since they are demoniac spirits, know some things both more quickly and more perfectly *than men;* for they are not retarded in their learning by the

heaviness of a body. And therefore they, as being spirits, know without delay and without difficulty what physicians attain after a long time and by much labour. It is not wonderful, therefore, if they know somewhat more than men do; but this is to be observed, that what they know they do not employ for the salvation of souls, but for the deception of them, that by means of it they may indoctrinate them in the worship of false religion. But God, that the error of so great deception might not be concealed, and that He Himself might not seem to be a cause of error in permitting them so great licence to deceive men by divinations, and cures, and dreams, has of His mercy furnished men with a remedy, and has made the distinction of falsehood and truth patent to those who desire to know. This, therefore, is that distinction: what is spoken by the true God, whether by prophets or by diverse visions, is always true; but what is foretold by demons is not always true. It is therefore an evident sign that those things are not spoken by the true God, in which at any time there is falsehood; for in truth there is never falsehood. But in the case of those who speak falsehoods, there may occasionally be a slight mixture of truth, to give as it were seasoning to the falsehoods.

CHAP. XXII. — WHY THEY SOMETIMES COME TRUE.

"But if any one say, What is the use of this, that they should be permitted even sometimes to speak truth, and thereby so much error be introduced amongst men? let him take this for answer: If they had never been allowed to speak any truth, then they would not foretell anything at all; while if they did not foretell, they would not be known to be demons. But if demons were not known to be in this world, the cause of our struggle and contest would be concealed from us, and we should suffer openly what was done in secret, that is, if the power were granted to them of only acting against us, and not of speaking. But now, since they sometimes speak truth, and sometimes falsehood, we ought to acknowledge, as I have said, that their responses are of demons, and not of God, with whom there is never falsehood.

CHAP. XXIII. — EVIL NOT IN SUBSTANCE.

"But if any one, proceeding more curiously, inquire: What then was the use of God's making these evil things, which should have so great a tendency to subvert the minds of men?[1] To one proposing such a question, we answer that we must first of all inquire whether there is any

---

[1] [Chaps. 23-26 have no exact parallel in the *Homilies;* comp. book iii. 16-26. The questions of the origin of evil and of free-will are more fully treated in the *Recognitions.* — R.]

evil in substance. And although it would be sufficient to say to him that it is not suitable that the creature judge the Creator, but that to judge the work of another belongs to him who is either of equal skill or equal power; yet, to come directly to the point, we say absolutely that there is no evil in substance. But if this be so, then the Creator of substance is vainly blamed.

CHAP. XXIV. — WHY GOD PERMITS EVIL.

"But you will meet me by saying, Even if it has come to this through freedom of will, was the Creator ignorant that those whom He created would fall away into evil? He ought therefore not to have created those who, He foresaw, would deviate from the path of righteousness. Now we tell those who ask such questions, that the purpose of assertions of the sort made by us is to show why the wickedness of those who as yet were not, did not prevail over the goodness of the Creator.[1] For if, wishing to fill up the number and measure of His creation, He had been afraid of the wickedness of those who were to be, and like one who could find no other way of remedy and cure, except only this, that He should refrain from His purpose of creating, lest the wickedness of those who were to be should be ascribed to Him; what else would this show but unworthy suffering and unseemly feebleness on the part of the Creator, who should so fear the actings of those who as yet were not, that He refrained from His purposed creation?

CHAP. XXV. — EVIL BEINGS TURNED TO GOOD ACCOUNT.

"But, setting aside these things, let us consider this earnestly, that God the Creator of the universe, foreseeing the future differences of His creation, foresaw and provided diverse ranks and different offices to each of His creatures, according to the peculiar movements which were produced from freedom of will; so that while all men are of one substance in respect of the method of creation, there should yet be diversity in ranks and offices, according to the peculiar movements of minds, to be produced from liberty of will. Therefore He foresaw that there would be faults in His creatures; and the method of His justice demanded that punishment should follow faults, for the sake of amendment. It behoved, therefore, that there should be ministers of punishment, and yet that freedom of will should draw them into that order. Moreover, those also must have enemies to conquer, who

had undertaken the contests for the heavenly rewards. Thus, therefore, neither are those things destitute of utility which are thought to be evil, since the conquered unwillingly acquire eternal rewards for those by whom they are conquered. But let this suffice on these points, for in process of time even more secret things shall be disclosed.

CHAP. XXVI. — EVIL ANGELS SEDUCERS.

"Now therefore, since you do not yet understand how great darkness of ignorance surrounds you, meantime I wish to explain to you whence the worship of idols began in this world. And by idols, I mean those lifeless images which you worship, whether made of wood, or earthenware, or stone, or brass, or any other metals: of these the beginning was in this wise. Certain angels, having left the course of their proper order, began to favour the vices of men,[2] and in some measure to lend unworthy aid to their lust, in order that by these means they might indulge their own pleasures the more; and then, that they might not seem to be inclined of their own accord to unworthy services, taught men that demons could, by certain arts — that is, by magical invocations — be made to obey men; and so, as from a furnace and workshop of wickedness, they filled the whole world with the smoke of impiety, the light of piety being withdrawn.

CHAP. XXVII. — HAM THE FIRST MAGICIAN.

"For these and some other causes, a flood was brought upon the world,[3] as we have said already, and shall say again; and all who were upon the earth were destroyed, except the family of Noah, who survived, with his three sons and their wives. One of these, by name Ham, unhappily discovered the magical act, and handed down the instruction of it to one of his sons, who was called Mesraim, from whom the race of the Egyptians and Babylonians and Persians are descended. Him the nations who then existed called Zoroaster,[3] admiring him as the first author of the magic art; under whose name also many books on this subject exist. He therefore, being much and frequently intent upon the stars, and wishing to be esteemed a god among them, began to draw forth, as it were, certain sparks from the stars, and to show them to men, in order that the rude and ignorant might be astonished, as with a miracle; and desiring to increase this estimation of him, he attempted these things again and again, until he was set on fire, and consumed by the demon himself, whom he accosted with too great importunity.

---

[1] There is considerable variety of reading in this sentence, and the precise meaning is somewhat obscure. The general sense, however, is sufficiently evident, that if God had refrained from creating those who, He foresaw, would fall into evil, this would have been to subject His goodness to their evil.

[2] [Comp. Homily VIII. 13. — R.]
[3] [With chaps. 27-31 compare Homily IX. 3-7. The resemblances are quite close. See also book i. 30, 31. — R.]

CHAP. XXVIII. — TOWER OF BABEL.

" But the foolish men who were then, whereas they ought to have abandoned the opinion which they had conceived of him, inasmuch as they had seen it confuted by his mortal punishment, extolled him the more. For raising a sepulchre to his honour, they went so far as to adore him as a friend of God, and one who had been removed to heaven in a chariot of lightning, and to worship him as if he were a living star. Hence also his name was called Zoroaster after his death — that is, *living star* — by those who, after one generation, had been taught to speak the Greek language. In fine, by this example, even now many worship those who have been struck with lightning, honouring them with sepulchres, and worshipping them as friends of God. But this man was born in the fourteenth generation, and died in the fifteenth, in which the tower was built, and the languages of men were divided into many.

CHAP. XXIX. — FIRE-WORSHIP OF THE PERSIANS.

" First among whom is named a certain king Nimrod, the magic art having been handed down to him as by a flash, whom the Greeks also called Ninus, and from whom the city of Nineveh took its name. Thus, therefore, diverse and erratic superstitions took their beginning from the magic art. For, because it was difficult to draw away the human race from the love of God, and attach them to deaf and lifeless images, the magicians made use of higher efforts, that men might be turned to erratic worship, by signs among the stars, and motions brought down as it were from heaven, and by the will of God. And those who had been first deceived, collecting the ashes of Zoroaster, — who, as we have said, was burnt up by the indignation of the demon, to whom he had been too troublesome, — brought them to the Persians, that they might be preserved by them with perpetual watching, as divine fire fallen from heaven, and might be worshipped as a heavenly God.

CHAP. XXX. — HERO-WORSHIP.

" By a like example, other men in other places built temples, set up statues, instituted mysteries and ceremonies and sacrifices, to those whom they had admired, either for some arts or for virtue, or at least had held in very great affection ; and rejoiced, by means of all things belonging to gods, to hand down their fame to posterity ; and that especially, because, as we have already said, they seemed to be supported by some phantasies of magic art, so that by invocation of demons something seemed to be done and moved by them towards the deception of men. To

these they add also certain solemnities, and drunken banquets, in which men might with all freedom indulge ; and demons, conveyed into them in the chariot of repletion, might be mixed with their very bowels, and holding a place there, might bind the acts and thoughts of men to their own will. Such errors, then, having been introduced from the beginning, and having been aided by lust and drunkenness, in which carnal men chiefly delight, the religion of God, which consisted in continence and sobriety, began to become rare amongst men, and to be well-nigh abolished.

CHAP. XXXI. — IDOLATRY LED TO ALL IMMORALITY.

" For whereas at first, men worshipping a righteous and all-seeing God, neither dared sin nor do injury to their neighbours, being persuaded that God sees the actions and movements of every one ; when religious worship was directed to lifeless images, concerning which they were certain that they were incapable of hearing, or sight, or motion, they began to sin licentiously, and to go forward to every crime, because they had no fear of suffering anything at the hands of those whom they worshipped as gods. Hence the madness of wars burst out ; hence plunderings, rapines, captivities, and liberty reduced to slavery ; each one, as he could, satisfied his lust and his covetousness, although no power can satisfy covetousness. For as fire, the more fuel it gets, is the more extensively kindled and strengthened, so also the madness of covetousness is made greater and more vehement by means of those things which it acquires.

CHAP. XXXII. — INVITATION.

" Wherefore begin now with better understanding to resist yourselves in those things which you do not rightly desire ; [1] if so be that you can in any way repair and restore in yourselves that purity of religion and innocence of life which at first were bestowed upon man by God, that thereby also the hope of immortal blessings may be restored to you. And give thanks to the bountiful Father of all, by Him whom He has constituted King of peace, and the treasury of unspeakable honours, that even at the present time your sins may be washed away with the water of the fountain, or river, or even sea : the threefold name of blessedness being called over you, that by it not only evil spirits may be driven out, if any dwell in you, but also that, when you have forsaken your sins, and have with entire faith and entire purity of mind believed in God, you may drive out wicked spirits and demons from others also, and may be able

[1] [To chaps. 32, 33, a close parallel is found in Homily IX. 19-21. — R.]

to set others free from sufferings and sicknesses. For the demons themselves know and acknowledge those who have given themselves up to God, and sometimes they are driven out by the mere presence of such, as you saw a little while ago, how, when we had only addressed to you the word of salutation, straightway the demons, on account of their respect for our religion, began to cry out, and could not bear our presence even for a little.

CHAP. XXXIII. — THE WEAKEST CHRISTIAN MORE POWERFUL THAN THE STRONGEST DEMON.

"Is it, then, that we are of another and a superior nature, and that therefore the demons are afraid of us? Nay, we are of one and the same nature with you, but we differ in religion. But if you will also be *like us*, we do not grudge it, but rather we exhort you, and wish you to be assured, that when the same faith and religion and innocence of life shall be in you that is in us, you will have equal and the same power and virtue against demons, through God rewarding your faith. For as he who has soldiers under him, although he may be inferior, and they superior to him in strength, yet 'says to this one, Go, and he goeth; and to another, Come, and he cometh; and to another, Do this, and he doeth it;'[1] and this he is able to do, not by his own power, but by the fear of Cæsar; so every faithful one commands the demons, although they seem to be much stronger than men, and that not by means of his own power, but by means of the power of God, who has put them in subjection. For even that which we have just spoken of, that Cæsar is held in awe by all soldiers, and in every camp, and in his whole kingdom, though he is but one man, and perhaps feeble in respect of bodily strength, this is not effected but by the power of God, who inspires all with fear, that they may be subject to one.

CHAP. XXXIV. — TEMPTATION OF CHRIST.

"This we would have you know assuredly, that a demon has no power against a man, unless one voluntarily submit himself to his desires.[2] Whence even that one who is the prince of wickedness, approached Him who, as we have said, is appointed of God King of peace, tempting Him, and began to promise Him all the glory of the world; because he knew that when he had offered this to others, for the sake of deceiving them, they had worshipped him. Therefore, impious as he was, and unmindful of himself, which indeed is the special peculiarity of wickedness, he presumed that he should be

worshipped by Him by whom he knew that he was to be destroyed. Therefore our Lord, confirming the worship of one God, answered him: 'It is written, Thou shalt worship the Lord thy God, and Him only shalt thou serve.'[3] And he, terrified by this answer, and fearing lest the true religion of the one and true God should be restored, hastened straightway to send forth into this world false prophets, and false apostles, and false teachers, who should speak indeed in the name of Christ, but should accomplish the will of the demon.

CHAP. XXXV. — FALSE APOSTLES.

"Wherefore observe the greatest caution, that you believe no teacher, unless he bring from Jerusalem the testimonial of James the Lord's brother, or of whosoever may come after him.[4] For no one, unless he has gone up thither, and there has been approved as a fit and faithful teacher for preaching the word of Christ, — unless, I say, he brings a testimonial thence, is by any means to be received. But let neither prophet nor apostle be looked for by you at this time, besides us. For there is one true Prophet, whose words we twelve apostles preach; for He is the accepted year of God, having us apostles as His twelve months. But for what reason the world itself was made, or what diversities have occurred in it, and why our Lord, coming for its restoration, has chosen and sent us twelve apostles, shall be explained more at length at another time. Meantime He has commanded us to go forth to preach, and to invite you to the supper of the heavenly King, which the Father hath prepared for the marriage of His Son, and that we should give you wedding garments, that is, the grace of baptism;[5] which whosoever obtains, as a spotless robe with which he is to enter to the supper of the King, ought to beware that it be not in any part of it stained with sin, and so he be rejected as unworthy and reprobate.

CHAP. XXXVI. — THE GARMENTS UNSPOTTED.

"But the ways in which this garment may be spotted are these: If any one withdraw from God the Father and Creator of all, receiving another teacher besides Christ, who alone is the faithful and true Prophet, and who has sent us twelve apostles to preach the word; if any one think otherwise than worthily of the substance of the Godhead, which excels all things; — these are the things which even fatally pollute the garment of baptism. But the things which pollute it in actions are these: murders, adulteries, hatreds, avarice, evil ambition. And the things which

---

[1] Matt. viii. 9. [Luke vii. 8. — R.]
[2] [The close of this discourse, chaps. 34-37, resembles that of the first at Tripolis, in Homily VIII. 21, 24. As already indicated, much of Homily IX. finds a parallel in this book. — R.]

[3] Matt. iv. 10. [Luke iv. 8. — R.]
[4] [This is peculiar in this connection. There is, at least, a suggestion of anti-Pauline spirit in its teaching. — R.]
[5] [Matt. xxii. 2-14.]

pollute at once the soul and the body are these : to partake of the table of demons, that is, to taste things sacrificed, or blood, or a carcase which is strangled,[1] and if there be aught else which has been offered to demons. Be this therefore the first step to you of three ; which step brings forth thirty commands, and the second sixty, and the third a hundred,[2] as we shall expound more fully to you at another time."

CHAP. XXXVII. — THE CONGREGATION DISMISSED.

When he had thus spoken, and had charged them to come to the same place in good time on the following day, he dismissed the crowds ; and when they were unwilling to depart, Peter said to them : " Do me this favour on account of the fatigue of yesterday's journey ; and now go away, and meet in good time to-morrow." And so they departed with joy. But Peter, commanding me to withdraw a little for the purpose of prayer,[3] afterwards ordered the couches to be spread in the part of the garden which was covered with shade ; and every one, according to custom, recognising the place of his own rank, we took food. Then, as there was still some portion of the day left, he conversed with us concerning the Lord's miracles ; and when evening was come, he entered his bed-chamber and went to sleep.

---

[1] [In Homily VII. 8 a similar injunction is given, at Sidon. The language in both places recalls Acts xv. 20 and 1 Cor. x. 21. But most of the chapter is peculiar to the *Recognitions.* — R.]

[2] Matt xiii. 23. [Comp. Mark iv. 8, 20, where the order of the numbers corresponds with that of the *Recognitions.* The interpretation is a fanciful one, indicating not only Judaistic legalism, but the notion of esoteric teaching. The passage shows Ebionitic tendencies. — R.]

[3] Clement, being not yet baptized, is represented as not permitted to join with the disciples, even in prayer. [Comp. i. 19, ii. 70–72. This separation is indicated in the *Homilies,* but more emphasis is placed upon it in the *Recognitions.* — R.]

BOOK V.

CHAP. I. — PETER'S SALUTATION.

BUT on the following day,[1] Peter rising a little earlier than usual, found us asleep ; and when he saw it, he gave orders that silence should be kept for him, as though he himself wished to sleep longer, that we might not be disturbed in our rest. But when we rose refreshed with sleep, we found him, having finished his prayer, waiting for us in his bed-chamber. And as it was already dawn, he addressed us shortly, saluting us according to his custom, and forthwith proceeded to the usual place for the purpose of teaching ; and when he saw that many had assembled there, having invoked peace upon them according to the first religious form, he began to speak as follows : —

CHAP. II. — SUFFERING THE EFFECT OF SIN.

" God, the Creator of all, at the beginning made man after His own image, and gave him dominion over the earth and sea, and over the air ; as the true Prophet has told us, and as the very reason of things instructs us : for man alone is rational, and it is fitting that reason should rule over the irrational. At first, therefore, while he was still righteous, he was superior to all disorders and all frailty ; but when he sinned, as we taught you yesterday, and became the servant of sin, he became at the same time liable to frailty. This therefore is written, that men may know that, as by impiety they have been made liable to suffer, so by piety they may be made free from suffering ; and not only free from suffering, but by even a little faith in God be able to cure the sufferings of others. For thus the true Prophet promised us, saying, ' Verily I say to you, that if ye have faith as a grain of mustard seed, ye shall say to this mountain, Remove hence, and it shall remove.' [2] Of this saying you have yourselves also had proofs ; for you saw yesterday how at our presence the demons removed and were put to flight, with those sufferings which they had brought upon men.

CHAP. III. — FAITH AND UNBELIEF.

" Whereas therefore some men suffer, and others cure those who suffer, it is necessary to know the cause at once of the suffering and the cure ; and this is proved to be nought else than unbelief on the part of the sufferers, and faith on the part of those who cure them. For unbelief, while it does not believe that there is to be a judgment by God, affords licence to sin, and sin makes men liable to sufferings ; but faith, believing that there is to be a judgment of God, restrains men from sin ; and those who do not sin are not only free from demons and sufferings, but can also put to flight the demons and sufferings of others.

---

[1] [Book v. has a partial parallel in Homily X., which is assigned to the second day at Tripolis. The matter here is more extensive. Chaps. 1, 2, show some resemblance to Homily X. 3–6. — R.]

[2] Matt. xvii. 20.

CHAP. IV. — IGNORANCE THE MOTHER OF EVILS.

" From [1] all these things, therefore, it is con-cluded that all evil springs from ignorance ; and ignorance herself, the mother of all evils, is sprung from carelessness and sloth, and is nour-ished, and increased, and rooted in the senses of men by negligence ; and if any one teach that she is to be put to flight, she is with difficulty and indignantly torn away, as from an ancient and hereditary abode. And therefore we must labour for a little, that we may search out the presumptions of ignorance, and cut them off by means of knowledge, especially in those who are preoccupied with some erroneous opinions, by means of which ignorance is the more firmly rooted in them, as under the appearance of a certain kind of knowledge ; for nothing is worse than for one to believe that he knows what he is ignorant of, and to maintain that to be true which is false. This is as if a drunk man should think himself to be sober, and should act indeed in all respects as a *drunk* man, and yet think himself to be sober, and should wish to be called so by others. Thus, therefore, are those also who do not know what is true, yet hold some appear-ance of knowledge, and do many evil things as if they were good, and hasten destruction as if it were to salvation.

CHAP. V. — ADVANTAGES OF KNOWLEDGE.

" Wherefore we must, above all things, hasten to the knowledge of the truth, that, as with a light kindled thereat, we may be able to dispel the darkness of errors : for ignorance, as we have said, is a great evil ; but because it has no substance, it is easily dispelled by those who are in earnest. For ignorance is nothing else than not knowing what is good for us ; once know this, and ignorance perishes. Therefore the knowl-edge of truth ought to be eagerly sought after ; and no one can confer it except the true Prophet. For this is the gate of life to those who will enter, and the road of good works to those going to the city of salvation.

CHAP. VI. — FREE-WILL.

" Whether any one, truly hearing the word of of the true Prophet, is willing or unwilling to receive it, and to embrace His burden, that is, the precepts of life, he has either in his power, for we are free in will.[2] For if it were so, that those who hear had it not in their power to do otherwise than they had heard, there were some power of nature in virtue of which it were not free to him to pass over to another opinion. Or

if, again, no one of the hearers could at all re-ceive it, this also were a power of nature which should compel the doing of some one thing, and should leave no place for the other course. But now, since it is free for the mind to turn its judgment to which side it pleases, and to choose the way which it approves, it is clearly manifest that there is in men a liberty of choice.

CHAP. VII. — RESPONSIBILITY OF KNOWLEDGE.

" Therefore, before any one hears what is good for him, it is certain that he is ignorant ; and being ignorant, he wishes and desires to do what is not good for him ; wherefore he is not judged for that. But when once he has heard the causes of his error, and has received the method of truth, then, if he remain in those errors with which he had been long ago preoc-cupied, he shall rightly be called into judgment, to suffer punishment, because he has spent in the sport of errors that portion of life which was given him to be spent in living well. But he who, hearing those things, willingly receives them, and is thankful that the teaching of good things has been brought to him, inquires more eagerly, and does not cease to learn, until he ascertains whether there be truly another world, in which rewards are prepared for the good. And when he is assured of this, he gives thanks to God because He has shown him the light of truth ; and for the future directs his actions in all good works, for which he is assured that there is a reward prepared in the world to come ; while he constantly wonders and is astonished at the errors of other men, and that no one sees the truth which is placed before his eyes. Yet he himself, rejoicing in the riches of wisdom which he hath found, desires insatiably to enjoy them, and is delighted with the practice of good works ; hastening to attain, with a clean heart and a pure conscience, the world to come, when he shall be able even to see God, the king of all.

CHAP. VIII. — DESIRES OF THE FLESH TO BE SUB-DUED.

" But the sole cause of our wanting and being deprived of all these things is ignorance. For while men do not know how much good there is in knowledge, they do not suffer the evil of ignorance to be removed from them ; for they know not how great a difference is involved in the change of one of these things for the other. Wherefore I counsel every learner willingly to lend his ear to the word of God, and to hear with love of the truth what we say, that his mind, receiving the best seed, may bring forth joyful fruits by good deeds. For if, while I teach the things which pertain to salvation, any one refuses to receive them, and strives to resist

---

[1] [Chaps. 4, 5, resemble somewhat Homily X. 2, which contains a preliminary discourse of the Apostle to his followers. — R.]
[2] [Here again the doctrine of free-will is pressed, the *Homilies* containing no parallel. Chaps. 6–13 have no corresponding passage in Homily X. — R.]

them with a mind occupied by evil opinions, he shall have the cause of his perishing, not from us, but from himself. For it is his duty to examine with just judgment the things which we say, and to understand that we speak the words of truth, that, knowing how things are, and directing his life in good actions, he may be found a partaker of the kingdom of heaven, subjecting to himself the desires of the flesh, and becoming lord of them, that so at length he himself also may become the pleasant possession of the Ruler of all.

CHAP. IX. — THE TWO KINGDOMS.

" For he who persists in evil, and is the servant of evil, cannot be made a portion of good so long as he persists in evil, because from the beginning, as we have said, God instituted two kingdoms, and has given to each man the power of becoming a portion of that kingdom to which he shall yield himself to obey. And since it is decreed by God that no one man can be a servant of both kingdoms, therefore endeavour with all earnestness to betake yourselves to the covenant and laws of the good King. Wherefore also the true Prophet, when He was present with us, and saw some rich men negligent with respect to the worship of God, thus unfolded the truth of this matter: ' No one,' said He, ' can serve two masters ; ye cannot serve God and mammon ; ' [1] calling riches, in the language of His country, *mammon*.

CHAP. X. — JESUS THE TRUE PROPHET.

" He therefore is the true Prophet, who appeared to us, as you have heard, in Judæa, who, standing in public places, by a simple command made the blind see, the deaf hear, cast out demons, restored health to the sick, and life to the dead ; and since nothing was impossible to Him, He even perceived the thoughts of men, which is possible for none but God only. He proclaimed the kingdom of God ; and we believed Him as a true Prophet in all that He spoke, deriving the confirmation of our faith not only from His words, but also from His works ; and also because the sayings of the law, which many generations before had set forth His coming, were fulfilled in Him ; and the figures of the doings of Moses, and of the patriarch Jacob before him, bore in all respects a type of Him. It is evident also that the time of His advent, that is, the very time at which He came, was foretold by them ; and, above all, it was contained in the sacred writings, that He was to be waited for by the Gentiles. And all these things were equally fulfilled in Him.

CHAP. XI. — THE EXPECTATION OF THE GENTILES.

" But that which a prophet of the Jews foretold, that He was to be waited for by the Gentiles,[2] confirms above measure the faith of truth in Him. For if he had said that He was to be waited for by the Jews, he would not have seemed to prophesy anything extraordinary, that He whose coming had been promised for the salvation of the world should be the object of hope to the people of the same tribe with Himself, and to His own nation : for that this would take place, would seem rather to be a matter of natural inference than one requiring the grandeur of a prophetic utterance. But now, whereas the prophets say that all that hope which is set forth concerning the salvation of the world, and the newness of the kingdom which is to be established by Christ, and all things which are declared concerning Him are to be transferred to the Gentiles ; the grandeur of the prophetic office is confirmed, not according to the sequence of things, but by an incredible fulfilment of the prophecy. For the Jews from the beginning had understood by a most certain tradition that this man should at some time come, by whom all things should be restored ; and daily meditating and looking out for His coming, when they saw Him amongst them, and accomplishing the signs and miracles, as had been written of Him, being blinded with envy, they could not recognise Him when present, in the hope of whom they rejoiced while He was absent ; yet the few of us who were chosen by Him understood it.

CHAP. XII. — CALL OF THE GENTILES.

" But this happened by the providence of God, that the knowledge of this good One should be handed over to the Gentiles, and those who had never heard of Him, nor had learned from the prophets, should acknowledge Him, while those who had acknowledged Him in their daily meditations should not know Him. For, behold, by you who are now present, and desire to hear the doctrine of His faith, and to know what, and how, and of what sort is His coming, the prophetic truth is fulfilled. For this is what the prophets foretold, that He is to be sought for by you, who never heard of Him.[3] And, therefore, seeing that the prophetic sayings are fulfilled even in yourselves, you rightly believe in Him alone, you rightly wait for Him, you rightly inquire concerning Him, that you not only may wait for Him, but also believing, you may obtain the inheritance of His kingdom ;

---

[1] Matt. vi. 24.

[2] Gen. xlix. 10. [This detailed statement of the call of the Gentiles is peculiar to the *Recognitions;* comp. i. 42. Such passages seem to indicate a tendency less anti-Pauline than that of the *Homilies*, yet the christology and soteriology are Ebionitic. — R].

[3] Isa. lxv. 1.

according to what Himself said, that every one is made the servant of him to whom he yields subjection.[1]

CHAP. XIII. — INVITATION OF THE GENTILES.

"Wherefore awake, and take to yourselves our Lord and God, even that Lord who is Lord both of heaven and earth, and conform yourselves to His image and likeness, as the true Prophet Himself teaches, saying, 'Be ye merciful, as also your heavenly Father is merciful, who makes His sun to rise upon the good and the evil, and rains upon the just and the unjust.'[2] Imitate Him, therefore, and fear Him, as the commandment is given to men, 'Thou shalt worship the Lord thy God, and Him only shalt thou serve.'[3] For it is profitable to you to serve this Lord alone, that through Him knowing the one God, ye may be freed from the many whom ye vainly feared. For he who fears not God the Creator of all, but fears those whom he himself with his own hands hath made, what does he do but make himself subject to a vain and senseless fear, and render himself more vile and abject than those very things, the fear of which he has conceived in his mind? But rather, by the goodness of Him who inviteth you, return to your former nobleness, and by good deeds show that you bear the image of your Creator, that by contemplation of His likeness ye may be believed to be even His sons.

CHAP. XIV. — IDOLS UNPROFITABLE.

"Begin,[4] therefore, to cast out of your minds the vain ideas of idols, and your useless and empty fears, that at the same time you may also escape the condition of unrighteous bondage. For those have become your lords, who could not even have been profitable servants to you. For how should lifeless images seem fit even to serve you, when they can neither hear, nor see, nor feel anything? Yea, even the material of which they are made, whether it be gold or silver, or even brass or wood, though it might have profited you for necessary uses, you have rendered wholly inefficient and useless by fashioning gods out of it. We therefore declare to you the true worship of God, and at the same time warn and exhort the worshippers, that by good deeds they imitate Him whom they worship, and hasten to return to His image and likeness, as we said before.

CHAP. XV. — FOLLY OF IDOLATRY.

"But I should like if those who worship idols would tell me if they wish to become like to those whom they worship? Does any one of you wish to see in such sort as they see? or to hear after the manner of their hearing? or to have such understanding as they have? Far be this from any of my hearers! For this were rather to be thought a curse and a reproach to a man, who bears in himself the image of God, although he has lost the likeness. What sort of gods, then, are they to be reckoned, the imitation of whom would be execrable to their worshippers, and to have whose likeness would be a reproach? What then? Melt your useless images, and make useful vessels. Melt the unserviceable and inactive metal, and make implements fit for the use of men. But, says one, human laws do not allow us.[5] He says well; for it is human laws, and not their own power, that prevents it. What kind of gods, then, are those which are defended by human laws, and not by their own energies? And so also they are preserved from thieves by watch-dogs and the protection of bolts, at least if they be of silver, or gold, or even of brass; for those that are of stone and earthenware are protected by their own worthlessness, for no one will steal a stone or a crockery god. Hence those seem to be the more miserable whose more precious metal exposes them to the greater danger. Since, then, they can be stolen, since they must be guarded by men, since they can be melted, and weighed out, and forged with hammers, ought men possessed of understanding to hold them as gods?

CHAP. XVI. — GOD ALONE A FIT OBJECT OF WORSHIP.

"Oh! into what wretched plight the understanding of men has fallen! For if it is reckoned the greatest folly to fear the dead, what shall we judge of those who fear something that is worse than the dead are? For those images are not even to be reckoned among the number of the dead, because they were never alive. Even the sepulchres of the dead are preferable to them, since, although they are now dead, yet they once had life; but those whom you worship never possessed even such base life as is in all, the life of frogs and owls. But why say more about them, since it is enough to say to him who adores them: Do you not see that he whom you adore sees not, hear that he whom you adore hears not, and understand that he understands not? — for he is the work of man's hand, and necessarily is void of understanding. You therefore worship a god without sense, whereas every one who has sense believes that not even those things are to be worshipped which have been made by God and have sense,[6] such as the sun, moon, and

[1] John viii. 34.
[2] Luke vi. 36; Matt. v. 45.
[3] Deut. vi. 13; Matt. iv. 10.
[4] [The parallel with Homily X. recurs at this chapter, and continues for several chapters. — R.]

[5] [This, with the more specific statement of Homily X. 8, points to an early date. — R.]
[6] It was a very prevalent opinion among the ancient philosophers, that the heavenly bodies have some kind of life and intelligence.

stars, and all things that are in heaven and upon earth. For they think it reasonable, that not those things which have been made for the service of the world, but the Creator of those things themselves, and of the whole world, should be worshipped. For even these things rejoice when He is adored and worshipped, and do not take it well that the honour of the Creator should be bestowed on the creature. For the worship of God alone is acceptable *to them*, who alone is uncreated, and all things also are His creatures. For as it belongs to him who alone is uncreated to be God, so everything that has been created is not truly God.

CHAP. XVII. — SUGGESTIONS OF THE OLD SERPENT.

"Above all, therefore, you ought to understand the deception of the old serpent [1] and his cunning suggestions, who deceives you as it were by prudence, and as by a sort of reason creeps through your senses ; and beginning at the head, he glides through your inner marrow, accounting the deceiving of you a great gain. Therefore he insinuates into your minds opinions of gods of whatsoever kinds, only that he may withdraw you from the faith of one God, knowing that your sin is his comfort. For he, for his wickedness, was condemned from the beginning to eat dust, for that he caused to be again resolved into dust him who had been taken from the dust, even till the time when your souls shall be restored, being brought through the fire ; as we shall instruct you more fully at another time. From him, therefore, proceed all the errors and doubts, by which you are driven from the faith and belief of one God.

CHAP. XVIII. — HIS FIRST SUGGESTION.

"And first of all he suggests to men's thoughts not to hear the words of truth, by which they might put to flight the ignorance of those things which are evils. And this he does, as by the presentation of another knowledge, making a show of that opinion which very many hold, to think that they shall not be held guilty if they have been in ignorance, and that they shall not be called to account for what they have not heard ; and thereby he persuades them to turn aside from hearing the word. But I tell you, in opposition to this, that ignorance is in itself a most deadly poison, which is sufficient to ruin the soul without any aid from without. And therefore there is no one who is ignorant who shall escape through his ignorance, but it is certain that he shall perish. For the power of sin

naturally destroys the sinner. But since the judgment shall be according to reason, the cause and origin of ignorance shall be inquired into, as well as of every sin. For he who is unwilling to know how he may attain to life, and prefers to be in ignorance lest he thereby be made guilty, from this very fact is judged as if he knew and had knowledge. For he knew what it was that he was unwilling to hear ; and the cunning obtained by the artifice of the serpent will avail him nothing for an excuse, for he will have to do with Him to whom the heart is open. But that you may know that ignorance of itself brings destruction, *I assure you that* when the soul departs from the body, if it leave it in ignorance of Him by whom it was created, and from whom in this world it obtained all things that were necessary for its uses, it is driven forth from the light of His kingdom as ungrateful and unfaithful.

CHAP. XIX. — HIS SECOND SUGGESTION.

"Again, the wicked serpent suggests another opinion to men, which many of you are in the habit of bringing forward, — that there is, as we say, one God, who is Lord of all ; but these also, they say, are gods. For as there is one Cæsar, and he has under him many judges, — for example, prefects, consuls, tribunes, and other officers, — in like manner we think, that while there is one God greater than all, yet still that these gods are ordained in this world, after the likeness of those officers of whom we have spoken, subject indeed to that greater God, yet ruling us and the things that are in this world. In answer to this, I shall show you how, in those very things which you propose for deception, you are confuted by the reasons of truth. You say that God occupies the place of Cæsar, and those who are called gods represent His judges and officers. Hold then, as you have adduced it, by the example of Cæsar ; and know that, as one of Cæsar's judges or administrators, as prefects, proconsuls, generals, or tribunes, may lawfully take the name of Cæsar, — or else both he who should take it and those who should confer it should be destroyed together, — so also in this case you ought to observe, that if any one give the name of God to any but Himself, and he accept it, they shall partake one and the same destruction, by a much more terrible fate than the servants of Cæsar. For he who offends against Cæsar shall undergo temporal destruction ; but he who offends against Him who is the sole and true God, shall suffer eternal punishment, and that deservedly, as having injured by a wrongful condition the name which is unique. [2]

---

[1] [Comp. book ii. 45. In Homily X. 10, etc., the influence of the serpent is spoken of, but the discourse here is much fuller. There is, however, a general agreement in outline between chaps. 17–22 here and Homily X. 10–21. — R.]

[2] The writer means, that insult is offered to that name which belongs to God alone by giving it to others, and thus placing it in a position which is unjust to it.

CHAP. XX. — EGYPTIAN IDOLATRY.

"Although this word God is not the *name* of God, but meantime that word is employed by men as His name; and therefore, as I have said, when it is used reproachfully, the reproach is referred to the injury of the true name. In short, the ancient Egyptians, who thought that they had discovered the theory of the heavenly revolutions and the nature of the stars, nevertheless, through the demon's blocking up their senses, subjected the incommunicable name to all kinds of indignity. For some taught that their ox, which is called Apis, ought to be worshipped; others taught that the he-goat, others that cats, the ibis, a fish also, a serpent, onions, drains, crepitus ventris, ought to be regarded as deities, and innumerable other things, which I am ashamed even to mention."

CHAP. XXI. — EGYPTIAN IDOLATRY MORE REASONABLE THAN OTHERS.

When Peter was speaking thus, all we who heard him laughed. Then said Peter: "You laugh at the absurdities of others, because through long custom you do not see your own. For indeed it is not without reason that you laugh at the folly of the Egyptians, who worship dumb animals, while they themselves are rational. But I will tell you how they also laugh at you; for they say, We worship living animals, though mortal; but you worship and adore things which never were alive at all. They add this also, that they are figures and allegories of certain powers by whose help the race of men is governed. Taking refuge in this for shame, they fabricate these and similar excuses, and so endeavour to screen their error. But this is not the time to answer the Egyptians, and leaving the care of those who are present to heal the disease of the absent. For it is a certain indication that you are held to be free from sickness of this sort, since you do not grieve over it as your own, but laugh at it as that of others.

CHAP. XXII. — SECOND SUGGESTION CONTINUED.

"But let us come back to you, whose opinion it is that God should be regarded as Cæsar, and the gods as the ministers and deputies of Cæsar. Follow me attentively, and I shall presently show you the lurking-places of the serpent, which lie in the crooked windings of this argument. It ought to be regarded by all as certain and beyond doubt, that no creature can be on a level with God, because He was made by none, but Himself made all things; nor indeed can any one be found so irrational, as to suppose that the thing made can be compared with the maker. If therefore the human mind, not only by reason, but even by a sort of natural instinct,

rightly holds this opinion, that that is called *God* to which nothing can be compared or equalled, but which exceeds all and excels all; how can it be supposed that that name which is believed to be above all, is rightly given to those whom you think to be employed for the service and comfort of human life? But we shall add this also. This world was undoubtedly made, and is corruptible, as we shall show more fully by and by; meantime it is admitted both that it has been made and that it is corruptible. If therefore the world cannot be called God, and rightly so, because it is corruptible, how shall parts of the world take the name of God? For inasmuch as the whole world cannot be God, much more its parts cannot. Therefore, if we come back to the example of Cæsar, you will see how far you are in error. It is not lawful for any one, though a man of the same nature with him, to be compared with Cæsar: do you think, then, that any one ought to be compared with God, who excels all in this respect, that He was made by none, but Himself made all things? But, indeed, you dare not give the name of Cæsar to any other, because he immediately punishes one who offends against him; you dare give that of God to others, because He delays the punishment of offenders against Him, in order to their repentance.

CHAP. XXIII. — THIRD SUGGESTION.

"Through the mouths of others also that serpent is wont to speak in this wise: We adore visible images in honour of the invisible God.[1] Now this is most certainly false. For if you really wished to worship the image of God, you would do good to man, and so worship the true image of God in him. For the image of God is in every man, though His likeness is not in all, but where the soul is benign and the mind pure. If, therefore, you wish truly to honour the image of God, we declare to you what is true, that you should do good to and pay honour and reverence to man, who is made in the image of God; that you minister food to the hungry, drink to the thirsty, clothing to the naked, hospitality to the stranger, and necessary things to the prisoner; and that is what will be regarded as truly bestowed upon God. And so far do these things go to the honour of God's image, that he who does not these things is regarded as casting reproach upon the divine image. What, then, is that honour of God which consists in running from one stone or wooden figure to another, in venerating empty and lifeless figures as deities, and despising men in whom the image of God is of a truth? Yea, rather be assured, that whoever commits murder or adultery, or anything

---

[1] [To chaps. 23–36 a parallel is afforded by Homily XI. 4–18. — R.]

that causes suffering or injury to men, in all these the image of God is violated. For to injure men is a great impiety towards God. Whenever, therefore, you do to another what you would not have another do to you, you defile the image of God with undeserved distresses. Understand, therefore, that that is the suggestion of the serpent lurking within you, which persuades you that you may seem to be pious when you worship insensible things, and may not seem impious when you injure sensible and rational beings.

CHAP. XXIV. — FOURTH SUGGESTION.

" But to these things the serpent answers us with another mouth, and says : If God did not wish these things to be, then they should not be. I am not telling you how it is that many contrary things are permitted to be in this world for the probation of every one's mind. But this is what is suitable to be said in the meantime : If, according to you, everything that was to be worshipped ôught not to have been, there would have been almost nothing in this world. For what is there that you have left without worshipping it? The sun, the moon, the stars, the water, the earth, mountains, trees, stones, men ; there is no one of these that ye have not worshipped. According to your saying, therefore, none of these ought to have been made by God, that you might not have anything that you could worship ! Yea, He ought not even to have made men themselves to be the worshippers ! But this is the very thing which that serpent which lurks within you desires : for he spares none of you ; he would have no one of you escape from destruction. But it shall not be so. For I tell you, that not that which is worshipped is in fault, but he who worships. For with God is righteous judgment ; and He judges in one way the sufferer, and in another way the doer, of wrong.

CHAP. XXV. — FIFTH SUGGESTION.

" But you say : Then those who adore what ought not to be adored, should be immediately destroyed by God, to prevent others doing the like. But are you wiser than God, that you should offer Him counsel?[1] He knows what to do. For with all who are placed in ignorance He exercises patience, because He is merciful and gracious ; and He foresees that many of the ungodly become godly, and that even some of those who worship impure statues and polluted images have been converted to God, and forsaking their sins and doing good works, attain to salvation. But it is said : We ought never to have come even to the thought of

[1] Rom. xi. 34.

doing these things. You do not know what freedom of will is, and you forget that he is good who is so by his own intention ; but. he who is retained in goodness by necessity cannot be called good, because it is not of himself that he is so. Because, therefore, there is in every one liberty to choose good or evil, he either acquires rewards, or brings destruction on himself. Nay, it is said, God brings to our minds whatsoever we think. What mean ye, O men? Ye blaspheme. For if He brings all our thoughts into our minds, then it is He that suggests to us thoughts of adultery, and covetousness, and blasphemy, and every kind of effeminacy. Cease, I entreat of you, these blasphemies, and understand what is the honour worthy of God. And say not, as some of you are wont to say, that God needs not honour from men. Indeed, He truly is in need of none ; but you ought to know that the honour which you bestow upon God is profitable to yourselves. For what is so execrable, as for a man not to render thanks to his Creator?

CHAP. XXVI. — SIXTH SUGGESTION.

" But it is said : We do better, who give thanks both to Himself, and to all with Him. In this you do not understand that there is the ruin of your salvation. For it is as if a sick man should call in for his cure at once a physician and poisoners ; since these could indeed injure him, but not cure him ; and the true physician would refuse to mix his remedies with their poisons, lest either the man's destruction should be ascribed to the good, or his recovery to the injurious. But you say : Is God then indignant or envious, if, when He benefits us, our thanks be rendered to others? Even if He be not indignant, at all events He does not wish to be the author of error, that by means of His work credit should be given to a vain idol. And what is so impious, so ungrateful, as to obtain a benefit from God, and to render thanks to blocks of wood and stone? Wherefore arise, and understand your salvation. For God is in need of no one, nor does He require anything, nor is He hurt by anything ; but we are either helped or hurt, in that we are grateful or ungrateful. For what does God gain from our praises, or what does He lose by our blasphemies? Only *this we must remember*, that God brings into proximity and friendship with Himself the soul that renders thanks to Him. But the wicked demon possesses the ungrateful soul.

CHAP. XXVII. — CREATURES TAKE VENGEANCE ON SINNERS.

" But this also I would have you know, that upon such souls God does not take vengeance directly, but His whole creation rises up and inflicts punishments upon the impious; and although in the present world the goodness of God bestows the light of the world and the services of the earth alike upon the pious and the impious, yet not without grief does the sun afford his light, and the other elements perform their service, to the impious. And, in short, sometimes even in opposition to the goodness of the Creator, the elements are wearied out by the crimes of the wicked; and thence it is that either the fruit of the earth is blighted, or the composition of the air is vitiated, or the heat of the sun is increased beyond measure, or there is an excessive amount of rain or of cold. Thence pestilence, and famine, and death in various forms stalk forth, for the creature hastens to take vengeance on the wicked; yet the goodness of God restrains it, and bridles its indignation against the wicked, and compels it to be obedient to His mercy, rather than to be inflamed by the sins and the crimes of men. For the patience of God waiteth for the conversion of men, as long as they are in this body.

CHAP. XXVIII. — ETERNITY OF PUNISHMENTS.

" But if any persist in impiety till the end of life, then as soon as the soul, which is immortal, departs, it shall pay the penalty of its persistence in impiety. For even the souls of the impious are immortal, though perhaps they themselves would wish them to end with their bodies. But it is not so; for they endure without end the torments of eternal fire, and to their destruction they have not the quality of mortality. But perhaps you will say to me, You terrify us, O Peter. And how shall we speak to you the things which are in reality? Can we declare to you the truth by keeping silence? We cannot state the things which are, otherwise than as they are. But if we were silent, we should make ourselves the cause of the ignorance that is ruinous to you, and should satisfy the serpent that lurks within you, and blocks up your senses, who cunningly suggests these things to you, that he may make you always the enemies of God. But we are sent for this end, that we may betray his disguises to you; and melting your enmities, may reconcile you to God, that you may be converted to Him, and may please Him by good works. For man is at enmity with God, and is in an unreasonable and impious state of mind and wicked disposition towards Him, especially when he thinks that he knows something, and is in ignorance. But when you lay aside these, and begin to be pleased and displeased with the same things which please and displease God, and to will what God willeth, then ye shall truly be called His friends.

CHAP. XXIX. — GOD'S CARE OF HUMAN THINGS.

" But perhaps some of you will say, God has no care of human things; and if we cannot even attain to the knowledge of Him, how shall we attain to His friendship? That God does concern Himself with the affairs of men, His government of the world bears witness: for the sun daily waits upon it, the showers minister to it; the fountains, rivers, winds, and all elements, attend upon it; and the more these things become known to men, the more do they indicate God's care over men. For unless by the power of the Most High, the more powerful would never minister to the inferior; and by this God is shown to have not only a care over men, but some great affection, since He has deputed such noble elements to their service. But that men may also attain to the friendship of God, is proved to us by the example of those to whose prayers He has been so favourable, that He has withheld the heaven from rain when they wished, and has again opened it when they prayed.[1] And many other things He has bestowed upon those who does His will, which could not be bestowed but upon His friends. But you will say, What harm is done to God if these things also are worshipped by us? If any one of you should pay to another the honour that is due to his father, from whom he has received innumerable benefits, and should reverence a stranger and foreigner as his father, should you not think that he was undutiful towards his father, and most deserving to be disinherited?

CHAP. XXX. — RELIGION OF FATHERS TO BE ABANDONED.

" Others say, It is wicked if we do not worship those *idols* which have come down to us from our fathers, and prove false to the religion bequeathed to us by our ancestors. On this principle, if any one's father was a robber or a base fellow, he ought not to change the manner of life handed down to him by his fathers, nor to be recalled from his father's errors to a better way; and it is reckoned impious if one do not sin with his parents, or does not persist in impiety with them. Others say, We ought not to be troublesome to God, and to be always burdening Him with complaints of our miseries, or with the exigencies of our petitions. How foolish and witless an answer! Do you think it is troublesome to God if you thank Him for His benefits, while you do not think it troublesome to Him if, for His gifts, you render thanks to stocks and stones? And how comes it, that when rain is withheld in a long drought, we all turn our eyes to heaven, and entreat the gift of rain from God Almighty, and all

---

[1] 1 Kings xvii., xviii.; Jas. v. 17, 18.

of us with our little ones pour out prayers on God, and entreat His compassion? But truly ungrateful souls, when they obtain the blessing, quickly forget: for as soon as they have gathered in their harvest or their vintage, straightway they offer the first-fruits to deaf and dumb images, and pay vows in temples or groves for those things which God has bestowed upon them, and then offer sacrifices to demons; and having received a favour, deny the bestower of the favour.[1]

CHAP. XXXI. — PAGANISM, ITS ENORMITIES.

" But some say, These things are instituted for the sake of joy, and for refreshing our minds; and they have been devised for this end, that the human mind may be relaxed for a little from cares and sorrows. See now what a charge you yourselves bring upon the things which you practise. If these things have been invented for the purpose of lightening sorrow and affording enjoyment, how is it that the invocations of demons are performed in groves and woods? What is the meaning of the insane whirlings, and the slashing of limbs, and the cutting off of members? How is it that mad rage is produced in them? How is insanity produced? How is it that women are driven violently, raging with dishevelled hair? Whence the shrieking and gnashing of teeth? Whence the bellowing of the heart and the bowels, and all those things which, whether they are pretended or are contrived by the ministration of demons, are exhibited to the terror of the foolish and ignorant? Are these things done for the sake of lightening the mind, or rather for the sake of oppressing it? Do ye not yet perceive nor understand, that these are the counsels of the serpent lurking within you, which draws you away from the apprehension of truth by irrational suggestions of errors, that he may hold you as slaves and servants of lust and concupiscence and every disgraceful thing?

CHAP. XXXII. — TRUE RELIGION CALLS TO SOBRIETY AND MODESTY.

" But I protest to you with the clear voice of preaching, that, on the contrary, the religion of God calls you to sobriety and modesty; orders you to refrain from effeminacy and madness, and by patience and gentleness to prevent the inroads of anger; to be content with your own possessions, and with the virtue of frugality; not even when driven by poverty to plunder the goods of others, but in all things to observe justice; to withdraw yourselves wholly from the idol sacrifices: for by these things you invite demons to you, and of your own accord give

them the power of entering into you; and so you admit that which is the cause either of madness or of unlawful love.

CHAP. XXXIII. — ORIGIN OF IMPIETY.

" Hence is the origin of all impiety; hence murders, adulteries, thefts; and a nursery is formed of all evils and wickednesses, while you indulge in profane libations and odours, and give to wicked spirits an opportunity of ruling and obtaining some sort of authority over you. For when they invade your senses, what do they else than work the things which belong to lust and injustice and cruelty, and compel you to be obedient to all things that are pleasing to them? God, indeed, permits you to suffer this at their hands by a certain righteous judgment, that from the very disgrace of your doings and your feelings you may understand how unworthy it is to be subject to demons and not to God. Hence also, by the friendship of demons, men are brought to disgraceful and base deeds; hence, men proceed even to the destruction of life, either through the fire of lust, or through the madness of anger through excess of grief, so that, as is well[2] known, some have even laid violent hands upon themselves. And this, as we have said, by a just sentence of God they are not prevented from doing, that they may both understand to whom they have yielded themselves in subjection, and know whom they have forsaken.

CHAP. XXXIV. — WHO ARE WORSHIPPERS OF GOD?

" But some one will say, These passions sometimes befall even those who worship God. It is not true. For we say that he is a worshipper of God, who does the will of God, and observes the precepts of His law. For in God's estimation he is not a Jew who is called a Jew among men (nor is he a Gentile that is called a Gentile), but he who, believing in God, fulfils His law and does His will, though he be not circumcised.[3] He is the true worshipper of God, who not only is himself free from passions, but also sets others free from them; though they be so heavy that they are like mountains, he removes them by means of the faith with which he believes in God. Yea, by faith he truly removes mountains with their trees, if it be necessary. But he who seems to worship God, but is neither fortified by a full faith, nor by obedience to the commandments, but is a sinner, has given a place in himself, by reason of his sins, to passions, which are appointed of God for the punishment of those

---

[1] Literally, " change the bestower of it for another."

[2] The original has here, " as is often known; " that is, as people know from many instances having occurred within their own knowledge.
[3] Rom. ii. 28; Rev. ii. 9.
[4] Matt. xvii. 20; Luke xvii. 6.

who sin, that they may exact from them the deserts of their sins by means of punishments inflicted, and may bring them purified to the general judgment of all, provided always that their faith do not fail them in their chastisement. For the chastisement of unbelievers in the present life is a judgment, by which they begin to be separated from future blessings; but the chastisement of those who worship God, while it is inflicted upon them for sins into which they have fallen, exacts from them the due of what they have done, that, preventing the judgment, they may pay the debt of their sin in the present life, and be freed, at least in half, from the eternal punishments which are there prepared.

CHAP. XXXV. — JUDGMENT TO COME.

" But he does not receive these things as true who does not believe that there is to be a judgment of God, and therefore, being bound by the pleasures of the present life, is shut out from eternal good things; and therefore we do not neglect to proclaim to you what we know to be necessary for your salvation, and to show you what is the true worship of God, that, believing in God, you may be able, by means of good works, to be heirs with us of the world to come. But if you are not yet convinced that what we say is true, meantime, in the first instance, you ought not to take it amiss and to be hostile to us because we announce to you the things which we consider to be good, and because we do not grudge to bestow also upon you that which we believe brings salvation to ourselves, labouring, as I have said, with all eagerness, that we may have you as fellow-heirs of the blessings which we believe are to befall ourselves. But whether those things which we declare to you are certainly true, you shall not be able to know otherwise than by rendering obedience to the things which are commanded, that you may be taught

by the issue of things, and the most certain end of blessedness.

CHAP. XXXVI. — CONCLUSION OF DISCOURSE.

" And, therefore, although the serpent lurking within you occupies your senses with a thousand arts of corruption, and throws in your way a thousand obstacles, by which he may turn you away from the hearing of saving instruction, all the more ought you to resist him, and despising his suggestions, to come together the more frequently to hear the word and receive instruction from us, because nobody can learn anything who is not taught." [1]

And when he had done speaking, he ordered those to be brought to him who were oppressed by sicknesses or demons, and laid his hands upon them with prayer; and so he dismissed the crowds, charging them to resort to the hearing of the word during the days that he was to remain there. Therefore, when the crowds had departed, Peter washed his body in the waters which ran through the garden, with as many of the others as chose to do so; and then ordered the couches to be spread on the ground under a very shady tree, and directed us to recline according to the order established at Cæsarea. And thus, having taken food and given thanks to God after the manner of the Hebrews, as there was yet some portion of the day remaining, he ordered us to question him on any matters that we pleased. And although we were with him twenty in all, he explained to every one whatever he pleased to ask of him; the particulars of which I set down in books and sent to you some time ago. And when evening came we entered with him into the lodging, and went to sleep, each one in his own place.

---

[1] [The latter half of this discourse, as already indicated (see note on chap. 23), finds a parallel in Homily XI. 4-18, which forms the first half of that discourse. — R.]

BOOK VI.

BUT as soon as day began to advance the dawn upon the retiring darkness, Peter having gone into the garden to pray, and returning thence and coming to us, by way of excuse for awaking and coming to us a little later than usual, said this: [1] " Now that the spring-time has lengthened the day, of course the night is

shorter; if, therefore, one desires to occupy some portion of the night in study, he must not keep the same hours [2] for waking at all seasons, but should spend the same length of time in sleeping, whether the night be longer or shorter, and be exceedingly careful that he do not cut off from the period which he is wont to have for study, and so add to his sleep and lessen his time of keeping awake. And this also is to be

---

[1] [Comp. book iii. 31. To this there is no parallel in the *Homilies*. — R.]

[2] It will be remembered that the *hours* were variable periods, and began to be reckoned from sunrise.

observed, lest haply if sleep be interrupted while the food is still undigested, the undigested mass load the mind, and by the exhalation of crude spirits render the inner sense confused and disturbed. It is right, therefore, that that part also be cherished with sufficient rest, so that, those things being sufficiently accomplished which are due to it, the body may be able in other things to render due service to the mind."

CHAP. II. — MUCH TO BE DONE IN A LITTLE TIME.

When he had said this, as very many had already assembled in the accustomed place of the garden to hear him, Peter went forth; and having saluted the crowds in his usual manner, began to speak as follows: [1] "Since, indeed, as land neglected by the cultivator necessarily produces thorns and thistles, so your sense, by long neglect, has produced a plentiful crop of noxious opinions of things and dogmas of false science; there is need now of much care in cultivating the field of your mind, that the word of truth, which is the true and diligent husbandman of the heart, may cultivate it with continual instructions. It is therefore your part to render obedience to it, and to lop off superfluous occupations and anxieties, lest a noxious growth choke the good seed of the word. For it may be that a short and earnest diligence may repair a long time's neglect; for the time of every one's life is uncertain, and therefore we must hasten to salvation, lest haply sudden death seize upon him who delays.

CHAP. III. — RIGHTEOUS ANGER.

"And all the more eagerly must we strive on this account, that while there is time, the collected vices of evil custom may be cut off. And this you shall not be able to do otherwise, than by being angry with yourselves on account of your profitless and base doings. For this is righteous and necessary anger, by which every one is indignant with himself, and accuses himself for those things in which he has erred and done amiss; and by this indignation a certain fire is kindled in us, which, applied as it were to a barren field, consumes and burns up the roots of vile pleasure, and renders the soil of the heart more fertile for the good seed of the word of God. And I think that you have sufficiently worthy causes of anger, from which that most righteous fire may be kindled, if you consider into what errors the evil of ignorance has drawn you, and how it has caused you to fall and rush headlong into sin, from what good things it has withdrawn you, and into what evils it has driven

you, and, what is of more importance than all the rest, how it has made you liable to eternal punishments in the world to come. Is not the fire of most righteous indignation kindled within you for all these things, now that the light of truth has shone upon you; and does not the flame of that anger which is pleasing to God rise within you, that every sprout may be burnt up and destroyed from the root, if haply any shoot of evil concupiscence has budded within you?

CHAP. IV. — NOT PEACE, BUT A SWORD.

Hence, also, He who hath sent us, when He had come,[2] and had seen that all the world had fallen into wickedness, did not forthwith give peace to him who is in error, lest He should confirm him in evil; but set the knowledge of truth in opposition to the ruins of ignorance of it, that, if haply men would repent and look upon the light of truth, they might rightly grieve that they had been deceived and drawn away into the precipices of error, and might kindle the fire of salutary anger against the ignorance that had deceived them. On this account, therefore, He said, 'I have come to send fire on the earth; and how I wish that it were kindled!'[3] There is therefore a certain fight, which is to be fought by us in this life; for the word of truth and knowledge necessarily separates men from error and ignorance, as we have often seen putrified and dead flesh in the body separated by the cutting knife from its connection with the living members. Such is the effect produced by knowledge of the truth. For it is necessary that, for the sake of salvation, the son, for example, who has received the word of truth, be separated from his unbelieving parents; or again, that the father be separated from his son, or the daughter from her mother. And in this manner the battle of knowledge and ignorance, of truth and error, arises between believing and unbelieving kinsmen and relations. And therefore He who has sent us said again, 'I am not come to send peace on earth, but a sword.'[4]

CHAP. V. — HOW THE FIGHT BEGINS.

"But if any one say, How does it seem right for men to be separated from their parents? I will tell you how. Because, if they remained with them in error, they would do no good to them, and they would themselves perish with them. It is therefore right, and very right, that he who will be saved be separated from him who will not. But observe this also, that this separa-

---

[1] [To chaps. 2, 3, there is a parallel in the corresponding chapters of Homily XI. Then follows a long passage similar to that in book v. 23–36. — R.]

[2] [The remaining chapters of this book (4–14) correspond with Homily XI. 19–33. The discourse here is somewhat fuller, but the order of topics is the same throughout. — R.]
[3] Luke xii. 49.
[4] Matt. x. 34.

tion does not come from those who understand aright; for they wish to be with their relatives, and to do them good, and to teach them better things. But it is the vice peculiar to ignorance, that it will not bear to have near it the light of truth, which confutes it; and therefore that separation originates with them. For those who receive the knowledge of the truth, because it is full of goodness, desire, if it be possible, to share it with all, as given by the good God; yea, even with those who hate and persecute them: for they know that ignorance is the cause of their sin. Wherefore, in short, the Master Himself, when He was being led to the cross by those who knew Him not, prayed the Father for His murderers, and said, 'Father, forgive their sin, for they know not what they do!'[1] The disciples also, in imitation of the Master, even when themselves were suffering, in like manner prayed for their murderers.[2] But if we are taught to pray even for our murderers and persecutors, how ought we not to bear the persecutions of parents and relations, and to pray for their conversion?

CHAP. VI. — GOD TO BE LOVED MORE THAN PARENTS.

"Then let us consider carefully, in the next place, what reason we have for loving our parents. For this cause, it is said, we love them, because they seem to be the authors of our life. But our parents are not authors of our life, but means of it. For they do not bestow life, but afford the means of our entering into this life; while the one and sole author of life is God. If therefore we would love the Author of our life, let us know that it is He that is to be loved. But then it is said, We cannot know Him; but them we know, and hold in affection. Be it so: you cannot know *what* God is, but you can very easily know what God is *not*. For how can any man fail to know that wood, or stone, or brass, or other such matter, is not God? But if you will not give your mind to consider the things which you might easily apprehend, it is certain that you are hindered in the knowledge of God, not by impossibility, but by indolence; for if you had wished it, even from these useless images you might have been set on the way of understanding.

CHAP. VII. — THE EARTH MADE FOR MEN.

"For it is certain that these images are made with iron tools; but iron is wrought by fire, which fire is extinguished by water. But water is moved by spirit; and spirit has its beginning from God. For thus saith the prophet Moses:

'In the beginning God made the heaven and the earth. But the earth was invisible, and unarranged; and darkness was over the deep: and the Spirit of God was upon the waters.'[3] Which Spirit, like the Creator's hand, by command of God separated light from darkness; and after that invisible heaven produced this visible one, that He might make the higher places a habitation for angels, and the lower for men. For your sake, therefore, by command of God, the water which was upon the face of the earth withdrew, that the earth might produce fruits for you; and into the earth also He inserted veins of moisture, that fountains and rivers might flow forth from it for you. For your sake it was commanded to bring forth living creatures, and all things which could serve for your use and pleasure. Is it not for you that the winds blow, that the earth, conceiving by them, may bring forth fruits? Is it not for you that the showers fall, and the seasons change? Is it not for you that the sun rises and sets, and the moon undergoes her changes? For you the sea offers its service, that all things may be subject to you, ungrateful as you are. For all these things shall there not be a righteous punishment of vengeance, because beyond all else you are ignorant of the bestower of all these things, whom you ought to acknowledge and reverence above all?

CHAP. VIII — NECESSITY OF BAPTISM.

"But now I lead you to understanding by the same paths. For you see that all things are produced from waters. But water was made at first by the Only-begotten; and the Almighty God is the head of the Only-begotten, by whom we come to the Father in such order as we have stated above. But when you have come to the Father, you will learn that this is His will, that you be born anew by means of waters, which were first created.[4] For he who is regenerated by water, having filled up the measure of good works, is made heir of Him by whom he has been regenerated in incorruption. Wherefore, with prepared minds, approach as sons to a father, that your sins may be washed away, and it may be proved before God that ignorance was their sole cause. For if, after the learning of these things, you remain in unbelief, the cause of your destruction will be imputed to yourselves, and not to ignorance. And do you suppose that you can have hope towards God, even if you cultivate all piety and all righteousness, but do not receive baptism. Yea rather, he will be worthy of greater punishment, who does good works not well; for merit accrues to men from good works, but only if they be done as God commands. Now God

---

[1] Luke xxiii. 34.
[2] Acts vii. 60.

[3] Gen i. 1, 2.
[4] [There is no exact parallel to these statements in the corresponding chapter of the *Homilies* (xi. 26). — R.]

has ordered every one who worships Him to be sealed by baptism ; but if you refuse, and obey your own will rather than God's, you are doubtless contrary and hostile to His will.

CHAP. IX. — USE OF BAPTISM.

"But you will perhaps say, What does the baptism of water contribute towards the worship of God? In the first place, because that which hath pleased God is fulfilled. In the second place, because, when you are regenerated and born again of water and of God, the frailty of your former birth, which you have through men, is cut off, and so at length you shall be able to attain salvation ; but otherwise it is impossible. For thus hath the true prophet testified to us with an oath : 'Verily I say to you, That unless a man is born again of water, he shall not enter into the kingdom of heaven.'[1] Therefore make haste ; for there is in these waters a certain power of mercy which was borne upon them at the beginning, and acknowledges those who are baptized under the name of the threefold sacrament, and rescues them from future punishments, presenting as a gift to God the souls that are consecrated by baptism. Betake yourselves therefore to these waters, for they alone can quench the violence of the future fire ; and he who delays to approach to them, it is evident that the idol of unbelief remains in him, and by it he is prevented from hastening to the waters which confer salvation. For whether you be righteous or unrighteous, baptism is necessary for you in every respect : for the righteous, that perfection may be accomplished in him, and he may be born again to God ; for the unrighteous, that pardon may be vouchsafed him of the sins which he has committed in ignorance. Therefore all should hasten to be born again to God without delay, because the end of every one's life is uncertain.

CHAP. X. — NECESSITY OF GOOD WORKS.

"But when you have been regenerated by water, show by good works the likeness in you of that Father who hath begotten you. Now you know God, honour Him as a father ; and His honour is, that you live according to His will. And His will is, that you so live as to know nothing of murder or adultery, to flee from hatred and covetousness, to put away anger, pride, and boasting, to abhor envy, and to count all such things entirely unsuitable to you. There is truly a certain peculiar observance of our religion, which is not so much imposed upon men, as it is sought out by every worshipper of God by reason of its purity. By reason of chastity, I say, of which there are many kinds, but first, that every one

be careful that he 'come not near a menstruous woman ;' for this the law of God regards as detestable. But though the law had given no admonition concerning these things, should we willingly, like beetles, roll ourselves in filth? For we ought to have something more than the animals, as reasonable men, and capable of heavenly senses, whose chief study it ought to be to guard the conscience from every defilement of the heart.

CHAP. XI. — INWARD AND OUTWARD CLEANSING.

"Moreover, it is good, and tends to purity, also to wash the body with water. I call it good, not as if it were that prime good of the purifying of the mind, but because this of the washing of the body is the sequel of that good. For so also our Master rebuked some of the Pharisees and scribes, who seemed to be better than others, and separated from the people, calling them hypocrites, because they purified only those things which were seen of men, but left defiled and sordid their hearts, which God alone sees. To some therefore of them — not to all — He said, 'Woe to you, scribes and Pharisees, hypocrites ! because ye cleanse the outside of the cup and platter, but the inside is full of pollution. O blind Pharisees, first make clean what is within, and what is without shall be clean also.'[2] For truly, if the mind be purified by the light of knowledge, when once it is clean and clear, then it necessarily takes care of that which is without a man, that is, his flesh, that it also may be purified. But when that which is without, the cleansing of the flesh, is neglected, it is certain that there is no care taken of the purity of the mind and the cleanness of the heart. Thus therefore it comes to pass, that he who is clean inwardly is without doubt cleansed outwardly also, but not always that he who is clean outwardly is also cleansed inwardly — to wit, when he does these things that he may please men.

CHAP. XII. — IMPORTANCE OF CHASTITY.

"But this kind of chastity is also to be observed, that sexual intercourse must not take place heedlessly and for the sake of mere pleasure, but for the sake of begetting children.[3] And since this observance is found even amongst some of the lower animals, it were a shame if it be not observed by men, reasonable, and worshipping God. But there is this further reason why chastity should be observed by those who hold the true worship of God, in those forms of it of which we have spoken, and others of like sort, that it is observed strictly even amongst those

---

[1] John iii. 5. [This passage is cited, with additions, in Homily XI. 26. — R.]

[2] Matt. xxiii. 25, 26.

[3] [This chapter is more specific in its statements than Homily XI. 30, to which it has a general resemblance. — R.]

who are still held by the devil in error, for even amongst them there is in some degree the observance of chastity. What then? Will you not observe, now that you are reformed, what you observed when you were in error?

CHAP. XIII. — SUPERIORITY OF CHRISTIAN MORALITY.

"But perhaps some one of you will say, Must we then observe all things which we did while we worshipped idols? Not all. But whatever things were done well, these you ought to observe even now; because, if anything is rightly done by those who are in error, it is certain that that is derived from the truth; whereas, if anything is not rightly done in the true religion, that is, without doubt, borrowed from error. For good is good, though it be done by those who are in error; and evil is evil, though it be done by those who follow the truth. Or shall we be so foolish, that if we see a worshipper of idols to be sober, we shall refuse to be sober, lest we should seem to do the same things which he does who worships idols? It is not so. But let this be our study, that if those who err do not commit murder, we should not even be angry; if they do not commit adultery, we should not even covet another's wife; if they love their neighbours, we should love even our enemies; if they lend to those who have the means of paying, we should give to those from whom we do not hope to receive anything. And in all things, we who hope for the inheritance of the eternal world ought to excel those who know only the present world; knowing that if their works, when compared with our works, be found like and equal in the day of judgment, there will be confusion to us, because we are found equal in our works to those who are condemned on account of ignorance, and had no hope of the world to come.

CHAP. XIV. — KNOWLEDGE ENHANCES RESPONSIBILITY.

"And truly confusion is our worthy portion, if we have done no more than those who are inferior to us in knowledge. But if it be confusion to us, to be found equal to them in works, what shall become of us if the examination that is to take place find us inferior and worse than them? Hear, therefore, how our true Prophet has taught us concerning these things; for, with respect to those who neglect to hear the words of wisdom, He speaks thus: 'The queen of the south shall rise in judgment with this generation, and shall condemn it, because she came from the ends of the earth to hear the wisdom of Solomon; and, behold, a greater than Solomon is here, and they

hear Him not.'[1] But with respect to those who refused to repent of their evil deeds, He spoke thus: 'The men of Nineve shall rise in the judgment with this generation, and shall condemn it; for they repented at the preaching of Jonas; and, behold, a greater than Jonas is here.'[2] You see, therefore, how He condemned those who were instructed out of the law, by adducing the example of those who came from Gentile ignorance, and showing that the former were not even equal to those who seemed to live in error. From all these things, then, the statement that He propounded is proved, that chastity, which is observed to a certain extent even by those who live in error, should be held much more purely and strictly, in all its forms, as we showed above, by us who follow the truth; and the rather because with us eternal rewards are assigned to its observance."

CHAP. XV. — BISHOPS, PRESBYTERS, DEACONS, AND WIDOWS ORDAINED AT TRIPOLIS.

When he had said these things, and others to the same effect, he dismissed the crowds; and having, according to his custom, supped with his friends, he went to sleep. And while in this manner he was teaching the word of God for three whole months, and converting multitudes to the faith, at the last he ordered me to fast; and after the fast he conferred on me the baptism of ever-flowing water, in the fountains which adjoin the sea.[3] And when, for the grace of regeneration divinely conferred upon me, we had joyfully kept holiday with our brethren, Peter ordered those who had been appointed to go before him, to proceed to Antioch, and there to wait three months more. And they having gone, he himself led down to the fountains, which, I have said, are near the sea, those who had fully received the faith of the Lord, and baptized them; and celebrating[4] the Eucharist with them, he appointed, as bishop over them, Maro, who had entertained him in his house, and who was now perfect in all things; and with him he ordained twelve presbyters and deacons at the same time. He also instituted the order of widows, and arranged all the services of the Church; and charged them all to obey Maro their bishop in all things that he should command them. And thus all things being suitably arranged, when the three months were fulfilled, we bade farewell to those who were at Tripolis, and set out for Antioch.

[1] Matt. xii. 42; Luke xi. 31.
[2] Matt. xii. 41; Luke xi. 32.
[3] [Comp. Homily XI. 35, 36, which, however, contain additional matter. — R.]
[4] Literally, "breaking the Eucharist."

BOOK VII.

CHAP. I. — JOURNEY FROM TRIPOLIS.

AT length leaving Tripolis,[1] a city of Phœnicia, we made our first halt at Ortosias, not far from Tripolis; and there we remained the next day also, because almost all those that had believed in the Lord, unable to part from Peter, followed him thus far. Thence we came to Antharadus. But because there were many in our company, Peter said to Niceta and Aquila: "As there are immense crowds of brethren with us, and we bring upon ourselves no little envy as we enter into every city, it seems to me that we must take means, without doing so unpleasing a thing as to prevent their following us, to secure that the wicked one shall not stir up envy against us on account of any display! I wish, therefore, that you, Niceta and Aquila, would go before us with them, so that you may lead the multitude divided into two sections, that we may enter every city of the Gentiles travelling apart, rather than in one assemblage.

CHAP. II. — DISCIPLES DIVIDED INTO TWO BANDS.

"But I know that you think it sad to be separated from me for the space of at least two days. Believe me, that in whatever degree you love me, my affection towards you is tenfold greater. But if, by reason of our mutual affection, we will not do the things that are right and honourable, such love will appear to be unreasonable. And therefore, without bating a tittle of our love, let us attend to those things which seem useful and necessary; especially since not a day can pass in which you may not be present at my discussions. For I purpose to pass through the most noted cities of the provinces one by one, as you also know, and to reside three months in each for the sake of teaching. Now, therefore, go before me to Laodicea, which is the nearest city, and I shall follow you after two or three days, so far as I purpose. But you shall wait for me at the inn nearest to the gate of the city; and thence again, when we have spent a few days there, you shall go before me to more distant cities. And this I wish you to do at every city, for the sake of avoiding envy as much as in us lies, and also that the brethren who are with us, finding lodgings prepared in the several cities by your foresight, may not seem to be vagabonds."

[1] [The narrative of book vii. is given in Homilies XII., XIII.; chap. 38 including some details of Homily XIV. 1. The variations in the narrative portions are unimportant; but the *Homilies* contain longer discourses of the Apostle. Chaps 1–24 here correspond quite exactly with Homily XII. 1–24: the topics of the respective chapters being the same, and the variations mainly in forms of expression. — R.]

CHAP. III. — ORDER OF MARCH.

When Peter thus spoke, they of course acquiesced, saying: "It does not greatly sadden us to do this, because we are ordered by you, who have been chosen by the foresight of Christ to do and to counsel well in all things; but also because, while it is a heavy loss not to see our lord Peter for one, or it may be two days, yet it is not intolerable. And we think of our twelve brethren who go before us, and who are deprived of the advantage of hearing and seeing you for a whole month out of the three that you stay in every city. Therefore we shall not delay doing as you order, because you order all things aright." And thus saying, they went forward, having received instructions that they should speak to the brethren who journeyed with them outside the city, and request them not to enter the cities in a crowd and with tumult, but apart, and divided into two bands.

CHAP. IV. — CLEMENT'S JOY AT REMAINING WITH PETER.

But when they were gone, I Clement rejoiced greatly because he had kept me with himself, and I said to him: "I give thanks to God that you have not sent me forward with the others, for I should have died through sadness." Then said Peter: "And what will happen if necessity shall demand that you be sent anywhere for the purpose of teaching? Would you die if you were separated from me for a good purpose? Would you not put a restraint upon yourself, to bear patiently what necessity has laid upon you? Or do you not know that friends are always together, and are joined in memory, though they be separated bodily; as, on the other hand, some persons are near to one another in body, but are separate in mind?"

CHAP. V. — CLEMENT'S AFFECTION FOR PETER.

Then I answered: "Think not, my lord, that I suffer these things unreasonably; but there is a certain cause and reason of this affection of mine towards you. For I have you alone as the object of all my affections, instead of father and mother, and brethren; but above all this, is the fact that you alone are the cause of my salvation and knowledge of the truth. And also this I do not count of least moment, that my youthful age is subject to the snares of lusts; and I am afraid to be without you, by whose sole presence all effeminacy, however irrational it be, is put to shame; although I trust, by the mercy of God, that even my mind, from what it has conceived through your instruction, shall be unable to receive aught else into its thoughts. Besides, I remember your saying at Cæsarea, 'If any one wishes to accompany me, without violating dutifulness, let him accompany me.' And by this you meant that he should not make any one sad, to whom he ought according to God's appointment to cleave; for example, that he should not leave a faithful wife, or parents, or the like. Now from these I am entirely free, and so I am fit for following you; and I wish you would grant me that I might perform to you the service of a servant."

CHAP. VI. — PETER'S SIMPLICITY OF LIFE.

Then Peter, laughing, said: "And do you not think, Clement, that very necessity must make you my servant? For who else can spread my sheets, and arrange my beautiful coverlets? Who will be at hand to keep my rings, and prepare my robes, which I must be constantly changing? Who shall superintend my cooks, and provide various and choice meats to be prepared by most recondite and various art; and all those things which are procured at enormous expense, and are brought together for men of delicate up-bringing, yea rather, for their appetite, as for some enormous beast? But perhaps, although you live with me, you do not know my manner of life. I live on bread alone, with olives, and seldom even with pot-herbs; and my dress is what you see, a tunic with a pallium: and having these, I require nothing more. This is sufficient for me, because my mind does not regard things present, but things eternal, and therefore no present and visible thing delights me. Whence I embrace and admire indeed your good mind towards me; and I commend you the more, because, though you have been accustomed to so great abundance, you have been able so soon to abandon it, and to accommodate yourself to this life of ours, which makes use of necessary things alone. For we — that is, I and my brother Andrew — have grown up from our childhood, not only orphans, but also extremely poor, and through necessity have become used to labour, whence now also we easily bear the fatigues of our journeyings. But rather, if you would consent and allow it, I, who am a working man, could more easily discharge the duty of a servant to you."

CHAP. VII. — PETER'S HUMILITY.

But I trembled when I heard this, and my tears immediately gushed forth, because so great a man, who is worth more than the whole world, had addressed such a proposal to me. Then he, when he saw me weeping, inquired the reason;

and I answered him: "How have I so sinned against you, that you should distress me with such a proposal?" Then Peter: "If it is evil that I said I should serve you, you were first in fault in saying the same thing to me." Then said I: "The cases are not alike: for it becomes me to do this to you; but it is grievous that you, who are sent as the herald of the Most High God to save the souls of men, should say it to me." Then said Peter: "I should agree with you, were it not that our Lord, who came for the salvation of the whole world, and who was nobler than any creature, submitted to be a servant, that He might persuade us not to be ashamed to perform the ministry of servants to our brethren." Then said I: "It were foolishness in me to suppose that I can prevail with you; nevertheless I give thanks to the providence of God, because I have merited to have you instead of parents."

CHAP. VIII. — CLEMENT'S FAMILY HISTORY.

Then said Peter: "Is there then no one of your family surviving?" I answered: "There are indeed many powerful men, coming of the stock of Cæsar; for Cæsar himself gave a wife to my father, as being his relative, and educated along with him, and of a suitably noble family. By her my father had twin sons, born before me, not very like one another, as my father told me; for I never knew them. But indeed I have not a distinct recollection even of my mother; but I cherish the remembrance of her face, as if I had seen it in a dream. My mother's name was Matthidia, my father's Faustinianus; my brothers', Faustinus and Faustus.[1] Now, when I was barely five years old, my mother saw a vision — so I learned from my father — by which she was warned that, unless she speedily left the city with her twin sons, and was absent for ten years, she and her children should perish by a miserable fate.

CHAP. IX. — DISAPPEARANCE OF HIS MOTHER AND BROTHERS.

"Then my father, who tenderly loved his sons, put them on board a ship with their mother, and sent them to Athens to be educated, with slaves and maid-servants, and a sufficient supply of money; retaining me only to be a comfort to him, and thankful for this, that the vision had not commanded me also to go with my mother. And at the end of a year my father sent men to Athens with money for them, desiring also to know how they did; but those who were sent

---

[1] [Comp. Homily XII. 8, where the names given are: Mattidia, Faustus (father); Faustinus and Faustinianus, the twin sons. With these names some connect the German legend of Faust; see Schaff, *History*, ii. 442. — R.]

never returned. Again, in the third year, my sorrowful father sent other men with money, who returned in the fourth year, and related that they had seen neither my mother nor my brothers, that they had never reached Athens, and that no trace had been found of any one of those who had been with them.

CHAP. X. — DISAPPEARANCE OF HIS FATHER.

" My father hearing this, and confounded with excessive sorrow, not knowing whither to go or where to seek, went down with me to the harbour, and began to ask of the sailors whether any of them had seen or heard of the bodies of a mother and two little children being cast ashore anywhere, four years ago ; when one told one story and another another, but nothing definite was disclosed to us searching in this boundless sea. Yet my father, by reason of the great affection which he bore to his wife and children, was fed with vain hopes, until he thought of placing me under guardians and leaving me at Rome, as I was now twelve years old, and himself going in quest of them. Therefore he went down to the harbour weeping, and going on board a ship, took his departure ; and from that time till now I have never received any letters from him, nor do I know whether he is alive or dead. But I rather suspect that he also has perished, either through a broken heart or by shipwreck ; for twenty years have now elapsed since then, and no tidings of him have ever reached me."

CHAP. XI. — DIFFERENT EFFECTS OF SUFFERING ON HEATHENS AND CHRISTIANS.

Peter, hearing this, shed tears of sympathy, and said to his friends who were present : " If any man who is a worshipper of God had endured what this man's father has endured, immediately men would assign his religion as the cause of his calamities ; but when these things happen to miserable Gentiles, they charge their misfortunes upon fate. I call them miserable, because they are both vexed with errors here, and are deprived of future hope ; whereas, when the worshippers of God suffer these things, their patient endurance of them contributes to their cleansing from sin."

CHAP. XII. — EXCURSION TO ARADUS.

After this, one of those present began to ask Peter, that early next day we should go to a neighbouring island called Aradus, which was not more than six furlongs off, to see a certain wonderful work that was in it, viz. vine-wood [1] columns of immense size. To this Peter assented, as he was very complaisant ; but he charged us

---

[1] Various reading, " glass."

that, when we left the ship, we should not rush all together to see it : " for," said he, " I do not wish you to be noticed by the crowd." When therefore, next day, we reached the island by ship in the course of an hour, forthwith we hastened to the place where the wonderful columns were. They were placed in a certain temple, in which there were very magnificent works of Phidias, on which every one of us gazed earnestly.

CHAP. XIII. — THE BEGGAR WOMAN.

But when Peter had admired only the columns, being no wise ravished with the grace of the painting, he went out, and saw before the gates a poor woman asking alms of those who went in ; and looking earnestly at her, he said : " Tell me, O woman, what member of your body is wanting, that you subject yourself to the indignity of asking alms, and do not rather gain your bread by labouring with your hands which God has given you." But she, sighing, said : " Would that I had hands which could be moved ; but now only the appearance of hands has been preserved, for they are lifeless, and have been rendered feeble and without feeling by my knawing of them." Then Peter said : " What has been the cause of your inflicting so great an injury upon yourself ? " " Want of courage," said she, " and nought else ; for if I had had any bravery in me, I could either have thrown myself from a precipice, or cast myself into the depths of the sea, and so ended my griefs."

CHAP. XIV. — THE WOMAN'S GRIEF.

Then Peter said : " Do you think, O woman, that those who destroy themselves are set free from torments, and not rather that the souls of those who lay violent hands upon themselves are subjected to greater punishments ? " Then said she : " I wish I were sure that souls live in the infernal regions, for I would gladly embrace the suffering of the penalty of suicide, only that I might see my darling children, if it were but for an hour." Then Peter : " What thing is it so great, that effects you with so heavy sadness ? I should like to know. For if you informed me of the cause, I might be able both to show you clearly, O woman, that souls do live in the infernal regions ; and instead of the precipice or the deep sea, I might give you some remedy, that you may be able to end your life without torment."

CHAP. XV. — THE WOMAN'S STORY.

Then the woman, hearing this welcome promise, began to say : " It is neither easy of belief, nor do I think it necessary to tell, what is my extraction, or what is my country. It is enough only to explain the cause of my grief, why I have rendered my hands powerless by gnawing them. Being born of noble parents, and having become the wife of a suitably powerful man, I had two twin sons, and after them one other. But my husband's brother was vehemently enflamed with unlawful love towards me; and as I valued chastity above all things, and would neither consent to so great wickedness, nor wished to disclose to my husband the baseness of his brother, I considered whether in any way I could escape unpolluted, and yet not set brother against brother, and so bring the whole race of a noble family into disgrace. I made up my mind, therefore, to leave my country with my two twins, until the incestuous love should subside, which the sight of me was fostering and inflaming; and I thought that our other son should remain to comfort his father to some extent.

CHAP. XVI. — THE WOMAN'S STORY CONTINUED.

" Now in order to carry out this plan, I pretended that I had had a dream, in which some deity stood by me in a vision, and told me that I should immediately depart from the city with my twins, and should be absent until he should command me to return; and that, if I did not do so, I should perish with all my children. And so it was done. For as soon as I told the dream to my husband, he was terrified; and sending with me my twin sons, and also slaves and maid-servants, and giving me plenty of money, he ordered me to sail to Athens, where I might educate my sons, and that I should stay there until he who commanded me to depart should give me leave to return. While I was sailing along with my sons, I was shipwrecked in the night by the violence of the winds, and, wretch that I am, was driven to this place; and when all had perished, a powerful wave caught me, and cast me upon a rock. And while I sat there with this only hope, that haply I might be able to find my sons, I did not throw myself into the deep, although then my soul, disturbed and drunk with grief, had both the courage and the power to do it.

CHAP. XVII. — THE WOMAN'S STORY CONTINUED.

" But when the day dawned, and I with shouting and howling was looking around, if I could even see the corpses of my unhappy sons anywhere washed ashore, some of those who saw me were moved with compassion, and searched, first over the sea, and then also along the shores, if they could find either of my children. But when neither of them was anywhere found, the women of the place, taking pity on me, began to comfort me, every one telling her own griefs, that I might take consolation from the likeness of their calamities to my own. But this saddened me all the more; for my disposition was not such that I could regard the misfortunes of others as comforts to me. And when many desired to receive me hospitably, a certain poor woman who dwells here constrained me to enter into her hut, saying that she had had a husband who was a sailor, and that he had died at sea while a young man, and that, although many afterwards asked her in marriage, she preferred widowhood through love of her husband. 'Therefore,' said she, 'we shall share whatever we can gain by the labour of our hands.'

CHAP. XVIII. — THE WOMAN'S STORY CONTINUED.

" And, not to detain you with a long and profitless story, I willingly dwelt with her on account of the faithful affection which she retained for her husband. But not long after, my hands (unhappy woman that I was!), long torn with gnawing, became powerless, and she who had taken me in fell into palsy, and now lies at home in her bed; also the affection of those women who had formerly pitied me grew cold. We are both helpless. I, as you see, sit begging; and when I get anything, one meal serves two wretches. Behold, now you have heard enough of my affairs; why do you delay the fulfilment of your promise, to give me a remedy, by which both of us may end our miserable life without torment?"

CHAP. XIX. — PETER'S REFLECTIONS ON THE STORY.

While she was speaking, Peter, being distracted with much thought, stood like one thunder-struck; and I Clement coming up, said: "I have been seeking you everywhere, and now what are we to do?" But he commanded me to go before him to the ship, and there to wait for him; and because he must not be gainsayed, I did as he commanded me. But he, as he afterwards told me the whole, being struck with a sort of suspicion, asked of the woman her family, and her country, and the names of her sons; "and straightway," he said, "if you tell me these things, I shall give you the remedy." But she, like one suffering violence, because she would not confess these things, and yet was desirous of the remedy, feigned one thing after another, saying that she was an Ephesian, and her husband a Sicilian, and giving false names to her sons. Then Peter, supposing that she had answered truly, said: "Alas! O woman, I thought that some great joy should spring up to us to-day; for I suspected that you were a certain woman, concerning whom I lately learned certain like things." But she adjured him, saying: "I entreat you to tell me what they are, that I may know if amongst women there be one more unfortunate than myself."

CHAP. XX. — PETER'S STATEMENT TO THE WOMAN.

Then Peter, incapable of deception, and moved with compassion, began to say : " There is a certain young man among those who follow me for the sake of religion and sect, a Roman citizen, who told me that he had a father and two twin brothers, of whom not one is left to him. ' My mother,' he said, ' as I learned from my father, saw a vision, that she should depart from the Roman city for a time with her twin sons, else they should perish by a dreadful death ; and when she had departed, she was never more seen.' And afterwards his father set out to search for his wife and sons, and was also lost."

CHAP. XXI. — A DISCOVERY.

When Peter had thus spoken, the woman, struck with astonishment, fainted. Then Peter began to hold her up, and to comfort her, and to ask what was the matter, or what she suffered. But she at length, with difficulty recovering her breath, and nerving herself up to the greatness of the joy which she hoped for, and at the same time wiping her face, said : " Is he here, the youth of whom you speak ? " But Peter, when he understood the matter, said : " Tell me first, or else you shall not see him." Then she said : " I am the mother of the youth." Then says Peter : " What is his name ? " And she answered : " Clement." Then said Peter : " It is himself ; and he it was that spoke with me a little while ago, and whom I ordered to go before me to the ship." Then she fell down at Peter's feet, and began to entreat him that he would hasten to the ship. Then Peter said : " Yes, if you will promise me that you will do as I say." Then she said : " I will do anything ; only show me my only son, for I think that in him I shall see my twins also." Then Peter said : " When you have seen him, dissemble for a little time, until we leave the island." " I will do so," she said.

CHAP. XXII. — A HAPPY MEETING.

Then Peter, holding her hand, led her to the ship. And when I saw him giving his hand to the woman, I began to laugh ; yet, approaching to do him honour, I tried to substitute my hand for his, and to support the woman. But as soon as I touched her hand, she uttered a loud scream, and rushed into my embrace, and began to devour me with a mother's kisses. But I, being ignorant of the whole matter, pushed her off as a mad woman ; and at the same time, though with reverence, I was somewhat angry with Peter.

CHAP. XXIII. — A MIRACLE.

But he said : " Cease : what mean you, O Clement, my son ? Do not push away your mother." But I, as soon as I heard these words, immediately bathed in tears, fell upon my mother, who had fallen down, and began to kiss her. For as soon as I heard, by degrees I recalled her countenance to my memory ; and the longer I gazed, the more familiar it grew to me. Meantime a great multitude assembled, hearing that the woman who used to sit and beg was recognised by her son, who was a good man.[1] And when we wished to sail hastily away from the island, my mother said to me : " My darling son, it is right that I should bid farewell to the woman who took me in ; for she is poor, and paralytic, and bedridden." When Peter and all who were present heard this, they admired the goodness and prudence of the woman ; and immediately Peter ordered some to go and to bring the woman in her bed as she lay. And when she had been brought, and placed in the midst of the crowd, Peter said, in the presence of all : " If I am a preacher of truth, for confirming the faith of all those who stand by, that they may know and believe that there is one God, who made heaven and earth, in the name of Jesus Christ, His Son, let this woman rise." And as soon as he had said this, she arose whole, and fell down at Peter's feet ; and greeting her friend and acquaintance with kisses, asked of her what was the meaning of it all. But she shortly related to her the whole proceeding of the *Recognition*,[2] so that the crowds standing around wondered.

CHAP. XXIV. — DEPARTURE FROM ARADUS.

Then Peter, so far as he could, and as time permitted, addressed the crowds on the faith of God, and the ordinances of religion ; and then added, that if any one wished to know more accurately about these things, he should come to Antioch, " where," said he, " we have resolved to stay three months, and to teach fully the things which pertain to salvation. For if," said he, " men leave their country and their parents for commercial or military purposes, and do not fear to undertake long voyages, why should it be thought burdensome or difficult to leave home for three months for the sake of eternal life ? " When he had said these things, and more to the same purpose, I presented a thousand drachmas to the woman who had entertained my mother, and who had recovered her health by means of Peter, and in the presence of all committed her to the charge of a certain good man, the chief person in that town, who promised that he would

[1] Perhaps, " a man in good position."
[2] [This is the title-word of the book, as is evident. Hence the italics here, and not in Homily XII. 23. — R.]

gladly do what we demanded of him. I also distributed a little money among some others, and among those women who were said formerly to have comforted my mother in her miseries, to whom I also expressed my thanks. And after this we sailed, along with my mother, to Antaradus.

CHAP. XXV. — JOURNEYINGS.

And when we had come to our lodging,[1] my mother began to ask of me what had become of my father; and I told her that he had gone to seek her, and never returned. But she, hearing this, only sighed; for her great joy on my account lightened her other sorrows. And the next day she journeyed with us, sitting with Peter's wife; and we came to Balaneæ, where we stayed three days, and then went on to Pathos, and afterwards to Gabala; and so we arrived at Laodicea, where Niceta and Aquila met us before the gates, and kissing us, conducted us to a lodging. But Peter, seeing that it was a large and splendid city, said that it was worthy that we should stay in it ten days, or even longer. Then Niceta and Aquila asked of me who was this unknown woman; and I answered: "It is my mother, whom God has given back to me by means of my lord Peter."

CHAP. XXVI. — RECAPITULATION.

And when I had said this, Peter began to relate the whole matter to them in order,[2] and said . "When we had come to Aradus,[3] and I had ordered you to go on before us, the same day after you had gone, Clement was led in the course of conversation to tell me of his extraction and his family, and how he had been deprived of his parents, and had had twin brothers older than himself, and that, as his father told him, his mother once saw a vision, by which she was ordered to depart from the city of Rome with her twin sons, else she and they should suddenly perish. And when she had told his father the dream, he, loving his sons with tender affection, and afraid of any evil befalling them, put his wife and sons on board a ship with all necessaries, and sent them to Athens to be educated. Afterwards he sent once and again persons to inquire after them, but nowhere found even a trace of them. At last the father himself went on the search, and until now he is nowhere *to be found*. When Clement had given me this narrative, there came one to us, asking us to go to the neighbouring island of Aradus,

to see vine-wood columns of wonderful size. I consented; and when we came to the place, all the rest went into the interior of the temple; but I — for what reason I know not — had no mind to go farther.

CHAP. XXVII. — RECAPITULATION CONTINUED.

"But while I was waiting outside for them, I began to notice this woman, and to wonder in what part of her body she was disabled, that she did not seek her living by the labour of her hands, but submitted to the shame of beggary. I therefore asked of her the reason of it. She confessed that she was sprung of a noble race, and was married to a no less noble husband, 'whose brother,' said she, 'being inflamed by unlawful love towards me, desired to defile his brother's bed. This I abhorring, and yet not daring to tell my husband of so great wickedness, lest I should stir up war between the brothers, and bring disgrace upon the family, judged it better to depart from my country with my two twin sons, leaving the younger boy to be a comfort to his father. And that this might be done with an honourable appearance, I thought good to feign a dream, and to tell my husband that there stood by me in a vision a certain deity, who told me to set out from the city immediately with my two twins, and remain until he should instruct me to return.' She told me that her husband, when he heard this, believed her, and sent her to Athens, with the twin children to be educated there; but that they were driven by a terrible tempest upon that island, where, when the ship had gone to pieces, she was lifted by a wave upon a rock, and delayed killing herself only for this, 'until,' said she, 'I could embrace at least the dead limbs of my unfortunate sons, and commit them to burial. But when the day dawned, and crowds had assembled, they took pity upon me, and threw a garment over me. But I, miserable, entreated them with many tears, to search if they could find anywhere the bodies of my unfortunate sons. And I, tearing all my body with my teeth, with wailing and howlings cried out constantly, Unhappy woman that I am, where is my Faustus? where my Faustinus?'"

CHAP. XXVIII. — MORE RECOGNITIONS.

And when Peter said this,[4] Niceta and Aquila suddenly started up, and being astonished, began to be greatly agitated, saying: "O Lord, Thou Ruler and God of all, are these things true, or are we in a dream?" Then Peter said: "Unless we be mad, these things are true." But they, after a short pause, and wiping their faces,

---

[1] [At this point a discourse of the Apostle on "philanthropy" is inserted in the *Homilies* (xii. 25–33). Homily XIII. 1 corresponds with this chapter. — R.]

[2] [This account is fuller than that in Homily XIII. 2. — R.]

[3] There is a confusion in the text between Aradus and Antaradus. [Aradus is the name of the island, Antaradus that of the neighbouring city. — R.]

[4] [With chaps. 28–36 the narrative in Homily XIII. 3–11 corresponds quite closely. — R.]

said : " We are Faustinus and Faustus: and even at the first, when you began this narrative, we immediately fell into a suspicion that the matters that you spoke of might perhaps relate to us ; yet again considering that many like things happen in men's lives, we kept silence, although our hearts were struck by some hope. Therefore we waited for the end of your story, that, if it were entirely manifest that it related to us, we might then confess it." And when they had thus spoken, they went in weeping to our mother. And when they found her asleep, and wished to embrace her, Peter prevented them, saying : " Permit me first to prepare your mother's mind, lest haply by the great and sudden joy she lose her reason, and her understanding be disturbed, especially as she is now stupefied with sleep."

CHAP. XXIX. — " NOTHING COMMON OR UNCLEAN."

Therefore, when our mother had risen from her sleep, Peter began to address her, saying : " I wish you to know, O woman, an observance of our religion. We worship one God, who made the world, and we keep His law, in which He commands us first of all to worship Him, and to reverence His name, to honour our parents, and to preserve chastity and uprightness. But this also we observe, not to have a common table with Gentiles, unless when they believe, and on the reception of the truth are baptized, and consecrated by a certain threefold invocation of the blessed name ; and then we eat with them.[1] Otherwise, even if it were a father or a mother, or wife, or sons, or brothers, we cannot have a common table with them. Since, therefore, we do this for the special cause of religion, let it not seem hard to you that your son cannot eat with you, until you have the same judgment of the faith that he has."

CHAP. XXX. — " WHO CAN FORBID WATER ? "

Then she, when she heard this, said : " And what hinders me to be baptized to-day? For even before I saw you I was wholly alienated from those whom they call gods, because they were not able to do anything for me, although I frequently, and almost daily, sacrificed to them. And as to chastity, what shall I say, when neither in former times did pleasures deceive me, nor afterwards did poverty compel me to sin? But I think you know well enough how great was my love of chastity, when I pretended that dream that I might escape the snares of unhallowed love, and that I might go abroad with my two twins. and when I left this my son Clement alone to be a comfort to his father. For if

two were scarcely enough for me, how much more it would have saddened their father, if he had had none at all? For he was wretched through his great affection towards our sons, so that even the authority of the dream could scarce prevail upon him to give up to me Faustinus and Faustus, the brothers of this Clement, and that himself should be content with Clement alone."

CHAP. XXXI. — TOO MUCH JOY.

While she was yet speaking, my brothers could contain themselves no longer, but rushed into their mother's embrace with many tears, and kissed her. But she said : " What is the meaning of this ? " Then said Peter : " Be not disturbed, O woman ; be firm. These are your sons Faustinus and Faustus, whom you supposed to have perished in the deep ; but how they are alive, and how they escaped in that horrible night, and how the one of them is called Niceta and the other Aquila, they will be able to explain to you themselves, and we also shall hear it along with you." When Peter had said this, our mother fainted, being overcome with excess of joy ; and after some time, being restored and come to herself, she said : " I beseech you, darling sons, tell me what has befallen you since that dismal and cruel night."

CHAP. XXXII. — " HE BRINGETH THEM UNTO THEIR DESIRED HAVEN."

Then Niceta began to say : " On that night, O mother, when the ship was broken up, and we were being tossed upon the sea, supported on a fragment of the wreck, certain men, whose business it was to rob by sea, found us, and placed us in their boat, and overcoming the power of the waves by rowing, by various stretches brought us to Cæsarea Stratonis. There they starved us, and beat us, and terrified us, that we might not disclose the truth ; and having changed our names, they sold us to a certain widow, a very honourable women, named Justa. She, having bought us, treated us as sons, so that she carefully educated us in Greek literature and liberal arts. And when we grew up, we also attended to philosophic studies, that we might be able to confute the Gentiles, by supporting the doctrines of the divine religion by philosophic disputations.

CHAP. XXXIII. — ANOTHER WRECK PREVENTED.

" But we adhered, for friendship's sake, and boyish companionship, to one Simon, a magician, who was educated along with us, so that we were almost deceived by him. For there is mention made in our religion of a certain Prophet, whose coming was hoped for by all who observe that

---

[1] [Comp. Homily XIII. 4. — R.]

religion, through whom immortal and happy life is promised to be given to those who believe in Him. Now we thought that this Simon was he. But these things shall be explained to you, O mother, at a more convenient season. Meanwhile, when we were almost deceived by Simon, a certain colleague of my lord Peter, Zacchæus by name, warned us that we should not be duped by the magician, but presented us to Peter on his arrival, that by him we might be taught the things which were sound and perfect. And this we hope will happen to you also, even as God has vouchsafed it to us, that we may be able to eat and have a common table with you. Thus therefore it was, O mother, that you believed that we were drowned in the sea, while we were stolen by pirates."

CHAP. XXXIV. — BAPTISM MUST BE PRECEDED BY FASTING.

When Niceta had spoken thus, our mother fell down at Peter's feet, entreating and beseeching him that both herself and her hostess might be baptized without delay; "that," said she, "I may not even for a single day suffer the loss of the company and society of my sons." In like manner, we her sons also entreated Peter. But he said: "What! Do you think that I alone am unpitiful, and that I do not wish you to enjoy your mother's society at meals? But she must fast at least one day first, and so be baptized; and this because I have heard from her a certain declaration, by which her faith has been made manifest to me, and which has given evidence of her belief; otherwise she must have been instructed and taught many days before she could have been baptized."

CHAP. XXXV. — DESIRING THE SALVATION OF OTHERS.

Then said I : "I pray you, my lord Peter, tell us what is that declaration which you say afforded you evidence of her faith?" Then Peter: "It is her asking that her hostess, whose kindnesses she wishes to requite, may be baptized along with her. Now she would not ask that this grace be bestowed upon her whom she loves, unless she believed that there is some great boon in baptism. Whence, also, I find fault with very many, who, when they are themselves baptized and believe, yet do nothing worthy of faith with those whom they love, such as wives, or children, or friends, whom they do not exhort to that which they themselves have attained, *as they would do* if indeed they believed that eternal life is thereby bestowed. In short, if they see them to be sick, or to be subject to any danger bodily, they grieve and mourn, because they are sure that in this destruction threatens them. So, then,

if they were sure of this, that the punishment of eternal fire awaits those who do not worship God, when would they cease warning and exhorting? Or, if they refused, how would they not mourn and bewail them, being sure that eternal torments awaited them? Now, therefore, we shall send for that woman at once, and see if she loves the faith of our religion; and as we find, so shall we act. But since your mother has judged so faithfully concerning baptism, let her fast only one day before baptism."

CHAP. XXXVI. — THE SONS' PLEADING.

But she declared with an oath, in presence of my lord Peter's wife, that from the time she recognised her son, she had been unable to take any food from excess of joy, excepting only that yesterday she drank a cup of water. Peter's wife also bore witness, saying that it was even so. Then Aquila said: "What, then, hinders her being baptized?" Then Peter, smiling, said: "But this is not the fast of baptism, for it was not done in order to baptism." Then Niceta said: "But perhaps God, wishing that our mother, on our recognition, should not be separated even for one day from participation of our table, pre-ordained this fasting. For as in her ignorance she preserved her chastity, that it might profit her in order to the grace of baptism; so she fasted before she knew the reason of fasting, that it might profit her in order to baptism, and that immediately, from the beginning of our acquaintance, she might enjoy communion of the table with us."

CHAP. XXXVII. — PETER INEXORABLE.

Then said Peter :[1] "Let not the wicked one prevail against us, taking occasion from a mother's love; but let you, and me with you, fast this day along with her, and to-morrow she shall be baptized: for it is not right that the precepts of truth be relaxed and weakened in favour of any person or friendship. Let us not shrink, then, from suffering along with her, for it is a sin to transgress any commandment. But let us teach our bodily senses, which are without us, to be in subjection to our inner senses; and not compel our inner senses, which savour the things that be of God, to follow the outer senses, which savour the things that be of the flesh. For to this end also the Lord commanded, saying: 'Whosoever shall look upon a woman to lust after her, hath committed adultery with her already in his heart.' And to this He added: 'If thy right eye offend thee, pluck it out, and cast it from thee: for it is profitable for thee

---

[1] [In Homily XIII. 12 the Apostle is represented as thus deferring the baptism; but a longer discourse on chastity (chaps. 13-21) is given, assigned to the evening of that day. — R.]

that one of thy members perish, rather than thy whole body be cast into hell-fire.'[1] He does not say, *has offended thee*, that you should then cast away the cause of sin after you have sinned; but *if it offend you*, that is, that before you sin you should cut off the cause of the sin that provokes and irritates you. But let none of you think, brethren, that the Lord commended the cutting off of the members. His meaning is, that the purpose should be cut off, not the members, and the causes which allure to sin, in order that our thought, borne up on the chariot of sight, may push towards the love of God, supported by the bodily senses;[2] and not give loose reins to the eyes of the flesh as to wanton horses, eager to turn their running outside the way of the commandments, but may subject the bodily sight to the judgment of the mind, and not suffer those eyes of ours, which God intended to be viewers and witnesses of His work, to become panders of evil desire. And therefore let the bodily senses as well as the internal thought be subject to the law of God, and let them serve His will, whose work they acknowledge themselves to be."

CHAP. XXXVIII. — REWARD OF CHASTITY.

Therefore, as the order and reason of the mystery demanded, on the following day she was baptized in the sea,[3] and returning to the lodging, was initiated in all the mysteries of religion

---

[1] Matt. v. 28, 29.
[2] Here a marginal reading is followed. The reading of the text is: " In order that our thought, borne on the chariot of contemplation, may hasten on, invisible to the bodily senses, towards the love of God." But the translation of *aspectus* by "contemplation" is doubtful.
[3] [The baptism is narrated in Homily XIV. 1. — R.]

in their order. And we her sons, Niceta and Aquila, and I Clement, were present. And after this we dined with her, and glorified God with her, thankfully acknowledging the zeal and teaching of Peter, who showed us, by the example of our mother, that the good of chastity is not lost with God;[4] "as, on the other hand," said he, "unchastity does not escape punishment, though it may not be punished immediately, but slowly. But so well pleasing," said he, " is chastity to God, that it confers some grace in the present life even upon those who are in error; for future blessedness is laid up for those only who preserve chastity and righteousness by the grace of baptism. In short, that which has befallen your mother is an example of this, for all this welfare has been restored to her in reward of her chastity, for the guarding and preserving of which continence alone is not sufficient; but when any one perceives that snares and deceptions are being prepared, he must straightway flee as from the violence of fire or the attack of a mad dog, and not trust that he can easily frustrate snares of this kind by philosophizing or by humouring them; but, as I have said, he must flee and withdraw to a distance, as your mother also did through her true and entire love of chastity. And on this account she has been preserved to you, and you to her; and in addition, she has been endowed with the knowledge of eternal life." When he had said this, and much more to the same effect, the evening having come, we went to sleep.

---

[4] [In Homily XIII. 20, 21, a longer discourse, to the same effect, is recorded; but it is addressed to the mother the evening before her baptism. — R.]

BOOK VIII.

CHAP. I. — THE OLD WORKMAN.

Now the next morning Peter took my brothers and me with him, and we went down to the harbour to bathe in the sea, and thereafter we retired to a certain secret place for prayer. But a certain poor old man, a workman, as he appeared by his dress, began to observe us eagerly, without our seeing him, that he might see what we were doing in secret.[1] And when he saw

---

[1] [From this point there are considerable variations in the two narratives. The old man becomes, in the *Recognitions*, a prominent participant in the discussions, arguing with Peter, and with Niceta, Aquila, and Clement. At the close of these discussions he is recognised first by the sons (ix. 35), and then by his wife, as Faustinianus (ix. 37). In the *Homilies* Peter tells of an interview with the old man (xiv. 2–8), and the recognition takes place immediately upon his appearance (xiv. 9). Some discussion with him follows (Homily XV.); but soon the main controversy is with Simon Magus (Homilies XVI.-XIX.), in the presence of the father, who is convinced by Peter. Book x. contains much matter introduced in Homilies IV.-VII. The correspondences will be indicated in the footnotes. — R.]

us praying, he waited till we came out, and then saluted us, and said: "If you do not take it amiss, and regard me as an inquisitive and importunate person, I should wish to converse with you; for I take pity on you, and would not have you err under the appearance of truth, and be afraid of things that have no existence; or if you think that there is any truth in them, then declare it to me. If, therefore, you take it patiently, I can in a few words instruct you in what is right; but if it be unpleasant to you, I shall go on, and do my business." To him Peter answered: "Speak what you think good, and we will gladly hear, whether it be true or false; for you are to be welcomed, because, like a father anxious on behalf of his children, you wish to put us in possession of what you regard as good."

CHAP. II. — GENESIS.

Then the old man proceeded to say : " I saw you bathe in the sea, and afterwards retire into a secret place ; wherefore observing, without your noticing me, what you were doing, I saw you praying. Therefore, pitying your error, I waited till you came out, that I might speak to you, and instruct you not to err in an observance of this sort ; because there is neither any God, nor any worship, neither is there any providence in the world, but all things are done by fortuitous chance and *genesis*, as I have discovered most clearly for myself, being accomplished beyond others in the discipline of learning.[1] Do not err, therefore : for whether you pray, or whether you do not pray, whatever your *genesis* contains, that shall befall you." Then I Clement was affected, I know not how, in my heart, recollecting many things in him that seemed familiar to me ; for some one says well, that that which is sprung from any one, although it may be long absent, yet a spark of relationship is never extinguished.[2] Therefore I began to ask of him who and whence he was, and how descended. But he, not wishing to answer these questions, said : " What has that to do with what I have told you? But first, if you please, let us converse of those matters which we have propounded ; and afterwards, if circumstances require, we can disclose to one another, as friends to friends, our names, and families, and country, and other things connected with these." Yet we all admired the eloquence of the man, and the gravity of his manners, and the calmness of his speech.

CHAP. III. — A FRIENDLY CONFERENCE.

But Peter, walking along leisurely while conversing, was looking out for a suitable place for a conference. And when he saw a quiet recess near the harbour, he made us sit down ; and so he himself first began. Nor did he hold the old man in any contempt, nor did he look down upon him because his dress was poor and mean. He said, therefore : " Since you seem to me to be a learned man, and a compassionate, inasmuch as you have come to us, and wish that to be known to us which you consider to be good, we also wish to expound to you what things we believe to be good and right ; and if you do not think them true, you will take in good part our good intentions towards you, as we do yours towards us." While Peter was thus speaking, a great multitude assembled. Then said the old man : " Perhaps the presence of a multitude disconcerts you." Peter replied : " Not at all, except only on this account, that I am afraid lest haply, when the truth is made manifest in the course of our discussion, you be ashamed in presence of the multitude to yield and assent to the things which you may have understood to be spoken truly." To this the old man answered : " I am not such a fool in my old age, that, understanding what is true, I should deny it for the favour of the rabble."

CHAP. IV. — THE QUESTION STATED.

Then Peter began to say : " Those who speak the word of truth, and who enlighten the souls of men, seem to me to be like the rays of the sun, which, when once they have come forth and appeared to the world, can no longer be concealed or hidden, while they are not so much seen by men, as they afford sight to all. Therefore it was well said by One to the heralds of the truth, ' Ye are the light of the world, and a city set upon a hill cannot be hid ; neither do men light a candle and put it under a bushel, but upon a candlestick, that it may enlighten all who are in the house.' "[3] Then said the old man : " He said well, whoever he is. But let one of you state what, according to his opinion, ought to be followed, that we may direct our speech to a definite aim. For, in order to find the truth, it is not sufficient to overthrow the things that are spoken on the other side, but also that one should himself bring forward what he who is on the other side may oppose. Therefore, in order that both parties may be on an equal footing, it seems to me to be right that each of us should first enunciate what opinion he holds. And, if you please, I shall begin first. I say, then, that the world is not governed according to the providence of God, because we see that many things in it are done unjustly and disorderly ; but I say that it is *genesis* that does and regulates all things."

CHAP. V. — FREEDOM OF DISCUSSION ALLOWED.

When Peter was about to reply to this, Niceta, anticipating him, said :[4] " Would my lord Peter allow me to answer to this ; and let it not be thought forward that I, a young man, should have an encounter with an old man, but rather let me converse as a son with a father." Then said the old man : " Not only do I wish, my son, that you should set forth your opinions ; but also if any one of your associates, if any one

---

[1] [In Homily XIV. 2–5 there is a discussion somewhat similar to the beginning of this one, but reported by the Apostle to the family of Clement. — R.]

[2] [There are a number of indications, like this, in the narrative, foreshadowing the recognition of the old man as the father. In the *Homilies* nothing similar appears. — R.]

[3] Matt. v. 14, 15.

[4] [The whole arrangement, introducing the brothers as disputants, is peculiar to the *Recognitions*. The several discourses are constructed with much skill. The courtesy of the discussion is in sharp contrast with the tone of those in the *Homilies*, especially those with Simon Magus. — R.]

even of the bystanders, thinks that he knows anything, let him unhesitatingly state it: we shall gladly hear it; for it is by the contribution of many that the things that are unknown are more easily found out." Then Niceta therefore answered: " Do not deem me to have done rashly, my father, because I have interrupted the speech of my lord Peter; but rather I meant to honour him by doing this. For he is a man of God, full of all knowledge, who is not ignorant even of Greek learning, because he is filled with the Spirit of God, to whom nothing is unknown. But because it is suitable to him to speak of heavenly things, I shall answer concerning those things which pertain to the babbling of the Greeks. But after we have disputed in the Grecian manner, and we have come to that point where no issue appears, then he himself, as filled with the knowledge of God, shall openly and clearly disclose to us the truth on all matters, so that not we only, but also all who are around us as hearers, shall learn the way of truth. And therefore now let him sit as umpire; and when either of us shall yield, then let him, taking up the matter, give an unquestionable judgment."

CHAP. VI. — THE OTHER SIDE OF THE QUESTION STATED.

When Niceta had thus spoken, those who had assembled conversed among themselves: " Is this that Peter of whom we heard, the most approved disciple of Him who appeared in Judæa, and wrought many signs and miracles?" And they stood gazing upon him with great fear and veneration, as conferring upon the Lord the honour of His good servant. Which when Peter observed, he said to them: " Let us hear with all attention, holding an impartial judgment of what shall be said by each; and after their encounter we also shall add what may seem necessary." And when Peter had said this, the crowds rejoiced. Then Niceta began to speak as follows: " You have laid down, my father, that the world is not governed by the providence of God, but that all things are subject to genesis, whether the things which relate to the dispositions, or those which relate to the doings of every one. This I could answer immediately; but because it is right to observe order, we also lay down what we hold, as you yourself requested should be done. I say that the world is governed by the providence of God, at least in those things which need His government. For He it is alone who holds all things in His hand, who also made the world; the just God, who shall at some time render to every one according to his deeds. Now, then, you have our position; go on as you please, either overthrowing mine or establishing your own, that I may meet your

statements. Or if you wish me to speak first, I shall not hesitate."

CHAP. VII. — THE WAY CLEARED.

Then the old man answered: " Whether it pleases you, my son, to speak first, or whether you prefer that I should speak, makes no difference, especially with those who discuss in a friendly spirit. However, speak you first, and I will gladly hear; and I wish you may be able even to follow out those things that are to be spoken by me, and to put in opposition to them those things that are contrary to them, and from the comparison of both to show the truth." Niceta answered: " If you wish it, I can even state your side of the argument, and then answer it." Then the old man: " Show me first how you can know what I have not yet spoken, and so I shall believe that you can follow out my side of the argument." Then Niceta: " Your sect is manifest, even by the proposition which you have laid down, to those who are skilled in doctrines of this sort; and its consequence is certain. And because I am not ignorant what are the propositions of the philosophers, I know what follows from those things which you have propounded; especially because I have frequented the schools of Epicurus in preference to the other philosophers. But my brother Aquila has attended more to the Pyrrhonists, and our other brother to the Platonists and Aristotelians; therefore you have to do with learned hearers."[1] Then said the old man: " You have well and logically informed us how you perceived the things that follow from the statements which have been enunciated. But I professed something more than the tenet of Epicurus; for I introduced the genesis, and asserted that it is the cause of all the doings of men."

CHAP. VIII. — INSTINCTS.

When the old man had said this, I Clement said to him: " Hear, my father: if my brother Niceta bring you to acknowledge that the world is not governed without the providence of God, I shall be able to answer you in that part which remains concerning the genesis; for I am well acquainted with this doctrine." And when I had thus spoken, my brother Aquila said: " What is the use of our calling him father, when we are commanded to call no man father upon earth?"[2] Then, looking to the old man, he said, " Do not take it amiss, my father, that I have found fault with my brother for calling you father, for we have a precept not to call any one by that name." When Aquila said that, all the assembly of the bystanders, as well as the old man and Peter,

---

[1] [Comp. Homily XIII. 7. — R.]
[2] Matt. xxiii. 9.

laughed. And when Aquila asked the reason of their all laughing, I said to him: "Because you yourself do the very thing which you find fault with in another; for you called the old man *father.*" But he denied it, saying: "I am not aware that I called him *father.*" Meantime Peter was moved with certain suspicions,[1] as he told us afterwards; and looking to Niceta, he said, "Go on with what you have proposed."

CHAP. IX. — SIMPLE AND COMPOUND.

Then Niceta began as follows:[2] "Everything that is, is either simple or compound. That which is simple is without number, division, colour, difference, roughness, smoothness, weight, lightness, quality, quantity, and therefore without end. But that which is compound is either compounded of two, or of three, or even of four *elements*, or at all events of several; and things which are compounded can also of necessity be divided." The old man, hearing this, said: "You speak most excellently and learnedly, my son." Then Niceta went on: "Therefore that which is simple, and which is without any of those things by which that which subsists can be dissolved, is without doubt incomprehensible and infinite, knowing neither beginning nor end, and therefore is one and alone, and subsisting without an author. But that which is compound is subject to number, and diversity, and division, — is necessarily compounded by some author, and is a diversity collected into one species. That which is infinite is therefore, in respect of goodness, a Father; in respect of power, a Creator. Nor can the power of creating cease in the Infinite, nor the goodness be quiescent; but He is impelled by goodness to change existing things, and by power to arrange and strengthen them. Therefore some things, as we have said, are changed, and composed of two or three, some of four, others of more elements. But since our inquiry at present is concerning the method of the world and its substance, which, it is agreed, is compounded of four elements, to which all those ten differences belong which we have mentioned above, let us begin at these lower steps, and come to the higher. For a way is afforded us to intellectual and invisible things from those which we see and handle; as is contained in arithmetical instructions, where, when inquiry is made concerning divine things, we rise from the lower to the higher numbers; but when the method respecting present and visible things is expounded,

the order is directed from the higher to the lower numbers. Is it not so?"

CHAP. X. — CREATION IMPLIES PROVIDENCE.

Then the old man said: "You are following it out exceedingly well." Then Niceta: "Now, then, we must inquire concerning the method of the world; of which the first inquiry is divided into two parts. For it is asked whether it has been made or not? And if it has not been made, itself must be that Unbegotten from which all things are. But if it has been made, concerning this again the question is divided into two parts, whether it was made by itself, or by another. And if indeed it was made by itself, then without doubt providence is excluded. If providence is not admitted, in vain is the mind incited to virtue, in vain justice is maintained, if there be no one to render to the just man according to his merits. But even the soul itself will not appear to be immortal, if there be no dispensation of providence to receive it after its escape from the body.

CHAP. XI. — GENERAL OR SPECIAL PROVIDENCE.

"Now, if it be taught that there is a providence, and that the world was made by it, other questions meet us which must be discussed. For it will be asked, In what way providence acts, whether generally towards the whole, or specially towards the parts, or generally also towards the parts, or both generally towards the whole, and specially towards the parts? But by general providence we mean this: as if God, at first making the world, has given an order and appointed a course to things, and has ceased to take any further care of what is done. But special providence towards the parts is of this sort, that He exercises providence over some men or places, but not over others. But general over all, and at the same time special over the parts, is in this wise: if God made all things at first, and exercises providence over each individual even to the end, and renders to every one according to his deeds.

CHAP. XII. — PRAYER INCONSISTENT WITH GENESIS.

"Therefore that first proposition, which declares that God made all things in the beginning, and having imposed a course and order upon things, takes no further account of them, affirms that all things are done according to *genesis*. To this, therefore, we shall first reply; and especially to those who worship the gods and defend *genesis*. Assuredly, these men, when they sacrifice to the gods and pray to them, hope that they shall obtain something in opposition to *genesis*, and so they annul *genesis*. But when they laugh at those who incite to virtue and exhort to

---

[1] [Another foreshadowing of the approaching recognition; peculiar to this narrative. — R.]

[2] [The argument of Niceta (chaps. 9-34), while it necessarily includes statements occurring elsewhere in this literature, is, as a whole, peculiar to the *Recognitions*. In order of arrangement and logical force it is much superior to most of the discourses. — R.]

continence, and say that nobody can do or suffer anything unless what is decreed to him by fate, they assuredly cut up by the roots all worship of the Divinity. For why should you worship those from whom you can obtain nothing which the method of what is decreed does not allow? Let this suffice in the meantime, in opposition to these men. But I say that the world is made by God, and that it is at some time to be destroyed by Him, that that world may appear which is eternal, and which is made for this end, that it may be always, and that it may receive those who, in the judgment of God, are worthy of it. But that there is another and invisible world, which contains this visible world within itself,—after we have finished our discussion concerning the visible world, we shall come to it also.

CHAP. XIII. — A CREATOR NECESSARY.

" Now, in the meantime, that this visible world has been made, very many wise men among the philosophers do testify. But that we may not seem to make use of assertions as witnesses, as though we needed them, let us inquire, if you please, concerning its principles. That this visible world is material, is sufficiently evident from the fact that it is visible. But every body receives *one of* two DIFFERENTIÆ; for it is either compact and solid, or divided and separate. And if the body of which the world was made was compact and solid, and that body was parted and divided through diverse species and parts according to its differences, there must necessarily be understood to have been some one to separate the body which was compact and solid, and to draw it into many parts and diverse forms ; or if all this mass of the world was compounded and compacted from diverse and dispersed parts of bodies, still there must be understood to have been some one to collect into one the dispersed parts, and to invest these things with their different species.

CHAP. XIV. — MODE OF CREATION.

" And, indeed, I know that several of the philosophers were rather of this opinion, that God the Creator made divisions and distinctions from one body, which they call MATTER, which yet consisted of four elements, mingled into one by a certain tempering of divine providence. For I think that what some have said is vain, that the body of the world is simple, that is, without any conjunction ; since it is evident that what is simple can neither be a body, nor can be mixed, or propagated, or dissolved ; all which, we see, happen to the bodies of the world. For how could it be dissolved if it were simple, and had not within it that from which it might be

resolved and divided? But if bodies seem to be composed of two, or three, or even of four elements, — who that has even a small portion of sense does not perceive that there must have been some one who collected several into one, and preserving the measure of tempering, made a solid body out of diverse parts? This *some one*, therefore, we call God, the Creator of the world, and acknowledge Him as the author of the universe.

CHAP. XV. — THEORIES OF CREATION.

" For the Greek philosophers, inquiring into the beginnings of the world, have gone, some in one way and some in another. In short, Pythagoras says that numbers are the elements of its beginnings ; Callistratus, that qualities ; Alcmæon, that contrarieties ; Anaximander, that immensity ; Anaxagoras, that equalities of parts ; Epicurus, that atoms ; Diodorus, that $\dot{a}\mu\epsilon\rho\hat{\eta}$, that is, things in which there are no parts ; Asclepius, that $\ddot{o}\gamma\kappa o\iota$, which we may call tumours or swellings ; the geometricians, that ends ; Democritus, that ideas ; Thales, that water ; Heraclitus, that fire ; Diogenes, that air ; Parmenides, that earth ; Zeno, Empedocles, Plato, that fire, water, air, and earth. Aristotle also introduces a fifth element, which he called $\dot{a}\kappa a\tau ov\acute{o}\mu a\sigma\tau ov$; that is, that which cannot be named ; without doubt indicating Him who made the world, by joining the four elements into one. Whether, therefore, there be two, or three, or four, or more, or innumerable elements, of which the world consists, in every supposition there is shown to be a God, who collected many into one, and again drew them, when collected, into diverse species ; and by this it is proved that the machine of the world could not have subsisted without a maker and a disposer.

CHAP. XVI. — THE WORLD MADE OF NOTHING BY A CREATOR.

" But from this fact also, that in the conjunction of the elements, if one be deficient or in excess, the others are loosened and fall, is shown that they took their beginning from nothing. For if, for example, moisture be wanting in any body, neither will the dry stand ; for dry is fed by moisture, as also cold by heat ; in which, as we have said, if one be defective, the whole are dissolved. And in this they give indications of their origin, that they were made out of nothing. Now if matter itself is proved to have been made, how shall its parts and its species, of which the world consists, be thought to be unmade? But about matter and its qualities this is not the time to speak : only let it suffice to have taught this, that God is the Creator of all things, because neither, if the body of which the world consists was solid and united, could it be separated and distinguished without a Creator; nor, if it was collected into one from diverse and separate parts, could it be collected and mixed without a Maker. Therefore, if God is so clearly shown to be the Creator of the world, what room is there for Epicurus to introduce atoms, and to assert that not only sensible bodies, but even intellectual and rational minds, are made of insensible corpuscles?

CHAP. XVII. — DOCTRINE OF ATOMS UNTENABLE.

"But you will say, according to the opinion of Epicurus, that successions of atoms coming in a ceaseless course, and mixing with one another, and conglomerating through unlimited and endless periods of time, are made solid bodies. I do not treat this opinion as a pure fiction, and that, too, a badly contrived one; but let us examine it, whatever be its character, and see if what is said can stand. For they say that those corpuscles, which they call atoms, are of different qualities: that some are moist, and therefore heavy, and tending downwards; others dry and earthy, and therefore still heavy; but others fiery, and therefore always pushing upwards; others cold and inert, and always remaining in the middle. Since then some, as being fiery, always tend upward, and others, as being moist and dry, always downwards, and others keep a middle and unequal course, how could they meet together and form one body? For if any one throw down from a height small pieces of straw, for example, and pieces of lead of the same size, will the light straws be able to keep up with the pieces of lead, though they be equal in size? Nay; the heavier reach the bottom far more quickly. So also atoms, though they be equal in size, yet, being unequal in weight, the lighter will never be able to keep pace with the heavier; but if they cannot keep pace, certainly neither can they be mixed or form one body.

CHAP. XVIII. — THE CONCOURSE OF ATOMS COULD NOT MAKE THE WORLD.

"Then, in the next place, if they are ceaselessly borne about, and always coming, and being added to things whose measure is already complete, how can the universe stand, when new weights are always being heaped upon so vast weights? And this also I ask: If this expanse of heaven which we see was constructed by the gradual concurrence of atoms, how did it not collapse while it was in construction, if indeed the yawning top of the structure was not propped and bound by any stays? For as those who build circular domes, unless they bind the fastening of the central top, the whole falls at once; so also the circle of the world, which we see to

be brought together in so graceful a form, if it was not made at once, and under the influence of a single forth-putting of divine energy by the power of a Creator, but by atoms gradually concurring and constructing it, not as reason demanded, but as a fortuitous issue befell, how did it not fall down and crumble to pieces before it could be brought together and fastened? And further, I ask this: What is the pavement on which the foundations of such an immense mass are laid? And again, what you call the pavement, on what does it rest? And again that other, what supports it? And so I go on asking, until the answer comes to nothing and vacuity!

CHAP. XIX. — MORE DIFFICULTIES OF THE ATOMIC THEORY.

"But if any one say that atoms of a fiery quality, being joined together, formed a body, and because the quality of fire does not tend downwards, but upwards, that the nature of fire, always pushing upwards, supports the mass of the world placed upon it; to this we answer: How could atoms of a fiery quality, which always make for the highest place, descend to the lower, and be found in the lowest place of all, so as to form a foundation for all; whereas rather the heavier qualities, that is, the earthy or watery, always come before the lighter, as we have said; hence, also, they assert that the heaven, as the higher structure, is composed of fiery atoms, which are lighter, and always fly upwards? Therefore the world cannot have foundations of fire, or any other: nor can there be any association or compacting of the heavier atoms with the lighter, that is, of those which are always borne downwards, with those that always fly upwards. Thus it is sufficiently shown that the bodies of the world are consolidated by the union of atoms; and that insensible bodies, even if they could by any means concur and be united, could not give forms and measures to bodies, form limbs, or effect qualities, or express quantities; all which, therefore, by their exactness, attest the hand of a Maker, and show the operation of reason, which reason I call the Word, and God.

CHAP. XX. — PLATO'S TESTIMONY.

"But some one will say that these things are done by nature. Now, in this, the controversy is about a name. For while it is evident that it is a work of mind and reason, what you call nature, I call God the Creator. It is evident that neither the species of bodies, arranged with so necessary distinctions, nor the faculties of minds, could or can be made by irrational and senseless work. But if you regard the philosophers as fit witnesses, Plato testifies concerning these things in the *Timæus*, where, in a discussion on the making of the world, he asks, whether it has existed always, or had a beginning, and decides that it was made. ' For,' says he, ' it is visible and palpable, and corporeal; but it is evident that all things which are of this sort have been made; but what has been made has doubtless an author, by whom it was made. This Maker and Father of all, however, it is difficult to discover; and when discovered, it is impossible to declare Him to the vulgar.' Such is the declaration of Plato; but though he and the other Greek philosophers had chosen to be silent about the making of the world, would it not be manifest to all who have any understanding? For what man is there, having even a particle of sense, who, when he sees a house having all things necessary for useful purposes, its roof fashioned into the form of a globe, painted with various splendour and diverse figures, adorned with large and splendid lights; who is there, I say, that, seeing such a structure, would not immediately pronounce that it was constructed by a most wise and powerful artificer? And so, who can be found so foolish, as, when he gazes upon the fabric of the heaven, perceives the splendour of the sun and moon, sees the courses and beauty of the stars, and their paths assigned to them by fixed laws and periods, will not cry out that these things are made, not so much by a wise and rational artificer, as by wisdom and reason itself?

CHAP. XXI. — MECHANICAL THEORY.

" But if you would rather have the opinions of others of the Greek philosophers, — and you are acquainted with mechanical science, — you are of course familiar with what is their deliverance concerning the heavens. For they suppose a sphere, equally rounded in every direction, and looking indifferently to all points, and at equal distances in all directions from the centre of the earth, and so stable by its own symmetry, that its perfect equality does not permit it to fall off to any side; and so the sphere is sustained, although supported by no prop. Now if the fabric of the world really has this form, the divine work is evident in it. But if, as others think, the sphere is placed upon the waters, and is supported by them, or floating in them, even so the work of a great contriver is shown in it.

CHAP. XXII. — MOTIONS OF THE STARS.

" But lest the assertion may seem doubtful respecting things which are not manifest to all, let us come to those things of which nobody is ignorant. Who disposed the courses of the stars with so great reason, ordained their risings and settings, and appointed to each one to accomplish the circuit of the heavens in certain and regular times? Who assigned to some to be al-

ways approaching to the setting, and others to be returning to the rising? Who put a measure upon the courses of the sun, that he might mark out, by his diverse motions, hours, and days, and months, and changes of seasons? — that he might distinguish, by the sure measurement of his course, now winter, then spring, summer, and afterwards autumn, and always, by the same changes of the year, complete the circle with variety, without confusion? Who, I say, will not pronounce that the director of such order is the very wisdom of God? And these things we have spoken according to the relations given us by the Greeks respecting the science of the heavenly bodies.

CHAP. XXIII. — PROVIDENCE IN EARTHLY THINGS.

" But what of those things also which we see on the earth, or in the sea? Are we not plainly taught, that not only the work, but also the providence, of God is in them? For whereas there are on the earth lofty mountains in certain places, *the object of this is*, that the air, being compressed and confined by them through the appointment of God, may be forced and pressed out into winds, by which fruits may germinate, and the summer heat may be moderated when the Pleiades glow, fired with the blaze of the sun. But you still say, Why that blaze of the sun, that moderating should be required? How, then, should fruits be ripened which are necessary for the uses of men? But observe this also, that at the meridian axis,[1] where the heat is greatest, there is no great collection of clouds, nor an abundant fall of rain, lest disease should be produced among the inhabitants; for watery clouds, if they are acted on by rapid heat, render the air impure and pestilential. And the earth also, receiving the warm rain, does not afford nourishment to the crops, but destruction. In this who can doubt that there is the working of divine providence? In short, Egypt, which is scorched with the heat of Æthiopia, in its neighbourhood, lest its air should be incurably vitiated by the effects of showers, its plains do not receive rain furnished to them from the clouds, but, as it were, an earthly shower from the overflow of the Nile.

CHAP. XXIV. — RIVERS AND SEAS.

" What shall we say of fountains and rivers, which flow with perpetual motion into the sea? And, by the divine providence, neither does their abundant supply fail, nor does the sea, though it receives so great quantities of water, experience any increase, but both those elements which contribute to it and those which are thus contributed

---

[1] That is, the equator.

remain in the same proportion. But you will say to me : The salt water naturally consumes the fresh water which is poured into it. Well, in this is manifest the work of providence, that it made that element salt into which it turned the courses of all the waters which it had provided for the use of men. So that through so great spaces of time the channel of the sea has not been filled, and produced a deluge destructive to the earth and to men. Nor will any one be so foolish as to think that this so great reason and so great providence has been arranged by irrational nature.

CHAP. XXV. — PLANTS AND ANIMALS.

"But what shall I say of plants, and what of animals? Is it not providence that has ordained that plants, when they decay by old age, should be reproduced by the suckers or the seeds which they have themselves produced, and animals by propagation? And by a certain wonderful dispensation of providence, milk is prepared in the udders of the dams for the animals before they are born ; and as soon as they are born, with no one to guide them, they seek out the store of nourishment provided for them. And not only males are produced, but females also, that by means of both the race may be perpetuated. But lest this should seem, as some think, to be done by a certain order of nature, and not by the appointment of the Creator, He has, as a proof and indication of His providence, ordained a few animals to preserve their stock on the earth in an exceptional way : for example, the crow conceives through the mouth, and the weasel brings forth through the ear ; and some birds, such as hens, sometimes produce eggs conceived of wind or dust ; other animals convert the male into the female, and change their sex every year, as hares and hyænas, which they call monsters ; others spring from the earth, and get their bodies from it, as moles ; others from ashes, as vipers ; others from putrifying flesh, as wasps from horse-flesh, bees from ox-flesh ; others from cow-dung, as beetles ; others from herbs, as the scorpion from the basil ; and again, herbs from animals, as parsley and asparagus from the horn of the stag or the she-goat.

CHAP. XXVI. — GERMINATION OF SEEDS.

"And what occasion is there to mention more instances in which divine providence has ordained the production of animals to be effected in various ways, that order being superseded which is thought to be assigned by nature, from which not an irrational course of things, but one arranged by his own reason, might be evinced? And in this also is there not a full work of providence shown, when seeds sown are prepared by means of earth and water for the sustenance of men? For when these seeds are committed to the earth, the soil milks upon the seeds, as from its teats, the moisture which it has received into itself by the will of God. For there is in water a certain power of the spirit given by God from the beginning, by whose operation the structure of the body that is to be begins to be formed in the seed itself, and to be developed by means of the blade and the ear ; for the grain of seed being swelled by the moisture, that power of the spirit which has been made to reside in water, running as an incorporeal substance through certain strait passages of veins, excites the seeds to growth, and forms the species of the growing plants. By means, therefore, of the moist element in which that vital spirit is contained and inborn, it is caused that not only is it revived, but also that an appearance and form in all respects like to the seeds that had been sown is reproduced. Now, who that has even a particle of sense will think that this method depends upon irrational nature, and not upon divine wisdom? Lastly, also these things are done in a resemblance of the birth of men ; for the earth seems to take the place of the womb, into which the seed being cast, is both formed and nourished by the power of water and spirit, as we have said above.

CHAP. XXVII. — POWER OF WATER.

"But in this also the divine providence is to be admired, that it permits us to see and know the things that are made, but has placed in secrecy and concealment the way and manner in which they are done, that they may not be competent to the knowledge of the unworthy, but may be laid open to the worthy and faithful, when they shall have deserved it. But to prove by facts and examples that nothing is imparted to seeds of the substance of the earth, but that all depends upon the element of water, and the power of the spirit which is in it, — suppose, for example, that a hundred talents' weight of earth are placed in a very large trough, and that there are sown in it several kinds of seeds, either of herbs or of shrubs, and that water enough is supplied for watering them, and that that care is taken for several years, and that the seeds which are gathered are stored up, for example of corn or barley and other sorts separately from year to year, until the seeds of each sort amount to a hundred talents' weight, then also let the stalks be pulled up by the roots and weighed ; and after all these have been taken from the trough, let the earth be weighed, it will still give back its hundred talents' weight undiminished.[1] Whence, then, shall we say that all that weight, and all

---

[1] [De Maistre, *Soirées*, vi. 259.]

the quantity of different seeds and stalks, has come? Does it not appear manifestly that it has come from the water? For the earth retains entire what is its own, but the water which has been poured in all through is nowhere, on account of the powerful virtue of the divine condition, which by the one species of water both prepares the substances of so many seeds and shrubs, and forms their species, and preserves the kind while multiplying the increase.

CHAP. XXVIII. — THE HUMAN BODY.

" From all these things I think it is sufficiently and abundantly evident that all things are produced; and the universe consists by a designing sense, and not by the irrational operation of nature. But let us come now, if you please, to our own substance, that is, the substance of man, who is a small world, *a microcosm*, in the great world; and let us consider with what reason it is compounded: and from this especially you will understand the wisdom of the Creator. For although man consists of different substances, one mortal and the other immortal, yet, by the skilful contrivance of the Creator, their diversity does not prevent their union, and that although the substances be diverse and alien the one from the other. For the one is taken from the earth and formed by the Creator, but the other is given from immortal substances; and yet the honour of its immortality is not violated by this union. Nor does it, as some think, consist of reason, and concupiscence, and passion, but rather such affections seem to be in it, by which it may be moved in each of these directions. For the body, which consists of bones and flesh, takes its beginning from the seed of a man, which is extracted from the marrow by warmth, and conveyed into the womb as into a soil, to which it adheres, and is gradually moistened from the fountain of the blood, and so is changed into flesh and bones, and is formed into the likeness of him who injected the seed.

CHAP. XXIX. — SYMMETRY OF THE BODY.

" And mark in this the work of the Designer, how He has inserted the bones like pillars, on which the flesh might be sustained and carried. Then, again, how an equal measure is preserved on either side, that is, the right and the left, so that foot answers to foot, hand to hand, and even finger to finger, so that each agrees in perfect equality with each; and also eye to eye, and ear to ear, which not only are suitable to and matched with each other, but also are formed fit for necessary uses. The hands, for instance, are so made as to be fit for work; the feet for walking; the eyes, protected with sentinel eye-brows, to serve the purpose of sight; the ears so formed for hearing, that, like a cymbal, they vibrate the sound of the word that falls upon them, and send it inward, and transmit it even in the understanding of the heart; whereas the tongue, striking against the teeth in speaking, performs the part of a fiddle-bow. The teeth also are formed, some for cutting and dividing the food, and handing it over to the inner ones; and these, in their turn, bruise and grind it like a mill, that it may be more conveniently digested when it is conveyed into the stomach; whence also they are called grinders.

CHAP. XXX. — BREATH AND BLOOD.

" The nostrils also are made for the purpose of collecting, inspiring, and expiring air, that by the renewal of the breath, the natural heat which is in the heart may, by means of the lungs, be either warmed or cooled, as the occasion may require; while the lungs are made to abide in the breast, that by their softness they may soothe and cherish the vigour of the heart, in which the life seems to abide; — the life, I say, not the soul. And what shall I say of the substance of the blood, which, proceeding as a river from a fountain, and first borne along in one channel, and then spreading through innumerable veins, as through canals, irrigates the whole territory of the human body with vital streams, being supplied by the agency of the liver, which is placed in the right side, for effecting the digestion of food and turning it into blood? But in the left side is placed the spleen, which draws to itself, and in some way cleanses, the impurities of the blood.

CHAP. XXXI. — THE INTESTINES.

" What reason also is employed in the intestines, which are arranged in long circular windings, that they may gradually carry off the refuse of the food, so as neither to render places suddenly empty, and so as not to be hindered by the food that is taken afterwards! But they are made like a membrane, that the parts that are outside of them may gradually receive moisture, which if it were poured out suddenly would empty the internal parts; and not hindered by a thick skin, which would render the outside dry, and disturb the whole fabric of man with distressing thirst.

CHAP. XXXII. — GENERATION.

" Moreover, the female form, and the cavity of the womb, most suitable for receiving, and cherishing, and vivifying the germ, who does not believe that it has been made as it is by reason and foresight? — because in that part alone of her body the female differs from the male, in which the fœtus being placed, is kept and cherished. And again the male differs from the female only in that part of his body in which is the power of injecting seed and propagating mankind. And in this there is a great proof of providence, from the necessary difference of members; but more in this, where, under a likeness of form there is found to be diversity of use and variety of office. For males and females equally have teats, but only those of the female are filled with milk; that, as soon as they have brought forth, the infant may find nourishment suited to him. But if we see the members in man arranged with such method, that in all the rest there is seen to be similarity of form, and a difference only in those in which their use requires a difference, and we neither see anything superfluous nor anything wanting in man, nor in woman anything deficient or in excess, who will not, from all these things, acknowledge the operation of reason, and the wisdom of the Creator?

CHAP. XXXIII. — CORRESPONDENCES IN CREATION.

" With this agrees also the reasonable difference of other animals, and each one being suited to its own use and service. This also is testified by the variety of trees and the diversity of herbs, varying both in form and in juices. This also is asserted by the change of seasons, distinguished into four periods, and the circle closing the year with certain hours, days, months, and not deviating from the appointed reckoning by a single hour. Hence, in short, the age of the world itself is reckoned by a certain and fixed account, and a definite number of years.

CHAP. XXXIV. — TIME OF MAKING THE WORLD.

" But you will say, When was the world made? And why so late? This you might have objected, though it had been made sooner. For you might say, Why not also before this? And so, going back through unmeasured ages, you might still ask, And why not sooner? But we are not now discussing this, why it was not made sooner; but whether it was made at all. For if it is manifest that it was made, it is necessarily the work of a powerful and supreme Artificer; and if this is evident, it must be left to the choice and judgment of the wise Artificer, when He should please to make it; unless indeed you think that all this wisdom, which has constructed the immense fabric of the world, and has given to the several objects their forms and kinds, assigning to them a habit not only in accordance with beauty, but also most convenient and necessary for their future uses, — unless, I say, you think that this alone has escaped it, that it should choose a convenient season for so magnificent a work of creation. He has doubtless a certain reason and evident causes why, and when,

and how He made the world; but it were not proper that these should be disclosed to those who are reluctant to inquire into and understand the things which are placed before their eyes, and which testify of His providence. For those things which are kept in secret, and are hidden within the senses of Wisdom, as in a royal treasury, are laid open to none but those who have learned of Him, with whom these things are sealed and laid up. It is God, therefore, who made all things, and Himself was made by none. But those who speak of nature instead of God, and declare that all things were made by nature, do not perceive the mistake of the name which they use. For if they think that nature is irrational, it is most foolish to suppose that a rational creature can proceed from an irrational creator. But if it is Reason — that is, Logos [1] — by which it appears that all things were made, they change the name without purpose, when they make statements concerning the reason of the Creator. If you have anything to say to these things, my father, say on."

CHAP. XXXV. — A CONTEST OF HOSPITALITY.

When Niceta had thus spoken, the old man answered: " You indeed, my son, have conducted your argument wisely and vigorously; so much so, that I do not think the subject of providence could be better treated. But as it is now late, I wish to say some things to-morrow in answer to what you have argued; and if on these you can satisfy me, I shall confess myself a debtor to your favour." And when the old man said this, Peter rose up. Then one of those present, a chief man of the Laodiceans, requested of Peter and us that he might give the old man other clothes instead of the mean and torn ones that he wore. [2] This man Peter and we embraced; and praising him for his honourable and excellent intention, said: " We are not so foolish and impious as not to bestow the things which are necessary for bodily uses upon him to whom we have committed so precious words; and we hope that he will willingly receive them, as a father from his sons, and also we trust that he will share with us our house and our living." While we said this, and that chief man of the city strove to take the old man away from us with the greatest urgency and with many blandishments, while we the more eagerly strove to keep him with us, all the people cried out that it should rather be done as the old man himself pleased; and when silence was obtained, the old man, with an oath, said: " To-day I shall stay with no

---

[1] [Comp. John i. 1-3. The expression seems to be used here with a polemic purpose. — R.]
[2] [This incident is peculiar to the *Recognitions*. There seems to be a reminiscence of this chief man in Homily IV. 10, where a rich man provides a place for the discussion; comp. chap. 38 here. — R.]

one, nor take anything from any one, lest the choice of the one should prove the sorrow of the other ; afterwards these things may be, if so it seem right."

CHAP. XXXVI. — ARRANGEMENTS FOR TO-MORROW.

And when the old man had said this, Peter said to the chief man of the city : "Since you have shown your good-will in our presence, it is not right that you should go away sorrowful ; but we will accept from you favour for favour. Show us your house, and make it ready, so that the discussion which is to be to-morrow may be held there, and that any who wish to be present to hear it may be admitted." When the chief man of the city heard this, he rejoiced greatly ; and all the people also heard it gladly. And when the crowds had dispersed, he pointed out his house ; and the old man also was preparing to depart. But I commanded one of my attendants to follow the old man secretly, and find out where he stayed. And when we returned to our lodging, we told our brethren all our dealings with the old man ; and so, as usual, we supped and went to sleep.

CHAP. XXXVII. — "THE FORM OF SOUND WORDS, WHICH YE HAVE HEARD OF ME."

But on the following day Peter arose early and called us, and we went together to the secret place in which we had been on the previous day, for the purpose of prayer. And when, after prayer, we were coming thence to the appointed place, he exhorted us by the way, saying :[1] "Hear me, most beloved fellow-servants : It is good that every one of you, according to his ability, contribute to the advantage of those who are approaching to the faith of our religion ; and therefore do not shrink from instructing the ignorant, and teaching according to the wisdom which has been bestowed upon you by the providence of God, yet so that you only join the eloquence of your discourse with those things which you have heard from me, and which have been committed to you. But do not speak anything which is your own, and which has not been committed to you, though it may seem to yourselves to be true ; but hold forth those things, as I have said, which I myself have received from the true Prophet, and have delivered to you, although they may seem to be less full of authority. For thus it often happens that men turn away from the truth, while they believe that they have found out, by their own thoughts, a form of truth more true and powerful."

CHAP. XXXVIII. — THE CHIEF MAN'S HOUSE.

To these counsels of Peter we willingly assented, saying to him that we should do nothing but what was pleasing to him. Then said he : "That you may therefore be exercised without danger, each of you conduct the discussion in my presence, one succeeding another, and each one elucidating his own questions. Now, then, as Niceta discoursed sufficiently yesterday, let Aquila conduct the discussion to-day ; and after Aquila, Clement ; and then I, if the case shall require it, will add something." Meantime, while we were talking in this way, we came to the house ; and the master of the house welcomed us, and led us to a certain apartment, arranged after the manner of a theatre, and beautifully built. There we found great crowds waiting for us, who had come during the night, and amongst them the old man who had argued with us yesterday. Therefore we entered, having Peter in the midst of us, looking about if we could see the old man anywhere ; and when Peter saw him hiding in the midst of the crowd, he called him to him, saying : "Since you possess a soul more enlightened than most, why do you hide yourself, and conceal yourself in modesty? Rather come hither, and propound your sentiments."

CHAP. XXXIX. — RECAPITULATION OF YESTERDAY'S ARGUMENT.

When Peter had thus spoken, immediately the crowd began to make room for the old man.[2] And when he had come forward, he thus began : "Although I do not remember the words of the discourse which the young man delivered yesterday, yet I recollect the purport and the order of it ; and therefore I think it necessary, for the sake of those who were not present yesterday, to call up what was said, and to repeat everything shortly, that, although something may have escaped me, I may be reminded of it by him who delivered the discourse, who is now present. This, then, was the purport of yesterday's discussion : that all things that we see, inasmuch as they consist in a certain proportion, and art, and form, and species, must be believed to have been made by intelligent power ; but if it be mind and reason that has formed them, it follows that the world is governed by the providence of the same reason, although the things which are done in the world may seem to us to be not quite rightly done. But it follows, that if God and mind is the creator of all things, He must also be just ; but if

---

[1] [Peculiar to the *Recognitions;* there is probably here an anti-Pauline purpose. — R.]

[2] [The second day's discussion, in which Aquila is the main speaker, is also of a high order. It is, as already indicated, peculiar to the *Recognitions*, though with the usual incidental correspondences in the *Homilies*. — R.]

He is just, He necessarily judges. If He judges, it is of necessity that men be judged with respect to their doings; and if every one is judged in respect of his doings, there shall at some time be a righteous separation between righteous men and sinners. This, I think, was the substance of the whole discourse.

CHAP. XL. — GENESIS.

"If, therefore, it can be shown that mind and reason created all things, it follows that those things which come after are also managed by reason and providence. But if unintelligent and blind nature produces all things, the reason of judgment is undoubtedly overthrown; and there is no ground to expect either punishment of sin or reward of well-doing where there is no judge. Since, then, the whole matter depends upon this, and hangs by this head, do not take it amiss if I wish this to be discussed and handled somewhat more fully. For in this the first gate, as it were, is shut towards all things which are propounded, and therefore I wish first of all to have it opened to me. Now therefore hear what my doctrine is; and if any one of you pleases, let him reply to me: for I shall not be ashamed to learn, if I hear that which is true, and to assent to him who speaks rightly. The discourse, then, which you delivered yesterday, which asserted that all things consist by art, and measure, and reason, does not fully persuade me that it is mind and reason that has made the world; for I have many things which I can show to consist by competent measure, and form, and species, and which yet were not made by mind and reason. Then, besides, I see that many things are done in the world without arrangement, consequence, or justice, and that nothing can be done without the course of GENESIS. This I shall in the sequel prove most clearly from my own case."

CHAP. XLI. — THE RAINBOW.

When the old man had thus spoken, Aquila answered: "As you yourself proposed that any one who pleased should have an opportunity of answering to what you might say, my brother Niceta permits me to conduct the argument to-day." Then the old man: "Go on, my son, as you please." And Aquila answered: "You promised that you would show that there are many things in the world which have a form and species arranged by equal reason, which yet it is evident were not effected by God as their Creator. Now, then, as you have promised, point out these things." Then said the old man: "Behold, we see the bow in the heaven assume a circular shape, completed in all proportion, and have an appearance of reality, which per-

haps neither mind could have constructed nor reason described; and yet it is not made by any mind. Behold, I have set forth the whole in a word: now answer me."

CHAP. XLII. — TYPES AND FORMS.

Then said Aquila: "If anything is expressed from a type and form, it is at once understood that it is from reason, and that it could not be made without mind; since the type itself, which expresses figures and forms, was not made without mind. For example, if wax be applied to an engraved ring, it takes the stamp and figure from the ring, which undoubtedly is without sense; but then the ring, which expresses the figure, was engraven by the hand of a workman, and it was mind and reason that gave the type to the ring. So then the bow also is expressed in the air; for the sun, impressing its rays on the clouds in the process of rarefaction, and affixing the type of its circularity to the cloudy moisture, as it were to soft wax, produces the appearance of a bow; and this, as I have said, is effected by the reflection of the sun's brightness upon the clouds, and reproducing the brightness of its circle from them. Now this does not always take place, but only when the opportunity is presented by the rarefaction of moistened clouds. And consequently, when the clouds again are condensed and unite, the form of the bow is dissolved and vanishes. Finally, the bow never is seen without sun and clouds, just as the image is not produced, unless there be the type, and wax, or some other material. Nor is it wonderful if God the Creator in the beginning made types, from which forms and species may now be expressed. But this is similar to that, that in the beginning God created insensible elements, which He might use for forming and developing all other things. But even those who form statues, first make a mould of clay or wax, and from it the figure of the statue is produced. And then afterwards a shadow is also produced from the statue, which shadow always bears the form and likeness of the statue. What shall we say then? That the insensible statue forms a shadow finished with as diligent care as the statue itself? Or shall the finishing of the shadow be unhesitatingly ascribed to him who has also fashioned the statue?

CHAP. XLIII. — THINGS APPARENTLY USELESS AND VILE MADE BY GOD.

"If, then, it seems to you that this is so, and what has been said on this subject is enough, let us come to inquire into other matters; or if you think that something is still wanting, let us go over it again." And the old man said: "I wish you would go over this again, since there are many other things which I see to be made in like manner: for both the fruits of trees are produced in like manner, beautifully formed and wonderfully rounded; and the appearance of the leaves is formed with immense gracefulness, and the green membrane is woven with exquisite art: then, moreover, fleas, mice, lizards, and such like, shall we say that these are made by God? Hence, from these vile objects a conjecture is derived concerning the superior, that they are by no means formed by the art of mind." "You infer well," said Aquila, "concerning the texture of leaves, and concerning small animals, that from these belief is withdrawn from the superior creatures; but let not these things deceive you, that you should think that God, working as it were only with two hands, could not complete all things that are made; but remember how my brother Niceta answered you yesterday, and truly disclosed the mystery before the time, as a son speaking with his father, and explained why and how things are made which seem to be useless."

CHAP. XLIV. — ORDINATE AND INORDINATE.

Then the old man: "I should like to hear from you why those useless things are made by the will of that supreme mind?" "If," said he, "it is fully manifest to you that there is in them the work of mind and reason, then you will not hesitate to say also why they were made, and to declare that they have been rightly made." To this the old man answered: "I am not able, my son, to say that those things which seem formed by art are made by mind, by reason of other things which we see to be done unjustly and disorderly in the world." "If," says Aquila, "those things which are done disorderly do not allow you say that they are done by the providence of God, why do not those things which are done orderly compel you to say that they are done by God, and that irrational nature cannot produce a rational work? For it is certain, nor do we at all deny, that in this world some things are done orderly, and some disorderly. Those things, therefore, that are done rationally, believe that they are done by providence; but those that are done irrationally and inordinately, that they befall naturally, and happen accidentally. But I wonder that men do not perceive, that where there is sense things may be done ordinately and inordinately, but where there is no sense neither the one nor the other can be done; for reason makes order, and the course of order necessarily produces something inordinate, if anything contrary happen to disturb order." Then the old man: "This very thing I wish you to show me."

CHAP. XLV. — MOTIONS OF THE SUN AND MOON.

Says Aquila: "I shall do so without delay. Two visible signs are shown in heaven — one of the sun, the other of the moon; and these are followed by five other stars, each describing its own separate orbit. These, therefore, God has placed in the heaven, by which the temperature of the air may be regulated according to the seasons, and the order of vicissitudes and alternations may be kept. But by means of the very same *signs*, if at any time plague and corruption is sent upon the earth for the sins of men, the air is disturbed, pestilence is brought upon animals, blight upon crops, and a destructive year in every way upon men; and thus it is that by one and the same means order is both kept and destroyed. For it is manifest even to the unbelieving and unskilful, that the course of the sun, which is useful and necessary to the world, and which is assigned by providence, is always kept orderly; but the courses of the moon, in comparison of the course of the sun, seem to the unskilful to be inordinate and unsettled in her waxings and wanings. For the sun moves in fixed and orderly periods: for from him are hours, from him the day when he rises, from him also the night when he sets; from him months and years are reckoned, from him the variations of seasons are produced; while, rising to the higher regions, he tempers the spring; but when he reaches the top of the heaven, he kindles the summer's heats: again, sinking, he produces the temper of autumn; and when he returns to his lowest circle, he bequeaths to us the rigour of winter's cold from the icy binding of heaven.

CHAP. XLVI. — SUN AND MOON MINISTERS BOTH OF GOOD AND EVIL.

"But we shall discourse at greater length on these subjects at another time. Now, meantime, *we remark that* though he is that good servant for regulating the changes of the seasons, yet, when chastisement is inflicted upon men according to the will of God, he glows more fiercely, and burns up the world with more vehement fires. In like manner also the course of the moon, and that changing which seems to the unskilful to be disorderly, is adapted to the growth of crops, and cattle, and all living creatures; for by her waxings and wanings, by a certain wonderful contrivance of providence, everything that is born is nourished and grows; concerning which we could speak more at length and unfold the matter in detail, but that the method of the question proposed recalls us. Yet, by the very same appliances by which they are produced, all things are nourished and increased; but when, from any just cause, the regulation of the appointed order is changed, corruption and distemper arise, so that chastisement may come upon men by the will of God, as we have said above.

CHAP. XLVII. — CHASTISEMENTS ON THE RIGHTEOUS AND THE WICKED.

" But perhaps you will say, What of the fact that, in that common chastisement, like things befall the pious and the impious? It is true, and we confess it; but the chastisement turns to the advantage of the pious, that, being afflicted in the present life, they may come more purified to the future, in which perpetual rest is prepared for them, and that at the same time even the impious may somewhat profit from their chastisement, or else that the just sentence of the future judgment may be passed upon them; since in the same chastisements the righteous give thanks to God, while the unrighteous blaspheme. Therefore, since the opinion of things is divided into two parts, that some things are done by order and others against order, it ought, from those things which are done according to order, to be believed that there is a providence; but with respect to those things which are done against order, we should inquire their causes from those who have learned them by prophetic teaching: for those who have become acquainted with prophetic discourse know when, and for what reason, blight, hail, and pestilence, and such like, have occurred in every generation, and for what sins these have been sent as a punishment; whence causes of sadness, lamentations, and griefs have befallen the human race; whence also trembling sickness has ensued, and that this has been from the beginning the punishment of parricide.[1]

CHAP. XLVIII. — CHASTISEMENTS FOR SINS.

" For in the beginning of the world there were none of these evils, but they took their rise from the impiety of men; and thence, with the constant increase of iniquities, the number of evils has also increased. But for this reason divine providence has decreed a judgment with respect to all men, because the present life was not such that every one could be dealt with according to his deservings. Those things, therefore, which were well and orderly appointed from the beginning, when no causes of evil existed, are not to be judged of from the evils which have befallen the world by reason of the sins of men. In short, as an indication of the things which were from the beginning, some nations are found which are strangers to these evils. For the Seres, because they live chastely, are kept

free from them all; for with them it is unlawful to come at a woman after she has conceived, or while she is being purified. No one there eats unclean flesh, no one knows aught of sacrifices; all are judges to themselves according to justice. For this reason they are not chastened with those plagues which we have spoken of; they live to extreme old age, and die without sickness. But we, miserable as we are, dwelling as it were with deadly serpents[2] — I mean with wicked men — necessarily suffer with them the plagues of afflictions in this world, but we cherish hope from the comfort of good things to come."

CHAP. XLIX. — GOD'S PRECEPTS DESPISED.

" If," said the old man, " even the righteous are tormented on account of the iniquities of others, God ought, as foreseeing this, to have commanded men not to do those things from which it should be necessary that the righteous be afflicted with the unrighteous; or if they did them, He ought to have applied some correction or purification to the world."[3] " God," said Aquila, " did so command, and gave precepts by the prophets how men ought to live; but even these precepts they despised: yea, if any desired to observe them, them they afflicted with various injuries, until they drove them from their purposed observance, and turned them to the rabble of infidelity, and made them like unto themselves.

CHAP. L. — THE FLOOD.

" Wherefore, in short, at the first, when all the earth had been stained with sins, God brought a flood upon the world, which you say happened under Deucalion; and at that time He saved a certain righteous man, with his sons, in an ark, and with him the race of all plants and animals.[4] And yet even those who sprang from them, after a time, again did deeds like to those of their predecessors; for those things that had befallen them were forgotten, so that their descendants did not even believe that the flood had taken place. Wherefore God also decreed that there should not be another flood in the present world, else there should have been one in every generation, according to the account of their sins by reason of their unbelief; but He rather granted that certain angels who delight in evil should bear sway over the several nations — and to them was given power over individual men, yet only on this condition, if any one first had made himself subject to them by sinning — until He should come who delights in good, and by Him the number of the righteous should be completed, and by the increase of the number of

---

[1] Gen. iv. 12, in LXX.

[2] Ezek. ii. 6.
[3] This rendering is according to a marginal reading.
[4] [Comp. book iv. 12; Homily VIII. 17. — R.]

pious men all over the world impiety should be in some measure repressed, and it should be known to all that all that is good is done by God.

CHAP. LI. — EVILS BROUGHT IN BY SIN.

"But by the freedom of the will, every man, while he is unbelieving in regard to things to come, by evil deeds runs into evils. And these are the things in the world which seem to be done contrary to order, which owe their existence to unbelief. Therefore the dispensation of divine providence is withal to be admired, which granted to those men in the beginning, walking in the good way of life, to enjoy incorruptible good things; but when they sinned, they gave birth to evil by sin. And to every good thing evil is joined as by a certain covenant of alliance on the part of sin, since indeed the earth has been polluted with human blood, and altars have been lighted to demons, and they have polluted the very air by the filthy smoke of sacrifices; and so at length the elements, being first corrupted, have handed over to men the fault of their corruption, as roots *communicate their qualities* to the branches and the fruit.

CHAP. LII. — "NO ROSE WITHOUT ITS THORN."

"Observe therefore in this, as I have said, how justly divine providence comes to the help of things vitiated; that, inasmuch as evils which had derived their origin from sin were associated with the good things of God, He should assign two chiefs to these two departments.[1] And *accordingly* to Him who rejoices in good He has appointed the ordering of good things, that He might bring those who believe *in Him* to the faith of His providence; but to him who rejoices in evil, He has given over those things which are done without order and uselessly, from which of course the faith of His providence comes into doubt; and thus a just division has been made by a just God. Hence therefore it is, that whereas the orderly course of the stars produces faith that the world was made by the hand of a designer, on the other hand, the disturbance of the air, the pestilent breeze, the uncontrolled fire of the lightning, cast doubt upon the work of providence. For, as we have said, every good thing has its corresponding contrary evil thing joined with it; as hail is opposite to the fertilizing showers, the corruption of mildew is associated with the gentle dew, the whirlwinds of storms are joined with the soft winds, unfruitful trees with fruitful, noxious herbs with useful, wild and destructive animals with gentle ones. But all these things are arranged by God, because

[1] [Compare with chaps. 52–54 the doctrine of pairs as stated in book iii. 59–61; Homily II. 15, etc., iii. 23. — R.]

that the choice of men's will has departed from the purpose of good, and fallen away to evil.

CHAP. LIII. — EVERYTHING HAS ITS CORRESPONDING CONTRARY.

"Therefore this division holds in all the things of the world; and as there are pious men, so there are also impious; as there are prophets, so also there are false prophets; and amongst the Gentiles there are philosophers and false philosophers. Also the Arabian nations, and many others, have imitated the circumcision of the Jews for the service of their impiety. So also the worship of demons is contrary to the divine worship, baptism to baptism, laws to the law, false apostles to apostles, and false teachers to teachers. And hence it is that among the philosophers some assert providence, others deny it; some maintain that there is one God, others that there are more than one: in short, the matter has come to this, that whereas demons are expelled by the word of God, by which it is declared that there is a providence, the magical art, for the confirmation of infidelity, has found out ways of imitating this by contraries. Thus has been discovered the method of counteracting the poison of serpents by incantations, and the effecting of cures contrary to the word and power of God. The magic art has also found out ministries contrary to the angels of God, placing the calling up of souls and the figments of demons in opposition to these. And, not to prolong the discourse by a further enumeration, there is nothing whatever that makes for the belief of providence, which has not something, on the other hand, prepared for unbelief; and therefore they who do not know that division of things, think that there is no providence, by reason of those things in the world which are discordant from themselves. But do you, my father, as a wise man, choose from that division the part which preserves order and makes for the belief of providence, and do not only follow that part which runs against order and neutralizes the belief of providence."

CHAP. LIV. — AN ILLUSTRATION.

To this the old man answered: "Show me a way, my son, by which I may establish in my mind one or other of these two orders, the one of which asserts, and the other denies, providence." "To one having a right judgment," says Aquila, "the decision is easy. For this very thing that you say, order and disorder, may be produced by a contriver, but not by insensible nature. For let us suppose, by way of illustration, that a great mass were torn from a high rock, and cast down headlong, and when dashed upon the ground were broken into many pieces, could it in any way happen that, amongst that multitude of fragments, there should be found even one which should have any perfect figure and shape?" The old man answered: "It is impossible." "But," said Aquila, "if there be present a statuary, he can by his skilful hand and reasonable mind form the stone cut from the mountain into whatever figure he pleases." The old man said: "That is true." "Therefore," says Aquila, "when there is not a rational mind, no figure can be formed out of the mass; but when there is a designing mind, there may be both form and deformity: for example, if a workman cuts from the mountain a block to which he wishes to give a form, he must first cut it out unformed and rough; then, by degrees hammering and hewing it by the rule of his art, he expresses the form which he has conceived in his mind. Thus, therefore, from informity or deformity, by the hand of the workman form is attained, and both proceed from the workman. In like manner, therefore, the things which are done in the world are accomplished by the providence of a contriver, although they may seem not quite orderly. And therefore, because these two ways have been made known to you, and you have heard the divisions of them, flee from the way of unbelief, lest haply it lead you to that prince who delights in evils; but follow the way of faith, that you may come to that King who delighteth in good men."

CHAP. LV. — THE TWO KINGDOMS.

To this the old man answered: "But why was that prince made who delights in evil?[1] And from what was he made? Or was he not made?" Aquila said: "The treatment of that subject belongs to another time; but that you may not go away altogether without an answer to this, I shall give a few hints on this subject also. God, foreseeing all things before the creation of the world, knowing that the men who were to be would some of them indeed incline to good, but others to the opposite, assigned those who should choose the good to His own government and His own care, and called them His peculiar inheritance;[2] but He gave over the government of those who should turn to evil to those angels who, not by their substance, but by opposition, were unwilling to remain with God, being corrupted by the vice of envy and pride. Those, therefore, he made worthy princes of worthy subjects; yet he so delivered them over to those angels, that they have not the power of doing what they will against them, unless they transgress the bounds assigned to them from the

beginning. And this is the bound assigned, that unless one first do the will of the demons, the demons have no power over him."

CHAP. LVI. — ORIGIN OF EVIL.

Then the old man said: "You have stated it excellently, my son. It now remains only that you tell me whence is the substance of evil: for if it was made by God, the evil fruit shows that the root is in fault; for it appears that it also is of an evil nature. But if this substance was co-eternal with God, how can that which was equally unproduced and co-eternal be subject to the other?" "It was not always," said Aquila; "but neither does it necessarily follow, if it was made by God, that its Creator should be thought to be such as is that which has been made by Him. For indeed God made the substance of all things; but if a reasonable mind, which has been made by God, do not acquiesce in the laws of its Creator, and go beyond the bounds of the temperance prescribed to it, how does this reflect on the Creator? Or if there is any reason higher than this, we do not know it; for we cannot know anything perfectly, and especially concerning those things for our ignorance of which we are not to be judged. But those things for which we are to be judged are most easy to be understood, and are despatched almost in a word. For almost the whole rule of our actions is summed up in this, that what we are unwilling to suffer we should not do to others. For as you would not be killed, you must beware of killing another; and as you would not have your own marriage violated, you must not defile another's bed; you would not be stolen from, neither must you steal; and every matter of men's actions is comprehended within this rule."

CHAP. LVII. — THE OLD MAN UNCONVINCED.

Then the old man: "Do not take amiss, my son, what I am going to say. Though your words are powerful, yet they cannot lead me to believe that anything can be done apart from GENESIS. For I know that all things have happened to me by the necessity of GENESIS,[3] and therefore I cannot be persuaded that either to do well or to do ill is in our power; and if we have not our actions in our power, it cannot be believed that there is a judgment to come, by which either punishments may be inflicted on the evil, or rewards bestowed on the good. In short, since I see that you are initiated in this sort of learning, I shall lay before you a few things from the art itself." "If," says Aquila, "you wish to add anything from that science, my

---

[1] [On the creation of the evil one, see book x. 3, etc., and the discussion with Simon in Homily XIX. 2-18. — R.]
[2] 1 Deut. xxxii. 8, in LXX.

[3] [Comp. Homily XIV. 3, etc. — R.]

brother Clement will answer you with all care, since he has attended more fully to the science of mathematics. For I can maintain in other ways that our actions are in our own power; but I ought not to presume upon those things which I have not learned."[1]

CHAP. LVIII. — SITTING IN JUDGMENT UPON GOD.

When Aquila had thus spoken, then I Clement said: "To-morrow, my father, you shall speak as you please, and we will gladly hear you; for I suppose it will also be gratifying to you that you have to do with those who are not ignorant of the science which you profess." When, therefore, it had been settled between the old man and me, that on the following day we should hold a discussion on the subject of GENESIS — whether all things are done under its influence, or there be anything in us which is not done by GENESIS, but by the judgment of the mind — Peter rose up, and began to speak to the following effect:[1] "To me it is exceedingly wonderful, that things which can easily be found out men make difficult by recondite thoughts and words; and those especially who think themselves wise, and who, wishing to comprehend the will of God, treat God as if He were a man, yea, as if He were something less than a man: for no one can know the purpose or mind of a man unless he himself reveal his thoughts; and neither can any one learn a profession unless he be for a long time instructed by a master. How much more must it be, that no one can know the mind or the work of the invisible and incomprehensible God, unless He Himself send a prophet to declare His purpose, and expound the way of His creation, so far as it is lawful for men to learn it! Hence I think it ridiculous when men judge of the power of God in natural ways, and think that this is possible and that impossible to Him, or this greater and that less, while they are ignorant of everything; who, being unrighteous men, judge the righteous God; unskilled, judge the contriver; corrupt, judge the incorruptible; creatures, judge the Creator.

CHAP. LIX. — THE TRUE PROPHET.

But I would not have you think, that in saying this I take away the power of judging concerning things; but I give counsel that no one walk through devious places, and rush into errors without end. And therefore I advise not only wise men, but indeed all men who have a desire of knowing what is advantageous to them, that they seek after the true Prophet; for it is He alone who knoweth all things, and who knoweth what and how every man is seeking.[2] For He is within the mind of every one of us, but in those who have no desire of the knowledge of God and His righteousness, He is inoperative; but He works in those who seek after that which is profitable to their souls, and kindles in them the light of knowledge. Wherefore seek Him first of all; and if you do not find Him, expect not that you shall learn anything from any other. But He is soon found by those who diligently seek Him through love of the truth, and whose souls are not taken possession of by wickedness. For He is present with those who desire Him in the innocency of their spirits, who bear patiently, and draw sighs from the bottom of their hearts through love of the truth; but He deserts malevolent minds,[3] because as a prophet He knows the thoughts of every one. And therefore let no one think that he can find Him by his own wisdom, unless, as we have said, he empty his mind of all wickedness, and conceive a pure and faithful desire to know Him. For when any one has so prepared himself, He Himself as a prophet, seeing a mind prepared for Him, of His own accord offers Himself to his knowledge.

CHAP. LX. — HIS DELIVERANCES NOT TO BE QUESTIONED.

"Therefore, if any one wishes to learn all things, *he cannot do it by* discussing them one by one; for, being mortal, he shall not be able to trace the counsel of God, and to scan immensity itself. But if, as we have said, he desires to learn all things, let him seek after the true Prophet; and when he has found Him, let him not treat with Him by questions and disputations and arguments; but if He has given any response, or pronounced any judgment, it cannot be doubted that this is certain. And therefore, before all things, let the true Prophet be sought, and His words be laid hold of. In respect to these this only should be discussed by every one, that he may satisfy himself if they are truly His prophetic words; that is, if they contain undoubted faith of things to come, if they mark out definite times, if they preserve the order of things, if they do not relate as last those things which are first, nor as first those things which were done last, if they contain nothing subtle, nothing composed by magic art to deceive, or if they have not transferred to themselves things which were revealed to others, and have mixed them with falsehoods. And when, all these things having been discussed by

---

[1] [This discourse of Peter is peculiar to the *Recognitions;* it resembles somewhat the earlier discourse to Clement in book i. — R.]

[2] [The introduction of these chapters concerning the true Prophet shows a far more orderly method of constructing the entire discussion with the father than that of the *Homilies;* comp. book xi. 1, 2. — R.]

[3] Wisd. i. 4.

right judgment, it is established that they are prophetic words, so they ought to be at once believed concerning all things on which they have spoken and answered.

CHAP. LXI. — IGNORANCE OF THE PHILOS-OPHERS.

"For let us consider carefully the work of divine providence.[1] For whereas the philosophers have introduced certain subtile and difficult words, so that not even the terms that they use in their discourses can be known and understood by all, God has shown that those who thought themselves word-framers are altogether unskilful as respects the knowledge of the truth. For the knowledge of things which is imparted by the true Prophet is simple, and plain, and brief; which those men walking through devious places, and through the stony difficulties of words, are wholly ignorant of. Therefore, to modest and simple minds, when they see things come to pass which have been foretold, it is enough, and more than enough, that they may receive most certain knowledge from most certain prescience; and for the rest may be at peace, having received evident knowledge of the truth. For all other things are treated by opinion, in which there can be nothing firm. For what speech is there which may not be contradicted? And what argument is there that may not be overthrown by another argument? And hence it is, that by disputation of this sort men can never come to any end of knowledge and

learning, but find the end of their life sooner than the end of their questions.

CHAP. LXII. — END OF THE CONFERENCE.

"And, therefore, since amongst these *philosophers* are things uncertain, we must come to the true Prophet. Him God the Father wished to be loved by all, and accordingly He has been pleased wholly to extinguish those opinions which have originated with men, and in regard to which there is nothing like certainty — that He *the true Prophet* might be the more sought after, and that He whom[2] they had obscured should show to men the way of truth. For on this account also God made the world, and by Him the world is filled; whence also He is everywhere near to them who seek Him, though He be sought in the remotest ends of the earth. But if any one seek Him not purely, nor holily, nor faithfully, He is indeed within him, because He is everywhere, and is found within the minds of all men; but, as we have said before, He is dormant to the unbelieving, and is held to be absent from those by whom His existence is not believed." And when Peter had said this, and more to the same effect, concerning the true Prophet, he dismissed the crowds; and when he very earnestly entreated the old man to remain with us, he could prevail nothing; but he also departed, to return next day, as had been agreed upon. And after this, we also, with Peter, went to our lodging, and enjoyed our accustomed food and rest.

---

[1] [Comp. Homily XV. 5. — R.]

[2] If we were to read *quam* instead of *quem*, the sense would be: that He might lay open to men the way of truth which they had blocked up. So Whiston.

BOOK IX.

CHAP. I. — AN EXPLANATION.

ON the following day, Peter, along with us, hastened early to the place in which the discussion had been held the day before; and when he saw that great crowds had assembled there to hear, and saw the old man with them, he said to him:[1] "Old man, it was agreed yesterday that you should confer to-day with Clement; and that you should either show that nothing takes place apart from *genesis*, or that Clement should prove that there is no such thing as *genesis*, but that what we do is in our own power." To this the old man answered: "I both remember what was agreed upon, and I keep in

---

[1] [The discourses in book ix. are peculiar to the *Recognitions* not only in their position in the story, but to a remarkably large extent in the matter. — R.]

memory the words which you spoke after the agreement was made, in which you taught that it is impossible for man to know any thing, unless he learn from the true Prophet." Then Peter said: "You do not know what I meant; but I shall now explain to you. I spoke of the will and purpose of God, which He had before the world was, and by which purpose He made the world, appointed times, gave the law, promised a world to come to the righteous for the rewarding of their good deeds, and decreed punishments to the unjust according to a judicial sentence. I said that this counsel and this will of God cannot be found out by men, because no man can gather the mind of God from conjectures and opinion, unless a prophet sent by Him declare it. I did not therefore speak of any doctrines or studies, that they cannot be found out or known without a prophet ; for I know that both arts and sciences can be known and practised by men, which they have learned, not from the true Prophet, but from human instructors.

CHAP. II. — PRELIMINARIES.

"Since, therefore, you profess to be conversant with the position of the stars and the courses of the heavenly bodies, and that from these you can convince Clement that all things are subject to GENESIS, or that you will learn from him that all things are governed by providence, and that we have something in our own power, it is now time for you two to set about this." To this the old man answered : "Now indeed it was not necessary to raise questions of this kind, if it were possible for us to learn from the true Prophet, and to hear in a definite proposition, that anything depends on us and on the freedom of our will; for your yesterday's discourse affected me greatly, in which you disputed concerning the prophetic power.[1] Whence also I assent to and confirm your judgment, that nothing can be known by man with certainty, and without doubt, seeing that he has but a short period of life, and a brief and slender breath, by which he seems to be kept in life. However, since I am understood to have promised to Clement, before I heard anything of the prophetic power, that I should show that all things are subject to GENESIS, or that I should learn from him that there is something in ourselves, let him do me this favour, that he first begin, and propound and explain what may be objected : for I, ever since I heard from you a few words concerning the power of prophecy, have, I confess, been confounded, considering the greatness of prescience ; nor do I think that anything ought to be received which is collected from conjectures and opinion."

CHAP. III. — BEGINNING OF THE DISCUSSION.

When the old man had said this, I Clement began to speak as follows : "God by His Son created the world as a double house, separated by the interposition of this firmament, which is called heaven ; and appointed angelic powers to dwell in the higher, and a multitude of men to be born in this visible world, from amongst whom He might choose friends for His Son, with whom He might rejoice, and who might be prepared for Him as a beloved bride for a bridegroom. But even till the time of the marriage, which is the manifestation of the world to come, He has appointed a certain power, to choose out and watch over the good ones of those who

are born in this world, and to preserve them for His Son, set apart in a certain place of the world, which is without sin ; in which there are already some, who are there being prepared, as I said, as a bride adorned for the coming of the bridegroom. For the prince of this world and of the present age is like an adulterer, who corrupts and violates the minds of men, and, seducing them from the love of the true bridegroom, allures them to strange lovers.

CHAP. IV. — WHY THE EVIL PRINCE WAS MADE.

But some one will say, How then was it necessary that that prince should be made, who was to turn away the minds of men from the true prince?[2] Because God, who, as I have said, wished to prepare friends for His Son, did not wish them to be such as by necessity of nature could not be aught else, but such as should desire of their own choice and will to be good ; because neither is that praiseworthy which is not desirable, nor is that judged to be good which is not sought for with purpose. For there is no credit in being that from which the necessity of your nature does not admit of your changing. Therefore the providence of God has willed that a multitude of men should be born in this world, that those who should choose a good life might be selected from many. And because He foresaw that the present world could not consist except by variety and inequality, He gave to each mind freedom of motions, according to the diversities of present things, and appointed this prince, through his suggestion of those things which run contrary, that the choice of better things might depend upon the exercise of virtue?

CHAP. V. — NECESSITY OF INEQUALITY.

"But to make our meaning plainer, we shall explain it by particulars. Was it proper, for example, that all men in this world should be kings, or princes, or lords, or teachers, or lawyers, or geometers, or goldsmiths, or bakers, or smiths, or grammarians, or rich men, or farmers, or perfumers, or fishermen, or poor men? It is certain that all could not be these. Yet all these professions, and many more, the life of men requires, and without these it cannot be passed ; therefore inequality is necessary in this world. For there cannot be a king, unless he has subjects over whom he may rule and reign ; nor can there be a master, unless he has one over whom he may bear sway ; and in like manner of the rest.

---

1 [Comp. book viii. 58–62. — R.]

2 [Comp. book viii. 55, 56; Homily XIX. 2–18. — R.]
3 [The doctrine of free-will, and the necessity of evil in consequence, appears throughout. Comp. book iii. 21, v. 6. In the *Homilies* there is not so much emphasis laid upon this point; but see Homily XI. 8. — R.]

CHAP. VI. — ARRANGEMENTS OF THE WORLD FOR THE EXERCISE OF VIRTUE.

"Therefore the Creator, knowing that no one would come to the contest of his own accord, while labour is shunned, — that is, to the practice of those professions which we have mentioned, by means of which either the justice or the mercy of every one can be manifested, — made for men a body susceptible of hunger, and thirst, and cold, in order that men, being compelled for the sake of supporting their bodies, might come down to all the professions which we have mentioned, by the necessity of livelihood. For we are taught to cultivate every one of these arts, for the sake of food, and drink, and clothing. And in this the purpose of each one's mind is shown, whether he will supply the demands of hunger and cold by means of thefts, and murders, and perjuries, and other crimes of that sort; or whether, keeping justice and mercy and continence, he will fulfil the service of imminent necessity by the practice of a profession and the labour of his hands. For if he supply his bodily wants with justice, and piety, and mercy, he comes forth as a victor in the contest set before him, and is chosen as a friend of the Son of God. But if he serve carnal lusts, by frauds, iniquities, and crimes, he becomes a friend of the prince of this world, and of all demons; by whom he is also taught this, to ascribe to the courses of the stars the errors of his own evil doings, although he chose them of purpose, and willingly. For arts are learned and practised, as we have said, under the compulsion of the desire of food and drink; which desire, when the knowledge of the truth comes to any one, becomes weaker, and frugality takes its place. For what expense have those who use water and bread, and only expect it from God?

CHAP. VII. — THE OLD AND THE NEW BIRTH.

"There is therefore, as we have said, a certain necessary inequality in the dispensation of the world. Since indeed all men cannot know all things, and accomplish all works, yet all need the use and service of almost all. And on this account it is necessary that one work, and another pay him for his work; that one be servant, and another be master; that one be subject, another be king. But this inequality, which is a necessary provision for the life of men, divine providence has turned into an occasion of justice, mercy, and humanity: that while these things are transacted between man and man, every one may have an opportunity of acting justly with him to whom he has to pay wages for his work; and of acting mercifully to him who, perhaps through sickness or poverty, can-

not pay his debt; and of acting humanely towards those who by their creation seem to be subject to him; also of maintaining gentleness towards subjects, and of doing all things according to the law of God. For He has given a law, thereby aiding the minds of men, that they may the more easily perceive how they ought to act with respect to everything, in what way they may escape evil, and in what way tend to future blessings; and how, being regenerate in water, they may by good works extinguish the fire of their old birth. For our first birth descends through the fire of lust, and therefore, by the divine appointment, this second birth is introduced by water, which may extinguish the nature of fire; [1] and that the soul, enlightened by the heavenly Spirit, may cast away the fear of the first birth: provided, however, it so live for the time to come, that it do not at all seek after any of the pleasures of this world, but be, as it were, a pilgrim and a stranger,[2] and a citizen of another city.

CHAP. VIII. — USES OF EVILS.

"But perhaps you will say, that in those things indeed in which the necessity of nature demands the service of arts and works, any one may have it in his power to maintain justice, and to put what restraint he pleases either upon his desires or his actions; but what shall we say of the sicknesses and infirmities which befall men, and of some being harassed with demons, and fevers, and cold fits, and some being attacked with madness, or losing their reason, and all those things which overwhelm the race of man with innumerable misfortunes? To this we say, that if any one consider the reason of the whole mystery, he will pronounce these things to be more just than those that we have already explained. For God has given a nature to men, by which they may be taught concerning what is good, and to resist evil; that is, they may learn arts, and to resist pleasures, and to set the law of God before them in all things. And for this end He has permitted certain contrary powers to wander up and down in the world, and to strive against us,[3] for the reasons which have been stated before, that by striving with them the palm of victory and the merit of rewards may accrue to the righteous.

CHAP. IX. — "CONCEIVED IN SIN."

"From this, therefore, it sometimes happens, that if any persons have acted incontinently, and have been willing not so much to resist as to

---

[1] [Compare Homily XI. 26 on this view of baptism. — R.]
[2] Ps. xxxix. 12.
[3] [On the doctrine of demons compare book iv. 14-22; Homily IX. 8-18. — R.

yield, and to give harbour to these *demons* in themselves, by their noxious breath an intemperate, ill-conditioned, and diseased progeny is begotten. For while lust is wholly gratified, and no care is taken in the copulation, undoubtedly a weak generation is affected with the defects and frailties of those demons by whose instigation these things are done. And therefore parents are responsible for their children's defects of this sort, because they have not observed the law of intercourse. Though there are also more secret causes, by which souls are made subject to these evils, which it is not to our present purpose to state, yet it behoves every one to acknowledge the law of God, that he may learn from it the observance of generation, and avoid causes of impurity, that that which is begotten may be pure. For it is not right, while in the planting of shrubs and the sowing of crops a suitable season is sought for, and the land is cleaned, and all things are suitably prepared, lest haply the seed which is sown be injured and perish, that in the case of man only, who is over all these things, there should be no attention or caution in sowing his seed.

CHAP. X. — TOW SMEARED WITH PITCH.

" But what, it is said, of the fact that some who in their childhood are free from any bodily defect, yet in process of time fall into those evils, so that some are even violently hurried on to death? Concerning these also the account is at hand, and is almost the same : for those powers which we have said to be contrary to the human race, are in some way invited into the heart of every one by many and diverse lusts, and find a way of entrance ; and they have in them such influence and power as can only encourage and incite, but cannot compel or accomplish. If, therefore, any one consents to them, so as to do those things which he wickedly desires, his consent and deed shall find the reward of destruction and the worst kind of death. But if, thinking of the future judgment, he be checked by fear, and reclaim himself, so that he do not accomplish in action what he has conceived in his evil thought, he shall not only escape present destruction, but also future punishments. For every cause of sin seems to be like tow smeared over with pitch, which immediately breaks into flame as soon as it receives the heat of fire ; and the kindling of this fire is understood to be the work of demons. If, therefore, any one be found smeared with sins and lusts as with pitch, the fire easily gets the mastery of him. But if the tow be not steeped in the pitch of sin, but in the water of purification and regeneration, the fire of the demons shall not be able to be kindled in it.

CHAP. XI. — FEAR.

" But some one will say, And what shall we do now, whom it has already happened to us to be smeared with sins as with pitch? I answer: Nothing ; but hasten to be washed, that the fuel of the fire may be cleansed out of you by the invocation of the holy name, and that for the future you may bridle your lusts by fear of the judgment to come, and with all constancy beat back the hostile powers whenever they approach your senses. But you say, If any one fall into love, how shall he be able to contain himself, though he see before his eyes even that river of fire which they call Pyriphlegethon? This is the excuse of those who will not be converted to repentance. But now I would not have you talk of Pyriphlegethon. Place before you human punishments, and see what influence fear has. When any one is brought to punishment for the crime of love, and is bound to the stake to be burned, can he at that time conceive any desire of her whom he loved, or place her image before his eyes? By no means, you will say. You see, then, that present fear cuts off unrighteous desires. But if those who believe in God, and who confess the judgment to come, and the penalty of eternal fire, — if they do not refrain from sin, it is certain that they do not believe with full faith : for if faith is certain, fear also becomes certain ; but if there be any defect in faith, fear also is weakened, and then the contrary powers find opportunity of entering. And when they have consented to their persuasions, they necessarily become subject also to their power, and by their instigation are driven to the precipices of sin.

CHAP. XII. — ASTROLOGERS.

" Therefore the astrologers,[1] being ignorant of such mysteries, think that these things happen by the courses of the heavenly bodies: hence also, in their answers to those who go to them to consult them as to future things, they are deceived in very many instances. Nor is it to be wondered at, for they are not prophets ; but, by long practice, the authors of errors find a sort of refuge in those things by which they were deceived, and introduce certain CLIMACTERIC PERIODS, that they may pretend a knowledge of uncertain things. For they represent these CLIMACTERICS as times of danger, in which one sometimes is destroyed, sometimes is not destroyed, not knowing that it is not the course of the stars, but the operation of demons, that regulates these things ; and those demons, being anxious to confirm the error of astrology, de-

---

[1] [On the error of astrology compare book x. 7–12. In Homily XIV. 5 and elsewhere " genesis " and the science of astrology are identified.] — R.

ceive men to sin by mathematical calculations, so that when they suffer the punishment of sin, either by the permission of God or by legal sentence, the astrologer may seem to have spoken truth. And yet they are deceived even in this; for if men be quickly turned to repentance, and remember and fear the future judgment, the punishment of death is remitted to those who are converted to God by the grace of baptism.

CHAP. XIII. — RETRIBUTION HERE OR HEREAFTER.

"But some one will say, Many have committed even murder, and adultery, and other crimes, and have suffered no evil. This indeed rarely happens to men, but to those who know not the counsel of God it frequently seems to happen. But God, who knows all things, knows how and why he who sins does sin, and what cause leads each one to sin. This, however, is in general to be noticed, that if any are evil, not so much in their mind as in their doings, and are not borne to sin under the incitement of purpose, upon them punishment is inflicted more speedily, and more in the present life; for everywhere and always God renders to every one according to his deeds, as He judges to be expedient. But those who practise wickedness of purpose, so that they sometimes even rage against those from whom they have received benefits, and who take no thought for repentance — their punishment He defers to the future. For these men do not, like those of whom we spoke before, deserve to end the punishment of their crimes in the present life; but it is allowed them to occupy the present time as they will, because their correction is not such as to need temporal chastisements, but such as to demand the punishment of eternal fire in hell; and there their souls shall seek repentance, where they shall not be able to find it.

CHAP. XIV. — KNOWLEDGE DEADENS LUSTS.

"But if, while in this life, they had placed before their eyes the punishments which they shall then suffer, they would certainly have bridled their lusts, and would in nowise have fallen into sin. For the understanding in the soul has much power for cutting off all its desires, especially when it has acquired the knowledge of heavenly things, by means of which, having received the light of truth, it will turn away from all darkness of evil actions. For as the sun obscures and conceals all the stars by the brightness of his shining, so also the mind, by the light of knowledge, renders all the lusts of the soul ineffective and inactive, sending out upon them the thought of the judgment to come as its rays, so that they can no longer appear in the soul.

CHAP. XV. — FEAR OF MEN AND OF GOD.

"But as a proof that the fear of God has much efficacy for the repressing of lusts, take the example of human fear. Who is there among men that does not covet his neighbour's goods? And yet they are restrained, and act honestly, through fear of the punishment which is prescribed by the laws. Through fear, nations are subject to their kings, and armies obey with arms in their hands. Slaves, although they are stronger than their masters, yet through fear submit to their masters' rule. Even wild beasts are tamed by fear; the strongest bulls submit their necks to the yoke, and huge elephants obey their masters, through fear. But why do we use human examples, when even divine are not wanting? Does not the earth itself remain under the fear of precept, which it testifies by its motion and quaking? The sea keeps its prescribed bounds; the angels maintain peace; the stars keep their order, and the rivers their channels: it is certain also that demons are put to flight by fear. And not to lengthen the discourse by too many particulars, see how the fear of God restraining everything, keeps all things in proper harmony, and in their fixed order. How much more, then, may you be sure that the lusts of demons which arise in your hearts may be extinguished and wholly abolished by the admonition of the fear of God, when even the inciters of lust are themselves put to flight by the influence of fear? You know that these things are so; but if you have anything to answer, proceed."

CHAP. XVI. — IMPERFECT CONVICTION.

Then said the old man: "My son Clement has wisely framed his argument, so that he has left us nothing to say to these things; but all his discourse which he has delivered on the nature of men has this bearing, that along with the fact that freedom of will is in man, there is also some cause of evil without him, whereby men are indeed incited by various lusts, yet are not compelled to sin; and that for this reason, he said, because fear is much more powerful than they, and it resists and checks the violence of desires, so that, although natural emotions may arise, yet sin may not be committed, those demons being put to flight who incite and inflame these emotions. But these things do not convince me; for I am conscious of certain things from which I know well, that by the arrangement of the heavenly bodies men become murderers or adulterers, and perpetrate other evils; and in like manner honourable and modest women are compelled to act well.

CHAP. XVII. — ASTROLOGICAL LORE.[1]

" In short, when Mars, holding the centre in his house, regards Saturn quarterly, with Mercury towards the centre, the full moon coming upon him, in the daily GENESIS, he produces murderers, and those who are to fall by the sword,[2] bloody, drunken, lustful, devilish men, inquirers into secrets,[3] malefactors, sacrilegious persons, and such like ; especially when there was no one of the good stars looking on. But again Mars himself, having a quarterly position with respect to Venus, in a direction toward the centre, while no good star looks on, produces adulterers and incestuous persons. Venus with the Moon, in the borders and houses of Saturn, if she was with Saturn, and Mars looking on, produces women that are viragos, ready for agriculture, building, and every manly work, to commit adultery with whom they please, and not to be convicted by their husbands, to use no delicacy, no ointments, nor feminine robes and shoes, but to live after the fashion of men. But the unpropitious Venus makes men to be as women, and not to act in any respect as men, if she is with Mars in Aries ; on the contrary, she produces women if she is in Capricorn or Aquarius."

CHAP. XVIII. — THE REPLY.

And when the old man had pursued this subject at great length, and had enumerated every kind of mathematical figure, and also the position of the heavenly bodies, wishing thereby to show that fear is not sufficient to restrain lusts, I answered again : " Truly, my father, you have argued most learnedly and skilfully ; and reason herself invites me to say something in answer to your discourse, since indeed I am acquainted with the science of mathematics, and gladly hold a conference with so learned a man. Listen, therefore, while I reply to what you have said, that you may learn distinctly that GENESIS is not at all from the stars, and that it is possible for those to resist the assault of demons who have recourse to God ; and, as I said before, that not only by the fear of God can natural lusts be restrained, but even by the fear of men, as we shall now instruct you.

CHAP. XIX. — REFUTATION OF ASTROLOGY.

" There are, in every country or kingdom, laws imposed by men, enduring either by writing or simply through custom, which no one easily transgresses. In short, the first Seres, who dwell at the beginning of the world,[4] have a law not to know murder, nor adultery, nor whoredom, and not to commit theft, and not to worship idols ; and in all that country, which is very large, there is neither temple, nor image, nor harlot, nor adulteress, nor is any thief brought to trial. But neither is any man ever slain there ; and no man's liberty of will is compelled, according to your doctrine, by the fiery star of Mars, to use the sword for the murder of man ; nor does Venus in conjunction with Mars compel to adultery, although of course with them Mars occupies the middle circle of heaven every day. But amongst the Seres the fear of laws is more powerful than the configuration of GENESIS.

CHAP. XX. — BRAHMANS.

" There are likewise amongst the Bactrians, in the Indian countries, immense multitudes of Brahmans, who also themselves, from the tradition of their ancestors, and peaceful customs and laws, neither commit murder nor adultery, nor worship idols, nor have the practice of eating animal food, are never drunk, never do anything maliciously, but always fear God. And these things indeed they do, though the rest of the Indians commit both murders and adulteries, and worship idols, and are drunken, and practise other wickednesses of this sort. Yea, in the western parts of India itself there is a certain country, where strangers, when they enter it, are taken and slaughtered and eaten ; and neither have good stars prevented these men from such wickednesses and from accursed food, nor have malign stars compelled the Brahmans to do any evil. Again, there is a custom among the Persians to marry mothers, and sisters, and daughters. In all that district the Persians contract incestuous marriages.

CHAP. XXI. — DISTRICTS OF HEAVEN.

" And that those who study mathematics may not have it in their power to use that subterfuge by which they say that there are certain districts of heaven to which it is granted to have some things peculiar to themselves, some of that nation of Persians have gone to foreign countries, who are called Magusæi, of whom there are some to this day in Media, others in Parthia, some also in Egypt, and a considerable number in Galatia and Phrygia, all of whom maintain the form of this incestuous tradition without variation, and hand it down to their posterity to be observed, even although they have changed their district of heaven ; nor has Venus with the Moon in the confines and houses of Saturn, with

---

[1] Ch. 17 and ch. 19–29 are taken in an altered form from the writing ascribed to Bardesanes, *De Fato*. [These chapters have no parallel in the *Homilies*, but the argument of the old man respecting genesis implies the same position; comp. Homily XIV. 3–7, 11. — R.]
[2] Conjectural reading, " to kill with the sword."
[3] That is, violators of the sacred mysteries, which was regarded as one of the most horrid of crimes.

[4] That is, the farthest east, not, as some of the annotators suppose, from the beginning of the world.

Saturn also and Mars looking on, compelled them to have a GENESIS among other men.[1]

CHAP. XXII. — CUSTOMS OF THE GELONES.

" Amongst the Geli also there is a custom, that women cultivate the fields, build, and do every manly work ; and they are also allowed to have intercourse with whom they please, and are not found fault with by their husbands, or called adulteresses : for they have promiscuous intercourse everywhere, and especially with strangers ; they do not use ointments ; they do not wear dyed garments, nor shoes. On the other hand, the men of the Gelones are adorned, combed, clothed in soft and various-coloured garments, decked with gold, and besmeared with ointments, and that not through lack of manliness, for they are most warlike, and most keen hunters. Yet the whole women of the Gelones had not at their birth the unfavourable Venus in Capricornus or Aquarius ; nor had all their men Venus placed with Mars in Aries, by which configuration the Chaldean science asserts that men are born effeminate and dissolute.

CHAP. XXIII. — MANNERS OF THE SUSIDÆ.

" But, further, in Susæ the women use ointments, and indeed of the best sort, being decked with ornaments and precious stones ; also they go abroad supported by the aid of their maid-servants, with much greater ambition than the men. They do not, however, cultivate modesty, but have intercourse indifferently with whomsoever they please, with slaves and guests, such liberty being allowed them by their husbands ; and not only are they not blamed for this, but they also rule over their husbands. And yet the GENESIS of all the Susian women has not Venus with Jupiter and Mars in the middle of the heaven in the houses of Jupiter. In the remoter parts of the East, if a boy be treated unnaturally, when it is discovered, he is killed by his brothers, or his parents, or any of his relations, and is left unburied. And again, among the Gauls, an old law allows boys to be thus treated publicly ; and no disgrace is thought to attach to it. And is it possible, that all those who are so basely treated among the Gauls, have had Lucifer with Mercury in the houses of Saturn and the confines of Mars?

CHAP. XXIV. — DIFFERENT CUSTOMS OF DIFFERENT COUNTRIES.

" In the regions of Britain several men have one wife ; in Parthia many women have one husband ; and each part of the world adheres to its own manners and institutions. None of the Amazons have husbands, but, like animals, they go out from their own territories once a year about the vernal equinox, and live with the men of the neighbouring nation, observing a sort of solemnity the while, and when they have conceived by them they return ; and if they bring forth a male child, they cast him away, and rear only females. Now, since the birth of all is at one season, it is absurd to suppose that in the case of males Mars is at the time in equal portions with Saturn, but never in the GENESIS of females ; and that they have not Mercury placed with Venus in his own houses, so as to produce either painters, or sculptors, or money-changers ; or in the houses of Venus, so that perfumers, or singers, or poets might be produced. Among the Saracens, and Upper Libyans, and Moors, and the dwellers about the mouths of the ocean, and also in the remote districts of Germany, and among the Sarmatians and Scythians, and all the nations who dwell in the regions of the Pontic shore, and in the island Chrysea, there is never found a money-changer, nor a sculptor, nor a painter, nor an architect, nor a geometrician, nor a tragedian, nor a poet. Therefore the influence of Mercury and Venus must be wanting among them.

CHAP. XXV. — NOT GENESIS, BUT FREE-WILL.

" The Medes alone in all the world, with the greatest care, throw men still breathing to be devoured by dogs ; yet they have not Mars with the Moon placed in Cancer all through their daily GENESIS. The Indians burn their dead, and the wives of the dead voluntarily offer themselves, and are burned with them. But all the Indian women who are burned alive have not the Sun under the earth in nightly GENESIS, with Mars in the regions of Mars. Very many of the Germans end their lives by the halter ; but all have not therefore the Moon with Hora begirt by Saturn and Mars. From all this it appears that the fear of the laws bears sway in every country, and the freedom of will which is implanted in man by the Spirit complies with the laws ; and GENESIS can neither compel the Seres to commit murder, nor the Brahmans to eat flesh, nor the Persians to shun incest, nor the Indians to refrain from burning, nor the Medes from being devoured by dogs, nor the Parthians from having many wives, nor the women of Mesopotamia from preserving their chastity, nor the Greeks from athletic exercises, nor the Gallic boys from being abused ; nor can it compel the barbarous nations to be instructed in the studies of the Greeks ; but, as we have said, each nation observes its own laws according to free-will, and annuls the decrees of GENESIS by the strictness of laws.

---

[1] This is a literal translation of text. If we read *genesi* for *genesim*, we get: " nor has Venus, etc., compelled them to keep up this custom in the midst of others through the force of *genesis*." Eusebius reads: " And assuredly Venus, etc., is not found in the *genesis* of all of them."

CHAP. XXVI. — CLIMATES.

" But some one skilled in the science of mathematics will say that GENESIS is divided into seven parts, which they call climates, and that over each climate one of the seven heavenly bodies bears rule; and that those diverse laws to which we have referred are not given by men, but by those dominant stars according to their will, and that that which pleases the star is observed by men as a law. To this we shall answer, in the first place, that the world is not divided into seven parts; and in the second place, that if it were so, we find many different laws in one part and one country; and therefore there are neither seven *laws* according to the number of the heavenly bodies, nor twelve according to the number of the signs, nor thirty-six according to that of the divisions of ten degrees; but they are innumerable.

CHAP. XXVII. — DOCTRINE OF " CLIMATES " UNTENABLE.

" Moreover, we ought to remember the things which have been mentioned, that in the one country of India there are both persons who feed on human flesh, and persons who abstain even from the flesh of sheep, and birds, and all living creatures; and that the Magusæi marry their mothers and daughters not only in Persia, but that in every nation where they dwell they keep up their incestuous customs.[1] Then, besides, we have mentioned also innumerable nations, which are wholly ignorant of the studies of literature, and also some wise men have changed the laws themselves in several places; and some laws have been voluntarily abandoned, on account of the impossibility of observing them, or on account of their baseness. Assuredly we can easily ascertain how many rulers have changed the laws and customs of nations which they have conquered, and subjected them to their own laws. This is manifestly done by the Romans, who have brought under the Roman law and the civil decrees almost the whole world, and all nations who formerly lived under various laws and customs of their own. It follows, therefore, that the stars of the nations which have been conquered by the Romans have lost their climates and their portions.

CHAP. XXVIII. — JEWISH CUSTOMS.

" I shall add another thing which may satisfy even the most incredulous. All the Jews who live under the law of Moses circumcise their sons on the eighth day without fail, and shed the blood of the tender infant. But no one of the Gentiles has ever submitted to this on the eighth day; and, on the other hand, no one of the Jews has ever omitted it. How then shall the account of GENESIS stand with this, since Jews live in all parts of the world, mixed with Gentiles, and on the eighth day suffer the cutting of a member? And no one of the Gentiles, but only they themselves, as I have said, do this, induced to it not by the compulsion of any star, nor by the perfusion[2] of blood, but by the law of their religion; and in whatever part of the world they are, this sign is familiar to them. But also the fact that one name is among them all, wheresoever they are, does this also come through GENESIS? And also that no child born among them is ever exposed, and that on every seventh day they all rest, wherever they may be, and do not go upon a journey, and do not use fire?[3] Why is it, then, that no one of the Jews is compelled by GENESIS to go on a journey, or to build, or to sell or buy anything on that day?

CHAP. XXIX. — THE GOSPEL MORE POWERFUL THAN " GENESIS."

" But I shall give a still stronger proof of the matters in hand. For, behold, scarcely seven years have yet passed since the advent of the righteous and true Prophet; and in the course of these, men of all nations coming to Judæa, and moved both by the signs and miracles which they saw, and by the grandeur of His doctrine, received His faith; and then going back to their own countries, they rejected the lawless rites of the Gentiles, and their incestuous marriages. In short, among the Parthians — as Thomas, who is preaching the Gospel amongst them, has written to us — not many now are addicted to polygamy; nor among the Medes do many throw their dead to dogs; nor are the Persians pleased with intercourse with their mothers, or incestuous marriages with their daughters; nor do the Susian women practise the adulteries that were allowed them; nor has GENESIS been able to force those into crimes whom the teaching of religion restrained.

CHAP. XXX. — " GENESIS " INCONSISTENT WITH GOD'S JUSTICE.

" Behold, from the very matter in which we are now engaged,[4] draw an inference, and from the circumstances in which we are now placed deduce a conclusion, how, through a rumour only

---

[1] The text reads: " the incestuous customs of their evils, or of their evil persons." Hilgenfeld (*Bardesanes*, p. 113) notices that it should be, " of their ancestors."

[2] Probably we should read *perfusionem* instead of *perfusione*, and then the translation would be: " no star compelling, or even urging on them the shedding of blood." So Whiston translates.

[3] Ex. xxxv. 3.

[4] [This conclusion of the argument by a reference to the Prophet is much more dignified than the personal boast of miraculous power, which, in the *Homilies*, is placed in the mouth of the Apostle just before the recognition. — R.]

reaching the ears of men that a Prophet had appeared in Judæa to teach men with signs and miracles to worship one God, all were expecting with prepared and eager minds, even before the coming of my lord Peter, that some one would announce to them what He taught who had appeared. But lest I should seem to carry the enumeration too far, I shall tell you what conclusion ought to be drawn from the whole. Since God is righteous, and since He Himself made the nature of men, how could it be that He should place GENESIS in opposition to us, which should compel us to sin, and then that He should punish us when we do sin? Whence it is certain that God punishes no sinner either in the present life or in that to come, except because He knows that he could have conquered, but neglected victory. For even in the present world He takes vengeance upon men, as He did upon those who perished in the deluge, who were all destroyed in one day, yea, in one hour, although it is certain that they were not all born in one hour according to the order of *genesis*. But it is most absurd to say that it befalls us by nature to suffer evils, if sins had not gone before.

CHAP. XXXI. — VALUE OF KNOWLEDGE.

"And therefore, if we desire salvation, we ought above all to seek after knowledge, being sure that if our mind remain in ignorance, we shall endure not only the evils of *genesis*, but also whatever other evils from without the demons may please, unless fear of laws and of the judgment to come resist all our desires, and check the violence of sinning. For even human fear does much good, and also much evil, unknown to GENESIS, as we have shown above. Therefore our mind is subject to errors in a threefold manner: from those things which come to us through evil custom; or from those lusts which the body naturally stirs up in us; or from those which hostile powers compel us to. But the mind has it in its own nature to oppose and fight against these, when the knowledge of truth shines upon it, by which knowledge is imparted fear of the judgment to come, which is a fit governor of the mind, and which can recall it from the precipices of lusts. That these things, therefore, are in our power, has been sufficiently stated.

CHAP. XXXII. — STUBBORN FACTS.

"Now, old man, if you have any thing to say in answer to these things, say on." Then said the old man:[1] "You have most fully argued, my son; but I, as I said at first, am prevented by my own consciousness from according assent to all this incomparable statement of yours. For

I know both my own GENESIS and that of my wife, and I know that those things have happened which our GENESIS prescribed to each of us; and I cannot now be withdrawn by words from those things which I have ascertained by facts and deeds. In short, since I perceive that you are excellently skilled in this sort of learning, hear the horoscope of my wife, and you shall find the configuration whose issue has occurred. For she had Mars with Venus above the centre, and the Moon setting in the houses of Mars and the confines of Saturn. Now this configuration leads women to be adulteresses, and to love their own slaves, and to end their days in foreign travel and in waters. And this has so come to pass. For she fell in love with her slave, and fearing at once danger and reproach, she fled with him, and going abroad, where she satisfied her love, she perished in the sea."

CHAP. XXXIII. — AN APPROACHING RECOGNITION.

Then I answered: "How know you that she cohabited with her slave abroad, and died in his society?" Then the old man said: "I know it with perfect certainty; not indeed that she was married to the slave, as indeed I had not even discovered that she loved him. But after she was gone, my brother gave me the whole story, telling me that she first had loved himself; but he, being honourable as a brother, would not pollute his brother's bed with the stain of incest. But she, being both afraid of me, and unable to bear the unhappy reproaches (and yet she should not be blamed for that to which her GENESIS compelled her), pretended a dream, and said to me: 'Some one stood by me in a vision, who ordered me to leave the city without delay with my two twins.' When I heard this, being anxious for her safety and that of my sons, I immediately sent away her and the children, retaining with myself one who was younger. For this she said that he had permitted who had given her warning in her sleep."

CHAP. XXXIV. — THE OTHER SIDE OF THE STORY.

Then I Clement, understanding that he perchance was my father, was drowned in tears, and my brothers also were ready to rush forward and to disclose the matter; but Peter restrained them, saying: "Be quiet, until I give you permission." Therefore Peter, answering, said to the old man: "What was the name of your younger son?" And he said: "Clement." Then Peter: "If I shall this day restore to you your most chaste wife and your three sons, will you believe that a modest mind can overcome unreasonable impulses, and that all things that have been spoken by us are true, and that GENESIS is nothing?" Then said the old man: "As

---

[1] [To chaps. 32–37 a partial parallel is found in Homily XIV. 5–9. The arrangement is quite different, and the details vary. — R.]

it is impossible for you to perform what you have promised, so it is impossible that anything can take place apart from GENESIS." Then says Peter: "I wish to have all who are here present as witnesses that I shall this day hand over to you your wife, who is living most chastely, with your three sons. And now take a token of these things from this, that I know the whole story much more accurately than you do ; and I shall relate the whole occurrences in order, both that you may know them, and that those who are present may learn."

CHAP. XXXV. — REVELATIONS.

When he had said this, he turned to the crowds, and thus began : "This person whom you see, O men, in this poor garb, is a citizen of the city Rome, descended of the stock of Cæsar himself. His name is Faustinianus. He obtained as his wife a woman of the highest rank, Matthidia by name. By her he had three sons, two of whom were twins ; and the one who was the younger, whose name was Clement, is this man !" When he said this, he pointed to me with his finger. "And his twin sons are these men, Niceta and Aquila, the one of whom was formerly called Faustinus and the other Faustus." [1] But as soon as Peter pronounced our names, all the old man's limbs were weakened, and he fell down in a swoon. But we his sons rushed to him, and embraced and kissed him, fearing that we might not be able to recall his spirit. And while these things were going on, the people were confounded with very wonder.

CHAP. XXXVI. — NEW REVELATIONS.

But Peter ordered us to rise from embracing our father, lest we should kill him ; and he himself, laying hold of his hand, and lifting him up as from a deep sleep, and gradually reviving him, began to set forth to him the whole transactions as they had really happened : [2] how his brother had fallen in love with Matthidia, and how she, being very modest, had been unwilling to inform her husband of his brother's lawless love, lest she should stir up hostility between the brothers, and bring disgrace upon the family ; and how she had wisely pretended a dream, by which she was ordered to depart from the city with her twin sons, leaving the younger one with his father ; and how on their voyage they had suffered shipwreck through the violence of a storm ; and how, when they were cast upon an island called Antaradus, Matthidia was thrown by a wave upon a rock, but her twin children were seized by pirates and car-

ried to Cæsarea, and there sold to a pious woman, who treated them as sons, and brought them up, and caused them to be educated as gentlemen ; and how the pirates had changed their names, and called the one Niceta and the other Aquila ; and how afterwards, through *common* studies and acquaintanceship, they had adhered to Simon ; and how they had turned away from him when they saw him to be a magician and a deceiver, and had come to Zacchæus ; and how subsequently they had been associated with himself ; and how Clement also, setting out from the city for the sake of learning the truth, had, through his acquaintance with Barnabas, come to Cæsarea, and had become known to him, and had adhered to him, and how he had been taught by him the faith of his religion ; and also how he had found and recognised his mother begging at Antaradus, and how the whole island rejoiced at his recognition of her ; and also concerning her sojourn with her most chaste hostess, and the cure that he had wrought upon her, and concerning the liberality of Clement to those who had been kind to his mother ; and how afterwards, when Niceta and Aquila asked who the strange woman was, and had heard the whole story from Clement, they cried out that they were her twin sons Faustinus and Faustus ; and how they had unfolded the whole history of what had befallen them ; and how afterwards, by the persuasion of Peter himself, they were presented to their mother with caution, lest she should be cut off by the sudden joy.

CHAP. XXXVII. — ANOTHER RECOGNITION.

But while Peter was detailing these things in the hearing of the old man, in a narrative which was most pleasing to the crowd, so that the hearers wept through wonder at the events, and through compassion for sufferings incident to humanity,[3] my mother, hearing (I know not how) of the recognition of my father, rushed into the middle of us in breathless haste, crying out, and saying : "Where is my husband, my lord Faustinianus, who has been so long afflicted, wandering from city to city in search of me ?" While she shouted thus like one demented, and gazed around, the old man, running up, began to embrace and hug her with many tears.[4] And while these things were going on, Peter requested the crowds to disperse, saying that it was unseemly to remain longer ; but that opportunity must be afforded them of seeing one another more privately. "But to-morrow," said he, "if any of you wish it, let them assemble to hear the word."

---

[1] [Compare the account of the recognition in Homily XIV. 9. — R.]
[2] [This recapitulation is peculiar to the *Recognitions;* in Homily XV. 4 the main facts are cited as a proof of divine providence. — R.]

[3] Lit. "through pity of humanity."
[4] [Comp. Homily XIV. 9. The recognition of the mother is represented as occurring first; the variations are quite remarkable. — R.]

CHAP. XXXVIII. — "ANGELS UNAWARES."

When Peter had said this, the crowds dispersed; and when we also were intending to go to our lodging, the master of the house said to us:[1] "It is base and wicked that such and so great men should stay in a hostelry, when I have almost my whole house empty, and very many beds spread, and all necessary things provided." But when Peter refused, the wife of the householder prostrated herself before him with her children, and besought him, saying, "I entreat you, stay with us." But not even so did Peter consent, until the daughter of those people who asked him, who had been for a long time vexed with an unclean spirit, and bound with chains, who had been shut up in a closet, having had the demon expelled from her, and the door of the closet opened, came with her chains and fell down at Peter's feet, saying: "It is right, my lord, that you keep my deliverance-feast here to-day, and not sadden me or my parents." But when Peter asked what was the meaning of her chains and of her words, her parents, gladdened beyond hope by the recovery of their daughter, were, as it were, thunderstruck with astonish-

ment, and could not speak; but the servants who were in attendance said: "This girl has been possessed of a demon from her seventh year, and used to cut, and bite, and even to tear in pieces, all who attempted to approach her, and this she has never ceased to do for twenty years till the present time. Nor could any one cure her, or even approach her, for she rendered many helpless, and even destroyed some; for she was stronger than any man, being doubtless strengthened by the power of the demon. But now, as you see, the demon has fled from your presence, and the doors which were shut with the greatest strength have been opened, and she herself stands before you in her sound mind, asking of you to make the day of her recovery gladsome both to herself and her parents, and to remain with them." When one of the servants had made this statement, and the chains of their own accord were loosened from her hands and feet, Peter, being sure that it was by his means that soundness was restored to the girl, consented to remain with them. And he ordered those also who had remained in the lodging, with his wife, to come over; and every one of us having got a separate bed-chamber, we remained; and having taken food in the usual manner, and given praises to God, we went to sleep in our several apartments.

[1] [This chapter is peculiar to the *Recognitions*; the detailed description of the exorcism is a curious piece of literature. — R.]

BOOK X

CHAP. I. — PROBATION.

But in the morning, after sunrise, I Clement, and Niceta and Aquila, along with Peter, came to the apartment in which my father and mother were sleeping; and finding them still asleep, we sat down before the door, when Peter addressed us in such terms as these:[1] "Listen to me, most beloved fellow-servants: I know that you have a great affection for your father; therefore I am afraid that you will urge him too soon to take upon himself the yoke of religion, while he is not yet prepared for it; and to this he may perhaps consent, through his affection for you. But this is not to be depended on; for what is done for the sake of men is not worthy of approba-

tion, and soon falls to pieces. Therefore it seems to me, that you should permit him to live for a year according to his own judgment; and during that time he may travel with us, and while we are instructing others he may hear with simplicity; and as he hears, if he has any right purpose of acknowledging the truth, he will himself request that he may take up the yoke of religion; or if he do not please to take it, he may remain a friend. For those who do not take it up heartily, when they begin not to be able to bear it, not only cast off that which they had taken up, but by way of excuse, as it were, for their weakness, they begin to speak evil of the way of religion, and to malign those whom they have not been able to follow or to imitate."

[1] [In book x. the arrangement, to the close of chap. 51, differs from that of the *Homilies*. Here Peter proposes a delay. In Homily XV. an account is given of the attempt to convert the father immediately; the Apostle arguing with him, and urging the importance of being of the same mind with his family. Then in Homilies XVI.–XIX. a second discussion with Simon is given, occurring in the presence of the father of Clement. Here the argument is carried on by Clement (chaps. 7–28), Niceta (chaps. 30–34, 41), Aquila (chaps. 35–38), and concluded by Peter himself (chaps. 42–51). Much of the mythological matter finds a parallel in the discussion with Appion (Homily IV.–VI.), but there is no direct agreement in the two works from this point to chap. 52. Comp. Homily XX. 11. — R.]

CHAP. II. — A DIFFICULTY.

To this Niceta answered: "My lord Peter, I say nothing against your right and good counsels; but I wish to say one thing, that thereby I may learn something that I do not know. What if my father should die within the year during which you recommend that he should be put off? He will go down to hell helpless, and so be tormented for ever." Then said Peter: "I embrace your kindly purpose towards your father, and I forgive you in respect of things of which you are ignorant. For do you suppose that, if any one is thought to have lived righteously, he shall forthwith be saved? Do you not think that he must be examined by Him who knows the secrets of men, as to how he has lived righteously, whether perchance according to the rule of the Gentiles, obeying their institutions and laws; or for the sake of the friendship of men; or merely from custom, or any other cause; or from necessity, and not on account of righteousness itself, and for the sake of God? For those who have lived righteously, for the sake of God alone and His righteousness, they shall come to eternal rest, and shall receive the perpetuity of the heavenly kingdom. For salvation is not attained by force, but by liberty; and not through the favour of men, but by the faith of God. Then, besides, you ought to consider that God is prescient, and knows whether this man is one of His. But if He knows that he is not, what shall we do with respect to those things which have been determined by Him from the beginning? But wherein I can, I give counsel: when he is awake, and we sit down together, then do you, as if you wished to learn something, ask a question about those matters which it is fitting for him to learn; and while we speak to one another, he will gain instruction. But yet wait first to see if he himself ask anything; for if he do so, the occasion of discourse will be the fitter. But if he do not ask anything, let us by turns put questions to one another, wishing to learn something, as I have said. Such is my judgment, state what is yours."

CHAP. III. — A SUGGESTION.

And when we had commended his right counsel, I Clement said: "In all things, the end for the most part looks back upon the beginning, and the issue of things is similar to their commencement. I hope, therefore, with respect to our father also, since God by your means has given a good beginning, that He will bestow also an ending suitable to the beginning, and worthy of Himself. However, I make this suggestion, that if, as you have said, we begin to speak, in presence of my father, as if for the purpose of discussing some subject, or learning something from one another, you, my lord Peter, ought not to occupy the place of one who has anything to learn; for if he see this, he will rather be offended. For he is convinced that you fully know all things, as indeed you do. How then will it be, if he see you pretending igno-

rance? This, as I have said, will rather hurt him, being ignorant of your design. But if we brothers, while we converse among ourselves, are in any doubt, let a fitting solution be given by you to our inquiry. For if he see even you hesitating and doubting, then truly he will think that no one has knowledge of the truth."

CHAP. IV. — FREE INQUIRY.

To this Peter answered: "Let us not concern ourselves about this; and if indeed it is fitting that he enter the gate of life, God will afford a fitting opportunity; and there shall be a beginning from God, and not from man. And therefore, as I have said, let him journey with us, and hear our discussions; but because I saw you in haste, therefore I said that opportunity must be sought; and when God shall give it, do you comply with my advice in what I shall say." While we were thus talking, a boy came to tell us that our father was now awake; and when we were intending to go in to him, he himself came to us, and saluting us with a kiss, after we had sat down again, he said: "Is it permitted to one to ask a question, if he wishes it; or is silence enforced, after the manner of the Pythagoreans?" Then said Peter: "We do not compel those who come to us either to keep silence continually, or to ask questions; but we leave them free to do as they will, knowing that he who is anxious about his salvation, if he feels pain in any part of his soul, does not suffer it to be silent. But he who neglects his salvation, no advantage is conferred upon him if he is compelled to ask, excepting this only, that he may seem to be earnest and diligent. Wherefore, if you wish to get any information, ask on."

CHAP. V. — GOOD AND EVIL.

Then the old man said: "There is a saying very prevalent among the Greek philosophers, to the effect that there is in reality neither good nor evil in the life of man; but that men call things good or evil as they appear to them, prejudiced by the use and custom of life. For not even murder is really an evil, because it sets the soul free from the bonds of the flesh. Further, they say that even just judges put to death those who commit crimes; but if they knew homicide to be an evil, just men would not do that. Neither do they say that adultery is an evil; for if the husband does not know, or does not care, there is, they say, no evil in it. But neither, say they, is theft an evil; for it takes away what one does not possess from another who has it. And, indeed, it ought to be taken freely and openly; but in that it is done secretly, that is rather a reproof of his inhumanity from whom it is secretly taken. For all men ought to have the common use of all things that are in this world; but through injustice one says that this is his, and another that that is his, and so division is caused among men. In short, a certain man, the wisest among the Greeks,[1] knowing that these things are so, says that friends should have all things common. Now, in *all things* unquestionably wives are included. He says also that, as the air and the sunshine cannot be divided, so neither ought other things to be divided, which are given in this world to all to be possessed in common, but should be so possessed. But I wished to say this, because I am desirous to turn to well-doing, and I cannot act well unless I first learn what is good; and if I can understand that, I shall thereby perceive what is evil, that is, opposite to good.

CHAP. VI. — PETER'S AUTHORITY.

"But I should like that one of you, and not Peter, should answer what I have said; for it is not fitting to take words and instruction at his hand, with questions; but when he gives a deliverance on any subject, that should be held without answering again. And therefore let us keep him as an umpire; so that if at any time our discussion does not come to an issue, he may declare what seems good to him, and so give an undoubted end to doubtful matters. And now therefore I could believe, content with his sole opinion, if he expressed any opinion; and this is what I shall do at last. Yet I wish first to see if it is possible by discussion to find what is sought. My wish therefore is, that Clement should begin first, and should show if there is any good or evil in substance or in actions."

CHAP. VII. — CLEMENT'S ARGUMENT.

To this I answered: "Since indeed you wish to learn from me if there is any good or evil in nature or in act, or whether it is not rather that men, prejudiced by custom, think some things to be good, and others to be evil, forasmuch as they have made a division among themselves of common things, which ought, as you say, to be as common as the air and the sunshine; I think that I ought not to bring before you any statements from any other quarter than from those studies in which you are well versed, and which you support, so that what I say you will receive without hesitation. You assign certain boundaries of all the elements and the heavenly bodies, and these, you say, meet in some without hurt, as in marriages; but in others they are hurtfully united, as in adulteries. And you say that some things are general to all, but other things do not belong to all, and are not general. But not to

make a long discussion, I shall speak briefly of the matter. The earth which is dry is in need of the addition and admixture of water, that it may be able to produce fruits, without which man cannot live: this is therefore a legitimate conjunction. On the contrary, if the cold of hoar-frost be mixed with the earth, or heat with the water, a conjunction of this sort produces corruption; and this, in such things, is adultery."

CHAP. VIII. — ADMITTED EVILS.

Then my father answered: "But as the harmfulness of an inharmonious conjunction of elements or stars is immediately betrayed, so ought also adultery to be immediately shown that it is an evil." Then I: "First tell me this, whether, as you yourself have confessed, evils are produced from incongruous and inharmonious mixture; and then after that we shall inquire into the other matter." Then my father said: "The nature of things is as you say, my son." Then I answered: "Since, then, you wish to learn of these things, see how many things there are which no one doubts to be evils. Do you think that a fever, a fire, sedition, the fall of a house, murder, bonds, racks, pains, mournings, and such like, are evils?" Then said my father: "It is true, my son, that these things are evil, and very evil; or, at all events, whoever denies that they are evil, let him suffer them!"

CHAP. IX. — EXISTENCE OF EVIL ON ASTROLOGICAL PRINCIPLES.

Then I answered: "Since, therefore, I have to deal with one who is skilled in astrological science,[2] I shall treat the matter with you according to that science, that, taking my method from those things with which you are familiar, you may the more readily acquiesce. Listen now, therefore: you confess that those things which we have mentioned are evils, such as fevers, conflagrations, and such like. Now these, according to you, are said to be produced by malignant stars, such as the humid Saturn and the hot Mars; but things contrary to these are produced by benignant stars, such as the temperate Jupiter and the humid Venus. Is it not so?" My father answered: "It is so, my son; and it cannot be otherwise." Then said I: "Since you say, therefore, that good things are produced by good stars — by Jupiter and Venus, for example — let us see what is the product where any one of the evil stars is mixed with the good, and let us understand that that is evil. For you lay it down that Venus makes marriages, and if she have Jupiter in her configura-

[1] Allusion is made to Socrates and community of wives, as stated in the *Republic* of Plato.

[2] [Comp. book ix. 15, 17, etc. The question of astrology is much more prominent in the *Recognitions;* but comp. Homily XIV. 5, and elsewhere. — R.]

tion she makes the marriages chaste; but if Jupiter be not regarding, and Mars be present, then you pronounce that the marriages are corrupted by adultery." Then said my father: "It is even so." Then I answered: "Therefore adultery is an evil, seeing that it is committed through the admixture of evil stars; and, to state it in a word, all things that you say that the good stars suffer from the mixture of evil stars, are undoubtedly to be pronounced to be evil. Those stars, therefore, by whose admixture we have said that fevers, conflagrations, and other such like evils are produced, — those, according to you, work also murders, adulteries, thefts, and also produce haughty and stolid men."

CHAP. X. — HOW TO MAKE PROGRESS.

Then my father said: "Truly you have shown briefly and incomparably that there are evils in actions; but still I should wish to learn this, how God justly judges those who sin, as you say, if GENESIS compels them to sin?" Then I answered: "I am afraid to speak anything to you, my father, because it becomes me to hold you in all honour; else I have an answer to give you, if it were becoming." Then says my father: "Speak what occurs to you, my son; for it is not you, but the method of inquiry, that does the wrong, as a modest woman to an incontinent man, if she is indignant for her safety and her honour." Then I answered: "If we do not hold by the principles that we have acknowledged and confessed, but if those things which have been defined are always loosened by forgetfulness, we shall seem to be weaving Penelope's web, undoing what we have done. And therefore we ought either not to acquiesce too easily, before we have diligently examined the doctrine propounded; or if we have once acquiesced, and the proposition has been agreed to, then we ought to keep by what has been once determined, that we may go on with our inquiries respecting other matters." And my father said: "You say well, my son; and I know why you say this: it is because in the discussion yesterday on natural causes, you showed that some malignant power, transferring itself into the order of the stars, excites the lusts of men, provoking them in various ways to sin, yet not compelling or producing sins." To this I answered: "It is well that you remember it; and yet, though you do remember it, you have fallen into error." Then said my father: "Pardon me, my son; for I have not yet much practice in these things: for indeed your discourses yesterday, by their truth, shut me up to agree with you; yet in my consciousness there are, as it were, some remains of fevers, which for a little hold me back from faith, as from health.

For I am distracted, because I know that many things, yea, almost all things, have befallen me according to GENESIS."

CHAP. XI. — TEST OF ASTROLOGY.

Then I answered: "I shall therefore tell you, my father, what is the nature of mathematics, and do you act according to what I tell you. Go to a mathematician,[1] and tell him first that such and such evils have befallen you at such a time, and that you wish to learn of him whence, or how, or through what stars they have befallen you. He will no doubt answer you that a malignant Mars or Saturn has ruled your times, or that some one of them has been periodic; or that some one has regarded you diametrically, or in conjunction, or centrally; or some such answer will he give, adding that in all these some one was not in harmony with the malignant one, or was invisible, or was in the figure, or was beyond the division, or was eclipsed, or was not in contact, or was among the dark stars; and many other like things will he answer, according to his own reasons, and will condescend upon particulars. After him go to another mathematician, and tell him the opposite, that such and such good happened to you at that time, mentioning to him the same time, and ask him from what parts of your GENESIS this good has come to you, and take care, as I said, that the times are the same with those about which you asked concerning evils. And when you have deceived him concerning the times, see what figures he will invent for you, by which to show that good things ought to have befallen you at those very times. For it is impossible for those treating of the GENESIS of men not to find in every quarter, as they call it, of the heavenly bodies, some stars favourably placed, and some unfavourably; for the circle is equally complete in every part, according to mathematics, admitting of diverse and various causes, from which they can take occasion of saying whatever they please.

CHAP. XII. — ASTROLOGY BAFFLED BY FREE-WILL.

"For, as usually happens when men see unfavourable dreams, and can make nothing certain out of them, when any event occurs, then they adapt what they saw in the dream to what has occurred; so also is mathematics. For before anything happens, nothing is declared with certainty; but after something has happened, they gather the causes of the event. And thus often, when they have been at fault, and the thing has fallen out otherwise, they take the blame to themselves, saying that it was such and such a star which opposed, and that they did not see it; not

---

[1] [The connection of mathematics and astrology is indicated also in Homily XIV. 3. — R.]

knowing that their error does not proceed from their unskilfulness in their art, but from the inconsistency of the whole system. For they do not know what those things are which we indeed desire to do, but in regard to which we do not indulge our desires. But we who have learned the reason of this mystery know the cause, since, having freedom of will, we sometimes oppose our desires, and sometimes yield to them.[1] And therefore the issue of human doings is uncertain, because it depends upon freedom of will. For a mathematician can indeed indicate the desire which a malignant power produces; but whether the acting or the issue of this desire shall be fulfilled or not, no one can know before the accomplishment of the thing, because it depends upon freedom of will. And this is why ignorant astrologers have invented to themselves the talk about climacterics as their refuge in uncertainties, as we showed fully yesterday.

CHAP. XIII. — PEOPLE ADMITTED.

" If you have anything that you wish to say to this, say on." Then my father: "Nothing can be more true, my son, than what you have stated." And while we were thus speaking among ourselves, some one informed us that a great multitude of people were standing outside, having assembled for the purpose of hearing. Then Peter ordered them to be admitted, for the place was large and convenient. And when they had come in, Peter said to us: "If any one of you wishes, let him address the people, and discourse concerning idolatry." To whom I Clement answered: "Your great benignity and gentleness and patience towards all encourages us, so that we dare speak in your presence, and ask what we please; and therefore, as I said, the gentleness of your disposition invites and encourages all to undertake the precepts of saving doctrine. This I never saw before in any one else, but in you only, with whom there is neither envy nor indignation. Or what do you think?

CHAP. XIV. — NO MAN HAS UNIVERSAL KNOWLEDGE.

Then Peter said: "These things come not only from envy or indignation; but sometimes there is a bashfulness in some persons, lest haply they may not be able to answer fully the questions that may be proposed, and so they avoid the discovery of their want of skill. But no one ought to be ashamed of this, because there is no man who ought to profess that he knows all things; for there is only One who knows all things, even He who also made all things. For if our Master declared that He knew not the

day and the hour whose signs even He foretold, and referred the whole to the Father, how shall we account it disgraceful to confess that we are ignorant of some things, since in this we have the example of our Master? But this only we profess, that we know those things which we have learned from the true Prophet; and that those things have been delivered to us by the true Prophet, which He judged to be sufficient for human knowledge."

CHAP. XV. — CLEMENT'S DISCOURSE.

Then I Clement went on to speak thus: "At Tripolis, when you were disputing against the Gentiles, my lord Peter, I greatly wondered at you, that although you were instructed by your father according to the fashion of the Hebrews and in observances of your own law, and were never polluted by the studies of Greek learning, you argued so magnificently and so incomparably; and that you even touched upon some things concerning the histories of the gods, which are usually declaimed in the theatres. But as I perceived that their fables and blasphemies are not so well known to you, I shall discourse upon these in your hearing, repeating them from the very beginning, if it please you." Then says Peter: "Say on; you do well to assist my preaching." Then said I: "I shall speak, therefore, because you order me, not by way of teaching you, but of making public what foolish opinions the Gentiles entertain of the gods."

CHAP. XVI. — "WOULD THAT ALL GOD'S PEOPLE WERE PROPHETS."

But when I was about to speak, Niceta, biting his lip, beckoned to me to be silent. And when Peter saw him, he said: "Why would you repress his liberal disposition and noble nature, that you would have him be silent for my honour, which is nothing? Or do you not know, that if all nations, after they have heard from me the preaching of the truth, and have believed, would betake themselves to teaching, they would gain the greater glory for me, if indeed you think me desirous of glory? For what so glorious as to prepare disciples for Christ, not who shall be silent, and shall be saved alone, but who shall speak what they have learned, and shall do good to others? I wish indeed that both you, Niceta, and you, beloved Aquila, would aid me in preaching the word of God, and the rather because those things in which the Gentiles err are well known to you; and not you only, but all who hear me, I wish, as I have said, so to hear and to learn, that they may be able also to teach: for the world needs many helpers, by whom men may be recalled

---

[1] [This argument from human freedom is the favourite one throughout. — R.]

from error." When he had spoken thus, he said to me : "Go on then, Clement, with what you have begun."

CHAP. XVII. — GENTILE COSMOGONY.

And I immediately rejoined : "Seeing that when you were disputing at Tripolis, as I said, you discoursed much concerning the gods of the Gentiles profitably and convincingly, I desire to set forth in your presence the ridiculous legends concerning their origin, both that you may not be unacquainted with the falsehood of this vain superstition, and that the hearers who are present may know the disgraceful character of their error. The wise men, then, who are among the Gentiles, say that first of all things was chaos ;[1] that this, through a long time solidifying its outer parts, made bounds to itself and a sort of foundation, being gathered, as it were, into the manner and form of a huge egg, within which, in the course of a long time, as within the shell of the egg, there was cherished and vivified a certain animal ; and that afterwards, that huge globe being broken, there came forth a certain kind of man of double sex, which they call masculo-feminine. This they called Phanetas, from appearing, because when it appeared, they say, then also light shone forth. And from this, they say that there were produced substance, prudence, motion, and coition, and from these the heavens and the earth were made. From the heaven they say that six males were produced, whom they call Titans ; and in like manner, from the earth six females, whom they called Titanides. And these are the names of the males who sprang from the heaven : Oceanus, Cœus, Crios, Hyperion, Iapetus, Chronos, who amongst us is called Saturn. In like manner, the names of the females who sprang from the earth are these : Theia, Rhea, Themis, Mnemosyne, Tethys, Hebe.[2]

CHAP. XVIII. — FAMILY OF SATURN.

"Of all these, the first-born of the heaven took to wife the first-born of earth ; the second the second, and in like manner all the rest. The first male, therefore, who had married the first female, was on her account drawn downwards ; but the second female rose upwards, by reason of him to whom she was married ; and so each doing in their order, remained in those places which fell to their share by the nuptial lot. From their intercourse they assert that innumerable others sprang. But of these six males, the one who is called Saturn received in marriage Rhea, and having been warned by a certain

oracle that he who should be born of her should be more powerful than himself, and should drive him from his kingdom, he determined to devour all the sons that should be born to him. First, then, there is born to him a son called Aides, who amongst us is called Orcus ; and him, for the reason we have just stated, he took and devoured. After him he begot a second son, called Neptune ; and him he devoured in like manner. Last of all, he begot him whom they call Jupiter ; but him his mother Rhea pitying, by stratagem withdrew from his father when he was about to devour him. And first, indeed, that the crying of the child might not be noticed, she made certain Corybantes strike cymbals and drums, that by the deafening sound the crying of the infant might not be heard.

CHAP. XIX. — THEIR DESTINIES.

"But when he understood from the lessening of her belly that her child was born, he demanded it, that he might devour it ; then Rhea presented him with a large stone, and told him that that was what she had brought forth. And he took it, and swallowed it ; and the stone, when it was devoured, pushed and drove forth those sons whom he had formerly swallowed. Therefore Orcus, coming forth first, descended, and occupies the lower, that is, the infernal regions. The second, being above him — he whom they call Neptune — is thrust forth upon the waters. The third, who survived by the artifice of his mother Rhea, she put upon a she-goat and sent into heaven.

CHAP. XX. — DOINGS OF JUPITER.

"But enough of the old wife's fables and genealogy of the Gentiles ; for it were endless if I should set forth all the generations of those whom they call gods, and their wicked doings. But by way of example, omitting the rest, I shall detail the wicked deeds of him only whom they hold to be the greatest and the chief, and whom they call Jupiter.[3] For they say that he possesses heaven, as being superior to the rest ; and he, as soon as he grew up, married his own sister, whom they call Juno, in which truly he at once becomes like a beast. Juno bears Vulcan ; but, as they relate, Jupiter was not his father. However, by Jupiter himself she became mother of Medea ; and Jupiter having received a response that one who should be born of her should be more powerful than himself, and should expel him from his kingdom, took her and devoured her. Again Jupiter produced Minerva from his brain, and Bacchus from his thigh. After this, when he had fallen in love with Thetis, they say

---

[1] [With this cosmogony (chaps. 17-19, 30-34) compare the discourse of Appion, Homily VI. 3-10. — R.]
[2] [Comp. chap. 31 and Homily VI. 2. — R.]

[3] [Comp. Homily V. 12-15 for a parallel to chaps. 20-23. — R.]

that Prometheus informed him that, if he lay with her, he who should be born of her should be more powerful than his father; and for fear of this, he gave her in marriage to one Peleus. Subsequently he had intercourse with Persephone, who was his own daughter by Ceres; and by her he begot Dionysius,[1] who was torn in pieces by the Titans. But calling to mind, it is said, that perhaps his own father Saturn might beget another son, who might be more powerful than himself, and might expel him from the kingdom, he went to war with his father, along with his brothers the Titans; and having beaten them, he at last threw his father into prison, and cut off his genitals, and threw them into the sea. But the blood which flowed from the wound, being mixed with the waves, and turned into foam by the constant churning, produced her whom they call Aphrodite, and whom with us they call Venus. From his intercourse with her who was thus his own sister, they say that this same Jupiter begot Cypris, who, they say, was the mother of Cupid.

CHAP. XXI. — A BLACK CATALOGUE.

"Thus much of his incests; I shall now speak of his adulteries. He defiled Europa, the wife of Oceanus, of whom was born Dodonæus; Helen, the wife of Pandion, of whom Musæus; Eurynome, the wife of Asopus, of whom Ogygias; Hermione, the wife of Oceanus, of whom the Graces, Thalia, Euphrosyne, Aglaia; Themis, his own sister, of whom the Hours, Eurynomia, Dice, Irene; Themisto, the daughter of Inachus, of whom Arcas; Idæa, the daughter of Minos, of whom Asterion; Phœnissa, the daughter of Alphion, of whom Endymion; Io, the daughter of Inachus, of whom Epaphus; Hippodamia and Isione, daughters of Danaus, of whom Hippodamia was the wife of Olenus, and Isione of Orchomenus or Chryses; Carme, the daughter of Phœnix, of whom was born Britomartis, who was an attendant of Diana; Callisto, the daughter of Lycaon, of whom Orcas; Lybee, the daughter of Munantius, of whom Belus; Latona, of whom Apollo and Diana; Leandia, the daughter of Eurymedon, of whom Coron; Lysithea, the daughter of Evenus, of whom Helenus; Hippodamia, the daughter of Bellerophon, of whom Sarpedon; Megaclite, the daughter of Macarius, of whom Thebe and Locrus; Niobe, the daughter of Phoroneus, of whom Argus and Pelasgus; Olympias, the daughter of Neoptolemus, of whom Alexander; Pyrrha, the daughter of Prometheus, of whom Helmetheus; Protogenia and Pandora, daughters of Deucalion, of whom he begot Æthelius, and Dorus, and Melera, and

Pandorus; Thaicrucia, the daughter of Proteus, of whom was born Nympheus; Salamis, the daughter of Asopus, of whom Saracon; Taygete, Electra, Maia, Plutide, daughters of Atlas, of whom respectively he begot Lacedæmon, Dardanus, Mercury, and Tantalus; Phthia, the daughter of Phoroneus, of whom he begot Achæus; Chonia, the daughter of Aramnus, of whom he begot Lacon; Chalcea, a nymph, of whom was born Olympus; Charidia, a nymph, of whom Alcanus; Chloris, who was the wife of Ampycus, of whom Mopsus was born; Cotonia, the daughter of Lesbus, of whom Polymedes; Hippodamia, the daughter of Anicetus; Chrysogenia, the daughter of Peneus, of whom was born Thissæus.

CHAP. XXII. — VILE TRANSFORMATION OF JUPITER.

"There are also innumerable adulteries of his, of which no offspring was the result, which it were tedious to enumerate. But amongst those whom we have mentioned, he violated some being transformed, like a magician. In short, he seduced Antiope, the daughter of Nycteus, when turned into a satyr, and of her were born Amphion and Zethus; Alcmene, when changed into her husband Amphitryon, and of her was born Hercules; Ægina, the daughter of Asopus, when changed into an eagle, of whom Æacus was born. So also he defiled Ganymede, the son of Dardanus, being changed into an eagle; Manthea, the daughter of Phocus, when changed into a bear, of whom was born Arctos; Danæ, the daughter of Acrisius, being changed into gold, of whom Perseus; Europa, the daughter of Phœnix, changed into a bull, of whom were born Minos, Rhadamanthus, and Sarpedon; Eurymedusa, the daughter of Achelaus, being changed into an ant, of whom Myrmidon; Thalia, the nymph, being changed into a vulture, of whom were born the Palisci, in Sicily; Imandra, the daughter of Geneanus, at Rhodes, being changed into a shower; Cassiopeia, being changed into her husband Phœnix, and of her was born Anchinos; Leda, the daughter of Thestius, being changed into a swan, of whom was born Helen; and again the same, being changed into a star, and of her were born Castor and Pollux; Lamia, being changed into a lapwing; Mnemosyne, being changed into a shepherd, of whom were born the nine Muses; Nemesis, being changed into a goose; the Cadmian Semele, being changed into fire, and of her was born Dionysius. By his own daughter Ceres he begot Persephone, whom also herself he defiled, being changed into a dragon.

CHAP. XXIII. — WHY A GOD?

"He also committed adultery with Europa, the wife of his own uncle Oceanus, and with her

---

[1] Dionysius appears here and subsequently in the text for Dionysus, the Greek god corresponding to the Latin Bacchus. Some of the other names are more or less corrupt forms.

sister Eurynome, and punished their father; and he committed adultery with Plute, the daughter of his own son Atlas, and condemned Tantalus, whom she bore to him. Of Larisse, the daughter of Orchomenus, he begot Tityon, whom also he consigned to punishment. He carried off Dia, the wife of his own son Ixion, and subjected him to perpetual punishment; and almost all the sons who sprang from his adulteries he put to violent deaths; and indeed the sepulchres of almost all of them are well known. Yea, the sepulchre of this parricide himself, who destroyed his uncles and defiled their wives, who committed whoredom with his sisters, this magician of many transformations, is shown among the Cretans, who, although they know and acknowledge his horrid and incestuous deeds, and tell them to all, yet are not ashamed to confess him to be a god. Whence it seems to me to be wonderful, yea, exceeding wonderful, how he who exceeds all men in wickedness and crimes, has received that holy and good name which is above every name, being called the father of gods and men; unless perhaps he who rejoices in the evils of men has persuaded unhappy souls to confer honour above all others upon him whom he saw to excel all others in crimes, in order that he might allure all to the imitation of his evil deeds.

CHAP. XXIV. — FOLLY OF POLYTHEISM.

" But also the sepulchres of his sons, who are regarded amongst these *the Gentiles* as gods, are openly pointed out, one in one place, and another in another: that of Mercury at Hermopolis; that of the Cyprian Venus at Cyprus; that of Mars in Thrace; that of Bacchus at Thebes, where he is said to have been torn in pieces; that of Hercules at Tyre, where he was burnt with fire; that of Æsculapius in Epidaurus. And all these are spoken of, not only as men who have died, but as wicked men who have been punished for their crimes; and yet they are adored as gods by foolish men.[1]

CHAP. XXV. — DEAD MEN DEIFIED.

" But if they choose to argue, and affirm that these are rather the places of their birth than of their burial or death, the former and ancient doings shall be convicted from those at hand and still recent, since we have shown that they worship those whom they themselves confess to have been men, and to have died, or rather to have been punished; as the Syrians worship Adonis, and the Egyptians Osiris; the Trojans, Hector; Achilles is worshipped at Leuconesus, Patroclus at Pontus, Alexander the Macedonian

at Rhodes; and many others are worshipped, one in one place and another in another, whom they do not doubt to have been dead men. Whence it follows that their predecessors also, falling into a like error, conferred divine honour upon dead men, who perhaps had had some power or some skill, and especially if they had stupefied stolid men by magical phantasies.[2]

CHAP. XXVI. — METAMORPHOSES.

" Hence there has now been added, that the poets also adorn the falsehoods of error by elegance of words, and by sweetness of speech persuade that mortals have been made immortal; yea more, they say that men are changed into stars, and trees, and animals, and flowers, and birds, and fountains, and rivers. And but that it might seem to be a waste of words, I could even enumerate almost all the stars, and trees, and fountains, and rivers, which they assert to have been made of men; yet, by way of example, I shall mention at least one of each class. They say that Andromeda, the daughter of Cepheus, was turned into a star; Daphne, the daughter of the river Lado, into a tree; Hyacinthus, beloved of Apollo, into a flower; Callisto into the constellation which they call Arctos; Progne and Philomela, with Tereus, into birds; that Thysbe in Cilicia was dissolved into a fountain; and Pyramus, at the same place, into a river. And they assert that almost all the stars, trees, fountains, and rivers, flowers, animals, and birds, were at one time human beings."

CHAP. XXVII. — INCONSISTENCY OF POLYTHEISTS.

But Peter, when he heard this, said: "According to them, then, before men were changed into stars, and the other things which you mention, the heaven was without stars, and the earth without trees and animals; and there were neither fountains, nor rivers, nor birds. And without these, how did those men themselves live, who afterwards were changed into them, since it is evident that, without these things, men could not live upon the earth?" Then I answered: " But they are not even able to observe the worship of their own gods consistently; for every one of those whom they worship has something dedicated to himself, from which his worshippers ought to abstain: as they say the olive is dedicated to Minerva, the she-goat to Jupiter, seeds to Ceres, wine to Bacchus, water to Osiris, the ram to Hammon, the stag to Diana, the fish and the dove to the demon of the Syrians, fire to Vulcan; and to each one, as I have said, is there something specially consecrated, from which the worshippers are bound to abstain, for the honour

---

[1] [Comp. Homily V. 23, where these details appear in a letter, written by Clement as if from a woman; also Homily VI. 21. — R.]

[2] [Comp. Homily VI. 22. — R.]

of those to whom they are consecrated. But were one abstaining from one thing, and another from another, by doing honor to one of the gods, they incur the anger of all the rest; and therefore, if they would conciliate them all, they must abstain from all things for the honour of all, so that, being self-condemned by a just sentence before the day of judgment, they should perish by a most wretched death through starvation.

CHAP. XXVIII. — BUTTRESSES OF GENTILISM.

"But let us return to our purpose. What reason is there, yea, rather, what madness possesses the minds of men, that they worship and adore as a god, a man whom they not only know to be impious, wicked, profane — I mean Jupiter — incestuous, a parricide, an adulterer, but even proclaim him publicly as such in their songs in the theatres? Or if by means of these deeds he has deserved to be a god, then also, when they hear of any murderers, adulterers, parricides, incestuous persons, they ought to worship them also as gods. But I cannot understand why they venerate in him what they execrate in others." Then Peter answered: "Since you say that you cannot understand it, learn of me why they venerate wickedness in him. In the first place, it is that, when they themselves do like deeds, they may know that they shall be acceptable to him, inasmuch as they have but imitated him in his wickedness. In the second place, because the ancients have left these things skilfully composed in their writings, and elegantly engrafted in their verses. And now, by the aid of youthful education, since the knowledge of these things adheres to their tender and simple minds, it cannot without difficulty be torn from them and cast away."

CHAP. XXIX. — ALLEGORIES.

When Peter had said this, Niceta answered: "Do not suppose, my lord Peter, but that the learned men of the Gentiles have certain plausible arguments, by which they support those things which seem to be blameworthy and disgraceful. And this I state, not as wishing to confirm their error (for far be it from me that such a thing should ever come into my thought); but yet I know that there are amongst the more intelligent of them certain defences, by which they are accustomed to support and colour over those things which seem to be absurd. And if it please you that I should state some of them — for I am to some extent acquainted with them — I shall do as you order me." And when Peter had given him leave, Niceta proceeded as follows.

CHAP. XXX. — COSMOGONY OF ORPHEUS.

"All the literature among the Greeks which is written on the subject of the origin of antiquity, is based upon many authorities, but especially two, Orpheus and Hesiod.[1] Now their writings are divided into two parts, in respect of their meaning, — that is, the literal and the allegorical; and the vulgar crowd has flocked to the literal, but all the eloquence of the philosophers and learned men is expended in admiration of the allegorical. It is Orpheus, then, who says that at first there was chaos, eternal, unbounded, unproduced, and that from it all things were made. He says that this chaos was neither darkness nor light, neither moist nor dry, neither hot nor cold, but that it was all things mixed together, and was always one unformed mass; yet that at length, as it were after the manner of a huge egg, it brought forth and produced from itself a certain double form, which had been wrought through immense periods of time, and which they call masculo-feminine, a form concrete from the contrary admixture of such diversity; and that this is the principle of all things, which came of pure matter, and which, coming forth, effected a separation of the four elements, and made heaven of the two elements which are first, *fire and air*, and earth of the others, *earth and water;* and of these he says that all things now are born and produced by a mutual participation of them. So far Orpheus.

CHAP. XXXI. — HESIOD'S COSMOGONY.

"But to this Hesiod adds, that after chaos the heaven and the earth were made immediately, from which he says that those eleven were produced (and sometimes also he speaks of them as twelve) of whom he makes six males and five females. And these are the names that he gives to the males: Oceanus, Cœus, Crius, Hyperion, Iapetus, Chronos, who is also called Saturn. Also the names of the females are: Theia, Rhea, Themis, Mnemosyne, Tethys.[2] And these names they thus interpret allegorically. They say that the number is eleven or twelve: that the first is nature itself, which also they would have to be called Rhea, from FLOWING; and they say that the other ten are her accidents, which also they call qualities; yet they add a twelfth, namely Chronos, who with us is called Saturn, and him they take to be time.[3] Therefore they assert that Saturn and Rhea are time and matter; and these, when they are mixed with moisture and dryness, heat and cold, produce all things.

CHAP. XXXII. — ALLEGORICAL INTERPRETATION.

"She therefore (Rhea, or nature), it is said, produced, as it were, a certain bubble which had been collecting for a long time; and it being

---

[1] [Comp. chaps. 17-19 and Homily VI. 3-10, 12-19. — R.]
[2] [Comp. chap. 17 and Homily VI. 2. — R.]
[3] [Comp. Homily VI. 5, 12. — R.]

gradually collected from the spirit which was in the waters, swelled, and being for some time driven over the surface of matter, from which it had come forth as from a womb, and being hardened by the rigour of cold, and always increasing by additions of ice, at length was broken off and sunk into the deep, and drawn by its own weight, went down to the infernal regions; and because it became invisible it was called Aides, and is also named Orcus or Pluto.[1] And since it was sunk from the top to the bottom, it gave place to the moist element to flow together; and the grosser part, which is the earth, was laid bare by the retirement of the waters. They say, therefore, that this freedom of the waters, which was formerly restrained by the presence of the bubble, was called Neptune after the bubble attained the lowest place. After this, when the cold element had been sucked down to the lower regions by the concretion of the icy bubble, and the dry and the moist element had been separated, there being now no hindrance, the warm element rushed by its force and lightness to the upper regions of the air, being borne up by wind and storm. This storm, therefore, which in Greek is called καταιγίς, they called ÆGIS — that is, a she-goat; and the fire which ascended to the upper regions they called Jupiter; wherefore they say that he ascended to Olympus riding on a she-goat.

CHAP. XXXIII. — ALLEGORY OF JUPITER, ETC.

" Now this Jupiter the Greeks would have to be called from his living, or giving life, but our people from his giving succour.[2] They say, therefore, that this is the living substance, which, placed in the upper regions, and drawing all things to itself by the influence of heat, as by the convolution of the brain, and arranging them by the moderation of a certain tempering, is said from his head to have produced wisdom, whom they call Minerva, who was called Ἀθήνη by the Greeks on account of her immortality; who, because the father of all created all things by his wisdom, is also said to have been produced from his head, and from the principal place of all, and is represented as having formed and adorned the whole world by the regulated admixture of the elements.[3] Therefore the forms which were impressed upon matter, that the world might be made, because they are constrained by the force of heat, are said to be held together by the energy of Jupiter. And since there are enough of these, and they do not need anything new to be added to them, but each thing is repaired by the produce of its own seed, the hands of Saturn are said to be bound by Jupi-

ter; because, as I have said, time now produces from matter nothing new: but the warmth of seeds restores all things according to their kinds; and no birth of Rhea — that is, no increase of flowing matter — ascends further. And therefore they call that first division of the elements the mutilation of Saturn, because he cannot any more produce a world.

CHAP. XXXIV. — OTHER ALLEGORIES.

" And of Venus they give forth an allegory to this effect. When, say they, the sea was put under the air, and when the brightness of the heavens shone more pleasantly, being reflected from the waters, the loveliness of things, which appeared fairer from the waters, was called Venus; and she, *it*, being united with the air as with her, *its*, own brother, so as to produce beauty, which might be the object of desire, is said to have given birth to Cupid. In this way, therefore, as we have said, they teach that Chronos, who is Saturn, is allegorically time; Rhea is matter; Aides — that is, Orcus — is the depth of the infernal regions; Neptune is water; Jupiter is air — that is, the element of heat; Venus is the loveliness of things; Cupid is desire, which is in all things, and by which posterity is propagated, or even the reason of things, which gives delight when wisely looked into. Hera — that is, Juno — is said to be that middle air which descends from heaven to earth. To Diana, whom they call Proserpine, they hand over the air below. They say that Apollo is the Sun himself, which goes round the heaven; that Mercury is speech, by which a reason is rendered for everything; that Mars is unrestrained fire, which consumes all things. But not to delay you by enumerating everything, those who have the more abstruse intelligence concerning such things think that they give fair and just reasons, by applying this sort of allegory to every one of their objects of worship."

CHAP. XXXV. — USELESSNESS OF THESE ALLEGORIES.

When Niceta had thus spoken, Aquila answered :[4] " Whoever he was that was the author and inventor of these things, he seems to me to have been very impious, since he covered over those things which seem to be pleasant and seemly, and made the ritual of his superstition to consist in base and shameful observances, since those things which are written according to the letter are manifestly unseemly and base; and the whole observance of their religion consists in these, that by such crimes and impieties they may teach men to imitate their gods whom

1 [Comp. Homily VI. 6. — R.]
2 [Comp. Homily VI. 7. — R.]
3 [With chaps. 33, 34, compare Homily VI. 8-10. — R.]

4 [With this treatment of the allegories compare Homily VI. 17, 18. — R.]

they worship. For in these allegories what profit can there be to them? For although they are framed so as to be decent, yet no use is derived from them for worship, nor for amendment of morals.

CHAP. XXXVI. — THE ALLEGORIES AN AFTER-THOUGHT.

"Whence it is the more evident that prudent men, when they saw that the common superstition was so disgraceful, so base, and yet they had not learned any way of correcting it, or any knowledge, endeavoured with what arguments and interpretations they could to veil unseemly things under seemly speech, and not, as they say, to conceal seemly reasons under unseemly fables. For if this were the case, surely their statues and their pictures would never be made with *representations of* their vices and crimes. The swan, which committed adultery with Leda, would not be represented, nor the bull which committed adultery with Europa; nor would they turn into a thousand monstrous shapes, him whom they think better than all. And assuredly, if the great and wise men who are amongst them knew that all this is fiction and not truth, would not they charge with impiety and sacrilege those who should exhibit a picture or carve an image of this sort, to the injury of the gods? In short, let them present a king of their own time in the form of an ox, or a goose, or an ant, or a vulture, and let them write the name of their king upon it, and set up such a statue or figure in a public place, and they will soon be made to feel the wrong of their deed, and the greatness of its punishment.

CHAP. XXXVII. — LIKE GODS, LIKE WORSHIPPERS.

"But since those things rather are true which the public baseness testifies, and concealments have been sought and fabricated by prudent men to excuse them by seemly speeches, therefore are they not only not prohibited, but even in the very mysteries figures are produced of Saturn devouring his sons, and of the boy hidden by the cymbals and drums of the Corybantes; and with respect to the mutilation of Saturn, what better proof of its truth could there be, than that even his worshippers are mutilated, by a like miserable fate, in honour of their god? Since then these things are manifestly seen, who shall be found of so little sense, yea, of such stolidity, that he does not perceive that those things are true concerning the unfortunate gods, which their more unfortunate worshippers attest by the wounding and mutilation of their bodies?

CHAP. XXXVIII. — WRITINGS OF THE POETS.

"But if, as they say, these things, so creditably and piously done, are dispensed by so discredit-able and impious a ritual, assuredly he is sacrilegious, whoever either gave forth these things at first, or persists in fulfilling them, now that they have unhappily been given forth. And what shall we say of the books of the poets? Ought not they, if they have debased the honourable and pious deeds of the gods with base fables, to be forthwith cast away and thrown into the fire, that they may not persuade the still tender age of boys that Jupiter himself, the chief of the gods, was a parricide towards his parents, incestuous towards his sisters and his daughters, and even impure towards boys; that Venus and Mars were adulterers, and all those things which have been spoken of above? What do you think of this matter, my lord Peter?"

CHAP. XXXIX. — ALL FOR THE BEST.

Then he answered: "Be sure, beloved Aquila, that all things are done by the good providence of God, that the cause which was to be contrary to the truth should not only be infirm and weak, but also base. For if the assertion of error had been stronger and more truth-like, any one who had been deceived by it would not easily return to the path of truth. If even now, when so many wicked and disgraceful things are related concerning the gods of the Gentiles, scarce any one forsakes the base error, how much more if there had been in it anything seemly and truth-like? For the mind is with difficulty transferred from those things with which it has been imbued in early youth; and on this account, as I said, it has been effected by divine providence, that the substance of error should be both weak and base. But all other things also divine providence dispenses fitly and advantageously, although the method of the divine dispensation, as good, and the best possible, is not clear to us who are ignorant of the causes of things."

CHAP. XL. — FURTHER INFORMATION SOUGHT.

When Peter had thus said, I Clement asked Niceta that he would explain to us, for the sake of instruction, some things concerning the allegories of the Gentiles, which he had carefully studied; "for," said I, "it is useful that when we dispute with the Gentiles, we should not be unacquainted with these things." Then said Niceta: "If my lord Peter permits me, I can do as you ask me." Then said Peter: "To-day I have given you leave to speak in opposition to the Gentiles, as you know." And Niceta said: "Tell me then, Clement, what you would have me speak about." And I said to him: "Inform us how the Gentiles represent matters concerning the supper of the gods, which they had at the marriage of Peleus and Thetis.[1] What do

---

[1] [Comp. Homily VI. 2, 14, 15, on the supper of the gods. — R.]

they make of the shepherd Paris, and what of less Juno, Minerva, and Venus, between whom he acted as judge? What of Mercury? and what of the apple, and the other things which follow in order?"

CHAP. XLI. — EXPLANATION OF MYTHOLOGY.

Then Niceta: "The affair of the supper of the gods stands in this wise. They say that the banquet is the world, that the order of the gods sitting at table is the position of the heavenly bodies. Those whom Hesiod calls the first children of heaven and earth, of whom six were males and six females, they refer to the number of the twelve signs, which go round all the world. They say that the dishes of the banquet are the reasons and causes of things, sweet and desirable, which in the shape of inferences from the positions of the signs and the courses of the stars, explain how the world is ruled and governed. Yet they say these things exist after the free manner of a banquet, inasmuch as the mind of every one has the option whether he shall taste aught of this sort of knowledge, or whether he shall refrain; and as in a banquet no one is compelled, but every one is at liberty to eat, so also the manner of philosophizing depends upon the choice of the will. They say that discord is the lust of the flesh, which rises up against the purpose of the mind, and hinders the desire of philosophizing; and therefore they say that the time was that in which the marriage was celebrated. Thus they make Peleus and the nymph Thetis to be the dry and the moist element, by the admixture of which the substance of bodies is composed. They hold that Mercury is speech, by which instruction is conveyed to the mind; that Juno is chastity, Minerva courage, Venus lust, Paris the understanding. If therefore, say they, it happens that there is in a man a barbarous and uncultivated understanding, and ignorant of right judgment, he will despise chastity and courage, and will give the prize, which is the apple, to lust; and thereby ruin and destruction will come not only upon himself, but also upon his countrymen and the whole race. These things, therefore, it is in their power to compose from whatever matter they please; yet they can be adapted to every man; because if any one has a pastoral and rustic and uncultivated understanding, and does not wish to be instructed, when the heat of his body shall make suggestions concerning the pleasure of lust, straightway he despises the virtues of studies and the blessings of knowledge, and turns his mind to bodily pleasures. And hence it is that implacable wars arise, cities are destroyed, countries fall, even as Paris, by the abduction of Helen, armed the Greeks and the barbarians to their mutual destruction."

CHAP. XLII. — INTERPRETATION OF SCRIPTURE.

Then Peter, commending his statement, said: [1] "Ingenious men, as I perceive, take many verisimilitudes from the things which they read; and therefore great care is to be taken, that when the law of God is read, it be not read according to the understanding of our own mind. For there are many sayings in the divine Scriptures which can be drawn to that sense which every one has preconceived for himself; and this ought not to be done. For you ought not to seek a foreign and extraneous sense, which you have brought from without, which you may confirm from the authority of the Scriptures, but to take the sense of truth from the Scriptures themselves; and therefore it behoves you to learn the meaning of the Scriptures from him who keeps it according to the truth handed down to him from his fathers, so that he can authoritatively declare what he has rightly received. But when one has received an entire and firm rule of truth from the Scriptures, it will not be improper if he contribute to the establishment of true doctrine anything from common education and from liberal studies, which, it may be, he has attached himself to in his boyhood; yet so that, when he has learned the truth, he renounce falsehood and pretence."

CHAP. XLIII. — A WORD OF EXHORTATION.

And when he had said this, he looked to our father, and said: "You therefore, old man, if indeed you care for your soul's safety, that when you desire to be separated from the body, it may, in consequence of this short conversion, find eternal rest, ask about whatever you please, and seek counsel, that you may be able to cast off any doubt that remains in you. For even to young men the time of life is uncertain; but to old men it is not even uncertain, for there is no doubt that there is but little time remaining to them. And therefore both young and old ought to be very earnest about their conversion and repentance, and to be taken up with the adornment of their souls for the future with the worthiest ornaments, such as the doctrines of truth, the grace of chastity, the splendour of righteousness, the fairness of piety, and all other things with which it becomes a reasonable mind to be adorned. Then, besides, they should break off from unseemly and unbelieving companions, and keep company with the faithful, and frequent those assemblies in which subjects are handled relating to chastity, righteousness, and piety; to pray to God always heartily, and to ask of Him those things which ought to be asked of God; to give thanks to Him; to repent truly of their past

---

[1] [This discourse of the Apostle (chaps. 42–51) has no exact parallel in the *Homilies*. It is a fitting conclusion to the discussion. — R.]

doings; in some measure also, if possible, by deeds of mercy towards the poor, to help their penitence: for by these means pardon will be more easily bestowed, and mercy will be sooner shown to the merciful.

CHAP. XLIV. — EARNESTNESS.

"But if he who comes to repentance is of more advanced age, he ought the more to give thanks to God, because, having received the knowledge of the truth, after all the violence of carnal lust has been broken, there awaits him no fight of contest, by which to repress the pleasures of the body rising against the mind. It remains, therefore, that he be exercised in the learning of the truth, and in works of mercy, that he may bring forth fruits worthy of repentance; and that he do not suppose that the proof of conversion is shown by length of time, but by strength of devotion and of purpose. For minds are manifest to God; and He does not take account of times, but of hearts. For He approves if any one, on hearing the preaching of the truth, does not delay, nor spend time in negligence, but immediately, and if I may say so, in the same moment, abhorring the past, begins to desire things to come, and burns with love of the heavenly kingdom.

CHAP. XLV. — ALL OUGHT TO REPENT.

"Wherefore, let no one of you longer dissemble nor look backwards, but willingly approach to the Gospel of the kingdom of God. Let not the poor man say, When I shall become rich, then I shall be converted. God does not ask money of you, but a merciful heart and a pious mind. Nor let the rich man delay his conversion by reason of worldly care, while he thinks how he may dispose the abundance of his fruits; nor say within himself, 'What shall I do? where shall I bestow my fruits?' Nor say to his soul, 'Thou hast much goods laid up for many years; feast and rejoice.' For it shall be said to him, 'Thou fool, this night thy soul shall be taken from thee, and whose shall those things be which thou hast provided?'[1] Therefore let every age, every sex, every condition, haste to repentance, that they may obtain eternal life. Let the young be thankful that they put their necks under the yoke of discipline in the very violence of their desires. The old also are themselves praiseworthy, because they change for the fear of God, the custom of a long time in which they have been unhappily occupied.

CHAP. XLVI. — THE SURE WORD OF PROPHECY.

"Let no one therefore put off. Let no one delay. For what occasion is there for delaying

to do well? Or are you afraid, lest, when you have done well, you do not find the reward as you supposed? And what loss will you sustain if you do well without reward? Would not conscience alone be sufficient in this? But if you find as you anticipate, shall you not receive great things for small, and eternal for temporal? But I say this for the sake of the unbelieving. For the things which we preach are as we preach them; because they cannot be otherwise, since they have been promised by the prophetic word.

CHAP. XLVII. — "A FAITHFUL SAYING, AND WORTHY OF ALL ACCEPTATION."

"But if any one desires to learn exactly the truth of our preaching, let him come to hear, and let him ascertain what the true Prophet is; and then at length all doubtfulness will cease to him, unless with obstinate mind he resist those things which he finds to be true. For there are some whose only object it is to gain the victory in any way whatever, and who seek praise for this rather than their salvation. These ought not to have a single word addressed to them, lest both the noble word suffer injury, and condemn to eternal death him who is guilty of the wrong done to it. For what is there in respect of which any one ought to oppose our preaching? or in respect of which the word of our preaching is found to be contrary to the belief of what is true and honourable? It says that the God the Father, the Creator of all, is to be honoured, as also His Son, who alone knows Him and His will, and who alone is to be believed concerning all things which He has enjoined. For He alone is the law and the Lawgiver, and the righteous Judge, whose law decrees that God, the Lord of all, is to be honoured by a sober, chaste, just, and merciful life, and that all hope is to be placed in Him alone.

CHAP. XLVIII. — ERRORS OF THE PHILOSOPHERS.

"But some one will say that precepts of this sort are given by the philosophers also.[2] Nothing of the kind: for they do indeed give commandments concerning justice and sobriety, but they are ignorant that God is the recompenser of good and evil deeds; and therefore their laws and precepts only shun a public accuser, but cannot purify the conscience. For why should one fear to sin in secret, who does not know that there is a witness and a judge of secret things? Besides, the philosophers in their precepts add that even the gods, who are demons, are to be honoured; and this alone, even if in other respects they seemed worthy of approbation, is sufficient to convict them of the most dreadful im-

---

[1] Luke xii. 17, 19, 20.

[2] [Compare the argument of Clement, as a heathen inquirer, against the philosophers, in Homily VI. 20. — R.]

piety, and condemn them by their own sentence, since they declare indeed that there is one God, yet command that many be worshipped, by way of humouring human error. But also the philosophers say that God is not angry, not knowing what they say. For anger is evil, when it disturbs the mind, so that it loses right counsel. But that anger which punishes the wicked does not bring disturbance to the mind; but it is one and the same affection, so to speak, which assigned rewards to the good and punishment to the evil; for if He should bestow blessings upon the good and the evil, and confer equal rewards upon the pious and the impious, He would appear to be unjust rather than good.

CHAP. XLIX. — GOD'S LONG-SUFFERING.

"But you say, Neither ought God to do evil. You say truly; nor does He. But those who have been created by Him, while they do not believe that they are to be judged, indulging their pleasures, have fallen away from piety and righteousness. But you will say, If it is right to punish the wicked, they ought to be punished immediately when they do wickedly. You indeed do well to make haste; but He who is eternal, and from whom nothing is secret, inasmuch as He is without end, in the same proportion is His patience extended, and He regards not the swiftness of vengeance, but the causes of salvation. For He is not so much pleased with the death as with the conversion of a sinner.[1] Therefore, in short, He has bestowed upon men holy baptism, to which, if any one makes haste to come, and for the future remains without stain, all his sins are thenceforth blotted out, which were committed in the time of his ignorance.

CHAP. L. — PHILOSOPHERS NOT BENEFACTORS OF MEN.

"For what have the philosophers contributed to the life of man, by saying that God is not angry with men? Only to teach them to have no fear of any punishment or judgment, and thereby to take away all restraint from sinners. Or what have they benefited the human race, who have said that there is no God, but that all things happen by chance and accident? What but that men, hearing this, and thinking that there is no judge, no guardian of things, are driven headlong, without fear of any one, to every deed which either rage, or avarice, or lust may dictate. For they truly have much benefited the life of man who have said that nothing can be done apart from GENESIS; that is, that every one, ascribing the cause of his sin to GENESIS,

might in the midst of his crimes declare himself innocent, while he does not wash out his guilt by repentance, but doubles it by laying the blame upon fate. And what shall I say of those philosophers who have maintained that the gods are to be worshipped, and such gods as were described to you a little while ago? What else was this but to decree that vices, crimes, and base deeds should be worshipped? I am ashamed of you, and I pity you, if you have not yet discovered that these things were unworthy of belief, and impious, and execrable, or if, having discovered and ascertained them to be evil, ye have nevertheless worshipped them as if they were good, yea, even the best.

CHAP. LI. — CHRIST THE TRUE PROPHET.

"Then, besides, of what sort is that which some of the philosophers have presumed to speak even concerning God, though they are mortal, and can only speak by opinion concerning invisible things, or concerning the origin of the world, since they were not present when it was made, or concerning the end of it, or concerning the treatment and judgment of souls in the infernal regions, forgetting that it belongs indeed to a reasonable man to know things present and visible, but that it is the part of prophetic prescience alone to know things past, and things future, and things invisible? These things, therefore, are not to be gathered from conjectures and opinions, in which men are greatly deceived, but from faith in prophetic truth, as this doctrine of ours is. For we speak nothing of ourselves, nor announce things gathered by human judgment; for this were to deceive our hearers. But we preach the things which have been committed and revealed to us by the true Prophet. And concerning His prophetic prescience and power, if any one, as I have said, wishes to receive clear proofs, let him come instantly and be alert to hear, and we shall give evident proofs by which he shall seem not only to hear the power of prophetic prescience with his ears, but even to see it with his eyes and handle it with his hand; and when he has entertained a sure faith concerning Him, he will without any labour take upon him the yoke of righteousness and piety;[2] and so great sweetness will he perceive in it, that not only will he not find fault with any labour being in it, but will even desire something further to be added and imposed upon him."

CHAP. LII. — APPION AND ANUBION.

And when he had said this, and more to the same purpose, and had cured some who were present who were infirm and possessed of de-

---

[1] Ezek. xviii. 33.

[2] Matt. xi 30.

mons, he dismissed the crowds, while they gave thanks and praised God, charging them to come to the same place on the following days also for the sake of hearing. And when we were together at home, and were preparing to eat, one entering told us that Appion Pleistonices,[1] with Anubion, were lately come from Antioch, and were lodging with Simon.[2] Then my father, when he heard this, rejoiced, and said to Peter: "If you permit me, I should like to go and salute Appion and Anubion, for they are great friends of mine; and perhaps I shall be able to persuade Anubion to dispute with Clement on the subject of GENESIS." Then Peter said: "I consent; and I commend you, because you respect your friends. But consider how all things occur to you according to your wish by God's providence; for, behold, not only have *the objects of* proper affection been restored to you by the appointment of God, but also the presence of your friends is arranged for you." Then said my father: "Truly I consider that it is so as you say." And when he had said this, he went away to Anubion.

CHAP. LIII. — A TRANSFORMATION.

But we, sitting with Peter the whole night, asking questions, and learning of him on many subjects, remained awake through very delight in his teaching and the sweetness of his words; and when it was daybreak, Peter, looking at me and my brothers, said: "I wonder what has befallen your father." And while he was speaking my father came in, and found Peter speaking to us about him. And when he had saluted he began to apologize, and to explain the reason why he had remained abroad. But we, looking at him, were horrified; for we saw on him the face of Simon, yet we heard the voice of our father. And when we shrank from him, and cursed him, my father was astonished at our treating him so harshly and barbarously. Yet Peter was the only one who saw his natural countenance; and he said to us: "Why do you curse your father?" And we, along with our mother, answered him: "He appears to us to be Simon, though he has our father's voice." Then Peter: "You indeed know only his voice, which has not been changed by the sorceries; but to me also his face, which to others appears changed by Simon's art, is known to be that of your father Faustinianus." And looking at my

father, he said: "The cause of the dismay of your wife and your sons is this, — the appearance of your countenance does not seem to be as it was, but the face of the detestable Simon appears in you."

CHAP. LIV. — EXCITEMENT IN ANTIOCH.

And while he was thus speaking, one of those returned who had gone before to Antioch, and said to Peter: "I wish you to know, my lord Peter, that Simon at Antioch, doing many signs and prodigies in public, has inculcated upon the people nothing but what tends to excite hatred against you, calling you a magician, a sorcerer, a murderer; and to such an extent has he stirred up hatred against you, that they greatly desire, if they can find you anywhere, even to devour your flesh. And therefore we who were sent before, seeing the city greatly moved against you, met together in secret, and considered what ought to be done.

CHAP. LV. — A STRATAGEM.

"And when we saw no way of getting out of the difficulty, there came Cornelius the centurion, being sent by Cæsar to the president of Cæsarea on public business. Him we sent for alone, and told him the reason why we were sorrowful, and entreated him that, if he could do anything, he should help us. Then he most readily promised that he would straightway put him to flight, if only we would aid his plans. And when we promised that we would be active in doing everything, he said, 'Cæsar has ordered sorcerers to be sought out and destroyed in the city of Rome and through the provinces, and a great number of them have been already destroyed. I shall therefore give out, through my friends, that I am come to apprehend that magician, and that I am sent by Cæsar for this purpose, that he may be punished with the rest of his fraternity. Let your people, therefore, who are with him in disguise, intimate to him, as if they had heard it from some quarter, that I am sent to apprehend him; and when he hears this, he is sure to take to flight. Or if you think of anything better, tell me. Why need I say more?' It was so done by those of ours who were with him, disguised for the purpose of acting as spies on him. And when Simon learned that this was come upon him, he received the information as a great kindness conferred upon him by them, and took to flight. He therefore departed from Antioch, and, as we have heard, came hither with Athenodorus.

CHAP. LVI. — SIMON'S DESIGN IN THE TRANSFORMATION.

"All we, therefore, who went before you, considered that in the meantime you should not go

---

[1] The name is generally written Apion. The meaning of Pleistonices is doubtful, some supposing that it indicates his birthplace, some his father; but generally it is taken as an epithet, and it will then refer to his frequent victories in literary contests. [See Homily IV. 3. and the discussions with Appion which follow in that homily and in V., VI. — R.]

[2] [From this point the resemblance to the close of Homily XX. (chaps. 11-22) is quite marked. But in the *Recognitions* the conclusion is more detailed and complete; see chap. 65. This is in accordance with the general design of this narrative, which gives greater prominence to the family of Clement. — R.]

up to Antioch, till we see if the hatred of you which he has sown among the people be in any degree lessened by his departure." When he who had come from Antioch had imparted this information, Peter, looking to our father, said, "Faustinianus, your countenance has been transformed by Simon Magus, as is evident; for he, thinking that he was being sought for by Cæsar for punishment, has fled in terror, and has placed his own countenance upon you, if haply you might be apprehended instead of him, and put to death, that so he might cause sorrow to your sons." But my father, when he heard this, crying out, said with tears: "You have judged rightly, O Peter: for Anubion also, who is very friendly with me, began to inform me in a certain mysterious way of his plots; but unhappily I did not believe him, because I had done him no harm."

CHAP. LVII. — GREAT GRIEF.

And when all of us, along with my father, were agitated with sorrow and weeping, meantime Anubion came to us, intimating to us that Simon had fled during the night, making for Judæa. But seeing our father lamenting and bewailing himself, and saying, "Wretch that I am, not to believe when I heard that he is a magician! What has befallen wretched me, that on one day, being recognised by my wife and my sons, I have not been able to rejoice with them, but have been rolled back to the former miseries which I endured in my wandering!" — but my mother, tearing her dishevelled hair, bewailed much more bitterly, — we also, confounded at the change of our father's countenance, were, as it were, thunderstruck and beside ourselves, and could not understand what was the matter. But Anubion, seeing us all thus afflicted, stood like one dumb. Then Peter, looking at us his sons, said: "Believe me that this is your very father; wherefore also I charge you that you respect him as your father. For God will afford some opportunity on which he shall be able to put off the countenance of Simon, and to recover the manifest figure of your father — that is, his own."

CHAP. LVIII. — HOW IT ALL HAPPENED.

Then, turning to my father, he said: "I gave you leave to salute Appion and Anubion, who, you said, were your friends from boyhood, but not that you should speak with Simon." Then my father said: "I confess I have sinned." Then said Anubion: "I also with him beg and entreat of you to pardon the old man — good and noble man as he is. He was unhappily seduced and imposed upon by the magician in question; for I will tell you how the thing was done. When he came to salute us, it happened that at that very time we were standing around him, hearing him tell that he intended to flee away that night, for that he had heard that some persons had come even to this city of Laodicea to apprehend him by command of the emperor, but that he wished to turn all their rage against this Faustinianus, who has lately come hither. And he said to us: 'Only you make him sup with us, and I shall compound a certain ointment, with which, when he has supped, he shall anoint his face, and from that time he shall seem to all to have my countenance. But you first anoint your faces with the juice of a certain herb, that you may not be deceived as to the change of his countenance, so that to all except you he shall seem to be Simon.'

CHAP. LIX. — A SCENE OF MOURNING.

"And when he said this, I said to him, 'And what advantage will you gain from this deed?' Then Simon said: 'In the first place, that those who are seeking me may lay hold on him, and so give over the search for me. But if he be punished by Cæsar, that his sons may have much sorrow, who forsook me, and fled to Peter, and are now his assistants.' Now I confess to you, Peter, what is true. I did not dare then tell Faustinianus; but neither did Simon give us opportunity of speaking with him in private, and disclosing to him fully Simon's design. Meantime, about the middle of the night, Simon has fled away, making for Judæa. And Athenodorus and Appion have gone to convoy him; but I pretended bodily indisposition, that I might remain at home, and make him return quickly to you, if haply he may in any way be concealed with you, lest, being seized by those who are in quest of Simon, he be brought before Cæsar, and perish without cause. And now, in my anxiety about him, I have come to see him, and to return before those who have gone to convoy Simon come back." And turning to us, Anubion said: "I, Anubion, indeed see the true countenance of your father, because I was previously anointed by Simon himself, as I have told you, that the real face of Faustinianus might appear to my eyes; whence I am astonished and wonder at the art of Simon Magus, because you standing here do not recognise your father." And while my father and mother, and all of us, wept for the things which had befallen, Anubion, moved with compassion, also wept.

CHAP. LX. — A COUNTERPLOT.

Then Peter, moved with compassion, promised that he would restore the face of our father, saying to him: "Listen, Faustinianus: As soon as the error of your transformed countenance shall have conferred some advantage on us, and shall have subserved the designs which we have in view, then I shall restore to you the true form of your countenance; on condition, however, that you first despatch what I shall command you." And when my father promised that he would with all his might fulfil everything that he might charge him with, provided only that he might recover his own countenance, Peter thus began: "You have heard with your own ears, that one of those who had been sent before has returned from Antioch, and told us how Simon, while he was there, stirred up the multitudes against me, and inflamed the whole city into hatred of me, declaring that I am a magician, and a murderer, and a deceiver, so that they are eager, if they see me, even to eat my flesh. Do therefore what I tell you: leave Clement with me, and go before us to Antioch, with your wife, and your sons Faustus and Faustinus. And I shall also send others with you, whom I think fit, who shall observe whatsoever I command them.

CHAP. LXI. — A MINE DUG.

"When therefore you come with them to Antioch, as you will be thought to be Simon, stand in a public place, and proclaim your repentance, and say: 'I Simon declare to you, and confess that all that I said concerning Peter was false: for he is neither a seducer, nor a magician, nor a murderer, nor any of the things that I spoke against him; but I said all these things under the instigation of madness. I therefore entreat you, even I myself, who erewhile gave you causes of hatred against him, that you think no such thing concerning him. But lay aside your hatred; cease from your indignation; because he is truly sent by God for the salvation of the world—a disciple and apostle of the true Prophet. Wherefore I advise, exhort, and charge you that you hear him, and believe him when he preaches to you the truth, lest haply, if you despise him, your very city suddenly perish. But I will tell you why I now make this confession to you. This night an angel of God rebuked me for my wickedness, and scourged me terribly, because I was an enemy to the herald of the truth. Therefore I entreat you, that even if I myself should ever again come to you, and attempt to say anything against Peter, you will not receive nor believe me. For I confess to you, I was a magician, a seducer, a deceiver; but I repent, for it is possible by repentance to blot out former evil deeds.'"

CHAP. LXII. — A CASE OF CONSCIENCE.

When Peter made this intimation to my father, he answered: "I know what you wish; do not trouble yourself further: for I understand and know what I am to undertake when I come to the place." And Peter gave him further instruction, saying: "When therefore you come to the place, and see the people turned by your discourse, and laying aside their hatred, and returning to their longing for me, send and tell me, and I shall come immediately; and when I come, I shall without delay set you free from this strange countenance, and restore to you your own, which is known to all your friends." And having said this, he ordered my brothers to go with him, and at the same time our mother Matthidia, and some of our friends. But my mother refused to go along with him, and said: "It seems as if I should be an adulteress if I were to associate with the countenance of Simon; but if I be compelled to go along with him, it is at all events impossible that I can lie in the same bed with him; but I do not know if I can consent even to go with him." And when she stoutly refused, Anubion began to exhort her, saying: "Believe me and Peter. But does not even his voice persuade you that he is your husband Faustinianus, whom truly I love not less than you do? And, in short, I also myself shall come with you." And when Anubion had said this, my mother promised that she would go with him.

CHAP. LXIII. — A PIOUS FRAUD.

Then said I: "God arranges our affairs to our liking; for we have with us Anubion an astrologer, with whom, if we come to Antioch, we shall dispute with all earnestness on the subject of GENESIS." And when our father had set out, after the middle of the night, with those whom Peter had ordered to accompany him, and with Anubion; in the morning, before Peter went to the discussion, those men returned who had convoyed Simon, namely Appion and Athenodorus, and came to us inquiring after my father. But Peter, when he was informed of their coming, ordered them to enter. And when they were seated, they asked, "Where is Faustinianus?" Peter answered: "We do not know; for since the evening that he went to you, no one of his friends has seen him. But yesterday morning Simon came inquiring for him; and because we gave him no answer, I know not what he meant, but he said that he was Faustinianus. But when nobody believed him, he went and lamented, and threatened that he would destroy himself; and afterwards he went away towards the sea."

CHAP. LXIV. — A COMPETITION IN LYING.

When Appion heard this, and those who were with him, they raised a great howling, saying: "Why have you done this? Why did you not receive him?" And when Athenodorus was going to tell me that it was my father Faustinianus himself, Appion prevented him, and said:

"We have learned from some one that he has gone with Simon, and that at the entreaty of Faustinianus himself, being unwilling to see his sons, because they are Jews. When therefore we heard this, we came to inquire after him here; but since he is not here, it appears that he must have spoken truly who told us that he has gone with Simon. This, therefore, we tell you." But I Clement, when I understood the designs of Peter, that he wished to make them suppose that the old man would be required at their hands, so that they might be afraid and flee away, I began to aid his design, and said to Appion: "Listen, dear Appion: what we believe to be good, we wish to deliver to our father also; but if he will not receive it, but rather, as you say, flees away through abhorrence of us — it may perhaps be harsh to say so — we care nothing about him." And when I had said this, they departed, cursing my cruelty, and followed the track of Simon, as we learned on the following day.

CHAP. LXV. — SUCCESS OF THE PLOT.

Meantime, while Peter was daily, according to his custom, teaching the people, and working many miracles and cures, after ten days came one of our people from Antioch, sent by my father, informing us how my father stood in public, accusing Simon, whose face indeed he seemed to wear, and extolling Peter with unmeasured praises, and commending him to all the people, and making them long for him, so that all were changed by his speech, and longed to see him; and that many had come to love Peter so much, that they raged against my father in his character of Simon, and thought of laying hands on him, because he had done such wrong to Peter! "Wherefore," said he, "make haste, lest haply he be murdered; for he sent me with speed to you, being in great fear, to ask you to come without delay, that you may find him alive, and also that you may appear at the favourable moment, when the city is growing in affection towards you."[1] He also told us how, as soon as my father entered the city of Antioch, the whole people were gathered to him, supposing him to be Simon; and he began to make public confession to them all, according to what the restoration of the people demanded: for all, as many as came, both noble and common, both rich and poor, hoping that some prodigies would be wrought by him in his usual way, he addressed thus: —

CHAP. LXVI. — TRUTH TOLD BY LYING LIPS.

"It is long that the divine patience bears with me, Simon the most unhappy of men; for what-

ever you have wondered at in me was done, not by means of truth, but by the lies and tricks of demons, that I might subvert your faith and condemn my own soul. I confess that all things that I said about Peter were lies; for he never was either a magician or a murderer, but has been sent by God for the salvation of you all; and if from this hour you think that he is to be despised, be assured that your very city may suddenly be destroyed. But, *you will ask*, what is the reason that I make this confession to you of my own accord? I was vehemently rebuked by an angel of God this night, and most severely scourged, because I was his enemy. I therefore entreat you, that if from this hour even I myself shall ever open my mouth against him, you will drive me from your sight; for that foul demon, who is an enemy to the salvation of men, speaks against him through my mouth, that you may not attain to life by his means. For what miracle could the magic art show you through me? I made brazen dogs bark, and statues move, men change their appearances, and suddenly vanish from men's sight; and for these things you ought to have cursed the magic art, which bound your souls with devilish fetters, that I might show you a vain miracle, that you might not believe Peter, who cures the sick in the name of Him by whom he is sent, and expels demons, and gives sight to the blind, and restores health to the palsied, and raises the dead."

CHAP. LXVII. — FAUSTINIANUS IS HIMSELF AGAIN.

Whilst he made these and similar statements, the people began to curse him, and to weep and lament because they had sinned against Peter, believing him to be a magician or wicked man. But the same day, at evening, Faustinianus had his own face restored to him, and the appearance of Simon Magus left him. Now Simon, hearing that his face on Faustinianus had contributed to the glory of Peter, came in haste to anticipate Peter, and intending to cause by his art that his likeness should be taken from Faustinianus, when Christ had already accomplished this according to the word of His apostle. But Niceta and Aquila, seeing their father's face restored after the necessary proclamation, gave thanks to God, and would not suffer him to address the people any more.

CHAP. LXVIII. — PETER'S ENTRY INTO ANTIOCH.

But Simon began, though secretly, to go amongst his friends and acquaintances, and to malign Peter more than before. Then all spat in his face, and drove him from the city, saying: "You will be chargeable with your own death, if you think of coming hither again, speaking against Peter." These things being known *at*

---

[1] [At this point the narrative in the *Homilies* virtually ends; a sentence follows, resembling a passage in chap. 68. See note on Homily XX. 23. — R.]

Laodicea, Peter ordered the people to meet on the following day; and having ordained one of those who followed him as bishop over them, and others as presbyters, and having baptized multitudes, and restored to health all who were troubled with sicknesses or demons, he stayed there three days longer; and all things being properly arranged, he bade them farewell, and set out from Laodicea, being much longed for by the people of Antioch.[1] And the whole city began to hear, through Niceta and Aquila, that Peter was coming. Then all the people of the city of Antioch, hearing of Peter's arrival, went to meet him, and almost all the old men and the nobles came with ashes sprinkled on their heads, in this way testifying their repentance, because they had listened to the magician Simon, in opposition to his preaching.

CHAP. LXIX. — PETER'S THANKSGIVING.

Stating these and such like things, they bring to him those distressed with sicknesses, and tormented with demons, paralytics also, and those suffering diverse perils; and there was an infinite number of sick people collected. And when Peter saw that they not only repented of the evil thoughts they had entertained of him through means of Simon, but also that they showed so entire faith in God, that they believed that all who suffered from every sort of ailment could be healed by him, he spread out his hands towards heaven, pouring out prayers with tears, and gave thanks to God, saying: " I bless thee, O Father, worthy of all praise, who hast deigned to fulfil every word and promise of Thy Son, that every creature may know that Thou alone art God in heaven and in earth."

CHAP. LXX. — MIRACLES.

With such sayings, he went up on a height, and ordered all the multitude of sick people to be ranged before him, and addressed them all in these words: " As you see me to be a man like to yourselves, do not suppose that you can recover your health from me, but through Him who, coming down from heaven, has shown to those who believe in Him a perfect medicine for body and soul. Hence let all this people be witnesses to your declaration, that with your whole heart you believe in the Lord Jesus Christ, that they may know that themselves also may be saved by Him." And when all the multitude of the sick with one voice cried out that He is the true God whom Peter preaches, suddenly an overpowering light of the grace of God appeared in the midst of the people; and the paralytics

being cured, began to run to Peter's feet, the blind to shout on the recovery of their sight, the lame to give thanks on regaining the power of walking, the sick to rejoice in restored health; some even who were barely alive, being already without consciousness or the power of speech, were raised up; and all the lunatics, and those possessed of demons, were set free.

CHAP. LXXI. — SUCCESS.

So great grace of His power did the Holy Spirit show on that day, that all, from the least to the greatest, with one voice confessed the Lord; and not to delay you with many words, within seven days, more than ten thousand men, believing in God, were baptized and consecrated by sanctification: so that Theophilus,[2] who was more exalted than all the men of power in that city, with all eagerness of desire consecrated the great palace of his house under the name of a church, and a chair was placed in it for the Apostle Peter by all the people; and the whole multitude assembling daily to hear the word, believed in the healthful doctrine which was avouched by the efficacy of cures.

CHAP. LXXII. — HAPPY ENDING.

Then I Clement, with my brothers and our mother, spoke to our father, asking him whether any remnants of unbelief remained in him. And he said: " Come, and you shall see, in the presence of Peter, what an increase of faith has grown in me." Then Faustinianus approached, and fell down at Peter's feet, saying: " The seeds of your word, which the field of my mind has received, are now sprung up, and have so advanced to fruitful maturity, that nothing is wanting but that you separate me from the chaff by that spiritual reaping-hook of yours, and place me in the garner of the Lord, making me partaker of the divine table." Then Peter, with all alacrity grasping his hand, presented him to me Clement, and my brothers, saying: " As God has restored your sons to you, their father, so also your sons restore their father to God." And he proclaimed a fast to all the people, and on the next Lord's day he baptized him; and in the midst of the people, taking occasion from his conversion, he related all his fortunes, so that the whole city received him as an angel, and paid him no less honour than they did to the apostle.[3]

---

[1] [The substance of this sentence forms the somewhat abrupt conclusion of the *Homilies*; xx. 23. — R.]

[2] [It is possible that this character was suggested to the writer by the well-known Theophilus of Antioch. But, in view of the evident anachronism, it seems more probable that he had in mind the " Theophilus " named in the prologue to the Gospel of Luke (i. 1-4) and in Acts i. 1. — R.]

[3] [The work probably closes with these words: the added sentence is not in harmony with the general plan of the *Recognitions*, which skilfully treats the material so as to give prominence to the family of Clement. Some scribe, zealous for the authority of the Apostle Peter, has doubtless contributed the unnecessary sentence

And these things being known, Peter ordered the people to meet on the following day ; and having ordained one of his followers as bishop, and others as presbyters, he baptized also a great number of people, and restored to health all who had been distressed with sicknesses.[1]

which follows. See next note. The ordination of a bishop at Antioch by Peter is simply an absurdity. It is unlikely that even the writer of the *Recognitions* would venture to ignore the previous existence of a Christian church in that city. — R.]

[1] This sentence occurs only in one MS.

INTRODUCTORY NOTICE TO THE CLEMENTINE HOMILIES

[BY THE REV. THOMAS SMITH, D.D.]

WE have already given an account of the *Clementines* in the Introductory Notice to the *Recognitions*.[1] All that remains for us to do here, is to notice the principal editions of the *Homilies*. The first edition was published by Cotelerius in his collection of the *Apostolic Fathers*, from a manuscript in the Royal Library at Paris, the only manuscript of the work then known to exist. He derived assistance from an epitome of the work which he found in the same library. The text of Cotelerius was revised by Clericus in his edition of Cotelerius, but more carefully by Schwegler, Stuttgart, 1847. The Paris MS. breaks off in the middle of the fourteenth chapter of of the nineteenth book.

In 1853 (Göttingen) Dressel published a new recension of the *Homilies*, having found a complete manuscript of the twenty Homilies in the Ottobonian Library in Rome. In 1859 (Leipzig) he published an edition of two Epitomes of the Homilies, — the one previously edited by Turnebus and Cotelerius being given more fully, and the other appearing for the first time. To these Epitomes were appended notes by Frederic Wieseler on the Homilies. The last edition of the *Clementines* is by Paul de Lagarde (Leipzig, 1865), which has no new sources, is pretentious, but far from accurate.

---

[1] [The reader is referred to the Introductory Notice prefixed to this edition of the Clementine literature for a brief summary of the views respecting the relations of the two principal works. The footnotes throughout will aid in making a comparison. The preparation of these notes has strengthened the conviction of the writer that the *Recognitions* are not dependent on the *Homilies*, but that the reverse may be true. — R.]

EPISTLE OF PETER TO JAMES

PETER to James, the lord and bishop of the holy Church, under the Father of all, through Jesus Christ, wishes peace always.[1]

CHAP. I. — DOCTRINE OF RESERVE.

Knowing, my brother, your eager desire after that which is for the advantage of us all, I beg and beseech you not to communicate to any one of the Gentiles the books of my preachings which I sent to you, nor to any one of our own tribe before trial; but if any one has been proved and found worthy, then to commit them to him, after the manner in which Moses delivered *his books* to the Seventy who succeeded to his chair. Wherefore also the fruit of that caution appears even till now. For his countrymen keep the same rule of monarchy and polity everywhere, being unable in any way to think otherwise, or to be led out of the way of the much-indicating Scriptures. For, according to the rule delivered to them, they endeavour to correct the discordances of the Scriptures, if any one, haply not knowing the traditions, is confounded at the various utterances of the prophets. Wherefore they charge no one to teach, unless he has first learned how the Scriptures must be used. And thus they have amongst them one God, one law, one hope.

CHAP. II. — MISREPRESENTATION OF PETER'S DOCTRINE.

In order, therefore, that the like may also happen to those among us as to these Seventy, give the books of my preachings to our brethren, with the like mystery of initiation, that they may indoctrinate those who wish to take part in teaching; for if it be not so done, our word of truth will be rent into many opinions. And this I know, not as being a prophet, but as already seeing the beginning of this very evil. For some from among the Gentiles have rejected my legal preaching, attaching themselves to certain lawless and trifling preaching of the man who is my enemy.[2] And these things some have attempted while I am still alive, to transform my words by certain various interpretations, in order to the dissolution of the law; as though I also myself were of such a mind, but did not freely proclaim it, which God forbid! For such a thing were to act in opposition to the law of God which was spoken by Moses, and was borne witness to by our Lord in respect of its eternal continuance; for thus he spoke: "The heavens and the earth shall pass away, but one jot or one tittle shall in no wise pass from the law."[3] And this He has said, that all things might come to pass. But these men, professing, I know not how, to know my mind, undertake to explain my words, which they have heard of me, more intelligently than I who spoke them, telling their catechumens that this is my meaning, which indeed I never thought of. But if, while I am still alive, they dare thus to misrepresent me, how much more will those who shall come after me dare to do so!

CHAP. III. — INITIATION.

Therefore, that no such thing may happen, for this end I have prayed and besought you not to communicate the books of my preaching which I have sent you to any one, whether of our own nation or of another nation, before trial; but if any one, having been tested, has been found worthy, then to hand them over to him, according to the initiation of Moses, by which he delivered *his books* to the Seventy who succeeded to his chair; in order that thus they may keep the faith, and everywhere deliver the rule of truth, explaining all things after our tradition; lest being themselves dragged down by ignorance, being drawn into error by conjectures after their mind, they bring others into the like pit of destruction. Now the things that seemed good to me, I have fairly pointed out to you; and what seems good to you, do you, my lord, becomingly perform. Farewell.

---

[1] [The object of this apocryphal epistle is to account for the late appearance of the *Homilies*. It would seem to be the latest portion of the literature. — R.]

[2] [This is one of the strongest anti-Pauline insinuations in the entire literature. — R.]

[3] Matt. v. 18; comp. Matt. xxiv. 35; Mark xiii. 31; Luke xxii. 33. [This is a fair specimen of the loose method of Scripture citation characteristic of the Clementine literature. Sometimes the meaning is perverted. — R.]

CHAP. IV. — AN ADJURATION CONCERNING THE RECEIVERS OF THE BOOK.

1. Therefore James, having read the epistle, sent for the elders; and having read it to them, said: "Our Peter has strictly and becomingly charged us concerning the establishing of the truth, that we should not communicate the books of his preachings, which have been sent to us, to any one at random, but to one who is good and religious, and who wishes to teach, and who is circumcised, and faithful. And these are not all to be committed to him at once; that, if he be found injudicious in the first, the others may not be entrusted to him. Wherefore let him be proved not less than six years. And then according to the initiation of Moses, he *that is to deliver the books* should bring him to a river or a fountain, which is living water, where the regeneration of the righteous takes place, and should make him, not swear — for that is not lawful — but to stand by the water and adjure, as we ourselves, when we were re-generated,[1] were made to do for the sake of not sinning.

2. "And let him say: 'I take to witness heaven, earth, water, in which all things are comprehended, and in addition to all these, that air also which pervades all things, and without which I cannot breathe, that I shall always be obedient to him who gives me the books of the preachings; and those same books which he may give me, I shall not communicate to any one in any way, either by writing them, or giving them in writing, or giving them to a writer, either myself or by another, or through any other initiation, or trick, or method, or by keeping them carelessly, or placing them before *any one*, or granting him permission *to see them*, or in any way or manner whatsoever communicating them to another; unless I shall ascertain one to be worthy, as I myself have been judged, or even more so, and that after a probation of not less than six years; but to one who is religious and good, chosen to teach, as I have received them, so I will commit them, doing these things also according to the will of my bishop.

3. "'But otherwise, though he were my son or my brother, or my friend, or otherwise in any way pertaining to me by kindred, if he be unworthy, that I will not vouchsafe the favour to him, as is not meet; and I shall neither be terrified by plot nor mollified by gifts. But if even it should ever seem to me that the books of the preachings given to me are not true, I shall not so communicate them, but shall give them back. And when I go abroad, I shall carry them with me, whatever of them I happen to possess. But if I be not minded to carry them about with me, I shall not suffer them to be in my house, but shall deposit them with my bishop, having the same faith, and setting out from the same persons *as myself*.[2] But if it befall me to be sick, and in expectation of death, and if I be childless, I shall act in the same manner. But if I die having a son who is not worthy, or not yet capable, I shall act in the same manner. For I shall deposit them with my bishop, in order that if my son, when he grows up, be worthy of the trust, he may give them to him as his father's bequest, according to the terms of this engagement.

4. "'And that I shall thus do, I again call to witness heaven, earth, water, in which all things are enveloped, and in addition to all these, the all-pervading air, without which I cannot breathe, that I shall always be obedient to him who giveth me these books of the preachings, and shall observe in all things as I have engaged, or even something more. To me, therefore, keeping this covenant, there shall be a part with the holy ones; but to me doing anything contrary to what I have covenanted, may the universe be hostile to me, and the all-pervading ether, and the God who is over all, to whom none is superior, than whom none is greater. But if even I should come to the acknowledgment of another God, I now swear by him also, be he or be he not, that I shall not do otherwise. And in addition to all these things, if I shall lie, I shall be accursed living and dying, and shall be punished with everlasting punishment.'

"And after this, let him partake of bread and salt with him who commits them to him."

CHAP. V. — THE ADJURATION ACCEPTED.

James having thus spoken, the elders were in an agony of terror. Therefore James, perceiving that they were greatly afraid, said: "Hear me, brethren and fellow-servants. If we should give the books to all indiscriminately, and they should be corrupted by any daring men, or be perverted by interpretations, as you have heard that some have already done, it will remain even for those who really seek the truth, always to wander in error. Wherefore it is better that they should be with us, and that we should communicate them with all the fore-mentioned care to those who wish to live piously, and to save others. But if any one, after taking this adjuration, shall act otherwise, he shall with good reason incur eternal punishment. For why should not he who is the cause of the destruction of

---

[1] [The form of adjuration has some points of resemblance with the baptismal forms given by Hippolytus, as those of the Elkesaites. See Introductory Notice to *Recognitions*, and comp. *Recognitions*, i. 45-48. — R.]

[2] Unless the reading be corrupt here, I suppose the reference must be to episcopal succession.

others not be destroyed himself?" The elders, therefore, being pleased with the sentiments of James, exclaimed, "Blessed be He who, as foreseeing all things, has graciously appointed thee as our bishop;" and when they had said this, we all rose up, and prayed to the Father and God of all, to whom be glory for ever. Amen.[1]

---

[1] [Rufinus, in his preface to the *Recognitions*, makes no allusion to this letter. — R.]

EPISTLE OF CLEMENT TO JAMES

CLEMENT to James, the lord,[1] and the bishop of bishops, who rules Jerusalem, the holy church of the Hebrews, and the churches everywhere excellently founded by the providence of God, with the elders and deacons, and the rest of the brethren, peace be always.

CHAP. I. — PETER'S MARTYRDOM.

Be it known to you, my lord, that Simon, who, for the sake of the true faith, and the most sure foundation of his doctrine, was set apart to be the foundation of the Church, and for this end was by Jesus Himself, with His truthful mouth, named Peter, the first-fruits of our Lord, the first of the apostles; to whom first the Father revealed the Son; whom the Christ, with good reason, blessed; the called, and elect, and associate at table and in the journeyings *of Christ;* the excellent and approved disciple, who, as being fittest of all, was commanded to enlighten the darker part of the world, namely the West, and was enabled to accomplish it, — and to what extent do I lengthen my discourse, not wishing to indicate what is sad, which yet of necessity, though reluctantly, I must tell you, — he himself, by reason of his immense love towards men, having come as far as Rome, clearly and publicly testifying, in opposition to the wicked one who withstood him, that there is to be a good King over all the world, while saving men by his God-inspired doctrine, himself, by violence, exchanged this present existence for life.

CHAP. II. — ORDINATION OF CLEMENT.

But about that time, when he was about to die, the brethren being assembled together, he suddenly seized my hand, and rose up, and said in presence of the church: "Hear me, brethren and fellow-servants. Since, as I have been taught by the Lord and Teacher Jesus Christ, whose apostle I am, the day of my death is approaching, I lay hands upon this Clement as your bishop; and to him I entrust my chair of discourse,

---

[1] More probably "the Lord's brother." So it must have been in the text from which Rufinus translated. [That this means "James the Lord's brother" is quite certain, but it is not necessary to adopt this reading here; comp. chap. 20 and the opening sentence of the previous epistle. In *Recognitions,* iii. 74, Clement is represented as writing "my lord James." — R.]

218

even to him who has journeyed with me from the beginning to the end, and thus has heard all my homilies — who, in a word, having had a share in all my trials, has been found stedfast in the faith; whom I have found, above all others, pious, philanthropic, pure, learned, chaste, good, upright, large-hearted, and striving generously to bear the ingratitude of some of the catechumens. Wherefore I communicate to him the power of binding and loosing, so that with respect to everything which he shall ordain in the earth, it shall be decreed in the heavens. For he shall bind what ought to be bound, and loose what ought to be loosed, as knowing the rule of the Church. Therefore hear him, as knowing that he who grieves the president of the truth, sins against Christ, and offends the Father of all. Wherefore he shall not live; and therefore it becomes him who presides to hold the place of a physician, and not to cherish the rage of an irrational beast."

CHAP. III. — NOLO EPISCOPARI.

While he thus spoke, I knelt to him, and entreated him, declining the honour and the authority of the chair. But he answered: "Concerning this matter do not ask me; for it has seemed to me to be good that thus it be, and all the more if you decline it. For this chair has not need of a presumptuous man, ambitious of occupying it, but of one pious in conduct and deeply skilled in the word *of God.* But show me a better *than yourself,* who has travelled more with me, and has heard more of my discourses, and has learned better the regulations of the Church, and I shall not force you to do well against your will. But it will not be in your power to show me your superior; for you are the choice first-fruits of the multitudes saved through me. However, consider this further, that if you do not undertake the administration of the Church, through fear of the danger of sin, you may be sure that you sin more, when you have it in your power to help the godly, who are, as it were, at sea and in danger, and will not do so, providing only for your own interest, and not for the common advantage of all. But that it behoves you altogether to undertake the danger, while I do not cease to ask it of you for the help of all, you well understand. The sooner, therefore, you consent, so much the sooner will you relieve me from anxiety.

CHAP. IV.—THE RECOMPENSE OF THE REWARD.

"But I myself also, O Clement, know the griefs and anxieties, and dangers and reproaches, that are appointed you from the uninstructed multitudes; and these you will be able to bear nobly, looking to the great reward of patience bestowed on you by God. But also consider this fairly with me: When has Christ need of your aid? Now, when the wicked one has sworn war against His bride; or in the time to come, when He shall reign victorious, having no need of further help? Is it not evident to any one who has even the least understanding, that it is now? Therefore with all good-will hasten in the time of the present necessity to do battle on the side of this good King, whose character it is to give great rewards after victory. Therefore take the oversight gladly; and all the more in good time, because you have learned from me the administration of the Church, for the safety of the brethren who have taken refuge with us.

CHAP. V.—A CHARGE.

"However, I wish, in the presence of all, to remind you, for the sake of all, of the things belonging to the administration. It becomes you, living without reproach, with the greatest earnestness to shake off all the cares of life, being neither a surety, nor an advocate, nor involved in any other secular business. For Christ does not wish to appoint you either a judge or an arbitrator in business, or negotiator of the secular affairs of the present life, lest, being confined to the present cares of men, you should not have leisure by the word of truth to separate the good among men from the bad. But let the disciples perform these offices to one another, and not withdraw *you* from the discourses which are able to save. For as it is wicked for you to undertake secular cares, and to omit the doing of what you have been commanded to do, so it is sin for every layman, if they do not stand by one another even in secular necessities. And if all do not understand to take order that you be without care in respect of the things in which you ought to be, let them learn it from the deacons; that you may have the care of the Church always, in order both to your administering it well, and to your holding forth the words of truth.

CHAP. VI.—THE DUTY OF A BISHOP.

"Now, if you were occupied with secular cares, you should deceive both yourself and your hearers. For not being able, on account of occupation, to point out the things that are advantageous, both you should be punished, as not having taught what was profitable, and they, not having learned, should perish by reason of ignorance. Wherefore do you indeed preside over them without occupation, so as to send forth seasonably the words that are able to save them; and so let them listen to you, knowing that whatever the ambassador of the truth shall bind upon earth is bound also in heaven, and what he shall loose is loosed. But you shall bind what ought to be bound, and loose what ought to be loosed. And these, and such like, are the things that relate to you as president.

CHAP. VII.—DUTIES OF PRESBYTERS.

"And with respect to the presbyters, take these *instructions*. Above all things, let them join the young betimes in marriage, anticipating the entanglements of youthful lusts. But neither let them neglect the marriage of those who are already old; for lust is vigorous even in some old men. Lest, therefore, fornication find a place among you, and bring upon you a very pestilence, take precaution, and search, lest at any time the fire of adultery be secretly kindled among you. For adultery is a very terrible thing, even such that it holds the second place in respect of punishment, the first being assigned to those who are in error, even although they be chaste. Wherefore do you, as elders of the Church, exercise the spouse of Christ to chastity (by the spouse I mean the body of the Church); for if she be apprehended to be chaste by her royal Bridegroom, she shall obtain the greatest honour; and you, as wedding guests, shall receive great commendation. But if she be caught having sinned, she herself indeed shall be cast out; and you shall suffer punishment, if at any time her sin has been through your negligence.

CHAP. VIII.—"DO GOOD UNTO ALL."

"Wherefore above all things be careful about chastity; for fornication has been marked out as a bitter thing in the estimation of God. But there are many forms of fornication, as also Clement himself will explain to you. The first is adultery, that a man should not enjoy his own wife alone, or a woman not enjoy her own husband alone. If any one be chaste, he is able also to be philanthropic, on account of which he shall obtain eternal mercy. For as adultery is a great evil, so philanthropy is the greatest good. Wherefore love all your brethren with grave and compassionate eyes, performing to orphans the part of parents, to widows that of husbands, affording them sustenance with all kindliness, arranging marriages for those who are in their prime, and for those who are without a profession, the means of necessary support through employment; giving work to the artificer, and alms to the incapable.

CHAP. IX. — "LET BROTHERLY LOVE CONTINUE."

"But I know that ye will do these things if you fix love into your minds; and for its entrance there is one only fit means, viz., the common partaking of food.[1] Wherefore see to it that ye be frequently one another's guests, as ye are able, that you may not fail of it. For it is the cause of well-doing, and well-doing of salvation. Therefore all of you present your provisions in common to all your brethren in God, knowing that, giving temporal things, you shall receive eternal things. Much more feed the hungry, and give drink to the thirsty, and clothing to the naked; visit the sick; showing yourselves to those who are in prison, help them as ye are able, and receive strangers into your houses with all alacrity. However, not to speak in detail, philanthropy will teach you to do everything that is good, as misanthropy suggests ill-doing to those who will not be saved.

CHAP. X. — "WHATSOEVER THINGS ARE HONEST."

"Let the brethren who have causes to be settled not be judged by the secular authorities; but let them by all means be reconciled by the elders of the church, yielding ready obedience to them. Moreover, also, flee avarice, inasmuch as it is able, under pretext of temporal gain, to deprive you of eternal blessings. Carefully keep your balances, your measures, your weights, and the things belonging to your traffic, just. Be faithful with respect to your trusts. Moreover, you will persevere in doing these things, and things similar to these, until the end, if you have in your hearts an ineradicable remembrance of the judgment that is from God. For who would sin, being persuaded that at the end of life there is a judgment appointed of the righteous God, who only now is long-suffering and good,[2] that the good may in future enjoy for ever unspeakable blessings; but the sinners being found as evil, shall obtain an eternity of unspeakable punishment. And, indeed, that these things are so, it would be reasonable to doubt, were it not that the Prophet of the truth has said and sworn that it shall be.

CHAP. XI. — DOUBTS TO BE SATISFIED.

"Wherefore, being disciples of the true Prophet, laying aside double-mindedness, from which comes ill-doing, eagerly undertake well-

doing. But if any of you doubt concerning the things which I have said are to be, let him confess it without shame, if he cares for his own soul, and he shall be satisfied by the president. But if he has believed rightly, let his conversation be with confidence, as fleeing from the great fire of condemnation, and entering into the eternal good kingdom of God.

CHAP. XII. — DUTIES OF DEACONS.

"Moreover let the deacons of the church, going about with intelligence, be as eyes to the bishop, carefully inquiring into the doings of each member of the church, *ascertaining* who is about to sin, in order that, being arrested with admonition by the president, he may haply not accomplish the sin. Let them check the disorderly, that they may not desist from assembling to hear the discourses, so that they may be able to counteract by the word of truth those anxieties that fall upon the heart from every side, by means of worldly casualties and evil communications; for if they long remain fallow, they become fuel for the fire. And let them learn who are suffering under bodily disease, and let them bring them to the notice of the multitude who do not know of them, that they may visit them, and supply their wants according to the judgment of the president. Yea, though they do this without his knowledge, they do nothing amiss. These things, then, and things like to these, let the deacons attend to.

CHAP. XIII. — DUTIES OF CATECHISTS.

"Let the catechists instruct, being first instructed; for it is a work relating to the souls of men. For the teacher of the word must accommodate himself to the various judgments of the learners. The catechists must therefore be learned, and unblameable, of much experience, and approved, as you will know that Clement is, who is to be your instructor after me. For it were too much for me now to go into details. However, if ye be of one mind, you shall be able to reach the haven of rest, where is the peaceful city of the great King.

CHAP. XIV. — THE VESSEL OF THE CHURCH.

"For the whole business of the Church is like unto a great ship, bearing through a violent storm men who are of many places, and who desire to inhabit the city of the good kingdom. Let, therefore, God be your shipmaster; and let the pilot be likened to Christ, the mate[3] to the bishop, and the sailors to the deacons, the midshipmen to the catechists, the multitude of the brethren to the passengers, the world to the

---

1 Literally, "of salt."
2 The common reading would give "who alone is now long-suffering;" but the change of a letter gives the reading which we have adopted.

3 It is impossible to translate these terms very accurately. I suppose the πρωρεύς was rather the "bow-oarsman" in the galley.

sea ; the foul winds to temptations, persecutions, and dangers ; and all manner of afflictions to the waves ; the land winds and their squalls to the discourses of deceivers and false prophets ; the promontories and rugged rocks to the judges in high places threatening terrible things ; the meetings of two seas, and the wild places, to unreasonable men and those who doubt of the promises of truth. Let hypocrites be regarded as like to pirates. Moreover, account the strong whirlpool, and the Tartarean Charybdis, and murderous wrecks, and deadly founderings, to be nought but sins. In order, therefore, that, sailing with a fair wind, you may safely reach the haven of the hoped-for city, pray so as to be heard. But prayers become audible by good deeds.

CHAP. XV. — INCIDENTS OF THE VOYAGE.

"Let therefore the passengers remain quiet, sitting in their own places, lest by disorder they occasion rolling or careening. Let the midshipmen give heed to the fare. Let the deacons neglect nothing with which they are entrusted ; let the presbyters, like sailors, studiously arrange what is needful for each one. Let the bishop, as the mate, wakefully ponder the words of the pilot alone. Let Christ, even the Saviour, be loved as the pilot, and alone believed in the matters of which He speaks ; and let all pray to God for a prosperous voyage. Let those sailing expect every tribulation, as travelling over a great and troubled sea, the world : sometimes, indeed, disheartened, persecuted, dispersed, hungry, thirsty, naked, hemmed in ; and, again, sometimes united, congregated, at rest ; but also sea-sick, giddy, vomiting, that is, confessing sins, like disease-producing bile,—I mean the sins proceeding from bitterness, and the evils accumulated from disorderly lusts, by the confession of which, as by vomiting, you are relieved of your disease, attaining healthful safety by means of carefulness.

CHAP. XVI. — THE BISHOP'S LABOURS AND REWARD.

"But know all of you that the bishop labours more than you all ; because each of you suffers his own affliction, but he his own and that of every one. Wherefore, O Clement, preside as a helper to every one according to your ability, being careful of the cares of all. Whence I know that in your undertaking the administration, I do not confer, but receive, a favour. But take courage and bear it generously, as knowing that God will recompense you when you enter the haven of rest, the greatest of blessings, a reward that cannot be taken from you, in proportion as you have undertaken more labour for the safety of all. So that, if many of the brethren

should hate you on account of your lofty righteousness, their hatred shall nothing hurt you, but the love of the righteous God shall greatly benefit you. Therefore endeavour to shake off the praise that arises from injustice, and to attain the profitable praise that is from Christ on account of righteous administration."

CHAP. XVII. — THE PEOPLE'S DUTIES.

Having said this, and more than this, he looked again upon the multitude, and said : "And you also, my beloved brethren and fellow-servants, be subject to the president of the truth in all things, knowing this, that he who grieves him has not received Christ, with whose chair he has been entrusted ; and he who has not received Christ shall be regarded as having despised the Father ; wherefore he shall be cast out of the good kingdom. On this account, endeavour to come to all the assemblies, lest as deserters you incur the charge of sin through the disheartening of your captain. Wherefore all of you think before all else of the things that relate to him, knowing this, that the wicked one, being the more hostile on account of every one of you, wars against him alone. Do you therefore strive to live in affection towards him, and in kindliness towards one another, and to obey him, in order that both he may he comforted and you may be saved.

CHAP. XVIII. — "AS A HEATHEN MAN AND A PUBLICAN."

"But some things also you ought of yourselves to consider, on account of his not being able to speak openly by reason of the plots. Such as : if he be hostile to any one, do not wait for his speaking ; and do not take part with that man, but prudently follow the bishop's will, being enemies to those to whom he is an enemy, and not conversing with those with whom he does not converse, in order that every one, desiring to have you all as his friends, may be reconciled to him and be saved, listening to his discourse. But if any one remain a friend of those to whom he is an enemy, and speak to those with whom he does not converse, he also himself is one of those who would waste the church. For, being with you in body, but not with you in judgment, he is against you ; and is much worse than the open enemies from without, since with seeming friendship he disperses those who are within."

CHAP. XIX. — INSTALLATION OF CLEMENT.

Having thus spoken, he laid his hands upon me in the presence of all, and compelled me to sit in his own chair. And when I was seated, he immediately said to me : "I entreat you, in the presence of all the brethren here, that whensoever I depart from this life, as depart I must, you send to James the brother of the Lord a brief account of your reasonings from your boyhood, and how from the beginning until now you have journeyed with me, hearing the discourses preached by me in every city, and *seeing* my deeds. And then at the end you will not fail to inform him of the manner of my death, as I said before. For that event will not grieve him very much, when he knows that I piously went through what it behoved me to suffer. And he will get the greatest comfort when he learns, that not an unlearned man, or one ignorant of life-giving words, or not knowing the rule of the Church, shall be entrusted with the chair of the teacher after me. For the discourse of a deceiver destroys the souls of the multitudes who hear."

CHAP. XX. — CLEMENT'S OBEDIENCE.

Whence I, my lord James, having promised as I was ordered, have not failed to write in books by chapters the greater part of his discourses in every city, which have been already written to you, and sent by himself, as for a token ; and thus I despatched them to you,[1] inscribing them " Clement's Epitome of the Popular Sermons of Peter." However, I shall begin to set them forth, as I was ordered.

---

[1] [Compare with this the remarkable chapter, *Recognitions*, iii. 75, where a summary is given of previous writings sent to James. The design of this letter, evidently known to Rufinus, was to authenticate the work which follows. The language of Rufinus may fairly imply that this letter, known to be of later origin, was sometimes prefixed to the *Recognitions* also. The entire literature gives James of Jerusalem a marked supremacy. This is an evidence of Jewish-Christian origin. — R.]

THE CLEMENTINE HOMILIES

BOOKS I. TO V. HAVE BEEN TRANSLATED BY REV. THOMAS SMITH, D.D.; BOOKS VI.-XII. BY
PETER PETERSON, M.A.; AND BOOKS XIII.-XX. BY DR. DONALDSON.

HOMILY I.

CHAP. I. — BOYISH QUESTIONINGS.

I CLEMENT, being a Roman citizen,[1] even from my earliest youth was able to live chastely, my mind from my boyhood drawing away the lust that was in me to dejection and distress. For I had a habit of reasoning — how originating I know not — making frequent cogitations concerning death : When I die, shall I neither exist, nor shall any one ever have any remembrance of me, while boundless time bears all things of all men into forgetfulness? and shall I then be without being, or acquaintance with those who are ; neither knowing nor being known, neither having been nor being? And has the world ever been made? and was there anything before it was made? For if it has been always, it shall also continue to be ; but if it has been made, it shall also be dissolved. And after its dissolution, shall there ever be anything again, unless, perhaps, silence and forgetfulness? Or perhaps something shall be which is not possible now to conceive.

CHAP. II. — GOOD OUT OF EVIL.

As I pondered without ceasing these and such like questions — I know not whence arising — I had such bitter grief, that, becoming pale, I wasted away ; and, what was most terrible, if at any time I wished to drive away this meditation as unprofitable, my suffering became all the more severe ; and I grieved over this, not knowing that I had a fair inmate, even my thought, which was to·be to me the cause of a blessed immortality, as I afterwards knew by experience, and gave thanks to God, the Lord of all. For it was by this thought, which at first afflicted me, that I was compelled to come to the search and the finding of things ; and then I pitied those whom at first, through ignorance, I ventured to call blessed.

---

[1] [The first six chapters agree closely with the corresponding passage in the *Recognitions*. — R.]

CHAP. III. — PERPLEXITY.

From my boyhood, then, being *involved* in such reasonings, in order to learn something definite, I used to resort to the schools of the philosophers. But nought else did I see than the setting up and the knocking down of doctrines, and strifes, and seeking for victory, and the arts of syllogisms, and the skill of assumptions ; and sometimes one *opinion* prevailed, — as, for example, that the soul is immortal, and sometimes that it is mortal. If, therefore, at any time the doctrine prevailed that it is immortal, I was glad ; and when the doctrine prevailed that it is mortal, I was grieved. And again, I was the more disheartened because I could not establish either doctrine to my satisfaction. However, I perceived that the opinions on subjects under discussion are taken as true or false, according to their defenders, and do not appear as they really are. Perceiving, therefore, now that the acceptance does not depend on the real nature of the subjects discussed, but that opinions are proved to be true or false, according to ability of those who defend them, I was still more than ever at a loss in regard of things. Wherefore I groaned from the depth of my soul. For neither was I able to establish anything, nor could I shake off the consideration of such things, though, as I said before, I wished it. For although I frequently charged myself to be at peace, in some way or other thoughts on these subjects, accompanied with a feeling of pleasure, would come into my mind.

CHAP. IV. — MORE PERPLEXITY.

And again, living in doubt, I said to myself, Why do I labour in vain, when the matter is clear, that if I lose existence when I die, it is not fitting that I should distress myself now while I. do exist? Wherefore I shall reserve my grief till that *day*, when, ceasing to exist, I shall not be affected with grief. But if I am to exist, what does it profit me now to distress myself gratuitously? And immediately after this another reasoning assailed me; for I said, Shall I not have something worse to suffer then than that which distresses me now, if I have not lived piously; and shall I not be delivered over, according to the doctrines of some philosophers, to Pyriphlegethon and Tartarus, like Sisyphus, or Tityus, or Ixion, or Tantalus, and be punished for ever in Hades? But again I replied, saying: But there are no such things as these. Yet again I said: But if there be? Therefore, said I, since the matter is uncertain, the safer plan is for me rather to live piously. But how shall I be able, for the sake of righteousness, to subdue bodily pleasures, looking, as I do, to an uncertain hope? But I am neither fully persuaded what is that righteous thing that is pleasing to God, nor do I know whether the soul is immortal or mortal. Neither can I find any well-established doctrine, nor can I abstain from such debatings.

CHAP. V. — A RESOLUTION.

What, then, am I to do, unless this? I shall go into Egypt, and I shall become friendly with the hierophants of the shrines, and with the prophets; and I shall seek and find a magician, and persuade him with large bribes to effect the calling up of a soul, which is called necromancy, as if I were going to inquire of it concerning some business. And the inquiry shall be for the purpose of learning whether the soul is immortal. But the answer of the soul that it is immortal shall not give me the knowledge from its speaking or my hearing, but only from its being seen; so that, seeing it with my very eyes, I may have a self-sufficient and fit assurance, from the very fact of its appearing, that it exists; and never again shall the uncertain words of hearing be able to overturn the things which the eyes have made their own. However, I submitted this very plan to a certain companion who was a philosopher; and he counselled me not to venture upon it, and that on many accounts. "For if," said he, "the soul shall not listen to the magician, you will live with an evil conscience, as having acted against the laws which forbid the doing of these things. But if it shall listen to him, then, besides your living with an evil conscience, I think that matters of piety will not be promoted to you on account of your making this attempt. For they say that the Deity is angry with those who disturb souls after their release from the body."[1] And I, when I heard this, became indeed more backward to undertake such a thing, but I did not abandon my original plan; but I was distressed, as being hindered in the execution of it.

CHAP. VI. — TIDINGS FROM JUDÆA.

And, not to discuss such matters to you in a long speech, while I was occupied with such reasonings and doings, a certain report, taking its rise in the spring-time,[2] in the reign of Tiberius Cæsar, gradually grew everywhere, and ran through the world as truly the good tidings of God, being unable to stifle the counsel of God in silence. Therefore it everywhere became greater and louder, saying that a certain One in Judæa, beginning in the spring season, was preaching to the Jews the kingdom of the invisible God, and saying that whoever of them would reform his manner of living should enjoy it. And in order that He might be believed that He uttered these things full of the Godhead, He wrought many wonderful miracles and signs by His mere command, as having received power from God. For He made the deaf to hear, the blind to see, the lame to walk, raised up the bowed down, drove away every disease, put to flight every demon; and even scabbed lepers, by only looking on Him from a distance, were sent away cured by Him; and the dead being brought to Him, were raised; and there was nothing which He could not do. And as time advanced, so much the greater, through the arrival of more persons, and the stronger grew — I say not now the report, but — the truth of the thing; for now at length there were meetings in various places for consultation and inquiry as to who He might be that had appeared, and what was His purpose.

CHAP. VII. — THE GOSPEL IN ROME.

And then in the same year, in the autumn season, a certain one, standing in a public place, cried and said, "Men of Rome, hearken. The Son of God is come in Judæa, proclaiming eternal life to all who will, if they shall live according to the counsel of the Father, who hath sent Him. Wherefore change your manner of life from the worse to the better, from things temporal to things eternal; for know ye that there is one God, who is in heaven, whose world ye unrighteously dwell in before His righteous eyes. But if ye be changed, and live according to His counsel, then, being born into the other world, and becoming eternal, ye shall enjoy His unspeakable good things. But if ye be unbelieving, your souls, after the dissolution of the body, shall be thrown into the place of fire, where, being punished eternally, they shall repent of their unprofitable deeds. For every one, the term of repentance is the present life." I therefore, when I heard these things, was grieved, because no one among so great multitudes, hear-

---

[1] This rendering is from the text in the corresponding passage of the *Epitome de gestis S. Petri.*

[2] [This clause is represented in the *Recognitions* as follows: "which took its rise in the regions of the East." — R.]

ing such an announcement, said : I shall go into Judæa, that I may know if this man who tells us these things speaks the truth, that the Son of God has come into Judæa, for the sake of a good and eternal hope, revealing the will of the Father who sent Him. For it is no small matter which they say that He preaches : for He asserts that the souls of some, being *themselves* immortal, shall enjoy eternal good things ; and that those of others, being thrown into unquenchable fire, shall be punished for ever.

CHAP. VIII. — DEPARTURE FROM ROME.

While I spoke thus concerning others, I also lectured myself, saying, Why do I blame others, being myself guilty of the very same crime of heedlessness? But I shall hasten into Judæa, having first arranged my affairs.[1] And when I had thus made up my mind, there occurred a long time of delay, my worldly affairs being difficult to arrange. Therefore, meditating further on the nature of life, that by involving[2] men in hope it lays snares for those who are making haste, yea, and how much time I had been robbed of while tossed by hopes, and that we men die while thus occupied, I left all my affairs as they were, and sped to Portus ;[3] and coming to the harbour, and being taken on board a ship, I was borne by adverse winds to Alexandria instead of Judæa ; and being detained there by stress of weather, I consorted with the philosophers, and told them about the rumour and the sayings of him who had appeared in Rome. And they answered that indeed they knew nothing of him who had appeared in Rome ; but concerning Him who was born in Judæa, and who was said by the report to be the Son of God, they had heard from many who had come from thence, and had learned respecting all the wonderful things that He did with a word.

CHAP. IX. — PREACHING OF BARNABAS.

And when I said that I wished I could meet with some one of those who had seen Him, they immediately brought me to one, saying, " There is one here who not only is acquainted with Him, but is also of that country, a Hebrew, by name Barnabas, who says that he himself is one of His disciples ; and hereabouts he resides, and readily announces to those who will the terms of His promise." Then I went with them ; and when I came, I stood listening to his words with the crowd that stood round him ; and I perceived that he was speaking the truth not with dialectic art, but was setting forth simply and

without preparation what he had heard and seen the manifested Son of God do and say. And even from the crowd who stood around him he produced many witnesses of the miracles and discourses which he narrated.

CHAP. X. — CAVILS OF THE PHILOSOPHERS.

But while the multitudes were favourably disposed towards the things that he so artlessly spoke, the philosophers, impelled by their worldly learning, set upon laughing at him and making sport of him, upbraiding and reproaching him with excessive presumption, making use of the great armoury of syllogisms. But he set aside their babbling, and did not enter into their subtle questioning, but without embarrassment went on with what he was saying. And then one of them asked, Wherefore it was that a gnat, although it be so small, and has six feet, has wings also ; while an elephant, the largest of beasts, is wingless, and has but four feet? But he, after the question had been put, resuming his discourse, which had been interrupted, as though he had answered the question, resumed his original discourse, only making use of this preface after each interruption : " We have a commission only to tell you the words and the wondrous doings of Him who sent us ; and instead of logical demonstration, we present to you many witnesses from amongst yourselves who stand by, whose faces I remember, as living images. These sufficient testimonies it is left to your choice to submit to, or to disbelieve.[4] But I shall not cease to declare unto you what is for your profit ; for to be silent were to me a loss, and to disbelieve is ruin to you. But indeed I could give answers to your frivolous questions, if you asked them through love of truth. But the reason of the different structure of the gnat and elephant it is not fitting to tell to those who are ignorant of the God of all."

CHAP. XI. — CLEMENT'S ZEAL.

When he said this, they all, as in concert, set up a shout of laughter, trying to silence him and put him out, as a barbarous madman. But I, seeing this, and seized, I know not how, with enthusiasm, could no longer keep silence with righteous indignation, but boldly cried out, saying, " Well has God ordained that His counsel should be incapable of being received by you, foreseeing you to be unworthy, as appears manifestly to such of those who are now present as have minds capable of judging. For whereas now heralds of His counsel have been sent forth, not making a show of grammatical art, but set-

---

[1] [The narrative here varies from that of the *Recognitions;* comp. book i. chaps. 7-11. — R.]
[2] For ἐκπλοκῶν Wieseler proposes ἐκκλέπτων, " that deceiving by hopes it lays snares," etc.
[3] Portus, the port of Rome. One MS. reads πόντον, " the sea."

[4] We have here adopted a conjectural reading of Davis. The common text is thus translated: " whose faces I remember, and who as being living images are satisfactory testimonies. These it is left," etc.

ting forth His will in simple and inartificial words, so that whosoever hear can understand what is spoken, and not with any invidious feeling, as though unwilling to offer it to all; you come here, and besides your not understanding what is for your advantage, to your own injury you laugh at the truth, which, to your condemnation, consorts with the barbarians, and which you will not entertain when it visits you, by reason of your wickedness and the plainness of its words, lest you be convicted of being merely lovers of words, and not lovers of truth and lovers of wisdom. How long will you be learning to speak, who have not the power of speech?[1] For many sayings of yours are not worth one word. What, then, will your Grecian multitude say, being of one mind, if, as he says, there shall be a judgment? "Why, O God, didst Thou not proclaim to us Thy counsel?" Shall you not, if you be thought worthy of an answer at all, be told this? "I, knowing before the foundation of the world all characters that were to be, acted towards each one by anticipation according to his deserts without making it known;[2] but wishing to give full assurance to those who have fled to me that this is so, and to explain why from the beginning, and in the first ages, I did not suffer my counsel to be publicly proclaimed; I now, in the end of the world,[3] have sent heralds to proclaim my will, and they are insulted and flouted by those who will not be benefited, and who wilfully reject my friendship. Oh, great wrong! The preachers are exposed to danger even to the loss of life,[4] and that by the men who are called to salvation.

CHAP. XII. — CLEMENT'S REBUKE OF THE PEOPLE.

"And this wrongful treatment of my heralds would have been against all from the beginning, if from the beginning the unworthy had been called to salvation. For that which is now done wrongfully by these men serves to the vindication of my righteous foreknowledge, that it was well that I did not choose from the beginning to expose uselessly to public contempt the word which is worthy of honour; but determined to suppress it, as being honourable, not indeed from those who were worthy from the beginning — for to them also I imparted it — but from those, and such as those, unworthy, as you see them to be, — those who hate me, and who will not love themselves. And now, give over laughing at this man, and hear me with respect to his announcement, or let any one of the hearers who

pleases answer. And do not bark like vicious dogs, deafening with disorderly clamour the ears of those who would be saved, ye unrighteous and God-haters, and perverting the saving method to unbelief. How shall you be able to obtain pardon, who scorn him who is sent to speak to you of the Godhead of God? And this you do towards a man whom you ought to have received on account of his good-will towards you, even if he did not speak truth."

CHAP. XIII. — CLEMENT INSTRUCTED BY BARNABAS.

While I spake these words, and others to the same effect, there arose a great excitement among the crowd; and some as pitying Barnabas, sympathized with me; but others, being senseless, terribly gnashed their teeth against me. But, as the evening had already come, I took Barnabas by the hand, and by force conducted him, against his will, to my lodging, and constrained him to remain there, lest some one might lay hands on him. And having spent several days, and instructed him briefly in the true doctrine, as well as he could in a few days, he said that he should hasten into Judæa for the observance of the festival, and also because he wished for the future to consort with those of his own nation.

CHAP. XIV. — DEPARTURE OF BARNABAS.

But it plainly appeared to me that he was disconcerted. For when I said to him, "Only set forth to me the words which you have heard of the Man who has appeared, and I will adorn them with my speech, and preach the counsel of God; and if you do so, within a few days I will sail with you, for I greatly desire to go to the land of Judæa, and perhaps I shall dwell with you all my life;" — when he heard this, he answered: "If you wish to inquire into our affairs, and to learn what is for your advantage, sail with me at once. But if you will not, I shall now give you directions to my house, and that of those whom you wish *to meet*, that when you choose to come you may find us. For I shall set out to-morrow for my home." And when I saw that he could not be prevailed upon, I went with him as far as the harbour; and having learned of him the directions which he had promised to give me for finding the dwellings, I said to him, "Were it not that to-morrow I am to recover a debt that is due to me, I should straightway set sail with you. But I shall soon overtake you." And having said this, and having given him in charge to those who commanded the ship, I returned grieving, remembering him as an excellent and dear friend.

---

[1] The Vatican MS. and Epit. have "the power of speaking well."
[2] Lit., "I met each one beforehand secretly." The Latin has, "unicuique prævius occurri."
[3] The Greek is βίου, "life."
[4] The Paris MS. reads φθόνου, "envy," instead of φόνου, "murder."

CHAP. XV. — INTRODUCTION TO PETER.

But having spent *some* days, and not having been able to recover the whole debt, for the sake of speed I neglected the balance, as being a hindrance, and myself also set sail for Judæa, and in fifteen days arrived at Cæsarea Stratonis.[1] And when I had landed, and was seeking for a lodging, I learned that one named Peter, who was the most esteemed disciple of the Man who had appeared in Judæa, and had done signs and wonders, was going to have a verbal controversy next day with Simon, a Samaritan of Gitthi. When I heard this, I begged to be shown his lodging; and as soon as I learned it, I stood before the door. And those who were in the house, seeing me, discussed the question who I was, and whence I had come. And, behold, Barnabas came out; and as soon as he saw me he embraced me, rejoicing greatly, and weeping. And he took me by the hand, and conducted me to where Peter was, saying to me, " This is Peter, of whom I told you as being the greatest in the wisdom of God, and I have spoken to him of you continually. Therefore enter freely,[2] for I have told him your excellent qualities, without falsehood; and, at the same time, have disclosed to him your intention, so that he himself also is desirous to see you. Therefore I offer him a great gift when by my hands I present you to him." Thus saying, he presented me, and said, " This, O Peter, is Clement."

CHAP. XVI. — PETER'S SALUTATION.

Then the blessed man, springing forward as soon as he heard my name, kissed me ; and making me sit down, straightway said, " You acted nobly in entertaining Barnabas, a herald of the truth, to the honour of the living God, being magnanimously not ashamed, nor fearing the resentment of the rude multitude. Blessed shall you be. For as you thus with all honour entertained the ambassador of the truth, so also truth herself shall constitute you, who are a stranger, a citizen of her own city. And thus you shall greatly rejoice, because you have now lent a small favour; I mean the kindness of good words. You shall be heir of blessings which are both eternal and cannot possibly be taken from you. And do not trouble yourself to detail to me your manner of life ; for the veracious Barnabas has detailed to us everything relating to you, making favourable mention of you almost every day. And in order that I may tell to you briefly, as to a genuine friend, what is in hand, travel with us, unless anything hinders you, partaking of the words of truth which I am going

to speak from city to city, as far as Rome itself. And if you wish *to say* anything, speak on."

CHAP. XVII. — QUESTIONS PROPOUNDED.

Then I set forth my purpose from the beginning, and how I had spent myself upon difficult questions, and all the things that I disclosed to you at the outset, so that I need not write the same things again. Then I said, " I hold myself in readiness to journey with you ; for this, I know not how, I gladly wish. However, I wish first to be convinced concerning the truth, that I may know whether the soul is mortal or immortal ; and whether, if it is eternal, it is to be judged concerning the things which it hath done here. Also, whether there is anything that is righteous and well-pleasing to God ; and whether the world was made, and for what end it was made ; and whether it shall be dissolved ; and if it shall be dissolved, whether it shall be made better, or shall not be at all." And not to mention them in detail, I said that I wished to learn these things, and things consequent upon these. And to this he answered : " I shall shortly convey to you, O Clement, the knowledge of the things that are ; and even now listen.

CHAP. XVIII. — CAUSES OF IGNORANCE.

"The will of God has been *kept* in obscurity in many ways. In the first place, there is evil instruction, wicked association, terrible society, unseemly discourses, wrongful prejudice. Thereby is error, then fearlessness, unbelief, fornication, covetousness, vainglory ; and ten thousand other such evils, filling the world as a quantity of smoke fills a house, have obscured the sight of the men inhabiting the world, and have not suffered them to look up and become acquainted with God the Creator from the delineation *of Himself which He has given*, and to know what is pleasing to Him. Wherefore it behoves the lovers of truth, crying out inwardly from their breasts, to call for aid, with truth-loving reason, that some one living within the house[3] which is filled with smoke may approach and open the door, so that the light of the sun which is without may be admitted into the house, and the smoke of the fire which is within may be driven out.

CHAP. XIX. — THE TRUE PROPHET.

" Now the Man who is the helper I call the true Prophet ; and He alone is able to enlighten the souls of men, so that with our own eyes we may be able to see the way of eternal salvation. But otherwise it is impossible, as you also know, since you said a little while ago that every doctrine is set up and pulled down, and the same is

---

[1] [Here the two accounts become again closely parallel. — R.]
[2] The text is corrupt. Dressel's reading is adopted in the text, being based on Rufinus's translation. Some conjecture, " as you will know of your own accord."

[3] A conjectural reading, " being without the house," seems preferable.

thought true or false, according to the power of him who advocates it ; so that doctrines do not appear as they are, but take the appearance of being or not being truth or falsehood from those who advocate them.¹ On this account the whole business of religion needed a true prophet, that he might tell us things that are, as they are, and how we must believe concerning all things. So that it is first necessary to test the prophet by every prophetic sign, and having ascertained that he is true, thereafter to believe him in every thing, and not to sit in judgment upon his several sayings, but to receive them as certain, being accepted indeed by seeming faith, yet by sure judgment. For by our initial proof, and by strict inquiry on every side, all things are received with right reason. Wherefore before all things it is necessary to seek after the true Prophet, because without Him it is impossible that any certainty can come to men."

CHAP. XX. — PETER'S SATISFACTION WITH CLEMENT.

And, at the same time, he satisfied me by expounding to me who He is, and how He is found, and holding Him forth to me as truly to be found, showing that the truth is more manifest to the ear by the discourse of the prophet than things that are seen with the eye ; so that I was astonished, and wondered that no one sees those things which are sought after by all, though they lie before him. However, having written this discourse concerning the Prophet by his order, he caused the volume to be despatched to you from Cæsarea Stratonis, saying that he had a charge from you to send his discourses and his acts year by year.² Thus, on the very first day, beginning only concerning the prophet of the truth, he confirmed me in every respect; and then he spoke thus : " Henceforth give heed to the discussions that take place between me and those on the other side ; and even if I come off at a disadvantage, I am not afraid of your ever doubting of the truth that has been delivered to you, knowing well that I seem to be beaten, but not the doctrine that has been delivered to us by the Prophet. However, I hope not to come off in our inquiries at a disadvantage with men who have understanding — I mean lovers of truth, who are able to know what discourses are specious, artificial, and pleasant, and what are unartificial and simple, trusting only to the truth *that is conveyed* through them."

¹ [Comp. *Recognitions*, i. 16, where the discourse is more fully given. — R.]
² The text is probably corrupt or defective. As it stands, grammatically Peter writes the discourse and sends it, and yet " by his order " must also apply to Peter. The *Recognitions* make Clement write the book and send it. The passage is deemed important, and is accordingly discussed in Schliemann, p. 83; Hilgenfeld, p. 37; and Uhlhorn, p. 101. [See *Recognitions*, i. 17. Both passages, despite the variation, may be urged in support of the existence of an earlier document as the common basis of the Clementine literature. — R.]

CHAP. XXI. — UNALTERABLE CONVICTION.

When he had thus spoken, I answered : " Now do I thank God ; for as I wished to be convinced, so He has vouchsafed to me. However, so far as concerns me, be you so far without anxiety that I shall never doubt ; so much so, that if you yourself should ever wish to remove me from the prophetic doctrine, you should not be able, so well do I know what I have received. And do not think that it is a great thing that I promise you that I shall never doubt ; for neither I myself, nor any man who has heard your discourse concerning the Prophet, can ever doubt of the true doctrine, having first heard and understood what is the truth of the prophetic announcement. Wherefore have confidence in the God-willed dogma ; for every art of wickedness has been conquered. For against prophecy, neither arts of discourses, nor tricks of sophisms, nor syllogisms, nor any other contrivance, can prevail anything ; that is, if he who has heard the true Prophet really is desirous of truth, and does not give heed to aught else under pretext of truth. So that, my lord Peter, be not disconcerted, as though you had presented the greatest good to a senseless person ; for you have presented it to one sensible of the favour, and who cannot be seduced from the truth that has been committed to him. For I know that it is one of those things which one wishes to receive quickly, and not to attain slowly. Therefore I know that I should not despise, on account of the quickness *with which I have got it*, what has been committed to me, what is incomparable, and what alone is safe."

CHAP. XXII. — THANKSGIVING.

When I had thus spoken, Peter said : " I give thanks to God, both for your salvation and for my satisfaction. For I am truly pleased to know that you apprehend what is the greatness of prophecy. Since, then, as you say, if I myself should ever wish — which God forbid — to transfer you to another doctrine, I shall not be able to persuade you, begin from to-morrow to attend upon me in the discussions with the adversaries. And to-morrow I have one with Simon Magus." And having spoken thus, and he himself having partaken of food in private, he ordered me also to partake ;³ and having blessed the food, and having given thanks after being satisfied, and having giving me an account of this matter, he went on to say : " May God grant you in all things to be made like unto me, and having been baptized, to partake of the same table with me." And having thus spoken, he enjoined me to go to rest ; for now indeed my bodily nature demanded sleep.

³ [Comp. Homily XIII. 4 and *Recognitions*, i. 19. — R.]

HOMILY II.

CHAP. I. — PETER'S ATTENDANTS.

THEREFORE the next day, I Clement, awaking from sleep before dawn, and learning that Peter was astir, and was conversing with his attendants concerning the worship of God (there were sixteen of them,[1] and I have thought good to set forth their names, as I subsequently learned them, that you may also know who they were. The first of them was Zacchæus, who was once a publican, and Sophonias his brother; Joseph and his foster-brother Michaias; also Thomas and Eliezer the twins; also Æneas and Lazarus the priests; besides also Elisæus, and Benjamin the son of Saphrus; as also Rubilus and Zacharias the builders; and Ananias and Haggæus the Jamminians; and Nicetas and Aquila the friends), —accordingly I went in and saluted him, and at his request sat down.

CHAP. II. — A SOUND MIND IN A SOUND BODY.

And he, breaking off the discourse in which he was engaged, assured me, by way of apology, why he had not awakened me that I might hear his discourses, assigning as the reason the discomfort of my voyage. As he wished this to be dispelled,[2] he had suffered me to sleep. "For," said he, "whenever the soul is distracted concerning some bodily want, it does not properly approach the instructions that are presented to it. On this account I am not willing to converse, either with those who are greatly grieving through some calamity, or are immoderately angry, or are turned to the frenzy of love, or are suffering under bodily exhaustion, or are distressed with the cares of life, or are harassed with any other sufferings, whose soul, as I said, being downcast, and sympathizing with the suffering body, occupies also its own intelligence therewith.

CHAP. III. — FOREWARNED IS FOREARMED.

"And let it not be said, Is it not, then, proper to present comforts and admonitions to those who are in any bad case? To this I answer, that if, indeed, any one is able, let him present them; but if not, let him bide his time. For I know[3] that all things have their proper season. Wherefore it is proper to ply men with words which strengthen the soul in anticipation of evil; so that, if at any time any evil comes upon them, the mind, being forearmed with the right argument, may be able to bear up under that which befalls it : for then the mind knows in the crisis of the struggle to have recourse to him who succoured it by good counsel.

CHAP. IV. — A REQUEST.

"However, I have learned, O Clement, how that in Alexandria Barnabas perfectly expounded to you the word respecting prophecy. Was it not so?" I answered, "Yes, and exceeding well." Then Peter: "Therefore it is not necessary now to occupy with the instructions which you know, the time which may serve us for other instructions which you do not know." Then said I : "You have rightly said, O Peter. But vouchsafe this to me, who purpose always to attend upon you, continuously to expound to me, a delighted hearer, the doctrine of the Prophet. For, apart from Him, as I learned from Barnabas, it is impossible to learn the truth."

CHAP. V. — EXCELLENCE OF THE KNOWLEDGE OF THE TRUE PROPHET.

And Peter, being greatly pleased with this, answered : "Already hath the rectifying process taken its end, as regards you, knowing as you do the greatness of the infallible prophecy, without which it is impossible for any one to receive that which is supremely profitable. For of many and diverse blessings which are in the things which are or which may be, the most blessed of all—whether it be eternal life, or perpetual health, or a perfect understanding, or light, or joy, or immortality, or whatever else there is or that can be supremely good in the nature of things — cannot be possessed without first knowing things as they are; and this knowledge cannot be otherwise obtained than by first becoming acquainted with the Prophet of the truth.

CHAP. VI. — THE TRUE PROPHET.

"Now the Prophet of the truth is He who always knows all things — things past as they were, things present as they are, things future as they shall be; sinless, merciful, alone entrusted with the declaration of the truth. Read, and you shall find that those *were deceived*[4] who thought that they had found the truth of themselves. For this is peculiar to the Prophet, to declare the truth, even as it is peculiar to the sun to bring the day. Wherefore, as many as have even desired to know the truth, but have not had the good fortune to learn it from Him, have not

---

[1] [With but two exceptions, these names, or their equivalents, occur in *Recognitions*, iii. 68, where importance is attached to the number twelve. Comp. also *Recognitions*, ii. 1. A comparison of these lists favours the theory of a common documentary basis. — R.]

[2] Literally, " to be boiled out of me."

[3] Eccles. iii. 1.

[4] "Were deceived" is not in the text, but the sense demands that some such expression should be supplied.

found it, but have died seeking it. For how can he find the truth who seeks it from his own ignorance? And even if he find it, he does not know it, and passes it by as if it were not. Nor yet shall he be able to obtain possession of the truth from another, who, in like manner, promises to him knowledge from ignorance; excepting only the knowledge of morality and things of that sort, which can be known through reason, which affords to every one the knowledge that he ought not to wrong another, through his not wishing *himself* to be wronged.

CHAP. VII. — UNAIDED QUEST OF TRUTH PROFITLESS.

"All therefore who ever sought the truth, trusting to themselves to be able to find it, fell into a snare. This is what both the philosophers of the Greeks, and the more intelligent of the barbarians, have suffered. For, applying themselves to things visible, they have given decisions by conjecture on things not apparent, thinking that that was truth which at any time presented itself to them *as such*. For, like persons who know the truth, they, still seeking the truth, reject some of the suppositions that are presented to them, and lay hold of others, as if they knew, while they do not know, what things are true and what are false. And they dogmatize concerning truth, even those who are seeking after truth, not knowing that he who seeks truth cannot learn it from his own wandering. For not even, as I said, can he recognise her when she stands by him, since he is unacquainted with her.

CHAP. VIII. — TEST OF TRUTH.

"And it is by no means that which is true, but that which is pleasing, which persuades every one who seeks to learn from himself. Since, therefore, one thing is pleasing to one, and another to another, one thing prevails over one as truth, and another thing over another. But the truth is that which is approved by the Prophet, not that which is pleasant to each individual. For that which is one would be many, if the pleasing were the true; which is impossible. Wherefore also the Grecian philologers — rather than philosophers [1] — going about matters by conjectures, have dogmatized much and diversely, thinking that the apt sequence of hypotheses is truth, not knowing that when they have assigned to themselves false beginnings, their conclusion has corresponded with the beginning.

CHAP. IX. — "THE WEAK THINGS OF THE WORLD."

"Whence a man ought to pass by all else, and commit himself to the Prophet of the truth alone.

[1] φιλόλογοι, οὐ φιλόσοφοι, "lovers of words, not lovers of wisdom."

And we are all able to judge of Him, whether he is a prophet, even although we be wholly unlearned, and novices in sophisms, and unskilled in geometry, and uninitiated in music. For God, as caring for all, has made the discovery concerning Himself easier to all, in order that neither the barbarians might be powerless, nor the Greeks unable to find Him. Therefore the discovery concerning Him is easy; and thus it is:—

CHAP. X. — TEST OF THE PROPHET.

"If he is a Prophet, and is able to know how the world was made, and the things that are in it, and the things that shall be to the end, if He has foretold us anything, and we have ascertained that it has been perfectly accomplished, we easily believe that the things shall be which *He says* are to be, from the things that have been already; we believe Him, I say, as not only knowing, but foreknowing. To whom then, however limited an understanding he may have, does it not appear, that it behoves us, with respect to the things that are pleasing to God, to believe beyond all others Him who beyond all men knows, even though He has not learned? Wherefore, if any one should be unwilling to concede the power of knowing the truth to such an one — I mean to Him who has foreknowledge through the divinity of the Spirit that is in Him — conceding the power of knowing to any one else, is he not void of understanding, in conceding to him who is no prophet, that power of knowing which he would not concede to the Prophet?

CHAP. XI. — IGNORANCE, KNOWLEDGE, FOREKNOWLEDGE.

"Wherefore, before all things, we must test the Prophet with all judgment by means of the prophetic promise; and having ascertained Him to be the Prophet, we must undoubtingly follow the other words of His teaching; and having confidence concerning things hoped for, we must conduct ourselves according to the first judgment, knowing that He who tells us these things has not a nature to lie. Wherefore, if any of the things that are afterwards spoken by Him do not appear to us to be well spoken, we must know that it is not that it has been spoken amiss, but that it is that we have not conceived it aright. For ignorance does not judge knowledge, and so neither is knowledge competent truly to judge foreknowledge; but foreknowledge affords knowledge to the ignorant.

CHAP. XII. — DOCTRINE OF THE TRUE PROPHET.

"Hence, O beloved Clement, if you would know the things pertaining to God, you have to learn them from Him alone, because He alone knows the truth. For if any one else knows anything, he has received it from Him or from His disciples. And this is His doctrine and true proclamation, that there is one God, whose work the world is; who being altogether righteous, shall certainly at some time render to every one according to his deeds.

CHAP. XIII. — FUTURE REWARDS AND PUNISHMENTS.

"For there is every necessity, that he who says that God is by His nature righteous, should believe also that the souls of men are immortal: for where would be His justice, when some, having lived piously, have been evil-treated, and sometimes violently cut off, while others who have been wholly impious, and have indulged in luxurious living, have died the common death of men? Since therefore, without all contradiction, God who is good is also just, He shall not otherwise be known to be just, unless the soul after its separation from the body be immortal, so that the wicked man, being in hell,[1] as having here received his good things, may there be punished for his sins; and the good man, who has been punished here for his sins, may then, as in the bosom of the righteous, be constituted an heir of good things. Since therefore God is righteous, it is fully evident to us that there is a judgment, and that souls are immortal.

CHAP. XIV. — RIGHTEOUSNESS AND UNRIGHTEOUSNESS.

"But if any one, according to the opinion of this Simon the Samaritan, will not admit that God is just, to whom then can any one ascribe justice, or the possibility of it? For if the Root of all have it not, there is every necessity to think that it must be impossible to find it in human nature, which is, as it were, the fruit. And if it is to be found in man, how much more in God! But if righteousness can be found nowhere, neither in God nor in man, then neither can unrighteousness. But there is such a thing as righteousness, for unrighteousness takes its name from the existence of righteousness; for it is called unrighteousness, when righteousness is compared with it, and is found to be opposite to it.

CHAP. XV. — PAIRS.

"Hence therefore God, teaching men with respect to the truth of existing things, being Himself one, has distinguished all principles into pairs and opposites,[2] Himself being one and sole God from the beginning, having made heaven and earth, day and night, light and fire, sun and moon, life and death. But man alone amongst these He made self-controlling, having

a fitness to be either righteous or unrighteous. To him also he hath varied the figures of combinations, placing before him small things first, and great ones afterwards, such as the world and eternity. But the world that now is, is temporary; that which shall be, is eternal. First is ignorance, then knowledge. So also has He arranged the leaders of prophecy. For, since the present world is female, as a mother bringing forth the souls of her children, but the world to come is male, as a father receiving his children *from their mother*, therefore in this world there come a succession of prophets, as being sons of the world to come, and having knowledge of men. And if pious men had understood this mystery, they would never have gone astray, but even now they should have known that Simon, who now enthralls all men, is a fellow-worker of error and deceit. Now, the doctrine of the prophetic rule is as follows.

CHAP. XVI. — MAN'S WAYS OPPOSITE TO GOD'S.

"As in the beginning God, who is one, like a right hand and a left, made the heavens first and then the earth, so also He constituted all the combinations in order; but upon men He no more does this, but varies all the combinations. For whereas from Him the greater things come first, and the inferior second, we find the opposite in men — the first worse, and the second superior. Therefore from Adam, who was made after the image of God, there sprang first the unrighteous Cain, and then the righteous Abel. Again, from him who amongst you is called Deucalion,[3] two forms of spirits were sent forth, the impure namely, and the pure, first the black raven, and then the white dove. From Abraham also, the patriarchs of our nation, two firsts[4] sprang — Ishmael first, then Isaac, who was blessed of God. And from Isaac himself, in like manner, there were again two — Esau the profane, and Jacob the pious. So, first in birth, as the first born in the world, was the high priest *Aaron*, then the lawgiver *Moses*.

CHAP. XVII. — FIRST THE WORSE, THEN THE BETTER.

"In like manner, the combination with respect to Elias, which behoved to have come, has been willingly put off to another time, having determined to enjoy it conveniently hereafter.[5] Wherefore, also, he who was among those born of woman came first; then he who was among

---

[1] Lit. Hades.
[2] Literally, "twofoldly and oppositely." [On the doctrine of pairs compare chap. 33, iii. 23; *Recognitions*, iii. 61. — R.]

[3] Noah.
[4] For "first" Wieseler conjectures "different," — two different persons.
[5] In this sentence the text is probably corrupted. The general meaning seems to be, that he does not enter fully at present into the subject of Elias, or John the Baptist, the greatest of those born of woman, coming first, and Christ, the greatest among the sons of men, coming after, but that he will return to the subject on a fitting occasion.

the sons of men came second   It were possible, following this order, to perceive to what series Simon belongs, who came before me to the Gentiles, and to which I belong who have come after him, and have come in upon him as light upon darkness, as knowledge upon ignorance, as healing upon disease.   And thus, as the true Prophet has told us, a false prophet must first come from some deceiver; and then, in like manner, after the removal of the holy place, the true Gospel must be secretly sent abroad for the rectification of the heresies that shall be.   After this, also, towards the end, Antichrist must first come, and then our Jesus must be revealed to be indeed the Christ; and after this, the eternal light having sprung up, all the things of darkness must disappear.

CHAP. XVIII. — MISTAKE ABOUT SIMON MAGUS.

"Since, then, as I said, some men do not know the rule of combination, thence they do not know who is my precursor Simon.   For if he were known, he would not be believed; but now, not being known, he is improperly believed; and though his deeds are those of a hater, he is loved; and though an enemy, he is received as a friend; and though he be death, he is desired as a saviour; and though fire, he is esteemed as light; and though a deceiver, he is believed as a speaker of truth."

Then I Clement, when I heard this, said, "Who then, I pray you, is this who is such a deceiver? I should like to be informed."   Then said Peter: "If you wish to learn, it is in your power to know it from those from whom I also got accurate information on all points respecting him.

CHAP. XIX. — JUSTA, A PROSELYTE.

"There is amongst us one Justa, a Syro-Phœnician, by race a Canaanite, whose daughter was oppressed with a grievous disease.[1]   And she came to our Lord, crying out, and entreating that He would heal her daughter.   But He, being asked also by us, said, 'It is not lawful to heal the Gentiles, who are like to dogs on account of their using various[2] meats and practices, while the table in the kingdom has been given to the sons of Israel.'   But she, hearing this, and begging to partake like a dog of the crumbs that fall from this table, having changed what she was,[3] by living like the sons of the kingdom, she obtained healing for her daughter, as she asked.   For she being a Gentile, and remaining in the same course of life, He would

not have healed had she remained a Gentile, on account of its not being lawful to heal her as a Gentile.[4]

CHAP. XX. — DIVORCED FOR THE FAITH.

"She, therefore, having taken up a manner of life according to the law, was, with the daughter who had been healed, driven out from her home by her husband, whose sentiments were opposed to ours.   But she, being faithful to her engagements, and being in affluent circumstances, remained a widow herself, but gave her daughter in marriage to a certain man who was attached to the true faith, and who was poor.   And, abstaining from marriage for the sake of her daughter, she bought two boys and educated them, and had them in place of sons.   And they being educated from their boyhood with Simon Magus, have learned all things concerning him.   For such was their friendship, that they were associated with him in all things in which he wished to unite with them.

CHAP. XXI. — JUSTA'S ADOPTED SONS, ASSOCIATES WITH SIMON.

"These men having fallen in with Zacchæus, who sojourned here, and having received the word of truth from him, and having repented of their former innovations, and immediately denouncing Simon as being privy with him in all things, as soon as I came to sojourn here, they came to me with their foster-mother, being presented to me by him, *Zacchæus*, and ever since they continue with me, enjoying instructions in the truth."   When Peter had said this, he sent for them, and charged them that they should accurately relate to me all things concerning Simon.   And they, having called God to witness that in nothing they would falsify, proceeded with the relation.

CHAP. XXII. — DOCTRINES OF SIMON.

First Aquila began to speak in this wise: "Listen, O dearest brother, that you may know accurately everything about this man, whose he is, and what, and whence; and what the things are which he does, and how and why he does them.[5] This Simon is the son of Antonius and Rachel, a Samaritan by race, of the village of Gitthæ, which is six schoeni distant from the city.   He having disciplined himself greatly in Alexandria,[6] and being very powerful in magic, and being ambitious, wishes to be accounted a certain supreme power, greater even than the God who created the world.   And sometimes intimating

---

[1] [Chaps. 19–21 are peculiar to the *Homilies*, though in the *Recognitions*, vii. 32, Justa is named as having purchased and educated Niceta and Aquila. — R.]

[2] For διαφόροις Duncker proposes ἀδιαφόροις, "meats without distinction."

[3] That is, having ceased to be a Gentile, by abstaining from forbidden foods.

[4] There are several various readings in this sentence, and none of them can be strictly construed; but the general sense is obvious.

[5] [For the parallel account of Simon, given also by Aquila, see *Recognitions*, ii. 7–15. — R.]

[6] The Vatican MS. adds, "which is in Egypt (or, on the Nile), in Greek culture."

that he is Christ, he styles himself the Standing One.[1] And this epithet he employs, as intimating that he shall always stand, and as not having any cause of corruption so that his body should fall. And he neither says that the God who created the world is the Supreme, nor does he believe that the dead will be raised. He rejects Jerusalem, and substitutes Mount Gerizzim for it. Instead of our Christ, he proclaims himself. The things of the law he explains by his own presumption; and he says, indeed, that there is to be a judgment, but he does not expect it. For if he were persuaded that he shall be judged by God, he would not dare be impious towards God Himself. Whence some not knowing that, using religion as a cloak, he spoils the things of the truth, and faithfully believing the hope and the judgment which in some way he says are to be, are ruined.

CHAP. XXIII. — SIMON A DISCIPLE OF THE BAPTIST.

"But that he came to deal with the doctrines of religion happened on this wise. There was one John, a day-baptist,[2] who was also, according to the method of combination, the forerunner of our Lord Jesus; and as the Lord had twelve apostles, bearing the number of the twelve months of the sun, so also he, *John*, had thirty chief men, fulfilling the monthly reckoning of the moon, in which number was a certain woman called Helena,[3] that not even this might be without a dispensational significance. For a woman, being half a man, made up the imperfect number of the triacontad; as also in the case of the moon, whose revolution does not make the complete course of the month.[4] But of these thirty, the first and the most esteemed by John was Simon; and the reason of his not being chief after the death of John was as follows : —

CHAP. XXIV. — ELECTIONEERING STRATAGEMS.

"He being absent in Egypt for the practice of magic, and John being killed, Dositheus desiring the leadership,[5] falsely gave out that Simon was dead, and succeeded to the seat. But Simon, returning not long after, and strenuously holding by the place as his own, when he met with Dositheus did not demand the place, knowing that a man who has attained power beyond his expectations cannot be removed from it. Wherefore with pretended friendship he gives himself for a while to the second place, under Dositheus. But taking his place after a few days among the thirty fellow-disciples, he began to malign Dositheus as not delivering the instructions correctly. And this he said that he did, not through unwillingness to deliver them correctly, but through ignorance. And on one occasion, Dositheus, perceiving that this artful accusation of Simon was dissipating the opinion of him with respect to many, so that they did not think that he was the Standing One, came in a rage to the usual place of meeting, and finding Simon, struck him with a staff. But it seemed to pass through the body of Simon as if he had been smoke. Thereupon Dositheus, being confounded, said to him, 'If you are the Standing One, I also will worship you.' Then Simon said that he was; and Dositheus, knowing that he himself was not the Standing One, fell down and worshipped; and associating himself with the twenty-nine chiefs, he raised Simon to his own place of repute; and thus, not many days after, Dositheus himself, while he (Simon) stood, fell down and died.

CHAP. XXV. — SIMON'S DECEIT.

"But Simon is going about in company with Helena, and even till now, as you see, is stirring up the people. And he says that he has brought down this Helena from the highest heavens to the world; being queen, as the all-bearing being, and wisdom, for whose sake, says he, the Greeks and barbarians fought, having before their eyes but an image of truth ;[6] for she, who really is the truth, was then with the chiefest god. Moreover, by cunningly explaining certain things of this sort, made up from Grecian myths, he deceives many ; especially as he performs many signal marvels, so that if we did not know that he does these things by magic, we ourselves should also have been deceived. But whereas we were his fellow-labourers at the first, so long as he did such things without doing wrong to the interests of religion ; now that he has madly begun to attempt to deceive those who are religious, we have withdrawn from him.

CHAP. XXVI. — HIS WICKEDNESS.

"For he even began to commit murder,[7] as himself disclosed to us, as a friend to friends, that, having separated the soul of a child from its own body by horrid incantations, as his assistant for the exhibition of anything that he pleased, and having drawn the likeness of the boy, he has it set up in the inner room where he sleeps, saying that he once formed the boy of air, by divine arts, and having painted his likeness, he gave him back again to the air. And

---

[1] [Comp. *Recognitions*, i. 72. — R.]
[2] A day-baptist is taken to mean "one who baptizes every day."
[3] [Called "Luna" in the *Recognitions*. — R.]
[4] [Peculiar, in this detailed form, to the *Homilies*. — R.]
[5] [Compare the varied account in *Recognitions*, ii. 8. — R.]

[6] We have here an allusion to the tradition that it was only an image of Helen that was taken to Troy, and not the real Helen herself.
[7] [With the account of Simon's doings in chaps. 26–32 compare *Recognitions*, ii. 9, 10, 13–15; iii. 47. — R.]

he explains that he did the deed thus. He says that the first soul of man, being turned into the nature of heat, drew to itself, and sucked in the surrounding air, after the fashion of a gourd;[1] and then that he changed it into water, when it was within the form of the spirit; and he said that he changed into the nature of blood the air that was in it, which could not be poured out on account of the consistency of the spirit, and that he made the blood solidified into flesh; then, the flesh being thus consolidated, that he exhibited a man not *made* from earth, but from air. And thus, having persuaded himself that he was able to make a new *sort of* man, he said that he reversed the changes, and again restored him to the air. And when he told this to others, he was believed; but by us who were present at his ceremonies he was religiously disbelieved. Wherefore we denounced his impieties, and withdrew from him."

CHAP. XXVII. — HIS PROMISES.

When Aquila had thus spoken, his brother Nicetas said: "It is necessary, O Clement our brother, for me to mention what has been left out by Aquila. For, in the first place, God is witness that we assisted him in no impious work, but that we looked on while he wrought; and as long as he did harmless things, and exhibited them, we were also pleased. But when, in order to deceive the godly, he said that he did, by means of godhead, the things that were done by magic, we no longer endured him, though he made us many promises, especially that our statues should be thought worthy of *a place in* the temple,[2] and that we should be thought to be gods, and should be worshipped by the multitude, and should be honoured by kings, and should be thought worthy of public honours, and enriched with boundless wealth.

CHAP. XXVIII. — FRUITLESS COUNSEL.

" These things, and things reckoned greater than these, he promised us, on condition only that we should associate with him, and keep silence as to the wickedness of his undertaking, so that the scheme of his deceit might succeed. But still we would not consent, but even counselled him to desist from such madness, saying to him: 'We, O Simon, remembering our friendship towards you from our childhood, and out of affection for you, give you good counsel. Desist from this attempt. You cannot be a God. Fear Him who is really God. Know that you are a man, and that the time of your life is short; and though you should get great riches, or even

become a king, few things accrue to the short time of your life for enjoyment, and things wickedly gotten soon flee away, and procure everlasting punishment for the adventurer. Wherefore we counsel you to fear God, by whom the soul of every one must be judged for the deeds that he hath done here.'

CHAP. XXIX. — IMMORTALITY OF THE SOUL.

" When he heard this he laughed; and when we asked him why he laughed at us for giving him good counsel, he answered: 'I laugh at your foolish supposition, because you believe that the soul of man is immortal.' Then I said: 'We do not wonder, O Simon, at your attempting to deceive us, but we are confounded at the way in which you deceive even yourself. Tell me, O Simon, even if no one else has been fully convinced that the soul is immortal, at all events you and we *ought to be so:* you as having separated one from a human body, and conversed with it, and laid your commands upon it; and we as having been present, and heard your commands, and clearly witnessed *the performance of* what was ordered.' Then said Simon: 'I know what you mean; but you know nothing of the matters concerning which you reason.' Then said Nicetas: 'If you know, speak; but if you do not know, do not suppose that we can be deceived by your saying that you know, and that we do not. For we are not so childish, that you can sow in us a shrewd suspicion that we should think that you know some unutterable things, and so that you should take and hold us in subjection, by holding us in restraint through means of desire.'

CHAP. XXX. — AN ARGUMENT.

" Then Simon said: 'I am aware that you know that I separated a soul from a human body; but I know that you are ignorant that it is not the soul of the dead person that ministers to me, for it does not exist; but a certain demon works, pretending to be the soul.' Then said Nicetas: 'Many incredible things we have heard in our lifetime, but aught more senseless than this speech we do not expect ever to hear. For if a demon pretends to be the soul of the dead person, what is the use of the soul at all, that it should be separated from the body? Were not we ourselves present, and heard you conjuring the soul from the body? And how comes it that, when one is conjured, another who is not conjured obeys, as if it were frightened? And you yourself, when at any time we have asked you why the conferences sometimes cease, did not you say that the soul, having fulfilled the time upon earth which it was to have passed in the body, goes to Hades? And you added, that

---

[1] Which was used by the ancients as cupping-glasses are now used.

[2] The Vatican MS. and *Epitome* read, " that a shrine and statues should be erected in honour of us."

the souls of those who commit suicide are not easily permitted to come, because, having gone home into Hades, they are guarded.'"

CHAP. XXXI. — A DILEMMA.

Nicetas having thus spoken, Aquila himself in turn said : "This only should I wish to learn of you, Simon, whether it is the soul or whether it is a demon that is conjured : what is it afraid of, that it does not despise the conjuration? Then Simon said : 'It knows that it should suffer punishment if it were disobedient.' Then said Aquila : 'Therefore, if the soul comes when conjured, there is also a judgment. If, therefore, souls are immortal, assuredly there is also a judgment. As you say, then, that those which are conjured on wicked business are punished if they disobey, how are you not afraid to compel them, when those that are compelled are punished for disobedience? For it is not wonderful that you do not already suffer for your doings, seeing the judgment has not yet come, when you are to suffer the penalty of those deeds which you have compelled others to do, and when that which has been done under compulsion shall be pardoned, as having been out of respect for the oath which led to the evil action.'[1] And he hearing this was enraged, and threatened death to us if we did not keep silence as to his doings."

CHAP. XXXII. — SIMON'S PRODIGIES.

Aquila having thus spoken, I Clement inquired : "What, then, are the prodigies that he works?" And they told me that he makes statues walk, and that he rolls himself on the fire, and is not burnt; and sometimes he flies; and he makes loaves of stones; he becomes a serpent; he transforms himself into a goat; he becomes two-faced; he changes himself into gold; he opens lockfast gates; he melts iron; at banquets he produces images of all manner of forms. In his house he makes dishes be seen as borne of themselves to wait upon him, no bearers being seen. I wondered when I heard them speak thus; but many bore witness that they had been present, and had seen such things.

CHAP. XXXIII. — DOCTRINE OF PAIRS.

These things having been thus spoken, the excellent Peter himself also proceeded to speak :[2] "You must perceive, brethren, the truth of the rule of conjunction, from which he who departs not cannot be misled. For since, as we have said, we see all things in pairs and contraries, and as the night is first, and then the day; and

first ignorance, then knowledge; first disease, then healing, so the things of error come first into our life, then truth supervenes, as the physician upon the disease. Therefore straightway, when our God-loved nation was about to be ransomed from the oppression of the Egyptians, first diseases were produced by means of the rod turned into a serpent, which was given to Aaron, and then remedies were superinduced by the prayers of Moses. And now also, when the Gentiles are about to be ransomed from the superstition with respect to idols, wickedness, which reigns over them, has by anticipation sent forth her ally like another serpent, even this Simon whom you see, who works wonders to astonish and deceive, not signs of healing to convert and save. Wherefore it behoves you also from the miracles that are done to judge the doers, what is the character of the performer, and what that of the deed. If he do unprofitable miracles, he is the agent of wickedness; but if he do profitable things, he is a leader of goodness.

CHAP. XXXIV. — USELESS AND PHILANTHROPIC MIRACLES.

"Those, then, are useless signs, which you say that Simon did. But I say that the making statues walk, and rolling himself on burning coals, and becoming a dragon, and being changed into a goat, and flying in the air, and all such things, not being for the healing of man, are of a nature to deceive many. But the miracles of compassionate truth are philanthropic, such as you have heard that the Lord did, and that I after Him accomplish by my prayers; at which most of you have been present, some being freed from all kinds of diseases, and some from demons, some having their hands restored, and some their feet, some recovering their eyesight, and some their hearing, and whatever else a man can do, being of a philanthropic spirit."

CHAP. XXXV. — DISCUSSION POSTPONED.

When Peter had thus spoken, towards dawn Zacchæus entered and saluted us, and said to Peter : "Simon puts off the inquiry till to-morrow; for to-day is his Sabbath, which occurs at intervals of eleven days." To him Peter answered : "Say to Simon, Whenever thou wishest; and know thou that we are always in readiness to meet thee, by divine providence, when thou desirest." And Zacchæus hearing this, went out to return the answer.

CHAP. XXXVI. — ALL FOR THE BEST.

But he (Peter) saw me disheartened, and asked the reason; and being told that it proceeded from no cause but the postponement of

---

[1] The Latin translates: "as having preferred the oath to the evil action."

[2] [Chaps. 33, 34, find a parallel in *Recognitions*, iii. 59, 60, at the close of the discussion with Simon. — R.]

the inquiry,[1] he said : "He who has apprehended that the world is regulated by the good providence of God, O beloved Clement, is not vexed by things howsoever occurring, considering that things take their course advantageously under the providence of the Ruler. Whence, knowing that He is just, and living with a good conscience, he knows how by right reason to shake off from his soul any annoyance that befalls him, because, when complete, it must come to some unknown good. Now then, let not Simon the magician's postponement of the inquiry grieve you ; for perhaps it has happened from the providence of God for your profit. Wherefore I shall not scruple to speak to you as being my special friend.

CHAP. XXXVII. — SPIES IN THE ENEMY'S CAMP.

"Some[2] of our people attend feignedly upon Simon as companions, as if they were persuaded by his most atheistic error, in order that they may learn his purpose and disclose it to us, so that we may be able to encounter this terrible man on favourable terms. And now I have learned from them what arguments he is going to employ in the discussion. And knowing this, I give thanks to God on the one hand, and I congratulate you on the other, on the postponement of the discussion ; for you, being instructed by me before the discussion, of the arguments that are to be used by him for the destruction of the ignorant, will be able to listen without danger of falling.

CHAP. XXXVIII. — CORRUPTION OF THE LAW.

"For the Scriptures have had joined to them many falsehoods against God on this account. The prophet Moses having by the order of God delivered the law, with the explanations, to certain chosen men, some seventy in number, in order that they also might instruct such of the people as chose, after a little the written law had added to it certain falsehoods contrary to the law of God,[3] who made the heaven and the earth, and all things in them ; the wicked one having dared to work this for some righteous purpose. And this took place in reason and judgment, that those might be convicted who should dare to listen to the things written against God, and those who, through love towards Him, should not only disbelieve the things spoken against Him, but should not even endure to hear them at all, even if they should happen to be true, judging it much safer to incur danger with respect to religious faith, than to live

with an evil conscience on account of blasphemous words.

CHAP. XXXIX. — TACTICS.

" Simon, therefore, as I learn, intends to come into public, and to speak of those chapters against God that are added to the Scriptures, for the sake of temptation, that he may seduce as many wretched ones as he can from the love of God. For we do not wish to say in public that these chapters are added to the Bible, since we should thereby perplex the unlearned multitudes, and so accomplish the purpose of this wicked Simon. For they not having yet the power of discerning, would flee from us as impious ; or, as if not only the blasphemous chapters were false, they would even withdraw from the word. Wherefore we are under a necessity of assenting to the false chapters, and putting questions in return to him concerning them, to draw him into a strait, and to give in private an explanation of the chapters that are spoken against God to the well-disposed after a trial of their faith ; and of this there is but one way, and that a brief one. It is this.[4]

CHAP. XL. — PRELIMINARY INSTRUCTION.

" Everything that is spoken or written against God is false. But that we say this truly, not only for the sake of reputation, but for the sake of truth, I shall convince you when my discourse has proceeded a little further. Whence you, my most beloved Clement, ought not to be sorry at Simon's having interposed a day between this and the discussion. For to-day, before the discussion, you shall be instructed concerning chapters added to the Scriptures ; and then in the discussion concerning the only one and good God, the Maker also of the world, you ought not to be distracted. But in the discussion you will even wonder how impious men, overlooking the multitudes of things that are spoken in the Scriptures for God, and looking at those that are spoken against Him, gladly bring these forward ; and thus the hearers, by reason of ignorance, believing the things against God, become outcasts from His kingdom. Wherefore you, by advantage of the postponement, learning the mystery of the Scriptures, and gaining the *means of* not sinning against God, will incomparably rejoice."

CHAP. XLI. — ASKING FOR INFORMATION, NOT CONTRADICTION.

Then I Clement, hearing this, said : " Truly I rejoice, and I give thanks to God, who in all things doeth well. However, he knows that I shall be able to think nothing other than that all

---

[1] [Comp. *Recognitions*, i. 21. — R.]
[2] [From chap. 27 to iii. 28 the matter is peculiar to the *Homilies*. The views stated are obviously coloured by the Gnostic Ebionism of the author. — R.]
[3] The Vatican MS. reads: " against the only God."

[4] [This view of the Scriptures, as held by Peter, is one of the marked characteristics of the *Homilies*. — R.]

things are for God. Wherefore do not suppose that I ask questions, as doubting the words concerning God,[1] or those that are to be spoken, but rather that I may learn, and so be able myself to instruct another who is ingenuously willing to learn. Wherefore tell me what are the falsehoods added to the Scriptures, and how it comes that they are really false." Then Peter answered : " Even although you had not asked me, I should have gone on in order, and afforded you the exposition of these matters, as I promised. Learn, then, how the Scriptures misrepresent Him in many respects, that you may know when you happen upon them.

CHAP. XLII. — RIGHT NOTIONS OF GOD ESSENTIAL TO HOLINESS.

" But what I am going to tell you will be sufficient by way of example. But I do not think, my dear Clement, that any one who possesses ever so little love to God and ingenuousness, will be able to take in, or even to hear, the things that are spoken against Him. For how is it that he can have a monarchic[2] soul, and be holy, who supposes that there are many gods, and not one only? But even if there be but one, who will cherish zeal to be holy, that finds in Him many defects, since he will hope that the Beginning of all things, by reason of the defects of his own nature, will not visit the crimes of others?

CHAP. XLIII. — A PRIORI ARGUMENT ON THE DIVINE ATTRIBUTES.

" Wherefore, far be it from us to believe that the Lord of all, who made the heaven and the earth, and all things that are in them, shares His government with others, or that He lies. For if He lies, then who speaks truth? Or that He makes experiments as in ignorance ; for then who foreknows? And if He deliberates, and changes His purpose, who is perfect in understanding and permanent in design? If He envies, who is above rivalry? If He hardens hearts, who makes wise? If He makes blind and deaf, who has given sight and hearing? If He commits pilfering, who administers justice? If He mocks, who is sincere? If He is weak, who is omnipotent? If He is unjust, who is just? If He makes evil things, who shall make good things? If He does evil, who shall do good?

CHAP. XLIV. — THE SAME CONTINUED.

" But if He desires the fruitful hill,[3] whose then are all things? If He is false, who then is

true? If He dwells in a tabernacle, who is without bounds? If He is fond of fat, and sacrifices, and offerings, and drink-offerings, who then is without need, and who is holy, and pure, and perfect? If He is pleased with candles and candlesticks, who then placed the luminaries in heaven? If He dwells in shadow, and darkness, and storm, and smoke, who is the light that lightens the universe? If He comes with trumpets, and shoutings, and darts, and arrows, who is the looked-for tranquillity of all? If He loves war, who then wishes peace? If He makes evil things, who makes good things? If He is without affection, who is a lover of men? If He is not faithful to His promises, who shall be trusted? If He loves the wicked, and adulterers, and murderers, who shall be a just judge? If He changes His mind, who is stedfast? If He chooses evil men, who then takes the part of the good?

CHAP. XLV. — HOW GOD IS TO BE THOUGHT OF.

" Wherefore, Clement, my son, beware of thinking otherwise of God, than that He is the only God, and Lord, and Father, good and righteous, the Creator, long-suffering, merciful, the sustainer, the benefactor, ordaining love of men, counselling purity, immortal and making immortal, incomparable, dwelling in the souls of the good, that cannot be contained and yet is contained,[4] who has fixed the great world as a centre in space, who has spread out the heavens and solidified the earth, who has stored up the water, who has disposed the stars in the sky, who has made the fountains flow in the earth, has produced fruits, has raised up mountains, hath set bounds to the sea, has ordered winds and blasts, who by the spirit of counsel has kept safely the body comprehended in a boundless sea.

CHAP. XLVI. — JUDGMENT TO COME.

" This is our Judge, to whom it behoves us to look, and to regulate our own souls, thinking all things in His favour, speaking well of Him, persuaded that by His long-suffering He brings to light the obstinacy of all, and is alone good. And He, at the end of all, shall sit as a just Judge upon every one of those who have attempted what they ought not."

CHAP. XLVII. — A PERTINENT QUESTION.

When I Clement heard this, I said, " Truly, this is a godliness ; truly this is piety." And again I said : " I would learn, therefore, why the Bible has written anything of this sort? For I remember that you said that it was for the con-

---

[1] The text has ὑπό, " by," which has been altered into ὑπέρ. Davis would read σου, " by you."

[2] Cotelerius doubts whether this expression means a soul ruling over his body, or a soul disposed to favour monarchical rule. The former explanation seems to us more probable.

[3] Wieseler considers this corrupt, and amends : " if He desires more."

[4] The Latin has here, " imperceptus et perceptus ; " but Wieseler points out that χωρούμενος has reference to God's dwelling in the souls of the good, and thus He is contained by them.

viction of those who should dare to believe anything that was spoken against God. But since you permit us, we venture to ask, at your command: If any one, most beloved Peter, should choose to say to us, 'The Scriptures are true, although to you the things spoken against God seem to be false,' how should we answer him?"

CHAP. XLVIII.— A PARTICULAR CASE.

Then Peter answered: "You speak well in your inquiry; for it will be for your safety. Therefore listen: Since there are many things that are spoken by the Scriptures against God, as time presses on account of the evening, ask with respect to any one matter that you please, and I will explain it, showing that it is false, not only because it is spoken against God, but because it is really false." Then I answered: "I wish to learn how, when the Scriptures say that God is ignorant, you can show that He knows?"

CHAP. XLIX.— REDUCTIO AD ABSURDUM.

Then Peter answered: "You have presented us with a matter that can easily be answered. However, listen, how God is ignorant of nothing, but even foreknows. But first answer me what I ask of you. He who wrote the Bible, and told how the world was made, and said that God does not foreknow, was he a man or not?" Then I said: "He was a man." Then Peter answered: "How, then, was it possible for him, being a man, to know assuredly how the world was made, and that God does not foreknow?"

CHAP. L.— A SATISFACTORY ANSWER.

Then I, already perceiving the explanation, smiled, and said that he was a prophet. And Peter said: "If, then, he was a prophet, being a man, he was ignorant of nothing, by reason of his having received foreknowledge from God; how then, should He, who gave to man the gift of foreknowledge, being God, Himself be ignorant?" And I said: "You have spoken rightly." Then Peter said: "Come with me one step further. It being acknowledged by us that God foreknows all things, there is every necessity that the scriptures are false which say that He is ignorant, and those are true which say that He knows." Then said I: "It must needs be so."

CHAP. LI.— WEIGH IN THE BALANCE.

Then Peter said: "If, therefore, some of the Scriptures are true and some false, with good reason said our Master, 'Be ye good money-changers,' [1] inasmuch as in the Scriptures there are some true sayings and some spurious. And to those who err by reason of the false scriptures He fitly showed the cause of their error, saying, 'Ye do therefore err, not knowing the true things of the Scriptures; [2] for this reason ye are ignorant also of the power of God.'" Then said I: "*You have spoken* very excellently."

CHAP. LII.— SINS OF THE SAINTS DENIED.

Then Peter answered: "Assuredly, with good reason, I neither believe anything against God, nor against the just men recorded in the law, taking for granted that they are impious imaginations. For, as I am persuaded, neither was Adam a transgressor, who was fashioned by the hands of God; nor was Noah drunken, who was found righteous above all the world; [3] nor did Abraham live with three wives at once, who, on account of his sobriety, was thought worthy of a numerous posterity; nor did Jacob associate with four — of whom two were sisters — who was the father of the twelve tribes, and who intimated the coming of the presence of our Master; nor was Moses a murderer, nor did he learn to judge from an idolatrous priest — he who set forth the law of God to all the world, and for his right judgment has been testified to as a faithful steward.

CHAP. LIII.— CLOSE OF THE CONFERENCE.

"But of these and such like things I shall afford you an explanation in due time. But for the rest, since, as you see, the evening has come upon us, let what has been said be enough for to-day. But whenever you wish, and about whatever you wish, ask boldly of us, and we shall gladly explain it at once." Thus having spoken, he rose up. And then, having partaken of food, we turned to sleep, for the night had come upon us.

---

[1] This is quoted three times in the *Homilies* as a saying of our Lord, viz., here and in Homily III. chap. 50, and Homily XVIII. chap. 20. It is probably taken from one of the apocryphal Gospels. In Homily XVIII. chap. 20 the meaning is shown to be, that as it is the part of a money-changer to distinguish spurious coins from genuine, so it is the part of a Christian to distinguish false statements from true.

[2] A corruption of the texts, Matt. xxii. 29, Mark xii. 24.

[3] Gen. vii. 1.

HOMILY III.

CHAP. I. — THE MORNING OF THE DISCUSSION.

Two days, therefore, having elapsed, and while the third was dawning, I Clement, and the rest of our companions, being roused about the second cock-crowing, in order to the discussion with Simon, found the lamp still alight, and Peter kneeling in prayer. Therefore, having finished his supplication, and turning round, and seeing us in readiness to hear, he said : [1] —

CHAP. II. — SIMON'S DESIGN.

" I wish you to know that those who, according to our arrangement, associate with Simon that they may learn his intentions, and submit them to us, so that we may be able to cope with his variety of wickedness, these men have sent to me, and informed me that Simon to-day is, as he arranged, prepared to come before all, and show from the Scriptures that He who made the heaven and the earth, and all things in them, is not the Supreme God, but that there is another, unknown and supreme, as being in an unspeakable manner God of gods ; and that He sent two gods, one of whom is he who made the world, and the other he who gave the law. And these things he contrives to say, that he may dissipate the right faith of those who would worship the one and only God who made heaven and earth.

CHAP. III. — HIS OBJECT.

" When I heard this, how was I not disheartened ! Wherefore I wished you also, my brethren, who associate with me, to know that I am beyond measure grieved in my soul, seeing the wicked one awake for the temptation of men, and men wholly indifferent about their own salvation. For to those from amongst the Gentiles who were about being persuaded respecting the earthly images that they are no gods, he has contrived to bring in opinions of many other gods, in order that, if they cease from the polytheo-mania, they may be deceived to speak otherwise, and even worse *than they now do*, against the sole government of God, so that they may not yet value the truths connected with that monarchy, and may never be able to obtain mercy. And for the sake of this attempt Simon comes to do battle with us, armed with the false chapters of the Scriptures. And what is more dreadful, he is not afraid to dogmatize thus against the true God from the prophets whom he does not *in fact* believe.

[1] [The first twenty-eight chapters of this homily have no exact parallel in the *Recognitions ;* much of the matter is peculiar to this work. — R.]

CHAP. IV. — SNARES LAID FOR THE GENTILES.

" And with us, indeed, who have had handed down from our forefathers the worship of the God who made all things, and also the mystery of the books which are able to deceive, he will not prevail ; but with those from amongst the Gentiles who have the polytheistic fancy bred in them, and who know not the falsehoods of the Scriptures, he will prevail much. And not only he ; but if any other shall recount to those from among the Gentiles any vain, dreamlike, richly set out story against God, he will be believed, because from their childhood their minds are accustomed to take in things spoken against God. And few there shall be of them, as a few out of a multitude, who through ingenuousness shall not be willing so much as to hear an evil word against the God who made all things. And to these alone from amongst the Gentiles it shall be vouchsafed to be saved. Let not any one of you, therefore, altogether complain of Simon, or of any one else ; for nothing happens unjustly, since even the falsehoods of Scripture are with good reason presented for a test."

CHAP. V. — USE OF ERRORS.

Then I Clement, hearing this, said : " How say you, my lord, that even the falsehoods of the Scriptures are set forth happily for the proof of men ? " And he answered : " The falsehoods of the Scriptures have been permitted to be written for a certain righteous reason, at the demand of evil. And when I say happily, I mean this : In the account of God, the wicked one, not loving God less than the good one, is exceeded by the good in this one thing only, that he, not pardoning those who are impious on account of ignorance, through love towards that which is profound, desires the destruction of the impious ; but the good one desires to present them with a remedy. For the good one desires all to be healed by repentance, but saves those only who know God. But those who know Him not He does not heal : not that He does not wish to do so, but because it is not lawful to afford to those who, through want of judgment, are like to irrational animals, the good things which have been prepared for the children of the kingdom.

CHAP. VI. — PURGATORY AND HELL.

" Such is the nature of the one and only God, who made the world, and who created us, and who has given us all things, that as long as any one is within the limit of piety, and does not blaspheme His Holy Spirit, through His love towards him He brings the soul to Himself by reason of His love towards it. And although it be sinful, it is His nature to save it, after it has been suitably punished for the deeds it hath done. But if any one shall deny Him, or in any other way be guilty of impiety against Him, and then shall repent, he shall be punished indeed for the sins he hath committed against Him, but he shall be saved, because he turned and lived. And perhaps excessive piety and supplication shall even be delivered from punishment, ignorance being admitted as a reason for the pardon of sin after repentance.[1] But those who do not repent shall be destroyed by the punishment of fire, even though in all other things they are most holy. But, as I said, at an appointed time a fifth[2] part, being punished with eternal fire, shall be consumed. For they cannot endure for ever who have been impious against the one God.

CHAP. VII. — WHAT IS IMPIETY?

" But impiety against Him is, in the matter of religion, to die saying there is another God, whether superior or inferior, or in any way saying that there is one besides Him who really is. For He who truly is, is He whose form the body of man bears ; for whose sake the heaven and all the stars, though in their essence superior, submit to serve him who is in essence inferior, on account of the form of the Ruler. So much has God blessed man above all, in order that, loving the Benefactor in proportion to the multitude of His benefits, by means of this love he may be saved for the world to come.

CHAP. VIII. — WILES OF THE DEVIL.

" Therefore the love of men towards God is sufficient for salvation. And this the wicked one knows ; and while we are hastening to sow the love towards Him which makes immortal in the souls of those who from among the Gentiles are ready to believe in the one and only God, this wicked one, having sufficient armour against the ignorant for their destruction, hastens to sow the supposition of many gods, or at least of one greater, in order that men, conceiving and being persuaded of what is not wisdom, may die, as in the crime of adultery, and be cast out from His kingdom.

CHAP. IX. — UNCERTAINTY OF THE SCRIPTURES.

"Worthy, therefore, of rejection is every one who is willing so much as to hear anything against the monarchy of God ; but if any one dares to hear anything against God, as trusting in the Scriptures, let him first of all consider with me that

if any one, as he pleases, form a dogma agreeable to himself, and then carefully search the Scriptures, he will be able to produce many testimonies from them in favour of the dogma that he has formed. How, then, can confidence be placed in them against God, when what every man wishes is found in them ?

CHAP. X. — SIMON'S INTENTION.

"Therefore Simon, who is going to discuss in public with us to-morrow, is bold against the monarchy of God, wishing to produce many statements from these Scriptures, to the effect that there are many gods, and a certain one who is not He who made this world, but who is superior to Him ; and, at the same time, he is going to offer many scriptural proofs. But we also can easily show many passages from them that He who made the world alone is God, and that there is none other besides Him. But if any one shall wish to speak otherwise, he also shall be able to produce proofs from them at his pleasure. For the Scriptures say all manner of things, that no one of those who inquire ungratefully may find the truth, but *simply* what he wishes to find, the truth being reserved for the grateful ; now gratitude is to preserve our love to Him who is the cause of our being.

CHAP. XI. — DISTINCTION BETWEEN PREDICTION AND PROPHECY.

"Whence it must before all things be known, that nowhere can truth be found unless from a prophet of truth. But He is a true Prophet, who always knows all things, and even the thoughts of all men, who is without sin, as being convinced respecting the judgment of God. Wherefore we ought not simply to consider respecting His foreknowledge, but whether His foreknowledge can stand, apart from other cause. For physicians predict certain things, having the pulse of the patient as matter submitted to them ; and some predict by means of having fowls, and some by having sacrifices, and others by having many various matters submitted to them ; yet these are not prophets.

CHAP. XII. — THE SAME.

"But if any one should say that the foreknowledge *shown* by these predictions is like to that foreknowledge which is really implanted, he were much deceived. For he only declares such things as being present, and that if he speaks truth. However, even these things are serviceable to me, for they establish that there is such a thing as foreknowledge. But the foreknowledge of the one true Prophet does not only know things present, but stretches out prophecy without limit as far as the world to

---

[1] The text manifestly corrupt.
[2] Perhaps, rather, " the greater part."

come, and needs nothing for its interpretation, not prophesying darkly and ambiguously, so that the things spoken would need another prophet for the interpretation of them; but clearly and simply, as our Master and Prophet, by the inborn and ever-flowing Spirit, always knew all things.

CHAP. XIII. — PROPHETIC KNOWLEDGE CONSTANT.

"Wherefore He confidently made statements respecting things that are to be — I mean sufferings, places, limits. For, being a faultless Prophet, and looking upon all things with the boundless eye of His soul, He knows hidden things. But if we should hold, as many do, that even the true Prophet, not always, but sometimes, when He has the Spirit, and through it, foreknows, but when He has it not is ignorant, — if we should suppose thus, we should deceive ourselves and mislead others. For such a matter belongs to those who are madly inspired by the spirit of disorder — to those who are drunken beside the altars, and are gorged with fat.

CHAP. XIV. — PROPHETIC SPIRIT CONSTANT.

"For if it were permitted to any one who will profess prophecy to have it believed in the cases in which he was found false, that then he had not the Holy Spirit of foreknowledge, it will be difficult to convict him of being a false prophet; for among the many things that he speaks, a few come to pass, and then he is believed to have the Spirit, although he speaks the first things last, and the last first; speaks of past events as future, and future as already past; and also without sequence; or things borrowed from others and altered, and some that are lessened, unformed, foolish, ambiguous, unseemly, obscure, proclaiming all unconscientiousness.

CHAP. XV. — CHRIST'S PROPHECIES.

"But our Master did not prophesy after this fashion; but, as I have already said, being a prophet by an inborn and ever-flowing Spirit, and knowing all things at all times, He confidently set forth, plainly as I said before, sufferings, places, appointed times, manners, limits. Accordingly, therefore, prophesying concerning the temple, He said: 'See ye these buildings? Verily I say to you, There shall not be left here one stone upon another which shall not be taken away; and this generation shall not pass until the destruction begin. For they shall come, and shall sit here, and shall besiege it, and shall slay your children here.'[1] And in like manner He spoke in plain words the things that were straightway to happen, which we can now see with our eyes, in order that the accomplishment

might be among those to whom the word was spoken. For the Prophet of truth utters the word of proof in order to the faith of His hearers.

CHAP. XVI. — DOCTRINE OF CONJUNCTION.

"However, there are many proclaimers of error, having one chief, even the chief of wickedness, just as the Prophet of truth, being one, and being also the chief of piety, shall in His own times have as His prophets all who are found pure. But the chief cause of men being deceived is this, their not understanding beforehand the doctrine of conjunction, which I shall not fail to expound to you in private every day, summarily; for it were too long to speak in detail. Be you therefore to me truth-loving judges of the things that are spoken.

CHAP. XVII. — WHETHER ADAM HAD THE SPIRIT.

"But I shall begin the statement now. God having made all things, if any one will not allow to a man, fashioned by His hands, to have possessed His great and Holy Spirit of foreknowledge, how does not he greatly err who attributes it to another born of a spurious stock![2] And I do not think that he will obtain pardon, though he be misled by spurious scripture to think dreadful things against the Father of all. For he who insults the image and the things belonging to the eternal King, has the sin reckoned as committed against Him in whose likeness the image was made. But then, says he, the Divine Spirit left him when he sinned. In that case *the Spirit* sinned along with him; and how can he escape peril who says this? But perhaps he received the Spirit after he sinned. Then it is given to the unrighteous; and where is justice? But it was afforded to the just and the unjust. This were most unrighteous of all. Thus every falsehood, though it be aided by ten thousand reasonings, must receive its refutation, though after a long time.

CHAP. XVIII. — ADAM NOT IGNORANT.

"Be not deceived. Our father was ignorant of nothing; since, indeed, even the law publicly current, though charging him with the crime of ignorance for the sake of the unworthy, sends to him those desirous of knowledge, saying, 'Ask your father, and he will tell you; your elders, and they will declare to you.'[3] This father, these elders ought to be inquired of. But you have not inquired whose is the time of the kingdom, and whose is the seat of prophecy, though He Himself points out Himself, saying, 'The

---

[1] Matt. xxiv. 2, 34; Luke xix. 43, 44.

[2] [Here we find another view, suggesting the speculative opinions for which the author desires the indorsement of Peter. — R.]
[3] Deut. xxxii. 7.

scribes and the Pharisees sit in Moses' seat; all things whatsoever they say to you, hear them.'[1] Hear *them*, He said, as entrusted with the key of the kingdom, which is knowledge, which alone can open the gate of life, through which alone is the entrance to eternal life. But truly, He says, they possess the key, but those wishing to enter they do not suffer to do so.

CHAP. XIX. — REIGN OF CHRIST.

"On this account, I say, He Himself, rising from His seat as a father for his children, proclaiming the things which from the beginning were delivered in secret to the worthy, extending mercy even to the Gentiles, and compassionating the souls of all, neglected His own kindred. For He, being thought worthy to be King of the world to come, *fights against*[2] him who, by predestination, has usurped the kingdom that now is. And the thing which exceedingly grieved Him is this, that by those very persons for whom, as for sons, he did battle, He was assailed, on account of their ignorance. And yet He loved even those who hated Him, and wept over the unbelieving, and blessed those who slandered Him, and prayed for those who were in enmity against Him.[3] And not only did He do this as a father, but also taught His disciples to do the like, bearing themselves as · towards brethren.[4] This did our Father, this did our Prophet. This is reasonable, that He should be King over His children; that by the affection of a father towards his children, and the engrafted respect of children towards their father, eternal peace might be produced. For when the good man reigneth, there is true joy among those who are ruled over, on account of him who rules.

CHAP. XX. — CHRIST THE ONLY PROPHET HAS APPEARED IN DIFFERENT AGES.

"But give heed to my first discourse of the truth. If any one do not allow the man fashioned by the hands of God to have had the Holy Spirit of Christ, how is he not guilty of the greatest impiety in allowing another born of an impure stock to have it? But he would act most piously, if he should not allow to another to have it, but should say that he alone has it, who has changed his forms and his names from the beginning of the world, and so reappeared again and again in the world, until coming upon his own times, and being anointed with mercy for the works of God, he shall enjoy rest for ever. His honour it is to bear rule and lordship over all things, in air, earth, and waters.

But in addition to these, himself having made man, he had breath, the indescribable garment of the soul, that he might be able to be immortal.

CHAP. XXI. — THE EATING OF THE FORBIDDEN FRUIT DENIED.

"He himself being the only true prophet, fittingly gave names to each animal, according to the merits of its nature, as having made it. For if he gave a name to any one, that was also the name of that which was made, being given by him who made it.[5] How, then had he still need to partake of a tree, that he might know what is good and what is evil, if he was commanded not to eat of it? But this senseless men believe, who think that a reasonless beast was more powerful than the God who made these things.

CHAP. XXII. — MALE AND FEMALE.

"But a companion was created along with him, a female nature, much differing from him, as quality from substance, as the moon from the sun, as fire from light. She, as a female ruling the present world as her like,[6] was entrusted to be the first prophetess, announcing prophecy with all amongst those born of woman.[7] But the other, as the son of man, being a male, prophesies better things to the world to come as a male.

CHAP. XXIII. — TWO KINDS OF PROPHECY.

"Let us then understand that there are two kinds of prophecy:[8] the one male; and let it be defined that the first, being the male, has been ranked after the other in the order of advent; but the second, being female, has been appointed to come first in the advent of the pairs. This second, therefore, being amongst those born of woman, as the female superintendent of this present world, wishes to be thought masculine.[9] Wherefore, stealing the seeds of the male, and sowing them with her own seeds of the flesh, she brings forth the fruits — that is, words — as wholly her own. And she promises that she will give the present earthly riches as a dowry, wishing to change the slow for the swift, the small for the greater.

CHAP. XXIV. — THE PROPHETESS A MISLEADER.

"However, she, not only presuming to say and to hear that there are many gods, but also believing herself to be one, and in hope of being

---

[1] Matt. xxiii. 2, 3.
[2] From a conjectural reading by Neander.
[3] Matt. xxiii. 37; Luke xiii. 34; Luke xxiii. 34.
[4] Matt. v. 44.

[5] Gen. ii. 20.
[6] That is, the present world is female, and is under the rule of the female: the world to come is male, and is under the rule of the male.
[7] The allusion is to the fact that John the Baptist is called the greatest of those born of woman, while Christ is called the Son of man.
[8] Literally, "Let there be to us two genuine prophecies."
[9] [The doctrine of these chapters is tinged with Gnostic dualism; much of the matter might, according to tradition, have been equally well put in the mouth of Simon. — R.]

that which she had not a nature to be, and throwing away what she had, and as a female being in her courses at the offering of sacrifices, is stained with blood; and then she pollutes those who touch her. But when she conceives and brings forth temporary kings, she stirs up wars, shedding much blood; and those who desire to learn truth from her, by telling them all things contrary, and presenting many and various services, she keeps them always seeking and finding nothing, even until death. For from the beginning a cause of death lies upon blind men; for she, prophesying deceit, and ambiguities, and obliquities, deceives those who believe her.

CHAP. XXV. — CAIN'S NAME AND NATURE.

"Hence the ambiguous name which she gave to her first-born son, calling him CAIN, which has a capability of interpretation in two ways;[1] for it is interpreted both POSSESSION and ENVY, as signifying that in the future he was to envy either a woman, or possessions, or the love of the parents towards her.[2] But if it be none of these, then it will befall him to be called the POSSESSION. For she possessed him first, which also was advantageous to him. For he was a murderer and a liar, and with his sins was not willing to be at peace with respect to the government. Moreover, those who came forth by succession from him were the first adulterers. And there were psalteries, and harps, and forgers of instruments of war. Wherefore also the prophecy of his descendants being full of adulterers and of psalteries, secretly by means of pleasures excites to wars.

CHAP. XXVI. — ABEL'S NAME AND NATURE.

"But he who amongst the sons of men had prophecy innate to his soul as belonging to it, expressly, as being a male, indicating the hopes of the world to come, called his own son Abel, which without any ambiguity is translated GRIEF. For he assigns to his sons to grieve over their deceived brethren. He does not deceive them when he promises them comfort in the world to come. When he says that we must pray to one only God, he neither himself speaks of gods, nor does he believe another who speaks of them. He keeps the good which he has, and increases more and more. He hates sacrifices, bloodshed, and libations; he loves the chaste, the pure, the holy. He quenches the fire of altars, represses wars, teaches pious preachers wisdom, purges sins, sanctions marriage, approves temperance, leads all to chastity, makes men liberal, prescribes justice, seals those of them who are perfect, publishes the word of peace, prophesies

---

[1] [Note the fantastic mysticism of the interpretations here given. — R.]
[2] Qu. " towards Abel" ?

explicitly, speaks decidedly, frequently makes mention of the eternal fire of punishment, constantly announces the kingdom of God, indicates heavenly riches, promises unfading glory, shows the remission of sins by works.

CHAP. XXVII. — THE PROPHET AND THE PROPHETESS.

"And what need is there to say more? The male is wholly truth, the female wholly falsehood. But he who is born of the male and the female, in some things speaks truth, in some falsehood. For the female, surrounding the white seed of the male with her own blood, as with red fire, sustains her own weakness with the extraneous supports of bones, and, pleased with the temporary flower of flesh, and spoiling the strength of the judgment by short pleasures, leads the greater part into fornication, and thus deprives them of the coming excellent Bridegroom. For every person is a bride, whenever, being sown with the true Prophet's whole word of truth, he is enlightened in his understanding.

CHAP. XXVIII. — SPIRITUAL ADULTERY.

"Wherefore, it is fitting to hear the one only Prophet of the truth, knowing that the word that is sown by another bearing the charge of fornication, is, as it were, cast out by the Bridegroom from His kingdom. But to those who know the mystery, death is also produced by spiritual adultery. For whenever the soul is sown by others, then it is forsaken by the Spirit, as guilty of fornication or adultery; and so the living body, the life-giving Spirit being withdrawn, is dissolved into dust, and the rightful punishment of sin is suffered at the time of the judgment by the soul, after the dissolution of the body; even as, among men, she who is caught in adultery is first cast out from the house, and then afterwards is condemned to punishment."

CHAP. XXIX. — THE SIGNAL GIVEN.

While Peter was about to explain fully to us this mystic word, Zacchæus came, saying: "Now indeed, O Peter, is the time for you to go out and engage in the discussion; for a great crowd awaits you, packed together in the court; and in the midst of them stands Simon, like a warchieftain attended by his spearmen." And Peter, hearing this, ordered me to withdraw for prayer, as not yet having received baptism for salvation, and then said to those who were already perfected: "Let us rise and pray that God, by His unfailing mercies, may help me striving for the salvation of the men whom He has made." And having thus said, and having prayed, he went out into the uncovered portion of the court, which was a large space; and there were many come together for the purpose of seeing him, his pre-eminence having made them more eagerly hasten to hear.[1]

CHAP. XXX. — APOSTOLIC SALUTATION.

Therefore, standing and seeing all the people gazing upon him in profound silence, and Simon the magician standing in the midst, he began to speak thus : " Peace be to all you who are in readiness to give your right hands to the truth of God,[2] which, being His great and incomparable gift in the present world, He who sent us, being an infallible Prophet of that which is supremely profitable, gave us in charge, by way of salutation before our words of instruction, to announce to you, in order that if there be any son of peace among you, peace may take hold of him through our teaching ; but if any of you will not receive it, then we, shaking off for a testimony the road-dust of our feet, which we have borne through our toils, and brought to you that you may be saved, will go to the abodes and the cities of others.[3]

CHAP. XXXI. — FAITH IN GOD.

" And we tell you truly, it shall be more tolerable in the day of judgment to dwell in the land of Sodom and Gomorrah, than in the place of unbelief. In the first place, because you have not preserved of yourselves what is reasonable ; in the second place, because, hearing the things concerning us, you have not come to us ; and in the third place, because you have disbelieved us when we have come to you. Wherefore, being concerned for you, we pray of our own accord that our peace may come upon you. If therefore ye will have it, you must readily promise not to do injustice, and generously to bear wrong ; which the nature of man would not sustain, unless it first received the knowledge of that which is supremely profitable, which is to know the righteous nature of Him who is over all, that He defends and avenges those who are wronged, and does good for ever to the pious.

CHAP. XXXII. — INVITATION.

" Do you, therefore, as thankful servants of God, perceiving of yourselves what is reasonable, take upon you the manner of life that is pleasing to Him, that so, loving Him, and being loved of Him, you may enjoy good for ever. For to Him alone is it most possible to bestow it, who gave being to things that were not, who created the

heavens, settled the earth, set bounds to the sea, stored up the things that are in Hades, and filled all places with air.

CHAP. XXXIII. — WORKS OF CREATION.

" He alone turned into the four contrary elements[4] the one, first, simple substance. Thus combining them, He made of them myriads of compounds, that, being turned into opposite natures, and mingled, they might effect the pleasure of life from the combination of contraries. In like manner, He alone, having created races of angels and spirits by the FIAT of His will, peopled the heavens ; as also He decked the visible firmament with stars, to which also He assigned their paths and arranged their courses. He compacted the earth for the production of fruits. He set bounds to the sea, marking out a dwelling-place on the dry land.[5] He stores up the things in Hades, designating it as the place of souls ; and He filled all places with air, that all living creatures might be able to breathe safely in order that they might live.

CHAP. XXXIV. — EXTENT OF CREATION.

" O the great hand of the wise God, which doeth all in all ! For a countless multitude of birds have been made by Him, and those various, differing in all respects from one another ; I mean in respect of their colours, beaks, talons, looks, senses, voices, and all else. And how many different species of plants, distinguished by boundless variety of colours, qualities, and scents ! And how many animals on the land and in the water, of which it were impossible to tell the figures, forms, habitats, colour, food, senses, natures, multitude ! Then also the multitude and height of mountains, the varieties of stones, awful caverns, fountains, rivers, marshes, seas, harbours, islands, forests, and all the inhabited world, and places uninhabited !

CHAP. XXXV. — " THESE ARE A PART OF HIS WAYS."

" And how many things besides are unknown, having eluded the sagacity of men ! And of those that are within our comprehension, who of mankind knows the limit? I mean, how the heaven rolls, how the stars are borne in their courses, and what forms they have, and the subsistence of their being,[6] and what are their ethereal paths. And whence the blasts of winds are borne around, and have different energies ; whence the fountains ceaselessly spring, and the rivers, being ever flowing, run down into the sea,

---

[1] [For a general comparison of the discussions with Simon, see *Recognitions*, ii. 19. Comp. Homily XVI. 1. — R.]

[2] [In *Recognitions*, ii. 20, this sentence occurs : but the opening discourse of Peter is quite different, far more dignified and consistent with the real character of the Apostle. — R.]

[3] Matt. x. 12, etc.; Mark. vi. 11, etc.; Luke. x. 5, etc. [Comp. *Recognitions*, ii. 20, where the exordium is quite different, presenting the righteousness of God. — R.]

[4] This is rather a paraphrase than a strict translation.

[5] Various reading, " assigned it *the sea* as a habitation for aquatic animals."

[6] Literally, " of their life," according to the idea prevalent of old, that the heavenly bodies were living creatures.

and neither is that *fountain* emptied whence they come, nor do they fill that *sea* whither they come ! How far reaches the unfathomable depth of the boundless Tartarus ! Upon what the heaven is upborne which encircles all ! How the clouds spring from air, and are absorbed into air ! What is the nature of thunder and lightning, snow, hail, mist, ice, storms, showers, hanging clouds ! And how He makes plants and animals ! And these things, with all accuracy, continually perfected in their countless varieties !

CHAP. XXXVI. — DOMINION OVER THE CREATURES.

"Therefore, if any one shall accurately scan the whole with reason, he shall find that God has made them for the sake of man. For showers fall for the sake of fruits, that man may partake of them, and that animals may be fed, that they may be useful to men. And the sun shines, that he may turn the air into four seasons, and that each time may afford its peculiar service to man. And the fountains spring, that drink may be given to men. And, moreover, who is lord over the creatures, so far as is possible? Is it not man, who has received wisdom to till the earth, to sail the sea : to make fishes, birds, and beasts his prey ; to investigate the course of the stars, to mine the earth, to sail the sea ; to build cities, to define kingdoms, to ordain laws, to execute justice, to know the invisible God, to be cognizant of the names of angels, to drive away demons, to endeavour to cure diseases by medicines, to find charms against poison-darting serpents, to understand antipathies?

CHAP. XXXVII. — "WHOM TO KNOW IS LIFE ETERNAL."

But if thou art thankful, O man, understanding that God is thy benefactor in all things, thou mayest even be immortal, the things that are made for thee having continuance through thy gratitude. And now thou art able to become incorruptible, if thou acknowledge Him whom thou didst not know, if thou love Him whom thou didst forsake, if thou pray to Him alone who is able to punish or to save thy body and soul. Wherefore, before all things, consider that no one shares His rule, no one has a name in common with Him — that is, is called God. For He alone is both called and is God. Nor is it lawful to think that there is any other, or to call any other by that name. And if any one should dare do so, eternal punishment of soul is his."

CHAP. XXXVIII. — SIMON'S CHALLENGE.

When Peter had thus spoken, Simon, at the outside of the crowd, cried aloud :[1] "Why would you lie, and deceive the unlearned multitude standing around you, persuading them that it is unlawful to think that there are gods, and to call them so, when the books that are current among the Jews say that there are many gods?[2] And now I wish, in the presence of all, to discuss with you from these books on the necessity of thinking that there are gods ; first showing respecting him whom you call God, that he is not the supreme and omnipotent *Being*, inasmuch as he is without foreknowledge, imperfect, needy, not good, and underlying many and innumerable grievous passions. Wherefore, when this has been shown from the Scriptures, as I say, it follows that there is another, not written of, foreknowing, perfect, without want, good, removed from all grievous passions. But he whom you call the Creator is subject to the opposite *evils*.

CHAP. XXXIX. — DEFECTS ASCRIBED TO GOD.

"Therefore also Adam, being made at first after his likeness, is created blind, and is said not to have knowledge of good or evil, and is found a transgressor, and is driven out of paradise, and is punished with death. In like manner also, he who made him, because he sees not in all places, says with reference to the overthrow of Sodom, 'Come, and let us go down, and see whether they do according to their cry which comes to me ; or if not, that I may know.'[3] Thus he shows himself ignorant. And in his saying respecting Adam, 'Let us drive him out, lest he put forth his hand and touch the tree of life, and eat, and live for ever ;'[4] in saying LEST he is ignorant ; and in driving him out lest he should eat and live for ever, he is also envious. And whereas it is written that 'God repented that he had made man,'[5] this implies both repentance and ignorance. For this reflection is a view by which one, through ignorance, wishes to inquire into the result of the things which he wills, or it is the act of one repenting on account of the event not being according to his expectation. And whereas it is written, 'And the Lord smelled a scent of sweetness,'[6] it is the part of one in need ; and his being pleased with the fat of flesh is the part of one who is not good. But his tempting, as it is written, 'And God did tempt Abraham,'[7] is the part of one who is wicked, and who is ignorant of the issue of the experiment."

---

[1] [The reply of Simon in the *Recognitions* is quite different, though the substance of this attack is given in the progress of this discussion ; see *Recognitions*, ii. 39. — R.]

[2] [The Ebionitic tendency appears in this representation of Simon, as opposing the monotheism of the Old Testament. Comp. *Recognitions*, ii. 38. — R.]
[3] Gen. xviii. 21.
[4] Gen. iii. 22.
[5] Gen. vi. 6.
[6] Gen. viii. 21.
[7] Gen. xxii. 1. [These objections from the anthropomorphism of the Jewish Scriptures are not found in the *Recognitions*. — R.]

CHAP. XL. — PETER'S ANSWER.

In like manner Simon, by taking many passages from the Scriptures, seemed to show that God is subject to every infirmity. And to this Peter said : "Does he who is evil, and wholly wicked, love to accuse himself in the things in which he sins? Answer me this." Then said Simon : "He does not." Then said Peter : "How, then, can God be evil and wicked, seeing that those evil things which have been commonly written regarding Him, have been added by His own will !" Then said Simon : "It may be that the charge against Him is written by another power, and not according to His choice." Then said Peter : "Let us then, in the first place, inquire into this. If, indeed, He has of His own will accused Himself, as you formerly acknowledged, then He is not wicked ; but if it is done by another power, it must be inquired and investigated with all energy who hath subjected to all evils Him who alone is good."

CHAP. XLI. — "STATUS QUÆSTIONIS."

Then said Simon : "You are manifestly avoiding the hearing of the charge from the Scriptures against your God." Then Peter : "You yourself appear to me to be doing this ; for he who avoids the order of inquiry, does not wish a true investigation to be made. Hence I, who proceed in an orderly manner, and wish that the writer should first be considered, am manifestly desirous to walk in a straight path." Then Simon : "First confess that if the things written against the Creator are true, he is not above all, since, according to the Scriptures, he is subject to all evil ; then afterwards we shall inquire as to the writer." Then said Peter : "That I may not seem to speak against your want of order through unwillingness to enter upon the investigation,[1] I answer you. I say that if the things written against God are true, they do not show that God is wicked." Then said Simon : "How can you maintain that?"

CHAP. XLII. — WAS ADAM BLIND?

Then said Peter : "Because things are written opposite to those sayings which speak evil of him ; wherefore neither the one nor the other can be confirmed." Then Simon : "How, then, is the truth to be ascertained, of those Scriptures that say he is evil, or of those that say he is good?" Then Peter : "Whatever sayings of the Scriptures are in harmony with the creation that was made by Him are true, but whatever are contrary to it are false."[2] Then Simon said :

"How can you show that the Scriptures contradict themselves?" And Peter said : "You say that Adam was created blind, which was not so ; for He would not have pointed out the tree of the knowledge of good and evil to a blind man, and commanded him not to taste of it." Then said Simon : "He meant that his mind was blind." Then Peter : "How could he be blind in respect of his mind, who, before tasting of the tree, in harmony with Him who made him, imposed appropriate names on all the animals?" Then Simon : "If Adam had foreknowledge, how did he not foreknow that the serpent would deceive his wife?" Then Peter : "If Adam had not foreknowledge, how did he give names to the sons of men as they were born with reference to their future doings, calling the first Cain (which is interpreted ' envy '), who through envy killed his brother Abel (which is interpreted ' grief ') ; for his parents grieved over him, the first slain?

CHAP. XLIII. — GOD'S FOREKNOWLEDGE.

"But if Adam, being the work of God, had foreknowledge, much more the God who created him. And that is false which is written that God reflected, as if using reasoning on account of ignorance ; and that the Lord tempted Abraham, that He might know if he would endure it ; and that which is written, ' Let us go down, and see if they are doing according to the cry of them which cometh to me ; and if not, that I may know.' And, not to extend my discourse too far, whatever sayings ascribe ignorance to Him, or anything else that is evil, being upset by other sayings which affirm the contrary, are proved to be false. But because He does indeed foreknow, He says to Abraham, ' Thou shalt assuredly know that thy seed shall be sojourners in a land that is not their own ; and they shall enslave them, and shall evil entreat them, and humble them four hundred years. But the nation to which they shall be in bondage will I judge, and after that they shall come out hither with much property ; but thou shalt depart to thy fathers with peace, being nourished in a good old age ; and in the fourth generation they shall return hither, for the sins of the Amorites are hitherto not filled up.'[3]

CHAP. XLIV. — GOD'S DECREES.

"But what? Does not Moses pre-intimate the sins of the people, and predict their dispersion among the nations? But if He gave foreknowledge to Moses, how can it be that He had it not Himself? But He has it. And if He has it, as we have also shown, it is an extravagant saying that He reflected, and that He repented,

---

[1] The text of this passage in all the editions is meaningless. It becomes clear by change of punctuation.

[2] [Comp. ii. 38 and many other passages for this view of the errors of Scripture. The test of truth as here stated is noteworthy. It suggests some modern affinities. — R.]

[3] Gen. xv. 13-16.

and that He went down to see, and whatever else of this sort. Whatsoever things being foreknown before they come to pass as about to befall, take issue by a wise economy, without repentance.

CHAP. XLV. — SACRIFICES.

" But that He is not pleased with sacrifices, is shown by this, that those who lusted after flesh were slain as soon as they tasted it, and were consigned to a tomb, so that it was called the grave of lusts.[1] He then who at the first was displeased with the slaughtering of animals, not wishing them to be slain, did not ordain sacrifices as desiring them ; nor from the beginning did He require them. For neither are sacrifices accomplished without the slaughter of animals, nor can the first-fruits be presented. But how is it possible for Him to abide in darkness, and smoke, and storm (for this also is written), who created a pure heaven, and created the sun to give light to all, and assigned the invariable order of their revolutions to innumerable stars? Thus, O Simon, the handwriting of God — I mean the heaven — shows the counsels of Him who made it to be pure and stable.

CHAP. XLVI. — DISPARAGEMENTS OF GOD.

" Thus the sayings accusatory of the God who made the heaven are both rendered void by the opposite sayings which are alongside of them, and are refuted by the creation. For they were not written by a prophetic hand. Wherefore also they appear opposite to the hand of God, who made all things." Then said Simon : " How can you show this? "

CHAP. XLVII. — FOREKNOWLEDGE OF MOSES.

Then said Peter : " The law of God was given by Moses, without writing, to seventy wise men, to be handed down, that the government might be carried on by succession. But after that Moses was taken up, it was written by some one, but not by Moses. For in the law itself it is written, ' And Moses died ; and they buried him near the house of Phogor,[2] and no one knows his sepulchre till this day.' But how could Moses write that Moses died? And whereas in the time after Moses, about 500 years or thereabouts, it is found lying in the temple which was built, and after about 500 years more it is carried away, and being burnt in the time of Nebuchadnezzar it is destroyed ; and thus being written after Moses, and often lost, even this shows the foreknowledge of Moses, because he, foreseeing its disappearance, did not write it ; but those who wrote it, being convicted of ignorance

through their not foreseeing its disappearance, were not prophets." [3]

CHAP. XLVIII. — TEST OF TRUTH.

Then said Simon : " Since, as you say, we must understand the things concerning God by comparing them with the creation, how is it possible to recognise the other things in the law which are from the tradition of Moses, and are true, and are mixed up with these falsehoods?" Then Peter said : " A certain verse has been recorded without controversy in the written law, according to the providence of God, so as to show clearly which of the things written are true and which are false." Then said Simon : " Which is that? Show it us."

CHAP. XLIX. — THE TRUE PROPHET.

Then Peter said : " I shall tell you forthwith. It is written in the first book of the law, towards the end : ' A ruler shall not fail from Judah, nor a leader from his thighs, until He come whose it is ; and He is the expectation of the nations.' [4] If, therefore, any one can apprehend Him who came after the failure of ruler and leader from Judah, and who was to be expected by the nations, he will be able by this verse to recognise Him as truly having come ; [5] and believing His teaching, he will know what of the Scriptures are true and what are false." Then said Simon : " I understand that you speak of your Jesus as Him who was prophesied of by the scripture. Therefore let it be granted that it is so. Tell us, then, how he taught you to discriminate the Scriptures."

CHAP. L. — HIS TEACHING CONCERNING THE SCRIPTURES.

Then Peter : " As to the mixture of truth with falsehood,[6] I remember that on one occasion He, finding fault with the Sadducees, said, ' Wherefore ye do err, not knowing the true things of the Scriptures ; and on this account ye are ignorant of the power of God.' [7] But if He cast up to them that they knew not the true things of the Scriptures, it is manifest that there are false things in them. And also, inasmuch as He said, ' Be ye prudent money-changers,' [8] it is because there are genuine and spurious words. And whereas He said, ' Wherefore do ye not

---

[1] That is, Kibroth-Hattaavah; Num. xi. 34.
[2] Deut. xxxiv. 6, LXX.

[3] [It is curious to find the post-exilian theory of the Pentateuch in this place, put in the mouth of the Apostle Peter. — R.]
[4] Gen. xlix. 10.
[5] From the amended reading of Davis.
[6] [Comp. Homily II. 40. The attitude of Peter, as here represented, disparaging the Old Testament, appearing to exalt the authority of Christ's teaching, and yet ignoring the claims of His Person and Work, seeks its justification in rationalistic interpretation. The attitude is not an uncommon one at present. — R.]
[7] Matt. xxii. 29. [Misquoted and misapplied here, as in Homily II. 51. — R.]
[8] This is frequently quoted as a saying of Christ. It is probably from one of the apocryphal Gospels. [Comp. Homily II. 51. — R.]

perceive that which is reasonable in the Scriptures?' He makes the understanding of him stronger who voluntarily judges soundly.

CHAP. LI. — HIS TEACHING CONCERNING THE LAW.

" And His sending to the scribes and teachers of the existing Scriptures, as to those who knew the true things of the law that then was, is well known. And also that He said, 'I am not come to destroy the law,'[1] and yet that He appeared to be destroying it, is the part of one intimating that the things which He destroyed did not belong to the law. And His saying, 'The heaven and the earth shall pass away, but one jot or one tittle shall not pass from the law,'[2] intimated that the things which pass away before the heaven and the earth do not belong to the law in reality.

CHAP. LII. — OTHER SAYINGS OF CHRIST.

" Since, then, while the heaven and the earth still stand, sacrifices have passed away, and kingdoms, and prophecies among those who are born of woman, and such like, as not being ordinances of God ; hence therefore He says, 'Every plant which the heavenly Father has not planted shall be rooted up.'[3] Wherefore He, being the true Prophet, said, 'I am the gate of life ; [4] he who entereth through me entereth into life,' there being no other teaching able to save. Wherefore also He cried, and said, 'Come unto me, all who labour,'[5] that is, who are seeking the truth, and not finding it ; and again, 'My sheep hear my voice ; '[6] and elsewhere, 'Seek and find,'[7] since the truth does not lie on the surface.

CHAP. LIII. — OTHER SAYINGS OF CHRIST.

" But also a witnessing voice was heard from heaven, saying, 'This is my beloved Son, in whom I am well pleased ; hear Him.'[8] And in addition to this, willing to convict more fully of error the prophets from whom they asserted that they had learned, He proclaimed that they died desiring the truth, but not having learned it, saying, 'Many prophets and kings desired to see what ye see, and to hear what you hear ; and verily I say to you, they neither saw nor heard.'[9] Still further He said, ' I am he concerning whom Moses prophesied, saying, A Prophet shall the Lord our God raise unto you of your brethren, like unto me : Him hear in all things ; and whosoever will not hear that Prophet shall die.'[10]

CHAP. LIV. — OTHER SAYINGS.

" Whence it is impossible without His teaching to attain to saving truth, though one seek it for ever where the thing that is sought is not. But it was, and is, in the word of our Jesus. Accordingly, He, knowing the true things of the law, said to the Sadducees, asking on what account Moses permitted to marry seven,[11] " Moses gave you commandments according to your hard-heartedness ; for from the beginning it was not so : for He who created man at first, made him male and female.'[12]

CHAP. LV. — TEACHING OF CHRIST.

" But to those who think, as the Scriptures teach, that God swears, He said, ' Let your yea be yea, and nay, nay ; for what is more than these is of the evil one.'[13] And to those who say that Abraham and Isaac and Jacob are dead, He said, ' God is not of the dead, but of the living.'[14] And to those who suppose that God tempts, as the Scriptures say, He said, 'The tempter is the wicked one,'[15] who also tempted Himself. To those who suppose that God does not foreknow, He said, ' For your heavenly Father knoweth that ye need all these things before ye ask Him.'[16] And to those who believe, as the Scriptures say, that He does not see all things, He said, ' Pray in secret, and your Father, who seeth secret things, will reward you.'[17]

CHAP. LVI. — TEACHING OF CHRIST.

" And to those who think that He is not good, as the Scriptures say, He said, ' From which of you shall his son ask bread, and he will give him a stone ; or shall ask a fish, and he will give him a serpent? If ye then, being evil, know to give good gifts to your children, how much more shall your heavenly Father give good things to those who ask Him, and to those who do His will !'[18] But to those who affirmed that He was in the temple, He said, ' Swear not by heaven, for it is God's throne ; nor by the earth, for it is the footstool of His feet.'[19] And to those who supposed that God is pleased with sacrifices, He said, ' God wishes mercy, and not sacrifices '[20] — the knowledge of Himself, and not holocausts.

CHAP. LVII. — TEACHING OF CHRIST.

" But to those who are persuaded that He is evil, as the Scriptures say, He said, ' Call not

---

[1] Matt. v. 17.
[2] Matt. v. 18.
[3] Matt. xv. 13.
[4] John x. 9.
[5] Matt. xi. 28.
[6] John x. 3.
[7] Matt. vii. 7.
[8] Matt. xvii. 5.
[9] Matt. xiii. 17 ; Luke x. 24.
[10] Deut. xviii. 15-19 ; Acts iii. 22, vii. 37.

[11] [A curious confusion of two Gospel narratives, mistaking the significance of both. — R.]
[12] Matt. xix. 8; Mark x. 5, 6.
[13] Matt. v. 37.
[14] Matt. xxii. 32; Mark xii. 27: Luke xx. 38.
[15] Perhaps Matt. xiii. 39.
[16] Matt. vi. 8, 32.
[17] Matt. vi. 6.
[18] Matt. vii. 9-11.
[19] Matt. v. 34, 35.
[20] Matt. ix. 13, xii. 7. [Comp. Hos. vi. 6. — R.]

me good, for One *only* is good.'[1] And again, 'Be ye good and merciful, as your Father in the heavens, who makes the sun rise on good and evil men, and brings rain upon just and unjust.'[2] But to those who were misled to imagine many gods, as the Scriptures say, He said, 'Hear, O Israel; the Lord your God is one Lord.'"[3]

CHAP. LVIII. — FLIGHT OF SIMON.

Therefore Simon, perceiving that Peter was driving him to use the Scriptures as Jesus taught, was unwilling that the discussion should go into the doctrine concerning God, even although Peter had changed the discussion into question and answer, as Simon himself asked. However, the discussion occupied three days.[4] And while the fourth was dawning, he set off darkling as far as Tyre of Phœnicia.[5] And not many days after, some of the precursors came and said to Peter: "Simon is doing great miracles in Tyre, and disturbing many of the people there; and by many slanders he has made you to be hated."

CHAP. LIX. — PETER'S RESOLUTION TO FOLLOW.

Peter, hearing this, on the following night assembled the multitude of hearers; and as soon as they were come together, he said: "While I am going forth to the nations which say that there are many gods, to teach and to preach that God is one, who made heaven and earth, and all things that are in them, in order that they may love Him and be saved, evil has anticipated me, and by the very law of conjunction has sent Simon before me, in order that these men, if they shall cease to say that there are many gods, disowning those upon earth that are called gods, may think that there are many gods in heaven; so that, not feeling the excellency of the monarchy, they may perish with eternal punishment. And what is most dreadful, since true doctrine has incomparable power, he forestalls me with slanders, and persuades them to this, not even at first to receive me; lest he who is the slanderer be convicted of being himself in reality a devil, and the true doctrine be received and believed. Therefore I must quickly catch him up, lest the false accusation, through gaining time, wholly get hold of all men.

CHAP. LX. — SUCCESSOR TO BE APPOINTED.

"Since, therefore, it is necessary to set apart some one instead of me to fill my place, let us all with one consent pray to God, that He would make manifest who amongst us is the best, that, sitting in the chair of Christ, he may piously rule His Church. Who, then, shall be set apart? For by the counsel of God that man is set forth as blessed, 'whom his Lord shall appoint over the ministry of his fellow-servants, to give them their meat in their season, not thinking and saying in his heart, My Lord delayeth His coming, and who shall not begin to beat his fellow-servants, eating and drinking with harlots and drunkards. And the Lord of that servant shall come in an hour when he doth not look for Him, and in a day when he is not aware, and shall cut him in sunder, and shall assign his unfaithful part with the hypocrites.'[6]

CHAP. LXI. — MONARCHY.

"But if any one of those present, being able to instruct the ignorance of men, shrink from it, thinking only of his own ease, let him expect to hear this sentence: 'O wicked and slothful servant, thou oughtest to have given my money to the exchangers, and I at my coming should have got my own. Cast out the unprofitable servant into the outer darkness.'[7] And with good reason; 'for,' says He, 'it is thine, O man, to prove my words, as silver and money are proved among the exchangers.'[8] Therefore the multitude of the faithful ought to obey some one, that they may live in harmony. For that which tends to the government of one person, in the form of monarchy, enables the subjects to enjoy peace by means of good order; but in case of all, through desire of ruling, being unwilling to submit to one only, they must altogether fall by reason of division.

CHAP. LXII. — OBEDIENCE LEADS TO PEACE.

"But, further, let the things that are happening before your eyes persuade you; how wars are constantly arising through there being now many kings all over the earth. For each one holds the government of another as a pretext for war. But if one were universal superior, he, having no reason why he should make war, would have perpetual peace. In short, therefore, to those who are thought worthy of eternal life, God appoints one universal King in the world that shall then be, that by means of monarchy there may be unfailing peace. It behoves all, therefore, to follow some one as a leader, honouring him as the image of God; and it behoves the leader to be acquainted with the road that entereth into the holy city.

---

[1] Matt. xix. 17; Mark x. 18; Luke xviii. 19.
[2] Matt. v. 44, 45.
[3] Mark xii. 29. [Comp. Deut. vi. 4. — R.]
[4] [The three days' discussion is detailed in *Recognitions*, ii. 20–iii. 48; the account here is confined to the first day. — R.]
[5] [Comp. *Recognitions*, iii. 73. The historical incidents of the two narratives vary greatly from this point onward. — R.]

[6] Matt. xxiv. 45–50.
[7] Matt. xxv. 27–30.
[8] Probably from an apocryphal Gospel.

CHAP. LXIII. — ZACCHÆUS APPOINTED.

" But of those who are present, whom shall I choose but Zacchæus,[1] to whom also the Lord went in [2] and rested, judging him worthy to be saved?" And having said this, he laid his hand upon Zacchæus, who stood by, and forced him to sit down in his own chair. But Zacchæus, falling at his feet, begged that he would permit him to decline the rulership; promising, at the same time, and saying, "Whatever it behoves the ruler to do, I will do; only grant me not to have this name: for I am afraid of assuming the name of the rulership, for it teems with bitter envy and danger."

CHAP. LXIV. — THE BISHOPRIC.

Then Peter said : " If you are afraid of this, do not be called RULER, but THE APPOINTED ONE, the Lord having permitted you to be so called, when He said, 'Blessed is that man whom his Lord shall APPOINT to the ministry of his fellow-servants.' [3] But if you wish it to be altogether unknown that you have authority of administration, you seem to me to be ignorant that the acknowledged authority of the president has great influence as regards the respect of the multitude. For every one obeys him who has received authority, having conscience as a great constraint. And are you not well aware that you are not to rule as the rulers of the nations, but as a servant ministering to them, as a father to the oppressed, visiting them as a physician, guarding them as a shepherd, — in short, taking all care for their salvation? And do you think that I am not aware what labours I compel you to undertake, desiring you to be judged by multitudes whom it is impossible for any one to please? But it is most possible for him who does well to please God. Wherefore I entreat you to undertake it heartily, by God, by Christ, for the salvation of the brethren, for their ordering, and your own profit.

CHAP. LXV. — NOLO EPISCOPARI.

" And consider this other thing, that in proportion as there is labour and danger in ruling the Church of Christ, so much greater is the reward. And yet again the greater is also the punishment to him who can, and refuses. I wish, therefore, knowing that you are the best instructed of my attendants, to turn to account those noble powers of judging with which you have been entrusted by the Lord, in order that you may be saluted with the WELL DONE, GOOD AND FAITHFUL SERVANT, and not be found fault

with, and declared liable to punishment, like him who hid the one talent. But if you will not be appointed a good guardian of the Church, point out another in your stead, more learned and more faithful than yourself. But you cannot do this; for you associated with the Lord, and witnessed His marvellous doings, and learned the administration of the Church.

CHAP. LXVI. — DANGER OF DISOBEDIENCE.

" And your work is to order what things are proper; and that of the brethren is to submit, and not to disobey. Therefore submitting they shall be saved, but disobeying they shall be punished by the Lord, because the president is entrusted with the place of Christ. Wherefore, indeed, honour or contempt shown to the president is handed on to Christ, and from Christ to God. And this I have said, that these brethren may not be ignorant of the danger they incur by disobedience to you, because whosoever disobeys your orders, disobeys Christ; and he who disobeys Christ offends God.

CHAP. LXVII. — DUTIES OF CHURCH OFFICE-BEARERS.

" It is necessary, therefore, that the Church, as a city built upon a hill, have an order approved of God, and good government. In particular, let the bishop, as chief, be heard in the things which he speaks; and let the elders give heed that the things ordered be done. Let the deacons, going about, look after the bodies and the souls of the brethren, and report to the bishop. Let all the rest of the brethren bear wrong patiently; but if they wish judgment to be given concerning wrongs done to them, let them be reconciled in presence of the elders; and let the elders report the reconciliation to the bishop.

CHAP. LXVIII. — " MARRIAGE ALWAYS HONOURABLE."

" And let them inculcate marriage not only upon the young, but also upon those advanced in years, lest burning lust bring a plague upon the Church by reason of whoredom or adultery. For, above every other sin, the wickedness of adultery is hated by God, because it not only destroys the person himself who sins, but those also who eat and associate with him. For it is like the madness of a dog, because it has the nature of communicating its own madness. For the sake of chastity, therefore, let not only the elders, but even all, hasten to accomplish marriage. For the sin of him who commits adultery necessarily comes upon all. Therefore, to urge the brethren to be chaste, this is the first charity. For it is the healing of the soul. For the nourishment of the body is rest.

---

[1] [Comp. *Recognitions*, iii. 66. The account here is much fuller. — R.]
[2] Luke xix. 5, etc.
[3] Luke xii. 42.

CHAP. LXIX. — "NOT FORSAKING THE ASSEMBLING OF YOURSELVES TOGETHER."

"But if you love your brethren, take nothing from them, but share with them such things as ye have. Feed the hungry; give drink to the thirsty; clothe the naked; visit the sick; so far as you can, help those in prison; receive strangers gladly into your own abodes; hate no one. And how you must be pious, your own mind will teach you, judging rightly. But before all else, if indeed I need say it to you, come together frequently, if it were every hour, especially on the appointed days of meeting. For if you do this, you are within a wall of safety. For disorderliness is the beginning of perdition. Let no one therefore forsake the assembly on the ground of envy towards a brother. For if any one of you forsake the assembly, he shall be regarded as of those who scatter the Church of Christ, and shall be cast out with adulterers. For as an adulterer, under the influence of the spirit that is in him, he separates himself on some pretext, and gives place to the wicked one against himself, — a sheep for the stealing, as one found outside the fold.[1]

CHAP. LXX. — "HEAR THE BISHOP."

"However, hear your bishop, and do not weary of giving all honour to him; knowing that, by showing it to him, it is borne to Christ, and from Christ it is borne to God; and to him who offers it, is requited manifold.[2] Honour, therefore, the throne of Christ. For you are commanded even to honour the chair of Moses, and that although they who occupy it are accounted sinners.[3] And now I have said enough to you; and I deem it superfluous to say to him how he is to live unblameably, since he is an approved disciple of Him who taught me also.

CHAP. LXXI. — VARIOUS DUTIES OF CHRISTIANS.

"But, brethren, there are some things that you must not wait to hear, but must consider of yourselves what is reasonable. Zacchæus alone having given himself up wholly to labour for you, and needing sustenance, and not being able to attend to his own affairs, how can he procure necessary support? Is it not reasonable that you are to take forethought for his living? not waiting for his asking you, for this is the part of a beggar. But he will rather die of hunger than submit to do this. And shall not you incur punishment, not considering that the workman is worthy of his hire? And let no one say: Is, then, the word sold which was freely given? Far be it. For if any one has the means of living, and takes anything, he sells the word; but if he who has not takes support in order to live — as the Lord also took at supper and among His friends, having nothing, though He alone is the owner of all things — he sins not. Therefore suitably honour elders, catechists, useful deacons, widows who have lived well, orphans as children of the Church. But wherever there is need of any provision for an emergency, contribute all together. Be kind one to another, not shrinking from the endurance of anything whatever for your own salvation."

CHAP. LXXII. — ORDINATION.

And having thus spoken, he placed his hand upon Zacchæus, saying, "O Thou Ruler and Lord of all, Father and God, do Thou guard the shepherd with the flock. Thou art the cause, Thou the power. We are that which is helped; Thou the helper, the physician, the saviour, the wall, the life, the hope, the refuge, the joy, the expectation, the rest. In a word, Thou art all things to us. In order to the eternal attainment of salvation, do Thou co-operate, preserve, protect. Thou canst do all things. For Thou art the Ruler of rulers, the Lord of lords, the Governor of kings. Do Thou give power to the president to loose what ought to be loosed, to bind what ought to be bound. Do Thou make him wise. Do Thou, as by His name, protect the Church of Thy Christ as a fair bride. For Thine is eternal glory. Praise to the Father and the Son and the Holy Ghost to all ages. Amen."

CHAP. LXXIII. — BAPTISMS.

And having thus spoken, he afterwards said: "Whoever of you wish to be baptized, begin from to-morrow to fast, and have hands laid upon you day by day, and inquire about what matters you please. For I mean still to remain with you ten days." And after three days, having begun to baptize, he called me, and Aquila, and Nicetas, and said to us: "As I am going to set out for Tyre after seven days, I wish you to go away this very day, and to lodge secretly with Bernice the Canaanite, the daughter of Justa, and to learn from her, and write accurately to me what Simon is about. For this is of great consequence to me, that I may prepare myself accordingly. Therefore depart straightway in peace." And leaving him baptizing, as he commanded, we preceded him to Tyre of Phœnicia.

---

[1] There seems to be a corruption of the text here, but the general meaning is evident enough.
[2] There are several conjectural readings of this sentence. We have not exactly followed any one of them, but have ventured on a conjecture of our own.
[3] Matt. xxiii. 2, 3.

HOMILY IV.

CHAP. I. — BERNICE'S HOSPITALITY.

Thus I Clement, departing from Cæsarea Stratonis, together with Nicetas and Aquila, entered into Tyre of Phœnicia; [1] and according to the injunction of Peter, who sent us, we lodged with Bernice, the daughter of Justa the Canaanitess. She received us most joyfully; and striving with much honour towards me, and with affection towards Aquila and Nicetas, and speaking freely as a friend, through joy she treated us courteously, and hospitably urged us to take bodily refreshment. Perceiving, therefore, that she was endeavouring to impose a short delay upon us, I said: "You do well, indeed, to busy yourself in fulfilling the part of love; but the fear of our God must take the precedence of this. For, having a combat on hand on behalf of many souls, we are afraid of preferring our own ease before their salvation.

CHAP. II. — SIMON'S PRACTICES.

"For we hear that Simon the magician, being worsted at Cæsarea in the discussion with our lord Peter, immediately hastened hither, and is doing much mischief. For he is slandering Peter, in opposition to truth, to all the adversaries, and stealing away the souls of the multitude. For he being a magician, calls him a magician; and he being a deceiver, proclaims him as a deceiver. And although in the discussions he was beaten in all points, and fled, yet he says that he was victorious; and he constantly charges them that they ought not to listen to Peter, — as if, forsooth, he were anxious that they may not be fascinated by a terrible magician.

CHAP. III. — OBJECT OF THE MISSION.

"Therefore our lord Peter, having learned these things, has sent us to be investigators of the things that have been told him; that if they be so, we may write to him and let him know, so that he may come and convict him face to face of the accusations that he has uttered against him. Since, therefore, danger on the part of many souls lies before us, on this account we must neglect bodily rest for a short time; and we would learn truly from you who live here, whether the things which we have heard be true. Now tell us particularly."

CHAP. IV. — SIMON'S DOINGS.

But Bernice, being asked, said: "These things are indeed as you have heard; and I will tell you other things respecting this same Simon, which perhaps you do not know. For he astonishes the whole city every day, by making spectres and ghosts appear in the midst of the market-place; and when he walks abroad, statues move, and many shadows go before him, which, he says, are souls of the dead. And many who attempted to prove him an impostor he speedily reconciled to him; and afterwards, under pretence of a banquet, having slain an ox, and given them to eat of it, he infected them with various diseases, and subjected them to demons. And in a word, having injured many, and being supposed to be a god, he is both feared and honoured." [2]

CHAP. V. — DISCRETION THE BETTER PART OF VALOUR.

"Wherefore I do not think that any one will be able to quench such a fire as has been kindled. For no one doubts his promises; but every one affirms that this is so. Wherefore, lest you should expose yourselves to danger, I advise you not to attempt anything against him until Peter come, who alone shall be able to resist such a power, being the most esteemed disciple of our Lord Jesus Christ. For so much do I fear this man, that if he had not elsewhere been vanquished in disputing with my lord Peter, I should counsel you to persuade even Peter himself not to attempt to oppose Simon."

CHAP. VI. — SIMON'S DEPARTURE.

Then I said: "If our lord Peter did not know that he himself alone can prevail against this power, he would not have sent us before him with orders to get information secretly concerning Simon, and to write to him." Then, as evening had come on, we took supper,[3] and went to sleep. But in the morning, one of Bernice's friends came and said that Simon had set sail for Sidon, and that he had left behind him Appion Pleistonices,[4] — a man of Alexandria, a

---

[1] [In the *Recognitions* (iv. 1) mention is made of Clement and others accompanying Peter to Dora, Ptolemais, Tyre, Sidon, and Berytus (Beyrout), but no record is made of any discourses. In Homilies IV.-VII. the details of this journey are given, but with a variation in some particulars. These *Homilies* are peculiar, in form, to this work; but much of the matter occurs in the *Recognitions*, in the final discussion with the father of Clement. — R.]

[2] [Comp. Acts viii. 9-11. — R.]

[3] Literally, "partook of salt."

[4] This epithet means, "the conqueror of very many." Suidas makes Appion the son of Pleistonices. [Comp. *Recognitions*, x. 52. It is evident that the writer has in mind Apion, the opponent of the Jews, against whom Josephus wrote his treatise. Compare the statement of Homily V. 2. The entire discussion with Appion, extending over Homilies IV.-VI. is peculiar to this narrative, though much of the argument occurs in the discussion of Clement with his father (*Recognitions*, x.). Appion and Annubion are introduced in *Recognitions*, x. 52, but not as disputants. The discussion here is constructed with much skill. — R.]

grammarian by profession, whom I knew as being a friend of my father; and a certain astrologer, Annubion the Diospolitan, and Athenodorus the Athenian, attached to the doctrine of Epicurus. And we, having learned these things concerning Simon, in the morning wrote and despatched a letter to Peter, and went to take a walk.

CHAP. VII. — APPION'S SALUTATION.

And Appion met us, not only with the two companions just named, but with about thirty other men. And as soon as he saw me, he saluted and kissed me, and said, "This is Clement, of whose noble birth and liberal education I have often told you; for he, being related to the family of Tiberius Cæsar, and equipped with all Grecian learning, has been seduced by a certain barbarian called Peter to speak and act after the manner of the Jews. Wherefore I beg of you to strive together with me for the setting of him right. And in your presence I now ask him. Let him tell me, since he thinks that he has devoted himself to piety, whether he is not ,acting most impiously, in forsaking the customs of his country, and falling away to those of the barbarians."

CHAP. VIII. — A CHALLENGE.

I answered: "I accept, indeed, your kindly affection towards me, but I take exception to your ignorance. For your affection is kindly, because you wish to continue in those *customs* which you consider to be good. But your inaccurate knowledge strives to lay a snare for me, under the guise of friendship." Then said Appion: "Does it seem to you to be ignorance, that one should observe the customs of his fathers, and judge after the manner of the Greeks?" Then I answered: "It behoves one who desires to be pious not altogether to observe the customs of his fathers; but to observe them if they be pious, and to shake them off if they be impious. For it is possible that one who is the son of an impious father, if he wishes to be pious, should not desire to follow the religion of his father." [1] Then answered Appion: "What then? Do you say that your father was a man of an evil life?" Then said I: "He was not of an evil life, but of an evil opinion." Then Appion: "I should like to know what was his evil apprehension." Then said I: "Because he believed the false and wicked myths of the Greeks." Then Appion asked: "What are these false and evil myths of the Greeks?" Then I said: "The wrong opinion concerning the gods, which, if you will bear with me, you shall hear, with those who are desirous to learn.

CHAP. IX. — UNWORTHY ENDS OF PHILOSOPHERS.

"Wherefore, before beginning our conversation, let us now withdraw into some quieter place, and there I shall converse with you. And the reason why I wish to speak privately is this, because neither the multitude, nor even all the philosophers, approach honestly to the judgment of things as they are. For we know many, even of those who pride themselves on their philosophy, who are vainglorious, or who have put on the philosopher's robe for the sake of gain, and not for the sake of virtue itself; and they, if they do not find that for which they take to philosophy, turn to mockery. Therefore, on account of such as these, let us choose some place fit for private conference."

CHAP. X. — A COOL RETREAT.

And a certain one amongst them — a rich man, and possessing a garden of evergreen plants [2] — said: "Since it is very hot, let us retire for a little from the city to my gardens." Accordingly they went forth, and sat down in a place where there were pure streams of cool water, and a green shade of all sorts of trees. There I sat pleasantly, and the others round about me; and they being silent, instead of a verbal request made to me, showed by their eager looks to me that they required the proof of my assertion. And therefore I proceeded to speak thus : —

CHAP. XI. — TRUTH AND CUSTOM.

"There is a certain great difference, O men of Greece, between truth and custom. For truth is found when it is honestly sought; but custom, whatsoever be the character of the custom received, whether true or false, is strengthened by itself without the exercise of judgment; and he who has received it is neither pleased with it as being true, nor grieved with it as false. For such an one has believed not by judgment, but by prejudice, resting his own hope on the opinion of those who have lived before him on a mere peradventure. And it is not easy to cast off the ancestral garment, though it be shown to himself to be wholly foolish and ridiculous.

CHAP. XII. — GENESIS.

"Therefore I say that the whole learning of the Greeks is a most dreadful fabrication of a wicked demon. For they have introduced many

---

[1] We have adopted the emendation of Wieseler, who reads σεβάσματι for σεβάσματα. He also proposes ἔθει (habit) instead of σεβάσματι. The readings in the MSS. vary.

[2] The text here is corrupt. If we adopt Lobeck's emendation of παμμιούσων into παμπλουσιον, the literal translation is, " possessing a property around him continually rich in leaves." [The offer of this man has a partial parallel in *Recognitions*, viii. 35-38. — R.]

gods of their own, and these wicked, and subject to all kinds of passion; so that he who wishes to do the like things may not be ashamed, which belongs to a man, having as an example the wicked and unquiet lives of the mythological gods. And through his not being ashamed, such an one affords no hope of his repenting. And others have introduced fate, which is called genesis, contrary to which no one can suffer or do anything. This, therefore, also is like to the first. For any one who thinks that no one has aught to do or suffer contrary to genesis easily falls into sin; and having sinned, he does not repent of his impiety, holding it as his apology that he was borne on by genesis to do these things. And as he cannot rectify genesis, he has no reason to be ashamed of the sins he commits.[1]

CHAP. XIII. — DESTINY.

"And others introduce an unforeseeing destiny, as if all things revolved of their own accord, without the superintendence of any master. But thus to think these things is, as we have said, the most grievous of all opinions. For, as if there were no one superintending and fore-judging and distributing to every one according to his deserving, they easily do everything as they can through fearlessness. Therefore those who have such opinions do not easily, or perhaps do not at all, live virtuously; for they do not foresee the danger which might have the effect of converting them. But the doctrine of the barbarous Jews, as you call them, is most pious, introducing One as the Father and Creator of all this world, by nature good and righteous; good, indeed, as pardoning sins to those who repent; but righteous, as visiting to every one after repentance according to the worthiness of his doings.

CHAP. XIV. — "DOCTRINE ACCORDING TO GODLINESS."

"This doctrine, even if it also be mythical, being pious, would not be without advantage for this life. For every one, in expectation of being judged by the all-seeing God, receives the greater impulse towards virtue. But if the doctrine be also true, it withdraws him who has lived virtuously from eternal punishment, and endows him with eternal and unspeakable blessings from God.

CHAP. XV. — WICKEDNESS OF THE GODS.

"But I return to the foremost doctrine of the Greeks, that which states in stories[2] that there are gods many, and subject to all kinds of passions. And not to spend much time upon

things that are clear, referring to the impious deeds of every one of those who are called gods, I could not tell all their amours; those of Zeus and Poseidon, of Pluto and Apollo, of Dionysus and Hercules, and of them all singly.[3] And of these you are yourselves not ignorant, and have been taught their manners of life, being instructed in the Grecian learning, that, as competitors with the gods, you might do like things.

CHAP. XVI. — WICKEDNESS OF JUPITER.

"But I shall begin with the most royal Zeus, whose father Kronos, having, as you say, devoured his own children, and having shorn off the members of his father Uranus with a sickle of adamant, showed to those who are zealous for the mysteries of the gods an example of piety towards parents and of love towards children. And Jupiter himself bound his own father, and imprisoned him in Tartarus; and he also punishes the other gods.[4] And for those who wish to do things not to be spoken of, he begat Metis, and devoured her. But Metis was seed; for it is impossible to devour a child. And for an excuse to abusers of themselves with mankind, he carries away Ganymedes. And as a helper of adulterers in their adultery, he is often found an adulterer. And to those who wish to commit incest with sisters, he sets the example in his intercourse with his sisters Hera and Demeter, and the heavenly Aphrodite, whom some call Dodona.[5] And to those who wish to commit incest with their daughters, there is a wicked example from his story, in his committing incest with Persephone. But in myriads of instances he acted impiously, that by reason of his excessive wickedness the fable of his being a god might be received by impious men.

CHAP. XVII. — "THEIR MAKERS ARE LIKE UNTO THEM."

"You will hold it reasonable for ignorant men to be moderately indignant at these fancies. But what must we say to the learned, some of whom, professing themselves to be grammarians and sophists, affirm that these acts are worthy of gods? For, being themselves incontinent, they lay hold of this mythical pretext; and as imitators of the gods,[6] they practise unseemly things with freedom.

CHAP. XVIII. — SECOND NATURE.

"On this account, they who live in the country sin much less than they do, not having been

---

[1] [Compare the discussion on Genesis in Homily XIV. 3, etc., but especially the full arguments in *Recognitions*, viii., ix. — R.]
[2] μυθολογοῦσαν.

[3] [See Homily VI 11-15, and comp. *Recognitions*, x. 20. — R.]
[4] Wieseler proposes θείους instead of θεούς; and he punishes his uncles also, as in vi. 2, 21.
[5] This is properly regarded as a mistake for Dione, or Didone, which is another form of the name Dione.
[6] Lit. " of those who are superior or better."

indoctrinated in those things in which they have been indoctrinated who dare do these things, having learned from evil instruction to be impious. For they who from their childhood learn letters by means of such fables, while their soul is yet pliant. engraft the impious deeds of those who are called gods into their own minds; whence, when they are grown up, they ripen fruit, like evil seeds cast into the soul. And what is worst of all, the rooted impurities cannot be easily cut down, when they are perceived to be bitter by them when they have attained to manhood. For every one is pleased to remain in those habits which he forms in childhood; and thus, since custom is not much less powerful than nature, they become difficult to be converted to those good things which were not sown in their souls from the beginning.

CHAP. XIX. — "WHERE IGNORANCE IS BLISS."

"Wherefore it behoves the young not to be satisfied with those corrupting lessons, and those who are in their prime should carefully avoid listening to the mythologies of the Greeks. For lessons about their gods are much worse than ignorance, as we have shown from the case of those dwelling in the country, who sin less through their not having been instructed by Greeks. Truly, such fables of theirs, and spectacles, and books, ought to be shunned, and if it were possible, even their cities. For those who are full of evil learning, even with their breath infect as with madness those who associate with them, with their own passions. And what is worst, whoever is most instructed among them, is so much the more turned from the judgment which is according to nature.

CHAP. XX. — FALSE THEORIES OF PHILOSOPHERS.

"And some of those amongst them who even profess to be philosophers, assert that such sins are indifferent, and say that those who are indignant at such practices are senseless.[1] For they say that such things are not sins by nature, but have been proscribed by laws made by wise men in early times, through their knowing that men, through the instability of their minds, being greatly agitated on these accounts, wage war with one another; for which reason, wise men have made laws to proscribe such things as sins. But this is a ridiculous supposition. For how can they be other than sins, which are the cause of tumults, and murders, and every confusion? For do not shortcomings of life[2] and many more evils proceed from adultery?

CHAP. XXI. — EVILS OF ADULTERY.

"But why, it is said, if a man is ignorant of his wife's being an adulteress, is he not indignant, enraged, distracted? why does he not make war? Thus these things are not evil by nature, but the unreasonable opinion of men make them terrible. But I say, that even if these dreadful things do not occur, it is usual for a woman, through association with an adulterer, either to forsake her husband, or if she continue to live with him, to plot against him, or to bestow upon the adulterer the goods procured by the labour of her husband; and having conceived by the adulterer while her husband is absent, to attempt the destruction of that which is in her womb, through shame of conviction, and so to become a child-murderer; or even, while destroying it, to be destroyed along with it. But if while her husband is at home she conceives by the adulterer and bears a child, the child when he grows up does not know his father, and thinks that he is his father who is not; and thus he who is not the father, at his death leaves his substance to the child of another. And how many other evils naturally spring from adultery! And the secret evils we do not know. For as the mad dog destroys all that he touches, infecting them with the unseen madness, so also the hidden evil of adultery, though it be not known, effects the cutting off of posterity.

CHAP. XXII. — A MORE EXCELLENT WAY.

"But let us pass over this now. But this we all know, that universally men are beyond measure enraged on account of it, that wars have been waged, that there have been overthrows of houses, and captures of cities, and myriads of other evils. On this account I betook myself to the holy God and law of the Jews, putting my faith in the well-assured conclusion that the law has been assigned by the righteous judgment of God, and that the soul must at some time receive according to the desert of its deeds."

CHAP. XXIII. — "WHITHER SHALL I GO FROM THY PRESENCE?"

When I had thus spoken, Appion broke in upon my discourse. "What!" said he; "do not the laws of the Greeks also forbid wickedness, and punish adulterers?" Then said I: "Then the gods of the Greeks, who acted contrary to the laws, deserve punishment. But how shall I be able to restrain myself, if I suppose that the gods themselves first practised all wickednesses as well as adultery, and did not suffer punishment; whereas they ought the rather to have suffered, as not being slaves to lust? But if they were subject to it, how were they gods?"

---

[1] [Compare the argument against the philosophers, as put in the mouth of the Apostle, in *Recognitions*, x. 48-50. — R.]
[2] The Vatican MS. inserts here, "upturning of houses, magic practices, deceptions, perplexities."

Then Appion said : " Let us have in our eye not the gods, but the judges ; and looking to them, we shall be afraid to sin." Then I said : " This is not fitting, O Appion : for he who has his eye upon men will dare to sin, in hope of escaping detection ; but he who sets before his soul the all-seeing God, knowing that he cannot escape His notice, will refrain from sinning even in secret."

CHAP. XXIV. — ALLEGORY.

When Appion heard this, he said : " I knew, ever since I heard that you were consorting with Jews, that you had alienated your judgment. For it has been well said by some one, ' Evil communications corrupt good manners.' " Then said I : " Therefore good communications correct evil manners." And Appion said : " To-day I am fully satisfied to have learned your position ; therefore I permitted you to speak first. But to-morrow, in this place, if it is agreeable to you, I will show, in the presence of these friends when they meet, that our gods are neither adulterers, nor murderers, nor corrupters of children, nor guilty of incest with sisters or daughters. But the ancients, wishing that only lovers of learning should know the mysteries, veiled them with those fables of which you have spoken. For they speak physiologically of boil-ing substance under the name of Zen, and of time under that of Kronos, and of the ever-flowing nature of water under that of Rhea. However, as I have promised, I shall to-morrow exhibit the truth of things, explaining them one by one to you when you come together in the morning." [1] In reply to this I said : " To-morrow, as you have promised, so do. But now hear something in opposition to what you are going to say.

CHAP. XXV. — AN ENGAGEMENT FOR TO-MORROW.

" If the doings of the gods, being good, have been veiled with evil fables, the wickedness of him who wove the veil is shown to have been great, because he concealed noble things with evil narratives, that no one imitate them. But if they really did things impious, they ought, on the contrary, to have veiled them with good narratives, lest men, regarding them as their superiors, should set about sinning in like manner." As I spoke thus, those present were evidently beginning to be well-disposed towards the words spoken by me ; for they repeatedly and earnestly asked me to come on the following day, and departed.

---

[1] [See Homily VI. 1-10. Homily V. contains an account of Clement's previous acquaintance with Appion. — R.]

HOMILY V.

CHAP. I. — APPION DOES NOT APPEAR.

THE next day, therefore, in Tyre, as we had agreed, I came to the quiet place, and there I found the rest, with some others also. Then I saluted them. But as I did not see Appion, I asked the reason of his not being present ; and some one said that he had been unwell ever since last evening. Then, when I said that it was reasonable that we should immediately set out to visit him, almost all begged me first to discourse to them, and that then we could go to see him. Therefore, as all were of one opinion, I proceeded to say : [1] —

CHAP. II. — CLEMENT'S PREVIOUS KNOWLEDGE OF APPION.

" Yesterday, when I left this, O friends, I confess that, through much anxiety about the discussion that was to take place with Appion, I was not able to get any sleep. And while I was unable to sleep, I remembered a trick that I played upon him in Rome. It was this. From my boyhood I Clement was a lover of truth, and a seeker of the things that are profitable for the soul, and spending my time in raising and refuting theories ; but being unable to find anything perfect, through distress of mind I fell sick. And while I was confined to bed Appion came to Rome, and being my father's friend, he lodged with me ; and hearing that I was in bed, he came to me, as being not unacquainted with medicine, and inquired the cause of my being in bed. But I, being aware that the man exceedingly hated the Jews, as also that he had written many books against them, and that he had formed a friendship with this Simon, not through desire of learning, but because he knew that he was a Samaritan and a hater of the Jews, and that he had come forth in opposition to the Jews, therefore he had formed an alliance with him, that he might learn something from him against the Jews ; [2] —

---

[1] [The historical setting of Homily V. is peculiar to this narrative; most of the views appear in a different connection in the *Recognitions* (mainly book x.). — R.]

[2] [See Homily IV. 6, footnote. — R.]

CHAP. III. — CLEMENT'S TRICK.

"I, knowing this before concerning Appion, as soon as he asked me the cause of my sickness, answered feignedly, that I was suffering and distressed in my mind after the manner of young men. And to this he said, 'My son, speak freely as to a father: what is your soul's ailment?' And when I again groaned feignedly, as being ashamed to speak of love, by means of silence and down-looking I conveyed the impression of what I wished to intimate. But he, being persuaded that I was in love with a woman, said: 'There is nothing in life which does not admit of help. For indeed I myself, when I was young, being in love with a most accomplished woman, not only thought it impossible to obtain her, but did not even hope ever to address her. And yet, having fallen in with a certain Egyptian who was exceedingly well versed in magic, and having become his friend, I disclosed to him my love, and not only did he assist me in all that I wished, but, honouring me more bountifully, he hesitated not to teach me an incantation by means of which I obtained her; and as soon as I had obtained her, by means of his secret instruction, being persuaded by the liberality of my teacher, I was cured of love.

CHAP. IV. — APPION'S UNDERTAKING.

"'Whence, if you also suffer any such thing after the manner of men, use freedom with me with all security; for within seven days I shall put you fully in possession of her.' When I heard this, looking at the object I had in view, I said: 'Pardon me that I do not altogether believe in the existence of magic; for I have already tried many who have made many promises, and have deceived me. However, your undertaking influences me, and leads me to hope. But when I think of the matter, I am afraid that the demons are sometimes not subject to the magicians with respect to the things that are commanded them.'

CHAP. V. — THEORY OF MAGIC.

"Then Appion said: 'Admit that I know more of these things than you do. However, that you may not think that there is nothing in what you have heard from me in reference to what you have said, I will tell you how the demons are under necessity to obey the magicians in the matters about which they are commanded. For as it is impossible for a soldier to contradict his general, and impossible for the generals themselves to disobey the king — for if any one oppose those set over him, he is altogether deserving of punishment — so it is impossible for the demons not to serve the angels who

are their generals; and when they are adjured by them, they yield trembling, well knowing that if they disobey they shall be fully punished. But the angels also themselves, being adjured by the magicians in the name of their ruler, obey, lest, being found guilty of disobedience, they be destroyed. For unless all things that are living and rational foresaw vengeance from the ruler, confusion would ensue, all revolting against one another.'

CHAP. VI. — SCRUPLES.

"Then said I: 'Are those things correct, then, which are spoken by poets and philosophers, that in Hades the souls of the wicked are judged and punished for their attempts; such as those of Ixion, and Tantalus, and Tityus, and Sisyphus, and the daughters of Danaus, and as many others as have been impious here? And how, if these things are not so, is it possible that magic can subsist?' Then he having told me that these things are so in Hades, I asked him: 'Why are not we ourselves afraid of magic, being persuaded of the punishment in Hades for adultery? For I do not admit that it is a righteous thing to compel to adultery a woman who is unwilling; but if any one will engage to persuade her, I am ready for that, besides confessing my thanks.'

CHAP. VII. — A DISTINCTION WITH A DIFFERENCE.

"Then Appion said: 'Do you not think it is the same thing, whether you obtain her by magic, or by deceiving her with words?' Then said I: 'Not altogether the same; for these differ widely from one another. For he who constrains an unwilling woman by the force of magic, subjects himself to the most terrible punishment, as having plotted against a chaste woman; but he who persuades her with words, and puts the choice in her own power and will, does not force her. And I am of opinion, that he who has persuaded *a woman* will not suffer so great punishment as he who has forced her. Therefore, if you can persuade her, I shall be thankful to you when I have obtained her; but otherwise, I had rather die than force her against her will.'

CHAP. VIII. — FLATTERY OR MAGIC.

"Then Appion, being really puzzled, said: 'What am I to say to you? For at one time, as one perturbed with love, you pray to obtain her; and anon, as if you loved her not, you make more account of your fear than your desire: and you think that if you can persuade her you shall be blameless, as without sin; but obtaining her by the power of magic, you will incur punishment. But do you not know that it is the end of every action that is judged, the fact that it has been committed, and that no account is made of the means by which it has been effected? And if you commit adultery, being enabled by magic, shall you be judged as having done wickedly ; and if by persuasion, shall you be absolved from sin in respect of the adultery?' Then I said : 'On account of my love, there is a necessity for me to choose one or other of the means that are available to procure the object of my love ; and I shall choose, as far as possible, to cajole her rather than to use magic. But neither is it easy to persuade her by flattery, for the woman is very much of a philosopher.'

CHAP. IX. — A LOVE-LETTER.

"Then Appion said : 'I am all the more hopeful to be able to persuade her, as you wish, provided only we be able to converse with her.' 'That,' said I, 'is impossible.' Then Appion asked if it were possible to send a letter to her. Then I said : 'That indeed may be done.' Then Appion said : 'This very night I shall write a paper on encomiums of adultery, which you shall get from me and despatch to her ; and I hope that she shall be persuaded, and consent.' Appion accordingly wrote the paper, and gave it to me ; and I thought of it this very night, and I remembered that fortunately I have it by me, along with other papers which I carry about with me." Having thus spoken, I showed the paper to those who were present, and read it to them as they wished to hear it ; and having read it, I said : "This, O men, is the instruction of the Greeks, affording a bountiful licence to sin without fear.[1] The paper was as follows : —

CHAP. X. — THE LOVER TO THE BELOVED ONE.

" 'Anonymously, on account of the laws of foolish men. At the bidding of Love, the first-born of all, salutation : I know that you are devoted to philosophy, and for the sake of virtue you affect the life of the noble. But who are nobler than the gods among all, and philosophers among men? For these alone know what works are good or evil by nature, and what, not being so, are accounted so by the imposition of laws. Now, then, some have supposed that the action which is called adultery is evil, although it is in every respect good. For it is by the appointment of Eros for the increase of life. And Eros is the eldest of all the gods. For without Eros there can be no mingling or generation either of elements, or gods, or men, or irrational animals, or aught else. For we are all instruments of Eros. He, by means of us, is the fabricator of all that is begotten, the mind inhabiting our souls. Hence it is not when we ourselves wish it, but when we are ordered by him, that we desire to do his will. But if, while we desire according to his will, we attempt to restrain the desire for the sake of what is called chastity, what do we do but the greatest impiety, when we oppose the oldest of all gods and men?

CHAP. XI. — "ALL UNCLEANNESS WITH GREEDINESS."

" 'But let all doors be opened to him, and let all baneful and arbitrary laws be set aside, which have been ordained by fanatical men, who, under the power of senselessness, and not willing to understand what is reasonable, and, moreover, suspecting those who are called adulterers, are with good reason mocked with arbitrary laws by Zeus himself, through Minos and Rhadamanthus. For there is no restraining of Eros dwelling in our souls ; for the passion of lovers is not voluntary. Therefore Zeus himself, the giver of these laws, approached myriads of women ; and, according to some wise men, he sometimes had intercourse with human beings, as a benefactor for the production of children. But in the case of those to whom he knew that his being unknown would be a favour,[2] he changed his form, in order that he might neither grieve them, nor seem to act in opposition to the laws given by himself. It becomes you, therefore, who are debaters of philosophy, for the sake of a good life, to imitate those who are acknowledged to be the nobler, who have had sexual intercourse ten thousand times.

CHAP. XII. — JUPITER'S AMOURS.

" 'And not to spend the time to no purpose in giving more examples, I shall begin with mentioning some embraces of Zeus himself, the father of gods and men.[3] For it is impossible to mention all, on account of their multitude. Hear, therefore, the amours of this great Jupiter, which he concealed by changing his form, on account of the fanaticism of senseless men. For, in the first place, wishing to show to wise men that adultery is no sin, when he was going to marry, being, according to the multitude, knowingly an adulterer, in his first marriage, but not being so in reality, by means, as I said, of a seeming sin he accomplished a sinless marriage.[4] For he married his own sister Hera, assuming the likeness of a cuckoo's wing ; and of her were born Hebe and Ilithyia. For he gave birth to Metis without copulation with any one, as did also Hera to Vulcan.

---

[1] [The introduction of the letters is an ingenious literary artifice. Much of the mythological matter is given in *Recognitions*, x. — R.]

[2] We have adopted the punctuation of Wieseler.
[3] [Comp. *Recognitions*, x. 20-23, for a parallel to chaps. 12-15. — R.]
[4] I have no doubt that this is the general meaning ; but the text is hopelessly corrupt.

CHAP. XIII. — JUPITER'S AMOURS CONTINUED.

"'Then he committed incest with his sister, who was born of Kronos and Thalasse, after the dismemberment of Kronos, and of whom were born Eros and Cypris, whom they call also Dodone. Then, in the likeness of a satyr, he had intercourse with Antiope the daughter of Nycteus, of whom were born Amphion and Zethus. And he embraced Alcmene, the wife of Amphitryon, in the form of her husband Amphitryon, of whom was born Hercules. And, changed into an eagle, he approached Ægina, the daughter of Asclepius, of whom Æacus was born. And in the form of a bear he lay with Amalthea the daughter of Phocus ; and in a golden shower he fell upon Danae, the daughter of Acrisius, of whom sprang Perseus. He became wild as a lion to Callisto the daughter of Lycaon, and begat Arcus the second. And with Europa the daughter of Phœnix he had intercourse by means of a bull, of whom sprang Minos, and Rhadamanthus, and Sarpedon ; and with Eurymedusa the daughter of Achelous, changing himself into an ant, of whom was born Myrmidon. With a nymph of Hersæus, in the form of a vulture, from whom sprang the wise men of old in Sicily. He came to Juno the earth-born in Rhodes, and of her were born Pargæus, Kronius, Kytis. And he deflowered Ossia, taking the likeness of her husband Phœnix, of whom Anchinous was born to him. Of Nemesis the daughter of Thestius, who is also thought to be Leda, he begot Helena, in the form of a swan or goose ; and again, in the form of a star, he produced Castor and Polydeuces. With Lamia he was transformed into a hoopoo.

CHAP. XIV. — JUPITER'S UNDISGUISED AMOURS.

"'In the likeness of a shepherd he made Mnemosyne mother of the Muses. Setting himself on fire, he married Semele, the daughter of Cadmus, of whom he begat Dionysus. In the likeness of a dragon he deflowered his daughter Persephone, thought to be the wife of his brother Pluto. He had intercourse with many other women without undergoing any change in his form ; for the husbands had no ill-will to him as if it were a sin, but knew well that in associating with their wives he bountifully produced children for them, bestowing upon them the Hermeses, the Apollos, the Dionysi, the Endymions, and others whom we have spoken of, most excellent in beauty through his fatherhood.

CHAP. XV. — UNNATURAL LUSTS.

"'And not to spend the time in an endless exposition, you will find numerous unions with Jupiter of all the gods. But senseless men call these doings of the gods adulteries ; even of those gods who did not refrain from the abuse of males as disgraceful, but who practised even this as seemly. For instance, Jupiter himself was in love with Ganymede : Poseidon with Pelops ; Apollo with Cinyras, Zacyinthus, Hyacinthus, Phorbas, Hylas, Admetus, Cyparissus, Amyclas, Troilus, Branchus the Tymnæan, Parus the Potnian, Orpheus ; Dionysus with Laonis, Ampelus, Hymenæus, Hermaphrodites, Achilles ; Asclepius with Hippolytus, and Hephæstus with Peleus ; Pan with Daphnis ; Hermes with Perseus, Chrysas, Theseus, Odrysus ; Hercules with Abderus, Dryops, Jocastus, Philoctetes, Hylas, Polyphemus, Hæmon, Chonus, Eurystheus.

CHAP. XVI. — PRAISE OF UNCHASTITY.

"'Thus have I in part set before you the amours of all the more noted gods, beloved, that you may know that fanaticism respecting this thing is confined to senseless men. Therefore they are mortal, and spend their lives sadly, because through their zeal they proclaim those things to be evil which the gods esteem as excellent. Therefore for the future you will be blessed, imitating the gods, and not men. For men, seeing you preserving that which is thought to be chastity, on account of what they themselves feel, praise you indeed, but do not help you. But the gods, seeing you like unto themselves, will both praise and help.

CHAP. XVII. — THE CONSTELLATIONS.

"'For reckon to me how many mistresses they have rewarded, some of whom they have placed among the stars ; and of some they have blessed both the children and the associates. Thus Zeus made Callisto a constellation, called the Little Bear, which some also call the Dog's Tail. Poseidon also placed the dolphin in the sky for the sake of Amphitrite ; and he gave a place among the stars to Orion the son of Euryale, the daughter of Minos, for the sake of his mother Euryale. And Dionysus made a constellation of the crown of Ariadne, and Zeus invested the eagle which assisted him in the rape of Ganymede, and Ganymede himself with the honour of the Water-pourer. Also he honoured the bull for the sake of Europa ; and also having bestowed Castor, and Polydeuces, and Helena upon Leda, he made them stars. Also Perseus for the sake of Danae ; and Arcus for the sake of Callisto. The virgin who also is Dice, for the sake of Themis ; and Heracles for the sake of Alcmene. But I do not enlarge further ; for it were long to tell particularly how many others the gods have blessed for the sake of their many mistresses, in their intercourse with human beings, which senseless men repudiate as evil deeds, not knowing that pleasure is the great advantage among men.

CHAP. XVIII. — THE PHILOSOPHERS ADVOCATES OF ADULTERY.

" ' But why? Do not the celebrated philosophers extol pleasure, and have they not had intercourse with what women they would? Of these the first was that teacher of Greece, of whom Phœbus himself said, " Of all men, Socrates is the wisest." Does not he teach that in a well-regulated state women should be common?[1] and did he not conceal the fair Alcibiades under his philosopher's gown? And the Socratic Antisthenes writes of the necessity of not abandoning what is called adultery. And even his disciple Diogenes, did not he freely associate with Lais, for the hire of carrying her on his shoulders in public? Does not Epicurus extol pleasure? Did not Aristippus anoint himself with perfumes, and devote himself wholly to Aphrodite? Does not Zeno, intimating indifference, say that the deity pervades all things, that it may be known to the intelligent, that with whomsoever a man has intercourse, it is as with himself; and that it is superfluous to forbid what are called adulteries, or intercourse with mother, or daughter, or sister, or children. And Chrysippus, in his erotic epistles, makes mention of the statue in Argos, representing Hera and Zeus in an obscene position.

CHAP. XIX. — CLOSE OF THE LOVE-LETTER.

" ' I know that to those uninitiated in the truth these things seem dreadful and most base ; but not so to the gods and the philosophers of the Greeks, nor to those initiated in the mysteries of Dionysus and Demeter. But above all these, not to waste time in speaking of the lives of all the gods, and all the philosophers, let the two chief be your marks — Zeus the greatest of the gods, and Socrates of philosophic men. And the other things which I have mentioned in this letter, understand and attend to, that you may not grieve your lover ; since, if you act contrarily to gods and heroes, you will be judged wicked, and will subject yourself to fitting punishment. But if you offer yourself to every lover, then, as an imitator of the gods, you shall receive benefits from them. For the rest, dearest one, remember what mysteries I have disclosed to you, and inform me by letter of your choice. Fare thee well.'

CHAP. XX. — THE USE MADE OF IT.

" I therefore, having received this billet from Appion, as though I were really going to send it to a beloved one, pretended as if she had written in answer to it ; and the next day, when Appion came, I gave him the reply, as if from her, as follows : —

CHAP. XXI. — ANSWER TO APPION'S LETTER.

" ' I wonder how, when you commend me for wisdom, you write to me as to a fool. For, wishing to persuade me to your passion, you make use of examples from the mythologies of the gods, that Eros is the eldest of all, as you say, and above all gods and men, not being afraid to blaspheme, that you might corrupt my soul and insult my body. For Eros is not the leader of the gods, — he, I mean, who has to do with lusts. For if he lusts willingly, he is himself his own suffering and punishment ; and he who should suffer willingly could not be a god. But if against his will he lust for copulation, and, pervading our souls as through the members of our bodies, is borne into intermeddling with our minds, then he that impels him to love is greater than he. And again, he who impels him, being himself impelled by another desire, another greater than he is found impelling him. And thus we come to an endless succession of lovers,[2] which is impossible. Thus, neither is there an impeller nor an impelled ; but it is the lustful passion of the lover himself, which is increased by hope and diminished by despair.

CHAP. XXII. — LYING FABLES.

" ' But those who will not subdue base lusts belie the gods, that, by representing the gods as first doing the things which they do, they may be set free from blame. For if those who are called gods committed adulteries for the sake of begetting children, and not through lasciviousness, why did they also debauch males? But it is said they complimented their mistresses by making them stars. Therefore before this were there no stars, until such time as, by reason of wantonness, the heaven was adorned with stars by adulterers? And how is it that the children of those who have been made stars are punished in Hades, — Atlas loaded, Tantalus tortured with thirst, Sisyphus pushing a stone, Tityus thrust through the bowels, Ixion continually rolled round a wheel? How is it that these divine lovers made stars of the women whom they defiled, but gave no such grace to these?

CHAP. XXIII. — THE GODS NO GODS.

" ' They were not gods, then, but representations of tyrants. For a certain tomb is shown among the Caucasian mountains, not in heaven, but in

---

[1] This from a marginal reading.

[2] I suspect it should rather be *impellers*, reading φερόντων for ἐρώντων.

earth, as that of Kronos, a barbarous man and a devourer of children. Further, the tomb of the lascivious Zeus, so famed in story, who in like manner devoured his own daughter Metis, is to be seen in Crete, and those of Pluto and Poseidon in the Acherusian lake; and that of Helius in Astra, and of Selene in Carræ, of Hermes in Hermopolis, of Ares in Thrace, of Aphrodite in Cyprus, of Dionysus in Thebes, and of the rest in other places. At all events, the tombs are shown of those that I have named; for they were men, and in respect of these things, wicked men and magicians.[1] For else they should not have become despots—I mean Zeus, renowned in story, and Dionysus—but that by changing their forms they prevailed over whom they pleased, for whatever purpose they designed.

CHAP. XXIV. — IF A PRINCIPLE BE GOOD, CARRY IT OUT.

" ' But if we must emulate their lives, let us imitate not only their adulteries, but also their banquets. For Kronos devoured his own children, and Zeus in like manner his own daughter. And what must I say? Pelops served as a supper for all the gods. Wherefore let us also, before unhallowed marriages, perpetrate a supper like that of the gods; for thus the supper would be worthy of the marriages. But this you would never consent to; no more will I to adultery. Besides this, you threaten me with the anger of Eros as of a powerful god. Eros is not a god, as I conceive him, but a desire occurring from the temperament of the living creature in order to the perpetuation of life, according to the foresight of Him who worketh all things, that the whole race may not fail, but by reason of pleasure another may be produced out of the substance of one who shall die, springing forth by lawful marriage, that he may know to sustain his own father in old age. And this those born from adultery cannot do, not having the nature of affection towards those who have begotten them.

CHAP. XXV. — BETTER TO MARRY THAN TO BURN.

" ' Since, therefore, the erotic desire occurs for the sake of continuation and legitimate increasing, as I have said, it behoves parents providing for the chastity of their children to anticipate the desire, by imbuing them with instruction by means of chaste books, and to accustom them beforehand by excellent discourses; for custom is a second nature. And in addition to this, frequently to remind them of the punishments appointed by the laws, that, using fear as a bridle, they may not run on in wicked pleasures.

And it behoves them also, before the springing of the desire, to satisfy the natural passion of puberty by marriage, first persuading them not to look upon the beauty of another woman.

CHAP. XXVI. — CLOSE OF THE ANSWER.

" ' For our mind, whenever it is impressed delightfully with the image of a beloved one, always seeing the form as in a mirror, is tormented by the recollection; and if it do not obtain its desire, it contrives ways of obtaining it; but if it do obtain it, it is rather increased, like fire having a supply of wood, and especially when there is no fear impressed upon the soul of the lover before the rise of passion. For as water extinguishes fire, so fear is the extinguisher of unreasonable desire. Whence I, having learned from a certain Jew both to understand and to do the things that are pleasing to God, am not to be entrapped into adultery by your lying fables. But may God help you in your wish and efforts to be chaste, and afford a remedy to your soul burning with love.'

CHAP. XXVII. — A REASON FOR HATRED.

" When Appion heard the pretended answer, he said: " Is it without reason that I hate the Jews? Here now some Jew has fallen in with her, and has converted her to his religion, and persuaded her to chastity, and it is henceforth impossible that she ever have intercourse with another man; for these fellows, setting God before them as the universal inspector of actions, are extremely persistent in chastity, as being unable to be concealed from Him.'

CHAP. XXVIII. — THE HOAX CONFESSED.

" When I heard this, I said to Appion: ' Now I shall confess the truth to you. I was not enamoured of the woman, or of any one else, my soul being exceedingly spent upon other desires, and upon the investigation of true doctrines. And till now, although I have examined many doctrines of philosophers, I have inclined to none of them, excepting only that of the Jews,—a certain merchant of theirs having sojourned here in Rome, selling linen clothes, and a fortunate meeting having set simply before me the doctrine of the unity of God.'

CHAP. XXIX. — APPION'S RESENTMENT.

" Then Appion, having heard from me the truth, with his unreasonable hatred of the Jews, and neither knowing nor wishing to know what their faith is, being senselessly angry, forthwith quitted Rome in silence. And as this is my first meeting with him since then, I naturally expect his anger in consequence. However, I shall ask him in your presence what he has to say con-

---

[1] [Compare the different use of these details in *Recognitions*, x. 24; also in Homily VI. 21. — R.]

cerning those who are called gods, whose lives, fabled to be filled with all passions, are constantly celebrated to the people, in order to their imitation; while, besides their human passions as I have said, their graves are also shown in different places."

CHAP. XXX. — A DISCUSSION PROMISED.

The others having heard these things from me, and desiring to learn what would ensue, ac-companied me to visit Appion. And we found him bathed, and sitting at a table furnished. Wherefore we inquired but little into the matter concerning the gods. But he, understanding, I suppose, our wish, promised that next day he would have something to say about the gods, and appointed to us the same place where he would converse with us. And we, as soon as he had promised, thanked him, and departed, each one to his home.

HOMILY VI.

CHAP. I. — CLEMENT MEETS APPION.

AND on the third day, when I came with my friends to the appointed place in Tyre, I found Appion sitting between Anubion and Athenodorus, and waiting for us, along with many other learned men. But in no wise dismayed, I greeted them, and sat down opposite Appion. And in a little he began to speak : —

" I wish to start from the following point, and to come with all speed at once to the question. Before you, my son Clement, joined us, my friend Anubion here, and Athenodorus, who yesterday were among those who heard you discourse, were reporting to me what you said of the numerous false accusations I brought against the gods when I was visiting you in Rome, at the time you were shamming love, how I charged them with pæderasty, lasciviousness, and numerous incests of all kinds. But, my son, you ought to have known that I was not in earnest when I wrote such things about the gods, but was concealing the truth, from my love to you. That truth, however, if it so please you, you may hear from me now.

CHAP. II. — THE MYTHS ARE NOT TO BE TAKEN LITERALLY.

" The wisest of the ancients, men who had by hard labour learned all truth, kept the path of knowledge hid from those who were unworthy and had no taste for lessons in divine things.[1] For it is not really true that from Ouranos and his mother Ge were born twelve children, as the myth counts them : six sons, Okeanos, Koios, Krios, Hyperion, Japetos, Kronos; and six daughters, Thea, Themis, Mnemosyne, Demeter, Tethys, and Rhea.[2] Nor that Kronos, with the knife of adamant, mutilated his father Ouranos, as you say, and threw the part into the sea; nor that Aphrodite sprang from the drops of blood which flowed from it; nor that Kronos associated with Rhea, and devoured his first-begotten son Pluto, because a certain saying of Prometheus led him to fear that a child born from him would wax stronger than himself, and spoil him of his kingdom; nor that he devoured in the same way Poseidon, his second child; nor that, when Zeus was born next, his mother Rhea concealed him, and when Kronos asked for him that he might devour him, gave him a stone instead; nor that this, when it was devoured, pressed those who had been previously devoured, and forced them out, so that Pluto, who was devoured first, came out first, and after him Poseidon, and then Zeus;[3] nor that Zeus, as the story goes, preserved by the wit of his mother, ascended into heaven, and spoiled his father of the kingdom; nor that he punished his father's brothers; nor that he came down to lust after mortal women; nor that he associated with his sisters, and daughters, and sisters-in-law, and was guilty of shameful pæderasty; nor that he devoured his daughter Metis, in order that from her he might make Athene be born out of his own brain (and from his thigh might bear Dionysos, who is said to have been rent in pieces by the Titans); nor that he held a feast at the marriage of Peleus and Thetis;[5] nor that he excluded Eris (discord) from the marriage; nor that Eris on her part, thus dishonoured, contrived an occasion of quarrelling and discord among the feasters; nor that she took a golden apple from the gardens of the Hesperides, and wrote on it ' For the fair.' And then they fable how Hera, and Athena, and Aphrodite, found the apple, and quarrelling about it, came to Zeus; and he

---

[1] [Compare in general, with chaps. 2–22, the mythological statements in *Recognitions*, x. 17–41. — R.]
[2] [Comp. *Recognitions*, x. 17, 31. — R.]
[3] The passage seems to be corrupt.
[4] The common story about Dionysus is, that he was the unborn son, not of Metis, but of Semele. Wieseler supposes that some words have fallen out, or that the latter part of the sentence is a careless interpolation.
[5] [Compare, on " the supper of the gods," chap. 15, and *Recognitions*, x. 41. — R.]

did not decide it for them, but sent them by Hermes to the shepherd Paris, to be judged of their beauty. But there was no such judging of the goddesses; nor did Paris give the apple to Aphrodite; nor did Aphrodite, being thus honoured, honour him in return, by giving him Helen to wife. For the honour bestowed by the goddess could never have furnished a pretext for a universal war, and that to the ruin of him who was honoured, himself nearly related to the race of Aphrodite. But, my son, as I said, such stories have a peculiar and philosophical meaning, which can be allegorically set forth in such a way that you yourself would listen with wonder." And I said, "I beseech you not to torment me with delay." And he said, "Do not be afraid; for I shall lose no time, but commence at once.

CHAP. III. — APPION PROCEEDS TO INTERPRET THE MYTHS.

"There was once a time when nothing existed but chaos and a confused mixture of orderless elements, which were as yet simply heaped together.[1] This nature testifies, and great men have been of opinion that it was so. Of these great men I shall bring forward to you him who excelled them all in wisdom, Homer, where he says, with a reference to the original confused mass, 'But may you all become water and earth;'[2] implying that from these all things had their origin, and that all things return to their first state, which is chaos, when the watery and earthy substances are separated. And Hesiod in the THEOGONY says, 'Assuredly chaos was the very first to come into being.'[3] Now, by 'come into being,' he evidently means that chaos came into being, as having a beginning, and did not always exist, without beginning. And Orpheus likens chaos to an egg, in which was the confused mixture of the primordial elements. This chaos, which Orpheus calls an egg, is taken for granted by Hesiod, having a beginning, produced from infinite matter, and originated in the following way.

CHAP. IV. — ORIGIN OF CHAOS.

"This matter, of four kinds, and endowed with life, was an entire infinite abyss, so to speak, in eternal stream, borne about without order, and forming every now and then countless but ineffectual combinations (which therefore it dissolved again from want of order); ripe indeed, but not able to be bound so as to generate a living creature. And once it chanced that this infinite sea, which was thus by its own nature

driven about with a natural motion, flowed in an orderly manner from the same to the same (back on itself), like a whirlpool, mixing the substances in such a way that from each[4] there flowed down the middle of the universe (as in the funnel of a mould) precisely that which was most useful and suitable for the generation of a living creature. This was carried down by the all-carrying whirlpool, drew to itself the surrounding spirit, and having been so conceived that it was very fertile, formed a separate substance. For just as a bubble is usually formed in water, so everything round about contributed to the conception of this ball-like globe. Then there came forth to the light, after it had been conceived in itself, and was borne upwards by the divine spirit which surrounded it,[5] perhaps the greatest thing ever born; a piece of workmanship, so to speak, having life in it which had been conceived from that entire infinite abyss, in shape like an egg, and as swift as a bird.

CHAP. V. — KRONOS AND RHEA EXPLAINED.

"Now you must think of Kronos as time (CHRONOS), and Rhea as the flowing (RHEON) of the watery substance.[6] For the whole body of matter was borne about for some TIME, before it brought forth, like an egg, the sphere-like, all-embracing heaven (OURANOS), which at first was full of productive marrow, so that it was able to produce out of itself elements and colours of all sorts, while from the one substance and the one colour it produced all kinds of forms. For as a peacock's egg seems to have only one colour, while potentially it has in it all the colours of the animal that is to be, so this living egg, conceived out of infinite matter, when set in motion by the underlying and ever-flowing matter, produces many different forms. For within the circumference a certain living creature, which is both male and female, is formed by the skill of the indwelling divine spirit. This Orpheus calls Phanes, because when it appeared (PHANEIS) the universe shone forth from it, with the lustre of that most glorious of the elements, fire, perfected in moisture. Nor is this incredible, since in glowworms nature gives us to see a moist light.

CHAP. VI. — PHANES AND PLUTO.

"This egg, then, which was the first substance, growing somewhat hot, was broken by the living creature within, and then there took shape and came forth something;[7] such as Orpheus also speaks of, where he says, 'when the capacious

---

[1] [With this discourse and its cosmogony compare the discourse of Clement and his brothers in *Recognitions*, x. 17-19, 30-34. — R.]
[2] *Iliad*, vii. 99.
[3] L. 116.

[4] This is the emendation of Davisius. The Greek has ἐξ ἀκουστοῦ; the Latin, "mirum in modum." Wieseler suggests ἐξακοντιστόν.
[5] This is Wieseler's emendation for "received."
[6] [Comp. *Recognitions*, x. 17, 31, 32. — R.]
[7] Wieseler corrects to "some such being," etc.; and below, "of him who appeared," etc.; and "he took his seat."

egg was broken,'¹ etc. And so by the mighty power of that which appeared (PHANEIS) and came forth, the globe attained coherency, and maintained order, while it itself took its seat, as it were, on the summit of heaven, there in ineffable mystery diffusing light through endless ages. But the productive matter left inside the globe, separated the substances of all things. For first its lower part, just like the dregs, sank downwards of its own weight; and this they called Pluto from its gravity, and weight, and great quantity (POLU) of underlying matter, styling it the king of Hades and the dead.²

CHAP. VII. — POSEIDON, ZEUS, AND METIS.

"When, then, they say that this primordial substance, although most filthy and rough, was devoured by Kronos, that is, time, this is to be understood in a physical sense, as meaning that it sank downwards. And the water which flowed together after this first sediment, and floated on the surface of the first substance, they called Poseidon. And then what remained, the purest and noblest of all, for it was translucent fire, they called Zeus, from its glowing (ZEOUSA) nature. Now since fire ascends, this was not swallowed, and made to descend by time or Kronos; but, as I said, the fiery substance, since it has life in it, and naturally ascends, flew right up into the air, which from its purity is very intelligent. By his own proper heat, then, Zeus — that is, the glowing substance — draws up what is left in the underlying moisture, to wit, that very strong³ and divine spirit which they called Metis.

CHAP. VIII. — PALLAS AND HERA.

"And this, when it had reached the summit of the æther, was devoured by it (moisture being mixed with heat, so to say) ; and causing in it that ceaseless palpitation, it begat intelligence, which they call Pallas from this palpitating (PALLESTHAI).⁴ And this is artistic wisdom, by which the ætherial artificer wrought out the whole world. And from all-pervading Zeus, that is, from this very hot æther, air (AER) extends all the way to our earth; and this they call Hera. Wherefore, because it has come below the æther, which is the purest substance (just as a woman, as regards purity, is inferior), when the two were compared to see which was the better, she was rightly regarded as the sister of Zeus, in respect of her origin from the same substance, but as his spouse, as being inferior like a wife.

CHAP. IX. — ARTEMIS.

"And Hera we understand to be a happy tempering of the atmosphere, and therefore she is very fruitful; but Athena, as they call Pallas, was reckoned a virgin, because on account of the intense heat she could produce nothing. And in a similar fashion Artemis is explained : for her they take as the lowest depth of air, and so they called her a virgin, because she could not bear anything on account of the extreme cold. And that troubled and drunken composition which arises from the upper and lower vapours they called Dionysus, as troubling the intellect. And the water under the earth, which is in nature indeed one, but which flows through all the paths of earth, and is divided into many parts, they called Osiris, as being cut in pieces. And they understand Adonis as favourable seasons, Aphrodite as coition and generation, Demeter as the earth, the Girl (Proserpine) as seeds; and Dionysus some understand as the vine.

CHAP. X. — ALL SUCH STORIES ARE ALLEGORICAL.

"And I must ask you to think of all such stories as embodying some such allegory. Look on Apollo as the wandering Sun (PERI-POLÔN), a son of Zeus, who was also called Mithras, as completing the period of a year. And these said transformations of the all-pervading Zeus must be regarded as the numerous changes of the seasons, while his numberless wives you must understand to be years, or generations. For the power which proceeds from the æther and passes through the air unites with all the years and generations in turn, and continually varies them, and so produces or destroys the crops. And ripe fruits are called his children, the barrenness of some seasons being referred to unlawful unions."

CHAP. XI. — CLEMENT HAS HEARD ALL THIS BEFORE.

While Appion was allegorizing in this way, I became plunged in thought, and seemed not to be following what he was saying. So he interrupted his discourse, and said to me, "If you do not follow what I am saying, why should I speak at all?" And I answered, "Do not suppose that I do not understand what you say. I understand it thoroughly; and that the more that this is not the first time I have heard it. And that you may know that I am not ignorant of these things, I shall epitomize what you have said, and supply in their order, as I have heard them from others, the allegorical interpretations of those stories you have omitted." And Appion said : "Do so."

---

¹ The first word of this quotation gives no sense, and has been omitted in the translation. Lobeck suggests " at its prime:" Hermann, "Heracapeian;" Duentzer, "ancient;" and Wieseler, "white."
² [Comp. *Recognitions*, x. 32. — R.]
³ The Paris MS. has " very fine."
⁴ [With chaps. 8–10 compare *Recognitions*, x. 32, 34. — R.]

CHAP. XII. — EPITOME OF APPION'S EXPLANATION.

And I answered:[1] "I shall not at present speak particularly of that living egg, which was conceived by a happy combination out of infinite matter, and from which, when it was broken, the masculo-feminine Phanes leaped forth, as some say. I say little about all that, up to the point when this broken globe attained coherency, there being left in it some of its marrow-like matter; and I shall briefly run over the description of what took place in it by the agency of this matter, with all that followed. For from Kronos and Rhea were born, as you say — that is, by time and matter — first Pluto, who represents the sediment which settled down; and then Poseidon, the liquid substance in the middle,[2] which floated over the heavier body below; and the third child — that is, Zeus — is the æther, and is highest of all. It was not devoured; but as it is a fiery power, and naturally ascends, it flew up as with a bound to the very highest æther.

CHAP. XIII. — KRONOS AND APHRODITE.

"And the bonds of Kronos are the binding together of heaven and earth, as I have heard others allegorizing; and his mutilation is the separation and parting of the elements; for they all were severed and separated, according to their respective natures, that each kind might be arranged by itself. And time no longer begets anything; but the things which have been begotten of it, by a law of nature, produce their successors. And the Aphrodite who emerged from the sea is the fruitful substance which arises out of moisture, with which the warm spirit mixing, causes that sexual desire, and perfects the beauty of the world.

CHAP. XIV. — PELEUS AND THETIS, PROMETHEUS, ACHILLES, AND POLYXENA.

"And the marriage banquet, at which Zeus held the feast on the occasion of the marriage of the Nereid Thetis and the beautiful Peleus, has in it this allegory,[3] — that you may know, Appion, that you are not the only one from whom I have heard this sort of thing. The banquet, then, is the world, and the twelve are these heavenly props of the Fates,[4] called the Zodiac. Prometheus is foresight (PROMETHEIA), by which all things arose; Peleus is clay (PELOS), namely, that which was COLLECTED[5] from the earth and mixed with Nereis, or water, to produce man; and from the mixing of the two, i.e., water and

earth, the first offspring was not begotten, but fashioned complete, and called Achilles, because he never put his lips (CHEILE) to the breast.[6] Still in the bloom of life, he is slain by an arrow while desiring to have Polyxena, that is, something other than the truth, and foreign (XENE) to it, death stealing on him through a wound in his foot.

CHAP. XV. — THE JUDGMENT OF PARIS.

"Then Hera, and Athena, and Aphrodite, and Eris, and the apple, and Hermes, and the judgment, and the shepherd, have some such hidden meaning as the following: — Hera is dignity; Athena, manliness; Aphrodite, pleasure; Hermes, language, which interprets (HERMENEUTIKOS) thought; the shepherd Paris, unreasoned and brutish passion. Now if, in the prime of life, reason, that shepherd of the soul, is brutish, does not regard its own advantage, will have nothing to do with manliness and temperance, chooses only pleasure, and gives the prize to lust alone, bargaining that it is to receive in return from lust what may delight it, — he who thus judges incorrectly will choose pleasure to his own destruction and that of his friends. And Eris is jealous spite; and the golden apples of the Hesperides are perhaps riches, by which occasionally even temperate persons like Hera are seduced, and manly ones like Athena are made jealous, so that they do things which do not become them, and the soul's beauty like Aphrodite is destroyed under the guise of refinement. To speak briefly, in all men riches provoke evil discord.

CHAP. XVI. — HERCULES.

"And Hercules, who slew the serpent which led and guarded riches, is the true philosophical reason which, free from all wickedness, wanders all over the world, visiting the souls of men, and chastising all it meets, — namely, men like fierce lions, or timid stags, or savage boars, or multiform hydras; and so with all the other fabled labours of Hercules, they all have a hidden reference to moral valour. But these instances must suffice, for all our time would be insufficient if we were to go over each one.

CHAP. XVII. — THEY ARE BLAMEWORTHY WHO INVENTED SUCH STORIES.

"Now,[7] since these things can be clearly, profitably, and without prejudice to piety, set forth in an open and straightforward manner, I wonder you call those men sensible and wise who concealed them under crooked riddles, and over-

---

[1] [Comp. *Recognitions*, x. 17-19, 29-36, 41, for statements similar to those in chaps. 12-19. — R.]
[2] This is Wieseler's conjecture.
[3] [Comp. chap. 2, and *Recognitions*, 40, 41. — R.]
[4] The Latin takes "moira" in the sense of "district," and translates, "these props of the districts of the sky."
[5] This is Wieseler's conjecture for the reading of the mss., "contrived."

[6] This is Schwegler's restoration of the passage. Davisius proposes, "He is in the bloom of life, at which time if any one desires," etc.
[7] [Compare with the arguments here, *Recognitions*, x. 35-38. — R.]

laid them with filthy stories, and thus, as if impelled by an evil spirit, deceived almost all men. For either these things are not riddles, but real crimes of the gods, in which case they should not have been exposed to contempt, nor should these their needs have been set before men at all as models; or things falsely attributed to the gods were set forth in an allegory, and then, Appion, they whom you call wise erred, in that, by concealing under unworthy stories things in themselves worthy, they led men to sin, and that not without dishonouring those whom they believed to be gods.

CHAP. XVIII. — THE SAME.

"Wherefore do not suppose that they were wise men, but rather evil spirits, who could cover honourable actions with wicked stories, in order that they who wish to imitate their betters may emulate these deeds of so-called gods, which yesterday in my discourse I spoke so freely of, — namely, their parricides, their murders of their children, their incests of all kinds, their shameless adulteries and countless impurities. The most impious of them are those who wish these stories to be believed, in order that they may not be ashamed when they do the like. If they had been disposed to act reverently, they ought, as I said a little ago, even if the gods really did the things which are sung of them, to have veiled their indecencies under more seemly stories, and not, on the contrary, as you say they did, when the deeds of the gods were honourable, clothed them in wicked and indecent forms, which, even when interpreted, can only be understood by much labour; and when they were understood by some, they indeed got for their much toil the privilege of not being deceived, which they might have had without the toil, while they who were deceived were utterly ruined. (Those, however, who trace the allegories to a more honourable source I do not object to; as, for instance, those who explain one allegory by saying that it was wisdom which sprang from the head of Zeus.) On the whole, it seems to me more probable that wicked men, robbing the gods of their honour, ventured to promulgate these insulting stories.

CHAP. XIX. — NONE OF THESE ALLEGORIES ARE CONSISTENT.

"Nor do we find the poetical allegory about any of the gods consistent with itself. To go no further than the fashioning of the universe, the poets now say that nature was the first cause of the whole creation, now that it was mind. For, say they, the first moving and mixture of the elements came from nature, but it was the foresight of mind which arranged them in order. Even when they assert that it was nature which fash-

ioned the universe, being unable absolutely to demonstrate this on account of the traces of design in the work, they inweave the foresight of mind in such a way that they are able to entrap even the wisest. But we say to them: If the world arose from self-moved nature, how did it ever take proportion and shape, which cannot come but from a superintending wisdom, and can be comprehended only by knowledge, which alone can trace such things? If, on the other hand, it is by wisdom that all things subsist and maintain order, how can it be that those things arose from self-moved chance?

CHAP. XX. — THESE GODS WERE REALLY WICKED MAGICIANS.

"Then those who chose to make dishonourable allegories of divine things — as, for instance, that Metis was devoured by Zeus — have fallen into a dilemma, because they did not see that they who in these stories about the gods indirectly taught physics, denied the very existence of the gods, revolving all kinds of gods into mere allegorical representations of the various substances of the universe. And so it is more likely that the gods these persons celebrate were some sort of wicked magicians, who were in reality wicked men, but by magic assumed different shapes, committed adulteries, and took away life, and thus to the men of old who did not understand magic seemed to be gods by the things they did; and the bodies and tombs of these men are to be seen in many towns.

CHAP. XXI. — THEIR GRAVES ARE STILL TO BE SEEN.

"For instance, as I have mentioned already, in the Caucasian mountains there is shown the tomb of a certain Kronos, a man, and a fierce monarch who slew his children. And the son of this man, called Zeus, became worse *than his father;* and having by the power of magic been declared ruler of the universe, he committed many adulteries, and inflicted punishment on his father and uncles, and so died; and the Cretans show his tomb. And in Mesopotamia there lie buried a certain Helios at Atir, and a certain Selene at Carrhæ. A certain Hermes, a man, lies buried in Egypt; Ares in Thrace; Aphrodite in Cyprus; Æsculapius in Epidaurus; and the tombs of many other such persons are to be seen.[1]

CHAP. XXII. — THEIR CONTEMPORARIES, THEREFORE, DID NOT LOOK ON THEM AS GODS.

"Thus, to right-thinking men, it is clear that they were admitted to be mortals. And their contemporaries, knowing that they were mortal,

---

[1] [Comp. v. 23, and *Recognitions*, x. 24. — R.]

when they died paid them no more heed ; and it was length of time which clothed them with the glory of gods. Nor need you wonder that they who lived in the times of Æsculapius and Hercules were deceived, or the contemporaries of Dionysus or any other of the men of that time, when even Hector in Ilium, and Achilles in the island of Leuce, are worshipped by the inhabitants of those places ; and the Opuntines worship Patroclus, and the Rhodians Alexander of Macedon.[1]

CHAP. XXIII. — THE EGYPTIANS PAY DIVINE HONOURS TO A MAN.

" Moreover, among the Egyptians even to the present day, a man is worshipped as a god before his death. And this truly is a small impiety, that the Egyptians give divine honours to a man in his lifetime ; but what is of all things most absurd is, that they worship birds and creeping things, and all kinds of beasts. For the mass of men neither think nor do anything with discretion. But look, I pray you, at what is most disgracefnl of all : he who is with them the father of gods and men is said by them to have had intercourse with Leda ; and many of them set up in public a painting of this, writing above it the name Zeus. To punish this insult, I could wish that they would paint their own present king in such base embraces as they have dared to do with Zeus, and set it up in public, that from the anger of a temporary monarch, and him a mortal, they might learn to render honour where it is due. This I say to you, not as myself already knowing the true God ; but I am happy to say that even if I do not know who is God, I think I at least know clearly what God is.

CHAP. XXIV. — WHAT IS NOT GOD.

" And first, then, the four original elements cannot be God, because they have a cause. Nor can that mixing be God, nor that compounding, nor that generating, nor that globe which surrounds the visible universe ; nor the dregs which flow together in Hades, nor the water which floats over them ; nor the fiery substance, nor the air which extends from it to our earth. For the four elements, if they lay outside one another, could not have been mixed together so as to generate animal life without some great artificer. If they have always been united, even in this case they are fitted together by an artistic mind to what is requisite for the

limbs and parts of animals, that they may be able to preserve their respective proportions, may have a clearly defined shape, and that all the inward parts may attain the fitting coherency. In the same way also the positions suitable for each are determined, and that very beautifully, by the artificer mind. To be brief, in all other things which a living creature must have, this great being of the world is in no respect wanting.

CHAP. XXV. — THE UNIVERSE IS THE PRODUCT OF MIND.

" Thus we are shut up to the supposition that there is an unbegotten artificer, who brought the elements together, if they were separate ; or, if they were together, artistically blended them so as to generate life, and perfected from all one work. For it cannot be that a work which is completely wise can be made without a mind which is greater than it. Nor will it do to say that love is the artificer of all things, or desire, or power, or any such thing. All these are liable to change, and transient in their very nature. Nor can that be God which is moved by another, much less what is altered by time and nature, and can be annihilated."[2]

CHAP. XXVI. — PETER ARRIVES FROM CÆSAREA.

While I was saying these things to Appion, Peter drew near from Cæsarea, and in Tyre the people were flocking together, hurrying to meet him and unite in an expression of gratification at his visit. And Appion withdrew, accompanied by Anubion and Athenodorus only ; but the rest of us hurried to meet Peter, and I was the first to greet him at the gate, and I led him towards the inn. When we arrived, we dismissed the people ; and when he deigned to ask what had taken place, I concealed nothing, but told him of Simon's slanders, and the monstrous shapes he had taken, and all the diseases he had sent after the sacrificial feast, and that some of the sick persons were still there in Tyre, while others had gone on with Simon to Sidon just as I arrived, hoping to be cured by him, but that I had heard that none of them had been cured by him. I also told Peter of the controversy I had had with Appion ; and he, from his love to me, and desiring to encourage me, praised and blessed me. Then, having supped, he betook himself to the rest the fatigues of his journey rendered so necessary.

---

[1] [Comp. *Recognitions*, x. 25, where these facts are also used. — R.]

[2] [The conclusion of the discussion is noteworthy, not only from the fairness of the argument, but from the skill with which the position of Clement, as a heathen inquirer, is maintained. — R.]

HOMILY VII.

CHAP. I. — PETER ADDRESSES THE PEOPLE.

AND on the fourth day of our stay in Tyre,[1] Peter went out about daybreak, and there met him not a few of the dwellers round about, with very many of the inhabitants of Tyre itself, who cried out, and said, "God through you have mercy upon us, God through you heal us!" And Peter stood on a high stone, that all might see him; and having greeted them in a godly manner, thus began: —

CHAP. II. — REASON OF SIMON'S POWER.

" God, who created the heavens and the whole universe, does not want occasion for the salvation of those who would be saved. Wherefore let no one, in seeming evils, rashly charge Him with unkindness to man. For men do not know the issue of those things which happen to them, nay, suspect that the result will be evil; but God knows that they will turn out well. So is it in the case of Simon. He is a power of the left hand of God, and has authority to do harm to those who know not God, so that he has been able to involve you in diseases; but by these very diseases, which have been permitted to come upon you by the good providence of God, you, seeking and finding him who is able to cure, have been compelled to submit to the will of God on the occasion of the cure of the body, and to think of believing, in order that in this way you may have your souls as well as your bodies in a healthy state.

CHAP. III. — THE REMEDY.

" Now I have been told, that after he had sacrificed an ox he feasted you in the middle of the forum, and that you, being carried away with much wine, made friends with not only the evil demons, but their prince also, and that in this way the most of you were seized by these sicknesses, unwittingly drawing upon yourselves with your own hands the sword of destruction. For the demons would never have had power over you, had not you first supped with their prince. For thus from the beginning was a law laid by God, the Creator of all things, on each of the two princes, him of the right hand and him of the left, that neither should have power over any one whom they might wish to benefit or to hurt, unless first he had sat down at the same table with them. As, then, when you partook of meat offered to idols, you became servants to

the prince of evil, in like manner, if you cease from these things, and flee for refuge to God through the good Prince of His right hand, honouring Him without sacrifices, by doing whatsoever He wills, know of a truth that not only will your bodies be healed, but your souls also will become healthy. For He only, destroying with His left hand, can quicken with His right; He only can both smite and raise the fallen.

CHAP. IV. — THE GOLDEN RULE.

" Wherefore, as then ye were deceived by the forerunner Simon, and so became dead in your souls to God, and were smitten in your bodies; so now, if you repent, as I said, and submit to those things which are well-pleasing to God, you may get new strength to your bodies, and recover your soul's health. And the things which are well-pleasing to God are these: to pray to Him, to ask from Him, recognising that He is the giver of all things, and gives with discriminating law; to abstain from the table of devils, not to taste dead flesh, not to touch blood; to be washed from all pollution; and the rest in one word, — as the God-fearing Jews have heard, do you also hear, and be of one mind in many bodies; let each man be minded to do to his neighbour those good things he wishes for himself. And you may all find out what IS good, by holding some such conversation as the following with yourselves: You would not like to be murdered; do not murder another man: you would not like your wife to be seduced by another; do not you commit adultery: you would not like any of your things to be stolen from you; steal nothing from another. And so understanding by yourselves what is reasonable, and doing it, you will become dear to God, and will obtain healing; otherwise in the life which now is your bodies will be tormented, and in that which is to come your souls will be punished."[2]

CHAP. V. — PETER DEPARTS FOR SIDON.

After Peter had spent a few days in teaching them in this way, and in healing them, they were baptized. And after that,[3] all sat down together in the market-places in sackcloth and ashes, grieving because of his other wondrous works, and repenting their former sins. And

---

[1] [The historical details of this Homily also have no parallel in the *Recognitions*. — R.]

[2] [With this discourse respecting Simon, compare *Recognitions*, ii. 6–18. But the statements respecting Simon's power and the design of it are much stronger than here. — R.]

[3] We have adopted Wieseler's emendation. The text may be translated thus: "And after that, among his other wondrous deeds, all the rest (who had not been baptized) sat down," etc.

when they of Sidon heard it, they did likewise, and sent to beseech Peter, since they could not come themselves for their diseases. And Peter did not spend many days in Tyre; but when he had instructed all its inhabitants, and freed them from all manners of diseases and had founded a church, and set over it as bishop one of the elders who were with him, he departed for Sidon. But when Simon heard that Peter was coming, he straightway fled to Beyrout with Appion and his friends.

CHAP. VI. — PETER IN SIDON.

And as Peter entered Sidon, they brought many in couches, and laid them before him. And he said to them: "Think not, I pray you, that I can do anything to heal you, who am a mortal man, myself subject to many evils. But I shall not refuse to show you the way in which you must be saved. For I have learned from the Prophet of truth the conditions fore-ordained of God before the foundation of the world; that is to say, the evil deeds which if men do He has ordained that they shall be injured by the prince of evil, and in like manner the good deeds for which He has decreed that they who have believed in Him as their Physician shall have their bodies made whole, and their souls established in safety.

CHAP. VII. — THE TWO PATHS.

"Knowing, then, these good and evil deeds, I make known unto you as it were two paths,[1] and I shall show you by which travellers are lost and by which they are saved, being guided of God. The path of the lost, then, is broad and very smooth — it ruins them without troubling them; but the path of the saved is narrow, rugged, and in the end it saves, not without much toil, those who have journeyed through it. And these two paths are presided over by unbelief and faith; and these journey through the path of unbelief, those who have preferred pleasure, on account of which they have forgotten the day of judgment, doing that which is not pleasing to God, and not caring to save their souls by the word, and have not anxiously sought their own good. Truly they know not that the counsels of God are not like men's counsels; for, in the first place, He knows the thoughts of all men, and all must give an account not only of their actions, but also of their thoughts. And their sin is much less who strive to understand well and fail, than that of those who do not at all strive after good things. Because it has pleased God that he who errs in his knowledge of good, as men count errors, should be saved

after being slightly punished. But they who have taken no care at all to know the better way, even though they may have done countless other good deeds, if they have not stood in the service He has Himself appointed, come under the charge of indifference, and are severely punished, and utterly destroyed.

CHAP. VIII. — THE SERVICE OF GOD'S APPOINTMENT.

"And this is the service He has appointed: To worship Him only, and trust only in the Prophet of truth, and to be baptized for the remission of sins, and thus by this pure baptism to be born again unto God by saving water; to abstain from the table of devils, that is, from food offered to idols, from dead carcases, from animals which have been suffocated or caught by wild beasts, and from blood;[2] not to live any longer impurely; to wash after intercourse; that the women on their part should keep the law of purification; that all should be sober-minded, given to good works, refraining from wrong-doing, looking for eternal life from the all-powerful God, and asking with prayer and continual supplication that they may win it." Such was Peter's counsel to the men of Sidon also. And in few days many repented and believed, and were healed. And Peter having founded a church, and set over it as bishop one of the elders who were with him, left Sidon.

CHAP. IX. — SIMON ATTACKS PETER.

No sooner had he reached Beyrout than an earthquake took place; and the multitude, running to Peter, said, "Help us, for we are afraid we shall all utterly perish." Then Simon ventured, along with Appion and Anubion and Athenodorus, and the rest of his companions, to cry out to the people against Peter in public: "Flee, friends, from this man! he is a magician; trust us, he it was who caused this earthquake: he sent us these diseases to terrify us, as if he were God Himself." And many such false charges did Simon and his friends bring against Peter, as one who could do things above human power. But as soon as the people gave him a moment's quiet, Peter with surprising boldness gave a little laugh, and said, "Friends, I admit that I can do, God willing, what these men say; and more than that, I am ready, if you do not believe what I say, to overturn your city from top to bottom."

CHAP. X. — SIMON IS DRIVEN AWAY.

And the people were afraid, and promised to do whatever he should command. "Let none

---

[1] [Compare with this chapter the recently discovered " Teaching " and Apostolic Constitutions, book vii. chap. 1, in vol. vii. pp. 377, 465. — R.]

[2] [Comp. *Recognitions*, iv. 36. The language recalls Acts xv. 20 and 1 Cor. x. 21. — R.]

of you, then," said Peter, "either hold conversation with these sorcerers, or have any thing to do with them." And as soon as the people heard this concise command, they took up sticks, and pursued them till they had driven them wholly out of the town. And they who were sick and possessed with devils came and cast themselves at Peter's feet. And he seeing all this, and anxious to free them from their terror, said to them :—

CHAP. XI. — THE WAY OF SALVATION.

"Were I able to cause earthquakes, and do all that I wish, I assure you I would not destroy Simon and his friends (for not to destroy men am I sent), but would make him my friend, that he might no longer, by his slanders against my preaching the truth, hinder the salvation of many. But if you believe me, he himself is a magician; he is a slanderer; he is a minister of evil to them who know not the truth. Therefore he has power to bring diseases on sinners, having the sinners themselves to help him in his power over them. But I am a servant of God the Creator of all things, and a disciple of His Prophet who is at His right hand. Wherefore I, being His apostle, preach the truth : to serve a good man I drive away diseases, for I am His second messenger, since first the disease comes, but after that the healing. By that evil-working magician, then, you were stricken with disease because you revolted from God. By me, if you believe on Him ye shall be cured : and so having had experience that He is able, you may turn to good works, and have your souls saved."

CHAP. XII. — PETER GOES TO BYBLUS AND TRIPOLIS.

As he said these things, all fell on their knees before his feet. And he, lifting up his hands to heaven, prayed to God, and healed them all by his simple prayer alone. And he remained not many days in Beyrout; but after he had accustomed many to the service of the one God, and had baptized them, and had set over them a bishop from the elders who were with him, he went to Byblus. And when he came there, and learned that Simon had not waited for them for a day, but had gone straightway to Tripolis, he remained there only a few days; and after that he had healed not a few, and exercised them in the Scriptures, he followed in Simon's track to Tripolis, preferring to pursue him rather than flee from him.

HOMILY VIII.

CHAP. I. — PETER'S ARRIVAL AT TRIPOLIS.

Now, as Peter was entering Tripolis,[1] the people from Tyre and Sidon, Berytus and Byblus, who were eager[2] to get instruction, and many from the neighbourhood, entered along with him; and not least were there gatherings of the multitudes from the city itself wishing to see him. Therefore there met with us in the suburbs the brethren who had been sent forth by him to ascertain as well other particulars respecting the city, as the proceedings of Simon, and to come and explain them. They received him, and conducted him to the house of Maroones.[3]

CHAP. II. — PETER'S THOUGHTFULNESS.

But he, when he was at the very gate of his lodging, turned round, and promised to the multitudes that after the next day he would converse with them on the subject of religion. And when he had gone in, the forerunners assigned lodgings to those who had come with him. And the hosts and the entertainers did not fall short of the desire of those who sought hospitality. But Peter, knowing nothing of this, being asked by us to partake of food, said that he would not himself partake until those who had come with him were settled. And on our assuring him that this was already done, all having received them eagerly by reason of their affection towards him, so that those were grieved beyond measure who had no guests to entertain, — Peter hearing this, and being pleased with their eager philanthropy, blessed them and went out, and having bathed in the sea, partook of food with the forerunners; and then, the evening having come, he slept.

CHAP. III. — A CONVERSATION INTERRUPTED.

But awaking about the second cock-crowing, he found us astir. We were in all sixteen, viz., Peter himself, and I Clement, Nicetas and Aquila, and the twelve who had preceded us.[4] Having therefore saluted us, he said, "To-day,

---

[1] [For the general parallelism of Homilies VIII.-XI. with *Recognitions*, iv-vi., see footnote on *Recognitions*, iv. 1. Homilies VIII., IX., contain matter included in the single discourse of *Recognitions*, book iv. — R.]
[2] Lit.: More willing to learn *than the others*.
[3] ["Maro" in *Recognitions*, iv. The resemblance between that book and this Homily is quite marked. — R.]

[4] [Comp. *Recognitions*, iv. 3. — R.]

not being occupied with those without, we are free to be occupied with one another. Wherefore I shall tell you the things that happened after your departure from Tyre ; and do you minutely relate to me what have been the doings of Simon here." While, therefore, we were answering one another by narratives on either side, one of our friends entered, and announced to Peter that Simon, learning of his arrival, had set off for Syria, and that the multitudes, thinking this one night to be like a year's time, and not able to wait for the appointment which he had made, were standing before the doors conversing with one another in knots and circles about the accusation brought by Simon, and how that, having raised their expectations, and promised that he would charge Peter when he came with many evils, he had fled by night when he knew of his arrival. "However," said he, "they are eager to hear you ; and I know not whence some rumour has reached them to the effect that you are going to address them to-day. In order, therefore, that they may not when they are very tired be dismissed without reason, you yourself know what it is proper for you to do."

CHAP. IV. — MANY CALLED.

Then Peter, wondering at the eagerness of the multitudes, answered,[1] " You see, brethren, how the words of our Lord are manifestly fulfilled. For I remember His saying, " Many shall come from the east and from the west, the north and the south, and shall recline on the bosoms of Abraham, and Isaac, and Jacob.'[2] ' But many,' said He also, ' are called, but few chosen.'[3] The coming, therefore, of these called ones is fulfilled. But inasmuch as it is not of themselves, but of God who has called them and caused them to come, on this account alone they have no reward, since it is not of themselves but of Him who has wrought in them. But if, after being called, they do things that are excellent, for this is of themselves, then for this they shall have a reward.

CHAP. V. — FAITH THE GIFT OF GOD.

" For even the Hebrews who believe Moses, and do not observe the things spoken by him, are not saved, unless they observe the things that were spoken to them. For their believing Moses was not of their own will, but of God, who said to Moses, ' Behold, I come to thee in a pillar of cloud, that the people may hear me speaking to thee, and may believe thee for ever.'[4] Since, therefore, both to the Hebrews and to those who are called from the Gentiles, believing in the teachers of truth is of God, while excellent actions are left to every one to do by his own judgment, the reward is righteously bestowed upon those who do well. For there would have been no need of Moses, or of the coming of Jesus, if of themselves they would have understood what is reasonable. Neither is there salvation in believing in teachers and calling them lords.

CHAP. VI. — CONCEALMENT AND REVELATION.

" For on this account Jesus is concealed from the Jews, who have taken Moses as their teacher, and Moses is hidden from those who have believed Jesus. For, there being one teaching by both, God accepts him who has believed either of these. But believing a teacher is for the sake of doing the things spoken by God. And that this is so our Lord Himself says, ' I thank thee, Father of heaven and earth, because Thou hast concealed these things from the wise and elder, and hast revealed them to sucking babes.'[5] Thus God Himself has concealed a teacher from some, as foreknowing what they ought to do, and has revealed him to others, who are ignorant what they ought to do.

CHAP. VII. — MOSES AND CHRIST.

" Neither, therefore, are the Hebrews condemned on account of their ignorance of Jesus, by reason of Him who has concealed Him, if, doing the things *commanded* by Moses, they do not hate Him whom they do not know. Neither are those from among the Gentiles condemned, who know not Moses on account of Him who hath concealed him, provided that these also, doing the things spoken by Jesus, do not hate Him whom they do not know. And some will not be profited by calling the teachers lords, but not doing the works of servants. For on this account our Jesus Himself said to one who often called Him Lord, but did none of the things which He prescribed, ' Why call ye me Lord, Lord, and do not the things which I say?'[6] For it is not saying that will profit any one, but doing. By all means, therefore, is there need of good works. Moreover, if any one has been thought worthy to recognise both as preaching one doctrine, that man has been counted rich in God, understanding both the old things as new in time, and the new things as old."

CHAP. VIII. — A LARGE CONGREGATION.

While Peter was thus speaking, the multitudes, as if they had been called by some one, entered into the place where Peter was. Then he, seeing a great multitude, like the smooth current of a river gently flowing towards him, said to

---

[1] [With chaps. 4–11 compare the closely resembling passage, *Recognitions*, iv. 4–11. — R.]
[2] Matt. viii. 11; Luke xiii. 29.
[3] Matt. xx. 16.
[4] Ex. xix. 9.
[5] Matt. xi. 25; [Luke x. 21. — R]
[6] Luke vi. 46.

Maroones, "Have you any place here that is better able to contain the crowd?" Then Maroones conducted him to a garden-plot in the open air, and the multitudes followed. But Peter, standing upon a base of a statue which was not very high, as soon as he had saluted the multitude in pious fashion, knowing that many of the crowd that stood by were tormented with demons and many sufferings of long standing, and *hearing them* shrieking with lamentation, and falling down *before him* in supplication, rebuked them, and commanded them to hold their peace; and promising healing to them after the discourse,[1] began to speak on this wise : —

CHAP. IX. — "VINDICATE THE WAYS OF GOD TO MEN."

"While beginning to discourse on the worship of God to those who are altogether ignorant of everything, and whose minds have been corrupted by the accusations of our adversary Simon, I have thought it necessary first of all to speak of the blamelessness of the God who hath made all things, starting from the occasion seasonably afforded by Him according to His providence, that it may be known how with good reason many are held by many demons, and subjected to strange sufferings, that in this the justice of God may appear; and that those who through ignorance blame Him, now may learn by good speaking and well-doing what sentiments they ought to hold, and recall themselves from their previous accusation, assigning ignorance as the cause of their evil presumption, in order that they may be pardoned.

CHAP. X. — THE ORIGINAL LAW.

"But thus the matter stands. The only good God having made all things well, and having handed them over to man, who was made after His image, he who had been made breathing of the divinity of Him who made him, being a true prophet and knowing all things, for the honour of the Father who had given all things to him, and for the salvation of the sons born of him, as a genuine father preserving his affection towards the children born of him, and wishing them, for their advantage, to love God and be loved of Him, showed them the way which leads to His friendship, teaching them by what deeds of men the one God and Lord of all is pleased; and having exhibited to them the things that are pleasing to Him, appointed a perpetual law to all, which neither can be abrogated by enemies, nor is vitiated by any impious one, nor is concealed in any place, but which can be read by all. To them, therefore, by obedience to the law, all things were in abundance, — the fairest of fruits, fulness of years, freedom from grief and from disease, bestowed upon them without fear, with all salubrity of the air.

CHAP. XI. — CAUSE OF THE FALL OF MAN.

"But they, because they had at first no experience of evils, being insensible to the gift of good things, were turned to ingratitude by abundance of food and luxuries, so that they even thought that there is no Providence, since they had not by previous labour got good things as the reward of righteousness, inasmuch as no one of them had fallen into any suffering or disease, or any other necessity; so that, as is usual for men afflicted on account of wicked transgression, they should look about for the God who is able to heal them.[2] But immediately after their despite, which proceeded from fearlessness and secure luxury, a certain just punishment met them, as following from a certain arranged harmony, removing from them good things as having hurt them, and introducing evil things instead, as advantageous.

CHAP. XII. — METAMORPHOSES OF THE ANGELS.

"For of the spirits who inhabit the heaven,[3] the angels who dwell in the lowest region, being grieved at the ingratitude of men to God, asked that they might come into the life of men, that, really becoming men, by more intercourse they might convict those who had acted ungratefully towards Him, and might subject every one to adequate punishment. When, therefore, their petition was granted, they metamorphosed themselves into every nature; for, being of a more godlike substance, they are able easily to assume any form. So they became precious stones, and goodly pearl, and the most beauteous purple, and choice gold, and all matter that is held in most esteem. And they fell into the hands of some, and into the bosoms of others, and suffered themselves to be stolen by them. They also changed themselves into beasts and reptiles, and fishes and birds, and into whatsoever they pleased. These things also the poets among yourselves, by reason of fearlessness, sing, as they befell, attributing to one the many and diverse doings of all.

CHAP. XIII. — THE FALL OF THE ANGELS.

"But when, having assumed these forms, they convicted as covetous those who stole them, and

---

[1] [In *Recognitions*, iv. 7, the healing is represented as occurring at once. — R.]

[2] The general meaning seems to be as given; but the text is undoubtedly corrupt, and scarcely intelligible.

[3] [Chaps. 12–16 have no parallel in the corresponding discourse of the *Recognitions*. The doctrine here is peculiar. But compare *Recognitions*, iv. 26. — R.]

changed themselves into the nature of men, in order that, living holily, and showing the possibility of so living, they might subject the ungrateful to punishment, yet having become in all respects men, they also partook of human lust, and being brought under its subjection they fell into cohabitation with women;[1] and being involved with them, and sunk in defilement and altogether emptied of their first power, were unable to turn back to the first purity of their proper nature, their members turned away from their fiery substance:[2] for the fire itself, being extinguished by the weight of lust, *and changed* into flesh, they trode the impious path downward. For they themselves, being fettered with the bonds of flesh, were constrained and strongly bound; wherefore they have no more been able to ascend into the heavens.

CHAP. XIV. — THEIR DISCOVERIES.

"For after the intercourse, being asked to show what they were before, and being no longer able to do so, on account of their being unable to do aught else after their defilement, yet wishing to please their mistresses, instead of themselves, they showed the bowels[3] of the earth; I mean, the choice metals,[4] gold, brass, silver, iron, and the like, with all the most precious stones. And along with these charmed stones, they delivered the arts of the things pertaining to each, and imparted the discovery of magic, and taught astronomy, and the powers of roots, and whatever was impossible to be found out by the human mind; also the melting of gold and silver, and the like, and the various dyeing of garments. And all things, in short, which are for the adornment and delight of women, are the discoveries of these demons bound in flesh.

CHAP. XV. — THE GIANTS.

"But from their unhallowed intercourse spurious men sprang, much greater in stature than *ordinary* men, whom they afterwards called giants; not those dragon-footed giants who waged war against God, as those blasphemous myths of the Greeks do sing, but wild in manners, and greater than men in size, inasmuch as they were sprung of angels; yet less than angels, as they were born of women. Therefore God, knowing that they were barbarized to brutality, and that the world was not sufficient to satisfy them (for it was created according to the proportion of men and human use), that they might not through want of food turn, contrary to na-

ture, to the eating of animals, and yet seem to be blameless, as having ventured upon this through necessity, the Almighty God rained manna upon them, suited to their various tastes; and they enjoyed all that they would. But they, on account of their bastard nature, not being pleased with purity of food, longed only after the taste of blood. Wherefore they first tasted flesh.

CHAP. XVI. — CANNIBALISM.

"And the men who were with them there for the first time were eager to do the like. Thus, although we are born neither good nor bad, we become *one or the other;* and having formed habits, we are with difficulty drawn from them. But when irrational animals fell short, these bastard men tasted also human flesh. For it was not a long step to the consumption of flesh like their own, having first tasted it in other forms.

CHAP. XVII. — THE FLOOD.

"But by the shedding of much blood, the pure air being defiled with impure vapour, and sickening those who breathed it, rendered them liable to diseases, so that thenceforth men died prematurely. But the earth being by these means greatly defiled, these first teemed with poison-darting and deadly creatures. All things, therefore, going from bad to worse, on account of these brutal demons, God wished to cast them away like an evil leaven, lest each generation from a wicked seed, being like to that before it, and equally impious, should empty the world to come of saved men. And for this purpose, having warned a certain righteous man,[5] with his three sons, together with their wives and their children, to save themselves in an ark, He sent a deluge of water, that all being destroyed, the purified world might be handed over to him who was saved in the ark, in order to a second beginning of life. And thus it came to pass.

CHAP. XVIII. — THE LAW TO THE SURVIVORS.

"Since, therefore, the souls of the deceased giants were greater than human souls, inasmuch as they also excelled their bodies, they, as being a new race, were called also by a new name. And to those who survived in the world a law was prescribed of God through an angel, how they should live. For being bastards in race, of the fire of angels and the blood of women, and therefore liable to desire a certain race of their own, they were anticipated by a certain righteous law. For a certain angel was sent to them by God, declaring to them His will, and saying : —

---

[1] [Comp. *Recognitions*, i. 30. The details here are not only fuller, but apparently represent a more developed speculation. — R.]
[2] The text is somewhat obscure; but the following sentence shows this to be the meaning of it.
[3] Literally, " the marrow."
[4] Literally, " the flowers of metals."

[5] [Comp. *Recognitions*, v. 12. — R.]

CHAP. XIX. — THE LAW TO THE GIANTS OR DEMONS.

" ' These things seem good to the all-seeing God, that you lord it over no man ; that you trouble no one, unless any one of his own accord subject himself to you, worshipping you, and sacrificing and pouring libations, and partaking of your table, or accomplishing aught else that they ought not, or shedding blood, or tasting dead flesh, or filling themselves with that which is torn of beasts, or that which is cut, or that which is strangled, or aught else that is unclean. But those who betake themselves to my law, you not only shall not touch, but shall also do honour to, and shall flee from, their presence. For whatsoever shall please them, being just, respecting you, that you shall be constrained to suffer. But if any of those who worship me go astray, either committing adultery, or practising magic, or living impurely, or doing any other of the things which are not well-pleasing to me, then they will have to suffer something at your hands or those of others, according to my order. But upon them, when they repent, I, judging of their repentance, whether it be worthy of pardon or not, shall give sentence. These things, therefore, ye ought to remember and to do, well knowing that not even your thoughts shall be able to be concealed from Him.'

CHAP. XX. — WILLING CAPTIVES.

" Having charged them to this effect, the angel departed. But you are still ignorant of this law, that every one who worships demons, or sacrifices to them, or partakes with them of their table, shall become subject to them and receive all punishment from them, as being under wicked lords. And you who, on account of ignorance of this *law*, have been corrupted beside their altars,[1] and have been satiated with *food offered to* them, have come under their power, and do not know how you have been in every way injured in respect of your bodies. But you ought to know that the demons have no power over any one, unless first he be their table-companion ; since not even their chief can do anything contrary to the law imposed upon them by God, wherefore he has no power over any one who does not worship him ; but neither can any one receive from them any of the things that he wishes, nor in anything be hurt by them, as you may learn from the following statement.

CHAP. XXI. — TEMPTATION OF CHRIST.

" For once the king of the present time came to our King of righteousness, using no violence,

for this was not in his power, but inducing and persuading, because the being persuaded lies in the power of every one.[2] Approaching Him, therefore, as being king of things present, he said to the King of things future, 'All the kingdoms of the present world are subject to me ; also the gold and the silver and all the luxury of this world are under my power. Wherefore fall down and worship me, and I will give you all these things.' And this he said, knowing that after He worshipped him he would have power also over Him, and thus would rob Him of the future glory and kingdom. But He, knowing all things, not only did not worship him, but would not receive aught of the things that were offered by him. For He pledged Himself with those that are His, to the effect that it is not lawful henceforth even to touch the things that are given over to him. Therefore He answered and said, 'Thou shalt fear the Lord thy God, and Him only shalt thou serve.'[3]

CHAP. XXII. — THE MARRIAGE SUPPER.

" However, the king of the impious, striving to bring over to his own counsel the King of the pious, and not being able, ceased his efforts, undertaking to persecute Him for the remainder of His life. But you, being ignorant of the foreordained law, are under his power through evil deeds. Wherefore you are polluted in body and soul, and in the present life you are tyrannized over by sufferings and demons, but in that which is to come you shall have your souls to be punished. And this not you alone suffer through ignorance, but also some of our nation, who by evil deeds having been brought under the power of the prince of wickedness, like persons invited to a supper by a father celebrating the marriage of his son, have not obeyed.[4] But instead of those who through preoccupation disobeyed, the Father celebrating the marriage of his Son, has ordered us, through the Prophet of the truth, to come into the partings of the ways, that is, to you, and to invest you with the clean wedding-garment, which is baptism, which is for the remission of the sins done by you, and to bring the good to the supper of God by repentance, although at the first they were left out of the banquet.

CHAP. XXIII. — THE ASSEMBLY DISMISSED.

" If, therefore, ye wish to be the vesture of the Divine Spirit, hasten first to put off your base presumption, which is an unclean spirit and a

---

[1] τοῖς αὐτῶν βωμοῖς προσφθαρέντες καὶ αὐτῶν ἐκπληρωθέντες.

[2] [The conclusion of this homily resembles *Recognitions*, iv. 34-37, but much of the matter of that book is contained in Homily iX. ; see footnotes. — R.]
[3] Matt. iv. ; Luke iv.
[4] Matt. xxii.

foul garment. And this you cannot otherwise put off, than by being first baptized in good works. And thus being pure in body and in soul, you shall enjoy the future eternal kingdom. Therefore neither believe in idols, nor partake with them of the impure table, nor commit murder, nor adultery, nor hate those whom it is not right to hate, nor steal, nor set upon any evil deeds ; since, being deprived of the hope of future blessings in the present life, you shall be subjected to evil demons and terrible sufferings, and in the world to come you shall be punished with eternal fire. Now, then, what has been said is enough for to-day. For the rest, those of you who are afflicted with ailments remain for healing; and of the others, you who please go in peace."

CHAP. XXIV. — THE SICK HEALED.

When he had thus spoken, all of them remained, some in order to be healed, and others to see those who obtained cures. But Peter, only laying his hands upon them, and praying, healed them ; [1] so that those who were straightway cured were exceeding glad, and those who looked on exceedingly wondered, and blessed God, and believed with a firm hope, and with those who had been healed departed to their own homes, having received a charge to meet early on the following day. And when they had gone, Peter remained there with his associates, and partook of food, and refreshed himself with sleep.

---

[1] [Comp. *Recognitions*, iv. 7. — R.]

HOMILY IX.

CHAP. I. — PETER'S DISCOURSE RESUMED.

THEREFORE on the next day, Peter going out with his companions, and coming to the former place, and taking his stand, proceeded to say : [1] " God having cut off by water all the impious men of old, having found one alone amongst them all that was pious, caused him to be saved in an ark, with his three sons and their wives. Whence may be perceived that it is His nature not to care for a multitude of wicked, nor to be indifferent to the salvation of one pious. Therefore the greatest impiety of all is forsaking the sole Lord of all, and worshipping many, who are no gods, as if they were gods.

CHAP. II. — MONARCHY AND POLYARCHY.

" If, therefore, while I expound and show you that this is the greatest sin, which is able to destroy you all, it occur to your mind that you are not destroyed, being great multitudes, you are deceived. For you have the example of the old world deluged. And yet their sin was much less than that which is chargeable against you. For they were wicked with respect to their equals, murdering or committing adultery. But you are wicked against the God of all, worshipping lifeless images instead of Him or along with Him, and attributing His divine name to every kind of senseless matter. In the first place, therefore, you are unfortunate in not knowing the difference between monarchy and polyarchy — that monarchy, on the one hand, is productive of concord, but polyarchy is effec-

tive of wars. For unity does not fight with itself, but multitude has occasion of undertaking battle one against another.

CHAP. III. — FAMILY OF NOE.

" Therefore, straightway after the flood,[2] Noe continued to live three hundred and fifty years with the multitude of his descendants in concord, being a king according to the image of the one God. But after his death many of his descendants were ambitious of the kingdom, and being eager to reign, each one considered how it might be effected ; and one attempted it by war, another by deceit, another by persuasion, and one in one way and another in another ; one of whom was of the family of Ham, whose descendant was Mestren, from whom the tribes of the Egyptians and Babylonians and Persians were multiplied.

CHAP. IV. — ZOROASTER.

" Of this family there was born in due time a certain one, who took up with magical practices, by name Nebrod, who chose, giant-like, to devise things in opposition to God. Him the Greeks have called Zoroaster. He, after the deluge, being ambitious of sovereignty, and being a great magician, by magical arts compelled the world-guiding star of the wicked one who now rules, to the bestowal of the sovereignty *as a gift* from him. But he,[3] being a prince,

---

[1] [Much of the matter in this Homily is to be found in *Recognitions*, iv. — R.]

[2] [With this and the succeeding chapters compare *Recognitions*, i. 30, 31, but more particularly iv. 27–31, which furnish a close parallel. — R.]

[3] That is, I suppose, the wicked one.

and having authority over him who compelled him,[1] wrathfully poured out the fire of the kingdom, that he might both bring to allegiance, and might punish him who at first constrained him.

CHAP. V. — HERO-WORSHIP.

"Therefore the magician Nebrod, being destroyed by this lightning falling on earth from heaven, for this circumstance had his name changed to Zoroaster, on account of the living ($\zeta\tilde{\omega}\sigma\alpha\nu$) stream of the star ($\dot{\alpha}\sigma\tau\acute{\epsilon}\rho\sigma\varsigma$) being poured upon him. But the unintelligent amongst the men who then were, thinking that through the love of God his soul had been sent for by lightning, buried the remains of his body, and honoured his burial-place with a temple among the Persians, where the descent of the fire occurred, and worshipped him as a god. By this example also, others there bury those who die by lightning as beloved of God, and honour them with temples, and erect statues of the dead in their own forms. Thence, in like manner, the rulers in different places were emulous *of like honour*, and very many of them honoured the tombs of those who were beloved of them, though not dying by lightning, with temples and statues, and lighted up altars, and ordered them to be adored as gods. And long after, by the lapse of time, they were thought by posterity to be really gods.

CHAP. VI. — FIRE-WORSHIP.

"Thus, in this fashion, there ensued many partitions of the one original kingdom. The Persians, first taking coals from the lightning which fell from heaven, preserved them by ordinary fuel, and honouring the heavenly fire as a god, were honoured by the fire itself with the first kingdom, as its first worshippers. After them the Babylonians, stealing coals from the fire that was there, and conveying it safely to their own home, and worshipping it, they themselves also reigned in order. And the Egyptians, acting in like manner, and calling the fire in their own dialect PHTHAË, which is translated HEPHAISTUS or OSIRIS, he who first reigned amongst them is called by its name. Those also who reigned in different places, acting in this fashion, and making an image, and kindling altars in honour of fire, most of them were excluded from the kingdom.

CHAP. VII. — SACRIFICIAL ORGIES.

"But they did not cease to worship images,[2] by reason of the evil intelligence of the magicians, who found excuses for them, which had power to constrain them to the foolish worship. For, establishing this things by magical ceremonies, they assigned them feasts from sacrifices, libations, flutes, and shoutings, by means of which senseless men, being deceived, and their kingdom being taken from them, yet did not desist from the worship that they had taken up with. To such an extent did they prefer error, on account of its pleasantness, before truth. They also howl after their sacrificial surfeit, their soul from the depth, as it were by dreams, forewarning them of the punishment that is to befall such deeds of theirs.

CHAP. VIII. — THE BEST MERCHANDISE.

"Many forms of worship,[3] then, having passed away in the world, we come, bringing to you, as good merchantmen, the worship that has been handed down to us from our fathers, and preserved; showing you, as it were, the seeds of plants, and placing them under your judgment and in your power. Choose that which seems good unto you. If, therefore, ye choose our wares, not only shall ye be able to escape demons, and the sufferings which are inflicted by demons, but yourselves also putting them to flight, and having them reduced to make supplication to you, shall for ever enjoy future blessings.

CHAP. IX. — HOW DEMONS GET POWER OVER MEN.

"Since, on the other hand, you are oppressed by strange sufferings inflicted by demons, on your removal from the body you shall have your souls also punished for ever; not indeed by God's inflicting vengeance, but because such is the judgment of evil deeds. For the demons, having power by means of the food given to them, are admitted into your bodies by your own hands; and lying hid there for a long time, they become blended with your souls. And through the carelessness of those who think not, or even wish not, to help themselves, upon the dissolution of their bodies, their souls being united to the demon, are of necessity borne by it into whatever places it pleases. And what is most terrible of all, when at the end of all things the demon is first consigned to the purifying fire, the soul which is mixed with it is under the necessity of being horribly punished, and the demon of being pleased. For the soul, being made of light, and not capable of bearing the heterogeneous flame of fire, is tortured; but the demon, being in the substance of his own kind, is greatly pleased, becoming the strong chain of the soul that he has swallowed up.

---

[1] I suppose Nimrod, or Zoroaster.
[2] [Comp. *Recognitions*, iv. 13. — R.]

[3] [Compare with chaps. 8-18 the parallel passage in *Recognitions*, iv. 14-22. The resemblances are quite close. — R.]

CHAP. X. — HOW THEY ARE TO BE EXPELLED.

" But the reason why the demons delight in entering into men's bodies is this. Being spirits, and having desires after meats and drinks, and sexual pleasures, but not being able to partake of these by reason of their being spirits, and wanting organs fitted for their enjoyment, they enter into the bodies of men, in order that, getting organs to minister to them, they may obtain the things that they wish, whether it be meat, by means of men's teeth, or sexual pleasure, by means of men's members. Hence, in order to the putting of demons to flight, the most useful help is abstinence, and fasting, and suffering of affliction. For if they enter into men's bodies for the sake of sharing *pleasures*, it is manifest that they are put to flight by suffering. But inasmuch as some,[1] being of a more malignant kind, remain by the body that is undergoing punishment, though they are punished with it, therefore it is needful to have recourse to God by prayers and petitions, refraining from every occasion of impurity, that the hand of God may touch him for his cure, as being pure and faithful.

CHAP. XI. — UNBELIEF THE DEMON'S STRONGHOLD.

" But it is necessary in our prayers to acknowledge that we have had recourse to God, and to bear witness, not to the apathy, but to the slowness of the demon. For all things are done to the believer, nothing to the unbeliever. Therefore the demons themselves, knowing the amount of faith of those of whom they take possession, measure their stay proportionately. Wherefore they stay permanently with the unbelieving, tarry for a while with the weak in faith; but with those who thoroughly believe, and who do good, they cannot remain even for a moment. For the soul being turned by faith, as it were, into the nature of water, quenches the demon as a spark of fire. The labour, therefore, of every one is to be solicitous about the putting to flight of his own demon. For, being mixed up with men's souls, they suggest to every one's mind desires after what things they please, in order that he may neglect his salvation.

CHAP. XII. — THEORY OF DISEASE.

" Whence many, not knowing how they are influenced, consent to the evil thoughts suggested by the demons, as if they were the reasoning of their own souls. Wherefore they become less active to come to those who are able to save them, and do not know that they themselves are held captive by the deceiving demons. Therefore the demons who lurk in their souls induce them to think that it is not a demon that is distressing them, but a bodily disease, such as some acrid matter, or bile, or phlegm, or excess of blood, or inflammation of a membrane, or something else. But even if this were so, the case would not be altered of its being a kind of demon. For the universal and earthly soul, which enters on account of all kinds of food, being taken to excess by over-much food, is itself united to the spirit, as being cognate, which is the soul of man; and the material part of the food being united to the body, is left as a dreadful poison to it. Wherefore in all respects moderation is excellent.

CHAP. XIII. — DECEITS OF THE DEMONS.

" But some of the maleficent demons deceive in another way. For at first they do not even show their existence, in order that care may not be taken against them; but in due time, by means of anger, love, or some other affection, they suddenly injure the body, by sword, or halter, or precipice, or something else, and at last bring to punishment the deceived souls of those who have been mixed up with them, as we said, withdrawing into the purifying fire. But others, who are deceived in another way, do not approach us, being seduced by the instigations of maleficent demons, as if they suffered these things at the hands of the gods themselves, on account of their neglect of them, and were able to reconcile them by sacrifices, and that it is not needful to come to us, but rather to flee from and hate us. And at the same time[2] they hate and flee from those who have greater compassion for them, and who follow after them in order to do good to them.

CHAP. XIV. — MORE TRICKS.

" Therefore shunning and hating us they are deceived, not knowing how it happens that they devise things opposed to their health. For neither can we compel them against their will to incline towards health, since now we have no such power over them, nor are they able of themselves to understand the evil instigation of the demon; for they know not whence these evil instigations are suggested to them. And these are they whom the demons affright, appearing in such forms as they please. And sometimes they prescribe remedies for those who are diseased, and thus they receive divine honours from those who have previously been deceived. And they conceal from many that they are demons, but not from us, who know their mystery, and why

---

[1] The gender is here changed, but the sense shows that the reference is still to the demons. I suppose the author forgot that in the preceding sentences he had written δαίμονες (*masc.*) and not δαιμόνια (*neut.*).

[2] Some read οὕτως, thus.

they do these things, changing themselves in dreams against those over whom they have power; and why they terrify some, and give oracular responses to others, and demand sacrifices from them, and command them to eat with them, that they may swallow up their souls.

CHAP. XV. — TEST OF IDOLS.

" For as dire serpents draw sparrows to them by their breath, so also these draw to their own will those who partake of their table, being mixed up with their understanding by means of food and drink, changing themselves in dreams according to the forms of the images, that they may increase error. For the image is neither a living creature, nor has it a divine spirit, but the demon that appeared abused the form.[1] How many, in like manner, have been seen by others in dreams; and when they have met one another when awake, and compared them with what they saw in their dream, they have not accorded: so that the dream is not a manifestation, but is either the production of a demon or of the soul, giving forms to present fears and desire. For the soul, being struck with fear, conceives forms in dreams. But if you think that images, as being alive, can accomplish such things, place them on a beam accurately balanced, and place an equipoise in the other scale, then ask them to become either heavier or lighter; and if this be done, then they are alive. But it does not so happen. But if it were so, this would not prove them to be gods. For this might be accomplished by the finger of the demon. Even maggots move, yet they are not called gods.

CHAP. XVI. — POWERS OF THE DEMONS.

" But that the soul of each man embodies the forms of demons after his own preconceptions, and that those who are called gods do not appear, is manifest from the fact that they do not appear to the Jews. But some one will say, How then do they give oracular responses, forecasting future things? This also is false. But suppose it were true, this does not prove them to be gods; for it does not follow, if anything prophesies, that it is a god. For pythons prophesy, yet they are cast out by us as demons, and put to flight. But some one will say, They work cures for some persons. It is false. But suppose it were true, this is no proof of Godhead; for physicians also heal many, yet are not gods. But, says one, physicians do not completely heal those of whom they take charge, but these heal oracularly. But the demons know

the remedies that are suited to each disease. Wherefore, being skilful physicians, and able to cure those diseases which can be cured by men, and also being prophets, and knowing when each disease is healed of itself, they so arrange their remedies that they may gain the credit of producing the cure.

CHAP. XVII. — REASONS WHY THEIR DECEITS ARE NOT DETECTED.

" For why do they oracularly foretell cures after a long time? And why, if they are almighty, do they not effect cures without administering any medicine? And for what reason do they prescribe remedies to some of those who pray to them, while to some, and it may be more suitable cases, they give no response? Thus, whenever a cure is going to take place spontaneously, they promise, in order that they may get the credit of the cure; and others, having been sick, and having prayed, and having recovered spontaneously, attributed the cure to those whom they had invoked, and make offerings to them. Those, however, who, after praying, have failed, are not able to offer their sacrifices. But if the relatives of the dead, or any of their children, inquired into the losses, you would find the failures to be more than the successes. But no one who has been taken in by them is willing to exhibit an accusation against them, through shame or fear; but, on the other hand, they conceal the crimes which they believe them to be guilty of.

CHAP. XVIII. — PROPS OF THE SYSTEM.

" And how many also falsify the responses given and the cures effected by them, and confirm them with an oath! And how many give themselves up to them for hire, undertaking falsely to suffer certain things, and thus proclaiming their suffering, and being restored by remedial means, they say that they oracularly promised them healing, in order that they may assign as the cause the senseless worship! And how many of these things were formerly done by magical art, in the way of interpreting dreams, and divining! Yet in course of time these things have disappeared. And how many are there now, who, wishing to obtain such things, make use of charms! However, though a thing be prophetical or healing, it is not divine.

CHAP. XIX. — PRIVILEGES OF THE BAPTIZED.

" For God is almighty. For He is good and righteous, now long-suffering to all, that those who will, repenting of the evils which they have done, and living well, may receive a worthy reward in the day in which all things are judged. Wherefore now begin to obey God by reason of

---

[1] The meaning is: " the idols or images of the heathen deities are not living, but the demons adopt the forms of these images' when they appear to men in dreams."

good knowledge,[1] and to oppose your evil lusts and thoughts, that you may be able to recover the original saving worship which was committed to humanity. For thus shall blessings straightway spring up to you, which, when you receive, you will thenceforth quit the trial of evils. But give thanks to the Giver; being kings for ever of unspeakable good things, with the King of peace. But in the present life, washing in a flowing river, or fountain, or even in the sea, with the thrice-blessed invocation, you shall not only be able to drive away the spirits which lurk in you; but yourselves no longer sinning, and undoubtingly believing God, you shall drive out evil spirits and dire demons, with terrible diseases, from others. And sometimes they shall flee when you but look on them. For they know those who have given themselves up to God. Wherefore, honouring them, they flee affrighted, as you saw yesterday, how, when after the address I delayed praying for those who were suffering these maladies, through respect towards the worship they cried out, not being able to endure it for a short hour.

CHAP. XX. — "NOT ALMOST, BUT ALTOGETHER SUCH AS I AM."

"Do not then suppose that we do not fear demons on this account, that we are of a different nature *from you*. For we are of the same nature, but not of the same worship. Wherefore, being not only much but altogether superior to you, we do not grudge you becoming such *as we are;* but, on the other hand, counsel you, knowing that all these *demons* beyond measure honour and fear those who are reconciled to God.

CHAP. XXI. — THE DEMONS SUBJECT TO THE BELIEVER.

"For, in like manner as the soldiers who are put under one of Cæsar's captains know to honour him who has received authority on account of him who gave it, so that the commanders say to this one, Come, and he comes, and to another, Go, and he goes; so also he who has given himself to God, being faithful, is heard when he only speaks to demons and diseases; and the demons give place, though they be much stronger than they who command them. For with unspeakable power God subjects the mind of every one to whom He pleases. For as many captains, with whole camps and cities, fear Cæsar, who is but a man, every one's heart being eager to honour the image of all;[2] for by the will of

God, all things being enslaved by fear, do not know the cause; so also all disease-producing spirits, being awed in some natural way, honour and flee from him who has had recourse to God, and who carries right faith as His image in his heart.

CHAP. XXII. — "RATHER REJOICE."

"But still, though all demons, with all diseases, flee before you, you are not to rejoice in this only, but in that, through grace, your names, as of the ever-living, are written in heaven. Thus also the Divine Holy Spirit rejoices, because man hath overcome death; for the putting of the demons to flight makes for the safety of another. But this we say, not as denying that we ought to help others, but that we ought not to be inflated by this and neglect ourselves. It happens, also, that the demons flee before some wicked men by reason of the honoured name, and both he who expels the demon and he who witnesses it are deceived: he who expels him, as if he were honoured on account of righteousness, not knowing the wickedness of the demon. For he has at once honoured the name, and by his flight has brought the wicked man into a thought of his righteousness, and so deceived him away from repentance. But the looker-on, associating with the expeller as a pious man, hastens to a like manner of life, and is ruined. Sometimes also they pretend to flee before adjurations not made in the name of God, that they may deceive men, and destroy them whom they will.

CHAP. XXIII. — THE SICK HEALED.

"This then we would have you know, that unless any one of his own accord give himself over as a slave to demons, as I said before, the demon has no power against him. Choosing, therefore, to worship one God, and refraining from the table of demons, and undertaking chastity with philanthropy and righteousness, and being baptized with the thrice-blessed invocation for the remission of sins, and devoting yourselves as much as you can to the perfection of purity, you can escape everlasting punishment, and be constituted heirs of eternal blessings."

Having thus spoken, he ordered those to approach who were distressed with diseases;[3] and thus many approached, having come together through the experience of those who had been healed yesterday. And he having laid his hands upon them and prayed, and immediately healed them, and having charged them and the others to come earlier, he bathed and partook of food, and went to sleep.

---

[1] [With chaps. 19–21 compare *Recognitions*, iv. 32, 35, which closely resemble them. — R.]

[2] I prefer here the common text to any of the proposed emendations, and suppose that the author represents Cæsar, though but one man, as the image or personification of the whole empire.

[3] [Comp. *Recognitions*, iv. 7. — R.]

HOMILY X.

CHAP. I. — THE THIRD DAY IN TRIPOLIS.

THEREFORE on the third day in Tripolis,[1] Peter rose early and went into the garden, where there was a great water-reservoir, into which a full stream of water constantly flowed. There having bathed, and then having prayed, he sat down; and perceiving us sitting around and eagerly observing him, as wishing to hear something from him, he said: —

CHAP. II. — IGNORANCE AND ERROR.

"There seems to me to be a great difference between the ignorant and the erring. For the ignorant man seems to me to be like a man who does not wish to set out for a richly stored city, through his not knowing the excellent things that are there; but the erring man to be like one who has learned indeed the good things that are in the city, but who has forsaken the highway in proceeding towards it, and so has wandered. Thus, therefore, it seems to me that there is a great difference between those who worship idols and those who are faulty in the worship of God. For they who worship idols are ignorant of eternal life, and therefore they do not desire it; for what they do not know, they cannot love. But those who have chosen to worship one God, and who have learned of the eternal life given to the good, if they either believe or do anything different from what is pleasing to God, are like to those who have gone out from the city of punishment, and are desirous to come to the well-stored city, and on the road have strayed from the right path."

CHAP. III. — MAN THE LORD OF ALL.

While he was thus discoursing to us, there entered one of our people, who had been appointed to make the following announcement to him, and said: "My lord Peter, there are great multitudes standing before the doors." With his consent, therefore, a great multitude entered. Then he rose up, and stood on the basis, as he had done the day before; and having saluted them in religious fashion, he said: "God having formed the heaven and the earth, and having made all things in them, as the true Prophet has said to us, man, being made after the image and likeness of God, was appointed to be ruler and lord of things, I say, in air and

earth and water, as may be known from the very fact that by his intelligence he brings down the creatures that are in the air, and brings up those that are in the deep, hunts those that are on the earth, and that although they are much greater in strength than he; I mean elephants, and lions, and such like.

CHAP. IV. — FAITH AND DUTY.

"While, therefore, he was righteous, he was also superior to all sufferings, as being unable by his immortal body to have any experience of pain; but when he sinned, as I showed you yesterday and the day before, becoming as it were the servant of sin, he became subject to all sufferings, being by a righteous judgment deprived of all excellent things. For it was not reasonable, the Giver having been forsaken, that the gifts should remain with the ungrateful. Whence, of His abundant mercy, in order to our receiving, with the first, also future blessings, He sent His Prophet. And the Prophet has given in charge to us to tell you what you ought to think, and what to do. Choose, therefore; and this is in your power. What, therefore, you ought to think is this, to worship the God who made all things; whom if you receive in your minds, you shall receive from Him, along with the first excellent things, also the future eternal blessings.

CHAP. V. — THE FEAR OF GOD.

"Therefore you shall be able to persuade yourselves with respect to the things that are profitable, if, like charmers, you say to the horrible serpent which lurks in your heart, 'The Lord God thou shalt fear, and Him alone thou shalt serve.'[2] On every account it is advantageous to fear Him alone, not as an unjust, but as a righteous God. For one fears an unjust being, lest he be wrongfully destroyed, but a righteous one, lest he be caught in sin and punished. You can therefore, by fear towards Him, be freed from many hurtful fears. For if you do not fear the one Lord and Maker of all, you shall be the slaves of all evils to your own hurt, I mean of demons and diseases, and of everything that can in any way hurt you.

CHAP. VI. — RESTORATION OF THE DIVINE IMAGE.

"Therefore approach with confidence to God, you who at first were made to be rulers and

---

[1] [Book v. of the *Recognitions*, assigned to the second day at Tripolis, contains most of the matter in this Homily, but has many passages without a parallel here. — R.]

[2] Matt. iv. 10; [Luke iv. 8; Deut. vi. 13. — R.].

lords of all things: ye who have His image in your bodies, have in like manner the likeness of His judgment in your minds. Since, then, by acting like irrational animals, you have lost the soul of man from your soul, becoming like swine, you are the prey of demons. If, therefore, you receive the law of God, you become men. For it cannot be said to irrational animals, 'Thou shalt not kill, thou shalt not commit adultery, thou shalt not steal,' and so forth. Therefore do not refuse, when invited, to return to your first nobility; for it is possible, if ye be conformed to God by good works. And being accounted to be sons by reason of your likeness to Him, you shall be reinstated as lords of all.

CHAP. VII. — UNPROFITABLENESS OF IDOLS.

" Begin,[1] then, to divest yourselves of the injurious fear of vain idols, that you may escape unrighteous bondage. For they have become your masters, who even as servants are unprofitable to you. I speak of the material of the lifeless images, which are of no use to you as far as service is concerned. For they neither hear nor see nor feel, nor can they be moved. For is there any one of you who would like to see as they see, and to hear as they hear, and to feel as they feel, and to be moved as they are? God forbid that such a wrong should be done to any man bearing the image of God, though he have lost His likeness.

CHAP. VIII. — NO GODS WHICH ARE MADE WITH HANDS.

" Therefore reduce your gods of gold and silver, or any other material, to their original nature; I mean into cups and basins and all other utensils, such as may be useful to you for service; and those good things which were given you at first shall be able to be restored. But perhaps you will say, The laws of the emperors do not permit us to do this.[2] You say well that it is the law, and not the power of the vain idols themselves, which is nothing. How, then, have ye regarded them as gods, who are avenged by human laws, guarded by dogs, kept by multitudes?—and that if they are of gold, or silver, or brass. For those of wood or earthenware are preserved for their worthlessness, because no man desires to steal a wooden or earthenware god! So that your gods are exposed to danger in proportion to the value of the material of which they are made. How, then, can they be gods, which are stolen, molten, weighed, guarded?

CHAP. IX. — " EYES HAVE THEY, BUT THEY SEE NOT."

" Oh the minds of wretched men, who fear things deader than dead men! For I cannot call them even dead, which have never lived, unless they are the tombs of ancient men. For sometimes a person, visiting unknown places, does not know whether the temples which he sees are monuments of dead men, or whether they belong to the so-called gods; but on inquiring and hearing that they belong to the gods, he worships, without being ashamed that if he had not learned on inquiring, he would have passed them by as the monument of a dead man, on account of the strictness of the resemblance. However, it is not necessary that I should adduce much proof in regard to such superstition. For it is easy for any one who pleases to understand that it, *an idol*, is nothing, unless there be any one who does not see. However, now at least hear that it does not hear, and understand that it does not understand. For the hands of a man who is dead made it. If, then, the maker is dead, how can it be that that which was made by him shall not be dissolved? Why, then, do you worship the work of a mortal which is altogether senseless? whereas those who have reason do not worship animals, nor do they seek to propitiate the elements which have been made by God,—I mean the heaven, the sun, the moon, lightning, the sea, and all things in them,— rightly judging not to worship the things that He has made, but to reverence the Maker and Sustainer of them. For in this they themselves also rejoice, that no one ascribes to them the honour that belongs to their Maker.

CHAP. X. — IDOLATRY A DELUSION OF THE SERPENT.

" For His alone is the excellent glory of being alone uncreated, while all else is created. As, therefore, it is the prerogative of the uncreated to be God, so whatever is created is not God indeed. Before all things, therefore, you ought to consider the evil-working suggestion of the deceiving serpent that is in you, which seduces you by the promise of better reason, creeping from your brain to your spinal marrow, and setting great value upon deceiving you.[3]

CHAP. XI. — WHY THE SERPENT TEMPTS TO SIN.

" For he knows the original law, that if he bring you to the persuasion of the so-called gods, so that you sin against the one good of monarchy, your overthrow becomes a gain to him. And that for this reason, because he being

---

[1] [*Recognitions*, v. 14, is parallel to this chapter, and the resemblance is close throughout some of the succeeding chapters. — R.]

[2] [This, with the corresponding passage in *Recognitions*, v. 15, points to an early origin of the literature, under the heathen emperors. — R.]

[3] [Comp. *Recognitions*, ii. 45, and especially the full discussion about the serpent in *Recognitions*, v. 17-26. — R.]

condemned eats earth, he has power to eat him who through sin being dissolved into earth, has become earth, your souls going into his belly of fire. In order, therefore, that you may suffer these things, he suggests every thought to your hurt.

CHAP. XII. — IGNORANTIA NEMINEM EXCUSAT.

" For all the deceitful conceptions against the monarchy are sown in your mind by him to your hurt. First, that you may not hear the discourses of piety, and so drive away ignorance, which is the occasion of evils, he ensnares you by a pretence of knowledge, giving in the first instance, and using throughout this presumption, which is to think and to be unhappily advised, that if any one do not hear the word of piety, he is not subject to judgments. Wherefore also some, being thus deceived, are not willing to hear, that they may be ignorant, not knowing that ignorance is of itself a sufficient deadly drug. For if any one should take a deadly drug in ignorance, does he not die? So naturally sins destroy the sinner, though he commit them in ignorance of what is right.

CHAP. XIII. — CONDEMNATION OF THE IGNORANT.

" But if judgment follows upon disobedience to instruction, much more shall God destroy those who will not undertake His worship. For he who will not learn, lest that should make him subject to judgment, is already judged as knowing, for he knew what he will not hear; so that that imagination avails nothing as an apology in presence of the heart-knowing God. Wherefore avoid that cunning thought suggested by the serpent to your minds. But if any one end this life in real ignorance, this charge will lie against him, that, having lived so long, he did not know who was the bestower of the food supplied to him: and as a senseless, and ungrateful, and very unworthy servant, he is rejected from the kingdom of God.

CHAP. XIV. — POLYTHEISTIC ILLUSTRATION.

" Again, the terrible serpent suggests this supposition to you, to think and to say that very thing which most of you do say; viz., We know that there is one Lord of all, but there also are gods. For in like manner as there is one Cæsar, but he has under him procurators, proconsuls, prefects, commanders of thousands, and of hundreds, and of tens; in the same way, there being one great God, as there is one Cæsar, there also, after the manner of inferior powers, are gods, inferior indeed to Him, but ruling over us. Hear, therefore, ye who have been led away by this conception as by a terrible poison — I mean the evil conception of this

illustration — that you may know what is good and what is evil. For you do not yet see it, nor do you look into the things that you utter.

CHAP. XV. — ITS INCONCLUSIVENESS.

" For if you say that, after the manner of Cæsar, God has subordinate powers — those, namely, which are called gods — you do not thus go by your illustration. For if you went by it, you must of necessity know that it is not lawful to give the name of Cæsar to another, whether he be consul, or prefect, or captain, or any one else, and that he who gives such a name shall not live, and he who takes it shall be cut off. Thus, according to your own illustration, the name of God must not be given to another; and he who is tempted either to take or give it is destroyed. Now, if this insult of a man induces punishment, much more they who call others gods shall be subject to eternal punishment, as insulting God. And with good reason; because you subject to all the insult that you can the name which it was committed to you to honour, in order to His monarchy. For GOD is not properly His name; but you having in the meantime received it, insult what has been given you, that it may be accounted as done against the real name, according as you use that. But you subject it to every kind of insult.

CHAP. XVI. — GODS OF THE EGYPTIANS.

" Therefore you ringleaders among the Egyptians, boasting of meteorology, and promising to judge the natures of the stars, by reason of the evil opinion lurking in them, subjected that name to all manner of dishonour as far as in them lay. For some of them taught the worship of an ox called Apis, some that of a he-goat, some of a cat, some of a serpent; yea, even of a fish, and of onions, and rumblings in the stomach,[1] and common sewers, and members of irrational animals, and to myriads of other base abominations *they gave the name of god.*"

CHAP. XVII. — THE EGYPTIANS' DEFENCE OF THEIR SYSTEM.

On Peter's saying this, the surrounding multitude laughed. Then Peter said to the laughing multitude: " You laugh at their proceedings, not knowing that you are yourselves much more objects of ridicule to them. But you laugh at one another's proceedings; for, being led by evil custom into deceit, you do not see your own. But I admit that you have reason to laugh at the idols of the Egyptians, since they, being rational, worship irrational animals, and these altogether dying. But listen to what they say when they deride you. We, they say, though we worship

---

[1] γαστρῶν πνεύματα.

dying creatures, yet still such as have once had life : but you reverence things that never lived. And in addition to this, they say, We wish to honour the form of the one God, but we cannot find out what it is, and so we choose to give honour to every form. And so, making some such statements as these, they think that they judge more rightly than you do.

CHAP. XVIII. — ANSWER TO THE EGYPTIANS.

"Wherefore answer them thus : You lie, for you do not worship these things in honour of the true God, for then all of you would worship every form ; not as ye do. For those of you who suppose the onion to be the divinity, and those who worship rumblings in the stomach, contend with one another ; and thus all in like manner preferring some one thing, revile those that are preferred by others. And with diverse judgments, one reverences one and another another of the limbs of the same animal. Moreover, those of them who still have a breath of right reason, being ashamed of the manifest baseness, attempt to drive these things into allegories, wishing by another vagary to establish their deadly error. But we should confute the allegories, if we were there, the foolish passion for which has prevailed to such an extent as to constitute a great disease of the understanding. For it is not necessary to apply a plaster to a whole part of the body, but to a diseased part. Since then, you, by your laughing at the Egyptians, show that you are not affected with their disease, with respect to your own disease it were reasonable I should afford to you a present cure of your own malady.

CHAP. XIX. — GOD'S PECULIAR ATTRIBUTE.

"He who would worship God ought before all things to know what alone is peculiar to the nature of God, which cannot pertain to another, that, looking at His peculiarity, and not finding it in any other, he may not be seduced into ascribing godhead to another. But this is peculiar to God, that He alone is, as the Maker of all, so also the best of all. That which makes is indeed superior in power to that which is made ; that which is boundless is superior in magnitude to that which is bounded : in respect of beauty, that which is comeliest ; in respect of happiness, that which is most blessed ; in respect of understanding, that which is most perfect. And in like manner, in other respects, He has incomparably the pre-eminence. Since then, as I said, this very thing, viz., to be the best of all, is peculiar to God, and the all-comprehending world was made by Him, none of the things made by Him can come into equal comparison with Him.

CHAP. XX. — NEITHER THE WORLD NOR ANY OF ITS PARTS CAN BE GOD.

"But the world, not being incomparable and unsurpassable, and altogether in all respects without defect, cannot be God. But if the whole world cannot be God, in respect of its having been made, how much more should not its parts be reasonably called God ; I mean the parts that are by you called gods, being made of gold and silver, brass and stone, or of any other material whatsoever ; and they constructed by mortal hand. However, let us further see how the terrible serpent through man's mouth poisons those who are seduced by his solicitations.

CHAP. XXI. — IDOLS NOT ANIMATED BY THE DIVINE SPIRIT.

"For many say, We do not worship the gold or the silver, the wood or the stone, of the objects of our worship. For we also know that these are nothing but lifeless matter, and the art of mortal man. But the spirit that dwells in them, that we call God. Behold the immorality of those who speak thus ! For when that which appears is easily proved to be nothing, they have recourse to the invisible, as not being able to be convicted in respect of what is non-apparent. However, they agree with us in part, that one half of their images is not God, but senseless matter. It remains for them to show how we are to believe that these images have a divine spirit. But they cannot prove to us that it is so, for it is not so ; and we do not believe them *when they say that they* have seen it. We shall afford them proofs that they have not a divine spirit, that lovers of truth, hearing the refutation of the thought that they are animated, may turn away from the hurtful delusion.

CHAP. XXII. — CONFUTATION OF IDOL-WORSHIP.

"In the first place, indeed, if you worship them as being animated, why do you also worship the sepulchres of memorable men of old, who confessedly had no divine spirit ? Thus you do not at all speak truth respecting this. But if your objects of worship were really animated, they would move of themselves ; they would have a voice ; they would shake off the spiders that are on them ; they would thrust forth those that wish to surprise and to steal them ; they would easily capture those who pilfer the offerings. But now they do none of these things, but are guarded, like culprits, and especially the more costly of them, as we have already said. But what ? Is it not so, that the rulers demand of you imposts and taxes on their account, as if you were greatly benefited by them ? But what ? Have they not often been taken as plunder by enemies, and been broken and scattered ? And do not the priests, more than the outside worshippers, carry off many of the offerings, thus acknowledging the uselessness of their worship?

CHAP. XXIII. — FOLLY OF IDOLATRY.

" Nay, it will be said; but they are detected by their foresight. It is false; for how many of them have not been detected? And if on account of the capture of some it be said that they have power, it is a mistake. For of those who rob tombs, some are found out and some escape; but it is not by the power of the dead that those who are apprehended are detected. And such ought to be our conclusion with respect to those who steal and pilfer the gods. But it will be said, The gods that are in them take no care of their images. Why, then, do you tend them, wiping them, and washing them, and scouring them, crowning them, and sacrificing to them? Wherefore agree with me that you act altogether without right reason. For as you lament over the dead, so you sacrifice and make libations to your gods.

CHAP. XXIV. — IMPOTENCE OF IDOLS.

" Nor yet is that in harmony with the illustration of Cæsar, and of the powers under him, to call them administrators; whereas you take all care of them, as I said, tending your images in every respect. For they, having no power, do nothing. Wherefore tell us what do they administer? what do they of that sort which rulers in different places do? and what influence do they exert, as the stars of God? Do they show anything like the sun, or do you light lamps before them? Are they able to bring showers, as the clouds bring rain, — they which cannot even move themselves, unless men carry them? Do they make the earth fruitful to your labours, these to whom you supply sacrifices? Thus they can do nothing.

CHAP. XXV. — SERVANTS BECOME MASTERS.

" But if they were able to do something, you should not be right in calling them gods: for it

is not right to call the elements gods, by which good things are supplied; but only Him who ordereth them, to accomplish all things for our use, and who commandeth them to be serviceable to man, — Him alone we call God in propriety of speech, whose beneficence you do not perceive, but permit those elements to rule over you which have been assigned to you as your servants. And why should I speak of the elements, when you not only have made and do worship lifeless images, but deign to be subject to them in all respects as servants? Wherefore, by reason of your erroneous judgments, you have become subject to demons. However, by acknowledgment of God Himself, by good deeds you can again become masters, and command the demons as slaves, and as sons of God be constituted heirs of the eternal kingdom."

CHAP. XXVI. — THE SICK HEALED.

Having said this, he ordered the demoniacs, and those taken with diseases, to be brought to him; and when they were brought, he laid his hands on them, and prayed, and dismissed them healed, reminding them and the rest of the multitude to attend upon him there every day that he should discourse. Then, when the others had withdrawn, Peter bathed in the reservoir that was there, with those who pleased; and then ordering a table to be spread on the ground under the thick foliage of the trees, for the sake of shade, he ordered us each to recline, according to our worth; and thus we partook of food. Therefore having blessed and having given thanks to God for the enjoyment, according to the accustomed faith of the Hebrews; and there being still a long time before us, he permitted us to ask him questions about whatever we pleased; and thus, though there were twenty of us putting questions to him all round, he satisfied every one. And now evening having descended, we all went with him into the largest apartment of the lodging, and there we all slept.

HOMILY XI.

CHAP. I. — MORNING EXERCISES.

THEREFORE on the fourth day at Tripolis, Peter rising and finding us awake, saluted us and went out to the reservoir, that he might bathe and pray; and we also did so after him. To us, therefore, when we had prayed together, and

were set down before him, he gave a discourse touching the necessity of purity. And when thereafter it was day, he permitted the multitudes to enter. Then, when a great crowd had entered, he saluted them according to custom, and began to speak.

CHAP. II. — "GIVING ALL DILIGENCE."

"Inasmuch as, by long-continued neglect on your part, to your own injury, your mind has caused to sprout many hurtful conceptions about religion, and ye have become like land fallow by the carelessness of the husbandman, you need a long time for your purification, that your mind, receiving like good seed the true word that is imparted to you, may not choke it with evil cares, and render it unfruitful with respect to works that are able to save you. Wherefore it behoves those who are careful of their own salvation to hear more constantly, that their sins which have been long multiplying may, in the short time that remains, be matched with constant care for their purification. Since, therefore, no one knows the time of his end, hasten to pluck out the many thorns of your hearts ; but not by little and little, for then you cannot be purified, for you have been long fallow.[1]

CHAP. III. — "BEHOLD WHAT INDIGNATION."

"But not otherwise will you endure to undertake much care for your purification unless you be angry with yourselves, and chastise yourselves for those things with which, as unprofitable servants, you have been ensnared, consenting to your evil lusts, that you may be able to let in your righteous indignation upon your mind, as fire upon a fallow field. If, therefore, ye have not righteous fire, I mean indignation, against evil lusts, learn from what good things ye have been seduced, and by whom ye have been deceived, and for what punishment ye are prepared ; and thus, your mind being sober, and kindled into indignation like fire by the teaching of Him who sent us, may be able to consume the evil things of lust. Believe me, that if you will, you can rectify all things.

CHAP. IV. — THE GOLDEN RULE.

"Ye are the image of the invisible God.[2] Whence let not those who would be pious say that idols are images of God, and therefore that it is right to worship them. For the image of God is man. He who wishes to be pious towards God does good to man, because the body of man bears the image of God. But all do not as yet bear His likeness, but the pure mind of the good soul does. However, as we know that man was made after the image and after the likeness of God, we tell you to be pious towards him, that the favour may be accounted as done to God, whose image he is. Therefore it behoves you to give honour to the image of God, which is man

—in this wise : food to the hungry, drink to the thirsty, clothing to the naked, care to the sick, shelter to the stranger, and visiting him who is in prison, to help him as you can. And not to speak at length, whatever good things any one wishes for himself, so let him afford to another in need, and then a good reward can be reckoned to him as being pious towards the image of God. And by like reason, if he will not undertake to do these things, he shall be punished as neglecting the image.

CHAP. V. — FORASMUCH AS YE DID IT UNTO ONE OF THESE.

"Can it therefore be said that, for the sake of piety towards God, ye worship every form, while in all things ye injure man who is really the image of God, committing murder, adultery, stealing, and dishonouring him in many other respects? But you ought not to do even one evil thing on account of which man is grieved. But now you do all things on account of which man is disheartened, for wrong is also distress. Wherefore you murder and spoil his goods, and whatever else you know which you would not receive from another. But you, being seduced by some malignant reptile to malice, by the suggestion of polytheistic doctrine, are impious towards the real image, which is man, and think that ye are pious towards senseless things.

CHAP. VI. — WHY GOD SUFFERS OBJECTS OF IDOLATRY TO SUBSIST.

"But some say, Unless He wished these things to be, they should not be, but He would take them away. But I say this shall assuredly be the case, when all shall show their preference for Him, and thus there shall be a change of the present world. However, if you wished him to act thus, so that none of the things that are worshipped should subsist, tell me what of existing things you have not worshipped. Do not some of you worship the sun, and some the moon, and some water, and some the earth, and some the mountains, and some plants, and some seeds, and some also man, as in Egypt? Therefore God must have suffered nothing, not even you, so that there should have been neither worshipped nor worshipper. Truly this is what the terrible serpent which lurks in you would have, and spares you not. But so it shall not be. For it is not the thing that is worshipped that sins ; for it suffers violence at the hands of him who will worship it. For though unjust judgment is passed by all men, yet not by God. For it is not just that the sufferer and the disposer receive the same punishment, unless he willingly receive the honour which belongs only to the Most Honourable.

---

[1] [With chaps. 2, 3, the corresponding chapters in *Recognitions*, vi., agree. The parallel is resumed in chap. 19. — R.]
[2] [Most of the matter in chaps. 4–18 is found in *Recognitions*, v. 23–36. — R.]

CHAP. VII. — "LET BOTH GROW TOGETHER TILL THE HARVEST."

"But it will be said that the worshippers themselves ought to be taken away by the true God, that others may not do it. But you are not wiser than God, that you should give Him counsel as one more prudent than He. He knows what He does; for He is long-suffering to all who are in impiety, as a merciful and philanthropic father, knowing that impious men become pious. And of those very worshippers of base and senseless things, many becoming sober have ceased to worship these things and to sin, and many Greeks have been saved so as to pray to the true God.

CHAP. VIII. — LIBERTY AND NECESSITY.

"But, you say, God ought to have made us at first so that we should not have thought at all of such things. You who say this do not know what is free-will, and how it is possible to be really good; that he who is good by his own choice is really good; but he who is made good by another under necessity is not really good, because he is not what he is by his own choice.[1] Since therefore every one's freedom constitutes the true good, and shows the true evil, God has contrived that friendship or hostility should be in each man by occasions. But no, it is said: everything that we think He makes us to think. Stop! Why do you blaspheme more and more, in saying this? For if we are under His influence in all that we think, you say that He is the cause of fornications, lusts, avarice, and all blasphemy. Cease your evil-speaking, ye who ought to speak well of Him, and to bestow all honour upon Him. And do not say that God does not claim any honour; for if He Himself claims nothing, you ought to look to what is right, and to answer with thankful voice Him who does you good in all things.

CHAP. IX. — GOD A JEALOUS GOD.

"But, you say, we do better when we are thankful at once to Him and to all others. Now, when you say this, you do not know the plot that is formed against you. For as, when many physicians of no power promise to cure one patient, one who is really able to cure him does not apply his remedy, considering that, if he should cure him, the others would get the credit; so also God does not do you good, when He is asked along with many who can do nothing. What! it will be said, is God enraged at this, if, when He cures, another gets the credit? I answer: Although He be not indignant, at all events He will not be an accomplice in deceit;

for when He has conferred a benefit, the idol, which has done nothing, is credited with the power. But also I say to you, if he who crouches in adoration before senseless idols had not been injured naturally, perhaps He (God) would have endured even this. Wherefore watch ye that you may attain to a reasonable understanding on the matter of salvation.[2] For God being without want, neither Himself needs anything, nor receives hurt; for it belongs to us to be profited or injured. For in like manner as Cæsar is neither hurt when he is evil spoken of, nor profited when he is thanked, but safety accrues to the renderer of thanks, and ruin to the evil-speaker, so they who speak well of God indeed profit Him nothing, but save themselves; and in like manner, those who blaspheme Him do not indeed injure Him, but themselves perish.

CHAP. X. — THE CREATURES AVENGE GOD'S CAUSE.

"But it will be said that the cases are not parallel between God and man; and I admit that they are not parallel: for the punishment is greater to him who is guilty of impiety against the greater, and less to him who sins against the less. As, therefore, God is greatest of all, so he who is impious against Him shall endure greater punishment, as sinning against the greater; not through His defending Himself with His own hand, but the whole creation being indignant at him, and naturally taking vengeance on him. For to the blasphemer the sun will not give his light, nor the earth her fruits, nor the fountain its water, nor in Hades shall he who is there constituted prince give rest to the soul; since even now, while the constitution of the world subsists, the whole creation is indignant at him. Wherefore neither do *the clouds* afford sufficient rains, nor the earth fruits, whereby many perish; yea, even the air itself, inflamed with anger, is turned to pestilential courses. However, whatsoever good things we enjoy, He of His mercy compels the creature to our benefits. Still, against you who dishonour the Maker of all, the whole creation is hostile.

CHAP. XI. — IMMORTALITY OF THE SOUL.

"And though by the dissolution of the body you should escape punishment, how shall you be able by corruption to flee from your soul, which is incorruptible? For the soul even of the wicked is immortal, for whom it were better not to have it incorruptible. For, being punished with endless torture under unquenchable fire, and never dying, it can receive no end of its misery. But perhaps some one of you will say, 'You terrify us, O Peter.' Teach us then how we can be

---

[1] [Comp. *Recognitions*, iii. 21, etc. In that work the freedom of the will, as necessary to goodness, is more frequently affirmed. — R.]

[2] We have adopted the reading of Codex O. The reading in the others is corrupt.

silent *about these things, and yet* tell you things as they are, for not otherwise can we tell you them. But if we should be silent, you should be ensnared by evils through ignorance. But if we speak, we are suspected of terrifying you with a false theory. How then shall we charm that wicked *serpent* that lurks in your *soul*, and subtilely insinuates suspicions hostile to God, under the guise of love of God? Be reconciled with yourselves; for in order to your salvation recourse is to Him with well-doing. Unreasonable lust in you is hostile to God, for by conceit of wisdom it strengthens ignorance.

CHAP. XII. — IDOLS UNPROFITABLE.

"But others say, God does not care for us. This also is false. For if really He did not care, He would neither cause His sun to rise on the good and the evil, nor send His rain on the just and the unjust. But others say, We are more pious *than you*, since we worship both him and images. I do not think, if one were to say to a king, ' I give you an equal share of honour with that which I give to corpses and to worthless dung ' — I do not think that he would profit by it. But some one will say, Do you call our objects of worship dung? I say Yes, for you have made them useless to yourselves by setting them aside for worship, whereas their substance might perhaps have been serviceable for some other purpose, or for the purpose of manure. But now it is not useful even for this purpose, since you have changed its shape and worship it. And how do you say that you are more pious, you who are the most wicked of all, who deserve destruction of your souls by this very one incomparable sin, at the hands of Him who is true, if you abide in it? For as if any son having received many benefits from his father, give to another, who is not his father, the honour that is due to his father, he is certainly disinherited; but if he live according to the judgment of his father, and so thanks him for his kindnesses, he is with good reason made the heir.

CHAP. XIII. — ARGUMENTS IN FAVOUR OF IDOLATRY ANSWERED.

"But others say, We shall act impiously if we forsake the objects of worship handed down to us by our fathers; for it is like the guarding of a deposit. But on this principle the son of a robber or a debauchee ought not to be sober and to choose the better part, lest he should act impiously, and sin by doing differently from his parents! How foolish, then, are they who say, We worship these things that we may not be troublesome to Him; as if God were troubled by those who bless Him, and not troubled by those who ungratefully blaspheme Him. Why

is it, then, that when there is a withholding of rain, you look only to heaven and pour out prayers and supplications; and when you obtain it, you quickly forget? For when you have reaped your harvest or gathered your vintage, you distribute your first-fruits among those idols which are nothing, quickly forgetting God your benefactor; and thus you go into groves and temples, and offer sacrifices and feasts. Wherefore some of you say, These things have been excellently devised for the sake of good cheer and feasting.

CHAP. XIV. — HEATHEN ORGIES.

" Oh men without understanding ! Judge ye rightly of what is said. For if it were necessary to give one's self to some pleasure for the refreshment of the body, whether were it better to do so among the rivers and woods and groves, where there are entertainments and convivialities and shady places, or where there is the madness of demons, and cuttings of hands, and emasculations, and fury and mania, and dishevelling of hair, and shoutings and enthusiasms and howlings, and all those things which are done with hypocrisy for the confounding of the unthinking, when you offer your prescribed prayers and thanksgivings even to those who are deader than the dead?

CHAP. XV. — HEATHEN WORSHIPPERS UNDER THE POWER OF THE DEMON.

" And why do ye take pleasure in these doings? Since the serpent which lurks in you, which has sown in you fruitless lust, will not tell you, I shall speak and put it on record. Thus the case stands. According to the worship of God, the proclamation is made to be sober, to be chaste, to restrain passion, not to pilfer other men's goods, to live uprightly, moderately, fearlessly, gently; rather to restrain one's self in necessities, than to supply his wants by wrongfully taking away the property of another. But with the so-called gods the reverse is done. And ye renounce some things *as done by you*, in order to the admiration of *your* righteousness; whereas, although you did all that you are commanded, ignorance with respect to God is alone sufficient for your condemnation. But meeting together in the places which you have dedicated to them, you delight in making yourselves drunk, and you kindle your altars, of which the diffused odour through its influence attracts the blind and deaf spirits to the place of their fumigation. And thus, of those who are present, some are filled with inspirations, and some with strange fiends, and some betake themselves to lasciviousness, and some to theft and murder. For the exhalation of blood, and the libation of wine, satisfies even these unclean spirits, which lurk within you and cause you to take pleasure in the things that are transacted there, and in dreams surround you with false phantasies, and punish you with myriads of diseases. For under the show of the so-called sacred victims you are filled with dire demons, which, cunningly concealing themselves, destroy you, so that you should not understand the plot that is laid for you. For, under the guise of some injury, or love, or anger, or grief, or strangling you with a rope, or drowning you, or throwing you from a precipice, or by suicide, or apoplexy, or some other disease, they deprive you of life.

CHAP. XVI. — ALL THINGS WORK FOR GOOD TO THEM THAT LOVE GOD.

" But no one of us can suffer such a thing; but they themselves are punished by us, when, having entered into any one, they entreat us that they may go out slowly. But some one will say perhaps, Even some of the worshippers of God fall under such sufferings. I say that that is impossible. For he is a worshipper of God, of whom I speak, who is truly pious, not one who is such only in name, but who really performs the deeds of the law that has been given him. If any one acts impiously, he is not pious; in like manner as, if he who is of another tribe keeps the law, he is a Jew; but he who does not keep it is a Greek. For the Jew believes God and keeps the law, by which faith he removes also other sufferings, though like mountains and heavy.[1] But he who keeps not the law is manifestly a deserter through not believing God; and thus as no Jew, but a sinner, he is on account of his sin brought into subjection to those sufferings which are ordained for the punishment of sinners. For, by the will of God prescribed at the beginning, punishment righteously follows those who worship Him on account of transgressions; and this is so, in order that, having reckoned with them by punishment for sin as for a debt, he may set forth those who have turned to Him pure in the universal judgment. For as the wicked here enjoy luxury to the loss of eternal blessings, so punishments are sent upon the Jews who transgress for a settlement of accounts, that, expiating their transgression here, they may there be set free from eternal punishments.

CHAP. XVII. — SPEAKING THE TRUTH IN LOVE.

" But you cannot speak thus; for you do not believe that things are then as we say; I mean, when there is a recompense for all. And on this account, you being ignorant of what is advanta-geous, are seduced by temporal pleasures from taking hold of eternal things. Wherefore we attempt to make to you exhibitions of what is profitable, that, being convinced of the promises that belong to piety, you may by good deeds inherit with us the griefless world. Until then you know us, do not be angry with us, as if we spoke falsely of the good things which we desire for you. For the things which are regarded by us as true and good, these we have not scrupled to bring to you, but, on the contrary, have hastened to make you fellow-heirs of good things, which we have considered to be such. For thus it is necessary to speak to the unbelievers. But that we really speak the truth in what we say, you cannot know otherwise than by first listening with love of the truth.

CHAP. XVIII. — CHARMING OF THE SERPENT.

" Wherefore, as to the matter in hand, although in ten thousand ways the serpent that lurks in you suggesting evil reasonings and hindrances, wishes to ensnare you, therefore so much the more ought ye to resist him, and to listen to us assiduously. For it behoves you, consulting, as having been grievously deceived, to know how he must be charmed. But in no other way is it possible. But by charming I mean the setting yourselves by reason in opposition to their evil counsels, remembering that by promise of knowledge he brought death into the world at the first.[2]

CHAP. XIX. — NOT PEACE, BUT A SWORD.

" Whence the Prophet of the truth, knowing that the world was much in error, and seeing it ranged on the side of evil, did not choose that there should be peace to it while it stood in error. So that till the end he sets himself against all those who are in concord with wickedness, setting *truth* over against error, sending as it were fire upon those who are sober, namely wrath against the seducer, which is likened to a sword,[3] and by holding forth the word he destroys ignorance by knowledge, cutting, as it were, and separating the living from the dead. Therefore, while wickedness is being conquered by lawful knowledge, war has taken hold of all. For the submissive son, for the sake of salvation, separated from the unbelieving father, or the father from the son, or the mother from the daughter, or the daughter from the mother, and relatives from relatives, and friends from associates.

---

[1] Matt. xvii. 20.

[2] [At this point the first discourse in the *Recognitions* (v. 36) ends; the following chapters (19-33) agree with the discourse in *Recognitions*, vi. 4-14. — R.]

[3] Matt. x. 34.

CHAP. XX. — WHAT IF IT BE ALREADY KINDLED?

" And let not any one say, How is this just, that parents should be separated from their children, and children from their parents? It is just, even entirely. For if they remained with them, and, after profiting them nothing, were also destroyed along with them, how is it not just that he who wishes to be saved should be separated from him who will not, but who wishes to destroy him along with himself. Moreover, it is not those who judge better that wish to be separated, but they wish to stay with them, and to profit them by the exposition of better things ; and therefore the unbelievers, not wishing to hearken to them, make war against them, banishing, persecuting, hating them. But those who suffer these things, pitying those who are ensnared by ignorance, by the teaching of wisdom pray for those who contrive evil against them, having learned that ignorance is the cause of their sin. For the Teacher Himself, being nailed to *the cross*, prayed to the Father that the sin of those who slew Him might be forgiven, saying, ' Father, forgive them their sins, for they know not what they do.' [1] They also therefore, being imitators of the Teacher in their sufferings, pray for those who contrive them, as they have been taught. Therefore they are not separated as hating their parents, since they make constant prayers even for those who are neither parents nor relatives, but enemies, and strive to love them, as they have been commanded.

CHAP. XXI. — " IF I BE A FATHER, WHERE IS MY FEAR ? "

" But tell me, how do you love your parents? If, indeed, you do it as always regarding what is right, I congratulate you ; but if you love them as it happens, then not so, for then you may on a small occasion become their enemies. But if you love them intelligently, tell me, what are parents? You will say they are the sources of our being. Why, then, do ye not love the *source of the* being of all things, if indeed you have with right understanding elected to do this? But you will now say again, we have not seen Him. Why, then, do ye not seek for Him, but worship senseless things? But what? If it were even difficult for you to know what God is, you cannot fail to know what is not God, so as to reason that God is not wood, nor stone, nor brass, nor anything else made of corruptible matter.

CHAP. XXII. — " THE GODS THAT HAVE NOT MADE THE HEAVENS."

" For are not they graven with iron? And has not the graving iron been softened by fire? And

is not the fire itself extinguished with water? And has not the water its motion from the spirit? And has not the spirit the beginning of its course from the God who hath made all things? For thus said the prophet Moses : ' In the beginning God made the heaven and the earth. And the earth was unsightly, and unadorned ; and darkness was over the deep : and the Spirit of God was borne above the waters.' Which Spirit, at the bidding of God, as it were His hand, makes all things, dividing light from darkness, and after the invisible heaven spreading out the visible, that the places above might be inhabited by the angels of light, and those below by man, and all the creatures that were made for his use.

CHAP. XXIII. — " TO WHOM MUCH IS GIVEN."

" For on thy account, O man, God commanded the water to retire upon the face of the earth, that the earth might be able to bring forth fruits for thee. And He made water-courses, that He might provide for thee fountains, and that river-beds might be disclosed, that animals might teem forth ; in a word, that He might furnish thee with all things. For is it not for thee that the winds blow, and the rains fall, and the seasons change for the production of fruits? Moreover, it is for thee that the sun and moon, with the other heavenly bodies, accomplish their risings and settings ; and rivers and pools, with all fountains, serve thee. Whence to thee, O senseless one, as the greater honour has been given, so for thee, ungrateful, the greater punishment by fire has been prepared, because thou wouldest not know Him whom it behoved thee before all things to know.

CHAP. XXIV. — " BORN OF WATER."

" And now from inferior things learn the cause of all, reasoning that water makes all things, and water receives the production of its movement from spirit, and the spirit has its beginning from the God of all. And thus you ought to have reasoned, in order that by reason you might attain to God, that, knowing your origin, and being born again by the first-born water, you may be constituted heir of the parents who have begotten you to incorruption.

CHAP. XXV. — GOOD WORKS TO BE WELL DONE.

" Wherefore come readily, as a son to a father, that God may assign ignorance as the cause of your sins. But if after being called you will not, or delay, you shall be destroyed by the just judgment of God, not being willed, through your not willing. And do not think, though you were more pious than all the pious that ever were, but if you be unbaptized, that you shall ever obtain hope. For all the more, on this account, you

---

[1] Luke xxiii. 34.

shall endure the greater punishment, because you have done excellent works not excellently. For well-doing is excellent when it is done as God has commanded. But if you will not be baptized according to His pleasure, you serve your own will and oppose His counsel.

CHAP. XXVI. — BAPTISM.

" But perhaps some one will say, What does it contribute to piety to be baptized with water? In the first place, because you do that which is pleasing to God ; and in the second place, being born again to God of water, by reason of fear you change your first generation, which is of lust, and thus you are able to obtain salvation. But otherwise it is impossible. For thus the prophet has sworn to us, saying, " Verily I say to you, Unless ye be regenerated by living water into the name of Father, Son, and Holy Spirit, you shall not enter the kingdom of heaven.¹ Wherefore approach. For there is there something that is merciful from the beginning, borne upon the water, and rescues from the future punishment those who are baptized with the thrice blessed invocation, offering as gifts to God the good deeds of the baptized whenever they are done after their baptism. Wherefore flee to the waters, for this alone can quench the violence of fires.² He who will not now come to it still bears the spirit of strife, on account of which he will not approach the living water for his own salvation.

CHAP. XXVII. — ALL NEED BAPTISM.

" Therefore approach, be ye righteous or unrighteous. For if you are righteous, baptism alone is lacking in order to salvation. But if you are unrighteous, come to be baptized for the remission of the sins formerly committed in ignorance. And to the unrighteous man it remains that his well-doing after baptism be according to the proportion of his *previous* impiety. Wherefore, be ye righteous or unrighteous, hasten to be born to God, because delay brings danger, on account of the fore-appointment of death being unrevealed ; and show by well-doing your likeness to the Father, who begetteth you of water. As a lover of truth, honour the true God as your Father. But His honour is that you live as He, being righteous, would have you live. And the will of the righteous One is that you do no wrong. But wrong is murder, hatred, envy, and such like ; and of these there are many forms.

CHAP. XXVIII. — PURIFICATION.

" However, it is necessary to add something to these things which has not community with man,

but is peculiar to the worship of God. I mean purification, not approaching to a man's own wife when she is in separation, for so the law of God commands. But what? If purity be not added to the service of God, you would roll pleasantly like the dung-flies. Wherefore as man, having something more than the irrational animals, namely, rationality, purify your hearts from evil by heavenly reasoning, and wash your bodies in the bath. For purification according to the truth is not that the purity of the body precedes purification after the heart, but that purity follows goodness. For our Teacher also, *dealing with* certain of the Pharisees and Scribes among us, who are separated, and as Scribes know the matters of the law more than others, still He reproved them as hypocrites, because they cleansed only the things that appear to men, but omitted purity of heart and the things seen by God alone.

CHAP. XXIX. — OUTWARD AND INWARD PURITY.

" Therefore He made use of this memorable expression, speaking the truth with respect to the hypocrites of them, not with respect to all. For to some He said that obedience was to be rendered, because they were entrusted with the chair of Moses. However, to the hypocrites he said, ' Woe to you, Scribes and Pharisees, hypocrites, for ye make clean the outside of the cup and the platter, but the inside is full of filth. Thou blind Pharisee, cleanse first the inside of the cup and the platter, that their outsides may be clean also.' And truly : for when the mind is enlightened by knowledge, the disciple is able to be good, and thereupon purity follows ; for from the understanding within a good care of the body without is produced. As from negligence with respect to the body, care of the understanding cannot be produced, so the pure man can purify both that which is without and that which is within. And he who, purifying the things without, does it looking to the praise of men, and by the praise of those who look on, he has nothing from God.

CHAP. XXX. — " WHATSOEVER THINGS ARE PURE."

" But who is there to whom it is not manifest that it is better not to have intercourse with a woman in her separation, but purified and washed. And also after copulation it is proper to wash. But if you grudge to do this, recall to mind how you followed after the parts of purity when you served senseless idols ; and be ashamed that now, when it is necessary to attain, I say not more, but to attain the one and whole of purity, you are more slothful. Consider, therefore, Him who made you, and you will understand who He is that casts upon you this sluggishness with respect to purity.

---

¹ Altered from John iii. 5.
² [Comp. *Recognitions*, ix. 7. — R.]

CHAP. XXXI. — "WHAT DO YE MORE THAN OTHERS?"

" But some one of you will say, Must we then do whatsoever things we did while we were idolaters? I say to you, Not all things; but whatsoever you did well, you must do now, and more: for whatsoever is well done in error hangs upon truth, as if anything be ill done in the truth it is from error. Receive, therefore, from all quarters the things that are your own, and not those that are another's, and do not say, If those who are in error do anything well we are not bound to do it. For, on this principle, if any one who worships idols do not commit murder, we ought to commit murder, because he who is in error does not commit it.

CHAP. XXXII. — "TO WHOM MUCH IS GIVEN."

" No; but rather, if those who are in error do not kill, let us not be angry; if he who is in error do not commit adultery, let us not lust even in the smallest degree; if he who is in error loves him who loves him, let us love even those who hate us; if he who is in error lends to those who have, let us *give* to those who have not. Unquestionably we ought — we who hope to inherit eternal life — to do better things than the good things that are done by those who know only the present life, knowing that if their works, being judged with ours in the day of judgment, be found equal in goodness, we shall have shame, and they perdition, having acted against themselves through error. And I say that we shall be put to shame on this account, because we have not done more than they, though we have known more than they. And if we shall be put to shame if we show well-doing equal to theirs, and no more, how much more if we show less than their well-doing?

CHAP. XXXIII. — THE QUEEN OF THE SOUTH AND THE MEN OF NINEVEH.

" But that indeed in the day of judgment the doings of those who have known the truth are compared with the good deeds of those who have been in error, the unlying One Himself has taught us, saying to those who neglected to come and listen to Him, ' The queen of the south shall rise up with this generation, and shall condemn it; because she came from the extremities of the earth to hear the wisdom of Solomon: and behold, a greater than Solomon is here,'[1] and ye do not believe Him. And to those amongst the people who would not repent at His preaching He said, ' The men of Nineveh shall rise up with this generation and shall condemn it, for they heard and repented on the preaching of

Jonas: and behold, a greater is here, and no one believes.'[2] And thus, setting over against all their impiety those from among the Gentiles who have done *well*, in order to condemn those who, possessing the true religion, had not acted so well as those who were in error, he exhorted those having reason not only to do equally with the Gentiles whatsoever things are excellent, but more than they. And this speech has been suggested to me, taking occasion from the necessity of respecting the separation, and of washing after copulation, and of not denying such purity, though those who are in error do the same, since those who in error do well, without being saved, are for the condemnation of those who are in the worship of God, *and do ill;* because their respect for purity is through error, and not through the worship of the true Father and God of all."

CHAP. XXXIV. — PETER'S DAILY WORK.

Having said this, he dismissed the multitudes; and according to his custom, having partaken of food with those dearest to him, he went to rest. And thus doing and discoursing day by day, he strongly buttressed the law of God, challenging the reputed gods with the reputed GENESIS,[3] and arguing that there is no automatism, but that the world is governed according to providence.

CHAP. XXXV. — " BEWARE OF FALSE PROPHETS."

Then after three months were fulfilled, he ordered me to fast for several days, and then brought me to the fountains that are near to the sea, and baptized me as in ever-flowing water. Thus, therefore, when our brethren rejoiced at my God-gifted regeneration, not many days after he turned to the elders in presence of all the church, and charged them, saying : " Our Lord and Prophet, who hath sent us, declared to us that the wicked one, having disputed with Him forty days, and having prevailed nothing against Him, promised that he would send apostles from amongst his subjects, to deceive. Wherefore, above all, remember to shun apostle or teacher or prophet who does not first accurately compare his preaching with *that of* James, who was called the brother of my Lord, and to whom was entrusted to administer the church of the Hebrews in Jerusalem, — and that even though he come to you with witnesses :[4] lest the wickedness which disputed forty days with the Lord, and prevailed nothing, should afterwards, like lightning falling from heaven upon the earth,

---

[1] Matt. xii. 42; [Luke xi. 31. — R.].

[2] [Matt. xii 41]: Luke xi. 32. [The order of the two citations suggests that they were taken from Luke. — R.].
[3] [Comp. Homily IV. 12 and the full discussion in XIV. 3-11. In the *Recognitions* there is no reference to " genesis" before book viii. 2, etc., which is parallel with the passage just referred to. — R.]
[4] A conjectural reading, which seems probable, is, Unless he come to you with credentials, viz., from James. [The whole charge is peculiar to the *Homilies.* — R.].

send a preacher to your injury, as now he has sent Simon upon us, preaching, under pretence of the truth, in the name of the Lord, and sowing error. Wherefore He who hath sent us, said, 'Many shall come to me in sheep's clothing, but inwardly they are ravening wolves. By their fruits ye shall know them.'"

CHAP. XXXVI. — FAREWELL TO TRIPOLIS.

Having spoken thus, he sent the harbingers into Antioch of Syria, bidding them expect him there forthwith. Then when they had gone, Peter having driven away diseases, sufferings, and demons from great multitudes who were persuaded, and having baptized them in the foun-

tains which are near to the sea, and having celebrated [1] the Eucharist, and having appointed Maroones, who had received him into his house, and was now perfected, as their bishop, and having set apart twelve elders, and having designated deacons, and arranged matters relating to widows, and having discoursed on the common good what was profitable for the ordering of the church, and having counselled them to obey the bishop Maroones, three months being now fulfilled, he bade those in Tripolis of Phœnicia farewell, and took his journey to Antioch of Syria, all the people accompanying us with due honour.

[1] Literally, "having broken."

HOMILY XII.

CHAP. I. — TWO BANDS.

THEREFORE starting from Tripolis of Phœnicia to go to Antioch of Syria, on the same day we came to Orthasia, and there stayed.[1] And on account of its being near the city which we had left, almost all having heard the preaching before, we stopped there only one day, and set out to Antaradus. And as there were many who journeyed with us, Peter, addressing Nicetus and Aquila, said, "Inasmuch as the great crowd of those who journey with us draws upon us no little envy as we enter city after city, I have thought that we must of necessity arrange, so that neither, on the one hand, these may be grieved at being prevented from accompanying us, nor, on the other hand, we, by being so conspicuous, may fall under the envy of the wicked.[2] Wherefore I wish you, Nicetus and Aquila, to go before me in two separate bodies, and enter secretly into the Gentile cities.

CHAP. II. — LOVE OF PREACHERS AND THEIR CONVERTS.

"I know, indeed, that you are distressed at being told to do this, being separated from me by a space of two days. I would have you know, therefore, that we the persuaders love you the persuaded much more than you love us who have persuaded you. Therefore loving one another as we do by not unreasonably doing what we wish, let us provide, as much as in us lies, for safety. For I prefer, as you also know,

to go into the more notable cities of the provinces, and to remain some days, and discourse. And for the present lead the way into the neighbouring Laodicea, and, after two or three days, so far as it depends upon my choice, I shall overtake you. And do you alone receive me at the gates, on account of the confusion, that thus we may enter along with you without tumult. And thence, in like manner, after some days' stay, others in your stead will go forward by turns to the places beyond, preparing lodgings for us."

CHAP. III. — SUBMISSION.

When Peter had thus spoken they were compelled to acquiesce, saying, "It does not altogether grieve us, my lord, to do this on account of its being your command; in the first place, indeed, because you have been chosen by the providence of God, as being worthy to think and counsel well in all things; and in addition to this, for the most part we shall be separated from you only for two days by the necessity of preceding you. And that were indeed a long time to be without sight of thee, O Peter, did we not consider that they will be more grieved who are sent much farther forward, being ordered to wait for thee longer in every city, distressed that they are longer deprived of the sight of thy longed-for countenance. And we, though not less distressed than they, make no opposition, because you order us to do it for profit." Thus, having spoken, they went forward, having it in charge that at the first stage they should address the accompanying multitude that they should enter the cities apart from one another.

[1] [On the correspondence of Homilies XII., XIII., with *Recognitions*, vii., see note on vii. 1. Chaps. 1–24 here agree quite closely, even in the divisions of chapters, with *Recognitions*, vii. 1–24. — R.]
[2] Literally, "of wickedness."

CHAP. IV. — CLEMENT'S JOY.

When, therefore, they had gone, I, Clement, rejoiced greatly that he had ordered me to remain with himself. Then I answered and said, " I thank God that you have not sent me away as you have done the others, as I should have died of grief." But he said, " But what? If there shall ever be any necessity that you be sent away for the sake of teaching, would you, on account of being separated for a little while from me, and that for an advantageous purpose, would you die for that? Would you not rather impress upon yourself the duty of bearing the things that are arranged for you through necessity, and cheerfully submit? And do you not know that friends are present with one another in their memories, although they are separated bodily; whereas some, being bodily present, wander from their friends in their souls, by reason of want of memory?"

CHAP. V. — CLEMENT'S OFFICE OF SERVICE.

Then I answered, " Do not think, my lord, that I should endure that grief foolishly, but with some good reason. For since I hold you, my lord, in place of all, father, mother, brothers, relatives, you who are the means through God of my having the saving truth, holding you in place of all, I have the greatest consolation. And in addition to this, being afraid of my natural youthful lust, I was concerned lest, being left by you (being but a young man, and having now such a resolution that it would be impossible to desert you without incurring the anger of God,) [1] I should be overcome by lust. But since it is much better and safer for me to remain with you, when my mind is with good reason set upon venerating, therefore I pray that I may always remain with you. Moreover, I remember you saying in Cæsarea, ' If any one wishes to journey with me, let him piously journey.' And by PIOUSLY you meant, that those who are devoted to the worship of God should grieve no one in respect of God, such as by leaving parents, an attached wife, or any others. [2] Whence I am in all respects a fitting fellow-traveller for you, to whom, if you would confer the greatest favour, you would allow to perform the functions of a servant."

CHAP. VI. — PETER'S FRUGALITY.

Then Peter, hearing, smiled and said, " What think you, then, O Clement? Do you not think that you are placed by very necessity in the position of my servant? For who else shall take care of those many splendid tunics, with all my changes of rings and sandals? And who shall make ready those pleasant and artistic dainties, which, being so various, need many skilful cooks, and all those things which are procured with great eagerness, and are prepared for the appetite of effeminate men as for some great wild beast? However, such a choice has occurred to you, perhaps, without you understanding or knowing my manner of life, that I use only bread and olives, and rarely pot-herbs; and that this is my only coat and cloak which I wear; and I have no need of any of them, nor of aught else : for even in these I abound. For my mind, seeing all the eternal good things that are there, regards none of the things that are here. However, I accept of your good will; and I admire and commend you, for that you, a man of refined habits, have so easily submitted your manner of living to your necessities. For we, from our childhood, both I and Andrew, my brother, who is also my brother as respects God, not only being brought up in the condition of orphans, but also accustomed to labour through poverty and misfortune, easily bear the discomforts of our present journeys. Whence, if you would obey me, you would allow me, a working man, to fulfil the part of a servant to you."

CHAP. VII. — " NOT TO BE MINISTERED UNTO, BUT TO MINISTER."

But I, when I heard this, fell a-trembling and weeping, that such a word should be spoken by a man to whom all the men of this generation are inferior in point of knowledge and piety. But he, seeing me weeping, asked the cause of my tears. Then I said, " In what have I sinned so that you have spoken to me such a word?" Then Peter answered, " If it were wrong of me to speak of being your servant, you were first in fault in asking to be mine." Then I said, " The cases are not parallel; for to do this indeed becomes me well; but it is terrible for you, the herald of God, and who savest our souls, to do this to me." Then Peter answered, " I should agree with you, but that [3] our Lord, who came for the salvation of all the world, being alone noble above all, submitted to the condition of a servant, that He might persuade us not to be ashamed to perform the ministrations of servants to our brethren, however well-born we may be." Then I said, " If I think to overcome you in argument, I am foolish. However, I thank the providence of God, that I have been thought worthy to have you instead of parents."

---

[1] Here the text is hopelessly corrupt, and the meaning can only be guessed at.

[2] I have ventured to make a very slight change on the reading here, so as to bring out what I suppose to be the sense.

[3] A negative particle seems to be dropped from the text.

CHAP. VIII. — FAMILY HISTORY.

Then Peter inquired, "Are you really, then, alone in your family?" Then I answered, "There are indeed many and great men, being of the kindred of Cæsar. Wherefore Cæsar himself gave a wife of his own family to my father, who was his foster-brother; and of her three sons of us were born, two before me, who were twins and very like each other, as my father told me. But I scarcely know either them or our mother, but bear about with me an obscure image of them, as through dreams. My mother's name was Mattidia, and my father's, Faustus; and of my brothers one was called Faustinus, and the other Faustinianus.[1] Then after I, their third son, was born, my mother saw a vision — so my father told me — *which told her*, that unless she immediately took away her twin sons, and left the city of Rome for exile for twelve years, she and they must die by an all-destructive fate.

CHAP. IX. — THE LOST ONES.

"Therefore my father, being fond of his children, supplying them suitably for the journey with male and female servants, put them on board ship, and sent them to Athens with her to be educated, and kept me alone of his sons with him for his comfort; and for this I am very thankful, that the vision had not ordered me also to depart with my mother from the city of Rome. Then, after the lapse of a year, my father sent money to them to Athens, and at the same time to learn how they did. But those who went on this errand did not return. And in the third year, my father being distressed, sent others in like manner with supplies, and they returned in the fourth year with the tidings that they had seen neither my mother nor my brothers, nor had they ever arrived at Athens, nor had they found any trace of any one of those who set out with them.

CHAP. X. — THE SEEKER LOST.

"Then my father, hearing this, and being stupefied with excessive grief, and not knowing where to go in quest of them, used to take me with him and go down to the harbour, and inquire of many where any one of them had seen or heard of a shipwreck four years ago. And one turned one place, and another another. Then he inquired whether they had seen the body of a woman with *two* children cast ashore. And when they told him they had seen many corpses in many places, my father groaned at the information. But, with his bowels yearning, he asked

unreasonable questions, that he might try to search so great an extent of sea. However, he was pardonable, because, through affection towards those whom he was seeking for, he fed on vain hopes. And at last, placing me under guardians, and leaving me at Rome when I was twelve years old, he himself, weeping, went down to the harbour, and went on board ship, and set out upon the search. And from that day till this I have neither received a letter from him, nor do I know whether he be alive or dead. But I rather suspect that he is dead somewhere, either overcome by grief, or perished by shipwreck. And the proof of that is that it is now the twentieth year that I have heard no true intelligence concerning him."

CHAP. XI. — THE AFFLICTIONS OF THE RIGHTEOUS.

But Peter, hearing this, wept through sympathy, and immediately said to the gentlemen who were present: "If any worshipper of God had suffered these things, such as this man's father hath suffered, he would immediately have assigned the cause of it to be his worship of God, ascribing it to the wicked one. Thus also it is the lot of the wretched Gentiles to suffer; and we worshippers of God know it not. But with good reason I call them wretched, because here they are ensnared, and the hope that is thine they obtain not. For those who in the worship of God suffer afflictions, suffer them for the expiation of their transgressions."

CHAP. XII. — A PLEASURE TRIP.

When Peter had spoken thus, a certain one amongst us ventured to invite him, in the name of all, that next day, early in the morning, he should sail to Aradus, an island opposite, distant, I suppose, not quite thirty stadia, for the purpose of seeing two pillars of vine-wood that were there, and that were of very great girth. Therefore the indulgent Peter consented, saying, "When you leave the boat, do not go many of you together to see the things that you desire to see; for I do not wish that the attention of the inhabitants should be turned to you." And so we sailed, and in short time arrived at the island. Then landing from the boat, we went to the place where the vine-wood pillars were, and along with them we looked at several of the works of Phidias.

CHAP. XIII. — A WOMAN OF A SORROWFUL SPIRIT.

But Peter alone did not think it worth while to look at the sights that were there; but noticing a certain woman sitting outside before the doors, begging constantly for her support, he said to her, "O woman, is any of your limbs

---

[1] [The family names as given in the *Recognitions* are: Matthidia; Faustinianus (the father); Faustinus and Faustus, the twin sons. — Comp. *Recognitions*, viii. 8, and *passim*. — R.]

defective, that you submit to such disgrace — I mean that of begging, — and do not rather work with the hands which God has given you, and procure your daily food?" But she, groaning, answered, "Would that I had hands able to work! But now they retain only the form of hands, being dead and rendered useless by my gnawing of them." Then Peter asked her, "What is the cause of your suffering so terribly?" And she answered, "Weakness of soul; and nought else. For if I had the mind of a man, there was a precipice or a pool whence I should have thrown myself, and have been able to rest from my tormenting misfortunes."

CHAP. XIV. — BALM IN GILEAD.

Then said Peter, "What then? Do you suppose, O woman, that those who destroy themselves are freed from punishment? Are not the souls of those who thus die punished with a worse punishment in Hades for their suicide?" But she said, "Would that I were persuaded that souls are really found alive in Hades; then I should love death, making light of the punishment, that I might see, were it but for an hour, my longed-for sons!" Then said Peter, "What is it that grieves you? I should like to know, O woman. For if you inform me, in return for this favour, I shall satisfy you that souls live in Hades; and instead of precipice or pool, I shall give you a drug, that you may live and die without torment."

CHAP. XV. — THE WOMAN'S STORY.

Then the woman, not understanding what was spoken ambiguously, being pleased with the promise, began to speak thus: — "Were I to speak of my family and my country, I do not suppose that I should be able to persuade any one. But of what consequence is it to you to learn this, excepting only the reason why in my anguish I have deadened my hands by gnawing them? Yet I shall give you an account of myself, so far as it is in your power to hear it. I, being very nobly born, by the arrangement of a certain man in authority, became the wife of a man who was related to him. And first I had twins sons, and afterwards another son. But my husband's brother, being thoroughly mad, was enamoured of wretched me, who exceedingly affected chastity. And I, wishing neither to consent to my lover nor to expose to my husband his brother's love of me, reasoned thus: that I may neither defile myself by the commission of adultery nor disgrace my husband's bed, nor set brother at war with brother, nor subject the whole family, which is a great one, to the reproach of all, as I said. I reasoned that it was best for me to leave the city for some time with my twin children, until the impure love should cease of him who flattered me to my disgrace. The other son, however, I left with his father, to remain for a comfort to him.

CHAP. XVI. — THE SHIPWRECK.

"However, that matters might be thus arranged, I resolved to fabricate a dream, to the effect that some one stood by me by night, and thus spoke: 'O woman, straightway leave the city with your twin children for some time, until I shall charge you to return hither again; otherwise you forthwith shall die miserably, with your husband and all your children.' And so I did. For as soon as I told the false dream to my husband, he being alarmed, sent me off by ship to Athens with my two sons, and with slaves, maids, and abundance of money, to educate the boys, until, said he, it shall please the giver of the oracle that you return to me. But, wretch that I am, while sailing with my children, I was driven by the fury of the winds into these regions, and the ship having gone to pieces in the night, I was wrecked. And all the rest having died, my unfortunate self alone was tossed by a great wave and cast upon a rock; and while I sat upon it in my misery, I was prevented, by the hope of finding my children alive, from throwing myself into the deep then, when I could easily have done it, having my soul made drunk by the waves.

CHAP. XVII. — THE FRUITLESS SEARCH.

"But when the day dawned, I shouted aloud, and howled miserably, and looked around, seeking for the dead bodies of my hapless children. Therefore the inhabitants took pity on me, and seeing me naked, they first clothed me and then sounded the deep, seeking for my children. And when they found nothing of what they sought, some of the hospitable women came to me to comfort me, and every one told her own misfortunes, that I might obtain comfort from the occurrences of similar misfortunes. But this only grieved me the more; for I said that I was not so wicked that I could take comfort from the misfortunes of others. And so, when many of them asked me to accept their hospitality, a certain poor woman with much urgency constrained me to come into her cottage, saying to me, 'Take courage, woman, for my husband, who was a sailor, also died at sea, while he was still in the bloom of his youth; and ever since, though many have asked me in marriage, I have preferred living as a widow, regretting the loss of my husband. But we shall have in common whatever we can both earn with our hands.'

CHAP. XVIII. — TROUBLE UPON TROUBLE.

" And not to lengthen out unnecessary details, I went to live with her, on account of her love to her husband. And not long after, my hands were debilitated by my gnawing of them; and the woman who had taken me in, being wholly seized by some malady, is confined in the house. Since then the former compassion of the women has declined, and I and the woman of the house are both of us helpless. For a long time I have sat here, as you see, begging; and whatever I get I convey to my fellow-sufferer for our support. Let this suffice about my affairs. For the rest, what hinders your fulfilling of your promise to give me the drug, that I may give it to her also, who desires to die; and thus I also, as you said, shall be able to escape from life?"

CHAP. XIX. — EVASIONS.

While the woman thus spoke, Peter seemed to be in suspense on account of many reasonings. But I came up and said, "I have been going about seeking you for a long time. And now, what is in hand?" But Peter ordered me to lead the way, and wait for him at the boat; and because there was no gainsaying when he commanded, I did as I was ordered. But Peter, as he afterwards related the whole matter to me, being struck in his heart with some slight suspicion, inquired of the woman, saying, "Tell me, O woman, your family, and your city, and the names of your children, and presently I shall give you the drug." But she, being put under constraint, and not wishing to speak, yet being eager to obtain the drug, cunningly said one thing for another. And so she said that she was an Ephesian, and her husband a Sicilian; and in like manner she changed the names of the three children. Then Peter, supposing that she spoke the truth, said, "Alas! O woman, I thought that this day was to bring you great joy, suspecting that you are a certain person of whom I was thinking, and whose affairs I have heard and accurately know." But she adjured him, saying, "Tell me, I entreat of you, that I may know if there is among women any one more wretched than myself."

CHAP. XX. — PETER'S ACCOUNT OF THE MATTER.

Then Peter, not knowing that she had spoken falsely, through pity towards her, began to tell her the truth: "There is a certain young man in attendance upon me, thirsting after the discourses on religion, a Roman citizen, who told me how that, having a father and two twin brothers, he has lost sight of them all. For," says he, "my mother, as my father related to me, having seen a vision, left the city Rome for a time with her twin children, lest she should perish by an evil fate, and having gone away with them, she cannot be found; and her husband, the young man's father, having gone in search of her, he also cannot be found."

CHAP. XXI. — A DISCLOSURE.

While Peter thus spoke, the woman, who had listened attentively, swooned away as if in stupor. But Peter approached her, and caught hold of her, and exhorted her to restrain herself, persuading her to confess what was the matter with her. But she, being powerless in the rest of her body, as through intoxication, turned her *head* round, being able to sustain the greatness of the hoped-for joy, and rubbing her face: "Where," said she, "is this youth?" And he, now seeing through the whole affair, said, "Tell me first; for otherwise you cannot see him." Then she earnestly said, "I am that youth's mother." Then said Peter, "What is his name?" And she said, "Clement." Then Peter said, "It is the same, and he it was that spoke to me a little while ago, whom I ordered to wait for me in the boat. And she, falling at Peter's feet, entreated him to make haste to come to the boat." Then Peter, "If you will keep terms with me, I shall do so." Then she said, "I will do anything; only show me my only child. For I shall seem to see in him my two children who died here." Then Peter said, "When ye see him, be quiet, until we depart from the island." And she said, "I will."

CHAP. XXII. — THE LOST FOUND.

Peter, therefore, took her by the hand, and led her to the boat. But I, when I saw him leading the woman by the hand, laughed, and approaching, offered to lead her instead of him, to his honour. But as soon as I touched her hand, she gave a motherly shout, and embraced me violently, and eagerly kissed me as her son. But I, being ignorant of the whole affair, shook her off as a madwoman. But, through my respect for Peter, I checked myself.

CHAP. XXIII. — REWARD OF HOSPITALITY.

But Peter said, "Alas! What are you doing, my son Clement, shaking off your real mother?" But I, when I heard this, wept, and falling down by my mother, who had fallen, I kissed her. For as soon as this was told me, I in some way recalled her appearance indistinctly. Then great crowds ran together to see the beggar woman, telling one another that her son had recognised her, and that he was a man of consideration. Then, when we would have straightway left the island with my mother, she said to us, "My much longed-for son, it is right that I should bid farewell to the woman who entertained me, who, being poor and wholly debilitated, lies in the house." And Peter hearing this, and all the multitude who stood by, admired the good disposition of the woman. And immediately Peter ordered some persons to go and bring the woman on her couch. And as soon as the couch was brought and set down, Peter said, in the hearing of the whole multitude, "If I be a herald of the truth, in order to the faith of the bystanders, that they may know that there is one God, who made the world, let her straightway rise whole." And while Peter was still speaking, the woman arose healed, and fell down before Peter, and kissed her dear associate, and asked her what it all meant. Then she briefly detailed to her the whole business of the recognition,[1] to the astonishment of the hearers. Then also my mother, seeing her hostess cured, entreated that she herself also might obtain healing. And his placing his hand upon her, cured her also.

CHAP. XXIV. — ALL WELL ARRANGED.

And then Peter having discoursed concerning God and the service accorded to Him, he concluded as follows : "If any one wishes to learn these things accurately, let him come to Antioch, where I have resolved to remain some length of time, and learn the things that pertain to his salvation. For if you are familiar with leaving your country for the sake of trading or of warfare, and coming to far-off places, you should not be unwilling to go three days' journey for the sake of eternal salvation." Then, after the address of Peter, I presented the woman who had been healed, in the presence of all the multitude, with a thousand drachmas, for her support, giving her in charge to a certain good man, who was the chief man of the city, and who of his own accord joyfully undertook the charge. Further, having distributed money amongst many other women, and thanked those who at any time had comforted my mother, I sailed away to Antaradus, along with my mother, and Peter, and the rest of our companions ; and thus we proceeded to our lodging.

CHAP. XXV. — PHILANTHROPY AND FRIENDSHIP.

And when we were arrived and had partaken of food, and given thanks according to our custom, there being still time,[2] I said to Peter: "My lord Peter, my mother has done a work of philanthropy in remembering the woman her hostess." And Peter answered, "Have you indeed, O Clement, thought truly that your mother did a work of philanthropy in respect of her treatment of the woman who took her in after her shipwreck, or have you spoken this word by way of greatly complimenting your mother? But if you spoke truly, and not by way of compliment, you seem to me not to know what the greatness of philanthropy is, which is affection towards any one whatever in respect of his being a man, apart from physical persuasion. But not even do I venture to call the hostess who received your mother after her shipwreck, philanthropic ; for she was impelled by pity, and persuaded to become the benefactress of a woman who had been shipwrecked, who was grieving for her children, — a stranger, naked, destitute, and greatly deploring her misfortunes. When, therefore, she was in such circumstances, who that saw her, though he were impious, could but pity her? So that it does not seem to me that even the stranger-receiving woman did a work of philanthropy, but to have been moved to assist her by pity for her innumerable misfortunes. And how much more is it true of your mother, than when she was in prosperous circumstances and requited her hostess, she did a deed, not of philanthropy, but of friendship ! for there is much difference between friendship and philanthropy, because friendship springs from requital. But philanthropy, apart from physical persuasion, loves and benefits every man as he is a man. If, therefore, while she pitied her hostess, she also pitied and did good to her enemies who have wronged her, she would be philanthropic ; but if, on one account she is friendly or hostile, and on another account is hostile or friendly, such an one is the friend or enemy of some quality, not of man as man."

CHAP. XXVI. — WHAT IS PHILANTHROPY.

Then I answered, "Do you not think, then, that even the stranger-receiver was philanthropic, who did good to a stranger whom she did not know?" Then Peter said, "Compassionate, indeed, I can call her, but I dare not call her philanthropic, just as I cannot call a mother philoteknic, for she is prevailed on to have an affection for them by her pangs, and by her rearing of them. As the lover also is gratified by the company and enjoyment of his mistress, and the friend by return of friendship, so also the compassionate man by misfortune. However the compassionate man is near to the philanthropic, in that he is impelled, apart from hunting after the receipt of anything, to do the kindness. But he is not yet philanthropic." Then I said, "By what deeds, then, can any one be philanthropic?" And Peter answered, "Since I see that you are eager to hear what is the work of philanthropy, I shall not object to telling you. He is the philanthropic man who does good even to

---

[1] [Comp. *Recognitions*, vii. 23, where the translator prints the word in italics. — R.]
[2] [The remainder of this Homily has no parallel in the *Recognitions*. The views presented are peculiar, and indicate a speculative tendency, less marked in the *Recognitions*. — R.]

his enemies. And that it is so, listen: Philanthropy is masculo-feminine; and the feminine part of it is called COMPASSION, and the male part is named love to our neighbour. But every man is neighbour to every man, and not merely this man or that; for the good and the bad, the friend and the enemy, are alike men. It behoves, therefore, him who practises philanthropy to be an imitator of God, doing good to the righteous and the unrighteous, as God Himself vouchsafes His sun and His heavens to all in the present world. But if you will do good to the good, but not to the evil, or even will punish them, you undertake to do the work of a judge, you do not strive to hold by philanthropy."

CHAP. XXVII. — WHO CAN JUDGE.

Then I said, "Then even God, who, as you teach us, is at some time to judge, is not philanthropic." Then said Peter, "You assert a contradiction; for because He shall judge, on that very account He is philanthropic. For he who loves and compassionates those who have been wronged, avenges those who have wronged them." Then I said, "If, then, I also do good to the good, and punish the wrong-doers in respect of their injuring men, am I not philanthropic?" And Peter answered, "If along with knowledge [1] you had also authority to judge, you would do this rightly on account of your having received authority to judge those whom God made, and on account of your knowledge infallibly justifying some as the righteous, and condemning some as unrighteous. Then I said, "You have spoken rightly and truly; for it is impossible for any one who has not knowledge to judge rightly. For sometimes some persons seem good, though they perpetrate wickedness in secret, and some good persons are conceived to be bad through the accusation of their enemies. But even if one judges, having the power of torturing and examining, not even so should he altogether judge righteously. For some persons, being murderers, have sustained the tortures, and have come off as innocent; while others, being innocent, have not been able to sustain the tortures, but have confessed falsely against themselves, and have been punished as guilty."

CHAP. XXVIII. — DIFFICULTY OF JUDGING.

Then said Peter, "These things are ordinary: now hear what is greater. There are some men whose sins or good deeds are partly their own, and partly those of others; but it is right that each one be punished for his own sins, and rewarded for his own merits. But it is impossible

for any one except a prophet, who alone has omniscience, to know with respect to the things that are done by any one, which are his own, and which are not; for all are seen as done by him." Then I said, "I would learn how some of men's wrong-doings or right-doings are their own, and some belong to others."

CHAP. XXIX. — SUFFERINGS OF THE GOOD.

Then Peter answered, "The prophet of the truth has said, 'Good things must needs come, and blessed, said he, is he by whom they come; in like manner evil things must needs come, but woe to him through whom they come.' [2] But if evil things come by means of evil men, and good things are brought by good men, it must needs be in each man as his own to be either good or bad, and proceeding from what he has proposed, in order to the coming of the subsequent good or evil,[3] which, being of his own choice, are not arranged by the providence of God to come from him. This being so, this is the judgment of God, that he who, as by a combat, comes through all misfortune and is found blameless, he is deemed worthy of eternal life; for those who by their own will continue in goodness, are tempted by those who continue in evil by their own will, being persecuted, hated, slandered, plotted against, struck, cheated, accused, tortured, disgraced, — suffering all these things by which it seems reasonable that they should be enraged and stirred up to vengeance.

CHAP. XXX. — OFFENCES MUST COME.

"But the Master knowing that those who wrongfully do these things are guilty by means of their former sins, and that the spirit of wickedness works these things by means of the guilty, has counselled to compassionate men, as they are men, and as being the instruments of wickedness through sin; *and this counsel* He has given to His disciples as claiming philanthropy, and, as much as in us lies, to absolve the wrong-doers from condemnation, that, as it were, the temperate may help the drunken, by prayers, fastings, and benedictions, not resisting, not avenging, lest they should compel them to sin more. For when a person is condemned by any one to suffer, it is not reasonable for him to be angry with him by whose means the suffering comes; for he ought to reason, that if he had not ill-used him, yet because he was to be ill-used, he must have suffered it by means of another. Why, then, should I be angry with the dispenser, when I was condemned at all events to suffer? But yet, further: if we do these same things to the evil on pretence of

---

[1] The word repeatedly rendered *knowledge* and once *omniscience* in this passage, properly signifies *foreknowledge*. The argument shows clearly that it means omniscience, of which foreknowledge is the most signal manifestation.

[2] An incorrect quotation from Matt. xviii. 7; Luke xvii. 1.
[3] This from a various reading.

revenge, we who are good do the very things which the evil do, excepting that they do them first, and we second; and, as I said, we ought not to be angry, as knowing that in the providence of God, the evil punish the good. Those, therefore, who are bitter against their punishers, sin, as disdaining the messengers of God; but those who honour them, and set themselves in opposition to those who think to injure them,[1] are pious towards God who has thus decreed."

CHAP. XXXI. — "HOWBEIT, THEY MEANT IT NOT."

To this I answered, "Those, therefore, who do wrong are not guilty, because they wrong the just by the judgment of God." Then Peter said, "They indeed sin greatly, for they have given themselves to sin. Wherefore knowing this, *God* chooses from among them *some* to punish those who righteously repented of their former sins, that the evil things done by the just before their repentance may be remitted through this punishment. But to the wicked who punish and desire to ill-use them, and will not repent, it is permitted to ill-use the righteous for the filling up of their own punishment. For without the will of God, not even a sparrow can fall into a girn.[2] Thus even the hairs of the righteous are numbered by God.

CHAP. XXXII. — THE GOLDEN RULE.

" But he is righteous who for the sake of what is reasonable fights with nature. For example, it is natural to all to love those who love them. But the righteous man tries also to love his enemies and to bless those who slander him, and even to pray for his enemies, and to compassionate those who do him wrong. Wherefore also he refrains from doing wrong, and blesses those who curse him, pardons those who strike him, and submits to those who persecute him, and salutes those who do not salute him, shares such things as he has with those who have not, persuades him that is angry with him, conciliates his enemy, exhorts the disobedient, instructs the unbelieving, comforts the mourner; being distressed, he endures; being ungratefully treated, he is not angry. But having devoted himself to love his neighbour as himself, he is not afraid of poverty, but becomes

poor by sharing his possessions with those who have none. But neither does he punish the sinner. For he who loves his neighbour as himself, as he knows that when he has sinned he does not wish to be punished, so neither does he punish those who sin. And as he wishes to be praised, and blessed, and honoured, and to have all his sins forgiven, thus he does to his neighbour, loving him as himself.[3] In one word, what he wishes for himself, he wishes also for his neighbour. For this is the law of God and of the prophets;[4] this is the doctrine of truth. And this perfect love towards every man is the male part of philanthropy, but the female part of it is compassion; that is, to feed the hungry, to give drink to the thirsty, to clothe the naked, to visit the sick, to take in the stranger, to show herself to, and help to the utmost of her power, him who is in prison,[5] and, in short, to have compassion on him who is in misfortune."

CHAP. XXXIII. — FEAR AND LOVE.

But I, hearing this, said: "These things, indeed, it is impossible to do; but to do good to enemies, bearing all their insolences, I do not think can possibly be in human nature." Then Peter answered: "You have said truly; for philanthropy, being the cause of immortality, is given for much." Then I said, "How then is it possible to get it in the mind?" Then Peter answered: "O beloved Clement, the way to get it is this: if any one be persuaded that enemies, ill-using for a time those whom they hate, become the cause to them of deliverances from eternal punishment; and forthwith he will ardently love them as benefactors. But the way to get it, O dear Clement, is but one, which is the fear of God. For he who fears God cannot indeed from the first love his neighbour as himself; for such an order does not occur to the soul. But by the fear of God he is able to do the things of those who love; and thus, while he does the deeds of love, the bride LOVE is, as it were, brought to the bridegroom FEAR. And thus this bride, bringing forth philanthropic thoughts, makes her possessor immortal, as an accurate image of God, which cannot be subject in its nature to corruption." Thus while he expounded to us the doctrine of philanthropy, the evening having set in, we turned to sleep.

---

[1] That is, I suppose, who render good for evil.
[2] See Luke xii. 6, 7; [Matt. x. 29, 30.—R.].
[3] Matt. xxii. 39.
[4] Matt. vii. 12
[5] Matt. xxv. 35, 36.

HOMILY XIII.

CHAP. I. — JOURNEY TO LAODICEA.

Now at break of day Peter entered, and said : [1] " Clement, and his mother Mattidia, and my wife, must take their seats immediately on the waggon." And so they did straightway. And as we were hastening along the road to Balanææ, my mother asked me how my father was ; and I said : " My father went in search of you, and of my twin brothers Faustinus and Faustinianus, and is now nowhere to be found. But I fancy he must have died long ago, either perishing by shipwreck, or losing his way,[2] or wasted away by grief." When she heard this, she burst into tears, and groaned through grief ; but the joy which she felt at finding me, mitigated in some degree the painfulness of her recollections. And so we all went down together to Balanææ. And on the following day we went to Paltus, and from that to Gabala ; and on the next day we reached Laodicea. And, lo ! before the gates of the city Nicetas and Aquila met us, and embracing us, brought us to our lodging. Now Peter, seeing that the city was beautiful and great, said : " It is worth our while to stay here for some days ; for, generally speaking, a populous place is most capable of yielding us those whom we seek."[3] Nicetas and Aquila asked me who that strange woman was ; and I said : " My mother, whom God, through my lord Peter, has granted me to recognise."

CHAP. II. — PETER RELATES TO NICETAS AND AQUILA THE HISTORY OF CLEMENT AND HIS FAMILY.

On my saying this, Peter gave them a summary account[4] of all the incidents, — how, when they had gone on before, I Clement had explained to him my descent, the journey undertaken by my mother with her twin children on the false pretext of the dream ; and furthermore, the journey undertaken by my father in search of her ; and then how Peter himself, after hearing this, went into the island, met with the woman, saw her begging, and asked the reason of her so doing ; and then ascertained who she was, and her mode of life, and the feigned dream, and the names of her children — that is, the name borne by me, who was left with my father, and the names of the twin children who travelled along with her, and who, she supposed, had perished in the deep.

CHAP. III. — RECOGNITION OF NICETAS AND AQUILA.

Now when this summary narrative had been given by Peter, Nicetas and Aquila in amazement said : " Is this indeed true, O Ruler and Lord of the universe, or is it a dream ? " And Peter said : " Unless we are asleep, it certainly is true." On this they waited for a little in deep meditation, and then said : " We are Faustinus and Faustinianus. From the commencement of your conversation we looked at each other, and conjectured much with regard to ourselves, whether what was said had reference to us or not ; for we reflected that many coincidences take place in life. Wherefore we remained silent while our hearts beat fast. But when you came to the end of your narrative, we saw clearly[5] that your statements referred to us, and then we avowed who we were." And on saying this, bathed in tears, they rushed in to see their mother ; and although they found her asleep, they were yet anxious to embrace her. But Peter forbade them, saying : " Let me bring you and present you to your mother, lest she should, in consequence of her great and sudden joy, lose her reason, as she is slumbering, and her spirit is held fast by sleep."

CHAP. IV. — THE MOTHER MUST NOT TAKE FOOD WITH HER SON. THE REASON STATED.

As soon as my mother had enough of sleep, she awoke, and Peter at once began first to talk to her of *true* piety, saying : " I wish you to know, O woman, the course of life involved in our religion.[6] We worship one God, who made the world which you see ; and we keep His law, which has for its chief injunctions to worship Him alone, and to hallow His name, and to honour our parents, and to be chaste, and to live piously. In addition to this, we do not live with all indiscriminately ; nor do we take our food from the same table as Gentiles, inasmuch as we cannot eat along with them, because they live impurely. But when we have persuaded them to have true thoughts, and to follow a right course of action, and have baptized them with a thrice blessed invocation, then we dwell with them. For not even if it were our father, or mother, or wife, or child, or brother, or

---

[1] [Comp. *Recognitions*, vii. 25. Here the narrative is somewhat fuller in detail. — R.]

[2] Cotelerius conjectured σφαγέντα for σφαλέντα — " being slain on our journey."

[3] The first *Epitome* explains " those whom we seek " as those who are worthy to share in Christ or in Christ's Gospel

[4] [In *Recognitions*, vii. 26, 27, the recapitulation is more extended. — R.]

[5] The text is somewhat doubtful. We have given the meaning contained in the first *Epitome*.

[6] θρήσκεια.

any other one having a claim by nature on our affection, can we venture to take our meals with him; for our religion compels us to make a distinction. Do not, therefore, regard it as an insult if your son does not take his food along with you, until you come to have the same opinions and adopt the same course of conduct as he follows."

CHAP. V. — MATTIDIA WISHES TO BE BAPTIZED.

When she heard this, she said: "What, then, prevents me from being baptized this day? for before I saw you I turned away from the so-called gods, induced by the thought that, though I sacrificed much to them almost every day, they did not aid me in my necessities. And with regard to adultery, what need I say? for not even when I was rich was I betrayed into this sin by luxury, and the poverty which succeeded has been unable to force me into it, since I cling to my chastity as constituting the greatest beauty,[1] on account of which I fell into so great distress. But I do not at all imagine that you, my lord Peter, are ignorant that the greatest temptation[2] arises when everything looks bright. And therefore, if I was chaste in my prosperity, I do not in my despondency give myself up to pleasures. Yea, indeed, you are not to suppose that my soul has now been freed from distress, although it has received some measure of consolation by the recognition of Clement. For the gloom which I feel in consequence of the loss of my two children rushes in upon me, and throws its shadow to some extent over my joy; for I am grieved, not so much because they perished in the sea, but because they were destroyed, both soul and body, without possessing true[3] piety towards God. Moreover, my husband, their father, as I have learned from Clement, went away in search of me and his sons, and for so many years has not been heard of; and, without doubt, he must have died. For the miserable man, loving me as he did in chastity, was fond of his children; and therefore the old man, deprived of all of us who were dear to him above everything else, died utterly broken-hearted."

CHAP. VI. — THE SONS REVEAL THEMSELVES TO THE MOTHER.

The sons, on hearing their mother thus speak, could no longer, in obedience to the exhortation of Peter, restrain themselves, but rising up, they clasped her in their arms, showering down upon her tears and kisses. But she said: "What is

the meaning of this?" And Peter answered: "Courageously summon up your spirits, O woman, that you may enjoy your children; for these are Faustinus and Faustinianus, your sons, who, you said, had perished in the deep. For how they are alive, after they had in your opinion died on that most disastrous night, and how one of them now bears the name of Nicetas, and the other that of Aquila, they will themselves be able to tell you; for we, as well as you, have yet to learn this." When Peter thus spoke, my mother fainted away through her excessive joy, and was like to die. But when we had revived her she sat up, and coming to herself, she said: "Be so good, my darling children, as tell us what happened to you after that disastrous night."

CHAP. VII. — NICETAS TELLS WHAT BEFELL HIM.

And Nicetas, who in future is to be called Faustinus, began to speak. "On that very night when, as you know, the ship went to pieces, we were taken up by some men, who did not fear to follow the profession of robbers on the deep. They placed us in a boat, and brought us along the coast, sometimes rowing and sometimes sending for provisions, and at length took us to Cæsarea Stratonis,[4] and there tormented us by hunger, fear, and blows, that we might not recklessly disclose anything which they did not wish us to tell; and, moreover, changing our names, they succeeded in selling us. Now the woman who bought us was a proselyte of the Jews, an altogether worthy person, of the name of Justa. She adopted us as her own children, and zealously brought us up in all the learning of the Greeks. But we, becoming discreet with our years, were strongly attached to her religion, and we paid good heed to our culture, in order that, disputing with the other nations, we might be able to convince them of their error. We also made an accurate study of the doctrines of the philosophers, especially the most atheistic, — I mean those of Epicurus and Pyrrho, — in order that we might be the better able to refute them.[5]

CHAP. VIII. — NICETAS LIKE TO BE DECEIVED BY SIMON MAGUS.

"We were brought up along with one Simon, a magician; and in consequence of our friendly intercourse with him, we were in danger of being

---

[1] One MS. and the first *Epitome* read, "as being the greatest blessing."

[2] Lit., "desire."

[3] The Greek has, "apart from divine piety towards God." As Wieseler remarks, the epithet "divine" is corrupt. The meaning may be, "without having known the proper mode of worshipping God."

[4] This clause, literally translated, is, "and sometimes impelling it with oars, they brought us along the land; and sometimes sending for provisions, they conveyed us to Cæsarea Stratonis." The Latin translator renders "to land," not "along the land." The passage assumes a different form in the *Recognitions*, the first *Epitome*, and the second *Epitome;* and there is, no doubt, some corruption in the text. The text has δακρύοντας, which makes no sense. We have adopted the rendering given in the *Recognitions*. Various attempts have been made to amend the word.

[5] [Comp *Recognitions*, viii. 7, where the studies of the brothers are more fully indicated, as a preface to the discussions in which they appear as disputants. — R.]

led astray. Now there is a report in regard to some man, that, when he appears, the mass of those who have been pious are to live free from death and pain in his kingdom. This matter, however, mother, will be explained more fully at the proper time. But when we were going to be led astray by Simon, a friend of our lord Peter, by name Zacchæus, came to us and warned us not to be led astray by the magician; and when Peter came, he brought us to him that he might give us full information, and convince us in regard to those matters that related to piety. Wherefore we beseech you, mother, to partake of those blessings which have been vouchsafed to us, that we may unite around the same table!¹ This, then, is the reason, mother, why you thought we were dead. On that disastrous night we had been taken up in the sea by pirates, but you supposed that we had perished."

CHAP. IX. — THE MOTHER BEGS BAPTISM FOR HERSELF AND HER HOSTESS.

When Faustinus had said this, our mother fell down at Peter's feet, begging and entreating him to send for her and her hostess, and baptize them immediately, in order that, says she, not a single day may pass after the recovery of my children, without my taking food with them. When we united with our mother in making the same request, Peter said: "What can you imagine? Am I alone heartless, so as not to wish that you should take your meals with your mother, baptizing her this very day? But yet it is incumbent on her to fast one day before she be baptized. And it is only one day, because, in her simplicity, she said something in her own behalf, which I looked on as a sufficient indication of her faith; otherwise, her purification must have lasted many days."

CHAP. X. — MATTIDIA VALUES BAPTISM ARIGHT.

And I said: "Tell us what it was that she said which made her faith manifest." And Peter said: "Her request that her hostess and benefactress should be baptized along with her. For she would not have besought this to be granted to her whom she loves, had she not herself first felt that baptism was a great gift. And for this reason I condemn many that, after being baptized, and asserting that they have faith, they yet do nothing worthy of faith; nor do they urge those whom they love — I mean their wives, or sons, or friends — to be baptized.² For if they had believed that God grants eternal life with good works on the acceptance of baptism,³ they without delay would urge those whom they loved

to be baptized. But some one of you will say, 'They do love them, and care for them.' That is nonsense. For do they not, most assuredly, when they see them sick, or led away along the road that ends in death, or enduring any other trial, lament over them and pity them? So, if they believed that eternal fire awaits those who worship not God, they would not cease admonishing them, or being in deep distress for them as unbelievers, if they saw them disobedient, being fully assured that punishment awaits them. But now I shall send for the hostess, and question her as to whether she deliberately accepts the law which is proclaimed through us;⁴ and so, according to her state of mind, shall we do what ought to be done.

CHAP. XI. — MATTIDIA HAS UNINTENTIONALLY FASTED ONE DAY.

"But since your mother has real confidence in the efficacy of baptism,⁵ let her fast at least one day before her baptism." But she swore: "During the two past days, while I related to the woman⁶ all the events connected with the recognition, I could not, in consequence of my excessive joy, partake of food: only yesterday I took a little water." Peter's wife bore testimony to her statement with an oath, saying: "In truth she did not taste anything." And Aquila, who must rather be called Faustinianus⁷ in future, said: "There is nothing, therefore, to prevent her being baptized." And Peter, smiling, replied: "But that is not a baptismal fast which has not taken place on account of the baptism itself." And Faustinus answered: "Perhaps God, not wishing to separate our mother a single day after our recognition from our table, has arranged beforehand the fast. For as she was chaste in the times of her ignorance, doing what the true religion inculcated,⁸ so even now perhaps God has arranged that she should fast one day before for the sake of the true baptism, that, from the first day of her recognising us, she might take her meals along with us."

CHAP. XII. — THE DIFFICULTY SOLVED.

And Peter said: "Let not wickedness have dominion over us, finding a pretext in Providence and your affection for your mother; but rather abide this day in your fast, and I shall join you in it, and to-morrow she will be baptized. And, besides, this hour of the day is not suitable for baptism." Then we all agreed that it should be so.

---

¹ Lit., "that we may be able to partake of common salt and table."
² Lit., "to this."
³ ἐπὶ τῷ βαπτίσματι; lit., "on the condition of baptism."

⁴ Lit., "the law which is by means of us." But the *Epitomes*, and a various reading in Cotelerius, give "our law."
⁵ Lit., "since your mother is faithfully disposed in regard to baptism."
⁶ The second *Epitome* makes her the wife of Peter: a various reading mentions also her hostess.
⁷ Dressel strangely prefers the reading "Faustinus."
⁸ Lit., "doing what was becoming to the truth."

CHAP. XIII. — PETER ON CHASTITY.

That same evening we all enjoyed the benefit of Peter's instruction. Taking occasion by what had happened to our mother, he showed us how the results of chastity are good, while those of adultery are disastrous, and naturally bring destruction on the whole race, if not speedily, at all events slowly.[1] "And to such an extent," he says, "do deeds of chastity please God, that in this life He bestows some small favour on account of it, even on those who are in error; for salvation in the other world is granted only to those who have been baptized on account of their trust[2] in Him, and who act chastely and righteously. This ye yourselves have seen in the case of your mother, that the results of chastity are in the end good. For perhaps she would have been cut off if she had committed adultery; but God took pity on her for having behaved chastely, rescued her from the death that threatened her, and restored to her her lost children.

CHAP. XIV. — PETER'S SPEECH CONTINUED.

"But some one will say, 'How many have perished on account of chastity!' Yes; but it was because they did not perceive the danger. For the woman who perceives that she is in love with any one, or is beloved by any one, should immediately shun all association with him as she would shun a blazing fire or a mad dog. And this is exactly what your mother did, for she really loved chastity as a blessing: wherefore she was preserved, and, along with you, obtained the full knowledge of the everlasting kingdom. The woman who wishes to be chaste, ought to know that she is envied by wickedness, and that because of love many lie in wait for her. If, then, she remain holy through a stedfast persistence in chastity, she will gain the victory over all temptations, and be saved; whereas, even if she were to do all that is right, and yet should once commit the sin of adultery, she must be punished, as said the prophet.

CHAP. XV. — PETER'S SPEECH CONTINUED.

"The chaste wife, doing the will of God, is a good reminiscence of His first creation; for God, being one, created one woman for one man. She is also still more chaste if she does not forget her own creation, and has future punishment before her eyes, and is not ignorant of the loss of eternal blessings. The chaste woman takes pleasure in those who wish to be saved, and is a pious example to the pious, for she is the model of a good life. She who wishes to be chaste,

cuts off all occasions for slander; but if she be slandered as by an enemy, though affording him no pretext, she is blessed and avenged by God. The chaste woman longs for God, loves God, pleases God, glorifies God; and to men she affords no occasion for slander. The chaste woman perfumes the Church with her good reputation, and glorifies it by her piety. She is, moreover, the praise of her teachers, and a helper to them in their chastity.[3]

CHAP. XVI. — PETER'S SPEECH CONTINUED.

"The chaste woman is adorned with the Son of God as with a bridegroom. She is clothed with holy light. Her beauty lies in a well-regulated soul; and she is fragrant with ointment, even with a good reputation. She is arrayed in beautiful vesture, even in modesty. She wears about her precious pearls, even chaste words. And she is radiant, for[4] her mind has been brilliantly lighted up. Into a beautiful mirror does she look, for she looks into God. Beautiful cosmetics[5] does she use, namely, the fear of God, with which she admonishes her soul. Beautiful is the woman, not because she has chains of gold on her,[6] but because she has been set free from transient lusts. The chaste woman is greatly desired by the great King;[7] she has been wooed, watched, and loved by Him. The chaste woman does not furnish occasions for being desired, except by her own husband. The chaste woman is grieved when she is desired by another. The chaste woman loves her husband from the heart, embraces, soothes, and pleases him, acts the slave to him, and is obedient to him in all things, except when she would be disobedient to God. For she who obeys God is without the aid of watchmen chaste in soul and pure in body.

CHAP. XVII. — PETER'S SPEECH CONTINUED.

"Foolish, therefore, is every husband who separates his wife from the fear of God; for she who does not fear God is not afraid of her husband. If she fear not God, who sees what is invisible, how will she be chaste in her unseen choice?[8] And how will she be chaste, who does not come to the assembly to hear chaste-making words? And how could she obtain admonition? And how will she be chaste without watchmen,

---

[1] [This detailed discourse is peculiar to the *Homilies*. In *Recognitions*, vii. 37, 38, there is, however, a briefer statement on the same topic. — R.]

[2] Lit., "hope."

[3] The Greek is αὐτοῖς σωφρονοῦσι. The Latin translator and Lehmann (*Die Clementinischen Schriften*, Gotha, 1869) render, "to those who are chaste, i.e., love or practise chastity," as if the reading were τοῖς σωφρονοῦσι.

[4] Lit., "when."

[5] κόσμῳ — properly ornaments; but here a peculiar meaning is evidently required.

[6] Lit., "as being chained with gold."

[7] Ps. xlv. 11.

[8] "In her unseen choice" means, in what course of conduct she really prefers in her heart. This reading occurs in one MS.; in the other MS. it is corrupt. Schwegler amended it into, How shall she be chaste towards him who does not see *what is invisible?*" and the emendation is adopted by Dressel.

if she be not informed in regard to the coming judgment of God, and if she be not fully assured that eternal punishment is the penalty for the slight pleasure? Wherefore, on the other hand, compel her even against her will always to come to hear the chaste-making word, yea, coax her to do so.

CHAP. XVIII. — PETER'S SPEECH CONTINUED.

"Much better is it if you will take her by the hand and come, in order that you yourself may become chaste; for you will desire to become chaste, that you may experience the full fruition of a holy marriage, and you will not scruple, if you desire it, to become a father,[1] to love your own children, and to be loved by your own children. He who wishes to have a chaste wife is also himself chaste, gives her what is due to a wife, takes his meals with her, keeps company with her, goes with her to the word that makes chaste, does not grieve her, does not rashly quarrel with her, does not make himself hateful to her, furnishes her with all the good things he can, and when he has them not, he makes up the deficiency by caresses. The chaste wife does not expect to be caressed, recognises her husband as her lord, bears his poverty when he is poor, is hungry with him when he is hungry, travels with him when he travels, consoles him when he is grieved, and if she have a large[2] dowry, is subject to him as if she had nothing at all. But if the husband have a poor wife, let him reckon her chastity a great dowry. The chaste wife is temperate in her eating and drinking, in order that the weariness of the body, thus pampered, may not drag the soul down to unlawful desires. Moreover, she never assuredly remains alone with young men, and she suspects[3] the old; she turns away from disorderly laughter, gives herself up to God alone; she is not led astray; she delights in listening to holy words, but turns away from those which are not spoken to produce chastity.

CHAP. XIX. — PETER'S SPEECH ENDED.

"God is my witness: one adultery is as bad as many murders; and what is terrible in it is this, that the fearfulness and impiety of its murders are not seen. For, when blood is shed, the dead body remains lying, and all are struck by the terrible nature of the occurrence. But the murders of the soul caused by adultery, though they are more frightful, yet, since they are not seen by men, do not make the daring a whit less eager in their impulse. Know, O man, whose breath it is that thou hast to keep thee in life,

and thou shalt not wish that it be polluted. By adultery alone is the breath of God polluted. And therefore it drags him who has polluted it into the fire; for it hastens to deliver up its insulter to everlasting punishment."

CHAP. XX. — PETER ADDRESSES MATTIDIA.

While Peter was saying this, he saw the good and chaste Mattidia weeping for joy; but thinking that she was grieved at having suffered so much in past times, he said :[4] "Take courage, O woman; for while many have suffered many evils on account of adultery, you have suffered on account of chastity, and therefore you did not die. But if you had died, your soul would have been saved. You left your native city of Rome on account of chastity, but through it you found the truth, the diadem of the eternal kingdom. You underwent danger in the deep, but you did not die; and even if you had died, the deep itself would have proved to you, dying on account of chastity, a baptism for the salvation of your soul. You were deprived of your children for a little; but these, the true offspring of your husband, have been found in better circumstances. When starving, you begged for food, but you did not defile your body by fornication. You exposed your body to torture, but you saved your soul; you fled from the adulterer, that you might not defile the couch of your husband: but, on account of your chastity, God, who knows your flight, will fill up the place of your husband. Grieved and left desolate, you were for a short time deprived of husband and children, but all these you must have been deprived of, some time or other, by death, the preordained lot of man. But better is it that you were willingly deprived of them on account of chastity, than that you should have perished unwillingly after a time, simply on account of sins.

CHAP. XXI. — THE SAME SUBJECT CONTINUED.

"Much better is it, then, that your first circumstances should be distressing. For when this is the case, they do not so deeply grieve you, because you hope that they will pass away, and they yield joy through the expectation of better circumstances. But, above all, I wish you to know how much chastity is pleasing to God. The chaste woman is God's choice, God's good pleasure, God's glory, God's child. So great a blessing is chastity,[5] that if there had not been a law that not even a righteous person should enter into the kingdom of God unbap-

---

[1] There seems to be some corruption in this clause. Literally it is, "and you will not scruple, if you love, I mean, to become a father."
[2] Lit., "larger" *than usual.*
[3] ὑποπτεύει. The Latin translator and Lehmann render "respects" or "reveres."

[4] [Something similar to chaps. 20, 21, occurs in *Recognitions*, vii. 38, addressed to the sons of Mattidia after her baptism. But this is much fuller. — R.]
[5] We have adopted an emendation of Wieseler's. The emendation is questionable; but the sense is the best that can be got out of the words.

tized, perhaps even the erring Gentiles might have been saved solely on account of chastity. Wherefore I am exceedingly sorry for those erring ones who are chaste because they shrink from baptism — thus choosing to be chaste without good hope. Wherefore they are not saved; for the decree of God is clearly set down, that an unbaptized person cannot enter into His kingdom." When he said this, and much more, we turned to sleep.

HOMILY XIV.

CHAP. I. — MATTIDIA IS BAPTIZED IN THE SEA.

MUCH earlier than usual Peter awoke, and came to us, and awaking us, said: "Let Faustinus and Faustinianus, along with Clement and the household, accompany me, that we may go to some sheltered spot by the sea, and there be able to baptize her without attracting observation." Accordingly, when we had come to the sea-shore, he baptized her betweeen some rocks, which supplied a place at once free from wind and dust.[1] But we brothers, along with our brother and some others, retired because of the women and bathed, and coming again to the women, we took them along with us, and thus we went to a secret place and prayed. Then Peter, on account of the multitude, sent the women on before, ordering them to go to their lodging by another way, and he permitted us alone of the men to accompany our mother and the rest of the women.[2] We went then to our lodging, and while waiting for Peter's arrival, we conversed with each other. Peter came several hours after, and breaking the bread for the Eucharist,[3] and putting salt upon it, he gave it first to our mother, and, after her, to us her sons. And thus we took food along with her and blessed God.

CHAP. II. — THE REASON OF PETER'S LATENESS.

Then,[4] at length, Peter seeing that the multitude had entered, sat down, and bidding us sit down beside him, he related first of all why he had sent us on before him after the baptism, and why he himself had been late in returning.[5] He said that the following was the reason: "At the time that you came up,"[6] he says, "an old man, a workman, entered along with you, concealing himself out of curiosity. He had watched us before, as he himself afterwards confessed, in order to see what we were doing when we entered into the sheltered place, and then he came out secretly and followed us. And coming up to me at a convenient place, and addressing me, he said, 'For a long time I have been following you and wishing to talk with you, but I was afraid that you might be angry with me, as if I were instigated by curiosity; but now I shall tell you, if you please, what I think is the truth.' And I replied, 'Tell us what you think is good, and we shall approve your conduct, even should what you say not be really good, since with a good purpose you have been anxious to state what you deem to be good.'

CHAP. III. — THE OLD MAN DOES NOT BELIEVE IN GOD OR PROVIDENCE.

"The old man began to speak as follows: 'When I saw you after you had bathed in the sea retire into the secret place, I went up and secretly watched what might be your object in entering into a secret place, and when I saw you pray, I retired;[7] but taking pity on you, I waited that I might speak with you when you came out, and prevail on you not to be led astray. For there is neither God nor providence; but all things are subject to Genesis.[8] Of this I am fully assured in consequence of what I have myself endured, having for a long time made a careful study of the science.[9] Do not therefore be deceived, my child. For whether you pray or not, you must endure what is assigned to you by Genesis. For if prayers could have

---

[1] Lit., "tranquil and clean." [The baptism is narrated in *Recognitions*, vii. 38. — R.]

[2] We have adopted an emendation of Schwegler's. The MSS. read either "these" or "the same" for "the rest of."

[3] The words "for the Eucharist" might be translated "after thanksgiving." But it is much the same which, for the Eucharist is plainly meant. The *Epitomes* have it: "taking the bread, giving thanks, blessing, and consecrating it, he gave it;" but no mention is made of salt. [The details here are more specific than in *Recognitions*, vii. 38. The mention of "salt" is peculiar. Compare "the salt" named as one of the "seven witnesses" in the baptismal form of the Elkesaites, Hippolytus, *Ante-Nicene Fathers*, v. pp. 132, 133. — R.]

[4] [For the extensive variations in the plan of the two narratives from this point to the end, see footnote on *Recognitions*, viii. 1. In the *Recognitions* the family of Clement are brought into greater prominence as disputants; in the *Homilies* Simon Magus, and Peter's discourses against him, are the main features; both, however, conserve the dramatic element of the re-united family, though the details are given differently in the two narratives. — R.]

[5] [The old man is introduced at once in *Recognitions*, viii. 1, and the subsequent discussion takes place in the presence of Clement and many others. — R.]

[6] We have adopted an emendation of Wieseler's. The text has, "at the time that you went away."

[7] Wieseler thinks that the reading should be: "I did not retire."

[8] Genesis is destiny determined by the stars which rule at each man's birth. [Comp. iv. 12. In *Recognitions*, viii. 2, the long discussion with the old man begins in the same way. — R.]

[9] μάθημα, mathematical science specially, which was closely connected with astrology. [Comp. *Recognitions*, x. 11-12. — R.]

done anything or any good, I myself should now be in better circumstances. And now, unless my needy garments mislead you, you will not refuse to believe what I say. I was once in affluent circumstances; I sacrificed much to the gods, I gave liberally to the needy; and yet, though I prayed and acted piously, I was not able to escape my destiny.' And I said: 'What are the calamities you have endured?' And he answered: 'I need not tell you now; perhaps at the end you shall learn who I am, and who are my parents, and into what straitened circumstances I have fallen. But at present I wish you to become fully assured that everything is subject to Genesis.'

CHAP. IV. — PETER'S ARGUMENTS AGAINST GENESIS.

"And I said: 'If all things are subject to Genesis, and you are fully convinced that this is the case, your thoughts and advice are contrary to your own opinion.[1] For if it is impossible even to think in opposition to Genesis, why do you toil in vain, advising me to do what cannot be done? Yea, moreover, even if Genesis subsists, do not make haste to prevail on me not to worship Him who is also Lord of the stars, by whose wish that a thing should not take place, that thing becomes an impossibility. For always that which is subject must obey that which rules. As far, however, as the worship of the common gods is concerned, that is superfluous, if Genesis has sway. For neither does anything happen contrary to what seems good to fate, nor are they themselves able to do anything, since they are subject to their own universal Genesis. If Genesis exists, there is this objection to it, that that which is not first has the rule; or, *in other words*, the uncreated cannot be subject, for the uncreated, as being uncreated, has nothing that is older than itself.'[2]

CHAP. V. — PRACTICAL REFUTATION OF GENESIS.

"While we were thus talking, a great multitude gathered round us. And then I looked to the multitude, and said: 'I and my tribe have had handed down to us from our ancestors the worship of God, and we have a commandment to give no heed to Genesis, I mean to the science of astrology;[3] and therefore I gave no attention to it. For this reason I have no skill in astrology, but I shall state that in which I have skill. Since I am unable to refute Genesis by an appeal to the science which relates to Genesis, I wish to prove in another way that the affairs *of this world* are managed by a providence, and that each one will receive reward or punishment according to his actions. Whether he shall do so now or hereafter, is a matter of no consequence to me; all I affirm is, that each one without doubt will reap the fruit of his deeds. The proof that there is no Genesis is this. If any one of you present has been deprived of eyes, or has his hand maimed, or his foot lame, or some other part of the body wrong, and if it is utterly incurable, and entirely beyond the range of the medical profession, — a case, indeed, which not even the astrologers profess to cure, for no such cure has taken place within the lapse of a vast period, — yet I praying to God will cure it,[4] although[5] it could never have been set right by Genesis.[6] Since this is so, do not they sin who blaspheme the God that fashioned all things?' And the old man answered: 'Is it then blasphemy to say that all things are subject to Genesis?' And I replied: 'Most certainly it is. For if all the sins of men, and all their acts of impiety and licentiousness, owe their origin to the stars, and if the stars have been appointed by God to do this work, so as to be the efficient causes of all evils, then the sins of all are traced up to Him who placed Genesis[7] in the stars.'

CHAP. VI. — THE OLD MAN OPPOSES HIS PERSONAL EXPERIENCE TO THE ARGUMENT OF PETER.

"And the old man answered:[8] 'You have spoken truly,[9] and yet, notwithstanding all your incomparable demonstration, I am prevented from yielding assent by my own personal knowledge. For I was an astrologer, and dwelt first at Rome; and then forming a friendship with one who was of the family of Cæsar, I ascertained accurately the genesis of himself and his wife. And tracing their history, I find all the deeds actually accomplished in exact accordance with their genesis, and therefore I cannot yield to your argument. For the arrangement[10] of her genesis was that which makes women commit adultery, fall in love with their own slaves, and perish abroad in the water. And this actually took place; for she fell in love with her own slave, and not being able to bear the reproach, she fled with him, hurried to a foreign land, shared his bed, and perished in the sea.'

---

[1] Lit., "thinking you counsel what is contrary to yourself."
[2] The argument here is obscure. Probably what is intended is as follows: Genesis means origination, coming into being. Origination cannot be the ruling power, for there must be something unoriginated which has given rise to the origination. The origination, therefore, as not being first, cannot have sway, and it must itself be subject to that which is unoriginated.
[3] [On the error of astrology compare the full discussion in *Recognitions*, ix. 12, x. 7-12. — R.]
[4] We have adopted the reading given in the two *Epitomes*.
[5] Lit., "when."
[6] [This method of proof, by appeal to the supernatural power of the Apostle, is peculiar to the *Homilies*. In the *Recognitions*, ix. 30, an argument is made by Clement, who appeals to the power of the true Prophet. — R.]
[7] That is, the power of origination.
[8] [With chaps. 6-9 there is a general correspondence in *Recognitions*, ix. 32-37. The arrangement is quite different. The old man's representation, that the story he tells is that of a friend, is peculiar to the *Homilies*. — R.]
[9] One MS. adds "greatly," and an *Epitome* "great things."
[10] That is, the position of the stars at her birth.

CHAP. VII.—THE OLD MAN TELLS HIS STORY.

"And I answered: 'How then do you know that she who fled and took up her residence in a foreign land married the slave, and marrying him died?' And the old man said: 'I am quite sure that this is true, not indeed that she married him, for I did not know even that she fell in love with him; but after her departure, a brother of her husband's told me the whole story of her passion, and how he acted as an honourable man, and did not, as being his brother, wish to pollute his couch, and how she the wretched woman (for she is not blameable, inasmuch as she was compelled to do and suffer all this in consequence of Genesis) longed for him, and yet stood in awe of him and his reproaches, and how she devised a dream, whether true or false I cannot tell; for he stated that she said, "Some one in a vision stood by me, and ordered me to leave the city of the Romans immediately with my children." But her husband being anxious that she should be saved with his sons, sent them immediately to Athens for their education, accompanied by their mother and slaves, while he kept the third and youngest son with himself, for he who gave the warning in the dream permitted this son to remain with his father. And when a long time had elapsed, during which[1] he received no letters from her, he himself sent frequently to Athens, and at length took me, as the truest of all his friends, and went in search of her. And much did I exert myself along with him in the course of our travels with all eagerness; for I remembered that, in the old times of his prosperity, he had given me a share of all he had, and loved me above all his friends. At length we set sail from Rome itself, and so we arrived in these parts of Syria, and we landed at Seleucia, and not many days after we had landed he died of a broken heart. But I came here, and have procured my livelihood from that day till this by the work of my hands.'

CHAP. VIII.—THE OLD MAN GIVES INFORMATION IN REGARD TO FAUSTUS THE FATHER OF CLEMENT.

"When the old man had thus spoken, I knew from what he said that the old man who he stated had died, was no other than your father. I did not wish, however, to communicate your circumstances to him until I should confer with you. But I ascertained where his lodging was, and I pointed out mine to him; and to make sure *that my conjecture was right*, I put this one question to him: 'What was the name of the old man?' And he said, 'Faustus.' 'And what

were the names of his twin sons?' And he answered, 'Faustinus and Faustinianus.' 'What was the name of the third son?' He said, 'Clement.' 'What was their mother's name?' He said, 'Mattidia.' Accordingly, from compassion, I shed tears along with him, and, dismissing the multitudes, I came to you, in order that I might take counsel with you after we had partaken of food[2] together. But I did not wish to disclose the matter to you before we had partaken of food, lest perchance you should be overcome by sorrow, and continue sad on the day of baptism, when even angels rejoice." At these statements of Peter we all fell a weeping along with our mother. But he beholding us in tears, said: "Now let each one of you, through fear of God, bear bravely what has been said; for certainly it was not to-day that your father died, but long ago, as you conjecturing said."

CHAP. IX.—FAUSTUS HIMSELF APPEARS.

When Peter said this, our mother could no longer endure it, but cried out, "Alas! my husband! loving us, you died by your own decision,[3] while we are still alive, see the light, and have just partaken of food." This one scream had not yet ceased, when, lo! the old man came in, and at the same time wishing to inquire into the cause of the cry, he looked on the woman and said, "What does this mean? Whom do I see?" And going up to her, and looking at her, and being looked at more carefully, he embraced her. But they were like to die through the sudden joy, and wishing to speak to each other, they could not get the power in consequence of their unsatisfied joy, for they were seized with speechlessness. But not long after, our mother said to him: "I now have you, Faustus, in every way the dearest being to me. How then are you alive, when we heard a short time ago that you were dead? But these are our sons, Faustinus, Faustinianus, and Clement." And when she said this, we all three fell on him, and kissed him, and in rather an indistinct way we recalled his form to our memory.[4]

CHAP. X.—FAUSTUS EXPLAINS HIS NARRATIVE TO PETER.

Peter seeing this, said: "Are you Faustus, the husband of this woman, and the father of her children?" And he said: "I am." And Peter said: "How, then, did you relate to me your own history as if it were another's; telling

---

[1] We have inserted ὡς from the *Epitomes*.

[2] Lit., " of salt."
[3] Lit., "you died by a judgment;" but it is thought that κρίσει is corrupt.
[4] [In the *Recognitions* the old man is not recognised until long discussions have been held; see book ix. 35, 37. Hints of the relationship are, however, given in advance. — R.]

me of your toils, and sorrow, and burial?" And our father answered: "Being of the family of Cæsar, and not wishing to be discovered, I devised the narrative in another's name, in order that it might not be perceived who I was. For I knew that, if I were recognised, the governors in the place would learn this, and recall me to gratify Cæsar, and would bestow upon me that former prosperity to which I had formerly bidden adieu with all the resolution I could summon. For I could not give myself up to a luxurious life when I had pronounced the strongest condemnation on myself, because I believed that I had been the cause of death to those who were loved by me." [1]

CHAP. XI. — DISCUSSION ON GENESIS.

And Peter said: "You did this according to your resolution. But in regard to Genesis, were you merely playing a part when you affirmed it, or were you in earnest in asserting that it existed?" Our father said: "I will not speak falsely to you. I was in earnest when I maintained that Genesis existed. For I am not uninitiated in the science; on the contrary, I associated with one who is the best of the astrologers, an Egyptian of the name of Annubion, who became my friend in the commencement of my travels, and disclosed to me the death of my wife and children." [2] And Peter said: "Are you not now convinced by facts, that the doctrine of Genesis has no firm foundation?" And my father answered: "I must lay before you all the ideas that occur to my mind, that listening to them I may understand your refutation of them.[3] I know, indeed, that astrologers both make many mistakes, and frequently speak the

[1] Lit., "Having judged the greatest things in regard to those who were loved by me, as having died." The text is doubtful; for the first *Epitome* has something quite different.
[2] [Comp. Homily IV. 6. Annubion and Appion are not introduced in the *Recognitions* until book x. 52. — R.]
[3] Here MSS. and *Epitomes* differ in their readings. The text adopted seems a combination of two ideas: "that you may listen and refute them, and that I may thus learn the truth."

truth. I suspect, therefore, that they speak the truth so far as they are accurately acquainted with the science, and that their mistakes are the result of ignorance; so that I conjecture that the science has a firm foundation, but that the astrologers themselves speak what is false solely on account of ignorance, because they cannot know all things with absolute [4] accuracy." And Peter answered: "Consider [5] whether their speaking of the truth is not accidental, and whether they do not make their declarations without knowing the matters accurately. For it must by all means happen that, when many prophecies are uttered, some of them should come true." And the old man said: "How, then, is it possible to be fully convinced of this, whether the science of Genesis has a sure foundation or not?"

CHAP. XII. — CLEMENT UNDERTAKES THE DISCUSSION.

When both were silent, I said: "Since I know accurately the science, but our lord and our father are not in this condition, I should like if Annubion himself were here, to have a discussion with him in the presence of my father. For thus would the matter be able to become public, when one practically acquainted with the subject has held the discussion with one equally informed." [6] And our father answered: "Where, then, is it possible to fall in with Annubion?" And Peter said: "In Antioch, for I learn that Simon Magus is there, whose inseparable companion Annubion is. When, then, we go there, if we come upon them, the discussion can take place." And so, when we had discussed many subjects, and rejoiced at the recognition and given thanks to God, evening came down upon us, and we turned to sleep.

[4] We have adopted the reading of Codex O, πάντως. The other MS. reads, "that all cannot know all things accurately."
[5] The MSS. read ἀπεχε, "hold back." The reading of the text is in an *Epitome*.
[6] Lit., "when artist has had discussion with fellow-artist."

HOMILY XV.

CHAP. I. — PETER WISHES TO CONVERT FAUSTUS.

AT break of day our father, with our mother and his three sons, entered the place where Peter was, and accosting him, sat down. Then we also did the same at his request; and Peter looking at our father, said: [1] "I am anxious that

[1] [In *Recognitions*, x. 1, after the father becomes known, the Apostle is represented as proposing delay in the attempt to convert him. — R.]

you should become of the same mind as your wife and children, in order that here you may live along with them, and in the other world,[2] after the separation of the soul from the body, you will continue to be with them free from sorrow. For does it not grieve you exceedingly that you should not associate with each other?" And my

[2] Lit., "there."

father said : " Most assuredly." And Peter said : " If, then, separation from each other here gives you pain, and if without doubt the penalty awaits you that after death you should not be with each other, how much greater will your grief be that you, a wise man, should be separated from your own family on account of your opinions? They too, must[1] feel the more distressed from the consciousness that eternal punishment awaits you because you entertain different opinions from theirs, and deny the established truth."[2]

CHAP. II. — REASON FOR LISTENING TO PETER'S ARGUMENTS.

Our father said : " But it is not the case, my very dear friend, that souls are punished in Hades, for the soul is dissolved into air as soon as it leaves the body." And Peter said : " Until we convince you in regard to this point, answer me, does it not appear to you that you are not grieved as having no faith in a *future* punishment, but they who have full faith in it must be vexed in regard to you?" And our father said : "You speak sense." And Peter said : "Why, then, will you not free them from the greatest grief they can have in regard to you by agreeing to their religion, not, I mean, through dread, but through kindly feeling, listening and judging about what is said by me, whether it be so or not? and if the truth is as we state it, then here you will enjoy life with those who are dearest to you, and in the other world you will have rest with them ; but if, in examining the arguments, you show that what is stated by us is a fictitious story,[3] you will thus be doing good service, for you will have your friends on your side, and you will put an end to their leaning upon false hopes, and you will free them from false fears."

CHAP. III. — OBSTACLES TO FAITH.

And our father said : "There is evidently much reason in what you say." And Peter said : "What is it, then, that prevents you from coming to our faith? Tell me, that we may begin our discussion with it. For many are the hindrances. The faithful are hindered by occupation with merchandise, or public business, or the cultivation of the soil, or cares, and such like ; the unbelievers, of whom you also are one, are hindered by ideas such as that the gods, which do not exist, really exist, or that all things are subject to Genesis, or chance,[4] or that souls are mortal, or

that our doctrines are false because there is no providence.

CHAP. IV. — PROVIDENCE SEEN IN THE EVENTS OF THE LIFE OF FAUSTUS AND HIS FAMILY.

" But I maintain, from what has happened to you,[5] that all things are managed by the providence of God, and that your separation from your family for so many years was providential ;[6] for since, if they had been with you, they perhaps would not have listened to the doctrines of the true religion, it was arranged that your children should travel with their mother, should be shipwrecked, should be supposed to have perished, and should be sold ;[7] moreover, that they should be educated in the learning of the Greeks, especially in the atheistic doctrines, in order that, as being acquainted with them, they might be the better able to refute them ; and in addition to this, that they should become attached to the true religion, and be enabled to be united with me, so as to help me in my preaching ; furthermore, that their brother Clement should meet in the same place, and that thus his mother should be recognised, and through her cure[8] should be fully convinced of the right worship of God ;[9] that after no long interval the twins should recognise and be recognised, and the other day should fall in with you, and that you should receive back your own. I do not think, then, that such a speedy filling in of circumstances, coming as it were from all quarters, so as to accomplish one design, could have happened without the direction of Providence."

CHAP. V. — DIFFERENCE BETWEEN THE TRUE RELIGION AND PHILOSOPHY.

And our father began to say : " Do not suppose, my dearest Peter, that I am not thinking of the doctrines preached by you. I was thinking of them. But during the past night, when Clement urged me earnestly to give in my adhesion to the truth preached by you, I at last answered, ' Why should I ? for what new commandment can any one give more than what the ancients urged us to obey?' And he, with a gentle smile, said, ' There is a great difference, father, between the doctrines of the true religion and those of philosophy ;[10] for the true religion receives its proof from prophecy, while philoso-

---

[1] We have inserted a δεῖ, probably omitted on account of the previous δέ.

[2] The words are peculiar. Lit., " eternal punishment awaits you thinking other things, through denial of the fixed dogma" (ῥητοῦ δόγματος). The Latin translator gives: " ob veri dogmatis negationem."

[3] μῦθόν τινα ψευδῆ.

[4] Properly, self-action.

[5] [The recapitulation of Peter in *Recognitions*, ix. 26, is in explanation to the sons, and not for a doctrinal purpose. — R.]

[6] We have adopted a reading suggested by the second *Epitome.*

[7] The word ἀπρασίαι is corrupt. We have adopted the emendation πρᾶσις. The word is not given in the MS. O, nor in the *Epitomes.*

[8] ὑπὸ θεραπείας, which Cotelerius translates *recuperata sanitate.*

[9] Lit., " convinced of the Godhead." " Godhead" is omitted in the *Epitomes.*

[10] [Compare the fuller statement in *Recognitions*, viii. 61; also *Recognitions*, x. 48-51. — R.]

phy, furnishing us with beautiful sentences, seems to present its proofs from conjecture.' On saying this, he took an instance, and set before us the doctrine of philanthropy,[1] which you had explained to him,[2] which rather appeared to me to be very unjust, and I shall tell you how. He alleged that it was right to present to him who strikes you on the one cheek the other[3] also, and to give to him who takes away your cloak your tunic also, and to go two miles with him who compels you to go one, and such like."[4]

CHAP. VI. — THE LOVE OF MAN.

And Peter answered : "You have deemed unjust what is most just. If you are inclined, will you listen to me?" And my father said : "With all my heart." And Peter said : "What is your opinion? Suppose that there were two kings, enemies to each other, and having their countries cut off from each other; and suppose that some one of the subjects of one of them were to be caught in the country of the other, and to incur the penalty of death on this account : now if he were let off from the punishment by receiving a blow instead of death, is it not plain that he who let him off is a lover of man?" And our father said : "Most certainly." And Peter said : "Now suppose that this same person were to steal from some one something belonging to him or to another; and if when caught he were to pay double, instead of suffering the punishment that was due to him, namely, paying four times the amount, and being also put to death, as having been caught in the territories of the enemy; is it not your opinion that he who accepts double, and lets him off from the penalty of death, is a lover of man?" And our father said : "He certainly seems so." And Peter said : "Why then? Is it not the duty of him who is in the kingdom of another, and that, too, a hostile and wicked monarch, to be pleasing to all[5] for the sake of life, and when force is applied to him, to yield still more, to accost those who do not accost him, to reconcile enemies, not to quarrel with those who are angry, to give his own property freely to all who ask, and such like?" And our father said : "He should with reason endure all things rather, if he prefers life to them."

CHAP. VII. — THE EXPLANATION OF A PARABLE ; THE PRESENT AND THE FUTURE LIFE.

And Peter[6] said : "Are not those, then, who you said received injustice, themselves transgressors, inasmuch as they are in the kingdom of the other, and is it not by overreaching that they have obtained all they possess? while those who are thought to act unjustly are conferring a favour on each subject of the hostile kingdom, so far as they permit him to have property. For these possessions belong to those who have chosen the present.[7] And they are so far kind as to permit the others to live. This, then, is the parable ; now listen to the actual truth. The prophet of the truth who appeared *on earth* taught us that the Maker and God of all gave two kingdoms to two,[8] good and evil ; granting to the evil the sovereignty over the present world along with law, so that he, *it*, should have the right to punish those who act unjustly ; but to the good He gave the eternal[9] age to come. But He made each man free with the power to give himself up to whatsoever he prefers, either to the present evil or the future good. Those men who choose the present have power to be rich, to revel in luxury, to indulge in pleasures, and to do whatever they can. For they will possess none of the future goods. But those who have determined to accept the blessings of the future reign have no right to regard as their own the things that are here, since they belong to a foreign king, with the exception only of water and bread, and those things procured with sweat to maintain life (for it is not lawful for them to commit suicide),[10] and also one garment, for they are not permitted to go naked on account of the all-seeing[11] Heaven.

CHAP. VIII. — THE PRESENT AND THE FUTURE.

"If, then, you wish to have an accurate account of the matter, listen. Those of whom you said a little before that they receive injustice, rather act unjustly themselves ; for they who have chosen the future blessings, live along with the bad in the present world, having many enjoyments the same as the bad, — such as life itself, light, bread, water, clothing, and others of a like nature. But they who are thought by you to act unjustly, shall not live with the good

---

1 Or "love of man" in all its phases — kindliness, gentleness, humanity, etc.

2 Hom. XII. 25 ff.

3 Matt. v. 39-41; Luke vi. 29. The writer of the *Homilies* changes the word χιτῶνα, "tunic," of the New Testament into μαφόριον, which Suicer describes "a covering for the head, neck, and shoulders, used by women." Wieseler is in doubt whether the writer of the *Homilies* uses μαφόριον as equivalent to χιτῶνα, or whether he intentionally changed the word, for the person who lost both cloak and tunic would be naked altogether; and this, the writer may have imagined, Christ would not have commanded.

4 [The larger part of the discussion in chaps. 5-11 is peculiar to the *Homilies*. There is little matter in it found in the longer arguments of *Recognitions*. — R.]

5 Lit., "to flatter."

6 The following words would be more appropriately put in the mouth of the father, as is done in fact by the *Epitomes*. Peter's address would commence, "And the parable is." The *Epitomes* differ much from each other and the text, and there seems to be confusion in the text.

7 This sentence would be more appropriate in the explanation of the parable.

8 The Greek leaves it uncertain whether it is two persons or two things, — whether it is a good being and an evil being, or good and evil. Afterwards, a good being and an evil are distinctly introduced.

9 The word ἀίδιος, properly and strictly "eternal," is used.

10 Lit., "to die willingly."

11 We have adopted an obvious emendation, πάντα for παντός.

men in [1] the coming age." And our father replied to this: " Now when you have convinced me that those who act unjustly suffer injustice themselves, while those who suffer injustice have by far the advantage, the whole affair seems to me still more the most unjust of transactions; for those who seem to act unjustly grant many things to those who have chosen the future blessings, but those who seem to receive injustice do themselves commit injustice, because they do not give in the other world, to those who have given them blessings here, the same advantages which these gave to them." And Peter said: " This is not unjust at all, because each one has the power to choose the present or the future goods, whether they be small or great. He who chooses by his own individual judgment and wish, receives no injustice, — I mean, not even should his choice rest on what is small, since the great lay within his choice, as in fact did also the small." And our father said: " You are right; for it has been said by one of the wise men of the Greeks, ' The blame rests with those who chose — God is blameless.' [2]

CHAP. IX. — POSSESSIONS ARE TRANSGRESSIONS.

" Will you be so good as to explain this matter also? I remember Clement saying to me, that we suffer injuries and afflictions for the forgiveness of our sins." Peter said: " This is quite correct. For we, who have chosen the future things, in so far as we possess more goods than these, whether they be clothing, or food or drink, or any other thing, possess sins, because we ought not to have anything, as I explained to you a little ago. To all of us possessions are sins.[3] The deprivation of these, in whatever way it may take place, is the removal of sins." And our father said: " That seems reasonable, as you explained that these were the two boundary lines of the two kings, and[4] that it was in the power of each to choose whatever he wished of what was under their authority. But why are the afflictions sent, or[5] do we suffer them justly?" And Peter said: " Most justly; for since the boundary line of the saved is, as I said, that no one should possess anything, but since many have many possessions, or in other words sins, for this reason the exceeding love of God

sends afflictions on those who do not act in purity of heart, that on account of their having some measure of the love of God, they might, by temporary inflictions, be saved from eternal punishments."

CHAP. X. — POVERTY NOT NECESSARILY RIGHTEOUS.

And our father said: " How then is this? Do we not see many impious men poor? Then do these belong to the saved on this account?" And Peter said: " Not at all; for that poverty is not acceptable which longs for what it ought not. So that some are rich as far as their choice goes, though poor in actual wealth, and they are punished because they desire to have more. But one is not unquestionably righteous because he happens to be poor. For he can be a beggar as far as actual wealth is concerned, but he may desire and even do what above everything he ought not to do. Thus he may worship idols, or be a blasphemer or fornicator, or he may live indiscriminately, or perjure himself, or lie, or live the life of an unbeliever. But our teacher pronounced the faithful poor blessed; [6] and he did so, not because they had given anything, for they had nothing, but because they were not to be condemned, as having done no sin, simply because they gave no alms, because they had nothing to give." And our father said: " In good truth all seems to go right as far as the subject of discussion is concerned; wherefore I have resolved to listen to the whole of your argument in regular order."

CHAP. XI. — EXPOSITION OF THE TRUE RELIGION PROMISED.

And Peter said: " Since, then, you are eager henceforth to learn what relates to our religion, I ought to explain it in order, beginning with God Himself, and showing that we ought to call Him alone God, and that we neither ought to speak of the others as gods nor deem them such, and that he who acts contrary to this will be punished eternally, as having shown the greatest impiety to Him who is the Lord of all." And saying this, he laid his hands on those who were vexed by afflictions, and were diseased, and possessed by demons; and, praying, he healed them, and dismissed the multitudes. And then entering in this way, he partook of his usual food, and went to sleep.

---

[1] We have translated Schwegler's emendation. He inserted ἐν.
[2] Plato, *Rep.*, x. 617 E.
[3] One MS. inserts before the sentence: " For if in all of us possessions are wont to occasion sins in those who have them."
[4] We have adopted Wieseler's emendation of τὰ into καί.
[5] We have changed εἰ into ἤ.

[6] Matt. v. 3. The *Epitomes* run thus: " Our Lord Jesus Christ, the Son of the living God, said." And then they quote the words of our Gospel.

HOMILY XVI.

CHAP. I. — SIMON WISHES TO DISCUSS WITH PETER
THE UNITY OF GOD.

AT break of day Peter went out, and reaching the place where he was wont to discourse, he saw a great multitude assembled. At the very time when he was going to discourse, one of his deacons entered, and said: "Simon has come from Antioch,[1] starting as soon as it was evening, having learned that you promised to speak on the unity[2] of God; and he is ready, along with Athenodorus the Epicurean, to come to hear your speech, in order that he may publicly oppose all the arguments ever adduced by you for the unity of God." Just as the deacon said this, lo! Simon himself entered, accompanied by Athenodorus and some other friends. And before Peter spoke at all, he took the first word, and said: —

CHAP. II. — THE SAME SUBJECT CONTINUED.

"I heard that you promised yesterday to Faustus to prove this day, giving out your arguments in regular order, and beginning with Him who is Lord of the universe, that we ought to say that He alone is God, and that we ought neither to say nor to think that there are other gods, because he that acts contrary to this will be punished eternally. But, above all, I am truly amazed at your madness in hoping to convert a wise man, and one far advanced in years, to your state of mind. But you will not succeed in your designs; and all the more that I am present, and can thoroughly refute your false arguments. For perhaps, if I had not been present, the wise old man might have been led astray, because he has no critical acquaintance[3] with the books publicly believed in amongst the Jews.[4] At present I shall omit much, in order that I may the more speedily refute that which you have promised to prove. Wherefore begin to speak what you promised to say before us, who know the Scriptures. But if, fearing our refutation, you are unwilling to fulfil

your promise in our presence, this of itself will be sufficient proof that you are wrong, because you did venture to speak in the presence of those who know the Scriptures. And now, why should I wait till you tell me, when I have a most satisfactory witness of your promise in the old man who is present?" And, saying this, he looked to my father, and said: "Tell me, most excellent of all men, is not this the man who promised to prove to you to-day that God is one, and that we ought not to say or think that there is any other god, and that he who acts contrary to this will be punished eternally, as committing the most heinous sin? Do you, then, refuse to reply to me?"

CHAP. III. — THE MODE OF THE DISCUSSION.

And our father said: "Well might you have demanded testimony from me, Simon, if Peter had first denied *that he had made the promise*. But now I shall feel no shame in saying what I am bound to say. I think that you wish to enter on the discussion inflamed with anger. Now this is a state of mind in which it is improper for you to speak and for us to listen to you; for we are no longer being helped on to the truth, but we are watching the progress of a contest. And now, having learned from Hellenic culture how those who seek *the truth* ought to act, I shall remind you. Let each of you give an exposition of his own opinion,[5] and let the right of speech pass from the one to the other.[6] For if Peter alone should wish to expound his thought, but you should be silent as to yours, it is possible that some argument adduced by you might crush both your and his opinion; and both of you, though defeated by this argument, would not appear defeated, but only the one who expounded his opinion; while he who did not expound his, though equally defeated, would not appear defeated, but would even be thought to have conquered." And Simon answered: "I will do as you say; but I am afraid lest you do not turn out a truth-loving judge, as you have been already prejudiced by his arguments."

CHAP. IV. — THE PREJUDICES OF FAUSTUS RATHER
ON THE SIDE OF SIMON THAN ON THAT OF
PETER.

Our father answered: "Do not compel me to agree with you without any exercise of my judgment in order that I may seem to be a

---

[1] [Homilies XVI.–XIX., giving the details of a second discussion with Simon at Laodicea, are peculiar to this narrative. Much of the matter finds a parallel in the longer account of the previous discussion at Cæsarea in *Recognitions*, ii. iii. (comp. Homily III.), but all the circumstances are different. Uhlhorn formerly regarded this portion of the *Homilies* as the nucleus of the entire literature. He has modified his view. An analysis of the discussion cannot be attempted; but in the footnote to *Recognitions*, ii. 19, a general comparison is given of the three accounts of discussions with Simon Magus. — R.]

[2] The word properly signifies the "sole government or monarchy of God." It means that God alone is ruler.

[3] ἰδιώτης.

[4] τῶν παρὰ Ἰουδαίοις δημοσίᾳ πεπιστευμένων βιβλων. The literal translation, given in the text, means that the Jews as a community believed in these books as speaking the truth. Cotelerius translates: "the books which were publicly entrusted to the Jews." One MS. reads, πεπιστωμένων, which might mean, "deemed trustworthy among the Jews."

[5] δόγμα.

[6] One MS. and an *Epitome* have: "And you must address your arguments to another who acts as judge."

truth-loving judge ; but if you wish me to tell you the truth, my prepossessions are rather on the side of your opinions." And Simon said : "How is this the case, when you do not know what my opinions are?" And our father said : "It is easy to know this, and I will tell you how. You promised that you would convict Peter of error in maintaining the unity of God ; but if one undertakes to convict of error him who maintains the unity of God, it is perfectly plain that he, as being in the right,[1] does not hold the same opinion. For if he holds the same opinion as the man who is thoroughly in error, then he himself is in error ; but if he gives his proofs holding opposite opinions, then he is in the right. Not well[2] then do you assert that he who maintains the unity of God is wrong, unless you believe that there are many gods. Now I maintain that there are many gods. Holding, therefore, the same opinion as you before the discussion, I am prepossessed rather in your favour. For this reason you ought to have no anxiety in regard to me, but Peter ought, for I still hold opinions contrary to his. And so after your discussion I hope that, as a truth-loving judge, who has stripped himself of his prepossessions, I shall agree to that doctrine which gains the victory." When my father said this, a murmur of applause burst insensibly from the multitudes because my father had thus spoken.

CHAP. V. — PETER COMMENCES THE DISCUSSION.

Peter then said : " I am ready to do as the umpire of our discussion has said ; and straightway without any delay I shall set forth my opinion in regard to God. I then assert that there is one God who made the heavens and the earth, and all things that are in them. And it is not right to say or to think that there is any other." And Simon said : " But I maintain that the Scriptures believed in amongst the Jews say that there are many gods, and that God is not angry at this, because He has Himself spoken of many gods in His Scriptures.

CHAP. VI. — SIMON APPEALS TO THE OLD TESTAMENT TO PROVE THAT THERE ARE MANY GODS.

" For instance, in the very first words of the law, He evidently speaks of them as being like even unto Himself. For thus it is written, that, when the first man received a commandment from God to eat of every tree that was in the garden,[3] but not to eat of the tree of the knowledge of good and evil, the serpent having persuaded them by means of the woman, through the promise that they would become gods, made them look up ;[4] and then, when they had thus looked up, God said,[5] ' Behold, Adam is become as one of us.' When, then, the serpent said,[6] ' Ye shall be as gods,' he plainly speaks in the belief that gods exist ; all the more as God also added His testimony, saying, ' Behold, Adam is become as one of us.' The serpent, then, who said that there are many gods, did not speak falsely. Again, the scripture,[7] ' Thou shalt not revile the gods, nor curse the rulers of thy people,' points out many gods whom it does not wish even to be cursed. But it is also somewhere else written,[8] ' Did another god dare to enter and take him a nation from the midst of another nation, as did I the Lord God ? ' When He says, ' Did another God dare ? ' He speaks on the supposition that other gods exist. And elsewhere :[9] ' Let the gods that have not made the heavens and the earth perish ; ' as if those who had made them were not to perish. And in another place, when it says,[10] ' Take heed to thyself lest thou go and serve other gods whom thy fathers knew not,' it speaks as if other gods existed whom they were not to follow. And again :[11] ' The names of other gods shall not ascend upon thy lips.' Here it mentions many gods whose names it does not wish to be uttered. And again it is written,[12] ' Thy God is the Lord, He is God of gods.' And again :[13] ' Who is like unto Thee, O Lord, among the Gods ? ' And again :[14] ' God is Lord of gods.' And again :[15] ' God stood in the assembly of gods : He judgeth among the gods.' Wherefore I wonder how, when there are so many passages in writing which testify that there are many gods, you have asserted that we ought neither to say nor to think that there are many.[16] Finally, if you have anything to say against what has been spoken so distinctly, say it in the presence of all."

CHAP. VII. — PETER APPEALS TO THE OLD TESTAMENT TO PROVE THE UNITY OF GOD.

And Peter said : " I shall reply briefly to what you have said. The law, which frequently speaks of gods, itself says to the Jewish multitude,[17] ' Be-

---

[1] The words translated "error," ψεῦσμα, and "to be in the right," ἀληθεύειν, are, properly rendered, "falsehood," and "to speak the truth."
[2] The MSS. read : " not otherwise." The reading of the text is found in an *Epitome.*
[3] παραδείσῳ, " paradise." Gen. ii. 16, 17.
[4] ἀναβλέψαι. It signifies either to look up, or to recover one's sight. Possibly the second meaning is the one intended here, corresponding to the words of our version: " Then your eyes shall be opened."
[5] Gen. iii. 22.
[6] Gen. iii. 5.
[7] Ex. xxii. 28.
[8] Deut. iv. 34.
[9] Jer. x. 11.
[10] Deut. xiii. 6.
[11] Josh. xxiii. 7, LXX.
[12] Deut. x. 17.
[13] Ps. xxxv. 10, lxxxvi. 8.
[14] Ps. l. 1.
[15] Ps. lxxxii. 1.
[16] [Comp. *Recognitions,* ii. 39. — R.]
[17] Deut. x. 14.

hold, the heaven of heavens is the Lord's thy God, with all that therein is ; ' implying that, even if there are gods, they are under Him, that is, under the God of the Jews. And again : [1] ' The Lord thy God, He is God in heaven above, and upon the earth beneath, and there is none other except Him.' And somewhere else the Scripture says to the Jewish multitude,[2] ' The Lord your God is God of gods ; ' so that, even if there are gods, they are under the God of the Jews. And somewhere else the Scripture says in regard to Him,[2] ' God, the great and true, who regardeth not persons, nor taketh reward, He doth execute the judgment of the fatherless and widow.' The Scripture, in calling the God of the Jews great and true, and executing judgment, marked out the others as small, and not true. But also somewhere else the Scripture says,[3] ' As I live, saith the Lord, there is no other God but me. I am the first, I am after this ; except me there is no God.' And again : [4] ' Thou shalt fear the Lord thy God, and Him only shalt thou serve.' And again : [5] ' Hear, O Israel, the Lord your God is one Lord.' And many passages besides seal with an oath that God is one, and except Him there is no God. Whence I wonder how, when so many passages testify that there is one God, you say that there are many."

CHAP. VIII. — SIMON AND PETER CONTINUE THE DISCUSSION.

And Simon said : ' My original stipulation with you was that I should prove from the Scriptures that you were wrong in maintaining that we ought not to speak of many gods. Accordingly I adduced many written passages to show that the divine Scriptures themselves speak of many gods." And Peter said : " Those very Scriptures which speak of many gods, also exhorted us, saying, ' The names of other gods shall not ascend upon thy lips.'[6] Thus, Simon, I did not speak contrary to what was written." And Simon said : " Do you, Peter, listen to what I have to say. You seem to me to sin in speaking against them,[7] when the Scripture says,[8] ' Thou shalt not revile *the gods*, nor curse the rulers of thy people.'" And Peter said : " I am not sinning, Simon, in pointing out their destruction according to the Scriptures ; for thus it is written : [9] ' Let the gods who did not make the heavens and the earth perish.' And He said thus, not as though SOME had made the heavens and were not to perish,

as you interpreted the passage. For it is plainly declared that He who made them is one in the very first part of Scripture : [10] ' In the beginning God created the heaven and the earth.' And it did not say, ' the gods.' And somewhere else it says,[11] ' And the firmament showeth His handiwork.' And in another place it is written,[12] ' The heavens themselves shall perish, but Thou shalt remain for ever.' "

CHAP. IX. — SIMON TRIES TO SHOW THAT THE SCRIPTURES CONTRADICT THEMSELVES.

And Simon said : " I adduced clear passages from the Scriptures to prove that there are many gods ; and you, in reply, brought forward as many or more from the same Scriptures, showing that God is one, and He the God of the Jews. And when I said that we ought not to revile gods, you proceeded to show that He who created is one, because those who did not create will perish. And in reply to my assertion that we ought to maintain that there are gods, because the Scriptures also say so, you showed that we ought not to utter their names, because the same Scripture tells us not to utter the names of other gods. Since, then, these very Scriptures say at one time that there are many gods, and at another that there is only one ; and sometimes that they ought not to be reviled, and at other times that they ought ; what conclusion ought we to come to in consequence of this, but that the Scriptures themselves lead us astray ? "

CHAP. X. — PETER'S EXPLANATION OF THE APPARENT CONTRADICTIONS OF SCRIPTURE.

And Peter said : " They do not lead astray, but convict and bring to light the evil disposition against God which lurks like a serpent in each one. For the Scriptures lie before each one like many divers types. Each one, then, has his own disposition like wax, and examining the Scriptures and finding everything in them, he moulds his idea of God according to his wish, laying upon them, as I said, his own disposition, which is like wax.[13] Since, then, each one finds in the Scriptures whatever opinion he wishes to have in regard to God, for this reason he, *Simon*, moulds from them the forms[14] of many gods, while we moulded the form of Him who truly exists, coming to the knowledge of the true type from our own shape.[15] For assuredly the soul within us is clothed with His image for immortality. If I abandon the parent

---

1 Deut. iv. 39.
2 Deut. x. 17.
3 Isa. xlix. 18, xlv. 21, xliv. 6.
4 Deut. vi. 13.
5 Deut. vi. 4.
6 Josh. xxiii. 7, LXX.
7 Namely, the gods.
8 Ex. xxii. 28. The MSS. omit θεούς, though they insert it in the passage as quoted a little before this. One MS. reads " the ruler " with our version.
9 Jer. x. 11.

10 Gen. i. 1.
11 Ps. xix. 1.
12 Ps. cii. 26, 27.
13 [This statement of the subjective method of interpretation is in curious harmony with the prevalent theory of this work respecting the mixture of error and truth in the Scriptures. — R.]
14 ἰδέας.
15 μορφῆς.

of this soul, it also will abandon me to just judgment, making known the injustice by the very act of daring;[1] and as coming from one who is just, it will justly abandon me; and so, as far as the soul is concerned, I shall, after punishment, be destroyed, having abandoned the help that comes from it. But if there is another *god*, first let him put on another form, another shape, in order that by the new shape of the body I may recognise the new god. But if he should change the shape, does he thereby change the substance of the soul? But if he should change it also, then I am no longer myself, having become another both in shape and in substance. Let him, therefore, create others, if there is another. But there is not. For if there had been, he would have created. But since he has not created, then let him, as non-existent, leave him who is really existent.[2] For he is nobody,[3] except only in the opinion of Simon. I do not accept of any other god but Him alone who created me."

CHAP. XI. — GEN. I. 26 APPEALED TO BY SIMON.

And Simon said: "Since I see that you frequently speak of the God who created you, learn from me how you are impious even to him. For there are evidently two who created, as the Scripture says:[4] 'And God said, Let us make man in our image, after our likeness.' Now 'let us make,' implies two or more; certainly not one only."

CHAP. XII. — PETER'S EXPLANATION OF THE PASSAGE.

And Peter answered: "One is He who said to His Wisdom, 'Let us make a man.' But His Wisdom[5] was that with which He Himself always rejoiced[6] as with His own spirit. It is united as soul to God, but it is extended by Him, as hand, fashioning the universe. On this account, also, one man was made, and from him went forth also the female. And being a unity generically, it is yet a duality, for by expansion and contraction the unity is thought to be a duality. So that I act rightly in offering up all the honour to one God as to parents." And Simon said: "What then? Even if the Scriptures say that there are other gods, will you not accept the opinion?"

CHAP. XIII. — THE CONTRADICTIONS OF THE SCRIPTURES INTENDED TO TRY THOSE WHO READ THEM.

And Peter answered:[7] "If the Scriptures or prophets speak of gods, they do so to try those who hear. For thus it is written:[8] 'If there arise among you a prophet, giving signs and wonders, and that sign and wonder shall then come to pass, and he say to thee, Let us go after and worship other gods which thy fathers have not known, ye[9] shall not hearken to the words of that prophet; let thy hands be among the first to stone him. For he hath tried to turn thee from the Lord thy God. But if thou say in thy heart, How did he do that sign or wonder? thou shalt surely know that he who tried thee, tried thee to see if thou dost fear the Lord thy God.' The words 'he who tried thee, tried thee,' have reference to the earliest times;[10] but it appears to be otherwise after the removal to Babylon. For God, who knows all things, would not, as can be proved by many arguments, try in order that He Himself might know, for He foreknows all things. But, if you like, let us discuss this point, and I shall show that God foreknows. But it has been proved that the opinion is false that He does not know, and that this was written to try us. Thus we, Simon, can be led astray[11] neither by the Scriptures nor by any one else; nor are we deceived into the admission of many gods, nor do we agree to any statement that is made against God.

CHAP. XIV. — OTHER BEINGS CALLED GODS.

"For we ourselves also know that angels are called gods by the Scriptures, — as, for instance, He who spake at the bush, and wrestled with Jacob, — and the name is likewise applied to Him who is born Emmanuel, and who is called the mighty God.[12] Yea, even Moses became a god to Pharaoh, though in reality he was a man. The same is the case also with the idols of the Gentiles. But we have but one God, one who made creation and arranged the universe, whose Son is the Christ. Obeying Christ,[13] we learn to know what is false from the Scriptures. Moreover, being furnished by our ancestors with the truths of the Scriptures, we know that there is only one who has made the heavens and the earth, the God of the Jews, and of all who

---

[1] Probably τολμήματι should be changed into ὁρμήματι, or some such word: making known that an act of injustice has been committed by taking its departure.

[2] This might possibly be translated, " let him leave him who exists to him who exists; " i.e., let him leave the real God to man, who really exists.

[3] Wieseler proposes, " for he exists to no one."

[4] Gen. i. 26.

[5] This is the only passage in the *Homilies* relating to the σοφία. The text is in some parts corrupt. It is critically discussed by Uhlhorn, some of whose emendations are adopted by Dressel and translated here.

[6] Prov. viii. 30.

[7] [On the theory of the Scriptures which is here set forth, compare ii. 38, etc., iii. 42, etc. — R.]

[8] Deut. xiii. 1 ff.

[9] The change from the singular to the plural is in the Greek.

[10] Lit., " But it had been said that he who tried, tried." The idea seems to be, Before the removal to Babylon true prophets tested the people by urging them to worship these gods; but after that event false prophets arose who really wished to seduce the Jews from the worship of the true God.

[11] Lit., " nor can we be made to stumble from the Scriptures nor by any one else *or anything else.*"

[12] Isa. ix. 6.

[13] Lit., " whom obeying: " the " whom " might refer to God.

choose to worship Him. Our fathers, with pious thought, setting down a fixed belief in Him as the true God, handed down this belief to us, that we may know that if any thing is said against God, it is a falsehood. I shall add this remark over and above what I need say : If the case be not as I have said, then may I, and all who love the truth, incur danger in regard to the praise of the God who made us."

CHAP. XV. — CHRIST NOT GOD, BUT THE SON OF GOD.

When Simon heard this, he said : " Since you say that we ought not to believe even the prophet that gives signs and wonders if he say that there is another god, and that you know that he even incurs the penalty of death, therefore your teacher also was with reason cut off for having given signs and wonders." And Peter answered : " Our Lord neither asserted that there were gods except the Creator of all, nor did He proclaim Himself to be God, but He with reason pronounced blessed him who called Him the Son of that God who has arranged the universe." And Simon answered : " Does it not seem to you, then, that he who comes from God is God?"[1] And Peter said : " Tell us how this is possible ; for we cannot affirm this, because we did not hear it from Him.

CHAP. XVI. — THE UNBEGOTTEN AND THE BEGOTTEN NECESSARILY DIFFERENT FROM EACH OTHER.

" In addition to this, it is the peculiarity of the Father not to have been begotten, but of the Son to have been begotten ; but what is begotten cannot be compared with that which is unbegotten or self-begotten." And Simon said : " Is it not the same on account of its origin?"[2] And Peter said : " He who is not the same in all respects as some one, cannot have all the same appellations applied to him as that person." And Simon said : " This is to assert, not to prove." And Peter said : " Why, do you not see that if[3] the one happens to be self-begotten or unbegotten, they cannot be called the same ; nor can it be asserted of him who has been begotten that he is of the same substance as he is who has begotten him?[4] Learn this also : The bodies of men have immortal souls, which have been clothed with the breath of God ; and having come forth from God, they are of

the same substance, but they are not gods. But if they are gods, then in this way the souls of all men, both those who have died, and those who are alive, and those who shall come into being, are gods. But if in a spirit of controversy you maintain that these also are gods, what great matter is it, then, for Christ to be called God? for He has only what all have.

CHAP. XVII. — THE NATURE OF GOD.

" We call Him God whose peculiar attributes cannot belong to the nature of any other ; for, as He is called the Unbounded because He is boundless on every side, it must of necessity be the case that it is no other one's peculiar attribute to be called unbounded, as another cannot in like manner be boundless. But if any one says that it is possible, he is wrong ; for two things boundless on every side cannot co-exist, for the one is bounded by the other. Thus it is in the nature[5] of things that the unbegotten is one. But if he possesses a figure, even in this case the figure is one and incomparable.[6] Wherefore He is called the Most High, because, being higher than all, He has the universe subject to Him."

CHAP. XVIII. — THE NAME OF GOD.

And Simon said : Is this word ' God ' His ineffable name, which all use, because you maintain so strongly in regard to a name that it cannot be given to another?" And Peter said : ' I know that this is not His ineffable name, but one which is given by agreement among men ; but if you give it to another, you will also assign to this other that which is not used ; and that, too, deliberately.[7] The name which is used is the forerunner of that which is not used. In this way insolence is attributed even to that which has not yet been spoken, just as honour paid to that which is known is handed on to that which has not yet been known."

CHAP. XIX. — THE SHAPE OF GOD IN MAN.

And Simon said : " I should like to know, Peter, if you really believe that the shape of man has been moulded after the shape of God."[8] And Peter said : " I am really quite certain, Simon, that this is the case." And Simon said : " How can death dissolve the body, impressed as it has thus been with the greatest seal?" And Peter said : " It is the shape of the just God. When, then, the body begins to act unjustly, the form which is in it takes to flight, and thus the body

---

[1] [Here we encounter marked evidence of Ebionism. Compare with these chapters the letter of Rufinus prefixed to the *Recognitions.* — R.]

[2] The word γένεσις, " arising, coming into being," is here used, not γέννησις, " begetting." The idea fully expressed is: " Is not that which is begotten identical in essence with that which begets it?"

[3] We have inserted εἰ. The passage is amended in various ways; this seems to be the simplest.

[4] [The very ancient variant in John i. 18, " God only begotten," indicates the distinction between the Unbegotten God and the Son. Even the Arians use the phrase, " Only-begotten God." — R.]

[5] Lit., " thus it is nature."

[6] We have adopted an emendation here. The text has: " Even thus the incomparable is one."

[7] Wieseler proposes to join this clause with the following: " And in point of choice the name which."

[8] Lit., " of that one, of Him." [The chapter is peculiar to the *Homilies* ; comp. xvii. 7, 8. — R.]

is dissolved, by the shape disappearing, in order that an unjust body may not have the shape of the just God. The dissolution, however, does not take place in regard to the seal, but in regard to the sealed body. But that which is sealed is not dissolved without Him who sealed it. And thus it is not permitted to die without judgment." And Simon said : " What necessity was there to give the shape of such a being to man, who was raised from the earth?" And Peter said : " This was done because of the love of God, who made man. For while, as far as substance is concerned, all things are superior to the flesh of man, — I mean the ether, the sun, the moon, the stars, the air, the water, the fire — in a word, all the other things which have been made for the service of man, — yet, though superior in substance, they willingly endure to serve the inferior in substance, because of the shape of the superior. For as they who honour the clay image of a king have paid honour to the king himself, whose shape the clay happens to have, so the whole creation with joy serves man, who is made from earth, looking to the honour thus paid to God.

CHAP. XX. — THE CHARACTER OF GOD.

" Behold, then, the character of that God to whom you, Simon, wish to persuade us to be ungrateful, and the earth continues to bear you, perhaps wishing to see who will venture to entertain similar opinions to yours. For you were the first to dare what no other dared : you were the first to utter what we first heard. We first and alone have seen the boundless long-suffering of God in bearing with such great impiety as yours, and that God no other than the Creator of the world, against whom you have dared to act impiously. And yet openings of the earth took not place, and fire was not sent down from heaven and went not forth to burn up men, and rain was not poured out,[1] and a multitude of beasts was not sent from the thickets, and upon us ourselves the destructive wrath of God did not begin to show itself, on account of one who sinned the sin, as it were, of spiritual adultery, which is worse than the carnal. For it is not God the Creator of heaven and earth that in former times punished sins, since now, when He is blasphemed in the highest degree, He would

inflict the severest punishment.[2] But, on the contrary, He is long-suffering, calls to repentance, having the arrows which end in the destruction of the impious laid up in His treasures, which He will discharge like living animals when He shall sit down to give judgment to those that are His.[3] Wherefore let us fear the just God, whose shape the body of man bears for honour."

CHAP. XXI. — SIMON PROMISES TO APPEAL TO THE TEACHING OF CHRIST. PETER DISMISSES THE MULTITUDES.

When Peter said this, Simon answered : " Since I see you skilfully hinting that what is written in the books[4] against the framer[5] *of the world* does not happen to be true, to-morrow I shall show, from the discourses of your teacher, that he asserted that the framer *of the world* was not the highest God." And when Simon said this, he went out. But Peter said to the assembled multitudes : " If Simon can do no other injury to us in regard to God, he at least prevents you from listening to the words that can purify the soul." On Peter saying this, much whispering arose amongst the crowds, saying, " What necessity was there for permitting him to come in here, and utter his blasphemies against God?" And Peter heard, and said, " Would that the doctrines against God which are intended to try men[6] went no further than Simon ! For there will be, as the Lord said, false apostles, false prophets,[7] heresies, desires for supremacy, who, as I conjecture, finding their beginning in Simon, who blasphemes God, will work together in the assertion of the same opinions against God as those of Simon." And saying this with tears, he summoned the multitudes to him by his hand ; and when they came, he laid his hands upon them and prayed, and then dismissed them, telling them to come at an earlier hour next day. Saying this, and groaning, he entered and went to sleep, without taking food.

---

[1] One MS. reads, " was not restrained."

[2] We have inserted ἄν, and suppose the sentence to be ironical. The meaning might be the same without ἄν. The text of Dressel is as follows: " For is not He who then punished the sins God, Creator of heaven and earth; since even now, being blasphemed in the highest degree, He punished it in the highest degree ? "
[3] Cotelerius translates: " to His enemies."
[4] i.e., the Scriptures.
[5] A distinction has to be made between the Creator, or maker out of nothing, and the framer, or fashioner, or Demiurge, who puts the matter into shape.
[6] Lit., " the word against God for the trial of men."
[7] Comp. Matt. xxiv. 24.

HOMILY XVII.

CHAP. I. — SIMON COMES TO PETER.

THE next day, therefore, as Peter was to hold a discussion with Simon, he rose earlier than usual and prayed. On ceasing to pray, Zacchæus came in, and said: "Simon is seated without, discoursing with about thirty of his own special followers." And Peter said: "Let him talk until the multitude assemble, and then let us begin the discussion in the following way. We shall hear all that has been said by him, and having fitted our reply to this, we shall go out and discourse." And assuredly so it happened. Zacchæus, therefore, went out, and not long after entered again, and communicated to Peter the discourse delivered by Simon against him.[1]

CHAP. II. — SIMON'S SPEECH AGAINST PETER.

Now he said: "He accuses you, Peter, of being the servant of wickedness, of having great power in magic, and as charming the souls of men in a way worse than idolatry.[2] To prove that you are a magician, he seemed to me to adduce the following evidence, saying: 'I am conscious of this, that when I come to hold a discussion with him, I do not remember a single word of what I have been meditating on by myself. For while he is discoursing, and my mind is engaged in recollecting what it is that I thought of saying on coming to a conference with him, I do not hear anything whatsoever of what he is saying. Now, since I do not experience this in the presence of any other than in his alone, is it not plain that I am under the influence of his magic? And as to his doctrines being worse than those of idolatry, I can make that quite clear to any one who has understanding. For there is no other benefit than this, that the soul should be freed from images[3] of every kind. For when the soul brings an image before its eye, it is bound by fear, and it pines away through anxiety lest it should suffer some calamity; and being altered, it falls under the influence of a demon; and being under his influence, it seems to the mass to be wise.

CHAP. III. — SIMON'S ACCUSATION OF PETER.

"'Peter does this to you while promising to make you wise. For, under the pretext of proclaiming one God, he seems to free you from many lifeless images, which do not at all injure those who worship them, because they are seen by the eyes themselves to be made of stone, or brass, or gold, or of some other lifeless material. Wherefore the soul, because it knows that what is seen is nothing, cannot be spell-bound by fear in an equal degree by means of what is visible. But looking to a terrible God through the influence' of deceptive teaching, it has all its natural foundations overturned. And I say this, not because I exhort you to worship images, but because Peter, seeming to free your souls from terrible images,[4] drives mad the mind of each one of you by a more terrible image, introducing God in a shape, and that, too, a God extremely just, — an image which is accompanied by what is terrible and awful to the contemplative soul, by that which can entirely destroy the energy of a sound mind. For the mind, when in the midst of such a storm, is like the depth stirred by a violent wind, perturbed and darkened. Wherefore, if he comes to benefit you, let him not, while seeming to dissolve your fears which gently proceed from lifeless shapes, introduce in their stead the terrible shape of God. But has God a shape? If He has, He possesses a figure. And if He has a figure, how is He not limited? And if limited, He is in space. But if He is in space, He is less than the space which encloses Him. And if less than anything, how is He greater than all, or superior to all, or the highest of all? This, then, is the state of the case.

CHAP. IV. — IT IS ASSERTED THAT CHRIST'S TEACH-ING IS DIFFERENT FROM PETER'S.

"'And that he does not really believe even the doctrines proclaimed by his teacher is evident, for he proclaims doctrines opposite to his.[5] For he said to some one, as I learn,[6] "Call me not good, for the good is one." Now, in speaking of the good one, he no longer speaks of that just one,[7] whom the Scriptures proclaim, who kills and makes alive, — kills those who sin, and makes alive those who live according to His will. But that he did not really call Him who is the framer of the world good, is plain to any one who can reflect. For the framer of the world was known to Adam whom He had made, and to Enoch who pleased Him, and to Noah who was seen to be just by Him; likewise to Abraham, and Isaac, and Jacob; also to Moses, and the people, and the whole world. But Jesus, the

---

[1] The text has: "against Peter."
[2] [Comp. *Recognitions*, iii. 12, for a similar accusation made by Simon, at the beginning of the second day's discussion. — R.]
[3] εἰδώλων, idols.
[4] ἰδεῶν.
[5] [These chapters are peculiar to the *Homilies.* — R.]
[6] Matt. xix. 17.
[7] The Gnostic distinction between the God who is just and the God who is good, is here insisted on.

teacher of Peter himself, came and said,[1] "No one knew the Father except the Son, as no one knoweth[2] even the Son except the Father, and those to whom the Son may wish to reveal Him." If, then, it was the Son himself who was present, it was from the time of his appearance that he began to reveal to those to whom he wished, Him who was unknown to all. And thus the Father was unknown to all who lived before him, and could not thus be He who was known to all.

CHAP. V. — JESUS INCONSISTENT IN HIS TEACHING.

"'In saying this, Jesus is consistent not even with himself. For sometimes by other utterances, taken from the Scriptures, he presents God as being terrible and just, saying,[3] "Fear not him who killeth the body, but can do nothing to the soul; but fear Him who is able to cast both body and soul into the Gehenna of fire. Yea, I say unto you, fear Him." But that he asserted that He is really to be feared as being a just God, to whom he says those who receive injustice cry, is shown in a parable of which he gives the interpretation, saying:[4] "If, then, the unjust judge did so, because he was continually entreated, how much more will the Father avenge those who cry to Him day and night? Or do you think that, because He bears long with them, He will not do it? Yea, I say to you, He will do it, and that speedily." Now he who speaks of God as an avenging and rewarding God, presents Him as naturally just, and not as good. Moreover he gives thanks to the Lord of heaven and earth.[5] But if He is Lord of heaven and earth, He is acknowledged to be the framer of the world, and if framer, then He is just. When, therefore, he sometimes calls Him good and sometimes just, he is not consistent with himself in this point.[6] But his wise disciple maintained yesterday a third point, that real sight[7] is more satisfactory than vision, not knowing that real sight can be human, but that vision confessedly proceeds from divinity.'

CHAP. VI. — PETER GOES OUT TO ANSWER SIMON.

"These and such like were the statements, Peter, which Simon addressed to the multitudes while he stood outside; and he seems to me to be disturbing the minds of the greater number. Wherefore go forth immediately, and by the power of truth break down his false statements."

When Zacchæus said this, Peter prayed after his usual manner and went out, and standing in the place where he spoke the day before, and saluting the multitudes according to the custom enjoined by his religion, he began to speak as follows: "Our Lord Jesus Christ, who is the true prophet (as I shall prove conclusively at the proper time), made concise declarations in regard to those matters that relate to the truth, for these two reasons: first, because He was in the habit of addressing the pious, who had knowledge enough to enable them to believe the opinions uttered by Him by way of declaration; for His statements were not strange to their usual mode of thought; and in the second place, because, having a limited time assigned Him for preaching, He did not employ the method of demonstration in order that He might not spend all His limited time in arguments, for in this way it might happen that He would be fully occupied in giving the solutions of a few problems which might be understood by mental exertion, while He would not have given us to any great extent[8] those statements which relate to the truth. Accordingly He stated any opinions He wished, as to a people who were able to understand Him, to whom we also belong, who, whenever we did not understand anything of what had been said by Him, — a thing which rarely happened, — inquired of Him privately, that nothing said by Him might be unintelligible to us.

CHAP. VII. — MAN IN THE SHAPE OF GOD.

"Knowing therefore that we knew all that was spoken by Him, and that we could supply the proofs, He sent us to the ignorant Gentiles to baptize them for remission of sins, and commanded us to teach them first.[9] Of His commandments this is the first and great one, to fear the Lord God, and to serve Him only. But He meant us to fear that God whose angels they are who are the angels of the least of the faithful amongst us, and who stand in heaven continually beholding the face of the Father.[10] For He has shape, and He has every limb primarily and solely for beauty's sake, and not for use.[11] For He has not eyes that He may see with them; for He sees on every side, since He is incomparably more brilliant in His body than the visual spirit which is in us, and He is more splendid than everything, so that in comparison with Him the light of the sun may be reckoned as darkness. Nor has He ears that He may hear; for He hears, perceives, moves, energizes, acts on every side. But He has the most beautiful shape on account

---

1 Matt. xi. 27; [Luke x. 22. Comp. *Recognitions*, ii. 47. — R.].
2 One MS. reads, "saw."
3 Matt. x. 28.
4 Luke xviii. 6–8.
5 Matt. xi 25; [Luke x. 21].
6 [Comp. xviii. 1, etc.; also *Recognitions*, iii. 37, 38. — R.]
7 The MSS. read ἐνέργειαν, "activity." Clericus amended it into ἐνάργειαν, which means, vision or sight in plain open day with one's own eyes, in opposition to the other word ὀπτασία, vision in sleep, or ecstasy, or some similar unusual state.

8 Lit. "to a greater extent."
9 Matt. xxviii. 19, 20.
10 Matt. xviii. 10.
11 [Comp. xvi. 19. The theosophical views here presented are peculiar to the *Homilies*, though some traces of them appear in the *Recognitions*. — R.]

of man, that the pure in heart [1] may be able to see Him, that they may rejoice because they suffered. For He moulded man in His own shape as in the grandest seal, in order that he may be the ruler and lord of all, and that all may be subject to him. Wherefore, judging that He is the universe, and that man is His image (for He is Himself invisible, but His image man is visible), the man who wishes to worship Him honours His visible image, which is man. Whatsoever therefore any one does to man, be it good or bad, is regarded as being done to Him. Wherefore the judgment which proceeds from Him shall go before, giving to every one according to his merits. For He avenges His own shape.

CHAP. VIII. — GOD'S FIGURE: SIMON'S OBJECTION THEREFROM REFUTED.

"But someone will say, If He has shape, then He has figure also, and is in space; but if He is in space, and is, as being less, enclosed by it, how is He great above everything? How can He be everywhere if He has figure? The first remark I have to make to him who urges these objections is this: The Scriptures persuade us to have such sentiments and to believe such statements in regard to Him; and we know that their declarations are true, for witness is borne to them by our Lord Jesus Christ, by whose orders we are bound to afford proofs to you that such is the case. But first I shall speak of space. The space of God is the non-existent, but God is that which exists. But that which is non-existent cannot be compared with that which is existent. For how can space be existent? unless it be a second space, such as heaven, earth, water, air, and if there is any other body that fills up the vacuity, which is called vacuity on this account, that it is nothing. For 'nothing' is its more appropriate name. For what is that which is called vacuity but as it were a vessel which contains nothing, except the vessel itself? But being vacuity, it is not itself space; but space is that in which vacuity itself is, if indeed it is the vessel. For it must be the case that that which exists is in that which does not exist. But by this which is non-existent I mean that which is called by some, space, which is nothing. But being nothing, how can it be compared with that which is, except by expressing the contrary, and saying that it is that which does not exist, and that that which does not exist is called space? But even if it were something, there are many examples which I have at hand, but I shall content myself with one only, to show that that which encloses is not unquestionably superior to that which is enclosed. The sun is a circular figure, and is

entirely enclosed by air, yet it lightens up the air, it warms it, it divides it; and if the sun be away from it, it is enveloped in darkness; and from whatsoever part of it the sun is removed, it becomes cold as if it were dead; but again it is illuminated by its rising, and when it has been warmed up by it, it is adorned with still greater beauty. And it does this by giving a share of itself, though it has its substance limited. What, then, is there to prevent God, as being the Framer and Lord of this and everything else, from possessing figure and shape and beauty, and having the communication of these qualities proceeding from Himself extended infinitely?

CHAP. IX. — GOD THE CENTRE OR HEART OF THE UNIVERSE.

"One, then, is the God who truly exists, who presides in a superior shape, being the heart of that which is above and that which is below twice,[2] which sends forth from Him as from a centre the life-giving and incorporeal power; the whole universe with the stars and regions [3] of the heaven, the air, the fire, and if anything else exists, is proved to be a substance infinite in height, boundless in depth, immeasurable in breadth, extending the life-giving and wise nature from Him over three infinites.[4] It must be, therefore, that this infinite which proceeds from Him on every side exists,[5] having as its heart Him who is above all, and who thus possesses figure; for wherever He be, He is as it were in the centre of the infinite, being the limit of the universe. And the extensions taking their rise with Him, possess the nature of six infinites; of whom the one taking its rise with Him penetrates [6] into the height above, another into the depth below, another to the right hand, another to the left, another in front, and another behind; to whom He Himself, looking as to a number that is equal on every side,[7] completes the world in six temporal intervals,[8] Himself being the rest,[9] and having the infinite age to come as His image, being the beginning and the end. For in Him the six infinites end, and from Him they receive their extension to infinity.

CHAP. X. — THE NATURE AND SHAPE OF GOD.

"This is the mystery of the hebdomad. For He Himself is the rest of the whole who·grants

---

[1] Matt. v. 8.

[2] The whole of this chapter is full of corruption: "twice" occurs in one MS. Various attempts have been made to amend the passage.
[3] An emendation.
[4] The text is corrupt. We have translated ἐπ' ἀπείρους τρεῖς. Some think "three" should be omitted. The three infinites are in respect of height, depth, and breadth.
[5] As punctuated in Dressel, this reads, "that the infinite is the heart."
[6] The emendation of the transcriber of one of the MSS.
[7] This refers to the following mode of exhibiting the number: ∴. where each side presents the number three.
[8] The creation of the world in six days.
[9] The seventh day on which God rested, the type of the rest of the future age. See *Epistle of Barnabas*, c. xv.

Himself as a rest to those who imitate His greatness within their little measure. For He is alone, sometimes comprehensible, sometimes incomprehensible, *sometimes limitable,*[1] sometimes illimitable, having extensions which proceed from Him into infinity. For thus He is comprehensible and incomprehensible, near and far, being here and there, as being the only existent one, and as giving a share of that mind which is infinite on every hand, in consequence of which souls breathe and possess life;[2] and if they be separated from the body and be found with a longing for Him, they are borne along into His bosom, as in the winter time the mists of the mountains, attracted by the rays of the sun, are borne along immortal[3] to it. What affection ought therefore to arise within us if we gaze with our mind on His beautiful shape! But otherwise it is absurd *to speak of beauty.* For beauty cannot exist apart from shape; nor can one be attracted to the love of God, nor even deem that he can see Him, if God has no form.

CHAP. XI. — THE FEAR OF GOD.

"But some who are strangers to the truth, and who give their energies to the service of evil, on pretext of glorifying God, say that He has no figure, in order that, being shapeless and formless, He may be visible to no one, so as not to be longed for. For the mind, not seeing the form of God, is empty of Him. But how can any one pray if he has no one to whom he may flee for refuge, on whom he may lean? For if he meets with no resistance, he falls out into vacuity. Yea, says he, we ought not to fear God, but to love Him. I agree; but the consciousness of having done well in each good act will accomplish this. Now well-doing proceeds from fearing. But fear, says he, strikes death into the soul. Nay, but I affirm that it does not strike death, but awakens the soul, and converts it. And perhaps the injunction not to fear God might be right, if we men did not fear many other things; such, for instance, as plots against us by those who are like us, and wild beasts, serpents, diseases, sufferings, demons, and a thousand other ills. Let him, then, who asks us not to fear God, rescue us from these, that we may not fear them; but if he cannot, why should he grudge that we should be delivered from a thousand fears by one fear, the fear of the Just One, and that it should be possible by a slight[4] faith in Him to remove a thousand

afflictions from ourselves and others, and receive instead an exchange of blessings, and that, doing no ill in consequence of fear of the God who sees everything, we should continue in peace even in the present life.

CHAP. XII. — THE FEAR AND LOVE OF GOD.

"Thus, then, grateful service to Him who is truly Lord, renders us free from service to all other masters.[5] If, then, it is possible for any one to be free from sin without fearing God, let him not fear; for under the influence of love to Him one cannot do what is displeasing to Him. For, on the one hand, it is written that we are to fear Him, and we have been commanded to love Him, in order that each of us may use that prescription which is suitable to his constitution. Fear Him, therefore, because He is just; but whether you fear Him or love Him, sin not. And may it be the case that any one who fears Him shall be able to gain the victory over unlawful desires, shall not lust after what belongs to others, shall practise kindness, shall be sober, and act justly! For I see some who are imperfect in their fear of Him sinning very much. Let us therefore fear God, not only because He is just; for it is through pity for those who have received injustice that He inflicts punishment on those who have done the injustice. As water therefore quenches fire, so does fear extinguish the desire for evil practices. He who teaches fearlessness does not himself fear; but he who does not fear, does not believe that there will be a judgment, strengthens his lusts, acts as a magician, and accuses others of the deeds which he himself does."

CHAP. XIII. — THE EVIDENCE OF THE SENSES CONTRASTED WITH THAT FROM SUPERNATURAL VISION.

Simon, on hearing this, interrupted him, and said: "I know against whom you are making these remarks; but in order that I may not spend any time in discussing subjects which I do not wish to discuss, repeating the same statements to refute you, reply to that which is concisely stated by us. You professed that you had well understood the doctrines and deeds[6] of your teacher because you saw them before you with your own eyes,[7] and heard them with your

---

[1] The words in italics are inserted by conjecture. "Sometimes incomprehensible, sometimes illimitable," occur only in one MS.
[2] We have adopted Wieseler's suggestions.
[3] This word is justly suspected. The passage is in other respects corrupt.
[4] The word "slight" is not used in reference to the character of the faith, but to indicate that the act of faith is a small act compared with the results that flow from it.

[5] We have adopted an emendation of a passage which is plainly corrupt.
[6] Doctrines and deeds: lit., the things of your teacher.
[7] The MSS. have here ἐνεργείᾳ, "activity." This has been amended into ἐναργείᾳ, "with plainness, with distinctness." Ἐνάργεια is used throughout in opposition to ὀπτασία, ὅραμα, and ἐνύπνιον, and means the act of seeing and hearing by our own senses in plain daylight, when to doubt the fact observed is to doubt the senses; ὀπτασία is apparition or vision in ecstasy, or some extraordinary way but that of sleep; ὅραμα and ἐνύπνιον are restricted to visions in sleep. The last term implies this. The first means simply "a thing seen."

own ears, and that it is not possible for any other to have anything similar by vision or apparition. But I shall show that this is false. He who hears any one with his own ears, is not altogether fully assured of the truth of what is said; for his mind has to consider whether he is wrong or not, inasmuch as he is a man as far as appearance goes. But apparition not merely presents an object to view, but inspires him who sees it with confidence, for it comes from God. Now reply first to this."[1]

CHAP. XIV. — THE EVIDENCE OF THE SENSES MORE TRUSTWORTHY THAN THAT OF SUPERNATURAL VISION.

And Peter said: "You proposed to speak to one point, you replied to another.[2] For your proposition was, that one is better able to know more fully, *and to attain confidence*,[3] when he hears in consequence of an apparition, than when he hears with his own ears; but when you set about the matter, you were for persuading us that he who hears through an apparition is surer than he who hears with his own ears. Finally, you alleged that, on this account, you knew more satisfactorily the doctrines of Jesus than I do, because you heard His words through an apparition. But I shall reply to the proposition you made at the beginning. The prophet, because he is a prophet, having first given certain information with regard to what is objectively[4] said by him, is believed with confidence; and being known beforehand to be a true prophet, and being examined and questioned as the disciple wishes, he replies: But he who trusts to apparition or vision and dream is insecure. For he does not know to whom he is trusting. For it is possible either that he may be an evil demon or a deceptive spirit, pretending in his speeches to be what he is not. But if any one should wish to inquire of him who he is who has appeared, he can say to himself whatever he likes. And thus, gleaming forth like a wicked one, and remaining as long as he likes, he is at length extinguished, not remaining with the questioner so long as he wished him to do for the purpose of consulting him. For any one that sees by means of dreams cannot inquire about whatever he may wish. For reflection is not in the special power of one who is asleep. Hence we, desiring to have information in regard to something in our waking hours, inquire about something else in our dreams; or without inquiring, we hear about matters that do not concern us, and awaking from sleep we are dispirited because we have neither heard nor inquired about those matters which we were eager to know."

CHAP. XV. — THE EVIDENCE FROM DREAMS DISCUSSED.

And Simon said: "If you maintain that apparitions do not always reveal the truth, yet for all that, visions and dreams, being God-sent, do not speak falsely in regard to those matters which they wish to tell." And Peter said: "You were right in saying that, being God-sent, they do not speak falsely. But it is uncertain if he who sees has seen a God-sent dream." And Simon said: "If he who has had the vision is just, he has seen a true vision." And Peter said: "You were right. But who is just, if he stands in need of a vision that he may learn what he ought to learn, and do what he ought to do?" And Simon said: "Grant me this, that the just man alone can see a true vision, and I shall then reply to that other point. For I have come to the conclusion that an impious man does not see a true dream." And Peter said: "This is false; and I can prove it both apart from Scripture and by Scripture; but I do not undertake to persuade you. For the man who is inclined to fall in love with a bad woman, does not change his mind so as to care for a lawful union with another woman in every respect good; but sometimes they love the worse woman through prepossessions, though they are conscious that there is another who is more excellent. And you are ignorant, in consequence of some such state of mind." And Simon said: "Dismiss this subject, and discuss the matter on which you promised to speak. For it seems to me impossible that impious men should receive dreams from God in any way whatever.

CHAP. XVI. — NONE BUT EVIL DEMONS APPEAR TO THE IMPIOUS.

And Peter said: "I remember that I promised to prove this point, and to give my proofs in regard to it from Scripture and apart from Scripture. And now listen to what I say. We know that there are many (if you will pardon me the statement; and if you don't, I can appeal to those who are present as judges) who worship idols, commit adultery, and sin in every way, and yet they see true visions and dreams, and some of them have also apparitions of demons. For I maintain that the eyes of mortals cannot see the incorporeal form of the Father or Son, because it is illumined by exceeding great light. Wherefore it is not because God envies, but because He pities, that He cannot be seen by man who has been turned into flesh. For he who sees *God*

---

[1] [Comp. *Recognitions*, ii. 50, 51, 61–65. The emphasis laid upon supernatural visions in the remainder of the Homily has been supposed to convey an insinuation against the revelations to the Apostle Paul. — R.]

[2] Probably it should be ἀπεκλίνω instead of ἀπεκρίνω, "you turned aside to another."

[3] The words *in italics* are inserted conjecturally, to fill up a lacuna in the best MS.

[4] ἐναργῶς, "with reference to things palpable to our senses."

cannot live. For the excess of light dissolves the flesh of him who sees; unless by the secret power of God the flesh be changed into the nature of light, so that it can see light, or the substance of light be changed into flesh, so that it can be seen by flesh. For the power to see the Father, without undergoing any change, belongs to the Son alone. But the just shall also in like manner behold God;[1] for in the resurrection of the dead, when they have been changed, as far as their bodies are concerned, into light, and become like the angels, they shall be able to see Him. Finally, then, if any angel be sent that he may be seen by a man, he is changed into flesh, that he may be able to be seen by flesh. For no one can see the incorporeal power not only of the Son, but not even of an angel. But if one sees an apparition, he should know that this is the apparition of an evil demon.

CHAP. XVII. — THE IMPIOUS SEE TRUE DREAMS AND VISIONS.

"But it is manifest that the impious see true visions and dreams, and I can prove it from Scripture. Finally, then, it is written in the law, how Abimelech, who was impious, wished to defile the wife of just Abraham by intercourse, and how he heard the commandment from God in his sleep, as the Scripture saith, not to touch her,[2] because she was dwelling with her husband. Pharaoh, also an impious man, saw a dream in regard to the fulness and thinness of the ears of corn,[3] to whom Joseph said, when he gave the interpretation, that the dream had come from God.[4] Nebuchadnezzar, who worshipped images, and ordered those who worshipped God to be cast into fire, saw a dream[5] extending over the whole age of the world.[6] And let no one say, 'No one who is impious sees a vision when awake.' That is false. Nebuchadnezzar himself, having ordered three men to be cast into fire, saw a fourth when he looked into the furnace, and said, 'I see the fourth as the Son of God.'[7] And nevertheless, though they saw apparitions, visions, and dreams, they were impious. Thus, we cannot infer with absolute certainty that the man who has seen visions, and dreams, and apparitions, is undoubtedly pious. For in the case of the pious man, the truth gushes up natural and pure[8] in his mind, not worked up through dreams, but granted to the good through intelligence.

CHAP. XVIII. — THE NATURE OF REVELATION.

"Thus to me also was the Son revealed by the Father. Wherefore I know what is the meaning of revelation, having learned it in my own case. For at the very time when the Lord said, 'Who do they say that I am?'[9] and when I heard one saying one thing of Him, and another another, it came into my heart to say (and I know not, therefore, how I said it), 'Thou art the Son of the living God.'[10] But He, pronouncing me blessed, pointed out to me that it was the Father who had revealed it to me; and from this time I learned that revelation is knowledge gained without instruction, and without apparition and dreams. And this is indeed the case. For in the *soul*[11] which has been placed in us by[12] God, there is all the truth; but it is covered and revealed by the hand of God, who works so far as each one through his knowledge deserves.[13] But the declaration of anything by means of apparitions and dreams from without is a proof, not that it comes from revelation, but from wrath. Finally, then, it is written in the law, that God, being angry, said to Aaron and Miriam,[14] 'If a prophet arise from amongst you, I shall make myself known to him through visions and dreams, but not so as to my servant Moses; because I shall speak to him in an *outward* appearance, and not through dreams, just as one will speak to his own friend.' You see how the statements of wrath are made through visions and dreams, but the statements to a friend are made face to face, in *outward* appearance, and not through riddles and visions and dreams, as to an enemy.

CHAP. XIX. — OPPOSITION TO PETER UNREASONABLE.

"If, then, our Jesus appeared to you in a vision, made Himself known to you, and spoke to you, it was as one who is enraged with an adversary; and this is the reason why it was through visions and dreams, or through revelations that were from without, that He spoke to you. But can any one be rendered fit for instruction through apparitions? And if you will say, 'It is possible,' then I ask, 'Why did our teacher abide and discourse a whole year to those who were awake?' And how are we to believe your word, when you tell us that He appeared to you? And how did He appear to you, when you entertain opinions contrary to His teaching? But if you were seen and taught

---

[1] We have translated a bold conjecture. The text has, "The just not in like manner," without any verb, which Schwegler amended: "To the just this power does not belong in like manner."
[2] Gen. xx. 3.
[3] Gen. xli. 5, ff.
[4] Gen. xli. 25.
[5] Dan. ii. 31.
[6] Lit, of the whole length of the age.
[7] Dan. iii. 25.
[8] We have amended this passage. The text applies the words "natural *or innate* and pure" to the mind.

[9] Matt. xvi. 13.
[10] Matt. xvi. 16.
[11] This word is not in the text. Schliemann proposed the word "heart." Possibly "breath" or "spirit" may be the lost word. See above.
[12] "By" should properly be "from."
[13] Lit., "who produces according to the merit of each one knowing." Cotelerius translated, "who, knowing the merit of each man, does to him according to it." The idea seems to be, that God uncovers the truth hidden in the soul to each man according to his deserts.
[14] Num. xii. 6, 7; Ex. xxxiii. 11.

by Him, and became His apostle for a single hour, proclaim His utterances, interpret His sayings, love His apostles, contend not with me who companied with Him. For in direct opposition to me, who am a firm rock, the foundation of the Church,[1] you now stand. If you were not opposed to me, you would not accuse me, and revile the truth proclaimed by me, in order that I may not be believed when I state what I myself have heard with my own ears from the Lord, as if I were evidently a person that was condemned and in bad repute.[2] But if you say that I am condemned, you bring an accusation against God, who revealed the Christ to me, and you inveigh against Him who pronounced me blessed on account of the revelation. But if, indeed, you really wish to work in the cause of truth, learn first of all from us what we have learned from Him, and, becoming a disciple of the truth, become a fellow-worker with us."

---

[1] Matt. xvi. 18.
[2] We have adopted an emendation of Schwegler's. The text reads, "in good repute." [The word "condemned" is supposed to be borrowed from the account of the contest at Antioch in Gal. ii. 11, where it is applied to the Apostle Peter. This passage has therefore been regarded as a covert attack upon the Apostle Paul. — R.]

CHAP. XX. — ANOTHER SUBJECT FOR DISCUSSION PROPOSED.

When Simon heard this, he said : " Far be it from me to become his or your disciple. For I am not ignorant of what I ought to know ; but the inquiries which I made as a learner were made that I may see if you can prove that actual sight is more distinct than apparition.[3] But you spoke according to your own pleasure ; you did not prove. And now, to-morrow I shall come to your opinions in regard to God, whom you affirmed to be the framer of the world ; and in my discussion with you, I shall show that he is not the highest, nor good, and that your teacher made the same statements as I now do ; and I shall prove that you have not understood him." On saying this he went away, not wishing to listen to what might be said to the propositions which he had laid down.

---

[3] This passage is corrupt in the text. Dressel reads, "that activity is more distinct than apparition." By activity would be meant, "acting while one is awake, and in full possession of his senses;" and thus the meaning would be nearly the same as in our translation.

HOMILY XVIII.

CHAP. I. — SIMON MAINTAINS THAT THE FRAMER OF THE WORLD IS NOT THE HIGHEST GOD.

At break of day, when Peter went forth to discourse, Simon anticipated him, and said : "When I went away yesterday, I promised to you to return to-day, and in a discussion show that he who framed the world is not the highest God, but that the highest God is another who alone is good, and who has remained unknown up to this time. At once, then, state to me whether you maintain that the framer of the world is the same as the lawgiver or not? If, then, he is the lawgiver, he is just ; but if he is just, he is not good. But if he is not good, then it was another that Jesus proclaimed, when he said,[1] ' Do not call me good ; for one is good, the Father who is in the heavens.' Now a lawgiver cannot be both just and good, for these qualities do not harmonize."[2] And Peter said : " First tell us what are the actions which in your opinion constitute a person good, and what are those which constitute him just, in order that thus we may address our words to the same mark." And Simon said : " Do you state first what in your opinion is goodness, and what justice."

---

[1] Matt. xix. 17.
[2] [Comp. xvii. 5, and *Recognitions*, iii. 37, 38. — R.]

CHAP. II. — DEFINITION OF GOODNESS AND JUSTICE.

And Peter said : " That I may not waste my time in contentious discussions, while I make the fair demand that you should give answers to my propositions, I shall myself answer those questions which I put, as is your wish. I then affirm that the man who bestows[3] *goods* is good, just as I see the Framer of the world doing when He gives the sun to the good, and the rain to the just and unjust." And Simon said : " It is most unjust that he should give the same things to the just and the unjust." And Peter said : " Do you, then, in your turn state to us what course of conduct would constitute Him good." And Simon said : " It is you that must state this." And Peter said : " I will. He who gives the same things to the good and just, and also to the evil and unjust, is not even just according to you ; but you would with reason call Him just if He gave goods to the good and evils to the evil. What course of conduct, then, would He adopt, if He does not adopt the plan of giving things temporal to the evil, if perchance they should be converted, and things eternal to the good, if at least they remain *good?* And thus by giving to all, but by gratifying the more

---

[3] There is a lacuna in one of the MSS. here, which is supplied in various ways. We have inserted the word " goods."

excellent,[1] His justice is good; and all the more long-suffering in this, that to sinners who repent He freely grants forgiveness of their sins, and to those who have acted well He assigns even eternal life. But judging at last, and giving to each one what he deserves, He is just. If, then, this is right, confess it; but if it appears to you not to be right, refute it."

CHAP. III. — GOD BOTH GOOD AND JUST.

And Simon said: "I said once for all, 'Every lawgiver, looking to justice, is just.'" And Peter said: "If it is the part of him who is good not to lay down a law, but of him who is just to lay down a law, in this way the Framer of the world is both good and just. He is good, inasmuch as it is plain that He did not lay down a law in writing from the times of Adam to Moses; but inasmuch as He had a written law from Moses to the present times,[2] He is just also." And Simon said: "Prove to me from the utterances of your teacher that it is within the power of the same man to be good and just; for to me it seems impossible that the lawgiver who is good should also be just." And Peter said: "I shall explain to you how goodness itself is just. Our teacher Himself first said to the Pharisee who asked Him,[3] 'What shall I do to inherit eternal life?' 'Do not call me good; for one is good, even the Father who is in the heavens;' and straightway He introduced these words, 'But if thou shalt wish to enter into life, keep the commandments.' And when he said, 'What commandments?' He pointed him to those of the law. Now He would not, if He were indicating some other good being, have referred him to the commandments of the Just One. That indeed justice and goodness are different I allow, but you do not know that it is within the power of the same being to be good and just. For He is good, in that He is now long-suffering with the penitent, and welcomes them; but just, when acting as judge He will give to every one according to his deserts."

CHAP. IV. — THE UNREVEALED GOD.

And Simon said: "How, then, if the framer of the world, who also fashioned Adam, was known, and known too by those who were just according to the law, and moreover by the just and unjust, and the whole world, does your teacher, coming after all these, say,[4] 'No one has known the Father but the Son, even as no one knoweth the Son but the Father, and those to whom the Son may wish to reveal Him?' But he would not have made this statement, had he not proclaimed a Father who was still unrevealed, whom the law speaks of as the highest, and who has not given any utterance either good or bad (as Jeremiah testifies in the Lamentations[5]); who also, limiting the nations to seventy languages, according to the number of the sons of Israel who entered Egypt, and according to the boundaries of these nations, gave to his own Son, who is also called Lord, and who brought into order the heaven and the earth, the Hebrews as his portion, and defined him to be God of gods, that is, of the gods who received the other nations as their portions. Laws, therefore, proceeded from all the so-called gods to their own divisions, which consist of the other nations. In like manner also from the Son of the Lord of all came forth the law which is established among the Hebrews. And this state of matters was determined on, that if any one should seek refuge in the law of any one, he should belong to the division of him whose law he undertook to obey. No one knew the highest Father, who was unrevealed, just as they did not know that his Son was his Son. Accordingly at this moment you yourself, in assigning the special attributes of the unrevealed Most High to the Son, do not know that he is the Son, being the Father of Jesus, who with you is called the Christ.

CHAP. V. — PETER DOUBTS SIMON'S HONESTY.

When Simon had made these statements, Peter said to him: "Can you call to witness that these are your beliefs that being Himself, — I do not mean Him whom you speak of now as being unrevealed, but Him in whom you believe, though you do not confess Him? For you are talking nonsense when you define one thing instead of another. Wherefore, if you call Him to witness that you believe what you say, I shall answer you. But if you continue discussing with me what you do not believe, you compel me to strike the empty air." And Simon said: "It is from some of your own disciples that I have heard *that this is the truth*."[6] And Peter said: "Do not bear false witness?" And Simon said: "Do not rebuke me, most insolent man." And Peter said: "So long as you do not tell who it was who said so, *I affirm that* you are a liar." And Simon said: "Suppose that I myself have got up these doctrines, or that I heard them from some other, give me your answer to them. For if they cannot be overturned, then I have learned that this is the truth." And Peter said: "If it is a human invention, I will not reply to

---

[1] This translation of Cotelerius is doubtful. More correctly it would be, "by gratifying different people," which does not make sense. Wieseler proposes, "by gratifying in different ways."

[2] The text seems corrupt here. Literally it is, "from Moses to the present times, as has been written, He is just also."

[3] Luke xviii. 18, ff.; Matt. xix. 16, ff.

[4] Matt. xi. 27; [Luke x. 22. Comp. Homily XVII. 4: *Recognitions*, ii. 47, 48. The discussion here is much fuller. — R.].

[5] Lam. iii. 38.

[6] The words in italics are inserted to fill up a lacuna which occurs here in the Vatican MS.

it; but if you are held fast by the supposition that it is the truth, acknowledge to me that this is the case, and I can then myself say something in regard to the matter." And Simon said: "Once for all, then, these doctrines seem to me to be true. Give me your reply, if you have aught to say against them."

CHAP. VI. — THE NATURE OF REVELATION.

And Peter said: "If this is the case, you are acting most impiously. For if it belongs to the Son, who arranged heaven and earth, to reveal His unrevealed Father to whomsoever He wishes, you are, as I said, acting most impiously in revealing Him to those to whom He has not revealed Him." And Simon said: "But he himself wishes me to reveal him." And Peter said: "You do not understand what I mean, Simon. But listen and understand. When it is said that the Son will reveal Him to whom He wishes, it is meant that such an one is to learn of Him not by instruction, but by revelation only. For it is revelation when that which lies secretly veiled in all the hearts of men is revealed *unveiled* by His *God's* own will without any utterance. And thus knowledge comes to one, not because he has been instructed, but because he has understood. And yet the person who understands it cannot demonstrate it to another, since he did not himself receive it by instruction; nor can he reveal it, since he is not himself the Son, unless he maintains that he is himself the Son. But you are not the standing Son. For if you were the Son, assuredly you would know those who are worthy of such a revelation. But you do not know them. For if you knew them, you would do as they do who know."

CHAP. VII. — SIMON CONFESSES HIS IGNORANCE.

And Simon said: "I confess I have not understood what you mean by the expression, 'You would do as they do who know.'" And Peter said: "If you have not understood it, then you cannot know the mind of every one; and if you are ignorant of this, then you do not know those who are worthy of the revelation. You are not the Son, for[1] the Son knows. Wherefore He reveals *Him* to whomsoever He wishes, because they are worthy." And Simon said: "Be not deceived. I know those who are worthy, and I am not the Son. And yet I have not understood what meaning you attach to the words, 'He reveals *Him* to whomsoever He wishes.' But I said that I did not understand it, not because I did not know it, but because I knew that those who were present did not understand it, in order

that you may state it more distinctly, so that they may perceive what are the reasons why we are carrying on this discussion." And Peter said: "I cannot state the matter more clearly: explain what meaning you have attached to the words." And Simon said: "There is no necessity why I should state your opinions." And Peter said: "You evidently, Simon, do not understand it, and yet you do not wish to confess, that you may not be detected in your ignorance, and thus be proved not to be the standing Son. For you hint this, though you do not wish to state it plainly; and, indeed, I who am not a prophet, but a disciple of the true Prophet, know well from the hints you have given what your wishes are. For you, though you do not understand even what is distinctly said, wish to call yourself son in opposition to us." And Simon said: "I will remove every pretext from you. I confess I do not understand what can be the meaning of the statement, 'The Son reveals *Him* to whomsoever He wishes.' State therefore what is its meaning more distinctly."

CHAP. VIII. — THE WORK OF REVELATION BELONGS TO THE SON ALONE.

And Peter said: "Since, at least in appearance, you have confessed that you do not understand it, reply to the question I put to you, and you will learn the meaning of the statement. Tell me, do you maintain that the Son, whoever he be, is just, or that he is not just?" And Simon said: "I maintain that he is most just." And Peter said: "Seeing He is just, why does He not make the revelation to all, but only to those to whom He wishes?" And Simon said: "Because, being just, he wishes to make the revelation only to the worthy." And Peter said: "Must He not therefore know the mind of each one, in order that He may make the revelation to the worthy?" And Simon said: "Of course he must." And Peter said: "With reason, therefore, has the work of giving the revelation been confined to Him alone, for He a*one knows the mind of every one; and it has not been given to you, who are not able to understand even that which is stated by us."

CHAP. IX. — HOW SIMON BEARS HIS EXPOSURE.

When Peter said this, the multitudes applauded.[2] But Simon, being thus exposed,[3] blushed through shame, and rubbing his forehead, said: "Well, then, do they declare that I, a magician, yea, even I who syllogize, am conquered by Peter? It is not so. But if one should syllogize, though carried away and conquered, he still re-

---

[1] The Greek has "but."

[2] [The remainder of the Homily is without a close parallel in the *Recognitions*. — R.]
[3] Lit., "caught in the act."

tains the truth that is in him. For the weakness in the defender is not identical with the truth in the conquered man.[1] But I assure you that I have judged all those who are bystanders worthy to know the unrevealed Father. Wherefore, because I publicly reveal him to them, you yourself, through envy, are angry with me who wish to confer a benefit on them."

CHAP. X. — PETER'S REPLY TO SIMON.

And Peter said : " Since you have thus spoken to please the multitudes who are present, I shall speak to them, not to please them, but to tell them the truth. Tell me how you know all those who are present to be worthy, when not even one of them agreed with your exposition of the subject ; for the giving of applause to me in opposition to you is not the act of those who agree with you, but of those who agree with me, to whom they gave the applause for having spoken the truth. But since God, who is just, judges the mind of each one — a doctrine which you affirm to be true — He would not have wished this to be given through the left hand to those on the right hand, exactly as the man who receives anything from a robber is himself guilty. So that, on this account, He did not wish them to receive what is brought by you ; but they are to receive the revelation through the Son, who has been set apart for this work. For to whom is it reasonable that the Father should give a revelation, but to His only Son, because He knows Him to be worthy of such a revelation ? And so this is a matter which one cannot teach or be taught, but it must be revealed by the ineffable hand to him who is worthy to know it."

CHAP. XI. — SIMON PROFESSES TO UTTER HIS REAL SENTIMENTS.

And Simon said : " It contributes much to victory, if the man who wars uses his own weapons ; for what one loves he can in real earnest defend, and that which is defended with genuine earnestness has no ordinary power in it. Wherefore in future I shall lay before you my real opinions. I maintain that there is some unrevealed power, unknown to all, even to the Creator himself, as Jesus himself has also declared, though he did not know what he said. For when one talks a great deal he sometimes hits

the truth, not knowing what he is saying. I am referring to the statement which he uttered, ' No one knows the Father.' " And Peter said : " Do not any longer profess that you know His doctrines. And Simon said : " I do not profess to believe his doctrines ; but I am discussing points in which he was by accident right." And Peter said : " Not to give you any pretext for escape, I shall carry on the discussion with you in the way you wish. At the same time, I call all to witness that you do not yet believe the statement which you just now made. For I know your opinions. And in order that you may not imagine that I am not speaking the truth, I shall expound your opinions, that you may know that you are discussing with one who is well acquainted with them.

CHAP. XII. — SIMON'S OPINIONS EXPOUNDED BY PETER.

" We, Simon, do not assert that from the great power, which is also called the dominant [2] power, two angels were sent forth, the one to create the world, the other to give the law ; nor that each one when he came proclaimed himself, on account of what he had done, as the sole creator ; nor that there is one who stands, will stand, and is opposed.[3] Learn how you disbelieve even in respect to this subject. If you say that there is an unrevealed power, that power is full of ignorance. For it did not foreknow the ingratitude of the angels who were sent by it." And Simon became exceedingly angry with Peter for saying this, and interrupted his discourse, saying : " What nonsense is this you speak, you daring and most impudent of men, revealing plainly before the multitudes the secret doctrines, so that they can be easily learned ? " And Peter said : " Why do you grudge that the present audience should receive benefit ? " And Simon said : " Do you then allow that such knowledge is a benefit ? " And Peter said : " I allow it : for the knowledge of a false doctrine is beneficial, inasmuch as you do not fall into it because of ignorance." And Simon said : " You are evidently not able to reply to the propositions I laid before you. I maintain that even your teacher affirms that there is some Father unrevealed.

CHAP. XIII. — PETER'S EXPLANATION OF THE PASSAGE.

And Peter said : " I shall reply to that which you wish me to speak of, — namely, the passage, ' No one knows the Father but the Son, nor does any one know the Son but the Father, and they to

---

[1] This passage is deemed corrupt by commentators. We have made no change in the reading of the MSS., except that of νενικημένην into νενικμένος, and perhaps even this is unnecessary. The last sentence means : " A man may overcome the weakness of his adversary ; but he does not therefore strip him of the truth, which he possesses even when he is conquered." The Latin translation of Cotelerius, with some emendations from later editors, yields this : " But they say that I, a magician, am not merely conquered by Peter, but reduced to straits by his reasonings. But not even though one be reduced to straits by reasonings, has he the truth which is in him conquered. For the weakness of the defender is not the truth of the conqueror."

[2] Κυρία.

[3] The text is corrupt. Various emendations have been proposed, none of which are satisfactory. Uhlhorn proposes, " That there is a standing one, one who will stand. You who are opposed, learn how you disbelieve, and that this subject which you say is the power unrevealed is full of ignorance." P. 328, note 1.

whom the Son may wish to reveal Him.' First, then, I am astonished that, while this statement admits of countless interpretations, you should have chosen the very dangerous position of maintaining that the statement is made in reference to the ignorance of the Creator (Demiurge), and all who are under him. For, first, the statement can apply to all the Jews who think that David is the father of Christ, and that Christ himself is his son, and do not know that He is the Son of God. Wherefore it is appropriately said, 'No one knows the Father,' since, instead of God, they affirmed David to be His father; and the additional remark, that no one knows even the Son, is quite correct, since they did not know that He was the Son. The statement also, 'to whomsoever the Son may wish to reveal Him,' is also correct; for He being the Son from the beginning, was alone appointed to give the revelation to those to whom He wishes to give it. And thus the first man (protoplast) Adam must have heard of Him; and Enoch, who pleased *God*, must have known Him; and Noah, the righteous one, must have become acquainted with Him; and Abraam His friend must have understood Him; and Isaac must have perceived Him; and Jacob, who wrestled with Him, must have believed in Him; and the revelation must have been given to all among the people who were worthy.

CHAP. XIV. — SIMON REFUTED.

"But if, as you say, it will be possible to know Him, because He is now revealed to all through Jesus,[1] are you not stating what is most unjust, when you say that these men did not know Him, who were the seven pillars of the world, and who were able to please the most just God, and that so many now from all nations who were impious know Him in every respect? Were not those who were superior to every one not deemed worthy to know Him?[2] And how can that be good which is not just? unless you wish to give the name of ' good,' not to him who does good to those who act justly, but to him who loves the unjust, even though they do not believe, and reveals to them the secrets which he would not reveal to the just. But such conduct is befitting neither in one who is good nor just, but in one who has come to hate the pious. Are not you, Simon, the standing one, who have the boldness to make these statements which never have been so made before?"

CHAP. XV. — MATTHEW XI. 25 DISCUSSED.

And Simon, being vexed at this, said: "Blame your own teacher, who said, 'I thank Thee, Lord

of heaven and earth, that what was concealed from the wise, Thou hast revealed to suckling babes.' "[3] And Peter said: "This is not the way in which the statement was made; but I shall speak of it as if it had been made in the way that has seemed good to you. Our Lord, even if He had made this statement, 'What was concealed from the wise, the Father revealed to babes,' could not even thus be thought to point out another God and Father in addition to Him who created the world. For it is possible that the concealed things of which He spoke may be those of the Creator (Demiurge) himself; because Isaiah[4] says, 'I will open my mouth in parables, and I will belch forth things concealed from the foundation of the world.' Do you allow, then, that the prophet was not ignorant of the things concealed, which Jesus says were concealed from the wise, but revealed to babes? And how was the Creator (Demiurge) ignorant of them, if his prophet Isaiah was not ignorant of them? But our Jesus did not in reality say 'what was concealed,' but He said what seems a harsher statement; for He said, ' *Thou hast concealed these things from the wise*, and[5] hast revealed them to sucking babes.' Now the word 'Thou hast concealed' implies that they had once been known to them; for the key of the kingdom of heaven, that is, the knowledge of the secrets, lay with them.

CHAP. XVI. — THESE THINGS HIDDEN JUSTLY FROM THE WISE.

"And do not say He acted impiously towards the wise in hiding these things from them. Far be such a supposition from us. For He did not act impiously; but since they hid the knowledge of the kingdom,[6] and neither themselves entered nor allowed those who wished to enter, on this account, and justly, inasmuch as they hid the ways from those who wished, were in like manner the secrets hidden from them, in order that they themselves might experience what they had done to others, and with what measure they had measured, an equal measure might be meted out to them.[7] For to him who is worthy to know, is due that which he does not know; but from him who is not worthy, even should he seem to have any thing, it is taken away,[8] even if he be wise in other matters; and it is given to the worthy, even should they be babes as far as the times of their discipleship are concerned.

[1] The text is corrupt. We have placed διὰ τὸ after εἰδέναι.
[2] Another reading is: "Were not those deemed better worthy than any one else to know Him?"

[3] Matt. xi. 25; [Luke x. 21; comp. *Recognitions*, iv. 5].
[4] The passage does not occur in Isaiah, but in Ps. lxxviii. 2. The words are quoted not from the LXX., but from the Gospel of Matthew (xiii. 35), where in some MSS. they are attributed to Isaiah. See Uhlhorn, p. 119.
[5] The words in italics are omitted in the MSS.; but the context leaves no doubt that they were once in the text.
[6] Luke xi. 52.
[7] Matt. vii. 2; [Luke vi. 38].
[8] Luke viii. 18.

CHAP. XVII. — THE WAY TO THE KINGDOM NOT CONCEALED FROM THE ISRAELITES.

"But if one shall say nothing was concealed from the sons of Israel, because it is written,[1] 'Nothing escaped thy notice, O Israel (for do not say, O Jacob, The way is hid from me),' he ought to understand that the things that belong to the kingdom had been hid from them, but that the way that leads to the kingdom, that is, the mode of life, had not been hid from them. Wherefore it is that He says, 'For say not that the way has been hid from me.' But by the way is meant the mode of life ; for Moses says,[2] 'Behold, I have set before thy face the way of life and the way of death.' And the Teacher spoke in harmony with this :[3] 'Enter ye through the strait and narrow way, through which ye shall enter into life.' And somewhere else, when one asked Him,[4] 'What shall I do to inherit eternal life?' He pointed out to him the commandments of the law.

CHAP. XVIII. — ISAIAH I. 3 EXPLAINED.

"From the circumstance that Isaiah said, in the person of God,[7] 'But Israel hath not known me, and the people hath not understood me,' it is not to be inferred that Isaiah indicated another God besides Him who is known ;[6] but he meant that the known God was in another sense unknown, because the people sinned, being ignorant of the just character of the known God, and imagined that they would not be punished by the good God. Wherefore, after he said, 'But Israel hath not known me, and the people hath not understood me,' he adds, 'Alas ! a sinful nation, a people laden with sins.' For, not being afraid, in consequence of their ignorance of His justice, as I said, they became laden with sins, supposing that He was merely good, and would not therefore punish them for their sins.

CHAP. XIX. — MISCONCEPTION OF GOD IN THE OLD TESTAMENT.

"And some sinned thus, on account of imagining that there would be no judgment[7] because of His goodness. But others took an opposite course. For, supposing the expressions of the Scriptures which are against God, and are unjust and false, to be true, they did not know His real divinity and power. Therefore, in the belief that He was ignorant and rejoiced in murder, and let off the wicked in consequence of the gifts of sacrifices ; yea, moreover, that He deceived and spake falsely, and did every thing that is unjust, they themselves did things like to what their God did, and thus sinning, asserted that they were acting piously. Wherefore it was impossible for them to change to the better, and when warned they took no heed. For they were not afraid, since they became like their God through such actions.

CHAP. XX. — SOME PARTS OF THE OLD TESTAMENT WRITTEN TO TRY US.

"But one might with good reason maintain that it was with reference to those who thought Him to be such that the statement was made, 'No one knoweth the Father but the Son, as no one knoweth even the Son, but the Father.' And reasonably. For if they had known, they would not have sinned, by trusting to the books written against God, really for the purpose of trying. But somewhere also He says, wishing to exhibit the cause of their error more distinctly to them, 'On this account ye do err, not knowing the true things of the Scriptures, on which account ye are ignorant also of the power of God.'[8] Wherefore every man who wishes to be saved must become, as the Teacher said, a judge of the books written to try us. For thus He spake : 'Become experienced bankers.' Now the need of bankers arises from the circumstance that the spurious is mixed up with the genuine."

CHAP. XXI. — SIMON'S ASTONISHMENT AT PETER'S TREATMENT OF THE SCRIPTURES.

When Peter said this, Simon pretended to be utterly astonished at what was said in regard to the Scriptures ; and as if in great agitation, he said : " Far be it from me, and those who love me, to listen to your discourses. And, indeed, as long as I did not know that you held these opinions in regard to the Scriptures, I endured you, and discussed with you ; but now I retire. Indeed, I ought at the first to have withdrawn, because I heard you say, ' I, for my part, believe no one who says anything against Him who created the world, neither angels, nor prophets, nor Scriptures, nor priests, nor teachers, nor any one else, even though one should work signs and miracles, even though he should lighten brilliantly in the air, or should make a revelation through visions or through dreams.' Who, then, can succeed in changing your mind, whether well or ill, so as that you should hold opinions different from what you have determined on, seeing that you abide so persistently and immoveably in your own decision?"

[1] Isa. xl. 26, 27.
[2] Deut. xxx. 15.
[3] Matt. vii. 13, 14.
[4] Luke xviii. 18, ff.; Matt. xix. 16, ff.
[5] Isa. i. 3.
[6] Cotelerius' MS. inserts " the Creator " (Demiurge).
[7] We have adopted the Latin translation here, as giving the meaning which was intended by the writer; but the Greek will scarcely admit of such a translation. Probably the text is corrupt, or something is omitted. The literal translation is, " in consequence of the unjudging supposition on account of the goodness."

[8] Mark xii. 24.

CHAP. XXII. — PETER WORSHIPS ONE GOD.

When Simon said this, and was going to depart, Peter said : " Listen to this one other remark, and then go where you like." Whereupon Simon turned back and remained, and Peter said : " I know how you were then astonished when you heard me say, 'Whosoever says anything whatever against God who created the world, I do not believe him.' But listen now to something additional, and greater than this. If God who created the world has in reality such a character as the Scriptures assign Him, and if somehow or other He is incomparably wicked, more wicked [1] than either the Scriptures were able to represent Him, or any other can even conceive Him to be, nevertheless [2] I shall not give up worshipping Him alone, and doing His will. For I wish you to know and to be convinced, that he who has not affection for his own Creator, can never have it towards another. And if he has it towards another, he has it contrary to nature, and he is ignorant that he has this passion for the unjust from the evil one. Nor will he be able to retain even it stedfastly. And, indeed, if there is another above the Creator (Demiurge), he will welcome me, since he is good, all the more that I love my own Father ; and he will not welcome you, as he knows that you have abandoned your own natural Creator : for I do not call Him Father, influenced by a greater hope, and not caring for what is reasonable. Thus, even if you find one who is superior to Him, he knows that you will one day abandon him ; and the more

so that he has not been your father, since you have abandoned Him who was really your Father.

CHAP. XXIII. — SIMON RETIRES.

" But you will say, ' He knows that there is no other above him, and on this account he cannot be abandoned.' Thanks, then, to there being no other ; but He knows that the state of your mind is one inclined to ingratitude. But if, knowing you to be ungrateful, He welcomes you, and knowing me to be grateful, He does not receive me, He is inconsiderate, according to your own assertion, and does not act reasonably. And thus, Simon, you are not aware that you are the servant of wickedness." And Simon answered : " Whence, then, has evil arisen ? tell us." And Peter said : " Since to-day you were the first to go out, and you declared that you would not in future listen to me as being a blasphemer, come to-morrow, if indeed you wish to learn, and I shall explain the matter to you, and I will permit you to ask me any questions you like, without any dispute." And Simon said : " I shall do as shall seem good to me." And saying this, he went away. Now, none of those who entered along with him went out along with him ; but, falling at Peter's feet, they begged that they might be pardoned for having been carried away with Simon, and on repenting, to be welcomed. But Peter, admitting those persons who repented, and the rest of the multitudes, laid his hands upon them, praying, and healing those who were sick amongst them ; and thus dismissing them, he urged them to return early about dawn. And saying this, and going in with his intimate friends, he made the usual preparations for immediate repose, for it was now evening.

---

[1] " Incomparably wicked, more wicked than ; " literally, " incomparably wicked as."
[2] The Greek has ὁμοίως, " in like manner." We have translated ὅμως.

HOMILY XIX.

CHAP. I. — SIMON UNDERTAKES TO PROVE THAT THE CREATOR OF THE WORLD IS NOT BLAMELESS.

THE next day Peter came forth earlier than usual ; and seeing Simon with many others waiting for him, he saluted the multitude, and began to discourse. But no sooner did he begin than Simon interrupted him, and said : " Pass by these long introductions of yours, and answer directly the questions I put to you. Since I perceive that you [1] (as I know from what I heard at the

beginning, that you have no other purpose, than by every contrivance to show that the Creator himself is alone the blameless God), — since, as I said, I perceive that you have such a decided desire to maintain this, that you venture to declare to be false some portions of the Scriptures that clearly speak against him, for this reason I have determined to-day to prove that it is impossible that he, being the Creator of all, should be blameless. But this proof I can now begin, if you reply to the questions which I put to you.

---

[1] This passage is corrupt. Wieseler has proposed to amend it by bold transposition of the clauses. We make one slight alteration in the text.

CHAP. II. — THE EXISTENCE OF THE DEVIL AFFIRMED.

"Do you maintain that there is any prince of evil or not?[1] For if you say that there is not, I can prove to you from many statements, and those too of your teacher, that there is; but if you honestly allow that the evil one exists, then I shall speak in accordance with this belief." And Peter said: "It is impossible for me to deny the assertion of my Teacher. Wherefore I allow that the evil one exists, because my Teacher, who spoke the truth in all things, has frequently asserted that he exists. For instance, then, he acknowledges that he conversed with Him, and tempted Him for forty days.[2] And I know that He has said somewhere else, 'If Satan casts out Satan, he is divided against himself: how then is his kingdom to stand?'[3] And He pointed out that He saw the evil one like lightning falling down from heaven.[4] And elsewhere He said, 'He who sowed the bad seed is the devil.'[5] And again, 'Give no pretext to the evil one.' Moreover, in giving advice, He said, 'Let your yea be yea, and your nay nay; for what is more than these is of the evil one.'[7] Also, in the prayer which He delivered to us, we have it said, 'Deliver us from the evil one.'[8] And in another place, He promised that He would say to those who are impious, 'Go ye into outer darkness, which the Father prepared for the devil and his angels.'[9] And not to prolong this statement further, I know that my Teacher often said that there is an evil one. Wherefore I also agree in thinking that he exists. If, then, in future you have anything to say in accordance with this belief, say it, as you promised."

CHAP. III. — PETER REFUSES TO DISCUSS CERTAIN QUESTIONS IN REGARD TO THE DEVIL.

And Simon said: "Since, then, you have honestly confessed, on the testimony of the Scriptures, that the evil one exists, state to us how he has come into existence, if indeed he has come into existence, and by whom, and why."[10] And Peter said: "Pardon me, Simon, if I do not dare to affirm what has not been written. But if you say that it has been written, prove it. But if, since it has not been written, you cannot prove it, why should we run risk in stating our opinions in regard to what has not been written?

For if we discourse too daringly in regard to God, it is either because we do not believe that we shall be judged, or that we shall be judged only in respect to that which we do, but not also in regard to what we believe and speak."[11] But Simon, understanding that Peter referred to his own madness, said: "Permit me to run the risk; but do not you make what you assert to be blasphemy a pretext for retiring. For I perceive that you wish to withdraw, in order that you may escape refutation before the masses, sometimes as if you were afraid to listen to blasphemies, and at other times by maintaining that, as nothing has been written as to how, and by whom, and why the evil one came into existence, we ought not to dare to assert more than the Scripture. Wherefore also as a pious man you affirm this only, that he exists. But by these contrivances you deceive yourself, not knowing that, if it is blasphemy to inquire accurately regarding the evil one, the blame rests with me, the accuser, and not with you, the defender of God. And if the subject inquired into is not in Scripture,[12] and on this account you do not wish to inquire into it, there are some satisfactory methods which can prove to you what is sought not less effectively than the Scriptures. For instance, must it not be the case that the evil one, who you assert exists, is either originated or unoriginated?"[13]

CHAP. IV. — SUPPOSITIONS IN REGARD TO THE DEVIL'S ORIGIN.

And Peter said: "It must be so." And Simon: "Therefore, if he is originated, he has been made by that very God who made all things, being either born as an animal, or sent forth substantially, and resulting from an external mixture of elements. For either[14] the matter, being living or lifeless, from which he was made was outside of Him,[15] or he came into being through God Himself, or through his own self, or he resulted from things non-existent, or he is a mere relative thing, or he always existed. Having thus, as I think, clearly pointed out all the possible ways by which we may find him, in going along some one of these we must find him. We must therefore go along each one of these in search of his origin; and when we find him who is his author, we must perceive that he is to blame. Or how does the matter seem to you?"

---

[1] [Compare with this discussion respecting the origin of the evil one, *Recognitions*, ix. 55, 56; x. 3, etc. In *Recognitions*, iii. 15–23, the existence of evil is discussed. — R.]
[2] Mark i. 13.
[3] Matt. xii. 26.
[4] Luke x. 18.
[5] Matt. xiii. 39.
[6] This passage is not found in the New Testament. It resembles Eph. iv. 27.
[7] Matt. v. 37; Jas. v. 12.
[8] Matt. vi. 13.
[9] Matt. xxv. 41.
[10] [Comp. Homily XX. 8, 9. — R.]

[11] This passage is probably corrupt. We have adopted the readings of Cotelerius — ἤ, ἤ, instead of εἰ and μή.
[12] Lit., "unwritten."
[13] The words γενητός and ἀγένητος are difficult to translate. The first means one who has somehow or other come into being; the second, one who has never *come* into being; but has always been. The MSS. confound γενητός with γεννητός, begotten, and ἀγένητος with ἀγέννητος, unbegotten.
[14] We have changed εἰ into ἤ.
[15] By "Him" is understood God, though it may mean the devil.

CHAP. V. — GOD NOT DESERVING OF BLAME IN PERMITTING THE EXISTENCE OF THE DEVIL.

And Peter said : " It is my opinion that, even if it be evident that he was made by God, the Creator who made him should not be blamed ; for it might perchance be found that the service he performs [1] was an absolute necessity. But if, on the other hand, it should be proved that he was not created, inasmuch as he existed for ever, not even is the Creator to be blamed in this respect, since He is better than all *others*, even if He has not been able to put an end to a being who had no beginning, because his nature did not admit of it ; or if, being able, He does not make away with him, deeming it unjust to put an end to that which did not receive a beginning, and pardoning that which was by nature wicked, because he could not have become anything else, even if he were to wish to do so.[2] But if, wishing to do good, He is not able, even in this case He is good in that He has the will, though He has not the power ; and while He has not the power, He is yet the most powerful of all, in that the power is not left to another. But if there is some other that is able, and yet does not accomplish it, it must be allowed that, in so far as, being able, he does not accomplish it, he is wicked in not putting an end to him, as if he took pleasure in the deeds done by him. But if not even he is able, then he is better who, though unable, is yet not unwilling to benefit us according to his ability."

CHAP. VI. — PETER ACCUSES SIMON OF BEING WORSE THAN THE DEVIL.

And Simon said : " When you have discussed all the subjects which I have laid before you, I shall show you the cause of evil. Then I shall also reply to what you have now said, and prove that that God whom you affirm to be blameless is blameable." And Peter said : " Since I perceive from what you say at the commencement that you are striving after nothing else than to subject God, as being the author of evil, to blame, I have resolved to go along with you all the ways you like, and to prove that God is entirely free from blame." And Simon said : " You say this as loving God, whom you suppose you know ; but you are not right." And Peter said : " But you, as being wicked, and hating God whom you have not known, utter blasphemous words." And Simon said : " Remember that you have likened me to the author of evil." And Peter said : " I confess it, I was wrong in comparing you to the evil one ; for I was compelled to do so, because I have not

found one who is your equal, or worse than you. For this reason I likened you to the evil one ; for you happen to be much more wicked than the author of evil. For no one can prove that the evil one spoke against God ; but all of us who are present see you speaking daringly against Him." And Simon said : " He who seeks the truth ought not to gratify any one in any respect contrary to what is really true. For why does he make the inquiry at all? Why, I ask? for I am not also able, laying aside the accurate investigation of things, to spend all my time in the praise of that God whom I do not know." [3]

CHAP. VII. — PETER SUSPECTS SIMON OF NOT BELIEVING EVEN IN A GOD.

And Peter said : " You are not so blessed as to praise Him, nor indeed can you do such a good deed as this ; for then you would be full of Him. For thus said our Teacher, who always spoke the truth : ' Out of the abundance of the heart the mouth speaketh.' [4] Whence you, abounding in evil purposes, through ignorance speak against the only good God. And not yet suffering what you deserve to suffer for the words which you have dared to utter,[5] you either imagine that there will be no judgment, or perchance you think that there is not even a God. Whence, not comprehending such long-suffering as His, you are moving on to still greater madness." And Simon said : " Do not imagine that you will frighten me into not investigating the truth of your examples. For I am so eager for the truth, that for its sake I will not shrink from undergoing danger. If, then, you have anything to say in regard to the propositions made by me at the commencement, say it now."

CHAP. VIII. — PETER UNDERTAKES TO DISCUSS THE DEVIL'S ORIGIN.

And Peter said : " Since you compel us, after we have made accurate investigations into the contrivances of God, to venture to state them, and that, too, to men who are not able to comprehend thoroughly the contrivances of their fellow-men, for the sake at least of those who are present, I, instead of remaining silent — a course which would be most pious — shall discuss the subjects of which you wish me to speak. I agree with you in believing that there is a prince of evil, of whose origin the Scripture has ventured to say nothing either true or false. But let us follow out the inquiry in many ways, as to how he has come into existence, if it is the fact that he has come into existence ; and of the

---

[1] Lit., " his usefulness was most necessary of all."
[2] This sentence is obscure in the original. We have, with Wieseler, read ἐπεί, omitting ἀρχῇ. Instead of supplying μή, we have turned συγγνῶναι into the participle.

[3] We have adopted the pointing of Wieseler.
[4] Matt. xii. 34.
[5] We have altered the punctuation. Editors connect this clause with the previous sentence, and change ἤ of the MS. into εἰ.

opinions which present themselves, let us select that which is most reverential, since, in the case of probable opinions, that one is assumed with confidence which *is based on the principle* that we ought to attribute to God that which is more reverential; and all the more so, if, when all other suppositions are removed, there still remains one which is adequate and involves less danger.[1] But I promise you, before I proceed with the investigation, that every method in the investigation can show that God alone is blameless.

CHAP. IX. — THEORIES IN REGARD TO THE ORIGIN OF THE DEVIL.

"But, as you said, if the evil one is created, either he has been begotten as an animal, or he has been sent forth substantially by Him,[2] or he has been compounded externally, or his will has arisen through composition; or it happened that he came into existence from things non-existent, without composition and the will of God; or he has been made by God from that which in no manner and nowhere exists; or the matter, being lifeless or living, from which he has arisen was outside of God; or he fashioned himself, or he was made by God, or he is a relative thing, or he ever existed: for we cannot say that he does not exist, since we have agreed in thinking that he does exist." And Simon said: "Well have you distinguished all the methods of accounting for his existence in a summary manner. Now it is my part to examine these various ideas, and to show that the Creator is blameable. But it is your business to prove, as you promised, that he is free from all blame. But I wonder if you will be able. For, first, if the devil has been begotten from God as an animal, the vice which is his is accordingly the same as that of him who sends him forth." And Peter said: "Not at all. For we see many men who are good the fathers of wicked children, and others who are wicked the fathers of good children, and others again who are wicked producing both good *and wicked*[3] children, and others who are good having both wicked and good children. For instance, the first man who was created produced the unrighteous Cain and the righteous Abel." To this Simon said: "You are acting foolishly, in using human examples when dis-

coursing about God." And Peter said: "Speak you, then, to us about God without using human examples, and yet so that what you say can be understood; but you are not able to do so.

CHAP. X. — THE ABSOLUTE GOD ENTIRELY INCOMPREHENSIBLE BY MAN.

"For instance, then, what did you say in the beginning? If the wicked one has been begotten of God, being of the same substance as He, then God is wicked. But when I showed you, from the example which you yourself adduced, that wicked beings come from good, and good from wicked, you did not admit the argument, for you said that the example was a human one. Wherefore I now do not admit that the term 'being begotten'[4] can be used with reference to God; for it is characteristic of man, and not of God, to beget. Not only so; but God cannot be good or evil, just or unjust. Nor indeed can He have intelligence, or life, or any of the other attributes which can exist in man; for all these are peculiar to man. And if we must not, in our investigations in regard to God, give Him the good attributes which belong to man, it is not possible for us to have any thought or make any statement in regard to God; but all we can do is to investigate one point alone, — namely, what is His will which He has Himself allowed us to apprehend, in order that, being judged, we might be without excuse in regard to those laws which we have not observed, though we knew them."

CHAP. XI. — THE APPLICATION OF THE ATTRIBUTES OF MAN TO GOD.

And Simon, hearing this, said: "You will not force me through shame to remain silent in regard to His substance, and to inquire into His will alone. For it is possible both to think and to speak of His substance. I mean from the good attributes that belong to man. For instance, life and death are attributes of man; but death is not an attribute of God, but life, and eternal life. Furthermore, men may be both evil and good; but God can be only incomparably good. And, not to prolong the subject too much, the better attributes of man are eternal attributes of God." And Peter said: "Tell me, Simon, is it an attribute of man to beget evil and good, and to do evil and good?" And Simon said: "It is." And Peter said: "Since you made this assertion, we must assign the better attributes of man to God; and so, while men beget evil and good, God can beget good only; and while men do evil and good, God rejoices only in doing good. Thus, with regard

---

[1] This sentence is regarded as corrupt by Wieseler. We have retained the reading of the Paris MS., ὁ, and understand λαμβάνεται after it. Δέ would naturally be inserted after ταύτῃ, but it is not necessary. Καθαρθεισῶν is translated in the Latin *purgatis*, which may mean the same as in our translation if we take it in the sense of "washed away;" but καθαιρεθεισῶν would be a better reading. The translation of Cotelerius gives, " Since this is reasonably assumed with firmness, — namely, that it is right to give to God," etc.

[2] The text here is evidently corrupt in many places. If the reading "by him" is to be retained, we must suppose, with Wieseler, that "by God" is omitted in the previous clause. Probably it should be, "by himself."

[3] "And bad" is not in the MSS., but is required by the context.

[4] The text is corrupt here. Literally it is, "I do not admit that God had been begotten."

to God, we must either not predicate any of the attributes of man and be silent, or it is reasonable that we should assign the best of the good attributes to Him. And thus He alone is the cause of all good things."

CHAP. XII. — GOD PRODUCED THE WICKED ONE, BUT NOT EVIL.

And Simon said: "If, then, God is the cause only of what is good, what else can we think than that some other principle begot the evil one;[1] or is evil unbegotten?" And Peter said: "No other power begot the wicked one, nor is evil unbegotten, as I shall show in the conclusion; for now my object is to prove, as I promised in the commencement, that God is blameless in every[2] respect. We have granted, then, that God possesses in an incomparable way the better attributes that belong to men. Wherefore also it is possible for Him to have been the producer of the four substances, — heat, I mean, and cold, moist and dry. These, as being at first simple and unmixed, were naturally indifferent in their desire;[3] but being produced by God, and mixed externally, they would naturally become a living being, possessing the free choice to destroy those who are evil. And thus, since all things have been begotten from Him, the wicked one is from no other source. Nor has he derived his evil from the God who has created all things (with whom it is impossible that evil should exist), because the substances were produced by Him in a state of indifference, and carefully separated from each other; and when they were externally blended through his art, there arose through volition the desire for the destruction of the evil ones. But the good cannot be destroyed by the evil that arose, even though it should wish to do so: for it exercises its power only[4] against those who sin. Ignorant, then, of the character of each,[5] he makes his attempt against him, and convicting him, he punishes him." And Simon said: "God being able to mingle the elements, and to make His mixtures so as to produce any dispositions that He may wish, why did He not make the composition of each such as that it would prefer what is good?"

CHAP. XIII. — GOD THE MAKER OF THE DEVIL.

And Peter said: "Now indeed our object is to show how and by whom the evil one came into being, since he did come into being; but we shall show if he came into being blamelessly,

when we have finished the subject now in hand. Then I shall show how and on account of what he came into being, and I shall fully convince you that his Creator is blameless.[6] We said, then, that the four substances were produced by God. And thus, through the volition of Him who mingled them, arose, as He wished, the choice of evils. For if it had arisen contrary to His determination, or from some other substance or cause, then God would not have had firmness of will: for perchance, even though He should not wish it, leaders of evil might continually arise, who would war against His wishes. But it is impossible that this should be the case. For no living being, and especially one capable of giving guidance, can arise from accident: for everything that is produced must be produced by some one."

CHAP. XIV. — IS MATTER ETERNAL?

And Simon said: "But what if matter, being coeval with Him, and possessing equal power, produces as His foe leaders who hinder His wishes?" And Peter said: "If matter is eternal, then it is the foe of no one: for that which exists for ever is impassible, and what is impassible is blessed; but what is blessed cannot be receptive of hatred, since, on account of its eternal creation,[7] it does not fear that it will be deprived of anything. But how does not matter rather love the Creator, when[8] it evidently sends forth its fruits to nourish all who are made by Him? And how does it not fear Him as superior, as trembling through earthquakes it confesses, and as, though its billows ran high, yet, when the Teacher was sailing on it and commanded a calm, it immediately obeyed and became still?[9] What! did not the demons go out through fear and respect for Him, and others of them desired to enter into swine; but they first entreated Him before going, plainly because they had no power to enter even into swine without His permission?"[10]

CHAP. XV. — SIN THE CAUSE OF EVIL.

And Simon said: "But what if, being lifeless, it possesses a nature capable of producing what is evil and what is good?" And Peter said: "According to this statement, it is neither good nor evil, because it does not act by free choice, being lifeless and insensible. Wherefore it is possible to perceive distinctly in this matter, how, being lifeless, it produces as if it were liv-

---

[1] "Evil" is not in the MSS. It is inserted from the next sentence.
[2] "Every" is inserted by a conjecture of Schwegler's.
[3] Lit., "naturally had their desire towards neither."
[4] The MSS. have "by law." We have changed νόμῳ into μόνον.
[5] The devil is plainly meant by the "he."

[6] This passage is evidently corrupt. But it is not easy to amend it.
[7] Probably "eternity" should be read, instead of "eternal creation."
[8] At this word the MS. of Cotelerius breaks off; and we have the rest only in the Ottobonian MS., first edited by Dressel.
[9] Matt. xxvii. 51, viii. 24–26.
[10] Matt. viii. 31.

ing ; [1] and being insensible, it yet plainly fashions artistic shapes both in animals and plants." And Simon said : "What ! if God Himself gave it life, is not He, then, the cause of the evils which it produces ? " And Peter said : " If God gave it life according to His own will, then it is His Spirit that produces it, and no longer is it anything hostile to God, or of equal power with Him ; or it is impossible that everything made by Him is made according as He wishes. But you will say, He Himself is the cause of evil, since He Himself produces the evils through it. What sort, then, are the evils of which you speak ? Poisonous serpents and deadly plants, or demons, or any other of those things that can disturb men ? — which things would not have been injurious had not man sinned, for which reason [2] death came in. For if man were sinless, the poison of serpents would have no effect, nor the activities of injurious plants, nor would there be the disturbances of demons, nor would man naturally have any other suffering ; but losing his immortality on account of his sin, he has become, as I said, capable of every suffering. But if you say, Why, then, was the nature of man made at the beginning capable of death ? I tell you, because of free-will ; for if we were not capable of death, we could not, as being immortal, be punished on account of our voluntary sin.[3] And thus, on account of our freedom from suffering, righteousness would be still more weakened if we were wicked by choice ; for those who should have evil purposes could not be punished, on account of their being incapable of suffering.[4]

CHAP. XVI. — WHY THE WICKED ONE IS ENTRUSTED WITH POWER.

And Simon said to this : " I have one thing more to say in regard to the wicked one. Assuredly, since God made him out of nothing, he is in this respect wicked,[5] especially since he was able to make him good, by giving him at his creation a nature in no way capable of selecting wickedness." And Peter said : " The statement that He created him out of nothing, with a power of choice, is like the statement we have made above, that, having made such a constitution as can rejoice in evils, He Himself appears to be the cause of what took place. But since there is one explanation of both statements, we shall show afterwards why it was that He made him rejoice in the destruction of the wicked." And Simon said : " If he made the angels also

voluntary agents, and the wicked one departed from a state of righteousness, why has he been honoured with a post of command ? Is it not plain that he who thus honoured him takes pleasure in the wicked, in that he has thus honoured him ? " [6] And Peter said : " If God set him by law, when he rebelled, to rule over those who were like him, ordering him to inflict punishment on those who sin, He is not unjust. But if it be the case that He has honoured him even after his revolt, He who honoured him saw beforehand his usefulness ; for the honour is temporary, and it is right that the wicked should be ruled by the wicked one, and that sinners should be punished by him."

CHAP. XVII. — THE DEVIL HAS NOT EQUAL POWER WITH GOD.

And Simon said : " If, then, he exists for ever, is not the fact of the sole government *of God* thus destroyed, since there is another power, namely, that concerned with matter, which rules along with Him ? " And Peter said : " If they are different in their substances, they are different also in their powers, and the superior rules the inferior. But if they are of the same substance, then they are equal in power, and they are in like manner good or bad. But it is plain that they are not equal in power ; for the Creator put matter into that shape of a world into which He willed to put it. Is it then at all possible to maintain that it always existed, being a substance ; and is not matter, as it were, the storehouse of God ? For it is not possible to maintain that there was a time [7] when God possessed nothing, but He always was the only ruler of it. Wherefore also He is an eternal sole ruler ; [8] and on this account it would justly be said to belong to Him who exists, and rules, and is *eternal*." [9] And Simon said : " What then ? Did the wicked one make himself ? And was God good in such a way, that, knowing he would be the cause of evil, he yet did not destroy him at his origination, when he could have been destroyed, as not yet being perfectly made ? For if he came into being suddenly and complete, then on that account [10] he is at war with the Creator, as having come suddenly into being, possessed of equal power with him."

CHAP. XVIII. — IS THE DEVIL A RELATION ?

And Peter said : " What you state is impossible ; for if he came into existence by degrees,

---

[1] Possibly the right reading is ἐμψύχους, " it produces living beings."
[2] Or, " on whose account."
[3] [Comp. xi. 8; *Recognitions*, iii. 21, 26, etc. — R.]
[4] The text is corrupt.
[5] The MS. reads: " In this respect he who made him is wicked, who gave existence to what was non-existent."

[6] The Greek is either ungrammatical or corrupt, but the sense is evident.
[7] This passage is supposed by most to be defective, and various words have been suggested to supply the lacuna.
[8] Or, " monarch." But only two letters of the word are in the MS.; the rest is filled in by conjecture.
[9] Supplied by conjecture.
[10] Three words are struck out of the text of the MS. by all editors, as being a repetition.

He could have cut him off as a foe by His own free choice. And knowing beforehand that he was coming into existence, He would not have allowed him as a good, had He not known that by reason of him what was useful was being brought into existence.[1] And he could not have come into existence suddenly, complete, of his own power. For he who did not exist could not fashion himself; and he neither could become complete out of nothing, nor could any one justly say that he had substance,[2] so as always to be equal in power if he were begotten." And Simon said: "Is he then a mere relation, and in this way wicked?[3] — being injurious, as water is injurious to fire, but good for the seasonably thirsty land; as iron is good for the cultivation of the land, but bad for murders; and lust is not evil in respect of marriage, but bad in respect of adultery; as murder is an evil, but good for the murderer so far as his purpose is concerned; and cheating is an evil, but pleasant to the man who cheats; and other things of a like character are good and bad in like manner. In this way, neither is evil evil, nor good good; for the one produces the other. For does not that which seems to be done injuriously rejoice the doer, but punish the sufferer? And though it seems unjust that a man should, out of self-love, gratify himself by every means in his power, to whom, on the other hand, does it not seem unjust that a man should suffer severe punishments at the hand of a just judge for having loved himself?"

CHAP. XIX. — SOME ACTIONS REALLY WICKED.

And Peter said: "A man ought to punish himself through self-restraint,[4] when his lust wishes to hurry on to the injury of another, knowing that[5] the wicked one can destroy the wicked, for he has received power over them from the beginning. And not yet is this an evil to those who have done evil; but that their souls should remain punished after the destruction, you are right in thinking to be really harsh, though the man who has been fore-ordained for evil should say that it is right.[6] Wherefore, as I said, we ought to avoid doing injury[7] to another for the sake of a shortlived pleasure, that we may not involve ourselves in eternal punishment for the sake of a little pleasure." And Simon said:

"Is it the case, then, that there is nothing either bad or good by nature, but the difference arises through law and custom? For is it not[8] the the habit of the Persians to marry their own mothers, sisters and daughters, while marriage with other women is prohibited[9] as most barbarous? Wherefore, if it is not settled what things are evil, it is not possible for all to look forward to the judgment of God." And Peter said: "This cannot hold; for it is plain to all that cohabitation with mothers is abominable, even though the Persians, who are a mere fraction of the whole, should under the effects of a bad custom fail to see the iniquity of their abominable conduct. Thus also the Britons publicly cohabit in the sight of all, and are not ashamed; and some men eat the flesh of others, and feel no disgust; and others eat the flesh of dogs; and others practice other unmentionable deeds. Thus, then, we ought not to form our judgments with a perception which through habit has been perverted from its natural action. For to be murdered is an evil, even if all were to deny it; for no one wishes to suffer it himself, and in the case of theft[10] no one rejoices at his own punishment. If, then, no one[11] were at all ever to confess that these are sins, it is right even then to look forward of necessity to a judgment in regard to sins." When Peter said this, Simon answered: "Does this, then, seem to you to be the truth in regard to the wicked one? Tell me."

CHAP. XX. — PAIN AND DEATH THE RESULT OF SIN.

And Peter said: "We remember that our Lord and Teacher, commanding us, said, 'Keep the mysteries for me and the sons of my house.' Wherefore also He explained to His disciples privately the mysteries of the kingdom of heaven.[12] But to you who do battle with us, and examine into nothing else but our statements, whether they be true or false, it would be impious to state the hidden truths. But that none of the bystanders may imagine that I am contriving excuses,[13] because I am unable to reply to the assertions made by you, I shall answer you by first putting the question, If there had been a state of painlessness, what is the meaning of the statement, 'The evil one was?'" And Simon said: "The words have no meaning." And Peter: "Is then evil the same as pain and death?" And Simon: "It seems so." And Peter said: "Evil, then, does not exist always, yea, it can-

---

[1] The editors punctuate differently, thus: "And knowing beforehand that he was becoming not good, He would not have allowed him, unless He knew that he would be useful to Himself." We suppose the reference in the text to be to Gen. i. 31.

[2] Or, "self-subsistence." We have supposed a transposition of the words in the text. The text is without doubt corrupt.

[3] We have adopted an emendation of Lagarde's.

[4] Dressel translates *viriliter*, "manfully."

[5] This word is supplied by conjecture.

[6] This passage is hopelessly corrupt. We have changed δικαίως into δικαίοις, the verb, and τὸν προδιωρισμένον into τοῦ προδιωρισμένου.

[7] We have adopted Wieseler's emendation of ἄδικον into ἀδικεῖν.

[8] This is a conjectural filling up of a blank.

[9] This is partly conjecture, to fill up a blank.

[10] The text is likely corrupt.

[11] Uhlhorn changed οὖν ἑνός into οὐδενός. We have changed καὶ τρίτην into καὶ τότε τήν. Various emendations have been proposed.

[12] Mark iv. 34. [More probably, Matt. xiii. 11. — R.]

[13] We have adopted an emendation of Wieseler's.

not even exist at all substantially; for pain and death belong to the class of accidents, neither of which can co-exist with abiding strength. For what is pain but the interruption of harmony? And what is death but the separation of soul from body? There is therefore no pain when there is harmony. For death does not even at all belong to those things which substantially exist: for death is nothing, as I said, but the separation of soul from body; and when this takes place, the body, which is by nature incapable of sensation, is dissolved; but the soul, being capable of sensation, remains in life and exists substantially. Hence, when there is harmony there is no pain, no death, no, not even deadly plants nor poisonous reptiles, nor anything of such a nature that its end is death. And hence, where immortality reigns, all things will appear to have been made with reason. And this will be the case when, on account of righteousness, man becomes immortal through the prevalence of the peaceful reign of Christ, when his composition will be so well arranged as not *to give rise*[1] to sharp impulses; and his knowledge, moreover, will be unerring, so as that he shall not *mistake*[1] evil for good; and he will suffer no pain, so that he will not be mortal."[2]

CHAP. XXI. — THE USES OF LUST, ANGER, GRIEF.

And Simon said:[3] "You were right in saying this; but in the present world does not man seem to you to be capable of every kind of affection,—as, for instance, of lust, anger, grief, and the like?" And Peter said: "Yes, these belong to the things that are accidental, not to those that always exist, and it will be found that they now occur with advantage to the soul. For lust has, by the will of Him who created all things well, been made to arise within the living being, that, led by it to intercourse, he may increase humanity, from a selection of which a multitude of superior beings arise who are fit for eternal life. But if it were not for lust, no one would trouble himself with intercourse with his wife; but now, for the sake of pleasure, and, as it were, gratifying himself, man carries out His will. Now, if a man uses lust for lawful marriage, he does not act impiously; but if he rushes to adultery, he acts impiously, and he is punished because he makes a bad use of a good ordinance. And in the same way, anger has been made by God to be lighted up naturally within us, in order that we may be induced by it to ward off injuries. Yet if any one indulges it without restraint, he acts unjustly; but if he uses it within due bounds, he does what is right. Moreover, we

are capable of grief, that we may be moved with sympathy at the death of relatives, of a wife, or children, or brothers, or parents, or friends, or some others, since, if we were not capable of sympathy, we should be inhuman. In like manner, all the other affections will be found to be adapted for us, if at least the reason for their existence[4] be considered."

CHAP. XXII. — SINS OF IGNORANCE.

And Simon: "Why is it, then, that some die prematurely, and periodical diseases arise; and that there are, moreover, attacks of demons, and of madness, and all other kinds of afflictions which can greatly punish?" And Peter said: "Because men, following their own pleasure in all things, cohabit without observing the proper times; and thus the deposition of seed, taking place unseasonably, naturally produces a multitude of evils. For they ought to reflect, that as a season has been fixed suitable for planting and sowing,[5] so days have been appointed as appropriate for cohabitation, which are carefully to be observed. Accordingly some one well instructed in the doctrines taught by Moses, finding fault with the people for their sins, called them sons of the new moons and the sabbaths.[6] Yet in the beginning of the world men lived long, and had no diseases. But when through carelessness they neglected the observation of the proper times, then the sons in succession cohabiting through ignorance at times when[7] they ought not, place their children under innumerable afflictions. Whence our Teacher, when we inquired of Him[8] in regard to the man who was blind from his birth, and recovered his sight, if this man sinned, or his parents, that he should be born blind, answered, 'Neither did he sin at all, nor his parents, but that the power of God might be made manifest through him in healing the sins of ignorance.'[9] And, in truth, such afflictions arise because of ignorance; as, for instance, by not knowing when one ought to cohabit with his wife, as if she be pure from her discharge. Now the afflictions which you mentioned before are the result of ignorance, and not, assuredly, of any wickedness that has been perpetrated. Moreover, give me the man who sins not, and I will show you the man who suffers not; and you will find that he not only does not suffer himself, but that he is able[10] to heal others. For instance, Moses, on account of his

---

[1] The words in italics supplied by conjecture.
[2] This last sentence has two blanks, which are filled up by conjectures; and one emendation has been adopted.
[3] [With chaps. 21, 22, compare Homily XX. 4. — R.]

[4] We have adopted an emendation of Lagarde's.
[5] Eccles. iii. 2.
[6] Lit., " new moons that are according to the moon." Gal. iv. 10.
[7] " At times when " is supplied by conjecture.
[8] We have followed an emendation of Wieseler's.
[9] John ix. 2, 3. [This clear instance of citation from the Gospel of John is found in that portion of the text recovered by Dressel. It is of importance, since writers of the Tübingen school previously denied that this author uses the fourth Gospel. — R.]
[10] We have adopted an obvious emendation of Wieseler's.

piety, continued free from suffering all his life, and by his prayers he healed the Egyptians when they suffered on account of their sins."

CHAP. XXIII. — THE INEQUALITIES OF LOT IN HU-
MAN LIFE.

And Simon said : " Let me grant that this is the case : does not the inequality of lot amongst men seem to you most unjust ? For one is in penury, another is rich ; one is sick, another is in good health : and there are innumerable differences of a like character in human life." [1] And Peter said : " Do you not perceive, Simon, that you are again shooting your observations beyond the mark ? For while we were discussing evil, you have made a digression, and introduced the question of the anomalies that appear in this world. But I shall speak even to this point. The world is an instrument artistically contrived, that for the male who is to exist eternally, the female may bear eternal righteous sons. Now they could not have been rendered perfectly pious here, had there been no needy ones for them to help. In like manner there are the sick, that they may have objects for their care. And the other afflictions admit of a like explanation." And Simon said : " Are not those in humble circumstances unfortunate ? for they are subjected to distress, that others may be made righteous." And Peter said : " If their humiliation were eternal, their misfortune would be very great. But the humiliations and exaltations of men take place according to lot ; and he who is not pleased with his lot can appeal,[2] and by trying his case according to law, he can exchange his mode of life for another." And Simon said : " What do you mean by this lot and this appeal ? " And Peter said : " You are now demanding the exposition of another topic ; but if you permit me, we can show you how, being born again, and changing your origin, and living according to law, you will obtain eternal salvation."

CHAP. XXIV. — SIMON REBUKED BY FAUSTUS.

And Simon hearing this, said : " Do not imagine that, when I, while questioning you, agreed with you in each topic, I went to the next, as being fully assured of the truth of the previous ; but I appeared to yield to your ignorance, that you might go on to the next topic, in order that, becoming acquainted with the whole range of your ignorance, I might condemn you, not through mere conjecture, but from full knowledge.[3] Allow me now to retire for three days, and I shall come back and show that you

know nothing." When Simon said this, and was on the point of going out, my father said : " Listen to me, Simon, for a moment, and then go wherever you like. I remember that in the beginning, before the discussion, you accused me of being prejudiced, though as yet you had had no experience of me. But now, having heard you discuss in turn, and judging that Peter has the advantage, and now assigning to him the merit of speaking the truth, do I appear to you to judge correctly, and with knowledge ;[4] or is it not so ? For if you should say that I have judged correctly, but do not agree, then you are plainly prejudiced, inasmuch as you do not wish to agree, after confessing your defeat. But if I was not correct in maintaining that Peter has the advantage in the discussion, do you convince us how we have not judged correctly, or you will cease[5] to discuss with him before all, since you will always be defeated and agree, and in consequence your own soul will suffer pain, condemned as you will be, and in disgrace, through your own conscience, even if you do not feel shame before all the listeners as the greatest torture ; for we have seen you conquered, in fact, and we have heard your own lips confess it. Finally, therefore, I am of opinion that you will not return to the discussion, as you promised ; but that you may seem not to have been defeated,[6] you have promised, when going away, that you will return."

CHAP. XXV. — SIMON RETIRES. SOPHONIAS ASKS
PETER TO STATE HIS REAL OPINIONS IN RE-
GARD TO EVIL.

And Simon hearing this, gnashed his teeth for rage, and went away in silence. But Peter (for a considerable portion of the day still remained) laid his hands on the large multitude to heal them ; and having dismissed them, went into the house with his more intimate friends, and sat down. And one of his attendants, of the name of Sophonias, said : " Blessed is God, O Peter, who selected you and instructed[7] you for the comfort of the good. For, in truth, you discussed with Simon with dignity and great patience. But we beg of you to discourse to us of evil ; for we expect that you will state to us your own genuine belief in regard to it, — not, however at the present moment, but to-morrow, if it seems good to you : for we spare you, because of the fatigue you feel on account of your discussion." And Peter said : " I wish you to know, that he who does anything with pleasure, finds rest in the very toils themselves ; but he

---

1 [Comp. *Recognitions*, iii. 40, 41. — R.]
2 An amendment of Wieseler's.
3 The whole of this sentence is corrupt. We have adopted the conjectures of Wieseler, though they are not entirely satisfactory.

4 Possibly something is corrupt here. The words may be translated : " Is it not plain that I know how to judge correctly ? "
5 The MS. has, " do not cease." We have omitted μὴ, and changed παύσῃ into παύσει. We have inserted the μή after ἤ, changed into εἰ before αἰδεῖσθαι.
6 We have adopted an emendation of Wieseler's.
7 An emendation of Wieseler's

who does not do what he wishes, is rendered exceedingly weary by the very rest he takes. Wherefore you confer on me a great rest when you make me discourse on topics which please me." Content, then, with his disposition, and sparing him on account of his fatigue, we requested him to put the discussion off till the night, when it was his custom to discourse to his genuine friends. And partaking of salt, we turned to sleep.

HOMILY XX.

CHAP. I. — PETER IS WILLING TO GRATIFY SOPHONIAS.

In the night-time Peter rose up and wakened us, and then sat down in his usual way, and said : "Ask me questions about anything you like."[1] And Sophonias was the first to begin to speak to him : "Will you explain to us who are eager to learn what is the real truth in regard to evil?" And Peter said : "I have already explained it in the course of my discussion with Simon ; but because I stated the truth in regard to it in combination with other topics, it was not altogether clearly put ; for many topics that seem to be of equal weight with the truth afford some kind of knowledge of the truth to the masses. So that, if now I state what I formerly stated to Simon along with many topics, do not imagine that you are *not*[2] honoured with honour equal to his." And Sophonias said : "You are right ; for if you now separate it for us from many of the topics that were then discussed, you will make the truth more evident."

CHAP. II. — THE TWO AGES.

And Peter said : "Listen, therefore, to the truth of the harmony in regard to the evil one. God appointed two kingdoms, and established two ages, determining that the present world should be given to the evil one, because it is small, and passes quickly away ; but He promised to preserve for the good one the age to come, as it will be great and eternal. Man, therefore, He created with free-will, and possessing the capability of inclining to whatever actions he wishes. And his body consists of three parts, deriving its origin from the female ; for it has lust, anger, and grief, and what is consequent on these. But the spirit not being uniform,[3] but consisting of three parts, derives its origin from the male ; and it is capable of reasoning, knowledge, and fear, and what is consequent on these. And each of these triads has one root, so that man is a compound of two mixtures, the female and the male. Wherefore also two ways have been laid before him — those of obedience and disobedience to law ; and two kingdoms have been established, — the one called[4] the kingdom of heaven, and the other the kingdom of those who are now kings upon earth. Also two kings have been appointed, of whom the one is selected to rule by law over the present and transitory world, and his composition is such that he rejoices in the destruction of the wicked. But the other and good[5] one, who is the King of the age to come, loves the whole nature of man ; but not being able to have boldness in the present world, he counsels what is advantageous, like one who tries to conceal who he really is.[6]

CHAP. III. — THE WORK OF THE GOOD ONE AND OF THE EVIL ONE.

"But of these two, *the one*[7] acts violently towards the other by the command of God. Moreover, each man has power to obey whichever of them he pleases for the doing of good or evil. But if any one chooses to do what is good, he becomes the possession of the future good king ; but if any one should do evil, he becomes the servant of the present evil one, who, having received power over him by just judgment on account of his sins, and wishing *to use it*[8] before the coming age, rejoices in punishing him in the present life, and thus by gratifying, as it were, his own private passion, he accomplishes the will of God. But the other, being made to rejoice in power over the righteous, when he finds a righteous man, is exceedingly glad, and saves him with eternal life ; and he also, as if gratifying himself, traces the gratification which he feels on account of these to God. Now it is within the power of every unrighteous man to repent and be saved ; and every righteous man may have to undergo punishment for sins committed at the end of his career. Moreover,

---

[1] [Chaps. 1-10 are also peculiar to the *Homilies*, though there are incidental resemblances to passages in the *Recognitions*, particularly in the presentation of free-will. — R.]
[2] "Not" is supplied by conjecture.
[3] A doubtful emendation of Wieseler's for the senseless τριτογενές. Possibly it may be for πρωτογενές, original, and is underived.

[4] An obvious correction of the MS. is adopted.
[5] We have changed αὐτός into ἀγαθός.
[6] [With these views compare the doctrine of pairs, as repeatedly set forth: Homily II. 33, 34; *Recognitions*, iii. 59, 60, etc. — R.]
[7] "One" is supplied by Dressel's conjecture.
[8] The words in italics are supplied by Dressel's conjecture.

these two leaders are the swift hands of God, eager to anticipate Him so as to accomplish His will. But that this is so, has been said even by the law in the person of God : ' I will kill, and I will make alive ; I will strike, and I will heal.' [1] For, in truth, He kills and makes alive. He kills through the left hand, that is, through the evil one, who has been composed so as to rejoice in afflicting the impious. And he saves and bene-fits through the right hand, that is, through the good one, who has been made to rejoice in the good deeds and salvation of the righteous. Now these have not their substances outside of God : for there is no other primal source. Nor, indeed, have they been sent forth as animals from God, for they were of the same mind with Him ; nor are they accidental,[2] arising sponta-neously in opposition to His will, since thus the greatest exercise of His power would have been destroyed. But from God have been sent forth the four first elements — heat and cold, moist and dry. In consequence of this, He is the father of every substance, but not of the dispo-sition [3] which may arise from the combination of the elements ; for when these were combined from without, disposition was begotten in them as a child. The wicked one, then, having served God blamelessly to the end of the present world, can become good by a change in his compo-sition,[4] since he assuredly is not of one uniform substance whose sole bent is towards sin. For not even more does he do evil, although he is evil, since he has received power to afflict law-fully."

CHAP. IV. — MEN SIN THROUGH IGNORANCE.

When Peter said this, Micah, who was himself one of his followers, asked : " What, then, is the reason why men sin ? " And Peter said : " It is because they are ignorant that they will without doubt be punished for their evil deeds when judgment takes place.[5] For this reason they, having lust, as I elsewhere said, for the continu-ance of life, gratify it in any accidental way, it may be by the vitiation of boys,[6] or by some other flattering sin. For in consequence of their ignorance, as I said before, they are urged on through fearlessness to satisfy their lust in an unlawful manner. Wherefore God is not evil, who has rightly placed lust within man, that there may be a continuance of life, but they are most impious who have used the good of lust badly. The same considerations apply to anger

also, that if one uses it righteously, as is within his power, he is pious ; but going beyond meas-ure, and taking judgment to himself,[7] he is im-pious."

CHAP. V. — SOPHONIAS MAINTAINS THAT GOD CAN-NOT PRODUCE WHAT IS UNLIKE HIMSELF.

And Sophonias said again : " Your great pa-tience, my lord Peter, gives us boldness to ask you many questions for the sake of accuracy. Wherefore we make our inquiries with confi-dence in every direction. I remember, then, that Simon said yesterday, in his discussion with you, that the evil one, if he was born of God, pos-sesses in consequence the same substance as He does who sent him forth, and he ought to have been good, and not wicked. But you answered that this was not always the case, since many wicked sons are born of good parents, as from Adam two unlike [8] sons were begotten, one of whom was bad and the other good. And when Simon found fault with you for having used human examples, you answered that in this way we ought not to admit that God begets at all ; for this also is a human example. And I, So-phonias, admit that God begets ; but I do not allow that He begets what is bad, even though the good among men beget bad children. And do not imagine [8] that I am without reason attrib-uting to God some of the qualities that distin-guish men, and refusing to attribute others, when I grant that He begets, but do not allow that He begets what is unlike Himself. For men, as you might expect, beget sons who are unlike them in their dispositions for the following reason. Being composed of four parts, they change their bodies variously, according to the various changes of the year ; and thus, the appropriate change either of increase or decrease taking place in the human body, each season destroys the har-monious combination. Now, when the combi-nations do not always remain exactly in the same position, the seeds, having sometimes one combination, sometimes another, are sent off ; and these are followed, according to the combi-nation belonging to the season, by dispositions either good or bad. But in the case of God we cannot suppose any such thing ; for, being un-changeable and always existing, whenever He wishes to send forth, there is an absolute neces-sity that what is sent forth should be in all respects in the same position as that which has begotten, I mean in regard to substance and disposition. But if any one should wish to maintain that He is changeable, I do not know how it is possible for him to maintain that He is immortal."

---

[1] Deut. xxxii. 39.
[2] We have adopted an obvious emendation of Wieseler's.
[3] We have changed οὔσης into οὐ τῆς.
[4] We have given a meaning to μετασυγκριθείς not found in dic-tionaries, but warranted by etymology, and demanded by the sense.
[5] Part of this is supplied by Dressel's conjecture.
[6] There is a lacuna, which has been filled up in various ways. We have supposed ἠμ to be for ἠ μ., possibly μητέρων ἠ. Wieseler supposes "immature boys."

[7] Dressel translates, " drawing judgment on himself."
[8] An emendation of Wieseler's.

CHAP. VI. — GOD'S POWER OF CHANGING HIMSELF.

When Peter heard this, he thought for a little, and said : " I do not think that any one can converse about evil without doing the will of the evil one. Therefore knowing this, I do not know what I shall do, whether I shall be silent or speak. For if I be silent, I should incur the laughter of the multitude, because, professing to proclaim the truth, I am ignorant of the explanation of vice. But if I should state my opinion, I am afraid lest it be not at all pleasing to God that we should seek after evil, for only seeking after good is pleasing to Him. However, in my reply to the statements of Sophonias, I shall make my ideas more plain. I then agree with him in thinking that we ought not to attribute to God all the qualities of men. For instance, men not having bodies that are convertible are not converted ; but they have a nature that admits of alteration by the lapse of time through the seasons of the year. But this is not the case with God ; for through His inborn[1] Spirit He becomes, by a power which cannot be described, whatever body He likes. And one can the more easily believe this, as the air, which has received such a nature from Him, is converted into dew by the incorporeal mind permeating it, and being thickened becomes water, and water being compacted becomes stone and earth, and stones through collision light up fire. According to such[2] a change and conversion, air becomes first water, and ends in being fire through conversions, and the moist is converted into its natural opposite. Why? Did not God convert the rod of Moses into an animal, making it a serpent,[3] which He reconverted into a rod? And by means of this very converted rod he converted the water of the Nile[4] into blood, which again he reconverted into water. Yea, even man, who is dust, He changed by the inbreathing of His breath[5] into flesh, and changed him back again into dust.[6] And was not Moses,[7] who himself was flesh, converted into the grandest light, so that the sons of Israel could not look him in the face? Much more, then, is God completely able to convert Himself into whatsoever He wishes.

CHAP. VII. — THE OBJECTION ANSWERED, THAT ONE CANNOT CHANGE HIMSELF.

"But perhaps some one of you thinks that one may become something under the influence of one, and another under the influence of another, but no one can change himself into

whatever he wishes, and that it is the characteristic of one who grows old, and who must die according to his nature,[8] to change, but we ought not to entertain such thoughts of immortal beings. For were not angels, who are free from old age, and of a fiery substance,[9] changed into flesh, — those, for instance, who received the hospitality of Abraham,[10] whose feet men washed, as if they were the feet of men of like substance?[11] Yea, moreover, with Jacob,[12] who was a man, there wrestled an angel, converted into flesh that he might be able to come to close quarters with him. And, in like manner, after he had wrestled by his own will, he was converted into his own natural form ; and now, when he was changed into fire, he did not burn up the broad sinew of Jacob, but he inflamed it, and made him lame. Now, that which cannot become anything else, whatever it may wish, is mortal, inasmuch as it is subject to its own nature ; but he who can become whatever he wishes, whenever he wishes, is immortal, returning to a new condition, inasmuch as he has control over his own nature. Wherefore much more does the power of God change the substance of the body into whatever He wishes, and whenever He wishes ; and by the change that takes place[13] He sends forth what, on the one hand, is of similar substance, but, on the other, is not of equal power. Whatever, then, he who sends forth turns into a different substance, that he can again turn back into his own ;[14] but he who is sent forth, arising in consequence of the change which proceeds from him, and being his child, cannot become anything else without the will of him who sent him forth, unless he wills it."

CHAP. VIII. — THE ORIGIN OF THE GOOD ONE DIFFERENT FROM THAT OF THE EVIL ONE.

When Peter said this, Micah,[15] who was himself also one of the companions that attended on him, said : " I also should like to learn from you if the good one has been produced in the same way that the evil one came into being. But if they came into being in a similar manner, then they are brothers in my opinion." And Peter said : " They have not come into being in a similar way : for no doubt you remember what I said in the beginning, that the substance of the body of the wicked one, being fourfold in origin, was carefully selected and sent forth by God ;

---

[1] ἐμφύτου.
[2] We have changed τοιοῦτον into τοιαύτην.
[3] Ex. iv. 3, 4.
[4] Ex. vii. 19, 20.
[5] Gen. ii. 7.
[6] Eccles. iii. 20.
[7] Ex. xxxiv. 29.

[8] One word of this is supplied conjecturally by Dressel.
[9] Gen. vi. 2. [Comp. Ps. civ. 4.]
[10] Part of this is conjectural.
[11] Gen. xviii. 4.
[12] Gen. xxxii. 24.
[13] We have adopted Wieseler's emendation of μή into μέν.
[14] This passage is corrupt. We have changed ὅτι into ὅ, τι, and supplied τρέπει.
[15] Dressel remarks that this cannot be the true reading. Some other name mentioned in Hom. II. c. 1 must be substituted here or in c. 4.

but when it was combined externally, according to the will of Him who sent it forth, there arose, in consequence of the combination, the disposition which rejoices in evils : [1] so that you may see that the substance, fourfold in origin, which was sent forth by Him, and which also always exists, is the child of God ; but that the accidentally arising disposition which rejoices in evils has supervened when the substance [2] was combined externally by him. And thus this disposition has not been begotten by God, nor by any one else, nor indeed has it been sent forth by Him, nor has it come forth spontaneously,[3] nor did it always exist, like the substance before the combination ; but it has come on as an accident by external combination, according to the will of God. And we have often said that it must be so. But the good one having been begotten from the most beautiful change of God, and not having arisen accidentally through an external combination, is really His Son. Yet, since these doctrines are unwritten, and are confirmed to us only by conjecture, let us by no means deem it as absolutely certain that this is the true state of the case. For if we act otherwise, our mind will cease from investigating the truth, in the belief that it has already fully comprehended it. Remember these things, therefore ; for I must not state such things to all, but only to those who are found after trial most trustworthy. Nor ought we rashly to maintain such assertions towards each other, nor ought ye to dare to speak as if you were accurately acquainted with the discovery of secret truths, but you ought simply to reflect over them in silence ; for in stating, perchance, that a matter is so,[4] he who says it will err, and he will suffer punishment for having dared to speak even to himself what has been honoured with silence."

CHAP. IX. — WHY THE WICKED ONE IS APPOINTED OVER THE WICKED BY THE RIGHTEOUS GOD.

When Peter said this, Lazarus, who also was one of his followers, said : " Explain to us the harmony, how it can be reasonable that the wicked one should be appointed by the righteous God to be the punisher of the impious, and yet should himself afterwards be sent into lower darkness along with his angels and with sinners : for I remember that the Teacher Himself said this."[5] And Peter said : " I indeed allow that the evil one does no evil, inasmuch as he is accomplishing the law given to him. And although he has an evil disposition, yet through fear of God he does nothing unjustly ; but, ac-

cusing the teachers of truth so as to entrap the unwary, he is himself named the accuser (the devil). But the statement of our unerring Teacher, that he and his angels, along with the deluded sinners, shall go into lower darkness, admits of the following explanation. The evil one, having obtained the lot[6] of rejoicing in darkness according to his composition, delights to go down to the darkness of Tartarus along with angels who are his fellow-slaves ; for darkness is dear to fire. But the souls of men, being drops of pure light, are absorbed by the substance fire, which is of a different class ; and not possessing a nature capable of dying, they are punished according to their deserts. But if he who is the leader of men[7] into vice is not sent into darkness, as not rejoicing in it, then his composition, which rejoices in evils, cannot be changed by another combination into the disposition for good. And thus he will be adjudged to be with the good,[8] all the more because, having obtained a composition which rejoices in evils, through fear of God he has done nothing contrary to the decrees of the law of God. And did not the Scripture by a mysterious hint[9] point out by the statement[10] that the rod of the high priest Aaron became a serpent, and was again converted into a rod, that a change in the composition of the wicked one would afterwards take place ? "

CHAP. X. — WHY SOME BELIEVE, AND OTHERS DO NOT.

And after Lazarus, Joseph, who also was one of his followers, said : " You have spoken all things rightly. Teach me also this, as I am eager to know it, why, when you give the same discourses to all, some believe and others disbelieve ? " And Peter said : " It is because my discourses are not charms, so that every one that hears them must without hesitation believe them. The fact that some believe, and others do not, points out to the intelligent the freedom of the will." And when he said this, we all blessed him.

CHAP. XI. — ARRIVAL OF APPION AND ANNUBION.

And as as we were going to take our meals,[11] some one ran in and said : " Appion Pleistonices has just come with Annubion from Antioch, and he is lodging with Simon." And my father hearing this, and rejoicing, said to Peter : " If you permit me, I shall go to salute Appion and

---

[1] This passage is corrupt. We have adopted Wieseler's emendations for the most part.
[2] We have read τῆς with Wieseler for τις.
[3] Wieseler translates " accidentally."
[4] We have changed οὐχ ὡς ἔχον into οὕτως ἔχειν.
[5] Matt. xxv. 41.
[6] We have adopted an emendation of Wieseler's.
[7] Wieseler's emendation.
[8] We have changed ἀγαθός into ἀγαθοῖς.
[9] An emendation of Wieseler's.
[10] Ex. vii. 9.
[11] [Chaps. 11–22 are almost identical with *Recognitions*, x. 52–64. But the conclusion of that narrative is fuller, giving prominence to the re-united family ; comp. also chap. 23 here. — R.]

Annubion, who have been my friends from childhood. For perchance I shall persaude Annubion to discuss genesis with Clement." And
Peter said : " I permit you, and I praise you
for fulfilling the duties of a friend. But now
consider how in the providence of God there
come together from all quarters considerations
which contribute to your full assurance, rendering the harmony complete. But I say this because the arrival of Annubion happens advantageously for you." And my father : " In truth,
I see that this is the case." And saying this, he
went to Simon.

CHAP. XII. — FAUSTUS APPEARS TO HIS FRIENDS WITH THE FACE OF SIMON.

Now all of us who were with Peter asked each
other questions the whole of the night, and
continued awake, because of the pleasure and
joy we derived from what was said. But when
at length the dawn began to break, Peter, looking at me and my brothers, said : " I am puzzled
to think what your father has been about." And
just as he was saying this, our father came in and
caught Peter talking to us of him ; and seeing
him displeased, he accosted him, and rendered
an apology for having slept outside. But we
were amazed when we looked at him : for we
saw the form of Simon, but heard the voice of
our father Faustus. And when we were fleeing
from him, and abhorring him, our father was
astonished at receiving such harsh and hostile
treatment from us. But Peter alone saw his
natural shape, and said to us : " Why do you in
horror turn away from your own father ? " But we
and our mother said : " It is Simon that we see
before us, with the voice of our father." And
Peter said : " You recognise only his voice,
which is unaffected by magic ; but as my eyes
also are unaffected by magic, I can see his form as
it really is, that he is not Simon, but your father
Faustus." Then, looking to my father, he said :
" It is not your own true form that is seen by
them, but that of Simon, our deadliest foe, and
a most impious man." [1]

CHAP. XIII. — THE FLIGHT OF SIMON.

While Peter was thus talking, there entered
one of those who had gone before to Antioch,
and who, coming back from Antioch, said to
Peter : " I wish you to know, my lord, that
Simon, by doing many miracles publicly in Antioch, and calling you a magician and a juggler
and a murderer,[2] has worked them up to such
hatred against you, that every man is eager to

taste your very flesh if you should sojourn there.[3]
Wherefore we who went before, along with our
brethren who were in pretence attached by you
to Simon, seeing the city raging wildly against
you, met secretly and considered what we ought
to do. And assuredly, while we were in great
perplexity, Cornelius the centurion arrived, who
had been sent by the emperor to the governor
of the province. He was the person whom our
Lord cured when he was possessed of a demon
in Cæsarea. This man we sent for secretly ; and
informing him of the cause of our despondency,
we begged his help. He promised most readily
that he would alarm Simon, and make him take
to flight, if we should assist him in his effort.
And when we all promised that we should readily do everything, he said, ' I shall spread abroad
the news [4] through many friends that I have secretly come to apprehend him ; and I shall pretend that I am in search of him, because the
emperor, having put to death many magicians,
and having received information in regard to
him, has sent me to search him out, that he may
punish him as he punished the magicians before
him ; while those of your party who are with him
must report to him, as if they had heard it from
a secret source, that I have been sent to apprehend him. And perchance when he hears it from
them, he will be alarmed and take to flight.'
When, therefore, we had intended to do something
else, nevertheless the affair turned out in the following way. For when he heard the news from
many strangers who gratified him greatly by secretly informing him, and also from our brethren
who pretended to be attached to him, and took
it as the opinion of his own followers, he resolved on retiring. And hastening away from
Antioch, he has come here with Athenodorus, as
we have heard. Wherefore we advise you not
yet to enter that city, until we ascertain whether
they can forget in his absence the accusations
which he brought against you."

CHAP. XIV. — THE CHANGE IN THE FORM OF FAUS-TUS CAUSED BY SIMON.

When the person who had gone before gave
this report, Peter looked to my father, and said :
" You hear, Faustus ; the change in your form
has been caused by Simon the magician, as is
now evident. For, thinking that *a servant* [5] of
the emperor was seeking him to punish him, he
became afraid and fled, putting you into his own
shape, that if you were put to death, your children might have sorrow." When my father heard
this, he wept and lamented, and said : " You
have conjectured rightly, Peter. For Annubion,

---

[1] There are some blanks here, supplied from the *Epitome*.
[2] Supplied from *Epitome*. The passage in *Epitome Second* renders it likely that the sentence ran : " But Simon, while doing many
miracles publicly in Antioch, did nothing else by his discourses than
excite hatred amongst them against you, and by calling you," etc.

[3] This passage is amended principally according to Wieseler and
the *Recognitions*.
[4] An emendation of Wieseler's.
[5] Inserted by conjecture.

who is my dear friend,[1] hinted his design to me ; but I did not believe him, *miserable man that I am*,[2] since I deserved to suffer."

CHAP. XV. — THE REPENTANCE OF FAUSTUS.

When my father said this, after no long time *Annubion came*[3] to us to announce to us the flight of Simon, and how that very night he had hurried to Judæa. And he found our father wailing, and with lamentations saying : " Alas, alas ! unhappy man ! I' did not believe when I was told that he was a magician. Miserable man that I am ! I have been recognised for one day by my wife and children, and have speedily gone back to my previous sad condition when I was still ignorant." And my mother lamenting, plucked her hair ; and we groaned in distress on account of the transformation of our father, and could not comprehend what in the world it could be. But Annubion stood speechless, seeing and hearing these things ; while Peter said to us, his children, in the presence of all : " Believe me, this is Faustus your father. Wherefore I urge you to attend to him as being your father. For God will vouchsafe some occasion for his putting off the shape of Simon, and exhibiting again distinctly that of your father." And saying this, and looking to my father, he said : " I permitted you to salute Appion and Annubion, since you asserted that they were your friends from childhood, but I did not permit you to associate with the magician Simon."

CHAP. XVI. — WHY SIMON GAVE TO FAUSTUS HIS OWN SHAPE.

And my father said : " I have sinned ; I confess it." And Annubion said : " I also along with him beg you to forgive the noble and good old man who has been deceived : for the unfortunate man has been the sport of that notorious fellow. But I shall tell you how it took place.[4] The good old man came to salute us. But at that very hour he who were there happened to be listening to Simon, who wished to run away that night, for he had heard that some people had come to Laodicea in search of him by the command of the emperor. But as Faustus was entering, he *turned*[5] his own rage on him, and thus addressed us : ' Make him, when he comes, share your meals ; and I will prepare an ointment, so that, when he has supped, he may take some of it, and anoint his face with it, and then he will appear to all to have my shape. But I will anoint you with the juice[6] of some plant,

and then you will not be deceived by his new[7] shape ; but to all others Faustus will seem to be Simon.'

CHAP. XVII. — ANNUBION'S SERVICES TO FAUSTUS.

" And while he stated this beforehand, I said, ' What, then, is the advantage you now expect to get from such a contrivance ? ' And Simon said, ' First, those who seek me, when they apprehend him, will give up the search after me. But if he be executed by the hand of the emperor, very great sorrow will fall upon his children, who left me, and fleeing *to Peter*, now aid him in his work.' And now, Peter, I confess the truth to you : I was prevented by fear *of Simon* from informing *Fau*stus of this. But Simon did not give us an opportunity for private conversation, *lest* some one of us might reveal[8] to him the wicked design of Simon. Simon then rose up in the middle of the night and fled to Judæa, convoyed by Appion and Athenodorus. Then I pretended that I was sick, in order that, remaining after they had gone, I might make Faustus go back immediately to his own people, if by any chance he might be able, by being concealed with you, to escape observation, lest, being caught as Simon by those who were in search of Simon, he might be put to death through the wrath of the emperor. At the dead of night, therefore, I sent him away to you ; and in my anxiety for him I came by night to see him, with the intention of returning before those who convoyed Simon should return." And looking to us, he said : " I, Annubion, see the true shape of your father ; for I was anointed, as I related to you before, by Simon himself, that the true shape of Faustus might be seen by my eyes. Astonished, therefore, I exceedingly wonder at the magic power of Simon, in that standing[9] you do not recognise your own father." And while our father and our mother and we ourselves wept on account of the calamity common to all of us, Annubion also through sympathy wept with us.

CHAP. XVIII. — PETER PROMISES TO RESTORE TO FAUSTUS HIS OWN SHAPE.

Then Peter promised to us to restore the shape of our father, and he said to him : " Faustus, you heard how matters stand with us. When, therefore, the deceptive shape which invests you has been useful to us, and you have assisted us in doing what I shall tell you to do, then I shall restore to you your true form, when

---

[1] Part of this is supplied from the *Recognitions*.
[2] Inserted from the *Recognitions*.
[3] These words are taken from the *Recognitions*.
[4] An emendation of Dressel's.
[5] Supplied by Dressel from the *Recognitions*.
[6] An emendation of Wieseler's.

[7] MS. reads " empty." Wieseler proposed " new " or " assumed."
[8] An emendation of Wieseler's. The parts in italics are supplied by conjecture.
[9] We should have expected " standing near " or something similar, as Weiseler remarks; but the Latin of the *Recognitions* agrees with the Greek in having the simple " standing."

you have first performed my commands." And when my father said, " I shall do everything that is in my power most willingly; only restore to my own people my own form;" Peter answered, "You yourself heard with your own ears how those who went before me came back from Antioch, and said that Simon had been there, and had strongly excited the multitudes against me by calling me a magician and a murderer, a deceiver and a juggler, to such an extent that all the people there were eager to taste my flesh. You will do, then, as I tell you. You will leave Clement with me, and you will go before us into Antioch with your wife, and your sons Faustinus and Faustinianus. And some others will accompany you whom I deem capable of helping forward my design.

CHAP. XIX. — PETER'S INSTRUCTIONS TO FAUSTUS.

"When *you are* with these in Antioch, while you look like Simon, proclaim publicly your *repentance*, saying, ' I Simon proclaim this to you: I confess [1] that all my statements in regard to Peter are *utterly false;* [2] *for he is not* a deceiver, nor a murderer, nor a juggler; nor are any of the evil things true which I, urged on by wrath, said previously in regard to him. I myself therefore beg of you, I who have been the cause of your hatred to him, cease from hating him; for he is the true apostle of the true Prophet that was sent by God for the salvation of the world. Wherefore also I counsel you to believe what he preaches; [3] for if you do not, your whole city will be utterly destroyed. Now I wish you to know for what reason I have made this confession to you. This night angels of God scourged me, the impious one, terribly, as being an enemy to the herald of the truth. I beseech you, therefore, do not listen to me, even if I myself should come at another time and attempt to say anything against Peter. For I confess to you I am a magician, I am a deceiver, I am a juggler. Yet perhaps it is possible for me by repentance to wipe out the sins which were formerly committed by me.' "

CHAP. XX. — FAUSTUS, HIS WIFE, AND SONS, PREPARE TO GO TO ANTIOCH.

When Peter suggested this, my father said: " I know what you want; wherefore take no trouble. For assuredly I shall take good care, when I reach that place, to make such statements in regard to you as I ought to make." And Peter again suggested: "When, then, you perceive the city changing from its hatred of me, and longing to see me, send information to me

of this, and I shall come to you immediately. And when I arrive there, that same day I shall remove the strange shape which now invests you, and I shall make your own unmistakeably visible to your own people and to all others." Saying this, he made his sons, my brothers, and our mother Mattidia to go along with him; and he also commanded some of his more intimate acquaintances to accompany him. But my mother was [4] unwilling to go with him, and said: " I seem to be an adulteress if I associate with the shape of Simon; but if I shall be compelled to go along with him, [5] it is impossible for me to recline on the same couch with him ! But I do not know if I shall be persuaded to go along with him." And while she was very unwilling to go, Annubion urged her, saying: " Believe me and Peter, and the very voice itself, that this is *Faustus* your husband, whom I love not less than you. And I myself *will go* [6] along with him." When Annubion said this, our mother promised to go with him.

CHAP. XXI. — APPION AND ATHENODORUS RETURN IN QUEST OF FAUSTUS.

But Peter said: " God arranges our affairs in a most satisfactory manner; [7] for we have with us Annubion the *astro*loger. [8] For when we arrive at Antioch, he will in future discourse regarding genesis, giving us his genuine opinions as a friend." Now when, after midnight, our father hurried with those whom Peter had ordered to go along with him and with Annubion to Antioch, which was near, early next day, before Peter went forth to discourse, Appion and Athenodorus, who had convoyed Simon, returned to Laodicea in search of our father. But Peter, ascertaining the fact, urged them to enter. And when they came in and sat down, and said, "Where is Faustus?" Peter answered: "We know not; for since the evening, when he went to you, he has not been seen by his kinsmen. But yesterday morning Simon came in search of him; and when we made no reply to him, something seemed to come over him, [9] for he called himself Faustus; but not being believed, he wept and lamented, and threatened to kill himself, and then rushed out in the direction of the sea."⁷

CHAP. XXII. — APPION AND ATHENODORUS RETURN TO SIMON.

When Appion and those who were with him heard this, they howled and lamented, saying:

---

[1] Amended according to *Epitome.*
[2] Partly filled up from *Epitome* and *Recognitions.*
[3] MS. reads, " I preach."

[4] We have changed εἶδε into εἶχε, and added καὶ εἶπε, according to the *Recognitions.*
[5] One word, τύχης, is superfluous.
[6] Supplied from the *Recognitions.*
[7] We read ἐπιτηδειότατα, in harmony with the *Recognitions.*
[8] Part in italics supplied from *Recognitions.*
[9] The Greek is probably corrupt here; but there can scarcely be a doubt about the meaning.

"Why did you not receive him?" And when at the same time Athenodorus wished to say to me, "It was Faustus, your father;" Appion anticipated him, and said, "We learned from some one that Simon, finding him, urged him *to go along with him,*[1] Faustus himself entreating him, since he did not wish to see his sons after they had become Jews. And hearing this, we came, for his own sake, in search of him. But since he is not here, it is plain that he spake the truth who gave us the information which we, hearing it from him, have given to you." And I Clement, perceiving the design of Peter, that he wished to beget a suspicion in them that he intended to look out among them for the old man, that they might be afraid and take to flight, assisted in his design, and said to Appion: "Listen to me, my dearest Appion. We were eager to give to him, as being our father, what we ourselves deemed to be good. But if he himself did not wish to receive it, but, on the contrary, fled from us in horror, I shall make a somewhat harsh remark, 'Nor do we care for him.'" And when I said this, they went away, as if irritated by my savageness; and, as we learn next day, they went to Judæa in the track of Simon.

---

[1] This is supplied purely by conjecture.

CHAP. XXIII. — PETER GOES TO ANTIOCH.

Now, when ten days had passed away, *there came one of our people*[2] from our father to announce to us how our father *stood forward* publicly *in the* shape *of Simon,* accusing him;[3] and how by praising Peter he had made the whole city of Antioch long for him: and in consequence of this, all said that they were eager to see him, and that there were some who were angry with him as being Simon, on account of their surpassing affection for Peter, and wished to lay hands on Faustus, believing he was Simon. Wherefore he, fearing that he might be put to death, had sent to request Peter to come immediately if he wished to meet him alive, and to appear at the proper time to the city, when it was at the height of its longing for him.[4] Peter, hearing this, called the multitude together to deliberate, and appointed one of his attendants bishop; and having remained three days in Laodicea baptizing and healing, he hastened to the neighboring city of Antioch. Amen.

---

[2] Supplied from the *Recognitions.*
[3] This part is restored by means of the *Recognitions.*
[4] [The narrative in the *Recognitions* (x. 65) is the same up to this point. But, instead of this somewhat abrupt conclusion of this chapter, we find there several chapters (from the close of chap. 65 to the end, chap. 72), which round out the story: the confession of the father in his metamorphosis, his restoration, the Apostle's entry into Antioch, his miracles there, with the happy re-union of the entire family of Clement as believers. It should be added, as indicating the close relation of the two narratives, that the closing sentence of the *Homilies* is found, with slight variations, in *Recognitions,* x. 18. — R.]

APOCRYPHA OF THE NEW TESTAMENT

TRANSLATED BY ALEXANDER WALKER, ESQ., ONE OF HER MAJESTY'S INSPECTORS OF
SCHOOLS FOR SCOTLAND.

INTRODUCTORY NOTICE

TO

APOCRYPHA OF THE NEW TESTAMENT

By PROFESSOR M. B. RIDDLE, D.D.

THE translations which follow have been made from the critical edition of Tischendorf (see Bibliography at close of this volume). The text varies greatly from that of Fabricius. It was found impossible to introduce the various readings and to cite the manuscript evidence supporting them. Those who are interested in such study will have recourse to the volumes of Tischendorf.

The general character of the writings here grouped as "Apocrypha of the New Testament" will appear from even a cursory perusal of them. It did not require any great discernment to distinguish between these and the canonical books of the New Testament. The negative internal evidence thus furnished in support of the authority of the latter need not be emphasized. But attention may well be called to certain historical facts in regard to these apocryphal writings : —

1. No one of them ever obtained any general recognition among Christians ; still less, a place in the Canon of the New Testament. A few so-called Gospels are referred to by early writers ; some obtained local recognition ; others, written for a purpose, were pressed into notice by the advocates of the tendency they were written to support : but, as a rule, the books were soon rejected, and never obtained extensive circulation.

2. Though a few of the Apocryphal Gospels are of comparatively early origin (see Translator's Introduction), there is no evidence that any Gospels purporting to be what our four Gospels are, existed in the first century, or that any other than fragmentary literature of this character existed even in the second century. The Canon of the New Testament was not formed out of a mass of writings possessing some claim to recognition, though there is a popular impression to this effect.

3. Here the character of the writings comes in as confirmatory evidence. Of the Apocryphal Gospels in general, R. Hofmann [1] well says : "The method employed in these compositions is always the same, whether the author intended simply to collect and arrange what was floating in the general tradition, or whether he intended to produce a definite dogmatical effect. Rarely he threw himself on his own invention ; but generally he elaborated what was only hinted at in the Canonical Gospels, or transcribed words of Jesus into action, or described the literal fulfilment of some Jewish expectation concerning the Messiah, or repeated the wonders of the Old Testament in an inhanced form, etc. The work done, he took care to conceal his own name, and inscribed his book with the name of some apostle or disciple, in order to give it authority." As a rule, therefore, the Apocryphal Gospels give details regarding those periods of our Lord's life about which the New Testament is wisely silent.

---

[1] Schaff-Herzog, i. p. 105.

The genesis of much of the literature resembles that of modern " Lives of Christ" written to present a view of the Person of our Lord which is not in accordance with the obvious sense of the New Testament. Probably some of the Apocryphal Gospels and Acts were not intended to be forgeries, but only novels with a purpose.[1]

4. But while the early Church exercised proper discernment, and the Canon of the New Testament was soon definitely recognised and universally accepted, the apocryphal writings were not without influence. The sacred legends, the ecclesiastical traditions, all too potent in their effect, are in many cases to be traced to these writings. Much that Rome inculcates is derived from these books, which the Western Church constantly rejected. It is, therefore, not strange that modern Protestant scholarship has been most active in the investigation of this literature. The study of these works furnishes not only a defence of the canonical books of the New Testament, but an effective weapon against that "tradition" which would overbear the authority of Holy Scripture. No attempt has been made to annotate the various works in illustration of the above positions, although the temptation to do so was very great. A few notes have been appended, but it was felt that in most cases the intelligent reader would not fail to draw the proper conclusions from the documents themselves. Those who desire to investigate further will find the best helps indicated either in the Introduction of the translator or in the Bibliography which closes this volume and series.

It will be noticed that no Apocryphal Epistles are included in the literature which follows. Such forgeries were less common, and the Apocryphal Acts furnished a more convenient channel for heretical opinions and argument. Of the few in existence, some appear, in connection with other works, in the Acts of Thaddæus, in the Pseudo-Ignatian Epistles, in the Clementine Homilies (Epistles of Peter to James), and in Eusebius. The forged letters of Paul, to the Laodiceans and a third to the Corinthians, deserve little attention, being made to supply the supposed loss suggested by Col. iv. 16 and 1 Cor. v. 9. The correspondence of Paul and Seneca (six letters from the former and eight from the latter) has a certain interest, but scarcely deserves a place even among the apocryphal writings.

---

[1] In most cases the vocabulary of the books furnishes positive evidence of the late origin. A great number of terms can be traced to a particular period of ecclesiastical development, while the dogmatic tendencies which point to a given (and comparatively late) period of controversy are frequent and obvious.

TRANSLATOR'S INTRODUCTORY NOTICE

OUR aim in these translations has been to give a rendering of the original as literal as possible; and to this we have adhered even in cases — and they are not a few — in which the Latin or the Greek is not in strict accordance with grammatical rule. It was thought advisable in all cases to give the reader the means of forming an accurate estimate of the style as well as the substance of these curious documents.

PART I. — APOCRYPHAL GOSPELS.

The portion of the volume, extending from page 361 to page 476, comprising the Apocryphal Gospels properly so called, consists of twenty-two separate documents, of which ten are written in Greek and twelve in Latin. These twenty-two may be classed under three heads: (*a*) those relating to the history of Joseph and of the Virgin Mary, previous to the birth of Christ; (*b*) those relating to the infancy of the Saviour; and (*c*) those relating to the history of Pilate. The *origines* of the traditions are the Protevangelium of James, the Gospel of Thomas, and the Acts of Pilate. All or most of the others can be referred to these three, as compilations, modifications, or amplifications.

There is abundant evidence of the existence of many of these traditions in the second century, though it cannot be made out that any of the books were then in existence in their present form. The greater number of the authorities on the subject, however, seem to agree in assigning to the first four centuries of the Christian era, the following five books: 1. The Protevangelium of James; 2. The Gospel of Pseudo-Matthew; 4. The History of Joseph the Carpenter; 5. The Gospel of Thomas; 9. The Gospel of Nicodemus.

We proceed to give a very brief notice of each of them.

I. *The Protevangelium of James.* — The name of Protevangelium was first given to it by Postel, whose Latin version was published in 1552. The James is usually referred to St. James the Less, the Lord's brother; but the titles vary very much.[1] Origen, in the end of the second century, mentions a book of James, but it is by no means clear that he refers to the book in question. Justin Martyr, in two passages, refers to the cave in which Christ was born; and from the end of the fourth century down, there are numerous allusions in ecclesiastical writings to statements made in the Protevangelium.

For his edition Tischendorf made use of seventeen MSS., one of them belonging to the ninth century. The Greek is good of the kind, and free from errors and corruptions. There are translations of it into English by Jones (1722) and Cowper (1867).

II. *The Gospel of Pseudo-Matthew.* — The majority of the MSS. attribute this book to Matthew, though the titles vary much. The letters prefixed, professing to be written to and by St. Jerome, exist in several of the MSS.; but no one who is acquainted with the style of Jerome's letters will think this one authentic. There are, however, in his works many allusions to some of the legends mentioned in this book. Chapters i.–xxiv. were edited by Thilo, chapters xxv. to the end are edited

---

[1] [James the Lord's brother, in the earliest Christian literature, is not identified with James the son of Alphæus, one of the twelve. On the titles, see footnote on first page of text. — R.]

351

for the first time by Tischendorf. It is not very clear whether the Latin be original, or a direct translation from the Greek. In most part it seems to be original. The list of epithets, however, applied to the triangles of the Alpha in chapter xxxi. are pretty obviously mistranslations of Greek technical terms, which it might not be difficult to reproduce.

III. *Gospel of the Nativity of Mary.* — This work, which is in substance the same as the earlier part of the preceding, yet differs from it in several important points, indicating a later date and a different author. It has acquired great celebrity from having been transferred almost entire to the *Historia Lombardica* or *Legenda Aurea* in the end of the thirteenth century. Mediæval poetry and sacred art have been very much indebted to its pages.

The original is in Latin, and is not a direct translation from the Greek. In many passages it follows very closely the Vulgate translation.

IV. *The History of Joseph the Carpenter.* — The original language of this history is Coptic. From the Coptic it was translated into Arabic. The Arabic was published by Wallin in 1722, with a Latin translation and copious notes. Wallin's version has been republished by Fabricius, and later in a somewhat amended form by Thilo. This amended form of Wallin's version is the text adopted by Tischendorf. Chapters xiv.–xxiii. have been published in the Sahidic text by Zoega in 1810 with a Latin translation, and more correctly by Dulaurier in 1835 with a French translation.

Tischendorf employs various arguments in support of his opinion that the work belongs to the fourth century. It is found, he says, in both dialects of the Coptic: the eschatology of it is not inconsistent with an early date: the feast of the thousand years of chapter xxvi. had become part of heretical opinion after the third century. The death of the Virgin Mary in chapter v. is consistent with the doctrine of the assumption, which began to prevail in the fifth century.

V., VI., VII. *The Gospel of Thomas.* — Like the Protevangelium of James, the Gospel of Thomas is of undoubted antiquity. It is mentioned by name by Origen, quoted by Irenæus and the author of the Philosophumena, who says that it was used by the Nachashenes, a Gnostic sect of the second century. Cyril of Jerusalem (*d.* 386) attributes the authorship not to the apostle, but to a Thomas who was one of the three disciples of Manes. This fact, of course, indicates that Cyril knew nothing of the antiquity of the book he was speaking of. This Manichæan origin has been adopted by many writers, of whom the best known are in recent times R. Simon and Mingarelli.

The text of the first Greek form is obtained from a Bologna MS. published by Mingarelli with a Latin translation in 1764, a Dresden MS. of the sixteenth century edited by Thilo, a Viennese fragment edited by Lambecius, and a Parisian fragment first brought to light by Coteler in his edition of the Apostolical Constitutions, and translated into English by Jones.

The second Greek form is published for the first time by Tischendorf, who got the MS., which is on paper, of the fourteenth or fifteenth century, from one of the monasteries on Mount Sinai.

The Latin form is also published for the first time, from a Vatican MS. There is another Latin text existing in a palimpsest, which Tischendorf assigns to the fifth century, and asserts to be much nearer the ancient Greek copy than any of the other MSS.

It seems pretty clear, from the contents of the book, that its author was a Gnostic, a Docetist, and a Marcosian; and it was held in estimation by the Nachashenes and the Manichæans. Its bearing upon Christian art, and to some extent Christian dogma, is well known.

The Greek of the original is by no means good, and the Latin translator has in many cases mistaken the meaning of common Greek words.

VIII. *Arabic Gospel of the Saviour's Infancy.* — Chapters i.–ix. are founded on the Gospels of Luke and Matthew, and on the Protevangelium of James; chapters xxxvi. to the end are compiled from the Gospel of Thomas ; the rest of the book, chapters x. to xxxv., is thoroughly Oriental in its character, reminding one of the tales of the *Arabian Nights,* or of the episodes in the *Golden Ass* of Apuleius.

It is evident that the work is a compilation, and that the compiler was an Oriental. Various arguments are adduced to prove that the original language of it was Syriac.

It was first published, with a Latin translation and copious notes, by Professor Sike of Cambridge in 1697, afterwards by Fabricius, Jones, Schmid, and Thilo. Tischendorf's text is Sike's Latin version amended by Fleischer.

There are not sufficient data for fixing with any accuracy the time at which it was composed or compiled.

IX.–XIV. *The Gospel of Nicodemus.*[1] — The six documents inserted under this name are various forms of two books — two in Greek and one in Latin of the Acts of Pilate ; one in Greek and two in Latin of the Descent of Christ to the world below. Of twelve MSS., only two or three give the second part consecutively with the first, nor does it so appear in the Coptic translation. The title of Gospel of Nicodemus does not appear before the thirteenth century.

Justin Martyr mentions a book called the Acts of Pilate, and Eusebius informs us that the Emperor Maximim allowed or ordered a book, composed by the pagans under this title, to be published in a certain portion of the empire, and even to be taught in the schools ; but neither of these could have been the work under consideration.

Tischendorf attributes it to the second century, which is probably too early, though without doubt the legend was formed by the end of the second century. Maury (*Mém. de la Société des Antiq. de France,* t. xx.) places it in the beginning of the fifth century, from 405 to 420 ; and Renan (*Études d'Hist. Relig.,* p. 177) concurs in this opinion. An able writer in the *Quarterly Review* (vol. cxvi.) assigns it to 439 ; the author of the article Pilate, in Smith's *Bible Dictionary,* gives the end of the third century as the probable date.

The author was probably a Hellenistic Jew converted to Christianity, or, as Tischendorf and Maury conclude, a Christian imbued with Judaic and Gnostic beliefs. The original language was most probably Greek, though, as in the case of Pseudo-Matthew, the History of Joseph the Carpenter, etc., the original language is, in many of the prefaces, stated to have been Hebrew. Some think that Latin was the original language, on the ground that Pilate would make his report to the Emperor in that, the official, language. The Latin text we have, however, is obviously a translation, made, moreover, by a man to whom Greek was not very familiar, as is obvious from several instances specified in our notes to the text.

The *editio princeps* of the Latin text is without place or date, and it has been re-edited by Jones, Birch, Fabricius, Thilo, and others. The Greek text of Part I., and of a portion of Part II., was first published by Birch, and afterwards in a much improved form, with the addition of copious notes and prolegomena, by Thilo. The latter part of his prolegomena contains a full account of the English, French, Italian, and German translations. For his edition Tischendorf consulted thirty-nine ancient documents, of which a full account is given in his prolegomena, pp. lxxi.–lxxvi.

For an interesting account of these documents, see the introduction to Mr. B. H. Cowper's translation of the Apocryphal Gospels, pp. lxxxv.–cii.

XV. *The Letter of Pontius Pilate.* — The text is formed from four authorities, none of them ancient. A translation of the Greek text of the same letter will be found at p. 480.

XVI., XVII. *The Report of Pilate.* — The first of these documents was first published by Fabricius with a Latin translation ; the second by Birch, and then by Thilo. Tischendorf has

---

[1] [The numbers here correspond with those of Tischendorf in his *prolegomena.* In his table of contents, however, he gives a separate number to the letter of Pilate, which closes XIII. Hence the enumeration differs from that point. — R.]

made use of five MSS., the earliest of the twelfth century. It does not seem possible to assign the date.

XVIII. *The Paradosis of Pilate.* — It has been well remarked by the author of the article in the *Quarterly Review* above referred to, that the early Church looked on Pilate with no unfavourable eye ; that he is favourably shown in the catacombs ; that the early Fathers interpreted him as a figure of the early Church, and held him to be guiltless of Christ's death ; that the creeds do not condemn him, and the Coptic Church has even made him a saint. He remarks also that Dante finds punishments for Caiaphas and Annas, but not for Pilate.

The text was first edited by Birch, and afterwards by Thilo. Tischendorf makes use of five MSS., of which the earliest belongs to the twelfth century.

XIX. *The Death of Pilate.* — This is published for the first time by Tischendorf from a Latin MS. of the fourteenth century. The language shows it to be of a late date. It appears almost entire in the *Legenda Aurea.*

XX. *The Narrative of Joseph.* — This history seems to have been popular in the middle ages, if we may judge from the number of the Greek MSS. of it which remain.

It was first published by Birch, and after him by Thilo. For his edition Tischendorf made use of three MSS., of which the oldest belongs to the twelfth century.

XXI. *The Avenging of the Saviour.* — This version of the Legend of Veronica is written in very barbarous Latin, probably of the seventh or eighth century. An Anglo-Saxon version, which Tischendorf concludes to be derived from the Latin, was edited and translated for the Cambridge Antiquarian Society, by C. W. Goodwin, in 1851. The Anglo-Saxon text is from a MS. in the Cambridge Library, one of a number presented to the Cathedral of Exeter by Bishop Leofric in the beginning of the eleventh century.

The reader will observe that there are in this document two distinct legends, somewhat clumsily joined together — that of Nathan's embassy, and that of Veronica.[1]

PART II. — THE APOCRYPHAL ACTS OF THE APOSTLES.

This portion of the volume, extending from page 477 to page 564, presents us with documents written in a style considerably different from that of the Apocryphal Gospels properly so called. There we have without stint the signs that the Jews desired ; here we begin to have some glimpses of the wisdom which the Greeks sought after, along with a considerable share of

> Quidquid Græcia mendax
> Audet in historia.

We have less of miracle, more of elaborate discourse. The Apocryphal Gospels were suited to the *vilis plebecula,* from which, as Jerome said, the Church originated ; the Apocryphal Acts appeal more to the *Academia.*

We have in ancient literature, especially Greek literature, a long series of fabulous histories attached to the names of men who made themselves famous either in arts or arms. This taste for the marvellous became general after the expedition of Alexander ; and from that time down we have numerous examples of it in the lives of Alexander, of Pythagoras, of Apollonius of Tyana, of Homer, of Virgil, and others without number ; and we all know how much fabulous matter is apt to gather round the names of popular heroes even in modern times.

---

[1] [For a full list of fragments and titles of other Apocryphal Gospels, see Schaff-Herzog, i. p. 106. Twenty-nine are given, but in some cases the same work probably appears under two titles. — R.]

It is not to be wondered at, then, that round the names of Christ and His apostles, who had brought about social changes greater than those effected by the exploits of any hero of old, there should gather, as the result of the wondering awe of simple-minded men, a growth of the romantic and the fabulous.

These stories came at length to form a sort of apostolic cycle, of which the documents following are portions. They exists also in a Latin form in the ten books of the Acts of the Apostles, compiled probably in the sixth century, and falsely attributed to Abdias, the first bishop of Babylon, by whom it was, of course, written in Hebrew.[1]

We shall now give a brief account of each of the thirteen documents which make up this part of the volume.

I. *The Acts of Peter and Paul.* — This book was first published in a complete form by Thilo in 1837 and 1838. A portion of it had already been translated into Latin by the famous Greek scholar Constantine Lascaris in 1490, and had been made use of in the celebrated controversy as to the situation of the island Melita, upon which St. Paul was shipwrecked. For his edition Tischendorf collated six MSS., the oldest of the end of the ninth century.

Some portions at least of the book are of an early date. The *Domine quo vadis* story, p. 485, is referred to by Origen, and others after him. A book called the Acts of Peter is condemned in the decree of Pope Gelasius.

II. *Acts of Paul and Thecla.* — This book is of undoubted antiquity. There seems reason to accept the account of it given by Tertullian, that it was written by an Asiatic presbyter in glorification of St. Paul (who, however, unquestionably occupies only a secondary place in it), and in support of the heretical opinion that women may teach and baptize. It is expressly mentioned and quoted by a long line of Latin and Greek Fathers. The quotations are inserted in Tischendorf's *Prolegomena*, p. xxiv.

The text was first edited in 1698 by Grabe from a Bodleian MS., republished by Jones in 1726. A blank in the Bodleian MS. was supplied in 1715 by Thomas Hearne from another Oxford MS. Tischendorf's text is from a recension of three Paris MSS., each of the eleventh century.

III. *Acts of Barnabas.* — This book has more an air of truth about it that any of the others. There is not much extravagance in the details, and the geography is correct, showing that the writer knew Cyprus well. It seems to have been written at all events before 478, in which year the body of Barnabas is said to have been found in Cyprus.

Papebroche first edited the book in the *Acta Sanctorum* in 1698, with a Latin translation. The Vatican MS. which he used was an imperfect one. Tischendorf's text is from a Parisian MS. of the end of the ninth century.

IV. *Acts of Philip.* — A book under this name was condemned in the decree of Pope Gelasius ; and that the traditions about Philip were well known from an early date, is evident from the abundant references to them in ancient documents. The writings of the Hagiographers also, both Greek and Latin, contain epitomes of Philip's life.

The Greek text, now first published, is a recension of two MSS., — a Parisian one of the eleventh century, and a Venetian one. The latter is noticeable, from being superscribed *From the Fifteenth Act to the end*, leaving us to infer that we have only a portion of the book.

V. *Acts of Philip in Hellas.* — This also is published for the first time by Tischendorf. It is obviously a later document than the preceding, though composed in the same style. It is from a Parisian MS. of the eleventh century.

---

[1] [That is, this is the tradition. Of such Hebrew original there is no trace. — R.]

VI. *Acts of Andrew.* — In the decree of Pope Gelasius (*d.* 496), a book under this name is condemned as apocryphal. Epiphanius (*d.* 403) states that the Acts of Andrew were in favour with the Encratites, the Apostolics, and the Origenians; Augustine (*d.* 430) mentions that the Acts of the Apostles written by Leucius Charinus — *discipulus diaboli*, as Pope Gelasius calls him — were held in estimation by the Manichæans. The authorship generally is attributed to Leucius by early writers; Innocentius I. (*d.* 417), however, says that the Acts of Andrew were composed by the philosophers Nexocharis and Leonidas. This book is much the same in substance with the celebrated *Presbyterorum et Diaconorum Achaiæ de martyrio S. Andreæ apostoli epistola encyclica,* first edited in Greek by Woog in 1749, and by him considered to be a genuine writing of the apostolic age, composed about A.D. 80. Thilo, while dissenting from this opinion of Woog's, concludes that it is a fragment from the Acts of Leucius, expurgated of most of its heresy, and put into its present shape by an orthodox writer. Cardinals Baronius and Bellarmine assign the epistle to the apostolic age; Fabricius thinks it much later.

The probability is that the book was written by Leucius, following earlier traditions, and that it was afterwards revised and fitted for general reading by an orthodox hand.

Though some of the traditions mentioned in the book are referred to by authors of the begin- ing of the fifth century, there does not seem to be any undoubted quotation of it before the eighth and the tenth centuries. Some portions of Pseudo-Abdias, however, are almost in the words of our Greek Acts.

The text is edited chiefly from two MSS., — the one of the eleventh, the other of the four- teenth century.

The Greek of the original is good of the kind, and exhibits considerable rhetorical skill.

VII. *Acts of Andrew and Matthias.* — Thilo assigns the authorship of these Acts also to Leucius, and the use of them to the Gnostics, Manichæans, and other heretics. Pseudo-Abdias seems to have derived his account of Andrew and Matthias from the same source. Epiphanius the monk, who wrote in the tenth century, gives extracts from the history. There is, besides, an old English — commonly called Anglo-Saxon — poem, Andrew and Helene, published by Jacob Grimm in 1840, the argument of which in great part coincides with that of the Acts of Andrew and Matthias.

There is considerable doubt as to whether it is Matthias or Matthew that is spoken of. Pseudo-Abdias, followed by all the Latin writers on the subject, calls him Matthew. The Greek texts hesitate between the two. Tischendorf edits Matthias, on the authority of his oldest MS. There is also some discrepancy as to the name of the town. Some MSS. say Sinope, others Myrmene or Myrna : they generally, however, coincide in calling it a town of Æthiopia.

Thilo, and Tischendorf after him, made use chiefly of three MSS., only one of which, of the fifteenth century, contains the whole book. The oldest is an uncial MS. of about the eighth century.

The Acts of Peter and Andrew, from the Bodleian MS., are inserted as an appendix to the Acts of Andrew and Matthias.

VIII. *Acts of Matthew.* — This book is edited by Tischendorf for the first time. It is a much later production than the last, written in bad Greek, and in a style rendered very cumbrous by the use of participial phrases.

On the authority of the oldest MS., Matthew, not Matthias, is the name here. It is probably owing to this confusion between the names, that there is much uncertainty in the traditions regard- ing St. Matthew.

Tischendorf gives, in his *Prolegomena*, a long extract from Nicephorus, which shows that he was acquainted with this book, or something very like it.

The text is edited from two MSS., — a Parisian of the eleventh century, and a Viennese of a later date.

IX. *Acts of Thomas.* — The substance of this book is of great antiquity, and in its original form it was held in great estimation by the heretics of the first and second centuries. The main heresy which it contained was that the Apostle Thomas baptized, not with water, but with oil only. It is mentioned by Epiphanius, Turribius, and Nicephorus, condemned in the decree of Gelasius, and in the Synopsis of Scripture ascribed to Athanasius, in which it is placed, along with the Acts of Peter, Acts of John, and other books, among the *Antilegomena*. St. Augustine in three passages refers to the book in such a way as to show that he had it in something very like its present form. Two centuries later, Pseudo-Abdias made a recension of the book, rejecting the more heretical portions, and adapting it generally to orthodox use. Photius attributes the authorship of this document, as of many other apocryphal Acts, to Leucius Charinus.

The Greek text was first edited, with copious notes ånd prolegomena, by Thilo in 1823. The text from which the present translation is made is a recension of five MSS., the oldest of the tenth century.

X. *Consummation of Thomas.* — This is properly a portion of the preceding book. Pseudo-Abdias follows it very closely, but the Greek of some chapters of his translation or compilation has not yet been discovered.

The text, edited by Tischendorf for the first time, is from a MS. of the eleventh century.

XI. *Martyrdom of Bartholomew.* — This Greek text, now for the first time edited by Tischendorf, is very similar to the account of Bartholomew in Pseudo-Abdias. The editor is inclined to believe, not that the Greek text is a translation of Abdias, which it probably is, but that both it and Abdias are derived from the same source. Tischendorf seems inclined to lay some weight upon the mention made by Abdias of a certain Crato, said to be a disciple of the Apostles Simon and Judas, having written a voluminous history of the apostles, which was translated into Latin by Julius Africanus. The whole story, however, is absurd. It is very improbable that Julius Africanus knew any Latin ; it is possible, however, that he may have compiled some stories of the apostles, that these may have been translated into Latin, and that Pseudo-Crato and Pseudo-Abdias may have derived some of their materials from this source.

The Greek text is edited from a Venetian MS. of the thirteenth century.

XII. *Acts of Thaddæus.* — This document, of which our text is the *editio princeps*, is of some consequence, as giving in another form the famous letters of Christ to Abgarus. Eusebius (*H. E.*, i. 13) says that he found in the archives of Edessa the letters written by their own hands, and that he translated them from the Syriac. The story of the portrait was a later invention. It is found in Pseudo-Abdias (x. 1), and with great detail in Nicephorus (*H. E.*, ii. 7). There is considerable variety in the texts of the letters. They were probably written in Syriac in the third century by some native of Edessa, who wished to add to the importance of his city and the antiquity of his church. See the whole subject discussed in Dr. Cureton's *Ancient Syriac Documents relative to the earliest establishment of Christianity in Edessa.*

The Greek text, which is probably of the sixth or seventh century, seems, from allusions to the synagogue, the hours of prayer, the Sabbath-day, etc., to have been written by a Jew. It is edited from a Paris MS. of the eleventh century, and a Vienna one of a later date.

XIII. *Acts of John.* — A book under this title is mentioned by Eusebius, Epiphanius, Photius, among Greek writers ; Augustine, Philastrius, Innocent I., and Turribius among Latin writers. The two last named and Photius ascribe the authorship to Leucius, *discipulus diaboli*, who got the credit of all these heretical *brochures*. It is not named in the decree of Gelasius.

Augustine (*Tractat. 124 in Johannem*) relates at length the story of John going down alive into his grave, and of the fact of his being alive being shown by his breath stirring about the dust on the tomb. This story, which has some resemblance to the Teutonic legend of Barbarossa, is reputed by Photius.

There is a Latin document published by Fabricius, *Pseudo-Melitonis liber de Passione S. Johannis Evangelistæ*, which the author professed to write with the original of Leucius before his eyes. It has considerable resemblances in some passages to the present text. The only passages in Pseudo-Abdias that appear to have any connection with the present document are those which refer to the apostle's burial.

The text is edited from a Paris MS. of the eleventh century, and a Vienna one, to which no date is assigned.

It is doubtful whether the narrative part of the Acts of John be by the same hand as the discourses.

PART III. — APOCRYPHAL APOCALYPSES.

This portion of the volume, extending from page 565 to page 598, consists of seven documents, four of which are called Apocalypses by their authors. Of these, the Greek text of the first three is edited for the first time ; the fourth, the Apocalypse of John, has appeared before. The fifth, The Falling Asleep of Mary, appears for the first time in its Greek form, and in the first Latin recension of it.

The MSS. of these documents are characterized by extreme variety of readings ; and in some of them, especially the earlier portion of the Apocalypse of Esdras, the text is in a very corrupt state.

I. *The Apocalypse of Moses.* — This document belongs to the Apocrypha of the Old Testament rather than that of the New. We have been unable to find in it any reference to any Christian writing. In its form, too, it appears to be a portion of some larger work. Parts of it at least are of an ancient date, as it is very likely from this source that the writer of the Gospel of Nicodemus took the celebrated legend of the Tree of Life and the Oil of Mercy. An account of this legend will be found in Cowper's *Apocryphal Gospels*, xcix.–cii. ; in Maury, *Croyances et Légendes de l'Antiquité*, p. 294 ; in Renan's commentary to the Syriac text of the Penitence of Adam, edited and translated by Renan in the *Journal Asiatique* for 1853. There appeared a poetical rendering of the legend in *Blackwood's Magazine* ten or twelve years ago.

Tischendorf's text is made from four MSS. : A, a Venice MS. of the thirteenth century ; B and C, Vienna MSS. of the thirteenth and twelfth centuries respectively ; and D, a Milan MS. of about the eleventh century.

II. *The Apocalypse of Esdras.* — This book is a weak imitation of the apocryphal fourth book of Esdras. Thilo, in his prolegomena to the Acts of Thomas, p. lxxxii., mentions it, and doubts whether it be the fourth book of Esdras or not. Portions of it were published by Dr. Hase of the Paris Library, and it was then seen that it was a different production. The MS. is of about the fifteenth century, and in the earlier portions very difficult to read.

III. *The Apocalypse of Paul.* — There are two apocryphal books bearing the name of Paul mentioned by ancient writers : The Ascension of Paul, adopted by the Cainites and the Gnostics ; and the Apocalypse of Paul, spoken of by Augustine and Sozomen. There seems to be no doubt that the present text, discovered by Tischendorf in 1843, and published by him in 1866, is the book mentioned by Augustine and Sozomen. It is referred to by numerous authorities, one of whom, however, ascribes it to the heretic Paul of Samosata, the founder of the sect of the Paulicians.

There appear to be versions of it in Coptic, Syriac, and Arabic. One of the Syriac versions, from an Urumiyeh MS., was translated into English by an American missionary in 1864. This translation, or the greater portion of it, is printed by Tischendorf along with his edition of the text.

Tischendorf, upon what seems to be pretty good evidence, ascribes it to the year 380. It is from a Milan MS. of not earlier than the fifteenth century. There is another MS. two centuries older; but they both seem to be copied from the same original. The Syriac seems to be later than the Greek, and, according to Eastern fashion, fuller in details.

IV. *The Apocalypse of John.* — In the scholia to the Grammar of Dionysius the Thracian, ascribed to the ninth century, immediately after the ascription of the Apocalypse of Paul to Paul of Samosata, there occurs the following statement: ' And there is another called the Apocalypse of John the Theologian. We do not speak of that in the island of Patmos, God forbid, for it is most true ; but of a supposititious and spurious one.' This is the oldest reference to this Apocalypse. Asseman says he found the book in Arabic in three MSS.

The document was first edited by Birch in 1804, from a Vatican MS., collated with a Vienna MS. For his edition Tischendorf collated other five MSS., two of Paris, three of Vienna, of from the fourteenth to the sixteenth century.

Of other Apocalypses, Tischendorf in his *Prolegomena* gives an abstract of the Apocalypse of Peter, the Apocalypse of Bartholomew, the Apocalypse of Mary, and the Apocalypse of Daniel. The Apocalypse of Peter professes to be written by Clement. There is an Arabic MS. of it in the Bodleian Library. It is called the Perfect Book, or the Book of Perfection, and consists of eighty-nine chapters, comprising a history of the world as revealed to Peter, from the foundation of the world to the appearing of Antichrist.

The Apocalypse of Bartholomew, from a MS. in the Paris Library, was edited and translated by Dulaurier in 1835. The translation appears in Tischendorf's *Prolegomena.*

The Apocalypse of Mary, containing her descent to the lower world, appears in several Greek MSS. It is of a late date, the work of some monk of the middle ages.

The Apocalypse of Daniel, otherwise called the Revelation of the Prophet Daniel about the consummation of the world, is also of a late date. About the half of the Greek text is given in the *Prolegomena.* We have not thought it necessary to translate it.

V., VI., VII. *The Assumption of Mary.* — It is somewhat strange that the Greek text of this book, which has been translated into several languages both of the East and the West, is edited by Tischendorf for the first time. He assigns it to a date not later than the fourth century. A book under this title is condemned in the decree of Gelasius. The author of the Second Latin Form (see p. 595, note), writing under the name of Melito, ascribes the authorship of a treatise on the same subject to Leucius. This, however, cannot be the book so ascribed to Leucius, as Pseudo-Melito affirms that his book, which is in substance the same as the Greek text, was written to condemn Leucius' heresies.

There are translations or recensions of our text in Syriac, Sahidic, and Arabic. The Syriac was edited and translated by Wright in 1865, in his *Contributions to the Apocryphal Literature of the New Testament.* Another recension of it was published in the *Journal of Sacred Literature* for January and April, 1864. An Arabic version of it, resembling more the Syriac than the Greek or Latin, was edited and translated by Enger in 1854. The Sahidic recension, published and translated by Zoega and Dulaurier, is considerably different from our present texts. The numerous Latin recensions also differ considerably from each other, as will be seen from a comparison of the First Latin Form with the Second. They are all, however, from the same source, and that probably the Greek text which we have translated. The Greek texts, again, exhibit considerable variations, especially in the latter portions.

In the end of the seventh century, John Archbishop of Thessalonica wrote a discourse on the falling asleep of Mary, mainly derived from the book of Pseudo-John ; and in some MSS. this treatise of John of Thessalonica is ascribed to John the Apostle. Epiphanius, however, makes distinctive mention of both treatises.

For his edition of the Greek text, Tischendorf made use of five MSS., the oldest of the eleventh century.

The First Latin Form is edited from three Italian MSS., the oldest of the thirteenth century.

The Second Latin Form, which has been previously published elsewhere, is from a Venetian MS. of the fourteenth century.

We have now concluded our notices, compiled chiefly from Tischendorf's *Prolegomena*, of the Apocryphal Literature of the New Testament.

While these documents are of considerable interest and value, as giving evidence of a widespread feeling in early times of the importance of the events which form the basis of our belief, and as affording us curious glimpses of the state of the Christian conscience, and of modes of Christian thought, in the first centuries of our era, the predominant impression which they leave on our minds is a profound sense of the immeasurable superiority, the unapproachable simplicity and majesty, of the Canonical Writings.

ST. ANDREWS, 26th March, 1870.

THE PROTEVANGELIUM OF JAMES

THE BIRTH OF MARY THE HOLY MOTHER OF GOD, AND VERY GLORIOUS MOTHER OF JESUS CHRIST.[1]

1. IN the records of the twelve tribes of Israel was Joachim, a man rich exceedingly; and he brought his offerings double,[2] saying: There shall be of my superabundance to all the people, and there shall be the offering for my forgiveness[3] to the Lord for a propitiation for me.[4] For the great day of the Lord was at hand, and the sons of Israel were bringing their offerings. And there stood over against him Rubim, saying: It is not meet for thee first to bring thine offerings, because thou hast not made seed in Israel.[5] And Joachim was exceedingly grieved, and went away to the registers of the twelve tribes of the people, saying: I shall see the registers of the twelve tribes of Israel, as to whether I alone have not made seed in Israel. And he searched, and found that all the righteous had raised up seed in Israel. And he called to mind the patriach Abraham, that in the last day[6] God gave him a son Isaac. And Joachim was exceedingly grieved, and did not come into the presence of his wife; but he retired to the desert,[7] and there pitched his tent, and fasted forty days and forty nights,[8] saying in himself: I will not go down either for food or for drink until the Lord my God shall look upon me, and prayer shall be my food and drink.

2. And his wife Anna[9] mourned in two mournings, and lamented in two lamentations, saying:

I shall bewail my widowhood; I shall bewail my childlessness. And the great day of the Lord was at hand; and Judith[10] her maid-servant said: How long dost thou humiliate thy soul? Behold, the great day of the Lord is at hand, and it is unlawful for thee to mourn. But take this head-band, which the woman that made it gave to me; for it is not proper that I should wear it, because I am a maid-servant, and it has a royal appearance.[11] And Anna said: Depart from me; for I have not done such things, and the Lord has brought me very low. I fear that some wicked person has given it to thee, and thou hast come to make me a sharer in thy sin. And Judith said: Why should I curse thee, seeing that[12] the Lord hath shut thy womb, so as not to give thee fruit in Israel? And Anna was grieved exceedingly, and put off her garments of mourning, and cleaned her head, and put on her wedding garments, and about the ninth hour went down to the garden to walk. And she saw a laurel, and sat under it, and prayed to the Lord, saying: O God of our fathers, bless me and hear my prayer, as Thou didst bless the womb of Sarah, and didst give her a son Isaac.[13]

3. And gazing towards the heaven, she saw a sparrow's nest in the laurel,[14] and made a lamentation in herself, saying: Alas! who begot me? and what womb produced me? because I have become a curse in the presence of the sons of Israel, and I have been reproached, and they have driven me in derision out of the temple of the Lord. Alas! to what have I been likened? I am not like the fowls of the heaven, because even the fowls of the heaven are productive before Thee, O Lord. Alas! to what have I been likened? I am not like the beasts of the earth, because even the beasts of the earth are productive before Thee, O Lord. Alas! to what have I been likened? I am not like these waters, because

---

[1] [This title is taken by Tischendorf from a manuscript of the eleventh century (Paris). At least seventeen other forms exist. The book is variously named by ancient writers. In the decree of Gelasius (A.D. 495) he condemns it as *Evangelium nomine Jacobi minoris apocryphum.*
　The text of Tischendorf, here translated, is somewhat less diffuse than that of Fabricius, and is based on manuscript evidence. The variations are verbal and formal rather than material. — R.]

[2] Susanna i. 4.

[3] The readings vary, and the sense is doubtful. Thilo thinks that the sense is: What I offer over and above what the law requires is for the benefit of the whole people; but the offering I make for my own forgiveness (according to the law's requirements) shall be to the Lord, that He may be rendered merciful to me.

[4] The Church of Rome appoints March 20 as the Feast of St. Joachim. His liberality is commemorated in prayers, and the lessons to be read are Wisd. xxxi. and Matt. i.

[5] 1 Sam. i. 6, 7; Hos. ix. 14.

[6] Another reading is: In his last days.

[7] Another reading is: Into the hill-country.

[8] Moses: Ex. xxiv. 18, xxxiv. 28; Deut. ix. 9. Elijah: 1 Kings xix. 8. Christ: Matt. iv. 2.

[9] The 26th of July is the Feast of St. Anna in the Church of Rome.

[10] Other forms of the name are Juth, Juthin.

[11] Some MSS. have: For I am thy maid-servant, and thou hast a regal appearance.

[12] Several MSS. insert: Thou hast not listened to my voice; for.

[13] Comp. 1 Sam. i. 9-18.

[14] Tobit ii. 10.

even these waters are productive before Thee, O Lord. Alas! to what have I been likened? I am not like this earth, because even the earth bringeth forth its fruits in season, and blesseth Thee, O Lord.[1]

4. And, behold, an angel of the Lord stood by, saying: Anna, Anna, the Lord hath heard thy prayer, and thou shalt conceive, and shalt bring forth; and thy seed shall be spoken of in all the world. And Anna said: As the Lord my God liveth, if I beget either male or female, I will bring it as a gift to the Lord my God; and it shall minister to Him in holy things all the days of its life.[2] And, behold, two angels came, saying to her: Behold, Joachim thy husband is coming with his flocks.[3] For an angel of the Lord went down to him, saying: Joachim, Joachim, the Lord God hath heard thy prayer Go down hence; for, behold, thy wife Anna shall conceive. And Joachim went down and called his shepherds, saying: Bring me hither ten she-lambs without spot or blemish, and they shall be for the Lord my God; and bring me twelve tender calves, and they shall be for the priests and the elders; and a hundred goats for all the people. And, behold, Joachim came with his flocks; and Anna stood by the gate, and saw Joachim coming, and she ran and hung upon his neck, saying: Now I know that the Lord God hath blessed me exceedingly; for, behold, the widow no longer a widow, and I the child-less shall conceive. And Joachim rested the first day in his house.

5. And on the following day he brought his offerings, saying in himself: If the Lord God has been rendered gracious to me, the plate[4] on the priest's forehead will make it manifest to me. And Joachim brought his offerings, and observed attentively the priest's plate when he went up to the altar of the Lord, and he saw no sin in himself. And Joachim said: Now I know that the Lord has been gracious unto me, and has remitted all my sins. And he went down from the temple of the Lord justified, and departed to his own house. And her months were fulfilled, and in the ninth[5] month Anna brought forth. And she said to the midwife: What have I brought forth? and she said: A girl. And said Anna: My soul has been magnified this day. And she laid her down. And the days having been fulfilled, Anna was purified, and gave the breast to the child,[6] and called her name Mary.

6. And the child grew strong day by day; and when she was six[7] months old, her mother set her on the ground to try whether she could stand, and she walked seven steps and came into her bosom; and she snatched her up, saying: As the Lord my God liveth, thou shalt not walk on this earth until I bring thee into the temple of the Lord. And she made a sanctuary in her bed-chamber, and allowed nothing common or unclean to pass through her. And she called the undefiled daughters of the Hebrews, and they led her astray.[8] And when she was a year old, Joachim made a great feast, and invited the priests, and the scribes, and the elders, and all the people of Israel. And Joachim brought the child to the priests; and they blessed her, saying: O God of our fathers, bless this child, and give her an everlasting name to be named in all generations. And all the people said: So be it, so be it, amen. And he brought her to the chief priests; and they blessed her, saying: O God most high, look upon this child, and bless her with the utmost blessing, which shall be for ever. And her mother snatched her up, and took her into the sanctuary of her bed-chamber, and gave her the breast. And Anna made a song to the Lord God, saying: I will sing a song to the Lord my God, for He hath looked upon me, and hath taken away the reproach of mine enemies; and the Lord hath given me the fruit of His right-eousness, singular in its kind, and richly endowed before Him. Who will tell the sons of Rubim that Anna gives suck? Hear, hear, ye twelve tribes of Israel, that Anna gives suck. And she laid her to rest in the bed-chamber of her sanctuary, and went out and ministered unto them. And when the supper was ended, they went down rejoicing, and glorifying the God of Israel.[9]

7. And her months were added to the child. And the child was two years old, and Joachim said: Let us take her up to the temple of the Lord, that we may pay the vow that we have vowed, lest perchance the Lord send to us,[10] and our offering be not received. And Anna said: Let us wait for the third year, in order that the child may not seek for father or mother. And Joachim said: So let us wait. And the child was three years old, and Joachim said: Invite the daughters of the Hebrews that are undefiled, and let them take each a lamp, and let them stand with the lamps burning, that the

---

[1] Many of the mss. here add: Alas! to what have I been likened? I am not like the waves of the sea, because even the waves of the sea, in calm and storm, and the fishes in them, bless Thee, O Lord.

[2] 1 Sam. i. 11.

[3] One of the mss.: With his shepherds, and sheep, and goats, and oxen.

[4] Ex. xxviii. 36–38. For traditions about the *petalon*, see Euseb., H. E., ii. 23, iii. 31, v. 24; Epiph., *Hær.*, 78.

[5] Various readings are: Sixth, seventh, eighth.

[6] One of the mss inserts: On the eighth day.

[7] One of the mss. has nine.

[8] This is the reading of most mss.; but it is difficult to see any sense in it. One ms. reads: They attended on her. Fabricius proposed: They bathed her.

[9] Two of the mss. add: And they gave her the name of Mary, because her name shall not fade for ever. This derivation of the name — from the root *mar*, fade — is one of a dozen or so.

[10] This is taken to mean: Send someone to us to warn us that we have been too long in paying our vow. One ms. reads, lest the Lord depart from us; another, lest the Lord move away from us.

child may not turn back, and her heart be captivated from the temple of the Lord. And they did so until they went up into the temple of the Lord. And the priest received her, and kissed her, and blessed her, saying: The Lord has magnified thy name in all generations. In thee, on the last of the days, the Lord will manifest His redemption to the sons of Israel. And he set her down upon the third step of the altar, and the Lord God sent grace upon her; and she danced with her feet, and all the house of Israel loved her.

8. And her parents went down marvelling, and praising the Lord God, because the child had not turned back. And Mary was in the temple of the Lord as if she were a dove that dwelt there, and she received food from the hand of an angel. And when she was twelve [1] years old there was held a council of the priests, saying: Behold, Mary has reached the age of twelve years in the temple of the Lord. What then shall we do with her, lest perchance she defile the sanctuary of the Lord? And they said to the high priest: Thou standest by the altar of the Lord; go in, and pray concerning her; and whatever the Lord shall manifest unto thee, that also will we do. And the high priest went in, taking the robe [2] with the twelve bells into the holy of holies; and he prayed concerning her. And behold an angel of the Lord stood by him, saying unto him: Zacharias, Zacharias, go out and assemble the widowers of the people, and let them bring each his rod; and to whomsoever the Lord shall show a sign, his wife shall she be. And the heralds went out through all the circuit of Judæa, and the trumpet of the Lord sounded, and all ran.

9. And Joseph, throwing away his axe, went out to meet them; and when they had assembled, they went away to the high priest, taking with them their rods. And he, taking the rods of all of them, entered into the temple, and prayed; and having ended his prayer, he took the rods and came out, and gave them to them: but there was no sign in them, and Joseph took his rod last; and, behold, a dove came out of the rod, and flew upon Joseph's head. And the priest said to Joseph, Thou hast been chosen by lot to take into thy keeping the virgin of the Lord. But Joseph refused, saying: I have children, and I am an old man, and she is a young girl. I am afraid lest I become a laughing-stock to the sons of Israel. And the priest said to Joseph: Fear the Lord thy God, and remember what the Lord did to Dathan, and Abiram, and Korah; [3] how the earth opened, and they were swallowed up on account of their contradiction.

And now fear, O Joseph, lest the same things happen in thy house. And Joseph was afraid, and took her into his keeping. And Joseph said to Mary: Behold, I have received thee from the temple of the Lord; and now I leave thee in my house, and go away to build my buildings, and I shall come to thee. The Lord will protect thee.

10. And there was a council of the priests, saying: Let us make a veil for the temple of the Lord. And the priest said: Call to me the undefiled virgins of the family of David. And the officers went away, and sought, and found seven virgins. And the priest remembered the child Mary, that she was of the family of David, and undefiled before God. And the officers went away and brought her. And they brought them into the temple of the Lord. And the priest said: Choose for me by lot who shall spin the gold, and the white, [4] and the fine linen, and the silk, and the blue, [5] and the scarlet, and the true purple. [6] And the true purple and the scarlet fell to the lot of Mary, and she took them, and went away to her house. And at that time Zacharias was dumb, and Samuel was in his place until the time that Zacharias spake. And Mary took the scarlet, and span it.

11. And she took the pitcher, and went out to fill it with water. And, behold, a voice saying: Hail, thou who hast received grace; the Lord is with thee; blessed art thou among women! [7] And she looked round, on the right hand and on the left, to see whence this voice came. And she went away, trembling, to her house, and put down the pitcher; and taking the purple, she sat down on her seat, and drew it out. And, behold, an angel of the Lord stood before her, saying: Fear not, Mary; for thou hast found grace before the Lord of all, and thou shalt conceive, according to His word. And she hearing, reasoned with herself, saying: Shall I conceive by the Lord, the living God? and shall I bring forth as every woman brings forth? And the angel of the Lord said: Not so, Mary; for the power of the Lord shall overshadow thee: wherefore also that holy thing which shall be born of thee shall be called the Son of the Most High. And thou shalt call His name Jesus, for He shall save His people from their sins. And Mary said: Behold, the servant of the Lord before His face: let it be unto me according to thy word.

12. And she made the purple and the scarlet, and took them to the priest. And the priest blessed her, and said: Mary, the Lord God hath

---

[1] Or, fourteen. Postel's Latin version has *ten*.
[2] Ex. xxviii. 28; Sirach xlv. 9; Justin, *Tryph.*, xlii.
[3] Num. xvi. 31–33.

[4] Lit., undefiled. It is difficult to say what colour is meant, or if it is a colour at all The word is once used to mean the sea, but with no reference to colour. It is also the name of a stone of a greenish hue.
[5] Lit., hyacinth.
[6] Ex. xxv. 4.
[7] Luke i. 28.

magnified thy name, and thou shalt be blessed in all the generations of the earth. And Mary, with great joy, went away to Elizabeth her kins-woman,[1] and knocked at the door. And when Elizabeth heard her, she threw away the scarlet,[2] and ran to the door, and opened it; and seeing Mary, she blessed her, and said: Whence is this to me, that the mother of my Lord should come to me? for, behold, that which is in me leaped and blessed thee.[3] But Mary had forgotten the mysteries of which the archangel Gabriel had spoken, and gazed up into heaven, and said: Who am I, O Lord, that all the generations of the earth should bless me?[4] And she remained three months with Elizabeth; and day by day she grew bigger. And Mary being afraid, went away to her own house, and hid herself from the sons of Israel. And she was sixteen[5] years old when these mysteries happened.

13. And she was in her sixth month; and, behold, Joseph came back from his building, and, entering into his house, he discovered that she was big with child. And he smote[6] his face,[7] and threw himself on the ground upon the sackcloth, and wept bitterly, saying: With what face shall I look upon the Lord my God? and what prayer shall I make about this maiden? because I received her a virgin out of the temple of the Lord, and I have not watched over her. Who is it that has hunted me[8] down? Who has done this evil thing in my house, and defiled the virgin? Has not the history of Adam been repeated in me? For just as Adam was in the hour of his singing praise,[9] and the serpent came, and found Eve alone, and completely deceived her, so it has happened to me also. And Joseph stood up from the sackcloth, and called Mary, and said to her: O thou who hast been cared for by God, why hast thou done this, and forgotten the Lord thy God? Why hast thou brought low thy soul, thou that wast brought up in the holy of holies, and that didst receive food from the hand of an angel? And she wept bitterly, saying: I am innocent, and have known no man. And Joseph said to her: Whence then is that which is in thy womb? And she said: As the Lord my God liveth, I do not know whence it is to me.

14. And Joseph was greatly afraid, and re-tired from her, and considered what he should do in regard to her.[10] And Joseph said: If I conceal her sin, I find myself fighting against the law of the Lord; and if I expose her to the sons of Israel, I am afraid lest that which is in her be from an angel,[11] and I shall be found giving up innocent blood to the doom of death. What then shall I do with her? I will put her away from me secretly. And night came upon him; and, behold, an angel of the Lord appears to him in a dream, saying: Be not afraid for this maiden, for that which is in her is of the Holy Spirit; and she will bring forth a Son, and thou shalt call His name Jesus, for He will save His people from their sins.[12] And Joseph arose from sleep, and glorified the God of Israel, who had given him this grace; and he kept her.

15. And Annas the scribe came to him, and said: Why hast thou not appeared in our assem-bly? And Joseph said to him: Because I was weary from my journey, and rested the first day. And he turned, and saw that Mary was with child. And he ran away to the priest,[13] and said to him: Joseph, whom thou didst vouch for, has committed a grievous crime. And the priest said: How so? And he said: He has defiled the virgin whom he received out of the temple of the Lord, and has married her by stealth, and has not revealed it to the sons of Israel. And the priest answering, said: Has Joseph done this? Then said Annas the scribe: Send offi-cers, and thou wilt find the virgin with child. And the officers went away, and found it as he had said; and they brought her along with Jo-seph to the tribunal. And the priest said: Mary, why hast thou done this? and why hast thou brought thy soul low, and forgotten the Lord thy God? Thou that wast reared in the holy of holies, and that didst receive food from the hand of an angel, and didst hear the hymns, and didst dance before Him, why hast thou done this? And she wept bitterly, saying: As the Lord my God liveth, I am pure before Him, and know not a man. And the priest said to Joseph: Why hast thou done this? And Joseph said: As the Lord liveth, I am pure concerning her. Then said the priest: Bear not false witness, but speak the truth. Thou hast married her by stealth, and hast not revealed it to the sons of Israel, and hast not bowed thy head under the strong hand, that thy seed might be blessed. And Joseph was silent.

16. And the priest said: Give up the virgin whom thou didst receive out of the temple of the Lord. And Joseph burst into tears. And the priest said: I will give you to drink of the water of the ordeal of the Lord,[14] and He shall make manifest your sins in your eyes. And the

---

[1] Luke i. 39, 40.
[2] Other readings are: the wool — what she had in her hand.
[3] Luke i. 43, 44.
[4] Luke i. 48.
[5] Six MSS. have *sixteen;* one, *fourteen;* two, *fifteen;* and one, *seventeen.*
[6] The Latin translation has *hung down.*
[7] Ezek. xxi. 12; Jer. xxxi. 19.
[8] Two MSS.: *her.*
[9] Another reading is: As Adam was in Paradise, and in the hour of the singing of praise (doxology) to God was with the angels, the serpent, etc
[10] Matt. i. 19.

[11] Lit., *angelic;* one MS. has *holy;* the Latin translation, follow-ing a slightly different reading, *that it would not be fair to her.*
[12] Matt. i. 20.
[13] Three MSS. have *high priest.*
[14] Num. v. 11, ff.

priest took the water, and gave Joseph to drink, and sent him away to the hill-country; and he returned unhurt. And he gave to Mary also to drink, and sent her away to the hill-country; and she returned unhurt. And all the people wondered that sin did not appear in them. And the priest said: If the Lord God has not made manifest your sins, neither do I judge you. And he sent them away. And Joseph took Mary, and went away to his own house, rejoicing and glorifying the God of Israel.

17. And there was an order from the Emperor Augustus, that all in Bethlehem of Judæa should be enrolled.[1] And Joseph said: I shall enrol my sons, but what shall I do with this maiden? How shall I enrol her? As my wife? I am ashamed. As my daughter then? But all the sons of Israel know that she is not my daughter. The day of the Lord shall itself bring it to pass[2] as the Lord will. And he saddled the ass, and set her upon it; and his son led it, and Joseph followed.[3] And when they had come within three miles, Joseph turned and saw her sorrowful; and he said to himself: Likely that which is in her distresses her. And again Joseph turned and saw her laughing. And he said to her: Mary, how is it that I see in thy face at one time laughter, at another sorrow? And Mary said to Joseph: Because I see two peoples with my eyes; the one weeping and lamenting, and the other rejoicing and exulting. And they came into the middle of the road, and Mary said to him: Take me down from off the ass, for that which is in me presses to come forth. And he took her down from off the ass, and said to her: Whither shall I lead thee, and cover thy disgrace? for the place is desert.

18. And he found a cave[4] there, and led her into it; and leaving his two sons beside her, he went out to seek a widwife in the district of Bethlehem.

And I Joseph was walking, and was not walking; and I looked up into the sky, and saw the sky astonished; and I looked up to the pole of the heavens, and saw it standing, and the birds of the air keeping still. And I looked down upon the earth, and saw a trough lying, and work-people reclining: and their hands were in the trough. And those that were eating did not eat, and those that were rising did not carry it up, and those that were conveying anything to their mouths did not convey it; but the faces of all were looking upwards. And I saw the sheep walking, and the sheep stood still; and the shepherd raised his hand to strike them, and his hand remained up. And I looked upon the current of the river, and I saw the mouths of the kids resting on the water and not drinking, and all things in a moment were driven from their course.

19. And I saw a woman coming down from the hill-country, and she said to me: O man, whither art thou going? And I said: I am seeking an Hebrew midwife. And she answered and said unto me: Art thou of Israel? And I said to her: Yes. And she said: And who is it that is bringing forth in the cave? And I said: A woman betrothed to me. And she said to me: Is she not thy wife? And I said to her: It is Mary that was reared in the temple of the Lord, and I obtained her by lot as my wife. And yet she is not my wife, but has conceived of the Holy Spirit.

And the widwife said to him: Is this true? And Joseph said to her: Come and see. And the midwife went away with him. And they stood in the place of the cave, and behold a luminous cloud overshadowed the cave. And the midwife said: My soul has been magnified this day, because mine eyes have seen strange things — because salvation has been brought forth to Israel. And immediately the cloud disappeared out of the cave, and a great light shone in the cave, so that the eyes could not bear it. And in a little that light gradually decreased, until the infant appeared, and went and took the breast from His mother Mary. And the midwife cried out, and said: This is a great day to me, because I have seen this strange sight. And the midwife went forth out of the cave, and Salome met her. And she said to her: Salome, Salome, I have a strange sight to relate to thee: a virgin has brought forth — a thing which her nature admits not of. Then said Salome: As the Lord my God liveth, unless I thrust in my finger, and search the parts, I will not believe that a virgin has brought forth.

20. And the midwife went in, and said to Mary: Show thyself; for no small controversy has arisen about thee. And Salome put in her finger, and cried out, and said: Woe is me for mine iniquity and mine unbelief, because I have tempted the living God; and, behold, my hand is dropping off as if burned with fire. And she bent her knees before the Lord, saying: O God of my fathers, remember that I am the seed of Abraham, and Isaac, and Jacob; do not make a show of me to the sons of Israel, but restore me to the poor; for Thou knowest, O Lord, that in Thy name I have performed my services, and that I have received my reward at Thy

---

[1] Luke ii. 1.
[2] Or: On this day of the Lord I will do, etc.
[3] Another reading is: And his son Samuel led it, and James and Simon followed.
[4] Bethlehem . . . used to be overshadowed by a grove of Thammuz, i.e., Adonis; and in the cave where Christ formerly wailed as an infant, they used to mourn for the beloved of Venus (*Jerome to Paulinus*). In his letter to Sabinianus the cave is repeatedly mentioned: "That cave in which the Son of God was born;" "that venerable cave," etc, "within the door of what was once the Lord's manger, now the altar." "Then you run to the place of the shepherds." There appears also to have been above the altar the figure of an angel, or angels. See also Justin, *Tryph.*, 78.

hand. And, behold, an angel of the Lord stood by her, saying to her : Salome, Salome, the Lord hath heard thee. Put thy hand to the infant, and carry it, and thou wilt have safety and joy. And Salome went and carried it, saying : I will worship Him, because a great King has been born to Israel. And, behold, Salome was immediately cured, and she went forth out of the cave justified. And behold a voice saying : Salome, Salome, tell not the strange things thou hast seen, until the child has come into Jerusalem.

21. And, behold, Joseph was ready to go into Judæa. And there was a great commotion in Bethlehem of Judæa, for Magi came, saying : Where is he that is born king of the Jews? for we have seen his star in the east, and have come to worship him. And when Herod heard, he was much disturbed, and sent officers to the Magi. And he sent for the priests, and examined them, saying : How is it written about the Christ? where is He to be born? And they said : In Bethlehem of Judæa, for so it is written.[1] And he sent them away. And he examined the Magi, saying to them : What sign have you seen in reference to the king that has been born? And the Magi said : We have seen a star of great size shining among these stars, and obscuring their light, so that the stars did not appear ; and we thus knew that a king has been born to Israel, and we have come to worship him. And Herod said : Go and seek him ; and if you find him, let me know, in order that I also may go and worship him. And the Magi went out. And, behold, the star which they had seen in the east went before them until they came to the cave, and it stood over the top of the cave. And the Magi saw the infant with His mother Mary ; and they brought forth from their bag gold, and frankincense, and myrrh. And having been warned by the angel not to go into Judæa, they went into their own country by another road.[2]

22. And when Herod knew that he had been mocked by the Magi, in a rage he sent murderers, saying to them : Slay the children[3] from two years old and under. And Mary, having heard that the children were being killed, was afraid, and took the infant and swaddled Him, and put Him into an ox-stall. And Elizabeth, having heard that they were searching for John, took him and went up into the hill-country, and kept looking where to conceal him. And there was no place of concealment. And Elizabeth, groaning with a loud voice, says : O mountain of God, receive mother and child. And immediately the mountain was cleft, and received her. And a light shone about them, for an angel of the Lord was with them, watching over them.

23. And Herod searched for John, and sent officers to Zacharias, saying : Where hast thou hid thy son? And he, answering, said to them : I am the servant of God in holy things, and I sit constantly in the temple of the Lord : I do not know where my son is. And the officers went away, and reported all these things to Herod. And Herod was enraged, and said : His son is destined to be king over Israel. And he sent to him again, saying : Tell the truth ; where is thy son? for thou knowest that thy life is in my hand. And Zacharias said : I am God's martyr, if thou sheddest my blood ; for the Lord will receive my spirit, because thou sheddest innocent blood at the vestibule of the temple of the Lord. And Zacharias was murdered about daybreak. And the sons of Israel did not know that he had been murdered.[4]

24. But at the hour of the salutation the priests went away, and Zacharias did not come forth to meet them with a blessing, according to his custom.[5] And the priests stood waiting for Zacharias to salute him at the prayer,[6] and to glorify the Most High. And he still delaying, they were all afraid. But one of them ventured to go in, and he saw clotted blood beside the altar ; and he heard a voice saying : Zacharias has been murdered, and his blood shall not be wiped up until his avenger come. And hearing this saying, he was afraid, and went out and told it to the priests. And they ventured in, and saw what had happened ; and the fretwork of the temple made a wailing noise, and they rent their clothes[7] from the top even to the bottom. And they found not his body, but they found his blood turned into stone. And they were afraid, and went out and reported to the people that Zacharias had been murdered. And all the tribes of the people heard, and mourned, and lamented for him three days and three nights. And after the three days, the priests consulted as to whom they should put in his place ; and the lot fell upon Simeon. For it was he who had been warned by the Holy Spirit that he should not see death until he should see the Christ in the flesh.[8]

And I James that wrote this history in Jerusalem, a commotion having arisen when Herod died, withdrew myself to the wilderness until the commotion in Jerusalem ceased, glorifying

---

[1] Two MSS. here add: And thou Bethlehem, etc., from Mic. v. 2.
[2] Matt. ii. 1-12. One of the MSS. here adds Matt. ii. 13-15, with two or three slight variations.
[3] Four MSS. have *all the male children*, as in Matt. ii. 16.

[4] Another reading is: And Herod, enraged at this, ordered him to be slain in the midst of the altar before the dawn, that the slaying of him might not be prevented by the people. [This incident was probably suggested by the reference to "Zacharias the son of Barachias" in Matt. xxiii. 35, Luke xi. 51; but comp 2 Chron. xxiv. 20-22. — R.]
[5] Lit., the blessing of Zacharias did not come forth, etc.
[6] Or, with prayer.
[7] Another reading is: And was rent from the top, etc.
[8] Luke ii. 26. One of the MSS. here adds Matt. ii. 19-23, with two or three verbal changes.

the Lord God, who had given me the gift and the wisdom to write this history.[1] And grace shall be with them that fear our Lord Jesus Christ, to whom be glory to ages of ages. Amen.[2]

[1] [Assuming that this is among the most ancient of the Apocryphal Gospels, it is noteworthy that the writer abstains from elaborating his statements on points fully narrated in the Canonical Gospels. The *supplementary* character of the earliest of these writings is obvious. But what a contrast between the impressive silence of the New-Testament narratives, and the garrulity, not to say indelicacy, of these detailed descriptions of the Nativity! — R.]

[2] The MSS. vary much in the doxology.

THE GOSPEL OF PSEUDO-MATTHEW

HERE beginneth the book of the Birth of the Blessed Mary and the Infancy of the Saviour. Written in Hebrew by the Blessed Evangelist Matthew, and translated into Latin by the Blessed Presbyter Jerome.

To their well-beloved brother Jerome the Presbyter, Bishops Cromatius and Heliodorus in the Lord, greeting.

The birth of the Virgin Mary, and the nativity and infancy of our Lord Jesus Christ, we find in apocryphal books. But considering that in them many things contrary to our faith are written, we have believed that they ought all to be rejected, lest perchance we should transfer the joy of Christ to Antichrist.[1] While, therefore, we were considering these things, there came holy men, Parmenius and Varinus, who said that your Holiness had found a Hebrew volume, written by the hand of the most blessed Evangelist Matthew, in which also the birth of the virgin mother herself, and the infancy of our Saviour, were written. And accordingly we entreat your affection by our Lord Jesus Christ Himself, to render it from the Hebrew into Latin,[2] not so much for the attainment of those things which are the insignia of Christ, as for the exclusion of the craft of heretics, who, in order to teach bad doctrine, have mingled their own lies with the excellent nativity of Christ, that by the sweetness of life they might hide the bitterness of death. It will therefore become your purest piety, either to listen to us as your brethren entreating, or to let us have as bishops exacting, the debt of affection which you may deem due.

REPLY TO THEIR LETTER BY JEROME.

To my lords the holy and most blessed Bishops Cromatius and Heliodorus, Jerome, a humble servant of Christ, in the Lord greeting.

He who digs in ground where he knows that there is gold,[3] does not instantly snatch at whatever the uptorn trench may pour forth ; but, before the stroke of the quivering spade raises aloft the glittering mass, he meanwhile lingers over the sods to turn them over and lift them up, and especially he who has not added to his gains. An arduous task is enjoined upon me, since what your Blessedness has commanded me, the holy Apostle and Evangelist Matthew himself did not write for the purpose of publishing. For if he had not done it somewhat secretly, he would have added it also to his Gospel which he published. But he composed this book in Hebrew ; and so little did he publish it, that at this day the book written in Hebrew by his own hand is in the possession of very religious men, to whom in successive periods of time it has been handed down by those that were before them. And this book they never at any time gave to any one to translate. And so it came to pass, that when it was published by a disciple of Manichæus named Leucius, who also wrote the falsely styled Acts of the Apostles, this book afforded matter, not of edification, but of perdition ; and the opinion of the Synod in regard to it was according to its deserts, that the ears of the Church should not be open to it. Let the snapping of those that bark against us now cease ; for we do not add this little book to the canonical writings, but we translate what was written by an Apostle and Evangelist, that we may disclose the falsehood of heresy. In this work, then, we obey the commands of pious bishops as well as oppose impious heretics. It is the love of Christ, therefore, which we fulfil, believing that they will assist us by their prayers, who through our obedience attain to a knowledge of the holy infancy of our Saviour.

There is extant another letter to the same bishops, attributed to Jerome : —

You ask me to let you know what I think of a book held by some to be about the nativity of St. Mary. And so I wish you to know that there is much in it that is false. For one Seleucus, who wrote the Sufferings of the Apostles, composed this book. But, just as he wrote what was true about their powers, and the miracles they worked, but said a great deal that was false about their doctrine ; so here too he has invented many untruths out of his own head. I shall take care to render it word for word, exactly as it is in the

---

368

Hebrew, since it is asserted that it was composed by the holy Evangelist Matthew, and written in Hebrew, and set at the head of his Gospel. Whether this be true or not, I leave to the author of the preface and the trustworthiness of the writer: as for myself, I pronounce them doubtful; I do not affirm that they are clearly false. But this I say freely — and I think none of the faithful will deny it — that, whether these stories be true or inventions, the sacred nativity of St. Mary was preceded by great miracles, and succeeded by the greatest; and so by those who believe that God can do these things, they can be believed and read without damaging their faith or imperilling their souls. In short, so far as I can, following the sense rather than the words of the writer, and sometimes walking in the same path, though not in the same footsteps, sometimes digressing a little, but still keeping the same road, I shall in this way keep by the style of the narrative, and shall say nothing that is not either written there, or might, following the same train of thought, have been written.

CHAP. 1.[1] — In those days there was a man in Jerusalem, Joachim by name, of the tribe of Judah. He was the shepherd of his own sheep, fearing the Lord in integrity and singleness of heart. He had no other care than that of his herds, from the produce of which he supplied with food all that feared God, offering double gifts in the fear of God to all who laboured in doctrine, and who ministered unto Him. Therefore his lambs, and his sheep, and his wool, and all things whatsoever he possessed, he used to divide into three portions: one he gave to the orphans, the widows, the strangers, and the poor; the second to those that worshipped God; and the third he kept for himself and all his house.[2] And as he did so, the Lord multiplied to him his herds, so that there was no man like him in the people of Israel. This now he began to do when he was fifteen years old. And at the age of twenty he took to wife Anna, the daughter of Achar, of his own tribe, that is, of the tribe of Judah, of the family of David. And though they had lived together for twenty years, he had by her neither sons nor daughters.[3]

CHAP. 2. — And it happened that, in the time of the feast, among those who were offering incense to the Lord, Joachim stood getting ready his gifts in the sight of the Lord. And the priest, Ruben by name, coming to him, said: It is not lawful for thee to stand among those who are doing sacrifice to God, because God has not blessed thee so as to give thee seed in Israel. Being therefore put to shame in the sight of the people, he retired from the temple of the Lord weeping, and did not return to his house, but went to his flocks, taking with him his shepherds into the mountains to a far country, so that for five months his wife Anna could hear no tidings of him. And she prayed with tears, saying: O Lord, most mighty God of Israel, why hast Thou, seeing that already Thou hast not given me children, taken from me my husband also? Behold, now five months that I have not seen my husband; and I know not where he is tarrying;[4] nor, if I knew him to be dead, could I bury him. And while she wept excessively, she entered into the court of His house; and she fell on her face in prayer, and poured out her supplications before the Lord. After this, rising from her prayer, and lifting her eyes to God, she saw a sparrow's nest in a laurel tree,[5] and uttered her voice to the Lord with groaning, and said: Lord God Almighty, who hast given offspring to every creature, to beasts wild and tame, to serpents, and birds, and fishes, and they all rejoice over their young ones, Thou hast shut out me alone from the gift of Thy benignity. For Thou, O God, knowest my heart, that from the beginning of my married life I have vowed that, if Thou, O God, shouldst give me son or daughter, I would offer them to Thee in Thy holy temple. And while she was thus speaking, suddenly an angel of the Lord appeared before her, saying: Be not afraid, Anna, for there is seed for thee in the decree of God; and all generations even to the end shall wonder at that which shall be born of thee. And when he had thus spoken, he vanished out of her sight. But she, in fear and dread because she had seen such a sight, and heard such words, at length went into her bed-chamber, and threw herself on the bed as if dead. And for a whole day and night she remained in great trembling and in prayer. And after these things she called to her servant, and said to her: Dost thou see me deceived in my widowhood and in great perplexity, and hast thou been unwilling to come in to me? Then she, with a slight murmur, thus answered and said: If God hath shut up thy womb, and hath taken away thy husband from thee, what can I do for thee? And when Anna heard this, she lifted up her voice, and wept aloud.

---

[1] Two of the MSS. have this prologue: I James, the son of Joseph, living in the fear of God, have written all that with my own eyes I saw coming to pass in the time of the nativity of the holy virgin Mary, or of the Lord the Saviour; giving thanks to God, who has given me wisdom in the accounts of His Advent, showing His abounding grace to the twelve tribes of Israel.

[2] Tobit i. 7.

[3] One of the MSS. has: Only they vowed that, if God should give them offspring, they would devote it to the service of the temple; and because of this, they were wont to go to the temple of the Lord at each of the yearly festivals.

[4] Another reading is: Where he has died — reading *mortuus* for *moratus.*

[5] Comp. Tobit ii. 10.

CHAP. 3. — At the same time there appeared a young man on the mountains to Joachim while he was feeding his flocks, and said to him : Why dost thou not return to thy wife? And Joachim said : I have had her for twenty years, and it has not been the will of God to give me children by her. I have been driven with shame and reproach from the temple of the Lord: why should I go back to her, when I have been once cast off and utterly despised? Here then will I remain with my sheep ; and so long as in this life God is willing to grant me light, I shall willingly, by the hands of my servants, bestow their portions upon the poor, and the orphans, and those that fear God. And when he had thus spoken, the young man said to him : I am an angel of the Lord, and I have to-day appeared to thy wife when she was weeping and praying, and have consoled her ; and know that she has conceived a daughter from thy seed, and thou in thy ignorance of this hast left her. She will be in the temple of God, and the Holy Spirit shall abide in her ; and her blessedness shall be greater than that of all the holy women, so that no one can say that any before her has been like her, or that any after her in this world will be so. Therefore go down from the mountains, and return to thy wife, whom thou wilt find with child. For God hath raised up seed in her, and for this thou wilt give God thanks ; and her seed shall be blessed, and she herself shall be blessed, and shall be made the mother of eternal blessing. Then Joachim adored the angel, and said to him : If I have found favour in thy sight, sit for a little in my tent, and bless thy servant.[1] And the angel said to him : Do not say servant, but fellow-servant ; for we are the servants of one Master.[2] But my food is invisible, and my drink cannot be seen by a mortal. Therefore thou oughtest not to ask me to enter thy tent ; but if thou wast about to give me anything,[3] offer it as a burnt-offering to the Lord. Then Joachim took a lamb without spot, and said to the angel : I should not have dared to offer a burnt-offering to the Lord, unless thy command had given me the priest's right of offering.[4] And the angel said to him : I should not have invited thee to offer unless I had known the will of the Lord. And when Joachim was offering the sacrifice to God, the angel and the odour of the sacrifice went together straight up to heaven with the smoke.[5]

Then Joachim, throwing himself on his face, lay in prayer from the sixth hour of the day even until evening. And his lads and hired servants who were with him saw him, and not knowing why he was lying down, thought that he was dead ; and they came to him, and with difficulty raised him from the ground. And when he recounted to them the vision of the angel, they were struck with great fear and wonder, and advised him to accomplish the vision of the angel without delay, and to go back with all haste to his wife. And when Joachim was turning over in his mind whether he should go back or not, it happened that he was overpowered by a deep sleep ; and, behold, the angel who had already appeared to him when awake, appeared to him in his sleep, saying : I am the angel appointed by God as thy guardian : go down with confidence, and return to Anna, because the deeds of mercy which thou and thy wife Anna have done have been told in the presence of the Most High ; and to you will God give such fruit as no prophet or saint has ever had from the beginning, or ever will have. And when Joachim awoke out of his sleep, he called all his herdsmen to him, and told them his dream. And they worshipped the Lord, and said to him : See that thou no further despise the words of the angel. But rise and let us go hence, and return at a quiet pace, feeding our flocks.

And when, after thirty days occupied in going back, they were now near at hand, behold, the angel of the Lord appeared to Anna, who was standing and praying, and said :[6] Go to the gate which is called Golden,[7] and meet thy husband in the way, for to-day he will come to thee. She therefore went towards him in haste with her maidens, and, praying to the Lord, she stood a long time in the gate waiting for him. And when she was wearied with long waiting, she lifted up her eyes and saw Joachim afar off coming with his flocks ; and she ran to him and hung on his neck, giving thanks to God, and saying : I was a widow, and behold now I am not so : I was barren, and behold I have now conceived. And so they worshipped the Lord, and went into their own house. And when this was heard of, there was great joy among all their neighbours and acquaintants, so that the whole land of Israel congratulated them.

CHAP. 4. — After these things, her nine months being fulfilled, Anna brought forth a daughter, and called her Mary. And having weaned her in her third year, Joachim, and Anna his wife, went together to the temple of the Lord to offer sacrifices to God, and placed the infant, Mary by name, in the community of virgins, in which the virgins remained day and night praising God. And when she was put down before the doors of

---

[1] Gen. xviii. 3.
[2] Rev. xix. 10.
[3] Judg. xiii. 16.
[4] Faustus the Manichæan said that Joachim was of the tribe of Levi (August. xxiii. 4, *Contra Faustum*). As belonging to the tribe of Judah, he had not the right of sacrifice.
[5] Comp Judg. xiii. 20.

[6] Comp. Acts ix. 11.
[7] This is the Beautiful gate of Acts iii. 2, to which, according to Josephus, there was an ascent by many steps from the valley of Kedron.

the temple, she went up the fifteen steps[1] so swiftly, that she did not look back at all; nor did she, as children are wont to do, seek for her parents. Whereupon her parents, each of them anxiously seeking for the child, were both alike astonished, until they found her in the temple, and the priests of the temple themselves wondered.

Chap. 5. — Then Anna, filled with the Holy Spirit, said before them all: The Lord Almighty, the God of Hosts, being mindful of His word, hath visited His people with a good and holy visitation, to bring down the hearts of the Gentiles who were rising against us, and turn them to Himself. He hath opened His ears to our prayers: He hath kept away from us the exulting of all our enemies. The barren hath become a mother, and hath brought forth exultation and gladness to Israel. Behold the gifts which I have brought to offer to my Lord, and mine enemies have not been able to hinder me. For God hath turned their hearts to me, and Himself hath given me everlasting joy.

Chap. 6. — And Mary was held in admiration by all the people of Israel; and when she was three years old, she walked with a step so mature, she spoke so perfectly, and spent her time so assiduously in the praises of God, that all were astonished at her, and wondered; and she was not reckoned a young infant, but as it were a grown-up person of thirty years old. She was so constant in prayer, and her appearance was so beautiful and glorious, that scarcely any one could look into her face. And she occupied herself constantly with her wool-work, so that she in her tender years could do all that old women were not able to do. And this was the order that she had set for herself:[2] From the morning to the third hour she remained in prayer; from the third to the ninth she was occupied with her weaving; and from the ninth she again applied herself to prayer. She did not retire from praying until there appeared to her the angel of the Lord, from whose hand she used to receive food; and thus she became more and more perfect in the work of God. Then, when the older virgins rested from the praises of God, she did not rest at all; so that in the praises and vigils of God none were found before her, no one more learned in the wisdom of the law of God, more lowly in humility, more elegant in singing, more perfect in all virtue. She was indeed stedfast, immove-

able, unchangeable, and daily advancing to perfection. No one saw her angry, nor heard her speaking evil. All her speech was so full of grace, that her God was acknowledged to be in her tongue. She was always engaged in prayer and in searching the law, and she was anxious lest by any word of hers she should sin with regard to her companions. Then she was afraid lest in her laughter, or the sound of her beautiful voice, she should commit any fault, or lest, being elated, she should display any wrong-doing or haughtiness to one of her equals.[3] She blessed God without intermission; and lest perchance, even in her salutation, she might cease from praising God; if any one saluted her, she used to answer by way of salutation: Thanks be to God. And from her the custom first began of men saying, Thanks be to God, when they saluted each other. She refreshed herself only with the food which she daily received from the hand of the angel; but the food which she obtained from the priests she divided among the poor. The angels of God were often seen speaking with her, and they most diligently obeyed her. If any one who was unwell touched her, the same hour he went home cured.

Chap. 7. — Then Abiathar the priest offered gifts without end to the high priests, in order that he might obtain her as wife to his son. But Mary forbade them, saying: It cannot be that I should know a man, or that a man should know me. For all the priests and all her relations kept saying to her: God is worshipped in children and adored in posterity, as has always happened among the sons of Israel. But Mary answered and said unto them: God is worshipped in chastity, as is proved first of all.[4] For before Abel there was none righteous among men, and he by his offerings pleased God, and was without mercy slain by him who displeased Him. Two crowns, therefore, he received — of oblation and of virginity, because in his flesh there was no pollution. Elias also, when he was in the flesh, was taken up in the flesh, because he kept his flesh unspotted. Now I, from my infancy in the temple of God, have learned that virginity can be sufficiently dear to God. And so, because I can offer what is dear to God, I have resolved in my heart that I should not know a man at all.

Chap. 8. — Now it came to pass, when she was fourteen[5] years old, and on this account there was occasion for the Pharisees' saying that it was now a custom that no woman of that age

---

[1] Corresponding with the fifteen Songs of Degrees, Ps. cxx.-cxxxiv. See Smith's *Dict.* — art. Songs of Degrees. Another reading is: And there were about the temple, according to the fifteen Psalms of Degrees, fifteen steps of ascent: the temple was on a mountain, and there had been there built the altar of burnt-offering, which could not be reached but by steps.

[2] For the hours of prayer, see *Apost. Const.*, ch. xl.; Jerome's letters to Læta, Demetrias, etc.

[3] One of the MSS. has: She was anxious about her companions, lest any of them should sin even in one word, lest any of them should raise her voice in laughing, lest any of them should be in the wrong, or proud to her father or her mother.

[4] Or, by the first of all.

[5] Or, twelve.

should abide in the temple of God, they fell upon the plan of sending a herald through all the tribes of Israel, that on the third day all should come together into the temple of the Lord. And when all the people had come together, Abiathar the high priest rose, and mounted on a higher step, that he might be seen and heard by all the people ; and when great silence had been obtained, he said : Hear me, O sons of Israel, and receive my words into your ears. Ever since this temple was built by Solomon, there have been in it virgins, the daughters of kings and the daughters of prophets, and of high priests and priests ; and they were great, and worthy of admiration. But when they came to the proper age they were given in marriage, and followed the course of their mothers before them, and were pleasing to God. But a new order of life has been found out by Mary alone, who promises that she will remain a virgin to God. Wherefore it seems to me, that through our inquiry and the answer of God we should try to ascertain to whose keeping she ought to be entrusted. Then these words found favour with all the synagogue. And the lot was cast by the priests upon the twelve tribes, and the lot fell upon the tribe of Judah. And the priest said : To-morrow let every one who has no wife come, and bring his rod in his hand. Whence it happened that Joseph [1] brought his rod along with the young men. And the rods having been handed over to the high priest, he offered a sacrifice to the Lord God, and inquired of the Lord. And the Lord said to him : Put all their rods into the holy of holies of God, and let them remain there, and order them to come to thee on the morrow to get back their rods ; and the man from the point of whose rod a dove shall come forth, and fly towards heaven, and in whose hand the rod, when given back, shall exhibit this sign, to him let Mary be delivered to be kept.

On the following day, then, all having assembled early, and an incense-offering having been made, the high priest went into the holy of holies, and brought forth the rods. And when he had distributed the rods,[2] and the dove came forth out of none of them, the high priest put on the twelve bells [3] and the sacerdotal robe ; and entering into the holy of holies, he there made a burnt-offering, and poured forth a prayer. And the angel of the Lord appeared to him, saying : There is here the shortest rod, of which thou hast made no account : thou didst bring it in with the rest, but didst not take it out with them. When thou hast taken it out, and hast

given it him whose it is, in it will appear the sign of which I spoke to thee. Now that was Joseph's rod ; and because he was an old man, he had been cast off, as it were, that he might not receive her, but neither did he himself wish to ask back his rod.[4] And when he was humbly standing last of all, the high priest cried out to him with a loud voice, saying : Come, Joseph, and receive thy rod ; for we are waiting for thee. And Joseph came up trembling, because the high priest had called him with a very loud voice. But as soon as he stretched forth his hand, and laid hold of his rod, immediately from the top of it came forth a dove whiter than snow, beautiful exceedingly, which, after long flying about the roofs of the temple, at length flew towards the heavens. Then all the people congratulated the old man, saying : Thou hast been made blessed in thine old age, O father Joseph, seeing that God hath shown thee to be fit to receive Mary. And the priests having said to him, Take her, because of all the tribe of Judah thou alone hast been chosen by God ; Joseph began bashfully to address them, saying : I am an old man, and have children ; why do you hand over to me this infant, who is younger than my grandsons ? Then Abiathar the high priest said to him : Remember, Joseph, how Dathan and Abiron and Core perished, because they despised the will of God. So will it happen to thee, if thou despise this which is commanded thee by God. Joseph answered him : I indeed do not despise the will of God ; but I shall be her guardian until I can ascertain concerning the will of God, as to which of my sons can have her as his wife. Let some virgins of her companions, with whom she may meanwhile spend her time, be given for a consolation to her. Abiathar the high priest answered and said : Five virgins indeed shall be given her for consolation, until the appointed day come in which thou mayst receive her ; for to no other can she be joined in marriage.

Then Joseph received Mary, with the other five virgins who were to be with her in Joseph's house. These virgins were Rebecca, Sephora, Susanna, Abigea, and Cael ; to whom the high priest gave the silk, and the blue,[5] and the fine linen, and the scarlet, and the purple, and the fine flax. For they cast lots among themselves what each virgin should do, and the purple for the veil of the temple of the Lord fell to the lot of Mary. And when she had got it, those virgins said to her : Since thou art the last, and humble, and younger than all, thou hast deserved to receive and obtain the purple. And thus saying,

---

[1] One of the MSS. adds: Seeing that he had not a wife, and not wishing to slight the order of the high priest.
[2] One of the MSS. inserts: To the number of three thousand.
[3] See Protev. James 8.

[4] Another and more probable reading is: And this was Joseph's rod; and he was of an abject appearance, seeing that he was old, and he would not ask back his rod, lest perchance he might be forced to receive her.
[5] Or, hyacinth.

as it were in words of annoyance, they began to call her queen of virgins. While, however, they were so doing, the angel of the Lord appeared in the midst of them, saying: These words shall not have been uttered by way of annoyance, but prophesied as a prophecy most true. They trembled, therefore, at the sight of the angel, and at his words, and asked her to pardon them, and pray for them.

CHAP. 9. — And on the second day, while Mary was at the fountain to fill her pitcher, the angel of the Lord appeared to her, saying: Blessed art thou, Mary; for in thy womb thou hast prepared an habitation for the Lord. For, lo, the light from heaven shall come and dwell in thee, and by means of thee will shine over the whole world.

Again, on the third day, while she was working at the purple with her fingers, there entered a young man of ineffable beauty. And when Mary saw him, she exceedingly feared and trembled. And he said to her: Hail, Mary, full of grace; the Lord is with thee: blessed art thou among women, and blessed is the fruit of thy womb.[1] And when she heard these words, she trembled, and was exceedingly afraid. Then the angel of the Lord added: Fear not, Mary; for thou hast found favour with God: Behold, thou shalt conceive in thy womb, and shalt bring forth a King, who fills not only the earth, but the heaven, and who reigns from generation to generation.

CHAP. 10. — While these things were doing, Joseph was occupied with his work, house-building, in the districts by the sea-shore; for he was a carpenter. And after nine months he came back to his house, and found Mary pregnant. Wherefore, being in the utmost distress, he trembled and cried out, saying: O Lord God, receive my spirit; for it is better for me to die than to live any longer. And the virgins who were with Mary said to him: Joseph, what art thou saying? We know that no man has touched her; we can testify that she is still a virgin, and untouched. We have watched over her; always has she continued with us in prayer; daily do the angels of God speak with her; daily does she receive food from the hand of the Lord. We know not how it is possible that there can be any sin in her. But if thou wishest us to tell thee what we suspect, nobody but the angel of the Lord[2] has made her pregnant. Then said Joseph: Why do you mislead me, to believe that an angel of the Lord has made her pregnant? But it is possible that some one has pretended to be an angel of the Lord, and has beguiled her. And thus speaking, he wept, and said:

With what face shall I look at the temple of the Lord, or with what face shall I see the priests of God? What am I to do? And thus saying, he thought that he would flee, and send her away.

CHAP. 11. — And when he was thinking of rising up and hiding himself, and dwelling in secret, behold, on that very night, the angel of the Lord appeared to him in sleep, saying: Joseph, thou son of David, fear not; receive Mary as thy wife: for that which is in her womb is of the Holy Spirit. And she shall bring forth a son, and His name shall be called Jesus, for He will save His people from their sins. And Joseph, rising from his sleep, gave thanks to God, and spoke to Mary and the virgins who were with her, and told them his vision. And he was comforted about Mary, saying: I have sinned, in that I suspected thee at all.

CHAP. 12. — After these things there arose a great report that Mary was with child. And Joseph was seized by the officers of the temple, and brought along with Mary to the high priest. And he with the priests began to reproach him, and to say: Why hast thou beguiled so great and so glorious a virgin, who was fed like a dove in the temple by the angels of God, who never wished either to see or to have a man, who had the most excellent knowledge of the law of God? If thou hadst not done violence to her, she would still have remained in her virginity. And Joseph vowed, and swore that he had never touched her at all. And Abiathar the high priest answered him: As the Lord liveth, I will give thee to drink of the water of drinking of the Lord, and immediately thy sin will appear.

Then was assembled a multitude of people which could not be numbered, and Mary was brought to the temple. And the priests, and her relatives, and her parents wept, and said to Mary: Confess to the priests thy sin, thou that wast like a dove in the temple of God, and didst receive food from the hands of an angel. And again Joseph was summoned to the altar, and the water of drinking of the Lord was given him to drink. And when any one that had lied drank this water, and walked seven times round the altar, God used to show some sign in his face. When, therefore, Joseph had drunk in safety, and had walked round the altar seven times, no sign of sin appeared in him. Then all the priests, and the officers, and the people justified him, saying: Blessed art thou, seeing that no charge has been found good against thee. And they summoned Mary, and said: And what excuse canst thou have? or what greater sign can appear in thee than the conception of thy womb, which betrays thee? This only we require of thee, that since Joseph is pure

---

[1] Luke i. 28.
[2] Another reading is: The Holy Spirit.

regarding thee, thou confess who it is that has beguiled thee. For it is better that thy confession should betray thee, than that the wrath of God should set a mark on thy face, and expose thee in the midst of the people. Then Mary said, stedfastly and without trembling: O Lord God, King over all, who knowest all secrets, if there be any pollution in me, or any sin, or any evil desires, or unchastity, expose me in the sight of all the people, and make me an example of punishment to all. Thus saying, she went up to the altar of the Lord boldly, and drank the water of drinking, and walked round the altar seven times, and no spot was found in her.

And when all the people were in the utmost astonishment, seeing that she was with child, and that no sign had appeared in her face, they began to be disturbed among themselves by conflicting statements : some said that she was holy and unspotted, others that she was wicked and defiled. Then Mary, seeing that she was still suspected by the people, and that on that account she did not seem to them to be wholly cleared, said in the hearing of all, with a loud voice, As the Lord Adonai liveth, the Lord of Hosts before whom I stand, I have not known man ; but I am known by Him to whom from my earliest years I have devoted myself. And this vow I made to my God from my infancy, that I should remain unspotted in Him who created me, and I trust that I shall so live to Him alone, and serve Him alone ; and in Him, as long as I shall live, will I remain unpolluted. Then they all began to kiss her feet and to embrace her knees, asking her to pardon them for their wicked suspicions. And she was led down to her house with exultation and joy by the people, and the priests, and all the virgins. And they cried out, and said : Blessed be the name of the Lord for ever, because He hath manifested thy holiness to all His people Israel.

CHAP. 13. — And it came to pass some little time after, that an enrolment was made according to the edict of Cæsar Augustus, that all the world was to be enrolled, each man in his native place. This enrolment was made by Cyrinus, the governor of Syria.[1] It was necessary, therefore, that Joseph should enrol with the blessed Mary in Bethlehem, because to it they belonged, being of the tribe of Judah, and of the house and family of David. When, therefore, Joseph and the blessed Mary were going along the road which leads to Bethlehem, Mary said to Joseph : I see two peoples before me, the one weeping, and the other rejoicing. And Joseph answered : Sit still on thy beast, and do not speak superfluous words. Then there appeared before them

a beautiful boy, clothed in white raiment, who said to Joseph : Why didst thou say that the words which Mary spoke about the two peoples were superfluous ? For she saw the people of the Jews weeping, because they have departed from their God ; and the people of the Gentiles rejoicing, because they have now been added and made near to the Lord, according to that which He promised to our fathers Abraham, Isaac, and Jacob : for the time is at hand when in the seed of Abraham all nations shall be blessed.[2]

And when he had thus said, the angel ordered the beast to stand, for the time when she should bring forth was at hand ; and he commanded the blessed Mary to come down off the animal, and go into a recess under a cavern, in which there never was light, but always darkness, because the light of day could not reach it. And when the blessed Mary had gone into it, it began to shine with as much brightness as if it were the sixth hour of the day. The light from God so shone in the cave, that neither by day nor night was light wanting as long as the blessed Mary was there. And there she brought forth a son, and the angels surrounded Him when He was being born. And as soon as He was born, He stood upon His feet, and the angels adored Him, saying : Glory to God in the highest, and on earth peace to men of good pleasure.[3] Now, when the birth of the Lord was at hand, Joseph had gone away to seek midwives. And when he had found them, he returned to the cave, and found with Mary the infant which she had brought forth. And Joseph said to the blessed Mary : I have brought thee two midwives — Zelomi[4] and Salome ; and they are standing outside before the entrance to the cave, not daring to come in hither, because of the exceeding brightness. And when the blessed Mary heard this, she smiled ; and Joseph said to her : Do not smile ; but prudently allow them to visit thee, in case thou shouldst require them for thy cure. Then she ordered them to enter. And when Zelomi had come in, Salome having stayed without, Zelomi said to Mary : Allow me to touch thee. And when she had permitted her to make an examination, the midwife cried out with a loud voice, and said : Lord, Lord Almighty, mercy on us ! It has never been heard or thought of, that any one should have her breasts full of milk, and that the birth of a son should show his mother to be a virgin. But there has been no spilling of blood in his birth, no pain in bringing him forth. A virgin has conceived, a virgin has

---

[1] Luke ii. 1-6.

[2] Gen. xii. 3.
[3] See Alford's Greek Testament on Luke ii. 14. [So Rev. Version, following the weight of manuscript authority. — R.]
[4] Or Zelemi.

brought forth, and a virgin she remains. And hearing these words, Salome said : Allow me to handle thee, and prove whether Zelomi have spoken the truth. And the blessed Mary allowed her to handle her. And when she had withdrawn her hand from handling her, it dried up, and through excess of pain she began to weep bitterly, and to be in great distress, crying out, and saying : O Lord God, Thou knowest that I have always feared Thee, and that without recompense I have cared for all the poor; I have taken nothing from the widow and the orphan, and the needy have I not sent empty away. And, behold, I am made wretched because of mine unbelief, since without a cause I wished to try Thy virgin.

And while she was thus speaking, there stood by her a young man in shining garments, saying : Go to the child, and adore Him, and touch Him with thy hand, and He will heal thee, because He is the Saviour of the world, and of all that hope in Him. And she went to the child with haste, and adored Him, and touched the fringe of the cloths in which He was wrapped, and instantly her hand was cured. And going forth, she began to cry aloud, and to tell the wonderful things which she had seen, and which she had suffered, and how she had been cured ; so that many through her statements believed.

And some shepherds also affirmed that they had seen angels singing a hymn at midnight, praising and blessing the God of heaven, and saying : There has been born the Saviour of all, who is Christ the Lord, in whom salvation shall be brought back to Israel.[1]

Moreover, a great star, larger than any that had been seen since the beginning of the world, shone over the cave from the evening till the morning. And the prophets who were in Jerusalem said that this star pointed out the birth of Christ, who should restore the promise not only to Israel, but to all nations.

CHAP. 14. — And on the third day after the birth of our Lord Jesus Christ, the most blessed Mary went forth out of the cave, and entering a stable, placed the child in the stall, and the ox and the ass adored Him. Then was fulfilled that which was said by Isaiah the prophet, saying : The ox knoweth his owner, and the ass his master's crib.[2] The very animals, therefore, the ox and the ass, having Him in their midst, incessantly adored Him. Then was fulfilled that which was said by Abacuc the prophet, saying :[3] Between two animals thou art made manifest. In the same place Joseph remained with Mary three days.

CHAP. 15. — And on the sixth day they entered Bethlehem, where they spent the seventh day. And on the eighth day they circumcised the child, and called His name Jesus ; for so He was called by the angel before He was conceived in the womb.[4] Now, after the days of the purifiation of Mary were fulfilled according to the law of Moses, then Joseph took the infant to the temple of the Lord. And when the infant had received parhithomus, [5] — parhithomus, that is, circumcision — they offered for Him a pair of turtle-doves, or two young pigeons.[6]

Now there was in the temple a man of God, perfect and just, whose name was Symeon, a hundred and twelve years old. He had received the answer from the Lord, that he should not taste of death till he had seen Christ, the Son of God, living in the flesh. And having seen the child, he cried out with a loud voice, saying : God hath visited His people, and the Lord hath fulfilled His promise. And he made haste, and adored Him. And after this he took Him up into his cloak and kissed His feet, and said : Lord, now lettest Thou Thy servant depart in peace, according to Thy word : for mine eyes have seen Thy salvation, which Thou hast prepared before the face of all peoples, to be a light to lighten the Gentiles, and the glory of Thy people Israel.[7]

There was also in the temple of the Lord, Anna, a prophetess, the daughter of Phanuel, of the tribe of Asher, who had lived with her husband seven years from her virginity ; and she had now been a widow eighty-four years. And she never left the temple of the Lord, but spent her time in fasting and prayer. She also likewise adored the child, saying : In Him is the redemption of the world.[8]

CHAP. 16. — And when the second year was past,[9] Magi came from the east to Jerusalem, bringing great gifts. And they made strict inquiry of the Jews, saying : Where is the king who has been born to you? for we have seen his star in the east, and have come to worship him. And word of this came to King Herod, and so alarmed him that he called together the scribes and the Pharisees, and the teachers of the people, asking of them where the prophets had foretold that Christ should be born. And they said : In Bethlehem of Judah. For it is written : And thou Bethlehem, in the land of Judah, art by no means the least among the princes of Judah ; for out of thee shall come forth a Leader who shall

---

[1] Luke ii. 8–12.
[2] Isa. i. 3.
[3] Hab. iii. 2, according to the LXX. reading, שָׁנִים חַיִּים two living creatures, for שָׁנִים חַיֵּיהוּ, years make alive.

[4] Luke ii 21–24.
[5] This shows the extent of the writer's, or transcriber's knowledge of Greek.
[6] Lev. xii. 8.
[7] Luke ii. 22–35.
[8] Luke ii. 36–38.
[9] One MS. has: When two days were past. Another: On the thirteenth day.

rule my people Israel.[1] Then King Herod summoned the magi to him, and strictly inquired of them when the star appeared to them. Then, sending them to Bethlehem, he said : Go and make strict inquiry about the child ; and when ye have found him, bring me word again, that I may come and worship him also. And while the magi were going on their way, there appeared to them the star, which was, as it were, a guide to them, going before them until they came to where the child was. And when the magi saw the star, they rejoiced with great joy ; and going into the house, they saw the child Jesus sitting in His mother's lap. Then they opened their treasures, and presented great gifts to the blessed Mary and Joseph. And to the child Himself they offered each of them a piece of gold.[2] And likewise one gave gold, another frankincense, and the third myrrh.[3] And when they were going to return to King Herod, they were warned by an angel in their sleep not to go back to Herod ; and they returned to their own country by another road.[4]

CHAP. 17.—And when Herod[5] saw that he had been made sport of by the magi, his heart swelled with rage, and he sent through all the roads, wishing to seize them and put them to death. But when he could not find them at all, he sent anew to Bethlehem and all its borders, and slew all the male children whom he found of two years old and under, according to the time that he had ascertained from the magi.[6]

Now the day before this was done Joseph was warned in his sleep by the angel of the Lord, who said to him : Take Mary and the child, and go into Egypt by the way of the desert. And Joseph went according to the saying of the angel.[7]

CHAP. 18.—And having come to a certain cave, and wishing to rest in it, the blessed[8] Mary dismounted from her beast, and sat down with the child Jesus in her bosom. And there were with Joseph three boys, and with Mary a girl, going on the journey along with them. And, lo, suddenly there came forth from the cave many dragons ; and when the children saw them, they cried out in great terror. Then Jesus went down from the bosom of His mother, and stood on His feet before the dragons ; and they adored Jesus, and thereafter retired. Then was fulfilled that which was said by David the prophet, saying : Praise the Lord from the earth, ye dragons ; ye dragons, and all ye deeps.[9] And the young child Jesus, walking before them, commanded them to hurt no man. But Mary and Joseph were very much afraid lest the child should be hurt by the dragons. And Jesus said to them : Do not be afraid, and do not consider me to be a little child ; for I am and always have been perfect ; and all the beasts of the forest must needs be tame before me.

CHAP. 19.—Lions and panthers adored Him likewise, and accompanied them in the desert. Wherever Joseph and the blessed Mary went, they went before them showing them the way, and bowing their heads ; and showing their submission by wagging their tails, they adored Him with great reverence. Now at first, when Mary saw the lions and the panthers, and various kinds of wild beasts, coming about them, she was very much afraid. But the infant Jesus looked into her face with a joyful countenance, and said : Be not afraid, mother ; for they come not to do thee harm, but they make haste to serve both thee and me. With these words He drove all fear from her heart. And the lions kept walking with them, and with the oxen, and the asses, and the beasts of burden which carried their baggage, and did not hurt a single one of them, though they kept beside them ; but they were tame among the sheep and the rams which they had brought with them from Judæa, and which they had with them. They walked among wolves, and feared nothing ; and no one of them was hurt by another. Then was fulfilled that which was spoken by the prophet : Wolves shall feed with lambs ; the lion and the ox shall eat straw together.[10] There were together two oxen drawing a waggon with provision for the journey, and the lions directed them in their path.

CHAP. 20.—And it came to pass on the third day of their journey, while they were walking, that the blessed Mary was fatigued by the excessive heat of the sun in the desert ; and seeing a palm tree, she said to Joseph : Let me rest a little under the shade of this tree. Joseph therefore made haste, and led her to the palm, and made her come down from her beast. And as the blessed Mary was sitting there, she looked up to the foliage of the palm, and saw it full of fruit, and said to Joseph : I wish it were possible to get some of the fruit of this palm. And Joseph said to her : I wonder that thou sayest this, when

---

[1] Mic. v. 2.
[2] The *siclus aureus*, or gold shekel, was worth £1, 16s. 6d.
[3] One MS. has: Gaspar gave Myrrh, Melchior frankincense, Balthusar gold.
[4] Matt. ii. 1–12.
[5] One MS. has: And when Herod, coming back from Rome the year after, saw.
[6] Matt. ii. 16.
[7] Matt. ii. 14.
[8] One of the MSS. has: Then Joseph put the blessed virgin and the boy upon a beast, and himself mounted another, and took the road through the hill country and the desert, that he might get safe to Egypt ; for they did not want to go by the shore, for fear of being waylaid.

[9] Ps. cxlviii. 7.
[10] Isa. lxv. 25.

thou seest how high the palm tree is; and that thou thinkest of eating of its fruit. I am thinking more of the want of water, because the skins are now empty, and we have none wherewith to refresh ourselves and our cattle. Then the child Jesus, with a joyful countenance, reposing in the bosom of His mother, said to the palm: O tree, bend thy branches, and refresh my mother with thy fruit. And immediately at these words the palm bent its top down to the very feet of the blessed Mary; and they gathered from it fruit, with which they were all refreshed. And after they had gathered all its fruit, it remained bent down, waiting the order to rise from Him who had commanded it to stoop. Then Jesus said to it: Raise thyself, O palm tree, and be strong, and be the companion of my trees, which are in the paradise of my Father; and open from thy roots a vein of water which has been hid in the earth, and let the waters flow, so that we may be satisfied from thee. And it rose up immediately, and at its root there began to come forth a spring of water exceedingly clear and cool and sparkling. And when they saw the spring of water, they rejoiced with great joy, and were satisfied, themselves and all their cattle and their beasts. Wherefore they gave thanks to God.

CHAP. 21. — And on the day after, when they were setting out thence, and in the hour in which they began their journey, Jesus turned to the palm, and said: This privilege I give thee, O palm tree, that one of thy branches be carried away by my angels, and planted in the paradise of my Father. And this blessing I will confer upon thee, that it shall be said of all who conquer in any contest, You have attained the palm of victory. And while He was thus speaking, behold, an angel of the Lord appeared, and stood upon the palm tree; and taking off one of its branches, flew to heaven with the branch in his hand. And when they saw this, they fell on their faces, and became as it were dead. And Jesus said to them: Why are your hearts possessed with fear? Do you not know that this palm, which I have caused to be transferred to paradise, shall be prepared for all the saints in the place of delights, as it has been prepared for us in this place of the wilderness? And they were filled with joy; and being strengthened, they all rose up.

CHAP. 22. — After this, while they were going on their journey, Joseph said to Jesus: Lord, it is a boiling heat; if it please Thee, let us go by the sea-shore, that we may be able to rest in the cities on the coast. Jesus said to him: Fear not, Joseph; I will shorten the way for you, so that what you would have taken thirty days to go over, you shall accomplish in this one day. And

while they were thus speaking, behold, they looked forward, and began to see the mountains and cities of Egypt.

And rejoicing and exulting, they came into the regions of Hermopolis, and entered into a certain city of Egypt which is called Sotinen;[1] and because they knew no one there from whom they could ask hospitality, they went into a temple which was called the Capitol of Egypt. And in this temple there had been set up three hundred and fifty-five idols,[2] to each of which on its own day divine honours and sacred rites were paid. For the Egyptians belonging to the same city entered the Capitol, in which the priests told them how many sacrifices were offered each day, according to the honour in which the god was held.

CHAP. 23. — And it came to pass, when the most blessed Mary went into the temple with the little child, that all the idols prostrated themselves on the ground, so that all of them were lying on their faces shattered and broken to pieces;[3] and thus they plainly showed that they were nothing. Then was fulfilled that which was said by the prophet Isaiah: Behold, the Lord will come upon a swift cloud, and will enter Egypt, and all the handiwork of the Egyptians shall be moved at His presence.[4]

CHAP. 24. — Then Affrodosius, that governor of the city, when news of this was brought to him, went to the temple with all his army. And the priests of the temple, when they saw Affrodosius with all his army coming into the temple, thought that he was making haste only to see vengeance taken on those on whose account the gods had fallen down. But when he came into the temple, and saw all the gods lying prostrate on their faces, he went up to the blessed Mary, who was carrying the Lord in her bosom, and adored Him, and said to all his army and all his friends: Unless this were the God of our gods, our gods would not have fallen on their faces before Him; nor would they be lying prostrate in His presence: wherefore they silently confess that He is their Lord. Unless we, therefore, take care to do what we have seen our gods doing, we may run the risk of His anger, and all come to destruction, even as it happened to Pharaoh king of the Egyptians, who, not believing in powers so mighty, was drowned in the sea, with all his army.[5] Then all the people of that same city believed in the Lord God through Jesus Christ.

---

[1] Or, Sotrina.
[2] No nation was so given to idolatry, and worshipped such a countless number of monsters, as the Egyptians. — *Jerome on Isaiah.*
[3] Cf. 1 Sam. v. 3.
[4] Isa. xix. 1.
[5] Ex. xv. 4.

CHAP. 25.—After no long time the angel said to Joseph: Return to the land of Judah, for they are dead who sought the child's life.[1]

CHAP. 26.—And it came to pass, after Jesus had returned out of Egypt, when He was in Galilee, and entering on the fourth year of His age, that on a Sabbath-day He was playing with some children at the bed of the Jordan. And as He sat there, Jesus made to Himself seven pools of clay, and to each of them He made passages, through which at His command He brought water from the torrent into the pool, and took it back again. Then one of those children, a son of the devil, moved with envy, shut the passages which supplied the pools with water, and overthrew what Jesus had built up. Then said Jesus to him: Woe unto thee, thou son of death, thou son of Satan! Dost thou destroy the works which I have wrought? And immediately he who had done this died. Then with great uproar the parents of the dead boy cried out against Mary and Joseph, saying to them: Your son has cursed our son, and he is dead. And when Joseph and Mary heard this, they came forthwith to Jesus, on account of the outcry of the parents of the boy, and the gathering together of the Jews. But Joseph said privately to Mary: I dare not speak to Him; but do thou admonish Him, and say: Why hast Thou raised against us the hatred of the people; and why must the troublesome hatred of men be borne by us? And His mother having come to Him, asked Him, saying: My Lord, what was it that he did to bring about his death? And He said: He deserved death, because he scattered the works that I had made. Then His mother asked Him, saying: Do not so, my Lord, because all men rise up against us. But He, not wishing to grieve His mother, with His right foot kicked the hinder parts of the dead boy, and said to him: Rise, thou son of iniquity; for thou art not worthy to enter into the rest of my Father, because thou didst destroy the works which I had made. Then he who had been dead rose up, and went away. And Jesus, by the word of His power, brought water into the pools by the aqueduct.

CHAP. 27.—And it came to pass, after these things, that in the sight of all Jesus took clay from the pools which He had made, and of it made twelve sparrows. And it was the Sabbath when Jesus did this, and there were very many children with Him. When, therefore, one of the Jews had seen Him doing this, he said to Joseph: Joseph, dost thou not see the child

Jesus working on the Sabbath at what it is not lawful for him to do? for he has made twelve sparrows of clay. And when Joseph heard this, he reproved him, saying: Wherefore doest thou on the Sabbath such things as are not lawful for us to do? And when Jesus heard Joseph, He struck His hands together, and said to His sparrows: Fly! And at the voice of His command they began to fly. And in the sight and hearing of all that stood by, He said to the birds: Go and fly through the earth, and through all the world, and live. And when those that were there saw such miracles, they were filled with great astonishment. And some praised and admired Him, but others reviled Him. And certain of them went away to the chief priests and the heads of the Pharisees, and reported to them that Jesus the son of Joseph had done great signs and miracles in the sight of all the people of Israel. And this was reported in the twelve tribes of Israel.

CHAP. 28.—And again the son of Annas, a priest of the temple, who had come with Joseph, holding his rod in his hand in the sight of all, with great fury broke down the dams which Jesus had made with His own hands, and let out the water which He had collected in them from the torrent. Moreover, he shut the aqueduct by which the water came in, and then broke it down. And when Jesus saw this, He said to that boy who had destroyed His dams: O most wicked seed of iniquity! O son of death! O workshop of Satan! verily the fruit of thy seed shall be without strength, and thy roots without moisture, and thy branches withered, bearing no fruit. And immediately, in the sight of all, the boy withered away, and died.

CHAP. 29.—Then Joseph trembled, and took hold of Jesus, and went with Him to his own house, and His mother with Him. And, behold, suddenly from the opposite direction a boy, also a worker of iniquity, ran up and came against the shoulder of Jesus, wishing to make sport of Him, or to hurt Him, if he could. And Jesus said to him: Thou shalt not go back safe and sound from the way that thou goest. And immediately he fell down, and died. And the parents of the dead boy, who had seen what happened, cried out, saying: Where does this child come from? It is manifest that every word that he says is true; and it is often accomplished before he speaks. And the parents of the dead boy came to Joseph, and said to him: Take away that Jesus from this place, for he cannot live with us in this town; or at least teach him to bless, and not to curse. And Joseph came up to Jesus, and admonished Him, saying: Why doest thou such things? For already many are in grief

---

[1] Matt. ii. 26. One of the MSS. here has: And Joseph and Mary went to live in the house of a certain widow, and spent a year there: and for the events of the year it gives a number of the miracles recorded in the early chapters of the Latin Gospel of Thomas.

and against thee, and hate us on thy account, and we endure the reproaches of men because of thee. And Jesus answered and said unto Joseph: No one is a wise son but he whom his father hath taught, according to the knowledge of this time; and a father's curse can hurt none but evil-doers. Then they came together against Jesus, and accused him to Joseph. When Joseph saw this, he was in great terror, fearing the violence and uproar of the people of Israel. And the same hour Jesus seized the dead boy by the ear, and lifted him up from the earth in the sight of all: and they saw Jesus speaking to him like a father to his son. And his spirit came back to him, and he revived. And all of them wondered.

CHAP. 30. — Now a certain Jewish schoolmaster named Zachyas[1] heard Jesus thus speaking; and seeing that He could not be overcome, from knowing the power that was in Him,[2] he became angry, and began rudely and foolishly, and without fear, to speak against Joseph. And he said: Dost thou not wish to entrust me with thy son, that he may be instructed in human learning and in reverence? But I see that Mary and thyself have more regard for your son than for what the elders of the people of Israel say against him. You should have given more honour to us, the elders of the whole church of Israel, both that he might be on terms of mutual affection with the children, and that among us he might be instructed in Jewish learning. Joseph, on the other hand, said to him: And is there any one who can keep this child, and teach him? But if thou canst keep him and teach him, we by no means hinder him from being taught by thee those things which are learned by all. And Jesus, having heard what Zachyas had said, answered and said unto him: The precepts of the law which thou hast just spoken of, and all the things that thou hast named, must be kept by those who are instructed in human learning; but I am a stranger to your law-courts, because I have no father after the flesh. Thou who readest the law, and art learned in it, abidest in the law; but I was before the law. But since thou thinkest that no one is equal to thee in learning, thou shalt be taught by me, that no other can teach anything but those things which thou hast named. But he alone can who is worthy.[3] For when I shall be exalted on earth, I will cause to cease all mention of your genealogy. For thou know-

est not when thou wast born: I alone know when you were born, and how long your life on earth will be. Then all who heard these words were struck with astonishment, and cried out: Oh! oh! oh! this marvellously great and wonderful mystery. Never have we heard the like! Never has it been heard from any one else, nor has it been said or at any time heard by the prophets, or the Pharisees, or the scribes. We know whence he is sprung, and he is scarcely five years old; and whence does he speak these words? The Pharisees answered: We have never heard such words spoken by any other child so young. And Jesus answered and said unto them: At this do ye wonder, that such things are said by a child? Why, then, do ye not believe me in those things which I have said to you? And you all wonder because I said to you that I know when you were born. I will tell you greater things, that you may wonder more. I have seen Abraham, whom you call your father, and have spoken with him; and he has seen me.[4] And when they heard this they held their tongues, nor did any of them dare to speak. And Jesus said to them: I have been among you with children, and you have not known me; I have spoken to you as to wise men, and you have not understood my words; because you are younger than I am,[5] and of little faith.

CHAP. 31. — A second time the master Zachyas, doctor of the law, said to Joseph and Mary: Give me the boy, and I shall hand him over to master Levi, who shall teach him his letters and instruct him. Then Joseph and Mary, soothing Jesus, took Him to the schools, that He might be taught His letters by old Levi. And as soon as He went in He held His tongue. And the master Levi said one letter to Jesus, and, beginning from the first letter Aleph, said to Him: Answer. But Jesus was silent, and answered nothing. Wherefore the preceptor Levi was angry, and seized his storax-tree rod, and struck Him on the head. And Jesus said to the teacher Levi: Why dost thou strike me? Thou shalt know in truth, that He who is struck can teach him who strikes Him more than He can be taught by him. For I can teach you those very things that you are saying. But all these are blind who speak and hear, like sounding brass or tinkling cymbal, in which there is no perception of those things which are meant by their sound.[6] And Jesus in addition said to Zachyas: Every letter from Aleph even to Thet[7] is known by its arrangement. Say thou first, therefore,

---

[1] Other forms of the name are: Zachias, Zachameus, Zacheus, Zachæus.
[2] Or, seeing that there was in Him an insuperable knowledge of virtue.
[3] Tischendorf thinks that the text is corrupt. But the meaning seems to be: You are not a whit better than your neighbours; for all of you teach what you have named, and you can teach nothing else. But he alone (*ipse*, i.e., Christ) can teach more who is worthy.

[4] Comp. John viii. 56–58.
[5] Or, literally, inferior to me.
[6] 1 Cor. xiii. 1, xiv. 7.
[7] Tau, and not Teth, is the last letter of the Hebrew alphabet.

what Thet is, and I will tell thee what Aleph is. And again Jesus said to them: Those who do not know Aleph, how can they say Thet, the hypocrites? Tell me what the first one, Aleph, is; and I shall then believe you when you have said Beth. And Jesus began to ask the names of the letters one by one, and said: Let the master of the law tell us what the first letter is, or why it has many triangles, gradate, subacute, mediate, obduced, produced, erect, prostrate, curvistrate.[1] And when Levi heard this, he was thunderstruck at such an arrangement of the names of the letters. Then he began in the hearing of all to cry out, and say: Ought such a one to live on the earth? Yea, he ought to be hung on the great cross. For he can put out fire, and make sport of other modes of punishment. I think that he lived before the flood, and was born before the deluge. For what womb bore him? or what mother brought him forth? or what breasts gave him suck? I flee before him; I am not able to withstand the words from his mouth, but my heart is astounded to hear such words. I do not think that any man can understand what he says, except God were with him. Now I, unfortunate wretch, have given myself up to be a laughing-stock to him. For when I thought I had a scholar, I, not knowing him, have found my master. What shall I say? I cannot withstand the words of this child: I shall now flee from this town, because I cannot understand them. An old man like me has been beaten by a boy, because I can find neither beginning nor end of what he says. For it is no easy matter to find a beginning of himself.[2] I tell you of a certainty, I am not lying, that to my eyes the proceedings of this boy, the commencement of his conversation, and the upshot of his intention, seem to have nothing in common with mortal man. Here then I do not know whether he be a wizard or a god; or at least an angel of God speaks in him. Whence he is, or where he comes from, or who he will turn out to be, I know not. Then Jesus, smiling at him with a joyful countenance, said in a commanding voice to all the sons of Israel standing by and hearing: Let the unfruitful bring forth fruit, and the blind see, and the lame walk right, and the poor enjoy the good things of this life,

and the dead live, that each may return to his original state, and abide in Him who is the root of life and of perpetual sweetness. And when the child Jesus had said this, forthwith all who had fallen under malignant diseases were restored. And they did not dare to say anything more to Him, or to hear anything from Him.

CHAP. 32.—After these things, Joseph and Mary departed thence with Jesus into the city of Nazareth; and He remained there with His parents. And on the first of the week, when Jesus was playing with the children on the roof of a certain house, it happened that one of the children pushed another down from the roof to the ground, and he was killed. And the parents of the dead boy, who had not seen this, cried out against Joseph and Mary, saying: Your son has thrown our son down to the ground, and he is dead. But Jesus was silent, and answered them nothing. And Joseph and Mary came in haste to Jesus; and His mother asked Him, saying: My lord, tell me if thou didst throw him down. And immediately Jesus went down from the roof to the ground, and called the boy by his name, Zeno. And he answered Him: My lord. And Jesus said to him: Was it I that threw thee down from the roof to the ground? And he said: No, my lord. And the parents of the boy who had been dead wondered, and honoured Jesus for the miracle that had been wrought. And Joseph and Mary departed thence with Jesus to Jericho.

CHAP. 33.—Now Jesus was six years old, and His mother sent Him with a pitcher to the fountain to draw water with the children. And it came to pass, after He had drawn the water, that one of the children came against Him, and struck the pitcher, and broke it. But Jesus stretched out the cloak which He had on, and took up in His cloak as much water as there had been in the pitcher, and carried it to His mother. And when she saw it she wondered, and reflected within herself, and laid up all these things in her heart.[3]

CHAP. 34.—Again, on a certain day, He went forth into the field, and took a little wheat from His mother's barn, and sowed it Himself. And it sprang up, and grew, and multiplied exceedingly. And at last it came to pass that He Himself reaped it, and gathered as the produce of it three kors,[4] and gave it to His numerous acquaintances.[5]

CHAP. 35.—There is a road going out of Jericho and leading to the river Jordan, to the place

---

[1] The original —*triangulos gradatos, subacutos, mediatos, obductos, productos, erectos, stratos, curvistratos*— is hopelessly corrupt. Compare the passages in the following Apocrypha. [The Gospel of Thomas, first Greek form, chaps. 6, 7, and parallel passages. —R.] It obviously, however, refers to the Pentalpha, Pentacle, or Solomon's Seal, celebrated in the remains of the magical books that have come down to us under the names of Hermes and the Pythagoreans. The Pentalpha was formed by joining by straight lines the alternate angles of a regular pentagon, and thus contained numerous triangles. The Pythagoreans called it the *Hygiea* or symbol of health, and it was frequently engraved on amulets and coins. It is still, if the books are to be trusted, a symbol of power in the higher grades of freemasonry.

[2] i.e., It is not wonderful that we do not understand what he says, for we do not know what he is.

[3] Luke ii. 19.
[4] The kor or chomer was, according to Jahn, equal to 32 pecks 1 pint.
[5] *Multiplicibus suis.*

where the children of Israel crossed : and there the ark of the covenant is said to have rested. And Jesus was eight years old, and He went out of Jericho, and went towards the Jordan. And there was beside the road, near the bank of the Jordan, a cave where a lioness was nursing her cubs ; and no one was safe to walk that way. Jesus then, coming from Jericho, and knowing that in that cave the lioness had brought forth her young, went into it in the sight of all. And when the lions saw Jesus, they ran to meet Him, and adored Him. And Jesus was sitting in the cavern, and the lion's cubs ran hither and thither round His feet, fawning upon Him, and sporting. And the older lions, with their heads bowed down, stood at a distance, and adored Him, and fawned upon Him with their tails. Then the people who were standing afar off, not seeing Jesus, said : Unless he or his parents had committed grievous sins, he would not of his own accord have offered himself up to the lions. And when the people were thus reflecting within themselves, and were lying under great sorrow, behold, on a sudden, in the sight of the people, Jesus came out of the cave, and the lions went before Him, and the lion's cubs played with each other before His feet. And the parents of Jesus stood afar off, with their heads bowed down, and watched ; likewise also the people stood at a distance, on account of the lions ; for they did not dare to come close to them. Then Jesus began to say to the people : How much better are the beasts than you, seeing that they recognise their Lord, and glorify Him ; while you men, who have been made after the image and likeness of God, do not know Him ! Beasts know me, and are tame ; men see me, and do not acknowledge me.

CHAP. 36. — After these things Jesus crossed the Jordan, in the sight of them all, with the lions ; and the water of the Jordan was divided on the right hand and on the left.[1] Then He said to the lions, in the hearing of all : Go in peace, and hurt no one ; but neither let man injure you, until you return to the place whence you have come forth. And they, bidding Him farewell, not only with their gestures but with their voices, went to their own place. But Jesus returned to His mother.

CHAP. 37. — Now Joseph[2] was a carpenter, and used to make nothing else of wood but ox-yokes, and ploughs, and implements of husbandry, and wooden beds. And it came to pass that a certain young man ordered him to make for him a couch six cubits long. And Joseph commanded his servant[3] to cut the wood with an iron saw, according to the measure which he had sent. But he did not keep to the prescribed measure, but made one piece of wood shorter than the other. And Joseph was in perplexity, and began to consider what he was to do about this. And when Jesus saw him in this state of cogitation, seeing that it was a matter of impossibility to him, He addresses him with words of comfort, saying : Come, let us take hold of the ends of the pieces of wood, and let us put them together, end to end, and let us fit them exactly to each other, and draw to us, for we shall be able to make them equal. Then Joseph did what he was bid, for he knew that He could do whatever He wished. And Joseph took hold of the ends of the pieces of wood, and brought them together against the wall next himself, and Jesus took hold of the other ends of the pieces of wood, and drew the shorter piece to Him, and made it of the same length as the longer one. And He said to Joseph : Go and work, and do what thou hast promised to do. And Joseph did what he had promised.[4]

CHAP. 38. — And it came to pass a second time, that Joseph and Mary were asked by the people that Jesus should be taught His letters in school. They did not refuse to do so ; and according to the commandment of the elders, they took Him to a master to be instructed in human learning. Then the master began to teach Him in an imperious tone, saying : Say Alpha.[5] And Jesus said to him : Do thou tell me first what Betha is, and I will tell thee what Alpha is. And upon this the master got angry and struck Jesus ; and no sooner had he struck Him, than he fell down dead.

And Jesus went home again to His mother. And Joseph, being afraid, called Mary to him, and said to her : Know of a surety that my soul is sorrowful even unto death on account of this child. For it is very likely that at some time or other some one will strike him in malice, and he will die. But Mary answered and said : O man of God ! do not believe that this is possible. You may believe to a certainty that He who has sent him to be born among men will Himself guard him from all mischief, and will in His own name preserve him from evil.

CHAP. 39. — Again the Jews asked Mary and Joseph a third time to coax Him to go to another master to learn. And Joseph and Mary, fearing the people, and the overbearing of the

---

[1] Josh. iii. 16; 2 Kings ii. 8.
[2] One of the MSS. tells the story, not of Joseph, but of a certain builder, a worker in wood.
[3] Lit., boy.
[4] One of the MSS. here inserts: And when Jesus was with other children He repeatedly went up and sat down upon a balcony, and many of them began to do likewise, and they fell down and broke their legs and arms. And the Lord Jesus healed them all.
[5] Note that the letters are Greek here.

princes, and the threats of the priests, led Him again to school, knowing that He could learn nothing from man, because He had perfect knowledge from God only. And when Jesus had entered the school, led by the Holy Spirit, He took the book out of the hand of the master who was teaching the law, and in the sight and hearing of all the people began to read, not indeed what was written in their book ; but He spoke in the Spirit of the living God, as if a stream of water were gushing forth from a living fountain, and the fountain remained always full. And with such power He taught the people the great things of the living God, that the master himself fell to the ground and adored Him. And the heart of the people who sat and heard Him saying such things was turned into astonishment. And when Joseph heard of this, he came running to Jesus, fearing that the master himself was dead. And when the master saw him, he said to him : Thou hast given me not a scholar, but a master ; and who can withstand his words ? Then was fulfilled that which was spoken by the Psalmist : The river of God is full of water : Thou hast prepared them corn, for so is the provision for it.[1]

CHAP. 40. — After these things Joseph departed thence with Mary and Jesus to go into Capernaum by the sea-shore, on account of the malice of his adversaries. And when Jesus was living in Capernaum, there was in the city a man named Joseph, exceedingly rich. But he had wasted away under his infirmity, and died, and was lying dead in his couch. And when Jesus heard them in the city mourning, and weeping, and lamenting over the dead man, He said to Joseph : Why dost thou not afford the benefit of thy favour to this man, seeing that he is called by thy name? And Joseph answered him : How have I any power or ability to afford him a benefit? And Jesus said to him : Take the handkerchief which is upon thy head, and go and put it on the face of the dead man, and say to him : Christ heal thee ; and immediately the dead man will be healed, and will rise from his couch. And when Joseph heard this, he went away at the command of Jesus, and ran, and entered the house of the dead man, and put the handkerchief which he was wearing on his head upon the face of him who was lying in the couch, and said : Jesus heal thee. And forthwith the dead man rose from his bed, and asked who Jesus was.[2]

CHAP. 41. — And they went away from Capernaum into the city which is called Bethlehem ; and Joseph lived with Mary in his own house, and Jesus with them. And on a certain day Joseph called to him his first-born son James,[3] and sent him into the vegetable garden to gather vegetables for the purpose of making broth. And Jesus followed His brother James into the garden ; but Joseph and Mary did not know this. And while James was collecting the vegetables, a viper suddenly came out of a hole and struck his hand,[4] and he began to cry out from excessive pain. And, becoming exhausted, he said, with a bitter cry : Alas ! alas ! an accursed viper has struck my hand. And Jesus, who was standing opposite to him, at the bitter cry ran up to James, and took hold of his hand ; and all that He did was to blow on the hand of James, and cool it : and immediately James was healed, and the serpent died. And Joseph and Mary did not know what had been done ; but at the cry of James, and the command of Jesus, they ran to the garden, and found the serpent already dead, and James quite cured.

CHAP. 42. — And Joseph having come to a feast with his sons, James, Joseph, and Judah, and Simeon and his two daughters, Jesus met them, with Mary His mother, along with her sister Mary of Cleophas, whom the Lord God had given to her father Cleophas and her mother Anna, because they had offered Mary the mother of Jesus to the Lord. And she was called by the same name, Mary, for the consolation of her parents.[5] And when they had come together, Jesus sanctified and blessed them, and He was the first to begin to eat and drink ; for none of them dared to eat or drink, or to sit at table, or to break bread, until He had sanctified them, and first done so. And if He hap-

---

[3] According to the tradition preserved by Hegesippus and Tertullian, James and Judas were husbandmen. See *Apost. Const.*, ch. lxvii.

[4] Comp. Acts xxviii.

[5] One of the MSS. has : And when Joseph, worn out with old age, died and was buried with his parents, the blessed Mary *lived* with her nephews, or with the children of her sisters ; for Anna and Emerina were sisters. Of Emerina was born Elizabeth, the mother of John the Baptist. And as Anna, the mother of the blessed Mary, was very beautiful, when Joachim was dead she was married to Cleophas, by whom she had a second daughter. She called her Mary, and gave her to Alphæus to wife; and of her was born James the son of Alphæus, and Philip his brother. And her second husband having died, Anna was married to a third husband named Salome, by whom she had a third daughter. She called her Mary likewise, and gave her to Zebedee to wife; and of her were born James the son of Zebedee, and John the Evangelist.

Another passage to the same effect is prefixed to the Gospel. It reads Emeria for Emerina, and Joseph for Philip. It ends with a quotation from Jerome's sermon upon Easter: — We read in the Gospels that there were four Marys — first, the mother of the Lord the Saviour; second, His maternal aunt, who was called Mary of Cleophas; third, Mary the mother of James and Joseph; fourth, Mary Magdalene — though some maintain that the mother of James and Joseph was His aunt.

The same MS. thus concludes: The holy Apostle and Evangelist John with his own hand wrote this little book in Hebrew, and the learned doctor Jerome rendered it from Hebrew into Latin.

---

[1] Ps. lxv. 9.

[2] In place of this chapter, one of the MSS. has a number of miracles copied from the canonical Gospels — the walking on the sea, the feeding of the five thousand, the healing of a blind man, the raising of Lazarus, and the raising of a certain young man.

pened to be absent, they used to wait until He should do this. And when He did not wish to come for refreshment, neither Joseph nor Mary, nor the sons of Joseph, His brothers, came. And, indeed, these brothers, keeping His life as a lamp before their eyes, observed Him, and feared Him. And when Jesus slept, whether by day or by night, the brightness of God shone upon Him. To whom be all praise and glory for ever and ever. Amen, amen.

THE GOSPEL OF THE NATIVITY OF MARY

CHAP. 1. — The blessed and glorious ever-virgin Mary, sprung from the royal stock and family of David, born in the city of Nazareth, was brought up at Jerusalem in the temple of the Lord. Her father was named Joachim, and her mother Anna. Her father's house was from Galilee and the city of Nazareth, but her mother's family from Bethlehem. Their life was guileless and right before the Lord, and irreproachable and pious before men. For they divided all their substance into three parts. One part they spent upon the temple and the temple servants; another they distributed to strangers and the poor; the third they reserved for themselves and the necessities of their family. Thus, dear to God, kind to men, for about twenty years they lived in their own house, a chaste married life, without having any children. Nevertheless they vowed that, should the Lord happen to give them offspring, they would deliver it to the service of the Lord; on which account also they used to visit the temple of the Lord at each of the feasts during the year.

CHAP. 2. — And it came to pass that the festival of the dedication [1] was at hand; wherefore also Joachim went up to Jerusalem with some men of his own tribe. Now at that time Issachar [2] was high priest there. And when he saw Joachim with his offering among his other fellow-citizens, he despised him, and spurned his gifts, asking why he, who had no offspring, presumed to stand among those who had; saying that his gifts could not by any means be acceptable to God, since He had deemed him unworthy of offspring: for the Scripture said, Cursed is every one who has not begot a male or a female in Israel. [3] He said, therefore, that he ought first to be freed from this curse by the begetting of children; and then, and then only, that he should come into the presence of the Lord with his offerings. And Joachim, covered with shame from this reproach that was thrown in his teeth,

retired to the shepherds, who were in their pastures with their flocks; nor would he return home, lest perchance he might be branded with the same reproach by those of his own tribe, who were there at the time, and had heard this from the priest.

CHAP. 3. — Now, when he had been there for some time, on a certain day when he was alone, an angel of the Lord stood by him in a great light. And when he was disturbed at his appearance, the angel who had appeared to him restrained his fear, saying: Fear not, Joachim, nor be disturbed by my appearance; for I am the angel of the Lord, sent by Him to thee to tell thee that thy prayers have been heard, and that thy charitable deeds have gone up into His presence. [4] For He hath seen thy shame, and hath heard the reproach of unfruitfulness which has been unjustly brought against thee. For God is the avenger of sin, not of nature: and, therefore, when He shuts up the womb of any one, He does so that He may miraculously open it again; so that that which is born may be acknowledged to be not of lust, but of the gift of God. For was it not the case that the first mother of your nation — Sarah — was barren up to her eightieth year? [5] And, nevertheless, in extreme old age she brought forth Isaac, to whom the promise was renewed of the blessing of all nations. Rachel also, so favoured of the Lord, and so beloved by holy Jacob, was long barren; and yet she brought forth Joseph, who was not only the lord of Egypt, but the deliverer of many nations who were ready to perish of hunger. Who among the judges was either stronger than Samson, or more holy than Samuel? And yet the mothers of both were barren. If, therefore, the reasonableness of my words does not persuade thee, believe in fact that conceptions very late in life, and births in the case of women that have been barren, are usually attended with something wonderful. Accordingly thy wife Anna will bring forth a daughter to thee, and thou shalt call her name Mary: she shall be, as you have vowed, consecrated to the Lord from her infancy, and

---

[1] 1 Macc. iv. 52-59; 2 Macc. x. 1-8; John x. 22; Josephus, *Antiq.* xii. 7.

[2] The spelling in the text is that in the Hebrew, the Samaritan Codex, the Targums, and the Textus Receptus. There is no Issachar in the list of high priests.

[3] This statement does not occur in Scripture in so many words; but sterility was looked upon as a punishment from God.

[4] Comp. Acts x. 4.

[5] Gen. xvii. 17. Sarah was ninety years old.

she shall be filled with the Holy Spirit, even from her mother's womb. She shall neither eat nor drink any unclean thing, nor shall she spend her life among the crowds of the people without, but in the temple of the Lord, that it may not be possible either to say, or so much as to suspect, any evil concerning her. Therefore, when she has grown up, just as she herself shall be miracu-lously born of a barren woman, so in an incomparable manner she, a virgin, shall bring forth the Son of the Most High, who shall be called Jesus, and who, according to the etymology of His name, shall be the Saviour of all nations. And this shall be the sign to thee of those things which I announce : When thou shalt come to the Golden gate in Jerusalem, thou shalt there meet Anna thy wife, who, lately anxious from the delay of thy return, will then rejoice at the sight of thee. Having thus spoken, the angel departed from him.

CHAP. 4. — Thereafter he appeared to Anna his wife, saying : Fear not, Anna, nor think that it is a phantom which thou seest. For I am that angel who has presented your prayers and alms before God ; and now have I been sent to you to announce to you that thou shalt bring forth a daughter, who shall be called Mary, and who shall be blessed above all women. She, full of the favour of the Lord even from her birth, shall remain three years in her father's house until she be weaned. Thereafter, being delivered to the service of the Lord, she shall not depart from the temple until she reach the years of discretion. There, in fine, serving God day and night in fastings and prayers, she shall abstain from every unclean thing ; she shall never know man, but alone, without example, immaculate, uncorrupted, without intercourse with man, she, a virgin, shall bring forth a son ; she, His handmaiden, shall bring forth the Lord — both in grace, and in name, and in work, the Saviour of the world. Wherefore arise, and go up to Jerusalem ; and when thou shalt come to the gate which, because it is plated with gold, is called Golden, there, for a sign, thou shalt meet thy husband, for whose safety thou hast been anxious. And when these things shall have so happened, know that what I announce shall without doubt be fulfilled.

CHAP. 5. — Therefore, as the angel had commanded, both of them setting out from the place where they were, went up to Jerusalem ; and when they had come to the place pointed out by the angel's prophecy, there they met each other. Then, rejoicing at seeing each other, and secure in the certainty of the promised offspring, they gave the thanks due to the Lord, who exalteth the humble. And so, having wor-shipped the Lord, they returned home, and awaited in certainty and in gladness the divine promise. Anna therefore conceived, and brought forth a daughter ; and according to the command of the angel, her parents called her name Mary.

CHAP. 6. — And when the circle of three years had rolled round, and the time of her weaning was fulfilled, they brought the virgin to the temple of the Lord with offerings. Now there were round the temple, according to the fifteen Psalms of Degrees,[1] fifteen steps going up ; for, on account of the temple having been built on a mountain, the altar of burnt-offering, which stood outside, could not be reached except by steps. On one of these, then, her parents placed the little girl, the blessed virgin Mary. And when they were putting off the clothes which they had worn on the journey, and were putting on, as was usual, others that were neater and cleaner, the virgin of the Lord went up all the steps, one after the other, without the help of any one leading her or lifting her, in such a manner that, in this respect at least, you would think that she had already attained full age. For already the Lord in the infancy of His virgin wrought a great thing, and by the indication of this miracle foreshowed how great she was to be. Therefore, a sacrifice having been offered according to the custom of the law, and their vow being perfected, they left the virgin within the enclosures of the temple, there to be educated with the other virgins, and themselves returned home.

CHAP. 7. — But the virgin of the Lord advanced in age and in virtues ; and though, in the words of the Psalmist, her father and mother had forsaken her, the Lord took her up.[2] For daily was she visited by angels, daily did she enjoy a divine vision, which preserved her from all evil, and made her to abound in all good. And so she reached her fourteenth year ; and not only were the wicked unable to charge her with anything worthy of reproach, but all the good, who knew her life and conversation, judged her to be worthy of admiration. Then the high priest publicly announced that the virgins who were publicly settled in the temple, and had reached this time of life, should return home and get married, according to the custom of the nation and the ripeness of their years. The others readily obeyed this command ; but Mary alone, the virgin of the Lord, answered that she could not do this, saying both that her parents had devoted her to the service of the Lord, and

---

[1] Ps. cxx.–cxxxiv. The fifteen steps led from the court of the women to that of the men.
[2] Ps. xxvii. 10.

that, moreover, she herself had made to the Lord a vow of virginity, which she would never violate by any intercourse with man. And the high priest, being placed in great perplexity of mind, seeing that neither did he think that the vow should be broken contrary to the Scripture, which says, Vow and pay,[1] nor did he dare to introduce a custom unknown to the nation, gave order that at the festival, which was at hand, all the chief persons from Jerusalem and the neighbourhood should be present, in order that from their advice he might know what was to be done in so doubtful a case. And when this took place, they resolved unanimously that the Lord should be consulted upon this matter. And when they all bowed themselves in prayer, the high priest went to consult God in the usual way. Nor had they long to wait: in the hearing of all a voice issued from the oracle and from the mercy-seat, that, according to the prophecy of Isaiah, a man should be sought out to whom the virgin ought to be entrusted and espoused. For it is clear that Isaiah says: A rod shall come forth from the root of Jesse, and a flower shall ascend from his root; and the Spirit of the Lord shall rest upon him, the spirit of wisdom and understanding, the spirit of counsel and strength, the spirit of wisdom and piety; and he shall be filled with the spirit of the fear of the Lord.[2] According to this prophecy, therefore, he predicted that all of the house and family of David that were unmarried and fit for marriage should bring there rods to the altar; and that he whose rod after it was brought should produce a flower, and upon the end of whose rod the Spirit of the Lord should settle in the form of a dove, was the man to whom the virgin ought to be entrusted and espoused.

CHAP. 8. — Now there was among the rest Joseph, of the house and family of David, a man of great age: and when all brought there rods, according to the order, he alone withheld his. Wherefore, when nothing in conformity with the divine voice appeared, the high priest thought it necessary to consult God a second time; and He answered, that of those who had been designated, he alone to whom the virgin ought to be espoused had not brought his rod. Joseph, therefore, was found out. For when he had brought his rod, and the dove came from heaven and settled upon the top of it, it clearly appeared to all that he was the man to whom the virgin should be espoused. Therefore, the usual ceremonies of betrothal having been gone through, he went back to the city of Bethlehem to put his house in order, and to procure things necessary for the marriage. But Mary, the virgin of

the Lord, with seven other virgins of her own age, and who had been weaned at the same time, whom she had received from the priest, returned to the house of her parents in Galilee.

CHAP. 9. — And in those days, that is, at the time of her first coming into Galilee, the angel Gabriel was sent to her by God, to announce to her the conception of the Lord, and to explain to her the manner and order of the conception. Accordingly, going in, he filled the chamber where she was with a great light; and most courteously saluting her, he said: Hail, Mary! O virgin highly favoured by the Lord, virgin full of grace, the Lord is with thee; blessed art thou above all women, blessed above all men that have been hitherto born.[3] And the virgin, who was already well acquainted with angelic faces, and was not unused to the light from heaven, was neither terrified by the vision of the angel, nor astonished at the greatness of the light, but only perplexed by his words; and she began to consider of what nature a salutation so unusual could be, or what it could portend, or what end it could have. And the angel, divinely inspired, taking up this thought, says: Fear not, Mary, as if anything contrary to thy chastity were hid under this salutation. For in choosing chastity, thou hast found favour with the Lord; and therefore thou, a virgin, shalt conceive without sin, and shalt bring forth a son. He shall be great, because He shall rule from sea to sea, and from the river even to the ends of the earth;[4] and He shall be called the Son of the Most High, because He who is born on earth in humiliation, reigns in heaven in exaltation; and the Lord God will give Him the throne of His father David, and He shall reign in the house of Jacob for ever, and of His kingdom there shall be no end;[5] forasmuch as He is King of kings and Lord of lords,[6] and His throne is from everlasting to everlasting. The virgin did not doubt these words of the angel; but wishing to know the manner of it, she answered: How can that come to pass? For while, according to my vow, I never know man, how can I bring forth without the addition of man's seed? To this the angel says: Think not, Mary, that thou shalt conceive in the manner of mankind: for without any intercourse with man, thou, a virgin, wilt conceive; thou, a virgin, wilt bring forth; thou, a virgin, wilt nurse: for the Holy Spirit shall come upon thee, and the power of the Most High shall overshadow thee,[7] without any of the heats of lust; and therefore that which shall be born of thee shall alone be holy, because it

[1] Ps. lxxvi. 11.
[2] Isa. xi. 1, 2.

[3] Luke i. 26–38.
[4] Ps. lxxii. 8.
[5] Luke i. 32, 33.
[6] Rev. xix. 16.
[7] Luke i. 35.

alone, being conceived and born without sin, shall be called the Son of God. Then Mary stretched forth her hands, and raised her eyes to heaven, and said: Behold the hand-maiden of the Lord, for I am not worthy of the name of lady; let it be to me according to thy word.

It will be long, and perhaps to some even tedious, if we insert in this little work every thing which we read of as having preceded or followed the Lord's nativity: wherefore, omitting those things which have been more fully written in the Gospel, let us come to those which are held to be less worthy of being narrated.

CHAP. 10. — Joseph therefore came from Judæa into Galilee, intending to marry the virgin who had been betrothed to him; for already three months had elapsed, and it was the beginning of the fourth since she had been betrothed to him. In the meantime, it was evident from her shape that she was pregnant, nor could she conceal this from Joseph. For in consequence of his being betrothed to her, coming to her more freely and speaking to her more familiarly, he found out that she was with child. He began then to be in great doubt and perplexity, because he did not know what was best for him to do. For, being a just man, he was not willing to expose her; nor, being a pious man, to injure her fair fame by a suspicion of fornication.

He came to the conclusion, therefore, privately to dissolve their contract, and to send her away secretly. And while he thought on these things, behold, an angel of the Lord appeared to him in his sleep, saying: Joseph, thou son of David, fear not; that is, do not have any suspicion of fornication in the virgin, or think any evil of her; and fear not to take her as thy wife: for that which is begotten in her, and which now vexes thy soul, is the work not of man, but of the Holy Spirit. For she alone of all virgins shall bring forth the Son of God, and thou shalt call His name Jesus, that is, Saviour; for He shall save His people from their sins. Therefore Joseph, according to the command of the angel, took the virgin as his wife; nevertheless he knew her not, but took care of her, and kept her in chastity.[1] And now the ninth month from her conception was at hand, when Joseph, taking with him his wife along with what things he needed, went to Bethlehem, the city from which he came. And it came to pass, while they were there, that her days were fulfilled that she should bring forth; and she brought forth her first-born son, as the holy evangelists have shown, our Lord Jesus Christ, who with the Father and the Son[2] and the Holy Ghost lives and reigns God from everlasting to everlasting.

[1] Matt. i. 18–24.
[2] Thus in the original.

THE HISTORY OF JOSEPH THE CARPENTER

In the name of God, of one essence and three persons.

The History of the death of our father, the holy old man, Joseph the carpenter.

May his blessings and prayers preserve us all, O brethren! Amen.

His whole life was one hundred and eleven years, and his departure from this world happened on the twenty-sixth of the month Abib, which answers to the month Ab. May his prayer preserve us! Amen. And, indeed, it was our Lord Jesus Christ Himself who related this history to His holy disciples on the Mount of Olives, and all Joseph's labour, and the end of his days. And the holy apostles have preserved this conversation, and have left it written down in the library at Jerusalem. May their prayers preserve us! Amen.[1]

1. It happened one day, when the Saviour, our Master, God, and Saviour Jesus Christ, was sitting along with His disciples, and they were all assembled on the Mount of Olives, that He said to them: O my brethren and friends, sons of the Father who has chosen you from all men, you know that I have often told you that I must be crucified, and must die for the salvation of Adam and his posterity, and that I shall rise from the dead. Now I shall commit to you the doctrine of the holy gospel formerly announced to you, that you may declare it throughout the whole world. And I shall endow you with power from on high, and fill you with the Holy Spirit.[2] And you shall declare to all nations repentance and remission of sins.[3] For a single cup of water,[4] if a man shall find it in the world to come, is greater and better than all the wealth of this whole world. And as much ground as one foot can occupy in the house of my Father, is greater and more excellent than all

the riches of the earth. Yea, a single hour in the joyful dwelling of the pious is more blessed and more precious than a thousand years among sinners:[5] inasmuch as their weeping and lamentation shall not come to an end, and their tears shall not cease, nor shall they find for themselves consolation and repose at any time for ever. And now, O my honoured members, go declare to all nations, tell them, and say to them: Verily the Saviour diligently inquires into the inheritance which is due, and is the administrator of justice. And the angels will cast down their enemies, and will fight for them in the day of conflict. And He will examine every single foolish and idle word which men speak, and they shall give an account of it.[6] For as no one shall escape death, so also the works of every man shall be laid open on the day of judgment, whether they have been good or evil.[7] Tell them also this word which I have said to you to-day: Let not the strong man glory in his strength, nor the rich man in his riches; but let him who wishes to glory, glory in the Lord.[8]

2. There was a man whose name was Joseph, sprung from a family of Bethlehem, a town of Judah, and the city of King David. This same man, being well furnished with wisdom and learning, was made a priest in the temple of the Lord. He was, besides, skilful in his trade, which was that of a carpenter; and after the manner of all men, he married a wife. Moreover, he begot for himself sons and daughters, four sons, namely, and two daughters. Now these are their names — Judas, Justus, James, and Simon. The names of the two daughters were Assia and Lydia. At length the wife of righteous Joseph, a woman intent on the divine glory in all her works, departed this life. But Joseph, that righteous man, my father after the flesh, and the spouse of my mother Mary, went away with his sons to his trade, practising the art of a carpenter.

3. Now when righteous Joseph became a widower, my mother Mary, blessed, holy, and pure, was already twelve years old. For her

[1] The Coptic has: The 26th day of Epep. This is the departure from the body of our father Joseph the carpenter, the father of Christ after the flesh, who was 111 years old. Our Saviour narrated all his life to His apostles on Mount Olivet; and His apostles wrote it, and put it in the library which is in Jerusalem. Also that the day on which the holy old man laid down his body was the 26th of the month Epep. In the peace of God, amen.
His day is the 19th of March in the Roman calendar.
[2] Luke xxiv. 49.
[3] Luke xxiv. 47.
[4] Comp. Matt. x. 42.

[5] Comp. Ps. lxxxiv. 10.
[6] Matt. xii. 36.
[7] 2 Cor. v. 10.
[8] Jer. ix. 23, 24; 1 Cor. i. 31; 2 Cor. x. 17.

parents offered her in the temple when she was three years of age, and she remained in the temple of the Lord nine years. Then when the priests saw that the virgin, holy and God-fearing, was growing up, they spoke to each other, saying : Let us search out a man, righteous and pious, to whom Mary may be entrusted until the time of her marriage ; lest, if she remain in the temple, it happen to her as is wont to happen to women, and lest on that account we sin, and God be angry with us.

4. Therefore they immediately sent out, and assembled twelve old men of the tribe of Judah. And they wrote down the names of the twelve tribes of Israel. And the lot fell upon the pious old man, righteous Joseph. Then the priests answered, and said to my blessed mother : Go with Joseph, and be with him till the time of your marriage. Righteous Joseph therefore received my mother, and led her away to his own house. And Mary found James the Less in his father's house, broken-hearted and sad on account of the loss of his mother, and she brought him up. Hence Mary was called the mother of James.[1] Thereafter Joseph left her at home, and went away to the shop where he wrought at his trade of a carpenter. And after the holy virgin had spent two years in his house her age was exactly fourteen years, including the time at which he received her.

5. And I chose her of my own will, with the concurrence of my Father, and the counsel of the Holy Spirit. And I was made flesh of her, by a mystery which transcends the grasp of created reason. And three months after her conception the righteous man Joseph returned from the place where he worked at his trade ; and when he found my virgin mother pregnant, he was greatly perplexed, and thought of sending her away secretly.[2] But from fear, and sorrow, and the anguish of his heart, he could endure neither to eat nor drink that day.

6. But at mid-day there appeared to him in a dream the prince of the angels, the holy Gabriel, furnished with a command from my Father ; and he said to him : Joseph, son of David, fear not to take Mary as thy wife : for she has conceived of the Holy Spirit ; and she will bring forth a son, whose name shall be called Jesus. He it is who shall rule all nations with a rod of iron.[3] Having thus spoken, the angel departed from him. And Joseph rose from his sleep, and did as the angel of the Lord had said to him ; and Mary abode with him.[4]

7. Some time after that, there came forth an order from Augustus Cæsar the king, that all the habitable world should be enrolled, each man in his own city. The old man therefore, righteous Joseph, rose up and took the virgin Mary and came to Bethlehem, because the time of her bringing forth was at hand. Joseph then inscribed his name in the list ; for Joseph the son of David, whose spouse Mary was, was of the tribe of Judah. And indeed Mary, my mother, brought me forth in Bethlehem, in a cave near the tomb of Rachel the wife of the patriarch Jacob, the mother of Joseph and Benjamin.

8. But Satan went and told this to Herod the Great, the father of Archelaus. And it was this same Herod[5] who ordered my friend and relative John to be beheaded. Accordingly he searched for me diligently, thinking that my kingdom was to be of this world.[6] But Joseph, that pious old man, was warned of this by a dream. Therefore he rose and took Mary my mother, and I lay in her bosom. Salome[7] also was their fellow-traveller. Having therefore set out from home, he retired into Egypt, and remained there the space of one whole year, until the hatred of Herod passed away.

9. Now Herod died by the worst form of death, atoning for the shedding of the blood of the children whom he wickedly cut off, though there was no sin in them. And that impious tyrant Herod being dead, they returned into the land of Israel, and lived in a city of Galilee which is called Nazareth. And Joseph, going back to his trade of a carpenter, earned his living by the work of his hands ; for, as the law of Moses had commanded, he never sought to live for nothing by another's labour.[8]

10. At length, by increasing years, the old man arrived at a very advanced age. He did not, however, labour under any bodily weakness, nor had his sight failed, nor had any tooth perished from his mouth. In mind also, for the whole time of his life, he never wandered ; but like a boy he always in his business displayed youthful vigour, and his limbs remained unimpaired, and free from all pain. His life, then, in all, amounted to one hundred and eleven years, his old age being prolonged to the utmost limit.

11. Now Justus and Simeon, the elder sons of Joseph, were married, and had families of their own. Both the daughters were likewise married, and lived in their own houses. So there remained in Joseph's house, Judas and James the Less, and my virgin mother. I moreover dwelt along with them, not otherwise than if I

---

[1] Luke xxiv. 10.
[2] Matt. i. 19.
[3] Ps. ii. 9; Rev. xii. 5, xix. 15.
[4] Matt. i. 20-24.

[5] It was Herod Antipas who ordered John to be beheaded.
[6] John xviii. 36.
[7] The Salome here mentioned was, according to two of the MSS. of Pseudo-Matthew, the third husband of Anna, Mary's mother, and the father of Mary the wife of Zebedee. But compare Matt. xxvii. 56 with Mark xv. 40.
[8] Gen. iii. 19.

had been one of his sons. But I passed all my life without fault. Mary I called my mother, and Joseph father, and I obeyed them in all that they said; nor did I ever contend against them, but complied with their commands, as other men whom earth produces are wont to do; nor did I at any time arouse their anger, or give any word or answer in opposition to them. On the contrary, I cherished them with great love, like the pupil of my eye.

12. It came to pass, after these things, that the death of that old man, the pious Joseph, and his departure from this world, were approaching, as happens to other men who owe their origin to this earth. And as his body was verging on dissolution, an angel of the Lord informed him that his death was now close at hand. Therefore fear and great perplexity came upon him. So he rose up and went to Jerusalem; and going into the temple of the Lord, he poured out his prayers there before the sanctuary, and said:

13. O God! author of all consolation, God of all compassion, and Lord of the whole human race; God of my soul, body, and spirit; with supplications I reverence thee, O Lord and my God. If now my days are ended, and the time draws near when I must leave this world, send me, I beseech Thee, the great Michael, the prince of Thy holy angels: let him remain with me, that my wretched soul may depart from this afflicted body without trouble, without terror and impatience. For great fear and intense sadness take hold of all bodies on the day of their death, whether it be man or woman, beast wild or tame, or whatever creeps on the ground or flies in the air. At the last all creatures under heaven in whom is the breath of life are struck with horror, and their souls depart from their bodies with strong fear and great depression. Now therefore, O Lord and my God, let Thy holy angel be present with his help to my soul and body, until they shall be dissevered from each other. And let not the face of the angel, appointed my guardian from the day of my birth,[1] be turned away from me; but may he be the companion of my journey even until he bring me to Thee: let his countenance be pleasant and gladsome to me, and let him accompany me in peace. And let not demons of frightful aspect come near me in the way in which I am to go, until I come to Thee in bliss. And let not the door-keepers hinder my soul from entering paradise. And do not uncover my sins, and expose me to condemnation before Thy terrible tribunal. Let not the lions rush in upon me; nor let the waves of the sea of fire overwhelm my soul — for this must every soul pass through[2] — before I have seen the glory of Thy Godhead. O God, most righteous Judge, who in justice and equity wilt judge mankind, and wilt render unto each one according to his works, O Lord and my God, I beseech Thee, be present to me in Thy compassion, and enlighten my path that I may come to Thee; for Thou art a fountain overflowing with all good things, and with glory for evermore. Amen.

14. It came to pass thereafter, when he returned to his own house in the city of Nazareth, that he was seized by disease, and had to keep his bed. And it was at this time that he died, according to the destiny of all mankind. For this disease was very heavy upon him, and he had never been ill, as he now was, from the day of his birth. And thus assuredly it pleased Christ[3] to order the destiny of righteous Joseph. He lived forty years unmarried; thereafter his wife remained under his care forty-nine years, and then died. And a year after her death, my mother, the blessed Mary, was entrusted to him by the priests, that he should keep her until the time of her marriage. She spent two years in his house; and in the third year of her stay with Joseph, in the fifteenth year of her age, she brought me forth on earth by a mystery which no creature can penetrate or understand, except myself, and my Father and the Holy Spirit, constituting one essence with myself.[4]

15. The whole age of my father, therefore, that righteous old man, was one hundred and eleven years, my Father in heaven having so decreed. And the day on which his soul left his body was the twenty-sixth of the month Abib. For now the fine gold began to lose its splendour, and the silver to be worn down by use — I mean his understanding and his wisdom. He also loathed food and drink, and lost all his skill in his trade of carpentry, nor did he any more pay attention to it. It came to pass, then, in the early dawn of the twenty-sixth day of Abib, that Joseph, that righteous old man, lying in his bed, was giving up his unquiet soul. Wherefore he opened his mouth with many sighs, and struck his hands one against the other, and with a loud

---

[1] On the subject of guardian angels, see *Shepherd of Hermas*, iii. 4; Justin, *Apol.*, ii. 5, *Tryph.*, 5; Athenagoras, *Legat.*, 10, 20; Clem. Alex., *Strom.*, vi. 17.

[2] This clause looks like an interpolation. But the doctrine of purgatory was held from an early date. Clem. Alex., *Pædag.*, iii. 9; *Strom.*, vii. 6; *Origen against Celsus*, v. 14, 15.

[3] Note the change from the first person.

[4] Here the Coptic has: This is the end of the life of my beloved father Joseph. When forty years old he married a wife, with whom he lived nine (? forty-nine) years. After her death he remained a widower one (or two) year; and my mother lived two years in his house before she was married to him, since he had been ordered by the priests to take charge of her until the time of her marriage. And my mother Mary brought me forth in the third year that she was in Joseph's house, in the fifteenth year of her age. My mother bore me in a cave (this seems a mistranslation for *mystery*), which it is unlawful either to name or seek, and there is not in the whole creation a man who knows it, except me and my Father and the Holy Spirit. It is to be noted that the last clause is omitted in the Coptic. The phrase *one essence* was first used in regard to the doctrine of the Trinity by Augustine.

voice cried out, and spoke after the following manner : —

16. Woe to the day on which I was born into the world ! Woe to the womb which bare me ! Woe to the bowels which admitted me ! Woe to the breasts which suckled me ! Woe to the feet upon which I sat and rested ! Woe to the hands which carried me and reared me until I grew up ! [1] For I was conceived in iniquity, and in sins did my mother desire me.[2] Woe to my tongue and my lips, which have brought forth and spoken vanity, detraction, falsehood, ignorance, derision, idle tales, craft, and hypocrisy ! Woe to mine eyes, which have looked upon scandalous things ! Woe to mine ears, which have delighted in the words of slanderers ! Woe to my hands, which have seized what did not of right belong to them ! Woe to my belly and my bowels, which have lusted after food unlawful to be eaten ! Woe to my throat, which like a fire has consumed all that it found ! Woe to my feet, which have too often walked in ways displeasing to God ! Woe to my body ; and woe to my miserable soul, which has already turned aside from God its Maker ! What shall I do when I arrive at that place where I must stand before the most righteous Judge, and when He shall call me to account for the works which I have heaped up in my youth ? Woe to every man dying in his sins ! Assuredly that same dreadful hour, which came upon my father Jacob,[3] when his soul was flying forth from his body, is now, behold, near at hand for me. Oh ! how wretched I am this day, and worthy of lamentation ! But God alone is the disposer of my soul and body ; He also will deal with them after His own good pleasure.

17. These are the words spoken by Joseph, that righteous old man. And I, going in beside him, found his soul exceedingly troubled, for he was placed in great perplexity. And I said to him : Hail ! my father Joseph, thou righteous man ; how is it with thee ? And he answered me : All hail ! my well-beloved son. Indeed, the agony and fear of death have already environed me ; but as soon as I heard Thy voice, my soul was at rest. O Jesus of Nazareth ! Jesus, my Saviour ! Jesus, the deliverer of my soul ! Jesus, my protector ! Jesus ! O sweetest name in my mouth, and in the mouth of all those that love it ! O eye which seest, and ear which hearest, hear me ! I am Thy servant ; this day I most humbly reverence Thee, and before Thy face I pour out my tears. Thou art altogether my God ; Thou art my Lord, as the angel has told me times without number, and especially on that day when my soul was driven about with perverse

thoughts about the pure and blessed Mary, who was carrying Thee in her womb, and whom I was thinking of secretly sending away. And while I was thus meditating, behold, there appeared to me in my rest angels of the Lord, saying to me in a wonderful mystery : O Joseph, thou son of David, fear not to take Mary as thy wife ; and do not grieve thy soul, nor speak unbecoming words of her conception, because she is with child of the Holy Spirit, and shall bring forth a son, whose name shall be called Jesus, for He shall save His people from their sins. Do not for this cause wish me evil, O Lord ! for I was ignorant of the mystery of Thy birth. I call to mind also, my Lord, that day when the boy died of the bite of the serpent. And his relations wished to deliver Thee to Herod, saying that Thou hadst killed him ; but Thou didst raise him from the dead, and restore him to them. Then I went up to Thee, and took hold of Thy hand, saying : My son, take care of thyself. But Thou didst say to me in reply : Art thou not my father after the flesh ? I shall teach thee who I am.[4] Now therefore, O Lord and my God, do not be angry with me, or condemn me on account of that hour. I am Thy servant, and the son of Thine handmaiden ; [5] but Thou art my Lord, my God and Saviour, most surely the Son of God.

18. When my father Joseph had thus spoken, he was unable to weep more. And I saw that death now had dominion over him. And my mother, virgin undefiled, rose and came to me, saying : O my beloved son, this pious old man Joseph is now dying. And I answered : Oh, my dearest mother, assuredly upon all creatures produced in this world the same necessity of death lies ; for death holds sway over the whole human race. Even thou, O my virgin mother, must look for the same end of life as other mortals. And yet thy death, as also the death of this pious man, is not death, but life enduring to eternity. Nay more, even I must die, as concerns the body which I have received from thee. But rise, O my venerable mother, and go in to Joseph, that blessed old man, in order that thou mayst see what will happen as his soul ascends from his body.

19. My undefiled mother Mary, therefore, went and entered the place where Joseph was. And I was sitting at his feet looking at him, for the signs of death already appeared in his countenance. And that blessed old man raised his head, and kept his eyes fixed on my face ; but he had no power of speaking to me, on account of the agonies of death, which held him in their

---

[1] Comp. Job iii.
[2] Comp. Ps. li. 5.
[3] Matt. i. 16.

[4] The Sahidic has : Joseph entreats Jesus to pardon him likewise, because when, once upon a time, He had recalled to life a boy bitten by a cerastes, he (Joseph) had pulled His right ear, advising Him to refrain from works that brought hatred upon Him. See Second Gospel of Thomas, chap. 5.
[5] Ps. cxvi. 16.

grasp. But he kept fetching many sighs. And I held his hands for a whole hour ; and he turned his face to me, and made signs for me not to leave him. Thereafter I put my hand upon his breast, and perceived his soul now near his throat, preparing to depart from its receptacle.

20. And when my virgin mother saw me touching his body, she also touched his feet. And finding them already dead and destitute of heat, she said to me : O my beloved son, assuredly his feet are already beginning to stiffen, and they are as cold as snow. Accordingly she summoned his sons and daughters, and said to them : Come, as many as there are of you, and go to your father ; for assuredly he is now at the very point of death. And Assia, his daughter, answered and said : Woe's me, O my brothers, this is certainly the same disease that my beloved mother died of. And she lamented and shed tears ; and all Joseph's other children mourned along with her. I also, and my mother Mary, wept along with them.[1]

21. And turning my eyes towards the region of the south, I saw Death already approaching, and all Gehenna with him, closely attended by his army and his satellites ; and their clothes, their faces, and their mouths poured forth flames. And when my father Joseph saw them coming straight to him, his eyes dissolved in tears, and at the same time he groaned after a strange manner. Accordingly, when I saw the vehemence of his sighs, I drove back Death and all the host of servants which accompanied him. And I called upon my good Father, saying : —

22. O Father of all mercy, eye which seest, and ear which hearest, hearken to my prayers and supplications in behalf of the old man Joseph ; and send Michael, the prince of Thine angels, and Gabriel, the herald of light, and all the light of Thine angels, and let their whole array walk with the soul of my father Joseph, until they shall have conducted it to Thee. This is the hour in which my father has need of compassion. And I say unto you, that all the saints, yea, as many men as are born in the world, whether they be just or whether they be perverse, must of necessity taste of death.

23. Therefore Michael and Gabriel came to the soul of my father Joseph, and took it, and wrapped it in a shining wrapper. Thus he committed his spirit into the hands of my good Father, and He bestowed upon him peace. But as yet none of his children knew that he had fallen asleep. And the angels preserved his soul from the demons of darkness which were in the way, and praised God even until they conducted it into the dwelling-place of the pious.

24. Now his body was lying prostrate and bloodless ; wherefore I reached forth my hand, and put right his eyes and shut his mouth, and said to the virgin Mary : O my mother, where is the skill which he showed in all the time that he lived in this world? Lo ! it has perished, as if it had never existed. And when his children heard me speaking with my mother, the pure virgin, they knew that he had already breathed his last, and they shed tears, and lamented. But I said to them : Assuredly the death of your father is not death, but life everlasting : for he has been freed from the troubles of this life, and has passed to perpetual and everlasting rest. When they heard these words, they rent their clothes, and wept.

25. And, indeed, the inhabitants of Nazareth and of Galilee, having heard of their lamentation, flocked to them, and wept from the third hour even to the ninth. And at the ninth hour they all went together to Joseph's bed. And they lifted his body, after they had anointed it with costly unguents. But I entreated my Father in the prayer of the celestials — that same prayer which with my own hand I made before I was carried in the womb of the virgin Mary, my mother. And as soon as I had finished it, and pronounced the amen, a great multitude of angels came up ; and I ordered two of them to stretch out their shining garments, and to wrap in them the body of Joseph, the blessed old man.

26. And I spoke to Joseph, and said : The smell or corruption of death shall not have dominion over thee, nor shall a worm ever come forth from thy body. Not a single limb of it shall be broken, nor shall any hair on thy head be changed. Nothing of thy body shall perish, O my father Joseph, but it will remain entire and uncorrupted even until the banquet of the thousand years.[2] And whosoever shall make an offering on the day of thy remembrance, him will I bless and recompense in the congregation of the virgins ; and whosoever shall give food to the wretched, the poor, the widows, and orphans from the work of his hands, on the day on which thy memory shall be celebrated, and in thy name, shall not be in want of good things all the days of his life. And whosoever shall have given a cup of water, or of wine, to drink to the widow or orphan in thy name, I will give him to thee, that thou mayst go in with him to the banquet of the thousand years. And every man who shall present an offering on the day of thy commemoration will I bless and recompense in the church of the virgins : for one I will render unto him thirty, sixty, and a hundred. And whosover shall

---

[1] The argument of the Sahidic is: He sends for Joseph's sons and daughters, of whom the oldest was Lysia the purple-seller. They all weep over their dying father.

[2] *Barnabas*, 15; *Hermas*, i. 3; Irenæus, *Contra Hær.*, v. 33; Justin, *Tryph.*, 81; Tertullian, *Adv. Marc.*, iii. 24. Caius and Dionysius imputed grossness and sensuality to Cerinthus, because he spoke of the wedding feast of the thousand years.

write the history of thy life, of thy labour, and thy departure from this world, and this narrative that has issued from my mouth, him shall I commit to thy keeping as long as he shall have to do with this life. And when his soul departs from the body, and when he must leave this world, I will burn the book of his sins, nor will I torment him with any punishment in the day of judgment; but he shall cross the sea of flames, and shall go through it without trouble or pain.[1] And upon every poor man who can give none of those things which I have mentioned this is incumbent: viz., if a son is born to him, he shall call his name Joseph. So there shall not take place in that house either poverty or any sudden death for ever.

27. Thereafter the chief men of the city came together to the place where the body of the blessed old man Joseph had been laid, bringing with them burial-clothes; and they wished to wrap it up in them after the manner in which the Jews are wont to arrange their dead bodies. And they perceived that he kept his shroud fast; for it adhered to the body in such a way, that when they wished to take it off, it was found to be like iron — impossible to be moved or loosened. Nor could they find any ends in that piece of linen, which struck them with the greatest astonishment. At length they carried him out to a place where there was a cave, and opened the gate, that they might bury his body beside the bodies of his fathers. Then there came into my mind the day on which he walked with me into Egypt, and that extreme trouble which he endured on my account. Accordingly, I bewailed his death for a long time; and lying upon his body, I said:—

28. O Death! who makest all knowledge to vanish away, and raisest so many tears and lamentations, surely it is God my Father Himself who hath granted thee this power. For men die for the transgression of Adam and his wife Eve, and Death spares not so much as one. Nevertheless, nothing happens to any one, or is brought upon him, without the command of my Father. There have certainly been men who have prolonged their life even to nine hundred years; but they died. Yea, though some of them have lived longer, they have, notwithstanding, succumbed to the same fate; nor has any one of them ever said: I have not tasted death. For the Lord never sends the same punishment more than once, since it hath pleased my Father to bring it upon men. And at the very moment when it, going forth, beholds the command descending to it from heaven, it says: I will go forth against

that man, and will greatly move him. Then, without delay, it makes an onset on the soul, and obtains the mastery of it, doing with it whatever it will. For, because Adam did not the will of my Father, but transgressed His commandment, the wrath of my Father was kindled against him, and He doomed him to death; and thus it was that death came into the world. But if Adam had observed my Father's precepts, death would never have fallen to his lot. Think you that I can ask my good Father to send me a chariot of fire,[2] which may take up the body of my father Joseph, and convey it to the place of rest, in order that it may dwell with the spirits? But on account of the transgression of Adam, that trouble and violence of death has descended upon all the human race. And it is for this cause that I must die according to the flesh, for my work which I have created, that they may obtain grace.

29. Having thus spoken, I embraced the body of my father Joseph, and wept over it; and they opened the door of the tomb, and placed his body in it, near the body of his father Jacob. And at the time when he fell asleep he had fulfilled a hundred and eleven years. Never did a tooth in his mouth hurt him, nor was his eyesight rendered less sharp, nor his body bent, nor his strength impaired; but he worked at his trade of a carpenter to the very last day of his life; and that was the six-and-twentieth of the month Abib.

30. And we apostles, when we heard these things from our Saviour, rose up joyfully, and prostrated ourselves in honour of Him, and said: O our Saviour, show us Thy grace. Now indeed we have heard the word of life: nevertheless we wonder, O our Saviour, at the fate of Enoch and Elias, inasmuch as they had not to undergo death. For truly they dwell in the habitation of the righteous even to the present day, nor have their bodies seen corruption. Yet that old man Joseph the carpenter was, nevertheless, Thy father after the flesh. And Thou hast ordered us to go into all the world and preach the holy Gospel; and Thou hast said: Relate to them the death of my father Joseph, and celebrate to him with annual solemnity a festival and sacred day. And whosoever shall take anything away from this narrative, or add anything to it, commits sin.[3] We wonder especially that Joseph, even from that day on which Thou wast born in Bethlehem, called Thee his son after the flesh. Wherefore, then, didst Thou not make him immortal as well as them, and Thou sayest that he was righteous and chosen?

31. And our Saviour answered and said: In-

---

[1] All the fathers placed the purgatorial fires, as the Greek Church does now, at the day of judgment. Augustine was the first who brought forward the supposition that the purification took place in Hades before the day of judgment. Haag, *Histoire des Dogmes*, ii. 323.

[2] 2 Kings ii. 11.
[3] Rev. xxii. 18, 19.

deed, the prophecy of my Father upon Adam, for his disobedience, has now been fulfilled. And all things are arranged according to the will and pleasure of my Father. For if a man rejects the commandment of God, and follows the works of the devil by committing sin, his life is prolonged; for he is preserved in order that he may perhaps repent, and reflect that he must be delivered into the hands of death. But if any one has been zealous of good works, his life also is prolonged, that, as the fame of his old age increases, upright men may imitate him. But when you see a man whose mind is prone to anger, assuredly his days are shortened; for it is these that are taken away in the flower of their age. Every prophecy, therefore, which my Father has pronounced concerning the sons of men, must be fulfilled in every particular. But with reference to Enoch and Elias, and how they remain alive to this day, keeping the same bodies with which they were born; and as to what concerns my father Joseph, who has not been allowed as well as they to remain in the body: indeed, though a man live in the world many myriads of years, nevertheless at some time or other he is compelled to exchange life for death.

And I say to you, O my brethren, that they also, Enoch and Elias,[1] must towards the end of time return into the world and die — in the day, namely, of commotion, of terror, of perplexity, and affliction. For Antichrist will slay four bodies, and will pour out their blood like water, because of the reproach to which they shall expose him, and the ignominy with which they, in their lifetime, shall brand him when they reveal his impiety.

32. And we said: O our Lord, our God and Saviour, who are those four whom Thou hast said Antichrist will cut off from the reproach they bring upon him? The Lord answered: They are Enoch, Elias, Schila, and Tabitha.[2] When we heard this from our Saviour, we rejoiced and exulted; and we offered all glory and thanksgiving to the Lord God, and our Saviour Jesus Christ. He it is to whom is due glory, honour, dignity, dominion, power, and praise, as well as to the good Father with Him, and to the Holy Spirit that giveth life, henceforth and in all time for evermore. Amen.

---

[1] Comp. Rev. xi. 3-12.
[2] Acts ix. 36. Schila is probably meant for the widow of Nain's son.

THE GOSPEL OF THOMAS

FIRST GREEK FORM.

THOMAS THE ISRAELITE PHILOSOPHER'S ACCOUNT OF THE INFANCY OF THE LORD.

1. I Thomas, an Israelite, write you this account, that all the brethren from among the heathen may know the miracles of our Lord Jesus Christ in His infancy, which He did after His birth in our country. The beginning of it is as follows : —

2. This child Jesus, when five years old, was playing in the ford of a mountain stream ; and He collected the flowing waters into pools, and made them clear immediately, and by a word alone He made them obey Him. And having made some soft clay, He fashioned out of it twelve sparrows. And it was the Sabbath when He did these things. And there were also many other children playing with Him. And a certain Jew, seeing what Jesus was doing, playing on the Sabbath, went off immediately, and said to his father Joseph : Behold, thy son is at the stream, and has taken clay, and made of it twelve birds, and has profaned the Sabbath. And Joseph, coming to the place and seeing, cried out to Him, saying : Wherefore doest thou on the Sabbath what it is not lawful to do? And Jesus clapped His hands, and cried out to the sparrows, and said to them : Off you go ! And the sparrows flew, and went off crying. And the Jews seeing this were amazed, and went away and reported to their chief men what they had seen Jesus doing.[1]

3. And the son of Annas the scribe was standing there with Joseph ; and he took a willow branch, and let out the waters which Jesus had collected. And Jesus, seeing what was done, was angry, and said to him : O wicked, impious, and foolish ! what harm did the pools and the waters do to thee ? Behold, even now thou shalt be dried up like a tree, and thou shalt not bring forth either leaves, or root,[2] or fruit. And straightway that boy was quite dried up. And Jesus departed, and went to Joseph's house.

But the parents of the boy that had been dried up took him up, bewailing his youth, and brought him to Joseph, and reproached him because, *said they,* thou hast such a child doing such things.[3]

4. After that He was again passing through the village ; and a boy ran up against Him, and struck His shoulder. And Jesus was angry, and said to him : Thou shalt not go back the way thou camest. And immediately he fell down dead. And some who saw what had taken place, said : Whence was this child begotten, that every word of his is certainly accomplished ? And the parents of the dead boy went away to Joseph, and blamed him, saying : Since thou hast such a child, it is impossible for thee to live with us in the village ; or else teach him to bless, and not to curse :[4] for he is killing our children.

5. And Joseph called the child apart, and admonished Him, saying : Why doest thou such things, and these people suffer, and hate us, and persecute us ? And Jesus said : I know that these words of thine are not thine own ;[5] nevertheless for thy sake I will be silent ; but they shall bear their punishment. And straightway those that accused Him were struck blind. And those who saw it were much afraid and in great perplexity, and said about Him : Every word which he spoke, whether good or bad, was an act, and became a wonder. And when they saw that Jesus had done such a thing, Joseph rose and took hold of His ear, and pulled it hard. And the child was very angry, and said to him : It is enough for thee to seek, and not to find ; and most certainly thou hast not done wisely. Knowest thou not that I am thine ? Do not trouble me.[6]

---

[1] Pseudo-Matt. 26, etc.
[2] Another reading is, *branches.*

[3] One MS has: And Jesus, at the entreaty of all of them, healed him.
[4] Or, either teach him to bless, and not to curse, or depart with him from this place; for, etc.
[5] Or, are not mine, but thine.
[6] Pseudo-Matt. 29. [The numerous references to the latter part of Pseudo-Matthæi, see pp. 378–383, shows the close relationship. But it is generally agreed that this narrative is the older, and one of the sources of Pseudo-Matthæi. — R.]

6. And a certain teacher, Zacchæus by name, was standing in a certain place, and heard Jesus thus speaking to his father; and he wondered exceedingly, that, being a child, he should speak in such a way. And a few days thereafter he came to Joseph, and said to him: Thou hast a sensible child, and he has some mind. Give him to me, then, that he may learn letters; and I shall teach him along with the letters all knowledge, both how to address all the elders, and to honour them as forefathers and fathers, and how to love those of his own age. And He said to him all the letters from the Alpha even to the Omega, clearly and with great exactness. And He looked upon the teacher Zacchæus, and said to him: Thou who art ignorant of the nature of the Alpha, how canst thou teach others the Beta? Thou hypocrite! first, if thou knowest, teach the A, and then we shall believe thee about the B. Then He began to question the teacher about the first letter, and he was not able to answer Him. And in the hearing of many, the child says to Zacchæus: Hear, O teacher, the order of the first letter, and notice here how it has lines, and a middle stroke crossing those which thou seest common; (lines) brought together; the highest part supporting them, and again bringing them under one head; with three points *of intersection;* of the same kind; principal and subordinate; of equal length. Thou hast the lines of the A.[1]

7. And when the teacher Zacchæus heard the child speaking such and so great allegories of the first letter, he was at a great loss about such a narrative, and about His teaching. And He said to those that were present: Alas! I, wretch that I am, am at a loss, bringing shame upon myself by having dragged this child hither. Take him away, then, I beseech thee, brother Joseph. I cannot endure the sternness of his look; I cannot make out his meaning at all. That child does not belong to this earth; he can tame even fire. Assuredly he was born before the creation of the world. What sort of a belly bore him, what sort of a womb nourished him, I do not know. Alas! my friend, he has carried me away; I cannot get at his meaning: thrice wretched that I am, I have deceived myself. I made a struggle to have a scholar, and I was found to have a teacher. My mind is filled with shame, my friends, because I, an old man, have been conquered by a child. There is nothing for me but despondency and death on account

of this boy, for I am not able at this hour to look him in the face; and when everybody says that I have been beaten by a little child, what can I say? And how can I give an account of the lines of the first letter that he spoke about? I know not, O my friends; for I can make neither beginning nor end of him. Therefore, I beseech thee, brother Joseph, take him home. What great thing he is, either god or angel, or what I am to say, I know not.[2]

8. And when the Jews were encouraging Zacchæus, the child laughed aloud, and said: Now let thy learning bring forth fruit, and let the blind in heart see. I am here from above, that I may curse them, and call them to the things that are above, as He that sent me on your account has commanded me. And when the child ceased speaking, immediately all were made whole who had fallen under His curse. And no one after that dared to make Him angry, lest He should curse him, and he should be maimed.

9. And some days after, Jesus was playing in an upper room of a certain house, and one of the children that were playing with Him fell down from the house, and was killed. And, when the other children saw this, they ran away, and Jesus alone stood still. And the parents of the dead child coming, reproached[3] . . . and they threatened Him. And Jesus leaped down from the roof, and stood beside the body of the child, and cried with a loud voice, and said: Zeno — for that was his name — stand up, and tell me; did I throw thee down? And he stood up immediately, and said: Certainly not, my lord; thou didst not throw me down, but hast raised me up. And those that saw this were struck with astonishment. And the child's parents glorified God on account of the miracle that had happened, and adored Jesus.[4]

10. A few days after, a young man was splitting wood in the corner,[5] and the axe came down and cut the sole of his foot in two, and he died from loss of blood. And there was a great commotion, and people ran together, and the child Jesus ran there too. And He pressed through the crowd, and laid hold of the young man's wounded foot, and he was cured immediately. And He said to the young man: Rise up now, split the wood, and remember me. And the crowd seeing what had happened, adored the child, saying: Truly the Spirit of God dwells in this child.

---

[1] Pseud.-Matt. 30, 31. Various explanations have been given of this difficult passage by annotators, who refer it to the A of the Hebrew, or of the Greek, or of the Armenian alphabet. It seems, however, to answer very closely to the old Phenician A, which was written ◁ or ⩔.

The Paris MS. has: And he sat down to teach Jesus the letters, and began the first letter Aleph; and Jesus says the second, Beth, Gimel, and told him all the letters to the end. And shutting the book, He taught the master the prophets.

[2] Instead of this chapter, the Paris MS. has: And he was ashamed and perplexed, because he knew not whence he knew the letters. And he arose, and went home, in great astonishment at this strange thing.

It then goes on with a fragment of the history of the dyer's shop, as given in the Arabic Gospel of the Infancy, ch. 37.

[3] One of the MSS. of the Latin Gospel inserts here — Jesus, saying: Indeed, you made him fall down. And Jesus said: I never made him fall.

[4] Pseud.-Matt. 32.

[5] A better reading would be ἐν τῇ γειτονίᾳ, in the neighbourhood, for ἐν τῇ γωνίᾳ, in the corner.

11. And when He was six years old, His mother gave Him a pitcher, and sent Him to draw water, and bring it into the house. But He struck against some one in the crowd, and the pitcher was broken. And Jesus unfolded the cloak which He had on, and filled it with water, and carried it to His mother. And His mother, seeing the miracle that had happened, kissed Him, and kept within herself the mysteries which she had seen Him doing.[1]

12. And again in seed-time the child went out with His father to sow corn in their land. And while His father was sowing, the child Jesus also sowed one grain of corn. And when He had reaped it, and threshed it, He made a hundred kors ;[2] and calling all the poor of the village to the threshing-floor, He gave them the corn, and Joseph took away what was left of the corn. And He was eight years old when He did this miracle.[3]

13. And His father was a carpenter, and at that time made ploughs and yokes. And a certain rich man ordered him to make him a couch. And one of what is called the cross pieces being too short, they did not know what to do. The child Jesus said to His father Joseph : Put down the two pieces of wood, and make them even in the middle. And Joseph did as the child said to him. And Jesus stood at the other end, and took hold of the shorter piece of wood, and stretched it, and made it equal to the other. And His father Joseph saw it, and wondered, and embraced the child, and blessed Him, saying : Blessed am I, because God has given me this child.[4]

14. And Joseph, seeing that the child was vigorous in mind and body, again resolved that He should not remain ignorant of the letters, and took Him away, and handed Him over to another teacher. And the teacher said to Joseph : I shall first teach him the Greek letters, and then the Hebrew. For the teacher was aware of the trial that had been made of the child, and was afraid of Him. Nevertheless he wrote out the alphabet, and gave Him all his attention for a long time, and He made him no answer. And Jesus said to him : If thou art really a teacher, and art well acquainted with the letters, tell me the power of the Alpha, and I will tell thee the power of the Beta. And the teacher was enraged at this, and struck Him on the head. And the child, being in pain, cursed him ; and immediately he swooned away, and fell to the ground on his face. And the child returned to Joseph's house ; and Joseph was grieved, and gave orders to His mother, saying : Do not let him go out-side of the door, because those that make him angry die.[5]

15. And after some time, another master again, a genuine friend of Joseph, said to him : Bring the child to my school; perhaps I shall be able to flatter him into learning his letters. And Joseph said : If thou hast the courage, brother, take him with thee. And he took Him with him in fear and great agony ; but the child went along pleasantly. And going boldly into the school, He found a book lying on the reading-desk ; and taking it, He read not the letters that were in it, but opening His mouth, He spoke by the Holy Spirit, and taught the law to those that were standing round. And a great crowd having come together, stood by and heard Him, and wondered at the ripeness of His teaching, and the readiness of His words, and that He, child as He was, spoke in such a way. And Joseph hearing of it, was afraid, and ran to the school, in doubt lest this master too should be without experience.[6] And the master said to Joseph : Know, brother, that I have taken the child as a scholar, and he is full of much grace and wisdom ; but I beseech thee, brother, take him home. And when the child heard this, He laughed at him directly, and said : Since thou hast spoken aright, and witnessed aright, for thy sake he also that was struck down shall be cured. And immediately the other master was cured. And Joseph took the child, and went away home.[7]

16. And Joseph sent his son James to tie up wood and bring it home, and the child Jesus also followed him. And when James was gathering the fagots, a viper bit James' hand. And when he was racked *with pain*, and at the point of death, Jesus came near and blew upon the bite ; and the pain ceased directly, and the beast burst, and instantly James remained safe and sound.[8]

17. And after this the infant of one of Joseph's neighbours fell sick and died, and its mother wept sore. And Jesus heard that there was great lamentation and commotion, and ran in haste, and found the child dead, and touched his breast, and said : I say to thee, child, be not dead, but live, and be with thy mother. And directly it looked up and laughed. And He said to the woman : Take it, and give it milk, and remember me. And seeing this, the crowd that was standing by wondered, and said : Truly this child was either God or an angel of God, for every word of his is a certain fact. And Jesus went out thence, playing with the other children.[9]

---

[1] Pseudo-Matt. 33.
[2] The kor or chomer was, according to Jahn, 32 pecks 1 pint.
[3] Pseudo-Matt. 34.
[4] Pseudo-Matt. 37.

[5] Pseudo-Matt. 38.
[6] Tischendorf suggests ἀνάπηρος, maimed, for ἄπειρος.
[7] Pseudo-Matt. 39.
[8] Pseudo-Matt. 41.
[9] Pseudo-Matt. 40.

18. And some time after there occurred a great commotion while a house was building, and Jesus stood up and went away to the place. And seeing a man lying dead, He took him by the hand, and said: Man, I say to thee, arise, and go on with thy work. And directly he rose up, and adored Him. And seeing this, the crowd wondered, and said: This child is from heaven, for he has saved many souls from death, and he continues to save during all his life.

19. And when He was twelve years old His parents went as usual to Jerusalem to the feast of the passover with their fellow-travellers. And after the passover they were coming home again. And while they were coming home, the child Jesus went back to Jerusalem. And His parents thought that He was in the company. And having gone one day's journey, they sought for Him among their relations; and not finding Him, they were in great grief, and turned back to the city seeking for Him. And after the third day they found Him in the temple, sitting in the midst of the teachers, both hearing the law and asking them questions. And they were all at-tending to Him, and wondering that He, being a child, was shutting the mouths of the elders and teachers of the people, explaining the main points of the law and the parables of the prophets. And His mother Mary coming up, said to Him: Why hast thou done this to us, child? Behold, we have been seeking for thee in great trouble. And Jesus said to them: Why do you seek me? Do you not know that I must be about my Father's business?[1] And the scribes and the Pharisees said: Art thou the mother of this child? And she said: I am. And they said to her: Blessed art thou among women, for God hath blessed the fruit of thy womb; for such glory, and such virtue and wisdom, we have neither seen nor heard ever. And Jesus rose up, and followed His mother, and was subject to His parents. And His mother observed all these things that had happened. And Jesus advanced in wisdom, and stature, and grace.[2] To whom be glory for ever and ever. Amen.

[1] [This may be rendered, as in R. V., Luke ii. 49, "in my Father's house." The words are the same as in that passage. — R.]
[2] Luke ii. 41-52.

SECOND GREEK FORM

THE WRITING OF THE HOLY APOSTLE THOMAS CONCERNING THE CHILDHOOD OF THE LORD.

1. I Thomas the Israelite have deemed it necessary to make known to all the brethren of the heathen the great things which our Lord Jesus Christ did in His childhood, when He dwelt in the body in the city of Nazareth, going in the fifth year of His age.

2. On one of the days, there being a rainstorm, He went out of the house where His mother was, and played on the ground where the waters were flowing. And He made pools, and brought in the waters, and the pools were filled with water. Then He says: It is my will that you become clear and excellent waters. And they became so directly. And a certain boy, the son of Annas the scribe, came past, and with a willow branch which he was carrying threw down the pools, and the water flowed out. And Jesus turning, said to him: O impious and wicked, how have the pools wronged thee, that thou hast emptied them? Thou shalt not go on thy way, and thou shalt be dried up like the branch which thou art carrying. And as he went along, in a short time he fell down and died. And when the children that were playing with him saw this, they wondered, and went away and told the father of the dead boy. And he ran and found his child dead, and he went away and reproached Joseph.

3. And Jesus made of that clay twelve sparrows, and it was the Sabbath. And a child ran and told Joseph, saying: Behold, thy child is playing about the stream, and of the clay he has made sparrows, which is not lawful. And when he heard this, he went, and said to the child: Why dost thou do this, profaning the Sabbath? But Jesus gave him no answer, but looked upon the sparrows, and said: Go away, fly, and live, and remember me. And at this word they flew, and went up into the air. And when Joseph saw it, he wondered.

4. And some days after, when Jesus was going through the midst of the city, a boy threw a stone at Him, and struck Him on the shoulder. And Jesus said to him: Thou shalt not go on thy way. And directly falling down, he also died. And they that happened to be there were struck with astonishment, saying: Whence is this child, that every word he says is certainly accomplished? And they also went and reproached Joseph, saying: It is impossible for

thee to live with us in this city: but if thou wishest to do so, teach thy child to bless, and not to curse: for he is killing our children, and everything that he says is certainly accomplished.

5. And Joseph was sitting in his seat, and the child stood before him; and he took hold of Him by the ear, and pinched it hard. And Jesus looked at him steadily, and said: It is enough for thee.

6. And on the day after he took Him by the hand, and led Him to a certain teacher, Zacchæus by name, and says to him: O master, take this child, and teach him his letters. And he says: Hand him over to me, brother, and I shall teach him the Scripture; and I shall persuade him to bless all, and not to curse. And Jesus hearing, laughed, and said to them: You say what you know; but I know more than you, for I am before the ages. And I know when your fathers' fathers were born; and I know how many are the years of your life. And hearing this, they were struck with astonishment. And again Jesus said to them: You wonder because I said to you that I knew how many are the years of your life. Assuredly I know when the world was created. Behold, you do not believe me now. When you see my cross, then will ye believe that I speak the truth. And they were struck with astonishment when they heard these things.

7. And Zacchæus, having written the alphabet in Hebrew, says to Him: Alpha. And the child says: Alpha. And again the teacher: Alpha; and the child likewise. Then again the teacher says the Alpha for the third time. Then Jesus, looking in the master's face, says: How canst thou, not knowing the Alpha, teach another the Beta? And the child, beginning from the Alpha, said by Himself the twenty-two letters. Then also He says again: Hear, O teacher, the order of the first letter, and know how many entrances and lines it has, and strokes common, crossing and coming together.[1] And when Zacchæus heard such an account of the one letter, he was so struck with astonishment, that he could make no answer. And he turned and said to Joseph: This child assuredly, brother, does not belong to the earth. Take him, then, away from me.

8. And after these things, on one of the days Jesus was playing with other children on the roof of a house. And one boy was pushed by another, and hurled down upon the ground, and he died. And seeing this, the boys that were playing with him ran away; and Jesus only was left standing upon the roof from which the boy had been hurled down. And when the news was brought to the parents of the dead boy, they ran weeping; and finding their boy lying dead upon the ground, and Jesus standing above, they supposed that their boy had been thrown down by Him; and fixing their eyes upon Him, they reviled Him. And seeing this, Jesus directly came down from the roof, and stood at the head of the dead body, and says to him: Zeno, did I throw thee down? Stand up, and tell us. For this was the name of the boy. And at the word the boy stood up and adored Jesus, and said: My lord, thou didst not throw me down, but thou hast brought me to life when I was dead.

9. And a few days after, one of the neighbours, when splitting wood, cut away the lower part of his foot with the axe, and was on the point of death from loss of blood. And a great number of people ran together, and Jesus came with them to the place. And He took hold of the young man's wounded foot, and cured him directly, and says to him: Rise up, split thy wood. And he rose up and adored Him, giving thanks, and splitting the wood. Likewise also all that were there wondered, and gave thanks to Him.

10. And when He was six years old, Mary His mother sent Him to bring water from the fountain. And as He went along, the pitcher was broken. And going to the fountain He unfolded His overcoat, and drew water from the fountain, and filled it, and took the water to His mother. And seeing this, she was struck with astonishment, and embraced Him, and kissed Him.

11. And when Jesus had come to the eighth year of His age, Joseph was ordered by a certain rich man to make him a couch. For he was a carpenter. And he went out into the field to get wood; and Jesus went with him. And having cut two pieces of wood, and smoothed them with the axe, he put the one beside the other; and in measuring he found it too short. And when he saw this he was grieved, and sought to find another piece. And seeing this, Jesus says to him: Put these two pieces together, so as to make both ends even. And Joseph, in doubt as to what the child should mean, did as he was told. And He says to him again: Take a firm hold of the short piece. And Joseph, in astonishment, took hold of it. Then Jesus also, taking hold of the other end, drew it towards Himself, and make it equal to the other piece of wood. And He says to Joseph: Grieve no more, but do thy work without hindrance. And seeing this, he wondered greatly, and says to himself: Blessed am I, because God has given me such a boy. And when they came back to the city, Joseph gave an account of the matter to Mary. And when she heard and saw the strange miracles of her son, she rejoiced and glorified Him, with the Father and the Holy Spirit, now and ever, and for evermore. Amen.

---

[1] [Compare the account in the version of the first Greek form, chap. 6, and the footnote. — R.]

LATIN FORM

HERE BEGINNETH THE TREATISE OF THE BOYHOOD OF JESUS ACCORDING TO THOMAS.

CHAP. I. — HOW MARY AND JOSEPH FLED WITH HIM INTO EGYPT.

WHEN a commotion took place in consequence of the search made by Herod for our Lord Jesus Christ to kill Him, then an angel said to Joseph: Take Mary and her boy, and flee into Egypt from the face of those who seek to kill Him. And Jesus was two years old when He went into Egypt.

And as He was walking through a field of corn, He stretched forth His hand, and took of the ears, and put them over the fire, and rubbed them, and began to eat.

And when they had come into Egypt, they received hospitality in the house of a certain widow, and they remained in the same place one year.

And Jesus was in His third year. And seeing boys playing, He began to play with them. And He took a dried fish, and put it into a basin, and ordered it to move about. And it began to move about. And He said again to the fish: Throw out thy salt ⋅ which thou hast, and walk into the water. And it so came to pass. And the neighbours, seeing what had been done, told it to the widow woman in whose house Mary His mother lived. And as soon as she heard it, she thrust them out of her house with great haste.

CHAP. II. — HOW A SCHOOLMASTER THRUST HIM OUT OF THE CITY.

And as Jesus was walking with Mary His mother through the middle of the city marketplace, He looked and saw a schoolmaster teaching his scholars. And behold twelve sparrows that were quarrelling fell over the wall into the bosom of that schoolmaster, who was teaching the boys. And seeing this, Jesus was very much amused, and stood still. And when that teacher saw Him making merry, he said to his scholars with great fury: Go and bring him to me. And when they had carried Him to the master, he seized Him by the ear, and said: What didst thou see, to amuse thee so much? And He said to him: Master, see my hand full of wheat. I showed it to them, and scattered the wheat among them, and they carry it out of the middle of the street where they are in danger; and on this account they fought among themselves to divide the wheat. And Jesus did not pass from the place until it was accomplished. And this being done, the master began to thrust Him out of the city, along with His mother.

CHAP. III. — HOW JESUS WENT OUT OF EGYPT.

And, lo, the angel of the Lord met Mary, and said to her: Take up the boy, and return into the land of the Jews, for they who sought His life are dead. And Mary rose up with Jesus; and they proceeded into the city of Nazareth, which is among the possessions of her father. And when Joseph went out of Egypt after the death of Herod, he kept Him in the desert until there should be quietness in Jerusalem on the part of those who were seeking the boy's life. And he gave thanks to God because He had given him understanding, and because he had found favour in the presence of the Lord God. Amen.

CHAP. IV. — WHAT THE LORD JESUS DID IN THE CITY OF NAZARETH.

It is glorious that Thomas the Israelite and apostle of the Lord gives an account also of the works of Jesus after He came out of Egypt into Nazareth. Understand all of you, my dearest brethren, what the Lord Jesus did when He was in the city of Nazareth; the first chapter of which is as follows: —

And when Jesus was five years old, there fell a great rain upon the earth, and the boy Jesus walked up and down through it. And there was a terrible rain, and He collected it into a fishpond, and ordered it by His word to become clear. And immediately it became so. Again He took of the clay which was of that fish-pond, and made of it to the number of twelve sparrows. And it was the Sabbath when Jesus did this among the boys of the Jews. And the boys of the Jews went away, and said to Joseph His father: Behold, thy son was playing along with us, and he took clay and made sparrows, which it was not lawful to do on the Sabbath; and he has broken it. And Joseph went away to the boy Jesus, and said to Him: Why hast thou done this, which it was not lawful to do on the Sabbath? And Jesus opened His hands, and ordered the sparrows, saying: Go up into the air, and fly; nobody shall kill you. And they flew, and began to cry out, and praise God Almighty. And the Jews seeing what had happened, wondered, and went away and told the miracles which Jesus had done. But a Pharisee who was with Jesus took an olive branch, and began to let the water out of the fountain which Jesus had made. And when Jesus saw this, He said to him in a rage : Thou impious and ignorant Sodomite, what harm have my works the fountains of water done thee? Behold, thou shalt become like a dry tree, having neither roots, nor leaves, nor fruit. And immediately he dried up, and fell to the ground, and died. And his parents took him away dead, and reproached Joseph, saying : See what thy son has done ; teach him to pray, and not to blaspheme.

CHAP. V. — HOW THE CITIZENS WERE ENRAGED AGAINST JOSEPH ON ACCOUNT OF THE DOINGS OF JESUS.

And a few days after, as Jesus was walking through the town with Joseph, one of the children ran up and struck Jesus on the arm. And Jesus said to him : So shalt thou not finish thy journey. And immediately he fell to the ground, and died. And those who saw these wonderful things cried out, saying : Whence is that boy? And they said to Joseph : It is not right for such a boy to be among us. And Joseph went and brought Him. And they said to him : Go away from this place ; but if thou must live with us, teach him to pray, and not to blaspheme : but our children have been killed. Joseph called Jesus, and reproved Him, saying : Why dost thou blaspheme? For these people who live here hate us And Jesus said : I know that these words are not mine, but thine ; but I will hold my tongue for thy sake : and let them see to it in their wisdom. And immediately those who were speaking against Jesus became blind. And they walked up and down, and said : All the words which proceed from his mouth are accomplished. And Joseph seeing what Jesus had done, in a fury seized Him by the ear ; and Jesus said to Joseph in anger : It is enough for thee to see me, not to touch me. For thou knowest not who I am ; but if thou didst know, thou wouldst not make me angry. And although just now I am with thee, I was made before thee.

CHAP. VI. — HOW JESUS WAS TREATED BY THE SCHOOLMASTER.

Therefore a certain man named Zacheus [1] listened to all that Jesus was saying to Joseph, and in great astonishment said to himself : Such a boy speaking in this way I have never seen. And he went up to Joseph, and said : That is an intelligent boy of thine ; hand him over to me to learn his letters ; and when he has thoroughly learned his letters, I shall teach him honourably, so that he may be no fool. But Joseph answered and said to him : No one can teach him but God alone. You do not believe that that little boy will be of little consequence? And when Jesus heard Joseph speaking in this way, He said to Zacheus : Indeed, master, whatever proceeds from my mouth is true. And before all I was Lord, but you are foreigners. To me has been given the glory of the ages, to you has been given nothing ; because I am before the ages. And I know how many years of life thou wilt have, and that thou wilt be carried into exile : and my Father hath appointed this, that thou mayest understand that whatever proceeds from my mouth is true. And the Jews who were standing by, and hearing the words which Jesus spoke, were astonished, and said : We have seen such wonderful things, and heard such words from that boy, as we have never heard, nor are likely to hear from any other human being, — either from the high priests, or the masters, or the Pharisees. Jesus answered and said to them : Why do you wonder? Do you consider it incredible that I have spoken the truth? I know when both you and your fathers were born, and to tell you more, when the world was made ; I know also who sent me to you.[2] And when the Jews heard the words which the child had spoken, they wondered, because that they were not able to answer. And, communing with Himself, the child exulted and said : I have told you a proverb ; and I know that you are weak and ignorant.

And that schoolmaster said to Joseph : Bring him to me, and I shall teach him letters. And Joseph took hold of the boy Jesus, and led Him to the house of a certain schoolmaster, where other boys were being taught. Now the master in soothing words began to teach Him His letters, and wrote for Him the first line, which is from A to T,[3] and began to stroke Him and teach Him. And that teacher struck the child on the head ; and when He had received the blow, the child said to him : I should teach thee, and not thou me ; I know the letters which thou wishest to teach me, and I know that you are to me like vessels from which there come forth only sounds, and no wisdom. And, beginning the line, He said the letters from A to T in full, and very fast. And He looked at the master, and said to him : Thou indeed canst not tell us what A and B are ; how dost thou wish to teach others? O hypocrite, if thou knowest and will tell me about the A, then will I tell thee about the B. And when that teacher began to tell[4] about the first letter, he was unable to give any answer. And

---

[1] [In this book the name Zacheus is given in different form, following the Latin. — R.]

[2] A slight alteration is here made upon the punctuation of the original.

[3] This refers to the Hebrew alphabet.

[4] Better, perhaps: And when He began to tell that teacher.

Jesus said to Zacheus: Listen to me, master; understand the first letter. See how it has two lines; advancing in the middle, standing still, giving, scattering, varying, threatening; triple intermingled with double; at the same time homogeneous, having all common.[1]

And Zacheus, seeing that He so divided the first letter, was stupefied about the first letter, and about such a human being and such learning; and he cried out, and said: Woe's me, for I am quite stupefied; I have brought disgrace upon myself through that child. And he said to Joseph: I earnestly entreat thee, brother, take him away from me, because I cannot look upon his face, nor hear his mighty words. Because that child can tame fire and bridle the sea: for he was born before the ages. What womb brought him forth, or what mother[2] nursed him, I know not. Oh, my friends, I am driven out of my senses; I have become a wretched laughing-stock. And I said that I had got a scholar; but he has been found to be my master. And my disgrace I cannot get over, because I am an old man; and what to say to him I cannot find. All I have to do is to fall into some grievous illness, and depart from this world; or to leave this town, because all have seen my disgrace. An infant has deceived me. What answer can I give to others, or what words can I say, because he has got the better of me in the first letter? I am struck dumb, O my friends and acquaintances; neither beginning nor end can I find of an answer to him. And now I beseech thee, brother Joseph, take him away from me, and lead him home, because he is a master, or the Lord, or an angel. What to say I do not know. And Jesus turned to the Jews who were with Zacheus, and said to them: Let all not seeing see, and not understanding understand; let the deaf hear, and let those who are dead through me rise again; and those who are exalted, let me call to still higher things, as He who sent me to you hath commanded me. And when Jesus ceased speaking, all who had been affected with any infirmity through His words were made whole. And they did not dare to speak to Him.

CHAP. VII. — HOW JESUS RAISED A BOY TO LIFE.

One day, when Jesus was climbing on a certain house, along with the children, He began to play with them. And one of the boys fell down through a back-door, and died immediately. And when the children saw this, they all ran away; but Jesus remained in the house.[3] And

when the parents of the boy who had died had come, they spoke against Jesus: Surely it was thou who made him fall down; and they reviled Him. And Jesus, coming down from the house, stood over the dead child, and with a loud voice called out the name of the child: Sinoo, Sinoo, rise and say whether it was I that made thee fall down. And suddenly he rose up, and said: No, my lord. And his parents, seeing such a great miracle done by Jesus, glorified God, and adored Jesus.

CHAP. VIII. — HOW JESUS HEALED A BOY'S FOOT.

And a few days thereafter, a boy in that town was splitting wood, and struck his foot. And a great crowd went to him, and Jesus too went with them. And He touched the foot which had been hurt, and immediately it was made whole. And Jesus said to him: Rise, and split the wood, and remember me. And when the crowd saw the miracles that were done by Him, they adored Jesus, and said: Indeed we most surely believe that Thou art God.

CHAP. IX. — HOW JESUS CARRIED WATER IN A CLOAK.

And when Jesus was six years old, His mother sent Him to draw water. And when Jesus had come to the fountain, or to the well, there were great crowds there, and they broke His pitcher. And He took the cloak which He had on, and filled it with water, and carried it to His mother Mary. And His mother, seeing the miracles which Jesus had done, kissed Him, and said: O Lord, hear me, and save my son.

CHAP. X. — HOW JESUS SOWED WHEAT.

In the time of sowing, Joseph went out to sow wheat, and Jesus followed him. And when Joseph began to sow, Jesus stretched out His hand, and took as much wheat as He could hold in His fist, and scattered it. Joseph therefore came at reaping-time to reap his harvest. Jesus came also, and collected the ears which He had scattered, and they made a hundred pecks[4] of the best grain; and he called the poor, and the widows, and the orphans, and distributed to them the wheat which He had made. Joseph also took a little of the same wheat, for the blessing of Jesus to his house.

CHAP. XI. — HOW JESUS MADE A SHORT PIECE OF WOOD OF THE SAME LENGTH AS A LONGER ONE.

And Jesus reached the age of eight years. Joseph was a master builder,[5] and used to make ploughs and ox-yokes. And one day a rich man

---

[1] This passage is hopelessly corrupt. The writer of this Gospel knew very little Greek, and probably the text from which he was translating was also here in a bad state. [Compare the accounts in the versions from the Greek forms. — R.]
[2] The Greek original has μήτρα, which he seems to have confounded with μήτηρ.
[3] Or, on the house.

[4] The *modius* or *modium* was almost exactly two gallons.
[5] But probably *architector* here is equal to τέκτων, a carpenter.

said to Joseph : Master, make me a couch, both useful and beautiful. And Joseph was in distress, because the wood which he had brought [1] for the work was too short. And Jesus said to him : Do not be annoyed. Take hold of this piece of wood by one end, and I by the other ; and let us draw it out. And they did so ; and immediately he found it useful for that which he wished. And He said to Joseph : Behold, do the work which thou wishest. And Joseph, seeing what He had done, embraced Him, and said : Blessed am I, because God hath given me such a son.

CHAP. XII. — HOW JESUS WAS HANDED OVER TO LEARN HIS LETTERS.

And Joseph, seeing that He had such favour, and that He was increasing in stature, thought it right to take Him to learn His letters. And he handed Him over to another teacher to be taught. And that teacher said to Joseph : What letters dost thou wish me to teach that boy? Joseph answered and said : First teach him the Gentile letters, and then the Hebrew. For the teacher knew that He was very intelligent, and willingly took Him in hand. And writing for Him the first line, which is A and B, he taught Him for some hours.[2] But Jesus was silent, and made him no answer. Jesus said to the master : If thou art indeed a master, and if thou indeed knowest the letters, tell me the power [3] of the A, and I shall tell thee the power of the B. Then His master was filled with fury, and struck Him on the head. And Jesus was angry, and cursed him ; and he suddenly fell down, and died.

And Jesus returned home. And Joseph gave orders to Mary His mother, not to let Him go out of the court of his house.

CHAP. XIII. — HOW HE WAS HANDED OVER TO ANOTHER MASTER.

Many days after came another teacher, a friend of Joseph, and said to him : Hand him over to me, and I with much sweetness will teach him his letters. And Joseph said to him : If thou art able, take him and teach him. May it be attended with joy. When the teacher had taken Him, he went along in fear and in great firmness, and held Him with exultation. And when He had come to the teacher's house, He found a book lying there, and took it and opened it, and did not read what was written in the book ; but opened His mouth, and spoke from the Holy Spirit, and taught the law. And, indeed, all who were standing there listened to Him attentively ;

and the master sat down beside Him, and listened to Him with pleasure, and entreated Him to teach them more. And a great crowd being gathered together, they heard all the holy teaching which He taught, and the choice words which came forth from the mouth of Him who, child as He was, spake such things.

And Joseph, hearing of this, was afraid, and running [4] . . . the master, where Jesus was, said to Joseph : Know, brother, that I have received thy child to teach him or train him ; but he is filled with much gravity and wisdom. Lo, now, take him home with joy, my brother ; because the gravity which he has, has been given him by the Lord. And Jesus, hearing the master thus speaking, became cheerful, and said : Lo, now, master, thou hast truly said. For thy sake, he who is dead shall rise again. And Joseph took Him home.

CHAP. XIV. — HOW JESUS DELIVERED JAMES FROM THE BITE OF A SERPENT.

And Joseph sent James to gather straw, and Jesus followed him. And while James was gathering the straw, a viper bit him ; and he fell to the ground, as if dead from the poison. And Jesus seeing this, blew upon his wound ; and immediately James was made whole, and the viper died.

CHAP. XV. — HOW JESUS RAISED A BOY TO LIFE.

A few days after, a child, His neighbour, died, and his mother mourned for him sore. Jesus, hearing this, went and stood over the boy, and knocked upon his breast, and said : I say to thee, child, do not die, but live. And immediately the child rose up. And Jesus said to the boy's mother : Take thy son, and give him the breast, and remember me. And the crowd, seeing this miracle, said : In truth, this child is from heaven ; for already has he freed many souls from death, and he has made whole all that hope in him.

The scribes and Pharisees said to Mary : Art thou the mother of this child? And Mary said : Indeed I am. And they said to her : Blessed art thou among women,[5] since God hath blessed the fruit of thy womb, seeing that He hath given thee such a glorious child, and such a gift of wisdom, as we have never seen nor heard of. Jesus rose up and followed His mother. And Mary kept in her heart all the great miracles that Jesus had done among the people, in healing many that were diseased. And Jesus grew in stature and wisdom ; and all who saw Him glo-

---

[1] Perhaps *sectum*, cut, is the true reading, and not *actum*.
[2] This is his translation of ἐπὶ πολλὴν ὡραν.
[3] Here again he makes a mistranslation — δύναμις, *fortitudo*.

[4] Some words have been omitted here in the MS., but the sense is obvious enough.
[5] Luke i. 28.

rified God the Father Almighty, who is blessed for ever and ever.   Amen.

And all these things I Thomas the Israelite have written what I have seen, and have recounted them to the Gentiles and to our brethren, and many other things done by Jesus, who was born in the land of Judah.   Behold, the house of Israel has seen all, from the first even to the last; how great signs and wonders Jesus did among them, which were exceedingly good,

and invisible to their father,[1] as holy Scripture relates, and the prophets have borne witness to His works in all the peoples of Israel.   And He it is who is to judge the world according to the will of immortality, since He is the Son of God throughout all the world.   To Him is due all glory and honour for ever, who lives and reigns God through all ages of ages.   Amen.

---

[1] This, I think, means: and which their father Israel, i.e. their fathers generally, had not seen.

THE ARABIC GOSPEL OF THE INFANCY OF
THE SAVIOUR

In the name of the Father, and the Son, and the Holy Spirit, one God.

With the help and favour of the Most High we begin to write a book of the miracles of our Lord and Master and Saviour Jesus Christ, which is called the Gospel of the Infancy: in the peace of the Lord. Amen.

———

1. We find [1] what follows in the book of Joseph the high priest, who lived in the time of Christ. Some say that he is Caiaphas.[2] He has said that Jesus spoke, and, indeed, when He was lying in His cradle said to Mary His mother: I am Jesus, the Son of God, the Logos, whom thou hast brought forth, as the Angel Gabriel announced to thee ; and my Father has sent me for the salvation of the world.

2. In the three hundred and ninth year of the era of Alexander, Augustus put forth an edict, that every man should be enrolled in his native place. Joseph therefore arose, and taking Mary his spouse, went away to [3] Jerusalem, and came to Bethlehem, to be enrolled along with his family in his native city. And having come to a cave, Mary told Joseph that the time of the birth was at hand, and that she could not go into the city ; but, said she, let us go into this cave. This took place at sunset. And Joseph went out in haste to go for a woman to be near her. When, therefore, he was busy about that, he saw an Hebrew old woman belonging to Jerusalem, and said : Come hither, my good woman, and go into this cave, in which there is a woman near her time.

3. Wherefore, after sunset, the old woman, and Joseph with her, came to the cave, and they both went in. And, behold, it was filled with lights more beautiful than the gleaming of lamps and candles,[4] and more splendid than the light of the sun. The child, enwrapped in swaddling clothes, was sucking the breast of the Lady Mary His mother, being placed in a stall. And when both were wondering at this light, the old woman asks the Lady Mary : Art thou the mother of this child? And when the Lady Mary gave her assent, she says : Thou art not at all like the daughters of Eve. The Lady Mary said : As my son has no equal among children, so his mother has no equal among women. The old woman replied : My mistress, I came to get payment ; I have been for a long time affected with palsy. Our mistress the Lady Mary said to her : Place thy hands upon the child. And the old woman did so, and was immediately cured. Then she went forth, saying : Henceforth I will be the attendant and servant of this child all the days of my life.

4. Then came shepherds ; and when they had lighted a fire, and were rejoicing greatly, there appeared to them the hosts of heaven praising and celebrating God Most High. And while the shepherds were doing the same, the cave was at that time made like a temple of the upper world, since both heavenly and earthly voices glorified and magnified God on account of the birth of the Lord Christ. And when that old Hebrew woman saw the manifestation of those miracles, she thanked God, saying : I give Thee thanks, O God, the God of Israel, because mine eyes have seen the birth of the Saviour of the world.

5. And the time of circumcision, that is, the eighth day, being at hand, the child was to be circumcised according to the law. Wherefore they circumcised Him in the cave. And the old Hebrew woman took the piece of skin ; but some say that she took the navel-string, and laid it past in a jar of old oil of nard. And she had a son, a dealer in unguents, and she gave it to him, saying : See that thou do not sell this jar of unguent of nard, even although three hundred denarii [5] should be offered thee for it. And this is that jar which Mary the sinner bought and poured upon the head and feet of our Lord

---

[1] Or, have found.
[2] He is called Joseph Caiaphas in Josephus, *Antiq.*, xviii. 2. 2.
[3] The Latin translation in Tischendorf has Hierosolyma, which, as the form in the rest of the translation is feminine, means "from Jerusalem." But as the Arabic can mean only "to Jerusalem," the acc. plural of the neut. form may be here intended.
[4] Or, with the lights of lamps and candles, more beautiful than lightning, and more splendid than sunlight.

[5] John xii. 5. The *denarius* was worth about 7¾d.

Jesus Christ, which thereafter she wiped with the hair of her head.[1] Ten days after, they took Him to Jerusalem; and on the fortieth day[2] after His birth they carried Him into the temple, and set Him before the Lord, and offered sacrifices for Him, according to the commandmeet of the law of Moses, which is: Every male that openeth the womb shall be called the holy of God.[3]

6. Then old Simeon saw Him shining like a pillar of light, when the Lady Mary, His virgin mother, rejoicing over Him, was carrying Him in her arms. And angels, praising Him, stood round Him in a circle, like life guards standing by a king. Simeon therefore went up in haste to the Lady Mary, and, with hands stretched out before her, said to the Lord Christ: Now, O my Lord, let Thy servant depart in peace, according to Thy word; for mine eyes have seen Thy compassion, which Thou hast prepared for the salvation of all peoples, a light to all nations, and glory to Thy people Israel. Hanna also, a prophetess, was present, and came up, giving thanks to God, and calling the Lady Mary blessed.[4]

7. And it came to pass, when the Lord Jesus was born at Bethlehem of Judæa, in the time of King Herod, behold, magi came from the east to Jerusalem, as Zeraduscht[5] had predicted; and there were with them gifts, gold, and frankincense, and myrrh. And they adored Him, and presented to Him their gifts. Then the Lady Mary took one of the swaddling-bands, and, on account of the smallness of her means, gave it to them; and they received it from her with the greatest marks of honour. And in the same hour there appeared to them an angel in the form of that star which had before guided them on their journey; and they went away, following the guidance of its light, until they arrived in their own country.[6]

8. And their kings and chief men came together to them, asking what they had seen or done, how they had gone and come back, what they had brought with them. And they showed them that swathing-cloth which the Lady Mary had given them. Wherefore they celebrated a feast, and, according to their custom, lighted a fire and worshipped it, and threw that swathing-cloth into it; and the fire laid hold of it, and enveloped it. And when the fire had gone out, they took out the swathing-cloth exactly as it had been before, just as if the fire had not touched it. Wherefore they began to kiss it, and to put it on their heads and their eyes, saying: This verily is the truth without doubt. Assuredly it is a great thing that the fire was not

able to burn or destroy it. Then they took it, and with the greatest honour laid it up among their treasures.

9. And when Herod saw that the magi had left him, and not come back to him, he summoned the priests and the wise men, and said to them: Show me where Christ is to be born. And when they answered, In Bethlehem of Judæa, he began to think of putting the Lord Jesus Christ to death. Then appeared an angel of the Lord to Joseph in his sleep, and said: Rise, take the boy and His mother, and go away into Egypt.[7] He rose, therefore, towards cockcrow, and set out.

10. While he is reflecting how he is to set about his journey, morning came upon him after he had gone a very little way. And now he was approaching a great city, in which there was an idol, to which the other idols and gods of the Egyptians offered gifts and vows. And there stood before this idol a priest ministering to him, who, as often as Satan spoke from that idol, reported it to the inhabitants of Egypt and its territories. This priest had a son, three years old, beset by several demons; and he made many speeches and utterances; and when the demons seized him, he tore his clothes, and remained naked, and threw stones at the people. And there was a hospital in that city dedicated to that idol. And when Joseph and the Lady Mary had come to the city, and had turned aside into that hospital, the citizens were very much afraid; and all the chief men and the priests of the idols came together to that idol, and said to it: What agitation and commotion is this that has arisen in our land? The idol answered them: A God has come here in secret, who is God indeed; nor is any god besides Him worthy of divine worship, because He is truly the Son of God. And when this land became aware of His presence, it trembled at His arrival, and was moved and shaken; and we are exceedingly afraid from the greatness of His power. And in the same hour that idol fell down, and at its fall all, inhabitants of Egypt and others, ran together.

11. And the son of the priest, his usual disease having come upon him, entered the hospital, and there came upon Joseph and the Lady Mary, from whom all others had fled. The Lady Mary had washed the cloths of the Lord Christ, and had spread them over some wood. That demoniac boy, therefore, came and took one of the cloths, and put it on his head. Then the demons, fleeing in the shape of ravens and serpents, began to go forth out of his mouth. The boy, being immediately healed at the command of the Lord Christ, began to praise God, and then to give thanks to the Lord who had healed him. And

---

[1] Luke vii. 37, 38.
[2] Lev. xii. 4.
[3] Ex. xiii. 2; Luke ii. 23.
[4] Luke ii. 25–38.
[5] For this prediction of Zoroaster, see Smith's *Dict. of the Bible*, art. Magi.
[6] Matt. ii. 1–12.

[7] Matt. ii. 13, 14.

when his father saw him restored to health, My son, said he, what has happened to thee? and by what means hast thou been healed? The son answered: When the demons had thrown me on the ground, I went into the hospital, and there I found an august woman with a boy, whose newly-washed cloths she had thrown upon some wood: one of these I took up and put upon my head, and the demons left me and fled. At this the father rejoiced greatly, and said: My son, it is possible that this boy is the Son of the living God who created the heavens and the earth: for when he came over to us, the idol was broken, and all the gods fell, and perished by the power of his magnificence.

12. Here was fulfilled the prophecy which says, Out of Egypt have I called my son.[1] Joseph indeed, and Mary, when they heard that that idol had fallen down and perished, trembled, and were afraid. Then they said: When we were in the land of Israel, Herod thought to put Jesus to death, and on that account slew all the children of Bethlehem and its confines; and there is no doubt that the Egyptians, as soon as they have heard that this idol has been broken, will burn us with fire.[2]

13. Going out thence, they came to a place where there were robbers who had plundered several men of their baggage and clothes, and had bound them. Then the robbers heard a great noise, like the noise of a magnificent king going out of his city with his army, and his chariots and his drums; and at this the robbers were terrified, and left all their plunder. And their captives rose up, loosed each other's bonds, recovered their baggage, and went away. And when they saw Joseph and Mary coming up to the place, they said to them: Where is that king, at the hearing of the magnificent sound of whose approach the robbers have left us, so that we have escaped safe? Joseph answered them: He will come behind us.

14. Thereafter they came into another city, where there was a demoniac woman whom Satan, accursed and rebellious, had beset, when on one occasion she had gone out by night for water. She could neither bear clothes, nor live in a house; and as often as they tied her up with chains and thongs, she broke them, and fled naked into waste places; and, standing in cross-roads and cemeteries, she kept throwing stones at people, and brought very heavy calamities upon her friends. And when the Lady Mary saw her, she pitied her; and upon this Satan immediately left her, and fled away in the form of a young man, saying: Woe to me from

thee, Mary, and from thy son. So that woman was cured of her torment, and being restored to her senses, she blushed on account of her nakedness; and shunning the sight of men, went home to her friends. And after she put on her clothes, she gave an account of the matter to her father and her friends; and as they were the chief men of the city, they received the Lady Mary and Joseph with the greatest honour and hospitality.

15. On the day after, being supplied by them with provision for their journey, they went away, and on the evening of that day arrived at another town, in which they were celebrating a marriage; but, by the arts of accursed Satan and the work of enchanters, the bride had become dumb, and could not speak a word. And after the Lady Mary entered the town, carrying her son the Lord Christ, that dumb bride saw her, and stretched out her hands towards the Lord Christ, and drew Him to her, and took Him into her arms, and held Him close and kissed Him, and leaned over Him, moving His body back and forwards. Immediately the knot of her tongue was loosened, and her ears were opened; and she gave thanks and praise to God, because He had restored her to health. And that night the inhabitants of that town exulted with joy, and thought that God and His angels had come down to them.

16. There they remained three days, being held in great honour, and living splendidly. Thereafter, being supplied by them with provision for their journey, they went away and came to another city, in which, because it was very populous, they thought of passing the night. And there was in that city an excellent woman: and once, when she had gone to the river to bathe, lo, accursed Satan, in the form of a serpent, had leapt upon her, and twisted himself round her belly; and as often as night came on, he tyrannically tormented her. This woman, seeing the mistress the Lady Mary, and the child, the Lord Christ, in her bosom, was struck with a longing for Him, and said to the mistress the Lady Mary: O mistress, give me this child, that I may carry him, and kiss him. She therefore gave Him to the woman; and when He was brought to her, Satan let her go, and fled and left her, nor did the woman ever see him after that day. Wherefore all who were present praised God Most High, and that woman bestowed on them liberal gifts.

17. On the day after, the same woman took scented water to wash the Lord Jesus; and after she had washed Him, she took the water with which she had done it, and poured part of it upon a girl who was living there, whose body was white with leprosy, and washed her with it. And as soon as this was done, the girl was cleansed from her leprosy. And the towns-

---

[1] Hos. xi. 1; Matt. ii. 15.
[2] Burning to death was the punishment of those convicted of sacrilege and the practice of magic. It was inflicted also on slaves for grave offences against their masters.

people said : There is no doubt that Joseph and Mary and that boy are gods, not men. And when they were getting ready to go away from them, the girl who had laboured under the leprosy came up to them, and asked them to let her go with them.

18. When they had given her permission, she went with them. And afterwards they came to a city, in which was the castle of a most illustrious prince, who kept a house for the entertainment of strangers. They turned into this place ; and the girl went away to the prince's wife ; and she found her weeping and sorrowful, and she asked why she was weeping. Do not be surprised, said she, at my tears ; for I am overwhelmed by a great affliction, which as yet I have not endured to tell it to any one. Perhaps, said the girl, if you reveal it and disclose it to me, I may have a remedy for it. Hide this secret, then, replied the princess, and tell it to no one. I was married to this prince, who is a king and ruler over many cities, and I lived long with him, but by me he had no son. And when at length I produced him a son, he was leprous ; and as soon as he saw him, he turned away with loathing, and said to me : Either kill him, or give him to the nurse to be brought up in some place from which we shall never hear of him more. After this I can have nothing to do with thee, and I will never see thee more. On this account I know not what to do, and I am overwhelmed with grief. Alas ! my son. Alas ! my husband. Did I not say so ? said the girl. I have found a cure for thy disease, and I shall tell it thee. For I too was a leper ; but I was cleansed by God, who is Jesus, the son of the Lady Mary. And the woman asking her where this God was whom she had spoken of, Here, with thee, said the girl ; He is living in the same house. But how is this possible ? said she. Where is he ? There, said the girl, are Joseph and Mary ; and the child who is with them is called Jesus ; and He it is who cured me of my disease and my torment. But by what means, said she, wast thou cured of thy leprosy ? Wilt thou not tell me that ? Why not ? said the girl. I got from His mother the water in which He had been washed, and poured it over myself ; and so I was cleansed from my leprosy. Then the princess rose up, and invited them to avail themselves of her hospitality. And she prepared a splendid banquet for Joseph in a great assembly of the men of the place. And on the following day she took scented water with which to wash the Lord Jesus, and thereafter poured the same water over her son, whom she had taken with her ; and immediately her son was cleansed from his leprosy. Therefore, singing thanks and praises to God, she said : Blessed is the mother who bore thee, O Jesus ; dost thou so cleanse

those who share the same nature with thee with the water in which thy body has been washed ? Besides, she bestowed great gifts upon the mistress the Lady Mary, and sent her away with great honour.

19. Coming thereafter to another city, they wished to spend the night in it. They turned aside, therefore, to the house of a man newly married, but who, under the influence of witchcraft, was not able to enjoy his wife ; and when they had spent that night with him, his bond was loosed. And at daybreak, when they were girding themselves for their journey, the bridegroom would not let them go, and prepared for them a great banquet.

20. They set out, therefore, on the following day ; and as they came near another city, they saw three women weeping as they came out of a cemetery. And when the Lady Mary beheld them, she said to the girl who accompanied her : Ask them what is the matter with them, or what calamity has befallen them. And to the girl's questions they made no reply, but asked in their turn : Whence are you, and whither are you going ? for the day is already past, and night is coming on apace. We are travellers, said the girl, and are seeking a house of entertainment in which we may pass the night. They said : Go with us, and spend the night with us. They followed them, therefore, and were brought into a new house with splendid decorations and furniture. Now it was winter ; and the girl, going into the chamber of these women, found them again weeping and lamenting. There stood beside them a mule, covered with housings of cloth of gold, and sesame was put before him ; and the women were kissing him, and giving him food. And the girl said : What is all the ado, my ladies, about this mule ? They answered her with tears, and said : This mule, which thou seest, was our brother, born of the same mother with ourselves. And when our father died, and left us great wealth, and this only brother, we did our best to get him married, and were preparing his nuptials for him, after the manner of men. But some women, moved by mutual jealousy, bewitched him unknown to us ; and one night, a little before daybreak, when the door of our house was shut, we saw that this our brother had been turned into a mule, as thou now beholdest him. And we are sorrowful, as thou seest, having no father to comfort us : there is no wise man, or magician, or enchanter in the world that we have omitted to send for ; but nothing has done us any good. And as often as our hearts are overwhelmed with grief, we rise and go away with our mother here, and weep at our father's grave, and come back again.

21. And when the girl heard these things, Be of

good courage, said she, and weep not: for the cure of your calamity is near; yea, it is beside you, and in the middle of your own house. For I also was a leper; but when I saw that woman, and along with her that young child, whose name is Jesus, I sprinkled my body with the water with which His mother had washed Him, and I was cured. And I know that He can cure your affliction also. But rise, go to Mary my mistress; bring her into your house, and tell her your secret; and entreat and supplicate her to have pity upon you. After the woman had heard the girl's words, they went in haste to the Lady Mary, and brought her into their chamber, and sat down before her weeping, and saying: O our mistress, Lady Mary, have pity on thy hand-maidens; for no one older than ourselves, and no head of the family, is left — neither father nor brother — to live with us; but this mule which thou seest was our brother, and women have made him such as thou seest by witchcraft. We beseech thee, therefore, to have pity upon us. Then, grieving at their lot, the Lady Mary took up the Lord Jesus, and put Him on the mule's back; and she wept as well as the women, and said to Jesus Christ: Alas! my son, heal this mule by Thy mighty power, and make him a man endowed with reason as he was before. And when these words were uttered by the Lady Mary, his form was changed, and the mule became a young man, free from every defect. Then he and his mother and his sisters adored the Lady Mary, and lifted the boy above their heads, and began to kiss Him, saying: Blessed is she that bore Thee, O Jesus, O Saviour of the world; blessed are the eyes which enjoy the felicity of seeing Thee.

22. Moreover, both the sisters said to their mother: Our brother indeed, by the aid of the Lord Jesus Christ, and by the salutary intervention of this girl, who pointed out to us Mary and her son, has been raised to human form. Now, indeed, since our brother is unmarried, it would do very well for us to give him as his wife this girl, their servant. And having asked the Lady Mary, and obtained her consent, they made a splendid wedding for the girl; and their sorrow being changed into joy, and the beating of their breasts into dancing, they began to be glad, to rejoice, to exult, and sing — adorned, on account of their great joy, in most splendid and gorgeous attire. Then they began to recite songs and praises, and to say: O Jesus, son of David, who turnest sorrow into gladness, and lamentations into joy! And Joseph and Mary remained there ten days. Thereafter they set out, treated with great honours by these people, who bade them farewell, and from bidding them farewell returned weeping, especially the girl.

23. And turning away from this place, they came to a desert; and hearing that it was infested by robbers, Joseph and the Lady Mary resolved to cross this region by night. But as they go along, behold, they see two robbers lying in the way, and along with them a great number of robbers, who were their associates, sleeping. Now those two robbers, into whose hands they had fallen, were Titus and Dumachus. Titus therefore said to Dumachus: I beseech thee to let these persons go freely, and so that our comrades may not see them. And as Dumachus refused, Titus said to him again: Take to thyself forty drachmas from me, and hold this as a pledge. At the same time he held out to him the belt which he had had about his waist, to keep him from opening his mouth or speaking. And the Lady Mary, seeing that the robber had done them a kindness, said to him: The Lord God will sustain thee by His right hand, and will grant thee remission of thy sins. And the Lord Jesus answered, and said to His mother: Thirty years hence, O my mother, the Jews will crucify me at Jerusalem, and these two robbers will be raised upon the cross along with me, Titus on my right hand and Dumachus on my left; and after that day Titus shall go before me into Paradise. And she said: God keep this from thee, my son. And they went thence towards a city of idols, which, as they came near it, was changed into sand-hills.

24. Hence they turned aside to that sycamore which is now called Matarea,[1] and the Lord Jesus brought forth in Matarea a fountain in which the Lady Mary washed His shirt. And from the sweat of the Lord Jesus which she sprinkled there, balsam was produced in that region.

25. Thence they came down to Memphis, and saw Pharaoh, and remained three years in Egypt; and the Lord Jesus did in Egypt very many miracles which are recorded neither in the Gospel of the Infancy nor in the perfect Gospel.

26. And at the end of the three years He came back out of Egypt, and returned. And when they had arrived at Judæa, Joseph was afraid to enter it; but hearing that Herod was dead, and that Archelaus his son had succeeded him, he was afraid indeed, but he went into Judæa. And an angel of the Lord appeared to him, and said: O Joseph, go into the city of Nazareth, and there abide.

Wonderful indeed, that the Lord of the world should be thus borne and carried about through the world!

---

[1] Matarea, or Matariyeh, the site of Heliopolis or On, is a little way to the N.E. of Cairo. Ismail Pasha is said to have presented, on his visit to the Paris Exhibition of 1867, the tree and the ground surrounding it to the Empress of the French. For some interesting particulars about the tree, see a paragraph, by B. H. C. (i.e., Mr. B. Harris Cowper, who has translated the Apocryphal Gospels), in the *Leisure Hour* for 2d November, 1867.

27. Thereafter, going into the city of Bethlehem, they saw there many and grievous diseases infesting the eyes of the children, who were dying in consequence. And a woman was there with a sick son, whom, now very near death, she brought to the Lady Mary, who saw him as she was washing Jesus Christ. Then said the woman to her: O my Lady Mary, look upon this son of mine, who is labouring under a grievous disease. And the Lady Mary listened to her, and said: Take a little of that water in which I have washed my son, and sprinkle him with it. She therefore took a little of the water, as the Lady Mary had told her, and sprinkled it over her son. And when this was done his illness abated; and after sleeping a little, he rose up from sleep safe and sound. His mother rejoicing at this, again took him to the Lady Mary. And she said to her: Give thanks to God, because He hath healed this thy son.

28. There was in the same place another woman, a neighbour of her whose son had lately been restored to health. And as her son was labouring under the same disease, and his eyes were now almost blinded, she wept night and day. And the mother of the child that had been cured said to her: Why dost thou not take thy son to the Lady Mary, as I did with mine when he was nearly dead? And he got well with that water with which the body of her son Jesus had been washed. And when the woman heard this from her, she too went and got some of the same water, and washed her son with it, and his body and his eyes were instantly made well. Her also, when she had brought her son to her, and disclosed to her all that had happened, the Lady Mary ordered to give thanks to God for her son's restoration to health, and to tell nobody of this matter.

29. There were in the same city two women, wives of one man, each having a son ill with fever. The one was called Mary, and her son's name was Cleopas. She rose and took up her son, and went to the Lady Mary, the mother of Jesus, and offering her a beautiful mantle, said: O my Lady Mary, accept this mantle, and for it give me one small bandage. Mary did so, and the mother of Cleopas went away, and made a shirt of it, and put it on her son. So he was cured of his disease; but the son of her rival died. Hence there sprung up hatred between them; and as they did the house-work week about, and as it was the turn of Mary the mother of Cleopas, she heated the oven to bake bread; and going away to bring the lump that she had kneaded, she left her son Cleopas beside the oven. Her rival seeing him alone — and the oven was very hot with the fire blazing under it — seized him and threw him into the oven, and took herself off. Mary coming back, and seeing her son Cleopas lying in the oven laughing, and the oven quite cold, as if no fire had ever come near it, knew that her rival had thrown him into the fire. She drew him out, therefore, and took him to the Lady Mary, and told her of what had happened to him. And she said: Keep silence, and tell nobody of the affair; for I am afraid for you if you divulge it. After this her rival went to the well to draw water; and seeing Cleopas playing beside the well, and nobody near, she seized him and threw him into the well, and went home herself. And some men who had gone to the well for water saw the boy sitting on the surface of the water; and so they went down and drew him out. And they were seized with a great admiration of that boy, and praised God. Then came his mother, and took him up, and went weeping to the Lady Mary, and said: O my lady, see what my rival has done to my son, and how she has thrown him into the well; she will be sure to destroy him some day or other. The Lady Mary said to her: God will avenge thee upon her. Thereafter, when her rival went to the well to draw water, her feet got entangled in the rope, and she fell into the well. Some men came to draw her out, but they found her skull fractured and her bones broken. Thus she died a miserable death, and in her came to pass that saying: They have digged a well deep, but have fallen into the pit which they had prepared.[1]

30. Another woman there had twin sons who had fallen into disease, and one of them died, and the other was at his last breath. And his mother, weeping, lifted him up, and took him to the Lady Mary, and said: O my lady, aid me and succour me. For I had two sons, and I have just buried the one, and the other is at the point of death. See how I am going to entreat and pray to God. And she began to say: O Lord, Thou art compassionate, and merciful, and full of affection. Thou gavest me two sons, of whom Thou hast taken away the one: this one at least leave to me. Wherefore Lady Mary, seeing the fervour of her weeping, had compassion on her, and said: Put thy son in my son's bed, and cover him with his clothes. And when she had put him in the bed in which Christ was lying, he had already closed his eyes in death; but as soon as the smell of the clothes of the Lord Jesus Christ reached the boy, he opened his eyes, and, calling upon his mother with a loud voice, he asked for bread, and took it and sucked it. Then his mother said: O Lady Mary, now I know that the power of God dwelleth in thee, so that thy son heals those that partake of the same nature with himself, as soon as they have touched his clothes. This boy that

[1] Ps. vii. 15, lvii. 6.

was healed is he who in the Gospel is called Bartholomew.

31. Moreover, there was there a leprous woman, and she went to the Lady Mary, the mother of Jesus, and said : My lady, help me. And the Lady Mary answered : What help dost thou seek ? Is it gold or silver ? or is it that thy body be made clean from the leprosy ? And that woman asked : Who can grant me this ? And the Lady Mary said to her : Wait a little, until I shall have washed my son Jesus, and put him to bed. The woman waited, as Mary had told her ; and when she had put Jesus to bed, she held out to the woman the water in which she had washed His body, and said : Take a little of this water, and pour it over thy body. And as soon as she had done so, she was cleansed, and gave praise and thanks to God.

32. Therefore, after staying with her three days, she went away ; and coming to a city, saw there one of the chief men, who had married the daughter of another of the chief men. But when he saw the woman, he beheld between her eyes the mark of leprosy in the shape of a star ; and so the marriage was dissolved, and became null and void. And when that woman saw them in this condition, weeping and overwhelmed with sorrow, she asked the cause of their grief. But they said : Inquire not into our condition, for to no one living can we tell our grief, and to none but ourselves can we disclose it. She urged them, however, and entreated them to entrust it to her, saying that she would perhaps be able to tell them of a remedy. And when they showed her the girl, and the sign of leprosy which appeared between her eyes, as soon as she saw it, the woman said : I also, whom you see here, laboured under the same disease, when, upon some business which happened to come in my way, I went to Bethlehem. There going into a cave, I saw a woman named Mary, whose son was he who was named Jesus ; and when she saw that I was a leper, she took pity on me, and handed me the water with which she had washed her son's body. With it I sprinkled my body, and came out clean. Then the woman said to her : Wilt thou not, O lady, rise and go with us, and show us the Lady Mary ? And she assented ; and they rose and went to the Lady Mary, carrying with them splendid gifts. And when they had gone in, and presented to her the gifts, they showed her the leprous girl whom they had brought. The Lady Mary therefore said : May the compassion of the Lord Jesus Christ descend upon you ; and handing to them also a little of the water in which she had washed the body of Jesus Christ, she ordered the wretched woman to be bathed in it. And when this had been done, she was immediately cured ; and they, and all standing by, praised God. Joyfully therefore they returned to their own city, praising the Lord for what He had done. And when the chief heard that his wife had been cured, he took her home, and made a second marriage, and gave thanks to God for the recovery of his wife's health.

33. There was there also a young woman afflicted by Satan ; for that accursed wretch repeatedly appeared to her in the form of a huge dragon, and prepared to swallow her. He also sucked out all her blood, so that she was left like a corpse. As often as he came near her, she, with her hands clasped over her head, cried out, and said : Woe, woe's me, for nobody is near to free me from that accursed dragon. And her father and mother, and all who were about her or saw her, bewailed her lot ; and men stood round her in a crowd, and all wept and lamented, especially when she wept, and said : Oh, my brethren and friends, is there no one to free me from that murderer ? And the daughter of the chief who had been healed of her leprosy, hearing the girl's voice, went up to the roof of her castle, and saw her with her hands clasped over her head weeping, and all the crowds standing round her weeping as well. She therefore asked the demoniac's husband whether his wife's mother were alive. And when he answered that both her parents were living, she said : Send for her mother to come to me. And when she saw that he had sent for her, and she had come, she said : Is that distracted girl thy daughter ? Yes, O lady, said that sorrowful and weeping woman, she is my daughter. The chief's daughter answered : Keep my secret, for I confess to thee that I was formerly a leper ; but now the Lady Mary, the mother of Jesus Christ, has healed me. But if thou wishest thy daughter to be healed, take her to Bethlehem, and seek Mary the mother of Jesus, and believe that thy daughter will be healed ; I indeed believe that thou wilt come back with joy, with thy daughter healed. As soon as the woman heard the words of the chief's daughter, she led away her daughter in haste ; and going to the place indicated, she went to the Lady Mary, and revealed to her the state of her daughter. And the Lady Mary hearing her words, gave her a little of the water in which she had washed the body of her son Jesus, and ordered her to pour it on the body of her daughter. She gave her also from the clothes of the Lord Jesus a swathing-cloth, saying : Take this cloth, and show it to thine enemy as often as thou shalt see him. And she saluted them, and sent them away.

34. When, therefore, they had gone away from her, and returned to their own district, and the time was at hand at which Satan was wont to attack her, at this very time that accursed one appeared to her in the shape of a huge dragon, and

the girl was afraid at the sight of him. And her mother said to her: Fear not, my daughter; allow him to come near thee, and then show him the cloth which the Lady Mary hath given us, and let us see what will happen. Satan, therefore, having come near in the likeness of a terrible dragon, the body of the girl shuddered for fear of him; but as soon as she took out the cloth, and placed it on her head, and covered her eyes with it, flames and live coals began to dart forth from it, and to be cast upon the dragon. O the great miracle which was done as soon as the dragon saw the cloth of the Lord Jesus, from which the fire darted, and was cast upon his head and eyes! He cried out with a loud voice: What have I to do with thee, O Jesus, son of Mary? Whither shall I fly from thee? And with great fear he turned his back and departed from the girl, and never afterwards appeared to her. And the girl now had rest from him, and gave praise and thanks to God, and along with her all who were present at that miracle.

35. Another woman was living in the same place, whose son was tormented by Satan. He, Judas by name, as often as Satan seized him, used to bite all who came near him; and if he found no one near him, he used to bite his own hands and other limbs. The mother of this wretched creature, then, hearing the fame of the Lady Mary and her son Jesus, rose up and brought her son Judas with her to the Lady Mary. In the meantime, James and Joses had taken the child the Lord Jesus with them to play with the other children; and they had gone out of the house and sat down, and the Lord Jesus with them. And the demoniac Judas came up, and sat down at Jesus' right hand: then, being attacked by Satan in the same manner as usual, he wished to bite the Lord Jesus, but was not able; nevertheless he struck Jesus on the right side, whereupon He began to weep. And immediately Satan went forth out of that boy, fleeing like a mad dog. And this boy who struck Jesus, and out of whom Satan went forth in the shape of a dog, was Judas Iscariot, who betrayed Him to the Jews; and that same side on which Judas struck Him, the Jews transfixed with a lance.[1]

36. Now, when the Lord Jesus had completed seven years from His birth, on a certain day He was occupied with boys of His own age. For they were playing among clay, from which they were making images of asses, oxen, birds, and other animals; and each one boasting of his skill, was praising his own work. Then the Lord Jesus said to the boys: The images that I have made I will order to walk. The boys asked Him

whether then he were the son of the Creator; and the Lord Jesus bade them walk. And they immediately began to leap; and then, when He had given them leave, they again stood still. And He had made figures of birds and sparrows, which flew when He told them to fly, and stood still when He told them to stand, and ate and drank when He handed them food and drink. After the boys had gone away and told this to their parents, their fathers said to them: My sons, take care not to keep company with him again, for he is a wizard: flee from him, therefore, and avoid him, and do not play with him again after this.

37. On a certain day the Lord Jesus, running about and playing with the boys, passed the shop of a dyer, whose name was Salem; and he had in his shop many pieces of cloth which he was to dye. The Lord Jesus then, going into his shop, took up all the pieces of cloth, and threw them into a tub full of indigo. And when Salem came and saw his cloths destroyed, he began to cry out with a loud voice, and to reproach Jesus, saying: Why hast thou done this to me, O son of Mary? Thou hast disgraced me before all my townsmen: for, seeing that every one wished the colour that suited himself, thou indeed hast come and destroyed them all. The Lord Jesus answered: I shall change for thee the colour of any piece of cloth which thou shalt wish to be changed. And immediately He began to take the pieces of cloth out of the tub, each of them of that colour which the dyer wished, until He had taken them all out. When the Jews saw this miracle and prodigy, they praised God.

38. And Joesph used to go about through the whole city, and take the Lord Jesus with him, when people sent for him in the way of his trade to make for them doors, and milk-pails, and beds, and chests; and the Lord Jesus was with him wherever he went. As often, therefore, as Joseph had to make anything a cubit or a span longer or shorter, wider or narrower, the Lord Jesus stretched His hand towards it; and as soon as He did so, it became such as Joseph wished. Nor was it necessary for him to make anything with his own hand, for Joseph was not very skilful in carpentry.

39. Now, on a certain day, the king of Jerusalem sent for him, and said: I wish thee, Joseph, to make for me a throne to fit that place in which I usually sit. Joseph obeyed, and began the work immediately, and remained in the palace two years, until he finished the work of that throne. And when he had it carried to its place, he perceived that each side wanted two spans of the prescribed measure. And the king, seeing this, was angry with Joseph; and Joseph, being in great fear of the king, spent the night without supper, nor did he taste any-

---

[1] John xix. 34.

thing at all. Then, being asked by the Lord Jesus why he was afraid, Joseph said: Because I have spoiled all the work that I have been two years at. And the Lord Jesus said to him: Fear not, and do not lose heart; but do thou take hold of one side of the throne; I shall take the other; and we shall put that to rights. And Joseph, having done as the Lord Jesus had said and each having drawn by his own side, the throne was put to rights, and brought to the exact measure of the place. And those that stood by and saw this miracle were struck with astonishment, and praised God. And the woods used in that throne were of those which are celebrated in the time of Solomon the son of David; that is, woods of many and various kinds.

40. On another day the Lord Jesus went out into the road, and saw the boys that had come together to play, and followed them; but the boys hid themselves from Him. The Lord Jesus, therefore, having come to the door of a certain house, and seen some women standing there, asked them where the boys had gone; and when they answered that there was no one there, He said again: Who are these whom you see in the furnace?[1] They replied that they were kids of three years old. And the Lord Jesus cried out, and said: Come out hither, O kids, to your Shepherd. Then the boys, in the form of kids, came out, and began to dance round Him; and the women, seeing this, were very much astonished, and were seized with trembling, and speedily supplicated and adored the Lord Jesus, saying: O our Lord Jesus, son of Mary, Thou art of a truth that good Shepherd of Israel; have mercy on Thy handmaidens who stand before Thee, and who have never doubted: for Thou hast come, O our Lord, to heal, and not to destroy. And when the Lord Jesus answered that the sons of Israel were like the Ethiopians among the nations, the women said: Thou, O Lord, knowest all things, nor is anything hid from Thee; now, indeed, we beseech Thee, and ask Thee of Thy affection to restore these boys Thy servants to their former condition. The Lord Jesus therefore said: Come, boys, let us go and play. And immediately, while these women were standing by, the kids were changed into boys.

41. Now in the month Adar, Jesus, after the manner of a king, assembled the boys together. They spread their clothes on the ground, and He sat down upon them. Then they put on His head a crown made of flowers, and, like chamber-servants, stood in His presence, on the right and on the left, as if He were a king. And whoever passed by that way was forcibly dragged by the boys, saying: Come hither, and adore the king; then go thy way.

42. In the meantime, while these things were going on, some men came up carrying a boy. For this boy had gone into the mountain with those of his own age to seek wood, and there he found a partridge's nest; and when he stretched out his hand to take the eggs from it, a venomous serpent bit him from the middle of the nest, so that he called out for help. His comrades accordingly went to him with haste, and found him lying on the ground like one dead. Then his relations came and took him up to carry him back to the city. And after they had come to that place where the Lord Jesus was sitting like a king, and the rest of the boys standing round Him like His servants, the boys went hastily forward to meet him who had been bitten by the serpent, and said to his relations: Come and salute the king. But when they were unwilling to go, on account of the sorrow in which they were, the boys dragged them by force against their will. And when they had come up to the Lord Jesus, He asked them why they were carrying the boy. And when they answered that a serpent had bitten him, the Lord Jesus said to the boys: Let us go and kill that serpent. And the parents of the boy asked leave to go away, because their son was in the agony of death; but the boys answered them, saying: Did you not hear the king saying: Let us go kill the serpent? and will you not obey him? And so, against their will, the couch was carried back. And when they came to the nest, the Lord Jesus said to the boys: Is this the serpent's place? They said that it was; and the serpent, at the call of the Lord, came forth without delay, and submitted itself to Him. And He said to it: Go away, and suck out all the poison which thou hast infused into this boy. And so the serpent crawled to the boy, and sucked out all its poison. Then the Lord Jesus cursed it, and immediately on this being done it burst asunder; and the Lord Jesus stroked the boy with his hand, and he was healed. And he began to weep; but Jesus said: Do not weep, for by and by thou shalt be my disciple. And this is Simon the Cananite,[2] of whom mention is made in the Gospel.[3]

43. On another day, Joseph sent his son James to gather wood, and the Lord Jesus went with him as his companion. And when they had come to the place where the wood was, and James had begun to gather it, behold, a venomous viper bit his hand, so that he began to cry out and weep. The Lord Jesus then, seeing him in this condition, went up to him, and blew upon the place where the viper had bitten him;

[1] Perhaps the correct reading is *fornice*, archway, and not *fornace*.

[2] [So the Latin: but the Greek word in the Gospels is equivalent to " zealot." See Rev. Vers. in the lists of the Apostles. — R.]
[3] Matt. x. 4, etc.

and this being done, he was healed immediately.

44. One day, when the Lord Jesus was again with the boys playing on the roof of a house, one of the boys fell down from above, and immediately expired. And the rest of the boys fled in all directions, and the Lord Jesus was left alone on the roof. And the relations of the boy came up and said to the Lord Jesus: It was thou who didst throw our son headlong from the roof. And when He denied it, they cried out, saying: Our son is dead, and here is he who has killed him. And the Lord Jesus said to them: Do not bring an evil report against me; but if you do not believe me, come and let us ask the boy himself, that he may bring the truth to light. Then the Lord Jesus went down, and standing over the dead body, said, with a loud voice: Zeno, Zeno, who threw thee down from the roof? Then the dead boy answered and said: My lord, it was not thou who didst throw me down, but such a one cast me down from it. And when the Lord commanded those who were standing by to attend to His words, all who were present praised God for this miracle.

45. Once upon a time the Lady Mary had ordered the Lord Jesus to go and bring her water from the well. And when He had gone to get the water, the pitcher already full was knocked against something, and broken. And the Lord Jesus stretched out His handkerchief, and collected the water, and carried it to His mother; and she was astonished at it. And she hid and preserved in her heart all that she saw.

46. Again, on another day, the Lord Jesus was with the boys at a stream of water, and they had again made little fish-ponds. And the Lord Jesus had made twelve sparrows, and had arranged them round His fish-pond, three on each side. And it was the Sabbath-day. Wherefore a Jew, the son of Hanan, coming up, and seeing them thus engaged, said in anger and great indignation: Do you make figures of clay on the Sabbath-day? And he ran quickly, and destroyed their fish-ponds. But when the Lord Jesus clapped His hands over the sparrows which He had made, they flew away chirping.

Then the son of Hanan came up to the fish-pond of Jesus also, and kicked it with his shoes, and the water of it vanished away. And the Lord Jesus said to him: As that water has vanished away, so thy life shall likewise vanish away. And immediately that boy dried up.

47. At another time, when the Lord Jesus was returning home with Joseph in the evening, He met a boy, who ran up against Him with so much force that He fell. And the Lord Jesus said to him: As thou hast thrown me down, so thou shalt fall, and not rise again. And the same hour the boy fell down, and expired.

48. There was, moreover, at Jerusalem, a certain man named Zacchæus, who taught boys. He said to Joseph: Why, O Joseph, dost thou not bring Jesus to me to learn his letters? Joseph agreed to do so, and reported the matter to the Lady Mary. They therefore took Him to the master; and he, as soon as he saw Him, wrote out the alphabet for Him, and told Him to say Aleph. And when He had said Aleph, the master ordered Him to pronounce Beth. And the Lord Jesus said to him: Tell me first the meaning of the letter Aleph, and then I shall pronounce Beth. And when the master threatened to flog Him, the Lord Jesus explained to him the meanings of the letters Aleph and Beth; also which figures of the letter were straight, which crooked, which drawn round into a spiral, which marked with points, which without them, why one letter went before another; and many other things He began to recount and to elucidate which the master himself had never either heard or read in any book. The Lord Jesus, moreover, said to the master: Listen, and I shall say them to thee. And He began clearly and distinctly to repeat Aleph, Beth, Gimel, Daleth, on to Tau. And the master was astonished, and said: I think that this boy was born before Noah. And turning to Joseph, he said: Thou hast brought to me to be taught a boy more learned than all the masters. To the Lady Mary also he said: This son of thine has no need of instruction.

49. Thereafter they took Him to another and a more learned master, who, when he saw Him, said: Say Aleph. And when He had said Aleph, the master ordered him to pronounce Beth. And the Lord Jesus answered him, and said: First tell me the meaning of the letter Aleph, and then I shall pronounce Beth. And when the master hereupon raised his hand and flogged Him, immediately his hand dried up, and he died. Then said Joseph, to the Lady Mary: From this time we shall not let him go out of the house, since every one who opposes him is struck dead.

50. And when He was twelve years old, they took Him to Jerusalem to the feast. And when the feast was finished, they indeed returned; but the Lord Jesus remained in the temple among the teachers and elders and learned men of the sons of Israel, to whom He put various questions upon the sciences, and gave answers in His turn.[1] For He said to them: Whose son is the Messias? They answered Him: The son of David. Wherefore then, said He, does he in the Spirit call him his lord, when he says, The Lord said to my lord,

---

[1] Luke ii. 42-47. [A comparison of the two narratives is very suggestive. The Evangelist Luke does not present any such monster of precocity, nor does he adventure into discussions "upon the sciences." — R.]

Sit at my right hand, that I may put thine ene-mies under thy footsteps?[1] Again the chief of the teachers said to Him: Hast thou read the books? Both the books, said the Lord Jesus, and the things contained in the books. And He explained the books, and the law, and the precepts, and the statutes, and the mysteries, which are contained in the books of the proph-ets — things which the understanding of no creature attains to. That teacher therefore said: I hitherto have neither attained to nor heard of such knowledge: Who, pray, do you think that boy will be?

51. And a philosopher who was there pres-ent, a skilful astronomer, asked the Lord Jesus whether He had studied astronomy. And the Lord Jesus answered him, and explained the number of the spheres, and of the heavenly bod-ies, their natures and operations; their opposi-tion; their aspect, triangular, square, and sextile; their course, direct and retrograde; the twenty-fourths,[2] and sixtieths of twenty-fourths; and other things beyond the reach of reason.

52. There was also among those philosophers one very skilled in treating of natural science, and he asked the Lord Jesus whether He had studied medicine. And He, in reply, explained to him physics and metaphysics, hyperphysics and hypophysics, the powers likewise and hu-mours of the body, and the effects of the same; also the number of members and bones, of veins, arteries, and nerves; also the effect of heat and dryness, of cold and moisture, and what these give rise to; what was the operation of the soul upon the body, and its perceptions and powers; what was the operation of the faculty of speech, of anger, of desire; lastly, their conjunction and disjunction, and other things beyond the reach of any created intellect. Then that philosopher rose up, and adored the Lord Jesus, and said: O Lord, from this time I will be thy disciple and slave.

53. While they were speaking to each other of these and other things, the Lady Mary came, after having gone about seeking Him for three days along with Joseph. She therefore, seeing Him sitting among the teachers asking them questions, and answering in His turn, said to Him: My son, why hast thou treated us thus? Behold, thy father and I have sought thee with great trouble. But He said: Why do you seek me? Do you not know that I ought to occupy myself in my Father's house? But they did not understand the words that He spoke to them. Then those teachers asked Mary whether He were her son; and when she signified that He was, they said: Blessed art thou, O Mary, who hast brought forth such a son. And returning with them to Nazareth, He obeyed them in all things. And His mother kept all these words of His in her heart. And the Lord Jesus ad-vanced in stature, and in wisdom, and in favour with God and man.[3]

54. And from this day He began to hide His miracles and mysteries and secrets, and to give attention to the law, until He completed His thirtieth year, when His Father publicly declared Him at the Jordan by this voice sent down from heaven: This is my beloved Son, in whom I am well pleased; the Holy Spirit being present in the form of a white dove.[4]

55. This is He whom we adore with supplica-tions, who hath given us being and life, and who hath brought us from our mothers' wombs; who for our sakes assumed a human body, and redeemed us, that He might embrace us in eter-ual compassion, and show to us His mercy ac-cording to His liberality, and beneficence, and generosity, and benevolence. To Him is glory, and beneficence, and power, and dominion from this time forth for evermore. Amen.

Here endeth the whole Gospel of the Infancy, with the aid of God Most High, according to what we have found in the original.

---

[1] Ps. cx. 1; Matt. xxii. 42-45. [The Latin reads: *vestigiis pedum tuorum*, "the footsteps of thy feet." The original term, "footstool," has evidently been misunderstood by some transcriber. — R.]

[2] The *scripulum* was the twenty-fourth part of the *as*. It is likely here put for the motion of a planet during one hour. Pliny, *N. H.*, ii. 10, uses the word to signify an undefined number of de-grees, or parts of a degree.

[3] Luke ii. 46-52.

[4] Matt. iii. 13-17; Luke iii. 21-23.

THE GOSPEL OF NICODEMUS

PART I. — THE ACTS OF PILATE

FIRST GREEK FORM.

MEMORIALS OF OUR LORD JESUS CHRIST, DONE IN THE TIME OF PONTIUS PILATE.

PROLOGUE. — I Ananias, of the proprætor's body-guard, being learned in the law, knowing our Lord Jesus Christ from the Holy Scriptures, coming to Him by faith, and counted worthy of the holy baptism, searching also the memorials written at that time of what was done in the case of our Lord Jesus Christ, which the Jews had laid up in the time of Pontius Pilate, found these memorials written in Hebrew, and by the favour of God have translated them into Greek for the information of all who call upon the name of our Master Jesus Christ, in the seventeenth year of the reign of our Lord Flavius Theodosius, and the sixth of Flavius Valentinianus, in the ninth indiction.[1]

All ye, therefore, who read and transfer into other books, remember me, and pray for me, that God may be merciful to me, and pardon my sins which I have sinned against Him.

Peace be to those who read, and to those who hear and to their households. Amen.

In the fifteenth year[2] of the government of Tiberius Cæsar, emperor of the Romans, and Herod being king of Galilee, in the nineteenth year of his rule, on the eighth day before the Kalends of April, which is the twenty-fifth of March, in the consulship of Rufus and Rubellio, in the fourth year of the two hundred and second Olympiad, Joseph Caiaphas being high priest of the Jews.

The account that Nicodemus wrote in Hebrew, after the cross and passion of our Lord Jesus Christ, the Saviour God, and left to those that came after him, is as follows : —

CHAP. I. — Having called a council, the high priests and scribes Annas and Caiaphas and Semes and Dathaes, and Gamaliel, Judas, Levi and Nephthalim, Alexander and Jaïrus,[3] and the rest of the Jews, came to Pilate accusing Jesus about many things, saying : We know this man to be the son of Joseph the carpenter, born of Mary ; and he says that he is the Son of God, and a king ; moreover, he profanes the Sabbath, and wishes to do away with the law of our fathers. Pilate says : And what are the things which he does, to show that he wishes to do away with it ?[4] The Jews say : We have a law not to cure any one on the Sabbath ; but this man[5] has on the Sabbath cured the lame and the crooked, the withered and the blind and the paralytic, the dumb and the demoniac, by evil practices. Pilate says to them : What evil practices ? They say to him : He is a magician, and by Beelzebul prince of the demons he casts out the demons, and all are subject to him. Pilate says to them : This is not casting out the demons by an unclean spirit, but by the god Æsculapius.

---

[1] [The works which precede sought to supplement the evangelical narrative in regard to the early life of our Lord, and Mary His mother; those which follow are also supplementary, but refer to the closing events. — R.]

[2] The 15th year of Tiberius, reckoning from the death of Augustus, was A.D. 29, A.U.C. 782, the *first* year of the 202d Olympiad, in the consulship of C. Fugus Geminus and L. Rubellius Geminus, and the 34th year of Herod Antipas. Other readings are: In the eighteenth year — In the nineteenth year. [Compare the Acts of Pilate in both forms. The variations here correspond with the various theories of the length of our Lord's ministry. The text seems to confuse the statement of Luke (iii. 1) respecting the beginning of the public ministry with the time of our Lord's death. — R.]

[3] There is in the MSS. great variation as to these names.

[4] Lit., and wishes to do away with it.

[5] Compare with this, Lactantius, iv. 17. The Jews brought charges against Jesus, that He did away with the law of God given by Moses; that is, that He did not rest on the Sabbath, etc.

416

The Jews say to Pilate : We entreat your highness that he stand at thy tribunal, and be heard.[1] And Pilate having called them, says : Tell me how I, being a procurator, can try a king? They say to him : We do not say that he is a king, but he himself says that he is. And Pilate having called the runner, says to him : Let Jesus be brought in with respect. And the runner going out, and recognising Him, adored Him, and took his cloak into his hand, and spread it on the ground, and says to him : My lord, walk on this, and come in, for the procurator calls thee. And the Jews seeing what the runner had done, cried out against Pilate, saying : Why hast thou ordered him to come in by a runner, and not by a crier? for assuredly the runner, when he saw him, adored him, and spread his doublet on the ground, and made him walk like a king.

And Pilate having called the runner, says to him : Why hast thou done this, and spread out thy cloak upon the earth, and made Jesus walk upon it? The runner says to him : My lord procurator, when thou didst send me to Jerusalem to Alexander,[2] I saw him sitting upon an ass, and the sons of the Hebrews held branches in their hands, and shouted ; and other spread their clothes under him, saying, Save now, thou who art in the highest : blessed is he that cometh in the name of the Lord.[3]

The Jews cry out, and say to the runner : The sons of the Hebrews shouted in Hebrew ; whence then hast thou the Greek? The runner says to them : I asked one of the Jews, and said, What is it they are shouting in Hebrew? And he interpreted it for me. Pilate says to them : And what did they shout in Hebrew? The Jews say to him : HOSANNA MEMBROME BARUCHAMMA ADONAÏ.[4] Pilate says to them : And this hosanna, etc., how is it interpreted? The Jews say to him : Save now in the highest ; blessed is he that cometh in the name of the Lord. Pilate says to them : If you bear witness to the words spoken by the children, in what has the runner done wrong? And they were silent. And the procurator says to the runner : Go out, and bring him in what way thou wilt. And the runner going out, did in the same manner as before, and says to Jesus : My lord, come in ; the procurator calleth thee.

And Jesus going in, and the standard-bearers holding their standards, the tops of the standards were bent down, and adored Jesus. And the Jews seeing the bearing of the standards, how they were bent down and adored Jesus, cried[5] out vehemently against the standard-bearers. And Pilate says to the Jews : Do you not wonder how the tops of the standards were bent down, and adored Jesus? The Jews say to Pilate : We saw how the standard-bearers bent them down, and adored him. And the procurator having called the standard-bearers, says to them : Why have you done this? They say to Pilate : We are Greeks and temple-slaves, and how could we adore him? and assuredly, as we were holding them up, the tops bent down of their own accord, and adored him.

Pilate says to the rulers of the synagogue and the elders of the people : Do you choose for yourselves men strong and powerful, and let them hold up the standards, and let us see whether they will bend down with them. And the elders of the Jews picked out twelve men powerful and strong, and made them hold up the standards six by six ; and they were placed in front of the procurator's tribunal. And Pilate says to the runner : Take him outside of the prætorium, and bring him in again in whatever way may please thee. And Jesus and the runner went out of the prætorium. And Pilate, summoning those who had formerly held up the standards, says to them : I have sworn by the health of Cæsar, that if the standards do not bend down when Jesus comes in, I will cut off your heads. And the procurator ordered Jesus to come in the second time. And the runner did in the same manner as before, and made many entreaties to Jesus to walk on his cloak. And He walked on it, and went in. And as He went in, the standards were again bent down, and adored Jesus.

CHAP. 2. — And Pilate seeing this, was afraid, and sought to go away from the tribunal ; but when he was still thinking of going away, his wife sent to him, saying : Have nothing to do with this just man, for many things have I suffered on his account this night.[6] And Pilate, summoning the Jews, says to them : You know that my wife is a worshipper of God, and prefers to adhere to the Jewish religion along with you. They say to him : Yes ; we know. Pilate says to them : Behold, my wife[7] has sent to me, saying, Have nothing to do with this just man, for many things have I suffered on account of him this night. And the Jews answering, say unto Pilate : Did we not tell thee that he was a sorcerer?[8] behold, he has sent a dream to thy wife.

---

[1] Another reading is: We entreat your highness to go into the prætorium, and question him. For Jesus was standing outside with the crowd.
[2] Probably the Alexander mentioned in Acts iv. 6.
[3] Matt. xxi. 8, 9.
[4] Ps. cxviii. 25: *Hosyah na bimromim baruch habbā* (*b'shem*) *Adonai.*

[5] Another reading is: Annas and Caiaphas and Joseph, the three false witnesses, began to cry out, etc.
[6] Matt. xxvii. 19.
[7] One MS. adds: Procla, — the traditional name of Pilate's wife.
[8] Three MSS. add: And by Beelzebul, prince of the demons, he casts out the demons, and they are all subject to him.

And Pilate, having summoned Jesus, says to Him: What do these witness against thee? Sayest thou nothing? And Jesus said: Unless they had the power, they would say nothing; for every one has the power of his own mouth to speak both good and evil. They shall see to it.[1]

And the elders of the Jews answered, and said to Jesus: What shall we see? first, that thou wast born of fornication; secondly, that thy birth in Bethlehem was the cause of the murder of the infants; thirdly, that thy father Joseph and thy mother Mary fled into Egypt because they had no confidence in the people.

Some of the bystanders, pious men of the Jews, say: We deny that he was born of fornication; for we know that Joseph espoused Mary, and he was not born of fornication. Pilate says to the Jews who said that he was of fornication: This story of yours is not true, because they were betrothed, as also these fellow-countrymen of yours say. Annas and Caiaphas say to Pilate: All the multitude of us cry out that he was born of fornication, and are not believed; these are proselytes, and his disciples. And Pilate, calling Annas and Caiaphas, says to them: What are proselytes? They say to him: They are by birth children of the Greeks, and have now become Jews. And those that said that He was not born of fornication, viz.—Lazarus, Asterius, Antonius, James, Amnes, Zeras, Samuel, Isaac, Phinees, Crispus, Agrippas, and Judas[2]—say: We are not proselytes, but are children of the Jews, and speak of the truth; for we were present at the betrothal of Joseph and Mary.

And Pilate, calling these twelve men who said that He was not born of fornication, says to them: I adjure you by the health of Cæsar, to tell me whether it be true that you say, that he was not born of fornication. They say to Pilate: We have a law against taking oaths, because it is a sin; but they will swear by the health of Cæsar,[3] that it is not as we have said, and we are liable to death. Pilate says to Annas and Caiaphas: Have you nothing to answer to this? Annas and Caiaphas say to Pilate: These twelve are believed when they say that he was not born of fornication; all the multitude of us cry out that he was born of fornication, and that he is a sorcerer, and he says that he is the Son of God and a king, and we are not believed.

And Pilate orders all the multitude to go out, except the twelve men who said that He was not born of fornication, and he ordered Jesus to be separated from them. And Pilate says to them: For what reason do they wish to put him to death? They say to him: They are angry be-

cause he cures on the Sabbath. Pilate says: For a good work do they wish to put him to death? They say to him: Yes.

CHAP. 3.—And Pilate, filled with rage, went outside of the prætorium, and said to them: I take the sun to witness[4] that I find no fault in this man. The Jews answered and said to the procurator: Unless this man were an evil-doer, we should not have delivered him to thee. And Pilate said, Do you take him, and judge him according to your law. The Jews said to Pilate: It is not lawful for us to put any one to death. Pilate said: Has God said that you are not to put to death, but that I am?

And Pilate went again into the prætorium, and spoke to Jesus privately, and said to Him: Art thou the king of the Jews? Jesus answered Pilate: Dost thou say this of thyself, or have others said it to thee of me? Pilate answered Jesus: Am I also a Jew?[5] Thy nation and the chief priests have given thee up to me. What hast thou done? Jesus answered: My kingdom is not of this world; for if my kingdom were of this world, my servants would fight in order that I should not be given up to the Jews: but now my kingdom is not from thence. Pilate said to Him: Art thou then a king? Jesus answered him: Thou sayest that I am a king. Because for this have I been born, and have I come, in order that every one who is of the truth might hear my voice. Pilate says to him: What is truth? Jesus says to him: Truth is from heaven. Pilate says: Is truth not upon earth? Jesus says to Pilate: Thou seest how those who speak the truth are judged by those that have the power upon earth.

CHAP. 4.—And leaving Jesus within the prætorium, Pilate went out to the Jews, and said to them: I find no fault in him. The Jews say to him: He said, I can destroy this temple, and in three days build it. Pilate says: What temple? The Jews say: The one that Solomon[6] built in forty-six years, and this man speaks of pulling it down and building it in three days. Pilate says to them: I am innocent of the blood of this just man. See you to it. The Jews say: His blood be upon us, and upon our children.

And Pilate having summoned the elders and priests and Levites, said to them privately: Do not act thus, because no charge that you bring against him is worthy of death; for your charge is about curing and Sabbath profanation. The elders and the priests and the Levites say: If

---

[1] i.e., let them see to it.
[2] There is considerable variation in the MSS. as to these names.
[3] Or, let them swear.

[4] See *Apost. Const.*, ii. 56. At last he who is going to pronounce sentence of death upon the culprit raises his hands aloft, and takes the sun to witness that he is innocent of his blood.
[5] The full force of the expression is: You do not mean to say that I too am a Jew?
[6] Comp. John ii. 20.

any one speak evil against Cæsar, is he worthy of death or not? Pilate says: He is worthy of death. The Jews say to Pilate: If any one speak evil against Cæsar, he is worthy of death; but this man has spoken evil against God.

And the procurator ordered the Jews to go outside of the prætorium; and summoning Jesus, he says to Him: What shall I do to thee? Jesus says to Pilate: As it has been given to thee. Pilate says: How given? Jesus says: Moses and the prophets have proclaimed beforehand of my death and resurrection. And the Jews noticing this, and hearing it, say to Pilate: What more wilt thou hear of this blasphemy? Pilate says to the Jews: If these words be blasphemous, do you take him for the blasphemy, and lead him away to your synagogue, and judge him according to your law. The Jews say to Pilate: Our law bears that a man who wrongs his fellow-men is worthy to receive forty save one; but he that blasphemeth God is to be stoned with stones.[1]

Pilate says to them: Do you take him, and punish him in whatever way you please. The Jews say to Pilate: We wish that he be crucified. Pilate says: He is not deserving of crucifixion.

And the procurator, looking round upon the crowds of the Jews standing by, sees many of the Jews weeping, and says: All the multitude do not wish him to die. The elders of the Jews say: For this reason all the multitude of us have come, that he should die. Pilate says to the Jews: Why should he die? The Jews say: Because he called himself Son of God, and King.

CHAP. 5. — And one Nicodemus, a Jew, stood before the procurator, and said: I beseech your honour, let me say a few words. Pilate says: Say on. Nicodemus says: I said to the elders and the priests and Levites, and to all the multitude of the Jews in the synagogue, What do you seek to do with this man? This man does many miracles and strange things, which no one has done or will do. Let him go, and do not wish any evil against him. If the miracles which he does are of God, they will stand; but if of man, they will come to nothing.[2] For assuredly Moses, being sent by God into Egypt, did many miracles, which the Lord commanded him to do before Pharaoh king of Egypt. And there were there Jannes and Jambres, servants of Pharaoh, and they also did not a few of the miracles which Moses did; and the Egyptians took them to be gods — this Jannes and this Jambres.[3] But, since the miracles which they did were not of God, both they and those who believed in

them were destroyed. And now release this man, for he is not deserving of death.

The Jews say to Nicodemus: Thou hast become his disciple, and therefore thou defendest him. Nicodemus says to them: Perhaps, too, the procurator has become his disciple, because he defends him. Has the emperor not appointed him to this place of dignity? And the Jews were vehemently enraged, and gnashed their teeth against Nicodemus. Pilate says to them: Why do you gnash your teeth against him when you hear the truth? The Jews say to Nicodemus: Mayst thou receive his truth and his portion. Nicodemus says: Amen, amen; may I receive it, as you have said.

CHAP. 6. — One of the Jews, stepping up, asked leave of the procurator to say a word. The procurator says: If thou wishest to say any thing, say on. And the Jew said: Thirty-eight years I lay in my bed in great agony. And when Jesus came, many demoniacs, and many lying ill of various diseases, were cured by him. And some young men, taking pity on me, carried me, bed and all, and took me to him. And when Jesus saw me, he had compassion on me, and said to me: Take up thy couch and walk. And I took up my couch, and walked. The Jews say to Pilate: Ask him on what day it was that he was cured. He that had been cured says: On a Sabbath.[4] The Jews say: Is not this the very thing that we said, that on a Sabbath he cures and casts out demons?

And another Jew stepped up and said: I was born blind; I heard sounds, but saw not a face. And as Jesus passed by, I cried out with a loud voice, Pity me, O son of David. And he pitied me, and put his hands upon my eyes, and I instantly received my sight.[5] And another Jew stepped up and said: I was crooked, and he straightened me with a word. And another said: I was a leper, and he cured me with a word.[6]

CHAP. 7. — And a woman[7] cried out from a distance, and said: I had an issue of blood, and I touched the hem of his garment, and the issue of blood which I had had for twelve years was stopped.[8] The Jews say: We have a law, that a woman's evidence is not to be received.[9]

CHAP. 8. — And others, a multitude both of men and women, cried out, saying: This man is a prophet, and the demons are subject to him. Pilate says to them who said that the demons

---

[1] Deut. xxv. 3; Lev. xxiv. 16.
[2] Acts v. 38.
[3] 2 Tim. iii. 8, 9.

[4] John v. 5–9.
[5] Mark x. 46, etc.
[6] Matt. viii. 1–4, etc.
[7] Some MSS. add the name Bernice, or Veronica.
[8] Matt. ix. 20–26.
[9] Jos. Ant., iv. 8, § 15.

were subject to Him : Why, then, were not your teachers also subject to him? They say to Pilate : We do not know. And others said : He raised Lazarus from the tomb after he had been dead four days.[1] And the procurator trembled, and said to all the multitude of the Jews : Why do you wish to pour out innocent blood?

CHAP. 9. — And having summoned Nicodemus and the twelve men that said He was not born of fornication, he says to them : What shall I do, because there is an insurrection among the people? They say to him : We know not ; let them see to it. Again Pilate, having summoned all the multitude of the Jews, says : You know that it is customary, at the feast of unleavened bread, to release one prisoner to you. I have one condemned prisoner in the prison, a murderer named Barabbas, and this man standing in your presence, Jesus, in whom I find no fault. Which of them do you wish me to release to you? And they cry out : Barabbas. Pilate says : What, then, shall we do to Jesus who is called Christ? The Jews say : Let him be crucified. And others said : Thou art no friend of Cæsar's if thou release this man, because he called himself Son of God and king. You wish, then, this man to be king, and not Cæsar?[2]

And Pilate, in a rage, says to the Jews : Always has your nation been rebellious, and you always speak against your benefactors. The Jews say : What benefactors? He says to them : Your God led you out of the land of Egypt from bitter slavery, and brought you safe through the sea as through dry land, and in the desert fed you with manna, and gave you quails, and quenched your thirst with water from a rock, and gave you a law ; and in all these things you provoked your God to anger, and sought a molten calf. And you exasperated your God, and He sought to slay you. And Moses prayed for you, and you were not put to death. And now you charge me with hating the emperor.[3]

And rising up from the tribunal, he sought to go out. And the Jews cry out, and say : We know that Cæsar is king, and not Jesus. For assuredly the magi brought gifts to him as to a king. And when Herod heard from the magi that a king had been born, he sought to slay him ; and his father Joseph, knowing this, took him and his mother, and they fled into Egypt. And Herod hearing of it, destroyed the children of the Hebrews that had been born in Bethlehem.[4]

And when Pilate heard these words, he was afraid ; and ordering the crowd to keep silence, because they were crying out, he said to them : So this is he whom Herod sought? The Jews say : Yes, it is he. And, taking water, Pilate washed his hands in the face of the sun, saying : I am innocent of the blood of this just man ; see you to it. Again the Jews cry out : His blood be upon us, and upon our children.

Then Pilate ordered the curtain of the tribunal where he was sitting to be drawn,[5] and says to Jesus : Thy nation has charged thee with being a king. On this account I sentence thee, first to be scourged, according to the enactment of venerable kings, and then to be fastened on the cross in the garden where thou wast seized. And let Dysmas and Gestas, the two malefactors, be crucified with thee.

CHAP. 10. — And Jesus went forth out of the prætorium, and the two malefactors with Him. And when they came to the place, they stripped Him of his clothes, and girded Him with a towel, and put a crown of thorns on Him round His head. And they crucified Him ; and at the same time also they hung up the two malefactors along with Him. And Jesus said : Father, forgive them, for they know not what they do. And the soldiers parted His clothes among them ; and the people stood looking at Him. And the chief priests, and the rulers with them, mocked Him, saying : He saved others ; let him save himself. If he be the Son of God, let him come down from the cross. And the soldiers made sport of Him, coming near and offering Him vinegar mixed with gall, and said : Thou art the king of the Jews ; save thyself.[6]

And Pilate, after the sentence, ordered the charge made against Him to be inscribed as a superscription in Greek, and Latin, and Hebrew, according to what the Jews had said : He is king of the Jews.

And one of the malefactors hanging up spoke to Him, saying : If thou be the Christ, save thyself and us. And Dysmas answering, reproved him, saying : Dost thou not fear God, because thou art in the same condemnation? And we indeed justly, for we receive the fit punishment of our deeds ; but this man has done no evil. And he said to Jesus : Remember me, Lord, in Thy kingdom. And Jesus said to him : Amen, amen ; I say to thee, To-day shalt thou be [7] with me in Paradise.

CHAP. 11. — And it was about the sixth hour, and there was darkness over the earth until the ninth hour, the sun being darkened ; and the

---

[1] John xi. 1-16.
[2] Matt. xxvii. 15-26, etc.
[3] Lit., king. Other readings are: with wishing another king; with seeking Jesus for king.
[4] One MS. adds: from two years old and under.

[5] This was customary before pronouncing sentence. See *Apost. Const.*, ii. 56.
[6] Some of the MSS. add: And the soldier Longinus, taking a spear, pierced His side, and there came forth blood and water.
[7] Lit., art.

curtain of the temple was split in the middle. And crying out with a loud voice, Jesus said: Father, BADDACH EPHKID RUEL, which is, interpreted: Into Thy hands I commit my spirit.[1] And having said this, He gave up the ghost. And the centurion, seeing what had happened, glorified God, and said: This was a just man. And all the crowds that were present at this spectacle, when they saw what had happened, beat their breasts and went away.

And the centurion reported what had happened to the procurator. And when the procurator and his wife heard it, they were exceedingly grieved, and neither ate nor drank that day. And Pilate sent for the Jews, and said to them: Have you seen what has happened? And they say: There has been an eclipse of the sun in the usual way.[2]

And His acquaintances were standing at a distance, and the women who came with Him from Galilee, seeing these things. And a man named Joseph, a councillor from the city of Arimathæa, who also waited for the kingdom of God, went to Pilate, and begged the body of Jesus. And he took it down, and wrapped it in clean linen, and placed it in a tomb hewn out of the rock, in which no one had ever lain.

CHAP. 12. — And the Jews, hearing that Joseph had begged the body of Jesus, sought him and the twelve who said that Jesus was not born of fornication, and Nicodemus, and many others who had stepped up before Pilate and declared His good works. And of all these that were hid, Nicodemus alone was seen by them, because he was a ruler of the Jews. And Nicodemus says to them: How have you come into the synagogue? The Jews say to him: How hast thou come into the synagogue? for thou art a confederate of his, and his portion is with thee in the world to come. Nicodemus says: Amen, amen. And likewise Joseph also stepped out and said to them: Why are you angry against me because I begged the body of Jesus? Behold, I have put him in my new tomb, wrapping him in clean linen; and I have rolled a stone to the door of the tomb. And you have acted not well against the just man, because you have not repented of crucifying him, but also have pierced him with a spear. And the Jews seized Joseph, and ordered him to be secured until the first day of the week, and said to him: Know that the time does not allow us to do anything against thee, because the Sabbath is dawning; and know that thou shalt not be deemed worthy of burial, but

we shall give thy flesh to the birds of the air. Joseph says to them: These are the words of the arrogant Goliath, who reproached the living God and holy David.[3] For God has said by the prophet, Vengeance is mine, and I will repay, saith the Lord.[4] And now he that is uncircumcised in flesh, but circumcised in heart, has taken water, and washed his hands in the face of the sun, saying, I am innocent of the blood of this just man; see ye to it. And you answered and said to Pilate, His blood be upon us, and upon our children. And now I am afraid lest the wrath of God come upon you, and upon your children, as you have said. And the Jews, hearing these words, were embittered in their souls, and seized Joseph, and locked him into a room where there was no window; and guards were stationed at the door, and they sealed the door where Joseph was locked in.

And on the Sabbath, the rulers of the synagogue,[5] and the priests and the Levites, made a decree that all should be found in the synagogue on the first day of the week. And rising up early, all the multitude in the synagogue consulted by what death they should slay him. And when the Sanhedrin was sitting, they ordered him to be brought with much indignity. And having opened the door, they found him not. And all the people were surprised, and struck with dismay, because they found the seals unbroken, and because Caiaphas had the key. And they no longer dared to lay hands upon those who had spoken before Pilate in Jesus' behalf.

CHAP. 13. — And while they were still sitting in the synagogue, and wondering about Joseph, there come some of the guard whom the Jews had begged of Pilate to guard the tomb of Jesus, that His disciples might not come and steal Him. And they reported to the rulers of the synagogue, and the priests and the Levites, what had happened: how there had been a great earthquake; and we saw an angel coming down from heaven, and he rolled away the stone from the mouth of the tomb, and sat upon it; and he shone like snow, and like lightning. And we were very much afraid, and lay like dead men; and we heard the voice of the angel saying to the women who remained beside the tomb, Be not afraid, for I know that you seek Jesus who was crucified. He is not here: He is risen, as He said. Come, see the place where the Lord lay: and go quickly, and tell His disciples that He is risen from the dead, and is in Galilee.[6]

---

[1] Luke xxiii. 46. Ps. xxxi. 5 is, *b'yadcha aphkid ruchi.*
[2] One MS. adds: Pilate said to them: You scoundrels! is this the way you tell the truth about everything? I know that that never happens but at new moon. Now you ate your passover yesterday, the fourteenth of the month, and you say that it was an eclipse of the sun.

[3] 1 Sam. xvii. 44.
[4] Deut. xxxii. 35; Rom. xii. 19; Heb. x. 30.
[5] [This is an evident blunder, one of many pointing to a late origin. — R.]
[6] Matt. xxviii. 5-7.

The Jews say: To what women did he speak? The men of the guard say: We do not know who they were. The Jews say: At what time was this? The men of the guard say: At midnight. The Jews say: And wherefore did you not lay hold of them? The men of the guard say: We were like dead men from fear, not expecting to see the light of day, and how could we lay hold of them? The Jews say: As the Lord liveth, we do not believe you. The men of the guard say to the Jews: You have seen so great miracles in the case of this man, and have not believed; and how can you believe us? And assuredly you have done well to swear that the Lord liveth, for indeed He does live. Again the men of the guard say: We have heard that you have locked up the man that begged the body of Jesus, and put a seal on the door; and that you have opened it, and not found him. Do you then give us the man whom you were guarding, and we shall give you Jesus. The Jews say: Joseph has gone away to his own city. The men of the guard say to the Jews: And Jesus has risen, as we heard from the angel, and is in Galilee.

And when the Jews heard these words, they were very much afraid, and said: We must take care lest this story be heard, and all incline to Jesus. And the Jews called a council, and paid down a considerable sum of money, and gave it to the soldiers, saying: Say, while we slept, his disciples came by night and stole him; and if this come to the ears of the procurator, we shall persuade him, and keep you out of trouble. And they took it, and said as they had been instructed.[1]

CHAP. 14. — And Phinees a priest, and Adas a teacher, and Haggai a Levite, came down from Galilee to Jerusalem, and said to the rulers of the synagogue, and the priests and the Levites: We saw Jesus and his disciples sitting on the mountain called Mamilch;[2] and he said to his disciples, Go into all the world, and preach to every creature: he that believeth and is baptized shall be saved, and he that believeth not shall be condemned. And these signs shall attend those who have believed: in my name they shall cast out demons, speak new tongues, take up serpents; and if they drink any deadly thing, it shall by no means hurt them; they shall lay hands on the sick, and they shall be well. And while Jesus was speaking to his disciples, we saw him taken up to heaven.[3]

The elders and the priests and Levites say: Give glory to the God of Israel, and confess to Him whether you have heard and seen those things of which you have given us an account. And those who had given the account said: As the Lord liveth, the God of our fathers Abraham, Isaac, and Jacob, we heard these things, and saw him taken up into heaven. The elders and the priests and the Levites say to them: Have you come to give us this announcement, or to offer prayer to God? And they say: To offer prayer to God. The elders and the chief priests and the Levites say to them: If you have come to offer prayer to God, why then have you told these idle tales in the presence of all the people?[4] Says Phinees the priest, and Adas the teacher, and Haggai the Levite, to the rulers of the synagogues, and the priests and the Levites: If what we have said and seen be sinful, behold, we are before you; do to us as seems good in your eyes. And they took the law, and made them swear upon it, not to give any more an account of these matters to any one. And they gave them to eat and drink, and sent them out of the city, having given them also money, and three men with them; and they sent them away to Galilee.

And these men having gone into Galilee, the chief priests, and the rulers of the synagogue, and the elders, came together into the synagogue, and locked the door, and lamented with a great lamentation, saying: Is this a miracle that has happened in Israel? And Annas and Caiaphas said: Why are you so much moved? Why do you weep? Do you not know that his disciples have given a sum of gold to the guards of the tomb, and have instructed them to say that an angel came down and rolled away the stone from the door of the tomb? And the priests and the elders said: Be it that his disciples have stolen his body; how is it that the life has come into his body, and that he is going about in Galilee? And they being unable to give an answer to these things, said, after great hesitation: It is not lawful for us to believe the uncircumcised.

CHAP. 15. — And Nicodemus stood up, and stood before the Sanhedrin, saying: You say well;[5] you are not ignorant, you people of the Lord, of these men that come down from Galilee, that they fear God, and are men of substance, haters of covetousness, men of peace; and they have declared with an oath, We saw Jesus upon the mountain Mamilch with his disciples, and he taught what we heard from him, and we saw him taken up into heaven. And no one asked them in what form he went up. For assuredly, as the book of the Holy Scriptures taught us, Helias also was taken up into heaven, and Elissæus cried out

---

[1] Three of the Latin versions say: And they took the money, but could not hide the truth. For they wanted to say, His disciples stole him while we slept, and could not utter it; but said, Truly the Lord Jesus Christ has risen from the dead; and we saw an angel of God coming down from heaven, and he rolled back the stone, and sat on it. And this saying has been spread abroad among the Jews even to this day.
[2] Other readings are: Malek, Mophek, Mambre, Mabrech. Comp. 2 Kings xxiii. 13.
[3] Mark xvi. 15-18.

[4] Lit., why then this trifling which ye have trifled, etc.
[5] Perhaps better as a question.

with a loud voice, and Helias threw his sheep-skin upon Elissæus, and Elissæus threw his sheepskin upon the Jordan, and crossed, and came into Jericho. And the children of the prophets met him, and said, O Elissæus, where is thy master Helias? And he said, He has been taken up into heaven. And they said to Elissæus, Has not a spirit seized him, and thrown him upon one of the mountains? But let us take our ser-vants [1] with us, and seek him. And they per-suaded Elissæus, and he went away with them. And they sought him three days, and did not find him; and they knew he had been taken up.[2] And now listen to me, and let us send into every district of Israel, and see lest perchance Christ has been taken up by a spirit, and thrown upon one of the mountains? And this proposal pleased all. And they sent into every district of Israel, and sought Jesus, and did not find Him; but they found Joseph in Arimathæa, and no one dared to lay hands on him.

And they reported to the elders, and the priests, and the Levites: We have gone round to every district of Israel, and have not found Jesus; but Joseph we have found in Arimathæa. And hearing about Joseph, they were glad, and gave glory to the God of Israel. And the rulers of the synagogue, and the priests and the Levites, having held a council as to the manner in which they should meet with Joseph, took a piece of paper, and wrote to Joseph as follows: —

Peace to thee! We know that we have sinned against God, and against thee; and we have prayed to the God of Israel, that thou shouldst deign to come to thy fathers, and to thy children, because we have all been grieved. For having opened the door, we did not find thee. And we know that we have counselled evil counsel against thee; but the Lord has defended thee, and the Lord Himself has scattered to the winds our counsel against thee, O honourable father Joseph.

And they chose from all Israel seven men, friends of Joseph, whom also Joseph himself was acquainted with; and the rulers of the synagogue, and the priests and the Levites, say to them: Take notice: if, after receiving our letter, he read it, know that he will come with you to us; but if he do not read it, know that he is ill-disposed towards us. And having saluted him in peace, return to us. And having blessed the men, they dismissed them. And the men came to Joseph, and did reverence to him, and said to him: Peace to thee! And he said: Peace to you, and to all the people of Israel! And they gave him the roll of the letter. And Joseph having received it, read the letter and rolled it

up, and blessed God, and said: Blessed be the Lord God, who has delivered Israel, that they should not shed innocent blood; and blessed be the Lord, who sent out His angel, and covered me under his wings. And he set a table for them; and they ate and drank, and slept there.

And they rose up early, and prayed. And Joseph saddled his ass, and set out with the men; and they came to the holy city Jerusalem. And all the people met Joseph, and cried out: Peace to thee in thy coming in! And he said to all the people: Peace to you! and he kissed them. And the people prayed with Joseph, and they were astonished at the sight of him. And Nico-demus received him into his house, and made a great feast, and called Annas and Caiaphas, and the elders, and the priests, and the Levites to his house. And they rejoiced, eating and drink-ing with Joseph; and after singing hymns, each proceeded to his own house. But Joseph re-mained in the house of Nicodemus.

And on the following day, which was the prep-aration, the rulers of the synagogue and the priests and the Levites went early to the house of Nicodemus; and Nicodemus met them, and said: Peace to you! And they said: Peace to thee, and to Joseph, and to all thy house, and to all the house of Joseph! And he brought them into his house. And all the Sanhedrin sat down, and Joseph sat down between Annas and Caia-phas: and no one dared to say a word to him. And Joseph said: Why have you called me? And they signalled to Nicodemus to speak to Joseph. And Nicodemus, opening his mouth, said to Joseph: Father, thou knowest that the honourable teachers, and the priests and the Levites, see to learn a word from thee. And Joseph said: Ask. And Annas and Caiaphas having taken the law, made Joseph swear, saying: Give glory to the God of Israel, and give Him confession; for Achar being made to swear by the prophet Jesus,[3] did not forswear himself, but declared unto him all, and did not hide a word from him. Do thou also accordingly not hide from us to the extent of a word. And Joseph said: I shall not hide from you one word. And they said to him: With grief were we grieved because thou didst beg the body of Jesus, and wrap it in clean linen, and lay it in a tomb. And on account of this we secured thee in a room where there was no windows: and we put locks and seals upon the doors, and guards kept watching where thou wast locked in. And on the first day of the week we opened, and found thee not, and were grieved exceedingly; and astonishment fell upon all the people of the Lord until yesterday. And now relate to us what has happened to thee.

And Joseph said: On the preparation, about

[1] Lit., boys.
[2] 2 Kings ii. 12-18.
[3] i.e., Joshua. Josh. vii. 19, 20.

the tenth hour, you locked me up, and I remained all the Sabbath. And at midnight, as I was standing and praying, the room where you locked me in was hung up by the four corners, and I saw a light like lightning into my eyes.[1] And I was afraid, and fell to the ground. And some one took me by the hand, and removed me from the place where I had fallen ; and moisture of water was poured from my head even to my feet, and a smell of perfumes came about my nostrils. And he wiped my face, and kissed me, and said to me, Fear not, Joseph ; open thine eyes, and see who it is that speaks to thee. And looking up, I saw Jesus. And I trembled, and thought it was a phantom ; and I said the commandments, and he said them with me.[2] Even so you are not ignorant that a phantom, if it meet anybody, and hear the commandments, takes to flight. And seeing that he said them with me, I said to him, Rabbi Helias. And he said to me, I am not Helias. And I said to him, Who art thou, my lord? And he said to me, I am Jesus, whose body thou didst beg from Pilate ; and thou didst clothe me with clean linen, and didst put a napkin on my face, and didst lay me in thy new tomb, and didst roll a great stone to the door of the tomb. And I said to him that was speaking to me, Show me the place where I laid thee. And he carried me away, and showed me the place where I laid him ; and the linen cloth was lying in it, and the napkin for his face. And I knew that it was Jesus. And he took me by the hand, and placed me, though the doors were locked, in the middle of my house, and led me away to my bed, and said to me, Peace to thee ! And he kissed me, and said to me, For forty days go not forth out of thy house ; for, behold, I go to my brethren into Galilee.

CHAP. 16. — And the rulers of the synagogue, and the priests and the Levites, when they heard these words from Joseph, became as dead, and fell to the ground, and fasted until the ninth hour. And Nicodemus, along with Joseph, exhorted Annas and Caiaphas, the priests and the Levites, saying : Rise up and stand upon your feet, and taste bread, and strengthen your souls, because to-morrow is the Sabbath of the Lord. And they rose up, and prayed to God, and ate and drank, and departed every man to his own house.

And on the Sabbath our teachers and the priests and Levites sat questioning each other, and saying : What is this wrath that has come upon us? for we know his father and mother. Levi, a teacher, says : I know that his parents fear God, and do not withdraw themselves from the prayers, and give the tithes thrice a year.[3] And when Jesus was born, his parents brought him to this place, and gave sacrifices and burnt-offerings to God. And when the great teacher Symeon took him into his arms, he said, Now Thou sendest away Thy servant, Lord, according to Thy word, in peace ; for mine eyes have seen Thy salvation, which Thou hast prepared before the face of all the peoples : a light for the revelation of the Gentiles, and the glory of Thy people Israel. And Symeon blessed them, and said to Mary his mother, I give thee good news about this child. And Mary said, It is well, my lord. And Symeon said to her, It is well ; behold, he lies for the fall and rising again of many in Israel, and for a sign spoken against ; and of thee thyself a sword shall go through the soul, in order that the reasoning of many hearts may be revealed.[4]

They say to the teacher Levi : How knowest thou these things? Levi says to them : Do you not know that from him I learned the law? The Sanhedrin say to him : We wish to see thy father. And they sent for his father. And they asked him ; and he said to them : Why have you not believed my son? The blessed and just Symeon himself taught him the law. The Sanhedrin says to Rabbi Levi : Is the word that you have said true? And he said : It is true. And the rulers of the synagogue, and the priests and the Levites, said to themselves : Come, let us send into Galilee to the three men that came and told about his teaching and his taking up, and let them tell us how they saw him taken up. And this saying pleased all. And they sent away the three men who had already gone away into Galilee with them ; and they say to them : Say to Rabbi Adas, and Rabbi Phinees, and Rabbi Haggai : Peace to you, and all who are with you ! A great inquiry having taken place in the Sanhedrin, we have been sent to you to call you to this holy place, Jerusalem.

And the men set out into Galilee, and found them sitting and considering the law ; and they saluted them in peace. And the men who were in Galilee said to those who had come to them : Peace upon all Israel ! And they said : Peace to you ! And they again said to them : Why you come? And those who had been sent said : The Sanhedrin call you to the holy city Jerusalem. And when the men heard that they were sought by the Sanhedrin, they prayed to God, and reclined with the men, and ate and drank, and rose up, and set out in peace to Jerusalem.

And on the following day the Sanhedrin sat in the synagogue, and asked them, saying : Did

---

[1] Comp. Acts x. 11.
[2] Or, and he spoke to me.

[3] This would seem to confirm the opinion that there were three tithes paid in the year. Comp. Smith's *Dict.*, *sub voce.*
[4] Luke ii. 25–35.

you really see Jesus sitting on the mountain Mamilch teaching his eleven disciples, and did you see him taken up? And the men answered them, and said : As we saw him taken up, so also we said.

Annas says : Take them away from one another, and let us see whether their account agrees. And they took them away from one another. And first they call Adas, and say to him : How didst thou see Jesus taken up? Adas says : While he was yet sitting on the mountain Mamilch, and teaching his disciples, we saw a cloud overshadowing both him and his disciples. And the cloud took him up into heaven, and his disciples lay upon their face upon the earth. And they call Phinees the priest, and ask him also, saying : How didst thou see Jesus taken up? And he spoke in like manner. And they again asked Haggai, and he spoke in like manner. And the Sanhedrin said : The law of Moses holds : At the mouth of two or three every word shall be established.[1] Buthem, a teacher, says : It is written in the law, And Enoch walked with God, and is not, because God took him.[2] Jairus, a teacher, said : And the death of holy Moses we have heard of, and have not seen it ; for it is written in the law of the Lord, And Moses died from the mouth of the Lord, and no man knoweth of his sepulchre unto this day.[3] And Rabbi Levi said : Why did Rabbi Symeon say, when he saw Jesus, " Behold, he lies for the fall and rising again of many in Israel, and for a sign spoken against?"[4] And Rabbi Isaac said : It is written in the law, Behold, I send my messenger before thy face, who shall go before thee to keep thee in every good way, because my name has been called upon him.[5]

Then Annas and Caiaphas said : Rightly have you said what is written in the law of Moses, that no one saw the death of Enoch, and no one has named the death of Moses ; but Jesus was tried before Pilate, and we saw him receiving blows and spittings on his face, and the soldiers put about him a crown of thorns, and he was scourged, and received sentence from Pilate, and was crucified upon the Cranium, and two robbers with him ; and they gave him to drink vinegar with gall, and Longinus the soldier pierced his side with a spear ; and Joseph our honourable father begged his body, and, as he says, he is risen ; and as the three teachers say, We saw him taken up into heaven ; and Rabbi Levi has given evidence of what was said by Rabbi Symeon, and that he said, Behold, he lies for the fall *and* rising again of many in Israel, and for a sign spoken against. And all the teachers said to all the people of the Lord : If this was from the Lord, and is wonderful in your eyes,[6] knowing you shall know, O house of Jacob, that it is written, Cursed is every one that hangeth upon a tree.[7] And another Scripture teaches : The gods which have not made the heaven and the earth shall be destroyed.[8] And the priests and the Levites said to each other : If his memorial be until the *year* that is called Jobel,[9] know that it shall it endure for ever, and he hath raised for himself a new people. Then the rulers of the synagogue, and the priests and the Levites, announced to all Israel, saying : Cursed is that man who shall worship the work of man's hand, and cursed is the man who shall worship the creatures more than the Creator. And all the people said, Amen, amen.[10]

And all the people praised[11] the Lord, and said : Blessed is the Lord, who hath given rest to His people Israel, according to all that He hath spoken ; there hath not fallen one word of every good word of His that He spoke to Moses His servant. May the Lord our God be with us, as He was with our fathers : let Him not destroy us. And let Him not destroy us, that we may incline our hearts to Him, that we may walk in all His ways, that we may keep His commandments and His judgments which He commanded to our fathers.[12] And the Lord shall be for a king over all the earth in that day ; and there shall be one Lord, and His name one.[13] The Lord is our king : He shall save us.[14] There is none like Thee, O Lord.[15] Great art Thou, O Lord, and great is Thy name. By Thy power heal us, O Lord, and we shall be healed : save us, O Lord, and we shall be saved ;[16] because we are Thy lot and heritage. And the Lord will not leave His people, for His great name's sake ; for the Lord has begun to make us into His people.[17]

And all, having sung praises, went away each man to his own house, glorifying God ; for His is the glory for ever and ever. Amen.

---

[1] Deut. xvii. 6.
[2] Gen. v. 24; Heb. xi. 5.
[3] Deut. xxxiv. 5, 6.
[4] Luke ii. 34.
[5] Ex. xxiii. 20, 21; Mal. iii. 1; Matt. xi. 10.

[6] Ps. cxviii. 23.
[7] Deut. xxi. 23; Gal. iii. 13.
[8] Jer. x. 11.
[9] i.e., the year of jubilee. The original, ἕως τοῦ σώμμου, is not Greek. It is not easy to see what the passage means. It may refer to Isa. lxi. 1-3.
[10] Deut. xxvii. 15; Rom. i. 25.
[11] Or, sang hymns to.
[12] 1 Kings viii. 56-58.
[13] Zech. xiv. 9.
[14] Isa. xxxiii. 22.
[15] Ps. lxxxvi. 8.
[16] Comp. Jer. xvii. 14.
[17] Comp. 1 Sam. xii. 22.

SECOND GREEK FORM.

A NARRATIVE about the suffering of our Lord Jesus Christ, and His holy resurrection.

Written by a Jew, Æneas by name, and translated out of the Hebrew tongue into the Romaic language by Nicodemus, a Roman toparch.

After the dissolution of the kingdom of the Hebrews, four hundred years having run their course, and the Hebrews also coming at last under the kingdom of the Romans, and the king of the Romans appointing them a king; when Tiberius Cæsar at last swayed the Roman sceptre, in the eighteenth year of his reign,[1] he appointed as king of Judæa, Herod, the son of the Herod who had formerly slaughtered the infants in Bethlehem, and he made Pilate procurator in Jerusalem; when Annas and Caiaphas held the high-priesthood of Jerusalem, Nicodemus, a Roman toparch, having summoned a Jew, Æneas by name, asked him to write an account of the things done in Jerusalem about Christ in the times of Annas and Caiaphas. The Jew accordingly did this, and delivered it to Nicodemus; and he, again, translated it from the Hebrew writing into the Romaic language. And the account is as follows:—

CHAP. I.—Our Lord Jesus Christ having wrought in Judæa many and great and extraordinary miracles, and on account of this being hated by the Hebrews, while Pilate was procurator in Jerusalem, and Annas and Caiaphas high priests, there came of the Jews to the chief priests, Judas, Levi, Nephthalim, Alexander, Syrus, and many others, speaking against Christ. And these chief priests sent them away to say these things to Pilate also. And they went away, and said to him: A man walks about in this city whose father is called Joseph, and his mother Mary; and he calls himself king and Son of God; and being a Jew, he overturns the Scriptures, and does away with the Sabbath. Pilate then asked, in order to learn from them in what manner he did away with the Sabbath. And they answered, saying: He cures the sick on the Sabbath. Pilate says: If he makes the sick whole, he does no evil. They say to him: If he effected the cures properly, small would be the evil; but by using magic he does these things, and by having the demons on his side. Pilate says: To cure a person that is ill is not a diabolic work, but a grace from God.

The Hebrews said: We beseech your highness to summon him, in order that thou mayst make accurate inquiry into what we say. Pilate therefore, throwing off his cloak, gave it to one of his officers,[2] saying: Go away, and show this to Jesus, and say to him, Pilate the procurator calls thee to come before him. The officer accordingly went away, and finding Jesus, summoned Him, having unfolded on the ground also Pilate's mantle, and urged Him to walk upon it. And the Hebrews, seeing this, and being greatly enraged, came to Pilate, murmuring against him, how he had deemed Jesus worthy of so great honour.

And he, having inquired of the officer who had been sent how he had done so, the officer answered: When thou didst send me to the Jew Alexander, I came upon Jesus entering the gate of the city, sitting upon an ass. And I saw that the Hebrews spread their garments in the way, and the ass walked upon the garments; and others cut branches, and they went forth to meet him, and cried out, Hosanna in the highest! Thus, therefore, it was necessary for me also to do.

The Jews, hearing these words, said to him: How didst thou, being a Roman, know what was said by the Hebrews? The officer answered: I asked one of the Hebrews, and he told me these things. Pilate said: What means Hosanna? The Jews said: Save us, O Lord. Pilate answered: Since you confess that your children said so, how now do you bring charges, and say against Jesus what you do say? The Jews were silent, and had nothing to answer.[3]

Now, as Jesus was coming to Pilate, the soldiers of Pilate adored Him. And others also were standing before Pilate holding standards. And as Jesus was coming, the standards also bowed down, and adored Him. As Pilate, therefore, was wondering at what had happened, the Jews said to him: My lord, it was not the standards that adored Jesus, but the soldiers who were holding them carelessly.

Pilate says to the ruler of the synagogue: Choose twelve powerful men, and give them the

---

[1] [Compare the first Greek form, prologue and footnote.—R.]

[2] One MS. inserts: by name Rachaab, the messenger.

[3] Instead of these four sections, MS. C has a minute account of the suicide of Judas, of which the following specimen may be given:—And he went home to make a halter to hang himself, and he found his wife roasting a cock on the coals. And he says to her: Rise, wife, and get a rope ready for me; for I mean to hang myself, as I deserve. And his wife said to him: Why do you speak like that? And Judas says: Know in truth that I unjustly betrayed my master, etc., and that he is going to rise on the third day; and woe to us! And his wife says: Do not speak or think in that way. It is just as likely as that this cock roasting on the coals will crow, that Jesus will rise, as you say. No sooner said than the cock flapped his wings, and crew thrice. This decided Judas, and he immediately made the halter, and hanged himself. [The MSS. of the "Second Greek Form" are designated by Tischendorf (*Evang. Apocry.*, pp. lxxii., lxxiii.) as follows: A, a Venice MS., comparatively recent; B, a Paris MS. of the fifteenth century; C, a Venice MS. of the same century.—R.]

standards, so that they may hold them firmly. And this having taken place, Pilate ordered the officer to take Jesus outside, and bring Him in again. And as He was coming in, the standards again bowed down, and adored Him. Pilate therefore wondered greatly. But the Jews said: He is a magician, and through that he does these things.

CHAP. 2. — Pilate says to Jesus: Hearest thou what these testify against thee, and answerest thou not?[1] And Jesus answered and said: Every man has power to speak either good or bad, as he wishes; these also, therefore, having power, say what they wish.[2]

The Jews said to Him: What have we to say about thee? First, that thou wast begotten from sin; second, that on account of thee, when thou wast born, the infants[3] were murdered; third, that thy father and thy mother fled into Egypt, because they had no confidence in the people.

To these the Jews who were there present, God-fearing men, answered and said: We say that his birth is not from sin; for we know that Joseph received into keeping his mother Mary, according to the practice of betrothal. Pilate said: Consequently you lie who say that his birth is from sin. They say again to Pilate: All the people testify that he is a magician. The God-fearing Jews answered and said: We also were at the betrothal of his mother, and we are Jews, and know all his daily life; but that he is a magician, that we do not know. And the Jews that thus said were these: Lazarus, Astharius, Antonius, James, Zaras, Samuel, Isaac, Phinees, Crispus, Dagrippus, Amese, and Judas.

Pilate therefore says to them: By the life of Cæsar, I wish you to swear whether the birth of this man is without sin. They answered: Our law lays down that we are to swear not at all, because an oath is great sin. Notwithstanding, by the life of Cæsar we swear that his birth is without sin; and if we lie, order us all to be beheaded. And when they had thus spoken, the Jews that were bringing the charge answered Pilate, and said: And dost thou believe these twelve single Jews more than all the multitude and us, who know for certain that he is a magician and blasphemer, and that he names himself Son of God?

Then Pilate ordered them all to go forth out of the prætorium except the said twelve alone. And when this had been done, Pilate says to them privately: As to this man, it appears that from envy and madness the Jews wish to murder him: for of one thing — that he does away with the Sabbath — they accuse him; but he then does a good work, because he cures the sick. For this, sentence of death is not upon the man. The twelve also say to him: Assuredly, my lord, it is so.

CHAP. 3. — Pilate therefore went outside in rage and anger, and says to Annas and Caiaphas, and to the crowd who brought Jesus: I take the sun to witness that I find no fault in this man. The crowd answered: If he were not a sorcerer, and a magician, and a blasphemer, we should not have brought him to your highness. Pilate said: Try him yourselves; and since you have a law, do as your law says. The Jews said: Our law permits to put no man to death.[4] Pilate says: If you are unwilling to put him to death, how much more am I!

Then Pilate returned to the palace, and says to Jesus: Tell me, art thou the king of the Jews? Jesus answered: Dost thou say this, or have the other Jews said this to thee, that thou mightst question me? Pilate said: Thou dost not think that I am a Hebrew? I am not a Hebrew. Thy people and the chief priests have delivered thee into my hands; and tell me if thou art king of the Jews? Jesus answered: My kingdom is not of this world; for if my kingdom were in this world, my soldiers would not be unconcerned at my being seized: wherefore my kingdom is not in this world. Pilate says: But art thou a king? Jesus said: Thou hast said: for this was I born, to bear witness to the truth; and if any one be a man of the truth, he believes my word, and does it. Pilate says: What is the truth?[5] Jesus answered: The truth is from the heavens. Pilate says: On earth, then, is there no truth? Christ says: I am the truth; and how is the truth judged on earth by those that have earthly power!

CHAP. 4. — Pilate therefore, leaving Christ alone, went outside, and says to the Jews: I find no fault in this man. The Jews answered: Let us tell your highness what he said. He said, I am able to destroy the temple of God, and in three days to build it. Pilate says: And what temple did he say that he was to destroy? The Hebrews say: The temple of Solomon, which Solomon built in forty-six years.[6]

Pilate says privately to the chief priests and the scribes and the Pharisees: I entreat you, do nothing evil against this man; for if you do evil against him, you will do unjustly: for it is not just that such a man should die, who has done great good to many men. They said to Pilate:

---

[1] Matt. xxvii. 13, 14.
[2] Comp. John xix. 11.
[3] MS. A, 14,000 infants; B, 44,000 infants.
[4] John xix. 6, 7.
[5] John xviii. 33–38.
[6] Comp. John ii. 20.

If, my lord, he who has dishonoured Cæsar is worthy of death, how much more this *man* who dishonours God!

Then Pilate dismissed them, and they all went outside. Thereupon he says to Jesus: What dost thou wish that I shall do to thee? Jesus says to Pilate: Do to me as is determined. Pilate says: How is it determined? Jesus answered: Moses and the prophets wrote about me being crucified, and rising again. The Hebrews, hearing *this*, said to Pilate: Why do you seek to hear a greater insult out of him against God? Pilate says: These words are not an insult against God, since they are written in the books of the prophets. The Hebrews said: Our Scripture says, If a man offend against a man, that is to say, if he insult him, he is worthy to receive forty strokes with a rod; but if any one insult God, to be stoned.[1]

Then came a messenger from Procle, the wife of Pilate, to him; and the message said: Take care that thou do not agree that any evil should happen to Jesus the good man; because during this night I have seen fearful dreams on account of him.[2] And Pilate spoke to the Hebrews, saying: If you hold as insult against God the words which you declare Jesus to have spoken, take and judge him yourselves according to your law.[3] The Jews said to Pilate: We wish that you should crucify him. Pilate says: This is not good.

And Pilate, turning towards the people, saw many weeping, and said: To me it seems that it is not the wish of all the people that this man should die. The priests and the scribes say: We on this account have brought all the people, that thou mightst have full conviction that all wish his death. Pilate says: For what evil hath he done? The Hebrews said: He says that he is a king, and the Son of God.

CHAP. 5.—A God-fearing Jew, therefore, Nicodemus by name, stood up in the midst, and said to Pilate: I entreat your highness to permit me to say a few words. Say on, said Pilate. Nicodemus says: I, being present in the synagogue, said to the priests, and the Levites, and the scribes, and the people, What have you to say against this man? This man does many miracles, such as man has never yet done nor will do. Let him go, therefore; and if indeed what he does be from God, it will stand; but if from man, it will be destroyed.[4] Just as happened also when God sent Moses into Egypt, and Pharoah king of Egypt told him to do a miracle, and he did it. Then Pharoah had also two magicians, Jannes and Jambres; and they also did miracles by the use of magic art, but not such as Moses did.[5]

And the Egyptians held these magicians to be gods; but because they were not from God, what they did was destroyed. This Jesus, then, raised up Lazarus, and he is alive. On this account I entreat thee, my lord, by no means to allow this man to be put to death.

The Hebrews were enraged against Nicodemus, and said: Mayst thou receive the truth of Jesus, and have a portion with him. Nicodemus says: Amen, amen; be it to me as you say.

CHAP. 6.—And when Nicodemus had thus spoken, another Hebrew rose up, and said to Pilate: I beg of thee, my lord Pilate, hear me also. Pilate answered: Say what thou wishest. The Hebrew says: I lay sick in bed thirty-eight years; and when he saw me he was grieved, and said to me, Rise, take up thy couch, and go into thine house. And while he was saying the word to me, I rose and walked about. The Hebrews say: Ask him on what day of the week this happened. He says: On Sabbath.[6] The Jews said: And consequently we say truly, that he does not keep the Sabbath.

Another, again, standing in the midst, said: I was born blind; and as Jesus was going along the road, I cried to him, saying, Have mercy upon me, Lord, thou son of David. And he took clay, and anointed mine eyes; and straightway I received my sight.[7] Another said: I was crooked; and seeing him, I cried, Have mercy upon me, O Lord. And he took me by the hand, and I was immediately raised.[8] Another said: I was a leper, and he healed me merely by a word.[9]

CHAP. 7.—There was found there also a woman named Veronica, and she said: Twelve years I was in an issue of blood, and I only touched the edge of his garment, and directly I was cured.[10] The Jews say: Our law does not admit the testimony of a woman.[11]

CHAP. 8.—Other men cried: This man is a prophet, and the demons are afraid of him. Pilate says: And how were the demons not at all thus afraid of your parents also? They say: We do not know. Others, again, said: Lazarus, after having been four days in the tomb, he raised by a single word.[12] Pilate therefore, hearing of the raising of Lazarus, was afraid, and said to the people: Why do you wish to shed the blood of a just man?

---

[1] Deut. xxv. 3; Lev. xxiv. 16.
[2] Matt. xxvii. 19.
[3] John xviii. 31.
[4] Comp. Acts v. 38.
[5] Ex. vii. 10–14.

[6] John v. 5–9.
[7] John ix. 6, 7.
[8] Comp. Acts iii. 7.
[9] Luke xvii. 11–19.
[10] Matt. ix. 20–22.
[11] See note 9, p. 419.
[12] John xi. 43.

CHAP. 9. — Then he summoned Nicodemus and the twelve God-fearing Jews, and said to them : What do you say that I should do? because the people are in commotion. They say : We do not know : do as thou wilt ; but what the people do, they do unjustly, in order to kill him. Pilate again went outside, and said to the people : You know that in the feasts of unleavened bread it is customary that I free on your account one of the criminals kept in custody. I have, then, one malefactor in the prison, a robber named Barabbas. I have also Jesus, who has never done any evil. Which of the two, then, do you wish that I release to you? The people answered : Release to us Barabbas. Pilate says : What then shall I do with Jesus? They say : Let him be crucified.[1] Again, others of them cried out : If thou release Jesus, thou art no friend of Cæsar,[2] because he calls himself Son of God, and king. And if thou free him, he becomes a king, and will take Cæsar's kingdom.

Pilate therefore was enraged, and said : Always has your nation been devilish[3] and unbelieving ; and ever have you been adversaries to your benefactors. The Hebrews say : And who were our benefactors? Pilate says : God, who freed you out of the hand of Pharaoh, and brought you through the Red Sea as upon dry land, and fed you with quails, and gave you water to drink out of the dry rock, and who gave you a law, which, denying God, you broke ; and if Moses had not stood and entreated God, you would have perished by a bitter death. All these, then, you have forgotten. Thus also, even now, you say that I do not at all love Cæsar, but hate him, and wish to plot against his kingdom.

And having thus spoken, Pilate rose up from the throne with anger, wishing to flee from them. The Jews therefore cried out, saying : We wish Cæsar to be king over us, not Jesus, because Jesus received gifts[4] from the Magi. And Herod also heard this — that there was going to be a king — and wished to put him to death, and for this purpose sent and put to death all the infants that were in Bethlehem. And on this account also his father Joseph and his mother fled from fear of him into Egypt.[5]

So then Pilate, hearing this, silenced all the people, and said : This, then, is the Jesus whom Herod then sought that he might put him to death? They say to him : Yes. Pilate therefore, having ascertained that he was of the jurisdiction of Herod, as being derived of the race of the Jews, sent Jesus to him. And Herod, seeing

Him, rejoiced greatly, because he had been long desiring to see Him, hearing of the miracles which He did. He put on Him, therefore, white garments. Then he began to question Him. But Jesus did not give him an answer. And Herod, wishing to see also some miracle or other done by Jesus, and not seeing it, and also because He did not answer him a single word, sent Him back again to Pilate.[6] Pilate, seeing this, ordered his officers to bring water. Washing, then, his hands with the water, he said to the people : I am innocent of the blood of this good man. See you to it, that he is unjustly put to death, since neither I have found a fault in him, nor Herod ; for because of this he has sent him back again to me. The Jews said : His blood be upon us, and upon our children.[7]

Then Pilate sat down upon his throne to pass sentence. He gave order, therefore, and Jesus came before him. And they brought a crown of thorns, and put it on His head, and a reed into His right hand.[8] Then he passed sentence, and said to Him : Thy nation says, and testifies against thee, that thou wishest to be a king. Therefore I decree that they shall beat thee first with a rod forty strokes, as the laws of the kings decree, and that they shall mock thee ; and finally, that they shall crucify thee.

CHAP. 10. — The sentence to this effect, then, having been passed by Pilate, the Jews began to strike Jesus, some with rods, others with *their* hands, others with *their* feet ; some also spat in His face. Immediately, therefore, they got ready the cross, and gave it to Him, and flew to take the road. And thus going along, bearing also the cross, He came as far as the gate of the city of Jerusalem. But as He, from the many blows and the weight of the cross, was unable to walk, the Jews, out of the eager desire they had to crucify Him as quickly as possible, took the cross from Him, and gave it to a man that met them, Simon by name, who had also two sons, Alexander and Rufus. And he was from the city of Cyrene.[9] They gave the cross, then, to him, not because they pitied Jesus, and wished to lighten Him of the weight, but because they eagerly desired, as has been said, to put Him to death more speedily.

Of His disciples, therefore, John followed Him there. Then he came fleeing to the mother of God,[10] and said to her : Where hast

[1] Matt. xxvii. 15-18, 21-23.
[2] John xix. 12.
[3] Or, slanderous.
[4] The word here, χάρισμα, is used in the New Testament only of gifts and graces bestowed by God, and specially of the miraculous gifts imparted to the early Christians by the Holy Ghost. The word in Matt. ii. 11 is δῶρα.
[5] Matt. ii. 14-16. [The writer seems to identify Herod the Great and Herod Antipas. — R.]

[6] Luke xxiii. 6-11. [The only passage directly interpolated into Luke's narrative is "as being derived of the race of the Jews." A curious blunder of the compiler! — R.]
[7] Matt. xxvii. 25.
[8] John xix. 2, 3; Matt. xxvii. 29.
[9] Mark xv. 21.
[10] Θεοτόκος — a word used several times by Athanasius (died 373), e.g., in Orat. iii. *Contra Arianos*, c. 14 and 29. The refusal of Nestorius to give this epithet to Mary was the commencement, in 428, of the long struggle between the rival sees of Constantinople and Alexandria. See Haag, *Histoire des Dogmes Chrétiens*, i. 190. The paragraphs about the Θεοτόκος in this chapter are interpolations.

thou been, that thou hast not come to see what has happened? She answered: What is it that has happened? John says: Know that the Jews have laid hold of my Master, and are taking Him away to crucify Him. Hearing this, His mother cried out with a loud voice, saying: My son, my son, what evil then hast thou done, that [1] they are taking thee away to crucify thee? And she rose up as if blinded,[2] and goes along the road weeping. And women followed her — Martha, and Mary Magdalene, and Salome, and other virgins. And John also was with her. When, therefore, they came to the multitude of the crowd, the mother of God says to John: Where is my son? John says: Seest thou Him bearing the crown of thorns, and having His hands bound? And the mother of God, hearing this, and seeing Him, fainted, and fell backwards to the ground, and lay a considerable time. And the women, as many as followed her, stood round her, and wept. And as soon as she revived and rose up, she cried out with a loud voice: My Lord, my son, where has the beauty of thy form sunk? how shall I endure to see thee suffering such things? And thus saying, she tore her face with her nails, and beat her breast. Where are they gone, said she, the good deeds which thou didst in Judæa? What evil hast thou done to the Jews? The Jews, then, seeing her thus lamenting and crying, came and drove her from the road; but she would not flee, but remained, saying: Kill me first, ye lawless Jews.

Then they got safe to the place called Cranium, which was paved with stone;[3] and there the Jews set up the cross. Then they stripped Jesus, and the soldiers took His garments, and divided them among themselves; and they put on Him a tattered robe of scarlet, and raised Him, and drew Him up on the cross at the sixth hour of the day. After this they brought also two robbers, the one on His right, the other on His left.

Then the mother of God, standing and looking, cried out with a loud voice, saying: My son! my son! And Jesus, turning to her, and seeing John near her, and weeping with the rest of the women, said: Behold thy son! Then He says also to John: Behold thy mother![4] And she wept much, saying: For this I weep, my son, because thou sufferest unjustly, because the lawless Jews have delivered thee to a bitter death. Without thee, my son, what will become of me? How shall I live without thee? What sort of life shall I spend? Where are thy disciples, who boasted that they would die with

thee? Where those healed by thee? How has no one been found to help thee? And looking to the cross, she said: Bend down, O cross, that I may embrace and kiss my son, whom I suckled at these breasts after a strange manner, as not having known man. Bend down, O cross; I wish to throw my arms round my son. Bend down, O cross, that I may bid farewell to my son like a mother. The Jews, hearing these words, came forward, and drove to a distance both her and the women and John.

Then Jesus cried out with a loud voice, saying: Father, let not this sin stand against them; for they know not what they do.[5] Then He says: I thirst. And immediately there ran one of the soldiers, and took a sponge, and filled it with gall and vinegar mixed, and put it on a reed, and gave Jesus to drink. And having tasted it, He would not drink it.[6] And the Jews standing and looking on laughed at Him, and said: If thou truly sayst that thou art the Son of God, come down from the cross, and immediately, that we may believe in thee. Others said mocking: Others he saved, others he cured, and he healed the sick, the paralytic, the lepers, the demoniacs, the blind, the lame, the dead; and himself he cannot cure.[7]

In the same manner also, the robber crucified on His left hand said to Him: If thou art the Son of God, come down and save both thyself and us. His name was Gistas. And he that was crucified on the right, Dysmas by name, reproved that robber, saying: O wretched and miserable man, dost thou not fear God? We suffer the due punishment of what we have done; but this man has done no evil at all. And turning to Jesus, he says to Him: Lord, when Thou shalt reign, do not forget me. And He said to him: To-day, I tell thee truth, I shall have thee in paradise with me.[8]

CHAP. 11. — Then Jesus, crying out with a loud voice, Father, into Thy hands I shall commit my spirit, breathed His last.[9] And immediately one could see the rocks rent: for there was an earthquake over all the earth; and from the earthquake being violent and great, the rocks also were rent. And the tombs of the dead were opened, and the curtain of the temple was rent, and there was darkness from the sixth hour till the ninth. And from all these things that had happened the Jews were afraid, and said: Certainly this was a just man. And Longinus, the centurion who stood by, said: Truly this was a son of God. Others coming and seeing

---

[1] Lit., and.
[2] Lit., darkened.
[3] A mistaken reference to John xix. 13.
[4] John xix. 26, 27.

[5] Luke xxiii. 34; cf. Acts vii. 60.
[6] John xix. 28; Matt. xxvii. 48.
[7] Comp. Matt. xxvii. 40–42.
[8] Luke xxiii. 39–43. MS. C here inserts the early history of the robber Dysmas. [See note 3, p. 426. — R.]
[9] Luke xxiii. 46.

Him, beat their breasts from fear, and again turned back.[1]

And the centurion having perceived all these so great miracles, went away and reported them to Pilate. And when he heard, he wondered and was astonished, and from his fear and grief would neither eat nor drink that day. And he sent notice, and all the Sanhedrin came to him as soon as the darkness was past; and he said to the people : You know how the sun has been darkened ; you know how the curtain has been rent. Certainly I did well in being by no means willing to put to death the good man. And the malefactors said to Pilate : This darkness is an eclipse of the sun, such as has happened also at other times. Then they say to him : We hold the feast of unleavened bread to-morrow ; and we entreat thee, since the crucified are still breathing, that their bones be broken, and that they be brought down. Pilate said : It shall be so. He therefore sent soldiers, and they found the two robbers yet breathing, and they broke their legs ; but finding Jesus dead, they did not touch Him at all, except that a soldier speared Him in the right side, and immediately there came forth blood and water.[2]

And as the *day of the* preparation [3] was drawing towards evening, Joseph, a man well-born and rich, a God-fearing Jew, finding Nicodemus, whose sentiments his foregoing speech had shown, says to him : I know that thou didst love Jesus when living, and didst gladly hear his words, and I saw thee fighting with the Jews on his account. If, then, it seem good to thee, let us go to Pilate, and beg the body of Jesus for burial, because it is a great sin for him to lie unburied. I am afraid, said Nicodemus, lest Pilate should be enraged, and some evil should befall me. But if thou wilt go alone, and beg the dead, and take him, then will I also go with thee, and help thee to do everything necessary for the burial. Nicodemus having thus spoken, Joseph directed his eyes to heaven, and prayed that he might not fail in his request; and he went away to Pilate, and having saluted him, sat down. Then he says to him : I entreat thee, my lord, not to be angry with me, if I shall ask anything contrary to what seems good to your highness. And he said : And what is it that thou askest ? Joseph says : Jesus, the good man whom through hatred the Jews have taken away to crucify, him I entreat that thou give me for burial. Pilate says : And what has happened, that we should deliver to be honoured again the dead body of him against whom evidence of sorcery was brought by his nation, and who was in suspicion of taking the kingdom of Cæsar,

and so was given up by us to death ? And Joseph, weeping and in great grief, fell at the feet of Pilate, saying : My lord, let no hatred fall upon a dead man ; for all the evil that a man has done should perish with him in his death. And I know your highness, how eager thou wast that Jesus should not be crucified, and how much thou saidst to the Jews on his behalf, now in entreaty and again in anger, and at last how thou didst wash thy hands, and declare that thou wouldst by no means take part with those who wished him to be put to death ; for all which *reasons* I entreat thee not to refuse my request. Pilate, therefore, seeing Joseph thus lying, and supplicating, and weeping, raised him up, and said : Go, I grant thee this dead man ; take him, and do whatever thou wilt.

And then Joseph, having thanked Pilate, and kissed his hands and his garments, went forth, rejoicing indeed in heart as having obtained his desire, but carrying tears in his eyes. Thus also, though grieved, he was glad. Accordingly he goes away to Nicodemus, and discloses to him all that had happened. Then, having bought myrrh and aloes a hundred pounds, and a new tomb,[4] they, along with the mother of God and Mary Magdalene and Salome, along with John, and the rest of the women, did what was customary for the body with white linen, and placed it in the tomb.[5]

And the mother of God said, weeping : How am I not to lament thee, my son ? How should I not tear my face with my nails ? This is that, my son, which Symeon the elder foretold to me when I brought thee, an infant of forty days old, into the temple. This is the sword which now goes through my soul.[6] Who shall put a stop to my tears, my sweetest son ? No one at all except thyself alone, if, as thou saidst, thou shalt rise again in three days.

Mary Magdalene said, weeping : Hear, O peoples, tribes, and tongues, and learn to what death the lawless Jews have delivered him who did them ten thousand good deeds. Hear, and be astonished. Who will let these things be heard by all the world ? I shall go alone to Rome, to the Cæsar. I shall show him what evil Pilate hath done in obeying the lawless Jews. Likewise also, Joseph lamented, saying : Ah, me ! sweetest Jesus, most excellent of men, if indeed it be proper to call thee man, who hast wrought such miracles as no man has ever done. How shall I enshroud thee ? How shall I entomb thee ? There should now have been here those whom thou fedst with a few loaves ; for thus should I not have seemed to fail in what is due.

Then Joseph, along with Nicodemus, went

---

[1] Comp. Luke xxiii. 44–49.
[2] John xix. 31–34.
[3] [Or simply, "the Preparation;" comp. Matt. xxvii. 62, and elsewhere, in the Rev. Vers. — R.]

[4] Comp. Matt. xxvii. 60.
[5] John xix. 38–42.
[6] Luke ii. 35.

home ; and likewise also the mother of God, with the women, John [1] also being present with them.

CHAP. 12. — When the Jews were made acquainted with these things done by Joseph and Nicodemus, they were greatly stirred up against them. And the chief priests Annas and Caiaphas sent for Joseph, and said : Why hast thou done this service to Jesus? Joseph says : I know that Jesus was a man just, and true, and good in all respects ; and I know also that you, through hatred, managed to murder him : and therefore I buried him. Then the high priests were enraged, and laid hold of Joseph, and threw him into prison, and said to him : If we had not to-morrow the feast of unleavened bread, to-morrow also should we have put thee, like him, to death ; but being kept in the meantime, early in the morning of the Lord's day [2] thou shalt be given up to death. Thus they spoke, and affixed their seal to the prison, having secured it by fastenings of all sorts.

Thus, therefore, when the Preparation was ended, early on the Sabbath the Jews went away to Pilate, and said to him : My lord, that deceiver said, that after three days he should rise again. Lest, therefore, his disciples should steal him by night, and lead the people astray by such deceit, order his tomb to be guarded. Pilate therefore, upon this, gave them five hundred soldiers, who also sat round the sepulchre so as to guard it, after having put seals upon the stone of the tomb. [3]

The Lord's day, then, having dawned, the chief priests, along with the Jews, called a council, and sent to take Joseph out of the prison, in order to put him to death. But having opened it, they found him not. And they were astonished at this — how, with the doors shut, and the bolts safe, and the seals unbroken, Joseph had disappeared.

CHAP. 13. — And upon this there came up one of the soldiers guarding the tomb, and he said in the synagogue : Learn that Jesus has risen. The Jews say : How? And he said : First there was an earthquake ; then an angel of the Lord, clothed with lightning, came from heaven, and rolled the stone from the tomb, and sat upon it. And from fear of him, all of us soldiers became as dead, and were able neither to flee nor speak. And we heard the angels saying to the women who came there to see the tomb : Be not you afraid, for I know that you seek Jesus. He is not here, but is risen, as He told you before.

Bend down and see the tomb where His body lay ; but go and tell His disciples that He is risen from the dead, and let them go into Galilee, for there shall they find Him. For this reason I tell you this first. [4]

The Jews say to the soldiers : What sort of women were they who came to the tomb? and why did you not lay hold of them? The soldiers say : From the fear and the mere sight of the angel, we were able neither to speak nor move. The Jews said : As the God of Israel liveth, we do not believe a word you say. The soldiers say : Jesus did so great wonders, and you believed not, and are you going to believe us? You say truly that God liveth ; and certainly he whom you crucified truly liveth. But we have heard that you had Joseph shut up in the prison, and that you afterwards opened the doors, and did not find him. Do you then present Joseph, and so we also shall present Jesus. The Jews say : Joseph, that fled from the prison, you will find in Arimathæa, his own country. And the soldiers say : Go you too into Galilee, and you will find Jesus, as the angel said to the women.

At these *words* the Jews were afraid, and said to the soldiers : See that you tell this story to nobody, or all will believe in Jesus. And for this reason they gave them also much money. And the soldiers said : We are afraid lest by any chance Pilate hear that we have taken money, and he will kill us. And the Jews said : Take it ; and we pledge ourselves that we shall speak to Pilate in your defence. Only say that you were asleep, and in your slumber the disciples of Jesus came and stole him from the tomb. The soldiers therefore took the money, and said as they were bid. And up to this day this same lying tale is told among the Jews. [5]

CHAP. 14. — And a few days after there came from Galilee to Jerusalem three men. One of them was a priest, by name Phinees ; the second a Levite, by name Aggai ; and the third a soldier, by name Adas. These came to the chief priests, and said to them and to the people : Jesus, whom you crucified, we have seen in Galilee with his eleven disciples upon the Mount of Olives, teaching them, and saying, Go into all the world, and proclaim the good news ; and whosoever will believe and be baptized shall be saved ; but whosoever will not believe shall be condemned. And having thus spoken, he went up into heaven. [6] And both we and many others of the five hundred [7] besides were looking on.

And when the chief priests and the Jews heard these things, they said to these three : Give glory

---

[1] It is to be observed that John's Gospel is much more frequently quoted in this book than any of the others.
[2] Observe the anachronism.
[3] Matt. xxvii. 62-66.

[4] Matt. xxviii. 1-8.
[5] Matt. xxviii. 11-15.
[6] Mark xvi. 16.
[7] 1 Cor. xv. 6.

to the God of Israel, and repent of these lies that you have told. They answered: As the God of our fathers Abraham, Isaac, and Jacob liveth, we do not lie, but tell you the truth. Then the high priest spoke, and they brought the old *covenant* of the Hebrews out of the temple, and he made them swear, and giving them also money, he sent them into another place, in order that they might not proclaim in Jerusalem the resurrection of Christ.

And when these stories had been heard by all the people, the crowd came together into the temple, and there was a great commotion. For many said: Jesus has risen from the dead, as we hear, and why did you crucify him? And Annas and Caiaphas said: Do not believe, ye Jews, what the soldiers say; and do not believe that they saw an angel coming down from heaven. For we have given money to the soldiers, in order that they should not tell such tales to any one; and thus also have the disciples of Jesus given them money, in order that they should say that Jesus has risen from the dead.

CHAP. 15. — Nicodemus says: O children of the inhabitants of Jerusalem, the prophet Helias went up into the height of heaven with a fiery chariot, and it is nothing incredible if Jesus too has risen; for the prophet Helias was a prototype of Jesus, in order that you, hearing that Jesus has risen, might not disbelieve. I therefore say and advise, that it is befitting that we send soldiers into Galilee, to that place where these men testify that they saw him with his disciples, in order that they may go round about and find him, and that thus we may ask pardon of him for the evil which we have done to him. This proposal pleased them; and they chose soldiers, and sent them away into Galilee. And Jesus indeed they did not find; but they found Joseph in Arimathæa.

When, therefore, the soldiers had returned, the chief priests, having ascertained that Joseph was found, brought the people together, and said: What shall we do to get Joseph to come to us? After deliberating, therefore, they wrote to him a letter to the following effect: — O father Joseph, peace *be* to thee and all thy house, and thy friends! We know that we have offended against God, and against thee His servant. On account of this, we entreat thee to come here to us thy children. For we have wondered much how thou didst escape from the prison, and we say in truth that we had an evil design against thee. But God, seeing that our designs against thee were unjust, has delivered thee out of our hands. But come to us, for thou art the honour of our people.

This letter the Jews sent to Arimathæa, with seven soldiers, friends of Joseph. And they went away and found him; and having respectfully saluted him, as they had been ordered, they gave him the letter. And after receiving it and reading it, he glorified God, and embraced the soldiers; and having set a table, ate and drank with them during all the day and the night.

And on the following day he set out with them to Jerusalem; and the people came forth to meet him, and embraced him. And Nicodemus received him into his own house. And the day after, Annas and Caiaphas, the chief priests, having summoned him to the temple, said to him: Give glory to the God of Israel, and tell us the truth. For we know that thou didst bury Jesus; and on this account we laid hold of thee, and locked thee up in the prison. Thereafter, when we sought to bring thee out to be put to death, we did not find thee, and we were greatly astonished and afraid. Moreover, we prayed to God that we might find thee, and ask thee. Tell us therefore the truth.

Joseph said to them: In the evening of the Preparation, when you secured me in prison, I fell a-praying throughout the whole night, and throughout the whole day of the Sabbath. And at midnight I see the prison-house that four angels lifted it up,[1] holding it by the four corners. And Jesus came in like lightning, and I fell to the ground from fear. Taking hold of me, therefore, by the hand, he raised me, saying, Fear not, Joseph. Thereafter, embracing me, he kissed me, and said, Turn thyself, and see who I am. Turning myself, therefore, and looking, I said, My lord, I know not who thou art. He says, I am Jesus, whom thou didst bury the day before yesterday. I say to him, Show me the tomb, and then I shall believe. He took me, therefore, by the hand, and led me away to the tomb, which had been opened. And seeing the linen and the napkin, and recognising him, I said, Blessed is he that cometh in the name of the Lord;[2] and I adored him. Then taking me by the hand, and accompanied by the angels, he brought me to my house in Arimathæa, and said to me, Sit here for forty days; for I go to my disciples, in order that I may enable them fully to proclaim my resurrection.

CHAP. 16. — When Joseph had thus spoken, the chief priests cried out to the people: We know that Jesus had a father and mother; how can we believe that he is the Christ? One of the Levites answered and said: I know the family of Jesus, noble-minded men,[3] great servants of God, and receiving tithes from the people of the Jews. And I know also Symeon the

---

[1] ἐσίκωσαν, which should be ἐσήκωσαν, is a modern Greek word, the aorist of σηκόνω.
[2] Ps. cxviii. 26; Matt. xxi. 9.
[3] Or, literally, men of good family.

elder, that he received him when he was an infant, and said to him : Now thou sendest away Thy servant, O Lord.

The Jews said : Let us now find the three men that saw him on the Mount of Olives, that we may question them, and learn the truth more accurately. They found them, and brought them before all, and made them swear to tell the truth. And they said : As the God of Israel liveth, we saw Jesus alive on the Mount of Olives, and going up into heaven.

Then Annas and Caiaphas took the three apart, one by one, and questioned them singly in private. They agreed with one another, therefore, and gave, even the three, one account. The chief priests answered, saying : Our Scripture says that every word shall be established by two or three witnesses.[1] Joseph, then, has confessed that he, along with Nicodemus, attended to his body, and buried him, and how it is the truth that he has risen.[2]

---

[1] Deut. xix. 15; Matt. xviii. 16.

[2] This last clause would be better as a question: And how is it the truth that he has risen?

THE GOSPEL OF NICODEMUS

PART II.—THE DESCENT OF CHRIST INTO HELL.

GREEK FORM.

CHAP. 1 (17).—JOSEPH says: And why do you wonder that Jesus has risen? But it is wonderful that He has not risen alone, but that He has also raised many others of the dead, who have appeared in Jerusalem to many.[1] And if you do not know the others, Symeon at least, who received Jesus, and his two sons whom He has raised up — them at least you know. For we buried them not long ago; but now their tombs are seen open *and* empty, and they are alive, and dwelling in Arimathæa. They therefore sent men, and they found their tombs open and empty. Joseph says: Let us go to Arimathæa and find them.

Then rose up the chief priests Annas and Caiaphas, and Joseph, and Nicodemus, and Gamaliel, and others with them, and went away to Arimathæa, and found those whom Joseph spoke of. They made prayer, therefore, and saluted each other. Then they came with them to Jerusalem, and brought them into the synagogue, and secured the doors, and placed in the midst the old *covenant* of the Jews; and the chief priests said to them: We wish you to swear by the God of Israel and Adonai, and so that you tell the truth, how you have risen, and who has raised you from the dead.

The men who had risen having heard this, made upon their faces the sign of the cross, and said to the chief priests: Give us paper and ink and pen. These therefore they brought. And sitting down, they wrote thus:—

CHAP. 2 (18).—O Lord Jesus Christ, the resurrection and the life of the world, grant us grace that we may give an account of Thy resurrection, and Thy miracles which Thou didst in Hades. We then were in Hades, with all

who had fallen asleep since the beginning of the world. And at the hour of midnight there rose a light as if of the sun, and shone into these dark *regions;* and we were all lighted up, and saw each other. And straightway our father Abraham was united with the patriarchs and the prophets, and at the same time they were filled with joy, and said to each other: This light is from a great source of light. The prophet Hesaias, who was there present, said: This light is from the Father, and from the Son, and from the Holy Spirit; about whom I prophesied when yet alive, saying, The land of Zabulon, and the land of Nephthalim, the people that sat in darkness, have seen a great light.[2]

Then there came into the midst another, an ascetic from the desert; and the patriarchs said to him: Who art thou? And he said: I am John, the last of the prophets, who made the paths of the Son of God straight,[3] and proclaimed to the people repentance for the remission of sins.[4] And the Son of God came to me; and I, seeing Him a long way off, said to the people: Behold the Lamb of God, who taketh away the sin of the world.[5] And with my hand I baptized Him in the river Jordan, and I saw like a dove also the Holy Spirit coming upon Him;[6] and I heard also the voice of God, even the Father,[7] thus saying: This is my beloved Son, in whom I am well pleased.[8] And on this account He sent me also to you, to proclaim how the only begotten Son of God is coming here, that whosoever shall believe in Him shall be saved, and whosoever shall not be-

---

[1] Matt. xxvii. 53.

[2] Isa. ix. 1, 2.
[3] Matt. iii. 3.
[4] Mark i. 4.
[5] John i. 29.
[6] Or: and I saw, as it were, a dove and the Holy Spirit, etc.
[7] Or, of the God and Father.
[8] Luke iii. 22.

lieve in Him shall be condemned.[1] On this account I say to you all, in order that when you see Him you all may adore Him, that now only is for you the time of repentance for having adored idols in the vain upper world, and for the sins you have committed, and that this is impossible at any other time.

CHAP. 3 (19). — While John, therefore, was thus teaching those in Hades, the first created and forefather Adam heard, and said to his son Seth : My son, I wish thee to tell the forefathers of the race of men and the prophets where I sent thee, when it fell to my lot to die. And Seth said : Prophets and patriarchs, hear. When my father Adam, the first created, was about to fall once upon a time into death, he sent me to make entreaty to God very close by the gate of paradise, that He would guide me by an angel to the tree of compassion, and that I might take oil and anoint my father, and that he might rise up from his sickness : which thing, therefore, I also did. And after the prayer an angel of the Lord came, and said to me : What, Seth, dost thou ask? Dost thou ask oil which raiseth up the sick, or the tree from which this oil flows, on account of the sickness of thy father? This is not to be found now. Go, therefore, and tell thy father, that after the accomplishing of five thousand five hundred years[2] from the creation of the world, then shall come into the earth the only begotten Son of God, being made man ; and He shall anoint him with this oil, and shall raise him up ; and shall wash clean, with water and with the Holy Spirit, both him and those out of him, and then shall he be healed of every disease ; but now this is impossible.[3]

When the patriarchs and the prophets heard these words, they rejoiced greatly.

CHAP. 4 (20). — And when all were in such joy, came Satan the heir of darkness, and said to Hades : O all-devouring and insatiable, hear my words. There is of the race of the Jews one named Jesus, calling himself the Son of God ; and being a man, by our working with them the Jews have crucified him : and now when he is dead, be ready that we may secure him here. For I know that he is a man, and I heard him also saying, My soul is exceeding sorrowful, even unto death.[4] He has also done me many evils when living with mortals in the upper world. For wherever he found my servants, he persecuted them ; and whatever men I made crooked, blind, lame, lepers, or any such thing, by a single word

he healed them ; and many whom I had got ready to be buried, even these through a single word he brought to life again.

Hades says : And is this *man* so powerful as to do such things by a single word? or if he be so, canst thou withstand him? It seems to me that, if he be so, no one will be able to withstand him. And if thou sayest that thou didst hear him dreading death, he said this mocking thee, and laughing, wishing to seize thee with the strong hand ; and woe, woe to thee, to all eternity !

Satan says : O all-devouring and insatiable Hades, art thou so afraid at hearing of our common enemy? I was not afraid of him, but worked in the Jews, and they crucified him, and gave him also to drink gall with vinegar.[5] Make ready, then, in order that you may lay fast hold of him when he comes.

Hades answered : Heir of darkness, son of destruction, devil, thou hast just now told me that many whom thou hadst made ready to be buried, he brought to life again by a single word. And if he has delivered others from the tomb, how and with what power shall he be laid hold of by us? For I not long ago swallowed down one dead, Lazarus by name ; and not long after, one of the living by a single word dragged him up by force out of my bowels : and I think that it was he of whom thou speakest. If, therefore, we receive him here, I am afraid lest perchance we be in danger even about the rest. For, lo, all those that I have swallowed from eternity I perceive to be in commotion, and I am pained in my belly. And the snatching away of Lazarus beforehand seems to me to be no good sign : for not like a dead body, but like an eagle, he flew out of me ; for so suddenly did the earth throw him out. Wherefore also I adjure even thee, for thy benefit and for mine, not to bring him here ; for I think that he is coming here to raise all the dead. And this I tell thee : by the darkness in which we live, if thou bring him here, not one of the dead will be left behind in it to me.

CHAP. 5 (21). — While Satan and Hades were thus speaking to each other, there was a great voice like thunder, saying : Lift up your gates, O ye rulers ; and be ye lifted up, ye everlasting gates ; and the King of glory shall come in.[6] When Hades heard, he said to Satan : Go forth, if thou art able, and withstand him. Satan therefore went forth to the outside. Then Hades says to his demons : Secure well and strongly the gates of brass and the bars of iron, and attend to my bolts, and stand in order,[7] and see to

---

[1] [Mark xvi. 16.] ; John iii. 18.
[2] 5500 B.C. was the date commonly assigned to the creation. See Clem., *Strom.*, i. ; Theoph. Ant., *ad Autol.*, iii. ; comp. Just., *Apol.*, xxxix.
[3] For this legend, see the Revelation of Moses.
[4] Mark xv. 34.

[5] Matt. xxvii. 34.
[6] Ps. xxiv. 7.
[7] Lit., erect.

everything; for if he come in here, woe will seize us.

The forefathers having heard this, began all to revile him, saying: O all-devouring and insatiable! open, that the King of glory may come in. David the prophet says: Dost thou not know, O blind, that I when living in the world prophesied this saying: Lift up your gates, O ye rulers? Hesaias said: I, foreseeing this by the Holy Spirit, wrote: The dead shall rise up, and those in their tombs shall be raised, and those in the earth shall rejoice.[1] And where, O death, is thy sting? where, O Hades, is thy victory?[2]

There came, then, again a voice saying: Lift up the gates. Hades, hearing the voice the second time, answered as if forsooth he did not know, and says: Who is this King of glory? The angels of the Lord say: The Lord strong and mighty, the Lord mighty in battle.[3] And immediately with these words the brazen gates were shattered, and the iron bars broken, and all the dead who had been bound came out of the prisons, and we with them. And the King of glory came in in the form of a man, and all the dark places of Hades were lighted up.

CHAP. 6 (22). — Immediately Hades cried out: We have been conquered: woe to us! But who art thou, that hast such power and might? and what art thou, who comest here without sin, who art seen to be small and yet of great power, lowly and exalted, the slave and the master, the soldier and the king, who hast power over the dead and the living? Thou wast nailed on the cross, and placed in the tomb; and now thou art free, and hast destroyed all our power. Art thou then the Jesus about whom the chief satrap Satan told us, that through cross and death thou art to inherit the whole world?

Then the King of glory seized the chief satrap Satan by the head, and delivered him to His angels, and said: With iron chains bind his hands, and his feet, and his neck, and his mouth. Then He delivered him to Hades, and said: Take him, and keep him secure till my second appearing.

CHAP. 7 (23). — And Hades receiving Satan, said to him: Beelzebul, heir of fire and punishment, enemy of the saints, through what necessity didst thou bring about that the King of glory should be crucified, so that he should come here and deprive us *of our power*? Turn and see that not one of the dead has been left in me, but all that thou hast gained through the tree of knowledge, all hast thou lost through the tree of the cross: and all thy joy has been turned into grief; and wishing to put to death the King of

glory, thou hast put thyself to death. For, since I have received thee to keep thee safe, by experience shalt thou learn how many evils I shall do unto thee. O arch-devil, the beginning of death, root of sin, end of all evil, what evil didst thou find in Jesus, that thou shouldst compass his destruction? how hast thou dared to do such evil? how hast thou busied thyself to bring down such a man into this darkness, through whom thou hast been deprived of all who have died from eternity?

CHAP. 8 (24). — While Hades was thus discoursing to Satan, the King of glory stretched out His right hand, and took hold of our forefather Adam, and raised him. Then turning also to the rest, He said: Come all with me, as many as have died through the tree which he touched; for, behold, I again raise you all up through the tree of the cross. Thereupon He brought them all out, and our forefather Adam seemed to be filled with joy, and said: I thank Thy majesty, O Lord, that Thou hast brought me up out of the lowest Hades.[4] Likewise also all the prophets and the saints said: We thank Thee, O Christ, Saviour of the world, that Thou hast brought our life up out of destruction.[5]

And after they had thus spoken, the Saviour blessed Adam with the sign of the cross on his forehead, and did this also to the patriarchs, and prophets, and martyrs, and forefathers; and He took them, and sprang up out of Hades. And while He was going, the holy fathers accompanying Him sang praises, saying: Blessed is He that cometh in the name of the Lord:[6] Alleluia; to Him be the glory of all the saints.

CHAP. 9 (25). — And setting out to paradise, He took hold of our forefather Adam by the hand, and delivered him, and all the just, to the archangel Michael. And as they were going into the door of paradise, there met them two old men, to whom the holy fathers said: Who are you, who have not seen death, and have not come down into Hades, but who dwell in paradise in your bodies and your souls? One of them answered, and said: I am Enoch, who was well-pleasing to God, and who was translated hither by Him; and this is Helias the Thesbite; and we are also to live until the end of the world; and then we are to be sent by God to withstand Antichrist, and to be slain by him, and after three days to rise again, and to be snatched up in clouds to meet the Lord.[7]

CHAP. 10 (26). — While they were thus speaking, there came another lowly man, carry-

---

[1] Isa. xxvi. 19, according to the LXX.
[2] Hos. xiii. 14.
[3] Ps. xxiv. 8.

[4] Ps. lxxxvi. 13.
[5] Comp. Ps. ciii. 4.
[6] Ps. cxviii. 26.
[7] 1 Thess. iv. 17; Rev. xi. 3-12.

ing also upon his shoulders a cross, to whom the holy fathers said : Who art thou, who hast the look of a robber ; and what is the cross which thou bearest upon thy shoulders ? He answered : I, as you say, was a robber and a thief in the world, and for these things the Jews laid hold of me, and delivered me to the death of the cross, along with our Lord Jesus Christ. While, then, He was hanging upon the cross, I, seeing the miracles that were done, believed in Him, and entreated Him, and said, Lord, when Thou shalt be King, do not forget me. And immediately He said to me, Amen, amen : to-day, I say unto thee, shalt thou be with me in paradise. Therefore I came to paradise carrying my cross ; and finding the archangel Michael, I said to him, Our Lord Jesus, who has been crucified, has sent me here ; bring me, therefore, to the gate of Eden. And the flaming sword, seeing the sign of the cross, opened to me, and I went in. Then the archangel says to me, Wait a little, for there cometh also the forefather of the race of men, Adam, with the just, that they too may come in. And now, seeing you, I came to meet you.

The saints hearing these things, all cried out with a loud voice : Great is our Lord, and great is His strength.[1]

CHAP. 11 (27).— All these things we saw and heard ; we, the two brothers, who also have been sent by Michael the archangel, and have been ordered to proclaim the resurrection of the Lord, but first to go away to the Jordan and to be baptized. Thither also we have gone, and have been baptized with the rest of the dead who have risen. Thereafter also we came to Jerusalem, and celebrated the passover of the resurrection. But now we are going away, being unable to stay here. And the love of God, even the Father, and the grace of our Lord Jesus Christ, and the communion of the Holy Spirit, be with you all.[2]

Having written these things, and secured the rolls, they gave the half to the chief priests, and the half to Joseph and Nicodemus. And they immediately disappeared : to the glory of our Lord Jesus Christ. Amen.

[1] Ps. cxlvii. 5.
[2] 2 Cor. xiii. 15.

THE GOSPEL OF NICODEMUS

PART I.—ACTS OF PILATE

LATIN FORM.

I ÆNEAS was at first a protector of the Hebrews, and follower of the law; then the grace of the Saviour and His great gift took possession of me. I recognised Christ Jesus in holy Scripture; I came to Him, and embraced His faith, so that I might become worthy of His holy baptism. First of all I searched for the memoirs written in those times about our Lord Jesus Christ, which the Jews published in the age of Pontius Pilate, and we found them in Hebrew writings, drawn up in the age of the Lord Jesus Christ; and I translated them into the language of the Gentiles, in the reign of the eminent Theodosius, who was fulfilling his seventeenth consulship, and of Valentinian, consul for the fifth time in the ninth indiction. Whosoever of you read this book, and transfer it to other copies, remember me, and pray for me, Æneas, least of the servants of God, that He be merciful to me, and pardon my sins which I have committed against Him. Peace be to all who shall read these, and to all their house, for ever! Amen.

Now it came to pass, in the nineteenth year of the reign of Tiberius Cæsar, emperor of the Romans, and of Herod, son of Herod king of Galilee, in the nineteenth year of his rule, on the eighth day before the kalends of April, which is the twenty-fifth day of the month of March, in the consulship of Rufinus and Rubellio, in the fourth year of the 202d Olympiad, under the rule of Joseph and Caiaphas, priests of the Jews: the things done by the chief priests and the rest of the Jews, which Nicodemus recorded after the cross and passion of the Lord, Nicodemus himself committed to Hebrew letters.

CHAP. I. — Annas and Caiaphas, Summas and Datam, Gamaliel, Judas, Levi, Neptalim, Alexarder and Jairus, and the rest of the Jews, came to Pilate, accusing the Lord Jesus Christ of many things, and saying: We know him *to be* the son of Joseph the carpenter, born of Mary; and he says that he is the Son of God, and a king. Not only so, but he also breaks the Sabbath, and wishes to do away with the law of our fathers. Pilate says: What is it that he does, and wishes to destroy the law? The Jews say: We have a law, not to heal any one on the Sabbath; but he, by evil arts, heals on the Sabbath the lame and the hunchbacked, the blind, the palsied, the lepers, and the demoniacs. Pilate says to them: By what evil arts? They say to him: He is a sorcerer; and by Beelzebub, prince of the demons, he casts out demons, and they are all subject to him. Pilate says to them: It is not in an unclean spirit to cast out demons, but in the god of Scolapius.

The Jews say: We pray thy majesty to set him before thy tribunal to be heard. Pilate, calling the Jews to him, says to them: How can I, seeing that I am a governor,[1] hear a king? They say to him: We do not say that he is a king, but he himself says he is. And Pilate, calling a runner, says to him: Let Jesus be brought in with kindness. And the runner, going out and recognising Him, adored Him, and spread on the ground the cloak which he carried in his hand, saying: My lord, walk upon this, and come in, because the governor calls thee. But the Jews, seeing what the runner did, cried out against Pilate, saying: Why didst not thou make him come in by the voice of a crier, but by a runner? for the runner, too, seeing him, has adored him, and has spread out before him on the ground the cloak which he held in his hand, and has said to him: My lord, the governor calls thee.

---

[1] The word in the original is the general term *præses*, which the Vulgate uses for procurator.

And Pilate, calling the runner, says to him: Wherefore hast thou done this, and honoured Jesus, who is called Christ? The runner says to him: When thou didst send me into Jerusalem to Alexander, I saw him sitting upon an ass, and the children of the Hebrews breaking branches from the trees, strewing them in the way; and others held branches in their hands; and others spread their garments in the way, shouting and saying, Save, therefore, Thou who art in the highest; blessed *is He* that cometh in the name of the Lord!

The Jews cried out, saying against the runner: The children of the Hebrews indeed cried out in Hebrew. How canst thou, a Gentile, know this? The runner says to them: I asked one of the Jews, and said, What is it that they cry out in Hebrew? and he explained to me. Pilate says to them: And how did they cry out in Hebrew? The Jews said: Osanna in the highest! Pilate says to them: What is the meaning of Osanna in the highest? They say to him: Save us, Thou who art in the highest. Pilate says to them: If you yourselves bear witness to the terms and words in which the children cried out, in what has the runner sinned? And they were silent. The governor says to the runner: Go out, and lead him in, in whatever way thou wilt. And the runner, going forth, did after the same form as before, and says to Jesus: My lord, go in, because the governor calls thee.

As Jesus, then, was going in, and the standard-bearers bearing the standards, the heads of the standards were bowed of themselves, and adored Jesus. And the Jews, seeing the standards, how they bowed themselves and adored Jesus, cried out the more against the standard-bearers. And Pilate says to the Jews: Do you not wonder at the way in which the standards have bowed themselves and adored Jesus? The Jews say to Pilate: We saw how the men carrying the standards bowed themselves and adored Jesus. And the governor, calling the standard-bearers, says to them: Why have you so done? They say to Pilate: We are Gentile men, and slaves of the temples: how had we[1] to adore him? for when we were holding the figures,[2] they themselves bowed and adored him.

Pilate says to the chiefs of the synagogue and the elders of the people: Choose ye men powerful and strong, and let them hold the standards, and let us see whether they will bow of themselves. And the elders of the Jews, taking twelve men very strong and powerful, made them hold the standards, six and six; and they stood before the governor's tribunal. Pilate says to the runner: Take out Jesus outside of the prætorium,

and bring him in again, in whatever way thou wilt. And Jesus and the runner went outside of the prætorium. And Pilate, calling those who had formerly held the standards, said to them: By the health of Cæsar, if the standards do not bow themselves when Jesus comes in, I will cut off your heads. And the governor ordered Jesus to come in a second time. And the runner did after the same form as before, and besought Jesus much that He would go up and walk upon his cloak. And He walked upon it, and went in. And as Jesus was going in, immediately the standards bowed themselves, and adored Jesus.

CHAP. 2. — And Pilate seeing, fear seized him, and immediately he wished to rise from the tribunal. And while he was thinking of this, *viz.*, to rise and go away, his wife sent to him, saying: Have nothing to do with that just man,[3] for I have suffered much on account of him this night. And Pilate, calling the Jews, said to them: Ye know that my wife is a worshipper of God, and in Judaism thinks rather with you. The Jews say to him: So it is, and we know. Pilate says to them: Lo, my wife has sent to me, saying: Have nothing to do with that just man,[3] for I have suffered much on account of him this night. And the Jews answering, said to Pilate: Did we not say to thee that he is a magician? Lo, he has sent a vision of dreams to thy wife.

Pilate called Jesus, and said to him: What is it that these witness against thee, and sayest thou nothing to them? And Jesus answered: If they had not the power, they would not speak. Every one has power over his own mouth to say good and evil; let them see[4] *to it.*

And the elders of the Jews answering, say to Jesus: What shall we see? First, that thou wast born of fornication; second, that at thy birth in Bethlehem there took place a massacre of infants; third, that thy father Joseph and thy mother Mary fled into Egypt, because they had no confidence in the people.

Some of the bystanders, kind *men* of the Jews, say: We say that he was not born of fornication; but we know that Mary was espoused to Joseph, and that he was not born of fornication. Pilate says to the Jews who said that he was of fornication: This speech of yours is not true, seeing that the betrothal took place, as these of your nation say. Annas and Caiaphas say to Pilate: We with all the multitude say that he was born of fornication, and that he is a magician; but these are proselytes, and his disciples. And Pilate, calling Annas and Caiaphas, says to them: What are proselytes? They say to him: They have been born sons of the Ger-

---

[1] i.e., was it possible for us.
[2] *Vultus.* He seems to have read προσωπα, and not προτομαι, as in the Greek.

[3] Lit., nothing to thee and that just man.
[4] Lit., they will see.

tiles, and then have become Jews. Then answered those who testified that Jesus was not born of fornication, Lazarus and Asterius, Antonius and James, Annes and Azaras, Samuel and Isaac, Finees and Crispus, Agrippa and Judas: We were not born proselytes, but are sons of the Jews, and we speak the truth; for we were present at the betrothal of Mary.

And Pilate, calling to him those twelve men who proved that Jesus had not been born of fornication, said to them: I adjure you by the health of Cæsar, tell me if it be true that Jesus was not born of fornication. They say to Pilate: We have a law not to swear, because it is a sin; but let them swear by the health of Cæsar that it is not as we say, and we are worthy of death. Then said Pilate to Annas and Caiaphas: Answer you nothing to those things which these testify? Annas and Caiaphas say to Pilate: Those twelve are believed that he is not born of fornication; we — all the people — cry out that he was born of fornication, and is a magician, and says that he himself is the Son of God and a king, and we are not believed.

And Pilate ordered all the multitude to go outside, except the twelve men who said that He was not born of fornication, and ordered to separate Jesus from them. And Pilate says to them: For what reason do the Jews wish to put Jesus to death? And they say to him: They are angry because he heals on the Sabbath. Pilate said: For a good work do they wish to put him to death? They say to him: Yes, my lord.

CHAP. 3. — Pilate, filled with fury, went forth outside of the prætorium, and says to them: I take the sun to witness that I find in this man not even one fault. The Jews answered and said to the governor: If he were not an evil-doer, we should never have delivered him to thee. Pilate says to them: Take him, and judge him according to your law. The Jews answered: It is not permitted to us to put any one to death. Pilate says to them: Has God said to you not to put any one to death? has He therefore said to me that I am to kill?

Pilate, having again gone into the prætorium, called Jesus to him privately, and said to Him: Art thou the king of the Jews? Jesus answered Pilate: Speakest thou this of thyself, or have others said *it* to thee of me? Pilate answered: Am I a Jew? Thy nation and the chief priests have delivered thee to me. What hast thou done? Jesus answering, said: My kingdom is not of this world. If my kingdom were of this world, my servants would assuredly strive that I should not be delivered to the Jews; but now my kingdom is not from hence. Pilate said to Him: Art thou then a king? Jesus said

to him: Thou sayest that I am a king. For I for this was born, and for this have I come, that I should bear witness to the truth; and every one who is of the truth hears my voice. Pilate says to him: What is truth? Jesus says: Truth is from heaven. Pilate says: Is not there truth upon earth? Jesus says to Pilate: Notice how the truth-speaking are judged by those who have power upon earth.

CHAP. 4. — Pilate therefore, leaving Jesus within the prætorium, went out to the Jews, and says to them: I find not even one fault in him. The Jews say to him: He said, I can destroy that temple, and in three days raise it again. Pilate said to them: What temple? The Jews say to him: *The temple* which Solomon built in forty and six years; and he says *that he can* destroy and build it in three days. Pilate says to them: I am innocent of the blood of this man; see ye *to it.* The Jews say to him: His blood *be* upon us, and upon our children.

And Pilate, calling the elders and priests and Levites, says to them privately: Do not do so; for in nothing, though you accuse him, do I find him deserving of death, not even about the healing and the breaking of the Sabbath. The priests and Levites and elders say: Tell us, if any one blaspheme Cæsar, is he deserving of death or not? Pilate says to them: He deserves to die. The Jews answered him: How much more is he who has blasphemed God deserving to die!

And the governor ordered the Jews to go outside of the prætorium; and calling Jesus, said to Him: What am I to do to thee? Jesus says to Pilate: As it has been given *thee.* Pilate says: How has it been given? Jesus says: Moses and the prophets made proclamation of my death and resurrection. And the Jews, hearing this, say to Pilate: Why do you desire any more to hear blasphemy? And Pilate said: If this speech is blasphemous, do you take him, and lead him to your synagogue, and judge him according to your law. The Jews say to Pilate: Our law holds, If a man have sinned against a man, he is worthy to receive forty less one; but he who has blasphemed against God, to be stoned.

Pilate says to them: Then judge him according to your law. The Jews say to Pilate: We wish that he be crucified. Pilate says to them: He does not deserve to be crucified.

And the governor, looking upon the people of the Jews standing round, saw very many of the Jews weeping, and said: All the multitude does not wish him to die. The elders say to Pilate: And for this reason have we come — the whole multitude — that he should die. Pilate said to the Jews: What has he done that he should die? They say: Because he said that he was the Son of God, and a king.

CHAP. 5. — But one Nicodemus, a Jew, stood before the governor, and said: I entreat, mercifully allow me to say a few words. Pilate says to him: Say on. Nicodemus says: I said to the elders and the priests and the Levites, and to all the multitude of the Jews, in the synagogue, What have you *to do* with this man? This man does many wonders and signs, which no one of men has done or can do. Let him go, and do not devise any evil against him: if the signs which he does are of God, they will stand; but if of men, they will come to nothing. For Moses also, being sent by God into Egypt, did many signs, which God told him to do before Pharaoh king of Egypt. And the sorcerers Jamnes and Mambres were there healing, and they did, they also, the signs which Moses did, but not all; and the Egyptians deemed them as gods, Jamnes and Mambres. And since the signs which they did were not of God, they perished, both they and those who believed in them. And now let this man go, for he is not deserving of death.

The Jews say to Nicodemus: Thou hast become his disciple, and takest his part.[1] Nicodemus says to them: Has the governor also become his disciple, and does he take his part? Has not Cæsar set him over that dignity? And the Jews were raging and gnashing with their teeth against Nicodemus. Pilate says to them: Why do you gnash with your teeth against him, *when you are* hearing the truth? The Jews say to Nicodemus: Mayst thou receive his truth, and a portion with him! Nicodemus says: Amen, amen, amen; may I receive *it*, as you have said!

CHAP. 6. — And of the Jews a certain other one, starting up, asks the governor that he might say a word. The governor says: What thou wishest to say, say. And he said: For thirty-eight years I lay in infirmity in my bed in very grievous pain. And at the coming of Jesus, many demoniacs, and *persons* held down by divers infirmities, were healed by him. And some young men had pity on me; and carrying me in my bed, laid me before him. And Jesus, seeing, had pity on me, and said the word to me, Take up thy bed, and walk. And immediately I was made whole; I took up my bed, and walked. The Jews say to Pilate: Ask him what was the day on which he was healed. He said: The Sabbath. The Jews say: Have we not so informed thee, that on the Sabbath he heals, and drives out demons?

And a certain other Jew starting up, said: I

was born blind; I heard a voice, and saw no man. And as Jesus was passing by, I cried out with a loud voice, Have pity upon me, thou son of David. And he had pity upon me, and laid his hands upon my eyes, and I saw immediately. And another Jew starting up, said: I was hunchbacked, and he straightened me with a word. And another said: I was leprous, and he healed me with a word.

CHAP. 7. — And also a certain woman, Veronica by name, from afar off cried out to the governor: I was flowing with blood for twelve years; and I touched the fringe of his garment, and immediately the flowing of my blood stopped. The Jews say: We have a law, that a woman does not come to bear witness.

CHAP. 8. — And certain others, a multitude of men and women, cried out, saying: That man is a prophet, and the demons are subject to him. Pilate says to those who said the demons are subject to him: And your masters, why are they not subject to him? They say to Pilate: We do not know. And others said to Pilate: He raised up dead Lazarus from the tomb after four days. The governor, hearing this, said trembling to all the multitude of the Jews: Why do you wish to shed innocent blood?

CHAP. 9. — And Pilate, calling Nicodemus and the twelve men who said that He was not born of fornication, says to them: What am I to do, seeing that there is a sedition among the people? They say to him: We do not know; let them see to it. Again Pilate, calling all the multitude of the Jews, said: You know that you have a custom during the day of unleavened bread, that I should release to you one that is bound. I have a notable one bound in the prison, a murderer who is called Barabbas, and Jesus who is called Christ, in whom I find no cause of death. Whom do you wish that I should release unto you? And they all cried out, saying: Release unto us Barabbas. Pilate says to them: What, then, am I to do with Jesus who is called Christ? They all say: Let him be crucified. Again the Jews said: Thou art no friend of Cæsar's if thou release this man, for he called himself the Son of God, and a king; unless, perhaps, thou wishest this man to be king, and not Cæsar.

Then, filled with fury, Pilate said to them: Always has your nation been seditious, and always have you been opposed to those who were for you. The Jews answered: Who are for us? Pilate says to them: Your God, — who rescued you from the hard slavery of the Egyptians, and led you forth out of Egypt through the sea as if through dry land, and fed you in the desert with manna and quail, and brought water to you out

---

[1] Lit., makest a word for him.

of the rock, and gave you to drink, and gave you a law ; and in all these things you provoked your God, and sought for yourselves a god, a molten calf. And you exasperated your God, and He wished to slay you ; and Moses made supplication for you, that ye should not die. And now you say that I hate the king.

And rising up from the tribunal, he wished to go outside. And the Jews cried out, and said to him : We know that Cæsar is king, and not Jesus. For the Magi also presented gifts to him as to a king ; and Herod, hearing from the Magi that a king was born, wished to slay him. But when this was known, his father Joseph took him and his mother, and fled into Egypt ; and Herod hearing, destroyed the infants of the Jews which were born in Bethlehem.

Pilate, hearing those words, was afraid. And silence being made among the people, who were crying out, Pilate said : This, then, is he whom Herod sought? They say to him : It is he. And taking water, Pilate washed his hands in presence of the people, saying : I am innocent of the blood of this just man ; see ye to it. Again the Jews cried out, saying : His blood *be* upon us, and upon our children.

Then Pilate ordered the veil to be loosened,[1] and said to Jesus : Thine own nation have brought charges against thee as a king ; and therefore I have sentenced thee first to be scourged on account of the statutes of the emperors, and then to be crucified on a cross.

CHAP. 10. — And when Jesus was scourged, he delivered Him to the Jews to be crucified, and two robbers with Him ; one by name Dismas, and the other by name Gestas. And when they came to the place, they stripped Him of His garments, and girt Him about with a linen cloth, and put a crown of thorns upon His head. Likewise also they hanged the two robbers with Him, Dismas on the right and Gestas on the left. And Jesus said : Father, forgive them, for they know not what they do. And the soldiers parted His garments among them. And the people stood waiting ; and their chief priests and judges mocked Him, saying among themselves : He saved others, now let him save himself ; if he is the Son of God, let him come down from the cross. And the soldiers mocked Him, falling prostrate[2] before Him, and offering vinegar with gall, and saying : If thou art the King of the Jews, set thyself free.

And Pilate, after sentence, ordered a title to be written in Hebrew, Greek, and Latin letters, according to what the Jews said : This is the King of the Jews.

And one of the robbers *who were* hanged,

by name Gestas, said to Him : If thou art the Christ, free thyself and us. And Dismas answering, rebuked him, saying : Dost not even thou fear God, who art in this condemnation? for we justly and deservedly have received those things which we endure ; but He has done no evil. And he kept saying to Jesus : Remember me, Lord, in Thy kingdom. And Jesus said to him : Verily I say unto thee, that to-day shalt thou be with me in paradise.

CHAP. 11. — And it was about the sixth hour, and there was darkness over the whole earth ; and the sun was obscured, and the veil of the temple was rent in the midst. And crying out with a loud voice, He said : Father, into Thy hands I commend my spirit. And thus saying, He gave up the ghost. And the centurion, seeing what was done, glorified God, saying : This was a just man. And all the people who were present at that spectacle, seeing what was done, beating their breasts, returned.

And the centurion reported to the governor what was done. And the governor and his wife hearing, were very sorrowful, and neither ate nor drank that day. And Pilate, calling together the Jews, said to them : Have you seen what has been done? And they said to the governor : There has been an eclipse of the sun, as is usual.

And his acquaintances also stood afar off, and the women who had followed Him from Galilee, seeing these things. And lo, a certain man, by name Joseph, holding office, a man good and just, who did not consent to their counsels nor their deeds, from Arimathæa,[3] a city of the Jews, waiting, he also, for the kingdom of God, went to Pilate and begged the body of Jesus. And taking Him down from the cross, he wrapped Him in clean linen, and laid Him in his own new tomb, in which no one had been laid.

CHAP. 12. — And the Jews, hearing that Joseph had begged the body of Jesus, sought for him ; and those twelve men who had said that He was not born of fornication, and Nicodemus, and many others, who had stood before Pilate and declared His good works. And all of them being hid, Nicodemus alone appeared to them, because he was a chief man of the Jews ; and he says to them : How have ye come into the synagogue? The Jews say to him : And thou, how hast thou come into the synagogue, seeing that thou consentest with him? May his portion be with thee in the world to come ! Nicodemus said : Amen, amen, amen. Likewise also Joseph, coming forth, said to them : Why are you enraged against me because I begged the body of Jesus? Lo, I have laid him in my own new

---

[1] See note 5, p. 420.
[2] *Procidentes;* but this, according to the Greek, should be *procedentes,* coming before Him.

[3] [The Latin has *Arimathia ;* and in the next clause there are variations in the MSS. — R.]

tomb, wrapping him in clean linen; and I have rolled a stone to the door of the cave. And ye have not acted well against a just man, since you have not borne in mind how you crucified him, and pierced him with a lance. The Jews therefore, laying hold of Joseph, ordered him to be imprisoned because of the Sabbath-day; and they say to him: Know that the hour compels us not to do anything against thee, because the Sabbath is dawning. But understand that thou art worthy not even of burial, but we will give thy flesh to the birds of the air and the beasts of the earth. Joseph says to them: That is the speech of proud Goliath, who reviled the living God against holy David. And God hath said, Vengeance is mine; I will repay, saith the Lord. And Pilate, intercepted[1] in his heart, took water, and washed his hands before the sun, saying, I am innocent of the blood of this just man; see ye to it. And you answered and said to Pilate, His blood be upon us, and upon our children. And now I fear that some time or other the wrath of God will come upon you and your childen, as you have said. And the Jews, hearing this, were embittered in heart; and taking Joseph, shut him up in a house where there was no window, and set guards at the gates, and sealed the gate where Joseph had been shut up.

And on the Sabbath morning they took counsel with the priests and the Levites, that they should all be assembled after the Sabbath-day. And awaking at dawn, all the multitude in the synagogue took counsel by what death they should slay him. And when the assembly was sitting, they ordered him to be brought with much indignity; and opening the gate, they found him not. All the people therefore were in terror, and wondered with exceeding astonishment, because they found the seals sealed, and because Caiaphas had the keys. And no longer did they dare to lay hand upon those who spoke before Pilate in Jesus' defence.

CHAP. 13. — And while they were sitting in the synagogue, and recriminating about Joseph, there came certain of the guards whom they had asked from Pilate to guard the sepulchre of Jesus, lest His disciples coming should steal Him. And they reported, saying to the rulers of the synagogue, and the priests and the Levites, what had happened: how there had happened a great earthquake, and we saw how an angel of the Lord came down from heaven, and rolled away the stone from the door of the tomb, and sat upon it; and his countenance was like lightning, and his raiment like snow. And for fear, we became as dead. And we heard the voice of the angel speaking to the women who had come to the sepulchre, and saying, Be not ye afraid; for I know that ye seek Jesus who was crucified: He is not here; He has risen, as He said: come and see the place where the Lord was laid. And go immediately and tell His disciples that He has risen from the dead, and will go before you into Galilee, as He said to you.

The Jews say: To what women was he speaking? The soldiers say: We do not know who the women were. The Jews say: At what hour was it? The guards say: At midnight. The Jews say: And why did you not detain them? The guards say: We became as dead from fear of the angel, not hoping now to see the light of day; and how could we detain them? The Jews says: *As* the Lord God liveth, we do not believe you. And the guards said to the Jews: You have seen so great signs in that man, and have not believed; and how can you believe us, that the Lord lives? For well have ye sworn that the Lord Jesus Christ lives. Again the guards say to the Jews: We have heard that you have shut up Joseph, who begged the body of Jesus, in the prison, and have sealed it with your rings; and on opening, that you have not found him. Give us Joseph, then, and we shall give you Jesus Christ. The Jews said: Joseph has gone to Arimathea, his own city. The guards say to the Jews: And Jesus, as we have heard from the angel, is in Galilee.

And the Jews, hearing these sayings, feared exceedingly, saying: Lest at some time or other this saying be heard, and all believe in Jesus. And the Jews, taking counsel among themselves, brought forth a sufficient number of silver pieces, and gave to the soldiers, saying: Say that, while we slept, his disciples came and stole him. And if this be heard by the governor, we shall persuade[2] him, and make you secure. And the soldiers, taking *the money*, said as they were advised by the Jews; and their saying was spread abroad among all.

CHAP. 14. — And Finees a certain priest, and Addas a teacher, and Egias a Levite, coming down from Galilee to Jerusalem, reported to the rulers of the synagogue, and the priests and the Levites, how they had seen Jesus sitting, and his disciples with him, on the Mount of Olivet, which is called Mambre or Malech. And he said to his disciples: Go into all the world, and declare to every creature the Gospel of the kingdom of God. He who believeth and is baptized shall be saved; but he who believeth not shall be condemned. And these signs shall follow them who believe: In my name shall they cast out demons; they shall speak in new tongues; they

---

[1] Another reading is *compunctus*, pricked. The reading in the text, *obstructus*, is a curious mistranslation of the word in the Greek, περιτετμημένος, cut away all round, i.e., *circumcised;* or, by an obvious transition, *hemmed in* — the meaning adopted in the version before us.

[2] *Confirmabimus.*

shall take up serpents; and if they have drunk any deadly thing, it shall not hurt them; they shall lay hands upon the sick, and they shall be well. And as Jesus was thus speaking to his disciples, we saw him taken up into heaven.[1]

The priests and the Levites and the elders say to them: Give glory to the God of Israel, and give confession to Him, whether you have both heard and seen those things which you have related. Those who had made the report say: As the Lord God of our fathers liveth, the God of Abraham, and the God of Isaac, and the God of Jacob, we have heard and seen. The Jews say to them: Have you come for this — to tell us? or have you come to give prayer to God? They said: We have come to give prayer to God. The elders and chief priests and Levites say to them: And if you have come to give prayer to God, why have you murmured before all the people about that foolish tale? Finees the priest, and Addas the teacher, and Egias the Levite, say to the rulers of the synagogue, and the priests and the Levites: If those words which we have spoken, which we have seen and heard, be sin, behold, we are in your presence; do unto us according to that which is good in your eyes. And they, taking the law, adjured them to report the words to no one thereafter. And they gave them to eat and drink, and put them outside of the city, giving them silver and pieces, and three men with them, who should conduct them as far as Galilee.

Then the Jews took counsel among themselves when those men had gone up into Galilee; and the rulers of the synagogue shut themselves in, and were cut up[2] with great fury, saying: What sign is this which hath come to pass in Israel? And Annas and Caiaphas say: Why are your souls sorrowful? Are we to believe the soldiers, that an angel of the Lord came down from heaven, and rolled away the stone from the door of the tomb? *No;* but that his disciples have given much gold to those who were guarding the sepulchre, and have taken Jesus away, and have taught them thus to say: Say ye that an angel of the Lord came down from heaven, and rolled away the stone from the door of the tomb. Do you not know that it is unlawful for Jews to believe foreigners in a single word, knowing that these same who received sufficient gold from us have said as we taught them?

CHAP. 15. — And Nicodemus rising up, stood in the midst of the counsel, and said: You have said rightly. And are not the men who have come down from Galilee God-fearing, men of peace, hating a lie? And they recounted with an oath, how "we saw Jesus sitting on Mount Mambre with his disciples, and he taught them in our hearing," and that they saw him taken up into heaven. And no one asked them this: How he was taken up into heaven. And, as the writing of the holy book teaches us, holy Elias too was taken up into heaven, and Elisæus cried out with a loud voice, and Elias threw his sheepskin over Elisæus; and again Elisæus threw that sheepskin over the Jordan, and went over and came to Jericho. And the sons of the prophets met him, and said to Elisæus, Where is thy master Elias? And he said, He has been taken up into heaven. And they said to Elisæus, Has a spirit snatched him away, and thrown him upon one of the mountains? But rather let us take our boys[3] with us and seek him. And they persuaded Elisæus, and he went with them. And they sought him for three days and three nights, and found him not, because he was taken up. And now, men, hear me, and let us send into all Israel, and see lest Jesus can have been taken up somewhere or other, and thrown upon one of the mountains. And that saying pleased all. And they sent to all the mountains of Israel to seek Jesus, and they found Him not; but they found Joseph of Arimathæa, and no one dared to lay hold of him.

And they reported to the elders and priests and Levites: We have gone round all the mountains of Israel, and not found Jesus; but we have found Joseph in Arimathæa. And hearing of Joseph, they rejoiced, and gave glory to the God of Israel. And the rulers of the synagogue, and the priests and the Levites, taking counsel in what manner they should send to Joseph, took paper, and wrote to Joseph: —

Peace to thee and all that is thine! We know that we have sinned against God, and against thee; and thou hast prayed to the God of Israel, and He has delivered thee out of our hands. And now deign to come to thy fathers and thy children, because we have been vehemently grieved. We have all sought for thee — we who opened the door, and found thee not. We know that we counselled evil counsel against thee; but the Lord hath supplanted our counsel against thee. Thou art worthy to be honoured, father Joseph, by all the people.

And they chose out of all Israel seven men friendly to Joseph, whom also Joseph knew to be friendly; and the rulers of the synagogue and the priests and the Levites say to them: See, if he take the letter and read it, for certain he will come with you to us; but if he do not read it, you may know that he is ill-disposed toward us, and, saluting him in peace, return to us. And blessing them, they sent them away. And they came to Arimathæa to Joseph, and

---

[1] [Comp. Mark xvi. 15-19; from the disputed ending of that Gospel. — R.]

[2] *Concidebantur*, a mistranslation from considering ἐκόπτοντο as passive, *they were cut*, instead of middle, *they beat their breasts.*

[3] i.e., servants.

adored him on their face upon the ground, and said : Peace to thee and all thine ! And Joseph said : Peace to you, and to all the people of Israel ! And they gave him the roll of the letter. And Joseph took and read it, and rolled up the letter, and blessed God, and said : Blessed *be* the Lord God, who hath delivered Israel from shedding innocent blood ; and blessed *be* God, who sent His angel, and covered me under his wings. And he kissed them, and set a table for them ; and they ate and drank, and slept there.

And they rose in the morning ; and Joseph saddled his ass, and travelled with them, and they came into the holy city Jerusalem. And there met them all the people, crying out, and saying : Peace *be* in thy coming in, father Joseph ! To whom he answered and said : The peace of the Lord *be* upon all the people ! And they all kissed him. And they prayed with Joseph, and were terrified at the sight of him. And Nicodemus took him into his house, and made a great feast, and called Annas and Caiaphas, and the elders and chief priests and Levites, to his house. And making merry, and eating and drinking with Joseph, they blessed God, and went every one to his own house. And Joseph remained in the house of Nicodemus.

And on the next day, which is the preparation, the priests and the rulers of the synagogue and the Levites rose early, and came to the house of Nicodemus. And Nicodemus met them, and said to them : Peace to you ! And they said to him : Peace to thee and Joseph, and to thy house and Joseph's house ! And Nicodemus brought them into his house. And the council sat ; and Joseph sat between Annas and Caiaphas, and no one dared to say a word. And Joseph said to them : Why have you called me ? And they made signs with their eyes to Nicodemus, that he should speak with Joseph. And Nicodemus, opening his mouth, said : Father Joseph, thou knowest that the reverend teachers, priests, and Levites seek to hear a word from thee. And Joseph said : Ask. And Annas and Caiaphas, taking up the law, adjured Joseph, saying : Give glory to the God of Israel, and give confession to Him, that thou wilt not hide any word [1] from us. And they said to him : With grief were we grieved that thou didst beg the body of Jesus, and wrap it in clean linen, and lay it in a tomb. Therefore we shut thee up in a house where there was no window, and put a lock and a seal on the gate ; and on the first day of the week we opened the gates, and found thee not. We were therefore exceedingly grieved, and astonishment came

over all the people of God. And therefore hast thou been sent for ; and now tell us what has happened.

Then said Joseph : On the day of the Preparation, about the tenth hour, you shut me in, and I remained there the whole Sabbath in full. And when midnight came, as I was standing and praying, the house where you shut me in was hung up by the four corners, and there was a flashing of light in mine eyes. And I fell to the ground trembling. Then some one lifted me up from the place where I had fallen, and poured over me an abundance of water from the head even to the feet, and put round my nostrils the odour of a wonderful ointment, and rubbed my face with the water itself, as if washing me, and kissed me, and said to me, Joseph, fear not ; but open thine eyes, and see who it is that speaks to thee. And looking, I saw Jesus ; and being terrified, I thought it was a phantom. And with prayer and the commandments I spoke to him, and he spoke with me. And I said to him : Art thou Rabbi Elias ? And he said to me : I am not Elias. And I said : Who art thou, my lord ? And he said to me : I am Jesus, whose body thou didst beg from Pilate, and wrap in clean linen ; and thou didst lay a napkin on my face, and didst lay me in thy new tomb, and roll a stone to the door of the tomb. Then I said to him that was speaking to me : Show me, Lord, where I laid thee. And he led me, and showed me the place where I laid him, and the linen which I had put on him, and the napkin which I had wrapped upon his face ; and I knew that it was Jesus. And he took hold of me with his hand, and put me in the midst of my house though the gates were shut, and put me in my bed, and said to me : Peace to thee ! And he kissed me, and said to me : For forty days go not out of thy house ; for, lo, I go to my brethren into Galilee.

CHAP. 16. — And the rulers of the synagogue, and the priests and the Levites, hearing these words from Joseph, became as it were dead, and fell to the ground, and fasted until the ninth hour. And Joseph and Nicodemus entreated them, saying : Arise and stand upon your feet, and taste bread, and comfort your souls, seeing that to-morrow is the Sabbath of the Lord. And they arose, and entreated the Lord, and ate and drank, and went every man to his own house.

And on the Sabbath the teachers and doctors sat questioning each other, and saying : What is this wrath that has come upon us ? because we know his father and mother. Levi the teacher said : I know that his parents fear God, and never depart from prayer, and give tithes thrice a-year. And when Jesus was born, his parents

---

[1] The Greek ῥῆμα means *thing* as well as *word*.

brought him up to this place, and gave to God sacrifices and burnt-offerings. And assuredly the great teacher Simeon took him into his arms, saying: Now Thou sendest away Thy servant, O Lord, according to Thy word, in peace; for mine eyes have seen Thy salvation, which Thou hast prepared before the face of all peoples, a light for the revealing of the nations, and the glory of Thy people Israel. And he blessed Mary his mother, and said, I make an announcement to thee concerning this child. And Mary said, Well, my lord.[1] And Simeon said, Well. And he said again, Lo, he has been set for the fall and rising again of many in Israel, and for a sign which shall be spoken against; and a sword shall pierce thine own soul, that the thoughts of many hearts may be revealed.

And the Jews said to Levi: And how knowest thou these things? Levi says: Do you not know that from him I learned the law? They of the council say: We wish to see thy father. And they searched out his father, and got information; for he said: Why did you not believe my son? The blessed and just Simeon taught him the law. The council says to Rabbi Levi: The saying which thou hast spoken is true. The chief priests and rulers of the synagogue, and Levites, said to each other: Come, let us send into Galilee to the three men who came hither and gave an account of his teaching and his being taken up, and let them tell us how they saw him taken up into heaven. And that saying pleased all. Then they sent three men into Galilee; and Go, said they, say to Rabbi Addas and Rabbi Finees and Rabbi Egias, Peace to you and yours! Many investigations have been made in the council concerning Jesus; therefore have we been instructed to call you to the holy place, to Jerusalem.

The men went to Galilee, and found them sitting, and meditating on the law. And they saluted them in peace. And they said: Why have you come? The messengers said: The council summon you to the holy city Jerusalem. And the men, hearing that they were sought for by the council, prayed to God, and reclined with the men, and ate and drank with them. And rising in the morning, they went to Jerusalem in peace.

And on the morrow the council sat; and they questioned them, saying: Did you plainly see Jesus sitting on Mount Mambre teaching his disciples, and taken up into heaven?

First Addas the teacher says: I really saw him sitting on Mount Mambre teaching his disciples; and a shining cloud overshadowed him and his disciples, and he went up into heaven;

and his disciples prayed upon their faces on the ground. And calling Finees the priest, they questioned him also, saying: How didst thou see Jesus taken up? And he said the same as the other. And again they called the third, Rabbi Egias, and questioned him, and he said the same as the first and second. And those who were in the council said: The law of Moses holds that by the mouth of two or three every word should stand. Abudem, a teacher, one of the doctors, says: It is written in the law, Enoch walked with God, and was translated; for God took him. Jairus, a teacher, said: And we have heard of the death of holy Moses, and have not seen it; for it is written in the law of the Lord, And Moses died according to the word[2] of the Lord, and no man knoweth of his burying even to the present day. Rabbi Levi said: What is it that Rabbi Simeon said: Lo, he lies for the fall and rising again of many in Israel, and for a sign which shall be spoken against? Rabbi Isaac said: It is written in the law, Lo, I send mine angel, who shall go before thy face to keep thee in every good way, because I have brought his[3] new name.

Then Annas and Caiaphas said: Rightly have ye said that these things are written in the law of Moses, that no one saw the death of Enoch, and no one has named the burying of holy Moses. And Jesus gave account to[4] Pilate, and we saw him scourged, and receiving spitting on his face; and the soldiers put a crown of thorns on him, and he received sentence from Pilate; and then he was crucified, and they gave him gall and vinegar to drink, and two robbers were crucified with him, and the soldier Longinus pierced his side with a lance; and our honourable father Joseph begged his body, and he has risen again, and, as they say, the three teachers have seen him taken up into heaven. And Rabbi Levi has borne witness to what was said by Simeon the elder — that he has been set for the fall and rising again of many in Israel, and for a sign which shall be spoken against.

Then Didas, a teacher, said to all the assembly: If all the things which these have borne witness to have come to pass in Jesus, they are from God, and let it not be wonderful in our eyes.[5] The chiefs of the synagogue, and the priests and the Levites, said to each other how our law holds, saying: His name shall be blessed for ever: His place endureth before the sun, and His seat before the moon: and all the tribes of earth shall be blessed in Him, and all nations shall serve Him; and kings shall come from far, adoring and magnifying Him.[6]

---

[1] Perhaps this would be better as a question: Is it good?

[2] Lit., mouth.
[3] Or, its. The text of the clause is corrupt.
[4] i.e., was tried before.
[5] Comp. Ps. cxviii. 23.
[6] Ps. lxxii. 11, 17.

THE GOSPEL OF NICODEMUS

PART II.—CHRIST'S DESCENT INTO HELL

LATIN. FIRST VERSION

CHAP. 1 (17).—And Joseph rose up and said to Annas and Caiaphas : Truly and well do you wonder, since you have heard that Jesus has been seen alive from the dead, ascending up into heaven. But it is more to be wondered at that he is not the only one who has risen from the dead ; but he has raised up alive out of their tombs many others of the dead, and they have been seen by many in Jerusalem. And hear me now, that we all know the blessed Simeon, the great priest, who took up with his hands Jesus, when an infant, in the temple. And Simeon himself had two sons, full brothers ; and we all were at their falling asleep, and at their burial. Go, therefore, and see their tombs : for they are open, because they have risen ; and, behold, they are in the city of Arimathæa, living together in prayers. And, indeed, they are heard crying out, but speaking with nobody, and they are silent as the dead. But come, let us go to them ; let us conduct them to us with all honour and respect. And if we adjure them, perhaps they will speak to us of the mystery of their resurrection.

At hearing this they all rejoiced. And Annas and Caiaphas, Nicodemus, and Joseph, and Gamaliel, went, and did not find them in their sepulchres ; but, walking into the city of Arimathea, they found them there, on their bended knees, and spending their time in prayer. And kissing them, they conducted them to Jerusalem, into the synagogue, with all veneration and fear of God. And shutting the doors, and lifting up the law of the Lord, they put it in their hands, adjuring them by the God Adonai, and the God of Israel, who by the law and the prophets spoke to our fathers, saying : Do you believe that it was Jesus who raised you from the dead ? Tell us how you have risen from the dead.

Karinus and Leucius, hearing this adjuration, trembled in their body, and groaned, being dis-turbed in heart. And together they looked towards heaven, and with their fingers made the sign of the cross on their tongues, and immediately they spoke together, saying : Give each of us sheets of paper, and let us write what we have seen and heard. And they gave it to them. And they sat down, and each of them wrote, saying : —

CHAP. 2 (18). — O Lord Jesus Christ, the resurrection and the life of the dead, permit us to speak mysteries through the death of Thy cross, because we have been adjured by Thee. For Thou didst order Thy servants to relate to no one the secrets of Thy divine majesty which Thou didst in Hades. And when we were, along with all our fathers, lying in the deep, in the blackness of darkness, suddenly there appeared a golden heat[1] of the sun, and a purple royal light shining upon us. And immediately the father of all the human race, with all the patriarchs and prophets, exulted, saying : That light is the source of eternal light, which hath promised to transmit to us co-eternal light. And Esaias cried out, and said : This is the light of the Father, the Son of God, as I predicted when I was alive upon earth : The land of Zabulon and the land of Nephthalim across Jordan, Galilee of the nations, the people who sat in darkness, have seen a great light ; and light was shining among those who are in the region of the shadow of death. And now it has come and shone upon us sitting in death.

And when we were all exulting in the light which shone over us, there came up to us our father Simeon ; and he said, exulting : Glorify the Lord Jesus Christ, the Son of God ; because I took Him up when born, an infant, in my hands

---

[1] *Calor;* another MS. has *color*, hue.

448

in the temple ; and instigated by the Holy Spirit, I said to Him, confessing : Now mine eyes have seen Thy salvation, which Thou hast prepared in the sight of all peoples, a light for the revealing of the nations, and the glory of Thy people Israel. When they heard this, all the multitude of the saints exulted more.

And after this there comes up, as it were, a dweller in the desert ; and he is asked by all : Who art thou ? To whom he says in answer : I am John, the voice and prophet of the Most High, going before the face of His coming to prepare His ways, to give the knowledge of salvation to His people for the remission of their sins. And seeing Him coming to me, instigated by the Holy Spirit, I said : Behold the Lamb of God ! behold Him who taketh away the sins of the world ! And I baptized Him in the river of Jordan, and I saw the Holy Spirit descending upon Him in the form of a dove ; and I heard a voice from the heavens saying, This is my beloved Son, in whom I am well pleased. And now I have gone before His face, and have descended to announce to you that the rising Son of God is close at hand to visit us, coming from on high to us sitting in darkness and the shadow of death.

CHAP. 3 (19). — And when the first created, father Adam, had heard this, that Jesus was baptized in Jordan, he cried out to his son Seth : Tell thy sons, the patriarchs and the prophets, all that thou heardest from Michael the archangel when I sent thee to the gates of paradise to implore God that he might send thee His angel to give thee oil from the tree of mercy, with which to anoint my body when I was sick. Then Seth, coming near to the holy patriarchs and prophets, said : When I, Seth, was praying to the Lord at the gates of paradise, behold Michael, the angel of the Lord, appeared to me, saying, I have been sent to thee by the Lord. I am set over the human race.[1] And to thee, Seth, I say, do not labour with tears in prayers and supplications on account of the oil of the tree of mercy to anoint thy father Adam for the pain of his body, because in no wise shalt thou receive of it, except in the last days and times, except when five thousand and five hundred years have been fulfilled : then will come upon the earth the most beloved Son of God, to raise up again the body of Adam, and the bodies of the dead ; and He, when He comes, will be baptized in Jordan. And when he shall have come out of the water of Jordan, then with the oil of His mercy shall He anoint all that believe on Him ; and that oil of mercy shall be for the generation of those who shall be born out of water and the Holy

Spirit into life eternal. Then, descending upon earth, Christ Jesus, the most beloved Son of God, will lead our father Adam into paradise to the tree of mercy.

And when they heard all these things from Seth, all the patriarchs and prophets exulted with great exultation.

CHAP. 4 (20). — And when all the saints were exulting, lo, Satan, the prince and leader of death, said to Hades : Make thyself ready to receive Jesus, who boasts himself to be the Son of God, and is a man fearing death, and saying, My soul is sorrowful, even unto death. And he has withstood me much, doing me evil ; and many whom I made blind, lame, deaf, leprous, and demoniac, he has healed with a word ; and those whom I have brought to thee dead, he has dragged away from thee.

Hades, answering, said to Prince Satan : Who is he that is so powerful, when he is a man in fear of death ? For all the powerful of the earth are kept in subjection by my power, whom thou hast brought into subjection by thy power. If, then, thou art powerful, what is that man Jesus like, who, though fearing death, withstands thy power ? If he is so powerful in humanity, verily I say unto thee, he is all-powerful in divinity, and his power can no one resist. And when he says that he fears death, he wishes to lay hold on thee, and woe will be to thee to the ages of eternity. And Satan, prince of Tartarus, answered and said : Why hast thou doubted, and feared to receive this Jesus, thy adversary and mine ? For I have tempted him, and I have roused up my ancient people the Jews with hatred and anger against him ; I have sharpened a lance to strike him ; I have mixed gall and vinegar to give him to drink ; and I have prepared wood to crucify him, and nails to pierce him, and his death is near at hand, that I may bring him to thee, subject to thee and me.

Tartarus answered and said : Thou hast told me that it is he himself who has dragged away the dead from me. Now there are many who are here kept by me, who, while they lived on earth, took the dead from me, not by their own powers, but by godly prayers, and their almighty God dragged them away from me. Who is that Jesus, who by his word has withdrawn the dead from me without prayers ? Perhaps he is the same who, by the word of his command, brought alive Lazarus, after he had been four days in stench and corruption, whom I kept dead. Satan, prince of death, answered and said : That Jesus is the same. And when Hades heard this, he said to him : I adjure thee by thy powers and mine, do not bring him to me. For I at that time, when I heard the command of his word, trembled with terror and dismay, and all

---

[1] Lit., body.

my officers at the same time were confounded along with me. Nor could we keep that Lazarus; but, shaking himself like an eagle, he sprang out, and went forth from us with all activity and speed, and the same ground which held the dead body of Lazarus immediately gave him forth alive. So now, I know that that man who could do these things is God, strong in authority, powerful in humanity, and He is the Saviour of the human race. But if thou bring Him to me, all who are here shut up in the cruelty of the prison, and bound by their sins in chains that cannot be loosened, He will let loose, and will bring to the life of His divinity for ever.

Chap. 5 (21). — And as Prince Satan and Hades were thus speaking to each other in turn, suddenly there was a voice as of thunders, and a shouting of spirits: Lift up your gates, ye princes; and be ye lifted up, ye everlasting gates; and the King of glory shall come in.[1] Hades hearing this, said to Prince Satan: Retire from me, and go outside of my realms: if thou art a powerful warrior, fight against the King of glory. But what hast thou to do with Him? And Hades thrust Satan outside of his realms. And Hades said to his impious officers: Shut the cruel gates of brass, and put up the bars of iron, and resist bravely, that we, holding captivity, may not take *Him* captive.[2]

And all the multitude of the saints, hearing this, said to Hades, with the voice of reproach: Open thy gates, that the King of glory may come in. And David cried out, saying: Did I not, when I was alive upon earth, prophesy to you: Let them confess to the Lord His tender mercies and His wonderful works to the children of men: for He has shattered the brazen gates, and burst the iron bars; He has taken them up out of the way of their iniquity?[3] And after this, in like manner, Esaias said: Did not I, when I was alive upon earth, prophesy to you: The dead shall rise up, and those who are in their tombs shall rise again, and those who are upon earth shall exult; because the dew, which is from the Lord, is their health?[4] And again I said, Where, O Death, is thy sting? where, O Hades, is thy victory?[5]

And when all the saints heard this from Esaias, they said to Hades: Open thy gates. Since thou art now conquered, thou wilt be weak and powerless. And there was a great voice, as of thunders, saying: Lift up your gates, ye princes; and be ye lifted up, ye infernal gates; and the King of glory shall come in. Hades, seeing that they

had twice shouted out this, says, as if not knowing: Who is the king of glory? David says, in answer to Hades: I recognise those words of the shout, since I prophesied the same by His Spirit. And now, what I have said above I say to thee, The Lord strong and mighty, the Lord mighty in battle; He is the King of glory.[6] And the Lord Himself hath looked down from heaven upon earth, to hear the groans of the prisoners, and to release the sons of the slain.[7] And now, most filthy and most foul Hades, open thy gates, that the King of glory may come in. While David was thus speaking, there came to Hades, in the form of a man, the Lord of majesty, and lighted up the eternal darkness, and burst asunder the indissoluble chains; and the aid of unconquered power visited us, sitting in the profound darkness of transgressions, and in the shadow of death of sins.[8]

Chap. 6 (22). — When this was seen by Hades and Death, and their impious officers, along with their cruel servants, they trembled at perceiving in their own dominions the clearness of so great a light, when they saw Christ suddenly in their abodes; and they cried out, saying: We have been overcome by thee. Who art thou, that to the Lord directest our confusion?[9] Who art thou, that, undestroyed by corruption, the uncorrupted proof of thy majesty, with fury condemnest our power? Who art thou, so great and little, lowly and exalted, soldier and commander, wonderful warrior in the form of a slave, and the king of glory dead and alive, whom slain the cross has carried? Thou, who didst lie dead in the sepulchre, hast come down to us alive; and in thy death every creature trembled, and the stars in a body were moved; and now thou hast been made free among the dead, and disturbest our legions. Who art thou, that settest free those who art held captive, bound by original sin, and recallest them to their former liberty? Who art thou, who sheddest a divine, and splendid, and illuminating light upon those who have been blinded by the darkness of their sins?

In like manner, also, all the legions of the demons, terror-stricken with like fear from their fearful overthrow, cried out, saying: Whence art thou, O Jesus, a man so powerful and splendid in majesty, so excellent, without spot, and free from guilt? For that world of earth which has been subject to us always until now, which used to pay tribute for our uses, has never sent us such a dead man, has never destined such gifts for the powers below. Who therefore art thou, that hast

---

[1] Ps. xxiv. 7.
[2] Ps. lxviii. 18. *Captivemus* in the text is probably a misprint for *captivemur*, may not be taken captive.
[3] Ps. cvii. 15-17, according to the LXX. and the Vulgate.
[4] Isa. xxvi. 19, according to the LXX.
[5] Hos. xiii. 14; 1 Cor. xv. 55.

[6] Ps. xxiv. 7, 8.
[7] Ps. cii. 19, 20.
[8] Comp. Isa. ix. 2; Luke i. 79.
[9] Some MSS. have: Who art thou, O man, that to God directest thy prayer to our confusion? The correct reading may be: Who art thou, that bringest confusion upon our master?

so intrepidly entered our bounds, and who hast not only no fear of our punishments, but, moreover, attemptest to take all away from our chains? Perhaps thou art that Jesus of whom our prince Satan said, that by thy death of the cross thou wast destined to receive the dominion of the whole world.

Then the King of glory, trampling on death by His majesty, and seizing Prince Satan, delivered him to the power of Hades, and drew Adam to His brightness.

CHAP. 7 (23). — Then Hades, receiving Prince Satan, said to him, with vehement revilings: O prince of perdition, and leader of extermination, Beelzebub, derision of angels, to be spit upon by the just, why didst thou wish to do this? Didst thou wish to crucify the King of glory, in whose death thou didst promise us so great spoils? Like a fool, thou didst not know what thou wast doing. For, behold, that Jesus by the splendour of His divinity is putting to flight all the darkness of death, and He has broken into the strong lowest depths of our dungeons, and has brought out the captives, and released those who were bound. And all who used to groan under our torments insult us, and by their prayers our dominions are taken by storm, and our realms conquered, and no race of men has now any respect for us. Moreover, also, we are grievously threatened by the dead, who have never been haughty to us, and who have not at any time been joyful as captives. O Prince Satan, father of all impious wretches and renegades, why didst thou wish to do this? Of those who from the beginning, even until now, have despaired of salvation and life, no bellowing after the usual fashion is now heard here; and no groaning of theirs resounds, nor in any of their faces is a trace of tears found. O Prince Satan, possessor of the keys of the lower regions, all thy riches which thou hadst acquired by the tree of transgression and the loss of paradise, thou hast now lost by the tree of the cross, and all thy joy has perished. When thou didst hang up that Christ Jesus the King of glory, thou wast acting against thyself and against me. Henceforth thou shalt know what eternal torments and infinite punishments thou art to endure in my everlasting keeping. O Prince Satan, author of death, and source of all pride, thou oughtest first to have inquired into the bad cause of that Jesus. Him in whom thou perceivedst no fault, why, without reason, didst thou dare unjustly to crucify? and why hast thou brought to our regions one innocent and just, and lost the guilty, the impious, and the unjust of the whole world?

And when Hades had thus spoken to Prince Satan, then the King of glory said to Hades: Satan the prince will be in thy power for ever, in place of Adam and his sons, my just ones.

CHAP. 8 (24). — And the Lord stretched out His hand, and said: Come to me, all my saints, who have my image and likeness. Do you, who have been condemned through the tree and the devil and death, now see the devil and death condemned through the tree. Immediately all the saints were brought together under the hand of the Lord. And the Lord, holding Adam by the right hand, said to him: Peace be to thee, with all thy children, my righteous ones! And Adam fell down at the knees of the Lord, and with tearful entreaty praying, said with a loud voice: I will extol Thee, O Lord; for Thou hast lifted me up, and hast not made my foes to rejoice over me. O Lord God, I cried unto Thee, and Thou hast healed me. O Lord, Thou hast brought out my soul from the powers below; Thou hast saved me from them that go down into the pit. Sing praises to the Lord, all His saints, and confess to the memory of His holiness; since there is anger in His indignation, and life in His goodwill.[1] In like manner also all the saints of God, falling on their knees at the feet of the Lord, said with one voice: Thou hast come, O Redeemer of the world: as Thou hast foretold by the law and Thy prophets, so hast Thou fulfilled by Thy deeds. Thou hast redeemed the living by Thy cross; and by the death of the cross Thou hast come down to us, to rescue us from the powers below, and from death, by Thy majesty. O Lord, as Thou hast set the title of Thy glory in heaven, and hast erected as the title of redemption Thy cross upon earth, so, O Lord, set in Hades the sign of the victory of Thy cross, that death may no more have dominion.

And the Lord, stretching forth His hand, made the sign of the cross upon Adam and upon all His saints; and holding Adam by the right hand, went up from the powers below: and all the saints followed Him. Then holy David cried out aloud, saying: Sing unto the Lord a new song, for He hath done wonderful things; His right hand and His holy arm have brought salvation to Himself. The Lord hath made known His salvation; His righteousness hath He revealed in the sight of the heathen.[2] And all the multitude of the saints answered, saying: This is glory to all His saints. Amen, alleluia.

And after this the prophet Habacuc cried out, saying: Thou wentest forth for the salvation of Thy people, to deliver Thine elect.[3] And all the saints answered, saying: Blessed is He who

---

[1] Ps. xxx. 1-6 (Vulg.).
[2] Ps. xcviii. 1, 2.
[3] Hab. iii. 13.

cometh in the name of the Lord; God is the Lord, and He hath shone upon us.[1] Amen, alleluia. In like manner after this the prophet Michæas also cried out, saying: Who is a God like unto thee, O Lord, taking away iniquities and passing by sins? And now Thou dost withhold Thine anger for a testimony *against us*, because Thou delightest in mercy. And Thou turnest again, and hast compassion upon us, and pardonest all our iniquities; and all our sins hast Thou sunk in the multitude of death,[2] as Thou hast sworn unto our fathers in the days of old.[3] And all the saints answered, saying: This is our God to eternity, and for ever and ever; and He will direct us for evermore.[4] Amen, alleluia. So also all the prophets, quoting the sacred *writings* concerning His praises,[5] and all the saints crying, Amen, alleluia, followed the Lord.

CHAP. 9 (25). — And the Lord, holding the hand of Adam, delivered him to Michael the archangel: and all the saints followed Michael the archangel, and he led them all into the glorious grace of paradise. And there met them two men, ancient of days. The saints asked them: Who are you, that have not yet been dead along with us in the regions below, and have been placed in paradise in the body? One of them answered, and said: I am Enoch, who by the word of the Lord have been translated hither; and he who is with me is Elias the Thesbite, who was taken up by a fiery chariot. Here also even until now we have not tasted death, but have been reserved to the coming of Antichrist, by divine signs and wonders to do battle with him, and, being killed by him in Jerusalem, after three days and half a day to be taken up alive again in the clouds.[6]

CHAP. 10 (26). — And while the saints Enoch and Elias were thus speaking, behold, there came up another man, most wretched, carrying on his shoulders the sign of the cross. And seeing him, all the saints said to him: Who art thou? because thy appearance is that of a robber. And what is the sign which thou carriest on thy shoulders? In answer to them, he said: Truly have you said that I was a robber, doing all sorts of evil upon the earth. And the Jews crucified me along with Jesus; and I saw the miracles in created things which were done through the cross of Jesus crucified, and I believed Him to be the Creator of all created things, and the

King omnipotent; and I entreated Him, saying, Be mindful of me, Lord, when Thou shalt have come into Thy kingdom. Immediately He accepted my entreaty, and said to me, Amen; I say to thee, To-day shalt thou be with me in paradise.[7] And He gave me this sign of the cross, saying, Walk into paradise carrying this; and if the guardian angel of paradise will not let thee go in, show him the sign of the cross, and thou shalt say to him, Jesus Christ, the Son of God, who has now been crucified, has sent me. Having done so, I said all this to the guardian angel of paradise. And when he heard this, he immediately opened, and led me in, and placed me at the right of paradise, saying, Lo, hold a little, and there will come in the father of the whole human race, Adam, with all his children, holy and just, after the triumph and glory of the ascension of Christ the crucified Lord. Hearing all these words of the robber, all the holy patriarchs and prophets with one voice said: Blessed art Thou, O Lord Almighty, Father of everlasting benefits, and Father of mercies, who hast given such grace to Thy sinners, and hast brought them back into the grace of paradise, and into Thy rich pastures; for this is spiritual life most sure. Amen, amen.

CHAP. 11 (27). — These are the divine and sacred mysteries which we saw and heard, I Karinus, and Leucius. More we are not allowed to tell of the other mysteries of God, as Michael the archangel adjured us, and said: You shall go into Jerusalem with your brethren, and continue in prayers, and you shall cry out, and glorify the resurrection of the Lord Jesus Christ, who has raised you up again from the dead with Himself. And with none of men shall you speak; and you shall sit as if dumb, until the hour shall come when the Lord Himself shall permit you to relate the mysteries of His divinity. And Michael the archangel ordered us to walk across Jordan into a place rich and fertile, where there are many who rose again along with us for an evidence of the resurrection of Christ the Lord; because only three days were allowed to us who have risen from the dead to celebrate in Jerusalem the passover of the Lord, with our living relations, for an evidence of the resurrection of Christ the Lord: and we have been baptized in the holy river of Jordan, receiving each of us white robes. And after three days, when we had celebrated the passover of the Lord, all who rose again along with us were snatched up into the clouds, and taken across the Jordan, and were no longer seen by any one. But we were told to remain in the city of Arimathæa in prayers.

---

[1] Ps. cxviii. 26, 27.
[2] So the text, *multitudine mortis ;* but the MSS. must have had *altitudine maris,* in the depth of the sea, with the LXX. and the Hebrew.
[3] Mic. vii. 18–20.
[4] Ps. xlviii. 14.
[5] Or, bringing sacred words from their praises.
[6] Rev. xi 3–12; 1 Thess. iv. 17.

[7] Luke xxiii. 42, 43.

These are the things which the Lord commanded us to relate to you. Give Him praise and confession, and be penitent, that He may have mercy upon you. Peace be to you from the same Lord Jesus Christ, and the Saviour of all of us! Amen.

And after they had finished all, writing on separate sheets of paper, they arose. And Karinus gave what he wrote into the hands of Annas and Caiaphas and Gamaliel; in like manner also Leucius gave what he wrote into the hands of Nicodemus and Joseph. And being suddenly transfigured, they became exceedingly white, and were seen no more. And their writings were found exactly the same, not one letter more or less.

All the synagogue of the Jews, hearing all these wonderful sayings of Karinus and Leucius, said to each other: Truly all these things have been done by the Lord, and blessed be the Lord for ever and ever. Amen. And they all went out with great anxiety, beating their breasts with fear and trembling; and they went away, each to his own house.

All these things which were said by the Jews in their synagogue Joseph and Nicodemus immediately reported to the proconsul. And Pilate himself wrote all which had been done and said concerning Jesus by the Jews, and he placed all the words in the public records of his prætorium.

CHAP. 12 (28). — After this, Pilate going into the temple of the Jews, assembled all the chief priests, and learned men, and scribes, and teachers of the law, and went in with them into the sanctuary of the temple, and ordered that all the gates should be shut, and said to them: We have heard that you have a certain great collection of books in this temple: therefore I ask you that it be presented before us. And when four officers brought in that collection of books, adorned with gold and precious gems, Pilate said to all: I adjure you by the God of your fathers, who ordered you to build this temple in the place of his sanctuary, not to conceal the truth from me. You all know what is written in that collection of books; but now say whether you have found in the writings that Jesus, whom you have crucified, to be the Son of God that was to come for the salvation of the human race, and in how many revolutions of the seasons he ought to come. Declare to me whether you crucified him in ignorance of this, or knowing it.

Being thus adjured, Annas and Caiaphas ordered all the others who were with them to go out of the sanctuary; and themselves shut all the gates of the temple and the sanctuary, and said to Pilate: We have been adjured by thee, O good judge, by the building of this temple, to give thee the truth, and a clear account *of this matter*. After we had crucified Jesus, not knowing Him to be the Son of God, thinking that He did miracles by means of some charm, we made a great synagogue in this temple. And conferring with each other of the signs of the miracles which Jesus had done, we found many witnesses of our nation who said that they had seen Jesus alive after suffering death, and that He had penetrated into the height of heaven. And we have seen two witnesses, whom Jesus raised up again from the dead, who told us many wonderful things that Jesus did among the dead, which we have in our hands, written out. And our custom is, every year before our synagogue, to open that holy collection of books, and seek out the testimony of God. And we have found in the first book of the LXX., where the archangel Michael spoke to the third son of Adam, the first man, of five thousand and five hundred years, in which the Christ, the most beloved Son of God, was to come from the heavens; and upon this we have considered that perhaps He was the God of Israel who said to Moses,[1] Make to thee the ark of the covenant, two cubits and a half in length, one cubit and a half in breadth, one cubit and a half in height. In these five and a half cubits we have understood and recognised, from the structure of the ark of the old covenant, that in five and a half thousands of years, Jesus Christ was to come in the ark of the body; and we have found Him to be the God of Israel, the Son of God. Because after His passion, we, the chief priests, wondering at the signs which happened on account of Him, opened this collection of books, searching out all the generations, even to the generation of Joseph, and reckoning that Mary the mother of Christ was of the seed of David; and we have found that from the time that God made the heaven and the earth and the first man, to the deluge, are two thousand two hundred and twelve[2] years; and from the deluge to the building of the tower, five hundred and thirty-one[3] years; and from the building of the tower to Abraham, six hundred and six[4] years; and from Abraham to the arrival of the children of Israel from Egypt, four hundred and seventy years; from the coming of the children of Israel out of Egypt to the building of the temple, five hundred and eleven years; and from the building of the temple to the destruction of the same temple, four hundred and sixty-four years. Thus far have we found in the book of Esdras. After searching, we find that from the burning of the temple to the advent of Christ, and His birth, there are six hundred and thirty-six[5] years, which together were five thousand five hundred years, as we have found written in the book that Michael the

---

[1] Ex. xxv. 10.
[2] Should be 2262 — βσοβ in place of βοιβ.
[3] This includes the second Cainan.
[4] Should be 676.
[5] Should be 586 — DLXXXVI. instead of DCXXXVI.

archangel foretold to Seth the third son of Adam, that in five and a half thousands of years Christ the Son of God would come.[1] Even until now we have told no one, that there might be no dissension in our synagogues. And now thou hast adjured us, O good judge, by this holy book of the testimonies of God, and we make it manifest to thee. And now we adjure thee, by thy life and safety, to make manifest these words to no one in Jerusalem.

CHAP. 13 (29). — Pilate, hearing these words of Annas and Caiaphas, laid them all up in the acts of our Lord and Saviour, in the public records of his prætorium, and wrote a letter to Claudius, king of the city of Rome,[2] saying : —

Pontius Pilate to Claudius his king, greeting. It has lately happened, as I myself have also proved, that the Jews, through envy, have punished themselves and their posterity by a cruel condemnation. In short, when their fathers had a promise that their God would send them from heaven his holy one, who should deservedly be called their king, and promised that he would send him by a virgin upon the earth : when, therefore, while I was procurator, he had come into Judæa, and when they saw him enlightening the blind, cleansing the lepers, curing the paralytics, making demons flee from men, even raising the dead, commanding the winds, walking dryshod upon the waves of the sea, and doing many other signs of miracles ; and when all the people of the Jews said that he was the Son of God, the chief priests felt envy against him, and seized him, and delivered him to me ; and, telling me one lie after another, they said that he was a sorcerer, and was acting contrary to their law.

And I believed that it was so, and delivered him to be scourged, according to their will. And they crucified him, and set guards over him when buried. And he rose again on the third day, while my soldiers were keeping guard. But so flagrant was the iniquity of the Jews, that they gave money to my soldiers, saying, Say that his disciples have stolen his body. But after receiving the money they could not keep secret what had been done ; for they bore witness both that he had risen again, that they had seen him,[3] and that they had received money from the Jews.

This accordingly I have done, lest any one should give a different and a false account of it, and lest thou shouldst think that the lies of the Jews are to be believed.

[1] Lit., has come.
[2] [Compare the other Latin form of this letter, as translated on p. 459; also the version of the Greek form of a similar letter, included in the *Acts of Peter and Paul.* — R.]

[3] Or, that they had seen that he rose from the dead.

LATIN. SECOND VERSION.

CHAP. I (17). — Then Rabbi Addas, and Rabbi Finees, and Rabbi Egias, the three men who had come from Galilee, testifying that they had seen Jesus taken up into heaven, rose up in the midst of the multitude of the chiefs of the Jews, and said before the priests and the Levites, who had been called together to the council of the Lord : When we were coming from Galilee, we met at the Jordan a very great multitude of men, fathers[1] who had been some time dead. And present among them we saw Karinus and Leucius. And they came up to us, and we kissed each other, because they were dear friends of ours ; and we asked them, Tell us, friends and brothers, what is this breath of life and flesh ? and who are those with whom you are going ? and how do you, who have been some time dead, remain in the body ?

And they said in answer : We have risen again along with Christ from the lower world, and He has raised us up again from the dead. And from this you may know that the gates of death and darkness have been destroyed, and the souls of the saints have been brought out thence, and have ascended into heaven along with Christ the Lord. And indeed to us it has been commanded by the Lord Himself, that for an appointed time we should walk over the banks of Jordan and the mountains ; not, however, appearing to every one, nor speaking to every one, except to those to whom He has permitted us. And just now we could neither have spoken nor appeared to you, unless it had been allowed to us by the Holy Spirit.

And when they heard this, all the multitude who were present in the council were struck with fear and trembling, and wondered whether these things had really happened which these Galilæans testified. Then Caiaphas and Annas said to the council : What these have testified, first and last, must shortly be altogether made clear : If it shall be found to be true that Karinus and Leucius remain alive in the body, and if we shall be able to behold them with our own eyes, then

[1] *Abbatorum.*

what they testify is altogether true; and if we find them, they will inform us of everything; but if not, you may know that it is all lies.

Then the council having suddenly risen, it pleased them to choose men fit for the duty, fearing God, and who knew when they died, and where they were buried, to inquire diligently, and to see whether it was as they had heard. The men therefore proceeded to the same place, fifteen in number, who through all were present at their falling asleep, and had stood at their feet when they were buried, and had beheld their tombs. And they came and found their tombs open, and very many others besides, and found a sign neither of their bones nor of their dust. And they returned in all haste, and reported what they had seen.

Then all their synagogue was in great grief and perplexity, and they said to each other: What shall we do? Annas and Caiaphas said: Let us turn to where we have heard that they are, and let us send to them men of rank, asking and entreating them: perhaps they will deign to come to us. Then they sent to them Nicodemus and Joseph, and the three men, the Galilæan rabbis who had seen them, asking that they should deign to come to them. And they went, and walked round all the region of Jordan and of the mountains, and they were coming back without finding them.

And, behold, suddenly there appeared coming down from Mount Amalech a very great number, as it were, twelve thousand men, who had risen with the Lord. And though they recognised very many there, they were not able to say anything to them for fear and the angelic vision; and they stood at a distance gazing and hearing them, how they walked along singing praises, and saying: The Lord has risen again from the dead, as He had said; let us all exult and be glad, since He reigns for ever. Then those who had been sent were astonished, and fell to the ground for fear, and received the answer from them, that they should see Karinus and Leucius in their own houses.

And they rose up and went to their houses, and found them spending their time in prayer. And going in to them, they fell on their faces to the ground, saluting them; and being raised up, they said: O friends of God, all the multitude of the Jews have directed us to you, hearing that you have risen from the dead, asking and beseeching you to come to them, that we all may know the great things of God which have happened around us in our times. And they immediately, at a sign from God, rose up, and came with them, and entered their synagogue. Then the multitude of the Jews, with the priests, put the books of the law in their hands, and adjured them by the God Heloi, and the God

Adonai, and by the law and the prophets, saying: Tell us how you have risen from the dead, and what are those wonderful things which have happened in our times, such as we have never heard to have happened at any other time; because already for fear all our bones have been benumbed, and have dried up, and the earth moves itself under our feet: for we have joined all our hearts to shed righteous and holy blood.

Then Karinus and Leucius signed to them with their hands to give them a sheet of paper and ink. And this they did, because the Holy Spirit did not allow them to speak to them. And they gave each of them paper, and put them apart, the one from the other in separate cells. And they, making with their fingers the sign of the cross of Christ, began to write on the separate sheets; and after they had finished, as if out of one mouth from the separate cells, they cried out, Amen. And rising up, Karinus gave his paper to Annas, and Leucius to Caiaphas; and saluting each other, they went out, and returned to their sepulchres.

Then Annas and Caiaphas, opening the sheet of paper, began each to read it in secret. But all the people took it ill, and so all cried out: Read these writings to us openly; and after they have been read through we shall keep them, lest perchance this truth of God be turned through wilful blindness, by unclean and deceitful men, into falsehood. At this Annas and Caiaphas fell a-trembling, and delivered the sheet of paper to Rabbi Addas, and Rabbi Finees, and Rabbi Egias, who had come from Galilee, and announced that Jesus had been taken up into heaven. All the multitude of the Jews trusted to them to read this writing. And they read the paper containing these words:—

CHAP. 2 (18).—I Karinus. O Lord Jesus Christ, Son of the living God, permit me to speak of Thy wonders which Thou hast done in the lower world. When, therefore, we were kept in darkness and the shadow of death in the lower world, suddenly there shone upon us a great light, and Hades and the gates of death trembled. And then was heard the voice of the Son of the Father most high, as if the voice of a great thunder; and loudly proclaiming, He thus charged them: Lift up your gates, ye princes; lift up the everlasting gates; the King of glory, Christ the Lord, will come up to enter in.

Then Satan, the leader of death, came up, fleeing in terror, saying to his officers and the powers below: My officers, and all the powers below, run together, shut your gates, put up the iron bars, and fight bravely, and resist, lest they lay hold of us, and keep us captive in chains. Then all his impious officers were perplexed, and began to shut the gates of death with all diligence, and by little and little to fasten the locks and the iron bars, and to hold all their weapons [1] grasped in their hands, and to utter howlings in a direful and most hideous voice.

CHAP. 3 (19). — Then Satan said to Hades: Make thyself ready to receive him whom I shall bring down to thee. Thereupon Hades thus replied to Satan: That voice was from nothing else than the cry of the Son of the Father most high, because the earth and all the places of the world below so trembled under it: wherefore I think that myself and all my dungeons are now lying open. But I adjure thee, Satan, head of all evils,[2] by thy power and my own, bring him not to me, lest, while we wish to take him, we be taken captive by him. For if, at his voice only, all my power has been thus destroyed, what do you think he will do when he shall come in person?

To him Satan, the leader of death, thus replied: What art thou crying out about? Do not be afraid, my old most wicked friend, because I have stirred up the people of the Jews against him; I have told them to strike him with blows on the face, and I have brought upon him betrayal by one of his disciples; and he is a man in great fear of death, because from fear he said, My soul is sorrowful even unto death; and I have brought him to this, that he has just been lifted up and hanged on the cross.

Then Hades said to him: If he be the same who, by the mere word of his command, made Lazarus fly away like an eagle from my bosom, when he had already been dead four days, he is not a man in humanity, but God in majesty. I entreat thee not to bring him to me. And Satan says to him: Make thyself ready nevertheless; be not afraid; because he is already hanging on the cross, I can do nothing else. Then Hades thus replied to Satan: If, then, thou canst do nothing else, behold, thy destruction is at hand. I, in short, shall remain cast down and dishonoured; thou, however, wilt be tortured under my power.

CHAP. 4 (20). — And the saints of God heard the wrangling of Satan and Hades. They, however, though as yet not at all recognising each other, were, notwithstanding, in the possession of their faculties. But our holy father Adam thus replied to Satan at once: O captain of death, why dost thou fear and tremble? Behold, the Lord is coming, who will now destroy all thy inventions; and thou shalt be taken by Him, and bound throughout eternity.

Then all the saints, hearing the voice of our father Adam, how boldly he replied to Satan in all points, were strengthened in joy; and all running together to father Adam, were crowded in one place. Then our father Adam, gazing on all that multitude, wondered greatly whether all of them had been begotten from him into the world. And embracing those who were standing everywhere around him, and shedding most bitter tears, he addressed his son Seth, saying: Relate, my son Seth, to the holy patriarchs and prophets what the guardian of paradise said to thee, when I sent thee to bring to me of that oil of compassion, in order to anoint my body when I was ill.

Then he answered: I, when thou sentest me before the gates of paradise, prayed and entreated the Lord with tears, and called upon the guardian of paradise to give me of it therefrom. Then Michael the archangel came out, and said to me, Seth, why then dost thou weep? Know, being informed beforehand, that thy father Adam will not receive of this oil of compassion now, but after many generations of time. For the most beloved Son of God will come down from heaven into the world, and will be baptized by John in the river Jordan; and then shall thy father Adam receive of this oil [3] of compassion, and all that believe in him. And of those who have believed in him, their kingdom will endure for ever.

CHAP. 5 (21). — Then all the saints, hearing this again, exulted in joy. And one of those standing round, Isaias by name, cried out aloud, and thundered: Father Adam, and all standing round, hear my declaration. When I was on earth, and by the teaching of the Holy Spirit, in prophecy I sang of this light: The people who sat in darkness have seen a great light; to them dwelling in the region of the shadow of death light has arisen. At these words father Adam, and all of them, turned and asked him: Who art thou? because what thou sayest is true. And he subjoined, and said: My name is Isaias.

Then appeared another near him, as if a hermit. And they asked him, saying: Who art thou, who bearest such an appearance in thy body?[4] And he firmly answered: I am John the Baptist, voice and prophet of the Most High. I went before the face of the same Lord, that I might make the waste and rough places into plain ways. I with my finger pointed out and made manifest the Lamb of the Lord, and Son of God, to the inhabitants of Jerusalem. I baptized Him in the river Jordan. I heard the voice of the Father from heaven thundering over Him, and proclaiming, This is my beloved Son, in whom I am well pleased. I received from Him the answer that He would descend to the lower world.

---

[1] *Ornamenta;* another MS. has *armamenta.*
[2] Or, of all the wicked.

[3] The text has *deo,* God, obviously a misprint for *oleo,* oil.
[4] Or, who wearest such (things) on thy body.

Then father Adam, hearing this, cried with a loud voice, exclaiming: Alleluia! which is, interpreted, The Lord is certainly coming.

CHAP. 6 (22). — After that, another standing there, pre-eminent as it were, with a certain mark of an emperor, David by name, thus cried out, and said: When I was upon earth, I made revelations to the people of the mercy of God and His visitation, prophesying future joys, saying through all ages, Let them make confession to the Lord of His tender mercy and His wonderful works to the sons of men, because He has shattered the gates of brass, and broken the bars of iron. Then the holy patriarchs and prophets began mutually to recognise each other, and each to quote his prophecies.

Then holy Jeremias, examining his prophecies, said to the patriarchs and prophets: When I was upon earth, I prophesied of the Son of God, that He was seen upon earth, and dwelt with men.

Then all the saints, exulting in the light of the Lord, and in the sight of father Adam, and in the answering of all the patriarchs and prophets, cried out, saying: Alleluia! blessed is He who cometh in the name of the Lord; so that at their crying out Satan trembled, and sought a way of escape. And he could not, because Hades and his satellites kept him bound in the lower regions, and guarded at all points. And they said to him: Why dost thou tremble? We by no means allow thee to go forth hence. But receive this, as thou art worthy, from Him whom thou didst daily assail; but if not, know that thou, bound by Him, shall be in my keeping.

CHAP. 7 (23). — And again there came the voice of the Son of the Father most high, as it were the voice of a great thunder, saying: Lift up your gates, ye princes; and be ye lifted up, ye everlasting gates, and the King of glory will come in. Then Satan and Hades cried out, saying: Who is the king of glory? And it was answered to them in the voice of the Lord: The Lord strong and mighty, the Lord mighty in battle.

After this voice there came a man, whose appearance was that of a robber, carrying a cross on his shoulder, crying from the outside of the door, and saying: Open to me, that I may come in. And Satan, opening to him a little, brought him inside into his dwelling,[1] and again shut the door after him. And all the saints saw him most clearly, and said to him forthwith: Thy appearance is that of a robber. Tell us what it is that thou carriest on thy back. And he answered, and said with humility: Truly I was a robber altogether; and the Jews hung me up on a cross, along with my Lord Jesus Christ, the Son of the Father most high. I, in fine, have come heralding[2] Him; He indeed is coming immediately behind me.

Then holy David, inflamed with anger against Satan, cried out aloud: Open thy gates, most vile wretch, that the King of glory may come in. In like manner also all the saints of God rose up against Satan, and would have seized him, and divided him among them. And again a cry was heard within: Lift up your gates, ye princes; and be ye lifted up, ye everlasting gates; and the King of glory shall come in. Hades and Satan, at that clear voice, again asked, saying: Who is this king of glory? And it was said to them by that wonderful voice: The Lord of powers, He is the King of glory.

CHAP. 8 (24). — And, behold, suddenly Hades trembled, and the gates of death and the bolts were shattered, and the iron bars were broken and fell to the ground, and everything was laid open. And Satan remained in the midst, and stood confounded and downcast, bound with fetters on his feet. And, behold, the Lord Jesus Christ, coming in the brightness of light from on high, compassionate, great, and lowly, carrying a chain in His hand, bound Satan by the neck; and again tying his hands behind him, dashed him on his back into Tartarus, and placed His holy foot on his throat, saying: Through all ages thou hast done many evils; thou hast not in any wise rested. To-day I deliver thee to everlasting fire. And Hades being suddenly summoned, He commanded him, and said: Take this most wicked and impious one, and have him in thy keeping even to that day in which I shall command thee. And he, as soon as he received him, was plunged under the feet of the Lord along with him into the depth of the abyss.

CHAP. 9 (25). — Then the Lord Jesus, the Saviour of all, affectionate and most mild, saluting Adam kindly, said to him: Peace be to thee, Adam, with thy children, through immeasurable ages of ages! Amen. Then father Adam, falling forward at the feet of the Lord, and being raised erect, kissed His hands, and shed many tears, saying, testifying to all: Behold the hands which fashioned me! And he said to the Lord: Thou hast come, O King of glory, delivering men, and bringing them into Thy everlasting kingdom. Then also our mother Eve in like manner fell forward at the feet of our Lord, and was raised erect, and kissed His hands, and poured forth tears in abundance, and

---

[1] *Hospitio.*

[2] *Præconcitus*, corrected to *præconatus* or *ans.*

said, testifying to all: Behold the hands which made me!

Then all the saints, adoring Him, cried out, saying: Blessed is He who cometh in the name of the Lord! The Lord God hath shone upon us — amen — through all ages. Alleluia for ever and ever! Praise, honour, power, glory! because Thou hast come from on high to visit us. Singing Alleluia continually, and rejoicing together concerning His glory, they ran together under the hands of the Lord. Then the Saviour, inquiring thoroughly about all, seized Hades,[1] immediately threw some down into Tartarus, and led some with Him to the upper world.

CHAP. 10 (26). — Then all the saints of God asked the Lord to leave as a sign of victory the sign of His holy cross in the lower world, that its most impious officers might not retain as an offender any one whom the Lord had absolved. And so it was done. And the Lord set His cross in the midst of Hades, which is the sign of victory, and which will remain even to eternity.

Then we all went forth thence along with the Lord, leaving Satan and Hades in Tartarus. And to us and many others it was commanded that we should rise in the body, giving in the world a testimony of the resurrection of our Lord Jesus Christ, and of those things which had been done in the lower world.

These are the things, dearest brethren, which

---

[1] *Momordidit infernum*, which is obviously corrupt. The translator may have read δέδηχε ᾅδην, bit Hades, for δέδειχε ᾅδην, brought Hades to light.

we have seen, and which, adjured by you, we testify, He bearing witness who died for us, and rose again; because, as it was written, so has it been done in all points.

CHAP. 11 (27). — And when the paper was finished and read through, all that heard it fell on their faces, weeping bitterly, and cruelly beating their breasts, crying out, and saying through all: Woe to us! Why has this happened to us wretched? Pilate flees; Annas and Caiaphas flee; the priests and Levites flee; moreover also the people of the Jews, weeping and saying, Woe to us wretched! we have shed sacred blood upon the earth.

For three days, therefore, and three nights, they did not taste bread and water at all; nor did any of them return to the synagogue. But on the third day again the council was assembled, and the other paper of Leucius was read through; and it was found neither more nor less, to a single letter, than that which the writing of Karinus contained. Then the synagogue was perplexed; and they all lamented forty days and forty nights, looking for destruction from God, and the vengeance of God. But He, pitier affectionate and most high, did not immediately destroy them, bountifully giving them a place of repentance. But they were not found worthy to be turned to the Lord.

These are the testimonies of Karinus and Leucius, dearest brethren, concerning Christ the Son of God, and His holy deeds in the lower world; to whom let us all give praise and glory through immeasurable age of ages. Amen.

THE LETTER OF PONTIUS PILATE

WHICH HE WROTE TO THE ROMAN EMPEROR, CONCERNING OUR LORD JESUS CHRIST.

Pontius Pilate to Tiberius Cæsar the emperor, greeting.[1]

Upon Jesus Christ, whose case I had clearly set forth to thee in my last, at length by the will of the people a bitter punishment has been inflicted, myself being in a sort unwilling and rather afraid. A man, by Hercules, so pious and strict, no age has ever had nor will have. But wonderful were the efforts of the people themselves, and the unanimity of all the scribes and chief men and elders, to crucify this ambassador of truth, notwithstanding that their own prophets, and after our manner the sibyls, warned them against it : and supernatural signs appeared while he was hanging, and, in the opinion of philosophers, threatened destruction to the whole world. His disciples are flourishing, in their work and the regulation of their lives not belying their master ; yea, in his name most beneficent. Had I not been afraid of the rising of a sedition among the people, who were just on the point of breaking out, perhaps this man would still have been alive to us ; although, urged more by fidelity to thy dignity than induced by my own wishes, I did not according to my strength resist that innocent blood free from the whole charge *brought against it*, but unjustly, through the malignity of men, should be sold and suffer, yet, as the Scriptures signify, to their own destruction. Farewell. 28th March.

---

[1] [Compare the translation of the letter of Pilate to Claudius, found in the *Acts of Peter and Paul ;* also a similar letter incorporated in *The Gospel of Nicodemus*, second part, Latin, first version, chap. 13 (29), p. 454. — R.]

THE REPORT OF PILATE THE PROCURATOR CONCERNING OUR LORD JESUS CHRIST

SENT TO THE AUGUST[1] CÆSAR IN ROME

FIRST GREEK FORM

IN those days, our Lord Jesus Christ having been crucified under Pontius Pilate, procurator of Palestine and Phœnicia, these records were made in Jerusalem as to what was done by the Jews against the Lord. Pilate therefore, along with his private report, sent them to the Cæsar in Rome, writing thus : —

To the most mighty, venerable, most divine, and most terrible, the august [1] Cæsar, Pilate the governor of the East *sends greeting*. I have, O most mighty, a narrative to give thee, on account of which I am seized with fear and trembling. For in this government of mine, of which one of the cities is called Jerusalem, all the people of the Jews have delivered to me a man named Jesus, bringing many charges against him, which they were not able to convict him of by the consistency of their evidence. And one of the heresies they had against him was, that Jesus said that their Sabbath should not be a day of leisure, and should not be observed. For he performed many cures on that day : he made the blind receive their sight, the lame walk ; he raised up the dead, he cleansed the lepers ; he healed paralytics that were not at all able to make any movement of their body, or to keep their nerves steady, but who had only speech and the modulation of their voice, and he gave them the power of walking and running, removing their illness by a single word. Another thing again, more powerful still, which is strange even with our gods : he raised up one that had been dead four days, summoning him by a single word, when the dead man had his blood corrupted, and when his body was destroyed by the worms produced in it, and when it had the stink of a dog And seeing him lying in the tomb, he ordered him to run. Nor had he anything of a dead body about him at all ; but as a bridegroom from the bridal chamber, so he came forth from the tomb filled with very great fragrance. And strangers that were manifestly demoniac, and that had their dwelling in deserts, and ate their own flesh, living like beasts and creeping things, even these he made to be dwellers in cities, and by his word restored them to soundness of mind, and rendered them wise and able and reputable, eating with all the enemies of the unclean spirits that dwelt in them for their destruction, which he cast down into the depths of the sea. And again there was another having a withered hand ; and not the hand only, but rather the half of the body of the man, was petrified, so that he had not the form of a man, or the power of moving his body. And him by a word he healed, and made sound. And a woman that had an issue of blood for many years, and whose joints [2] and veins were drained by the flowing of the blood, so that she did not present the appearance of a human being, but was like a corpse, and was speechless every day, so that all the physicians of the district could not cure her. For there was not any hope of life left to her. And when Jesus passed by, she mysteriously received strength through his overshadowing her ; and she took hold of his fringe behind, and immediately in the same hour power filled up what in her was empty, so that, no longer suffering any pain, she began to run swiftly to her own city Kepharnaum, so as to accomplish the journey in six days.

And these are the things which I lately had in my mind to report, which Jesus accomplished on the Sabbath. And other signs greater than these he did, so that I have perceived that the wonderful works done by him are greater than can be done by the gods whom we worship.

And him Herod and Archelaus and Philip, Annas and Caiaphas, with all the people, deliv-

---

[1] Or, Augustus.

[2] Codex A has a better reading — arteries. [The MS. here referred to is in Paris, of the fourteenth century (A.D. 1315). — R.]

ered to me, making a great uproar against me that I should try him. I therefore ordered him to be crucified, having first scourged him, and having found against him no cause of evil accusations or deeds.

And at the time he was crucified there was darkness over all the world, the sun being darkened at mid-day, and the stars appearing, but in them there appeared no lustre ; and the moon, as if turned into blood, failed in her light. And the world was swallowed up by the lower regions, so that the very sanctuary of the temple, as they call it, could not be seen by the Jews in their fall ; and they saw below them a chasm of the earth, with the roar of the thunders that fell upon it.[1] And in that terror dead men were seen that had risen, as the Jews themselves testified ; and they said that it was Abraham, and Isaac, and Jacob, and the twelve patriarchs, and Moses and Job, that had died, as they say, three thousand five hundred years before. And there were very many whom I also saw appearing in the body ; and they were making a lamentation about the Jews, on account of the wickedness that had come to pass through them, and the destruction of the Jews and of their law.

And the fear of the earthquake remained from the sixth hour of the preparation until the ninth hour. And on the evening of the first day of the week there was a sound out of the heaven, so that the heaven became enlightened sevenfold more than all the days. And at the third hour of the night also the sun was seen brighter than it had ever shone before, lighting up all the heaven. And as lightnings come suddenly in winter, so majestic men appeared[2] in glorious robes, an innumerable multitude, whose voice was heard as that of a very great thunder, crying out : Jesus that was crucified is risen : come up out of Hades, ye that have been enslaved in the underground regions of Hades. And the chasm of the earth was as if it had no bottom ; but it was as if the very foundations of the earth appeared along with those that cried out in the heavens, and walked about in the body in the midst of the dead that had risen. And he that raised up all the dead, and bound Hades, said : Say to my disciples, He goes before you into Galilee ; there shall you see him.

And all that night the light did not cease shining. And many of the Jews died, swallowed up in the chasm of the earth, so that on the following day most of those who had been against Jesus could not be found. Others saw the appearing of those that had risen, whom no one of us had ever seen.[3] And only one[4] synagogue of the Jews was left in this Jerusalem, since all disappeared in that fall.

With that terror, being in perplexity, and seized with a most frightful trembling, I have written what I saw at that time, and have reported to thy majesty. Having set in order also what was done by the Jews against Jesus, I have sent it, my lord, to thy divinity.

---

[1] The text here is very corrupt.

[2] Or, so men appeared on high.
[3] This sentence also is very corrupt.
[4] Another and more probable reading is, *not one.* [So B, a Paris MS. of the fourteenth century. — R.]

THE REPORT OF PONTIUS PILATE, PROCURATOR OF JUDÆA

SENT TO ROME TO TIBERIUS CÆSAR.

SECOND GREEK FORM.

To the most mighty, venerable, awful, most divine, the august, — Pilatus Pontius, the governor of the East: I have to report to thy reverence, through this writing of mine, being seized with great trembling and fear, O most mighty emperor, the conjuncture of the present times, as the end of these things has shown. For while I, my lord, according to the commandment of thy clemency, was discharging the duties of my government, which is one of the cities of the East, Jerusalem by name, in which is built the temple of the Jewish nation, all the multitude of the Jews came together, and delivered to me a certain man named Jesus, bringing against him many and groundless charges; and they were not able to convict him in anything. And one heresy of theirs against him was, that he said that the Sabbath was not their right rest. And that man wrought many cures, in addition to good works. He made the blind see; he cleansed lepers; he raised the dead; he healed paralytics who could not move at all, except that they only had their voice, and the joining of their bones; and he gave them the power of walking about and running, commanding *them* by a single word. And another mightier work he did, which was strange even with our gods: he raised up a dead man, Lazarus, who had been dead four days, by a single word ordering the dead man to be raised, although his body was already corrupted by the worms that grow in wounds; and that ill-smelling body lying in the tomb he ordered to run; and as a bridegroom from the bridal chamber, so he came forth out of the tomb, filled with exceeding fragrance. And some that were cruelly vexed by demons, and had their dwellings in deserts, and ate the flesh of their own limbs, and lived along with reptiles and wild beasts, he made to be dwellers in cities in their own houses, and by a word he rendered them sound-minded; and he made those that were troubled by unclean spirits to be intelligent and reputable; and sending away the demons in them into a herd of swine, he suffocated them in the sea. Another man, again, who had a withered hand, and lived in sorrow, and had not even the half of his body sound, he rendered sound by a single word. And a woman that had a flow of blood for many years, so that, in consequence of the flowing of her blood, all the joinings of her bones appeared, and were transparent like glass; and assuredly all the physicians had left her without hope, and had not cleansed her, for there was not in her a single hope of health: once, then, as Jesus was passing by, she took hold of the fringe of his clothes behind, and that same hour the power of her body was completely restored, and she became whole, as if nothing were the matter with her, and she began to run swiftly to her own city Paneas.[1]

And these things indeed were so. And the Jews gave information that Jesus did these things on the Sabbath. And I also ascertained that the miracles done by him were greater than any which the gods whom we worship could do.

Him then Herod and Archelaus and Philip, and Annas and Caiaphas, with all the people, delivered to me to try him. And as many were exciting an insurrection against me, I ordered him to be crucified.

And when he had been crucified, there was darkness over the whole earth, the sun having been completely hidden, and the heaven appearing dark though it was day, so that the stars appeared, but had at the same time their brightness darkened, as I suppose your reverence is not ignorant of, because in all the world they lighted lamps from the sixth hour until evening. And the moon, being like blood, did not shine the whole night, and yet she happened to be at

---

[1] This is a conjecture of Thilo's. The mss. have Spania.

the full. And the stars also, and Orion, made a lament about the Jews, on account of the wickedness that had been done by them.[1]

And on the first of the week, about the third hour of the night, the sun was seen such as it had never at any time shone, and all the heaven was lighted up. And as lightnings come on in winter, so majestic men of indescribable splendour of dress and of glory appeared in the air, and an innumerable multitude of angels crying out, and saying: Glory in the highest to God, and on earth peace, among men goodwill : come up out of Hades, ye who have been kept in slavery in the underground regions of Hades. And at their voice all the mountains and hills were shaken, and the rocks were burst asunder; and great chasms were made in the earth, so that also what was in the abyss appeared.

And there were seen in that terror dead men raised up,[2] as the Jews that saw them said : We have seen Abraham, and Isaac, and Jacob, and the twelve patriarchs, that died two thousand five hundred years ago ; and we have seen Noah manifestly in the body. And all the multitude walked about, and sang praises to God with a loud voice, saying : The Lord our God that has risen from the dead has brought to life all the dead, and has plundered Hades, and put him to death.

All that night therefore, my lord, O king, the light ceased not. And many of the Jews died, and were engulphed and swallowed up in the chasms in that night, so that not even their bodies appeared. Those, I say, of the Jews suffered that had spoken against Jesus. And one synagogue was left in Jerusalem, since all those synagogues that had been against Jesus were engulphed.

From that fear, then, being in perplexity, and seized with much trembling, at that same hour I ordered what had been done by them all to be written ; and I have reported it to thy mightiness.

---

[1] Instead of this last sentence, one of the MSS. has: And the whole world was shaken by unspeakable miracles, and all the creation was like to be swallowed up by the lower regions; so that also the sanctuary of their temple was rent from top to bottom. And again there was thunder, and a mighty noise from heaven, so that all our land shook and trembled. Another: And there began to be earthquakes in the hour in which the nails were fixed in Jesus' hands and feet, until evening.

[2] One MS. adds: To the number of five hundred.

THE GIVING UP OF PONTIUS PILATE

AND the writings having come to the city of the Romans, and having been read to the Cæsar, with not a few standing by, all were astounded, because through the wickedness of Pilate the darkness and the earthquake had come over the whole world. And the Cæsar, filled with rage, sent soldiers, and ordered them to bring Pilate a prisoner.

And when he was brought to the city of the Romans, the Cæsar, hearing that Pilate had arrived, sat in the temple of the gods, in the presence of all the senate, and with all the army, and all the multitude of his power; and he ordered Pilate to stand forward.[1] And the Cæsar says to him: Why hast thou, O most impious, dared to do such things, having seen so great miracles in that man? By daring to do an evil deed, thou hast destroyed the whole world.

And Pilate said: O almighty[2] king, I am innocent of these things; but the multitude of the Jews are violent and guilty. And the Cæsar said: And who are they? Pilate says: Herod, Archelaus, Philip, Annas and Caiaphas, and all the multitude of the Jews. The Cæsar says: For what reason didst thou follow out their counsel? And Pilate says: Their nation is rebellious and insubmissive, not submitting themselves to thy power. And the Cæsar said: When they delivered him to thee, thou oughtest to have made him secure, and to have sent him to me, and not to have obeyed them in crucifying such a man, righteous as he was, and one that did such good miracles, as thou hast said in thy report. For from such miracles Jesus was manifestly the Christ, the King of the Jews.

And as the Cæsar was thus speaking, when he named the name of Christ, all the multitude of the gods fell down in a body, and became as dust, where the Cæsar was sitting with the senate. And the people standing beside the Cæsar all began to tremble, on account of the speaking of the word, and the fall of their gods; and being seized with terror, they all went away, each to his own house, wondering at what had happened. And the Cæsar ordered Pilate to be kept in security, in order that he might know the truth about Jesus.

And on the following day, the Cæsar, sitting in the Capitol with all the senate, tried again to question Pilate. And the Cæsar says: Tell the truth, O most impious, because through thy impious action which thou hast perpetrated against Jesus, even here the doing of thy wicked deeds has been shown by the gods having been cast down. Say, then, who is he that has been crucified; because even his name has destroyed all the gods? Pilate said: And indeed the records of him are true; for assuredly I myself was persuaded from his works that he was greater than all the gods whom we worship. And the Cæsar said: For what reason, then, didst thou bring against him such audacity and such doings, if thou wert not ignorant of him, and altogether devising mischief against my kingdom? Pilate said: On account of the wickedness and rebellion of the lawless and ungodly Jews, I did this.

And the Cæsar, being filled with rage, held a council with all his senate and his power, and ordered a decree to be written against the Jews as follows: — To Licianus, the governor of the chief places of the East, greeting. The reckless deed which has been done at the present time by the inhabitants of Jerusalem, and the cities of the Jews round about, and their wicked action, has come to my knowledge, that they have forced Pilate to crucify a certain god named Jesus, and on account of this great fault of theirs the world has been darkened and dragged to destruction. Do thou then speedily, with a multitude of soldiers, go to them there, and make them prisoners, in accordance with this decree. Be obedient, and take action against them, and scatter them, and make them slaves among all the nations; and having driven them out of the whole of Judæa, make them the smallest of nations, so that it may not any longer be seen at all, because they are full of wickedness.[3]

And this decree having come into the region of the East, Licianus, obeying from fear of the decree, seized all the nation of the Jews; and those that were left in Judæa he scattered among the nations, and sold for slaves:[4] so that it was known to the Cæsar that these things had been

---

[1] Or, in the entrance.
[2] αὐτοκράτωρ.

[3] The text is very corrupt.
[4] Lit., he made to be slaves in the dispersion of the Gentiles.

done by Licianus against the Jews in the region of the East; and it pleased him.

And again the Cæsar set himself to question Pilate; and he orders a captain named Albius to cut off Pilate's head, saying: Just as he laid hands upon the just man named Christ, in like manner also shall he fall, and not find safety.

And Pilate, going away to the place, prayed in silence, saying: Lord, do not destroy me along with the wicked Hebrews, because I would not have laid hands upon Thee, except for the nation of the lawless Jews, because they were exciting rebellion against me. But Thou knowest that I did it in ignorance. Do not then destroy me for this my sin; but remember not evil against me, O Lord, and against Thy servant Procla, who is standing with me in this the hour of my death, whom Thou didst appoint to prophesy that Thou shouldest be nailed to the cross. Do not condemn her also in my sin; but pardon us, and make us to be numbered in the portion of Thy righteous.

And, behold, when Pilate had finished his prayer, there came a voice out of the heaven, saying: All the generations and families of the nations shall count thee blessed, because under thee have been fulfilled all those things said about me by the prophets; and thou thyself shalt be seen as my witness at my second appearing, when I shall judge the twelve tribes of Israel, and those that have not owned my name. And the prefect struck off the head of Pilate; and, behold, an angel of the Lord received it. And his wife Procla, seeing the angel coming and receiving his head, being filled with joy herself also, immediately gave up the ghost, and was buried along with her husband.[1]

---

[1] One of the MSS. adds: By the will and good pleasure of our Lord Jesus Christ, to whom be the glory of the Father, and the Son, and the Holy Ghost, now and ever, and to ages of ages. Amen.

THE DEATH OF PILATE, WHO CONDEMNED JESUS

AND when Tiberius Cæsar, the emperor of the Romans, was labouring under a grievous disease, and understanding that there was at Jerusalem a certain physician, Jesus by name, who by a single word cured all infirmities, he, not knowing that the Jews and Pilate had put Him to death, ordered a certain friend of his named Volusianus: Go as quickly as possible across the seas; and thou shalt tell Pilate, my servant and friend, to send me this physician, that he may restore me to my former health. And this Volusianus, having heard the emperor's command, immediately departed, and came to Pilate, as he had been commanded. And he related to the same Pilate what had been entrusted to him by Tiberius Cæsar, saying: Tiberius Cæsar, the emperor of the Romans, thy master, having heard that in this city there is a physician who by his word alone heals infirmities, begs thee earnestly to send him to him for the curing of his infirmity. Pilate, hearing this, was very much afraid, knowing that through envy he had caused Him to be put to death. Pilate answered the same messenger thus, saying: This man was a malefactor, and a man who drew to himself all the people; so a council of the wise men of the city was held, and I caused him to be crucified. And this messenger returning to his inn, met a certain woman named Veronica, who had been a friend of Jesus; and he said: O woman, a certain physician who was in this city, who cured the sick by a word alone, why have the Jews put him to death? And she began to weep, saying: Ah me! my lord, my God and my Lord, whom Pilate for envy delivered, condemned, and ordered to be crucified. Then he, being exceedingly grieved, said: I am vehemently grieved that I am unable to accomplish that for which my lord had sent me. And Veronica said to him: When my Lord was going about preaching, and I, much against my will, was deprived of His presence, I wished His picture to be painted for me, in order that, while I was deprived of His presence, the figure of His picture might at least afford me consolation. And when I was carrying the canvas to the painter to be painted, my Lord met me, and asked whither I was going. And when I had disclosed to Him the cause of my journey, He asked of me the cloth, and gave it back to me impressed with the image of His venerable face. Therefore, if thy lord will devoutly gaze upon His face,[1] he shall obtain forthwith the benefit of health. And he said to her: Is a picture of such a sort procurable by gold or silver? She said to him: No; but by the pious influence of devotion. I shall therefore set out with thee, and shall carry the picture to be seen by Cæsar, and shall come back again.

Volusianus therefore came with Veronica to Rome, and said to Tiberius the emperor: Jesus, whom thou hast been longing for, Pilate and the Jews have delivered to an unjust death, and have through envy affixed to the gibbet of the cross. There has therefore come with me a certain matron, bringing a picture of Jesus himself; and if thou wilt devoutly look upon it, thou shalt immediately obtain the benefit of thy health. Cæsar therefore ordered the way to be strewn with silk cloths, and the picture to be presented to him; and as soon as he had looked upon it, he regained his former health.

Pontius Pilate, therefore, by the command of Cæsar, is taken and brought through to Rome. Cæsar, hearing that Pilate had arrived at Rome, was filled with exceeding fury against him, and caused him to be brought to him. But Pilate brought down with him the seamless tunic of Jesus; and he wore it on him in presence of the emperor. And as soon as the emperor saw him, he laid aside all his anger, and forthwith rose up to meet him. Nor was he able to speak harshly to him in anything; and he who seemed so terrible and fierce in his absence, now in his presence is somehow found to be mild. And when he had sent him away, immediately he blazed out against him terribly, crying out that he was a wretch, inasmuch as he had not at all shown him the fury of his heart. And immediately he made him be called back, swearing and declaring that he was the son of death, and that it was infamous that he should live upon the earth. And as soon as he saw him, he forthwith saluted him,

---

[1] Or, upon the sight of this.

466

and threw away all the ferocity of his mind. All wondered; and he himself wondered that he should thus blaze out against Pilate when he was absent, and that while he was present he could say nothing to him roughly.   Then, by a divine impulse, or perhaps by the advice of some Christian,[1] he caused him to be stripped of that tunic, and immediately resumed against him his former ferocity of mind. And when at this the emperor wondered very much, it was told him that that tunic had belonged to the Lord Jesus.   Then the emperor ordered him to be kept in prison, until he should deliberate in a council of the wise men what ought to be done with him.   And a few days after, sentence was therefore passed upon Pilate, that he should be condemned to the most disgraceful death.   Pilate, hearing this, killed himself with his own knife, and by such a death ended his life.

When Cæsar knew of the death of Pilate, he said : Truly he has died by a most disgraceful death, whom his own hand has not spared.   He is therefore bound to a great mass, and sunk into the river Tiber.   But malignant and filthy spirits in his malignant and filthy body, all rejoicing together, kept moving themselves in the waters, and in a terrible manner brought lightnings and tempests, thunders and hail-storms, in the air, so that all men were kept in horrible fear.   Wherefore the Romans, drawing him out of the river Tiber, in derision carried him down to Vienna, and sunk him in the river Rhone. For Vienna is called, as it were, *Via Gehennæ*, the way of Gehenna, because it was then a place of cursing.   But there evil spirits were present, working the same things in the same place. Those men therefore, not enduring such a visitation of demons, removed from themselves that vessel of malediction, and sent him to be buried in the territory of Losania.[2]   And they, seeing that they were troubled by the aforesaid visitations, removed him from themselves, and sunk him in a certain pit surrounded by mountains, where to this day, according to the account of some, certain diabolical machinations are said to bubble up.

---

[1] This is the first appearance of the word Christian in these writings.

[2] Losonium was the Roman name of Lausanne.   For a discussion of this legend concerning Mont Pilate, near Lucerne, see Smith's *Dictionary of the Bible*, under Pilate.

THE NARRATIVE OF JOSEPH

NARRATIVE OF JOSEPH OF ARIMATHÆA, THAT BEGGED THE LORD'S BODY;
IN WHICH ALSO HE BRINGS IN THE CASES OF THE TWO ROBBERS.

CHAP. I. — I *am* Joseph of Arimathæa, who begged from Pilate the body of the Lord Jesus for burial, and who for this cause was kept close in prison by the murderous and God-fighting[1] Jews, who also, keeping to the law, have by Moses himself become partakers in tribulation; and having provoked their Lawgiver to anger, and not knowing that He was God, crucified Him, and made Him manifest to those that knew God. In those days in which they condemned the Son of God to be crucified, seven days before Christ suffered, two condemned robbers were sent from Jericho to the procurator Pilate; and their case was as follows: —

The first, his name Gestas, put travellers to death, murdering them with the sword, and others he exposed naked. And he hung up women by the heels, head down, and cut off their breasts, and drank the blood of infants' limbs, never having known God, not obeying the laws, being violent from the beginning, and doing such deeds.

And the case of the other was as follows: He was called Demas, and was by birth a Galilæan, and kept an inn. He made attacks upon the rich, but was good to the poor — a thief like Tobit, for he buried the bodies of the poor.[2] And he set his hand to robbing the multitude of the Jews, and stole the law[3] itself in Jerusalem, and stripped naked the daughter of Caiaphas, who was priestess of the sanctuary, and took away from its place the mysterious deposit itself placed there by Solomon. Such were his doings.

And Jesus also was taken on the third day before the passover, in the evening. And to Caiaphas and the multitude of the Jews it was not a passover, but it was a great mourning to them, on account of the plundering of the sanctuary by the robber. And they summoned Judas Iscariot, and spoke to him, for he was *son* of the brother[4] of Caiaphas the priest. He was not a disciple before the face of Jesus; but all the multitude of the Jews craftily supported him, that he might follow Jesus, not that he might be obedient to the miracles done by Him, nor that he might confess Him, but that he might betray Him to them, wishing to catch up some lying word of Him, giving him gifts for such brave, honest conduct to the amount of a half shekel of gold each day. And he did this for two years with Jesus, as says one of His disciples called John.

And on the third day, before Jesus was laid hold of, Judas says to the Jews: Come, let us hold a council; for perhaps it was not the robber that stole the law, but Jesus himself, and I accuse him. And when these words had been spoken, Nicodemus, who kept the keys of the sanctuary, came in to us, and said to all: Do not do such a deed. For Nicodemus was true, more than all the multitude of the Jews. And the daughter of Caiaphas, Sarah by name, cried out, and said: He himself said before all against this holy place, I am able to destroy this temple, and in three days to raise it. The Jews say to her: Thou hast credit with all of us. For they regarded her as a prophetess. And assuredly, after the council had been held, Jesus was laid hold of.

CHAP. 2. — And on the following day, the fourth day of the week, they brought Him at the ninth hour into the hall of Caiaphas. And Annas and Caiaphas say to Him: Tell us, why hast thou stolen our law, and renounced[5] the ordinances of Moses and the prophets? And Jesus answered nothing. And again a second time, the multitude also being present, they say to Him: The sanctuary which Solomon built in forty and six years, why dost thou wish to destroy in one moment? And to these things Jesus answered nothing. For the sanctuary of the synagogue had been plundered by the robber.

---

[1] MS. C has God-killing. [C is the designation given by Tischendorf to the MS. from which Birch made his edition of the text. It is in Paris; date A.D. 1315. The MSS. which Tischendorf himself collated are designated A (in the Ambrosian library at Milan, of about the twelfth century), B (Paris, fifteenth century), D (Harleian codex, of the same century). Only a small part of the last MS. was used by Tischendorf; see his *prolegomena*, p. lxxxi. — R.]

[2] Tobit i. 17, 18.

[3] Perhaps the true reading is ναόν, and not νόμον: plundered the temple.

[4] MS. B has: And they say that he was of the family of the sister, etc.

[5] Tischendorf suggests ἀέκρυψας, hidden, for ἀπεκήρυξας.

And the evening of the fourth day being ended, all the multitude sought to burn the daughter of Caiaphas, on account of the loss of the law; for they did not know how they were to keep the passover. And she said to them: Wait, my children, and let us destroy this Jesus, and the law will be found, and the holy feast will be fully accomplished. And secretly Annas and Caiaphas gave considerable money to Judas Iscariot, saying: Say as thou saidst to us before, I know that the law has been stolen by Jesus, that the accusation may be turned against him, and not against this maiden, who is free from blame. And Judas having received this command, said to them: Let not all the multitude know that I have been instructed by you to do this against Jesus; but release Jesus, and I persuade the multitude that it is so. And craftily they released Jesus.

And Judas, going into the sanctuary at the dawn of the fifth day, says to all the people: What will you give me, and I will give up to you the overthrower[1] of the law, and the plunderer of the prophets? The Jews say to him: If thou wilt give him up to us, we will give thee thirty pieces of gold. And the people did not know that Judas was speaking about Jesus, for many of them confessed that he was the Son of God. And Judas received the thirty pieces of gold.

And going out at the fourth hour, and at the fifth, he finds Jesus walking in the street. And as evening was coming on, Judas says to the Jews: Give me the aid of soldiers with swords and staves, and I will give him up to you. They therefore gave him officers for the purpose of seizing Him. And as they were going along, Judas says to them: Lay hold of the man whom I shall kiss, for he has stolen the law and the prophets. Going up to Jesus, therefore, he kissed Him, saying: Hail, Rabbi! it being the evening of the fifth day. And having laid hold of Him, they gave Him up to Caiaphas and the chief priests, Judas saying: This is he who stole the law and the prophets. And the Jews gave Jesus an unjust trial, saying: Why hast thou done these things? And he answered nothing.

And Nicodemus and I Joseph, seeing the seat of the plagues,[2] stood off from them, not wishing to perish along with the counsel of the ungodly.

CHAP. 3. — Having therefore done many and dreadful things against Jesus that night, they gave Him up to Pilate the procurator at the dawn of the preparation, that they might crucify Him; and for this purpose they all came together. After a trial, therefore, Pilate the procurator ordered Him to be nailed to the cross, along with the two robbers. And they were nailed up along with Jesus, Gestas on the left, and Demas on the right.

And he that was on the left began to cry out, saying to Jesus: See how many evil deeds I have done in the earth; and if I had known that thou wast the king, I should have cut off thee also. And why dost thou call thyself Son of God, and canst not help thyself in necessity? how canst thou afford it to another one praying for help? If thou art the Christ, come down from the cross, that I may believe in thee. But now I see thee perishing along with me, not like a man, but like a wild beast. And many other things he began to say against Jesus, blaspheming and gnashing his teeth upon Him. For the robber was taken alive in the snare of the devil.[3]

But the robber on the right hand, whose name was Demas, seeing the Godlike grace of Jesus, thus cried out: I know Thee, Jesus Christ, that Thou art the Son of God. I see Thee, Christ, adored by myriads of myriads of angels. Pardon me my sins which I have done. Do not in my trial make the stars come against me, or the moon, when Thou shalt judge all the world; because in the night I have accomplished my wicked purposes. Do not urge the sun, which is now darkened on account of Thee, to tell the evils of my heart, for no gift can I give Thee for the remission of my sins. Already death is coming upon me because of my sins; but Thine is the propitiation. Deliver me, O Lord of all, from Thy fearful judgment. Do not give the enemy power to swallow me up, and to become heir of my soul, as of that of him who is hanging on the left; for I see how the devil joyfully takes his soul, and his body disappears. Do not even order me to go away into the portion of the Jews; for I see Moses and the patriarchs in great weeping, and the devil rejoicing over them. Before, then, O Lord, my spirit departs, order my sins to be washed away, and remember me the sinner in Thy kingdom, when upon the great most lofty throne[4] thou shalt judge the twelve tribes of Israel.[5] For Thou hast prepared great punishment for Thy world on account of Thyself.

And the robber having thus spoken, Jesus says to him: Amen, amen; I say to thee, Demas, that to-day thou shalt be with me in paradise.[6] And the sons of the kingdom, the children of Abraham, and Isaac, and Jacob, and Moses, shall be cast out into outer darkness; there shall be weeping and gnashing of teeth.[7] And thou alone shalt dwell in paradise until my second appearing, when I am to judge those who do not

---

[1] Or, taker away.
[2] Following the reading of the LXX. in Ps. i. 1.

[3] 2 Tim. ii. 26.
[4] Or, upon the great throne of the Most High.
[5] Matt. xix. 28.
[6] Luke xxiii. 43.
[7] Matt. viii. 11, 12.

confess my name. And He said to the robber: Go away, and tell the cherubim and the powers, that turn the flaming sword, that guard paradise from the time that Adam, the first created, was in paradise, and sinned, and kept not my commandments, and I cast him out thence. And none of the first shall see paradise until I am to come the second time to judge living and dead. And He wrote thus: Jesus Christ the Son of God, who have come down from the heights of the heavens, who have come forth out of the bosom of the invisible Father without being separated from Him,[1] and who have come down into the world to be made flesh, and to be nailed to a cross, in order that I might save Adam, whom I fashioned, — to my archangelic powers, the gatekeepers of paradise, to the officers of my Father: I will and order that he who has been crucified along with me should go in, should receive remission of sins through me; and that he, having put on an incorruptible body, should go in to paradise, and dwell where no one has ever been able to dwell.

And, behold, after He had said this, Jesus gave up the ghost, on the day of the preparation, at the ninth hour. And there was darkness over all the earth; and from a great earthquake that happened, the sanctuary fell down, and the wing of the temple.

CHAP. 4. — And I Joseph begged the body of Jesus, and put it in a new tomb, where no one had been put. And of the robber on the right the body was not found; but of him on the left, as the form of a dragon, so was his body.

And after I had begged the body of Jesus to bury, the Jews, carried away by hatred and rage, shut me up in prison, where evil-doers were kept under restraint. And this happened to me on the evening of the Sabbath, whereby our nation transgressed the law. And, behold, that same nation of ours endured fearful tribulations on the Sabbath.

And now, on the evening of the first of the week, at the fifth hour of the night, Jesus comes to me in the prison, along with the robber who had been crucified with Him on the right, whom He sent into paradise. And there was a great light in the building. And the house was hung up by the four corners, and the place was opened, and I came out. Then I first recognised Jesus, and again the robber, bringing a letter to Jesus. And as we were going into Galilee, there shone a great light, which the creation did not produce. And there was also with the robber a great fragrance out of paradise.

And Jesus, having sat down in a certain place, thus read: We, the cherubim and the six-winged,

who have been ordered by Thy Godhead to watch the garden of paradise, make the following statement through the robber who was crucified along with Thee, by Thy arrangement: When we saw the print of the nails of the robber crucified along with Thee, and the shining light of the letter of Thy Godhead,[2] the fire indeed was extinguished, not being able to bear the splendour of the print;[3] and we crouched down, being in great fear. For we heard that the Maker of heaven and earth, and of the whole creation, had come down from on high to dwell in the lower parts of the earth, on account of Adam, the first created. And when we beheld the undefiled cross shining like lightning from the robber, gleaming with sevenfold the light of the sun, trembling fell upon us. We felt a violent shaking of the world below;[4] and with a loud voice, the ministers of Hades said, along with us: Holy, holy, holy is He who in the beginning was in the highest. And the powers sent up a cry: O Lord, Thou hast been made manifest in heaven and in earth, bringing joy to the world; and, a greater gift than this, Thou hast freed Thine own image from death by the invisible purpose of the ages.

CHAP. 5. — After I had beheld these things, as I was going into Galilee with Jesus and the robber, Jesus was transfigured, and was not as formerly, before He was crucified, but was altogether light; and angels always ministered to Him, and Jesus spoke with them. And I remained with Him three days. And no one of His disciples was with Him, except the robber alone.

And in the middle of the feast of unleavened bread, His disciple John comes, and we no longer beheld the robber as to what took place. And John asked Jesus: Who is this, that Thou hast not made me to be seen by him? But Jesus answered him nothing. And falling down before Him, he said: Lord, I know that Thou hast loved me from the beginning, and why dost Thou not reveal to me that man? Jesus says to him: Why dost thou seek what is hidden? Art thou still without understanding? Dost thou not perceive the fragrance of paradise filling the place? Dost thou not know who it is? The robber on the cross has become heir of paradise. Amen, amen; I say to thee, that it shall belong to him alone until that the great day shall come. And John said: Make me worthy to behold him.

And while John was yet speaking, the robber suddenly appeared; and John, struck with astonishment, fell to the earth. And the robber

---

[1] Lit., inseparably.

[2] Or, the shining light of the letter, the fire of the Godhead, we indeed were extinguished.
[3] i e., of the nails.
[4] The text is here corrupt; but this seems to be the meaning.

was not in his first form, as before John came; but he was like a king in great power, having on him the cross. And the voice of a great multitude was sent forth: Thou hast come to the place prepared for thee in paradise. We have been commanded by Him that has sent thee, to serve thee until the great day. And after this voice, both the robber and I Joseph vanished, and I was found in my own house; and I no longer saw Jesus.

And I, having seen these things, have written them down, in order that all may believe in the crucified Jesus Christ our Lord, and may no longer obey the law of Moses, but may believe in the signs and wonders that have happened through Him, and in order that we who have believed may inherit eternal life, and be found in the kingdom of the heavens. For to Him are due glory, strength, praise, and majesty for ever and ever. Amen.

THE AVENGING OF THE SAVIOUR

THIS version of the legend of Veronica is written in very barbarous Latin, probably of the seventh or eighth century. An Anglo-Saxon version, which Tischendorf concludes to be derived from the Latin, was edited and translated for the Cambridge Antiquarian Society, by C. W. Goodwin, in 1851. The Anglo-Saxon text is from a MS. in the Cambridge Library, one of a number presented to the Cathedral of Exeter by Bishop Leofric in the beginning of the eleventh century.

The reader will observe that there are in this document two distinct legends, somewhat clumsily joined together — that of Nathan's embassy, and that of Veronica.

HERE BEGINNETH THE AVENGING OF THE SAVIOUR.

IN the days of the Emperor Tiberius Cæsar, when Herod was tetrarch, Christ was delivered under Pontius Pilate by the Jews, and revealed by Tiberius.

In those days Titus [1] was a prince under Tiberius in the region of Equitania, in a city of Libia which is called Burgidalla. And Titus had a sore in his right nostril, on account of a cancer, and he had his face torn even to the eye. There went forth a certain man from Judæa, by name Nathan the son of Nahum; for he was an Ishmaelite who went from land to land, and from sea to sea, and in all the ends of the earth. Now Nathan was sent from Judæa to the Emperor Tiberius, to carry their treaty to the city of Rome. And Tiberius was ill, and full of ulcers and fevers, and had nine kinds of leprosy. And Nathan wished to go to the city of Rome. But the north wind blew and hindered his sailing, and carried him down to the harbour of a city of Libia. Now Titus, seeing the ship coming, knew that it was from Judæa; and they all wondered, and said that they had never seen any vessel so coming from that quarter. And Titus ordered the captain to come to him, and asked him who he was. And he said: I am Nathan the son of Nahum, of the race of the Ishmaelites, and I am a subject of Pontius Pilate in Judæa. And I have been sent to go to Tiberius the Roman emperor, to carry a treaty from Judæa. And a strong wind came down upon the sea, and has brought me to a country that I do not know.

And Titus says: If thou couldst at any time find anything either of cosmetics or herbs which could cure the wound that I have in my face, as thou seest, so that I should become whole, and regain my former health, I should bestow upon thee many good things. And Nathan said to him: I do not know, nor have I ever known, of such things as thou speakest to me about. But for all that, if thou hadst been some time ago in Jerusalem, there thou wouldst have found a choice prophet, whose name was Emanuel, for He will save His people from their sins. And He, as His first miracle in Cana of Galilee, made wine from water; and by His word He cleansed lepers, He enlightened the eyes of one born blind, He healed paralytics, He made demons flee, He raised up three dead; a woman caught in adultery, and condemned by the Jews to be stoned, He set free; and another woman, named Veronica, who suffered twelve years from an issue of blood, and came up to Him behind, and touched the fringe of His garment, He healed; and with five loaves and two fishes He satisfied five thousand men, to say nothing of little ones and women, and there remained of the fragments twelve baskets. All these things, and many others, were accomplished before His passion. After His resurrection we saw Him in the flesh as He had been before. And Titus said to Him: How did he rise again from the dead, seeing that he was dead? And Nathan answered

---

[1] The Saxon version has Titus.

and said : He was manifestly dead, and hung up on the cross, and again taken down from the cross, and for three days He lay in the tomb ; thereafter He rose again from the dead, and went down to Hades, and freed the patriarchs and the prophets, and the whole human race ; thereafter He appeared to His disciples, and ate with them ; thereafter they saw Him going up into heaven. And so it is the truth, all this that I tell you. For I saw it with my own eyes, and all the house of Israel. And Titus said in his own words : Woe to thee, O Emperor Tiberius, full of ulcers, and enveloped in leprosy, because such a scandal has been committed in thy kingdom ; because thou hast made such laws [1] in Judæa, in the land of the birth of our Lord Jesus Christ, and they have seized the King, and put to death the Ruler of the peoples ; and they have not made Him come to us to cure thee of thy leprosy, and cleanse me from mine infirmity : on which account, if they had been before my face, with my own hands I should have slain the carcases of those Jews, and hung them up on the cruel tree, because they have destroyed my Lord, and mine eyes have not been worthy to see His face. And when he had thus spoken, immediately the wound fell from the face of Titus, and his flesh and his face were restored to health. And all the sick who were in the same place were made whole in that hour. And Titus cried out, and all the rest with him, in a loud voice, saying : My King and my God, because I have never seen Thee, and Thou hast made me whole, bid me go with the ship over the waters to the land of Thy birth, to take vengeance on Thine enemies ; and help me, O Lord, that I may be able to destroy them, and avenge Thy death : do Thou, Lord, deliver them into my hand. And having thus spoken, he ordered that he should be baptized. And he called Nathan to him, and said to him : How hast thou seen those baptized who believe in Christ? Come to me, and baptize me in the name of the Father, and of the Son, and of the Holy Ghost. Amen.[2] For I also firmly believe in the Lord Jesus Christ with all my heart, and with all my soul ; because nowhere in the whole world is there another who has created me, and made me whole from my wounds.

And having thus spoken, he sent messengers to Vespasian to come with all haste with his bravest men, so prepared as if for war.

Then Vespasian brought with him five thousand armed men, and they went to meet Titus. And when they had come to the city of Libia,

he said to Titus : Why is it that thou hast made me come hither? And he said : Know that Jesus has come into this world, and has been born in Judæa, in a place which is called Bethlehem, and has been given up by the Jews, and scourged, and crucified on Mount Calvary,[3] and has risen again from the dead on the third day. And His disciples have seen Him in the same flesh in which he was born, and He has shown Himself to His disciples, and they have believed in Him. And we indeed wish to become His disciples. Now, let us go and destroy His enemies from the earth, that they may now know that there is none like the Lord our God on the face of the earth.

With this design, then, they went forth from the city of Libia which is called Burgidalla,[4] and went on board a ship, and proceeded to Jerusalem, and surrounded the kingdom of the Jews, and began to send them to destruction. And when the kings of the Jews heard of their doings, and the wasting of their land, fear came upon them, and they were in great perplexity. Then Archelaus[5] was perplexed in his words, and said to his son : My son, take my kingdom and judge it ; and take counsel with the other kings who are in the land of Judah, that you may be able to escape from our enemies. And having thus said, he unsheathed his sword and leant upon it ; and turned his sword, which was very sharp, and thrust it into his breast, and died. And his son allied himself with the other kings who were under him, and they took counsel among themselves, and went into Jerusalem with their chief men who were in their counsel, and stood in the same place seven years. And Titus and Vespasian took counsel to surround their city. And they did so. And the seven years being fulfilled, there was a very sore famine, and for want of bread they began to eat earth. Then all the soldiers who were of the four kings took counsel among themselves, and said : Now we are sure to die : what will God do to us? or of what good is our life to us, because the Romans have come to take our place and nation? It is better for us to kill each other, than that the Romans should say that they have slain us, and gained the victory over us. And they drew their swords and smote themselves, and died, to the number of twelve thousand men of them. Then there was a great stench in that city from the corpses of those dead men. And their kings feared with a very great fear even unto death ; and they could not bear the stench of them, nor bury them, nor throw them forth out of the city. And they

---

[1] *Reges*, kings, instead of *leges*, as suggested by Mr. Cowper, is a much better reading.
[2] Sax.: Then Nathan came, and baptized him in the name of the Father, and the Son, and the Holy Ghost, and took away from him his name of Tirus, and called him in his baptism Titus, which is in our language Pius.

[3] Note the popular but erroneous appellation of Mount.
[4] Sax. omits *which is called Burgidalla*.
[5] Sax.: And Herod the king was so terrified, that he said to Archelaus his son.

said to each other: What shall we do? We indeed gave up Christ to death, and now we are given up to death ourselves. Let us bow our heads, and give up the keys of the city to the Romans, because God has already given us up to death. And immediately they went up upon the walls of the city, and all cried out with a loud voice, saying: Titus and Vespasian, take the keys of the city, which have been given to you by Messiah, who is called Christ.

Then they gave themselves up into the hands of Titus and Vespasian, and said: Judge us, seeing that we ought to die, because we judged Christ; and he was given up without cause. Titus and Vespasian seized them, and some they stoned, and some they hanged on a tree, feet up and head down, and struck them through with lances; and others they gave up to be sold, and others they divided among themselves, and made four parts of them, just as they had done of the garments of the Lord. And they said: They sold Christ for thirty pieces of silver, and we shall sell thirty of them for one denarius. And so they did. And having done so, they seized all the lands of Judæa and Jerusalem.

Then they made a search about the face or portrait[1] of Jesus, how they might find it.[2] And they found a woman named Veronica who had it. Then they seized Pilate, and sent him to prison, to be guarded by four quaternions of soldiers at the door of the prison. Then they forthwith sent their messengers to Tiberius, the emperor of the city of Rome, that he should send Velosianus to them. And he said to him: Take all that is necessary for thee in the sea, and go down into Judæa, and seek out one of the disciples of him who is called Christ and Lord, that he may come to me, and in the name of his God cure me of the leprosy and the infirmities by which I am daily exceedingly burdened, and of my wounds, because I am ill at ease. And send upon the kings of the Jews, who are subject to my authority, thy forces and terrible engines, because they have put to death Jesus Christ our Lord, and condemn them to death. And if thou shalt there find a man as may be able to free me from this infirmity of mine, I will believe in Christ the Son of God, and will baptize myself in his name. And Velosianus said: My lord emperor, if I find such a man as may be able to help and free us, what reward shall I promise him? Tiberius said to him: The half of my kingdom, without fail, to be in his hand.

Then Velosianus immediately went forth, and went on board the ship, and hoisted the sail in the vessel, and went on sailing through the sea. And he sailed a year and seven days, after which he arrived at Jerusalem. And immediately he ordered some of the Jews to come to his power, and began carefully to ask what had been the acts of Christ. Then Joseph, of the city of Arimathæa, and Nicodemus, came at the same time. And Nicodemus said: I saw Him, and I know indeed that He is the Saviour of the world. And Joseph said to him: And I took Him down from the cross, and laid Him in a new tomb, which had been cut out of the rock. And the Jews kept me shut up on the day of the preparation, at evening; and while I was standing in prayer on the Sabbath-day, the house was hung up by the four corners, and I saw the Lord Jesus Christ like a gleam of light, and for fear I fell to the ground. And He said to me, Look upon me, for I am Jesus, whose body thou buriedst in thy tomb. And I said to Him, Show me the sepulchre where I laid Thee. And Jesus, holding my hand in His right hand, led me to the place where I buried Him.[3]

And there came also the woman named Veronica, and said to him: And I touched in the crowd the fringe of His garment, because for twelve years I had suffered from an issue of blood; and He immediately healed me. Then Velosianus said to Pilate: Thou, Pilate, impious and cruel, why hast thou slain the Son of God? And Pilate answered: His own nation, and the chief priests Annas and Caiaphas, gave him to me. Velosianus said: Impious and cruel, thou art worthy of death and cruel punishment. And he sent him back to prison. And Velosianus at last sought for the face or the countenance of the Lord. And all who were in that same place said: It is the woman called Veronica who has the portrait of the Lord in her house. And immediately he ordered her to be brought before his power. And he said to her: Hast thou the portrait of the Lord in thy house? But she said, No. Then Velosianus ordered her to be put to the torture, until she should give up the portrait of the Lord. And she was forced to say: I have it in clean linen, my lord, and I daily adore it. Velosianus said: Show it to me. Then she showed the portrait of the Lord. When Velosianus saw it, he prostrated himself on the ground; and with a ready heart and true faith he took hold of it, and wrapped it in cloth of gold, and placed it in a casket, and sealed it with his ring. And he swore with an oath, and said: As the Lord God liveth, and by the health

---

[1] Lit., countenance.
[2] Sax.: And they inquired diligently whether perchance there were there any one who had miraculous relics of the Saviour, of His clothing, or other precious things; and they sought so diligently, that they found a woman, etc.

[3] In the Saxon, Joseph's speech is: I know that they took Him down from the cross, and laid Him in the tomb which I had cut out of the rock. And I was one of those who guarded His tomb; and I bent my head and thought I should see Him, but I beheld nothing of Him, but saw two angels, one at the head and the other at the foot, and they asked me whom I was seeking. I answered and said to them, I seek Jesus who was crucified. Again they said to me, Go into Galilee; there shall you see Him, as He said to you before.

of Cæsar, no man shall any more see it upon the face of the earth, until I see the face of my lord Tiberius. And when he had thus spoken, the princes, who were the chief men of Judæa, seized Pilate to take him to a seaport. And he took the portrait of the Lord, with all His disciples, and all in his pay, and they went on board the ship the same day. Then the woman Veronica, for the love of Christ, left all that she possessed, and followed Velosianus. And Velosianus said to her: What dost thou wish, woman, or what dost thou seek? And she answered: I am seeking the portrait of our Lord Jesus Christ, who enlightened me, not for my own merits, but through His own holy affection.[1] Give back to me the portrait of my Lord Jesus Christ; for because of this I die with a righteous longing. But if thou do not give it back to me, I will not leave it until I see where thou wilt put it, because I, most miserable woman that I am, will serve Him all the days of my life; because I believe that He, my Redeemer, liveth for everlasting.

Then Velosianus ordered the woman Veronica to be taken down with him into the ship. And the sails being hoisted, they began to go in the vessel in the name of the Lord, and they sailed through the sea. But Titus, along with Vespasian, went up into Judæa, avenging all nations upon their land.[2] At the end of a year Velosianus came to the city of Rome, brought his vessel into the river which is called Tiberis, or Tiber, and entered the city which is called Rome. And he sent his messenger to his lord Tiberius the emperor in the Lateran about his prosperous arrival.

Then Tiberius the emperor, when he heard the message of Velosianus, rejoiced greatly, and ordered him to come before his face. And when he had come, he called him, saying: Velosianus, how hast thou come, and what hast thou seen in the region of Judæa of Christ the Lord and his disciples? Tell me, I beseech thee, that he is going to cure me of mine infirmity, that I may be at once cleansed from that leprosy which I have over my body, and I give up my whole kingdom into thy power and his.

And Velosianus said: My lord emperor, I found thy servants Titus and Vespasian in Judæa fearing the Lord, and they were cleansed from all their ulcers and sufferings. And I found that all the kings and rulers of Judæa have been hanged by Titus; Annas and Caiaphas have

been stoned, Archelaus has killed himself with his own lance; and I have sent Pilate to Damascus in bonds, and kept him in prison under safe keeping. But I have also found out about Jesus, whom the Jews most wickedly attacked with swords, and staves, and weapons; and they crucified him who ought to have freed and enlightened us, and to have come to us, and they hanged him on a tree. And Joseph came from Arimathæa, and Nicodemus with him, bringing a mixture of myrrh and aloes, about a hundred pounds, to anoint the body of Jesus; and they took him down from the cross, and laid him in a new tomb. And on the third day he most assuredly rose again from the dead, and showed himself to his disciples in the same flesh in which he had been born. At length, after forty days, they saw him going up into heaven. Many, indeed, and other miracles did Jesus before his passion and after. First, of water he made wine; he raised the dead, he cleansed lepers, he enlightened the blind, he cured paralytics, he put demons to flight; he made the deaf hear, the dumb speak; Lazarus, when four days dead, he raised from the tomb; the woman Veronica, who suffered from an issue of blood twelve years, and touched the fringe of his garment, he made whole. Then it pleased the Lord in the heavens, that the Son of God, who, sent into this world as the first-created, had died upon earth, should send his angel; and he commanded Titus and Vespasian, whom I knew in that place where thy throne is. And it pleased God Almighty that they went into Judæa and Jerusalem, and seized thy subjects, and put them under that sentence, as it were, in the same manner as they did when thy subjects seized Jesus and bound him. And Vespasian afterwards said: What shall we do about those who shall remain? Titus answered: They hanged our Lord on a green tree, and struck him with a lance; now let us hang them on a dry tree, and pierce their bodies through and through with the lance. And they did so. And Vespasian said: What about those who are left? Titus answered: They seized the tunic of our Lord Jesus Christ, and of it made four parts; now let us seize them, and divide them into four parts, — to thee one, to me one, to thy men another, and to my servants the fourth part. And they did so. And Vespasian said: But what shall we do about those who are left? Titus answered him: The Jews sold our Lord for thirty pieces of silver: now let us sell thirty of them for one piece of silver. And they did so. And they seized Pilate, and gave him up to me, and I put him in prison, to be guarded by four quaternions of soldiers in Damascus. Then they made a search with great diligence to seek the portrait of the Lord; and they found a woman named Veronica who had the portrait of the Lord. Then the

---

[1] A few lines of the text are here very corrupt, and are omitted by Tischendorf. The meaning of them is: And woe's me, because, contrary to the law, thou hast treated me most unjustly. Ah! woe's me, because thou hast taken my Lord from me; just as the Jews did contrary to the law in crucifying in this world the Lord Jesus Christ, whom the eyes of your Cæsar have not seen. But woe's me! have I done contrary to the law? Have I deserved to suffer this punishment?

[2] Or, taking vengeance upon all the nations of their land.

Emperor Tiberius said to Velosianus : How hast thou it? And he answered : I have it in clean cloth of gold, rolled up in a shawl. And the Emperor Tiberius said : Bring it to me, and spread it before my face, that I, falling to the ground and bending my knees, may adore it on the ground. Then Velosianus spread out his shawl with the cloth of gold on which the portrait of the Lord had been imprinted ; and the Emperor Tiberius saw it. And he immediately adored the image of the Lord with a pure heart, and his flesh was cleansed as the flesh of a little child. And all the blind, the lepers, the lame, the dumb, the deaf, and those possessed by various diseases, who were there present, were healed, and cured, and cleansed. And the Emperor Tiberius bowed his head and bent his knees, considering that saying : Blessed is the womb which bore Thee, and the breasts which Thou hast sucked ; and he groaned to the Lord, saying with tears : God of heaven and earth, do not permit me to sin, but confirm my soul and my body, and place me in Thy kingdom, because in Thy name do I trust always : free me from all evils, as Thou didst free the three children from the furnace of blazing fire.

Then said the Emperor Tiberius to Velosianus : Velosianus, hast thou seen any of those men who saw Christ? Velosianus answered : I have. He said : Didst thou ask how they baptize those who believed in Christ? Velosianus said : Here, my Lord, we have one of the disciples of Christ himself. Then he ordered Nathan to be summoned to come to him. Nathan therefore came and baptized him in the name of the Father, and of the Son, and of the Holy Ghost. Amen. Immediately the Emperor Tiberius, made whole from all his diseases, ascended upon his throne, and said : Blessed art Thou, O Lord God Almighty, and worthy to be praised, who hast freed me from the snare of death, and cleansed me from all mine iniquities ; because I have greatly sinned before Thee, O Lord my God, and I am not worthy to see Thy face. And then the Emperor Tiberius was instructed in all the articles of the faith, fully, and with strong faith.

May that same God Almighty, who is King of kings and Lord of lords, Himself shield us in His faith, and defend us, and deliver us from all danger and evil, and deign to bring us to life everlasting, when this life, which is temporary, shall fail ; who is blessed for ever and ever. Amen.

ACTS OF THE HOLY APOSTLES PETER AND PAUL

IT came to pass, after Paul went out of the island Gaudomeleta,[1] that he came to Italy; and it was heard of by the Jews who were in Rome, the elder of the cities, that Paul demanded to come to Cæsar. Having fallen, therefore, into great grief and much despondency, they said among themselves: It does not please him that he alone has afflicted all our brethren and parents in Judæa and Samaria, and in all Palestine; and he has not been pleased with these, but, behold, he comes here also, having through imposition asked Cæsar to destroy us.

Having therefore made an assembly against Paul, and having considered many proposals,[2] it seemed good to them to go to Nero the emperor, *to ask him* not to allow Paul to come to Rome. Having therefore got in readiness not a few presents, and having carried them with them, with supplication they came before him, saying: We beseech thee, O good emperor, send orders into all the governments of your worship, to the effect that Paul is not to come near these parts; because this Paul, having afflicted all the nation of our fathers, has been seeking to come hither to destroy us also. And the affliction, O most worshipful emperor, which we have from Peter is enough for us.

And the Emperor Nero, having heard these things, answered them: It is [3] according to your wish. And we write to all our governments that he shall not on any account come to anchor in the parts of Italy. And they also informed Simon the magian, having sent for him, that, as has been said, he should not come into the parts of Italy.

And while they were thus doing, some of those that had repented out of the nations, and that had been baptized at the preaching of Peter, sent elders to Paul with a letter to the following effect: Paul, dear servant of our Lord Jesus Christ, and brother of Peter, the first of the apostles, we have heard from the rabbis of the Jews that are in this Rome, the greatest of the cities, that they have asked Cæsar to send into all his governments, in order that, wherever thou mayst be found, thou mayst be put to death. But we have believed, and do believe, that as God does not separate the two great lights which He has made, so He is not to part you from each other, that is, neither Peter from Paul, nor Paul from Peter; but we positively believe in our Lord Jesus Christ, into whom we have been baptized, that we have become worthy also of your teaching.

And Paul, having received the two men sent with the letter on the twentieth of the month of May, became eager *to go*, and gave thanks to the Lord and Master Jesus Christ. And having sailed from Gaudomeleta, he did not now come through Africa to the parts of Italy, but ran to Sicily, until he came to the city of Syracuse with the two men who had been sent from Rome to him. And having sailed thence, he came to Rhegium of Calabria, and from Rhegium he crossed to Mesina, and there ordained a bishop, Bacchylus by name. And when he came out of Mesina he sailed to Didymus, and remained there one night. And having sailed thence, he came to Pontiole [4] on the second day.

And Dioscorus the shipmaster, who brought him to Syracuse, sympathizing with Paul because he had delivered his son from death, having left his own ship in Syracuse, accompanied him to Pontiole. And some of Peter's disciples having been found there, and having received Paul, exhorted him to stay with them. And he stayed a week, in hiding, because of the command of Cæsar. And all the toparchs were watching to seize and kill him. But Dioscorus the shipmaster, being himself also bald, wearing his shipmaster's dress, and speaking boldly, on the first day went out into the city of Pontiole. Thinking therefore that he was Paul, they seized him, and beheaded him, and sent his head to Cæsar.

Cæsar therefore, having summoned the first men of the Jews, announced to them, saying: Rejoice with great joy, for Paul your enemy is dead. And he showed them the head. Hav-

---

[1] Lambecius proposes to read Gaudos and Melita. In the Latin version of the famous Greek scholar Lascaris, 1490, it is *a Melita et Gaudisio insulis*. [Comp. Acts xxvii. 16, xxviii. 1. The two names are apparently combined here. — R.]

[2] τρακταίσαντες: from the Byzantine verb τρακταίζειν = tractare. The various readings in the MSS. are: Being very disorderly; having been much disturbed.

[3] Various reading: Let it be . . . and we will write, etc.

[4] Puteoli.

ing therefore made great rejoicing on that day, which was the fourteenth of the month of June, each of the Jews fully believed it.

And Paul, being in Pontiole, and having heard that Dioscorus had been beheaded, being grieved with great grief, gazing into the height of the heaven, said : O Lord Almighty in heaven, who hast appeared to me in every place whither I have gone on account of Thine only-begotten Word, our Lord Jesus Christ, punish this city, and bring out all who have believed in God and followed His word. He said to them therefore : Follow me : And going forth from Pontiole with those who had believed in the word of God, they came to a place called Baias ;[1] and looking up with their eyes, they all see that city called Pontiole sunk into the sea-shore about one fathom ; and there it is until this day, for a remembrance, under the sea.

And having gone forth from Baias, they went to Gaitas, and there he taught the word of God. And he stayed there three days in the house of Erasmus, whom Peter sent from Rome to teach the Gospel of God. And having come forth from Gaitas, he came to the castle called Taracinas, and stayed there seven days in the house of Cæsarius the deacon, whom Peter had ordained by the laying on of hands. And sailing thence, he came by the river to a place called Tribus Tabernes.

And those who had been saved out of the city of Pontiole, that had been swallowed up, reported to Cæsar in Rome that Pontiole had been swallowed up, with all its multitude. And the emperor, being in great grief on account of the city, having summoned the chief of the Jews, said to them : Behold, on account of what I heard from you, I have caused Paul to be beheaded, and on account of this the city has been swallowed up. And the chief of the Jews said to Cæsar : Most worshipful emperor, did we not say to thee that he troubled all the country of the East, and perverted our fathers ? It is better therefore, most worshipful emperor, that one city be destroyed, and not the seat of thine empire ; for this had Rome to suffer. And the emperor, having heard their words, was appeased.

And Paul stayed in Tribus Tabernes four days. And departing thence, he came to Appii Forum, which is called Vicusarape ; and having slept there that night, he saw one sitting on a golden chair, and a multitude of blacks standing beside him, saying : I have to-day made a son murder his father. Another said : And I have made a house fall, and kill parents with children. And they reported to him many evil deeds — some of one kind, some of another. And another coming, reported to him : I have managed that the bishop Juvenalius, whom Peter ordained, should

sleep with the abbess Juliana. And having heard all these things when sleeping in that Appii Forum, near Vicusarape, straightway and immediately he sent to Rome one of those who had followed him from Pontiole to the bishop Juvenalius, telling him this same thing which had just been done. And on the following day, Juvenalius, running, threw himself at the feet of Peter, weeping and lamenting, and saying what had just befallen ; and he recounted to him the matter, and said : I believe that this is the light which thou wast awaiting. And Peter said to him : How is it possible that it is he when he is dead ? And Juvenalius the bishop took to Peter him that had been sent by Paul, and he reported to him that he was alive, and on his way, and that he was at Appii Forum. And Peter thanked and glorified the God and Father of our Lord Jesus Christ.

Then having summoned his disciples that believed, he sent them to Paul as far as Tribus Tabernes. And the distance from Rome to Tribus Tabernes is thirty-eight miles.[2] And Paul seeing them, having given thanks to our Lord Jesus Christ, took courage ; and departing thence, they slept in the city called Aricia.

And a report went about in the city of Rome that Paul the brother of Peter was coming. And those that believed in God rejoiced with great joy. And there was great consternation among the Jews ; and having gone to Simon the magian, they entreated him, saying : Report to the emperor that Paul is not dead, but that he is alive, and has come. And Simon said to the Jews : What head is it, then, which came to Cæsar from Pontiole ? Was it not bald also ?

And Paul having come to Rome, great fear fell upon the Jews. They came together therefore to him, and exhorted him, saying : Vindicate the faith in which thou wast born ; for it is not right that thou, being a Hebrew, and of the Hebrews, shouldst call thyself teacher of Gentiles, and vindicator of the uncircumcised ; and, being thyself circumcised, that thou shouldst bring to nought the faith of the circumcision.[3] And when thou seest Peter, contend against his teaching, because he has destroyed all the bulwarks of our law ; for he has prevented the keeping of Sabbaths and new moons, and the holidays appointed by the law. And Paul, answering, said to them : That I am a true Jew, by this you can prove ; because also you have been able to keep the Sabbath, and to observe the true circumcision ; for assuredly on the day of the Sabbath God rested from all His works. We have fathers, and patriarchs, and the law. What, then,

---

[1] The geographical names are given in the peculiar forms of the text. Occasionally the usual forms, such as Baiæ, occur.

[2] The distance was thirty-three miles. In the *Antonine Itinerary*, " To Aricia is sixteen miles, to Tres Tabernæ seventeen miles, to Appii Forum ten miles."

[3] Or, do away with belief in circumcision.

does Peter preach in the kingdom of the Gentiles? But if he shall wish to bring in any new teaching, without any tumult, and envy, and trouble, send him word, that we may see, and in your presence I shall convict him. But if his teaching be true, supported by the book and testimony of the Hebrews, it becomes all of us to submit to him.

Paul saying these and such like things, the Jews went and said to Peter: Paul of the Hebrews has come, and entreats thee to come to him, since those who have brought him say that he cannot meet whomsoever he may wish until he appear before Cæsar. And Peter having heard, rejoiced with great joy; and rising up, immediately went to him. And seeing each other, they wept for joy; and long embracing each other, they bedewed each other with tears.

And when Paul had related to Peter the substance [1] of all his doings, and how, through the disasters of the ship, he had come, Peter also told him what he had suffered from Simon the magian, and all his plots. And having told these things, he went away towards evening.

And in the morning of the following day, at dawn, behold, Peter coming, finds a multitude of the Jews before Paul's door. And there was a great uproar between the Christian Jews and the Gentiles. For, on the one hand, the Jews said: We are a chosen race, a royal priesthood, the friends of Abraham, and Isaac, and Jacob, and all the prophets, with whom God spake, to whom He showed His own mysteries and His great wonders. But you of the Gentiles are no great thing in your lineage; if otherwise, you have become polluted and abominable by idols and graven images.

While the Jews were saying such things, and such-like, those of the Gentiles answered, saying: We, when we heard the truth, straightway followed it, having abandoned our errors. But you, both knowing the mighty deeds of your fathers, and seeing the signs of the prophets, and having received the law, and gone through the sea with dry feet, and seen your enemies sunk in its depths, and the pillar of fire by night and of cloud by day shining upon you, and manna having been given to you out of heaven, and water flowing to you out of a rock, — after all these things you fashioned to yourselves the idol of a calf, and worshipped the graven image. But we, having seen none of the signs, believe to be a Saviour the God whom you have forsaken in unbelief.

While they were contending in these and such-like words, the Apostle Paul said that they ought not to make such attacks upon each other, but that they should rather give heed to this,

that God had fulfilled His promises which He swore to Abraham our father, that in his seed he should inherit all the nations.[2] For there is no respect of persons with God.[3] As many as have sinned in law shall be judged according to law, and as many as have sinned without law shall perish without law.[4] But we, brethren, ought to thank God that, according to His mercy, He has chosen us to be a holy people to Himself: so that in this we ought to boast, whether Jews or Greeks; for you are all one in the belief of His name.

And Paul having thus spoken, both the Jews and they of the Gentiles were appeased. But the rulers of the Jews assailed Peter. And Peter, when they accused him of having renounced their synagogues, said: Hear, brethren, the holy Spirit about the patriarch David, promising, Of the fruit of thy womb shall He set upon thy throne.[5] Him therefore to whom the Father said, Thou art my Son, this day have I begotten Thee, the chief priests through envy crucified; but that He might accomplish the salvation of the world, it was allowed that He should suffer all these things.[6] Just as, therefore, from the side of Adam Eve was created, so also from the side of Christ was created the Church, which has no spot nor blemish. In Him,[7] therefore, God has opened an entrance to all the sons of Abraham, and Isaac, and Jacob, in order that they may be in the faith of profession towards Him,[8] and have life and salvation in His name. Turn, therefore, and enter into the joy of your father Abraham, because God hath fulfilled what He promised to him. Whence also the prophet says, The Lord hath sworn, and will not repent: Thou art a priest for ever, after the order of Melchizedec.[9] For a priest He became upon the cross, when He offered the whole burnt-offering of His own body and blood as a sacrifice for all the world.

And Peter saying this and such-like, the most part of the people believed. And it happened also that Nero's wife Libia, and the yoke-fellow of Agrippa the prefect, Agrippina by name, thus believed, so that also they went away from beside their own husbands. And on account of the teaching of Paul, many, despising military life, clung to God; so that even from the emperor's bed-chamber some came to him, and having become Christians, were no longer willing to return to the army or the palace.

When, consequently, the people were making

---

[1] Lit., web or tissue.

[2] Gen. xii. 3, xvii. 5.
[3] Rom. ii. 11; Eph. vi. 9; Col. iii. 25; Jas. ii. 1.
[4] Rom. ii. 12.
[5] Ps. cxxxii. 11.
[6] Or, He allowed Himself to suffer all these things.
[7] Or, by Him.
[8] i.e., That all may profess their faith in Him. For similar expressions, see 2 Cor. ix. 13, Heb. x. 23.
[9] Ps. cx. 4; Heb. vii. 21.

a seditious murmuring, Simon, moved with zeal, rouses himself, and began to say many evil things about Peter, saying that he was a wizard and a cheat. And they believed him, wondering at his miracles; for he made a brazen serpent move itself, and stone statues to laugh and move themselves, and himself to run and suddenly to be raised into the air. But as a set-off to these, Peter healed the sick by a word, by praying made the blind to see, put demons to flight by a command; sometimes he even raised the dead. And he said to the people that they should not only flee from Simon's deceit, but also that they should expose him, that they might not seem to be slaves to the devil.

And thus it happened that all pious men abhorred Simon the magian, and proclaimed him impious. But those who adhered to Simon strongly affirmed Peter to be a magian, bearing false witness as many of them as were with Simon the magian; so that the matter came even to the ears of Nero the Cæsar, and he gave order to bring Simon the magian before him. And he, coming in, stood before him, and began suddenly to assume different forms, so that on a sudden he became a child, and after a little an old man, and at other times a young man; for he changed himself both in face and stature into different forms, and was in a frenzy, having the devil as his servant. And Nero beholding this, supposed him to be truly the son of God; but the Apostle Peter showed him to be both a liar and a wizard, base and impious and apostate, and in all things opposed to the truth of God, and that nothing yet remained except that his wickedness, being made apparent by the command of God, might be made manifest to them all.

Then Simon, having gone in to Nero, said: Hear, O good emperor: I am the son of God come down from heaven. Until now I have endured Peter only calling himself an apostle; but now he has doubled the evil: for Paul also himself teaches the same things, and having his mind turned against me, is said to preach along with him; in reference to whom, if thou shalt not contrive their destruction, it is very plain that thy kingdom cannot stand.

Then Nero, filled with concern, ordered to bring them speedily before him. And on the following day Simon the magian, and Peter and Paul the apostles of Christ, having come in to Nero, Simon said: These are the disciples of the Nazarene, and it is not at all well that they should be of the people of the Jews, Nero said: What is a Nazarene? Simon said: There is a city of Judah which has always been opposed to us, called Nazareth, and to it the teacher of these men belonged. Nero said: God commands us to love every man; why, then, dost thou persecute them? Simon said: This is a race of men

who have turned aside all Judæa from believing in me. Nero said to Peter: Why are you thus unbelieving, according to your race?[1] Then Peter said to Simon: Thou hast been able to impose upon all, but upon me never; and those who have been deceived, God has through me recalled from their error. And since thou hast learned by experience that thou canst not get the better of me, I wonder with what face thou boastest thyself before the emperor, and supposest that through thy magic art thou shalt overcome the disciples of Christ. Nero said: Who is Christ? Peter said: He is what this Simon the magian affirms himself to be; but this is a most wicked man, and his works are of the devil. But if thou wishest to know, O good emperor, the things that have been done in Judæa about Christ, take the writings of Pontius Pilate sent to Claudius, and thus thou wilt know all. And Nero ordered them to be brought, and to be read in their presence; and they were to the following effect:[2] —

Pontius Pilate to Claudius, greeting. There has lately happened an event which I myself was concerned in. For the Jews through envy have inflicted on themselves, and those coming after them, dreadful judgments. Their fathers had promises that their God would send them his holy one from heaven, who according to reason should be called their king, and he had promised to send him to the earth by means of a virgin. He, then, when I was procurator, came into Judæa. And they saw[3] him enlightening the blind, cleansing lepers, healing paralytics, expelling demons from men, raising the dead, subduing the winds, walking upon the waves of the sea, and doing many other wonders, and all the people of the Jews calling him Son of God. Then the chief priests, moved with envy against him, seized him, and delivered him to me; and telling one lie after another, they said that he was a wizard, and did contrary to their law. And I, having believed that these things were so, gave him up, after scourging him, to their will;[4] and they crucified him, and after he was buried set guards over him. But he, while my soldiers were guarding him, rose on the third day. And to such a degree was the wickedness of the Jews inflamed against him, that they gave money to the soldiers, saying, Say his disciples have stolen his body. But they, having taken the money, were not able to keep silence as to what had happened; for they have testified that they have seen him (after he was) risen, and that they

---

[1] i.e., How do you happen, as a race, to be so unbelieving? The Latin translation has: against your race — κατὰ τοῦ γένους for κατὰ τὸ γένος.

[2] For another translation of this letter, see Latin Gospel of Nicodemus, chap. xiii. (xxix.) [This occurs on p. 454; there is another form on p. 459. — R.]

[3] Or, I saw.

[4] Or, to their council.

have received money from the Jews. These things, therefore, have I reported, that no one should falsely speak otherwise, and that thou shouldest not suppose that the falsehoods of the Jews are to be believed.

And the letter having been read, Nero said: Tell me, Peter, were all these things thus done by him? Peter said: They were, with your permission, O good emperor. For this Simon is full of lies and deceit, even if it should seem that he is what he is not — a god. And in Christ there is all excellent victory through God and through man,[1] which that incomprehensible glory assumed which through man deigned to come to the assistance of men. But in this Simon there are two essences, of man and of devil, who through man endeavours to ensnare men.

Simon said: I wonder, O good emperor, that you reckon this man of any consequence — a man uneducated, a fisherman of the poorest, and endowed with power neither in word nor by rank. But, that I may not long endure him as an enemy, I shall forthwith order my angels to come and avenge me upon him. Peter said: I am not afraid of thy angels; but they shall be much more afraid of me in the power and trust of my Lord Jesus Christ, whom thou falsely declarest thyself to be.

Nero said: Art thou not afraid, Peter, of Simon, who confirms his godhead by deeds? Peter said: Godhead is in Him who searcheth the hidden things of the heart.[2] Now then, tell me what I am thinking about, or what I am doing. I disclose to thy servants who are here what my thought is, before he tells lies about it, in order that he may not dare to lie as to what I am thinking about. Nero said: Come hither, and tell me what thou art thinking about. Peter said: Order a barley loaf to be brought, and to be given to me secretly. And when he ordered it to be brought, and secretly given to Peter, Peter said: Now tell us, Simon, what has been thought about, or what said, or what done.

Nero said: Do you mean me to believe that Simon does not know these things, who both raised a dead man, and presented himself on the third day after he had been beheaded, and who has done whatever he said he would do? Peter said: But he did not do it before me. Nero said: But he did all these before me. For assuredly he ordered angels to come to him, and they came. Peter said: If he has done what is very great, why does he not do what is very small? Let him tell what I had in my mind, and what I have done. Nero said: Between you, I do not know myself. Simon said: Let Peter say what I am thinking of, or what I am doing. Peter said: What Simon has in his

mind I shall show that I know, by my doing what he is thinking about. Simon said: Know this, O emperor, that no one knows the thoughts of men, but God alone. Is not, therefore, Peter lying? Peter said: Do thou, then, who sayest that thou art the Son of God, tell what I have in my mind; disclose, if thou canst, what I have just done in secret. For Peter, having blessed the barley loaf which he had received, and having broken it with his right hand and his left, had heaped it up in his sleeves. Then Simon, enraged that he was not able to tell the secret of the apostle, cried out, saying: Let great dogs come forth, and eat him up before Cæsar. And suddenly there appeared great dogs, and rushed at Peter. But Peter, stretching forth his hands[3] to pray, showed to the dogs the loaf which he had blessed; which the dogs seeing, no longer appeared. Then Peter said to Nero: Behold, I have shown thee that I knew what Simon was thinking of, not by words, but by deeds; for he, having promised that he would bring angels against me, has brought dogs, in order that he might show that he had not god-like but dog-like angels.

Then Nero said to Simon: What is it, Simon? I think we have got the worst of it. Simon said: This man, both in Judæa and in all Palestine and Cæsarea, has done the same to me;[4] and from very often striving with me, he has learned that this is adverse to them. This, then, he has learned how to escape from me; for the thoughts of men no one knows but God alone. And Peter said to Simon: Certainly thou feignest thyself to be a god; why, then, dost thou not reveal the thoughts of every man?

Then Nero, turning to Paul, said: Why dost thou say nothing, Paul? Paul answered and said: Know this, O emperor, that if thou permittest this magician to do such things, it will bring an access of the greatest mischief to thy country, and will bring down thine empire from its position. Nero said to Simon: What sayest thou? Simon said: If I do not manifestly hold myself out to be a god, no one will bestow upon me due reverence. Nero said: And now, why dost thou delay, and not show thyself to be a god, in order that these men may be punished? Simon said: Give orders to build for me a lofty tower of wood, and I, going up upon it, will call my angels, and order them to take me, in the sight of all, to my father in heaven; and these men, not being able to do this, are put to shame as[5] uneducated men. And Nero said to Peter: Hast thou heard, Peter, what has been said by Simon? From this will appear how much power either he or thy god has. Peter said: O most

---

[1] i.e., human nature.
[2] Jer. xvii. 10; Rev. ii. 23.

[3] Lam. iii. 41; Mark xi. 25; 1 Tim. ii. 8.
[4] See the *Clementines*, Homilies II., III., VI., XVI., XX.
[5] Or, are proved to be.

mighty emperor, if thou wert willing, thou mightst perceive that he is full of demons. Nero said: Why do you make to me roundabouts of circumlocutions? To-morrow will prove you.

Simon said: Dost thou believe, O good emperor, that I who was dead, and rose again, am a magician? For it had been brought about by his own cleverness that the unbelieving Simon had said to Nero: Order me to be beheaded in a dark place, and there to be left slain; and if I do not rise on the third day, know that I am a magician; but if I rise again, know that I am the Son of God.

And Nero having ordered this, in the dark, by his magic art he managed that a ram should be beheaded. And for so long did the ram appear to be Simon until he was beheaded. And when he had been beheaded in the dark, he that had beheaded him, taking the head, found it to be that of a ram; but he would not say anything to the emperor, lest he should scourge him, having ordered this to be done in secret. Thereafter, accordingly, Simon said that he had risen on the third day, because he took away the head of the ram and the limbs — but the blood had been there congealed — and on the third day he showed himself to Nero, and said: Cause to be wiped away my blood that has been poured out; for, behold, having been beheaded, as I promised, I have risen again on the third day.

And when Nero said, To-morrow will prove you, turning to Paul, he says: Thou Paul, why dost thou say nothing? Either who taught thee, or whom thou hast for a master, or how thou hast taught in the cities, or what things have happened through thy teaching? For I think that thou hast not any wisdom, and art not able to accomplish any work of power. Paul answered: Dost thou suppose that I ought to speak against a desperate man, a magician, who has given his soul up to death, whose destruction and perdition will come speedily? For he ought to speak who pretends to be what he is not, and deceives men by magic art. If thou consentest to hear his words, and to shield him, thou shalt destroy thy soul and thy kingdom, for he is a most base man. And as the Egyptians Jannes and Jambres led Pharaoh and his army astray until they were swallowed up in the sea, so also he, through the instruction of his father the devil, persuades men to do many evils to themselves, and thus deceives many of the innocent, to the peril of thy kingdom. But as for the word of the devil, which I see has been poured out through this man, with groanings of my heart I am dealing with the Holy Spirit, that it may be clearly shown what it is; for as far as he seems to raise himself towards heaven, so far will he be sunk down into the depth of Hades, where

there is weeping and gnashing of teeth. But about the teaching of my Master, of which thou didst ask me, none attain it except the pure, who allow faith to come into their heart.[1] For as many things as belong to peace and love, these have I taught. Round about from Jerusalem, and as far as Illyricum,[2] I have fulfilled the word of peace. For I have taught that in honour they should prefer one another;[3] I have taught those that are eminent and rich not to be lifted up, and hope in uncertainty of riches, but to place their hope in God;[4] I have taught those in a middle station to be content with food and covering;[5] I have taught the poor to rejoice in their own poverty; I have taught fathers to teach their children instruction in the fear of the Lord, children to obey their parents in wholesome admonition;[6] I have taught wives to love their own husbands, and to fear them as masters, and husbands to observe fidelity to their wives; I have taught masters to treat their slaves with clemency, and slaves to serve their own masters faithfully;[7] I have taught the churches of the believers to reverence one almighty, invisible, and incomprehensible God. And this teaching has been given me, not from men, nor through men, but through Jesus Christ,[8] who spoke to me out of heaven, who also has sent me to preach, saying to me, Go forth, for I will be with thee; and all things, as many as thou shalt say or do, I shall make just.

Nero said: What sayest thou, Peter? He answered and said: All that Paul has said is true.[9] For when he was a persecutor of the faith of Christ, a voice called him out of heaven, and taught him the truth; for he was not an adversary of our faith from hatred, but from ignorance. For there were before us false Christs, like Simon, false apostles, and false prophets, who, contrary to the sacred writings, set themselves to make void the truth; and against these it was necessary to have in readiness this man, who from his youth up set himself to no other thing than to search out the mysteries of the divine law, by which[10] he might become a vindicator of truth and a persecutor of falsehood. Since, then, his persecution was not on account of hatred, but on account of the vindication of the law, the very truth out of heaven held intercourse with him, saying, I am the truth which you persecutest; cease perse-

---

[1] Or, the pure in heart admitting the faith.
[2] Rom. xv. 19.
[3] Rom. xii. 10.
[4] 1 Tim. vi. 17.
[5] Or, those who have a moderate quantity of food and covering to be content (1 Tim. vi. 8).
[6] Or, in the admonition of the Saviour (Eph. vi. 4).
[7] Col. iii. 18-22.
[8] Gal. i. 1.
[9] Four of the MSS. and the Latin version here add: For assuredly I have for a long time past received letters from our bishops throughout all the world about the things done and said by him.
[10] i.e., mysteries.

cuting me. When, therefore, he knew that this was so, leaving off that which he was vindicating, he began to vindicate this way of Christ which he was persecuting.

Simon said: O good emperor, take notice that these two have conspired against me; for I am the truth, and they purpose evil against me. Peter said: There is no truth in thee; but all thou sayest is false.

Nero said: Paul, what sayest thou? Paul said: Those things which thou hast heard from Peter, believe to have been spoken by me also; for we purpose the same thing, for we have the same Lord Jesus the Christ. Simon said: Dost thou expect me, O good emperor, to hold an argument with these men, who have come to an agreement against me? And having turned to the apostles of Christ, he said: Listen, Peter and Paul: if I can do nothing for you here, we are going to the place where I must judge you. Paul said: O good emperor, see what threats he holds out against us. Peter said: Why was it necessary to keep from laughing outright at a foolish man, made the sport of demons, so as to suppose that he cannot be made manifest?

Simon said: I spare you until I shall receive my power. Paul said: See if you will go out hence safe. Peter said: If thou do not see, Simon, the power of our Lord Jesus Christ, thou wilt not believe thyself not to be Christ. Simon said: Most sacred emperor, do not believe them, for they are circumcised knaves. Paul said: Before we knew the truth, we had the circumcision of the flesh; but when the truth appeared, in the circumcision of the heart we both are circumcised, and circumcise. Peter said: If circumcision be a disgrace, why hast thou been circumcised, Simon?

Nero said: Has, then, Simon also been circumcised? Peter said: For not otherwise could he have deceived souls, unless he feigned himself to be a Jew, and made a show of teaching the law of God. Nero said: Simon, thou, as I see, being carried away with envy, persecutest these men. For, as it seems, there is great hatred between thee and their Christ; and I am afraid that thou wilt be worsted by them, and involved in great evils. Simon said: Thou art led astray, O emperor. Nero said: How am I led astray? What I see in thee, I say. I see that thou art manifestly an enemy of Peter and Paul and their master.

Simon said: Christ was not Paul's master. Paul said: Yes; through revelation He taught me also. But tell me what I asked thee — Why wast thou circumcised? Simon said: Why have you asked me this? Paul said: We have a reason for asking you this. Nero said: Why art thou afraid to answer them? Simon said: Listen, O emperor. At that time circumcision was

enjoined by God when I received it. For this reason was I circumcised.

Paul said: Hearest thou, O good emperor, what has been said by Simon? If, therefore, circumcision be a good thing, why hast thou, Simon, given up those who have been circumcised, and forced them, after being condemned, to be put to death? Nero said: Neither about you do I perceive anything good. Peter and Paul said: Whether this thought about us be good or evil has no reference to the matter; but to us it was necessary that what our Master promised should come to pass. Nero said: If I should not be willing? Peter said: Not as thou willest, but as He promised to us.

Simon said: O good emperor, these men have reckoned upon thy clemency, and have bound thee. Nero said: But neither hast thou yet made me sure about thyself. Simon said: Since so many excellent deeds and signs have been shown to thee by me, I wonder how thou shouldst be in doubt. Nero said: I neither doubt nor favour any of you; but answer me rather what I ask.

Simon said: Henceforward I answer thee nothing. Nero said: Seeing that thou liest, therefore thou sayest this. But if even I can do nothing to thee, God, who can, will do it. Simon said: I no longer answer thee. Nero said: Nor do I consider thee to be anything: for, as I perceive, thou art a liar in everything. But why do I say so much? The three of you show that your reasoning is uncertain; and thus in all things you have made me doubt, so that I find that I can give credit to none of you.[1]

Peter said: We preach one God and Father of our Lord Jesus Christ, that has made the heaven and the earth and the sea, and all that therein is, who is the true King; and of His kingdom there shall be no end.[2] Nero said: What king is lord? Paul said: The Saviour of all the nations. Simon said: I am he whom you speak of. Peter and Paul said: May it never be well with thee, Simon, magician, and full of bitterness.

Simon said: Listen, O Cæsar Nero, that thou mayst know that these men are liars, and that I have been sent from the heavens: to-morrow I go up into the heavens, that I may make those who believe in me blessed, and show my wrath upon those who have denied me. Peter and Paul said: Us long ago God called to His own glory; but thou, called by the devil, hastenest to punishment. Simon said: Cæsar Nero, listen to me. Separate these madmen from thee, in order that when I go into heaven to my father, I may be very merciful to thee. Nero said: And whence shall we prove this, that thou goest

---

[1] Or, to nothing.
[2] Luke i. 33.

away into heaven? Simon said: Order a lofty tower to be made of wood, and of great beams, that I may go up upon it, and that my angels may find me in the air; for they cannot come to me upon earth among the sinners. Nero said: I will see whether thou wilt fulfil what thou sayest.

Then Nero ordered a lofty tower to be made in the Campus Martius, and all the people and the dignities to be present at the spectacle. And on the following day, all the multitude having come together, Nero ordered Peter and Paul to be present, to whom also he said: Now the truth has to be made manifest. Peter and Paul said: We do not expose him, but our Lord Jesus Christ, the Son of God, whom he has falsely declared himself to be.

And Paul, having turned to Peter, said: It is my part to bend the knee, and to pray to God; and thine to produce the effect, if thou shouldst see him attempting anything, because thou wast first taken in hand[1] by the Lord. And Paul, bending his knees, prayed. And Peter, looking stedfastly upon Simon, said: Accomplish what thou hast begun; for both thy exposure and our call is at hand: for I see my Christ calling both me and Paul. Nero said: And where will you go to against my will? Peter said: Whithersoever our Lord has called us. Nero said: And who is your lord? Peter said: Jesus the Christ, whom I see calling us to Himself. Nero said: Do you also then intend to go away to heaven? Peter said: If it shall seem good to Him that calls us. Simon said: In order that thou mayst know, O emperor, that these are deceivers, as soon as ever I ascend into heaven, I will send my angels to thee, and will make thee come to me. Nero said: Do at once what thou sayest.

Then Simon went up upon the tower in the face of all, and, crowned with laurels, he stretched forth his hands, and began to fly. And when Nero saw him flying, he said to Peter: This Simon is true; but thou and Paul are deceivers. To whom Peter said: Immediately shalt thou know that we are true disciples of Christ; but that he is not Christ, but a magician, and a malefactor. Nero said: Do you still persist? Behold, you see him going up into heaven. Then Peter, looking stedfastly upon Paul, said: Paul, look up and see. And Paul, having looked up, full of tears, and seeing Simon flying, said: Peter, why art thou idle? finish what thou hast begun; for already our Lord Jesus Christ is calling us. And Nero hearing them, smiled a little, and said: These men see themselves worsted already, and are gone mad. Peter said: Now thou shalt know that

we are not mad. Paul said to Peter: Do at once what thou doest.

And Peter, looking stedfastly against Simon, said: I adjure you, ye angels of Satan, who are carrying him into the air, to deceive the hearts of the unbelievers, by the God that created all things, and by Jesus Christ, whom on the third day He raised from the dead, no longer from this hour to keep him up, but to let him go. And immediately, being let go, he fell into a place called Sacra Via, that is, Holy Way, and was divided into four parts, having perished by an evil fate.

Then Nero ordered Peter and Paul to be put in irons, and the body of Simon to be carefully kept three days, thinking that he would rise on the third day. To whom Peter said: He will no longer rise, since he is truly dead, being condemned to everlasting punishment. And Nero said to him: Who commanded thee to do such a dreadful deed? Peter said: His reflections and blasphemy against my Lord Jesus Christ have brought him into this gulf of destruction. Nero said: I will destroy you by an evil taking off. Peter said: This is not in thy power, even if it should seem good to thee to destroy us; but it is necessary that what our Master promised to us should be fulfilled.

Then Nero, having summoned Agrippa the proprætor, said to him: It is necessary that men introducing mischievous religious observances should die. Wherefore I order them to take iron clubs,[2] and to be killed in the sea-fight. Agrippa the proprætor said: Most sacred emperor, what thou hast ordered is not fitting for these men, since Paul seems innocent beside Peter. Nero said: By what fate, then, shall they die? Agrippa answered and said: As seems to me, it is just that Paul's head should be cut off, and that Peter should be raised on a cross as the cause of the murder. Nero said: Thou hast most excellently judged.

Then both Peter and Paul were led away from the presence of Nero. And Paul was beheaded on the Ostesian road.[3]

And Peter, having come to the cross, said: Since my Lord Jesus Christ, who came down from the heaven upon the earth, was raised upon the cross upright,[4] and He has deigned to call to heaven me, who am of the earth, my cross ought to be fixed head downmost, so as to direct my feet towards heaven; for I am not worthy to be crucified like my Lord. Then, having reversed the cross, they nailed his feet up.

---

[1] Or, chosen.

[2] The text has κινάρας, artichokes, for which I have read κορυνας, clubs. Sea-fights were a favourite spectacle of the Roman emperors (Suet., *Nero*, xii.; *Claud.*, xxi.; *Dom*, iv.). The combatants were captives, or persons condemned to death (Dion Cass , lx, 33).

[3] For the episode of Perpetua, contained in three of the Greek MSS., but not in the Latin versions, see the end of this book.

[4] i.e., head uppermost.

And the multitude was assembled reviling Cæsar, and wishing to kill him. But Peter restrained them, saying : [1] A few days ago, being exhorted by the brethren, I was going away; and my Lord Jesus Christ met me, and having adored Him, I said, Lord, whither art Thou going? And He said to me, I am going to Rome to be crucified. And I said to Him, Lord, wast Thou not crucified once for all? And the Lord answering, said, I saw thee fleeing from death, and I wish to be crucified instead of thee. And I said, Lord, I go; I fulfil Thy command. And He said to me, Fear not, for I am with thee.[2] On this account, then, children, do not hinder my going ; for already my feet are going on the road to heaven. Do not grieve, therefore, but rather rejoice with me, for to-day I receive the fruit of my labours. And thus speaking, he said : I thank Thee, good Shepherd, that the sheep which Thou hast entrusted to me, sympathize with me; I ask, then, that with me they may have a part in Thy kingdom.[3] And having thus spoken, he gave up the ghost.

And immediately there appeared men glorious and strange in appearance ; and they said : We are here, on account of the holy and chief apostles, from Jerusalem. And they, along with Marcellus, an illustrious man, who, having left Simon, had believed in Peter, took up his body secretly, and put it under the terebinth near the place for the exhibition of sea-fights in the place called the Vatican.[4]

And the men who had said that they came from Jerusalem said to the people : Rejoice, and be exceeding glad, because you have been deemed worthy to have great champions. And know that Nero himself, after these not many days, will be utterly destroyed, and his kingdom shall be given to another.

And after these things the people revolted against him ; and when he knew of it, he fled into desert places, and through hunger and cold he gave up the ghost, and his body became food for the wild beasts.

And some devout men of the regions of the East wished to carry off the relics of the saints, and immediately there was a great earthquake in the city;[5] and those that dwelt in the city having become aware of it, ran and seized the men, but they fled. But the Romans having taken them, put them in a place three miles from the city, and there they were guarded a year and seven months, until they had built the place in which they intended to put them. And after these things, all having assembled with glory and singing of praise, they put them in the place built for them.

And the consummation of the holy glorious Apostles Peter and Paul was on the 29th of the month of June — in Christ Jesus our Lord, to whom be glory and strength.

---

[1] One of the MSS. here inserts: Do not be hard upon him, for he is the servant of his father Satan; but I must fulfil the command of my Lord.
[2] Some of the MSS. insert: Until I bring thee into my Father's house.
[3] Several of the MSS. here add: I commend unto Thee the sheep whom Thou didst entrust unto me, that they may not feel that they are without me, having for a shepherd Thee, through whom I have been able to feed this flock.
[4] In three of the Greek MSS., but not in the Latin versions, the story of Perpetua is here continued.
[5] Several MSS. here add: And the people of the Romans ran, and took them into the place called the Catacombs on the Appian Way, at the third milestone; and there the bodies of the saints were guarded a year and six months, until places were built for them in which they might be put. And the body of St. Peter was put into the Vatican, near the place for the sea-fights, and that of St. Paul into the Vostesian (or Ostesian) Way, two miles from the city; and in these places, through their prayers, many good deeds are wrought to the faithful in the name of our Lord Jesus Christ.

THE STORY OF PERPETUA.

AND as Paul was being led away to be beheaded at a place about three miles from the city, he was in irons. And there were three soldiers guarding him who were of a great family. And when they had gone out of the gate about the length of a bow-shot, there met them a God-fearing woman ; and she, seeing Paul dragged along in irons, had compassion on him, and wept bitterly. And the name of the woman was called Perpetua ; and she was one-eyed. And Paul, seeing her weeping, says to her : Give me thy handkerchief, and when I turn back I shall give it to thee. And she, having taken the handkerchief, gave it to him willingly. And the soldiers laughed, and said to the woman : Why dost thou wish, woman, to lose thy handkerchief? Knowest thou not that he is going away to be beheaded? And Perpetua said to them : I adjure you by the health of Cæsar to bind his eyes with this handkerchief when you cut off his head. Which also was done. And they beheaded him at the place called Aquæ Salviæ, near the pine tree. And as God had willed, before the soldiers came back, the handkerchief, having on it drops of blood, was restored to the woman. And as she was carrying it, straightway and immediately her eye was opened.

CONTINUATION OF THE STORY OF PERPETUA.

And the three soldiers who had cut off the head of Saint Paul, when after three hours they came on the same day with the BULLA bringing it to Nero, having met Perpetua, they said to her: What is it, woman? Behold, by thy confidence thou hast lost thy handkerchief. But she said to them: I have both got my handkerchief, and my eye has recovered its sight. And as the Lord, the God of Paul, liveth, I also have entreated him that I may be deemed worthy to become the slave of his Lord. Then the soldiers who had the BULLA, recognising the handkerchief, and seeing that her eye had been opened, cried out with a loud voice, as if from one mouth, and said: We too are the slaves of Paul's master. Perpetua therefore having gone away, reported in the palace of the Emperor Nero that the soldiers who had beheaded Paul said: We shall no longer go into the city, for we believe in Christ whom Paul preached, and we are Christians. Then Nero, filled with rage, ordered Perpetua, who had informed him of the soldiers, to be kept fast in irons; and as to the soldiers, he ordered one to be beheaded outside of the gate about one mile from the city, another to be cut in two, and the third to be stoned. And Perpetua was in the prison; and in this prison there was kept Potentiana, a noble maiden, because she had said: I forsake my parents and all the substance of my father, and I wish to become a Christian. She therefore joined herself to Perpetua, and ascertained from her everything about Paul, and was in much anxiety about the faith in Christ. And the wife of Nero was Potentiana's sister; and she secretly informed her about Christ, that those who believe in Him see everlasting joy, and that everything here is temporary, but there eternal: so that also she fled out of the palace, and some of the senators' wives with her. Then Nero, having inflicted many tortures upon Perpetua, at last tied a great stone to her neck, and ordered her to be thrown over a precipice. And her remains lie at the Momentan[1] gate. And Potentiana also underwent many torments; and at last, having made a furnace one day, they burned her.

---

[1] This is a slip for Nomentan.

ACTS OF PAUL AND THECLA

As Paul was going up to Iconium after the flight from Antioch, his fellow-travellers were Demas and Ermogenes, full of hypocrisy; and they were importunate with Paul,[1] as if they loved him. But Paul, looking only to the goodness of Christ, did them no harm, but loved them exceedingly, so that he made the oracles of the Lord sweet to them in the teaching both of the birth and the resurrection of the Beloved; and he gave them an account, word for word, of the great things of Christ, how He[2] had been revealed to him.

And a certain man, by name Onesiphorus, hearing that Paul had come to Iconium, went out to meet him with his children Silas and Zeno, and his wife Lectra, in order that he might entertain him: for Titus had informed him what Paul was like in appearance: for he had not seen him in the flesh, but only in the spirit. And he went along the road to Lystra, and stood waiting for him, and kept looking at the passers-by according to the description of Titus. And he saw Paul coming, a man small in size, bald-headed, bandy-legged, well-built,[3] with eyebrows meeting, rather long-nosed, full of grace. For sometimes he seemed like a man, and sometimes he had the countenance of an angel. And Paul, seeing Onesiphorus, smiled; and Onesiphorus said: Hail, O servant of the blessed God! And he said: Grace be with thee and thy house. And Demas and Ermogenes were jealous, and showed greater hypocrisy; so that Demas said: Are not we of the blessed God, that thou hast not thus saluted us? And Onesiphorus said: I do not see in you the fruit of righteousness; but if such you be, come you also into my house and rest yourselves.

And Paul having gone into the house of Onesiphorus, there was great joy, and bending of knees, and breaking of bread, and the word of God about self-control and the resurrection; Paul saying: Blessed are the pure in heart, for they shall see God:[4] blessed are they that have kept the flesh chaste, for they shall become a temple of God:[5] blessed are they that control themselves, for God shall speak with them:

blessed are they that have kept aloof from this world, for they shall be called upright:[6] blessed are they that have wives as not having them, for they shall receive God for their portion:[7] blessed are they that have the fear of God, for they shall become angels of God:[8] blessed are they that have kept the baptism, for they shall rest beside the Father and the Son: blessed are the merciful, for they shall obtain mercy,[9] and shall not see the bitter day of judgment: blessed are the bodies of the virgins, for they shall be well pleasing to God, and shall not lose the reward of their chastity; for the word of the Father shall become to them a work of salvation against the day of His Son, and they shall have rest for ever and ever.[10]

And while Paul was thus speaking in the midst of the church in the house of Onesiphorus, a certain virgin Thecla, the daughter of Theocleia, betrothed to a man *named* Thamyris, sitting at the window close by, listened night and day to the discourse of virginity and prayer, and did not look away from the window, but paid earnest heed to the faith, rejoicing exceedingly. And when she still saw many women going in beside Paul, she also had an eager desire to be deemed worthy to stand in the presence of Paul, and to hear the word of Christ; for never had she seen his figure, but heard his word only.

And as she did not stand away from the window, her mother sends to Thamyris; and he comes gladly, as if already receiving her in marriage. And Theocleia said: I have a strange story to tell thee, Thamyris; for assuredly for three days and three nights Thecla does not rise from the window, neither to eat nor to drink; but looking earnestly as if upon some pleasant sight, she is so devoted to a foreigner teaching deceitful and artful discourses, that I wonder how a virgin of such modesty is so painfully put about. Thamyris, this man will overturn the city of the Iconians, and thy Thecla too besides; for

---

[1] Or, persisted in staying with Paul.
[2] Or, how they.
[3] Or, healthy.
[4] Matt. v. 8.
[5] Comp. 1 Cor. vi. 18, 19.

[6] Comp. Rom. xii. 2.
[7] Comp. 1 Cor. vii. 29.
[8] Comp. Luke xx. 36.
[9] Matt. v. 7.
[10] Some MSS. add the following beatitudes: Blessed are they that tremble at the words of God, for they shall be comforted: blessed are they that have received the wisdom of Jesus Christ, for they shall be called the sons of the Most High: blessed are they that through love of Christ have come out from conformity with the world, for they shall judge the angels, and shall be blessed at the right hand of the Father.

all the women and the young men go in beside him, being taught to fear God and to live in chastity. Moreover also my daughter, tied to the window like a spider, lays hold of what is said by Paul with a strange eagerness and awful emotion ; for the virgin looks eagerly at what is said by him, and has been captivated. But do thou go near and speak to her, for she has been betrothed to thee.

And Thamyris going near, and kissing her, but at the same time also being afraid of her overpowering emotion, said : Thecla, my betrothed, why dost thou sit thus? and what sort of feeling holds thee overpowered? Turn round to thy Thamyris, and be ashamed. Moreover also her mother said the same things : Why dost thou sit thus looking down, my child, and answering nothing, but like a mad woman? And they wept fearfully, Thamyris indeed for the loss of a wife, and Theocleia of a child, and the maidservants of a mistress : there was accordingly much confusion in the house of mourning.[1] And while these things were thus going on, Thecla did not turn round, but kept attending earnestly to the word of Paul.

And Thamyris starting up, went forth into the street, and kept watching those going in to him and coming out. And he saw two men bitterly contending with each other ; and he said : Men, tell me who this is among you, leading astray the souls of young men, and deceiving virgins, so that they do not marry, but remain as they are. I promise, therefore, to give you money enough if you tell me about him ; for I am the first man[2] of the city. And Demas and Ermogenes said to him : Who this is, indeed, we do not know ; but he deprives young men of wives, and maidens of husbands, saying, There is for you a resurrection in no other way, unless you remain chaste, and pullute not the flesh, but keep it chaste. And Thamyris said to them : Come into my house, and rest yourselves. And they went to a sumptuous dinner, and much wine, and great wealth, and a splendid table ; and Thamyris made them drink, from his love to Thecla, and his wish to get her as his wife. And Thamyris said during the dinner : Ye men, what is his teaching, tell me, that I also may know ; for I am no little distressed about Thecla, because she thus loves the stranger, and I am prevented from marrying.

Demas and Ermogenes said : Bring him before the governor Castelios on the charge of persuading the multitudes to embrace the new teaching of the Christians, and he will speedily destroy him, and thou shalt have Thecla as thy wife. And we shall teach thee that the resurrection of which this man speaks has taken place, be-cause it has already taken place in the children which we have ;[3] and we rose again when we came to the knowledge of the true God.

And Thamyris, hearing these things, being filled with anger and rage, rising up early, went to the house of Onesiphorus with archons and public officers, and a great crowd with batons, saying : Thou hast corrupted the city of tne Iconians, and her that was betrothed to me, so that she will not have me : let us go to the governor Castelios. And all the multitude said : Away with the magician ; for he has corrupted all our wives, and the multitudes have been persuaded *to change their opinions.*

And Thamyris, standing before the tribunal, said with a great shout : O proconsul, this man, who he is we know not, who makes virgins averse to marriage ; let him say before thee on what[4] account he teaches these things. And Demas and Ermogenes said to Thamyris : Say that he is a Christian, and thus thou wilt do away with him. But the proconsul stayed his intention, and called Paul, saying : Who art thou, and what dost thou teach? for they bring no small charges against thee. And Paul lifted up his voice, saying : Since I am this day examined as to what I teach, listen, O proconsul : A living God, a God of retributions, a jealous God, a God in need of nothing, consulting for the salvation of men, has sent me that I may reclaim them from corruption and uncleanness, and from all pleasure, and from death, that they may not sin. Wherefore God sent His own Son, whom ,I preach, and in whom I teach men to rest their hope, who alone has had compassion upon a world led astray, that they may be no longer under judgment, O proconsul, but may have faith, and the fear of God, and the knowledge of holiness, and the love of truth. If, therefore, I teach what has been revealed to me by God, wherein do I do wrong? And the proconsul having heard, ordered Paul to be bound, and sent to prison, until, said he, I, being at leisure, shall hear him more attentively.

And Thecla by night having taken off her bracelets, gave them to the gatekeeper ; and the door having been opened to her, she went into the prison ; and having given the jailor a silver mirror, she went in beside Paul, and, sitting at his feet, she heard the great things of God. And Paul was afraid of nothing, but ordered his life in the confidence of God. And her faith also was increased, and she kissed his bonds.

And when Thecla was sought for by her friends, and Thamyris, as if she had been lost, was running up and down the streets, one of the gatekeeper's fellow-slaves informed him that she had gone out by night. And having gone out, they examined

---

[1] Or, a great outpouring of lamentation in the house.
[2] Or, a chief man.

[3] i.e., we rise again in our children.
[4] Or, whose.

the gatekeeper; and he said to them: She has gone to the foreigner into the prison. And having gone, they found her, as it were, enchained by affection. And having gone forth thence, they drew the multitudes together, and informed the governor of the circumstance. And he ordered Paul to be brought to the tribunal; but Thecla was wallowing on the ground [1] in the place where he sat and taught her in the prison; and he ordered her too to be brought to the tribunal. And she came, exulting with joy. And the crowd, when Paul had been brought, vehemently cried out: He is a magician! away with him! But the proconsul gladly heard Paul upon the holy works of Christ. And having called a council, he summoned Thecla, and said to her: Why dost thou not obey Thamyris, according to the law of the Iconians? But she stood looking earnestly at Paul. And when she gave no answer, her mother cried out, saying: Burn the wicked *wretch;* burn in the midst of the theatre her that will not marry, in order that all the women that have been taught by this man may be afraid.

And the governor was greatly moved; and having scourged Paul, he cast him out of the city, and condemned Thecla to be burned. And immediately the governor went away to the theatre, and all the crowd went forth to the spectacle of Thecla. But as a lamb in the wilderness looks round for the shepherd, so she kept searching for Paul. And having looked upon the crowd, she saw the Lord sitting in the likeness of Paul, and said: As I am unable to endure my lot, Paul has come to see me. And she gazed upon him with great earnestness, and he went up into heaven. But the maid-servants [2] and virgins brought the faggots, in order that Thecla might be burned. And when she came in naked, the governor wept, and wondered at the power [3] that was in her. And the public executioners arranged the faggots for her to go up on the pile. And she, having made the sign of the cross, went up on the faggots; and they lighted them. And though a great fire was blazing, it did not touch her; for God, having compassion upon her, made an underground rumbling, and a cloud overshadowed them from above, full of water and hail; and all that was in the cavity of it was poured out, so that many were in danger of death. And the fire was put out, and Thecla saved.

And Paul was fasting with Onesiphorus and his wife, and his children, in a new tomb, as they were going from Iconium to Daphne. And when many days were past, the fasting children said to Paul: We are hungry, and we cannot buy loaves; for Onesiphorus had left the things of the world, and followed Paul, with all his house. And Paul, having taken off his cloak, said: Go, my child, buy more loaves, and bring them. And when the child was buying, he saw Thecla their neighbour, and was astonished, and said: Thecla, whither art thou going? And she said: I have been saved from the fire, and am following Paul. And the boy said: Come, I shall take thee to him; for he is distressed about thee, and is praying six days. And she stood beside the tomb where Paul was with bended knees, and praying, and saying: O Saviour Christ, let not the fire touch Thecla, but stand by her, for she is Thine. And she, standing behind him, cried out: O Father, who hast made the heaven and the earth, the Father of Thy holy Son, I bless Thee that Thou hast saved me that I may see Paul. And Paul, rising up, saw her, and said: O God, that knowest the heart, the Father of our Lord Jesus Christ, I bless Thee that Thou, having heard me, hast done quickly what I wished.

And they had five loaves, and herbs, and water; and they rejoiced in the holy works of Christ. And Thecla said to Paul: I shall cut my hair, and follow thee whithersoever thou mayst go. And he said: It is a shameless age, and thou art beautiful. I am afraid lest another temptation come upon thee worse than the first, and that thou withstand it not, but be cowardly. And Thecla said: Only give me the seal [4] in Christ, and temptation shall not touch me. And Paul said: Thecla, wait with patience, and thou shalt receive the water.

And Paul sent away Onesiphorus and all his house to Iconium; and thus, having taken Thecla, he went into Antioch. And as they were going in, a certain Syriarch, Alexander by name, seeing Thecla, became enamoured of her, and tried to gain over Paul by gifts and presents. But Paul said: I know not the woman whom thou speakest of, nor is she mine. But he, being of great power, himself embraced her in the street. But she would not endure it, but looked about for Paul. And she cried out bitterly, saying: Do not force the stranger; do not force the servant of God. I am one of the chief persons of the Iconians; and because I would not have Thamyris, I have been cast out of the city. And taking hold of Alexander, she tore his cloak, and pulled off his crown, and made him a laughing-stock. And he, at the same time loving her, and at the same time ashamed of what had happened, led her before the governor; and when she had confessed that she had done these things, he condemned her to the wild beasts. And the women were struck with astonishment, and cried

---

[1] i.e., in sign of grief.
[2] One ms. has, boys.
[3] Or, virtue.

[4] 2 Cor. i. 22; Eph. i. 13, iv. 30.

out beside the tribunal: Evil judgment! impious judgment! And she asked the governor, that, said she, I may remain pure until I shall fight with the wild beasts. And a certain Tryphæna,[1] whose daughter was dead, took her into keeping, and had her for a consolation.

And when the beasts were exhibited, they bound her to a fierce lioness; and Tryphæna accompanied her. But the lioness, with Thecla sitting upon her, licked her feet; and all the multitude was astonished. And the charge on her inscription was: Sacrilegious. And the women cried out from above: An impious sentence has been passed in this city! And after the exhibition, Tryphæna again receives her. For her daughter Falconilla had died, and said to her in a dream: Mother, thou shalt have this stranger Thecla in my place, in order that she may pray concerning me, and that I may be transferred to the place of the just.

And when, after the exhibition, Tryphæna received her, at the same time indeed she grieved that she had to fight with the wild beasts on the day following; and at the same time, loving her as much as her daughter Falconilla, she said: My second child Thecla, come and pray for my child, that she may live for ever; for this I saw in my sleep. And she, nothing hesitating, lifted up her voice, and said: God most high,[2] grant to this woman according to her wish, that her daughter Falconilla may live for ever. And when Thecla had thus spoken, Tryphæna lamented, considering so much beauty thrown to the wild beasts.

And when it was dawn, Alexander came to take her, for it was he that gave the hunt,[3] saying: The governor is sitting, and the crowd is in uproar against us. Allow me to take away her that is to fight with the wild beasts. And Tryphæna cried aloud, so that he even fled, saying: A second mourning for my Falconilla has come upon my house, and there is no one to help; neither child, for she is dead, nor kinsman, for I am a widow. God of Thecla, help her!

And immediately the governor sends an order that Thecla should be brought. And Tryphæna, taking her by the hand, said: My daughter Falconilla, indeed, I took away to the tomb; and thee, Thecla, I am taking to the wild-beast fight. And Thecla wept bitterly, saying: O Lord, the God in whom I believe, to whom I have fled for refuge, who deliveredst me from the fire, do Thou grant a recompense to Tryphæna, who has had compassion on Thy servant, and because she has kept me pure. Then a tumult arose, and a

cry of the people, and the women sitting together, the one saying: Away with the sacrilegious person! the others saying: Let the city be raised[4] against this wickedness. Take off all of us, O proconsul! Cruel sight! evil sentence!

And Thecla, having been taken out of the hand of Tryphæna, was stripped, and received a girdle,[5] and was thrown into the arena, and lions and bears and a fierce lioness were let loose upon her; and the lioness having run up to her feet, lay down; and the multitude of the women cried aloud. And a bear ran upon her; but the lioness, meeting the bear, tore her to pieces. And again a lion that had been trained against men, which belonged to Alexander, ran upon her; and she, *the lioness*, encountering the lion, was killed along with him. And the women made great lamentation, since also the lioness, her protector, was dead.

Then they send in many wild beasts, she standing and stretching forth her hands, and praying. And when she had finished her prayer, she turned and saw a ditch full of water, and said: Now it is time to wash myself. And she threw herself in, saying: In the name of Jesus Christ I am baptized on my last day. And the women seeing, and the multitude, wept, saying: Do not throw thyself into the water; so that also the governor shed tears, because the seals were going to devour such beauty. She then threw herself *in* in the name of Jesus Christ; but the seals having seen the glare of the fire of lightning, floated about dead. And there was round her, as she was naked, a cloud of fire; so that neither could the wild beasts touch her, nor could she be seen naked.

And the women, when other wild beasts were being thrown in, wailed. And some threw sweet-smelling herbs, others nard, others cassia, others amomum, so that there was abundance of perfumes. And all the wild beasts that had been thrown in, as if they had been withheld by sleep, did not touch her; so that Alexander said to the governor: I have bulls exceedingly terrible; let us bind to them her that is to fight with the beasts. And the governor, looking gloomy, turned, and said: Do what thou wilt. And they bound her by the feet between them, and put red-hot irons under the privy parts of the bulls, so that they, being rendered more furious, might kill her. They rushed about, therefore; but the burning flame consumed the ropes, and she was as if she had not been bound. But Tryphæna fainted standing beside the arena, so that the crowd said: Queen Tryphæna is dead. And the governor put a stop to the games, and the city was in dismay. And Alexander entreated the governor, saying: Have mercy both on me

---

[1] Some MSS. add: A widow, very rich.
[2] One MS. has: God of our fathers, Son of the Most High. Another: O Lord God, who hast made the heaven and the earth, Son of the Most High, Lord Jesus Christ.
[3] i.e., the exhibition of wild beasts.

[4] Or, be taken off, i.e., put to death.
[5] Or, drawers.

and the city, and release this woman. For if Cæsar hear of these things, he will speedily destroy the city also along with us, because his kinswoman Queen Tryphæna has died beside the ABACI.[1]

And the governor summoned Thecla out of the midst of the wild beasts, and said to her: Who art thou? and what is there about thee, that not one of the wild beasts touches thee? And she said: I indeed am a servant of the living God; and as to what there is about me, I have believed in the Son of God, in whom He is well pleased; wherefore not one of the beasts has touched me. For He alone is the end[2] of salvation, and the basis of immortal life; for He is a refuge to the tempest-tossed, a solace to the afflicted, a shelter to the despairing; and, once for all, whoever shall not believe on Him, shall not live for ever.

And the governor having heard this, ordered her garments to be brought, and to be put on. And Thecla said: He that clothed me naked among the wild beasts, will in the day of judgment clothe thee with salvation. And taking the garments, she put them on. The governor therefore immediately issued an edict, saying: I release to you the God-fearing Thecla, the servant of God. And the women shouted aloud, and with one mouth returned thanks to God, saying: There is one God, *the God* of Thecla; so that the foundations of the theatre were shaken by their voice. And Tryphæna having received the good news, went to meet the holy Thecla, and said: Now I believe that the dead are raised; now I believe that my child lives. Come within, and I shall assign to thee all that is mine. She therefore went in along with her, and rested eight days, having instructed her in the word of God, so that most even of the maid-servants believed. And there was great joy in the house.

And Thecla kept seeking Paul; and it was told her that he was in Myra of Lycia. And taking young men and maidens, she girded herself; and having sewed the tunic so as to make a man's cloak, she came to Myra, and found Paul speaking the word of God. And Paul was astonished at seeing her, and the crowd with her, thinking that some new trial was coming upon her. And when she saw him, she said: I have received the baptism, Paul; for He that wrought along with thee for the Gospel has wrought in me also for baptism. And Paul, taking her, led her to the house of Hermæus, and hears everything from her, so that those that heard greatly wondered, and were comforted, and prayed over Tryphæna. And she rose up, and said: I am going to Iconium. And Paul said: Go, and teach the word of God.

And Tryphæna sent her much clothing and gold, so that she left to Paul many things for the service of the poor.

And she went to Iconium. And she goes into the house of Onesiphorus, and fell upon the pavement where Paul used to sit and teach her, and wept, saying: God of myself and of this house, where Thou didst make the light to shine upon me, O Christ Jesus, the Son of the living God, my help in the fire, my help among the wild beasts, Thou art glorified for ever. Amen. And she found Thamyris dead, but her mother alive. And having sent for her mother, she said: Theocleia, my mother, canst thou believe that the Lord liveth in the heavens? For whether thou desirest wealth, God gives it to thee through me; or thy child, I am standing beside thee. And having thus testified, she departed to Seleucia, and dwelt in a cave seventy-two years, living upon herbs and water. And she enlightened many by the word of God.

And certain men of the city, being Greeks by religion, and physicians by profession, sent to her insolent young men to destroy[3] her. For they said: She is a virgin, and serves Artemis, and from this she has virtue in healing. And by the providence of God she entered into the rock alive, and went under ground. And she departed to Rome to see Paul, and found that he had fallen asleep.[4] And after staying there no long time, she rested in a glorious sleep; and she is buried about two or three stadia from the tomb of her master Paul.

She was cast, then, into the fire when seventeen years old, and among the wild beasts when eighteen. And she was an ascetic in the cave, as has been said, seventy-two years, so that all the years of her life were ninety. And having accomplished many cures, she rests in the place of the saints, having fallen asleep on the twenty-fourth of the month of September in Christ Jesus our Lord, to whom be glory and strength for ever and ever. Amen.

Instead of the last two sections, the MS. which Dr. Grabe used has the following:—

And a cloud of light guided her. And having come into Seleucia, she went forth outside of the city one stadium. And she was afraid of them also, for they worshipped idols. And it guided her to the mountain called Calamon or Rhodeon; and having there found a cave, she went into it. And she was there many years, and underwent many and grievous trials by the devil, and bore them nobly, being assisted by Christ. And some of the well-born women, having learned about the virgin Thecla,

[1] A part of the ancient theatres on or near the stage.
[2] Or, way.

[3] Or, corrupt.
[4] i.e., that he was dead.

went to her, and learned the oracles of God. And many of them bade adieu to the world, and lived an ascetic life with her. And a good report was spread everywhere concerning her, and cures were done by her. All the city, therefore, and country round, having known this, brought their sick to the mountain; and before they came near the door they were speedily released from whatever disease they were afflicted by; and the unclean spirits went out shrieking, and all received their own in health, glorifying God, who had given such grace to the virgin Thecla. The physicians, therefore, of the city of the Seleucians were thought nothing of, having lost their trade, and no one any longer had regard to them; and being filled with envy and hatred, they plotted against the servant of Christ, what they should do to her. The devil then suggests to them a wicked device; and one day, being assembled, and having taken counsel, they consult with each other, saying: This virgin is a priestess of the great goddess Artemis; and if she ask anything of her, she hears her as being a virgin, and all the gods love her. Come, then, let us take men of disorderly lives, and make them drunk with much wine, and let us give them much gold, and say to them, If you can corrupt and defile her, we shall give you even more money. The physicians therefore said to themselves, that if they should be able to defile her, neither the gods nor Artemis would listen to her in the case of the sick. They therefore did so. And the wicked men, having gone to the mountain, and rushed upon the cave like lions, knocked at the door. And the holy martyr Thecla opened, emboldened by the God in whom she believed; for she knew of their plot beforehand. And she says to them: What do you want, my children? And they said: Is there one here called Thecla? And she said: What do you want with her? They say to her: We want to sleep with her. The blessed Thecla says to them: I am a humble old woman, but the servant of my Lord Jesus Christ; and even though you want to do something to me out of place, you cannot. They say to her: It is impossible for us not to do to thee what we want. And having said this, they laid fast hold of her, and wished to insult her. And she says to them

with mildness: Wait, my children, that you may see the glory of the Lord. And being laid hold of by them, she looked up into heaven, and said: God, terrible and incomparable, and glorious to Thine adversaries, who didst deliver me out of the fire, who didst not give me up to Thamyris, who didst not give me up to Alexander, who didst deliver me from the wild beasts, who didst save me in the abyss, who hast everywhere worked with me, and glorified Thy name in me, now also deliver me from these lawless men, and let me not insult my virginity, which through Thy name I have preserved till now, because I love Thee, and desire Thee, and adore Thee, the Father, and the Son, and the Holy Ghost for ever. Amen. And there came a voice out of the heaven, saying: Fear not, Thecla, my true servant, for I am with thee. Look and see where an opening has been made before thee, for there shall be for thee an everlasting house, and there thou shalt obtain shelter. And the blessed Thecla regarding it, saw the rock opened as far as to allow a man to enter, and did according to what had been said to her: and nobly fleeing from the lawless ones, entered into the rock; and the rock was straightway shut together, so that not even a joining appeared. And they, beholding the extraordinary wonder, became as it were distracted; and they were not able to detain the servant of God, but only caught hold of her veil, and were able to tear off a certain part; and that by the permission of God for the faith of those seeing the venerable place, and for a blessing in the generations afterwards to those that believe in our Lord Jesus Christ out of a pure heart.

Thus, then, suffered the first martyr of God, and apostle, and virgin, Thecla, who came from Iconium at eighteen years old; and with the journeying, and the going round, and the retirement in the mountain, she lived other seventy-two years. And when the Lord took her, she was ninety years old. And thus is her consummation. And her holy commemoration is on the twenty-fourth of the month of September, to the glory of the Father, and the Son, and the Holy Spirit, now and ever, and to ages of ages. Amen.

THE ACTS OF BARNABAS

THE JOURNEYINGS AND MARTYRDOM OF ST. BARNABAS THE APOSTLE.

SINCE from the descent of the presence of our Saviour Jesus Christ, the unwearied and benevolent and mighty Shepherd and Teacher and Physician, I beheld and saw the ineffable and holy and unspotted mystery of the Christians, who hold the hope in holiness, and who have been sealed; and since I have zealously served Him, I have deemed it necessary to give an account of the mysteries which I have heard and seen.

I John, accompanying the holy apostles Barnabas and Paul, being formerly a servant of Cyrillus the high priest of Jupiter, but now having received the gift of the Holy Spirit through Paul and Barnabas and Silas, *who were* worthy of the calling, and who baptized me in Iconium. After I was baptized, then, I saw a certain man standing clothed in white raiment; and he said to me : Be of good courage, John, for assuredly thy name shall be changed to Mark, and thy glory shall be proclaimed in all the world. And the darkness in thee has passed away from thee, and there has been given to thee understanding to know the mysteries of God.

And when I saw the vision, becoming greatly terrified, I went to the feet of Barnabas, and related to him the mysteries which I had seen and heard from that man. And the Apostle Paul was not by when I disclosed the mysteries. And Barnabas said to me : Tell no one the miracle which thou hast seen. For by me also this night the Lord stood, saying, Be of good courage : for as thou hast given thy life for my name to death and banishment from thy nation, thus also shalt thou be made perfect. Moreover, as for the servaut who is with you, take him also with thyself; for he has certain mysteries. Now then, my child, keep to thyself the things which thou hast seen and heard; for a time will come for thee to reveal them.[1]

And I, having been instructed in these things by him, remained in Iconium[2] many days; for there was there a holy man and a pious, who also entertained us, whose house also Paul had sanctified. Thence, therefore, we came to Se-leucia, and after staying three days sailed away to Cyprus; and I was ministering to them until we had gone round all Cyprus. And setting sail from Cyprus, we landed in Perga of Pamphylia. And there I then stayed about two months, wishing to sail to the regions of the West; and the Holy Spirit did not allow me. Turning, therefore, I again sought the apostles; and having learned that they were in Antioch, I went to them.

And I found Paul in bed in Antioch from the toil of the journey, who also seeing me, was exceedingly grieved on account of my delaying in Pamphylia. And Barnabas coming, encouraged him, and tasted bread, and he took a little of it. And they preached the word of the Lord, and enlightened many of the Jews and Greeks. And I only attended to them, and was afraid of Paul to come near him, both because he held me as having spent much time in Pamphylia, and because he was quite enraged against me. And I gave repentance on my knees upon the earth to Paul, and he would not endure it. And when I remained for three Sabbaths in entreaty and prayer on my knees, I was unable to prevail upon him about myself; for his great grievance against me was on account of my keeping several parchments in Pamphylia.

And when it came to pass that they finished teaching in Antioch, on the first of the week they took counsel together to set out for the places of the East, and after that to go into Cyprus, and oversee all the churches in which they had spoken the word of God. And Barnabas entreated Paul to go first to Cyprus, and oversee his own in his village; and Lucius[3] entreated him to take the oversight of his city Cyrene. And a vision was seen by Paul in sleep, that he should hasten to Jerusalem, because the brethren expected him there. But Barnabas urged that they should go to Cyprus, and pass the winter, and then that they should go to Jerusalem at the feast. Great contention, therefore, arose between them.[4] And Barnabas urged me also to accompany them, on account of my being their servant from the beginning, and on account

---

[1] Or, will come to reveal thee.
[2] One MS. has *Jerusalem*, and adds, *and we came to Antioch*, which suits the geography better.
[3] Acts xiii. 1; Rom. xvi. 21.
[4] Acts xv. 39.

of my having served them in all Cyprus until they came to Perga of Pamphylia; and I there had remained many days. But Paul cried out against Barnabas, saying: It is impossible for him to go with us. And those who were with us there urged me also to accompany them, because there was a vow upon me to follow them to the end. So that Paul said to Barnabas: If thou wilt take John who also is surnamed Mark with thee, go another road; for he shall not come with us. And Barnabas coming to himself, said: The grace of God does not desert[1] him who has once served the Gospel and journeyed with us. If, therefore, this be agreeable to thee, Father Paul, I take him and go. And he said: Go thou in the grace of Christ, and we in the power of the Spirit.

Therefore, bending their knees, they prayed to God. And Paul, groaning aloud, wept, and in like manner also Barnabas, saying to one another: It would have been good for us, as at first, so also at last, to work in common among men; but since it has thus seemed good to thee, Father Paul, pray for me that my labour may be made perfect to commendation: for thou knowest how I have served thee also to the grace of Christ that has been given to thee. For I go to Cyprus, and hasten to be made perfect;[2] for I know that I shall no more see thy face, O Father Paul. And falling on the ground at his feet, he wept long. And Paul said to him: The Lord stood by me also this night, saying, Do not force Barnabas not to go to Cyprus, for there it has been prepared for him to enlighten many; and do thou also, in the grace that has been given to thee, go to Jerusalem to worship in the holy place, and there it shall be shown thee where thy martyrdom has been prepared. And we saluted one another, and Barnabas took me to himself.

And having come down to Laodiceia,[3] we sought to cross to Cyprus; and having found a ship going to Cyprus, we embarked. And when we had set sail, the wind was found to be contrary. And we came to Corasium;[4] and having gone down to the shore where there was a fountain, we rested there, showing ourselves to no one, that no one might know that Barnabas had separated from Paul. And having set sail from Corasium, we came to the regions of Isauria, and thence came to a certain island called Pityusa;[5] and a storm having come on, we remained there three days; and a certain pious man entertained us, by name Euphemus, whom also Barnabas instructed in many things in the faith, with all his house.

And thence we sailed past the Aconesiæ,[6] and came to the city of Anemurium; and having gone into it, we found two Greeks. And coming to us, they asked whence and who we were. And Barnabas said to them: If you wish to know whence and who we are, throw away the clothing which you have, and I shall put on you clothing which never becomes soiled; for neither is there in it anything filthy, but it is altogether splendid. And being astonished at the saying, they asked us: What is that garment which you are going to give us? And Barnabas said to them: If you shall confess your sins, and submit yourselves to our Lord Jesus Christ, you shall receive that garment which is incorruptible for ever. And being pricked at heart by the Holy Spirit, they fell at his feet, entreating and saying: We beseech thee, father, give us that garment; for we believe in the living and true God whom thou proclaimest. And leading them down to[7] the fountain, he baptized them into the name of Father, and Son, and Holy Ghost. And they knew that they were clothed with power, and a holy robe. And having taken from me one robe, he put it on the one; and his own robe he put on the other. And they brought money to him, and straightway Barnabas distributed it to the poor. And from them also the sailors were able to gain many things.[8]

And they having come down to the shore, he spoke to them the word of God; and he having blessed them, we saluted them, and went on board the ship. And the one of them who was named Stephanus wished to accompany us, and Barnabas did not permit him. And we, having gone across, sailed down to Cyprus by night; and having come to the place called Crommya-cita,[9] we found Timon and Ariston the temple servants, at whose house also we were entertained.

And Timon was afflicted by much fever. And having laid our hands upon him, we straightway removed his fever, having called upon the name of the Lord Jesus. And Barnabas had received documents from Matthew, a book of the word[10] of God, and a narrative of miracles and doctrines. This Barnabas laid upon the sick in each place that we came to, and it immediately made a cure of their sufferings.

And when we had come to Lapithus,[11] and an idol festival[12] being celebrated in the theatre, they did not allow us to go into the city, but we rested a little at the gate. And Timon, after he rose up from his disease, came with us. And having gone forth from Lapithus, we travelled

---

[1] Or, turn away.
[2] i.e., to finish my course.
[3] This is the Syrian Laodiceia, opposite Cyprus.
[4] Perhaps Corycus.
[5] Or, Pityussa, close to the Zephyrian promontory.
[6] Perhaps Aphrodisias.

[7] Or, into.
[8] To make much profit.
[9] Crommyon Pr.
[10] Lit., the voice.
[11] Lapethus.
[12] Lit., an idol-frenzy, — a term often applied to the worship of Bacchus.

through the mountains, and came to the city of Lampadistus, of which also Timon was a native; in addition to whom, having found also that Heracleius was there, we were entertained by him. He was of the city of Tamasus,[1] and had come to visit his relations; and Barnabas, looking stedfastly at him, recognised him, having met with him formerly at Citium with Paul; to whom also the Holy Spirit was given at baptism, and he changed his name to Heracleides. And having ordained him bishop over Cyprus, and having confirmed the church in Tamasus, we left him in the house of his brethren that dwelt there.

And having crossed the mountain called Chionodes,[2] we came to Old Paphos, and there found Rhodon, a temple servant, who also, having himself believed, accompanied us. And we met a certain Jew, by name Barjesus, coming from Paphos, who also recognised Barnabas, as having been formerly with Paul. He did not wish us to go into Paphos; but having turned away, we came to Curium.[3]

And we found that a certain abominable race was being performed[4] in the road near the city, where a multitude of women and men naked were performing the race. And there was great deception and error in that place. And Barnabas turning, rebuked it; and the western part fell, so that many were wounded, and many of them also died; and the rest fled to the temple of Apollo, which was close at hand in the *city* which was called sacred.[5] And when we came near the temple, a great multitude of Jews who were there, having been put up to it by Barjesus, stood outside of the city, and did not allow us to go into the city; but we spent the evening under a tree near the city, and rested there.

And on the following day we came to a certain village where Aristoclianus dwelt. He being a leper, had been cleansed in Antioch, whom also Paul and Barnabas sealed to be a bishop, and sent to his village in Cyprus, because there were many Greeks there. And we were entertained in the cave by him in the mountain, and there we remained one day. And thence we came to Amathus, and there was a great multitude of Greeks in the temple in the mountain, low women and men pouring libations. There also Barjesus, getting the start of us, gained over the nation of the Jews, and did not allow us to enter into the city; but a certain widow woman, eighty years old, being outside of the city, and she also not worshipping the idols, coming forward to us, took us into her house one hour.

And when we came out we shook the dust off our feet over against that temple where the libation of the abominable took place.

And having gone out thence, we came through desert places, and Timon also accompanied us. And having come to Citium, and there being a great uproar there also in their hippodrome, having learned this, we came forth out of the city, having all shaken the dust off our feet; for no one received us, except that we rested one hour in the gate near the aqueduct.

And having set sail in a ship from Citium, we came to Salamis, and landed in the so-called islands, where there was a place full of idols; and there there took place high festivals[6] and libations. And having found Heracleides there again, we instructed him to proclaim the Gospel of God, and to set up churches, and ministers in them. And having gone into Salamis, we came to the synagogue near the place called Biblia; and when we had gone into it, Barnabas, having unrolled the Gospel which he had received from Matthew his fellow-labourer, began to teach the Jews.

And Barjesus, having arrived after two days, after not a few Jews had been instructed, was enraged, and brought together all the multitude of the Jews; and they having laid hold of Barnabas, wished to hand him over to Hypatius, the governor of Salamis. And having bound him to take him away to the governor, and a pious Jebusite,[7] a kinsman of Nero, having come to Cyprus, the Jews, learning this, took Barnabas by night, and bound him with a rope by the neck; and having dragged him to the hippodrome from the synagogue, and having gone out of the city, standing round him, they burned him with fire, so that even his bones became dust. And straightway that night, having taken his dust, they cast it into a cloth; and having secured it with lead, they intended to throw it into the sea. But I, finding an opportunity in the night, and being able along with Timon and Rhodon to carry it. we came to a certain place, and having found a cave, put it down there, where the nation of the Jebusites formerly dwelt. And having found a secret place in it, we put it away, with the documents which he had received from Matthew. And it was the fourth hour of the night of the second of the week.[8]

And when we were hid in the place, the Jews made no little search after us; and having almost found us, they pursued us as far as the

---

[1] Tamassus.
[2] i.e., snowy, an epithet of Olympus, the mountain they crossed.
[3] Perhaps Curtium, which was nearer Palæo Paphos than Curias Pr. was.
[4] i.e., as a religious service.
[5] Another reading is: *In the city called Curium.*

[6] Lit., assemblies of the whole nation.
[7] Another reading is: *Eusebius the Jebusite.* There is a legend that the Jebusites colonized Cyprus after they were driven out of Palestine by King David.
[8] The Vatican MS. adds: on the 17th of the month Paiin according to the Egyptians, and according to the Romans the 11th of the month of June.

village of the Ledrians; and we, having found there also a cave near the village, took refuge in it, and thus escaped them. And we were hid in the cave three days; and the Jews having gone away, we came forth and left the place by night. And taking with us Ariston and Rhodon, we came to the village of Limnes.[1]

And having come to the shore, we found an Egyptian ship; and having embarked in it, we landed at Alexandria. And there I remained, teaching the brethren that came the word of the Lord, enlightening them, and preaching what I had been taught by the apostles of Christ, who also baptized me into the name of Father, and Son, and Holy Ghost; who also changed my name to Mark in the water of baptism, by which also I hope to bring many to the glory of God through His grace; because to Him is due honour and everlasting glory. Amen.

The journeyings and martyrdom of the holy apostle Barnabas have been fulfilled through God.

---

[1] This place does not appear on the ancient maps, but there is a modern C. Limniti.

THE ACTS OF PHILIP

OF THE JOURNEYINGS OF PHILIP THE APOSTLE.

FROM THE FIFTEENTH ACT UNTIL THE END, AND AMONG THEM THE MARTYRDOM.[1]

ABOUT the time when the Emperor Trajan received the government of the Romans, after Simon the son of Clopas, who was bishop of Jerusalem, had suffered martyrdom in the eighth year of his reign, being the second bishop of the church there after James who bore the name of brother of the Lord,[2] Philip the apostle, going through the cities and regions of Lydia and Asia, preached to all the Gospel of Christ.

And having come to the city of Ophioryma, which is called Hierapolis of Asia, he was entertained by a certain believer, Stachys by name. And there was with him also Bartholomew, one of the seventy disciples of the Lord, and his sister Mariamme, and his disciples that followed him. All the men of the city therefore, having left their work, ran to the house of Stachys, hearing about the works which Philip did. And many men and women having assembled in the house of Stachys, Philip along with Bartholomew taught them the things of Jesus.

And Philip's sister Mariamme, sitting in the entry of the house of Stachys, addressed herself to those coming, persuading them to listen to the apostles, saying to them: Our brethren, and sons of my Father in heaven, ye are the excellent riches, and the substance of the city above, the delight of the habitation which God has prepared for those that love Him. Trample under foot the snares of the enemy, the writhing serpent. For his path is crooked, since he is the son of the wicked one, and the poison of wickedness is in him; and his father is the devil, the author of death, and his mother corruption; rage in his eyes and destruction in his mouth, and his path is Hades. Wherefore flee from him that has no substance, the shapeless one that has no shape in all the creation, whether in the heaven or in the earth, whether in the flying creatures or the beasts. For everything is taken away from his shape; for among the beasts of the earth and the fowls of the heaven is the

knowledge of him, that the serpent trails his belly and his breast; and Tartarus is his dwelling-place, and he goes in the darkness, since he has confidence in nothing.[3] Flee therefore from him, that his poison may not be poured out into your mouth. But be rather believing, holy, of good works, having no deceit. Take away from yourselves the wicked disposition, that is, the evil desires through which the serpent, the wicked dragon, the prince of evil, has produced the pasture of destruction and death for the soul, since all the desire of the wicked has proceeded from him. And this is the root of iniquity, the maintenance of evils, the death of souls; for the desire of the enemy is armed against the believers, and comes forth from the darkness, and walks in the darkness, taking in hand to war with those who are in the light. For this is the beginning of concupiscence.[4] Wherefore you who wish to come to us, and the rather that God has come through us to you as a father to his own children, wishing to have mercy upon you, and to deliver you from the wicked snare of the enemy, flee from the evil lusts of the enemy, and cast them completely out of your mind, hating openly the father of evils, and loving Jesus, who is light, and life, and truth, and the Saviour of all who desire Him. Having run, therefore, to Him, take hold of Him in love, that He may bring you up out of the pit of the wicked, and having cleansed you, set you blameless, living in truth, in the presence of His Father.

And all these things Philip said to the multitudes that had come together to worship as in old times the serpents and the viper, of which also they set up images and worshipped them. Wherefore also they called Hierapolis Ophioryma.[5] And these things having been said by Philip, Bartholomew and Mariamme and his disciples, and Stachys being along with him, all the people gave ear, and a great multitude of

---

1 [This enlarged title is from the Venetian MS.; see p. 355. — R.]
2 Comp. Euseb., *H. E.*, iii, 32.

3 Or, in no one.
4 Or, covetousness.
5 i.e., Serpent's town.

them fleeing from the enemy were turned to Jesus, and were added to Philip and those about him. And the faithful were the more confirmed in the love of Christ.

And Nicanora, the wife of the proconsul, lying in bed under various diseases, especially of the eyes, having heard about the Apostle Philip and his teaching, believed in the Lord. For she had even before this heard about Him; and having called upon His name, she was released from the troubles that afflicted her. And rising up, she went forth out of her house through the side door, carried by her own slaves in a silver litter, and went into the house of Stachys, where the apostles were.

And when she came before the gate of the house, Mariamme, the sister of Philip the apostle, seeing her, spoke to her in the Hebrew tongue before Philip and Bartholomew, and all the multitude of those who had believed, saying: ALEMAKAN, IKASAME, MARMARE, NACHAMAN,[1] MASTRANAN, ACHAMAN; which is, Daughter of the father, thou art my mistress, thou hast been given as a pledge to the serpent; but Jesus our Redeemer has come to deliver thee through us, to break thy bands, and cut them, and to remove them from thee from their root, because thou art my sister, one mother brought us forth twins. Thou hast forsaken thy father, thou hast forsaken the path leading thee to the dwelling-place of thy mother, being in error; thou hast left the temple of that deception, and of the temporary glory, and hast come to us, fleeing from the enemy, because he is the dwelling-place of death. Behold, now thy Redeemer has come to redeem thee; Christ the Sun of righteousness has risen upon thee, to enlighten thee.[2]

And when Nicanora, standing before the door, heard these things, she took courage before all, crying out, and saying: I am a Hebrew, and a daughter of the Hebrews; speak with me in the language of my fathers. For, having heard the preaching of my fathers, I was straightway cured of the disease and the troubles that encompassed me. I therefore adore the goodness of God, who has caused you to be spoiled even to this city, on account of His true stone[3] held in honour, in order that through you we may receive the knowledge of Him, and may live with you, having believed in Him.

Nicanora having thus spoken, the Apostle Philip, along with Bartholomew and Mariamme and those with them, prayed for her to God, saying: Thou who bringest the dead to life, Christ Jesus the Lord, who hast freed us through baptism from the slavery of death,[4] completely deliver also this woman from the error, the enemy; make her alive in Thy life, and perfect her in Thy perfection, in order that she may be found in the country of her fathers in freedom, having a portion in Thy goodness, O Lord Jesus.

And all having sent up the amen along with the Apostle Philip, behold, there came the tyrant, the husband of Nicanora, raging like an unbroken horse; and having laid hold of his wife's garments, he cried out, saying: O Nicanora, did not I leave thee in bed? how hadst thou so much strength as to come to these magicians? And how hast thou been cured of the inflammation of thine eyes? Now, therefore, unless thou tell me who thy physician is, and what is his name, I shall punish thee with various punishments, and shall not have compassion upon thee. And she answering, says to him: O tyrant, cast out from thee this tyranny of thine, forsake this wickedness of thine; abandon this life lasting only for a season; run away from the brutality of thy worthless disposition; flee from the wicked dragon and his lusts; throw from thee the works and the dart of the man-slaying serpent; renounce the abominable and wicked sacrifices of the idols, which are the husbandry of the enemy, the hedge of darkness; make for thyself a life chaste and pure, that being in holiness thou mayst be able to know my Physician, and to get His name. If therefore thou wishest me to be beside thee, prepare thyself to live in chastity and self-restraint, and in fear of the true God, and I shall live with thee all my life; only cleanse thyself from the idols, and from all their filth.

And when the gloomy tyrant her husband heard these words of hers, he seized her by the hair of her head, and dragged her along, kicking her, and saying: It will be a fine thing for thee to be cut off by the sword, or to see thee from beside me committing fornication with these foreign magicians; for I see that thou hast fallen into the madness of these deceivers. Thee first of them, therefore, I shall cut off by an evil death; and then, not sparing them, I shall cut their sinews, and put them to a most cruel death. And having turned, he said to those about him: Bring out for me those impostors of magicians. And the public executioners having run into the house of Stachys, and laid hold of the Apostle Philip, and Bartholomew and Mariamme, dragged them along, leading them to where the proconsul was. And the most faithful Stachys followed, and all the faithful.

And the proconsul seeing them, gnashed his teeth, saying: Torture these deceivers that have deceived many women, and young men and girls, saying that they are worshippers of God, while they are an abomination. And he ordered thongs of raw hide to be brought, and Philip

[1] Or, iachaman.
[2] Comp. Mal. iv. 2.
[3] Isa. xxviii. 16; 1 Pet. ii. 4, etc.
[4] Comp. Rom. vi. 3, 4.

and Bartholomew and Mariamme to be beaten; and after they had been scourged with the thongs, he ordered their feet to be tied, and them to be dragged through the streets of the city as far as the gate of their temple. And a great crowd was assembled, so that scarcely any one stayed at home; and they all wondered at their patience, as they were being violently and inhumanly dragged along.

And the proconsul, having tortured the Apostle Philip and the saints who were with him, ordered them to be brought, and secured in the temple of the idol of the viper by its priests, until he should decide by what death he should destroy each of them. And many of the crowd believed in the grace of Christ, and were added to the Apostle Philip, and those with him, having renounced the idol of the viper, and were confirmed in the faith, being magnified by the endurance of the saints; and all together with their voice glorified God, saying the amen.

And when they were shut up in the temple of the viper — both Philip the Apostle, and Bartholomew and Mariamme — the priests of the viper assembled in the same place, and a great crowd, about seven thousand men; and having run to the proconsul, they cried out, saying: Avenge us of the foreigners, and magicians, and corrupters and seducers of men. For ever since they came to us, our city has been filled with every evil deed; and they have also killed the serpents, the sons of our goddess; and they have also shut the temple, and the altar has been desolated; and we have not found the wine which had been brought in order that the viper, having drunk of it, might go to sleep. But if thou wishest to know that they are really magicians, look and see how they wish to bewitch us, saying, Live in chastity and piety, after believing in God; and how also they have come into the city; and how also the dragons have not struck them blind, or even killed them; and how also they have not drunk their blood; but even they who keep our city from every foreigner have been cast down by these men.

And the proconsul, having heard these things, was the more inflamed with rage, and filled with wrath and threatening; and he was exceedingly enraged, and said to the priests: Why *need you speak*, when they have bewitched my own wife? And from that time she has spoken to me with strange words; and praying all the night through, she speaks in a strange tongue with a light shining round her; and groaning aloud, she says, Jesus the true light has come to me. And I, having gone forth from my chamber, wished to look down through the window and see Jesus, the light which she spoke of; and like lightning it came upon me, so that I was within a little of being blinded; and from that time forth I am afraid of my wife, on account of her luminous Jesus. Tell me, ye priests, what I am to do. And they said to him: O proconsul, assuredly we are no longer priests; for ever since thou didst shut them up, in consequence of them praying, not only has the temple been shaken from the foundations, but it is also assuredly falling down.

Then the proconsul ordered to bring Philip and those with him forth out of the temple, and to bring them up to the tribunal, saying to the public executioner: Strip Philip and Bartholomew and Mariamme, and search thoroughly to try to find their enchantments. Having therefore first stripped Philip, then Bartholomew, they came also to Mariamme; and dragging her along, they said: Let us strip her naked, that all may see her, how she follows men; for she especially deceives all the women. And the tyrant says to the priests: Proclaim throughout the whole city round about that all should come, men and women, that they may see her indecency, that she travels about with these magicians, and no doubt commits adultery with them. And he ordered Philip to be hanged, and his ankles to be pierced, and to bring also iron hooks, and his heels also to be driven through, and to be hanged head downwards, opposite the temple on a certain tree; and stretch out Bartholomew opposite Philip, having nailed his hands on the wall of the gate of the temple.

And both of them smiled, seeing each other, both Philip and Bartholomew; for they were as if they were not tortured: for their punishments were prizes and crowns. And when also they had stripped Mariamme, behold, straightway the semblance of her body was changed in the presence of all, and straightway there was about her a cloud of fire before all; and they could not longer look at all on the place in which the holy Mariamme was, but they all fled from her.

And Philip spoke with Bartholomew in the Hebrew tongue, saying: Where is our brother John? for, behold, I am being released from the body; and who is he that has prayed for us? Because they have also laid hands on our sister Mariamme, contrary to what is meet; and, behold, they have set fire to the house of Stachys, saying, Let us burn it, since he entertained them. Dost thou wish then, Bartholomew, fire to come from heaven, and that we should burn them up?

And as Philip was thus speaking, behold, also John entered into the city like one of their fellow-citizens; and moving about in the street, he asked: Who are these men, and why are they punished? And they say to him: It cannot be that thou art of our city, and askest about these men, who have wronged many: for they have shut up our gods, and by their magic have cut off both the serpents and the dragons; and they have also raised many of the dead, who have struck us with amazement, detailing many punishments *against us;* and they wish also, these strangers who are hanging, to pray for fire out of heaven, and to burn up us and our city.

Then says John: Let us go, and do you show me them. They led John, therefore, as their fellow-citizen, to where Philip was; and there was there a great crowd, and the proconsul, and the priests. And Philip, seeing John, said to Bartholomew in Hebrew: Brother, John has come, who was in Barek, where the living water is.[1] And John saw Philip hanging head downwards both by the ankles and the heels;[2] and he also saw Bartholomew stretched out on the wall of the temple; and he said to them: The mystery of him that was hanged between the heaven and the earth shall be with you.

And he said also to the men of that city: Ye men who dwell in Ophioryma Hierapolis, great is the ignorance which is among you, for you have erred in the path of error. The dragon breathing has breathed upon you, and blinded you in three ways; that is, he has made you blind in body, and blind in soul, and blind in spirit: and you have been struck by the destroyer. Look upon the whole creation, whether in the earth, or in the heaven, or in the waters, that the serpent has no resemblance to anything above;[3] but he is of the stock of corruption, and has been brought to nothing by God; and on this account he is twisted and crooked, and there is no life in him; and anger, and rage, and darkness, and fire, and smoke are in all his members. And now, therefore, why do you punish these men because they have told you that the serpent is your enemy?

And when they heard these words from John, they raised their hands against him, saying: We thought thee to be a fellow-citizen, but now thou hast shown thyself that thou art their companion. Like them, so also thou shalt be put to death; for the priests have intended to squeeze out your blood, and having mixed it with wine, to bring it to the viper to drink it. When, therefore, the priests attempted to lay hold of John, their hands were paralyzed. And John said to Philip: Let us not at all render evil for evil. And Philip said to John: Behold now, where is my Lord Jesus, who told me not to avenge myself? But for my part, I shall not endure it longer; but I will accomplish upon them my threat, and will destroy them all.[4]

And John and Bartholomew and Mariamme restrained him, saying: Our Master was beaten, was scourged, was extended *on the cross,* was made to drink gall and vinegar, and said, Father, forgive them, for they know not what they do.[5] And this He taught, saying: Learn of me, for I am meek and lowly in heart.[6] Let us also therefore be patient. Philip says: Go away, and do not mollify me; for I will not bear that they have hanged me head down, and pierced my ankles and my heels with irons. And thou, John, beloved of God, how much hast thou reasoned with them, and thou hast not been listened to! Wherefore go away from me, and I will curse them, and they shall be destroyed utterly to a man. And he began to curse them, invoking, and crying out in Hebrew: ABALO, AREMUN, IDUTHAEL, THARSELEON, NACHOTH, AIDUNAPH, TELETOLOI:[7] that is, O Father of Christ, the only and Almighty God; O God, whom all ages dread, powerful and impartial Judge, whose name is in Thy dynasty Sabaoth,[8] blessed art Thou for everlasting: before Thee tremble dominions and powers of the celestials, and the fire-breathing threats of the cherubic living ones; the King, holy in majesty, whose name came upon the wild beasts of the desert, and they were tamed, and praised Thee with a rational voice; who lookest upon us, and readily grantest our requests; who knewest us before we were fashioned; the Overseer of all: now, I pray, let the great Hades open its mouth; let the great abyss swallow up these the ungodly, who have not been willing to receive the word of truth in this city. So let it be, Sabaoth. And, behold, suddenly the abyss was opened, and the whole of the place in which the proconsul was sitting was swallowed up, and the whole of the temple, and the viper which they worshipped, and great crowds, and the priests of the viper, about seven thousand men, besides women and children, except where the apostles were: they remained unshaken. And the proconsul was swallowed up into the abyss; and their voices came up from beneath, saying, with weeping: Have mercy upon us, O God of Thy glorious apostles, because we now see the judgments of those who have not confessed the crucified One: behold, the cross illumines us. O Jesus Christ, manifest Thyself to us, because we are all coming down alive into Hades, and are being scourged because we have unjustly crucified Thine apostles. And a voice was heard of one, saying: I shall be merciful to you in the cross of light.

And there remained both Stachys and all his house, and the wife of the proconsul, and fifty other women who had believed with her upon

---

[1] Another and more probable reading is: He who is the son of Barek, which means living water.

[2] Or, hams.

[3] One of the MSS. has: has no resemblance to a man in anything.

[4] A Bodleian MS. adds: for because I am wrathful, Jesus named me Son of thunder. [This is the MS. from which Grabe derived his text of the *Acts of Paul and Thecla;* comp. pp. 355 and 491.—R.]

[5] Luke xxiii. 34.

[6] Matt. xi. 29.

[7] The Bodleian MS. has the Hebrew thus: *Saballon, prumeni, duthael, tharseli, annachathaei; adonab batelo teioe.*

[8] The Bodleian MS. has Ailoel.

the Lord, and a multitude besides, both of men and women, and a hundred virgins who had not been swallowed up because of their chastity, having been sealed with the seal of Christ.

Then the Lord, having appeared unto Philip, said: O Philip, didst thou not hear: Thou shalt not render evil for evil? and why hast thou inflicted such destruction? O Philip, whosoever putteth his hand to the plough, and looketh backwards,[1] is his furrow well set? or who gives up his own lamp to another, and himself sits in darkness? or who forsakes his own dwelling-place, and dwells on a dunghill himself? And who, giving away his own garment in winter, goes naked? or what enemy rejoices in the joy of the man that hates him? and what soldier goes to war without a full suit of armour? and what slave who has fulfilled his master's order will not be commended? and who in the race-course, having nobly run, does not receive the prize? and who that has washed his garments willingly defiles them? Behold, my bridechamber is ready; but blessed is he who has been found in it wearing the shining garment:[2] he it is who receives the crown upon his head. Behold, the supper is ready; and blessed is he who is invited, and is ready to go to Him that has invited him. The harvest of the field is much,[3] and blessed is the good labourer. Behold the lilies and all the flowers, and it is the good husbandman who is the first to get a share of them. And how hast thou become, O Philip, unmerciful, having cursed thine enemies in wrath?

Philip says: Why art Thou angry with me, Lord, because I have cursed mine enemies? for why dost Thou not tread them under foot, because they are yet alive in the abyss? And knowest Thou, Lord, that because of Thee I came into this city, and in Thy name I have persecuted all the error of the idols, and all the demons? The dragons have withered away, and the serpents. And since these men have not received Thy light, therefore have I cursed them, and they have gone down to Hades alive.

And the Saviour says to Philip: But since thou hast disobeyed me, and hast requited evil for evil, and hast not kept my commandment, on this account thou shalt finish thy course gloriously indeed, and shalt be led by the hand by my holy angels, and shalt come with them even to the paradise of delight; and they indeed shall come beside me into paradise, but thee will I order to be shut outside of paradise for forty days, in terror under the flaming and turning sword, and thou shalt groan because thou hast done evil to those who have done evil to thee. And after

forty days I shall send my archangel Michael; and he, having taken hold of the sword guarding paradise, shall bring thee into it, and thou shalt see all the righteous who have walked in their innocence, and then thou shalt worship the glory of my Father in the heavens. Nevertheless the sign of thy departure shall be glorified in my cross. And Bartholomew having gone away into Lycaonia, shall there also be himself crucified; and Mariamme shall lay her body in the river Jordan. But I, O Philip, will not endure thee, because thou hast swallowed up the men into the abyss; but, behold, my Spirit is in them, and I shall bring them up from the dead; and thus they, seeing thee, shall believe in the glory of Him that sent thee.

And the Saviour having turned, stretched up His hand, and marked a cross in the air coming down from above even to the abyss, and it was full of light, and had its form after the likeness of a ladder. And all the multitude that had gone down from the city into the abyss came up on the ladder of the luminous cross; but there remained below the proconsul, and the viper which they worshipped. And when the multitude had come up, having looked upon Philip hanging head downwards, they lamented with a great lamentation at the lawless action which they had done. And they also saw Bartholomew, and Mariamme having her former appearance. And, behold, the Lord went up into the heavens in the sight of Philip, and Bartholomew and Mariamme, and Stachys, and all the unbelieving people, and silently they glorified God in fear and trembling. And all the multitudes cried out, saying: He alone is God, whom these men proclaim in truth; He alone is God, who sent these men for our salvation. Let us therefore truly repent for our great error, because we are by no means worthy of everlasting life. Now we believe, because we have seen great wonders, because the Saviour has brought us up from the abyss. And they all fell upon their face, and adored Philip, and entreated him, ready to flee: Do not do another miracle, and again send us away into the abyss. And they prayed that they might become worthy of the appearing of Christ.

And Philip, yet hanging, addressed them, and said: Hear and learn how great are the powers of my God, remembering what you have seen below, and how your city has been overturned, with the exception of the house which received me; and now the sweetness of my God has brought you up out of the abyss, and I am obliged to walk round paradise for forty days on your account, because I was enraged against you into requiting you. And this commandment alone I have not kept, in that I did not give you good in return for evil. But I say unto you, From this time forth, in the goodness of God, re-

[1] Comp. Luke ix. 62.
[2] Comp. Matt. xxii. 11.
[3] Comp. Matt. ix. 37.

ject the evil, that you may become worthy of the thanksgiving [1] of the Lord.

And some of the faithful ran up to take down Philip, and take off him the iron grapnels, and the hooks out of his ankles. But Philip said: Do not, my children, do not come near me on account of this, for thus shall be my end. Listen to me, ye who have been enlightened in the Lord, that I came to this city, not to make any merchandise, or do any other thing; but I have been destined to go out of my body in this city in the case in which you see me. Grieve not, then, that I am hanging thus; for I bear the stamp [2] of the first man, who was brought to the earth head downwards, and again, through the wood of the cross brought to life out of the death of the transgression. And now I accomplish that which hath been enjoined upon me; for the Lord said to me, Unless you shall make that of you which is down to be up, and that which is on the left to be on the right, you shall not enter into my kingdom. Be ye not therefore likened to the unchanged type, for all the world has been changed, and every soul dwelling in a body is in forgetfulness of heavenly things; but let not us possessing the glory of the heavenly seek that which is without, which is the body and the house of slavery. Be not unbelieving, but believing, and forgive each other's faults. Behold, I hang six days, and I have blame from the true Judge, because I altogether requited you evil, and put a stumbling-block in the way of my rectitude. And now I am going up on high; be not sorrowful, but rather rejoice, because I am leaving this dwelling-place, my body, having escaped from the corruption of the dragon, who punishes every soul that is in sins.

And Philip, having looked round upon the multitudes, said: O ye who have come up out of the dead from Hades, and the swallowing up of the abyss, — and the luminous cross led you up on high, through the goodness of the Father, and the Son, and the Holy Ghost, — He being God became man, having been made flesh out of the Virgin Mary, immortal, abiding in flesh; and having died, He raised the dead, having had pity on mankind, having taken away the sting of sin. He was great, and became small for our sake, until He should enlarge the small, and bring them into His greatness. And He it is who has sweetness; and they spat upon Him, giving Him gall to drink, in order that He might make those who were bitter against Him to taste of His sweetness. Cleave then to Him, and do not forsake Him, for He is our life to everlasting.

And when Philip had finished this announcement, he says to them, Loose Bartholomew;

and having gone up, they loosed him. And after loosing him, Philip says to him: Bartholomew, my brother in the Lord, thou knowest that the Lord has sent thee with me to this city, and thou hast shared with me in all the dangers with our sister Mariamme; but I know that the going forth from thy body has been appointed in Lycaonia, and it has been decreed to Mariamme to go forth from the body in the river Jordan. Now therefore I command you, that when I have gone forth from my body, you shall build a church in this place; and let the leopard and the kid of the goats [3] come into the church, for a sign to those that believe; and let Nicanora provide for them until they shall go forth from the body; and when they shall have gone forth, bury them by the gate of the church. And lay your peace upon the house of Stachys, as Christ laid His peace on this city. And let all the virgins who believe stand in that house each day, watching over the sick, walking two and two; but let them have no communication with young men, that Satan may not tempt them: [4] for he is a creeping serpent, and he caused Adam by means of Eve to slip into death. Let it not be so again in this time as in the case of Eve. But do thou, O Bartholomew, look to them well; [5] and thou shalt give these injunctions to Stachys, and appoint him bishop. Do not entrust the place of the bishopric to a young man, that the Gospel of Christ may not be brought to shame; and let every one that teacheth have his works equal to his words. But I am going to the Lord, and take my body and prepare it for burial with Syriac sheets of paper; and do not put round me flaxen cloth, because the body of my Lord was wrapped in linen. And having prepared my body for burial in the sheets of paper, bind it tight with papyrus reeds, and bury it in the church; and pray for me [6] forty days, in order that the Lord may forgive me the transgression wherein I transgressed, in requiting those who did evil to me. See, O Bartholomew, where my blood shall drop upon the earth, a plant shall spring up from my blood, and shall become a vine, and shall produce fruit of a bunch of grapes; and having taken the cluster, press it into the cup; and having partaken of it on the third day, send up on high the Amen, in order that the offering may be complete.

And Philip, having said these things, prayed thus: O Lord Jesus Christ, Father of the ages, King of the light, who hast made us wise in Thy wisdom, and hast given us Thine understanding, and hast bestowed upon us the counsel of Thy

---

[1] Or, the Eucharist.
[2] Or, type.

[3] Alluding to Isa. xi. 6.
[4] Comp. 1 Cor. vii. 5.
[5] Lit., be a good trier.
[6] On the subject of the immemorial practice of prayers for the dead, see *Apostolical Constitutions*, vi. 30, viii. 47. Comp. 2 Macc. xii. 44 and 2 Tim. i. 18.

goodness, who hast never at any time left us, Thou art He who taketh away the disease of those who flee to Thee for refuge ; Thou art the Son of the living God, who hast given us Thy presence of wisdom, who hast given us signs and wonders, and hast turned those who have gone astray ; who crownest those who overcome the adversary, Thou excellent Judge.[1] Come now, Jesus, and give me the everlasting crown of victory against every adverse dominion and power, and do not let their dark air hide me when I shall cross the waters of fire and all the abyss. O my Lord Jesus Christ, let not the enemy have ground to accuse me at Thy tribunal : but put on me Thy glorious robe, Thy seal of light that ever shines, until I shall pass by all the powers of the world, and the wicked dragon that lieth in wait for us. Now therefore, my Lord Jesus Christ, make me to meet Thee in the air, having forgiven me the recompense which I recompensed to my enemies ; and transform the form of my body into angelic glory, and give me rest in Thy blessedness ; and let me receive the promise from Thee which Thou hast promised to Thy saints to everlasting.

And having thus spoken, Philip gave up the ghost, while all the multitudes were looking upon him, and weeping, and saying : The life of this spirit has been accomplished in peace. And they said the Amen.

And Bartholomew and Mariamme took down his body, and did as Philip had commanded

[1] Lit., president of the games.

them, and buried it in that place. And there was straightway a voice out of the heavens : Philip the apostle has been crowned with an incorruptible crown by Jesus Christ, the Judge of the contest. And all shouted out the Amen.

And after the three days the plant of the vine sprouted up where the blood of the holy Philip had dropped. And they did all that had been commanded them by him, offering an offering for forty days, praying without ceasing. And they built the church in that place, having appointed Stachys bishop in the church. And Nicanora and all the faithful assembled, and did not cease, all of them, glorifying God on account of the wonders that had happened among them. And all the city believed in the name of Jesus. And Bartholomew commanded Stachys to baptize those who believed into the name of the Father, and the Son, and the Holy Ghost.

And after the forty days, the Saviour, having appeared in the form of Philip, said to Bartholomew and Mariamme : My beloved brethren, do you wish to rest in the rest of God ? Paradise has been opened to me, and I have entered into the glory of Jesus. Go away to the place appointed for you ; for the plant that has been set apart and planted in this city shall bear excellent fruit. Having therefore saluted the brethren, and prayed for each of them, they departed from the city of Ophioryma, the Hierapolis of Asia ; and Bartholomew departed into Lycaonia ; and Mariamme proceeded to the Jordan ; and Stachys and those with him remained, maintaining the church in Christ Jesus our Lord, to whom be glory and strength for ever and ever. Amen.

ACTS OF SAINT PHILIP THE APOSTLE WHEN HE WENT TO UPPER HELLAS.

AND it came to pass in those days, when Philip entered into the city of Athens called Hellas, there assembled to him three hundred philosophers, saying : Let us go and see what his wisdom is ; for they say about the wise men of Asia, that their wisdom is great. For they thought that Philip was a philosopher, since he was travelling in the dress of a recluse ; and they did not know that he was an apostle of Christ. For the dress which Jesus gave to His disciples was a mantle only, and a linen cloth.[1] Thus, then, Philip was going about. On this account, therefore, when the philosophers of Hellas saw him, they were afraid. They assembled therefore into one place, and said to each other : Come, let us look into our books, lest somehow this stranger overcome us, and put us to shame.

[1] Comp. Matt. x. 10 ; Mark vi. 9.

And having done so, they came together to the same place, and say to Philip : We have doctrines of our fathers in which we are pleased, seeking after knowledge ; but if thou hast anything new, O stranger, show it to us without envy boldly : for we have need of nothing else, but only to hear something new.[2]

And Philip answering, said to them : O philosophers of Hellas, if you wish to hear some new thing, and are desirous of something new, you ought to throw away from you the disposition of the old man ; as my Lord said, It is impossible to put new wine into old bottles, since the bottle is burst, and the wine spilled, and the bottle destroyed.[3] But they put new wine into fresh bottles, so that both may be preserved. And these

[2] Acts xvii. 21.
[3] Comp. Matt. ix. 17, etc.

things the Lord said in parables, teaching us in His holy wisdom, that many will love the new wine, not having a bottle fresh and new. And I love you, O men of Hellas, and I congratulate you for having said, We love something new. For instruction really new and fresh my Lord has brought into the world, in order that He might sweep away all worldly instruction.

The philosophers say: Who is it that thou callest thy Lord? Philip says: My Lord is Jesus in heaven. And they said to him: Show him to our comprehension without envy, that we also may believe in him. And Philip said: He with whom I am about to make you acquainted as Lord, is above every name; there is no other.[1] And this only I say: As you have said, Do not refuse us through envy, let it not be that I should refuse you; but rather in great exultation and in great joy I have to reveal to you that name, for I have no other work in this world than this proclamation.[2] For when my Lord came into this world, He chose us, being twelve in number, having filled us with the Holy Spirit; from His light He made us know who He was, and commanded us to preach all salvation through Him, because there is no other name named out of heaven than this.[3] On this account I have come to you, to make you fully assured, not in word only, but also in the showing forth of wonderful works in the name of our Lord Jesus Christ.

And when the philosophers heard this, they say to Philip: This name that has been heard of by us from thee we have never found in the books of our fathers; now, therefore, how can we know about thy words? And moreover, in addition, they say to him: Allow us three days, that we may consult with each other about this name; for we lay no little stress upon this — to apostatize from our fathers' religion. Philip therefore says to them: Consult as you wish; for there is no deceit in the matter.

And the three hundred philosophers having assembled, spoke with each other, saying: You know that this man has brought a strange philosophy, and the words spoken by him bring us to distraction. What, then, shall we do about him, or about the name of him who is called Jesus, the king of the ages, whom he speaks of? And moreover they say to each other: Assuredly we cannot reason with him, but the high priest of the Jews can. If therefore it seem good, let us send to him, in order that he may stand up to this stranger, and that we may learn accurately the name that is preached.

They wrote therefore to Jerusalem after this manner: — The philosophers of Hellas to Ananias, the great high priest of the Jews in Jerusa-

lem. There being between thee and us at all times great [4] . . . as thou knowest that we Athenians are searchers after truth. A certain foreigner has come to Hellas, Philip by name; and, in a word, he has disturbed us exceedingly, both by words and by extraordinary miracles, and he introduces a glorious name, Jesus, professing himself to be his disciple. And he does also wonders of which we write to you, in that he has cast out demons that have been long in men, and makes the deaf hear, the blind see; and what is more wonderful — which also we should have first mentioned — he has raised up men after they were dead, that have fairly completed the number of their days.[5] And the fame of him has gone abroad into all Hellas and Macedonia; and there are many coming to him from the cities round about, bringing those who are ill with various diseases, and he heals them all through the name of Jesus. On this account, therefore, come to us without any reluctance, that thou thyself mayst announce to us what Jesus, this name which he teaches, means. For on this account also we have sent this letter to thee, O high priest.

And when he had read, he was filled with great wrath, and rent his clothes, and said: Has that deceiver gone even to Athens, among the philosophers, to lead them astray? And the Mansemat — that is, Satan — entered into Ananias unawares, and filled him with anger and rage; and he said: If I allow that Philip himself, and those with him, to live, the law will be entirely destroyed, and their teaching will likely fill the whole earth. And the high priest went into his own house, and the teachers of the law, and the Pharisees; and they consulted with each other, saying: What shall we do about these things?[6] And they say to the high priest Ananias: Stand up and arm thyself, and five hundred able men out of the people, and go away to Athens, and by all means kill Philip, and thus thou shalt overturn his teaching.

And having put on the high priest's robe, he came to Hellas in great pomp, with the five hundred men. And Philip was in the house of a certain chief man of the city, with the brethren who had believed. And the high priest and those with him, and the three hundred philosophers, went up to the gateway of the house where Philip was; and it was told Philip that they were outside. And he rose up and went out. And when the high priest saw him, he says to him: O Philip, sorcerer and magician, for I know thee, that in Jerusalem thy master the deceiver called thee Son of Thunder.[7] Was

---

[1] Eph. i. 21.
[2] Or, preaching.
[3] Acts iv. 12.

[4] There seems to be some omission in the MSS. here.
[5] Lit., of life.
[6] Or, these men.
[7] It was James and John who were called sons of thunder (Mark iii. 17).

not the whole of Judæa sufficient for you, but you have come here also to deceive men who are searchers after wisdom? And Philip said: Would that, O Ananias, thy covering of unbelief were taken away from thy heart, that thou mightst know my words, and from them learn whether I am a deceiver, or thou!

Ananias having heard this, said to Philip: I shall give answer to all. And Philip said: Speak. The high priest says: O men of Hellas, this Philip believes in a man called Jesus, who was born among us, who also taught this heresy, and destroyed the law and the temple, and brought to nought the purification through Moses, and the new moons, because he says, These have not been commanded by God. And when we saw that he thus destroyed the law, we stood up against him, and crucified him, that his teaching might not be fulfilled. For many changes were brought in by him; and he gave an evil testimony, for he ate all things in common, and mixed with blood, after the manner of the Gentiles.[1] And having given him up, we put him to death, and buried him in a tomb; and these disciples of his having stolen him, have proclaimed everywhere that he has risen from the dead, and have led astray a great multitude by professing that he is at the right hand of God in heaven.[2] But now these men, themselves having the circumcision as we also have, have not followed it, since they began to do many deeds of power in Jerusalem through the name of Jesus; and having been cast out of Jerusalem, they go about the world, and deceive all men by the magic of that Jesus, as also now this Philip has come to you to deceive you by the same means. But I shall carry him away with myself to Jerusalem, because Archelaus the king is also searching for him to kill him.

And when the multitude standing round heard this, those indeed who had been confirmed in the faith were not shaken nor made to waver; for they knew that Philip would conquer in the glory of Jesus. Philip therefore stated his case in the power of Christ with great boldness, exulting and saying: I, O men of Athens, and those of you who are philosophers, have come to you, not to teach you with words, but by the showing forth of miracles; and in part you have quickly seen[3] the things that have come to pass through me, in that name by which the high priest himself is cast off.[4] For, behold, I shall cry to my God, and teach you, and you will prove the words of both.

The high priest having heard this, ran to Philip, wishing to scourge him, and that same hour his whole hand was dried up, and his eyes were blinded; and in like manner also the five hundred who were with him were also themselves blinded. And they reviled and cursed the high priest, saying: Coming out of Jerusalem we said to thee, Refrain; for, being men, we cannot fight against God.[5] But we entreat thee, O Philip, apostle of the God Jesus, give us the light that is through him, that we also may truly be his slaves.

And Philip, having seen what had come to pass, said: O weak nature! which has thrown itself upon us, but straightway has been brought down low into itself; O bitter sea! which rouses its waves against us, and thinks to cast us out, but which by itself lulls its waves to rest. Now therefore, O our good steward Jesus, the holy light, Thou hast not overlooked us who are all together crying up to Thee in all good works, but hast come to finish them through us. Now therefore come, Lord Jesus; reprove the folly of these men.

The high priest says to Philip: Dost thou then think to turn us away from the traditions of our fathers, and the God of the desert, and Moses; and dost thou imagine that thou wilt make us followers of Jesus the Nazarene? Then Philip says to him: Behold, I shall pray to my God to come and manifest Himself before thee and the five hundred, and before all here; for perhaps thou wilt change thy mind, and believe. But if even to the end thou remain in unbelief, there is coming upon thee an extraordinary thing, which shall be spoken of to generations of generations — that also thou shalt go down alive, down into Hades, before the face of all seeing thee, because thou yet abidest in unbelief, because also thou seekest to turn away this multitude from the true life. And Philip prayed, saying: O holy Father of the holy Son Jesus Christ, who hast granted to me to believe in Him, send Thy beloved Son Jesus Christ to reprove the unbelieving high priest, that Thy name may be glorified in Christ the Beloved.

And while Philip was yet crying out this, suddenly the heavens were opened, and Jesus appeared coming down in most excellent glory, and in lightning; and His face was shining sevenfold more than the sun, and His garments were whiter than snow, so that also all the idols of Athens fell suddenly to the ground. And the people fled in anguish; and the demons dwelling among them cried out: Behold, we also flee because of Him who has appeared to the city, Jesus the Son of God. Then Philip says to the high priest: Hearest thou the demons crying out because of Him who has been seen, and believest thou not in Him who is present, that He

---

[1] This last sentence is very corrupt in the original. A few changes give it the meaning above.
[2] Rom. viii. 34, etc.
[3] Better ταχ᾽ ἂν θεάσεσθε — you will perhaps see.
[4] Or, which the high priest casts off for himself.

[5] Comp. Acts v. 39 and xxiii. 9 in Textus Receptus.

is Lord of all? The high priest says: I have no other God than the one in the desert.

And as Jesus was going up into heaven there happened a very great earthquake, so that the place on which they stood was cleft; and the crowds ran and fell at the feet of the apostle, crying out: Have mercy upon us, O man of God! In like manner also the five hundred men cried out themselves also again: Have mercy upon us, O Philip, that we may know thee, and through thee Jesus the light of life: for we said to this unbelieving high priest, Being sinful men, we cannot fight against God.

Then Philip says: There is no hatred in us, but the grace of Christ will make you receive your sight; but I will make the high priest receive his sight before you, that at this you may the more believe. And a voice out of heaven was brought to Philip: O Philip, son once of thunder, but now of meekness, whatever thou mayst ask of my Father, He shall do for thee. And all the crowd was terror-struck at the voice, for the sound of it was greater than that of thunder. Then Philip says to the high priest: In the name of the power of the voice of my Lord, receive thy sight, Ananias. And immediately he received his sight, and looked round, and said: What is there in the magic of Jesus, that this Philip within a short time has made me blind, and again within a short time has made me receive my sight? Dost thou then, said Philip, believe in Jesus? The high priest says: You do not think, do you, that you can bewitch me, and persuade me? And the five hundred who were with him, having heard that their high priest, having received his sight, was yet unbelieving, said to the bystanders to pray Philip that he should make them receive their sight, that, *said they*, we may cut off this unbelieving high priest.

And Philip said: Do not avenge yourselves upon the wicked. And he says to the high priest: There will be a certain great sign upon thee. He says to Philip: I know that thou art a sorcerer and a disciple of Jesus: thou dost not bewitch me. And the apostle said to Jesus: SABARTHAN, SABATHABT, BRAMANUCH, come quickly. And immediately the earth was cleft in the place where Ananias was, and swallowed him up as far as the knees. And Ananias cried out: O great *is the* power of the true witchcraft, because it has cleft the earth, when Philip threatened it in Hebrew, and adjured it; and it holds me even to the knees, and by the heels some hooks as it were drag me downwards, that I may believe in Philip; but he cannot persuade me, for from Jerusalem I know his magic tricks.

And Philip, enraged, said: O earth, lay fast hold of him, even to the navel. And immediately it dragged him down. And he said:

The one of my feet underneath is turned into ice, and the other is frightfully hot; but by thy magic, Philip, I will not be overcome. Except, therefore, that I am sore tortured underneath, I do not believe at all. And the crowds wished to stone him. And Philip says: Not so; for this has in the meantime happened, that he has been swallowed up as far as the navel, that the salvation of your souls may be effected, because he would almost have drawn you by his wicked words into unbelief. But if even he repented, I should bring him up out of the earth to the salvation of his soul; but assuredly he is not worthy of salvation. If, then, he remain in unbelief, you shall see him sunk down into the abyss, unless the Lord intends to raise those who are in Hades, that they may confess that Jesus is Lord. For in that day every tongue shall confess that Jesus is Lord,[1] and that there is one glory of the Father, and the Son, with the Holy Spirit for evermore.

And Philip, having said this, extended his right hand, stretching it through the air over the five hundred men in the name of Jesus. And their eyes were opened, and they all praised God with one mouth, saying: We bless Thee, O Christ Jesus, the God of Philip, that thou hast driven the blindness away from us, and hast given us Thy light, the Gospel. And Philip rejoiced exceedingly at their words, because they were thus confirmed in the faith. And after this, Philip, having turned to the high priest, said: Confess thou also in a pure heart that Jesus is Lord, that thou mayst be saved, like those with thee. But the high priest laughed at Philip, and remained in unbelief.

Philip then, seeing that he remained in unbelief, having looked at him, says to the earth: Open thy mouth, and swallow him up as far as his neck in the presence of those who have believed in Christ Jesus. And in the same hour the earth, having opened its mouth, received him as far as the neck. And the multitude communed with each other on account of the wonders that had happened.

A certain chief man of the city came crying out, and saying: O blessed apostle, a certain demon has assailed my son, and cried out, saying to me, Since thou hast allowed a foreigner to come into your city, thou who hast been the first to do away with[2] our worship and our sacrifices, what shall I do for thee, except to kill this thine only begotten son? And after he said this, he strangled my son. Now therefore, I beseech thee, O apostle of Christ, do not allow my joy to be turned into sorrow, because I also have believed thy words.

And the apostle, having heard this, said: I

---

[1] Phil. ii. 11.
[2] Or, thou being a chief man who has done away with.

wonder at the activity of the demons, that it is active in every place, and dares to assail those to whose help I have not been able to come,[1] as now they have tried you, wishing to cause you to offend. And he says to the man : Bring me thy son, and I will give him to thee alive, through my Christ. And rejoicing, he ran to bring his son. And when he came near his house, he cried out, saying : My son, I have come to thee to carry thee to the apostle, so that he may present thee to me living. And he ordered his slaves to carry the bed ; and his son was twenty-three years old. And when Philip saw him, he was moved ; and he turned to the high priest, and said : This has happened as a chance for thee : if, therefore, I shall raise him up, wilt thou henceforth believe? And he says : I know your magic arts, that thou wilt raise him up ; but I will not believe thee. And Philip, enraged, said : A curse upon thee ! then go down altogether into the abyss before the face of all these. And at the same hour he went down into Hades alive, except that the high priest's robe flew off from him ; and because of this, from that day, no one knew what became of the priest's robe. And the apostle turned round and prayed for the boy ; and having driven the demon away from him, he raised him up, and set him beside his father alive.

And the multitude having beheld this, cried out : The God of Philip is the only God, who has punished the unbelief of the high priest, and driven away the demon from the young man, and raised him up from the dead. And the five hundred having seen the high priest swallowed up into the abyss, and the other miracles, besought Philip, and he gave them the seal in Christ. And Philip abode in Athens two years ; and having founded a church, appointed a bishop and a presbyter, and so went away to Parthia, preaching Christ. To whom be glory for ever. Amen.

ADDITION TO ACTS OF PHILIP.
(From a Paris MS.)[2]

And he taught them thus : My brethren, sons of my Father — for you are of my family as to Christ, substance of my city, the Jerusalem above, the delight of my dwelling-place — why have you been taken captive by your enemy the serpent, twisted, crooked, and perverse, to whom God has given neither hands nor feet? And crooked is his going, since he is the son of the wicked one ; for his father is death, and his mother corruption, and ruin is in his body. Do not go then into his destruction ; for you are in bondage by the unbelief and deception of his son,

who is without order, and has no substance ;[3] formless, and has no form in the whole creation, either in the heaven or in the earth, or among the fishes that are in the waters. But if you see him, flee from him, since he has no resemblance to men : his dwelling is the abyss, and he walks in darkness. Flee, then, from him, that his venom may not be poured out upon you : if his venom be poured out upon your body, you walk in his wickedness. But remain rather in the true worship, being faithful, reverent, and good, without guile. Flee from Satan the dragon, and remove from you his wicked seed, namely desire, by which he begets disease in the soul, which is the venom of the serpent. For desire is of the serpent from the beginning, and she it is who arms herself against the faithful ; for she came forth out of the darkness, and returns to the darkness. You ought therefore, after coming to us, or rather through us to God, to throw out the venom of the devil from your bodies.

And as the apostle was saying this, behold, Nicanora came forth from her house, and went with her slaves into the house of Stachys. And when she came near the door of the house, behold, Mariamme spoke to her in the Syriac language : HELIKOMAEI, KOSMA, ETAA, MARIACHA. And she explained her words, saying : O daughter of the Spirit, thou art my lady, who hast been given in pledge to the serpent ; but I have come to deliver thee : I shall break thy bonds, and cut them from their root. Behold, the Deliverer that frees thee has come : behold, the Sun of righteousness has risen to enlighten thee.

And when she was thus speaking, the gloomy tyrant came running and panting. And Nicanora, who was before the door, heard this, and took courage before them all, crying out and saying : I am a Hebrew, a daughter of the Hebrews ; speak with me in the language of my fathers, because I have heard your preaching, and have been cured of this my disease. I reverence and glorify the goodness of God, in that He hath made you to be utterly spoiled in this earth.

And when she said this, the tyrant came, and took hold of her garments, and said : O Nicanora, did I not leave thee lying on the bed from thy disease? Whence, then, hast thou found this power and strength, so as to be able to come to these magicians ? Unless, then, thou tell who is the healer, I shall punish thee most severely. And Nicanora answered, and said : O rearer of tyrants, cast away from thyself this tyranny, and forget thy wicked works, and abandon this temporary life, and put away vainglory, because it passes like a shadow : seek rather what is everlasting, and take away from thyself the beastly

---

[1] There is some doubt about the reading here.
[2] [The Greek text of this addition is given by Tischendorf in the supplement appended to his volume containing *Apocalypses Apocryphæ*, pp. 141-150. The MS. from which it is taken is of the eleventh century. Tischendorf regards this form as of Gnostic origin. — R.]

[3] ὑπόστασιν.

and impious work of base desire, and reject vain intercourse, which is the husbandry of death, the dark prison; and overturn the middle wall of corruption, and prepare for thyself a life chaste and spotless, that we may altogether live in sanctity. If, then, thou wishest me to remain with thee, I will live with thee in continence.

And when the tyrant heard these words, he seized her by the hair of the head, and dragged her along, kicking her, and saying: It would be better for thee to be put to death by my sword, than to be seen with these foreign magicians and deceivers. I will punish thee, therefore, and put to death those who have deceived thee. And he turned in a rage to the executioners who followed him, and said: Bring me these impostors. And the executioners ran to the house of Stachys, and laid hold of Philip, and Bartholomew, and Mariamne, with the leopard and the kid of the goats, and dragged them along, and brought them.

When the tyrant saw them, he gnashed his teeth against them, and said: Drag along these magicians and deceivers that have deceived many souls of women by saying, We are worshippers of God. And he caused thongs to be brought, and bound their feet. And he ordered them to be dragged along from the gate as far as the temple. And great multitudes came together to that place. And they wondered exceedingly at the leopard and the kid; for they were speaking like men, and some of the multitude believed the words of the apostles.

And the priests said to the tyrant: These men are magicians. And when he heard that, he burned with rage, and was filled with anger; and he ordered Philip, and Bartholomew, and Mariamne to be stripped, saying: Search them. Perhaps you will find their sorcery. And the executioners stripped them, and laid hold of Mariamne, and dragged her along, saying: Uncover her, that they may learn that it is a woman who follows them. And he ordered to bring clubs and strong cords; and after piercing Philip's ankles they brought hooks, and put the cords through his ankles, and hung him head downwards on a tree that was before the door of the temple; and they fixed pegs into the temple wall, and left him. And after binding Bartholomew hand and foot, they extended him naked on the wall; and when they had stripped Mariamne, the appearance of her body was changed, and became a glass chest filled with light, and they could not come near her.

And Philip spoke with Bartholomew in Hebrew: Where is John to-day, in the day of our need? for, behold, we are being delivered from our bodies. And they have laid hands on Mariamne beyond what is seemly, and they have scourged the leopard and the kid of the goats,

and have set fire to the house of Stachys, because he took us in. . Let us therefore speak, that fire may come down from heaven and burn them up.

And as Philip was thus speaking, behold, John came into the city, and walked about the street, and asked those in the city: What is the commotion, and who are these men, and why are they punished? And they say to him: Art thou not of this city? And dost thou not know about these men, how they disturbed our houses, and the whole city? Moreover, they have even persuaded our wives to go away from us on the pretence of religion, proclaiming a foreign name, viz. Christ's; and they have also shut our temples by the sorcery they have, and they have put to death the serpents that are in the city by foreign names that we have never known. And they have fixed their abode in the house of Stachys the blind man, whom they made to recover his sight through the spittle of a woman who accompanies them; and it is perhaps she who has all the sorcery: and there accompany them a leopard and a kid, speaking like men. But if ever you have seen such doings, you will not be put about by them. And John answered, and said to them: Show me them. And they brought him to the temple where Philip was hanging. And when Philip saw John, he said to Bartholomew: O my brother, behold the son of Barega — that is, the living water — has come. And John saw Philip hanging head down, tied by his ankles; and saw Bartholomew also bound to the temple wall.

And he said to the men of the city: O children of the serpent, how great is your folly! for the way of deceit has deceived you, the wicked dragon breathing has breathed upon you: why do you punish these men for saying the serpent is your enemy?

And when they heard these words from John, they laid their hands upon him, saying: We called thee our fellow-citizen, but now thy speech has made thee manifest that thou also art in communion with them. Thou also, therefore, shalt be put to the same death as they, for the priests have decided thus: Let us drain out their blood as they hang head downward, and mix it with wine, and offer it to the viper.

And when they were thus speaking, behold, Mariamne rose up from the place in which she was, and came back to her former appearance.

And the priests reached forth their hands towards John, wishing to lay hold of him, and they could not. Then Philip with Bartholomew said to John: Where is Jesus, who enjoins upon us not to take into our own hands vengeance on those that torture us? for after this I will not endure them. And Philip spoke in Hebrew, and said: My Father Uthael, i.e., O Christ,

Father of majesty, whose name all the ages [1] fear, who art powerful, and the power of the universe, whose name goes forth in lordship,[2] Eloa: Blessed art Thou to the ages ; Thou whom dominions and powers fear, trembling before Thy face ; King of honour ! Father of majesty ! whose name has gone forth to the wild beasts of the desert, and they have become quiet because of Thee, and through Thee the serpents have departed from us : Hear us before we ask. Thou who seest us before we call, who knowest our thoughts, the All-surveyor [3] of all, who sends forth from Himself unnumbered compassions ; let the abyss open its mouth, and swallow up these godless persons who will not accept the word of Thy truth.

And in that very hour the abyss opened its mouth, and all that place was violently shaken, from the proconsul to all the multitude along with the priests ; and they were all sunk down. And the places where the apostles and all who were with them were remained unshaken, and the house of Stachys, and Nicanora the tyrant's wife, and the twenty-four wives who fled from their husbands, and the forty virgins who had not known men. These alone did not go down into the abyss, because they had become servants, and had received the word of God, and His seal ; but all the rest of the city were swallowed down into the abyss.

And the Saviour having appeared at that hour, said to Philip : Who is it that has put his hand to the plough, and has turned back from making the furrow straight? or who gives his light to others, and himself remains sitting in darkness? or who dwells in the dirt, and leaves his dwelling-place to strangers? or who lays down his garment, and goes out in the days of winter naked? or what slave that has done his master's service, shall not be called by him to supper? or who runs with zeal in the racecourse, and does not get the prize? Philip, behold my bridal chamber is ready, and blessed is he who has his own shining garment ; for he it is who gets the crown of joy upon his head. Behold, the supper is ready, and blessed is he who is called by the bridegroom. Great is the harvest of the field ; blessed is the able workman.

And when Philip heard these words from the Saviour, he answered and said to him : Thou didst give us leave, O Jesus of Nazareth, and dost Thou not enjoin us to smite those who do not wish Thee to reign over them? But this we know, that Thy name has not been proclaimed in all the world, and Thou hast sent us to this city. And I did not intend to come into this city, and Thou didst send me, after giving me

Thy true commandment, that I should drive away all deceit, and bring to nothing every idol and demon, and all the power of the unclean one. And when I came here, the demons fled from our faces through Thy name, and the dragons and the serpents withered away, but these men did not take to themselves Thy true light ; and for this reason I resolved to bring them low, according to their folly.

And the Saviour said : O Philip, since thou hast forsaken this commandment of mine, not to render evil for evil,[4] for this reason thou shalt be debarred in the next world for forty years from being in the place of my promise : besides, this is the end of thy departure from the body in this place ; and Bartholomew has his lot in Lycaonia, and shall be crucified there ; and Mariamne shall lay down her body in the river Jordan.

And the Saviour turned and stretched out His hand, and made the sign of the cross in the air ; and it was full of light, and had its form after the likeness of a ladder. And all the multitude of the men of the city who had gone down into the abyss came up upon the ladder of the cross of light, and none of them remained in the abyss, but only the tyrant and the priests, and the viper which they worshipped. And when the multitudes came up from the abyss, they looked and saw Philip hanging head down, and Bartholomew upon the wall of the temple, and they also found Mariamne in her first shape. And the Saviour went up into heaven in the sight of Philip and Bartholomew and Mariamne, and the leopard and the kid of the goats, and Nicanora and Stachys ; and they all with a loud voice glorified God with fear and trembling, crying out : There is one God who has sent us His salvation, whose name these men proclaim : we repent therefore of the error in which we were before yesterday, not being worthy of eternal life ; and we believe, having seen the wonderful things that have come to pass through us. And some of them threw themselves on their faces, and worshipped the apostles ; and others made ready to flee, saying : There may be another earthquake like the one that has just happened.

And stretching out his hands, the Apostle Philip, hanging head down, said : Men of the city, hear these words which I am going to say to you, hanging head down. Ye have learned how great are the powers of God, and the wonders which you saw when your city was destroyed by the earthquake which came upon it. And this was manifest to you, that the house of Stachys was not destroyed, and that he did not go down into the abyss, because he believed on the true God, and received us His servants.

---

[1] Or, æons.
[2] δυναστεία.
[3] πανεπίσκοπος.

---

[4] Matt. v. 39 ; 1 Pet. iii. 9.

And I, having fulfilled all the will of my God, am His debtor for what I requited to him that did evil to me.

And some of those who had been baptized ran to loose Philip hanging head down. And he answered and said to them: My brethren, . . .[1] those who are virgins in the members of their flesh and commit fornication in their hearts, and the fornication of their eyes, shall abound like the deluge. And they grow immoderate from listening to persuasive pleasures, forgetting the God of the knowledge of the Gospel; and their hearts are full of arrogance, eating and drinking in their worship, forgetting the holy commandment, and despising it. That generation is turned aside; but blessed is he that retires into his retreat, for he shall obtain rest in his departure. Knowest thou not, Bartholomew, that the word of our Lord is true life and knowledge? for the Lord said to us in His teaching, Every one who shall look upon a woman, and lust after her in his heart, has completed adultery.[2] And on this account our brother Peter fled from every place in which a woman was, and yet there was scandal on account of his own daughter; and he prayed to the Lord, and she had paralysis of her side, that she might not be deceived. Thou seest, brother, that the sight of the eyes brings gainsaying, and the beginning of sin, as it is written,[3] She looked, and saw the tree, that it was pleasing to her eyes, and good for food, and she was deceived. Let the hearing, then, of the virgins be holy; and in their going out let them walk two and two, for many are the wiles of the enemy. Let their walk and conversation be well ordered, that they may be saved; but if not, let their fruit be common.

My brother Bartholomew, give these promises to Stachys, and appoint him ruler and bishop in the Church, that he may be like thee, teaching well. Do not entrust the office to a man too young: appoint not such a one to the chair of the teachers, lest thou profane the witness of Christ. For he that teaches should have his works corresponding to his words, that the word may be ready on every occasion in its own glory. But I am being released from my body, hanging head down. Take, then, my body, and prepare it for burial in Syrian paper, and do not put about it linen cloth, since they put it upon the body of our Lord, and wrap it close in paper and papyrus, and put it in the vestibule of the holy church. And pray over me for forty days, that God may forgive the transgression which I did, in that I requited evil to him that did evil to me, and there may not be for me in the world to come the forty years.

And after thus speaking, Philip prayed, saying: My Lord Jesus Christ, Father of the ages, King of all light, who makest us wise in Thy wisdom, who hast given us the exalted knowledge, who hast graciously conferred upon us the counsel of Thy goodness, who hast never departed from us; Thou who takest away disease from those who take refuge in Thee; Thou who hast given us the Word, to turn unto Thee those who have been led astray; Thou who hast given us signs and wonders on behalf of those of little faith; Thou who presentest the crown to those who have conquered; Thou who art the judge of the games, who hast given us the crown of joy, who speakest with us, that we may be able to withstand those that hurt us; Thou art He who sows and reaps, and completes, and increases, and vivifies all Thine own servants: reproaches and threats are to us help and power through those who turn to Thee through us, who are Thy servants. Come, Lord, and give me the crown of victory in the presence of men. Let not their dark air envelope me, nor their smoke burn the shape of my soul, that I may cross the waters of the abyss, and not sink in them. My Lord Jesus Christ, let not the enemy find anything that he can bring against me in the presence of Thee, the true Judge, but clothe me in Thy shining robe, and . . . (The rest is wanting.)

---

[1] Here a good deal of the text is wanting. The Bodleian MS. fills up the blank to some extent: — Walking two and two, but let them not talk with the young men, lest Satan tempt them. For he is a creeping serpent, and made Adam be destroyed even to death. And thus shall it be again at this time, for the time and the season shall be wicked. Many women and men shall leave the work of marriage, and the women shall assume the name of virginity, but knowing nothing at all about it, and that it has a great and glorious seal. And there shall be many men in those days in word only, and not in its power; for they shall observe virginity in the members of their flesh, and commit fornication in their hearts, etc. [The MS. is that referred to on p. 500. Tischendorf gives large extracts from it; the Greek text of this paragraph may be found on pp. 154, 155, supplement to *Apocalypses Apocryphæ*. — R.]

[2] Matt. v. 28.

[3] Gen. iii. 6.

ACTS AND MARTYRDOM OF THE HOLY APOSTLE ANDREW

WHAT we have all, both presbyters and deacons of the churches of Achaia, beheld with our eyes, we have written to all the churches established in the name of Christ Jesus, both in the east and west, north and south. Peace to you, and to all who believe in one God, perfect Trinity, true Father unbegotten, true Son only-begotten, true Holy Spirit proceeding from the Father, and abiding in the Son, in order that there may be shown one Holy Spirit subsisting in the Father and Son in precious Godhead. This faith we have learned from the blessed Andrew, the apostle of our Lord Jesus Christ, whose passion also we, having seen it set forth before our eyes, have not hesitated to give an account of, according to the degree of ability we have.

Accordingly the proconsul Ægeates,[1] having come into the city of Patras, began to compel those believing in Christ to worship the idols ; to whom the blessed Andrew, running up, said : It behoved thee, being a judge of men, to acknowledge thy Judge who is in the heaven, and having acknowledged Him, to worship Him ; and worshipping Him who is the true God, to turn away thy thoughts from those which are not true gods.

To whom Ægeates said : Art thou Andrew, who destroyest the temples of the gods, and persuadest men about the religion which, having lately made its appearance, the emperors of the Romans have given orders to suppress?

The blessed Andrew said : The emperors of the Romans have never recognised the truth. And this the Son of God, who came on account of the salvation of men, manifestly teaches — that these idols are not only not gods, but also most shameful demons,[2] and hostile to the human race, teaching men to offend God, so that, by being offended, He turns away and will not hearken ; that therefore, by His turning away and not hearkening, they may be held captive by the devil ; and that they might work them to such a degree, that when they go out of the body

they may be found deserted and naked, carrying nothing with them but sins.

Ægeates said : These are superfluous and vain words : as for your Jesus, for proclaiming these things to the Jews they nailed him to the tree of the cross.

The blessed Andrew answering, said : Oh, if thou wouldst recognise the mystery of the cross, with what reasonable love the Author[3] of the life of the human race for our restoration endured this tree of the cross, not unwillingly, but willingly !

Ægeates said : Seeing that, betrayed by his own disciple, and seized by the Jews, he was brought before the procurator, and according to their request was nailed up by the procurator's soldiers, in what way dost thou say that he willingly endured the tree of the cross?

The holy Andrew said : For this reason I say willingly, since I was with Him when he was betrayed by His disciple. For before He was betrayed, He spoke to us to the effect that He should be betrayed and crucified for the salvation of men, and foretold that He should rise again on the third day. To whom my brother Peter said,[4] Far be it from thee, Lord ; let this by no means be. And so, being angry, He said to Peter, Get thee behind me, Satan ; for thou art not disposed to the things of God. And in order that He might most fully explain that He willingly underwent the passion, He said to us,[5] I have power to lay down my life, and I have power to take it again. And, last of all, while He was supping with us, He said,[6] One of you will betray me. At these words, therefore, all becoming exceedingly grieved, in order that the surmise might be free from doubt, He made it clear, saying, To whomsoever I shall give the piece of bread out of my hand, he it is who betrays me. When, therefore, He gave it to one of our fellow-disciples, and gave an account of things to come as if they were already present,

---

[1] Another reading is Ægeas. [This is the reading of the Bodleian MS., already frequently referred to (see p. 355). In most cases its text is followed in the Latin version collated by Tischendorf.—R.]
[2] Deut. xxxii. 17; 1 Cor. x. 20, 21.

[3] Or, Prince.
[4] Matt. xvi. 22.
[5] John x. 18.
[6] Matt. xxvi. 21.

He showed that He was to be willingly betrayed. For neither did He run away, and leave His betrayer at fault; but, remaining in the place in which He knew that he was, He awaited him.

Ægeates said: I wonder that thou, being a sensible man, shouldst wish to uphold him on any terms whatever; for, whether willingly or unwillingly, all the same, thou admittest that he was fastened to the cross.

The blessed Andrew said: This is what I said, if now thou apprehendest, that great is the mystery of the cross, which, if thou wishest, as is likely, to hear, attend to me.[1]

Ægeates said: A mystery it cannot be called, but a punishment.

The blessed Andrew said: This punishment is the mystery of man's restoration. If thou wilt listen with any attention, thou wilt prove it.

Ægeates said: I indeed will hear patiently; but thou, unless thou submissively obey me, shalt receive[2] the mystery of the cross in thyself.

The blessed Andrew answered: If I had been afraid of the tree of the cross, I should not have proclaimed the glory of the cross.

Ægeates said: Thy speech is foolish, because thou proclaimest that the cross is not a punishment, and through thy foolhardiness thou art not afraid of the punishment of death.

The holy Andrew said: It is not through foolhardiness, but through faith, that I am not afraid of the punishment of death; for the death of sins[3] is hard. And on this account I wish thee to hear the mystery of the cross, in order that thou perhaps, acknowledging it, mayst believe, and believing, mayst come somehow or other to the renewing of thy soul.

Ægeates said: That which is shown to have perished is for renewing. Do you mean that my soul has perished, that thou makest me come to the renewing of it through the faith, I know not what, of which thou hast spoken?

The blessed Andrew answered: This it is which I desired thee to learn, which also I shall teach and make manifest, that though the souls of men are destroyed, they shall be renewed through the mystery of the cross. For the first man through the tree of transgression brought in death; and it was necessary for the human race, that through the suffering of the tree, death, which had come into the world, should be driven out. And since the first man, who brought death into the world through the transgression of the tree, had been produced from the spotless earth, it was necessary that the Son of God should be begotten a perfect man from the spotless virgin, that He should restore eternal life, which men

had lost through Adam, and should cut off[4] the tree of carnal appetite through the tree of cross. Hanging upon the cross, He stretched out His blameless hands for the hands which had been incontinently stretched out; for the most sweet food of the forbidden tree He received gall for food; and taking our mortality upon Himself, He made a gift of His immortality to us.

Ægeates said: With these words thou shalt be able to lead away those who shall believe in thee; but unless thou hast come to grant me this, that thou offer sacrifices to the almighty gods, I shall order thee, after having been scourged, to be fastened to that very cross which thou commendest.

The blessed Andrew said: To God Almighty, who alone is true, I bring sacrifice day by day not the smoke of incense, nor the flesh of bellowing bulls, nor the blood of goats, but sacrificing a spotless lamb day by day on the altar of the cross; and though all the people of the faithful partake of His body and drink His blood, the Lamb that has been sacrificed remains after this entire and alive. Truly, therefore, is He sacrificed, and truly is His body eaten by the people, and His blood is likewise drunk; nevertheless, as I have said, He remains entire, and spotless, and alive.

Ægeates said: How can this be?

The blessed Andrew said: If thou wouldest know, take the form of a disciple, that thou mayst learn what thou art inquiring after.

Ægeates said: I will exact of thee through tortures the gift of this knowledge.

The blessed Andrew declared: I wonder that thou, being an intelligent man, shouldest fall into[5] the folly of thinking that thou mayst be able to persuade me, through thy tortures, to disclose to thee the sacred things of God. Thou hast heard the mystery of the cross, thou hast heard the mystery of the sacrifice. If thou believest in Christ the Son of God, who was crucified, I shall altogether disclose to thee in what manner the Lamb that has been slain may live, after having been sacrificed and eaten, remaining in His kingdom entire and spotless.

Ægeates said: And by what means does the lamb remain in his kingdom after he has been slain and eaten by all the people, as thou hast said?

The blessed Andrew said: If thou believest with all thy heart, thou shalt be able to learn: but if thou believest not, thou shalt not by any means attain to the idea of such truth.

Then Ægeates, enraged, ordered him to be shut up in prison, where, when he was shut up, a multitude of the people came together to him

---

[1] Another reading is: This is what I spoke of, as you know — that great is the mystery of the cross; and if so be that you are willing to listen, I will reveal it.
[2] Perhaps we should read ἀναδείξει, shalt exhibit, for ἀναδέξει.
[3] Two MSS., of sinners.

[4] Or, shut out.
[5] Lit., be rolled towards.

from almost all the province, so that they wished to kill Ægeates, and by breaking down the doors of the prison to set free the blessed Andrew the apostle.

Them the blessed Andrew admonished in these words, saying : Do not stir up the peace of our Lord Jesus Christ into seditious and devilish uproar. For my Lord, when He was betrayed, endured it with all patience ; He did not strive, He did not cry out, nor in the streets did any one hear Him crying out.[1] Therefore do ye also keep silence, quietness, and peace ; and hinder not my martyrdom, but rather get yourselves also ready beforehand as athletes to the Lord, in order that you may overcome threatenings by a soul that has no fear of man, and that you may get the better of injuries through the endurance of the body. For this temporary fall is not to be feared ; but that should be feared which has no end. The fear of men, then, is like smoke which, while it is raised and gathered together, disappears. And those torments ought to be feared which never have an end. For these torments, which happen to be somewhat light, any one can bear ; but if they are heavy, they soon destroy life. But those torments are everlasting, where there are daily weepings, and mournings, and lamentations, and never-ending torture, to which the proconsul Ægeates is not afraid to go. Be ye therefore rather prepared for this, that through temporary afflictions ye may attain to everlasting rest, and may flourish for ever, and reign with Christ.[2]

The holy Apostle Andrew having admonished the people with these and such like words through the whole night, when the light of day dawned, Ægeates having sent for him, ordered the blessed Andrew to be brought to him ; and having sat down upon the tribunal, he said : I have thought that thou, by thy reflection during the night, hast turned away thy thoughts from folly, and given up thy commendation of Christ, that thou mightst be able to be with us, and not throw away the pleasures of life ; for it is folly to come for any purpose to the suffering of the cross, and to give oneself up to most shameful punishments and burnings.

The holy Andrew answered : I shall be able to have joy with thee, if thou wilt believe in Christ, and throw away the worship of idols ; for Christ has sent me to this province, in which I have acquired for Christ a people not the smallest.

Ægeates said : For this reason I compel thee to make a libation, that these people who have been deceived by thee may forsake the vanity of thy teaching, and may themselves offer grateful libations to the gods ; for not even one city

has remained in Achaia in which their temples[3] have not been forsaken and deserted. And now, through thee, let them be again restored to the worship of the images, in order that the gods also, who have been enraged against thee, being pleased by this, may bring it about that thou mayst return to their friendship and ours. But if not, thou awaitest varied tortures, on account of the vengeance of the gods ; and after these, fastened to the tree of the cross which thou commendest, thou shalt die.

The holy Andrew said : Listen, O son of death and chaff made ready for eternal burnings,[4] to me, the servant of God and apostle of Jesus Christ. Until now I have conversed with thee kindly about the perfection of the faith, in order that thou, receiving the exposition of the truth, being made perfect as its vindicator, mightst despise vain idols, and worship God, who is in the heavens ; but since thou remainest in the same shamelessness at last, and thinkest me to be afraid because of thy threats, bring against me whatever may seem to thee greater in the way of tortures. For the more shall I be well pleasing to my King, the more I shall endure in tortures for the confession of His name.

Then the proconsul Ægeates, being enraged, ordered the apostle of Christ to be afflicted by tortures. Being stretched out, therefore, by seven times three[5] soldiers, and beaten with violence, he was lifted up and brought before the impious Ægeates. And he spoke to him thus : Listen to me, Andrew, and withdraw thy thoughts from the outpouring of thy blood ; but if thou wilt not hearken to me, I shall cause thee to perish on the tree of the cross.

The holy Andrew said : I am a slave of the cross of Christ, and I ought rather to pray to attain to the trophy of the cross than to be afraid ; but for thee is laid up eternal torment, which, however, thou mayst escape after thou hast tested my endurance, if thou wilt believe in my Christ. For I am afflicted about thy destruction, and I am not disturbed about my own suffering. For my suffering takes up a space of one day, or two at most ; but thy torment for endless ages shall never come to a close. Wherefore henceforward cease from adding to thy miseries, and lighting up everlasting fire for thyself.

Ægeates then being enraged, ordered the blessed Andrew to be fastened to the cross.[6] And he having left them all, goes up to the cross, and says to it with a clear voice : Rejoice, O cross, which has been consecrated by the body

---

[1] Matt. xii. 19.
[2] Comp. 2 Cor. iv. 17.

[3] Or, their sacred rites.
[4] Comp. Matt. iii. 12.
[5] Another reading is, seven quaternions.
[6] One of the mss. [the Bodleian] has here: Giving orders to the centurions that he should be bound hand and foot as if he were stretched on the rack, and not pierced with nails, that he might not die soon, but be tormented with long-continuing torture.

of Christ, and adorned by His limbs as if with pearls. Assuredly before my Lord went up on thee, thou hadst much earthly fear; but now invested with heavenly longing, thou art fitted up[1] according to my prayer. For I know, from those who believe, how many graces thou hast in Him, how many gifts prepared beforehand. Free from care, then, and with joy, I come to thee, that thou also exulting mayst receive me, the disciple of Him that was hanged upon thee; because thou hast been always faithful to me, and I have desired to embrace thee. O good cross, which hast received comeliness and beauty from the limbs of the Lord; O much longed for, and earnestly desired, and fervently sought after, and already prepared beforehand for my soul longing for thee, take me away from men, and restore me to my Master, in order that through thee He may accept me who through thee has redeemed me.

And having thus spoken, the blessed Andrew, standing on the ground, and looking earnestly upon the cross, stripped himself and gave his clothes to the executioners, having urged the brethren that the executioners should come and do what had been commanded them; for they were standing at some distance. And they having come up, lifted him on the cross; and having stretched his body across with ropes, they only bound his feet, but did not sever his joints,[2] having received this order from the proconsul: for he wished him to be in distress while hanging, and in the night-time, as he was suspended, to be eaten up alive by dogs.[3]

And a great multitude of the brethren stood by, nearly twenty thousand; and having beheld the executioners standing off, and that they had done to the blessed *one* nothing of what those who were hanged up suffer, they thought that they would again hear something from him; for assuredly, as he was hanging, he moved his head smiling. And Stratocles inquired of him: Why art thou smiling, Andrew, servant of God? Thy laughter makes us mourn and weep, because we are deprived of thee. And the blessed Andrew answered him: Shall I not laugh at all, my son Stratocles, at the empty stratagem of Ægeates, through which he thinks to take vengeance upon us? We have nothing to do with him and his plans. He cannot hear; for if he could, he would be aware, having learned it by experience, that a man of Jesus is unpunished.[4]

And having thus spoken, he discoursed to them all in common, for the people ran together enraged at the unjust judgment of Ægeates: Ye men standing by me, and women, and children, and elders, bond and free, and as many as will hear; I beseech you, forsake all this life, ye who have for my sake assembled here; and hasten to take upon you my life, which leads to heavenly things, and once for all despise all temporary things, confirming the purposes of those who believe in Christ. And he exhorted them all, teaching that the sufferings of this transitory life are not worthy to be compared with the future recompense of the eternal life.

And the multitude hearing what was said by him, did not stand off from the place, and the blessed Andrew continued the rather to say to them more than he had spoken. And so much was said by him, that a space of three days and nights was taken up, and no one was tired and went away from him. And when also on the fourth day they beheld his nobleness, and the unweariedness of his intellect, and the multitude of his words, and the serviceableness of his exhortations, and the stedfastness of his soul, and the sobriety of his spirit, and the fixedness of his mind, and the perfection of his reason, they were enraged against Ægeates; and all with one accord hastened to the tribunal, and cried out against Ægeates, who was sitting, saying: What is thy judgment, O proconsul? Thou hast judged wickedly; thy awards are impious. In what has the man done wrong; what evil has he done? The city has been put in an uproar; thou grievest us all; do not betray Cæsar's city. Grant willingly to the Achaians a just man; grant willingly to us a God-fearing man; do not put to death a godly man. Four days he has been hanging, and is alive; having eaten nothing, he has filled us all. Take down the man from the cross, and we shall all seek after wisdom; release the man, and to all Achaia will mercy be shown. It is not necessary that he should suffer this, because, though hanging, he does not cease proclaiming the truth.

And when the proconsul refused to listen to them, at first indeed signing with his hand to the crowd to take themselves off, they began to be emboldened against him, being in number about twenty thousand. And the proconsul having beheld that they had somehow become maddened, afraid that something frightful would befall him, rose up from the tribunal and went away with them, having promised to set free the blessed Andrew. And some went on before to tell the apostle the cause for which they came to the place.

While all the crowd, therefore, was exulting that the blessed Andrew was going to be set free, the proconsul having come up, and all the

---

[1] Another reading is: I am attached to thee.
[2] The original is obscure. The meaning seems to be that he was tied only, not nailed. The nailing, however, seems to have been an essential part of the punishment of crucifixion.
[3] It was common to let loose wild beasts on the crucified (Sueton., *Nero*, 49).
[4] Instead of this paragraph, one MS. [the Bodleian] has: And there ran up a great multitude, about twenty thousand in number, among whom was the brother of Ægeas, Stratocles by name; and he cried out with the people, It is an unjust judgment. And the holy Andrew, hitting upon the thoughts of the believers, exhorted them to endure the temporary trial, saying that the suffering counted for nothing when compared with the eternal recompense.

brethren rejoicing along with Maximilla,[1] the blessed Andrew, having heard this, said to the brethren standing by : What is it necessary for me to say to him, when I am departing to the Lord, that will I also say.   For what reason hast thou again come to us, Ægeates?   On what account dost thou, being a stranger to us,[2] come to us?   What wilt thou again dare to do, what to contrive?   Tell us.   Hast thou come to release us, as having changed thy mind?   I would not agree with thee that thou hadst really changed thy mind.   Nor would I believe thee, saying that thou art my friend.   Dost thou, O proconsul, release him that has been bound?   By no means.   For I have One with whom I shall be for ever ; I have One with whom I shall live to countless ages.   To Him I go ; to Him I hasten, who also having made thee known to me, has said to me, Let not that fearful man terrify thee ; do not think that he will lay hold of thee, who art mine : for he is thine enemy.   Therefore, having known thee through him who has turned towards me, I am delivered from thee.   But if thou wishest to believe in Christ, there will be opened up for thee, as I promised thee, a way of access ; but if thou hast come only to release me, I shall not be able after this to be brought down from this cross alive in the body.   For I and my kinsmen depart to our own, allowing thee to be what thou art, and what thou dost not know about thyself.   For already I see my King, already I worship Him, already I stand before Him, where the fellowship [3] of the angels is, where He reigns the only emperor, where there is light without night, where the flowers never fade, where trouble is never known, nor the name of grief heard, where there are cheerfulness and exultation that have no end.   O blessed cross ! without the longing for thee, no one enters into that place.   But I am distressed, Ægeates, about thine own miseries, because eternal perdition is ready to receive thee.   Run then, for thine own sake, O pitiable one, while yet thou canst, lest perchance thou shouldst wish then when thou canst not.

When, therefore, he attempted to come near the tree of the cross, so as to release the blessed Andrew, with all the city applauding him, the holy Andrew said with a loud voice : Do not suffer Andrew, bound upon Thy tree, to be released, O Lord ; do not give me who am in Thy mystery to the shameless devil.   O Jesus Christ, let not Thine adversary release me, who have been hanged by Thy favour ; O Father, let this insignificant man no longer humble him who has known Thy greatness.   The executioners, there-

fore, putting out their hands, were not able at all to touch him.   Others, then, and others endeavoured to release him, and no one at all was able to come near him ; for their arms were benumbed.

Then the blessed Andrew, having adjured the people, said : I entreat you earnestly, brethren, that I may first make one prayer to my Lord.   So then set about releasing me.   All the people therefore kept quiet because of the adjuration.   Then the blessed Andrew, with a loud cry, said : Do not permit, O Lord, Thy servant at this time to be removed from Thee ; for it is time that my body be committed to the earth, and Thou shalt order me to come to Thee.   Thou who givest eternal life, my Teacher whom I have loved, whom on this cross I confess, whom I know, whom I possess, receive me, O Lord ; and as I have confessed Thee and obeyed Thee, so now in this word hearken to me ; and, before my body come down from the cross, receive me to Thyself, that through my departure there may be access to Thee of many of my kindred, finding rest for themselves in Thy majesty.

When, therefore, he had said this, he became in the sight of all glad and exulting ; for an exceeding splendour like lightning coming forth out of heaven shone down upon him, and so encircled him, that in consequence of such brightness mortal eyes could not look upon him at all.   And the dazzling light remained about the space of half an hour.   And when he had thus spoken and glorified the Lord still more, the light withdrew itself, and he gave up the ghost, and along with the brightness itself he departed to the Lord in giving Him thanks.

And after the decease of the most blessed Andrew the apostle, Maximilla being the most powerful of the notable women,[4] and continuing among those who had come, as soon as she learned that the apostle had departed to the Lord, came up and turned her attention to the cross, along with Stratocles, taking no heed at all of those standing by, and with reverence took down the body of the most blessed apostle from the cross.   And when it was evening, bestowing upon him the necessary care, she prepared the body for burial with costly spices, and laid it in her own tomb.   For she had been parted from Ægeates on account of his brutal disposition and lawless conduct, having chosen for herself a holy and quiet life ; and having been united to the love of Christ, she spent her life blessedly along with the brethren.

Ægeates had been very importunate with her, and promised that he would make her mistress of his wealth ; but not having been able to persuade her, he was greatly enraged, and was determined to make a public charge against all

---

[1] One MS. calls her the proconsul's wife. [So Pseudo-Abdias ; but the Greek MSS., collated by Tischendorf, do not give this reading. — R.]

[2] i.e., having nothing to do with us.

[3] ὁμόνοιαι.

[4] Lit., females.

the people, and to send to Cæsar an accusation against both Maximilla and all the people. And while he was arranging these things in the presence of his officers, at the dead of night he rose up, and unseen by all his people, having been tormented by the devil, he fell down from a great height, and rolling into the midst of the market-place of the city, breathed his last.

And this was reported to his brother Stratocles; and he sent his servants, having told them that they should bury him among those who had died a violent death. But he sought nothing of his substance, saying: Let not my Lord Jesus Christ, in whom I have believed, suffer me to touch anything whatever of the goods of my brother, that

the condemnation of him who dared to cut off the apostle of the Lord may not disgrace me.

These things were done in the province of Achaia, in the city of Patras on the day before the kalends of December,[1] where his good deeds are kept in mind even to this day, to the glory and praise of our Lord Jesus Christ, to whom be glory for ever and ever. Amen.[2]

---

[1] i.e., 30th November, St. Andrew's day.
[2] One MS. thus ends: These things were done in the province of Achaia, in the city of Patras, on the day before the kalends of December; where also his glorious good deeds are shown even to this day; and so great fear came upon all, that no one remained who did not believe in God our Saviour, who wishes all to be saved, and to come to the knowledge of the truth. To Him be glory to ages of ages. Amen. [This is the ending of the Latin version (in Tischendorf); the Bodleian MS. has a similar conclusion, but the text is differently arranged. — R.]

ACTS OF ANDREW AND MATTHIAS[1]

IN THE CITY OF THE MAN–EATERS

ABOUT that time all the apostles had come together to the same place, and shared among themselves the countries, casting lots, in order that each might go away into the part that had fallen to him. By lot, then, it fell to Matthias to set out to the country of the man-eaters. And the men of that city used neither to eat bread nor drink wine; but they ate the flesh of men, and drank their blood. Every man, therefore, who came into their city they laid hold of, and digging they thrust out his eyes, and gave him a drug to drink, prepared by sorcery and magic; and from drinking the drug his heart was altered and his mind deranged.

Matthias then having come into the gate of their city, the men of that city laid hold of him, and thrust out his eyes; and after putting them out they made him drink the drug of their magical deception, and led him away to the prison, and put beside him grass to eat, and he ate it not. For when he had partaken of their drug, his heart was not altered, nor his mind deranged; but he kept praying to God, weeping, and saying: Lord Jesus Christ, for whose sake we have forsaken all things and have followed Thee, knowing that Thou art the helper of all who hope in Thee, attend then and behold what they have done to Matthias Thy servant, how they have made me nigh to the brutes; for Thou art He who knowest all things. If, therefore, Thou hast ordained that the wicked men in this city should eat me up, I will not by any means flee from Thy dispensation. Afford to me then, O Lord, the light of mine eyes, that at least I may behold what the wicked men in this city have in hand for me; do not forsake me, O my Lord Jesus Christ, and do not give me up to this bitter death.

While Matthias was thus praying in the prison, a light shone, and there came forth out of the light a voice saying: Beloved Matthias, receive thy sight. And immediately he received his sight. And again there came forth a voice saying: Be of good courage, our Matthias, and be not dismayed; for I shall not by any means forsake thee, for I shall deliver thee from all danger; and not only thee, but also all thy brethren who are with thee: for I am with thee everywhere and at all times. But remain here twenty-seven days for the edification[2] of many souls; and after that I shall send forth Andrew to thee, and he shall lead thee forth out of this prison; and not thee only, but also all who hear. Having said this, the Saviour said again to Matthias, Peace be to thee, our Matthias, and went into heaven. Then Matthias having beheld Him, said to the Lord: Let thy grace abide with me, O my Lord Jesus.

Then Matthias therefore[3] sat down in the prison, and sang. And it came to pass that, when the executioners came into the prison to bring forth the men to eat them, Matthias also shut his eyes, that they might not behold that he saw. And the executioners having come to him, read the ticket in his hand, and said among themselves: Yet three days, and we shall bring out this one also from the prison, and slay him. Because in the case of every man whom they laid hold of, they noted that day on which they laid hold of him, and tied a ticket to his right hand, that they might know the completion of the thirty days.

And it came to pass when the twenty-seven days were fulfilled since Matthias was seized, the Lord appeared in the country where Andrew was teaching, and said to him: Rise up, and set out with thy disciples to the country of the man-eaters, and bring forth Matthias out of that place; for yet three days, and the men of the city will bring him forth and slay him for their food. And Andrew answered and said: My Lord, I shall not be able to accomplish the journey thither before the limited period of the three days; but send Thine angel quickly, that he may bring him out thence: for thou knowest, Lord, that I also am flesh, and shall not be able to go there quickly. And He says to Andrew: Obey Him who made thee, and Him who is able to say in a word, and

---

[1] The oldest MS. has Matthias; the four or five others have Matthew.

[2] Lit., œconomy.
[3] One MS. inserts: having given thanks to God.

that city shall be removed thence, and all that dwell in it. For I command the horns of the winds,[1] and they drive it thence. But rise up early, and go down to the sea with thy disciples, and thou shalt find a boat upon the shore, and thou shalt go aboard with thy disciples. And having said this, the Saviour again said: Peace to thee, Andrew, along with those with thee! And He went into the heavens.

And Andrew having risen up early, proceeded to the sea along with his disciples; and having come down to the shore, he saw a little boat, and in the boat three men sitting. For the Lord by His own power had prepared a boat, and He it was in human shape a pilot in the boat; and He brought two angels whom He made to appear like men, and they were in the boat sitting.[2] Andrew, therefore, having beheld the boat, and the three who were in it, rejoiced with exceeding great joy; and having gone to them, he said: Where are you going, brethren, with this little boat? And the Lord answered and said to him: We are going to the country of the man-eaters. And Andrew having beheld Jesus, did not recognise Him; for Jesus was hiding His Godhead, and He appeared to Andrew like a pilot. And Jesus having heard Andrew saying, I too am going to the country of the man-eaters, says to him: Every man avoids that city, and how are you going there? And Andrew answered and said: We have some small business to do there, and we must get through with it; but if thou canst, do us this kindness to convey us to the country of the man-eaters, to which also you intend to go. Jesus answered and said to them: Come on board.

And Andrew said: I wish to make some explanation to thee, young man, before we come on board thy boat. And Jesus said: Say what thou wilt. And Andrew said to Him: We have no passage-money to give thee; we have not even bread for our nourishment. And Jesus answered and said to him: How, then, are you going away without giving us the passage-money, and without having bread for your nourishment? And Andrew said to Jesus, Listen, brother; do not think that it is through masterfulness that we do not give thee our passage-money, but we are disciples of our Lord Jesus Christ, the good God. For He chose for Himself us twelve, and gave us such a commandment, saying, When you go to preach, do not carry money in the journey, nor bread, nor bag, nor shoes, nor staff, nor two coats.[3] If, therefore, thou wilt do us the kindness, brother, tell us at once; if not, let us know, and we shall go and seek another boat

for ourselves. And Jesus answered and said to Andrew: If this is the commandment which you received, and you keep it, come on board my boat with all joy. For I really wish you, the disciples of Him who is called Jesus, to come on board my boat, rather than those who give me of their silver and gold; for I am altogether worthy that the apostle of the Lord should come on board my boat. And Andrew answered and said: Permit me, brother, may the Lord grant thee. glory and honour. And Andrew went on board the boat with his disciples.

And having gone on board, he sat down by the boat's sail. And Jesus answered and said to one of the angels: Rise and go down to the hold of the boat, and bring up three loaves, that the men may eat, lest perchance they be hungry, from having come to us off a long journey. And he rose and went down to the hold of the boat, and brought up three loaves, as the Lord commanded him; and he gave them the loaves. Then Jesus said to Andrew: Rise up, brother, with thy friends; partake of food, that you may be strong to bear the tossing of the sea. And Andrew answered and said to his disciples: My children, we have found great kindness from this man. Stand up, then, and partake of the nourishment of bread, that you may be strong to bear the tossing of the sea. And his disciples were not able to answer him a word, for they were in distress because of the sea. Then Jesus forced Andrew to partake himself also of the nourishment of bread along with his disciples. And Andrew answered and said to Jesus, not knowing that it was Jesus: Brother, may the Lord give thee heavenly bread out of His kingdom. Allow me then, brother; for thou seest the children, that they are distressed because of the sea. And Jesus answered and said to Andrew: Assuredly the brethren are without experience of the sea; but inquire of them whether they want to go to land, and thyself to remain, until thou shalt finish thy business, and again come back to them. Then Andrew said to his disciples: My children, do you wish to go to the land, and me to remain here until I shall finish my business for which I have been sent? And they answered and said to Andrew: If we go away from thee, may we become strangers to the good things which the Lord hath provided for us. Now, therefore, we are with thee, wherever thou mayst go.

Jesus answered and said to Andrew: If thou art truly a disciple of Him who is called Jesus, tell thy disciples the miracles which thy Teacher did, that their soul may rejoice, and that they may forget the fear of the sea; for, behold, we are going to take the boat off from the land. And immediately Jesus said to one of the angels: Let go the boat; and he let go the boat from

---

[1] The winds from the four quarters of the heavens.
[2] One MS. has: And the Lord prepared a small boat, and put angels in it for sailors; and Jesus was, as it were, the master of the boat.
[3] Matt. x. 10; Mark vi. 9.

the land. And Jesus came and sat down beside the rudder, and steered the boat. Then Andrew exhorted and comforted his disciples, saying: My children, who have given up your life to the Lord, fear not; for the Lord will not at all forsake you for ever. For at that time when I was alone with our Lord, we went on board the boat with Him, and He lay down to sleep in the boat, trying us; for He was not [1] fast asleep. And a great wind having arisen, and the sea being stormy, so that the waves were uplifted, and came under the sail of the boat, and when we were in great fear, the Lord stood up and rebuked the winds, and there was a calm in the sea; for all things feared Him, as being made by Him.[2] Now, therefore, my children, fear not. For the Lord Jesus will not at all forsake us. And having said this, the holy Andrew prayed in his heart that his disciples might be led to sleep. And as Andrew was praying, his disciples fell asleep.

And Andrew, turning round to the Lord, not knowing that it was the Lord, said to Him: Tell me, O man, and show me the skill of thy steering; for I have never seen any man so steering in the sea as I now see thee. For sixteen years have I sailed the sea, and behold this is the seventeenth, and I have not seen such skill; for truly the boat is just as if on land. Show me then, young man, thy skill. Then Jesus answered and said to Andrew: We also have often sailed the sea, and been in danger; but since thou art a disciple of Him called Jesus, the sea has recognised thee that thou art righteous, and has become calm, and has not lifted its waves against the boat. Then Andrew cried out with a loud voice, saying: I thank Thee, my Lord Jesus Christ, that I have met a man who glorifies Thy name.

And Jesus answered and said: O Andrew, tell me, thou disciple of Him called Jesus, wherefore the unbelieving Jews did not believe in Him, saying that He was not God, but man. Show me, O disciple of Him called Jesus; for I have heard that He showed His Godhead to His disciples. And Andrew answered and said: Truly, brother, He showed us that He was God. Do not think, then, that He is man. For He made the heaven, and the earth, and the sea, and all that is in them. And Jesus answered and said: How then did the Jews not believe Him? Perhaps He did not do miracles before them? Andrew said: Hast thou not heard of the miracles which He did before them? He made the blind see, the lame walk, the deaf hear; He cleansed lepers, He changed water into wine; and having taken five loaves and two fishes, He made a

crowd recline on the grass, and having blessed, He gave them to eat; and those that ate were five thousand men,[3] and they were filled: and they took up what was over to them twelve baskets of fragments.[4] And after all these things they did not believe Him.

And Jesus answered and said to Andrew: Perhaps He did these miracles before the people, and not before the chief priests, and because of this they did not believe Him.

And Andrew answered and said: Nay, brother, He did them also before the chief priests, not only openly, but also in secret, and they did not believe Him. Jesus answered and said: What are the miracles which He did in secret? Disclose them to me. And Andrew answered and said: O man, who hast the spirit of inquisitiveness, why dost thou put me to the test? And Jesus answered and said: I do not put thee to the test by saying this, O disciple of Him called Jesus; but my soul rejoices and exults, and not only mine, but also every soul that hears the wonders of Jesus.

And Andrew answered and said: O child, the Lord shall fill thy soul with all joy and all good, as thou hast persuaded me now to relate to thee the miracles which our Lord did in secret.

It came to pass as we, the twelve disciples, were going with our Lord into a temple of the Gentiles, that He might make known to us the ignorance of the devil, that the chief priests, having beheld us following Jesus, said to us, O wretches, why do you walk with him who says, I am the Son of God? Do you mean to say that God has a son? Which of you has ever at any time seen God associating with a woman? Is not this the son of Joseph the carpenter, and his mother is Mary, and his brothers James and Simon?[5] And when we heard these words, our hearts were turned into weakness. And Jesus, having known that our hearts were giving way, took us into a desert place, and did great miracles before us, and displayed to us all His Godhead. And we spoke to the chief priests, saying, Come ye also, and see; for, behold, He has persuaded us.

And the chief priests having come, went with us; and when we had gone into the temple of the Gentiles, Jesus showed us the heaven,[6] that we might know whether the things were true or not. And there went in along with us thirty men of the people, and four chief priests. And Jesus, having looked on the right hand and on the left of the temple, saw two sculptured sphinxes, one on the right and one on the left.

---

1 One MS. omits the negative.
2 Comp. Matt. viii. 26.

3 One MS. inserts, besides women and children.
4 Mark vi. 37-44.
5 Mark vi. 3.
6 There seems to be something wrong here. One MS. has, the structure of the temple, and omits the following clause.

And Jesus having turned to us, said, Behold the sign of the cross; for these are like the cherubim and the seraphim which are in heaven. Then Jesus, having looked to the right, where the sphinx was, said to it, I say unto thee, thou image of that which is in heaven, which the hands of craftsmen have sculptured, be separated from thy place, and come down, and answer and convict the chief priests, and show them whether I am God or man.

And immediately at that very time the sphinx removed from its place, and having assumed a human voice, said, O foolish sons of Israel, not only has the blinding of their own hearts not been enough for them, but they also wish others to be blind like themselves, saying that God is man, who in the beginning fashioned man, and put His breath into all, who gave motion to those things which moved not; He it is who called Abraham, who loved his son Isaac, who brought back his beloved Jacob into his land; He is the Judge of living and dead; He it is who prepareth great benefits for those who obey Him, and prepareth punishment for those who believe Him not. Heed not that I am an idol that can be handled; for I say unto you, that the sacred places of your synagogue are more excellent.[1] For though we are stones, the priests have given us only the name of a god; and those priests who serve the temple purify themselves, being afraid of the demons: for if they have had intercourse with women, they purify themselves seven days, because of their fear; so that they do not come into the temple because of us, because of the name which they have given us, that we are a god. But you, if you have committed fornication, take up the law of God, and go into the synagogue of God, and purify, and read, and do not reverence the glorious words of God. Because of this, I say unto you, that the holy things purify your synagogues, so that they also become churches of His only begotten Son. The sphinx having said this, ceased speaking.

And we said to the chief priests, Now it is fitting that you should believe, because even the stones have convicted you. And the Jews answered and said, By magic these stones speak, and do not you think that it is a god? For if you have tested what has been said by the stone, you have ascertained its deception. For where did he find Abraham, or how did he see him? For Abraham died many years before he was born, and how does he know him?

And Jesus, having again turned to the image, said to it, Because these believe not that I have spoken with Abraham, go away into the land of the Canaanites, and go away to the double[2] cave in the field of Mamre, where the body of Abraham is, and cry outside of the tomb, saying, Abraham, Abraham, whose body is in the tomb, and whose soul is in paradise, thus speaks He who fashioned man, who made thee from the beginning his friend, Rise up, thou and thy son Isaac, and the son of thy son Jacob, and come to the temples of the Jebusites, that we may convict the chief priests, in order that they may know that I am acquainted with thee, and thou with me. And when the sphinx heard these words, immediately she walked about in the presence of us all, and set out for the land of the Canaanites to the field of Mamre, and cried outside of the tomb, as God had commanded her. And straightway the twelve patriarchs[3] came forth alive out of the tomb, and answered and said to her, To which of us hast thou been sent? And the sphinx answered and said, I have been sent to the three patriarchs for testimony; but do ye go in, and rest until the time of the resurrection. And having heard, they went into the tomb and fell asleep. And the three patriarchs set out along with the sphinx to Jesus, and convicted the chief priests. And Jesus said to them, Go away to your places; and they went away. And He said also to the image, Go up to thy place; and straightway she went up and stood in her place. And He did also many other miracles, and they did not believe Him; which *miracles*, if I shall recount, thou wilt not be able to bear. And Jesus answered and said to him: I can bear it; for I prudently listen to profitable words.

And when the boat was about to come near the land, Jesus bent down His head upon one of His angels, and was quiet. And Andrew ceased speaking; and he also, reclining his head upon one of his disciples, fell asleep. And Jesus said to His angels: Spread your hands under him, and carry Andrew and his disciples, and go and put them outside of the city of the man-eaters; and having laid them on the ground, return to me. And the angels did as Jesus commanded them, and the angels returned to Jesus: and He went up into the heavens with His angels.

And when it was morning, Andrew, having awakened and looked up, found himself sitting on the ground; and having looked,[4] he saw his disciples sleeping on the ground; and he wakened them, and said to them: Rise up, my children, and know the great dispensation that has happened to us, and learn that the Lord was with us in the boat, and we knew Him not; for He transformed Himself as if He were a pilot in

---

[1] One MS. has: Do not say that I am a carved stone, and that you alone have a name, and are called high priests.

[2] Gen. xxiii. 9, 17, following the version of the LXX. and the older interpreters.

[3] Not one of the twelve patriarchs was buried in Machpelah.

[4] One MS. inserts: And he saw the gate of that city.

the boat, and humbled Himself, and appeared to us as a man, putting us to the test. And Andrew, recovering himself, said : Lord, I recognised Thy excellent words, but Thou didst not manifest Thyself to me, and because of this I did not know Thee. And his disciples answered and said to him : Father Andrew, do not think that we knew when thou wast speaking with Him in the boat, for we were weighed down by a most heavy sleep ; and eagles came down out of the heavens, and lifted up our souls, and took them away into the paradise in heaven, and we saw great wonders. For we beheld our Lord Jesus sitting on a throne of glory, and all the angels round about Him. We beheld also Abraham, and Isaac, and Jacob, and all the saints ; and David praised Him with a song upon his harp. And we beheld there you the twelve apostles standing by in the presence of our Lord Jesus Christ, and outside of you twelve angels round about you, and each angel standing behind each of you, and they were like you in appearance. And we heard the Lord saying to the angels, Listen to the apostles in all things whatsoever they shall ask you. These are the things which we have seen, father Andrew, until thou didst awake us ; and angels, who appeared like eagles, brought our souls into our bodies.

Then Andrew, having heard, rejoiced with great joy that his disciples had been deemed worthy to behold these wonderful things. And Andrew looked up into heaven, and said : Appear to me, Lord Jesus Christ ; for I know that Thou art not far from Thy servants. Pardon me, Lord, for what I have done ; for I have beheld Thee as a man in the boat, and I have conversed with Thee as with a man. Now therefore, Lord, manifest Thyself to me in this place.

And when Andrew had said this, Jesus appeared to him in the likeness of a most beautiful little child. And Jesus answered and said : Hail, our Andrew ! And Andrew, having beheld Him, worshipped Him, saying : Pardon me, Lord Jesus Christ, for I saw Thee like a man on the sea, and conversed with Thee. What is there, then, wherein I have sinned, my Lord Jesus, that Thou didst not manifest Thyself to me on the sea ? And Jesus answered and said to Andrew : Thou hast not sinned, but I did this to thee because thou saidst, I shall not be able to go to the city of the man-eaters in three days ; and I have showed thee that I am able to do all things, and to appear to every one as I wish. Now therefore rise up, go into the city to Matthias, and bring him forth out of the prison, and all the strangers that are with him. For, behold, I show thee, Andrew, what thou must suffer before going into this city. They will heap upon thee tortures and insults, and scatter thy flesh in the ways and the streets, and thy blood shall flow to the ground, but they are not able to put thee to death ; but endure, just as thou sawest me beaten, insulted, and crucified : for there are those who are destined to believe in this city. And having said this, the Saviour went into the heavens.

And Andrew went into the city along with his disciples, and no one beheld him. And when he came to the prison, he saw seven warders standing at the gate guarding, and he prayed within himself, and they fell down and expired ; and he marked the gate with the sign of the cross, and it opened of its own accord. And having gone in with his disciples, he found Matthias sitting and singing ; and seeing him, he stood up, and they saluted each other with a holy kiss ; and he said to Matthias : Brother, how hast thou been found here ? For yet three days, and they will bring thee out to be food for them. Where are the great mysteries which thou hast been taught, and the wonderful things which we have believed ? And Matthias said to him : Didst thou not hear the Lord saying, I shall send you like sheep into the midst of wolves ? They straightway brought me into the prison, and I prayed to the Lord ; and He said to me, Remain here twenty-seven days, and I shall send thee Andrew, and he will bring thee forth out of the prison. And now, behold, it has come to pass as the Lord said.

Then Andrew, having looked, saw three men shut up eating grass naked ; and he beat his breast, and said : Consider, O Lord, what the men suffer ; how have they made them like the irrational brutes ? And he says to Satan : Woe to thee, the devil, the enemy of God, and to thine angels, because the strangers here have done nothing to thee ; and how hast thou brought upon them this punishment ? how long dost thou war against the human race ? Thou didst bring forth Adam out of paradise, and didst cause men to be mixed up with transgression ; and the Lord was enraged, and brought on the deluge so as to sweep man away. And again hast thou made thy appearance in this city too, in order that thou mayst make those who are here eat men,[2] that the end of them also may be in execration and destruction, thinking in thyself that God will sweep away the work of His hands. Hast thou not heard that God said, I will not bring a deluge upon the earth ?[3] but if there is any punishment prepared, it is for the sake of taking vengeance upon thee.

Then he stood up, and Andrew and Matthias prayed ; and after the prayer Andrew laid his hands upon the faces of the blind men who were

---

[1] Matt. x. 16.
[2] Another MS. has: make men eat their like.
[3] Gen. ix. 11.

in the prison, and straightway they all received their sight. And again he laid his hand upon their hearts, and their minds were changed into human reason. Then Andrew answered them: Rise up, and go into the lower parts of the city, and you shall find in the way a great fig-tree, and sit under the fig-tree, and eat of its fruit, until I come to you; but if I delay coming there, you will find abundance of food for yourselves: for the fruit shall not fail from the fig-tree, but according as you eat it shall produce more fruit, and nourish you, as the Lord has said. And they answered and said to Andrew: Go along with us, O our master, lest perchance the wicked men of this city again see us, and shut us up, and inflict upon us greater and more dreadful tortures than they have inflicted upon us. And Andrew answered and said to them: Go; for in truth I say to you, that as you go, not a dog shall bark with his tongue against you. And there were in all two hundred and seventy men and forty-nine women [1] whom Andrew released from the prison. And the men went as the blessed Andrew said to them; and he made Matthias go along with his disciples out of the eastern gate of the city. And Andrew commanded a cloud, and the cloud took up Matthias and the disciples of Andrew; and the cloud set them down on the mountain where Peter was teaching,[2] and they remained beside him.

And Andrew, having gone forth from the prison, walked about in the city; and having seen a brazen pillar, and a statue standing upon it, he came and sat down behind that pillar until he should see what should happen. And it happened that the executioners went to the prison to bring out the men for their food,[3] according to the custom; and they found the doors of the prison opened, and the guards that guarded it lying dead upon the ground. And straightway they went, and reported to the rulers of the city, saying: We found the prison opened, and having gone inside we found nobody;[4] but we found the guards lying dead upon the ground. And the rulers having heard this, said among themselves: What, then, has happened? You do not mean to say that some persons have gone into the prison of the city, and have killed the warders, and taken away those that were shut up? And they spoke to the executioners, saying: Go to the prison, and bring the men that are dead, that we may eat them up to-day. And let us go to-morrow, and bring together all the old men of the city, that they may cast lots upon themselves, until the seven lots come, and we slay seven each day. And they shall be to us

for food until we may choose young men, and put them in boats as sailors, that they may go away to the countries round about, and attack them, and bring some men here, that they may be for food to us.

And the executioners went to the prison, and brought the seven men that were dead; and there was an oven built in the midst of the city, and there lay in the oven a large trough in which they killed the men, and their blood ran down into the trough, and they drew out of the blood and drank it. And they brought the men, and put them into the trough. And when the executioners were lifting their hands against them, Andrew heard a voice, saying: Behold, Andrew, what is happening in this city. And Andrew having beheld, prayed to the Lord, saying: Lord Jesus Christ, who didst order me to come into this city, do not suffer those in this city to do any evil, but let the knives go out of the hands of the wicked ones. And straightway the knives of the wicked men fell, and their hands were turned into stone. And the rulers, having seen what had happened, wept, saying: Woe unto us, for here are the magicians who have gone into the prison, and brought out the men; for, behold, they have bewitched these also. What, then, shall we do? Let us go now, and gather together the old men of the city, seeing that we are hungry.

And they went and gathered them together, and found two hundred and seventeen; and they brought them to the rulers, and they made them cast lots, and the lot came upon seven old men. And one of those taken by lot answered and said to the officers: I pray you, I have for myself one son; take him, and slay him instead of me, and let me go. And the officers answered and said to him: We cannot take thy son, unless we bring him first to our superiors. And the officers went and told the rulers. And the rulers answered and said to the officers: If he give us his son instead of himself, let him go. And the officers went and told the old man. And the old man answered and said to them: I have also a daughter along with my son; take them, and kill them, only let me go. And he gave his children to the officers, that they might kill them. And the children wept to each other, and prayed the officers, saying: We pray you do not kill us, as we are of so small a size; but let us complete our size, and so kill us. For it was a custom in that city, and they did not bury their dead, but ate them up. And the officers did not hearken to the children, nor take pity upon them, but carried them to the trough weeping and praying.

And it happened, as they were leading them away to kill them, that Andrew, having beheld what happened, shed tears; and weeping, he looked up to heaven and said: Lord Jesus

---

[1] Two MSS. have: two hundred and forty-nine men.
[2] Another reading is, praying.
[3] i.e., to be eaten by them.
[4] Comp. Acts v. 20-25.

Christ, as Thou didst hear me in the case of the dead men, and didst not suffer them to be eaten up, so also now hear me, that the executioners may not inflict death upon these children, but that the knives may be loosened out of the hands of the executioners.[1] And straightway the knives were loosened, and fell out of the hands of the executioners. And when this came to pass, the executioners, having beheld what had happened, were exceedingly afraid. And Andrew, seeing what had happened, glorified the Lord because He had listened to him in every work.

And the rulers, having beheld what had happened, wept with a great weeping, saying: Woe unto us! what are we to do? And, behold, the devil appeared in the likeness of an old man, and began to say in the midst of all: Woe unto you! because you are now dying, having no food; what can sheep and oxen do for you? They will not at all be enough for you. But rise up, and make a search here for one who has come to the city, a stranger named Andrew, and kill him; for if you do not, he will not permit you to carry on this practice longer: for it was he who let loose the men out of the prison. Assuredly the man is in this city, and you have not seen[2] him. Now, therefore, rise and make search for him, in order that henceforward you may be able to collect your food.

And Andrew saw the devil, how he was talking to the multitudes; but the devil did not see the blessed Andrew. Then Andrew answered the devil, and said: O Belial most fiendish, who art the foe of every creature;[3] but my Lord Jesus Christ will bring thee down to the abyss. And the devil, having heard this, said: I hear thy voice indeed, and I know thy voice, but where thou art standing I know not. And Andrew answered and said to the devil: Why, then, hast thou been called Amael?[4] is it not because thou art blind, not seeing all the saints? And the devil, having heard this, said to the citizens: Look round now for him speaking to me, for he is the man. And the citizens, having run in different directions, shut the gates of the city, and searched for the blessed one, and did not see him.[5] Then the Lord showed Himself to Andrew, and said to him; Andrew, rise up and show thyself to them, that they may learn my power, and the powerlessness of the devil working in them.

Then Andrew rose up, and said in presence of all: Behold, I am Andrew whom you seek. And the multitudes ran upon him, and laid hold of him, saying: What thou hast done to us, we also will do to thee. And they reasoned among themselves, saying: By what death shall we kill him? And they said to each other: If we take off his head, his death is not torture; and if we burn him, he will not be for food to us. Then one of them, the devil having entered into him, answered and said to the multitudes: As he has done to us, so let us also do to him. Let us rise up, then, and fasten a rope to his neck, and drag him through all the streets and lanes of the city; and when he is dead, we shall share his body. And they did as he said to them; and having fastened a rope round his neck, they dragged him through the streets and lanes of the city, and the flesh of the blessed Andrew stuck to the ground, and his blood flowed to the ground like water. And when it was evening they cast him into the prison, having bound his hands behind him; and he was in sore distress.

And in the morning again they brought him out, and having fastened a rope round his neck, they dragged him about; and again his flesh stuck to the ground, and his blood flowed. And the blessed one wept and prayed, saying: Do not forsake me, my Lord Jesus Christ; for I know that Thou art not far from Thy servants. And as he was praying, the devil walked behind, and said to the multitudes: Strike him on the mouth, that he may not speak.[6]

And when it was evening they took him again to the prison, having bound his hands behind him, and left him till the morrow again. And the devil having taken with himself seven demons[7] whom the blessed one had cast out of the countries round about, and having gone into the prison, they stood before him, wishing to kill him. And the demons answered and said to Andrew: Now hast thou fallen into our hands; where is thy glory and thy exultation, thou that raisest thyself up against us, and dishonourest us, and tellest our doings to the people in every place and country, and hast made our workshops and our temples to become desolate, in order that sacrifices may not be brought to them? Because of this, then, we shall also kill thee, like thy teacher called Jesus, and John whom Herod beheaded.[8]

And they stood before Andrew, wishing to kill him; and having beheld the seal upon his forehead which the Lord gave him, they were afraid, and did not come near him, but fled. And the devil said to them: Why have you fled from him, my children, and not killed him? And the de-

---

[1] One MS. adds: like wax before fire.
[2] Or, do not know.
[3] One MS. has: Thou art always warring against the race of the Christians.
[4] One of the MSS. has Samael.
[5] One MS. adds: And Andrew answered and said: O Belial! foe of the whole creation, thou hast always been a robber, warring against the race of men: thou in the beginning didst cause Adam to be cast out of paradise; thou didst cause the loaves upon the table to be turned into stones; and again thou hast appeared in this city, to cause the people here to eat up men.

[6] Comp. Acts xxiii. 2.
[7] Comp. Matt. xii. 45.
[8] One MS. adds: And the devil answered and said to the seven wicked demons, My children, kill him that dishonours us.

mons answered and said to the devil: We cannot kill him, but kill him if thou art able; for we knew him before he came into the distress of his humiliation. Then one of the demons answered and said: We cannot kill him, but come let us mock him in the distress of his humiliation. And the demons came and stood before him, and scoffed at him. And the blessed one hearing, wept; and there came to him a voice saying: Andrew, why weepest thou? And it was the voice of the devil changed. And Andrew answered and said: I am weeping because God commanded me, saying, Be patient toward them. And the devil said: If thou canst do anything, do it. And Andrew answered and said: Is it for this, then, that you do these things to me? But forbid it that I should disobey the commandment of my Lord; for if the Lord shall make for me a charge [1] in this city, I shall chastise you as you deserve. And having heard this, they fled.

And when it was morning they brought him out again, and having fastened a rope about his neck, they dragged him; and again his flesh stuck to the ground, and his blood flowed to the ground like water. And the blessed one, as he was being dragged along, wept, saying: Lord Jesus Christ, be not displeased with me; for Thou knowest, Lord, what the fiend has inflicted upon me, along with his demons. These tortures are enough, my Lord; for, behold, I am dragged about for three days. But do Thou, Lord, remember that Thou wast three hours upon the cross, and didst cry out to the Father, My Father, why hast Thou forsaken me? [2] Where are Thy words, Lord, which Thou spakest to us, confirming us, when we walked about with Thee, saying to us, Ye shall not lose one hair? [3] Consider, then, Lord, what has become of my flesh, and the hairs of my head. Then Jesus said to Andrew: O our Andrew, the heaven and the earth shall pass away, but my words shall not pass away. [4] Turn thyself then, Andrew, and behold thy flesh that has fallen, and thy hair, what has become of them. And Andrew turned, and saw great trees springing up, bearing fruit; and he glorified God.

And when it was evening they took him up again, and cast him into the prison, having bound his hands behind him; and he was exceedingly exhausted. And the men of the city said among themselves: Perhaps he dies in the night, and we do not find him alive on the following day; for he was languid, and his flesh was spent.

And the Lord appeared in the prison, and having stretched out His hand, said to Andrew:

Give me thy hand, and rise up whole. And Andrew, having beheld the Lord Jesus, gave Him his hand, and rose up whole. And falling down, he worshipped Him, and said: I thank Thee, my Lord Jesus Christ, that Thou hast speedily brought help to me. And Andrew, having looked into the middle of the prison, saw a pillar standing, and upon the pillar there stood an alabaster statue. And Andrew, having gone up to the statue, unfolded his hands seven times, and said to the pillar, and the statue upon it: Fear the sign of the cross, which the heaven and the earth dread; and let the statue set upon the pillar bring up much water through its mouth, until all who are in this city be punished. And say not, I am stone, and am not worthy to praise the Lord, for the Lord fashioned us from the earth; but you are pure, because that out of you He gave the tables of the law. [5] When the blessed Andrew had said this, straightway the stone statue cast out of its mouth water in abundance, as if out of a canal. And the water stood high upon the earth; and it was exceedingly acrid, eating into the flesh of men.

And when it was morning, the men of the city saw it, and began to flee, saying in themselves: Woe to us! because we are now dying. And the water killed their cattle and their children; and they began to flee out of the city. Then Andrew prayed, saying: Lord Jesus Christ, in whom I have hoped that this miracle should come upon this city, forsake me not, but send Michael Thy archangel in a cloud of fire, and be a wall round the city, that no one may be able to escape out of the fire. And straightway a cloud of fire came down and encircled the city like a wall; and the water was as high as the neck of those men, and it was eating them up exceedingly. And they wept, saying: Woe to us! for all these things have come upon us because of the stranger who is in the prison. Let us go and release him, lest perchance we die.

And they went out, crying with a loud voice: God of the stranger, take away from us this water. And the apostle knew that they were in great affliction, and said to the alabaster statue: Stop the water, for they have repented. And I say to thee, that if the citizens of this city shall believe, I will build a church, and place thee in it, because thou hast done me this service. And the statue ceased flowing, and no longer brought forth water. And the men of the city, having come out to the doors of the prison, cried out, saying: Have pity upon us, God of the stranger, and do not according to our unbelief, and according to what we have done to this man, but

---

[1] Or, a bishopric.
[2] Matt. xxvii. 46.
[3] Comp. Matt. x. 30.
[4] Matt. v. 18.

[5] One MS. has: Yea, for assuredly you have been honoured: for God did not write the law for His people on plates of gold or silver, but on plates of stone. Now therefore, O statue, do this that I require of thee.

take away from us this water. And Andrew came forth out of the prison; and the water ran this way and that from the feet of the blessed Andrew. Then all the multitude seeing him, all cried out: Have pity upon us.

And the old man having come who gave up his children that they should slay them instead of him, prayed at the feet of the blessed Andrew, saying: Have pity upon me. And the holy Andrew answered and said to the old man: I wonder how thou sayest, Have pity upon me; for thou hadst no pity upon thy children, but gavest them up to be slain instead of thee. Therefore I say unto thee, At what hour this water goes away, into the abyss shalt thou go, with the fourteen[1] executioners who slay the men every day. And he came to the place of the trough, where they used to slay the men. And the blessed one, having looked up to heaven, prayed before all the multitude; and the earth was opened, and swallowed up the water, along with the old man. He was carried down into the abyss, with the executioners. And the men, having seen what had happened, were exceedingly afraid, and began to say: Woe unto us! because this man is from God; and now he will kill us because of the afflictions which we have caused him. For, behold, what he said to the executioners and the old man has befallen them. Now, therefore, he will command the fire, and it will burn us. And Andrew, having heard, said to them: Fear not, children; for I shall not send these also to Hades; but those have gone, that you may believe in our Lord Jesus Christ.

Then the holy Andrew ordered to be brought up all who had died in the water. And they were not able to bring them; for there had died a great multitude both of men, and women, and children, and cattle.

Then Andrew prayed, and they all came to life. And after these things he drew a plan of a church, and he caused the church to be built. And he baptized them, and gave them the ordinances of our Lord Jesus Christ, saying to them: Stand by these, in order that you may know the mysteries of our Lord Jesus Christ. And they

all prayed him: We pray thee, stay with us a few days, that we may be filled with thy fountain, because we are newly planted.[2] And he did not comply with their request, but said to them: I shall go first to my disciples. And the children followed after, weeping and praying, with the men; and they cast ashes[3] upon their heads. And he did not comply with them, but said: I shall go to my disciples, and after that I shall come again to you. And he went his way.

And the Lord Jesus Christ came down, being like a comely little child, and met Andrew, and said: Andrew, why hast thou come out and left them without fruit, and hast not had compassion upon the children that followed after thee, and the men entreating thee, Stay with us a few days? For the cry of them and the weeping has come up to heaven. Now therefore return, and go into the city, and remain there seven days, until I shall confirm their souls in the faith; and then thou shalt go away into the country of the barbarians, thou and thy disciples. And after going into this city, thou shalt proclaim my Gospel, and bring up the men who are in the abyss. And thou shalt do what I command thee.

Then Andrew turned and went into the city, saying: I thank Thee, my Lord Jesus Christ, who wishest to save every soul, that Thou hast not allowed me to go forth out of this city in mine anger. And when he had come into the city, they, seeing him, rejoiced with exceeding great joy. And he stayed there seven days, teaching and confirming them in the Lord Jesus Christ. And the seven days having been fulfilled, it came to pass, while the blessed Andrew was going out, all came together to him, from the child even to the elder, and sent him on his way, saying: There is one God, *the God* of Andrew, and one Lord Jesus Christ, who alone doeth wonders; to whom[4] be glory and strength for ever. Amen.

---

[1] One MS. has, four.

[2] i.e., neophytes.
[3] Or, dust.
[4] One MS. adds: With the Father, and the Son, and the all-holy and good and life-giving and holy Spirit. Another MS. ends thus: Then the Apostle Andrew wished to go out again to preach. And they assembled from small to great of them, and said: *There is* one God and Father of all, one Lord, one faith, one baptism, which we have been taught by our father Andrew, the first called in (or by) Christ Jesus our Lord; to whom be glory for ever. Amen.

ACTS OF PETER AND ANDREW

FROM A BODLEIAN MS.[1]

ACTS OF THE HOLY APOSTLES PETER AND ANDREW.

IT came to pass when Andrew the apostle of Christ went forth from the city of the man-eaters, behold a luminous cloud snatched him up, and carried him away to the mountain where Peter and Matthew and Alexander were sitting. And when he saw them, they saluted him with great joy. Then Peter says to him: What has happened to thee, brother Andrew? Hast thou sown the word of truth in the country of the man-eaters or not? Andrew says to him: Yes, father Peter, through thy prayers; but the men of that city have done me many mischiefs, for they dragged me through their street three days, so that my blood stained the whole street. Peter says to him: Be a man in the Lord, brother Andrew, and come hither, and rest from thy labour. For if the good husbandman laboriously till the ground, it will also bear fruit, and straightway all his toil will be turned into joy; but if he toil, and his land bring forth no fruit, he has double toil.

And while he was thus speaking, the Lord Jesus Christ appeared to them in the form of a child, and said to them: Hail, Peter, bishop of the whole of my Church! hail, Andrew! My co-heirs, be courageous, and struggle for mankind; for verily I say unto you, you shall endure toils in this world for mankind. *But be bold; I will give you rest* in one hour of repose in the kingdom of my Father. Arise, then, and go into the city of the barbarians, and preach in it; and I will be with you in the wonders that shall happen in it by your hands. And the Lord Jesus, after saluting them, went up into the heavens in glory.

And Peter, and Andrew, and Alexander, and Rufus, and Matthias, went into the city of the barbarians. And after they had come near the city, Andrew answered and said to Peter: Father Peter, have we again to undergo toils in this city, as in the country of the man-eaters? Peter says to him: I do not know. But, behold, there is an old man before us sowing in his field:

if we go up to him, let us say to him, Give us bread; and if he give us bread, we may know that we are not to suffer in this city; but if he say to us, We have no bread, on the other hand, we shall know that suffering again awaits us. And when they came up to the old man, Peter says to him: Hail, farmer! And the farmer says to them: Hail you too, merchants! Peter says to him: Have you bread to give to these children, for we have been in want? The old man says to them: Wait a little, and look after the oxen, and the plough, and the land, that I may go into the city, and get you loaves. Peter says to him: If you provide hospitality for us, we shall look after the cattle and the field. The old man says: So be it. Peter says to him: Are the oxen your own? The old man says: No; I have them on hire. Peter says to him: Go into the city. And the old man went into the city. And Peter arose, and girded up his cloak and his under-garment, and says to Andrew: It is not right for us to rest and be idle; above all, when the old man is working for us, having left his own work. Then Peter took hold of the plough, and sowed the wheat. And Andrew was behind the oxen, and says to Peter: Father Peter, why dost thou bring toil upon us, especially when we have work enough already! Then Andrew took the plough out of Peter's hand, and sowed the wheat, saying: O seed cast into the ground in the field of the righteous, come up, and come to the light. Let the young men of the city therefore come forth, whom I found in the pit of destruction until to-day; for, behold, the apostles of Christ are coming into the city, pardoning the sins of those who believe in them, and healing every disease, and every sickness. Pray ye for me, that He may have mercy upon me, and that I may be delivered from this strait.

And many of the multitude believed in Christ, because of the saying of the woman;[2] and they fell at the feet of the apostles, and adored them.

---

[1] [This is the MS. frequently referred to in the previous pages. The Greek text of this fragment is given by Tischendorf in the supplement to *Apocalypses Apocr.*, pp. 161-167. — R.]

[2] Something seems to have fallen out here.

And they laid their hands upon them. And they healed those in the city that were sick, and gave sight to the blind and hearing to the deaf, and drove out the demons. All the multitude glorified the Father, and the Son, and the Holy Spirit.

And there was a certain rich man in the city, by name Onesiphorus. He, having seen the miracles done by the apostles, says to them: If I believe in your God, can I also do a miracle like you? Andrew says to him: If thou wilt forsake all that belongs to thee, and thy wife and thy children, as we also have done, then thou also shalt do miracles. When Onesiphorus heard this, he was filled with rage, and took his scarf and threw it over Andrew's neck, and struck him, and said to him: Thou art a sorcerer. How dost thou force me to abandon my wife, and my children, and my goods? Then Peter, having turned and seen him striking Andrew, says to him: Man, stop now striking Andrew. Onesiphorus says to him: I see that thou art more sensible than he. Do thou then tell me to leave my wife, and my children, and my goods. What dost thou say? Peter says to him: One thing I say unto thee: it is easier for a camel to go through the eye of a needle, than for a rich man to go into the kingdom of heaven.[1] When Onesiphorus heard this, he was even more filled with rage and anger, and took his scarf off the neck of Andrew, and threw it upon the neck of Peter; and so he dragged him along, saying: Verily thou art a great sorcerer, more than the other; for a camel cannot go through the eye of a needle. But if thou wilt show me this miracle, I will believe in thy God; and not only I, but also the whole city. But if not, thou shalt be grievously punished in the midst of the city. And when Peter heard this, he was exceedingly grieved, and stood and stretched forth his hands towards heaven, and prayed, saying: O Lord our God, listen to me at this time; for they will ensnare us from Thine own words: for no prophet has spoken to set forth this his explanation, and no patriarch that we might learn the interpretation of it; and now we seek for ourselves the explanation with boldness. Do Thou then, Lord, not overlook us: for thou art He who is praised by the cherubim.

And after he had said this, the Saviour appeared in the form of a child of twelve years old, wearing a linen garment; and He says to them: Be courageous, and tremble not, my chosen disciples; for I am with you always. Let the needle and the camel be brought. And after saying this, He went up into the heavens. And there was a certain merchant[2] in the city who had believed in the Lord through the Apostle Philip; and when he heard of this, he ran and searched for a needle with a big eye, to do a favour to the apostles. When Peter learned this, he said: My son, do not search for a big needle; for nothing is impossible with God: rather bring us a small needle. And after the needle had been brought, and all the multitude of the city were standing by to see, Peter looked up and saw a camel coming. And he ordered her to be brought. Then he fixed the needle in the ground, and cried out with a loud voice, saying: In the name of Jesus Christ, who was crucified under Pontius Pilate, I order thee, O camel, to go through the eye of the needle. Then the eye of the needle was opened like a gate, and the camel went through it, and all the multitude saw it. Again Peter says to the camel: Go again through the needle. And the camel went a second time. When Onesiphorus saw this, he said to Peter; Truly thou art a great sorcerer; but I do not believe unless I send and bring a camel and a needle. And he called one of his servants, and said to him privately: Go and bring me here a camel and a needle; find also a polluted woman, and force her to come here: for these men are sorcerers. And Peter having learned the mystery through the Spirit, says to Onesiphorus: Send and bring the camel, and the woman, and the needle. And when they brought them, Peter took the needle, and fixed it in the ground. And the woman was sitting on the camel. Then Peter says: In the name of our Lord Jesus Christ the crucified, I order thee, O camel, to go through this needle. And immediately the eye of the needle was opened, and became like a gate, and the camel went through it. Peter again says to the camel: Go through it again, that all may see the glory of our Lord Jesus Christ, in order that some may believe on Him. Then the camel again went through the needle. And Onesiphorus seeing it, cried out, and said: Truly great is the God of Peter and Andrew, and I from this time forth believe in the name of our Lord Jesus Christ. Now then, hear my words, O Peter. I have corn lands, vineyards, and fields; I have also twenty-seven pounds of gold, and fifty pounds of silver; and I have very many slaves. I give my possessions to the poor, that I also may do one miracle like you. And Peter was grieved lest the powers should not work in him, seeing that he had not received the seal in Christ. And while he was considering this, behold, a voice out of the heaven saying to him: Do to him what he wishes, because I will accomplish for him what he desires. Peter says to him: My son, come hither; do as we do. And Onesiphorus came up, and stood before the camel and the needle, and said: In the n . . . (Here the MS. ends.)

---

[1] Matt. xix. 24, etc.
[2] παντάπωλης.

ACTS AND MARTYRDOM OF ST. MATTHEW THE APOSTLE

About that time Matthew, the holy apostle and evangelist of Christ, was abiding in the mountain resting, and praying in his tunic and apostolic robes without sandals; and, behold, Jesus came to Matthew in the likeness of the infants who sing in paradise, and said to him: Peace to thee, Matthew! And Matthew having gazed upon Him, and not known who He was, said: Grace to thee, and peace, O child highly favoured! And why hast thou come hither to me, having left those who· sing in paradise, and the delights there? Because here the place is desert; and what sort of a table I shall lay for thee, O child, I know not, because I have no bread nor oil in a jar. Moreover, even the winds are at rest, so as not to cast down from the trees to the ground anything for food; because, for the accomplishing of my fast of forty days, I, partaking only of the fruits falling by the movement of the winds, am glorifying my Jesus. Now, therefore, what shall I bring thee, beautiful boy? There is not even water near, that I may wash thy feet.

And the child said: Why sayest thou, O Matthew? Understand and know that good discourse is better than a calf, and words of meekness better than every herb of the field, and a sweet saying as the perfume of love, and cheerfulness of countenance better that feeding, and a pleasant look is as the appearance of sweetness. Understand, Matthew, and know that I am paradise, that I am the comforter, I am the power of the powers above, I the strength of those that restrain themselves, I the crown of the virgins, I the self-control of the once married, I the boast of the widowed, I the defence of the infants, I the foundation of the Church, I the kingdom of the bishops, I the glory of the presbyters, I the praise of the deacons. Be a man, and be strong, Matthew, in· these words.

And Matthew said: The sight of thee hast altogether delighted me, O child; moreover also, thy words are full of life. For assuredly thy face shines more than the lightning, and thy words are altogether most sweet. And that indeed I saw thee in paradise when thou didst sing with the other infants who were killed in Bethlehem,

I know right well; but how thou hast suddenly come hither, this altogether astonishes me. But I shall ask thee one thing, O child: that impious Herod, where is he? The child says to him: Since thou hast asked, hear his dwelling-place. He dwells, indeed, in Hades; and there has been prepared for him fire unquenchable, Gehenna without end, bubbling mire, worm that sleeps not,[1] because he cut off three [2] thousand infants, wishing to slay the child Jesus, the ancient of the ages; but of all these ages I am father. Now therefore, O Matthew, take this rod of mine, and go down from the mountain, and go into Myrna, the city of the man-eaters, and plant it by the gate of the church which thou [3] and Andrew founded; and as soon as thou hast planted it, it shall be a tree, great and lofty and with many branches, and its branches shall extend to thirty cubits, and of each single branch the fruit shall be different both to the sight and the eating,[4] and from the top of the tree shall flow down much honey; and from its root there shall come forth a great fountain, giving drink to this country round about, and in it creatures that swim and creep; and in it the man-eaters shall wash themselves, and eat of the fruit of the trees of the vine and of the honey; and their bodies shall be changed, and their forms shall be altered so as to be like those of other men; and they shall be ashamed of the nakedness of their body, and they shall put on clothing of the rams of the sheep, and they shall no longer eat unclean things; and there shall be to them fire in superabundance, preparing the sacrifices for offerings, and they shall bake their bread with fire; and they shall see each other in the likeness of the rest of men, and they shall acknowledge me, and glorify· my Father who is in the heavens. Now therefore make haste, Matthew, and go down hence, because the departure from thy body through fire is at hand, and the crown of thy endurance.

---

[1] Or, that dies not.
[2] The other [Vienna] MS. has, eleven.
[3] In some of the MSS. of the previous book the name of Matthew appears in place of that of Matthias — Matthaios for Mattheias.
[4] Comp. Rev. xxii. 2.

528

And the child having said this, and given him the rod, was taken up into the heavens. And Matthew went down from the mountain, hastening to the city. And as he was about to enter into the city, there met him Fulvana the wife of the king, and his son Fulvanus and his wife Erva, who were possessed by an unclean spirit, and cried out shouting: Who has brought thee here again, Matthew? or who has given thee the rod for our destruction? for we see also the child Jesus, the Son of God, who is with thee. Do not go then, O Matthew, to plant the rod for the food, and for the transformation of the man-eaters: for I have found what I shall do to thee. For since thou didst drive me out of this city, and prevent me from fulfilling my wishes among the man-eaters, behold, I will raise up against thee the king of this city, and he will burn thee alive. And Matthew, having laid his hands on each one of the demoniacs, put the demons to flight, and made the people whole; and they followed him.

And thus the affair being made manifest, Plato the bishop, having heard of the presence of the holy Apostle Matthew, met him with all the clergy; and having fallen to the ground, they kissed his feet. And Matthew raised them, and went with them into the church, and the child Jesus was also with him. And Matthew, having come to the gate of the church, stood upon a certain lofty and immoveable stone; and when the whole city ran together, especially the brethren who had believed, began to say: Men and women who appear in our sight, heretofore believing in the universe,[1] but now knowing Him who has upheld and made the universe; until now worshipping the Satyr, and mocked by ten thousand false gods, but now through Jesus Christ acknowledging the one and only God, Lord, Judge; who have laid aside the immeasurable greatness of evil, and put on love, which is of like nature with affectionateness, towards men; once strangers to Christ, but now confessing Him Lord and God; formerly without form, but now transformed through Christ; — behold, the staff which you see in my hand, which Jesus, in whom you have believed and will believe, gave me; perceive now what comes to pass through me, and acknowledge the riches of the greatness which He will this day make for you. For, behold, I shall plant this rod in this place, and it shall be a sign to your generations, and it shall become a tree, great and lofty and flourishing, and its fruit beautiful to the view and good to the sight; and the fragrance of perfumes shall come forth from it, and there shall be a vine twining round it, full of clusters; and from the top of it honey coming down, and every flying creature shall find covert in its branches; and a fountain of water shall come forth from the root of it, having swimming and creeping things, giving drink to all the country round about.

And having said this, and called upon the name of the Lord Jesus, he fixed his rod in the ground, and straightway it sprung up to one cubit; and the sight was strange and wonderful. For the rod having straightway shot up, increased in size, and grew into a great tree, as Matthew had said. And the apostle said: Go into the fountain and wash your bodies in it, and then thus partake both of the fruits of the tree, and of the vine and the honey, and drink of the fountain, and you shall be transformed in your likeness to that of men; and after that, having gone into the church, you will clearly recognise that you have believed in the living and true God. And having done all these things, they saw themselves changed into the likeness of Matthew; then, having thus gone into the church, they worshipped and glorified God. And when they had been changed, they knew that they were naked; and they ran in haste each to his own house to cover their nakedness, because they were ashamed.

And Matthew and Plato remained in the church spending the night, and glorifying God. And there remained also the king's wife, and his son and his wife, and they prayed the apostle to give them the seal in Christ. And Matthew gave orders to Plato; and he, having gone forth, baptized them in the water of the fountain of the tree, in the name of the Father, and the Son, and the Holy Ghost. And so thereafter, having gone into the church, they communicated in the holy mysteries of Christ;[2] and they exulted and passed the night, they also, along with the apostle, many others having also come with them; and all in the church sang the whole night, glorifying God.

And when the dawn had fully come, the blessed Matthew, having gone along with the bishop Plato, stood in the place in which the rod had been planted, and he sees the rod grown into a great tree, and near it a vine twined round it, and honey coming down from above even to its root; and that tree was at once beautiful and flourishing, like the plants in paradise, and a river proceeded from its root watering[3] all the land of the city of Myrna.[4] And all ran together, and ate of the fruit of the tree and the vine, just as any one wished.

And when what had come to pass was reported in the palace, the king Fulvanus, having learned what had been done by Matthew about his wife,

---

[1] The other [Vienna] MS. has: heretofore worshipping every evil thing.

[2] The other [Paris] MS. has: having communicated in the Eucharist.

[3] Or, giving drink to.

[4] The other [Paris] MS. has Smyrna. Nicephorus calls it Myrmene.

and his son, and his daughter-in-law, rejoiced for a time at their purification; but seeing that they were inseparable from Matthew, he was seized with rage and anger, and endeavoured to put him to death by fire. And on that night [1] in which the king intended to lay hands on Matthew, Matthew saw Jesus saying to him: I am with thee always to save thee, Matthew; be strong, and be a man.

And the blessed Matthew, having awoke, and sealed himself over all the body, rose up at dawn, and proceeded into the church; and having bent his knees, prayed earnestly. Then the bishop having come, and the clergy, they stood in common in prayer, glorifying God. And after they had ended the prayer, the bishop Plato said: Peace to thee, Matthew, apostle of Christ! And the blessed Matthew said to him: Peace to you! And when they had sat down, the apostle said to the bishop Plato, and to all the clergy: I wish you, children, to know, Jesus having declared it to me, that the king of this city is going to send soldiers against me, the devil having entered into him, and manifestly armed him against us. But let us give ourselves up to Jesus, and He will deliver us from every trial, and all who have believed in Him.

And the king, plotting against the blessed Matthew how he should lay hands on him, and seeing also that the believers were very many, was very much at fault, and was in great difficulty. Therefore the wicked and unclean devil who had come forth from the king's wife, and his son, and his daughter-in-law, put to flight by Matthew, having transformed himself into the likeness of a soldier, stood before the king, and said to him: O king, why art thou thus put to the worse by this stranger and sorcerer? Knowest thou not that he was a publican, but now he has been called an apostle [2] by Jesus, who was crucified by the Jews? For, behold, thy wife, and thy son, and thy daughter-in-law, instructed by him, have believed in him, and along with him sing in the church. And now, behold, Matthew is going forth, and Plato with him, and they are going to the gate called Heavy; but make haste, and thou wilt find them, and thou shalt do to him all that may be pleasing in thine eyes.

The king having heard this, and being the more exasperated by the pretended soldier, sent against the blessed Matthew four soldiers, having threatened them, and said: Unless you bring Matthew to me, I shall burn you alive with fire; and the punishment which he is to undergo, you shall endure. And the soldiers, having been thus threatened by the king, go in arms to where the Apostle Matthew and the bishop Plato are. And when they came near them, they heard their speaking indeed, but saw no one. And having come, they said to the king: We pray thee, O king, we went and found no one, but only heard the voices of persons talking. And the king, being enraged, and having blazed up like fire, gave orders to send other ten soldiers — man-eaters — saying to them: Go stealthily to the place, and tear them in pieces alive, and eat up Matthew, and Plato, who is with him. And when they were about to come near the blessed Matthew, the Lord Jesus Christ, having come in the likeness of a most beautiful boy, holding a torch of fire, ran to meet them, burning out their eyes. And they, having cried out and thrown their arms from them, fled, and came to the king, being speechless.

And the demon who had before appeared to the king in the form of a soldier, being again transformed into the form of a soldier, stood before the king, and said to him: Thou seest, O king, this stranger has bewitched them all. Learn, then, how thou shalt take him. The king says to him: Tell me first wherein his strength is, that I may know, and then I will draw up against him with a great force. And the demon, compelled by an angel, says to the king: Since thou wishest to hear accurately about him, O king, I will tell thee all the truth. Really, unless he shall be willing to be taken by thee of his own accord, thou labourest in vain, and thou wilt not be able to hurt him; but if thou wishest to lay hands on him, thou wilt be struck by him with blindness, and thou wilt be paralyzed. And if thou send a multitude of soldiers against him, they also will be struck with blindness, and will be paralyzed. And we shall go, even seven unclean demons, and immediately make away with thee and thy whole camp, and destroy all the city with lightning, except those naming that awful and holy name of Christ; for wherever a footstep of theirs has come, thence, pursued, we flee. And even if thou shalt apply fire to him, to him the fire will be dew; and if thou shalt shut him up in a furnace, to him the furnace will be a church; and if thou shalt put him in chains in prison, and seal up the doors, the doors will open to him of their own accord, and all who believe in that name will go in, even they, and say, This prison is a church of the living God, and a holy habitation of those that live alone.[3] Behold, O king, I have told thee all the truth. The king therefore says to the pretended soldier: Since I do not know Matthew, come with me, and point him out to me from a distance, and take from me gold, as much as thou mayst wish, or go thyself, and with thy sword kill him, and Plato his associate.[4] The demon says to him: I cannot kill him. I dare

---

[1] Comp. Acts xviii. 9, xxiii. 11.
[2] Or, as an apostle.

[3] i.e., monks.
[4] Lit., of the same form with him.

not even look into his face, seeing that he has destroyed all our generation through the name of Christ, proclaimed through him.

The king says to him : And who art thou? And he says : I am the demon who dwelt in thy wife, and in thy son, and in thy daughter-in-law ; and my name is Asmodæus ; and this Matthew drove me out of them. And now, behold, thy wife, and thy son, and thy daughter-in-law sing along with him in the church. And I know, O king, that thou also after this wilt believe in him. The king says to him : Whoever thou art, spirit of many shapes, I adjure thee by the God whom he whom thou callest Matthew proclaims, depart hence without doing hurt to any one. And straightway the demon, no longer like a soldier, but like smoke, became invisible ; and as he fled he cried out : O secret name, armed against us, I pray thee, Matthew, servant of the holy God, pardon me, and I will no longer remain in this city. Keep thou thine own ; but I go away into the fire everlasting.

Then the king, affected with great fear at the answer of the demon, remained quiet that day. And the night having come, and he not being able to sleep because he was hungry,[1] leaped up at dawn, and went into the church, with only two soldiers without arms, to take Matthew by craft, that he might kill him. And having summoned two friends of Matthew, he said to them : Show to Matthew, says he, that I wish to be his disciple. And Matthew hearing, and knowing the craft of the tyrant, and having been warned also by the vision of the Lord to him, went forth out of the church, led by the hand by Plato, and stood in the gate of the church.

And they say to the king : Behold Matthew in the gate ! And he says : Who he is, or where he is, I see not. And they said to him : Behold, he is in sight of thee. And he says : All the while I see nobody. For he had been blinded by the power of God. And he began to cry out : Woe to me, miserable ! what evil has come upon me, for my eyes have been blinded, and all my limbs paralyzed ? O Asmodæus Beelzebul Satan ! all that thou hast said to me has come upon me. But I pray thee, Matthew, servant of God, forgive me as the herald of the good God ; for assuredly the Jesus proclaimed by thee three days ago through the night appeared to me altogether resplendent as with lightning, like a beautiful young man, and said to me, Since thou art entertaining evil counsels in the wickedness of thine heart in regard to my servant Matthew, know I have disclosed to him that through me there will be the release of his body. And straightway I saw him going up into heaven. If therefore he is thy God, and a true God, and

if he wishes thy body to be buried in our city for a testimony of the salvation of the generations after this, and for the banishing [2] of the demons, I shall know the truth for myself by this, by thee laying on hands upon me, and I shall receive my sight. And the apostle having laid his hands upon his eyes, and saying EPHPHATHA, Jesus,[3] he made him receive his sight instantly.

And straightway the king, laying hold of the apostle, and leading him by the right hand, brought him by craft into the palace ; and Plato was on Matthew's left hand, going along with him, and keeping hold of him.[4] Then Matthew says : O crafty tyrant, how long dost thou not fulfil the works of thy father the devil? And he was enraged at what had been said ; for he perceived that he would inflict upon him a more bitter death. For he resolved to put him to death by fire. And he commanded several executioners to come, and to lead him away to the place by the sea-shore, where the execution of malefactors was wont to take place, saying to the executioners : I hear, says he, that the God whom he proclaims delivers from fire those who believe in him. Having laid him, therefore, on the ground on his back, and stretched him out, pierce his hands and feet with iron nails, and cover him over with paper, having smeared it with dolphins' oil, and cover him up with brimstone and asphalt and pitch, and *put* tow and brushwood above. Thus apply the fire to him ; and if any of the same tribe with him rise up against you, he shall get the same punishment.

And the apostle exhorted the brethren to remain undismayed, and that they should rejoice, and accompany him with great meekness, singing and praising God, because they were deemed worthy to have the relics of the apostle. Having therefore come to the place, the executioners, like most evil wild beasts, pinned down to the ground Matthew's hands and feet with long nails ; and having done everything as they had been bid, applied the fire. And they indeed laboured [5] closely, kindling it all round ; but all the fire was changed into dew, so that the brethren, rejoicing, cried out : The only God is the Christians', who assists Matthew, in whom also we have believed : the only God is the Christians', who preserves His own apostle in the fire. And by the voice the city was shaken. And some of the executioners, having gone forth, said to the king : We indeed, O king, by every contrivance of vengeance, have kindled the fire ; but the sorcerer by a certain name puts it out, calling upon Christ, and invoking his cross ; and the

---

[1] The other [Vienna] MS. has: For he neither ate nor drank, in his concern about these things.

[2] The word thus translated is used by the LXX. in the sense of an asylum, or place of refuge.

[3] Comp. Mark vii 34. The addition of *Jesus* here shows that the writer did not know the meaning of the Aramaic word.

[4] Or, holding him back.

[5] I should be disposed to read ἔκαιον, set fire to, for ἔκαμνον, laboured.

Christians surrounding him play with the fire, and walking *in it* with naked feet, laugh at us,[1] and we have fled ashamed.

Then he ordered a multitude to carry coals of fire from the furnace of the bath in the palace, and the twelve gods of gold and silver; and place them, says he, in a circle round the sorcerer, lest he may even somehow bewitch the fire from the furnace of the palace. And there being many executioners and soldiers, some carried the coals; and others, bearing the gods, brought them. And the king accompanied them, watching lest any of the Christians should steal one of his gods, or bewitch the fire. And when they came near the place where the apostle was nailed down, his face was looking towards heaven, and all his body was covered over with the paper, and much brushwood over his body to the height of ten cubits. And having ordered the soldiers to set the gods in a circle round Matthew, five cubits off, securely fastened that they might not fall, again he ordered the coal to be thrown on, and to kindle the fire at all points.

And Matthew, having looked up to heaven, cried out, ADONAI ELOI SABAOTH MARMARI ·MARMUNTH; that is, O God the Father, O Lord Jesus Christ, deliver me, and burn down their gods which they worship; and let the fire also pursue the king even to his palace, but not to his destruction: for perhaps he will repent and be converted. And when he saw the fire to be monstrous in height, the king, thinking that Matthew was burnt up, laughed aloud, and said: Has thy magic been of any avail to thee, Matthew? Can thy Jesus now give thee any help?

And as he said this a dreadful wonder appeared; for all the fire along with the wood went away from Matthew, and was poured round about their gods, so that nothing of the gold or the silver was any more seen; and the king fled, and said: Woe's me, that my gods are destroyed by· the rebuke of Matthew, of which the weight was a thousand talents of gold and a thousand talents of silver. Better are the gods of stone and of earthenware, in that they are neither melted nor stolen.[2]

And when the fire had thus utterly destroyed their gods, and burnt up many soldiers, there came to pass again another stranger wonder. For the fire, in the likeness of a great and dreadful dragon, chased the tyrant as far as the palace, and ran hither and thither round the king, not letting him go into the palace. And the king, chased by the fire, and not allowed to go into his palace, turned back to where Matthew was, and cried out, saying: I beseech thee, whoever thou art, O man, whether magician or sorcerer

or god, or angel of God, whom so great a pyre has not touched, remove from me this dreadful and fiery dragon; forget the evil I have done, as also when thou madest me receive my sight. And Matthew, having rebuked the fire, and the flames having been extinguished, and the dragon having become invisible, stretching his eyes to heaven, and praying in Hebrew, and commending his spirit to the Lord, said: Peace to you! And having glorified the Lord, he went to his rest about the sixth hour.

Then the king, having ordered more soldiers to come, and the bed to be brought from the palace, which had a great show of gold, he ordered the apostle to be laid on it, and carried to the palace. And the body of the apostle was lying as if in sleep, and his robe and his tunic unstained by the fire; and sometimes they saw him on the bed, and sometimes following, and sometimes going before the bed, and with his right hand put upon Plato's head, and singing along with the multitude, so that both the king and the soldiers, with the crowd, were struck with astonishment. And many diseased persons and demoniacs, having only touched the bed, were made sound; and as many as were savage in appearance, in that same hour were changed into the likeness of other men.

And as the bed was going into the palace, we [3] all saw Matthew rising up, as it were, from the bed, and going into heaven, led by the hand by a beautiful boy; and twelve men in shining garments came to meet him, having never-fading and golden crowns on their head; and we saw how that child crowned Matthew, so as to be like them, and in a flash of lightning they went away to heaven.

And the king stood at the gate of the palace, and ordered that no one should come in but the soldiers carrying the bed. And having shut the doors,[4] he ordered an iron coffin to be made, put the body of Matthew into it, and sealed it up with lead; through the eastern gate of the palace at midnight put it into a boat, no one knowing of it, and threw it into the deep part of the sea.

And through the whole night the brethren remained before the gate of the palace, spending the night, and singing; and when the dawn rose there was a voice: O bishop Plato, carry the Gospel and the Psalter of David; go along with the multitude of the brethren to the east of the palace, and sing the Alleluia, and read the Gospel, and bring as an offering the holy bread; and having pressed three clusters from

---

[1] The other [Vienna] MS. has: at our gods.
[2] The other [Vienna] MS. adds: How my forefathers toiled, and with great trouble made the gods; and now, behold, they have been destroyed by one magician.

[3] The change of person is noticeable.
[4] In the other MS. the king prays: And now, since there is still in me a little unbelief, I beseech thee that thou wilt bring the body of Matthew from the sea. For, behold, I will order the body to be thrown into the depths of the sea; and if thou deliver it as thou didst deliver it in the funeral pile, I will forsake all my gods at once, and believe in thee alone. [The Vienna MS., here cited, interpolates still more. — R.]

the vine into a cup, communicate with me, as the Lord Jesus showed us how to offer up when He rose from the dead on the third day.

And the bishop having run into the church, and taken the Gospel and the Psalter of David, and having assembled the presbyters and the multitude of the brethren, came to the east of the palace at the hour of sunrise; and having ordered the one who was singing to go upon a certain lofty stone, he began to praise in singing of a song to God: Precious in the sight of God is the death of His saints.[1] And again: I laid me down and slept; I arose: because the Lord will sustain me.[2] And they listened to the singing of a song of David: Shall he that is dead not rise again? Now I shall raise him up for myself, saith the Lord. And all shouted out the Alleluia. And the bishop read the Gospel, and all cried out: Glory to Thee, Thou who hast been glorified in heaven and on earth. And so then they offered the gift of the holy offering for Matthew; and having partaken for thanksgiving[3] of the undefiled and life-giving mysteries of Christ, they all glorified God.

And it was about the sixth hour, and Plato sees the sea opposite about seven furlongs off; and, behold, Matthew was standing on the sea, and two men, one on each side, in shining garments, and the beautiful boy in front of them. And all the brethren saw these things, and they heard them saying Amen, Alleluia. And one could see the sea fixed like a stone of crystal, and the beautiful boy in front of them, when out of the depth of the sea a cross came up, and at the end of the cross the coffin going up in which was the body of Matthew; and in the hour of the piercing on the cross,[4] the boy placed the coffin on the ground, behind the palace towards the east, where the bishop had offered the offering for Matthew.

And the king having seen these things from the upper part of the house, and being terror-struck, went forth from the palace, and ran and worshipped towards the east at the coffin, and fell down before the bishop, and the presbyters, and the deacons, in repentance and confession, saying:[5] Truly I believe in the true God, Christ Jesus. I entreat, give me the seal in Christ, and I will give you my palace, in testimony of Matthew, and you shall put the coffin upon my golden bed, in the great dining-room; only, having baptized me in it, communicate to me the Eucharist of Christ. And the bishop having prayed, and ordered him to take off his clothes, and having examined him for a long time, and he having confessed and wept over what he had done, having sealed him, and anointed him with oil, put him down into the sea, in the name of Father, and Son, and Holy Ghost. And when he came up from the water he ordered him to put on himself splendid garments, and so then having given praise and thanks, communicating the holy bread and mixed cup, the bishop first gave them to the king, saying: Let this body of Christ, and this cup, His blood shed for us, be to thee for the remission of sins unto life. And a voice was heard from on high: Amen, amen, amen. And when he had thus communicated in fear and joy, the apostle appeared and said: King Fulvanus, thy name shall no longer be Fulvanus; but thou shalt be called Matthew. And thou, the son of the king, shalt no longer be called Fulvanus, but Matthew also; and thou Ziphagia, the wife of the king, shalt be called Sophia;[6] and Erva, the wife of your son, shall be called Synesis.[7] And these names of yours shall be written in the heavens, and there shall not fail of your loins from generation to generation. And in that same hour Matthew appointed the king a presbyter, and he was thirty-seven years old; and the king's son he appointed deacon, being seventeen years old; and the king's wife he appointed a presbyteress; and his son's wife he appointed a deaconess,[8] and she also was seventeen years old. And then he thus blessed them, saying: The blessing and the grace of our Lord Jesus Christ shall be with you to time everlasting.

Then the king, having awakened out of sleep, and rejoiced with all his house at the vision of the holy Apostle Matthew, praised God.

And the king, having gone into his palace, broke all the idols to pieces, and gave a decree to those in his kingdom, writing thus: King Matthew, to all those under my kingdom, greeting. Christ having appeared upon earth, and having saved the human race, the so-called gods have been found to be deceivers, and soul-destroyers, and plotters against the human race. Whence, divine grace having shone abroad, and come even to us, and we having come to the knowledge of the deception of the idols, that it is vain and false, it has seemed good to our divinity that there should not be many gods, but

---

[1] Ps cxvi. 15.
[2] Ps. iii. 5 according to the LXX.
[3] Or, of the Eucharist.
[4] The meaning is not clear. The other MS. has: After one hour he sees in that place an image of a cross coming up from the depth of the sea. [The Vienna MS. varies more than this extract indicates. — R.]
[5] The other [Vienna] MS. is much fuller here: And the cry of the multitude came to the king. And he asked: What is the uproar and shouting among the people? And he learned that Matthew's coffin had come of itself. Then, filled with great joy, the king straightway goes to the coffin, crying out, and saying with a loud voice: The God of Matthew is the only God, and there is none other but Him. And he fell on his face near the coffin, saying: Pardon me, Lord Jesus Christ, for what I have done against this holy man, for I was in ignorance. And the bishop, seeing the repentance and tears of the king, gave him a hand, and raised him from the ground, and said to him: Rise up, and be of good courage; for the Lord God hath accepted thy repentance and conversion through the good offices of His servant and apostle Thomas. And the king rose up from the ground, and fell at the bishop's feet, etc. — as in the text.

[6] Wisdom.
[7] Understanding.
[8] The other [Vienna] MS. has: And likewise his wife and his daughter-in-law deaconesses.

one, and one only, the God in the heavens. And you, having received this our decree, keep to the purport of it, and break to pieces and destroy every idol; and if any one shall be detected from this time forth serving idols, or concealing them, let such an one be subjected to punishment by the sword. Farewell all, because we also are well.

And when this order was given out, all, rejoicing and exulting, broke their idols to pieces, crying out and saying : There is one only God, He who is in the heavens, who does good to men.

And after all these things had come to pass, Matthew the apostle of Christ appeared to the bishop Plato, and said to him : Plato, servant of God, and our brother, be it known unto thee, that after three years shall be thy rest in the Lord, and exultation to ages of ages. And the king himself, whom after my own name I have called Matthew, shall receive the throne of thy bishopric, and after him his son. And he, having said Peace to thee and all the saints, went to heaven.

And after three years the bishop Plato rested in the Lord. And King Matthew succeeded him, having given up his kingdom willingly to another, whence there was given him grace against unclean demons, and he cured every affliction. And he advanced his son to be a presbyter, and made him second to himself.

And Saint Matthew finished his course in the country of the man-eaters, in the city of Myrna, on the sixteenth of the month of November, our Lord Jesus Christ reigning, to whom be glory and strength, now and ever, and to ages of ages. Amen.[1]

---

[1] The other [Paris] MS. ends differently: And there came a voice, Peace to you, and joy, for there shall not be war nor stroke of sword in this city, because of Matthew, mine elect, whom I have loved for ever. Blessed are they who observe his memory, for they shall be glorified to ages of ages.

And the day of his commemoration shall be the fourteenth of the month of Gorpiæus.[2] Glory, honour, and worship to God, and to the Son, and to the Holy Spirit, now and ever, and to the ages. [The Paris MS. is usually followed by Tischendorf. But in the three concluding paragraphs, as given in the text above, he follows the Vienna MS. — R.]

[2] Gorpiæus was the eleventh month of the Macedonian year, and fell partly in August and partly in September.

ACTS OF THE HOLY APOSTLE THOMAS

At that time we the apostles were all in Jerusalem — Simon called Peter, and Andrew his brother; James the son of Zebedee, and John his brother; Philip and Bartholomew; Thomas, and Matthew the tax-gatherer; James of Alphæus and Simon the Cananæan; and Judas of James;[1] — and we portioned out the regions of the world, in order that each one of us might go into the region that fell to him, and to the nation to which the Lord sent him. By lot, then, India fell to Judas Thomas,[2] also called Didymus. And he did not wish to go, saying that he was not able to go on account of the weakness of the flesh; and how can I, being an Hebrew man, go among the Indians to proclaim the truth? And while he was thus reasoning and speaking, the Saviour appeared to him through the night, and said to him: Fear not, Thomas; go away to India, and proclaim the word; for my grace shall be with thee. But he did not obey, saying: Wherever Thou wishest to send me, send me elsewhere; for to the Indians I am not going.

And as he was thus speaking and growing angry, there happened to be there a certain merchant come from India, by name Abbanes, sent from the king Gundaphoros, and having received an order from him to buy a carpenter and bring him to him. And the Lord, having seen him walking about in the market at noon, said to him: Dost thou wish to buy a carpenter? And he said to Him: Yes. And the Lord said to him: I have a slave a carpenter, and I wish to sell him. And having said this, He showed him Thomas at a distance, and agreed with him for three pounds of uncoined silver; and He wrote a bill of sale, saying: I Jesus, the son of Joseph the carpenter, declare that I have sold my slave, Judas by name, to thee Abbanes, a merchant of Gundaphoros, the king of the Indians. And the purchase[3] being completed, the Saviour taking Judas, who also is Thomas, led him to Abbanes the merchant; and Abbanes seeing him, said to him: Is this thy master? And the apostle answered and said: Yes, He is my Lord.

And he says: I have bought thee from him. And the apostle held his peace.

And at dawn of the following day, the apostle having prayed and entreated the Lord, said: I go wherever Thou wishest, O Lord Jesus; Thy will be done. And he went to Abbanes the merchant, carrying nothing at all with him, but only his price. For the Lord had given it to him, saying: Let thy worth also be with thee along with my grace, wherever thou mayst go. And the apostle came up with Abbanes, who was carrying his effects into the boat. He began therefore also to carry them along with him. And when they had gone on board and sat down, Abbanes questioned the apostle, saying: What kind of work dost thou know? And he said: In wood, ploughs, and yokes, and balances,[4] and boats, and boats' oars, and masts, and blocks; in stone, slabs,[5] and temples, and royal palaces. And Abbanes the merchant said to him: Of such a workman, to be sure, we have need. They began, therefore, to sail away. And they had a fair wind, and they sailed fast until they came to Andrapolis, a royal city.

And having gone out of the boat, they went into the city. And, behold, the voices of flute-players, and of water-organs, and trumpets, sounding round them; and the apostle inquired, saying: What festival is this in this city? And those who were there said to him: The gods have brought thee also, that thou mayst be feasted in this city. For the king has an only-begotten daughter, and he is now giving her to a husband in marriage: this festival, then, which thou seest to-day, is the rejoicing and public assembly for the marriage. And the king has sent forth heralds to proclaim everywhere that all are to come to the marriage, rich and poor, bond and free, strangers and citizens. And if any one shall refuse and not come to the marriage, he will be answerable to the king.[6] And Abbanes having heard, said to the apostle: Let us also go, then, that we may not offend the king, and especially as we are strangers. And he said: Let us go. And having turned into the inn, and

---

[1] This list is a transcript of Matt. x. 2–4, except in the last name.
[2] This double name is in accordance with a tradition preserved by Eusebius (*H. E.*, i. 13), that the true name of Thomas was Judas.
[3] Or, bill of sale.

[4] Or, scales.
[5] i.e., monuments.
[6] Comp. Matt. xxii. 3–14.

rested a little, they went to the marriage. And the apostle seeing them all reclining, reclined he also in the midst. And they all looked at him as a stranger, and coming from a foreign land. And Abbanes the merchant, as being a lord, reclined in another place.

And when they had dined and drunk, the apostle tasted nothing. Those, then, about him said to him: Why hast thou come hither, neither eating nor drinking? And he answered and said to them: For something greater than food or even drink have I come hither, even that I might accomplish the will of the King. For the heralds proclaim the wishes of the King, and whoever will not hear the heralds will be liable to the judgment of the King. When, therefore, they had dined and drunk, and crowns and perfumes had been brought, each took perfume, and one anointed his face, another his cheek,[1] and one one part of his body, and another another. And the apostle anointed the crown of his head, and put a little of the ointment in his nostrils, and dropped it also into his ears, and applied it also to his teeth, and carefully anointed the parts round about his heart; and having taken the crown that was brought to him wreathed of myrtle and other flowers, he put it on his head, and took a branch of reed in his hand, and held it.

And the flute-girl, holding the flutes in her hand, went round them all; and when she came to the place where the apostle was, she stood over him, playing the flute over his head a long time. And that flute-girl was Hebrew by race.

And as the apostle looked away to the ground, a certain one of the wine-pourers[2] stretched forth his hand and struck him. And the apostle, having raised his eyes, and regarded him who had struck him, said: My God will forgive thee this wrong in the world to come, but in this world He will show His wonders, and I shall soon see that hand that struck me dragged along by a dog. And having thus spoken, he began to sing and to repeat this song: —

Maiden, daughter of the light, in whom there exists and abides the majestic splendour of kings; and delightsome is the sight of her, resplendent with brilliant beauty. Her garments are like spring flowers, and the odour of a sweet smell is given forth from them; and on the crown of her head the king is seated, feeding with his own ambrosia those who are seated beside him; and truth rests upon her head, and she shows forth joy with her feet; and becomingly does she open her mouth; thirty-and-two are they who sing her praises, and their tongue

is like a curtain of the door which is drawn for them who go in; and her neck is made in the likeness of the stairs which the first Creator created; and her two hands signify and represent the choral dance of the blessed ages, proclaiming it; and her fingers represent the gates of the city. Her chamber lighted up breathes forth scent from balsam and every perfume, and gives forth a sweet odour of myrrh and savoury herbs; and within are strewn myrtles and sweet-smelling flowers of all kinds; and the bridal chambers are adorned with calamus.[3] And her groomsmen, of whom the number is seven, whom she has chosen for herself, surround her like a wall; and her bridesmaids are seven, who dance before her; and twelve are they in number who minister before her and are at her bidding, having their gaze and their sight upon the bridegroom, that through the sight of him they may be enlightened. And they shall be with him to everlasting in that everlasting joy, and they shall sit down in that wedding to which the great ones are gathered together, and they shall abide in the festivities of which the eternals are deemed worthy; and they shall be arrayed in royal raiment, and shall put on shining robes; and in joy and exultation both of them shall be, and they shall glorify the Father of the universe, whose majestic light they have received, and they have been enlightened by the sight of Him their Lord, whose ambrosial food they have received, of which there is no failing at all; and they have drunk also of the wine which brings to them no thirst, neither desire of the flesh; and they have with the living spirit glorified and praised the father of truth and the mother of wisdom.

And when he had sung and finished this song, all who were there present looked upon him and kept silence, and they also saw his form changed; and what had been said by him they did not understand, since he was a Hebrew, and what had been said by him had been said in Hebrew. But the flute-girl alone heard all, for she was Hebrew by race, and standing off from him she played the flute to the others; but at him she mostly turned her eyes and looked, for she altogether loved him as a man of the same nation with herself, and he was also beautiful in appearance above all who were there. And when the flute-girl had come to the end of all her flute-playing, she sat down opposite him, and looked and gazed upon him. But he looked at no one at all, neither did he regard any one, but only kept his eyes on the ground, waiting until he should depart thence. And that wine-pourer that struck him came down to the fountain to draw water; and there happened to be a lion

---

[1] Or, chin.
[2] Or, cup-bearers.

[3] Ex. xxx. 23; Cant. iv. 14; Ezek. xxvii. 19.

there, and it came forth and killed him, and left him lying in the place, after tearing up his limbs; and dogs immediately seized his limbs, among which also one black dog, laying hold of his right hand in his mouth, brought it to the place of the banquet.

And all seeing were terror-struck, inquiring which of them had been taken off. And when it was clear that it was the hand of the wine-pourer who had struck the apostle, the flute-girl broke her flutes in pieces, and threw them away, and went and sat down at the feet of the apostle, saying: This man is either God or God's apostle; for I heard him saying in Hebrew to the wine-pourer, I shall soon see the hand that struck me dragged about by dogs, which also you have now seen; for as he said, so also it has come to pass. And some believed her, and some not. And the king, having heard, came up and said to him: Rise up, and go with me, and pray for my daughter; for she is my only child, and to-day I give her away. And the apostle would not go with him; for his Lord had not at all been revealed to him there. And the king took him away against his will to the bridal-chamber, that he might pray for them.

And the apostle stood, and began to pray and speak thus: My Lord and my God, who accompanies His servants on their way, guiding and directing those who trust in Him, the refuge and the repose of the afflicted, the hope of the mourners, and the deliverer of the captives, the physician of the souls that are lying under disease, and Saviour of every creature, who gives life to the world, and invigorates our souls! Thou knowest what will come to pass, who also for our sakes makest these things perfect: Thou, Lord, who revealest hidden mysteries, and declarest unspeakable words; Thou, Lord, the planter of the good tree, also through the tree makest words to spring up; Thou, Lord, who art in all, and camest through all, and existest in all Thy works, and makest Thyself manifest through the working of them all; Jesus Christ, the Son of compassion, and perfect Saviour; Christ, Son of the living God, the undaunted Power which has overthrown the enemy; and the voice heard by the rulers,[1] which shook all their powers; the ambassador who was sent to them from on high, and who wentest down even to Hades; who also, having opened the doors, didst bring out thence those that had been shut in for many ages by the controller of the world, and didst show them the way up that leads up on high: I beseech Thee, Lord Jesus Christ, I offer Thee supplication for these young persons, that Thou mayst make what happens and befalls them to be for their good. And having laid his hands on them,

and said, The Lord will be with you, he left them in the place, and went away.[2]

And the king requested the groomsmen to go out of the bridal-chamber; and all having gone forth, and the doors having been shut, the bridegroom raised the curtain of the bridal-chamber, that he might bring the bride to himself. And he saw the Lord Jesus talking with the bride, and having the appearance of Judas Thomas, who shortly before had blessed them, and gone out from them; and he says to him: Didst thou not go out before them all? And how art thou found here? And the Lord said to him: I am not Judas, who also is Thomas; I am his brother. And the Lord sat down on the bed, and ordered them also to sit down on the seats;[3] and He began to say to them:—

Keep in mind, my children, what my brother said to you, and to whom he commended you; and this know, that if you refrain from this filthy intercourse, you become temples holy *and* pure, being released from afflictions and troubles, known and unknown, and you will not be involved in the cares of life, and of children, whose end is destruction; but if you get many children, for their sakes you become grasping and avaricious, plundering orphans, coveting the property of widows, and by doing this you subject yourselves to most grievous punishments. For many children become unprofitable, being harassed by demons, some openly and others secretly: for they become either lunatics, or half-withered, or lame, or deaf, or dumb, or paralytics, or idiots; and even if they be in good health, they will be again good-for-nothing, doing unprofitable and abominable works: for they will be detected either in adultery, or in murder, or in theft, or in fornication, and by all these you will be afflicted. But if you will be persuaded, and preserve your souls pure to God, there will be born to you living children, whom these hurtful things do not touch; and you will be without care, spending an untroubled life, free from grief and care, looking forward to receive that marriage incorruptible and true; and you will be in it companions of the bridegroom, going in along with Him into that bridal-chamber full of immortality and light.[4]

And when the young people heard this, they believed the Lord, and gave themselves over into His keeping, and refrained from filthy lust, and remained thus spending the night in the place. And the Lord went out from before them, having spoken thus to them: The grace of the Lord shall be with you. And the dawn having come on, the king arrived, and having

[1] Comp. Ps. xxiv. 7, according to the LXX.

[2] Three of the five MSS. either omit the prayer altogether, or give it very briefly.
[3] Or, couches.
[4] The text of this exhortation also varies much in the four MSS. which give it.

supplied the table, brought it in before the bridegroom and the bride; and he found them sitting opposite each other, and he found the face of the bride uncovered, and the bridegroom was quite cheerful. And the mother having come to the bride, said: Wherefore dost thou sit thus, child, and art not ashamed, but thus as if thou hadst for a long time lived with thine own husband? And her father said: Is it because of thy great love to thy husband that thou art uncovered?

And the bride answered and said: Truly, father, I am in great love, and I pray to my Lord to continue to me the love which I have experienced this night, and I shall beg for myself this husband whom I have experienced to-day. For this reason, then, I am no longer covered, since the mirror [1] of shame has been taken away from me, and I am no longer ashamed nor abashed, since the work of shame and bashfulness has been removed far from me; and because I am not under any violent emotion, since violent emotion does not abide in me; and because I am in cheerfulness and joy, since the day of joy has not been disturbed; and because I hold of no account this husband, and these nuptials that have passed away from before mine eyes, since I have been joined in a different marriage; and because I have had no intercourse with a temporary husband, whose end is with lewdness and bitterness of soul, since I have been united to a true Husband.

And when the bride is saying yet more, the bridegroom answers and says: I thank Thee, Lord, who hast been proclaimed by the stranger and found by us; [2] who hast put corruption far from me, and hast sown life in me; who hast delivered me from this disease, hard to heal, and hard to cure, and abiding for ever, and established in me sound health; who hast shown Thyself to me, and hast revealed to me all that concerns me, in which I am; who hast redeemed me from falling, and hast led me to something better, and who hast released me from things temporary, and hast deemed me worthy of things immortal and ever existing; who hast

brought Thyself down even to me and to my littleness, in order that, having placed me beside Thy greatness, Thou mightest unite me to Thyself; who hast not withheld Thine own compassion from me lost, but hast shown me how to search myself, and to know what [3] I was and what [3] and how I am now, in order that I may again become as I was; whom I indeed did not know, but Thou Thyself whom I knew not hast sought me out and taken me to Thyself; whom I have experienced, and am not now able to forget, whose love is fervent in me; and speak indeed as I ought I cannot. But what I have time to say about Him is short, and altogether little, and not in proportion to His glory; but He does not find fault with me for not being ashamed to say to Him even what I do not know; because it is through the love of Him that I say even this.

And the king, having heard these things from the bridegroom and the bride, rent his garments, and said to those standing near him: Go out quickly, and go round the whole city, and seize and bring me that man, the sorcerer, who has come for evil into this city: for I led him with my own hands into my house, and I told him to pray for my most unfortunate daughter; and whoever shall find him and bring him to me, whatever service he shall ask of me, I give him. They went away, therefore, and went round seeking him, and found him not; for he had sailed. They went, therefore, also into the inn where he had stayed, and found there the flute-girl weeping and in distress, because he had not taken her with him. And they having recounted what had happened in the case of the young people, she was altogether glad when she heard it, and dismissed her grief, and said: Now have I found, even I, repose here. And she arose and went to them, and was with them a long time, until they had instructed the king also. And many also of the brethren were gathered together there, until they heard word of the apostle, that he had gone down to the cities of India, and was teaching there. And they went away, and joined him.

---

[1] Or, look.
[2] Or, in us.

[3] Or, who.

ACTS OF THE HOLY APOSTLE THOMAS,
WHEN HE CAME INTO INDIA, AND BUILT THE PALACE IN THE HEAVENS.

AND when the apostle came into the cities of India, with Abbanes the merchant, Abbanes went away to salute Gundaphoros the king, and reported to him about the carpenter whom he had brought with him; and the king was glad, and ordered him to come in to himself. And when he had come in, the king said to him: What trade knowest thou? The apostle says to him: The carpenter's and housebuilder's. The king says to him: What work in wood knowest thou, then, and what in stone? The apostle says: In wood, ploughs, yokes, balances, pulleys, and boats, and oars, and masts; and in stone, monuments, temples, royal palaces. And the king said: Wilt thou build me a palace? And he answered: Yes, I shall build it, and finish it; for because of this I came, to build houses, and to do carpenter's work.

And the king having taken him, went forth out of the gates of the city, and began to talk with him on the way about the building of the palace, and about the foundations, how they should be laid, until they came to that place in which he wished the building to be. And he said: Here I wish the building to be. And the apostle says: Yes; for assuredly this place is convenient for the building. For the place was well wooded, and there was much water there. The king therefore says: Begin to build. And he said: I cannot begin to build at this time.

And the king says: When wilt thou be able? And he says: I shall begin in Dius and end in Xanthicus.[1] And the king wondering, said: Every building is built in summer; but canst thou build and make a palace in winter itself? And the apostle said: Thus it must be, and otherwise it is impossible. And the king said: If, therefore, this be thy opinion, mark out for me how the work is to be, since I shall come here after some time. And the apostle, having taken a reed, measured the place, and marked it out; and he set the doors towards the rising of the sun, to look to the light, and the windows towards its setting, to the winds; and he made the bakehouse to be towards the south, and the water-tank, for abundance, towards the north. And the king seeing this, said to the apostle: Thou art a craftsman indeed, and it is fitting that thou shouldst serve kings. And having left many things for him, he went away.

And from time to time he also sent the money that was necessary, for the living both of him and the other workmen. And he taking it, dispenses it all, going about the cities and the places round, distributing and doing kindnesses to the poor and the afflicted, and gave them rest,[2] saying: The king knows how to obtain royal recompense, and it is necessary for the poor to have repose for the present.

And after this, the king sent a messenger to the apostle, having written to him as follows: Show me what thou hast done, or what I am to send thee, or what thou needest. The apostle sends to him, saying: The palace is built, and only the roof remains to be done. And the king, having heard, sent him again gold and silver uncoined, and wrote to him: Let the palace, if it be done, be roofed. And the apostle said to the Lord: I thank Thee, Lord, as to all things, that Thou didst die for a short time, that I might live in Thee for ever; and hast sold me, so that Thou mayst deliver many through me. And he did not cease to teach and refresh the afflicted, saying: These things the Lord hath dispensed to us, and He gives to each his food; for He is the support of the orphans, and the provider of the widows, and to all that are afflicted He is rest and repose.

And when the king came into the city, he inquired of his friends about the palace which Judas, who also is Thomas, had built; and they said to him: He has neither built a palace, nor done anything else of what he promised to do; but he goes round the cities and the districts, and if he has anything he gives all to the poor, and teaches one new God,[3] and heals the diseased, and drives out demons, and does many other extraordinary things; and we think that he is a magician. But his acts of compassion, and the cures done by him as a free gift, and still more, his single-mindedness, and gentleness, and fidelity, show that he is a just man, or an apostle of the new God whom he preaches; for he continually fasts and prays, and eats only bread with salt, and his drink is water, and he carries one coat, whether in warm weather or in cold, and he takes nothing from any one, but gives to others even what he has. The king having heard this, stroked his face with his hands, shaking his head for a long time.

And he sent for the merchant that had brought him, and for the apostle, and said to him: Hast thou built me the palace? And he said: Yes, I have built it. And the king said: When, then, are we to go and see it? And he answered and said: Now thou canst not see it; but when thou hast departed this life, thou shalt see it. And the king, quite enraged, ordered both the merchant, and Judas who also is Thomas, to be put in chains, and to be cast into prison, until he should examine, and learn to whom he had given the king's property. And thus I shall destroy him along with the merchant. And the apostle went to prison rejoicing, and said to the merchant: Fear nothing at all, but only believe in the God proclaimed by me, and thou shalt be freed from this world, and thou shalt obtain life in the world to come.

And the king considered by what death he should kill them; and when it seemed good to him to flay them, and burn them with fire, on that very night Gad the king's brother fell ill,

---

[1] Dius was the first, and Xanthicus the sixth, of the twelve lunar months of the Macedonian calendar, which after the time of Alexander was adopted by the Greek cities of Asia generally. Dius fell partly in October and partly in November; Xanthicus answered generally to April. — *Smith's Dict. of Antiq., s. v. Mensis.*

Another reading is: I shall begin in Hyperberetæus — the twelfth month.

[2] Or, remission.

[3] One of the MSS. has: that there is one God, namely Jesus.

and through the grief and imposition which the king suffered he was grievously depressed ; and having sent for the king, he said to him : My brother the king, I commend to thee my house and my children ; for I, on account of the insult that has befallen thee, have been grieved, and am dying ; and if thou do not come down with vengeance upon the head of that magician, thou wilt give my soul no rest in Hades. And the king said to his brother : During the whole night I have considered this, how I shall put him to death ; and this has seemed good to me — to flay him and burn him up with fire, both him and with him the merchant that brought him.

And as they were talking together, the soul of Gad his brother departed. And the king mourned for Gad exceedingly, for he altogether loved him. And he ordered him to be prepared for burial in a royal and costly robe. And as this was being done, angels received the soul of Gad the king's brother, and took it up into heaven, showing him the places and dwellings there, asking him : In what sort of a place dost thou wish to dwell ? And when they came near the edifice of Thomas the apostle, which he had built for the king, Gad, seeing it, said to the angels, I entreat you, my lords, permit me to dwell in one of the underground chambers of this palace. And they said to him : Thou canst not dwell in this building.[1] And he said : Wherefore ? They say to him : This palace is the one which that Christian built for thy brother. And he said : I entreat you, my lords, permit me to go to my brother, that I may buy this palace from him ; for my brother does not know what it is like, and he will sell it to me.

Then the angels let the soul of Gad go. And as they were putting on him the burial robe, his soul came into him. And he said to those standing round him : Call my brother to me, that I may beg of him one request. Straightway, therefore, they sent the good news to their king, saying : Thy brother has come alive again. And the king started up, and along with a great multitude went to his brother, and went in and stood beside his bed as if thunderstruck, not being able to speak to him. And his brother said : I know and am persuaded, brother, that if any one asked of thee the half of thy kingdom, thou wouldst give it for my sake ; wherefore I entreat thee to grant me one favour, which I beg of thee to do me. And the king answered and said : And what is it that thou askest me to do for thee ? And he said : Assure me by an oath that thou wilt grant it me. And the king swore to him : Of what belongs to me, whatever thou shalt ask,

I will give thee. And he says to him : Sell me that palace which thou hast in the heavens. And the king said : Whence does a palace in the heavens belong to me ? And he said : That which the Christian who is now in the prison, whom the merchant bought from a certain Jesus, and brought to thee, built for thee. And as he was at a loss, he says to him again : I speak of that Hebrew slave whom thou didst wish to punish, as having suffered some imposition from him, on account of whom I also was grieved and died, and now have come alive again.

Then the king, having come to know, understood about the eternal benefits that were conferred upon him and destined for him, and said : That palace I cannot sell thee, but I pray thee to go into it, and dwell *there*, and become worthy to be of its inhabitants ; but if thou really wishest to buy such a palace, behold, the man is alive, and will build thee a better than that.[2] And having sent immediately, he brought out of the prison the apostle, and the merchant who had been shut up along with him, saying : I entreat thee, as a man entreating the servant of God, that thou wilt pray for me, and entreat him whose servant thou art, to pardon me, and overlook what I have done to thee, or even what I meant to do, and that I may be worthy to be an inhabitant of that house for which indeed I have laboured nothing, but which thou labouring alone hast built for me, the grace of thy God working with thee ; and that I may become a servant, I also, and slave of this God whom thou proclaimest. And his brother, falling down before the apostle, said : I entreat thee, and supplicate before thy God, that I may become worthy of this ministry and service, and may be allotted to become worthy of those things which were shown me by his angels.

And the apostle, seized with joy, said : I make full confession[3] to Thee, Lord Jesus, that Thou hast revealed Thy truth in these men : for Thou alone art a God of truth, and not another ; and Thou art He who knowest all things that are unknown to many : Thou art He, Lord, who in all things showest compassion and mercy to men ; for men, through the error that is in them, have overlooked Thee, but Thou hast not overlooked them. And now, when I am entreating and supplicating Thee, accept the king and his brother, and unite them into Thy fold, having

---

[1] One MS. has : But if thou buy it, thou shalt live in it. And he said to them : Can I buy it ? And they said to him : See that thou obtain one like this which thou seest, or better if thou wilt, that when thou comest hither again, thou mayst not be driven into the darkness.

[2] One of the MSS. here ends the history in these words : — And he sent, and brought out Thomas, and said to him : Pardon us if we have in ignorance been in any way harsh to thee ; and make us to be partakers of him whom thou preachest. And the apostle says : I too rejoice with you, that you are made partakers of His kingdom. And he took and enlightened them, having given them the washing of grace in the name of Father, and Son, and Holy Spirit, to whom is due all glory and kingdom without end. And when they had gone up straightway out of the water, the Saviour appeared to them, so that the apostle wondered, and a great light shone brighter than the rays of the sun. And having confirmed their faith, he went out, going on his way in the Lord.

[3] i.e., give thanks, as in Matt. xi. 25, Luke x. 21, etc.

cleansed them by Thy purification, and anointed them with Thy oil, from the error which encompasseth them; and protect them also from the wolves, bringing them into Thy meadows; and give them to drink of Thy ambrosial fountain, that is never muddy and never faileth: for they entreat Thee, and supplicate, and wish to become Thy ministers and servants; and on account of this they are well pleased even to be persecuted by Thine enemies, and for Thy sake to be hated by them, and insulted, and to die; as Thou also for our sakes didst suffer all these things, that Thou mightst gain us to Thyself, as being Lord. and truly a good shepherd. And do Thou grant them that they may have confidence in Thee alone, and aid from Thee, and hope of their salvation, which they obtain from Thee alone, and that they may be confirmed in Thy mysteries; and they shall receive the perfect benefits of Thy graces and gifts, and flourish in Thy service, and bear fruit to perfection in Thy Father.

King Gundaphoros, therefore, and Gad, having been altogether set apart by the apostle, followed him, not at all going back, they also providing for those that begged of them, giving to all, and relieving all. And they entreated him that they might also then receive the seal of baptism; and they said to him: As our souls are at ease, and as we are earnest about God, give us the seal; for we have heard thee saying that the God whom thou proclaimest recognises through his seal his own sheep. And the apostle said to them: And I am glad, and entreat you to receive this seal, and to communicate with me in this thanksgiving [1] and blessing of God, and to be made perfect in it; [2] for this Jesus Christ whom I proclaim is Lord and God of all, and He is the Father of truth, in whom I have taught you to believe. And he ordered to bring them oil, in order that through the oil they might receive the seal. They brought the oil, therefore, and lighted many lamps, for it was night. [3]

And the apostle arose, and sealed them; and the Lord was revealed to them, through a voice saying, Peace to you, brethren! And they heard His voice only, but His form they saw not; for they had not yet received the ratification [4] of the seal. And the apostle, having taken oil, and

poured it over their head, and salved and anointed them, began to say: Come, holy name of Christ, which is above every name; come, power of the Most High, and perfect compassion; come, grace most high; come, compassionate mother; come, thou that hast charge [6] of the male child; come, thou who revealest secret mysteries; come, mother of the seven houses, that there may be rest for thee in the eighth house; come, thou presbyter of the five members — intelligence, thought, purpose, reflection, reasoning — communicate with these young persons; come, Holy Spirit, and purify their reins and heart, and seal them in the name of Father, and Son, and Holy Spirit. And when they had been sealed, there appeared to them a young man holding a burning torch, so that their lamps were even darkened by the approach [6] of its light. And he went out, and disappeared from their sight. And the apostle said to the Lord: Thy light, Lord, is too great for us, and we cannot bear it; for it is too much for our sight. And when light came, and it was dawn, having broken bread, he made them partakers of the thanksgiving [7] of Christ. And they rejoiced and exulted; and many others also believed, and were added, and came to the refuge of the Saviour.

And the apostle ceased not proclaiming, and saying to them: Men and women, boys and girls, young men and maidens, vigorous and aged, both bond and free, withhold yourselves from fornication, and covetousness, and the service of the belly; for under these three heads all wickedness comes. For fornication maims the mind, and darkens the eyes of the soul, and becomes a hindrance of the due regulation of the body, changing the whole man into feebleness, and throwing the whole body into disease. And insatiableness puts the soul into fear and shame, existing by what pertains to the body, [8] and forcibly seizing what belongs to another; . . . and the service of the belly throws the soul into cares and troubles and griefs. . . . Since, therefore, you have been set free from these, you are without care, and without grief, and without fear; and there remains to you that which was said by the Saviour: Take no care for the morrow, for the morrow will take care of itself. [9] Keep in mind also that saying before mentioned: Look upon the ravens, and behold the fowls of the heaven, that they neither sow nor reap, nor gather into barns, and God takes care of them; how much more you, O ye of little faith! [10] But look for His appearing, and have your hopes in Him, and believe in His

---

[1] Or, Eucharist.
[2] i.e., by it.
[3] One MS. for this whole section has: The two brothers having been set apart by the apostle, said to him, Give us the seal in Christ. And he ordered them to bring him oil. And ends the history thus: And he arose. and sealed them in the name of Father, and Son, and Holy Spirit, and baptized them. And the Lord was revealed to them, through a voice saying to them, Peace unto you! And the apostle sealed also all that were with them. And they all believed in our Lord Jesus Christ; and the whole of India became believing.
The last sentence in the text seems to be an interpolation. The oil was not for the lamps, but for the ceremony of baptism. The practice of baptizing with oil instead of water — one of the "notable and execrable" heresies of the Manichæans — is said to have been founded on this passage.
[4] Lit., the sealing up.

[5] Lit., the administration.
[6] Perhaps for προσβολῇ we should read προβολῇ, projection or emanation.
[7] Or, communicants of the Eucharist.
[8] Or, arising from the things of the body.
[9] Comp. Matt. vi. 34.
[10] Luke xii. 24.

name : for He is the Judge of living and dead, and He requites to each one according to his deeds ; and at His coming and appearance at last no one will have as a ground of excuse, when he comes to be judged by Him, that he has not heard. For His heralds are proclaiming in the four quarters of the world. Repent, therefore, and believe the message,[1] and accept the yoke of gentleness and the light burden,[2] that you may live and not die. These things lay hold of, these things keep ; come forth from the darkness, that the light may receive you ; come to Him who is truly good, that from Him you may receive grace, and place His sign upon your souls.

When he had thus said, some of the bystanders said to him : It is time for this debtor to receive his debt. And he said to them : The creditor,[3] indeed, always wishes to receive more ; but let us give him what is proper. And having blessed them, he took bread and oil, and herbs and salt, and gave them to eat. But he continued in his fasting, for the Lord's day was about to dawn. And on the night following, while he was asleep, the Lord came and stood by his head, saying : Thomas, rise up early and bless them all ; and after the prayer and service go along the eastern road two miles, and there I shall show in thee my glory. For because thou goest away, many shall flee to me for refuge, and thou shalt reprove the nature and the power of the enemy. And having risen up from sleep, he said to the brethren who were with him : Children and brethren, the Lord wishes to do something or other to-day through me ; but let us pray and entreat Him that nothing may be a hindrance to us towards Him, but as at all times let it now also be done unto us according to His purpose and will. And having thus spoken, he laid his hands upon them and blessed them. And having broken the bread of the Eucharist, he gave it to them, saying : This Eucharist shall be[4] to you for compassion, and mercy, and recompense, and not for judgment. And they said : Amen.

ABOUT THE DRAGON AND THE YOUNG MAN.

And the apostle went forth to go where the Lord had bidden him. And when he came near the second milestone he turned a little out of the way, and saw the body of a beautiful youth lying ; and he said : Lord, was it for this that Thou broughtest me out to come here, that I might see this trial ? Thy will therefore be done, as Thou purposest. And he began to pray, and to say : Lord, Judge of the living, and of those that are lying dead, and Lord of all, and Father — Father not only of the souls that are in bodies,

but also of those that have gone out of them ; for of the souls that are in pollutions Thou art Lord and Judge — come at this time, when I call upon Thee, and show Thy glory upon him that is lying down here. And he turned and said to those that followed him : This affair has not happened idly ; but the enemy has wrought and effected this, that he might make an assault upon him ; and you see that he has availed himself of no other form, and has wrought through no other living being, but through his subject.

And when the apostle had thus spoken, behold, a great dragon came forth from his den, knocking his head, and brandishing his tail down to the ground, and, using a loud voice, said to the apostle : I shall say before thee for what cause I have put him to death, since thou art here in order to reprove my works. And the apostle says : Yes, say on. And the dragon : There is a certain woman in this place exceedingly beautiful ; and as she was once passing by, I saw her, and fell in love with her, and I followed and watched her ; and I found this young man kissing her, and he also had intercourse with her, and did with her other shameful things. And to me indeed it was pleasant to tell thee this, for I know that thou art the twin-brother of Christ, and always bringest our race to nought. But, not wishing to harass her, I did not at this time put him to death ; but I watched him passing by in the evening, and struck him, and killed him, and especially as he had dared to do this on the Lord's day.[5] And the apostle inquired of him, saying : Tell me, of what seed and of what race art thou?

And he said to him : I am the offspring of the race of the serpent, and hurtful of the hurtful ; I am son of him who hurt and struck the four brothers that stood ; I am son of him who sits on the throne of destruction, and takes his own from what he has lent ;[6] I am son of that apostate who encircles the globe ; I am kinsman to him who is outside of the ocean, whose tail lies in his mouth ; I am he who went into paradise through the hedge, and spoke with Eve what my father bade me speak to her ; I am he who inflamed and fired Cain to kill his brother, and through me thorns and prickles sprang up in the ground ; I am he who cast down the angels from above, and bound them down by the desires of women, that earth-born[7] children might be produced from them, and that I might work my will in them ;[8] I am he who hardened the heart of Pharaoh, that he should murder the children of Israel, and keep them down by the hard yoke of slavery ; I am he who caused the multitude to err in the desert when they made the

---

[1] Or, announcement.
[2] Matt. xi. 30.
[3] Lit., master of the debt.
[4] i.e , be.

[5] In this passage we have one of the data for fixing the date of the writing.
[6] Or, from those to whom he was lent.
[7] And, by implication, gigantic.
[8] Or, by them.

calf; I am he who inflamed Herod and incited Caiaphas to the lying tales of falsehood before Pilate, for this became me; I am he who inflamed Judas, and bought him, that he should betray Christ; I am he who inhabits and holds the abyss of Tartarus, and the Son of God has wronged me against my will, and has gathered his own out of me; I am the kinsman of him who is to come from the east, to whom also power has been given to do whatever he will upon the earth.

And that dragon having thus spoken in the hearing of all the multitude, the apostle raised his voice on high, and said: Cease henceforth, O thou most unabashed, and be ashamed and altogether put to death; for the end of thy destruction is at hand, and do not dare to say what thou hast done through thy dependants. And I order thee, in the name of that Jesus who even until now makes a struggle against you for the sake of His own human beings, to suck out the poison which thou hast put into this man, and to draw it forth, and take it out of him. And the dragon said: The time of our end is by no means at hand, as thou hast said. Why dost thou force me to take out what I have put into him, and to die before the time? Assuredly, when my father shall draw forth and suck out what he has put into the creation, then his end will come. And the apostle said to him: Show us, therefore, now the nature of thy father. And the dragon went up, and put his mouth upon the wound of the young man, and sucked the gall out of it. And in a short time the skin of the young man, which was like purple, grew white, and the dragon swelled. And when the dragon had drawn up all the gall into himself, the young man sprang up and stood, and ran and fell at the apostle's feet. And the dragon, being swelled up, shrieked out and died, and his poison and gall were poured forth; and in the place where his poison was poured forth there was made a great chasm, and that dragon was swallowed up. And the apostle said to the king and his brother: Take workmen, and fill up the place in which the dragon has been swallowed up, and lay foundations, and build houses above it, that it may be made a dwelling-place for the strangers.

And the young man said to the apostle, with many tears: I have sinned against the God proclaimed by thee, and against thee, but I ask pardon of thee; for thou art a man having two forms, and wherever thou wishest there art thou found, and thou art held in by no one, as I see. For I beheld that man, when I stood beside thee, who also said to thee, I have many wonders to show by means of thee, and I have great works to accomplish by means of thee, for which thou shalt obtain a reward; and thou shalt make

many to live, and they shall be in repose and eternal light as the children of God: do thou therefore bring alive — he says, speaking to thee about me — this young man who has been cast down by the enemy, and in all time be the overseer of him. Thou hast, then, well come hither, and again thou shalt well go away to him, he being not at all forsaken by thee. And I am without care and reproach, for the dawn has risen upon me from the care of the night, and I am at rest; and I have also been released from him who exasperated me to do these things: for I have sinned against Him who taught me the contrary, and I have destroyed him who is the kinsman of the night, who forced me to sin by his own practices; and I have found that kinsman of mine who is like the light. I have destroyed him who darkens and blinds those who are subject to him, lest they should know what they are doing, and, ashamed of their works, withdraw themselves from them, and their deeds have an end; and I have found Him whose works are light, and whose deeds are truth, of which whoever does them shall not repent. I have been set free also from him in whom falsehood abides, whom darkness as a covering goes before, and shame conducting herself impudently in idleness follows after. And I have found also Him who shows me what is beautiful, that I should lay hold of it, the Son of the truth, who is kinsman of concord, who, driving away the mist, enlightens His own creation, and heals its wounds, and overturns its enemies. But I entreat thee, O man of God, make me again to behold and see Him, now become hidden from me, that I may also hear His voice, the wonders of which I cannot declare: for it is not of the nature of this bodily organ.

And the apostle said to him: If, as thou hast also said, thou hast cast off the knowledge of those things which thou hast received, and if thou knowest who has wrought these things in thee, and if thou shalt become a disciple and hearer of Him of whom, through thy living love, thou now desirest the sight, thou shalt both see Him, and shalt be with Him for ever, and shalt rest in His rest, and shalt be in His joy. But if thou art rather carelessly disposed towards Him, and again returnest to thy former deeds, and lettest go that beauty and that beaming countenance which has now been displayed to thee, and if the splendour of the light of Him whom thou now desirest be forgotten by thee, thou shalt be deprived not only of this life, but also of that which is to come; and thou shalt go to him whom thou hast said thou hast destroyed, and shalt no longer behold Him whom thou hast said thou hast found.

And when the apostle had thus spoken, he went into the city, holding that young man by the hand, and saying to him : Those things which thou hast beheld, my child, are a few out of the many which God has : for it is not about these things that appear that the good news is brought to us, but greater things than these are promised to us ; but inasmuch as we are in the body, we cannot tell and speak out what He will do for our souls. If we say that He affords us light, it is seen by us, and we have it ; and if riches, they exist and appear in this world, and we name them, since it has been said, With difficulty will a rich man enter into the kingdom of the heavens.[1] And if we speak of fine clothing, which they who delight in this life put on, it has been said, They that wear soft things are in kings' palaces ;[2] and if costly dinners, about these we have received a commandment to keep away from them, not to be burdened by carousing and drunkenness and the cares of life ;[3] as also in the Gospel it has been said, Take no heed for your life, what ye shall eat, or what ye shall drink ; nor for your body, what ye shall put on : because the life is more than food, and the body than clothing.[4] And if we speak of this rest lasting only for a season, its judgment has also been ordained. But we speak about the upper world, about God and angels, about ambrosial food, about garments that last and become not old, about those things which eye hath not seen, nor ear heard, nor hath there come into the heart of sinful men what God has prepared for those that love Him.[5] Do thou also therefore believe in Him, that thou mayst live ; and have confidence in Him, and thou shalt never die. For He is not persuaded by gifts, that thou shouldst offer them to Him ; nor does He want sacrifices, that thou shouldst sacrifice to Him. But look to Him, and thou shalt not look in vain, for His comeliness and desirable beauty will ·make thee love Him ; and neither will He allow thee to turn thyself away from Him.

And when the apostle was thus speaking to that young man, a great multitude joined them. And the apostle looked, and saw them lifting themselves up that they might see him ; and they went up into elevated places. And the apostle said to them : Ye men who have come to the assembly of Christ, and who wish to believe in Jesus, take an example from this, and see that if you do not get high up, you cannot see me, who am small, and cannot get a look of me, who am like yourselves. If, then, you cannot see me, who am like yourselves, unless you raise yourselves a little from the earth, how can you see Him who lives above, and is now found below, unless you first raise yourselves out of

your former behaviour, and unprofitable deeds, and troublesome desires, and the riches that are left behind here, and create things that are of the earth, and that grow old, and the garments that are destroyed, and the beauty that ages and vanishes away, yea, even out of the whole body in which all these have been stored past, and which grows old, and becomes dust, returning into its own nature? for all these things the body itself sets up.[6] But rather believe in our Lord Jesus Christ, whom we proclaim to you, in order that your hope may be upon Him, and that you may have life in Him to ages of ages, that He may be your fellow-traveller in this land, and may release you from error, and may become [7] a haven for you in this troublous sea. And there shall be for you also a fountain welling out in this thirsty land, and a fold full of food in the place of the hungry, and rest for your souls, and also a physician for your bodies.

Then the multitude of those assembled that heard, wept, and said to the apostle : O man of God, as for the God whom thou proclaimest, we dare not say that we are his, because our works which we have done are alien from him, not pleasing to him ; but if he has compassion upon us, and pities us, and delivers us, overlooking our former doings ; and if he set us free from the evil things which we did when we were in error, and shall not take into account nor keep the recollection of our former sins, we shall become his servants, and we shall do his will to the end. And the apostle answered and said to them : He does not reckon against you the sins which you did, being in error ; but He overlooks your transgressions which you have done in ignorance.[8]

ABOUT THE DEMON THAT DWELT IN THE WOMAN.

And the apostle went into the city, all the multitude accompanying him ; and he thought of going to the parents of the young man whom, when killed by the dragon, he had brought to life ; for they earnestly entreated him to come to them, and to enter into their house.

And a certain woman, exceedingly beautiful, suddenly uttered a loud cry, saying : O apostle of the new God, who hast come into India, and servant of that holy and only good God — for through thee he is proclaimed the Saviour of the souls that come unto him, and through thee he heals the bodies of those that are punished by the enemy, and thou hast become the cause of life to all who turn to him — order me to be brought before thee, that I may declare to thee what has happened to me, and that perhaps there may be hope to me from thee, and those

---

[1] Matt. xix. 23.
[2] Matt. xi. 8.
[3] Rom. xiii. 13; Luke xxi. 34.
[4] Matt. vi. 25.
[5] 1 Cor. ii. 9; Isa. lxiv. 4.

[6] Or, establishes.
[7] Or, and that there may be.
[8] Comp. Acts xvii. 30.

who stand beside thee may have more and more hope in the God whom thou proclaimest. For I am not a little tormented by the adversary, who has assailed me for now a period of five years. As a woman, I formerly sat down in peace, and peace encompassed me on all sides; and I had nothing to trouble me, for of nothing else [1] had I a care. And it happened on one of the days as I was coming forth from the bath, there met me one like a man troubled and disturbed; and his voice and utterance seemed to me to be indistinct and very weak. And he said, standing over against me, Thou and I shall be in one love, and we shall have intercourse with each other, as a man is coupled with his wife. And I answered him, saying, To my betrothed I consented not, entreating him not to marry me; and to thee, wishing to have intercourse with me as it were in adultery, how shall I give myself up? And having thus spoken, I went away from him. And to my maid I said, Hast thou seen the young man and his shamelessness, how shamelessly and boldly he talks to me? And she said to me, It was an old man I saw talking with thee. And when I was in my own house, and had supped, my mind suggested to me some suspicion, and especially because he had appeared to me in two forms. I fell asleep, having this same thing in my thoughts. And he came that night, and made me share in his filthy commerce. And I saw him when it was day, and fled from him; but, according to his wont, he came at night and abused me. And now, as thou seest me, I have been tormented by him five years, and he has not departed from me. But I know and am persuaded that even demons, and spirits, and avenging deities, are subject to thee, and tremble at thy prayer. Pray, then, for me, and drive away from me the demon that torments me, that I also may become free, and may be brought to my former nature, and I shall receive the gift [2] that has been granted to my kindred.

And the apostle said: O irrepressible wickedness! O the shamelessness of the enemy! O the sorcerer that is never at rest! O the ill-favoured one, bring to subjection the well-favoured! O the many-formed one! He appears just as he may wish, but his essence cannot be changed. O offspring of the crafty and insatiable one! O bitter tree, which also his fruits are like! O thou who art of the devil, who fights over those who do not belong to him! O thou who art of the deceit that uses shamelessness! O thou who art of the wickedness that creeps like a serpent, and art thyself his kindred! And when the apostle had thus spoken the fiend stood before him, no one seeing him but the woman and the apostle,

and with a very loud voice he said in the hearing of all: What have we to do with thee, O apostle of the Most High? What have we to do with thee, O servant of Jesus Christ? What have we to do with thee, O thou that sittest in council with the Holy Spirit. Wherefore dost thou wish to destroy us, when our time has not yet come? On what account dost thou wish to take away our power? for until the present hour we have had hope and time left us.[3] What have we to do with thee? Thou hast power over thine own, and we over our own. Why dost thou wish to use tyranny against us, and especially thou who teachest others not to use tyranny? Why dost thou want those who do not belong to thee, as if thou wert not satisfied with thine own? Why dost thou liken thyself to the Son of God, who has done us hurt? For thou art like him altogether, just as if thou hadst been brought forth by him. For we thought to bring him also under the yoke, like the rest; but he turned, and held us under his hand. For we did not know him; but he deceived us by the form which he had put on, and his poverty and his want; for when we saw him such, we thought him to be a man clothed with flesh, not knowing that it was he who makes men live. And he gave us power over our own, and, in the time in which we live, not to let our own go, but to employ ourselves about them. But thou wishest to get more than is necessary, or than has been given thee, and to overpower us.

And having thus spoken, the demon wept, saying: I let thee go, my most lovely yoke-fellow,[4] whom I found long ago and was at rest; I leave thee, my beloved and trusty sister, in whom I was well pleased. What I shall do I know not, or whom I shall call upon to hear me and protect me. I know what I shall do. I shall go to some place where the fame of this man has not been heard, and perhaps I shall call thee, my beloved, by a new name.[5] And lifting up his voice, he said: Abide in peace, having received an asylum with a greater than I; but I, as I have said, will go away and seek thy like, and if I find her not I shall again return to thee: for I know that when thou art beside this man, thou hast an asylum in him; but when he has gone away, thou shalt be as thou wast before he made his appearance, and him indeed wilt thou forget, and to me there will again be opportunity and boldness; but now I am afraid of the name of him who has delivered thee. And having thus said, the demon disappeared. And just when he had disappeared, fire and smoke were seen there, and all there present were struck with amazement.

---

[1] Or, no one else.
[2] Or, grace.
[3] Comp. Matt. viii. 29.
[4] Or, wife.
[5] i.e., get another instead of thee, my beloved.

And the apostle seeing this, said to them: Nothing strange or unusual has that demon shown, but his own nature, in which also he shall be burnt up; for the fire shall consume him, and the smoke of him shall be scattered abroad. And he began to say: O Jesus Christ, the secret mystery which has been revealed to us, Thou art He who disclosest to us all manner of mysteries, who hast set me apart from all my companions, and who hast told me three words with which I am set on fire, and I cannot tell them to others; O Jesus, man slain, dead, buried; Jesus, God of God, and Saviour who bringest the dead to life, and healest those who are diseased; O Jesus, who appearest to be in want, and savest as if in want of nothing, catching the fishes for the morning and the evening meal, and establishing all in abundance with a little bread; Jesus, who didst rest from the toil of the journey as a man, and walk upon the waves as God; [1] Jesus Most High, voice arising from perfect compassion, Saviour of all, the right hand of the light overthrowing him that is wicked in his own kind, and bringing all his kind into one place; Thou who art only begotten, the first-born of many brethren, [2] God of God Most High, man despised until now; Jesus Christ, who overlookest us not when we call upon Thee; who hast been shown forth to all in Thy human life; who for our sakes hast been judged and kept in prison, and freest all that are in bonds; who hast been called a deceiver, [3] and who deliverest Thine own from deception: I entreat Thee in behalf of those standing and entreating Thee, and those that believe in Thee; for they pray to obtain Thy gifts, being of good hope in Thine aid, occupying Thy place of refuge in Thy majesty; they give audience, so as to hear from us the words that have been spoken to them. Let Thy peace come and dwell in them, that they may be purified from their former deeds, and may put off the old man with his deeds, and put on the new now declared to them by me. [4]

And having laid his hands on them, he blessed them, saying: The grace of our Lord Jesus Christ be upon you for ever! [5] And they said, Amen. And the woman begged of him, saying: Apostle of the Most High, give me the seal, that that foe may not come back upon me again. Then he made her come near him; and putting his hand upon her, he sealed her in the name of Father, and Son, and Holy Ghost. And many others also were sealed along with her. And the apostle ordered his servant [6] to set out a table; and they set out a bench [7] which they found there. And having spread a linen cloth upon it, he put on it the bread of the blessing. And the apostle standing by it, said: Jesus Christ, Son of God, who hast deemed us worthy to communicate of the Eucharist of Thy sacred body and honourable blood, behold, we are emboldened by the thanksgiving [8] and invocation of Thy sacred name; come now, and communicate with us. And he began to say: Come, perfect compassion; come, communion with mankind; come, Thou that knowest the mysteries of the chosen one; come, Thou that communicatest in all the combats [9] of the noble combatant; come, peace that revealest the great things of all greatness; come, Thou that disclosest secrets, and makest manifest things not to be spoken; the sacred dove which has brought forth twin young; come, thou secret mother; come, Thou who art manifest in Thy deeds, and givest joy and rest to those who are united to Thee; come and communicate with us in this Eucharist, which we make in Thy name, and in the love [10] in which we are united in calling upon Thee. [11] And having thus said, he made the sign of the cross upon the bread, and broke it, and began to distribute it. And first he gave it to the woman, saying: This shall be to thee for remission of sins, and the ransom of everlasting transgressions. And after her, he gave also to all the others who had received the seal.

ABOUT THE YOUNG MAN WHO KILLED THE MAIDEN.

And there was a certain young man who had done a nefarious deed; and having come to the apostle, he took the bread of the Eucharist into his mouth, and his two hands immediately withered, so that he could no longer bring them to his mouth. And those who were present and saw him told the apostle what had happened. And he, having summoned him, said: Tell me, my child, and be ashamed of nothing, [12] what thou hast done, and why thou hast come hither; for the Eucharist of the Lord has convicted thee. For this gracious gift coming to many is especially healing to those who approach it through faith and love; but thee it has withered away, and what has happened has happened not without some working cause. And the young man who had been convicted by the Eucharist of the Lord came up, and fell at the apostle's feet, and prayed him, saying: An evil deed has been done by me, yet I thought to do something good. I was

---

[1] Matt. xiv. 17; John xxi. 11; John iv. 6; Matt. xiv. 25.
[2] Rom. viii. 29.
[3] Matt. xxvii. 63.
[4] Col. iii. 9.
[5] Rom. xvi. 20.
[6] Or, deacon.

[7] συμψέλλιον, which is not Greek, is obviously the Latin subsellium.
[8] Or, Eucharist.
[9] Or, prizes.
[10] Or, love-feast.
[11] Or, in Thy calling.
[12] Or, stand in awe of no one.

in love with a certain woman living outside of the city in an inn, and she loved me. And I having heard from thee, and believed that thou proclaimest the living God, came and received the seal from thee along with the others; and thou saidst, Whoever shall indulge in filthy intercourse, and especially in adultery, shall not have life with the God whom I proclaim.[1] Since, then, I altogether loved her, I begged of her, and persuaded her to live with me in chaste and pure intercourse, as thou thyself teachest; but she would not. When therefore she would not, I took a sword and killed her; for I could not see her living in adultery with another.

The apostle, having heard this, said: O maddening intercourse, into what shamelessness dost thou lead! O unrestrained lust, how hast thou brought him into subjection to do this! O work of the serpent, how dost thou rage in thine own! And the apostle ordered water to be brought him in a dish. And when the water had been brought, he said: Come waters from the living waters, existing from the existing, and sent to us; the fountain sent to us from repose, the power of salvation coming from that power that subdues all things, and subjects them to its own will; come and dwell in these waters, that the gracious gift of the Holy Spirit may be fully perfected in them. And he said to the young man: Go, wash thy hands in these waters. And when he had washed, they were restored. And the apostle said to him: Dost thou believe in our Lord Jesus Christ, that He can do all things? And he said: Even though I am least of all, I believe; but this I did, thinking to do a good thing: for I implored her, as also I told thee; but she would not be persuaded by me to keep herself chaste.

And the apostle said to him: Come, let us go to the inn where thou didst this deed, and let us see what has happened. And the young man went before the apostle on the road; and when they came to the inn, they found her lying. And the apostle, seeing her, was disheartened, for she was a beautiful maiden; and he ordered her to be brought into the middle of the inn. And having put her on a couch, they brought it, and set it in the midst of the court-yard of the inn. And the apostle laid his hand on her, and began to say: Jesus, who always appearest to us — for this Thou always wishest, that we should seek Thee — and Thou Thyself hast given us this power of asking and receiving;[2] and not only hast Thou given us this, but hast also taught us how to pray;[3] who art not seen by bodily eyes, but who art not altogether hidden from those of our soul, and who art hidden in Thy form, but

manifested to us by Thy works; and by Thy many deeds we have recognised Thee as we go on, and Thou hast given us Thy gifts without measure, saying, Ask, and it shall be given you; seek, and ye shall find; knock, and it shall be opened unto you.[4] We pray, therefore, having suspicion of our sins;[5] and we ask of Thee not riches, nor gold, nor silver, nor possessions, nor any of those things that come from the earth and go into the earth again; but this we beg of Thee, and entreat that in Thy holy name Thou raise this woman lying here by Thy power, to the glory and faith of those standing by.

And when he had thus prayed, he sealed the young man, and said to him: Go, and take her by the hand, and say to her, I through my hands killed thee with the sword;[6] and again I raise thee by my hands, in the faith of our Lord Jesus Christ. And the young man went and stood by her, saying: I have believed in Thee, O Christ Jesus. And looking upon Judas Thomas the apostle, he said to him: Pray for me, that my Lord, upon whom also I call, may come to my help. And having laid his hand on her hand, he said: Come, Lord Jesus Christ, giving this woman life, and me the earnest of Thy faith. And immediately, as he drew her hand, she sprang up, and sat, looking at the great multitude standing round. And she also saw the apostle standing opposite to her; and having left the couch, she sprang up, and fell at his feet, and took hold of his garments, saying: I pray thee, my lord, where is that other who is with thee, who has not left me to remain in that fearful and grievous place, but has given me up to thee, saying, Do thou take her, that she may be made perfect, and thereafter brought into her own place?

And the apostle says to her: Tell us where thou hast been. And she answered: Dost thou, who wast with me, to whom also I was entrusted, wish to hear? And she began to say: A certain man received me, hateful in appearance, all black, and his clothing exceedingly filthy; and he led me away to a place where there were many chasms, and a great stench and most hateful odour were given forth thence; and he made me bend down into each chasm, and I saw in the chasm blazing fire; and wheels of fire ran there, and souls were hung upon those wheels, and were dashed against each other. And there was there crying and great lamentation, and there was none released. And that man said to me, These souls are of thine own nation, and for a certain number of days[7] they have been given over to punishment and torture; and then

---

[1] 1 Cor. vi. 9.
[2] Matt. vii. 7; Luke xi. 9.
[3] Matt. vi. 9; Luke xi. 2.

[4] Matt. vii. 7.
[5] Or, having our sins in view.
[6] Lit., with iron.
[7] Lit., days of number.

others are brought in instead of them; and likewise also these are again succeeded by others. These are they who have exchanged the intercourse of man and wife. And again I looked down, and saw infants heaped upon each other, and struggling and lying upon each other; and he answered and said to me, These are their children, and for this have they been placed here for a testimony against them.

And he brought me to another chasm, and I bent down and saw mud, and worms spouting forth, and souls wallowing there; and a great gnashing of teeth was heard thence from them. And that man said to me, These are the souls of women that left their own husbands, and went and committed adultery with others, and who have been brought to this torment. He showed me another chasm, into which I bent down and saw souls hung up, some by the tongue, some by the hair, some by the hands, some by the feet, head downwards, and smoked with smoke and sulphur; about whom that man who was with me answered me, These souls which are hung up by the tongue are slanderers, and such as have uttered false and disgraceful words; *those that are hung up by the hair* [1] are those that are shameless, and that have gone about with uncovered heads in the world; these hung up by the hands are those who have taken what belongs to others, and have stolen, and who have never given anything to the poor, nor assisted the afflicted; but they so acted, wishing to get everything, and giving no heed at all to justice and the laws; and these hung up by the feet are those who lightly and eagerly ran in wicked ways, and disorderly wickedness, not looking after the sick, and not aiding those departing this life, and on account of this each individual soul is requited for what has been done by it.

Again leading me away, he showed me a cavern, exceedingly dark, exhaling a great stench; and many souls were peeping out thence, wishing to get some share of the air, but their keepers would not let them peep out. And he who was with me said, This is the prison of those souls which thou seest; for when they shall complete their punishments for those things which each one has done, afterwards again others succeed them — and there are some also quite used up — and are given up to other punishments. Those, then, who guarded the souls that were in the dark cave said to the man that had charge of me, Give her to us, that we may take her in beside the others, until the time comes for her to be given up to punishment. And he answered them, I will not give her to you, for I am afraid of him who gave her up to me; for I

received no orders to leave her here, and I shall take her up with me until I get some injunction about her. And he took me and brought me to another place, in which were men who were bitterly tortured. And he that is like thee took me and gave me up to thee, having thus said to thee, Take her, since she is one of the creatures that have been led astray. And I was taken by thee, and am now before thee. I beg, therefore, and supplicate thee that I may not go into those places of punishment which I saw.

And the apostle said to the multitudes standing by: You have heard, brethren, what this woman has recounted; and these are not the only punishments, but there are others worse than these; and if you do not turn to this God whom I proclaim, and refrain from your former works and deeds which you have done without knowledge, in these punishments you shall have your end. Believe, therefore, in our Lord Jesus Christ, and He will forgive you the sins done by you heretofore, and will purify you from all the bodily desires that abide in the earth, and will heal you from the faults that follow after you, and go along with you, and are found before you. And let each of you put off the old man, and put on the new, and leave your former course of conduct and behaviour; and let those that steal steal no more, but let them live, labouring and working; [2] and let the adulterers no more commit adultery, lest they give themselves up to everlasting punishment; for adultery is with God an evil altogether grievous above other evils. Put away also from yourselves covetousness, and lying, and drunkenness, and slandering, and requiting evil for evil: for all these are alien and strange to the God proclaimed by us; but rather live in faith, and meekness, and holiness, and hope, in which God rejoices, that ye may become His servants, having received from Him gracious gifts, which few or none receive.

All the people therefore believed, and presented their souls obedient to the living God and Christ Jesus, enjoying His blessed works, and His holy service. And they brought much money for the service of the widows; for he had them collected in the cities, and he sent to all of them by his own servants [3] what was necessary, both clothing and food. But he did not cease proclaiming and saying to them, and showing that this is Jesus the Christ, concerning whom the Scriptures proclaimed that He should come, and be crucified, and be raised from the dead after three days. And he showed them a second time, beginning from the prophets, and explaining the things concerning Christ, and that it was necessary for Him to come, and for all things to

---

[1] Obviously omitted either in the MSS. or in the text.

[2] Eph. iv. 28.
[3] Or, deacons.

be fulfilled that had been said to us beforehand concerning Him.[1]

And the report of him ran through all the cities and countries; and all who had persons sick or tormented by unclean spirits brought them, and they were healed. Some also they laid on the road by which he was to pass, and he healed them all by the power of the Lord.[2] Then said all with one accord who had been healed by him, with one voice: Glory to Thee, Jesus, who givest Thy healing to all alike by means of Thy servant and apostle Thomas. And being in good health, and rejoicing, we pray Thee that we may be of Thy flock, and be numbered among Thy sheep; receive us, therefore, O Lord, and consider not our transgressions and former offences which we did, being in ignorance.

And the apostle said: Glory to the only-begotten from the Father;[3] glory to the first-born of many brethren;[4] Glory to Thee, the defender and helper of those who come to Thy place of refuge; Thou that sleepest not, and raisest those that are asleep; that livest and bringest to life those that are lying in death; O God Jesus Christ, Son of the living God, redeemer and helper, refuge and rest of all that labour in Thy work, who affordest health to those who for Thy name's sake bear the burden of the day, and the icy coldness of the night; we give thanks for the gracious gifts that have been given us by Thee, and for the help from Thee bestowed upon us, and Thy providential care that has come upon us from Thee. Perfect these things upon us, therefore, unto the end, that we may have confidence in Thee; look upon us, because for Thy sake we have left our homes, and for Thy sake have become strangers gladly and willingly; look upon us, O Lord, because for Thy sake we have abandoned our possessions, that we may have Thee for a possession that shall not be taken away; look upon us, O Lord, because we have left those related to us by ties of kindred in order that we may be united in relationship to Thee; look upon us, O Lord, who have left our fathers and mothers, and those that nourished us, that we may behold Thy Father, and be satisfied with His divine nourishment: look upon us, O Lord, because for Thy sake we have left our bodily yoke-fellows,[5] and our earthly fruit, in order that we may share in that intercourse which is lasting and true, and bring forth true fruits, whose nature is from above, the enjoyment of which no one can take away from us, with which we abide, and they abide with us.

---

[1] Comp. Luke xxiv. 46.
[2] Comp. Acts v. 15.
[3] John i. 14.
[4] Rom. viii. 29.

[5] i.e., wives.

CONSUMMATION OF THOMAS THE APOSTLE [1]

At the command of King Misdeus [2] the blessed Apostle Thomas was cast into prison; and he said: I glorify God, and I shall preach the word to the prisoners, so that all rejoiced at his presence. When, therefore, Juzanes the king's son, and Tertia his mother, and Mygdonia, and Markia, had become believers, but were not yet thought worthy of baptism, they took it exceedingly ill that the blessed one had been shut up. And having come to the prison, and given much money to the jailor,[3] they went in to him. And he, seeing them, was glad, and glorified the Lord, and blessed them. And they entreated and begged the seal in the Lord, a beautiful young man having appeared to them in a dream, and ordered the apostle into the house of Juzanes.

And again the beautiful young man coming to them and Thomas, bade them do this on the coming night. And he ran before them, and gave them light on the way, and without noise opened the doors that had been secured, until all the mystery was completed. And having made them communicate in the Eucharist, and having talked much with them, and confirmed them in the faith, and commended them to the Lord, he went forth thence, leaving the women, and again went to be shut up.[4] And they grieved and wept because Misdeus the king was to kill him.

And Thomas went and found the jailors fighting, and saying: What wrong have we done to that sorcerer, that, availing himself of his magic art, he has opened the doors of the prison, and wishes to set all the prisoners free? But let us go and let the king know about his wife and his son.[5] And when he came they stripped him, and girded him with a girdle; and thus they stood before the king.

---

[1] The following translation of a MS. in the Bodleian Library, transcribed by Tischendorf (*Apocal. Apocr.*, p. 158), gives a fuller account of the martyrdom of St. Thomas: —

MARTYRDOM OF THE HOLY AND ALL-RENOWNED APOSTLE THOMAS.

After the apostle had gone forth, according to the command of our Lord, and God, and Saviour Jesus Christ, the Lord appeared to him, saying: Peace to thee, my disciple and apostle! And the apostle fell on his face on the ground, and prayed the Lord to reveal to him the circumstances of his precious departure. And the Lord said to him: Misdæus is contriving a plan to destroy thee very soon; but, behold, he will come to me. And after having sealed him, He ascended into the heavens. And the apostle taught the people, and there was added unto the flock of Christ. But some men who hated Christ accused him before King Misdeus, saying: Destroy this sorcerer, who corrupts and deceives the people in this new one God whom he proclaims. Moreover, *he has deceived* thy lady and thy son. On hearing this, Misdeus, without inquiry, ordered him to be laid hold of, and shut up in prison. And they did quickly what they were ordered, and threw him into the prison, and sealed it. And when the women who believed in God had heard that Judas was shut up, they gave a great sum of money to the warders, and went in to him in the prison. And the apostle says to them: My daughters, handmaidens of Jesus Christ, listen to me. In my last day I address you, because I shall no more speak in the body; for, lo, I am taken up to my Lord Jesus Christ, who has had pity upon me, who humbled Himself even to my littleness. And I rejoice that the time is at hand for my change from this, that I may depart and receive my reward in the end; for my Lord is just. And at the end of his discourse to them, he said: O my Saviour, who hast endured much for our sake, let Thy mercies be upon us. And he sent them away, saying: The grace of the Holy Spirit be with you! And they grieved and wept, knowing that King Misdeus was going to put him to death. And Judas heard the warders contending with each other, and saying: Let us go and tell the king. Thy wife and thy son are going to the prison to this sorcerer, and for their sakes thou shouldst put him to death soon. And at dawn they arose and went to King Misdeus, and said: My lord, release that sorcerer, or cause him to be shut up elsewhere; for though we shut in the prisoners, and secure the doors, when we rise we find them opened. Nay, more; thy wife and son will not keep away from the man any more than the rest of them. And when the king heard this, he went to look at the seals. And he looked all about them on the doors, and found them as they were. Then he says to the jailors: What are you telling lies about? for certainly these seals are quite safe: and how do you say that Tertia, and Mygdonia, and my son go within the prison? And the warders said: We have told thee the truth, O king. And after this the king went into the prison, and sent for the apostle. And when he came, they took off his girdle, and set him before the tribunal. And the king said: Art thou a slave, or free? And Thomas said: I am One's slave. Thou hast no power over me whatever. And Misdæus says: Didst thou run away and come to this country? Thomas: I came here to save many, and I am to depart from my body by thy hands. Misdæus says to him: Who is thy master? and what is his name? and what country dost thou belong to? Thomas: Thou canst not hear His true name at this time; but I tell thee the name that has been given Him for the time: it is Jesus the Christ. And Misdæus says: I have been in no hurry to put thee to death, but have restrained myself; but thou hast made a display of thy works, so that thy sorceries have been heard of in every country. But no; I shall bring thee to an end, that thy sorceries may be destroyed, and our nation purified. And Thomas said: What thou callest sorceries shall abound in me, and never be removed from the people here. And after this was said, Misdeus reflected in what manner he should put the apostle to death, for he was afraid of the people standing by who believed. And he arose and took Thomas outside of the city; and he was accompanied by a few armed soldiers. And the multitude suspected that the king was plotting about him, and stood and addressed themselves to him. And when they had gone forth three stadia, he delivered him to four soldiers and one of the polemarchs, and ordered them to spear him on the mountain; and he returned to the city. And those who were present ran to Thomas, eager to rescue him. And he was led away, accompanied by the soldiers, two on each side. . . . And Thomas, walking along, said: O Thy secret mysteries, O Jesus! for even unto the end of life are they fulfilled in us. O the riches of Thy grace! . . . for, lo, how four have laid hold of me, since of four elements . . . (Here the fragment ends.) [The MS. in which this occurs is not that one which has been so frequently cited in the preceding Apocryphal Acts. — R.]

[2] Pseudo-Abdias, in his *Histories of the Apostles*, has as follows: Wherefore, in a rage, Mesdeus king of India thrust into prison the Apostle Thomas, and Zuganes his son, and several others.

[3] Abdias: Treptia, who was the king's wife, and Mygdonia the wife of Charisius, one of the king's friends, and Narchia the nurse, gave the jailor 360 pieces of silver, and were let in to the apostle.

[4] Abdias: Thomas stood in the prison, and said: Lord Jesus, who didst endure very much for us, let the gates be shut as they were before, and the seals be made again on the same doors.

[5] Abdias gives an account of the king going to the prison, and disbelieving the report of the warders, because he found the seals on the doors as he had left them.

And Misdeus said to him: Art thou a slave, or a freeman? And Thomas answered and said to him: I am not[1] a slave, and thou hast no power against me at all. And how, said Misdeus, hast thou run away and come to this country? And Thomas said: I came here that I might save many, and that I might by thy hands depart from this body. Misdeus says to him: Who is thy master? and what is his name? and of what country, and of whom is he? My Lord, says Thomas, is my Master and thine, being the Lord of heaven and earth. And Misdeus said: What is he called? And Thomas said: Thou canst not know His true name at this time; but I tell thee the name that has been given Him for a season — Jesus the Christ. And Misdeus said: I have not been in a hurry[2] to destroy thee, but have restrained myself; but thou hast made a display of works, so that thy sorceries have been heard of in all the country. But now this will I do,[3] that thy sorceries may also perish with thee, that our nation may be purified from them. And Thomas said: Dost thou call these things which will follow me sorceries? They shall never be removed from the people here.

And while these things were saying, Misdeus was considering in what manner he should put him to death; for he was afraid of the multitude standing round, many, even some of the chief men, having believed in him. And he arose, and took Thomas outside of the city; and a few soldiers accompanied him with their arms. And the rest of the multitude thought that the king was wishing to learn something from him; and they stood and observed him closely. And when they had gone forth three stadia, he delivered him to four soldiers, and to one of the chief officers,[4] and ordered them to take him up into the mountain and spear him; but he himself returned to the city.

And those present ran to Thomas, eager to rescue him; but he was led away by the soldiers who were with him. For there were two on each side having hold of him, because of sorcery. And the chief officer held him by the hand, and led him with honour. And at the same time the blessed apostle said: O the hidden mysteries of Thee, O Lord! for even to the close of life is fulfilled in us the riches of Thy grace, which does not allow us to be without feeling as to the body. For, behold, four have laid hold of me, and one leads me, since I belong to One, to whom I am going always invisibly. But now I learn that my Lord also, since He was a stranger, to whom I am going, who also is always present with me invisibly, was struck by one; but I am struck by four.[5]

And when they came to that place where they were to spear him, Thomas spoke thus to those spearing him: Hear me now, at least, when I am departing from my body; and let not your eyes be darkened in understanding, nor your ears shut up so as not to hear those things in which you have believed the God whom I preach, after being delivered in your souls from rashness; and behave in a manner becoming those who are free, being void of human glory, and live the life towards God. And he said to Juzanes: Son of an earthly king, but servant of Jesus Christ, give what is due to those who are to fulfil the command[6] of Misdeus, in order that I may go apart from them and pray. And Juzanes having paid the soldiers, the apostle betook himself to prayer; and it was as follows: —

My Lord, and my God, and hope, and leader, and guide in all countries, I follow Thee along with all that serve Thee, and do Thou guide me this day on my way to Thee. Let no one take my soul, which Thou hast given to me. Let not publicans and beggars look upon me, nor let serpents slander me, and let not the children of the dragon hiss at me. Behold, I have fulfilled Thy work, and accomplished what Thou gavest me to do. I have become a slave, that I might receive freedom from Thee; do then give it to me, and make me perfect. And this I say not wavering, but that they may hear who need to hear. I glorify Thee in all, Lord and Master; for to Thee is due glory for ever. Amen.

And when he had prayed, he said to the soldiers: Come and finish the work of him that sent you. And the four struck him at once, and killed him. And all the brethren wept, and wrapped him up in beautiful shawls, and many linen cloths, and laid him in the tomb in which of old the kings used to be buried.

And Syphor and Juzanes did not go to the city, but spent the whole day there, and waited during the night. And Thomas appeared to them, and said: I am not there; why do you sit watching? for I have gone up, and received the things I hoped for; but rise up and walk, and after no long time you shall be brought beside me. And Misdeus and Charisius[7] greatly afflicted Tertia and Mygdonia, but did not persuade them to abandon their opinions. And Thomas appeared, and said to them: Forget not the former things, for the holy and sanctifying Jesus Himself will aid you. And Misdeus and Charisius, when they could not persuade them not

---

[1] The *not* should, by the context, be omitted. [So Pseudo-Abdias. — R.]
[2] Reading ἠπείχθην for ἀπήχθην.
[3] i e., I will so act.
[4] Lit., polemarchs, who in the early times of Athens combined the duties of Foreign Secretary and War Secretary, and sometimes took the command in the field.

[5] Abdias: The apostle said that great and divine mysteries were revealed in his death, since he was led by four soldiers, because he consisted of four elements; and the Lord Jesus had been struck by one man, because He knew that one Father had begotten Him.
[6] Lit., the servants of the order.
[7] The husband of Mygdonia.

to be of this opinion, granted them their own will. And all the brethren assembled together For the blessed one had made Syphorus [1] a presbyter in the mountain, and Juzanius [1] a deacon, when he was led away to die. And the Lord helped them, and increased the faith by means of them.

And after a long time, it happened that one of the sons of Misdeus was a demoniac; and the demon being stubborn, no one was able to heal him. And Misdeus considered, and said: I shall go and open the tomb, and take a bone of the apostle's body, and touch my son with it, and I know that he will be healed. And he went to do what he had thought of. And the blessed apostle appeared to him, and said: Thou didst not believe in me when alive; how wilt thou believe in me when I am dead? Fear not. Jesus

Christ is kindly disposed to thee, through His great clemency. And Misdeus, when he did not find the bones (for one of the brethren had taken them, and carried them into the regions of the West [2]), took some dust from where the bones had lain, and touched his son with it, and said: I believe in Thee, Jesus, now when he has left me who always afflicts men, that they may not look to Thy light which giveth understanding, O Lord, kind to men. And his son being healed in this manner, he met with the rest of the brethren who were under the rule of Syphorus, and entreated the brethren to pray for him, that he might obtain mercy from our Lord Jesus Christ; to whom be glory for ever and ever. Amen.

---

[1] These names are slightly different in form in this paragraph.

[2] Abdias: and buried them in the city of Edessa. [The translator cites the readings of Pseudo-Abdias, as given by Tischendorf (from Fabricius), as those of "Abdias." The same form of citation appears in the footnotes to the *Martyrdom of Bartholomew*, pp. 553-557. — R.]

MARTYRDOM OF THE HOLY AND GLORIOUS APOSTLE BARTHOLOMEW

HISTORIANS declare that India is divided into three parts; and the first is said to end at Ethiopia, and the second at Media, and the third completes the country; and the one portion of it ends in the dark, and the other in the ocean. To this India, then, the holy Bartholomew the apostle of Christ went, and took up his quarters in the temple of Astaruth, and lived there as one of the pilgrims and the poor. In this temple, then, there was an idol called Astaruth, which was supposed to heal the infirm, but rather the more injured all. And the people were in entire ignorance of the true God; and from want of knowledge, but rather from the difficulty *of going to any other*, they all fled for refuge to the false god. And he brought upon them troubles, infirmities, damage, violence, and much affliction; and when any one sacrificed to him, the demon, retiring, appeared to give a cure to the person in trouble; and the foolish people, seeing this, believed in him. But the demons retired, not because they wished to cure men, but that they might the more assail them, and rather have them altogether in their power; and thinking that they were cured bodily, those that sacrificed to them were the more diseased in soul.

And it came to pass, that while the holy apostle of Christ, Bartholomew, stayed there, Astaruth gave no response, and was not able for curing. And when the temple was full of sick persons, who sacrificed to him daily, Astaruth could give no response; and sick persons who had come from far countries were lying there. When, therefore, in that temple not even one of the idols was able to give a response, and was of benefit neither to those that sacrificed to them nor to those who were in the agonies of death on their account, they were compelled to go to another city, where there was a temple of idols, where their great and most eminent god was called Becher.[1] And having there sacrificed, they demanded, asking why their god Astaruth had not responded to them. And the demon Becher answered and said to them: From the day and hour that the true God, who dwelleth in the heavens, sent his apostle Bartholomew into the regions here, your god Astaruth is held fast by chains of fire, and can no longer either speak or breathe. They said to him: And who is this Bartholomew? He answered: He is the friend of the Almighty God, and has just come into these parts, that he may take away all the worship of the idols in the name of his God. And the servants of the Greeks said to him: Tell us what he is like, that we may be able to find him.

And the demon answered and said: He has black hair, a shaggy head, a fair skin,[2] large eyes, beautiful nostrils, his ears hidden by the hair of his head, with a yellow beard, a few grey hairs, of middle height, and neither tall nor stunted, but middling, clothed with a white undercloak bordered with purple, and upon his shoulders a very white cloak; and his clothes have been worn twenty-six years, but neither are they dirty, nor have they waxed old. Seven times[3] a day he bends the knee to the Lord, and seven times[3] a night does he pray to God. His voice is like the sound of a strong trumpet; there go along with him angels of God, who allow him neither to be weary, nor to hunger, nor to thirst; his face, and his soul, and his heart are always glad and rejoicing; he foresees everything, he knows and speaks every tongue of every nation. And behold now, as soon as you ask me, and I answer you about him, behold, he knows; for the angels of the Lord tell him; and if you wish to seek him, if he is willing he will appear to you; but if he shall not be willing, you will not be able to find him. I entreat you, therefore, if you shall find him, entreat him not to come here, lest his angels do to me as they have done to my brother Astaruth.

And when the demon had said this, he held his peace. And they returned, and set to work to look into every face of the pilgrims and poor men, and for two days they could find him nowhere. And it came to pass, that one who was

---

[1] The history of Abdias gives the name as Berith, after Judg. ix. 46.

[2] Lit., white flesh.

[3] Pseudo-Abdias says: a hundred times.

a demoniac set to work to cry out: Apostle of the Lord, Bartholomew, thy prayers are burning me up. Then said the apostle to him: Hold thy peace, and come out of him. And that very hour, the man who had suffered from the demon for many years was set free.

And Polymius, the king of that country, happened to be standing opposite the apostle; and he had a daughter a demoniac, that is to say, a lunatic. And he heard about the demoniac that had been healed, and sent messengers to the apostle, saying: My daughter is grievously torn; I implore thee, therefore, as thou hast delivered him [1] who suffered for many years, so also to order my daughter to be set free. And the apostle rose up, and went with them. And he sees the king's daughter bound with chains, for she used to tear in pieces all her limbs; and if any one came near her, she used to bite, and no one dared to come near her. The servants say to him: And who is it that dares to touch her? The apostle answered them: Loose her, and let her go. They say to him again: We have her in our power when she is bound with all our force, and dost thou bid us loose her? The apostle says to them: Behold, I keep her enemy bound, and are you even now afraid of her? Go and loose her; and when she has partaken of food, let her rest, and early to-morrow bring her to me. And they went and did as the apostle had commanded them; and thereafter the demon was not able to come near her.

Then the king loaded camels with gold and silver, precious stones, pearls, and clothing, and sought to see the apostle; and having made many efforts, and not found him, he brought everything back to his palace.

And it happened, when the night had passed, and the following day was dawning, the sun having risen, the apostle appeared alone with the king in his bed-chamber, and said to him: Why didst thou seek me yesterday the whole day with gold and silver, and precious stones, pearls, and raiment? For these gifts those persons long for who seek earthly things; but I seek nothing earthly, nothing carnal. Wherefore I wish to teach thee that the Son of God deigned to be born as a man out of a virgin's womb. He was conceived in the womb of the virgin; He took to Himself her who was always a virgin, having within herself Him who made the heaven and the earth, the sea, and all that therein is. He, born of a virgin, like mankind, took to Himself a beginning in time, He who has a beginning neither of times nor days; but He Himself made every beginning, and everything created, whether in things visible or invisible. And as this virgin did not know man, so she, preserving her vir-

ginity, vowed a vow [2] to the Lord God. And she was the first who did so. For, from the time that man existed from the beginning of the world, no woman made a vow of this mode of life; but she, as she was the first among women who loved this in her heart, said, I offer to Thee, O Lord, my virginity. And, as I have said to thee, none of mankind dared to speak this word; but she being called for the salvation of many, observed this — that she might remain a virgin through the love of God, pure and undefiled. And suddenly, when she was shut up in her chamber, the archangel Gabriel appeared, gleaming like the sun; and when she was terrified at the sight, the angel said to her, Fear not, Mary; for thou hast found favour in the sight of Lord, and thou shalt conceive. And she cast off fear, and stood up, and said, How shall this be to me, since I know not man? The angel answered her, The Holy Ghost shall come upon thee, and the power of the Most High shall overshadow thee; wherefore also that holy thing which is born of thee shall be called Son of God.[3] Thus, therefore, when the angel had departed from her, she escaped the temptation of the devil, who deceived the first man when at rest. For, having tasted of the tree of disobedience, when the woman said to him, Eat, he ate; and thus the first man was cast out of paradise, and banished to this life. From him have been born the whole human race. Then the Son of God having been born of the virgin, and having become perfect man, and having been baptized, and after His baptism having fasted forty days, the tempter came and said to Him: If thou art the Son of God, tell these stones to become loaves. And He answered: Not on bread alone shall man live, but by every word of God.[4] Thus therefore the devil, who through eating had conquered the first man, was conquered through the fasting of the second man; and as he through want of self-restraint had conquered the first man, the son of the virgin earth, so we shall conquer through the fasting of the second Adam, the Son of the Virgin Mary.

The king says to him: And how is it that thou saidst just now that she was the first virgin of whom was born God and man? And the apostle answered: I give thanks to the Lord that thou hearest me gladly. The first man, then, was called Adam; he was formed out of the earth. And the earth, his mother out of which he was, was virgin, because it had neither been polluted by the blood of man nor opened for the burial of any one. The earth, then, was like the virgin, in order that he who conquered the

---

[1] Abdias calls him Pseustius.

[2] Or, prayed a prayer.
[3] Comp. Luke i. 26-38. Abdias goes on: He then, after His birth, suffered Himself to be tempted by that devil who had overcome the first man, persuading him to eat of the tree forbidden by God.
[4] Comp. Luke iv. 1-13.

son of the virgin earth might be conquered by the Son of the Virgin Mary. And, behold, he did conquer; for his wicked craft, through the eating of the tree by which man, being deceived, came forth from paradise, kept paradise shut. Thereafter this Son of the virgin conquered all the craft of the devil. And his craft was such, that when he saw the Son of the virgin fasting forty days, he knew in truth that He was the true God. The true God and man, therefore, hath not given Himself out to be known, except to those who are pure in heart,[1] and who serve Him by good works. The devil himself, therefore, when he saw that after the forty days He was again hungry, was deceived into thinking that He was not God, and said to Him, Why hast thou been hungry? tell these stones to become loaves, and eat. And the Lord answered him, Listen, devil; although thou mayst lord it over man, because he has not kept the commandment of God, I have fulfilled the righteousness of God in having fasted, and shall destroy thy power, so that thou shalt no longer lord it over man. And when he saw himself conquered, he again takes Jesus to an exceeding high mountain, and shows Him all the kingdoms of the world, and says, All these will I give thee, if thou wilt fall down and worship me. The Lord says to him, Get thee behind me, Satan; for it is written, Thou shalt worship the Lord thy God, and Him only shalt thou serve. And there was a third temptation for the Lord; for he takes Him up to the pinnacle of the temple, and says, If thou art the Son of God, cast thyself down. The Lord says to him, Thou shalt not tempt the Lord thy God. And the devil disappeared. And he indeed that once conquered Adam, the son of the virgin earth, was thrice conquered by Christ, the Son of the Virgin Mary.

And when the Lord had conquered the tyrant, He sent His apostles into all the world, that He might redeem His people from the deception of the devil; and one of these I am, an apostle of Christ. On this account we seek not after gold and silver, but rather despise them, because we labour to be rich in that place where the kingdom of Him alone endureth[2] for ever, where neither trouble, nor grief, nor groaning, nor death, has place; where there is eternal blessedness, and ineffable joy, and everlasting exultation, and perpetual repose. Wherefore also the demon sitting in your temple, who makes responses to you, is kept in chains through the angel of the Lord who has sent me. Because if thou shalt be baptized, and wishest thyself to be enlightened, I will make thee behold Him, and learn from how great evils thou hast been redeemed.

At the same time hear also by what means he injures all those who are lying sick in the temple. The devil himself by his own art causes the men to be sick, and again to be healed, in order that they may the more believe in the idols, and in order that he may have place the more in their souls, in order that they may say to the stock and the stone, Thou art our God.[3] But that demon who dwells in the idol is held in subjection, conquered by me, and is able to give no response to those who sacrifice and pray there. And if thou wishest to prove that it is so, I order him to return into the idol, and I will make him confess with his own mouth that he is bound, and able to give no response.

The king says to him: To-morrow, at the first hour of the day, the priests are ready to sacrifice in the temple, and I shall come there, and shall be able to see this wonderful work.

And it came to pass on the following day, as they were sacrificing, the devil began to cry out: Refrain, ye wretched ones, from sacrificing to me, lest ye suffer worse for my sake; because I am bound in fiery chains, and kept in subjection by an angel of the Lord Jesus Christ, the Son of God, whom the Jews crucified: for, being afraid of him, they condemned him to death. And he put to death Death himself, our king, and he bound our prince in chains of fire; and on the third day, having conquered death and the devil, rose in glory, and gave the sign of the cross to his apostles, and sent them out into the four quarters of the world; and one of them is here just now, who has bound me, and keeps me in subjection. I implore you, therefore, supplicate him on my account, that he may set me free to go into other habitations.

Then the apostle answered: Confess, unclean demon, who is it that has injured all those that are lying here from heavy diseases? The demon answered: The devil, our ruler, he who is bound, he sends us against men, that, having first injured their bodies, we may thus also make an assault upon their souls when they sacrifice to us. For then we have complete power over them, when they believe in us and sacrifice to us. And when, on account of the mischief done to them, we retire, we appear curing them, and are worshipped by them as gods; but in truth we are demons, and the servants of him who was crucified, the Son of the virgin, have bound us. For from that day on which the Apostle Bartholomew came I am punished, kept bound in chains of fire. And for this reason I speak, because he has commanded me. At the same time, I dare not utter more when the apostle is present, neither I nor our rulers.

The apostle says to him: Why dost thou not

---

[1] Matt. v. 8.
[2] Lit., reigneth.

[3] Jer. ii. 27.

save all that have come to thee? The demon says to him: When we injure their bodies, unless we first injure their souls, we do not let their bodies go. The apostle says to him: And how do you injure their souls? The demon answered him: When they believe that we are gods, and sacrifice to us, God withdraws from those who sacrifice, and we do not take away the sufferings of their bodies, but retire into their souls.

Then the apostle says to the people: Behold, the god whom you thought to cure you, does the more mischief to your souls and bodies. Hear even now your Maker who dwells in the heavens, and do not believe in lifeless stones and stocks. And if you wish that I should pray for you, and that all these may receive health, take down this idol, and break it to pieces; and when you have done this, I will sanctify this temple in the name of our Lord Jesus Christ; and having baptized all of you who are in it in the baptism of the Lord, and sanctified you, I will save all.

Then the king gave orders, and all the people brought ropes and crowbars, and were not at all able to take down the idol. Then the apostle says to them: Unfasten the ropes. And when they had unfastened them, he said to the demon dwelling in it: In the name of our Lord Jesus Christ, come out of this idol, and go into a desert place, where neither winged creature utters a cry, nor voice of man has ever been heard. And straightway he arose at the word of the apostle, and lifted it up from its foundations; and in that same hour all the idols that were in that place were broken to pieces.

Then all cried out with one voice, saying: He alone is God Almighty whom Bartholomew the apostle proclaims. Then the holy Bartholomew, having spread forth his hands to heaven, said: God of Abraham, God of Isaac, God of Jacob, who for the salvation of men hast sent forth Thine only begotten Son, our Lord Jesus Christ, in order that He might redeem by His own blood all of us enslaved by sin, and declare us to be Thy sons, that we may know Thee, the true God, that Thou existest always to eternity God without end: one God, the Father, acknowledged in Son and Holy Spirit; one God, the Son, glorified in Father and Holy Spirit; one God, the Holy Spirit, worshipped in Father and Son; and acknowledged to be truly one,[1] the Father unbegotten, the Son begotten, the Holy Spirit proceeding; and in Thee the Father, and in the Holy Spirit, Thine only begotten Son our Lord Jesus Christ is, in whose name Thou hast given us power to heal the sick, to cure paralytics, to expel demons, and raise the dead: for He said to us, Verily I say unto you, that whatever ye shall ask in my name ye shall re-

ceive.[2] I entreat, then, that in His name all this multitude may be saved, that all may know that Thou alone art God in heaven, and in the earth, and in the sea, who seekest the salvation of men through that same Jesus Christ our Lord, with whom Thou livest and reignest in unity of the Holy Spirit for ever and ever.

And when all responded to the Amen, suddenly there appeared an angel of the Lord, shining brighter than the sun, winged, and other four angels holding up the four corners of the temple; and with his finger the one sealed the temple and the people, and said: Thus saith the Lord who hath sent me, As you have all been purified from all your infirmity, so also this temple shall be purified from all uncleanness, and from the demons dwelling in it, whom the apostle of God has ordered to go into a desert place; for so hath God commanded me, that I may manifest Him to you. And when ye behold Him, fear nothing; but when I make the sign of the cross, so also do ye with your finger seal your faces, and these evil things will flee from you. Then he showed them the demon who dwelt in the temple, like an Ethiopian, black as soot; his face sharp like a dog's, thin-cheeked, with hair down to his feet, eyes like fire, sparks coming out of his mouth; and out of his nostrils came forth smoke like sulphur, with wings spined like a porcupine; and his hands were bound with fiery chains, and he was firmly kept in. And the angel of the Lord said to him: As also the apostle hath commanded, I let thee go; go where voice of man is not heard, and be there until the great day of judgment. And when he let him go, he flew away, groaning and weeping, and disappeared. And the angel of the Lord went up into heaven in the sight of all.

Then the king, and also the queen, with their two sons, and with all his people, and with all the multitude of the city, and every city round about, and country, and whatever land his kingdom ruled over, were saved, and believed, and were baptized in the name of the Father, and the Son, and the Holy Spirit. And the king laid aside his diadem, and followed Bartholomew the apostle of Christ.

And after these things the unbelievers of the Greeks, having come together to Astreges[3] the king, who was the elder brother of the king who had been baptized, say to him: O king, thy brother Polymius has become disciple to a certain magician, who has taken down our temples, and broken our gods to pieces. And while they were thus speaking and weeping, behold, again there came also some others from the cities round about, both priests[4] and people; and

---

[1] Or, unity.

[2] Matt. xxi. 22.

[3] Abdias calls him Astyages; elsewhere he is called Sanathrugus.

[4] Lit., no-priests — μιερεις for μη ιερεις — a name given in scorn to heathen priests by Christian writers.

they set about weeping and making accusations [1] before the king. Then King Astreges in a rage sent a thousand armed men along with those priests, in order that, wherever they should find the apostle, they might bring him to him bound. And when they had done so, and found him, and brought him, he says to him: Art thou he who has perverted my brother from the gods? To whom the apostle answered: I have not perverted him, but have converted him to God. The king says to him: Art thou he who caused our gods to be broken in pieces? The apostle says to him: I gave power to the demons who were in them, and they broke in pieces the dumb and senseless idols, that all men might believe in God Almighty, who dwelleth in the heavens. The king says to him: As thou hast made my brother deny his gods, and believe in thy God, so I also will make you reject thy God and believe in my gods. The apostle says to him: If I have bound and kept in subjection the god which thy brother worshipped, and at my order the idols were broken in pieces, if thou also art able to do the same to my God, thou canst persuade me also to sacrifice to thy gods; but if thou canst do nothing to my God, I will break all thy gods in pieces; but do thou believe in my God.

And when he had thus spoken, the king was informed that his god Baldad [2] and all the other idols had fallen down, and were broken in pieces. Then the king rent the purple in which he was clothed, and ordered the holy apostle Bartholo-mew to be beaten with rods; and after having been thus scourged, to be beheaded.

And innumerable multitudes came from all the cities, to the number of twelve thousand, who had believed in him along with the king; and they took up the remains of the apostle with singing of praise and with all glory, and they laid them in the royal tomb, and glorified God. And the king Astreges having heard of this, ordered him to be thrown into the sea; and his remains were carried into the island of Liparis.

And it came to pass on the thirtieth day after the apostle was carried away, that the king Astreges was overpowered by a demon and miserably strangled; and all the priests were strangled by demons, and perished on account of their rising against [3] the apostle, and thus died by an evil fate.

And there was great fear and trembling, and all came to the Lord, and were baptized by the presbyters who had been ordained by the holy apostle Bartholomew. And according to the commandment of the apostle, all the clergy of the people made King Polymius bishop; and in the name of our Lord Jesus Christ he received the grace of healing, and began to do signs. And he remained in the bishopric twenty years; and having prospered in all things, and governed the church well, and guided it in right opinions,[4] he fell asleep in peace, and went to the Lord: to whom be glory and strength for ever and ever. Amen.

---

[1] Lit., calling out.
[2] Abdias calls him Vualdath.

[3] Or it may mean: that the apostle might be established.
[4] Or, in orthodoxy.

ACTS OF THE HOLY APOSTLE THADDÆUS,

ONE OF THE TWELVE [1]

LEBBÆUS, who also is Thaddæus, was of the city of Edessa — and it is the metropolis of Osroene, in the interior of the Armenosyrians — an Hebrew by race, accomplished and most learned in the divine writings. He came to Jerusalem to worship in the days of John the Baptist; and having heard his preaching and seen his angelic life, he was baptized, and his name was called Thaddæus. And having seen the appearing of Christ, and His teaching, and His wonderful works, he followed Him, and became His disciple; and He chose him as one of the twelve, the tenth apostle according to the Evangelists Matthew and Mark.

In those times there was a governor of the city of Edessa, Abgarus by name. And there having gone abroad the fame of Christ, of the wonders which He did, and of His teaching, Abgarus having heard of it, was astonished, and desired to see Christ, and could not leave his city and government. And about the days of the Passion and the plots of the Jews, Abgarus, being seized by an incurable disease, sent a letter to Christ by Ananias the courier,[2] to the following effect: — To Jesus[3] called Christ, Abgarus the governor of the country of the Edessenes, an unworthy slave. The multitude of the wonders done by thee has been heard of by me, that thou healest the blind, the lame, and the paralytic, and curest all the demoniacs; and on this account I entreat thy goodness to come even to us, and escape from the plottings of the wicked Jews, which through envy they set in motion against thee. My city is small, but large enough for both. Abgarus enjoined Ananias to take accurate account of Christ, of what appearance He was, and His stature, and His hair, and in a word everything.

And Ananias, having gone and given the letter, was carefully looking at Christ, but was unable to fix Him in his mind. And He knew as knowing the heart, and asked to wash Himself; and a towel[4] was given Him; and when He had washed Himself, He wiped His face with it. And His image having been imprinted upon the linen, He gave it to Ananias, saying: Give this, and take back this message, to him that sent thee: Peace to thee and thy city! For because of this I am come, to suffer for the world, and to rise again, and to raise up the forefathers. And after I have been taken up into the heavens I shall send thee my disciple Thaddæus, who shall enlighten thee, and guide thee into all the truth, both thee and thy city.

And having received Ananias, and fallen down and adored the likeness, Abgarus was cured of his disease before Thaddæus came.

And after the passion, and the resurrection, and the ascension, Thaddæus went to Abgarus; and having found him in health, he gave him an account of the incarnation of Christ, and baptized him, with all his house. And having instructed great multitudes, both of Hebrews and Greeks, Syrians and Armenians, he baptized them in the name of the Father, and Son, and Holy Spirit, having anointed them with the holy perfume; and he communicated to them of the undefiled mysteries of the sacred body and blood of our Lord Jesus Christ, and delivered to them to keep and observe the law of Moses, and to give close heed to the things that had been said by the apostles in Jerusalem. For year by year they came together to the passover, and again he imparted to them the Holy Spirit.

And Thaddæus along with Abgarus destroyed idol-temples and built churches; ordained as bishop one of his disciples, and presbyters, and deacons, and gave them the rule of the psalmody and the holy liturgy. And having left them, he went to the city of Amis, great metropolis of the Mesechaldeans and Syrians, that is, of Mesopotamia-Syria, beside the river Tigris. And he having gone into the synagogue of the Jews along with his disciples on the Sabbath-day, after the

---

[1] [Curiously enough, the Vienna MS. has in the title: "one of the seventy," instead of "one of the twelve." The same confusion exists in the writings of Eusebius and Jerome. — R.]

[2] Lit., the swift runner.

[3] [Compare with this letter that found in Eusebius (*Hist. Eccl.*, i. 13), where the reply is also given. Eusebius claims that he had seen the original documents. — R.]

[4] Lit., doubled in four.

reading of the law the high priest said to Thaddæus and his disciples: Men, whence are you? and why are you here?

And Thaddæus said: No doubt you have heard of what has taken place in Jerusalem about Jesus Christ, and we are His disciples, and witnesses of the wonderful things which He did and taught, and how through hatred the chief priests delivered Him to Pilate the procurator of Judæa. And Pilate, having examined Him and found no case,[1] wished to let Him go; but they cried out, If thou let him go, thou art not Cæsar's friend, because he proclaims himself king. And he being afraid, washed his hands in the sight of the multitude, and said, I am innocent of the blood of this man; see ye to it. And the chief priests answered and said, His blood be upon us and our children. And Pilate gave him up to them. And they took Him, and spit upon Him, with the soldiers, and made a great mock of Him, and crucified Him, and laid Him in the tomb, and secured it well, having also set guards upon Him. And on the third day before dawn He rose, leaving His burial-clothes in the tomb. And He was seen first by His mother and other women, and by Peter and John first of my fellow disciples, and thereafter to us the twelve, who ate and drank with Him after His resurrection for many days. And He sent us in His name to proclaim repentance and remission of sins to all the nations, that those who were baptized, having had the kingdom of the heavens preached to them, would rise up incorruptible at the end of this age; and He gave us power to expel demons, and heal every disease and every malady, and raise the dead.

And the multitudes having heard this, brought together their sick and demoniacs. And Thaddæus, having gone forth along with his disciples, laid his hand upon each one of them, and healed them all by calling upon the name of Christ. And the demoniacs were healed before Thaddæus came near them, the spirits going out of them. And for many days the people ran together from different places, and beheld what was done by Thaddæus. And hearing his teaching, many believed, and were baptized, confessing their sins.

Having therefore remained with them for five years, he built a church; and having appointed as bishop one of his disciples, and presbyters, and deacons, and prayed for them, he went away, going round the cities of Syria, and teaching, and healing all the sick; whence he brought many cities and countries to Christ through His teaching. Teaching, therefore, and evangelizing along with the disciples, and healing the sick, he went to Berytus, a city of Phœnicia by the sea;[2] and there, having taught and enlightened many, he fell asleep on the twenty-first[3] of the month of August. And the disciples having come together, buried him with great honour; and many sick were healed, and they gave glory to the Father, and the Son, and the Holy Spirit, for ever and ever. Amen.

---

[1] Or, fault.

[2] The other [Vienna] MS. here adds: And having gone into it, he preached Christ, saying to them all with tears, Ye men who have ears to hear, hear from me the word of life: hear attentively, and understand. Cast off your many opinions, and believe and come to the one living and true God, the God of the Hebrews. For He only is the true God and Maker of the whole creation, searching the hearts of mankind, and knowing all about each one before their birth, as being the Maker of them all. To Him alone, fixing your eyes upon heaven, fall down evening and morning, and at noon, and to Him alone offer the sacrifice of praise, and give thanks always, refraining from what you yourselves hate; because God is compassionate and benevolent, and recompenses to each one according to his works.

[3] The Paris MS. has 20th.

ACTS OF THE HOLY APOSTLE AND EVANGELIST JOHN THE THEOLOGIAN

ABOUT HIS EXILE AND DEPARTURE.

WHEN Agrippa, whom, on account of his plotting against Peace, they stoned and put to death, was king of the Jews, Vespasian Cæsar, coming with a great army, invested Jerusalem; and some prisoners of war he took and slew, others he destroyed by famine in the siege, and most he banished, and at length scattered up and down. And having destroyed the temple, and put the holy vessels on board a ship, he sent them to Rome, to make for himself a temple of peace, and adorned it with the spoils of war.

And when Vespasian was dead, his son Domitian, having got possession of the kingdom, along with his other wrongful acts, set himself also to make a persecution against the righteous men. For, having learned that the city was filled with Jews, remembering the orders given by his father about them, he purposed casting them all out of the city of the Romans. And some of the Jews took courage, and gave Domitian a book, in which was written as follows : —

O Domitian, Cæsar and king of all the world, as many of us as are Jews entreat thee, as suppliants we beseech of thy power not to banish us from thy divine and benignant countenance; for we are obedient to thee, and the customs, and laws, and practices, and policy, doing wrong in nothing, but being of the same mind with the Romans. But there is a new and strange nation, neither agreeing with other nations nor consenting to the religious observances of the Jews, uncircumcised, inhuman, lawless, subverting whole houses, proclaiming a man as God, all assembling together[1] under a strange name, that of Christian. These men reject God, paying no heed to the law given by Him, and proclaim to be the Son of God a man born of ourselves, Jesus by name, whose parents and brothers and all his family have been connected with the Hebrews ; whom on account of his great blasphemy and his wicked fooleries we gave up to the cross. And they add another blasphemous lie to their first one : him that was nailed up and buried, they glorify as having risen from the dead ; and, more than this, they falsely assert that he has been taken up by[2] clouds into the heavens.

At all this the king, being affected with rage, ordered the senate to publish a decree that they should put to death all who confessed themselves to be Christians. Those, then, who were found in the time of his rage, and who reaped the fruit of patience, and were crowned in the triumphant contest against the works of the devil, received the repose of incorruption.

And the fame of the teaching of John was spread abroad in Rome ; and it came to the ears of Domitian that there was a certain Hebrew in Ephesus, John by name, who spread a report about the seat of empire of the Romans, saying that it would quickly be rooted out, and that the kingdom of the Romans would be given over to another. And Domitian, troubled by what was said, sent a centurion with soldiers to seize John, and bring him. And having gone to Ephesus, they asked where John lived. And having come up to his gate, they found him standing before the door ; and, thinking that he was the porter, they inquired of him where John lived. And he answered and said : I am he. And they, despising his common, and low, and poor appearance, were filled with threats, and said : Tell us the truth. And when he declared again that he was the man they sought, the neighbours moreover bearing witness to it, they said that he was to go, with them at once to the king in Rome. And, urging them to take provisions for the journey, he turned and took a few dates, and straightway went forth.

And the soldiers, having taken the public conveyances, travelled fast, having seated him in the midst of them. And when they came to the first change, it being the hour of breakfast, they

[1] Tischendorf gives a conjectural reading: who is present to them when they assemble; but the MSS. reading will bear the interpretation given above.

[2] Or, in.

entreated him to be of good courage, and to take bread, and eat with them. And John said: I rejoice in soul indeed, but in the meantime I do not wish to take any food. And they started, and were carried along quickly. And when it was evening they stopped at a certain inn; and as, besides, it was the hour of supper, the centurion and the soldiers being most kindly disposed, entreated John to make use of what was set before them. But he said that he was very tired, and in want of sleep more than any food. And as he did this each day, all the soldiers were struck with amazement, and were afraid lest John should die, and involve them in danger. But the Holy Spirit showed him to them as more cheerful. And on the seventh day, it being the Lord's day, he said to them: Now it is time for me also to partake of food. And having washed his hands and face, he prayed, and brought out the linen cloth, and took one of the dates, and ate it in the sight of all.

And when they had ridden a long time they came to the end of their journey, John thus fasting. And they brought him before the king, and said: Worshipful king, we bring to thee John, a god, not a man; for, from the hour in which we apprehended him, to the present, he has not tasted bread. At this Domitian being amazed, stretched out his mouth on account of the wonder, wishing to salute him with a kiss; but John bent down his head, and kissed his breast. And Domitian said: Why hast thou done this? Didst thou not think me worthy to kiss thee? And John said to him: It is right to adore the hand of God first of all, and in this way to kiss the mouth of the king; for it is written in the holy books, The heart of a king is in the hand of God.[1]

And the king said to him: Art thou John, who said that my kingdom would speedily be uprooted, and that another king, Jesus, was going to reign instead of me? And John answered and said to him: Thou also shalt reign for many years given thee by God, and after thee very many others; and when the times of the things upon earth have been fulfilled, out of heaven shall come a King, eternal, true, Judge of living and dead, to whom every nation and tribe shall confess, through whom every earthly power and dominion shall be brought to nothing, and every mouth speaking great things shall be shut. This is the mighty Lord and King of everything that hath breath and flesh,[2] the Word and Son of the living One, who is Jesus Christ.

At this Domitian said to him: What is the proof of these things? I am not persuaded by words only; words are a sight of the unseen.[3]

What canst thou show in earth or heaven by the power of him who is destined to reign, as thou sayest? For he will do it, if he is the Son of God. And immediately John asked for a deadly poison. And the king having ordered poison to be given to him, they brought it on the instant. John therefore, having taken it, put it into a large cup, and filled it with water, and mixed it, and cried out with a loud voice, and said: In Thy name, Jesus Christ, Son of God, I drink the cup which Thou wilt sweeten; and the poison in it do Thou mingle with Thy Holy Spirit, and make it become a draught of life and salvation, for the healing of soul and body, for digestion and harmless assimilation, for faith not to be repented of, for an undeniable testimony of death as the cup of thanksgiving.[4] And when he had drunk the cup, those standing beside Domitian expected that he was going to fall to the ground in convulsions. And when John stood, cheerful, and talked with them safe, Domitian was enraged against those who had given the poison, as having spared John. But they swore by the fortune and health of the king, and said that there could not be a stronger poison than this. And John, understanding what they were whispering to one another, said to the king: Do not take it ill, O king, but let a trial be made,[5] and thou shalt learn the power of the poison. Make some condemned criminal be brought from the prison. And when he had come, John put water into the cup, and swirled it round, and gave it with all the dregs to the condemned criminal. And he, having taken it and drunk, immediately fell down and died.

And when all wondered at the signs that had been done, and when Domitian had retired and gone to his palace, John said to him: O Domitian, king of the Romans, didst thou contrive this, that, thou being present and bearing witness, I might to-day become a murderer? What is to be done about the dead body which is lying? And he ordered it to be taken and thrown away. But John, going up to the dead body, said: O God, Maker of the heavens, Lord and Master of angels, of glories, of powers, in the name of Jesus Christ, Thine only begotten Son, give to this man who has died for this occasion a renewal of life, and restore him his soul, that Domitian may learn that the Word is much more powerful than poison, and is the ruler of life. And having taken him by the hand, he raised him up alive.

And when all were glorifying God, and wondering at the faith of John, Domitian said to him: I have put forth a decree of the senate, that all such persons should be summarily dealt with, without trial; but since I find from thee

---

[1] Prov. xxi. 1
[2] Lit., of all breath and flesh.
[3] Equal to our proverb, Seeing is believing.

[4] i.e., the Eucharist.
[5] Tischendorf conjectures this clause, as the original is illegible.

that they are innocent, and that their religion is rather beneficial, I banish thee to an island, that I may not seem myself to do away with my own decrees. He asked then that the condemned criminal should be let go; and when he was let go, John said: Depart, give thanks to God, who has this day delivered thee from prison and from death.

And while they were standing, a certain home-born slave of Domitian's, of those in the bed-chamber, was suddenly seized by the unclean demon, and lay dead; and word was brought to the king. And the king was moved, and entreated John to help her. And John said: It is not in man to do this; but since thou knowest how to reign, but dost not know from whom thou hast received it, learn who has the power over both thee and thy kingdom. And he prayed thus: O Lord, the God of every kingdom, and master of every creature, give to this maiden the breath of life. And having prayed, he raised her up. And Domitian, astonished at all the wonders, sent him away to an island, appointing for him a set time.

And straightway John sailed to Patmos, where also he was deemed worthy to see the revelation of the end. And when Domitian was dead, Nerva succeeded to the kingdom, and recalled all who had been banished; and having kept the kingdom for a year, he made Trajan his successor in the kingdom. And when he was king over the Romans, John went to Ephesus, and regulated all the teaching of the church, holding many conferences, and reminding them of what the Lord had said to them, and what duty he had assigned to each. And when he was old and changed, he ordered Polycarp to be bishop over the church.

And what like his end was, or his departure from men, who cannot give an account of? For on the following day, which was the Lord's day, and in the presence of the brethren, he began to say to them: Brethren, and fellow-servants, and co-heirs, and copartners of the kingdom of the Lord, know the Lord what miracles He hath shown you through me, what wonders, what cures, what signs, what gracious gifts, teachings, rulings, rests, services, glories, graces, gifts, faiths, communions; how many things you have seen with your eyes, that ear hath not heard. Be strong, therefore, in Him, remembering Him in all your doings, knowing the mystery of the dispensation that has come to men, for the sake of which the Lord has worked. He then, through me, exhorts you: Brethren, I wish to remain without grief, without insult, without treachery, without punishment. For He also knows insult from you, He knows also dishonour, He knows also treachery, He knows also punishment from those that dis-

obey His commandments. Let not therefore our God be grieved, the good, the compassionate, the merciful, the holy, the pure, the undefiled, the only, the one, the immutable, the sincere, the guileless, the slow to anger, He that is higher and more exalted than every name that we speak or think of — our God, Jesus Christ. Let Him rejoice along with us because we conduct ourselves well; let Him be glad because we live in purity; let Him rest because we behave reverently; let Him be pleased because we live in fellowship; let Him smile because we are sober-minded; let Him be delighted because we love. These things, brethren, I communicate to you, pressing on to the work set before me, already perfected for me by the Lord. For what else have I to say to you? Keep the sureties of your God; keep His presence, that shall not be taken away from you. And if then ye sin no more, He will forgive you what ye have done in ignorance; but if, after ye have known Him, and He has had compassion upon you, you return to the like courses, even your former offences will be laid to your charge, and ye shall have no portion or compassion before His face.[1]

And when he had said this to them, he thus prayed: Jesus, who didst wreathe this crown by Thy twining, who hast inserted these many flowers into the everlasting flower of Thy countenance, who hast sown these words among them, be Thou Thyself the protector and healer of Thy people. Thou alone art benignant and not haughty, alone merciful and kind, alone a Saviour, and just; Thou who always seest what belongs to all, and art in all, and everywhere present, God Lord Jesus Christ; who with Thy gifts and Thy compassion coverest those that hope in Thee; who knowest intimately those that everywhere speak against us, and blaspheme Thy holy name, do Thou alone, O Lord, help Thy servants with Thy watchful care. So be it, Lord.

And having asked bread, he gave thanks thus, saying: What praise, or what sort of offering, or what thanksgiving, shall we, breaking the bread, invoke, but Thee only? We glorify the name by which Thou hast been called by the Father; we glorify the name by which Thou hast been called through the Son; we glorify the resurrection which has been manifested to us through Thee; of Thee we glorify the seed,[2] the word, the grace, the true pearl, the treasure, the plough, the net,[3] the majesty, the diadem, Him called Son of man for our sakes, the truth, the rest, the knowledge, the freedom, the place of refuge in Thee. For Thou alone art Lord, the root of immortality, and the fountain of incorruption,

---

[1] Comp. Heb. x. 26.
[2] Or, sowing.
[3] Comp. Matt. xiii.

and the seat of the ages; Thou who hast been called all these for our sakes, that now we, calling upon Thee through these, may recognise Thine illimitable majesty, presented to us by Thy presence, that can be seen only by the pure, seen in Thine only Son.

And having broken the bread, he gave it to us, praying for each of the brethren, that he might be worthy of the Eucharist of the Lord. He also therefore, having likewise tasted it, said: To me also let there be a portion with you, and peace, O beloved. And having thus spoken, and confirmed the brethren, he said to Eutyches, also named Verus: Behold, I appoint thee a minister [1] of the Church of Christ, and I entrust to thee the flock of Christ. Be mindful, therefore, of the commandments of the Lord; and if thou shouldst fall into trails or dangers, be not afraid: for thou shalt fall under many troubles, and thou shalt be shown to be an eminent witness [2] of the Lord. Thus, then, Verus, attend to the flock as a servant of God, until the time appointed for thy testimony.

And when John had spoken this, and more than this, having entrusted to him the flock of Christ, he says to him: Take some brethren, with baskets and vessels, and follow me. And Eutyches, without considering, [3] did what he was bid. And the blessed John having gone forth from the house, went outside of the gates, having told the multitude to stand off from him. And having come to the tomb of one of our brethren, he told them to dig. And they dug. And he says: Let the trench be deeper. And as they dug, he conversed with those who had come out of the house with him, building them up, and furnishing them thoroughly into the majesty of the Lord. And when the young men had finished the trench, as he had wished, while we knew [4] nothing, he takes off the clothes he had on, and throws them, as if they were some bedding, into the depth of the trench; and, standing in only his drawers, [5] stretched forth his hands, and prayed.

O God, who hast chosen us for the mission [6] of the Gentiles, who hast sent us out into the world, who hast declared Thyself through the apostles; who hast never rested, but always savest from the foundation of the world; who hast made Thyself known through all nature; who hast made our wild and savage nature quiet and peaceable; who hast given Thyself to it when thirsting after knowledge; [7] who hast put to death its adversary, when it took refuge in Thee;

who hast given it Thy hand, and raised it from the things done in Hades; who hast shown it its own enemy; who hast in purity turned its thoughts upon Thee, O Christ Jesus, Lord of things in heaven, and law of things on earth, the course of things aerial, and guardian of things etherial, the fear of those under the earth, and grace of Thine own people, receive also the soul of Thy John, which has been certainly deemed worthy by Thee, Thou who hast preserved me also till the present hour pure to Thyself, and free from intercourse with woman; who, when I wished in my youth to marry, didst appear to me, and say, I am in need of thee, John; who didst strengthen for me beforehand my bodily weakness; who, when a third time I wished to marry, didst say to me at the third hour, in the sea, John, if thou wert not mine, I would let thee marry; who hast opened up the sight of my mind, and hast favoured my bodily [8] eyes; who, when I was looking about me, didst call even the gazing upon a woman hateful; who didst deliver me from temporary show, and preserve me for that which endureth for ever; who didst separate me from the filthy madness of the flesh; who didst stop up [9] the secret disease of the soul, and cut out its open actions; who didst afflict and banish him who rebelled in me; who didst establish my love to Thee spotless and unimpaired; who didst give me undoubting faith in Thee; who hast drawn out for me pure thoughts towards Thee; who hast given me the due reward of my works; who hast set it in my soul to have no other possession than Thee alone: for what is more precious than Thou? Now, O Lord, when I have accomplished Thy stewardship with which I was entrusted, make me worthy of Thy repose, having wrought that which is perfect in Thee, which is ineffable salvation. And as I go to Thee, let the fire withdraw, let darkness be overcome, let the furnace be slackened, let Gehenna be extinguished, let the angels follow, let the demons be afraid, let the princes be broken in pieces, let the powers of darkness fall, let the places on the right hand stand firm, let those on the left abide not, let the devil be muzzled, let Satan be laughed to scorn, let his madness be tamed, let his wrath be broken, let his children be trodden under foot, and let all his root be uprooted; and grant to me to accomplish the journey to Thee, not insulted, not despitefully treated, and to receive what Thou hast promised to those that live in purity, and that have loved a holy life.

And gazing towards heaven, he glorified God; and having sealed himself altogether, he stood and said to us, Peace and grace be with you,

---

1 Or, deacon.
2 i.e., martyr.
3 The other MSS. has: not without concern.
4 Or, saw.
5 The word διγρωσίῳ is not to be found in any of the dictionaries. Perhaps it is a misreading of διαζώστρᾳ.
6 Or, apostleship.
7 Lit., words or reasons.

8 Or, visible.
9 Or, muzzle.

brethren! and sent the brethren away. And when they went on the morrow they did not find him, but his sandals, and a fountain welling up. And after that they remembered what had been said to Peter by the Lord about him: For what does it concern thee if I should wish him to remain until I come?[1] And they glorified God for the miracle that had happened. And having thus believed, they retired praising and blessing the benignant God; because to Him is due glory now and ever, and to ages of ages. Amen.

[1] John xxi. 22.

REVELATION OF MOSES

ACCOUNT and life of Adam and Eve, the first-created, revealed by God to His servant Moses, when he received from the hand of the Lord the tables of the law of the covenant, instructed by the archangel Michael.

This is the account of Adam and Eve. After they went forth out of paradise, Adam took Eve his wife, and went up into the east. And he remained there eighteen years and two months; and Eve conceived and brought forth two sons, Diaphotus called Cain, and Amilabes[1] called Abel.

And after this, Adam and Eve were with one another; and when they lay down, Eve said to Adam her lord: My lord, I have seen in a dream this night the blood of my son Amilabes, who is called Abel, thrown into the mouth of Cain his brother, and he drank it without pity. And he entreated him to grant him a little of it, but he did not listen to him, but drank it all up; and it did not remain in his belly, but came forth out of his mouth. And Adam said to Eve: Let us arise, and go and see what has happened to them, lest perchance the enemy should be in any way warring against them.

And having both gone, they found Abel killed by the hand of Cain his brother. And God says to the archangel Michael: Say to Adam, Do not relate the mystery which thou knowest to thy son Cain, for he is a son of wrath. But grieve thyself not; for I will give thee instead of him another son, who shall show thee all things, as many as thou shalt do to him; but do thou tell him nothing. This God said to His angel; and Adam kept the word in his heart, and with him Eve also, having grief about Abel their son.

And after this, Adam knew his wife Eve, and she conceived and brought forth Seth. And Adam says to Eve: Behold, we have brought forth a son instead of Abel whom Cain slew; let us give glory and sacrifice to God.

And Adam had[2] thirty sons and thirty daughters.[3] And he fell into disease, and cried with a loud voice, and said: Let all my sons come to me, that I may see them before I die. And they were all brought together, for the earth was inhabited in three parts; and they all came to the door of the house into which he had entered to pray to God. And his son Seth said: Father Adam, what is thy disease? And he says: My children, great trouble has hold of me. And they say: What is the trouble and disease? And Seth answered and said to him: Is it that thou rememberest the *fruits* of paradise of which thou didst eat, and grievest thyself because of the desire of them? If it is so, tell me, and I will go and bring thee fruit from paradise. For I will put dung upon my head, and weep and pray, and the Lord will hearken to me, and send his angel; and I shall bring *it* to thee,[4] that thy trouble may cease from thee. Adam says to him: No, my son Seth; but I have disease and trouble. Seth says to him: And how have they come upon thee? Adam said to him: When God made us, me and your mother, for whose sake also I die, He gave us every plant in paradise; but about one he commanded us not to eat of it, because on account of it we should die. And the hour was at hand for the angels who guarded your mother to go up and worship the Lord; and the enemy gave to her, and she ate of the tree, knowing that I was not near her, nor the holy angels; then she gave me also to eat. And when we had both eaten, God was angry with us. And the Lord, coming into paradise, set His throne, and called with a dreadful voice, saying, Adam, where art thou? and why art thou hidden from my face? shall the house be hidden from him that built it? And He says, Since thou hast forsaken my covenant, I have brought upon thy body seventy strokes.[5] The trouble of the first stroke is the injury of the eyes; the trouble of the second stroke, of the hearing; and so in succession, all the strokes shall overtake thee.

And Adam thus speaking to his sons, groaned out loud, and said: What shall I do? I am in great grief. And Eve also wept, saying: My lord Adam, arise, give me the half of thy disease,

---

[1] There is great variety as to these names in the MSS. The true reading was probably διαφύτωρ or διαφυτευτής, a planter, and μηλατάς or μηλοβότης, a keeper of sheep.
[2] Lit., made.
[3] One MS. adds: And Adam lived 930 years; and when he came to his end he cried, etc.
[4] One MS. has: and he will bring to me of the tree in which compassion flows, and thy trouble shall cease from thee.
[5] Or, plagues.

and let me bear it, because through me this has happened to thee; through me thou art in distresses and troubles. And Adam said to Eve: Arise, and go with our son Seth near paradise, and put earth upon your heads, and weep, beseeching the Lord that He may have compassion upon me, and send His angel to paradise, and give me of the tree in which flows the oil out of it, and that thou mayest bring it to me; and I shall anoint myself, and have rest, and show thee the manner in which we were deceived at first.

And Seth and Eve went into the regions of paradise. And as they were going along, Eve saw her son, and a wild beast fighting with him. And Eve wept, saying: Woe's me, woe's me; for if I come to the day of the resurrection, all who have sinned will curse me, saying, Eve did not keep the commandment of God. And Eve cried out to the wild beast, saying: O thou evil wild beast, wilt thou not be afraid to fight with the image of God? How has thy mouth been opened? how have thy teeth been strengthened? how hast thou not been mindful of thy subjection, that thou wast formerly subject to the image of God? Then the wild beast cried out, saying: O Eve, not against us thy upbraiding nor thy weeping, but against thyself, since the beginning of the wild beasts was from thee. How was thy mouth opened to eat of the tree about which God had commanded thee not to eat of it? For this reason also our nature has been changed. Now, therefore, thou shalt not be able to bear up, if I begin to reproach thee. And Seth says to the wild beast: Shut thy mouth and be silent, and stand off from the image of God till the day of judgment. Then the wild beast says to Seth: Behold, I stand off, Seth, from the image of God. Then the wild beast fled, and left him wounded, and went to his covert.

And Seth went with his mother Eve near paradise: and they wept there, beseeching God to send His angel, to give [1] them the oil of compassion. And God sent to them the archangel Michael, and he said to them these words: Seth, man of God, do not weary thyself praying in this supplication about the tree in which flows the oil to anoint thy father Adam; for it will not happen to thee now, but at the last times. Then shall arise all flesh from Adam even to that great day, as many as shall be a holy people; then shall be given to them all the delight of paradise, and God shall be in the midst of them; and there shall not any more be sinners before Him, because the wicked heart shall be taken from them, and there shall be given to them a heart made to understand what is good, and to worship God only. Do thou again go to thy father, since the measure of his life has been

fulfilled, equal to [2] three days. And when his soul goes out, thou wilt behold its dreadful passage.

And the angel, having said this, went away from them. And Seth and Eve came to the tent where Adam was lying. And Adam says to Eve: Why didst thou work mischief against us, and bring upon us great wrath, which is death, holding sway over all our race? And he says to her: Call all our children, and our children's children, and relate to them the manner of our transgression.

Then Eve says to them: Listen, all my children, and my children's children, and I shall relate to you how our enemy deceived us. It came to pass, while we were keeping paradise, that we kept each the portion allotted to him by God. And I was keeping in my lot the south and west. And the devil went into the lot of Adam where were the male wild beasts; since God parted to us the wild beasts, and had given all the males to your father, and all the females He gave to me, and each of us watched his own. And the devil spoke to the serpent, saying, Arise, come to me, and I shall tell you a thing in which thou mayst be of service. Then the serpent came to him, and the devil says to him, I hear that thou art more sagacious than all the wild beasts, and I have come to make thy acquaintance; [3] and I have found thee greater than all the wild beasts, and they associate with thee; notwithstanding, thou doest reverence to one far inferior. Why eatest thou of the tares [4] of Adam and his wife, and not of the fruit of paradise? Arise and come hither, and we shall make him be cast out of paradise through his wife, as we also were cast out through him. The serpent says to him, I am afraid lest the Lord be angry with me. The devil says to him, Be not afraid; only become my instrument, and I will speak through thy mouth a word by which thou shalt be able to deceive him. Then straightway he hung by the walls of paradise about the hour when the angels of God went up to worship. Then Satan came in the form of an angel, and praised God as did the angels; and looking out from the wall, I saw him like an angel. And says he to me, Art thou Eve? And I said to him, I am. And says he to me, What doest thou in paradise? And I said to him, God has set us to keep it, and to eat of it. The devil answered me through the mouth of the serpent, Ye do well, but you do not eat of every plant. And I

---

[1] Lit., and he will give.

[2] Perhaps for ἰδού we should read εἴσω, within. Another reading is: for the days of his life have been fulfilled, and he will live from to-day three days, and he will die.

[3] C has: I take counsel with thee. [C is a Vienna manuscript of the twelfth century; see p. 358, and Tischendorf, *Apocalypses Apocryphæ*, pp. xi., xii. — R.]

[4] It seems to be settled that the *zizania* of the Greeks, the *zawân* of the Arabs, was darnel; but, from the associations connected with the word, it is better to keep the common translation.

say to him, Yes, of every plant we eat, but one only which is in the midst of paradise, about which God has commanded us not to eat of it, since you will die the death. Then says the serpent to me, As God liveth, I am grieved for you, because you are like cattle. For I do not wish you to be ignorant of this; but rise, come hither, listen to me, and eat, and perceive the value of the tree, as He told us. But I said to him, I am afraid lest God be angry with me. And he says to me, Be not afraid; for as soon as thou eatest, thine eyes shall be opened, and ye shall be as gods in knowing what is good and what is evil. And God, knowing this, that ye shall be like Him, has had a grudge against you, and said, Ye shall not eat of it. But do thou observe the plant, and thou shalt see great glory about it. And I observed the plant, and saw great glory about it. And I said to him, It is beautiful to the eyes to perceive; and I was afraid to take of the fruit. And he says to me, Come, I will give to thee: follow me. And I opened to him, and he came inside into paradise, and went through it before me. And having walked a little, he turned, and says to me, I have changed my mind, and will not give thee to eat. And this he said, wishing at last to entice and destroy me. And he says to me, Swear to me that thou wilt give also to thy husband. And I said to him, I know not by what oath I shall swear to thee; but what I know I say to thee, By the throne of the Lord, and the cherubim, and the tree of life, I will give also to my husband to eat. And when he had taken the oath from me, then he went and ascended upon it. And he put upon the fruit which he gave me to eat the poison of his wickedness, that is, of his desire; for desire is the head [1] of all sin. And I bent down the branch to the ground, and took of the fruit, and ate. And in that very hour mine eyes were opened, and I knew that I was stripped [2] of the righteousness with which I had been clothed; and I wept, saying, What is this thou hast done to me, because I have been deprived of the glory with which I was clothed? And I wept too about the oath. And he came down out of the tree, and went out of sight. And I sought leaves in my portion,[3] that I might cover my shame; and I did not find them from the plants of paradise, since, at the time that I ate, the leaves of all the plants in my portion fell, except of the fig alone. And having taken leaves off it, I made myself a girdle, and it is from those plants of which I ate. And I cried out with a loud voice, saying, Adam, Adam, where art thou? Arise, come to me, and I shall show thee a great mystery. And when your

father came, I said to him words of wickedness, which brought us down from great glory. For as soon as he came I opened my mouth, and the devil spoke; and I began to advise him, saying, Come hither, my lord Adam, listen to me, and eat of the fruit of the tree of which God said to us not to eat of it, and thou shalt be as God. And your father answered and said, I am afraid lest God be angry with me. And I said to him, Be not afraid, for as soon as thou shalt eat thou shalt know good and evil. And then I quickly persuaded him, and he ate; and his eyes were opened, and he was aware, he also, of his nakedness. And he says to me, O wicked woman, why hast thou wrought mischief in us? Thou hast alienated me from the glory of God. And that same hour we heard the archangel Michael sounding his trumpet, calling the angels, saying, Thus saith the Lord, Come with me to paradise, and hear the word in which I judge Adam. And when we heard the archangel sounding, we said, Behold, God is coming into paradise to judge us. And we were afraid, and hid ourselves. And God came up into paradise, riding upon a chariot of cherubim, and the angels praising Him. When God came into paradise, the plants both of Adam's lot and of my lot bloomed, and all lifted themselves up; and the throne of God was made ready where the tree of life was. And God called Adam, saying, Adam, where art thou hidden, thinking that I shall not find thee? Shall the house be hidden from him that built it? Then your father answered and said, Not, Lord, did we hide ourselves as thinking that we should not be found by Thee; but I am afraid, because I am naked, and stand in awe of Thy power, O Lord. God says to him, Who hath shown thee that thou art naked, unless it be that thou hast forsaken my commandment which I gave thee to keep it? Then Adam remembered the word which I spake to him when I wished to deceive him, I will put thee out of danger from God. And he turned and said to me, Why hast thou done this? And I also remembered the word of the serpent, and said, The serpent deceived me. God says to Adam, Since thou hast disobeyed my commandment, and obeyed thy wife, cursed is the ground in thy labours. For whenever thou labourest it, and it will not give its strength, thorns and thistles shall it raise for thee; and in the sweat of thy face shalt thou eat thy bread. And thou shalt be in distresses of many kinds. Thou shalt weary thyself, and rest not; thou shalt be afflicted by bitterness, and shalt not taste of sweetness; thou shalt be afflicted by heat, and oppressed by cold; and thou shalt toil much, and not grow rich; and thou shalt make haste,[4] and not attain

---

[1] C has, root and origin.
[2] Lit., naked.
[3] i.e., of the garden.

[4] I have read ταχυνθήσει for παχυνθήσει: thou shalt grow fat.

thine end; and the wild beasts, of which thou wast lord, shall rise up against thee in rebellion, because thou hast not kept my commandment. And having turned to me, the Lord says to me, Since thou hast obeyed the serpent, and disobeyed my commandment, thou shalt be in distresses [1] and unbearable pains; thou shalt bring forth children with great tremblings; and in one hour shalt thou come *to bring them forth*,[2] and lose thy life in consequence of thy great straits and pangs. And thou shalt confess, and say, Lord, Lord, save me; and I shall not return to the sin of the flesh. And on this account in thine own words I shall judge thee, on account of the enmity which the enemy hath put in thee; and thou shalt turn again to thy husband, and he shall be thy lord.[3] And after speaking thus to me, He spoke to the serpent in great wrath, saying to him, Since thou hast done this, and hast become an ungracious instrument until thou shouldst deceive those that were remiss in heart, cursed art thou of all the beasts. Thou shalt be deprived of the food which thou eatest; and dust shalt thou eat all the days of thy life; upon thy breast and belly shalt thou go, and thou shalt be deprived both of thy hands and feet; there shall not be granted thee ear, nor wing, nor one limb of all which those have whom thou hast enticed by thy wickedness, and hast caused them to be cast out of paradise. And I shall put enmity between thee and between his seed. He shall lie in wait for [4] thy head, and thou for his heel, until the day of judgment. And having thus said, He commands His angels that we be cast out of paradise. And as we were being driven along, and were lamenting, your father Adam entreated the angels, saying, Allow me a little, that I may entreat God, and that He may have compassion upon me, and pity me, for I only have sinned. And they stopped driving him. And Adam cried out with weeping, saying, Pardon me, Lord, what I have done. Then says the Lord to His angels, Why have you stopped driving Adam out of paradise? It is not that the sin is mine, or that I have judged ill? Then the angels, falling to the ground, worshipped the Lord, saying, Just art Thou, Lord, and judgest what is right. And turning to Adam, the Lord said, I will not permit thee henceforth to be in paradise. And Adam answered and said, Lord, give me of the tree of life, that I may eat before I am cast out. Then

the Lord said to Adam, Thou shalt not now take of it, for it has been assigned to the cherubim and the flaming sword, which turneth to guard it on account of thee, that thou mayst not taste of it and be free from death for ever, but that thou mayst have the war which the enemy has set in thee. But when thou art gone out of paradise, if thou shalt keep thyself from all evil, as being destined to die, I will again raise thee up when the resurrection comes, and then there shall be given thee of the tree of life, and thou shalt be free from death for ever. And having thus said, the Lord commanded us to be cast out of paradise. And your father wept before the angels over against paradise. And the angels say to him, What dost thou wish that we should do for thee, Adam? And your father answered and said to the angels, Behold, you cast me out. I beseech you, allow me to take sweet odours out of paradise, in order that, after I go out, I may offer sacrifice to God, that God may listen to me. And the angels, advancing, said to God, Jael, eternal King, order to be given to Adam sacrifices [5] of sweet odour out of paradise. And God ordered Adam to go, that he might take perfumes of sweet odour out of paradise for his food. And the angels let him go, and he gathered both kinds — saffron and spikenard, and calamus [6] and cinnamon, and other seeds for his food; and having taken them, he went forth out of paradise. And we came to the earth.[7]

Now, then, my children, I have shown you the manner in which we were deceived. But do ye watch over yourselves, so as not to forsake what is good.

And when she had thus spoken in the midst of her sons, and Adam was lying in his disease, and he had one other day before going out of the body, Eve says to Adam: Why is it that thou diest, and I live? or how long time have I to spend after thou diest? tell me. Then says Adam to Eve: Do not trouble thyself about matters; for thou wilt not be long after me, but we shall both die alike, and thou wilt be laid into my place.[8] And when I am dead you will leave [9] me, and let no one touch me, until the angel of the Lord shall say something about me; for God will not forget me, but will seek His own vessel which He fashioned. Arise, rather, pray to God until I restore my spirit into the hands of Him who has given it; because we know not how we shall meet Him who made us, whether He shall be angry with us, or turn and have mercy upon us. Then arose Eve, and went

---

[1] The text has ματαίοις, vain; the true reading is probably καμάτοις or μόχθοις.
[2] Inserted from MS. C.
[3] MS. B inserts: And Eve was twelve years old when the demon deceived her, and gave her evil desires. For night and day he ceased not to bear hatred against them, because he himself was formerly in paradise; and therefore he supplanted them, because he could not bear to see them in paradise. [B is a Vienna MS. of the thirteenth or fourteenth century; see Tischendorf, *Apocal. Apocr.*, p. xi. — R.]
[4] This is after the version of the LXX., and it is also the interpretation of Gesenius of the Hebrew *shúph*, Gen. iii. 15.

[5] Or, incense.
[6] This is the "sweet cane" of Isa. xliii. 24; Jer. vi. 20. See also Ex. xxx. 23; Cant. iv. 14; Ezek. xxvii. 19.
[7] Or, and we were upon the earth.
[8] Perhaps τάφον, tomb, would be better than τόπον.
[9] Or, anoint.

outside ; and falling to the ground, she said : I have sinned, O God ; I have sinned, O Father of all ; I have sinned to Thee, I have sinned against Thy chosen angels, I have sinned against the cherubim, I have sinned against Thine unshaken throne ; I have sinned, O Lord, I have sinned much, I have sinned before Thee, and every sin [1] through me has come upon the creation. And while Eve was still praying, being on her knees, behold, there came to her the angel of humanity, and raised her up, saying : Arise, Eve, from thy repentance ; for, behold, Adam thy husband has gone forth from his body ; arise and see his spirit carried up to Him that made [2] it, to meet Him.

And Eve arose, and covered her face with her hand ; and the angel says to her : Raise thyself from the things of earth. And Eve gazed up into heaven, and she saw a chariot of light going along under four shining eagles — and it was not possible for any one born of woman [3] to tell the glory of them, or to see the face of them — and angels going before the chariot. And when they came to the place where your father Adam was lying, the chariot stood still, and the seraphim between your father and the chariot. And I saw golden censers, and three vials ; and, behold, all the angels with incense, and the censers, and the vials, came to the altar, and blew them up, and the smoke of the incense covered the firmaments. And the angels fell down and worshipped God, crying out and saying : Holy Jael, forgive ; for he is Thine image, and the work of Thine holy hands.

And again, I Eve saw two great and awful mysteries standing before God. And I wept for fear, and cried out to my son Seth, saying : Arise, Seth, from the body of thy father Adam, and come to me, that thou mayst see what the eye of no one hath ever seen ; and they are praying for thy father Adam.[4]

Then Seth arose and went to his mother, and said to her : What has befallen thee ? and why weepest thou ? She says to him : Look up with thine eyes, and see the seven firmaments opened, and see with thine eyes how the body of thy father lies upon its face, and all the holy angels with him, praying for him, and saying : Pardon him, O Father of the universe ; for he is Thine image. What then, my child Seth, will this be ? and when will he be delivered into the hands of our invisible Father and God ? And who are the two dark-faced ones who stand by at the prayer of thy father ? And Seth says to his mother : These are the sun and the moon, and they are falling down and praying for my father

Adam. Eve says to him : And where is their light, and why have they become black-looking ? And Seth says to her : They cannot shine in the presence of the Light of the universe,[5] and for this reason the light from them has been hidden.

And while Seth was speaking to his mother, the angels lying upon their faces sounded their trumpets, and cried out with an awful voice, saying, Blessed be the glory of the Lord upon what He has made, for He has had compassion upon Adam, the work of His hands. When the angels had sounded this forth, there came one of the six-winged seraphim, and hurried Adam to the Acherusian lake, and washed him in presence of God. And he spent three hours [6] lying, and thus the Lord of the universe, sitting upon His holy throne, stretched forth His hands, and raised Adam, and delivered him to the archangel Michael, saying to him : Raise him into paradise, even to the third heaven, and let him be there until that great and dreadful day which I am to bring upon the world. And the archangel Michael, having taken Adam, led him away, and anointed him, as God said to him at the pardoning of Adam.

After all these things, therefore, the archangel asked about the funeral rites of the remains ; and God commanded that all the angels should come together into His presence, each according to his rank. And all the angels were assembled, some with censers, some with trumpets. And the Lord of Hosts went up,[7] and the winds drew Him, and cherubim riding upon the winds, and the angels of heaven went before Him ; and they came to where the body of Adam was, and took it. And they came to paradise, and all the trees of paradise were moved so that all begotten from Adam hung their heads in sleep at the sweet smell, except Seth, because he had been begotten according to the appointment of God.

The body of Adam, then, was lying on the ground in paradise, and Seth was grieved exceedingly about him. And the Lord God says : Adam, why hast thou done this ? If thou hadst kept my commandment, those that brought thee down to this place would not have rejoiced. Nevertheless I say unto thee, that I will turn their joy into grief, but I will turn thy grief into joy ; and having turned, I will set thee in thy kingdom, on the throne of him that deceived thee ; and he shall be cast into this place, that thou mayst sit upon him. Then shall be condemned, he and those who hear him ; and they shall be much grieved, and shall weep, seeing thee sitting upon his glorious throne.

---

[1] Or, all sin.
[2] The text has ποιήσαντα, a misprint for ποιήσαντα.
[3] Lit., of a womb.
[4] The last clause is not in C.

[5] MS. A here ends thus: the Father, and the Son, and the Holy Spirit, now and ever, and to ages of ages. Amen. [A is the Venice MS." of about the thirteenth century;" Tischendorf, *Apocal. Apocr.*, p. xi. — R.]
[6] The MSS. originally had *days*, and *hours* is substituted in another hand.
[7] i.e., mounted His chariot.

And then He said to the archangel Michael: Go into paradise, into the third heaven, and bring me three cloths of fine linen and silk. And God said to Michael, Gabriel, Uriel, and Raphael:[1] Cover Adam's body with the cloths, and bring olive oil of sweet odour, and pour upon him. And having thus done, they prepared his body for burial. And the Lord said: Let also the body of Abel be brought. And having brought other cloths, they prepared it also for burial, since it had not been prepared for burial since the day on which his brother Cain slew him. For the wicked Cain, having taken great pains to hide it, had not been able; for the earth did not receive it, saying: I will not receive a body into companionship[2] until that dust which was taken up and fashioned upon me come to me. And then the angels took it up, and laid it on the rock until his father died. And both were buried, according to the commandment of God, in the regions of paradise, in the place in which God found the dust.[3] And God sent seven angels into paradise, and they brought many sweet-smelling herbs, and laid them in the earth; and thus they took the two bodies, and buried them in the place which they had dug and built.

And God called Adam, and said: Adam, Adam. And the body answered out of the ground, and said: Here am I, Lord. And the Lord says to him: I said to thee, Dust[4] thou art, and unto dust thou shalt return. Again I promise thee the resurrection. I will raise thee up in the last day in the resurrection, with every man who is of thy seed.

And after these words God made a three-cornered seal, and sealed the tomb, that no one should do anything to him in the six days, until his rib should return to him. And the beneficent God and the holy angels having laid him in his place, after the six days Eve also died. And while she lived she wept about her falling asleep, because she knew not where her body was to be laid. For when the Lord was present in paradise when they buried Adam, both she and her children fell asleep, except Seth, as I said. And Eve, in the hour of her death, besought that she might be buried where Adam her husband was, saying thus: My Lord, Lord and God of all virtue, do not separate me, Thy servant, from the body of Adam, for of his members Thou madest me; but grant to me, even me, the unworthy and the sinner, to be buried by his body. And as I was along with him in paradise, and not separated from him after the transgression, so also let no one separate us. After having prayed, therefore, she looked up into heaven, and stood up, and said, beating her breast: God of all, receive my spirit. And straightway she gave up her spirit to God.

And when she was dead, the archangel Michael stood beside her; and there came three angels, and took her body, and buried it where the body of Abel was. And the archangel Michael said to Seth: Thus bury every man that dies, until the day of the resurrection. And after having given this law, he said to him: Do not mourn beyond six days. And on the seventh day, rest, and rejoice in it, because in it God and we the angels rejoice in the righteous soul that has departed from earth. Having thus spoken, the archangel Michael went up into heaven, glorifying, and saying the Alleluia:[5] Holy, holy, holy Lord, to the glory of God the Father, because to Him is due glory, honour, and adoration, with His unbeginning and life-giving Spirit, now and ever, and to ages of ages. Amen.

---

[1] According to a Jewish tradition, these were the four angels who stood round the throne of God.

[2] Probably the reading should be ἕτερον, another, and not ἑταῖρον. Or it may mean: I will not receive a friendly body, i.e., one upon which I have no claims.

[3] i.e., of which Adam was made.

[4] Lit., earth.

[5] MS. D ends here with: To whom be glory and strength to ages of ages. Amen. [D is the Milan manuscript which Tischendorf assigns to " about the eleventh century," *Apocalypses Apocryphæ*, p. xi.—R.]

REVELATION OF ESDRAS

WORD AND REVELATION OF ESDRAS, THE HOLY PROPHET AND BELOVED OF GOD.

It came to pass in the thirtieth year, on the twenty-second of the month, I was in my house. And I cried out and said to the Most High: Lord, give the glory,[1] in order that I may see Thy mysteries. And when it was night, there came an angel, Michael the archangel, and says to me: O Prophet Esdras, refrain from bread for seventy *weeks*.[2] And I fasted as he told me. And there came Raphael the commander of the host, and gave me a storax rod. And I fasted twice sixty[3] weeks. And I saw the mysteries of God and His angels. And I said to them: I wish to plead before God about the race of the Christians. It is good for a man not to be born rather than to come into the world. I was therefore taken up into heaven, and I saw in the first heaven a great army of angels; and they took me to the judgments. And I heard a voice saying to me: Have mercy on us, O thou chosen of God, Esdras. Then began I to say: Woe to sinners when they see one who is just more than the angels, and they themselves are in the Gehenna of fire! And Esdras said: Have mercy on the works of Thine hands, Thou who art compassionate, and of great mercy. Judge me rather than the souls of the sinners; for it is better that one soul should be punished, and that the whole world should not come to destruction. And God said: I will give rest in paradise to the righteous, and I have become[4] merciful. And Esdras said: Lord, why dost Thou confer benefits on the righteous? for just as one who has been hired out, and has served out his time, goes and again works as a slave when he come to his masters, so also the righteous has received his reward in the heavens. But have mercy on the sinners, for we know that Thou art merciful. And God said: I do not see how I can have mercy upon them. And Esdras said: They cannot endure

Thy wrath. And God said: This is *the fate* of such. And God said: I wish to have thee like Paul and John, as thou hast given me uncorrupted the treasure that cannot be stolen, the treasure of virginity, the bulwark[5] of men. And Esdras said: It is good for a man not to be born. It is good not to be in life. The irrational *creatures* are better than man, because they have no punishment; but Thou hast taken us, and given us up to judgment. Woe to the sinners in the world to come! because their judgment is endless, and the flame unquenchable. And while I was thus speaking to him, there came Michael and Gabriel, and all the apostles; and they said: Rejoice, O faithful man of God! And Esdras said:[6] Arise, and come hither with me, O Lord, to judgment. And the Lord said: Behold, I give thee my covenant between me and thee, that you may receive it. And Esdras said: Let us plead in Thy hearing.[7] And God said: Ask Abraham your father how a son pleads with his father,[8] and come plead with us. And Esdras said: As the Lord liveth, I will not cease pleading with Thee in behalf of the race of the Christians. Where are Thine ancient compassions, O Lord? Where is Thy long-suffering? And God said: As I have made night and day, I have made the righteous and the sinner; and he should have lived like the righteous. And the prophet said: Who made Adam the first-formed? And God said: My undefiled hands. And I put him in paradise to guard the food of the tree of life; and thereafter he became disobedient, and did this in transgression. And the prophet said: Was he not protected by an angel? and was not his life guarded by the cherubim to endless ages? and how was he deceived who was guarded by angels? for Thou didst command all to be present, and to attend to

---

[1] i.e., reveal.
[2] Supplied by Tischendorf. Perhaps it should be days.
[3] Perhaps this should be five — ϵ instead of ξ — which would make seventy days, as above.
[4] Or, I am.

[5] Lit., wall.
[6] Tischendorf supplies this clause from conjecture, and adds that some more seems to have fallen out.
[7] Lit., to Thine ear.
[8] This seems to be the meaning of the text, which is somewhat corrupt. It obviously refers to Abraham pleading for Sodom.

what was said by Thee.[1] But if Thou hadst not given him Eve, the serpent would not have deceived her;[2] but whom Thou wilt Thou savest, and whom Thou wilt Thou destroyest.[3] And the prophet said: Let us come, my Lord, to a second judgment. And God said: I cast fire upon Sodom and Gomorrah. And the prophet said: Lord, Thou dealest with us according to our deserts. And God said: Your sins transcend my clemency. And the prophet said: Call to mind the Scriptures, my Father, who hast measured out Jerusalem, and set her up again. Have mercy, O Lord, upon sinners; have mercy upon Thine own creatures;[4] have pity upon Thy works. Then God remembered those whom He had made, and said to the prophet: How can I have mercy upon them? Vinegar and gall did they give me to drink,[5] and not even then did they repent. And the prophet said: Reveal Thy cherubim, and let us go together to judgment; and show me the day of judgment, what like it is. And God said: Thou hast been deceived, Esdras; for such is the day of judgment as that in which there is no rain upon the earth; for it is a merciful tribunal as compared with that day. And the prophet said: I will not cease to plead with Thee, unless I see the day of the consummation. And God said:[6] Number the stars and the sand of the sea; and if thou shalt be able to number this, thou art also able to plead with me. And the prophet said: Lord, Thou knowest that I wear human flesh; and how can I count the stars of the heaven, and the sand of the sea? And God said: My chosen prophet, no man will know that great day and the appearing[7] that comes to judge the world. For thy sake, my prophet, I have told thee the day; but the hour have I not told thee. And the prophet said: Lord, tell me also the years. And God said: If I see the righteousness of the world, that it has abounded, I will have patience with them; but if not, I will stretch forth my hand, and lay hold of the world by the four quarters, and bring them all together into the valley of Jehoshaphat,[8] and I will wipe out the race of men, so that the world shall be no more. And the prophet said: And how can Thy right hand be glorified? And God said: I shall be glorified by my angels. And the prophet said: Lord, if Thou hast resolved to do this, why didst Thou make man? Thou didst say to our father Abraham,[9] Multiplying I will multiply thy seed as the stars of the heaven, and as the sand that is

by the sea-shore;[10] and where is Thy promise? And God said: First will I make an earthquake for the fall of four-footed beasts and of men; and when you see that brother gives up brother to death, and that children shall rise up against their parents, and that a woman forsakes her own husband, and when nation shall rise up against nation in war, then will you know that the end is near.[11] For then neither brother pities brother, nor man wife, nor children parents, nor friends friends, nor a slave his master; for he who is the adversary of men shall come up from Tartarus, and shall show men many things. What shall I make of thee, Esdras? and wilt thou yet plead with me? And the prophet said: Lord, I shall not cease to plead with Thee. And God said: Number the flowers of the earth. If thou shalt be able to number them, thou art able also to plead with me. And the prophet said: Lord, I cannot number *them*. I wear human flesh; but I shall not cease to plead with Thee. I wish, Lord, to see also the under parts of Tartarus. And God said: Come down and see. And He gave me Michael, and Gabriel, and other thirty-four angels; and I went down eighty-five steps, and they brought me down five hundred steps, and I saw a fiery throne, and an old man sitting upon it; and his judgment was merciless. And I said to the angels: Who is this? and what is his sin? And they said to me: This is Herod, who for a time was a king, and ordered to put to death the children from two years old and under.[12] And I said: Woe to his soul! And again they took me down thirty steps, and I there saw boilings up of fire, and in them *there was* a multitude of sinners; and I heard their voice, but saw not their forms. And they took me down lower many steps, which I could not measure. And I there saw old men, and fiery pivots turning in their ears. And I said: Who are these? and what is their sin? And they said to me: These are they who would not listen.[13] And they took me down again other five hundred steps, and I there saw the worm that sleeps not, and fire burning up the sinners. And they took me down to the lowest part of destruction, and I saw there the twelve plagues of the abyss. And they took me away to the south, and I saw there a man hanging by the eyelids; and the angels kept scourging him. And I asked: Who is this? and what is his sin? And Michael the commander said to me: This is one who lay with his mother; for having put into practice a small wish, he has been ordered to be hanged. And they took me away to the north, and I saw there a man bound with iron chains. And I asked: Who is this? And he said to me: This is he who

---

[1] This passage is very corrupt in the text; but a few emendations bring out the meaning above.
[2] Better, him.
[3] Comp. Ex. xxxiii. 19; Rom. ix. 18.
[4] Lit., framing, or fashioning.
[5] Matt. xxvii. 34.
[6] This is inserted by Tischendorf.
[7] Comp. 2 Tim. iv. 1, 8; Tit. ii. 13.
[8] Joel iii. 2, 12.
[9] Gen. xxii. 17.

[10] Lit., the lip of the sea.
[11] Comp. Matt. xxiv.
[12] Matt. ii. 16.
[13] Or, who heard wrong.

said, I am the Son of God, that made stones bread, and water wine. And the prophet said: My lord, let me know what is his form, and I shall tell the race of men, that they may not believe in him. And he said to me: The form of his countenance is like that of a wild beast; his right eye like the star that rises in the morning, and the other without motion; his mouth one cubit; his teeth span long; his fingers like scythes; the track of his feet of two spans; and in his face an inscription, Antichrist. He has been exalted to heaven; he shall go down to Hades.[1] At one time he shall become a child; at another, an old man. And the prophet said: Lord, and how dost Thou permit him, and he deceives the race of men? And God said: Listen, my prophet. He becomes both child and old man, and no one believes him that he is my beloved Son. And after this a trumpet, and the tombs shall be opened, and the dead shall be raised incorruptible.[2] Then the adversary, hearing the dreadful threatening, shall be hidden in outer darkness. Then the heaven, and the earth, and the sea shall be destroyed. Then shall I burn the heaven eighty cubits, and the earth eight hundred cubits. And the prophet said: And how has the heaven sinned? And God said: Since[3] . . . there is evil. And the prophet said: Lord, and the earth, how has it sinned? And God said: Since the adversary, having heard the dreadful threatening, shall be hidden, even on account of this will I melt the earth, and with it the opponent of the race of men. And the prophet said: Have mercy, Lord, upon the race of the Christians. And I saw a woman hanging, and four wild beasts sucking her breasts. And the angels said to me: She grudged to give her milk, but even threw her infants into the rivers. And I saw a dreadful darkness, and a night that had no stars nor moon; nor is there there young or old, nor brother with brother, nor mother with child, nor wife with husband. And I wept, and said: O Lord God, have mercy upon the sinners. And as I said this, there came a cloud and snatched me up, and carried me away again into the heavens. And I saw there many judgments; and I wept bitterly, and said: It is good for a man not to have come out of his mother's womb. And those who were in torment cried out, saying: Since thou hast come hither, O holy one of God, we have found a little remission. And the prophet said: Blessed are they that weep for their sins. And God said: Hear, O beloved Esdras. As a husbandman casts the seed of the corn into the ground, so also the man casts his seed into the parts of the woman. The first *month* it is all together; the

second it increases in size; the third it gets hair; the fourth it gets nails; the fifth it is turned into milk;[4] and the sixth it is made ready, and receives life;[5] the seventh it is completely furnished; the ninth the barriers of the gate of the woman are opened; and it is born safe and sound into the earth. And the prophet said: Lord, it is good for man not to have been born. Woe to the human race then, when Thou shalt come to judgment! And I said to the Lord: Lord, why hast Thou created man, and delivered him up to judgment? And God said, with a lofty proclamation: I will not by any means have mercy on those who transgress my covenant. And the prophet said: Lord, where is Thy goodness? And God said: I have prepared all things for man's sake, and man does not keep my commandments. And the prophet said: Lord, reveal to me the judgments and paradise. And the angels took me away towards the east, and I saw the tree of life. And I saw there Enoch, and Elias, and Moses, and Peter, and Paul, and Luke, and Matthias, and all the righteous, and the patriarchs. And I saw there the keeping of the air within bounds, and the blowing of the winds, and the storehouses of the ice, and the eternal judgments. And I saw there a man hanging by the skull. And they said to me: This man removed landmarks. And I saw there great judgments.[6] And I said to the Lord: O Lord God, and what man, then, who has been born has not sinned? And they took me lower down into Tartarus, and I saw all the sinners lamenting and weeping and mourning bitterly. And I also wept, seeing the race of men thus tormented. Then God says to me: Knowest thou, Esdras, the names of the angels at the end of the world? Michael, Gabriel, Uriel, Raphael, Gabuthelon, Aker, Arphugitonos, Beburos, Zebuleon. Then there came a voice to me: Come hither and die, Esdras, my beloved; give that which hath been entrusted to thee.[7] And the prophet said: And whence can you bring forth my soul? And the angels said: We can put it forth through the mouth. And the prophet said: Mouth to mouth have I spoken with God,[8] and it comes not forth thence. And the angels said: Let us bring it out through thy nostrils. And the prophet said: My nostrils have smelled the sweet savour of the glory of God. And the angels said: We can bring it out through thine eyes. And the prophet said: Mine eyes have seen the back parts of God.[9] And the angels said: We can bring it out through the crown of thy head.

---

[1] Comp. Matt. xi. 23.
[2] 1 Cor. xv. 52.
[3] There is something wanting here in the text.
[4] So in the text.
[5] Or, the soul.
[6] Or, tribunals.
[7] Or, thy trust, or pledge. Comp. 1 Tim. vi. 20; 2 Tim. i. 14, in Textus Receptus.
[8] Comp. Deut. xxxiv. 10.
[9] Comp. Ex. xxxiii. 23.

And the prophet said : I walked about with Moses also on the mountain, and it comes not forth thence. And the angels said : We can put it forth through the points of thy nails. And the prophet said : My feet also have walked about on the altar. And the angels went away without having done anything, saying : Lord, we cannot get his soul. Then He says to His only begotten Son : Go down, my beloved Son, with a great host of angels, and take the soul of my beloved Esdras. For the Lord, having taken a great host of angels, says to the prophet : Give me the trust which I entrusted to thee ; the crown has been prepared for thee.[1] And the prophet said : Lord, if Thou take my soul from me, who will be left to plead with Thee for the race of men? And God said : As thou art mortal, and of the earth, do not plead with me. And the prophet said : I will not cease to plead. And God said : Give up just now the trust ; the crown has been prepared for thee. Come and die, that thou mayst obtain it. Then the prophet began to say with tears : O Lord, what good have I done pleading with Thee, and I am going to fall down into the earth? Woe's me, woe's me, that I am going to be eaten up by worms ! Weep, all ye saints and ye righteous, for me, who have pleaded much, and who am delivered up to death. Weep for me, all ye saints and ye righteous, because I have gone to the pit of Hades. And God said to him : Hear, Esdras, my beloved. I, who am immortal, endured a cross ; I tasted vinegar and gall ; I was laid in a tomb, and I raised up my chosen ones ; I called Adam up out of Hades, that *I might save*[2] the race of men. Do not therefore be afraid of death : for that which is from me — that is to say, the soul — goes to heaven ; and that which is from the earth — that is to say, the body — goes to the earth, from which it was taken.[3] And the prophet said : Woe's me ! woe's me ! what shall I set about? what shall I do? I know not. And then the blessed Esdras began to say : O eternal God, the Maker of the whole creation, who hast measured the heaven with a span, and who holdest the earth as a handful,[4] who ridest upon the cherubim, who didst take the prophet Elias to the heavens in a chariot of fire,[5] who givest food to all flesh, whom all things dread and tremble at from the face of Thy power, — listen to me, who have pleaded much, and give to all who transcribe this book, and have it, and remember my name, and honour my memory, give them a blessing from heaven ; and bless him[6] in all things, as Thou didst bless Joseph at last, and remember not his former wickedness in the day of his judgment. And as many as have not believed this book shall be burnt up like Sodom and Gomorrah. And there came to him a voice, saying : Esdras, my beloved, all things whatever thou hast asked will I give to each one. And immediately he gave up his precious soul with much honour, in the month of October, on the twenty-eighth. And they prepared him for burial with incense and psalms ; and his precious and sacred body dispenses strength of soul and body perpetually to those who have recourse to him from a longing desire. To whom is due glory, strength, honour, and adoration, — to the Father, and to the Son, and to the Holy Spirit, now and ever, and to ages of ages. Amen.

---

[1] Comp. 2 Tim. iv. 8.
[2] The word is wanting in the MS.
[3] Eccles. xii. 7.
[4] Or, in a measure. Δρακήν in the text should be δρακά. Comp. Isa. xl. 12 in the LXX.
[5] Comp. 1 Kings ii. 11 ; Ecclus. xlviii. 9.
[6] So the MS. Perhaps *them* would be better.

REVELATION OF PAUL

REVELATION of the holy Apostle Paul: the things which were revealed to him when he went up even to the third heaven, and was caught up into paradise, and heard unspeakable words.[1]

There dwelt a certain nobleman in the city of Tarsus, in the house of St. Paul the apostle, in the government of Theodosius the worshipful king, and of the most illustrious Gratianus;[2] and there was revealed to him an angel of the Lord, saying: Upturn the foundation of this house, and lift up what thou shalt find. But he thought that he had had a dream. And the angel having persisted even to a third vision, the nobleman was compelled to upturn the foundation; and having dug, he found a marble[3] box containing this revelation; and having taken it, he showed it to the ruler of the city. And the ruler, seeing it sealed up with lead, sent it to the King Theodosius, thinking that it was something else.[4] And the king having received it, and transcribed it, sent the original writing to Jerusalem. And there was written in it thus:—

The word of the Lord came to me, saying: Say to this people, Till when do you sin, and add to your sin, and provoke to anger the God who made you, saying that you are children to Abraham,[5] but doing the works of Satan, going on in speaking against God, boasting only in your addressing *of God*, but poor on account of the substance of sin? Know, ye sons of men, that the whole creation has been made subject to God; but the human race alone, by sinning, provokes God to anger. For often the great light, the sun, has come before God, saying against men: Lord God Almighty, how long dost Thou endure all the sin of men? Command me, and I will burn them up. And there came a voice to him: My long-suffering endures them all, that they may repent; but if not, they shall come to me, and I will judge them. And often also the moon and the stars have come before God, saying: Lord God Almighty, Thou hast given us the dominion of the night, and we no longer

cover the thefts, and adulteries, and blood-sheddings of men; command us, and we shall do marvels against them. And there came a voice: My long-suffering bears with them, that they may turn to me; but if not, they shall come to me, and I will judge them. And in like manner also the sea cried out, saying: Lord God Almighty, the sons of men have profaned Thy holy name; command me, and I shall rise up and cover the earth, and wipe out from it[6] the sons of men. And there came a voice, saying: My long-suffering bears with them, that they may repent; but if not, they shall come to me, and I will judge them. You see, ye sons of men, that the whole creation has been made subject to God, but the human race alone sins before God. On account of all these things, bless God without ceasing, and yet more when the sun is setting. For at this hour all the angels come to God to adore Him, and they bring before Him the works of men, of each what he has done from morning even to evening, whether good or evil. And one angel goes rejoicing on account of man when he behaves well, and another goes with a sad countenance. All the angels at the appointed hour meet for the worship of God, to bring each day's works of men. But do ye men bless God without ceasing Whenever, therefore, at the appointed hour the angels of pious men come, rejoicing and singing psalms, they meet for the worship of the Lord; and, behold, the Spirit of God *says* to them: Whence do ye come rejoicing? And they answered and said: We are here from the pious men, who in all piety spend their life, fearing the name of God. Command them, Lord, to abide even to the end in Thy righteousness. And there came to them a voice: I have both kept and will keep them void of offence in my kingdom. And when it came to pass that they went away, there came other angels with a cheerful countenance, shining like the sun. And behold a voice to them: Whence have ye come? And they answered and said: We have come from those who have held themselves aloof from the world and the things in the world for Thy holy name's sake, who in deserts, and mountains, and caves, and the

---

[1] 2 Cor. xii. 4.
[2] The MSS. have Kontianus.
[3] Or, according to the primary meaning of the word, shining, sparkling. The translation of the Syriac version has, "a box of white glass."
[4] Syr., Thinking that there was something of gold within it.
[5] Syr., of the living God.

[6] Or, sweep off it.

dens of the earth, in beds on the ground, and in fastings, spend their life.[1] Command us to be with them. And there came a voice : Go with them in peace, guarding them. Moreover, when they went away, behold, there came other angels to worship before God, mourning and weeping. And the Spirit went forth to meet them, and there came a voice to them : Whence have ye come? And they answered and said : We have come from those who have been called by Thy name, and are slaves to the matter of sin.[2] Why, then, is it necessary to minister unto them? And there came a voice to them : Do not cease to minister unto them ; perhaps they will turn ; but if not, they shall come to me, and I will judge them. Know, sons of men, that all that is done by you day by day, the angels write in the heavens. Do you therefore cease not to bless God.

And I was in the Holy Spirit, and an angel says to me : Come, follow me, that I may show thee the place of the just, where they go after their end. And I went along with the angel, and he brought me up into the heavens under the firmament ; and I perceived and saw powers great and dreadful, full of wrath, and through the mouth of them a flame of fire coming out, and clothed in garments of fire. And I asked the angel : Who are these ? And he said to me : These are they who are sent away to the souls of the sinners in the hour of necessity ; for they have not believed that there is judgment and retribution. And I looked up into the heaven, and saw angels, whose faces shone like the sun, girded with golden girdles, having in their hands prizes, on which the name of the Lord was inscribed, full of all meekness and compassion. And I asked the angel : Who are these ? And he answered and said to me : These are they who are sent forth in the day of the resurrection to bring the souls of the righteous,[3] who intrepidly walk according to God.[4] And I said to the angel : I wish to see the souls of the righteous and of the sinners, how they go out of the world. And the angel said to me : Look to the earth. And I looked, and saw the whole world as nothing disappearing before me. And I said to the angel : Is this the greatness of men ? And he said to me : Yes ; for thus every unjust man disappears. And I looked, and saw a cloud of fire wrapped over all the world ; and I said : What is this, my lord ? And he said to me : This is the unrighteousness mingled with the destruction of the sinners. And I wept, and said to the angel : I wished to see the departures of the righteous and of the sinners, in what manner

they go out of the world. And the angel says to me : Paul, look down, and see what thou hast asked. And I looked, and saw one of the sons of men falling near death. And the angel says to me : This is a righteous man, and, behold, all his works stand beside him in the hour of his necessity.[5] And there were beside him good angels, and along with them also evil angels. And the evil angels indeed found no place in him, but the good took possession of[6] the soul of the righteous man, and said to it : Take note of the body whence thou art coming out ; for it is necessary for thee again to return to it in the day of the resurrection, that thou mayst receive what God hath promised to the righteous. And the good angels who had received the soul of the righteous man, saluted it, as being well known to them. And it went with them ; and the Spirit came forth to meet them, saying : Come, soul, enter into the place of the resurrection, which God hath prepared for His righteous ones. And the angel said to me : Look down to the earth, and behold the soul of the impious, how it goes forth from its tabernacle, which has provoked God to anger, saying, Let us eat and drink ;[7] for who is it that has gone down to Hades, and come up and announced that there is judgment and retribution? And take heed, and see all his works which he has done standing before him. And the evil angels came and the good. The good therefore found no place of rest in it, but the evil took possession of it, saying : O wretched soul, pay heed to thy flesh ; take note of that whence thou art coming forth, for thou must return into thy flesh in the day of the resurrection, that thou mayst receive the recompense of thy sins. And when it had gone forth from its tabernacle, the angel who had lived along with it ran up to it, saying to it : O wretched soul, whither goest thou ? I am he who each day wrote down thy sins. Thou hast destroyed the time of repentance ; be exceedingly ashamed. And when it came, all the angels saw it, and cried out with one voice, saying : Woe to thee, wretched soul ! what excuse hast thou come to give to God ? And the angel of that soul said : Weep for it, all of you, along with me. And the angel came up, and worshipped the Lord, saying : Lord, behold the soul which has dwelt in wickedness in its time, and in its temporary life ; do to it according to Thy decision. And there came a voice to that soul, saying : Where is the fruit of thy righteousness? And it was silent,[8] not being able to give an answer. And again there came a voice to it : He who has shown mercy will have mercy shown

---

[1] Comp. Heb. xi. 38.
[2] i.e., to sinful matter — ὕλη — the source of the σῶμα in the Gnostic doctrine.
[3] Comp. Matt. xiii. 41.
[4] Or, come to God.

[5] Comp. Rev. xiv. 13.
[6] Or, bare rule over.
[7] Isa. xxii. 13 ; 1 Cor. xv. 32.
[8] Lit., shut up.

to him ;[1] he who has not shown mercy will not have mercy shown to him. Let this soul be delivered to the merciless angel Temeluch, and let it be cast into outer darkness, where there is weeping and gnashing of teeth. And there was a voice as of tens of thousands, saying : Righteous art Thou, O Lord, and righteous is Thy judgment.[2] And moreover I saw, and, behold, another soul was led by an angel ; and it wept, saying : Have mercy upon me, O righteous Judge, and deliver me from the hand of this angel, because he is dreadful and merciless. And a voice came to it, saying : Thou wast altogether merciless, and for this reason thou hast been delivered up to such an angel. Confess thy sins which thou hast done in the world. And that soul said : I have not sinned, O righteous Judge. And the Lord said to that soul : Verily thou seemest as if thou wert in the world, and wert hiding thy deeds from men. Knowest thou not that whensoever any one dies, his deeds run before him, whether they are good or evil? And when it heard this, it was silent. And I heard the Judge saying : Let the angel come, having in his hands the record of thy sins. And the Judge says to the angel : I say to thee the angel, Disclose all. Say what he has done five years before his death. By myself I swear to thee, that in the first period of his life there was forgetfulness of all his former sins. And the angel answered and said : Lord, command the souls to stand beside their angels ; and that same hour they stood beside them. And the lord of that soul said : Take note of these souls, and whether thou hast in any way sinned against them. And it answered and said : Lord, a year has not been completed since I killed the one, and lived with the other. And not only this, but I also wronged it. And the Lord said to it : Knowest thou not that he who wrongs any one in the world is kept, as soon as he dies, in the place until he whom he has wronged come, and both shall be judged before me, and each receive according to his works? And I heard a voice saying : Let this soul be delivered to the angel Tartaruch, and guarded till the great day of judgment. And I heard a voice as of tens of thousands saying : Righteous art Thou, O Lord. and righteous Thy judgment.

And the angel says to me : Hast thou seen all these things? And I answered : Yes, my lord. And again he said to me : Come, follow me, and I shall show thee the place of the righteous. And I followed him, and he set me before the doors of the city. And I saw a golden gate, and two golden pillars before it, and two golden plates upon it full of inscriptions. And the angel said to me : Blessed is he who shall enter into these doors ; because not every one goeth in, but only those who have single-mindedness, and guiltlessness, and a pure heart.[3] And I asked the angel : For what purpose have the inscriptions been graven on these plates? And he said to me : These are the names of the righteous, and of those who serve God. And I said to him : Is it so that their names have been inscribed in heaven itself while they are yet alive? And the angel said to me : . . .[4] of the angels, such as serve Him well are acknowledged by God. And straightway the gate was opened, and there came forth a hoary-headed man to meet us ; and he said to me : Welcome, Paul, beloved of God! and, with a joyful countenance, he kissed me with tears. And I said to him : Father, why weepest thou? And he said to me : Because God hath prepared many good things for men, and they do not His will in order that they may enjoy them. And I asked the angel : My lord, who is this? And he said to me : This is Enoch, the witness of the last day.[5] And the angel says to me : See that whatever I show thee in this place thou do not announce, except what I tell thee. And he set me upon[6] the river whose source springs up in the circle of heaven ; and it is this river which encircleth the whole earth. And he says to me : This river is Ocean. And there was then a great light. And I said : My lord, what is this? And he said to me : This is the land of the meek. Knowest thou not that it is written, Blessed are the meek, for they shall inherit the earth?[7] The souls of the righteous, therefore, are kept in this place. And I said to the angel : When, then, will they be made manifest? And he said to me : When the Judge shall come in the day of the resurrection, and sit down. Then, accordingly, shall he command, and shall reveal the earth, and it shall be lighted up ; and the saints shall appear in it, and shall delight themselves in the good[8] that have been reserved from the foundation of the world. And there were by the bank of the river, trees planted, full of different fruits. And I looked towards the rising of the sun, and I saw there trees of great size full of fruits ; and that land was more brilliant than silver and gold ; and there were vines growing on those date-palms, and myriads of shoots, and myriads of clusters on each branch. And I said to the archangel : What is this, my lord? And

---

[1] Matt. v. 7.
[2] Ps. cxix. 137.
[3] Comp. Ps. xxiv. 3.
[4] The hiatus is thus filled up in the Syriac: Yes, not only are their names written, but their works from day to day: the angel their minister brings tidings of their works every day from morning to morning; they are known to God by their hearts and their works. And after they are recorded, if there happen to them a matter of sin or deficiency, it is purified by chastisement according to their sin, that there be not unto them any defect in their strivings.
[5] Rev. xi. 3-12. Enoch and Elijah were supposed to be the two witnesses there mentioned.
[6] Or, above.
[7] Matt. v. 5.
[8] Or, the good things.

he says to me : This is the Acherusian lake, and within it the city of God. All are not permitted to enter into it, except whosoever shall repent of his sins ; and as soon as he shall repent, and alter his life, he is delivered to Michael, and they cast him into the Acherusian lake, and then he brings him in the city of God, near the righteous. And I wondered and blessed God at all that I saw. And the angel said to me : Follow me, that I may bring thee into the city of God, and into its light. And its light was greater than the light of the world, and greater than gold, and walls encircled it. And the length and the breadth of it were a hundred stadia. And I saw twelve gates, exceedingly ornamented, leading into the city ; and four rivers encircled it, flowing with milk, and honey, and oil, and wine. And I said to the angel : My lord, what are these rivers ? And he said to me : These are the righteous who, when in the world, did not make use of these things, but humbled themselves for the sake of God ; and here they receive a recompense ten thousand fold.

And I, going into the city, saw a very lofty tree before the doors of the city, having no fruit, and a few men under it ; and they wept exceedingly, and the trees bent down to them. And I, seeing them, wept, and asked the angel : Who are these, that they have not turned to go into the city ? And he said to me : Yes, the root of all evils is vainglory. And I said : And these trees, why have they thus humbled themselves ? And the angel answered and said to me : For this reason the trees are not fruit-bearing, because they have not withheld themselves from vaunting. And I asked the angel : My lord, for what reason have they been put aside before the doors of the city ? And he answered and said to me : On account of the great goodness of God, since by this way Christ is going to come into the city, and that those who go along with Him may plead for these men, and that they may be brought in along with them. And I was going along, guided by the angel, and he set me upon the river. And I saw there all the prophets ; and they came and saluted me, saying : Welcome, Paul, beloved of God. And I said to the angel : My lord, who are these ? And he said to me : These are all the prophets, and these are the songs of all the prophecies,[1] and of whoever hath grieved his soul, not doing its will, for God's sake. Having departed, then, he comes here, and the prophets salute him. And the angel brought me to the south of the city, where the river of milk is. And I saw there all the infants that King Herod slew for the Lord's name's sake. And the angel took me again to the east of the city, and I saw there

Abraham, Isaac, Jacob. And I asked the angel : My lord, what place is this ? And he said to me : Every one who is hospitable to men comes hither when he comes out of the world, and they salute him as a friend of God on account of his love to strangers. And again he took me away to another place, and I saw there a river like oil on the north of the city, and I saw people there rejoicing and singing praises. And I asked : Who are these, my lord ? And he said to me : These are they who have given themselves up to God ; for they are brought into this city. And I looked, and saw in the midst of the city an altar, great and very lofty ; and there was one standing near the altar, whose face shone like the sun, and he had in his hands a psaltery and a harp, and he sung the Alleluia delightfully, and his voice filled all the city. And all with one consent accompanied him, so that the city was shaken by their shouting. And I asked the angel : Who is this that singeth delightfully, whom all accompany ? And he said to me : This is the prophet David ; this is the heavenly Jerusalem. When, therefore, Christ shall come in His second appearing, David himself goes forth with all the saints. For as it is in the heavens, so also upon earth : for it is not permitted without David to offer sacrifice even in the day of the sacrifice of the precious body and blood of Christ ; but it is necessary for David to sing the Alleluia. And I asked the angel : My lord, what is the meaning of Alleluia ? It is called in Hebrew, THEBEL MAREMATHA — speech to God who founded all things ; let us glorify Him in the same. So that every one who sings the Alleluia glorifies God.

When these things, therefore, had been thus said to me by the angel, he led me outside of the city, and the Acherusian lake, and the good land, and set me upon the river of the ocean that supports the firmament of the heaven, and said to me : Knowest thou where I am going ? And I said : No, my lord. And he said to me : Follow me, that I may show thee where the souls of the impious and the sinners are. And he took me to the setting of the sun, and *where* the beginning of the heaven had been founded upon the river of the ocean. And I saw beyond the river, and there was no light there, but darkness, and grief, and groaning ; and I saw a bubbling river, and a great multitude both of men and women who had been cast into it, some up to the knees, others up to the navel, and many even up to the crown of the head. And I asked : Who are these ? And he said to me : These are they who lived unrepenting in fornications and adulteries. And I saw at the south-west of the river another river, where there flowed a river of fire, and there was there a multitude of many souls. And I asked the angel : Who are these,

---

[1] Syr., This is the place of the prophets. A very slight change in the Greek text would give this reading.

my lord? And he said to me: These are the thieves, and slanderers, and flatterers, who did not set up God as their help, but hoped in the vanity of their riches. And I said to him: What is the depth of this river? And he said to me: Its depth has no measure, but it is immeasurable. And I groaned and wept because of mankind. And the angel said to me: Why weepest thou? Art thou more merciful than God? for, being holy, God, repenting over men, waits for their conversion and repentance; but they, deceived by their own will, come here, and are eternally punished. And I looked into the fiery river, and saw an old man dragged along by two, and they pulled him in up to the knee. And the angel Temeluch coming, laid hold of an iron with his hand, and with it drew up the entrails of that old man through his mouth. And I asked the angel: My lord, who is this that suffers this punishment? And he said to me: This old man whom thou seest was a presbyter; and when he had eaten and drunk, then he performed the service of God. And I saw there another old man carried in haste by four angels; and they threw him into the fiery river up to the girdle, and he was frightfully burnt by the lightnings. And I said to the angel: Who is this, my lord? And he said to me: This whom thou seest was a bishop, and that name indeed he was well pleased to have; but in the goodness of God he did not walk, righteous judgment he did not judge, the widow and the orphan he did not pity, he was neither affectionate nor hospitable;[1] but now he has been recompensed according to his works. And I looked, and saw in the middle of the river another man up to the navel, having his hands all bloody, and worms were coming up through his mouth. And I asked the angel: Who is this, my lord? And he said to me: This whom thou seest was a deacon, who ate and drank, and ministered to God. And I looked to another place where there was a brazen wall in flames, and within it men and women eating up their own tongues, dreadfully judged. And I asked the angel: Who are these, my lord? And he said to me: These are they who in the church speak against their neighbours, and do not attend to the word of God. And I looked, and saw a bloody pit. And I said: What is this pit? And he said to me: This is the place where are cast the wizards, and sorcerers, and the whoremongers, and the adulterers, and those that oppress widows and orphans. And I saw in another place women wearing black, and led away into a dark place. And I asked: Who are these, my lord? And he said to me: These are they who did not listen to their parents, but before their marriage defiled their virginity. And I saw women wearing white

robes, being blind, and standing upon obelisks of fire; and an angel was mercilessly beating them, saying: Now you know where you are; you did not attend when the Scriptures were read to you. And the angel said to me: These are they who corrupted themselves and killed their infants. Their infants therefore came crying out: Avenge us of our mothers. And they were given to an angel to be carried away into a spacious place, but their parents into everlasting fire.

And the angel took me up from these torments, and set me above a well, which had seven seals upon its mouth. And the angel who was with me said to the angel at the well of that place: Open the well, that Paul the beloved of God may see, because there has been given to him authority to see the torments. And the angel of the place said to me: Stand afar off, until I open the seals. And when he had opened them, there came forth a stench which it was impossible to bear. And having come near the place, I saw that well filled with darkness and gloom, and great narrowness of space in it. And the angel who was with me said to me: This place of the well which thou seest is cast off from the glory of God, and none of the angels is importunate in behalf of them; and as many as have professed that the holy Mary is not the mother of God, and that the Lord did not become man out of her, and that the bread of the thanksgiving and the cup of blessing are not His flesh and blood,[2] are cast into this well: and, as I said before, no angel is importunate in their behalf. And I saw towards the setting of the sun, where there is weeping and gnashing of teeth, many men and women there tormented. And I said to the angel: Who are these, my lord? And he said to me: These are they who say that there is no resurrection of the dead; and to them mercy never comes.

Having heard this, I wept bitterly; and looking up into the firmament, I saw the heaven opened, and the archangel Gabriel coming down with hosts of angels, who were going round about all the torments. And they who were judged in the torments seeing them, all cried out with one loud voice: Have mercy upon us, Gabriel, who standest in the presence of God; for we heard that there was a judgment: behold, we know it. And the archangel Gabriel answered and said: As the Lord liveth, beside whom I stand, night and day without ceasing I plead in behalf

---

[1] Comp. 1 Tim. iii. 1-4.

[2] The Syriac has: Those who do not confess Jesus Christ, nor His resurrection, nor His humanity, but consider Him as all mortal, and who say that the sacrament of the body of our Lord is bread.

The word θεοτόκος in the text was the occasion of the three years' struggle between Nestorius and Cyril of Alexandria, which ended by the condemnation of the former by the Council of Ephesus, A.D. 431.

The view of the Eucharist in the text is not inconsistent with an early date, though it must be remembered that the idea of a substantial presence became the orthodox doctrine only after the Second Council of Nicæa in A.D. 787.

of the race of men; but they did not do any good when in life, but spent the period of their life in vanity. And now I shall weep, even I, along with the beloved Paul; perhaps the good Lord may have compassion, and grant you remission. And they assented with one voice: Have mercy upon us, O Lord. And they fell down before God, and supplicated, saying: Have mercy, O Lord, upon the sons of men whom Thou hast made after Thine image. And the heaven was shaken like a leaf, and I saw the four and twenty elders lying on their face; and I saw the altar, and the throne, and the veil; and all of them entreated the glory of God; [1] and I saw the Son of God with glory and great power coming down to the earth.[2] And when the sound of the trumpet took place, all who were in the torments cried out, saying: Have mercy upon us, Son of God; for to Thee has been given power over things in heaven, and things on earth, and things under the earth. And there came a voice saying: What good work have you done, that you are asking for rest? For you have done as you wished, and have not repented, but you have spent your life in profligacy. But now for the sake of Gabriel, the angel of my righteousness, and for the sake of Paul my beloved, I give you a night and the day of the holy Lord's day, on which I rose from the dead, for rest. And all who were in the torments cried out, saying: We bless Thee, O Son of the living God; better for us is such rest than the life which we lived when spending our time in the world.

And after these things the angel says to me: Behold, thou hast seen all the torments: come, follow me, that I may lead thee away to paradise, and that thou mayst change thy soul by the sight of the righteous; for many desire to salute thee. And he took me by an impulse of the Spirit, and brought me into paradise. And he says to me: This is paradise, where Adam and Eve transgressed. And I saw there a beautiful tree of great size, on which the Holy Spirit rested; and from the root of it there came forth all manner of most sweet-smelling water, parting into four channels. And I said to the angel: My lord, what is this tree, that there comes forth from it a great abundance of this water, and where does it go? And he answered and said to me: Before the heaven and the earth existed, He divided them into four kingdoms and heads, of which the names are Phison, Gehon, Tigris, Euphrates. And having again taken hold of me by the hand, he led me near the tree of the knowledge of good and evil. And he says to me: This is the tree by means of which death came into the world, and Adam took of the fruit of it from his wife, and ate; and thereafter they were

cast out hence. And he showed me another, the tree of life, and said to me: This the cherubim and the flaming sword guard. And when I was closely observing the tree, and wondering, I saw a woman coming from afar off, and a multitude of angels singing praises to her. And I asked the angel: Who is this, my lord, who is in so great honour and beauty? And the angel says to me: This is the holy Mary, the mother of the Lord. And she came and saluted me, saying: Welcome, Paul, beloved of God, and angels, and men; thou hast proclaimed the word of God in the world, and established churches, and all bear testimony to thee who have been saved by means of thee: for, having been delivered from the deception of idols through thy teaching, they come here.

While they were yet speaking to me, I gazed, and saw other three men coming. And I asked the angel: Who are these, my lord? And he said to me: These are Abraham, Isaac, and Jacob, the righteous forefathers. And they came and saluted me, saying: Welcome, Paul, beloved of God. . . . God did not grieve us. But we know thee in the flesh, before thou camest forth out of the world. And in succession they told me their names from Abraham to Manasseh. And one of them, Joseph who was sold in Egypt, says to me: Hear me, Paul, friend of God: I did not requite my brethren who cursed me. For blessed is he who is able to endure trial, because the Lord will give him in requital sevenfold reward in the world to come.[3] And while he was yet speaking with me, I saw another coming afar off, and the appearance of him was as the appearance of an angel. And I asked the angel, saying: My lord, who is this? And he said to me: This is Moses the lawgiver, by whom God led forth the children of Israel out of the slavery of Egypt. And when he came near me, he saluted me weeping. And I said to him: Father, why weepest thou, being righteous and meek?[4] And he answered and said to me: I must weep for every man, because I brought trouble upon a people that does not understand, and they have not borne fruit; and I see the sheep of which I was shepherd scattered, and the toil which I toiled for the children of Israel has been counted for nothing; and they saw powers [5] and hosts in the midst of them, and they did not understand; and I see the Gentiles worshipping, and believing through thy word, and being converted, and coming here, and out of my people that was so great not one has understood. For, when the Jews hanged the Son of God upon the cross, all the angels and archangels, and the righteous, and the whole creation

---

[1] Rev. iv. 4.
[2] Matt. xxiv. 30.

[3] Comp. Matt. xix. 29.
[4] Num. xii. 3.
[5] Or, miracles.

of things in heaven, and things in earth, and things under the earth, lamented and mourned with a great lamentation, but the impious and insensate Jews did not understand; wherefore there has been prepared for them the fire everlasting, and the worm that dies not.

While he was yet speaking, there came other three, and saluted me, saying: Welcome, Paul, beloved of God, the boast of the churches, and model of angels. And I asked: Who are you? And the first said: I am Isaiah, whom Manasseh sawed with a wood saw.[1] And the second said: I am Jeremiah, whom the Jews stoned, but they remained burnt up with everlasting fire. And the third said: I am Ezekiel, whom the slayers of the Messiah pierced; all these things have we endured, and we have not been able to turn the stony heart of the Jews. And I threw myself on my face, entreating the goodness of God, because He had had mercy upon me, and had delivered me from the race of the Hebrews. And there came a voice saying: Blessed art thou, Paul, beloved of God; and blessed are those who through thee have believed in the name of our Lord Jesus Christ, because for them has been prepared everlasting life.

While this voice was yet speaking, there came another, crying: Blessed art thou, Paul. And I asked the angel: Who is this, my lord? And he said to me: This is Noah, who lived in the time of the deluge. And when we had saluted each other, I asked him: Who art thou? And he said to me: I am Noah, who in a hundred years built the ark, and without putting off the coat which I wore, or shaving my head; moreover, I practised continence, and did not come near my wife; and in the hundred years my coat was not dirtied, and the hair of my head was not diminished. And I ceased not to proclaim to men, Repent, for, behold, a deluge is coming. And no one paid heed; but all derided me, not refraining from their lawless deeds, until the water of the deluge came and destroyed them all.

And looking away, I saw other two from afar off. And I asked the angel: Who are these, my lord? And he said to me: These are Enoch and Elias. And they came and saluted me, saying: Welcome, Paul, beloved of God! And I said to them: Who are you? And Elias the prophet answered and said to me: I am Elias the prophet, who prayed to God, and He caused that no rain should come down upon the earth for three years and six months, on account of the unrighteousness of the sons of men. For often, of a truth, even the angel besought God on account of the rain; and I heard, Be patient until Elias my beloved shall pray, and I send rain upon the earth.[2]

---

[1] For this tradition, see the Bible Dictionaries under Manasseh. Comp. Heb. xi. 37.

[2] Here the [Greek] MS. abruptly ends. The Syriac thus continues: — And He gave not until I called upon Him again; then He gave unto them. But blessed art thou, O Paul, that thy generation and those thou teachest are the sons of the kingdom. And know thou, O Paul, that every man who believes through thee hath a great blessing, and a blessing is reserved for him. Then he departed from me.

And the angel who was with me led me forth, and said unto me: Lo, unto thee is given this mystery and revelation. As thou pleasest, make it known unto the sons of men. — And then follow details of the depositing of the revelation under the foundation of the house in Tarsus, — details which Tischendorf says the translator of the Syriac did not find in his original. [The close of the English translation of the Syriac version is given in full by Tischendorf (pp. 68, 69). It varies greatly from the above paragraph in the text, besides the addition of the details which Tischendorf regards as spurious. — R.]

REVELATION OF JOHN

REVELATION OF SAINT JOHN THE THEOLOGIAN.

AFTER the taking up of our Lord Jesus Christ, I John was alone upon Mount Tabor,[1] where also He showed us His undefiled Godhead; and as I was not able to stand, I fell upon the ground, and prayed to the Lord, and said: O Lord my God, who hast deemed me worthy to be Thy servant, hear my voice, and teach me about Thy coming. When Thou shalt come to the earth, what will happen? The heaven and the earth, and the sun and the moon, what will happen to them in those times? Reveal to me all; for I am emboldened, because Thou listenest to Thy servant.

And I spent seven days praying; and after this a cloud of light caught me up from the mountain, and set me before the face of the heaven. And I heard a voice saying to me: Look up, John, servant of God, and know. And having looked up, I saw the heaven opened, and there came forth from within the heaven a smell of perfumes of much sweet odour; and I saw an exceeding great flood of light, more resplendent than the sun. And again I heard a voice saying to me: Behold, righteous John. And I directed my sight, and saw a book lying, of the thickness, methought, of seven mountains;[2] and the length of it the mind of man cannot comprehend, having seven seals. And I said: O Lord my God, reveal to me what is written in this book. And I heard a voice saying to me: Hear, righteous John. In this book which thou seest there have been written the things in the heaven, and the things in the earth, and the things in the abyss, and the judgments and righteousness of all the human race.[3] And I said: Lord, when shall these things come to pass? and what do those times bring? And I heard a voice saying to me: Hear, righteous John.[4] There shall be in that time abundance of corn and wine, such as there hath never been upon the earth, nor shall ever be until those times come. Then the ear of corn shall produce a half chœnix,[5] and the bend of the branch shall produce a thousand clusters, and the cluster shall produce a half jar of wine; and in the following year there shall not be found upon the face of all the earth a half chœnix of corn or a half jar of wine.

And again I said: Lord, thereafter what wilt Thou do? And I heard a voice saying to me: Hear, righteous John. Then shall appear the denier, and he who is set apart in the darkness, who is called Antichrist. And again I said: Lord, reveal to me what he is like. And I heard a voice saying to me: The appearance of his face is dusky;[6] the hairs of his head are sharp, like darts; his eyebrows like a wild beast's; his right eye like the star which rises in the morning, and the other like a lion's; his mouth about one cubit; his teeth span long; his fingers like scythes; the print of his feet of two spans; and on his face an inscription, Antichrist; he shall be exalted even to heaven, and shall be cast down even to Hades, making false displays.[7] And then will I make the heaven brazen, so that it shall not give moisture[8] upon the earth; and I will hide the clouds in secret places, so that they shall not bring moisture upon the earth; and I will command the horns of the wind, so that the wind shall not blow upon the earth.[9]

And again I said: Lord, and how many years

---

[1] For the history of the tradition that the transfiguration occurred on Mount Tabor, see Robinson's *Researches*, ii. 358.

[2] One ms. has: 700 cubits.

[3] MS. B adds: And they shall be manifested at the consummation of the age, in the judgment to come. Just as the prophet Daniel saw the judgment, I sat, and the books were opened. Then also shall the twelve apostles sit, judging the twelve tribes of Israel. And when I heard this from my Lord, I again asked: Show me, my Lord, when these things shall come to pass, etc. [B is the designation of a Paris manuscript dated 1523. All the manuscripts are comparatively recent; see Tischendorf, pp. xviii., xix. — R.]

[4] MS. B here inserts Luke xxi. 11.

[5] The chœnix of corn was a man's daily allowance. It was equal to two pints according to some, a pint and a half according to others.

[6] Or, gloomy.

[7] MS. B adds: And he will love most of all the nation of the Hebrews; and the righteous shall hide themselves, and flee to mountains and caves. And he shall take vengeance on many of the righteous; and blessed is he who shall not believe in him.

[8] Or, dew.

[9] To the description of Antichrist, MS. E adds: He holds in his hand a cup of death; and all that worship him drink of it. His right eye is like the morning star, and his left like a lion's; because he was taken prisoner by the archangel Michael, and he took his godhead from him. And I was sent from the bosom of my Father, and I drew up the head of the polluted one, and his eye was consumed. And when they worship him, he writes on their right hands, that they may sit with him in the outer fire; and for all who have not been baptized, and have not believed, have been reserved all anger and wrath. And I said: My Lord, and what miracles does he do? Hear, righteous John: He shall remove mountains and hills, and he shall beckon with his polluted hand, Come all to me; and through his displays and deceits they will be brought together to his own place. He will raise the dead, and show in everything like God. [E is one of the Venice manuscripts. — R.]

will he do this upon the earth? And I heard a voice saying to me: Hear, righteous John. Three years shall those times be; and I will make the three years like three months, and the three months like three weeks, and the three weeks like three days, and the three days like three hours, and the three hours like three seconds, as said the prophet David, His throne hast Thou broken down to the ground; Thou hast shortened the days of his time; Thou hast poured shame upon him.[1] And then I shall send forth Enoch and Elias to convict him; and they shall show him to be a liar and a deceiver; and he shall kill them at the altar, as said the prophet, Then shall they offer calves upon Thine altar.[2]

And again I said: Lord, and after that what will come to pass? And I heard a voice saying to me: Hear, righteous John. Then all the human race shall die, and there shall not be a living man upon all the earth. And again I said: Lord, after that what wilt Thou do? And I heard a voice saying to me: Hear, righteous John. Then will I send forth mine angels, and they shall take the ram's horns that lie upon the cloud; and Michael and Gabriel shall go forth out of the heaven and sound with those horns, as the prophet David foretold, With the voice of a trumpet of horn.[3] And the voice of the trumpet shall be heard from the one quarter of the world to the other;[4] and from the voice of that trumpet all the earth shall be shaken, as the prophet foretold, And at the voice of the bird every plant shall arise;[5] that is, at the voice of the archangel all the human race shall arise.[6]

And again I said: Lord, those who are dead from Adam even to this day, and who dwell in Hades from the beginning of the world, and who die at the last ages, what like shall they arise? And I heard a voice saying to me: Hear, righteous John. All the human race shall arise thirty years old.

And again I said: Lord, they die male and female, and some old, and some young, and some infants. In the resurrection what like shall they arise? And I heard a voice saying to me: Hear, righteous John. Just as the bees are, and differ not one from another, but are all

of one appearance and one size, so also shall every man be in the resurrection. There is neither fair, nor ruddy, nor black, neither Ethiopian nor different countenances; but they shall all arise of one appearance and one stature. All the human race shall arise without bodies, as I told you that in the resurrection they neither marry nor are given in marriage, but are as the angels of God.[7]

And again I said: Lord, is it possible in that world to recognise each other, a brother his brother, or a friend his friend, or a father his own children, or the children their own parents? And I heard a voice saying to me: Hear, John. To the righteous there is recognition, but to the sinners not at all; they cannot in the resurrection recognise each other. And again I John said: Lord, is there there recollection of the things that are here, either fields or vineyards, or other things here? And I heard a voice saying to me: Hear, righteous John. The prophet David speaks, saying, I remembered that we are dust: as for man, his days are as grass; as a flower of the field, so he shall flourish: for a wind hath passed over it, and it shall be no more, and it shall not any longer know its place.[8] And again the same said: His spirit[9] shall go forth, and he returns to his earth; in that day all his thoughts shall perish.[10]

And again I said: Lord, and after that what wilt Thou do? And I heard a voice saying to me: Hear, righteous John. Then will I send forth mine angels over the face of all the earth, and they shall lift off the earth everything honourable, and everything precious, and the venerable and holy images, and the glorious and precious crosses, and the sacred vessels of the churches, and the divine and sacred books; and all the precious and holy things shall be lifted up by clouds into the air. And then will I order to be lifted up the great and venerable sceptre,[11] on which I stretched forth my hands, and all the orders of my angels shall do reverence to it. And then shall be lifted up all the race of men upon clouds, as the Apostle Paul foretold.[12] Along with them we shall be snatched up in[13] clouds to meet the Lord in the air. And then shall come forth every evil spirit, both in the earth and in the abyss, wherever they are on the face of all the earth, from the rising of the sun even to the setting, and they shall be united to him that is served by the devil, that is, Antichrist, and they shall be lifted up upon the clouds.

And again I said: Lord, and after that what wilt Thou do? And I heard a voice saying to

---

[1] Ps. lxxxix. 44, 45.
[2] Ps. li. 19.
[3] Ps. xcviii. 6 according to the LXX.
[4] Lit., from quarters even to quarters of the world.
[5] Adapted from Eccles. xii. 4.
[6] To this section MS. E adds many details: They that have gold and silver shall throw them into the streets, and into every place in the world, and no one will heed them. They shall throw into the streets ivory vessels, and robes adorned with stones and pearls; kings and rulers wasting away with hunger, patriarchs and governors (or abbots), elders and peoples. Where is the fine wine, and the tables, and the pomp of the world? They shall not be found in all the world; and men shall die in the mountains and in the streets, and in every place of the world. And the living shall die from the stink of the dead, etc. Whosoever shall not worship the beast and his pomp shall be called a witness (or martyr) in the kingdom of heaven, and shall inherit eternal life with my holy ones.

[7] Comp. Matt. xxii. 30, and parallel passages.
[8] Ps. ciii. 14–16 according to LXX.
[9] Or, breath.
[10] Ps. cxlvi. 4 according to LXX.
[11] Another reading is cross.
[12] 1 Thess. iv. 17.
[13] Or, by.

me : Hear, righteous John. Then shall I send forth mine angels over the face of all the earth, and they shall burn up the earth eight thousand five hundred [1] cubits, and the great mountains shall be burnt up, and all the rocks shall be melted and shall become as dust, and every tree shall be burnt up, and every beast, and every creeping thing creeping upon the earth, and every thing moving upon the face of the earth, and every flying thing flying in the air ; and there shall no longer be upon the face of all the earth anything moving, and the earth shall be without motion.

And again I said : Lord, and after that what wilt Thou do? And I heard a voice saying to me : Hear, righteous John. Then shall I uncover the four parts of the east, and there shall come forth four great winds, and they shall sweep [2] all the face of the earth from the one end of the earth to the other ; and the Lord shall sweep sin from off the earth, and the earth shall be made white like snow, and it shall become as a leaf of paper, without cave, or mountain, or hill, or rock ; but the face of the earth from the rising even to the setting of the sun shall be like a table, and white as snow ; and the reins of the earth shall be consumed by fire, and it shall cry unto me, saying, I am a virgin before thee, O Lord, and there is no sin in me ; as the prophet David said aforetime, Thou shalt sprinkle me with hyssop, and I shall be made pure ; Thou shalt wash me, and I shall be made whiter than snow.[3] And again he [4] said : Every chasm shall be filled up, and every mountain and hill brought low, and the crooked places shall be made straight, and the rough ways into smooth ; and all flesh shall see the salvation of God.[5]

And again I said : Lord, and after that what wilt Thou do? And I heard a voice saying to me : Hear, righteous John. Then shall the earth be cleansed from sin, and all the earth shall be filled with a sweet smell, because I am about to come down upon the earth ; and then shall come forth the great and venerable sceptre, with thousands of angels worshipping it, as I said before ; and then shall appear the sign of the Son of man from the heaven with power and great glory.[6] And then the worker of iniquity with his servants shall behold it, and gnash his teeth exceedingly, and all the unclean spirits shall be turned to flight. And then, seized by invisible power, having no means of flight, they shall gnash their teeth against him, saying to him : Where is thy power? How hast thou led us astray? and we

have fled away, and have fallen away from the glory which we had beside Him who is coming to judge us, and the whole human race. Woe to us ! because He banishes us into outer darkness.

And again I said : Lord, and after that what wilt Thou do? And I heard a voice saying to me : Then will I send an angel out of heaven, and he shall cry with a loud voice, saying, Hear, O earth, and be strong, saith the Lord ; for I am coming down to thee. And the voice of the angel shall be heard from the one end of the world even to the other, and even to the remotest part of the abyss. And then shall be shaken all the power of the angels and of the many-eyed ones, and there shall be a great noise in the heavens, and the nine regions of the heaven shall be shaken, and there shall be fear and astonishment upon all the angels. And then the heavens shall be rent from the rising of the sun even to the setting, and an innumerable multitude of angels shall come down to the earth ; and then the treasures of the heavens shall be opened, and they shall bring down every precious thing, and the perfume of incense, and they shall bring down to the earth Jerusalem robed like a bride.[7] And then there shall go before me myriads of angels and archangels, bearing my throne, crying out, Holy, holy, holy, Lord of Sabaoth ; heaven and earth are full of Thy glory.[8] And then will I come forth with power and great glory, and every eye in [9] the clouds shall see me ; and then every knee shall bend, of things in heaven, and things on earth, and things under the earth.[10] And then the heaven shall remain empty ; and I will come down upon the earth, and all that is in the air shall be brought down upon the earth, and all the human race and every evil spirit along with Antichrist, and they shall all be set before me naked, and chained by the neck.

And again I said : Lord, what will become of the heavens, and the sun, and the moon, along with the stars? And I heard a voice saying to me : Behold, righteous John. And I looked, and saw a Lamb having seven eyes and seven horns.[11] And again I heard a voice saying to me : I will bid the Lamb come before me, and will say, Who will open this book? And all the multitudes of the angels will answer, Give this book to the Lamb to open it. And then will I order the book to be opened. And when He shall open the first seal, the stars of the heaven shall fall, from the one end of it to the other. And when He shall open the second seal, the moon shall be hidden, and there shall be no light

---

[1] Two MSS. have this number; the other four have 500, 1800, 30, 60-100ths.
[2] Or, winnow.
[3] Ps. li. 7.
[4] MS. D has: Again another prophet has said. [D is another Paris manuscript of the fifteenth century. — R.]
[5] Isa. xl. 4.
[6] Comp. Matt. xxiv. 30.

[7] Rev. xxi. 2.
[8] Comp. Isa. vi. 3.
[9] Or, upon.
[10] Phil. ii. 10.
[11] Rev. v. 6.

in her. And when He shall open the third seal, the light of the sun shall be withheld, and there shall not be light upon the earth. And when He shall open the fourth seal, the heavens shall be dissolved, and the air shall be thrown into utter confusion, as saith the prophet: And the heavens are the works of Thy hands; they shall perish, but Thou endurest, and they shall all wax old as a garment.[1] And when He shall open the fifth seal, the earth shall be rent, and all the tribunals upon the face of all the earth shall be revealed. And when He shall open the sixth seal, the half of the sea shall disappear. And when He shall open the seventh seal, Hades shall be uncovered.

And I said: Lord, who will be the first to be questioned, and to receive judgment? And I heard a voice saying to me, The unclean spirits, along with the adversary. I bid them go into outer darkness, where the depths[2] are. And I said: Lord, and in what place does it lie? And I heard a voice saying to me: Hear, righteous John. As big a stone as a man of thirty years old can roll, and let go down into the depth, even falling down for twenty years will not arrive at the bottom of Hades; as the prophet David said before, And He made darkness His secret place.[3]

And I said: Lord, and after them what nation[4] will be questioned? And I heard a voice saying to me: Hear, righteous John. There will be questioned of Adam's race those nations, both the Greek and those who have believed in idols, and in the sun, and in the stars, and those who have defiled the faith by heresy, and who have not believed the holy[5] resurrection, and who have not confessed the Father, and the Son, and the Holy Ghost: then will I send them away into Hades, as the prophet David foretold, Let the sinners be turned into Hades, and all the nations that forget God.[6] And again he said: They were put in Hades like sheep; death shall be their shepherd.[7]

And again I said: Lord, and after them whom wilt Thou judge? And I heard a voice saying to me: Hear, righteous John. Then the race of the Hebrews shall be examined, who nailed me to the tree like a malefactor. And I said: And what punishment will these get, and in what place, seeing that they did such things to Thee? And I heard a voice saying to me: They shall go away into Tartarus, as the prophet David foretold, They cried out, and there was none to save; to the Lord, and He did not hearken to them.[8]

And again the Apostle Paul said: As many as have sinned without law shall also perish without law, and as many as have sinned in law shall be judged by means of law.[9]

And again I said: Lord, and what of those who have received baptism? And I heard a voice saying to me: Then the race of the Christians shall be examined, who have received baptism; and then the righteous shall come at my command, and the angels shall go and collect[10] them from among the sinners, as the prophet David foretold: The Lord will not suffer the rod of the sinners in the lot of the righteous;[11] and all the righteous shall be placed on my right hand,[12] and shall shine like the sun.[13] As thou seest, John, the stars of heaven, that they were all made together, but differ in light,[14] so shall it be with the righteous and the sinners; for the righteous shall shine as lights and as the sun, but the sinners shall stand in darkness.

And again I said: Lord, and do all the Christians go into one punishment? — kings, high priests, priests, patriarchs, rich and poor, bond and free? And I heard a voice saying to me: Hear, righteous John. As the prophet David foretold, The expectation of the poor shall not perish for ever.[15] Now about kings: they shall be driven like slaves, and shall weep like infants; and about patriarchs, and priests, and Levites, of those that have sinned, they shall be separated in their punishments, according to the nature[16] of the peculiar transgression of each, — some in the river of fire, and some to the worm that dieth not, and others in the seven-mouthed pit of punishment. To these punishments the sinners will be apportioned.

And again I said: Lord, and where will the righteous dwell? And I heard a voice saying to me: Then shall paradise be revealed, and the whole world and paradise shall be made one, and the righteous shall be on the face of all the earth with my angels, as the Holy Spirit foretold through the prophet David: The righteous shall inherit the earth, and dwell therein for ever and ever.[17]

And again I said: Lord, how great is the multitude of the angels? and which is the greater, that of angels or of men? And I heard a voice saying to me: As great as is the multitude of the angels, so great is the race of men, as the prophet has said, He set bounds to the nations according to the number of the angels of God.[18]

And again I said: Lord, and after that what

---

[1] Ps. cii. 26.
[2] Or, regions sunk in water.
[3] Ps. xviii. 11.
[4] Lit., tongue.
[5] MS. D inserts, *Trinity and*.
[6] Ps. ix. 17.
[7] Ps. xlix. 14.
[8] Ps. xviii. 41.

[9] Rom. ii. 12.
[10] Lit., heap up.
[11] Ps. cxxv. 3.
[12] Matt. xxv. 33.
[13] Matt. xiii. 43.
[14] 1 Cor. xv. 41.
[15] Ps. ix. 18.
[16] Lit., proportion or analogy.
[17] Ps. xxxvii. 29.
[18] Deut. xxxii. 8 according to the LXX.

wilt Thou do? and what is to become of the world? Reveal to me all. And I heard a voice saying to me: Hear, righteous John. After that there is no pain, there is no grief, there is no groaning; there is no recollection of evils, there are no tears, there is no envy, there is no hatred of brethren, there is no unrighteousness, there is no arrogance, there is no slander, there is no bitterness, there are none of the cares of life, there is no pain from parents or children, there is no pain from gold, there are no wicked thoughts, there is no devil, there is no death, there is no night, but all is day.[1] As I said before, And other sheep I have, which are not of this fold, that is, men who have been made like the angels through their excellent course of life; them also must I bring, and they will hear my voice, and there shall be one fold, one shepherd.[2]

And again I heard a voice saying to me: Behold, thou hast heard all these things, righteous John; deliver them to faithful men, that they also may teach others, and not think lightly of them,[3] nor cast our pearls before swine, lest perchance they should trample them with their feet.[4]

And while I was still hearing this voice, the cloud brought me down, and put me on Mount Thabor. And there came a voice to me, saying: Blessed are those who keep judgment and do righteousness in all time.[5] And blessed is the house where this description lies, as the Lord said, He that loveth me keepeth my sayings [6] in Christ Jesus our Lord; to Him be glory for ever. Amen.[7]

---

[1] Rev. vii. 17, xxi. 4.
[2] John x. 16. [The correct text of John x. 16 is: "one flock, one shepherd·" but it was altered quite early. — R.]
[3] i.e., the things heard.
[4] Matt. vii. 6.
[5] Ps. cvi. 3.
[6] John xiv. 23.
[7] As a specimen of the eschatology of these documents, Tischendorf gives the following extracts from the termination of MS. E: —

Hear, righteous John: All these shall be assembled, and they shall be in the pit of lamentation; and I shall set my throne in the place, and shall sit with the twelve apostles and the four and twenty elders, and thou thyself an elder on account of thy blameless life; and to finish three services thou shalt receive a white robe and an unfading crown from the hand of the Lord, and thou shalt sit with the four and twenty elders, etc. And after this the angels shall come forth, having a golden censer and shining lamps; and they shall gather together on the Lord's right hand those who have lived well, and done His will, and He shall make them to dwell for ever and ever in light and joy, and they shall obtain life everlasting. And when He shall separate the sheep from the goats, that is, the righteous from the sinners, the righteous on the right, and the sinners on the left; then shall He send the angel Raguel, saying: Go and sound the trumpet for the angels of cold and snow and ice, and bring together every kind of wrath upon those that stand on the left. Because I will not pardon them when they see the glory of God, the impious and unrepentant, and the priests who did not what was commanded. You who have tears, weep for the sinners. And Temeluch shall call out to Taruch: Open the punishments, thou keeper of the keys; open the judgments; open the worm that dieth not, and the wicked dragon; make ready Hades; open the darkness; let loose the fiery river, and the frightful darkness in the depths of Hades. Then the pitiful sinners, seeing their works, and having no consolation, shall go down weeping into streams as it were of blood. And there is none to pity them, neither father to help, nor mother to compassionate, but rather the angels going against them, and saying: Ye poor wretches, why are you weeping? In the world you had no compassion on the weak, you did not help them. And these go away into everlasting punishment. There you will not be able to bear the sight of Him who was born of the virgin; you lived unrepenting in the world, and you will get no pity, but everlasting punishment. And Temeluch says to Taruch: Rouse up the fat three-headed serpent; sound the trumpet for the frightful wild beasts to gather them together to feed upon them (i.e., the sinners); to open the twelve plagues, that all the creeping things may be brought together against the impious and unrepenting. And Temeluch will gather together the multitude of the sinners, and will kick the earth; and the earth will be split up in diverse places, and the sinners will be melted in frightful punishments. Then shall God send Michael, the leader of His hosts; and having sealed the place, Temeluch shall strike them with the precious cross, and the earth shall be brought together as before. Then their angels lamented exceedingly, then the all-holy *Virgin* and all the saints wept for them, and they shall do them no good. And John says: Why are the sinners thus punished? And I heard a voice saying to me: They walked in the world each after his own will, and therefore are they thus punished.

Blessed is the man who reads the writing: blessed is he who has transcribed it, and given it to other Catholic churches: blessed are all who fear God. Hear, ye priests, and ye readers; hear ye people, etc.

THE BOOK OF JOHN CONCERNING THE FALLING ASLEEP OF MARY

THE ACCOUNT OF ST. JOHN THE THEOLOGIAN[1] OF THE FALLING ASLEEP OF THE HOLY MOTHER OF GOD.

As the all-holy glorious mother of God and ever-virgin Mary, as was her wont, was going to the holy tomb of our Lord to burn incense, and bending her holy knees, she was importunate that Christ our God who had been born of her should return to her. And the Jews, seeing her lingering by the divine sepulchre, came to the chief priests, saying: Mary goes every day to the tomb. And the chief priests, having summoned the guards set by them not to allow any one to pray at the holy sepulchre, inquired about her, whether in truth it were so. And the guards answered and said that they had seen no such thing, God having not allowed them to see her when there. And on one of the days, it being the preparation, the holy Mary, as was her wont, came to the sepulchre; and while she was praying, it came to pass that the heavens were opened, and the archangel Gabriel came down to her, and said: Hail, thou that didst bring forth Christ our God! Thy prayer having come through to the heavens to Him who was born of thee, has been accepted; and from this time, according to thy request, thou having left the world, shalt go to the heavenly places to thy Son, into the true and everlasting life.

And having heard this from the holy archangel, she returned to holy Bethlehem, having along with her three virgins who ministered unto her. And after having rested a short time, she sat up and said to the virgins: Bring me a censer, that I may pray. And they brought it, as they had been commanded. And she prayed, saying: My Lord Jesus Christ, who didst deign through Thy supreme goodness to be born of me, hear my voice, and send me Thy apostle John, in order that, seeing him, I may partake of joy; and send me also the rest of Thy apostles, both those who have already gone to Thee, and those in the world that now is, in whatever

country they may be, through Thy holy commandment, in order that, having beheld them, I may bless Thy name much to be praised; for I am confident that Thou hearest Thy servant in everything.

And while she was praying, I John came, the Holy Spirit having snatched me up by a cloud from Ephesus, and set me in the place where the mother of my Lord was lying. And having gone in beside her, and glorified Him who had been born of her, I said: Hail, mother of my Lord, who didst bring forth Christ our God, rejoice that in great glory thou art going out of this life. And the holy mother of God glorified God, because I John had come to her, remembering the voice of the Lord, saying: Behold thy mother, and, Behold thy son.[2] And the three virgins came and worshipped. And the holy mother of God says to me: Pray, and cast incense. And I prayed thus: Lord Jesus Christ, who hast done wonderful things, now also do wonderful things before her who brought Thee forth; and let Thy mother depart from this life; and let those who crucified Thee, and who have not believed in Thee, be confounded. And after I had ended the prayer, holy Mary said to me: Bring me the censer. And having cast incense, she said, Glory to Thee, my God and my Lord, because there has been fulfilled in me whatsoever Thou didst promise to me before thou didst ascend into the heavens, that when I should depart from this world Thou wouldst come to me, and the multitude of Thine angels, with glory. And I John say to her: Jesus Christ our Lord and our God is coming, and thou seest[3] Him, as He promised to thee. And the holy mother of God answered and said to me: The Jews have sworn that after I have died they will burn my body. And I answered and said to her: Thy holy and precious body will by no means

[1] The titles vary considerably. In two MSS. the author is said to be James the Lord's brother; in one, John Archbishop of Thessalonica, who lived in the seventh century.

[2] John xix. 26, 27.
[3] i.e., wilt see.

see corruption. And she answered and said to me : Bring a censer, and cast incense, and pray. And there came a voice out of the heavens saying the Amen. And I John heard this voice; and the Holy Spirit said to me : John, hast thou heard this voice that spoke in the heaven after the prayer was ended? And I answered and said : Yes, I heard. And the Holy Spirit said to me : This voice which thou didst hear denotes that the appearance of thy brethren the apostles is at hand, and of the holy powers that they are coming hither to-day.

And at this I John prayed.

And the Holy Spirit said to the apostles : Let all of you together, having come by the clouds from the ends of the world, be assembled to holy Bethlehem by a whirlwind, on account of the mother of our Lord Jesus Christ; Peter from Rome, Paul from Tiberia,[1] Thomas from Hither India, James from Jerusalem. Andrew, Peter's brother, and Philip, Luke, and Simon the Cananæan, and Thaddæus who had fallen asleep, were raised by the Holy Spirit out of their tombs; to whom the Holy Spirit said : Do not think that it is now the resurrection; but on this account you have risen out of your tombs, that you may go to give greeting to the honour and wonder-working of the mother of our Lord and Saviour Jesus Christ, because the day of her departure is at hand, of her going up into the heavens. And Mark likewise coming round, was present from Alexandria; he also with the rest, as has been said before, from each country. And Peter being lifted up by a cloud, stood between heaven and earth, the Holy Spirit keeping him steady. And at the same time, the rest of the apostles also, having been snatched up in clouds, were found along with Peter. And thus by the Holy Spirit, as has been said, they all came together.

And having gone in beside the mother of our Lord and God, and having adored, we said : Fear not, nor grieve; God the Lord, who was born of thee, will take thee out of this world with glory. And rejoicing in God her Saviour, she sat up in the bed, and says to the apostles : Now have I believed that our Master and God is coming from heaven, and I shall behold Him, and thus depart from this life, as I have seen that you have come. And I wish you to tell me how you knew that I was departing and came to me, and from what countries and through what distance you have come hither, that you have thus made haste to visit me. For neither has He who was born of me, our Lord Jesus Christ, the God of the universe, concealed it; for I am persuaded even now that He is the Son of the Most High.

And Peter answered and said to the apostles :

Let us each, according to what the Holy Spirit announced and commanded us, give full information to the mother of our Lord. And I John answered and said : Just as I was going in to the holy altar in Ephesus to perform divine service, the Holy Spirit says to me, The time of the departure of the mother of thy Lord is at hand; go to Bethlehem to salute her. And a cloud of light snatched me up, and set me down in the door where thou art lying. Peter also answered : And I, living in Rome, about dawn heard a voice through the Holy Spirit saying to me, The mother of thy Lord is to depart, as the time is at hand; go to Bethlehem to salute her. And, behold, a cloud of light snatched me up; and I beheld also the other apostles coming to me on clouds, and a voice saying to me, Go all to Bethlehem. And Paul also answered and said : And I, living in a city at no great distance from Rome, called the country of Tiberia, heard the Holy Spirit saying to me, The mother of thy Lord, having left this world, is making her course to the celestial regions through her departure;[2] but go thou also to Bethlehem to salute her. And, behold, a cloud of light having snatched me up, set me down in the same place as you. And Thomas also answered and said : And I, traversing the country of the Indians, when the preaching was prevailing by the grace of Christ, and the king's sister's son, Labdanus by name, was about to be sealed by me in the palace, on a sudden the Holy Spirit says to me, Do thou also, Thomas, go to Bethlehem to salute the mother of thy Lord, because she is taking her departure to the heavens. And a cloud of light having snatched me up, set me down beside you. And Mark also answered and said : And when I was finishing the canon[3] of the third *day* in the city of Alexandria, just as I was praying, the Holy Spirit snatched me up, and brought me to you. And James also answered and said : While I was in Jerusalem, the Holy Spirit commanded me, saying, Go to Bethlehem, because the mother of thy Lord is taking her departure. And, behold, a cloud of light having snatched me up, set me beside you. And Matthew also answered and said : I have glorified and do glorify God, because when I was in a boat and overtaken by a storm, the sea raging with its waves, on a sudden a cloud of light overshadowing the stormy billow, changed it to a calm, and having snatched me up, set me down beside you. And those who had come before likewise answered, and gave an account of how they had come. And Bartholomew said : I was in the Thebais proclaiming the word, and behold the Holy Spirit says

---

[1] A place near Rome; one ms. calls it Tiberis.

[2] Or, dissolution.

[3] A canon is a part of the Church service consisting of nine odes. The canon of the third day is the canon for Tuesday.

to me, The mother of thy Lord is taking her departure ; go, then, to salute her in Bethlehem. And, behold, a cloud of light having snatched me up, brought me to you.

The apostles said all these things to the holy mother of God, why they had come, and in what way ; and she stretched her hands to heaven, and prayed, saying : I adore, and praise, and glorify Thy much to be praised name, O Lord, because Thou hast looked upon the lowliness of Thine handmaiden, and because Thou that art mighty hast done great things for me ; and, behold, all generations shall count me blessed.[1] And after the prayer she said to the apostles : Cast incense, and pray. And when they had prayed, there was thunder from heaven, and there came a fearful voice, as if of chariots ; and, behold, a multitude of a host of angels and powers, and a voice, as if of the Son of man, was heard, and the seraphim in a circle round the house where the holy, spotless mother of God and virgin was lying, so that all who were in Bethlehem beheld all the wonderful things, and came to Jerusalem and reported all the wonderful things that had come to pass. And it came to pass, when the voice was heard, that the sun and the moon suddenly appeared about the house ; and an assembly[2] of the first-born saints stood beside the house where the mother of the Lord was lying, for her honour and glory. And I beheld also that many signs came to pass, the blind seeing, the deaf hearing, the lame walking, lepers cleansed, and those possessed by unclean spirits cured ; and every one who was under disease and sickness, touching the outside of the wall of the house where she was lying, cried out : Holy Mary, who didst bring forth Christ our God, have mercy upon us. And they were straightway cured. And great multitudes out of every country living in Jerusalem for the sake of prayer, having heard of the signs that had come to pass in Bethlehem through the mother of the Lord, came to the place seeking the cure of various diseases, which also they obtained. And there was joy unspeakable on that day among the multitude of those who had been cured, as well as of those who looked on, glorifying Christ our God and His mother. And all Jerusalem from Bethlehem kept festival with psalms and spiritual songs.

And the priests of the Jews, along with their people, were astonished at the things which had come to pass ; and being moved[3] with the heaviest hatred, and again with frivolous reasoning, having made an assembly, they determine to send against the holy mother of God and the

holy apostles who were there in Bethlehem. And accordingly the multitude of the Jews, having directed their course to Bethlehem, when at the distance of one mile it came to pass that they beheld a frightful vision, and their feet were held fast ; and after this they returned to their fellow-countrymen, and reported all the frightful vision to the chief priests. And they, still more boiling with rage, go to the procurator, crying out and saying : The nation of the Jews has been ruined by this woman ; chase her from Bethlehem and the province of Jerusalem. And the procurator, astonished at the wonderful things, said to them : I will chase her neither from Bethlehem nor from any other place. And the Jews continued crying out, and adjuring him by the health of Tiberius Cæsar to bring the apostles out of Bethlehem. And if you do not do so, we shall report it to the Cæsar. Accordingly, being compelled, he sends a tribune of the soldiers[4] against the apostles to Bethlehem. And the Holy Spirit says to the apostles and the mother of the Lord : Behold, the procurator has sent a tribune against you, the Jews having made an uproar. Go forth therefore from Bethlehem, and fear not : for, behold, by a cloud I shall bring you to Jerusalem ; for the power of the Father, and the Son, and the Holy Spirit is with you. The apostles therefore rose up immediately, and went forth from the house, carrying the bed of the Lady the mother of God, and directed their course to Jerusalem ; and immediately, as the Holy Spirit had said, being lifted up by a cloud, they were found in Jerusalem in the house of the Lady. And they stood up, and for five days made an unceasing singing of praise. And when the tribune came to Bethlehem, and found there neither the mother of the Lord nor the apostles, he laid hold of the Bethlehemites, saying to them : Did you not come telling the procurator and the priests all the signs and wonders that had come to pass, and how the apostles had come out of every country? Where are they, then? Come, go to the procurator at Jerusalem. For the tribune did not know of the departure of the apostles and the Lord's mother to Jerusalem. The tribune then, having taken the Bethlehemites, went in to the procurator, saying that he had found no one. And after five days it was known to the procurator, and the priests, and all the city, that the Lord's mother was in her own house in Jerusalem, along with the apostles, from the signs and wonders that came to pass there. And a multitude of men and women and virgins came together, and cried out : Holy virgin, that didst bring forth Christ our God, do not forget the generation of men. And when these things came to pass, the people

---

[1] Luke i. 48.
[2] Or, a church.
[3] Burning — MS. B. [This MS. is in Venice; see Tischendorf, *Apocalypses Apocryphæ*, p. xliii., for designations of MSS. — R.]

[4] Lit., chiliarch, i.e., commander of a thousand.

of the Jews, with the priests also, being the more moved with hatred, took wood and fire, and came up, wishing to burn the house where the Lord's mother was living with the apostles. And the procurator stood looking at the sight from afar off. And when the people of the Jews came to the door of the house, behold, suddenly a power of fire coming forth from within, by means of an angel, burnt up a great multitude of the Jews. And there was great fear throughout all the city; and they glorified God, who had been born of her. And when the procurator saw what had come to pass, he cried out to all the people, saying: Truly he who was born of the virgin, whom you have thought of driving away, is the Son of God; for these signs are those of the true God. And there was a division among the Jews; and many believed in the name of our Lord Jesus Christ, in consequence of the signs that had come to pass.

And after all these wonderful things had come to pass through the mother of God, and evervirgin Mary the mother of the Lord, while we the apostles were with her in Jerusalem, the Holy Spirit said to us: You know that on the Lord's day the good news was brought to the Virgin Mary by the archangel Gabriel; and on the Lord's day the Saviour was born in Bethlehem; and on the Lord's day the children of Jerusalem came forth with palm branches to meet him, saying, Hosanna in the highest, blessed is [1] He that cometh in the name of the Lord; [2] and on the Lord's day He rose from the dead; and on the Lord's day He will come to judge the living and the dead; and on the Lord's day He will come out of heaven, to the glory and honour of the departure of the holy glorious virgin who brought Him forth. And on the same [3] Lord's day the mother of the Lord says to the apostles: Cast incense, because Christ is coming with a host of angels; and, behold, Christ is at hand, sitting on a throne of cherubim. And while we were all praying, there appeared innumerable multitudes of angels, and the Lord mounted upon cherubim in great power; and, behold, a stream of light [4] coming to the holy virgin, because of the presence of her only-begotten Son, and all the powers of the heavens fell down and adored Him. And the Lord, speaking to His mother, said: Mary. And she answered and said: Here am I, Lord. And the Lord said to her: Grieve not, but let thy heart rejoice and be glad; for thou hast found grace to behold the glory given to me by my Father. And the holy mother of God looked up, and saw in Him a glory which it is impos-

sible for the mouth of man to speak of, or to apprehend. And the Lord remained beside her, saying: Behold, from the present time thy precious body will be transferred to paradise, and thy holy soul to the heavens to the treasures of my Father in exceeding brightness, where there is peace and joy of the holy angels, — and other things besides. [5] And the mother of the Lord answered and said to him: Lay Thy right hand upon me, O Lord, and bless me. And the Lord stretched forth His undefiled right hand, and blessed her. And she laid hold of His undefiled right hand, and kissed it, saying: I adore this right hand, which created the heaven and the earth; and I call upon Thy much to be praised name Christ, O God, the King of the ages, the only-begotten of the Father, to receive Thine handmaid, Thou who didst deign to be brought forth by me, in a low estate, to save the race of men through Thine ineffable dispensation; do Thou bestow Thine aid upon every man calling upon, or praying to, or naming the the name of, Thine handmaid. And while she is saying this, the apostles, having gone up to her feet and adored, say: O mother of the Lord, leave a blessing to the world, since thou art going away from it. For thou hast blessed it, and raised it up when it was ruined, by bringing forth the Light of the world. And the mother of the Lord prayed, and in her prayer spoke thus: O God, who through Thy great goodness hast sent from the heavens Thine onlybegotten Son to dwell in my humble body, who hast deigned to be born of me, humble *as I am*, have mercy upon the world, and every soul that calls upon Thy name. And again she prayed, and said: O Lord, King of the heavens, Son of the living God, accept every man who calls upon Thy name, that Thy birth may be glorified. And again she prayed, and said: O Lord Jesus Christ, who art all-powerful in heaven and on earth, in this appeal I implore Thy holy name; in every time and place where there is made mention of my name, make that place holy, and glorify those that glorify Thee through my name, accepting of such persons all their offering, and all their supplication, and all their prayer. And when she had thus prayed, the Lord said to His mother: Let thy heart rejoice and be glad; for every favour [6] and every gift has been given to thee from my Father in heaven, and from me, and from the Holy Spirit: every soul that calls upon thy name shall not be ashamed, but shall find mercy, and comfort, and support, and confidence, both in the world that now is, and in that which is to come, in the presence of my Father in the heavens. And the

---

[1] Or, be.
[2] Matt. xxi. 9; Luke xix. 38; Ps. cxviii. 26.
[3] The holy — MS. A.
[4] Lit., a going forth of illumination.

[5] Perhaps the true reading is: thou shalt dwell where there is peace and joy of the holy angels.
[6] Or, grace.

Lord turned and said to Peter: The time has come to begin the singing of the hymn. And Peter having begun the singing of the hymn, all the powers of the heavens responded with the Alleluiah. And then the face of the mother of the Lord shone brighter than the light, and she rose up and blessed each of the apostles with her own hand, and all gave glory to God; and the Lord stretched forth His undefiled hands, and received her holy and blameless soul. And with the departure of her blameless soul the place was filled with perfume and ineffable light; and, behold, a voice out of the heaven was heard, saying: Blessed art thou among women. And Peter, and I John, and Paul, and Thomas, ran and wrapped up her precious feet for the consecration; and the twelve apostles put her precious and holy body upon a couch, and carried it. And, behold, while they were carrying her, a certain well-born Hebrew, Jephonias by name, running against the body, put his hands upon the couch; and, behold, an angel of the Lord by invisible power, with a sword of fire, cut off his two hands from his shoulders, and made them hang about the couch, lifted up in the air. And at this miracle which had come to pass all the people of the Jews who beheld it cried out: Verily, He that was brought forth by thee is the true God, O mother of God, ever-virgin Mary. And Jephonias himself, when Peter ordered him, that the wonderful things of God might be showed forth, stood up behind the couch, and cried out: Holy Mary, who broughtest forth Christ who is God, have mercy upon me. And Peter turned and said to him: In the name of Him who was born of her, thy hands which have been taken away from thee, will be fixed on again. And immediately, at the word of Peter, the hands hanging by the couch of the Lady came, and were fixed on Jephonias. And he believed, and glorified Christ, God who had been born of her.

And when this miracle had been done, the apostles carried [1] the couch, and laid down her precious and holy body in Gethsemane in a new tomb. And, behold, a perfume of sweet savour came forth out of the holy sepulchre of our Lady the mother of God; and for three days the voices of invisible angels were heard glorifying Christ our God, who had been born of her. And when the third day was ended, the voices were no longer heard; and from that time forth all knew that her spotless and precious body had been transferred to paradise.

And after it had been transferred, behold, we see Elisabeth the mother of St. John the Baptist, and Anna the mother of the Lady, and Abraham, and Isaac, and Jacob, and David, singing the Alleluiah, and all the choirs of the saints adoring the holy relics of the mother of the Lord, and the place full of light, than which light nothing could be more brilliant, and an abundance of perfume in that place to which her precious and holy body had been transferred in paradise, and the melody of those praising Him who had been born of her — sweet melody, of which there is no satiety, such as is given to virgins, and them only, to hear. We apostles, therefore, having beheld the sudden precious translation of her holy body, glorified God, who had shown us His wonders at the departure of the mother of our Lord Jesus Christ, whose [2] prayers and good offices may we all be deemed worthy to receive,[3] under her shelter, and support, and protection, both in the world that now is and in that which is to come, glorifying in every time and place her only-begotten Son, along with the Father and the Holy Spirit, for ever and ever. Amen.

---

[1] Four of the MSS. give a different account here: While the apostles were going forth from the city of Jerusalem carrying the couch, suddenly twelve clouds of light snatched up the apostles, with the body of our Lady, and translated them to paradise.

[2] i.e., the mother's.

[3] One MS. has: To find mercy and remission of sins from our Lord Jesus Christ.

THE PASSING OF MARY

FIRST LATIN FORM.

CONCERNING THE PASSING[1] OF THE BLESSED VIRGIN MARY.

In that time before the Lord came to His passion, and among many words which the mother asked of the Son, she began to ask Him about her own departure, addressing Him as follows : — O most dear Son, I pray Thy holiness, that when my soul goes out of my body, Thou let me know on the third day before ; and do Thou, beloved Son, with Thy angels, receive it.[2] Then He received the prayer of His beloved mother, and said to her : O palace and temple of the living God, O blessed mother,[3] O queen of all saints, and blessed above all women, before thou carriedst me in thy womb, I always guarded thee, and caused thee to be fed daily with my angelic food,[4] as thou knowest : how can I desert thee, after thou hast carried me, and nourished me, and brought me down in flight into Egypt, and endured many hardships for me ? Know, then, that my angels have always guarded thee, and will guard thee even until thy departure. But after I undergo suffering for men, as it is written, and rise again on the third day, and after forty days ascend into heaven, when thou shalt see me coming to thee [5] with angels and archangels, with saints and with virgins, and with my disciples, know for certain that thy soul will be separated from the body, and I shall carry it into heaven, where it shall never at all have tribulation or anguish. Then she joyed and gloried, and kissed the knees of her Son, and blessed the Creator of heaven and earth, who gave her such a gift through Jesus Christ her Son.

In the second year, therefore, after the ascension of our Lord Jesus Christ, the most blessed Virgin Mary continued always in prayer day and night. And on the third day before she passed away, an angel of the Lord came to her, and saluted her, saying : Hail, Mary, full of grace ! the Lord be with thee. And she answered, saying : Thanks to God. Again he said to her : Receive this palm which the Lord promised to thee. And she, giving thanks to God, with great joy received from the hand of the angel the palm sent to her. The angel of the Lord said to her : Thy assumption will be after three days. And she answered : Thanks to God.[6]

Then she called Joseph of the city of Arimathæa, and the other[7] disciples of the Lord ; and when they, both relations and acquaintances, were assembled, she announced her departure to all standing there. Then the blessed Mary washed[8] herself, and dressed herself like a queen, and waited the advent of her Son, as He had promised to her. And she asked all her relations to keep beside[9] her, and give her comfort. And she had along with her three virgins, Sepphora, Abigea, and Zaël ; but the disciples of our Lord Jesus Christ had been already dispersed throughout the whole world to preach to the people of God.

Then at the third hour[10] there were great thunders, and rains, and lightnings, and tribulation, and an earthquake,[11] while queen Mary was standing in her chamber. John the evangelist and apostle was suddenly brought from Ephesus, and entered the chamber of the blessed Mary, and saluted her, and said to her : Hail, Mary, full of grace ! the Lord be with thee. And she answered : Thanks to God. And raising herself up, she kissed Saint John. And the blessed Mary said to him : O my dearest son, why hast

---

[1] MS. B, the assumption. [For the list of MSS. used by Tischendorf, see his *Apocal. Apocr.*, p. xliii. — R.]

[2] MS. C adds: And cause all the apostles to be present at my departure.

[3] Puerpera.

[4] *Protevangelium of James*, ch. 8, p. 363.

[5] MS. C has: When, therefore, thou shalt see my archangel Gabriel coming to thee with a palm which I shall send to thee from heaven, know that I shall soon come to thee, my disciples, and angels, etc.

[6] MS. C: And she began to give great thanks to God in these words: My soul doth magnify the Lord, and my spirit hath rejoiced in God my Saviour.

[7] Or, other.

[8] MS. A, raised. *Levavit* instead of *lavit.*

[9] Lit., guard.

[10] MS. C inserts: of the second day after the angel had come to her with the palm.

[11] Or, earthquakes.

thou left me at such a time, and hast not paid heed to the commands of thy Master, to take care of me, as He commanded thee while He was hanging on the cross? And he asked pardon with bended knee. Then the blessed Mary gave him her benediction, and again kissed him. And when she meant to ask him whence he came, and for what reason he had come to Jerusalem, behold, all the disciples of the Lord, except Thomas who is called Didymus, were brought by a cloud to the door of the chamber of the blessed Mary. They stood and went in, and saluted the queen with the following words, and adored her: Hail, Mary, full of grace! the Lord be with thee. And she eagerly rose quickly, and bowed herself, and kissed them, and gave thanks to God. These are the names of the disciples of the Lord who were brought thither in the cloud: John the evangelist and James his brother, Peter and Paul, Andrew, Philip, Luke, Barnabas, Bartholomew and Matthew, Matthias who is called Justus,[1] Simon the Chananæan, Judas and his brother, Nicodemus and Maximianus, and many others who cannot be numbered. Then the blessed Mary said to her brethren: What is this, that you have all come to Jerusalem? Peter, answering, said to her: We had need to ask this of thee, and dost thou question us? Certainly, as I think, none of us knows why we have come here to-day with such rapidity. I was at Antioch, and now I am here. All declared plainly the place where they had been that day. And they all wondered that they were there when they heard these things. The blessed Mary said to them: I asked my Son, before He endured the passion, that He and you should be at my death; and He granted me this gift. Whence you may know that my departure will be to-morrow.[2] Watch and pray with me, that when the Lord comes to receive my soul, He may find you watching. Then all promised that they would watch. And they watched and prayed the whole night, with psalms and chants, with great illuminations.

And when the Lord's day came, at the third hour, just as the Holy Spirit descended upon the apostles in a cloud,[3] so Christ descended with a multitude of angels, and received the soul of His beloved mother. For there was such splendour and perfume of sweetness, and angels singing the songs of songs, where the Lord says, As a lily among thorns, so is my love among the daughters,[4] that all who were there present fell on their faces, as the apostles fell when Christ transfigured Himself before them on Mount Thabor, and for a whole hour and a half no one was able to rise. But when the light went away, and at the same time with the light itself, the soul of the blessed virgin Mary was taken up into heaven with psalms, and hymns, and songs of songs. And as the cloud went up the whole earth shook, and in one moment all the inhabitants of Jerusalem openly saw the departure of St. Mary.

And that same hour Satan entered into them, and they began to consider what they were to do with her body. And they took up weapons, that they might burn her body and kill the apostles, because from her had gone forth the dispersions of Israel, on account of their sins and the gathering together of the Gentiles. But they were struck with blindness, striking their heads against the walls, and striking each other.[5] Then the apostles, alarmed by so much brightness, arose, and with psalms carried the holy body down from Mount Zion to the valley of Jehoshaphat. But as they were going in the middle of the road, behold, a certain Jew,[6] Reuben by name, wishing to throw to the ground the holy bier with the body of the blessed Mary. But his hands dried up, even to the elbow; whether he would or not, he went down even to the Valley of Jehoshaphat, weeping and lamenting because his hands were raised to the bier, and he was not able to draw back his hands to himself. And he began to ask the apostles[7] that by their prayer he might be saved and made a Christian. Then the apostles, bending their knees, asked the Lord to let him loose. And he, being healed that same hour, giving thanks to God and kissing the feet of the queen of all the saints and apostles, was baptized in that same place, and began to preach the name of our God Jesus Christ.

Then the apostles with great honour laid the body in the tomb, weeping and singing through exceeding love and sweetness. And suddenly there shone round them a light from heaven, and they fell to the ground, and the holy body was taken up by angels into heaven.

Then the most blessed Thomas was suddenly brought to the Mount of Olivet, and saw the most blessed body going up to heaven, and began to cry out and say: O holy mother, blessed mother, spotless mother, if I have now found grace because I see thee, make thy servant joyful through thy compassion, because thou art going to heaven. Then the girdle with which the

---

[1] It was Joseph, the other candidate for the apostleship, who was called Justus (Acts i. 23).
[2] MS. C adds: And she showed them the palm which the Lord had sent her from heaven by His angel.
[3] MS. C has: just as the Holy Spirit appeared in a cloud to His disciples, viz., Peter, James, and John, when He was transfigured, so, etc.
[4] Cant. ii. 2.

[5] MS. C: By the divine vengeance, at that very instant they began to strike and slay each other with their weapons, and struck their heads against the walls like madmen.
[6] MS. C inserts: a scribe of the tribe of Dan.
[7] MS. C adds: and firmly to promise that, if he were made whole by their prayers, he would become a Christian.

apostles had encircled the most holy body was thrown down from heaven to the blessed Thomas. And taking it, and kissing it, and giving thanks to God, he came again into the Valley of Jehoshaphat. He found all the apostles and another great crowd there beating their breasts on account of the brightness which they had seen. And seeing and kissing each other, the blessed Peter said to him : Truly thou hast always been obdurate and unbelieving, because for thine unbelief it was not pleasing to God that thou shouldst be along with us at the burial of the mother of the Saviour. And he, beating his breast, said : I know and firmly believe that I have always been a bad and an unbelieving man ; therefore I ask pardon of all of you for my obduracy and unbelief. And they all prayed for him. Then the blessed Thomas said : Where have you laid her body? And they pointed out the sepulchre with their finger. And he said : The body which is called most holy is not there. Then the blessed Peter said to him : Already on another occasion thou wouldst not believe the resurrection of our Master and Lord at our word, unless thou went to touch Him with thy fingers, and see Him ; how wilt thou believe us that the holy body is here? Still he persists saying : It is not here. Then, as it were in a rage, they went to the sepulchre, which was a new one hollowed out in the rock, and took up the stone ; but they did not find the body, not knowing what to say, because they had been convicted by the words of Thomas. Then the blessed Thomas told them how he was singing mass in India — he still had on his sacerdotal robes. He, not knowing the word of God, had been brought to the Mount of Olivet, and saw the most holy body of the blessed Mary going up into heaven, and prayed her to give him a blessing. She heard his prayer, and threw him her girdle which she had about her. And the apostles seeing the belt which they had put about her, glorifying God, all asked pardon of the blessed Thomas, on account of the benediction which the blessed Mary had given him, and because he had seen the most holy body going up into heaven. And the blessed Thomas gave them his benediction, and said : Behold how good and how pleasant it is for brethren to dwell together in unity ! [1]

[1] Ps. cxxxiii. 1.

And the same cloud by which they had been brought carried them back each to his own place, just like Philip when he baptized the eunuch, as is read in the Acts of the Apostles ; [2] and as Habakkuk the prophet carried food to Daniel, who was in the lions' den, and quickly returned to Judæa.[3] And so also the apostles quickly returned to where they had at first been, to preach to the people of God. Nor is it to be wondered at that He should do such things, who went into the virgin and came out of her though her womb was closed ; who, though the gates were shut, went in to His disciples ; [4] who made the deaf to hear, raised the dead, cleansed the lepers, gave sight to the blind,[5] and did many other wonderful things. To believe this is no doubtful matter.

I am Joseph who laid the Lord's body in my sepulchre, and saw Him rising again ; and who, before the ascension and after the ascension of the Lord, always kept his most sacred temple the blessed ever-virgin Mary, and *who have kept* in writing and in my breast the things which came forth from the mouth of God, and how the things mentioned above were done by the judgment of God. And I have made known to all, Jews and Gentiles, those things which I saw with my eyes, and heard with my ears ; and as long as I live I shall not cease to declare them. And her, whose assumption is at this day venerated and worshipped throughout the whole world, let us assiduously entreat that she be mindful of us in the presence of her most pious Son in heaven, to whom is praise and glory through endless ages of ages. Amen.[6]

[2] Acts viii. 39.
[3] Bel and the Dragon, vers. 33-39.
[4] John xx. 19.
[5] MS. C adds: and in Cana of Galilee made wine out of water.
[6] MS. C has this last section as follows: For I am Joseph, who laid the body of our Lord Jesus Christ in my sepulchre, and saw Him and spoke with Him after His resurrection; who afterwards kept His most pious mother in my house until her assumption into the heavens, and served her according to my power; who also was deemed worthy to hear and see from her holy mouth many secrets, which I have written and keep in my heart. That which I saw with mine eyes, and heard with mine ears, of her holy and glorious assumption, I have written for faithful Christians, and those that fear God; and while I live I shall not cease to preach, speak, and write them to all nations. And let every Christian know, that if he keep this writing by him, even in his house, whether he be cleric, or lay, or a woman, the devil will not hurt him; his son will not be lunatic, or demoniac, or deaf, or blind; no one will die suddenly in his house; in whatever tribulation he cries to her, he will be heard; and in the day of his death he will have her with her holy virgins for his help. I beseech continually that the same most pious and merciful queen may be always mindful of me; and all who believe in her and hope before her most pious Son, our Lord Jesus Christ, who, with the Father and the Holy Spirit, lives and reigns God through endless ages of ages. Amen.

SECOND LATIN FORM.

HERE BEGINNETH THE PASSING OF THE BLESSED MARY.

1.[1] THEREFORE, when the Lord and Saviour Jesus Christ was hanging on the tree fastened by the nails of the cross for the life of the whole world, He saw about the cross His mother standing, and John the evangelist, whom He peculiarly loved above the rest of the apostles, because he alone of them was a virgin in the body. He gave him, therefore, the charge of holy Mary, saying to him: Behold thy mother! and saying to her: Behold thy son![2] From that hour the holy mother of God remained specially in the care of John, as long as she had her habitation in this life. And when the apostles had divided the world by lot for preaching, she settled in the house of his parents near Mount Olivet.

2. In the second year, therefore, after Christ had vanquished death, and ascended up into heaven, on a certain day, Mary, burning with a longing for Christ, began to weep alone, within the shelter of her abode. And, behold, an angel, shining in a dress of great light, stood before her, and gave utterance to[3] the words of salutation, saying: Hail! thou blessed by the Lord, receive the salutation of Him who commanded safety to Jacob by His prophets. Behold, said He, a palm branch — I have brought it to thee from the paradise of the Lord — which thou wilt cause to be carried before thy bier, when on the third day thou shalt be taken up from the body. For, lo, thy Son awaits thee with thrones and angels, and all the powers of heaven. Then Mary said to the angel: I beg that all the apostles of the Lord Jesus Christ be assembled to me. To whom the angel said: Behold, to-day, by the power of my Lord Jesus Christ, all the apostles

will come to thee. And Mary says to him: I ask that thou send upon me thy blessing, that no power of the lower world may withstand me in that hour in which my soul shall go out of my body, and that I may not see the prince of darkness. And the angel said: No power indeed of the lower world will hurt thee; and thy Lord God, whose servant and messenger I am, hath given thee eternal blessing; but do not think that the privilege of not seeing the prince of darkness is to be given thee by me, but by Him whom thou hast carried in thy womb; for to Him belongeth power over all for ever and ever. Thus saying, the angel departed with great splendour. And that palm shone with exceeding great light. Then Mary, undressing herself, put on better garments. And, taking the palm which she had received from the hands of the angel, she went out to the mount of Olivet, and began to pray, and say: I had not been worthy, O Lord, to bear Thee, unless Thou hadst had compassion on me; but nevertheless I have kept the treasure which Thou entrustedst to me. Therefore I ask of Thee, O King of glory, that the power of Gehenna hurt me not. For if the heavens and the angels daily tremble before Thee, how much more man who is made from the ground, who possesses no good thing, except as much as he has received from Thy benignant bounty! Thou art, O Lord, God always blessed for ever. And thus saying, she went back to her dwelling.

3. And, behold, suddenly, while St. John was preaching in Ephesus, on the Lord's day, at the third hour of the day, there was a great earthquake, and a cloud raised him and took him up from the eyes of all, and brought him before the door of the house where Mary was. And knocking at the door, he immediately went in. And when Mary saw him, she exulted in joy, and said: I beg of thee, my son John, be mindful of the words of my Lord Jesus Christ, in which He entrusted me to thee. For, behold, on the third day, when I am to depart from the body,[4] I have heard the plans of the Jews, saying, Let us wait for the day when she who bore that seducer shall die, and let us burn her body with fire. She therefore called St. John, and led him into the secret chamber of the house, and showed him the robe of her burial, and that palm of light which she had received from the

---

[1] The other MS. has the following introductory chapter: Melito, servant of Christ, bishop of the church of Sardis, to the venerable brethren in the Lord appointed at Laodicea, in peace greeting. I remember that I have often written of one Leucius, who, having along with ourselves associated with the apostles, turned aside through alienated feelings and a rash soul from the path of rectitude, and inserted very many things in his books about the acts of the apostles. Of their powers, indeed, he said many and diverse things; but of their teaching he gave a very false account, affirming that they taught otherwise than they did, and establishing his own impious statements, as it were, by their words. Nor did he think this to be enough; but he even vitiated, by his impious writing, the assumption of the blessed ever-virgin Mary, the mother of God, to such a degree that it would be impious not only to read it in the church of God, but even to hear it. When you ask us, therefore, what we heard from the Apostle John, we simply write this, and have directed it to your brotherhood; believing, not the strange dogmas hatched by heretics, but the Father in the Son, the Son in the Father, while the threefold person of the Godhead and undivided substance remains; *believing* not that two human natures were created, a good and a bad, but that one good nature was created by a good God, which by the craft of the serpent was vitiated through sin, and restored through the grace of Christ. [Tischendorf gives this from *Maxima Bibliotheca vet. patr.*, ii. 2, pp. 212 sqq. (ed. Sugdun). — R.]

[2] John xix. 26, 27.

[3] Lit., sprung forward to.

[4] The other MS. has a better reading: For, behold, on the third day I am to depart from the body; and I have heard, etc.

angel, instructing him that he should cause it to be carried before her couch when she was going to her tomb.

4. And St. John said to her: How shall I alone perform thy funeral rites, unless my brethren and fellow-apostles of my Lord Jesus Christ come to pay honour to thy body? And, behold, on a sudden, by the command of God, all the apostles were snatched up, raised on a cloud, from the places in which they were preaching the word of God, and set down before the door of the house in which Mary dwelt. And, saluting each other, they wondered, saying: What is the cause for which the Lord hath assembled us here? [1]

5. Then all the apostles, rejoicing [2] with one mind, finished their prayer. And when they had said the Amen, behold, on a sudden, there came the blessed John, and told them all these things. The apostles then, having entered the house, found Mary, and saluted her, saying: Blessed art thou by the Lord, who hath made heaven and earth. And she said to them: Peace be with you, most beloved brethren! How have you come hither? And they recounted to her how they had come, each one raised on a cloud by the Spirit of God, and set down in the same place. And she said to them: God hath not deprived me of the sight of you. Behold, I shall go the way of all the earth, and I doubt not that the Lord hath now conducted you hither to bring me consolation for the anguish which is just coming upon me. Now therefore I implore you, that without intermission you all with one mind watch, even till that hour in which the Lord will come, and I shall depart from the body.

6. And when they had sat down in a circle consoling her, when they had spent three days in the praises of God, behold, on the third day, about the third hour of the day, a deep sleep seized upon all who were in that house, and no one was at all able to keep awake but the apostles alone, and only the three virgins who were there. And, behold, suddenly the Lord Jesus Christ came with a great multitude of angels; and a great brightness came down upon that place, and the angels were singing a hymn, and praising God together. Then the Saviour spoke, saying: Come, most precious pearl, within the receptacle of life eternal.

7. Then Mary prostrated herself on the pavement, adoring God, and said: Blessed be the name of Thy glory, O Lord my God, who hast deigned to choose me Thine handmaid, and to entrust to me Thy hidden mystery. Be mindful of me, therefore, O King of glory, for Thou knowest that I have loved Thee with all my heart, and kept the treasure committed to me. Therefore receive me, Thy servant, and free me from the power of darkness, that no onset of Satan may oppose me, and that I may not see filthy spirits standing in my way. And the Saviour answered her: When I, sent by my Father for the salvation of the world, was hanging on the cross, the prince of darkness came to me; but when he was able to find in me no trace of his work, [3] he went off vanquished and trodden under foot. But when thou shalt see him, thou shalt see him indeed by the law of the human race, in accordance with which thou hast come to the end of thy life; but he cannot hurt thee, because I am with thee to help thee. Go in security, because the heavenly host is waiting for thee to lead thee in to the joys of paradise. And when the Lord had thus spoken, Mary, rising from the pavement, reclined upon her couch, and giving thanks to God, gave up the ghost. And the apostles saw that her soul was of such whiteness, that no tongue of mortals can worthily utter it; for it surpassed all the whiteness of snow, and of every metal, and of gleaming silver, by the great brightness of its light.

8. Then the Saviour spoke, saying: Rise, Peter, and take the body of Mary, and send it to the right hand of the city towards the east, and thou wilt find there a new tomb, in which you will lay her, and wait until I come to you. And thus saying, the Lord delivered the soul of St. Mary to Michael, who was the ruler of paradise, and the prince of the nation of the Jews; [4] and Gabriel went with them. And immediately the Saviour was received up into heaven along with the angels.

9. And the three virgins, who were in the same place, and were watching, took up the body of the blessed Mary, that they might wash it after the manner of funeral rites. And when they had taken off her clothes, that sacred body shone with so much brightness, that it could be touched indeed for preparation for burial, but the form of it could not be seen for the excessive flashing light: except that the splendour of the Lord appeared great, and nothing was perceived, the body, when it was washed, was perfectly clean, and stained by no moisture of filth. [5] And when they had put the dead-clothes on her, that light

---

[1] The other MS. here adds: And there came with them Paul, converted from the circumcision, who had been selected along with Barnabas for the ministry of the Gentiles. And when there was a pious contention among them as to which of them should be the first to pray to the Lord to show them the reason, and Peter was urging Paul to pray first, Paul answered and said: That is thy duty, to begin first, especially seeing that thou hast been chosen by God a pillar (Gal. ii. 9) of the Church, and thou hast precedence of all in the apostleship; but it is by no means mine, for I am the least of you all, and Christ was seen by me as one born out of due time (1 Cor. xv. 8); nor do I presume to make myself equal to you: nevertheless by the grace of God I am what I am (1 Cor. xv. 10).

[2] The other MS. adds: at the humility of Paul.

[3] Comp. John xiv. 30.

[4] Comp. Dan. x. 21, xii. 1.

[5] This does not seem to make very good sense. Another reading is: And the splendour appeared great, and nothing was perceived, while the body, perfectly clean, and unstained by any horror of filth, was being washed.

was gradually obscured. And the body of the blessed Mary was like lily flowers; and an odour of great sweetness came forth from it, so that no sweetness could be found like it.

10. Then, accordingly, the apostles laid the holy body on the bier, and said to each other: Who is to carry this palm before her bier? Then John said to Peter: Thou, who hast precedence of us in the apostleship, shouldst carry this palm before her couch. And Peter answered him: Thou wast the only virgin among us chosen by the Lord, and thou didst find so great favour that thou didst recline upon His breast.[1] And He, when for our salvation He was hanging upon the stem of the cross, entrusted her to thee with His own mouth. Thou therefore oughtest to carry this palm, and let us take up that body to carry it even to the place of sepulture.[2] After this, Peter, raising *it, and saying*, Take the body, began to sing and say: Israel hath gone forth out of Egypt. Alleluiah. And the other apostles along with him carried the body of the blessed Mary, and John bore the palm of light before the bier. And the other apostles sang with a most sweet voice.

11. And, behold, a new miracle. There appeared above the bier a cloud exceeding great, like the great circle which is wont to appear beside the splendour of the moon; and there was in the clouds an army of angels sending forth a sweet song,[3] and from the sound of the great sweetness the earth resounded. Then the people, having gone forth from the city, about fifteen thousand, wondered, saying: What is that sound of so great sweetness? Then there stood up one who said to them: Mary has departed from the body, and the disciples of Jesus are singing[4] praises around her. And looking, they saw the couch crowned with great glory, and the apostles singing with a loud voice. And, behold, one of them, who was chief of the priests of the Jews in his rank, filled with fury and rage, said to the rest: Behold, the tabernacle of him who disturbed us and all our race, what glory has it received? And going up, he wished to overturn the bier, and throw the body down to the ground. And immediately his hands dried up from his elbows, and stuck to the couch. And when the apostles raised the bier, part of him hung, and part of him adhered to the couch; and he was vehemently tormented with pain, while the apostles were walking and singing. And the angels who were in the clouds smote the people with blindness.

12. Then that chief cried out, saying: I im-plore thee, Saint Peter, do not despise me, I beseech thee, in so great an extremity, because I am exceedingly tortured by great torments. Bear in mind that when, in the prætorium, the maid that kept the door[5] recognised thee, and told the others to revile thee, then I spoke good words in thy behalf. Then Peter answering, said: It is not for me to give other to thee; but if thou believest with thy whole heart on the Lord Jesus Christ, whom she carried in her womb, and remained a virgin after the birth, the compassion of the Lord, which with profuse benignity saves[6] the unworthy, will give thee sal-vation.[7]

To this he replied: Do we not believe? But what shall we do? The enemy of the human race has blinded our hearts, and confusion has covered our face, lest we should confess the great things of God, especially when we ourselves uttered maledictions against Christ, shouting: His blood be upon us, and upon our children.[8] Then Peter said: Behold, this malediction will hurt him who has remained unfaithful to Him; but to those who turn themselves to God mercy is not denied. And he said: I believe all that thou sayest to me; only I implore, have mercy upon me, lest I die.

13. Then Peter made the couch stand still, and said to him: If thou believest with all thy heart upon the Lord Jesus Christ, thy hands will be released from the bier. And when he had said this,[9] his hands were immediately released from the bier, and he began to stand on his feet; but his arms were dried up, and the torture did not go away from him. Then Peter said to him: Go up to the body, and kiss the couch, and say: I believe in God, and in the Son of God, Jesus Christ, whom she bore, and I believe all what-soever Peter the apostle of God has said to me. And going up, he kissed the couch, and im-mediately all pain went away from him, and his hands were healed. Then he began greatly to bless God, and from the books of Moses to ren-der testimony to the praises of Christ, so that even the apostles themselves wondered, and wept for joy, praising the name of the Lord.

14. And Peter said to him: Take this palm from the hand of our brother John, and going into the city thou wilt find much people blinded, and declare to them the great things of God; and whosoever shall believe in the Lord Jesus Christ, thou shalt put this palm upon their eyes, and they shall see; but those who will not believe shall remain blind. And when he had done so, he found much people blinded, lamenting thus: Woe unto us, because we have been made like

---

[1] John xiii. 23.
[2] The other MS. inserts: And Paul said to him: And I, who am younger than any of you, will carry along with thee. And when all had agreed, Peter, raising the bier at the head, began to sing and say.
[3] Lit., a song of sweetness.
[4] Lit., saying.

[5] John xviii. 17.
[6] Or, heals.
[7] Or, health.
[8] Matt. xxvii. 25.
[9] The other MS. has: And when he had said this, " I believe."

the Sodomites struck with blindness.[1] Nothing now is left to us but to perish. But when they heard the words of the chief who had been cured speaking, they believed in the Lord Jesus Christ; and when he put the palm over their eyes, they recovered sight. Five of them remaining in hardness of heart died. And the chief of the priests going forth, carried back the palm to the apostles, reporting all things whatsoever had been done.

15. And the apostles, carrying Mary, came to the place of the Valley of Jehoshaphat which the Lord had showed them; and they laid her in a new tomb, and closed the sepulchre. And they themselves sat down at the door of the tomb, as the Lord had commanded them; and, behold, suddenly the Lord Jesus Christ came with a great multitude of angels, with a halo of great brightness gleaming, and said to the apostles: Peace be with you! And they answered and said: Let Thy mercy, O Lord, be upon us, as we have hoped in Thee.[2] Then the Saviour spoke to them, saying: Before I ascended to my Father I promised to you, saying that you who have followed me in the regeneration, when the Son of man shall sit upon the throne of His majesty, will sit, you also, upon twelve thrones, judging the twelve tribes of Israel.[3] Her, therefore, did I choose out of the tribes of Israel by the command of my Father, that I should dwell in her. What, therefore, do you wish that I should do to her? Then Peter and the other apostles said: Lord, Thou didst choose beforehand this Thine handmaid to become a spotless chamber for Thyself, and us Thy servants to minister unto Thee. Before the ages Thou didst foreknow all things along with the Father, with whom to Thee and the Holy Spirit there is one Godhead, equal and infinite power. If, therefore, it were possible to be done in the presence of the power of Thy grace, it had seemed to us Thy servants to be right that, just as Thou, having vanquished death, reignest in glory, so, raising up again the body of Thy mother, Thou shouldst take her with Thee in joy into heaven.

16. Then the Saviour said: Let it be according to your opinion. And He ordered the archangel Michael to bring the soul of St. Mary. And, behold, the archangel Michael [4] rolled back the stone from the door of the tomb; and the Lord said: Arise, my beloved and my nearest *relation;* thou who hast not put on corruption by intercourse with man, suffer not destruction of the body in the sepulchre. And immediately Mary rose from the tomb, and blessed the Lord, and falling forward at the feet of the Lord, adored Him, saying: I cannot render sufficient thanks to Thee, O Lord, for Thy boundless benefits which Thou hast deigned to bestow upon me Thine handmaiden. May Thy name, O Redeemer of the world, God of Israel, be blessed for ever.

17. And kissing her, the Lord went back, and delivered her soul to the angels, that they should carry it into paradise. And He said to the apostles: Come up to me. And when they had come up He kissed them, and said: Peace be to you! as I have always been with you, so will I be even to the end of the world. And immediately, when the Lord had said this, He was lifted up on a cloud, and taken back into heaven, and the angels along with Him, carrying the blessed Mary into the paradise of God. And the apostles being taken up in the clouds, returned each into the place allotted [5] for his preaching, telling the great things of God, and praising our Lord Jesus Christ, who liveth and reigneth with the Father and the Holy Spirit, in perfect unity, and in one substance of Godhead, for ever and ever. Amen.

---

[1] Gen. xix. 11; Wisd. xix. 17.
[2] Ps. xxxiii. 22.
[3] Matt. xix. 28.

[4] The other ms. has Gabriel.
[5] Lit., the lot.

THE DECRETALS

[TRANSLATED BY THE REV. S. D. F. SALMOND.]

INTRODUCTORY NOTICE

TO

THE DECRETALS

THE learned editors of the Edinburgh series have given us only a specimen of these frauds, which, pretending to be a series of "papal edicts" from Clement and his successors during the *ante-Nicene ages*, are, in fact, the manufactured product of the *ninth century*, — the most stupendous imposture of the world's history, the most successful and the most stubborn in its hold upon enlightened nations. Like the mason's framework of lath and scantlings, on which he turns an arch of massive stone, the Decretals served their purpose, enabling Nicholas I. to found the Papacy by their insignificant aid. That swelling arch of vanity once reared, the framework might be knocked out; but the fabric stood, and has borne up every weight imposed upon it for ages. Its strong abutments have been ignorance and despotism. Nicholas produced his flimsy framework of imposture, and amazed the whole Church by the audacity of the claims he founded upon it. The age, however, was unlearned and uncritical; and, in spite of remonstrances from France under lead of Hincmar, bishop of Rheims, the West patiently submitted to the overthrow of the ancient Canons and the Nicene Constitutions, and bowed to the yoke of a new canon-law, of which these frauds were not only made an integral, but the essential, part. The East never accepted them for a moment: her great patriarchates retain the Nicene System to this day. But, as the established religion of the "Holy Roman Empire," the national churches of Western Europe, one by one, succumbed to this revolt from historic Catholicity. The Eastern churches were the more numerous. They stood by the Constitutions confirmed by all the Œcumenical Synods; they altered not a word of the Nicene Creed; they stood up for the great Catholic law, "Let the ancient customs prevail;" and they were, and are to this day, *the grand historic stem of Christendom*. The Papacy created the Western schism, and contrived to call it "the schism of the Greeks." The Decretals had created the Papacy, and they enabled the first Pope to assume that communion with himself was the test of Catholic communion: hence his excommunication of the Easterns, which, after brief intervals of relaxation, settled into the chronic schism of the Papacy, and produced the awful history of the mediæval Church in Western Europe.

In naming Nicholas I. as the founder of the Papacy, and the first Pope, I merely reach the logical consequence of admitted facts and demonstrated truths. I merely apply the recognised principles of modern thought and scientific law to the science of history, and dismiss the technology of empiricism in this science, as our age has abolished similar empiricisms in the exact sciences. For ages after Copernicus, even those who basked in the light of the true system of the universe went on in the old ruts, *talking* as if the Ptolemaic theory were yet a reality: and so the very historians whose lucid pages explode the whole fabric of the Papal communion, still go on, in the language of fable, giving to the early Bishops of Rome the title of "Popes;" counting St. Peter as the first Pope; bewildering the student by many confusions of fact with fable; and conceding to the modern fabric of Romanism the name of "the Catholic Church," with all the immense advantages that accrue to falsehood by such a surrender of truth, and the consequent endowment of imposture with the raiment and the domain of Apostolic antiquity.

The student of this series must have noted the following fundamental facts : —

1. That the name *papa* was common to all bishops, and signified no pre-eminence in those who bore it.

2. That the Apostolic Sees were all equally accounted *matrices* of unity, and the *roots* of other Catholic churches.

3. That, down to the Council of Nicæa, the whole system of the Church was framed on this principle, and that these were the " ancient customs " which that council ordained to be perpetual.

4. That " because it was the old capital of the empire," and *for no other reason* (the Petrine idea never once mentioned), the primacy of *honour* was conceded to Old Rome, and *equal* honour to New Rome, because it was the new capital.[1] It was to be named second on the list of patriarchates, but to be in no wise inferior to Old Rome ; while the ancient and all-command-ing patriarchate of Alexandria yielded this credit to the *parvenu* of Byzantium only on the prin-ciple of the Gospel, " in honour preferring one another," and only because the imperial capital must be the centre of Catholic concourse.

Now, the rest of the story must be sought in post-Nicene history. The salient points are as follows : —

1. The mighty centralization about Constantinople ; the three councils held within its walls ; the virtual session of the other councils under its eaves ; the inconsiderable figure of " Old Rome " in strictly ecclesiastical history ; her barrenness of literature, and of great heroic sons, like Atha-nasius and Chrysostom in the East, and Cyprian and Augustine in the West ; and her decadence as a capital, — had led Leo I., and others after him, to dwell much upon " St. Peter," and to favour new ideas of his personal greatness, and of a transmitted grandeur as the inheritance of his suc-cessors. As yet, these were but " great swelling words of vanity ; " but they led to the formulated fraud of the Decretals.

2. Ambition once entering the pale of Catholicity, we find a counter idea to that of the coun-cils at the root of the first usurpation of unscriptural dignity. John " the Faster," bishop of New Rome, conceived himself not merely equal (as the councils had decreed) to the bishop of Old Rome, but his superior, in view of the decrepitude of the latter, and its occupation by the Goths, while the imperial dignity of Constantinople was now matured. He called himself " Œcumenical Bishop."

3. Gregory was then bishop of " Old Rome," and that was the time to assert the principle of the Decretals, had any such idea ever been heard of. How did he meet his brother's arrogance ? Not appealing to decretals, not by asserting that such was his own dignity derived from St. Peter, but by protesting against such abasement of all the other patriarchs and all other bishops (who were all equals), and by pronouncing the impious assumption of such a nefarious title to denote a " forerunner of Antichrist." Plainly, then, there was no " Pope " known to Christen-dom at the close of the sixth century.

4. But hardly was Gregory in his grave when court policy led the Emperor Phocas (one of the most infamous of men) to gratify the wicked ambition of the new Bishop of Rome by giving to him the titular honour of being a " forerunner of Antichrist." Boniface III. (607 A.D.) assumed the daring title of " Universal Bishop." But it was a mere court-title : the Church never recog-nised it ; and so it went down to his successors as mere " sounding brass and a tinkling cymbal " till the days of Charlemagne.

5. In his times the Petrine fable had grown upon the Western mind. All Western Europe had but one Apostolic See. As " *the* Apostolic See " it was known throughout the West, just as " *the* Post-Office " means that which is nearest to one's own dwelling. What was geographically true, had grown to be theologically false, however ; and the Bishop of Rome began to consider himself the only inheritor of Apostolic precedency, if not of all Apostolic authority and power.

---

[1] Compare these Canons: Nicæa, vi.; Constantinople, ii., iii.; Ephesus, viii.; and Chalcedon, xxviii.

6. The formation of the Western Empire favoured this assumption : but it did not take definite shape while Charlemagne lived, for he regarded himself, like Constantine, the "head of the Church ; " [1] and in his day he acted as supreme pontiff, called the Council of Frankfort, overruled the Roman bishop, and, in short, was a lay-Pope throughout his empire. That nobody refused him all he claimed, that Adrian " couched like a strong ass " under the burden of his rebukes, and that Leo paid him bodily "homage," demonstrated that no such character as a " Pope " was yet in existence. Leo III. had personally "adored" Charlemagne with the homage afterwards rendered to the pontiffs, and Adrian had set him the example of personal submission.

7. But, Charlemagne's feeble sons and successors proving incapable of exercising his power, the West only waited for an ambitious and original genius to come to the See of Rome, to yield him all that Charlemagne had claimed, and to invest him with the more sacred character of the Apostolic head to the whole Church.

8. Such a character arose in Nicholas I. He found the Decretals made to his hand by some impostor, and he saw a benighted age ready to accept his assumptions. He therefore used them, and passed them into the organic canon-law of the West. The " Holy Roman Empire " reluctantly received the impious frauds : [2] the East contemptuously resisted. Thus the Papacy was formed on the base of the " Holy Roman Empire," and arrogated to itself the right to cut off and anathematize the greater part of Christendom, with the old patriarchal Sees. So we have in Nicholas the first figure in history in whose person is concentrated what Rome means by the Papacy. No " Pope " ever existed previously, in the sense of her canon-law ; and it was not till two centuries longer that even a " Pope " presumed to pronounce that title *peculiar* to the Bishop of Rome.[3]

Such, then, are the historical facts, which render vastly important some study of the Decretals. I shall give what follows exclusively from " Roman-Catholic " sources. Says the learned Dupin : [4]—

" 1. All these *Decretals* were unknown to all the ancient Fathers, to all the Popes and all the ecclesiastical authors *that wrote before the ninth century*. Now, what rational man can believe that so vast a number of letters, composed by so many holy Popes, containing so many important points in relation to the discipline of the Church, could be unknown to Eusebius, to St. Jerome, to St. Augustine, to St. Basil, and, in short, to all those authors that have spoken of their writings, or who have written upon the discipline of the Church? Could it possibly happen that the Popes, to whom these epistles are so very favourable, would never have cited and alleged them to aggrandize their own reputation? Who could ever imagine that the decisions of these Decretals *should be never so much as quoted* in any council or in any canon? He that will seriously consider with himself, that, since these Decretals have been imposed upon the world, *they have been cited in an infinite number of places by Popes, by councils, and as often by canonists*, will be readily convinced that they would have acquired immense credit, and been very often quoted by antiquity, if they had been genuine and true."

Here I must direct attention to the all-important fact, that whatever may have been the authorship of these forgeries, the Roman pontiffs, and the " Roman Catholic " communion as such, have committed themselves over and over again to the fraud, as Dupin remarks above, and that, long after the imposture was demonstrated and exposed ; in proof of which I cite the following, from one whose eyes were opened by his patient investigation of such facts, but who, while a member of the Roman communion, wrote to his co-religionist Cardinal Manning as follows : [5]—

" Is it credible that the Papacy should have so often appealed to these forgeries for its extended claims, had it any better authorities — *distinctive* authorities — to fall back upon? Every disputant on the Latin side finds in these forgeries a convincing argument against the Greeks. 'To prove this,' the universal jurisdiction of the Pope, said Abbot Barlaam, himself converted by them from the Greek Church, to convert his countrymen, ' one need only look through the decretal epistles of the Roman pontiffs from St. Clement to St. Sylvester.' In the

---

[1] *Episcopus ab extra ;* i.e., head of temporalities.
[2] Hincmar of Rheims opposed them as he could. See Prichard's *Hincmar*, Oxford, 1849.
[3] See vol. v. p. 154, Elucidation III.
[4] See his *Eccles. History*, Cent. iii. p. 173, ed. London, 1693.
[5] Ed. Hayes, London, 1868.

twenty-fifth session of the Council of Florence the provincial of the Dominicans is ordered to address the Greeks on the rights of the Pope, the Pope being present. Twice he argues from the pseudo-decretal of St. Anacletus, at another time from a synodical letter of St. Athanasius to Felix, at another time from a letter of Julius to the Easterns, *all forgeries*. Afterwards, in reply to objections taken by Bessarion, in conference, to their authority, apart from any question of their authenticity, his position in another speech is, 'that *those decretal epistles of the Popes*, being synodical epistles in each case, are entitled to the same authority as the Canons themselves.' Can we need further evidence of the weight attached to them on the Latin side?

"Popes appealed to them in their official capacity, as well as private doctors; (1) Leo IX., for instance, to the pseudo-donation in the prolix epistle written by him, or in his name, to Michael Cerularius, patriarch of Constantinople, on the eve of the schism. (2) Eugenius IV. to the pseudo-decretals of St. Alexander and Julius, during the negotiations for healing it, in his instructions to the Armenians. (3) But why, my lord, need I travel any further for proofs, when in the Catechism of the Council of Trent, that has been for three, centuries *the accredited instructor of the clergy themselves, recommended authoritatively by so many Popes, notwithstanding the real value of these miserable impostures* had been for three centuries before the world, I find these words : [1] 'On the primacy of the Supreme Pontiff, see the third epistle (that is, pseudo-decretal) of Anacletus'! Such is, actually, the authority to which the clergy of our own days are referred, *in the first instance*, for sound and true views on the primacy. (4) Afterwards, when they have mastered what is said there, they may turn to three more authorities, all culled likewise from Gratian, which they will not fail to interpret in accordance with the ideas they have already imbibed. Nor can I refrain from calling attention to a much more flagrant case. On the sacrament of confirmation there had been many questions raised by the Reformers, calculated to set people thinking, and anxious to know the strict truth respecting it. On this the Catechism proceeds as follows : [2] —

"'Since it has been already shown how necessary it would be tó teach generally respecting all the sacraments, by whom they were instituted, so there is need of similar instruction respecting confirmation, that the faithful may be the more attracted by the holiness of this sacrament. *Pastors must therefore explain* that not only was Christ our Lord the author of it, but that, on the authority of the Roman pontiff St. Fabian (i.e., the pseudo-decretal attributed to him), He instituted the rite of the chrism, and the words used by the Catholic Church in its administration.'

"Strange phenomenon, indeed, that the asseverations of such authorities should be still *ordered to be taught as Gospel* from our pulpits in these days, when everybody that is acquainted with the merest rudiments of ecclesiastical history knows how absolutely unauthenticated they are in point of fact, and how unquestionably the authorities cited to prove them are forgeries.

"Absolutely, my lord, with such evidence before me, I am unable to resist the inference that *truthfulness* is not one of the strongest characteristics of the teaching of even the modern Church of Rome ; for is not this a case palpably where its highest living authorities are both indifferent to having possible untruths preached from the pulpit, and something more than indifferent to having forgeries, after their detection as such, adduced from the pulpit to authenticate facts?

"This, again, strongly reminds me of a conversation I had with the excellent French priest who received me into the Roman-Catholic Church, some time subsequently to that event. I had, as an Anglican, inquired very laboriously into the genuineness of the *Santa Casa ;* and having visited Nazareth and Loretto since, and plunged into the question anew at each place, came back more thoroughly convinced than ever of its utterly fictitious character, notwithstanding the privileges bestowed upon it by so many Popes. On stating my convictions to him, his only reply was : 'There are many things in the Breviary which I do not believe, myself.' Oh the stumbling-blocks of a system in the construction of which forgeries have been so largely used, in which it is still thought possible for the clergy to derive edification from legends which they cannot believe, and the people instruction from works of acknowledged imposture!"

Further, Dupin remarks : [3] —

"The first man that published them, if we may believe Hincmar, was one Riculphus, bishop of Mentz, who died about the ninth century. It is commonly believed, seeing the collection bears the name of Isidore, that he brought them from Spain. But it never could have been composed by the great Archbishop of Seville; and there is great reason to believe that no Spaniard, but rather some German or Frenchman, began this imposture.

"It likewise seems probable that some of these Decretals have been foisted in since the time of Riculphus. Benedict, a deacon of the church of Mentz, who made a collection of canons for the successors of Riculphus, may have put the last hand to this collection of false Decretals attributed to one Isidore, a different person from the famous Bishop of Seville, and surnamed Peccator, or Mercator. About his time a certain Isidore did come from Spain, along with some merchants, and then withdrew to Mentz. Not improbably, therefore, this man's name was given to the collection, and it was naturally believed that it was brought from Spain.

"And since these letters first appeared in an unlearned, dark age, what wonder is it that they were received

---

[1] *De Ord. Sacram.*, § 49.   [2] § 5.   [3] P. 173, as above.

with very little opposition? And yet Archbishop Hincmar of Rheims, with other French bishops, made great difficulty in accepting them, even in that time. Soon after, however, they acquired some authority, owing to the support of the court of Rome, the pretensions of which they mightily favoured."

On the twin imposture of the " Donation of Constantine," it may be well to cite the same learned authority. But this shall be found elsewhere.[1]

Let me now recur to the same candid Gallican doctor, Dupin, who remarks as follows : —

"2. The imposture of these letters is invincibly proved from hence: because they are made up of a *contexture* of passages out of Fathers, councils, papal epistles, and imperial ordinances, which have appeared after the third century, *down to the middle of the ninth.*

"3. The citations of Scripture in all these letters *follow the Vulgate* of St. Jerome, which demonstrates that they are since his time (A.D. 420), and consequently do not proceed from Popes who lived long before St. Jerome.

"4. The matter of these letters is not at all in keeping with the ages when those to whom they are attributed were living.

"5. These *Decretals* are full of anachronisms. The consulships and names of consuls mentioned in them are confused and out of order; and, moreover, the true dates of the writers themselves, as Bishops of Rome, do not agree with those assumed in these letters.

"6. Their style is extremely barbarous, full of solecisms; and in them we often meet with certain words *never used till the later ages.* Also, they are all of one style! How does it happen that so many different Popes, living in divers centuries, should all write in the same manner?"

Dupin then goes on to examine the whole series with learning and candour, showing that *every single one of them.*" carries with it unequivocal signs of lying and imposture." To his pages let the student recur, therefore. I follow him in the following enumeration of the frauds he calmly exposes with searching logic and demonstration : —

1. *St. Clement to St. James the Lord's Brother.* — Plainly spurious.

2. *The Second Epistle of Clement to the Same.* — Equally so.

3. *St. Clement to all Suffragan Bishops, Priests, Deacons, and Others of the Clergy: to all Princes Great and Small, and to all the Faithful.*

Dupin remarks : " This very title suffices to prove the forgery, as, in the days of St. Clement, there were no " princes great or small " in the Church. He adds that it speaks of " subdeacons," an order not then existing, and that it is patched up from scraps of the apocryphal *Recognitions.*

4. *A Fourth Letter of the Same.* It is self-refuted by " the same reasons."

5. *The Fifth Letter to St. James of St. Clement, Bishop of Rome and Successor of St. Peter.*

" But," says Dupin, " as St. James died before St. Peter, it necessarily follows, that this epistle cannot have been written by St. Clement." Further, " We have one genuine epistle of St. Clement, the style of which is wholly different from that of these Decretals."

6. *The Epistle of Anacletus.* — Barbarous, full of solecisms and falsehoods.

7. *A Second Epistle of Anacletus.* — Filled with passages out of authors who lived long after the times of Anacletus.

8. *A Third Letter, etc.* — Spurious for the same reasons.

9. *An Epistle of Evaristus.* — Patched up out of writings of Innocent in the fifth century, dated under consuls not contemporaries of the alleged writer.

10. *A Second Epistle of the Same.* — Stuffed with patchwork of later centuries.

11. *An Epistle of Alexander.* — Contains passages from at least one author of the eighth century.

12. *A Second Epistle of the Same.* — Refers to the Council of Laodicea, which was held (A.D. 365) after Alexander was dead.

13. *A Third Epistle, etc.* — Quotes an author of the fifth century.

14. *An Epistle of Xystus.* — Dated under a consul that lived in another age, and quotes authors of centuries later than his own day.

15. *A Second Epistle of the Same.* — Subject to the same objections, anachronisms, etc.

---

[1] Elucidation II., *infra.*

16. *An Epistle of Telesphorus.* — False dates, patched from subsequent authors, etc.

17. *An Epistle of Hyginus.* — Anachronisms, etc.

18. *A Second of the Same.* — Stuffed with anachronisms, and falsely dated by consuls not of his age.

19. *An Epistle of Pius I.* — Full of absurdities, and quotes " the Theodosian Code " !

20. *A Second.* — It is addressed to Justus, etc. Bad Latin, and wholly unknown to antiquity, though Baronius has tried to sustain it.

21. *A Third Letter, etc.* — Addressed to Justus, bishop of Vienna. False for the same reasons.

22. *An Epistle of Anicetus.* — Full of blunders as to dates, etc. Mentions names, titles, and the like, unheard of till later ages.

23. *An Epistle of Soter.* — Dated under consuls who lived before Soter was bishop of Rome.

24. *A Second Letter, etc.* — Speaks of " monks," " palls," and other things of later times ; is patched out of writings of subsequent ages, and dated under consuls not his contemporaries.

25. *An Epistle of Eleutherus.* — Subject to like objections.

26. *A Second Letter, etc.* — Anachronisms.

27. *A Third Letter, etc.* — Addressed to " Desiderius, bishop of Vienna." There was no such bishop till the sixth century.

28. *A Fourth Letter, etc.* — Quotes later authors, and is disproved by its style.

29. *An Epistle of Zephyrinus.* — Little importance to be attached to anything from such a source ; but Dupin (who lived before his bad character came to light in the writings of Hippolytus) convicts it of ignorance, and shows that it is a patchwork of later ideas and writers.

30. *A Second Letter.* — " Yet more plainly an imposture," says Dupin.

31. *An Epistle of St. Callistus.* — What sort of a " saint " he was, our readers are already informed. This epistle is like the preceding ones of Zephyrinus.

32. *A Second Epistle, etc.* — Quotes from writings of the eighth century.

33. *An Epistle of Urban.* — Quotes the Vulgate, the Theodosian Code, and Gregory the Fourth.

34. *An Epistle of Pontianus.* — Anachronisms.

35. *A Second Epistle, etc.* — Barbarous and impossible.

36. *An Epistle of Anterus.* — Equally impossible ; stuffed with anachronisms.

37. *An Epistle of Fabianus.* — Contradicts the facts of history touching Cyprian, Cornelius, and Novatus.

38. *A Second Epistle, etc.* — Self-refuted by its monstrous details of mistake and the like.

39. *A Third Epistle, etc.* — Quotes authors of the sixth century.

40. *An Epistle of Cornelius.* — Contradicts historical facts, etc.

41. *A Second Epistle, etc.* — Equally full of blunders. " But nothing," says Dupin, " shows the imposture of these two letters more palpably than the difference of style from those truly ascribed to Cornelius in Cyprian's works."

42. *A Third Letter, etc.* — Equally false on its face. Dupin, with his usual candour, remarks : " We find in it the word ' Mass,' which was unknown to the contemporaries of Cornelius."

43. *An Epistle of Lucius.* — It is dated six months before he became Bishop of Rome, and quotes authors who lived ages after he was dead.

44. *An Epistle of Stephen.* — " Filled with citations out of subsequent authors."

45. *A Second Epistle, etc.* — Open to the like objection ; it does not harmonize with the times to which it is referred.

Here Dupin grows weary, and winds up his review as follows : —

"For like reasons, we must pass judgment, in like manner, on the two Epistles of Sixtus II.; the two of Dionysius; the three of St. Felix I.; the two of Eutychianus; one of Caius; two of Marcellinus and those of Marcellus; the three of Eusebius; those of Miltiades, and the rest of Isidore's collection: they are full of passages out of Fathers, Popes, and councils, more modern than the very Popes by whom they are pretended to be written. In them are many things that clash with the known history of those times, and were *purposely framed to favour the court of Rome, and to sustain her pretensions against the rights of bishops and the liberties of churches.* But it would take up too much time to show the gross falsehood of these monuments. They are now rejected by common consent, and even by those authors who are most favourable to the court of Rome, who are obliged to abandon the patronage of these epistles, though they have done a great deal of service in developing the greatness of the court of Rome, and *ruining the ancient discipline of the Church*, especially with reference to the rights of bishops and ecclesiastical decisions."

The following is the TRANSLATOR'S PREFACE to these frauds: —

IN regard to these Decretals, Dean Milman says: "Up to this period the Decretals, the letters or edicts of the Bishops of Rome, according to the authorized or common collection of Dionsysius, commenced with Pope Siricius, towards the close of the fourth century. To the collection of Dionysius was added that of the authentic councils, which bore the name of Isidore of Seville. On a sudden was promulgated, unannounced, without preparation, not absolutely unquestioned, but apparently overawing at once all doubt, a new code, which to the former authentic documents added fifty-nine letters and decrees of the twenty oldest popes from Clement to Melchiades,[1] and the donation of Constantine;[2] and in the third part, among the decrees of the popes and of the councils from Sylvester to Gregory II., thirty-nine false decrees, and the acts of several unauthentic councils."[3]

In regard to the authorship and date of the False Decretals, Dean Milman says: "The author or authors of this most audacious and elaborate of pious frauds are unknown; the date and place of its compilation are driven into such narrow limits that they may be determined within a few years, and within a very circumscribed region. The False Decretals came not from Rome; the time of their arrival at Rome, after they were known beyond the Alps, appears almost certain. In one year Nicholas I. is apparently ignorant of their existence; the next he speaks of them with full knowledge. They contain words manifestly used at the Council of Paris, A.D. 829, consequently are of later date. They were known to the Levite Benedict of Mentz, who composed a supplement to the collection of capitularies by Ansegise, between A.D. 840–847. The city of Mentz is designated with nearly equal certainty as the place in which, if not actually composed, they were first promulgated as the canon law of Christendom."[4]

---

[1] [Elucidation I.]
[2] [Elucidation II.]
[3] *History of Latin Christianity*, vol. iii. p. 191.
[4] *History of Latin Christianity*, vol. iii. p. 193. [In the marvellous confusion of vol. ix. of the Edinburgh series, these Decretals are mixed up with genuine works as "Fragments of the Third Century."]

THE EPISTLES OF ZEPHYRINUS [1]

THE FIRST EPISTLE.

TO ALL THE BISHOPS OF SICILY.

OF THE FINAL DECISION OF THE TRIALS OF BISHOPS, AND GRAVER ECCLESIASTICAL CASES IN THE SEAT OF THE APOSTLES.

ZEPHYRINUS, archbishop of the city of Rome, to all the bishops settled in Sicily, in the Lord, greeting.

We ought to be mindful of the grace of God to us, which in His own merciful regard has raised us for this purpose to the summit of priestly honour, that, abiding by His commandments, and appointed in a certain supervision of His priests, we may prohibit things unlawful, and teach those that are to be followed. As night does not extinguish the stars of heaven, so the unrighteousness of the world does not blind the minds of the faithful that hold by the sure support of Scripture. Therefore we ought to consider well and attend carefully to the Scriptures, and the divine precepts which are contained in these Scriptures, in order that we may show ourselves not transgressors, but fulfillers of the law of God.

Now patriarchs and primates, in investigating the case of an accused bishop, should not pronounce a final decision until, supported by the authority of the apostles, they find that the person either confesses himself guilty, or is proved so by witnesses trustworthy and regularly examined, who should not be fewer in number than were those disciples whom the Lord directed to be chosen for the help of the apostles — that is, seventy-two. Detractors also, who are to be rooted out by divine authority, and the advisers of enemies (*auctores inimicorum*), we do not admit in the indictment of bishops or in evidence against them; nor should any one of superior rank be indicted or condemned on the accusations of inferiors. Nor in a doubtful case

should a decisive judgment be pronounced; nor should any trial be held valid unless it has been conducted according to order. No one, moreover, should be judged in his absence, because both divine and human laws forbid that. The accusers of those persons should also be free of all suspicion, because the Lord has chosen that His pillars should stand firm, and not be shaken by any one who will. For a sentence should not bind any of them if it is not given by their proper judge, because even the laws of the world ordain that that be done. For any accused bishop may, if it be necessary, choose twelve judges by whom his case may be justly judged. Nor should he be heard or excommunicated or judged until these be chosen by him; and on his being regularly summoned at first to a council of his own bishops, his case should be justly heard by them, and investigated on sound principles. The end of his case, however, should be remitted to the seat of the apostles, that it may be finally decided there. Nor should it be finished, as has been decreed of old by the apostles or their successors, until it is sustained by its authority. To it also all, and especially the oppressed, should appeal and have recourse as to a mother, that they may be nourished by her breasts, defended by her authority, and relieved of their oppressions, because " a mother cannot," and should not, " forget her son." [2] For the trials of bishops and graver ecclesiastical cases, as the apostles and their holy successors have decreed, are to be finally decided along with other bishops [3] by the seat of the apostles, and by no other; because, although they may be transferred to other bishops, it was yet to the blessed Apostle Peter these terms were addressed : " Whatsoever thou shalt bind on earth shall be bound in heaven, and whatsoever thou shalt loose on earth shall be loosed in heaven." [4] And the other privileges which have

---

[1] The little that is known of Zephyrinus is derived from Eusebius. That historian states that Zephyrinus succeeded Victor in the presidency of the Roman church "about the ninth year of the reign of Severus" (A.D. 201), and that he died in the first year of the reign of Antoninus (Heliogabalus, A.D. 218). He is several times alluded to in the fragments ascribed to Caius, or in connection with them.

The two letters bearing his name are forgeries. They belong to the famous collection of False Decretals forged in the ninth century.

[2] Isa. xlix. 15.
[3] The word " bishops " is omitted in MS.
[4] Matt. xvi. 19.

been granted to this holy seat alone are found embodied both in the constitutions of the apostles [1] and their successors, and in very many others in harmony with these. For the apostles have prefixed seventy [2] decrees, together with very many other bishops, and have appointed them to be kept. For to judge rashly of the secrets of another's heart is sin ; and it is unjust to reprove him on suspicion whose works seem not other than good, since God alone is Judge of those things which are unknown to men. He, however, "knoweth the secrets of the heart," [3] and not another. For unjust judgments are to be guarded against by all, especially however by the servants of God. "And the servant of the Lord must not strive," [4] nor harm any one. For bishops are to be borne by laity and clergy, and masters by servants, in order that, under the exercise of endurance, things temporal may be maintained, and things eternal hoped for. For that increases the worth of virtue, which does not violate the purpose of religion. You should be

earnestly intent that none of your brothers be grievously injured or undone. Therefore you ought to succour the oppressed, and deliver them from the hand of their persecutors, in order that with the blessed Job you may say : "The blessing of him that was ready to perish will come upon me, and I consoled the widow's heart. I put on righteousness, and clothed myself with a robe and a diadem, my judgment. I was eye to the blind, and foot to the lame. I was a father to the poor, and the cause which I knew not I searched out most carefully. I brake the grinders of the wicked, and plucked the spoil out of his teeth ; " [5] and so forth. You, therefore, who have been placed in eminence by God, ought with all your power to check and repel those who prepare snares for brethren, or raise seditions and offences against them. For it is easy by word to deceive man, not however God. Therefore you ought to keep these off, and be on your guard against them, until such darkness is done away utterly, and the morning star shines upon them, and gladness arises, most holy brethren. Given on the 20th September, in the consulship of the most illustrious Saturninus and Gallicanus. [6]

---

[1] This means the seventy-third apostolic canon, in which it is ordained that episcopal cases be not decided but by superior bishops, councils, or the Roman pontiff. [See note 1, p. 612.]

[2] Another reading has sixty, and another fifty. Whatever be the reading, it is true that by these decrees are meant the apostolic canons; and although their number was only fifty, yet, because sometimes several decrees are comprehended in one canon, there would be no inconsistency between the number of sixty or seventy apostolic decrees and the number of fifty apostolic canons (Sev. Bin.).

[3] Ps. xliv. 21.

[4] 2 Tim. ii. 24.

---

[5] Job xxix. 13-17, according to the Vulgate version.

[6] Or, Gallus. But Saturninus and Gallus were consuls in the year 198, while Victor was yet alive.

THE SECOND EPISTLE.

TO THE BISHOPS OF THE PROVINCE OF EGYPT.

ZEPHYRINUS, archbishop of the city of Rome, to the most beloved brethren who serve the Lord in Egypt.

So great trust have we received from the Lord, the Founder of this holy seat and of the apostolic church, and from the blessed Peter, chief of the apostles, that we may labour with unwearied affection [1] for the universal Church which has been redeemed by the blood of Christ, and aid all who serve the Lord, and give help to all who live piously by apostolic authority. All who will live [2] piously in Christ must needs endure reproaches from the impious and aliens, and be despised as fools and madmen, that they may be made better and purer who lose the good things of time that they may gain those of eternity. But the contempt and ridicule of those who afflict and scorn them will be cast back upon them-

selves, when their abundance shall change to want, and their pride to confusion.

I.

On the Spoliation or Expulsion of certain Bishops.

It has been reported at the seat of the apostles by your delegates, [3] that certain of our brethren, bishops to wit, are being expelled from their churches and seats, and deprived of their goods, and summoned, thus destitute and spoiled, to trial ; a thing which is void of all reason, since the constitutions of the apostles and their successors, and the statutes of emperors, and the regulations of laws, prohibit it, and the authority of the seat of the apostles forbids it to be done.

---

[1] Or, diligence. [See note 2, p. 612.]

[2] 2 Tim. ii. 24.

---

[3] By these apocrisarii are meant the deputies of the bishops, and their locum tenentes, as it were, who manage the affairs of the Church, hear the cases of individuals, and refer them to the bishops. They are therefore called apocrisarii, i.e., responders, from ἀποκρίνομαι, to respond. Mention is made of them in Justinian Novell., Quomodo oporteat Episcopos, chap. xii. Albericus understands by them the legates of the Pope. [Note 3.]

It has been ordained, indeed, in the ancient statutes, that bishops who have been ejected and spoiled of their property should recover their churches, and, in the first place, have all their property restored to them; and then, in the second place, that if any one may desire to accuse them justly, he should do so at the like risk; that the judges should be discreet, the bishops right-minded and harmonious in the Church, where they should be witnesses for every one who seemed to be oppressed; and that they should not answer till all that belonged to them was restored to them, and to their churches by law without detriment. Nor is it strange, brethren, if they persecute you, when they persecuted even to death your Head, Christ our Lord. Yet even persecutions are to be endured patiently, that ye may be known to be His disciples, for whom also ye suffer. Whence, too, he says Himself, "Blessed are they which are persecuted for righteousness' sake."[1] Sustained by these testimonies, we ought not greatly to fear the reproach of men, nor be overcome by their upbraidings, since the Lord gives us this command by Isaiah the prophet, saying, "Hearken unto me, ye that know righteousness, my people, in whose heart is my law; fear ye not the reproach of men, neither be ye afraid of their revilings;"[2] considering what is written in the Psalm, "Shall not God search this out? for He knoweth the secrets of the heart,[3] and the thoughts of such men, that they are vanity."[4] "They spoke vanity every one with his neighbour: with deceitful lips in their heart, and with an evil heart they spoke. But the Lord shall cut off all deceitful lips, and the tongue that speaketh proud things; who have said, Our lips are our own; who is Lord over us?"[5] For if they kept these things in memory, they would by no means break forth into so great wickedness. For they do not this by laudable and paternal instruction (*probabili et paterna doctrina*), but that they may wreak their vengeful feeling against the servants of God. For it is written, "The way of a fool is right in his eyes;"[6] and, "There are ways which seem right unto a man, but the end thereof leads to death."[7] Now we who suffer these things ought to leave them to the judgment of God, who will render to every man according to his works;[8] who also has thundered through His servants, saying, "Vengeance is mine, I will repay."[9] Assist ye, therefore, one another in good faith, and by deed and with a hearty will; nor let any one

remove his hand from the help of a brother, since "by this," saith the Lord, "shall all men know that ye are my disciples, if ye have love one to another."[10] Whence, too, He speaks by the prophet, saying, "Behold how good and how pleasant it is for brethren to dwell together in unity!"[11] In a spiritual dwelling, I interpret it, and in a concord which is in God, and in the unity of the faith which distinguishes this pleasant dwelling according to truth, which indeed was more beauteously illustrated in Aaron and the priests[12] clothed with honour, as ointment upon the head, nurturing the highest understanding, and leading even to the end of wisdom. For in this dwelling the Lord has promised blessing and eternal life. Apprehending, therefore, the importance of this utterance of the prophet, we have spoken this present brotherly word for love's sake, and by no means seeking, or meaning to seek, our own things. For it is not good to repay detraction with detraction, or *according to the common proverb* to cast out a beam with a beam (*excutere palum palo*). Be it far from us. Such manners are not ours. May the Godhead indeed forbid it. By the just judgment of God, power is given sometimes to sinners to persecute His saints, in order that they who are aided and borne on by the Spirit of God may become more glorious through the discipline of sufferings. But to those very persons who persecute, and reproach, and injure them, there will doubtless be woe. Woe, woe to those who injure the servants of God; for injury done to them concerns Him whose service they discharge, and whose function they execute. But we pray that a door of enclosure be placed upon their mouths, as we desire that no one perish or be defiled by their lips, and that they think or publish with their mouth no hurtful word. Whence also the Lord speaks by the prophet, "I said I will take heed to my ways, that I sin not with my tongue."[13] May the Lord Almighty, and His only-begotten Son and our Saviour Jesus Christ, give you this incitement, that with all means in your power you aid all the brethren under whatsoever tribulations they labour, and esteem, as is meet, their sufferings your own. Afford them the utmost assistance by word and deed, that ye may be found His true disciples, who enjoined all to love the brethren as themselves.

II.

On the Ordination of Presbyters and Deacons.

Ordinations of presbyters and Levites, moreover, solemnly perform on a suitable occasion, and in the presence of many witnesses; and to

---

[1] Matt. v. 10.
[2] Isa. li. 7.
[3] Ps. xliv. 21.
[4] Ps. xciv. 11.
[5] Ps. xii. 2–4.
[6] Prov. xii. 15.
[7] Prov. xiv. 12.
[8] Matt. xvi. 27.
[9] Rom. xii. 19.

[10] John xiii. 35.
[11] Ps. cxxxiii. 1.
[12] The MS reads, "and those wearing the priestly dignity."
[13] Ps. xxxix. 1.

this duty advance tried and learned men, that ye may be greatly gladdened by their fellowship and help. Place the confidence of your hearts without ceasing on the goodness of God, and declare these and the other divine words to succeeding generations: " For this is our God for ever and ever, and He will guide us to eternity." [1] Given on the 7th November, in the consulship of the most illustrious Saturninus and Gallicanus. [2]

[1] Ps. xlviii. 14.
[2] Or, Gallus. [See note 5, p. 610.]

NOTES BY THE AMERICAN EDITOR.

1. The translator's reference to Canon 73 is a mistake, and quite misleading. See vol. vii. Canon 74, p. 504.

2. It is worth while to recall who and what Zephyrinus was. See vol. v. p. 156, Elucidation V.; also same volume of this series, p. 157, Elucidation VI. This unhappy prelate was a heretic; and his decrees and opinions are worthless, as Hippolytus shows. Hence this letter, even were it genuine, would be of no value whatever. Consult also vol. v. p. 156, in Elucidation IV.; also same volume, Elucidation III.

3. On p. 610, Ep. 2, sec. 1, observe the reference to the " statutes of Emperors," where the wily forger forgot himself, as if the Cæsars of this date had legislated for the Christian Church. On the spirit of the ancient Canons, refuting all these Decretals, compare the Canons of Nicæa, 4, 5, 6, 7, and 15; of Constantinople, 2 and 3; of Ephesus, 8; and of Chalcedon, 9 and 28. To these Canons, against the claims of the Paparchy, the Church of England appealed at her Restoration.

THE EPISTLES OF POPE CALLISTUS[1]

THE FIRST EPISTLE.[2]

TO BISHOP BENEDICTUS.

ON THE FASTS OF THE FOUR SEASONS, AND THAT NO ONE SHOULD TAKE UP AN ACCUSATION AGAINST A DOCTOR (TEACHER).

CALLISTUS, archbishop of the Church Catholic in the city of Rome, to Benedictus, our brother and bishop, greeting in the Lord.

By the love of the brotherhood wè are bound, and by our apostolic rule we are constrained, to give answer to the inquiries of the brethren, according to what the Lord has given us, and to furnish them with the authority of the seal of the apostles.

I.

(Of the seasons for fasting.)

Fasting, which ye have learned to hold three times in the year among us, we decree now to take place, as more suitable, in four seasons; so that even as the year revolves through four seasons, we too may keep a solemn fast quarterly in the four seasons of the year. And as we are replenished with corn, and wine, and oil for the nourishment of our bodies, so let us be replenished with fasting for the nourishment of our souls, in accordance with the word of the prophet Zechariah, who says, " The word of the Lord came to me, saying, Thus saith the Lord of hosts, As I thought to punish you, when your fathers provoked me to wrath, and I repented not; so again have I thought in these days to do well unto Jerusalem, and to the house of Judah: fear ye not. These are the things that ye shall do: Speak ye every man the truth to his neighbour; judge the truth and the judgment of peace in your gates; and let none of you imagine evil in your hearts against his neighbour, and love no false oath: for all these are things that I hate, saith the Lord of hosts.

And the word of the Lord of hosts came unto me, saying, Thus saith the Lord of hosts, The fast of the fourth month, and the fast of the fifth, and the fast of the seventh, and the fast of the tenth, shall be to the house of the Lord joy and gladness, and cheerful feasts; only love the truth and peace, saith the Lord of hosts." [3] In this, then, we ought to be all of one mind, so that, according to apostolic teaching, we may all say the same thing, and that there be no divisions among us. Let us then be perfect in the same mind, and in the same judgment;[4] in ready zeal for which work we congratulate ourselves on having your affection as our partner. For it is not meet for the members to be at variance with the head; but, according to the testimony of sacred Scripture,[5] all the members should follow the head. It is matter of doubt, moreover, to no one, that the church of the apostles is the mother of all the churches, from whose ordinances it is not right that you should deviate to any extent. And as the Son of God came to do the Father's will, so shall ye fulfil the will of your mother, which is the Church, the head of which, as has been stated already, is the church of Rome. Wherefore, whatsoever may be done against the discipline of this church, without the decision of justice, cannot on any account be permitted to be held valid.

II.

(Of accusations against doctors.)

Moreover, let no one take up an accusation against a doctor (*teacher*), because it is not right for sons to find fault with fathers, nor for slaves to wound their masters. Now, all those whom they instruct are sons of doctors; and as sons ought to love their fathers after the flesh, so ought they to love their spiritual fathers. For he does not live rightly who does not believe rightly, or who reprehends fathers, or calumniates

---

[1] Callistus succeeded Zephyrinus in the bishopric of Rome, and discharged the duties of that office for five years. This is all the information which Eusebius (in his *Chronicon* and *Hist. Eccl.*, vi. 21) gives us in regard to Callistus. Later writers make many other statements. [See note, p. 618.]
    The letters attributed to him form part of the False Decretals of the pseudo-Isidorus, mentioned in the notice of Zephyrinus.
[2] Mansi, *Concil.*, i. 737.

[3] Zech. viii. 1-19.
[4] 1 Pet. iii.
[5] 1 Cor. xii.

them.   Doctors therefore, who are also called fathers, are rather to be borne with than reprehended, unless they err from the true faith.   Let no one, consequently, accuse a doctor by writing (*per scripta*) ; neither let him answer to any accuser, unless he be one who is trustworthy and recognised by law, and who leads also a life and conversation free from reproach.   For it is a thing unworthy that a doctor should reply to a foolish and ignorant person, and one who leads a reprehensible life, according to the man's folly ; as Scripture says, Answer not a fool according to his folly.[1]   He does not live rightly who does not believe rightly.   He means nothing evil who is faithful.   If any one is faithful (*a believer*), let him see to it that he make no false allegations, nor lay a snare for any man.   The faithful man acts always in faith ; and the unfaithful man plots cunningly, and strives to work the ruin of those who are faithful, and who live in piety and righteousness, because like seeks like.   The unfaithful man is one dead in the living body. And on the other hand, the discourse of the man of faith guards the life of his hearers.   For as the Catholic doctor, and especially the priest of the Lord, ought to be involved in no error, so ought he to be wronged by no machination or passion.   Holy Scripture indeed says, Go not after thy lusts, but refrain thyself from thine appetites ;[2] and we must resist many allurements of this world, and many vanities, in order that the integrity of a true continence may be obtained, whereof the first blemish is pride, the beginning of transgression and the origin of sin ; for the mind with lustful will knows neither to abstain nor to give itself to piety.   No good man has an enemy except in the wicked, who are permitted to be such only in order that the good man may be corrected or exercised through their means.   Whatever, therefore, is faultless is defended by the Church Catholic.   Neither for prince, nor for any one who observes piety, is it lawful to venture anything contrary to the divine injunctions.   Consequently an unjust judgment, or an unjust decision (*diffinitio*), instituted or enforced by judges under the fear or by the command of a prince, or any bishop or person of influence, cannot be valid.   The religious man ought not to hold it enough merely to refrain from entering into the enmities of others, or increasing them by evil speech, unless he also make it his study to extinguish them by good speech.[3]   Better is a humble confession in evil deeds, than a proud boasting in good deeds.[4] Moreover, all who live the blessed life, choose rather to run that course in the proper estate of peace and righteousness, than to involve themselves in the avenging pains of our sins.[5]   For I am mindful that I preside over the Church under the name of him whose confession was honoured by our Lord Jesus Christ, and whose faith ever destroys all errors.   And I understand that I am not at liberty to act otherwise than to expend all my efforts on that cause in which the well-being of the universal Church is at stake (*infestatur*).   I hope, too, that the mercy of God will so favour us, that, with the help of His clemency, every deadly disease may be removed, God Himself expelling it, and that whatever may be done wholesomely, under His inspiration and help, may be accomplished to the praise of thy faith and devotion.   For all things cannot otherwise be safe, unless, as far as pertains to the service of the divine office, sacerdotal authority upholds them.   Given on the 21st day of November in the consulship of the most illustrious Antoninus and Alexander.[6]

[1] Prov. xxvi. 4.
[2] Ecclus. xviii. 30.

[3] See Augustine's *Confessions*, book ix. ch. ix.
[4] See Augustine on Ps. xciii.
[5] See Ambrose, Epistle xxi.
[6] In the year 222.

THE SECOND EPISTLE.

TO ALL THE BISHOPS OF GAUL.

(OF CONSPIRACIES AND OTHER ILLICIT PURSUITS, THAT THEY BE NOT ENGAGED IN, AND OF THE RESTORATION OF THE LAPSED AFTER PENITENCE.)

CALLISTUS to our most dearly beloved brethren, all the bishops settled throughout Gaul.

By the report of very many, we learn that your love, by the zeal of the Holy Spirit, holds and guides the helm of the Church so firmly in the face of all assaults, that by God's will it is conscious neither of shipwreck nor of the losses of shipwreck.   Rejoicing, therefore, in such testimonies, we beg you not to permit anything to be done in those parts contrary to the apostolic statutes ; but, supported by our authority, do ye check what is injurious, and prohibit what is unlawful.

I.

(Of those who conspire against bishops, or who take part with such.)

Now we have heard that the crime of conspiracies prevails in your parts, and it has been shown us that the people are conspiring against their bishops; of which crime the craft is hateful, not only among Christians, but even among the heathen, and it is forbidden by foreign laws. And therefore the laws not only of the Church, but of the world, condemn those who are guilty of this crime; and not only those indeed who actually conspire, but those also who take part with such.[1] Our predecessors, moreover, together with a very numerous body of bishops, ordained that any *guilty of this offence* among those who are set in the honour of the priesthood, and who belong to the clergy, should be deprived of the honour which they enjoy; and they ordered that others should be cut off from communion, and expelled from the Church; and they decreed, at the same time, that all men of both orders should be infamous (*infames*); and that, too, not only for those who did the deed, but for those also who took part with such. For it is but equitable that those who despise the divine mandates, and prove themselves disobedient to the ordinances of the fathers, should be chastised with severer penalties, in order that others may fear to do such things, and that all may rejoice in brotherly concord, and all take to themselves the example of severity and goodness. For if (which may God forbid) we neglect the care of the Church, and are regardless of its strength, our slothfulness will destroy discipline, and injury will be done assuredly to the souls of the faithful. Such persons, moreover, are not to be admitted to accuse any one: neither can their voice, nor that of those who are under the ban, injure or criminate any man.

II.

(Of those who have intercourse with excommunicated persons, or with unbelievers.)

Those, too, who are excommunicated by the priests, let no one receive previous to the just examination of both sides; nor let him have any intercourse with such in speech, or in eating or drinking, or in the salutation with the kiss, nor let him greet such; because, whosoever wittingly holds intercourse with the excommunicated in these or other prohibited matters, will subject himself, according to the ordinance of the apostles,[2] to like excommunication. From these, therefore, let clergy and laity keep themselves if they would not have the same penalty to endure. Also do not join the unbelievers, neither have any fellowship with them. They who do such things, indeed, are judged not as believers, but as unbelievers. Whence the apostle says: " What part hath he that believeth with an infidel? or what fellowship hath righteousness with unrighteousness?"[3]

III.

(That no bishop should presume in anything pertaining to another's parish, and of the transference of bishops.)

Let no one, again, trespass upon the boundaries of another, nor presume to judge or excommunicate one belonging to another's parish; because such judgment or ordination, or excommunication or condemnation, shall neither be ratified nor have any virtue; since no one shall be bound by the decision of another judge than his own, neither shall he be condemned by such. Whence also the Lord speaks to this effect: " Pass not the ancient landmarks which thy fathers have set."[4] Moreover, let no primate or metropolitan *invade* the church or parish of a diocesan (*diœcesani*), or presume to excommunicate or judge any one belonging to his parish, or do anything without his counsel or judgment; but let him observe this law, which has been laid down by the apostles[5] and fathers, and our predecessors, and has been ratified by us: to wit, that if any metropolitan bishop, except in that which pertains to his own proper parish alone, shall attempt to do anything without the counsel and good-will of all the comprovincial bishops, he will do it at the risk of his position, and what he does in this manner shall be held null and void; but whatever it may be necessary to do or to arrange with regard to the cases of the body of provincial bishops, and the necessities of their churches and clergy and laity, this should be done by consent of all the pontiffs of the same province, and that too without any pride of lordship, but with the most humble and harmonious action, even as the Lord says: " I came not to be ministered unto, but to minister."[6] And in another passage He says: " And whosoever of you is the greater, shall be your servant,"[7] and so forth. And in like manner the bishops of the same province themselves should do all things in counsel with him, except so much as pertains to their own proper parishes, in accordance with the statutes of the holy fathers (who, although they have preceded us by a certain interval of time, have yet drawn the light of truth and faith from one and the same fountain of purity, and have sought the prosperity of the Church of God and the common advantage of all Christians by the same enlightening and guiding Spirit), that

---

[1] Comp. Rom. i. 32.
[2] The reference is to the 11th and 12th of the canons of the apostles. [Vol. vii. p. 501, this series.]
[3] 2 Cor. vi 14, 15.
[4] Prov. xxii. 28.
[5] Canons 35 and 36. [Vol. vii. p. 503.]
[6] Matt. xx. 28.
[7] Mark x. 44.

with one mind, and one mouth, and one accord, the Holy Trinity may be glorified for ever. No primate, no metropolitan, nor any of the other bishops, is at liberty to enter the seat of another, or to occupy a possession which does not pertain to him, and which forms part of the parish of another bishop, at the direction of any one, unless he is invited by him to whose jurisdiction it is acknowledged to belong; nor can he set about any arrangement or ordinance, or judgment there, if he wishes to keep the honour of his station. But if he presume to do otherwise, he shall be condemned; and not only he, but those who co-operate and agree with him: for just as the power of making appointments (*ordinatio*) is interdicted in such circumstances, so also is the power of judging or of disposing of other matters. For if a man has no power to appoint, how shall he judge? Without doubt, he shall in no wise judge or have power to judge: for just as another man's wife cannot intermarry with any one (*adulterari*), nor be judged or disposed of by any one but by her own husband so long as he liveth; so neither can it in anywise be allowed that the wife of a bishop, by whom undoubtedly is meant his church or parish, should be judged or disposed of by another without his (the bishop's) judgment and good-will so long as he liveth, or enjoy another's embrace, that is, his ordaining. Wherefore the apostle says: "The wife is bound by the law so long as her husband liveth; but if he be dead, she is loosed from the law of her husband."[1] In like manner also, the spouse of a bishop (for the church is called his spouse and wife) is bound to him while he liveth; but when he is dead she is loosed, and may be wedded to whomsoever she will, only in the Lord, that is, according to order. For if, while he is alive, she marry another, she shall be judged to be an adulteress. And in the same manner, he too, if he marry another of his own will, shall be held to be an adulterer, and shall be deprived of the privilege of communion. If, however, he is persecuted in his own church, he must flee to another, and attach himself to it, as the Lord says: "If they persecute you in one city, flee ye into another."[2] If, however, the change be made for the sake of the good *of the church*, he may not do this of himself, but only on the invitation of the brethren, and with the sanction of this holy seat, and not for ambition's sake, but for the public good.

IV.

(Of marriages among blood-relations, and of those who are born of them; and of accusations which the laws reject.)

Moreover, marriages among blood-relations are forbidden, since all laws, both sacred and secular, forbid such. Wherefore the divine laws not only expel, but even anathematize, those who do so, and those who spring from them. Secular laws, again, call such persons infamous, and interdict them from inheriting. And we too, following our fathers, and keeping close by their footsteps, brand such with infamy, and hold them to be infamous, because they are sprinkled with the stains of infamy. Neither ought we to admit those men or their accusations, that secular laws reject. (For who doubts that human laws, when they are not inconsistent with reason and honour, are to be embraced, especially when they either further the public good or defend the authority of the ecclesiastical office, and uphold it as a help?) And we call those blood-relations whom divine laws, and those of the emperors, both Roman and Greek, name blood-relations, and whom they admit to the right of inheriting, and cannot exclude from that. Marriages, then, between such are neither lawful nor capable of holding good, but are to be rejected. (And if any such are attempted in rash daring, they come to be rescinded by apostolic authority.)

V.

(Of those who ought not to be admitted to prefer an accusation, or to bear witness; and that evidence is not to be given but on things happening in the person's presence)

Whosoever, therefore, has not been lawfully married, or has been united without the dotal title (*dotali titulo*) and the blessing of a priest, cannot by any means bring a charge against priests, or those who are lawfully married, or bear witness against them, since every one who is polluted with the stain of incest is infamous, and is not allowed to accuse the above-named. And consequently not only they, but all those too who agree with them, are to be rejected, and are rendered infamous. We hold that the same should also be the case with robbers, or with those who assault the elderly. The laws of the world, indeed, put such persons to death; but we, with whom mercy has the first place, receive them under the mark of infamy to repentance. That infamy also with which they are stained, we are not able to remove; but our desire is to heal their souls by public penitence, and by satisfaction made to the Church: for public sins are not to be purged by secret correction. Those, again, who are suspected in the matter of the right faith, should by no means be admitted to prefer charges against priests, and against those of whose faith there is no doubt; and such persons should be held of doubtful authority in matters of human testimony. Their voice, consequently, should be reckoned invalid whose faith is doubted; and no credit should be given to those who are ignorant of the right faith. Accordingly, in judg-

---

[1] Rom. vii. 2.
[2] Matt. x. 23.

ment, inquiry should be made as to the conversation and faith of the person who accuses, and of him who is accused ; since those who are not of correct conversation and faith, and whose life is open to impeachment, are not allowed to accuse their elders, neither can such permission be given to those whose faith and life and liberty are unknown. Nor should vile persons be admitted to accuse them. But a clear examination is to be made as to what kind of persons the accusers are (*rimandæ sunt enucleatim personæ accusatorum*) ; for they are not to be admitted readily without writing, and are never to be admitted *as accusers* on mere writing. For no one may either accuse or be accused by mere writing, but with the living voice ; and every one must lay his accusation in the presence of him whom he seeks to accuse. And no credit should be given to any accuser in the absence of him whom he seeks to accuse. In like manner, witnesses must not prefer their evidence by writing only ; but they must give their testimony truthfully in their own persons, and in matters which they have seen and do know. And they are not to give evidence in any other cases or matters but in those which are known to have happened in their presence. Accusers, moreover, of one blood, are not to bear witness against those who are not related to the family, nor is that to be the case with domestics (*familiares*) or those proceeding from the house ; but if it is their wish, and they agree among themselves, the parents only should give evidence in such cases, and not others. Neither accusers nor witnesses should be admitted who are open to any suspicion ; for the feeling of relationship, or friendship, or lordship, is wont to impede the truth. \ Carnal love, and fear, and avarice, commonly blunt the perceptions of men, and pervert their opinions ; so that they look on gain as godliness, and on money as the reward of prudence. Let no one, then, speak deceitfully to his neighbour.[1] The mouth of the malevolent is a deep pit. The innocent man, while he believes easily, falls readily ; but though he falls, he rises ; and the shuffler, with all his arts, goes headlong to ruin, whence he can never rise or escape. Therefore let every one weigh well his words, and let him not say to another what he would not say to himself. Whence the sacred Scripture says well : "Do not that to another which thou wouldest not have done to thyself."[2] For we need time to do anything perfectly (*maturius*) ; and let us not be precipitate in our counsels or our works, neither let us violate order. But if any one has fallen in anything, let us not consign him to ruin ; but let us reprove him with brotherly affection, as the

blessed apostle says : "If a man be overtaken in any fault, ye which are spiritual restore such an one in the spirit of meekness ; considering thyself, lest thou also be tempted. Bear ye one another's burden, and so will ye fulfil the law of Christ."[3] Furthermore, the sainted David had deadly crimes to repent of, and yet he was continued in honour. The blessed Peter also shed the bitterest tears when he repented of having denied the Lord ; but still he abode an apostle. And the Lord by the prophet makes this promise to the sinning : "In the day that the sinner is converted, and repenteth, I will not mention any more against him all his transgressions."[4]

VI.

(As to whether a priest may minister after a lapse.)

For those are in error who think that the priests of the Lord, after a lapse, although they may have exhibited true repentance, are not capable of ministering to the Lord, and engaging their honourable offices, though they may lead a good life thereafter, and keep their priesthood correctly. And those who hold this opinion are not only in error, but also seem to dispute and act in opposition to *the power of* the keys committed to the Church, whereof it is said : "Whatsoever ye shall loose on earth, shall be loosed in heaven."[5] And in short, this opinion either is not the Lord's, or it is true. But *be that as it may*, we believe without hesitation, that both the priests of the Lord and other believers may return to their honours after a proper satisfaction for their error, as the Lord Himself testifies by His prophet : "Shall he who falls not also rise again ? and shall he who turns away not return ?"[6] And in another passage the Lord says : "I desire not the death of the sinner, but that he may turn, and live."[7] And the prophet David, on his repentance, said : "Restore unto me the joy of Thy salvation, and uphold me with Thy free Spirit."[8] And he indeed, after his repentance, taught others also, and offered sacrifice to God, giving thereby an example to the teachers of the holy Church, that if they have fallen, and thereafter have exhibited a right repentance to God, they may do both things in like manner. For he taught when he said : "I will teach transgressors Thy ways, and sinners shall be converted unto Thee."[9] And he offered sacrifice for himself, while he said : "The sacrifice for God is a broken spirit."[10] For the prophet, seeing his own transgressions purged by repentance, had no doubt as

---

[1] Ps. xxiv. 4.
[2] Comp. Tobit iv. 15.

[3] Gal. vi. 1, 4.
[4] Ezek. xviii. 21, 22.
[5] Matt. xviii. 18.
[6] Jer. viii. 4.
[7] Ezek. xviii. 32 and xxxiii. 11.
[8] Ps. li. 12.
[9] Ps. li. 13.
[10] Ps. li. 17.

to healing those of others by preaching, and by making offering to God. Thus the shedding of tears moves the mind's feeling (*passionem*). And when the satisfaction is made good, the mind is turned aside from anger. For how does that man think that mercy will be shown to himself, who does not forgive his neighbour? If offences abound, then, let mercy also abound; for with the Lord there is mercy, and with Him is plenteous redemption.[1] In the Lord's hand there is abundance of all things, because He is the Lord of powers (*virtutum*) and the King of glory.[2] For the apostle says: "All have sinned, and come short of the glory of God; being justified freely by His grace, through the redemption that is in Jesus Christ: whom God hath set forth to be a propitiation through faith in His blood, to declare His righteousness for the remission of sins that are past, through the forbearance of God; to declare, 'I say,' at this time His righteousness, that He might be just, and the justifier of him which believeth in Jesus."[3] And David says: "Blessed are they whose iniquities are forgiven, and whose sins are covered."[4] Man, therefore, is cleansed of his sin, and rises again by the grace of God though he has fallen, and abides in his first position, according to the above-cited authorities. Let him see to it that he sin no more, that the sentence of the Gospel may abide in him: "Go, and sin no more."[5] Whence the apostle says: "Let not sin therefore reign in your mortal body, that ye should obey the lusts thereof: neither yield ye your members as instruments of unrighteousness unto sin: but yield yourselves unto God, as those that are alive from the dead, and your members as instruments of righteousness unto God. For sin shall not have dominion over you: for ye are not under the law, but under grace. What then? shall we sin because we are not under the law, but under grace? God forbid. Know ye not, that to whom ye yield yourselves servants to obey, his servants ye are to whom ye obey; whether of sin unto death, or of obedience unto righteousness? But God be thanked, that ye were the servants of sin; but ye have obeyed from the heart that form of doctrine which was delivered you. Being then made free from sin, ye became the servants of righteousness. I speak after the manner of men."[6] For greater is the sin of him who judgeth, than of him who is judged. "Thinkest thou," says the apostle, "O man, that judgest them that do such things, and doest the same, that thou shalt escape the judgment of God? or despisest thou the riches of His goodness, and forbearance, and long-suffering? Dost thou not know that the goodness of God leadeth thee to repentance? But, after thy hardness and impenitent heart, thou treasurest up unto thyself wrath against the day of wrath and revelation of the righteous judgment of God; who will render to every man according to his deeds: to them who, by patient continuance in well-doing, seek for glory, and honour, and immortality, eternal life; but unto them that are contentious, and do not obey the truth, but obey unrighteousness, indignation and wrath, tribulation and anguish, upon every soul of man that doeth evil, of the Jew first, and *also* of the Greek: but glory, honour, and peace, to every man that worketh good."[7] My brethren, shun not only the holding, but even the hearing, of the judgment that bans mercy; for better is mercy than all whole burnt-offerings and sacrifices.[8] We have replied to your interrogations shortly, because your letter found us burdened overmuch, and preoccupied with other judgments. Given on the 8th day of October, in the consulship of the most illustrious Antonine and Alexander."[9]

---

[1] Ps. cxxx. 7.
[2] Ps. xxiv. 10.
[3] Rom. iii. 23-26.
[4] Ps. xxxii. 1.
[5] John viii. 11.

[6] Rom. vi. 12-19.
[7] Rom. iii. 3-10.
[8] Mark xii. 33.
[9] In the year 222.

NOTE BY THE AMERICAN EDITOR.

See p. 613, note 1. For Callistus and his times, see the testimony of Hippolytus, vol. v. pp. 158, 159, 160; Elucidations X., XI., XII., XIII., XIV., XV. It must be owned that the forgery is better than the genuine productions of this forerunner of the Popes of the ninth and tenth centuries. The title "Pope," in its later sense, seems not inappropriate to such a character.

THE EPISTLE OF POPE URBAN FIRST[1]

TO ALL CHRISTIANS

OF THE CHURCH'S RECEIVING ONLY THE PROPERTY OF THE FAITHFUL, AND NOT THE PRICE OF THE SAME, AS IN THE TIMES OF THE APOSTLES; AND AS TO WHY ELEVATED SEATS SHOULD BE PREPARED IN THE CHURCHES FOR THE BISHOPS; AND AS TO THE FACT THAT NO ONE SHOULD HAVE INTERCOURSE WITH THOSE WHOM THE BISHOPS EXCOMMUNICATE, AND THAT NO ONE SHOULD RECEIVE THOSE WHOM THEY HAVE CAST OUT IN ANY MANNER WHATEVER.[2]

URBAN, bishop, to all Christians, in sanctification of the spirit, in obedience and sprinkling of the blood of Jesus Christ our Lord, greeting.

It becomes all Christians, most dearly beloved, to imitate Him whose name they have received. "What doth it profit, my brethren," says the Apostle James, "though a man say he hath faith, and have not works?"[3] "My brethren, be not many masters, knowing that ye receive (*sumitis*) the greater condemnation; for in many things we offend all."[4] "Let him who is a wise man, and endued with knowledge among you, show out of a good conversation his works with meekness of wisdom."[5]

I.

Of the life in common, and of the reason why the Church has begun to hold property.

We know that you are not ignorant of the fact that hitherto the principle of living with all things in common has been in vigorous operation among good Christians, and is still so by the grace of God; and most of all among those who have been chosen to the lot of the Lord, that is to say, the clergy, even as we read in the Acts of the Apostles: "And the multitude of them that believed were of one heart and of one soul: neither said any of them that ought of the things which he possessed was his own; but they had all things common. And with great power gave the apostles witness of the resurrection of Jesus Christ: and great grace was upon them all. Neither was there any among them that lacked: for as many as were possessors of lands or houses sold them, and brought the prices of the things that were sold, and laid them down at the apostles' feet: and distribution was made unto every man according as he had need. And Joseph, who by the apostles was surnamed Barnabas (which is, being interpreted, the son of consolation), a Levite, and of the country of Cyprus, having land, sold it, and brought the money, and laid it at the apostles' feet;"[6] and so forth. Accordingly, as the chief priests and others, and the Levites, and the rest of the faithful, perceived that it might be of more advantage if they handed over to the churches over which the bishops presided the heritages and fields which they were in the way of selling, inasmuch as they might furnish a larger and better maintenance for the faithful who hold the common faith, not only in present but also in future times, out of the revenues of such property than out of the money for which they might at once be sold, they began to consign to the mother churches the property and lands which they were wont to sell, and got into the manner of living on the revenues of these.

II.

Of the persons by whom, and the uses for which, ecclesiastical property should be managed, and of the invaders thereof.

The property, moreover, in the possession of the several parishes was left in the hands of the bishops, who hold the place of the apostles; and it is so to this day, and ought to be so in all future time. And out of those possessions the bishops and the faithful as their stewards ought to furnish to all who wish to enter the life in common all necessaries as they best can, so that none may be found in want among them. For the possessions of the faithful are also called oblations, because they are offered to the Lord.

---

[1] Urban was the successor of Callistus. The letter ascribed to him is one of the pseudo-Isidorian forgeries.
[2] Mansi, *Concil. Collect.*, i. p. 748.
[3] Jas ii. 14.
[4] Jas. iii. 1, 2.
[5] Jas. iii. 13.

[6] Acts iv. 32-37.

619

They ought not therefore to be turned to any other uses than those of the Church, and in behoof of Christian brethren before mentioned, and of the poor; for they are the offerings of the faithful, and they are redemption moneys for sins (*pretia peccatorum*), and the patrimony of the poor, and are given over to the Lord for the purpose already named. But if any one act otherwise (which may God forbid), let him take care lest he meet the condemnation of Ananias and Sapphira, and be found guilty of sacrilege, as those were who lied as to the price of the property designated, of whom we read thus in the before-cited passage of the Acts of the Apostles: "But a certain man named Ananias, with Sapphira his wife, sold land (*agrum*), and kept back part of the price, his wife also being privy to it, and brought a certain part, and laid it at the apostles' feet. But Peter said to Ananias, Why hath Satan tempted (*tentavit*) thine heart to lie to the Holy Ghost, and to keep back part of the price of the land? Whilst it remained, was it not thine own? and after it was sold, was it not in thine own power? Why hast thou conceived this thing in thine heart? Thou hast not lied unto men, but unto the Lord. And Ananias, hearing these words, fell down, and gave up the ghost. And great fear came on all them that heard *these things*. And the young men arose, and removed him (*amoverunt*), and carried him out, and buried him. And it was about the space of three hours after, when his wife, not knowing what was done, came in. And Peter answered unto her, and said, Tell me whether ye sold the land for so much? And she said, Yea, for so much. Then Peter said unto her, How is it that ye have agreed together to tempt the Spirit of the Lord? Behold, the feet of them which have buried thy husband are at the door, and shall carry thee out. Then fell she down straightway at his feet, and yielded up the ghost. And the young men came in, and found her dead, and, carrying her forth, buried her by her husband. And great fear came upon all the Church, and upon as many as heard these things." [1] These things, brethren, are carefully to be guarded against, and greatly to be feared. For the property of the Church, not being like personal, but like common property, and property offered to the Lord, is to be dispensed with the deepest fear, in the spirit of faithfulness, and for no other objects than the above-named, lest those should incur the guilt of sacrilege who divert it from the hands to which it was consigned, and lest they should come under the punishment and death of Ananias and Sapphira, and lest (which is yet worse) they should become anathema maranatha, and lest, though their body

may not fall dead like that of Ananias and Sapphira, their soul, which is nobler than the body, should fall dead, and be cut off from the company of the faithful, and sink into the depths of the pit. Wherefore all must give heed to this matter, and watch in faithfulness, and avert the dishonour of such usurpation, lest possessions dedicated to the uses of things secret (or sacred) and heavenly be spoiled by any parties invading them. And if any one do so, then, after the sharp vengeance which is due to such a crime, and which is justly to be carried out against the sacrilegious, let him be condemned to perpetual infamy, and cast into prison or consigned to life-long exile. For, according to the apostle,[2] we ought to deliver such a man to Satan, that the spirit may be saved in the day of the Lord.

III.

As to any one's attempting to take from the Church the right of holding property.

By the increase, therefore, and the mode of life which have been mentioned, the churches over which the bishops preside have grown so greatly with the help of the Lord, and the greater part of them are now in possession of so much property, that among them there is not a man who, selecting the life in common, is kept in poverty; but such an one receives all necessaries from the bishop and his ministers. Therefore, if any one in modern or in future time shall rise up and attempt to divert that property, let him be smitten with the judgment which has been already mentioned.

IV.

Of the seats of the bishops.

Furthermore, as to the fact that in the churches of the bishops there are found elevated seats set up and prepared like a throne, they show by these that the power of inspection and of judging, and the authority to loose and bind, are given to them by the Lord. Whence the Saviour Himself says in the Gospel, "Whatsoever ye shall bind on earth shall be bound in heaven; and whatsoever ye shall loose on earth shall be loosed in heaven." [3] And elsewhere: "Receive ye the Holy Ghost. Whose soever sins ye remit, are remitted unto them; and whose soever sins ye retain, they are retained." [4]

V.

That no one should have intercourse with those with whom the bishop has no intercourse, or receive those whom he rejects.

These things, then, we have set before you, most dearly beloved, in order that ye may un-

---

[1] Acts v. 1-11.

[2] 1 Cor. v. 5.
[3] Matt. xviii. 18.
[4] John xx. 22, 23.

derstand the power of your bishops, and give reverence to God in them, and love them as your own souls ; and in order that ye may have no communication with those with whom they have none, and that ye may not receive those whom they have cast out. For the judgment of a bishop is greatly to be feared, although he may bind one unjustly, which, however, he ought to guard against with the utmost care.

VI.

Of the engagement made in baptism, and of those who have given themselves to the life in common.

And in exhorting you, we also admonish all who have embraced the faith of Christ, and who have taken from Christ the name of Christian, that ye make your Christianity vain in no respect, but keep stedfastly the engagement which ye took upon yourselves in baptism, so that ye may be found not reprobate, but worthy in His presence. And if any one of you has entered the life which has all things common, and has taken the vow to hold no private property, let him see to it that he make not his promise vain, but let him keep with all faithfulness this engagement which he has made to the Lord, so that he may acquire for himself not damnation, but a reward ; for it is better for a man not to take a vow at all, than not to discharge to the best of his ability the vow that he has made. For they who have made a vow, or taken on them the faith, and have not kept their vow, or have carried out their life in things evil, are punished more severely than those who have carried out their life without a vow, or have died without faith, but not without doing good works. For to this end have we received a reasonable mind by the gift of nature, and the renewal also of the second birth, that, according to the apostle, we may discern (*sapiamus*) rather things above, and not things on the earth ; [1] for the wisdom of this world is foolishness with God.[2] For to what, most dearly beloved, does the wisdom of this world urge us, but to seek things that are hurtful, and to love things that are to perish, and to neglect things that are healthful, and to esteem as of no value things that are lasting? It commends the love of money, of which it is said,

The love of money is the root of all evil ; [3] and which has this evil in especial, that while it obtrudes the transitory, it hides from view the eternal ; and while it looks on things that are outside, it does not look in upon things that lurk within ; and while it seeks after strange things, it is an evil that makes itself strange to him who does it.[4] Behold, to what does the wisdom of this world urge a man? To live in pleasures. Whence it is said : A widow that liveth in pleasure, is dead while she liveth.[5] It urges a man to feed the flesh with the softest delights, with sins, and vices, and flames, to press the soul with intemperance in food and wine, and to check the life of the spirit, and to put into his enemy's hand the sword to be used against himself. Behold, what is the counsel which the wisdom of this world gives? That those who are good should choose rather to be evil, and that in error of mind they should be zealous to be sinners, and should not bethink themselves of that terrible voice of God, when the wicked shall be burned up like grass.[6]

VII.

Of the imposition of the bishop's hand.

For all the faithful ought to receive the Holy Spirit after baptism by imposition of the hand of the bishops, so that they may be found to be Christians fully ; because when the Holy Spirit is shed upon them, the believing heart is enlarged for prudence and stedfastness. We receive of the Holy Spirit in order that we may be made spiritual ; for the natural man receiveth not the things of the Spirit of God.[7] We receive of the Holy Spirit in order that we may be wise to discern between good and evil, to love the just, and to loathe the unjust, so as to withstand malice and pride, and resist luxury and divers allurements, and impure and unworthy lust. We receive of the Holy Spirit in order that, fired with the love of life and the ardour of glory, we may be able to raise our mind from things earthly to things heavenly and divine. — Given on the Nones of September, — that is, on the fifth day of the same month, in the consulship of the most illustrious Antonine and Alexander.

---

[1] Col. iii. 2.
[2] 1 Cor. iii. 19.

[3] 1 Tim. vi. 10.
[4] "Sectatori," for which read "factori."
[5] 1 Tim. v. 6.
[6] Ps. xcii. 7.
[7] 1 Cor. ii. 14.

THE EPISTLES OF POPE PONTIANUS[1]

THE FIRST EPISTLE.[2]

TO FELIX SUBSCRIBONIUS

ON THE HONOUR TO BE BESTOWED ON PRIESTS.

PONTIANUS, bishop, to Felix Subscribonius, greeting.

Our heart is exceedingly rejoiced with your goodness, in that you strive by all means in your power to carry out the practice of holy religion, and strengthen sad and destitute brethren in faith and religion. Wherefore we implore the mercy of our Redeemer, that His grace may support us in all things, and that He may grant us to carry out in effect what He has given us to aspire after. In this good thing, therefore, the benefits of recompense are multiplied just in proportion as our zeal for the work increases. And because in all these things we need the assistance of divine grace, we implore with constant prayers the clemency of Omnipotent God, that He may both grant us the desire for these good works which should ever be wrought by us, and give us power also to perform them, and direct us in that way, for the fruit of well-doing — which *way* the Pastor of pastors declared Himself to be — so that ye may be able to carry out through Him, without whom nothing can be done, those good works which you have begun. Moreover, with respect to the priests of the Lord whom we have heard you aid against the plots of wicked men, and whose cause you sustain, know ye that in so doing ye please God greatly, who has called them to the service of Himself, and has honoured them with so intimate a fellowship with Him, that through them He accepts the oblations of others, and pardons their sins, and reconciles them with Him. They also make the body of the Lord with their own mouth (*proprio ore corpus Domini conficiunt*), and give it to the people. For of them it is said : He that hurteth you, hurteth me ; and he that doeth you an injury, shall receive again that which he hath done unrighteously.[3] And elsewhere : He that heareth you, heareth me ; and he that despiseth you, despiseth me ; and he that despiseth me, despiseth Him that sent me.[4] Hence they are not to be molested, but honoured. And in them the Lord Himself is honoured, whose commission they execute. They accordingly, if they happen to fall, are to be raised up and sustained by the faithful. And again, they are not to be accused by the infamous, or the wicked, or the hostile, or by the members of another sect or religion. If they sin, they are to be arraigned by the other priests ; further, they are to be held in check (*constringantur*) by the chief pontiffs, and they are not to be arraigned or restrained by seculars or by men of evil life. Not slight, therefore, is our grief in hearing that you have to sorrow for your brother's passing away (*transitu*). For which reason we beseech Almighty God to console you by the breathing (*aspiratione*) of His grace, and keep you with heavenly guardianship from evil spirits and perverse men. For if ye have to bear any turmoil of certain adversaries after his disease, do not think it strange though ye, who seek to enjoy good in your own country — that is, in the land of the living — have to bear evil things at the hands of men in a strange country. For the present life is a sojourning ; and to him who sighs after the true fatherland, the place of his sojourning is a trial, however pleasant it may seem. And as to you who seek the fatherland, among the sighs which ye heave I hear the groans also of human oppression rising. And this happens by the wonderful dispensation of Almighty God, in order that, while the truth calls you in love, this present world may cast back your affection from itself through the tribulations which it brings on, and that the mind may be so much the more easily delivered from the love of this world, as it is also impelled while it is called. Therefore, as you have begun, give heed to the duty of hospitality ; labour most urgently in prayer and tears ; devote yourselves more liberally and freely

---

[1] Eusebius tells us that Pontianus was bishop of the Roman church five or six years (230-235 A.D.). He succeeded Urbanus. The letters are the forgeries of the pseudo-Isidorus.
[2] Mansi, *Concil. Collect.*, i. 735.
[3] Perhaps Zech. ii. 8.

[4] Luke x. 16.

now to those almsgivings which you have ever loved, in order that in the recompense the profit to you for your work may be greater in proportion as your zeal for the labour has risen to higher degrees here.

Furthermore, hailing your goodness with paternal pleasantness, we beg you not to fail in the good works which ye have begun. And may no one be able to turn you from them; but may the clergy and servants of God, and all Christians who sojourn in those parts, fully discover by the love of Christ and Saint Peter the disposition of your charity in all things, and obtain the comforts of your favour in every necessity that may arise; to the end that all may be defended and helped by your aid, and that we, too, may owe you thanks, and that our Lord Jesus Christ may make good *to you* eternal glory, and that the blessed Apostle Peter, the chief of the apostles, in whose cause you spend yourselves, may open the gate of that same glory. — Given on the 10th day before the kalends of February (the 23d of January), in the consulship of the most illustrious Severus and Quintianus.[1]

[1] In the year 235.

THE SECOND EPISTLE.

TO ALL BISHOPS.

ON BROTHERLY LOVE, AND ON AVOIDING THE EVIL.

Pontianus, bishop of the holy and universal Church, to all who worship the Lord aright, and love the divine worship, greeting.

Glory to God in the highest, and on earth peace to men of good will.[1] These words, most beloved, are not the words of men, but of angels; and they were not devised by human sense, but were uttered by angels at the birth of the Saviour. And from these words it can be understood without doubt by all that peace is given by the Lord, not to men of evil will, but to men of good will. Whence the Lord, speaking by the prophet, says: "How good is God to Israel, even to such as are of a clean heart! But as for me, my feet were almost gone; my steps had well-nigh slipped: for I was envious at the unrighteous, when I saw the prosperity of the wicked."[2] Of the good, however, the Truth says in His own person, "Blessed are the pure in heart, for they shall see God."[3] And they are not the pure in heart who think evil things, or things hurtful to their brethren; for he who is the faithful man devises nothing evil. The faithful man, accordingly, loves rather to hear things which are becoming, than to speak things which are not becoming. And if any one is faithful, let him see to it that he speak no evil, and lay no snares in the way of any one. In this, then, are the children of God distinguished from the children of the devil. For the children of God always think and strive to do things which are of God, and give help unceasingly to their brethren, and wish to injure no one. But, on the other hand, the children of the devil are always meditating things evil and hurtful, because their deeds are evil. And of them the Lord, speaking by the prophet Jeremiah, says: "I will utter my judgments against them touching all their wickedness."[4] "Wherefore I will yet plead with you, saith the Lord; and with your children's children will I plead."[5] "Behold, I frame evil against you, and devise a device against you."[6] These things, brethren, are greatly to be feared, and to be guarded against by all; for the man on whom the judgment of God may fall will not depart unhurt. And therefore let every one see to it carefully that he neither contrive nor do against a brother what he would not wish to have to endure himself. And let not the man of faith come under the suspicion even of saying or doing what he would not wish to have to endure himself. Wherefore persons suspected, or hostile or litigious, and those who are not of good conversation, or whose life is reprehensible, and those who do not hold and teach the right faith, have been debarred from being either accusers or witnesses by our predecessors with apostolic authority; and we too remove them from that function, and exclude them from it in times to come, lest those lapse wilfully whom we ought to keep in and save; lest not only (which may God forbid!) the predicted judgment of God should fall upon both, but we also should perish (which may God forbid!) through their fault. For it is written, "Have they made thee the master *of a feast?* Take care for them, that thou mayst be merry on their account, and receive as thy crown the ornament of esteem, and find approbation of

[1] Luke i. 14.
[2] Ps. lxxiii. 1–3.
[3] Matt. v. 8.

[4] Jer. i. 16.
[5] Jer. ii. 9.
[6] Jer. xviii. 11.

thine election."[1] For the evil word affects the heart, out of which proceed these four objects, good and evil, life and death ; and the tongue in its assiduous action is what determines these. Wherefore the before-named parties are altogether to be avoided ; and until the before-noted matters are investigated, and the parties are found to be clear of such, they are not to be received : for the right sacrifice is to give heed to the commandments, and to depart from all iniquity. "To depart from wickedness is a thing pleasing to the Lord, and to forsake unrighteousness is *a sacrifice of* praise."[2] For it is written, "Love thy friend, and be faithful unto him. But if thou bewrayest his secrets, follow no more after him. For as a man who destroyeth his friend, so is he who destroys (loseth) the friendship of his neighbour. And as one that letteth a bird go out of his hand, so art thou that has let thy neighbour go and shalt not get him again. Follow after him no more, for he is far off. For he has escaped like a roe out of the snare, because his soul is wounded. Thou wilt not be able to bind him any more, and there is reconciliation for the reviled. But to bewray the secrets of a friend is the desperation of a wretched soul. He that winketh with the eye worketh evil, and no one will cast him off. When thou art present, he will despise his own mouth, and express his wonder at thy discourse ; but at the last he will writhe his mouth, and slander thy sayings. I have hated many things, but nothing like him ; and the Lord will hate him. Whoso casteth a stone on high, it will fall upon his own head, and a deceitful stroke of the deceitful will make wounds. Whoso diggeth a pit shall fall therein ; and he that setteth a stone in his neighbour's way will fall thereon ; and he that placeth a snare for another will perish therein. He that worketh mischief, it shall fall upon him, and he shall not know whence it cometh on him. Mockery and reproach are from the proud ; and vengeance, as a lion, shall be in wait for them. They that rejoice at the fall of the righteous shall perish in the snare, and anguish shall consume them before they die. Anger and wrath are both abominations, and the sinful man shall have them both."[3] "He that will be avenged shall find vengeance from the Lord, and he will surely keep his sins. Forgive thy neighbour the hurt that he hath done unto thee, and then shall thy sins be forgiven thee when thou prayest. One man beareth hatred against another ; and doth he ask redress of God? He showeth no mercy to a man which is like himself ; and doth he ask forgiveness of the Most High for his own sins? He, though he is flesh, nourisheth hatred ; and

doth he ask pardon of God? Who will entreat for his sins? Remember thy end, and let enmity cease ; for corruption and death impend on commandments. Remember the fear of God, and bear no malice to thy neighbour. Remember the covenant of the Highest, and look down upon (*despice*) the ignorance of thy neighbour. Abstain from strife, and thou shalt diminish thy sins. For a furious man kindleth strife ; and a sinful man will disquiet friends, and make enmity among them that be at peace. For even as the trees of the wood are, so will the fire burn ; and as a man's strength is, so will his anger be ; and as his riches are, so will he make his anger rise. An hastened contention will kindle a fire, and an hastening quarrel will shed blood, and a testifying (*testificans*) tongue will bring death. If thou blow upon the spark, it will burn like a fire ; and if thou spit upon it, it will be extinguished : and both these come out of the mouth. Cursed be the whisperer and doubled-tongued, for such have troubled many that were at peace. A third (*tertia*) tongue hath disquieted many, and driven them from nation to nation : the fortified cities of the rich it hath pulled down, and overthrown the houses of great men. It has subverted the virtues of peoples, and has destroyed strong nations. A third tongue hath cast out truthful[4] women, and deprived them of their labours. Whoso hearkeneth unto it shall never find rest, and never dwell quietly. The stroke of the whip maketh marks in the flesh, but the stroke of the tongue will break bones. Many have fallen by the edge of the sword, but not in such manner as those who have perished by their tongue. Well is he that is defended from the evil tongue, who hath not passed into the anger thereof, and who hath not drawn the yoke thereof, nor hath been bound with the bands of it ; for the yoke thereof is a yoke of iron, and the band thereof is a band of brass. The death thereof is the vilest death, and the grave were better than it. The perseverance thereof shall not abide ; but it shall hold the ways of the unrighteous, and its flame shall not burn the righteous. Such as forsake the Lord shall fall into it, and it shall burn in them, and not be quenched ; and it shall be sent upon them as a lion, and hurt them as a leopard. Hedge thine ears about with thorns, and listen not to the evil tongue ; and make a door for thy mouth, and bars for thine ears. Smelt (*confla*) thy gold and silver, and make a balance for thy words, and right curbs for thy mouth. And beware that thou slide not perchance in thy tongue, and fall before thine enemies that lie in wait for thee, and thy fall be irremediable even to death."[5] "Make no tarrying to turn to the

---

[1] Ecclus. xxxii. 1–3.
[2] Ecclus. xxxv. 1–3.
[3] Ecclus. xxvii. 17–30.

[4] Veridicas. The text reads "Viratas."
[5] Ecclus. xxviii.

Lord, and put not off from day to day. For suddenly shall His wrath come, and in the time of vengeance He will destroy thee. Set not thine heart upon goods unjustly gotten, for they shall not profit thee in the day of veiling (for execution, *obductionis*) and vengeance. Move not with every wind, and go not into every way; for so is the sinner proved with the double-tongue. Be stedfast in the way of the Lord, and in the truth of thine understanding, and in knowledge; and let the word of peace and righteousness attend thee. Be courteous in hearing the word, that thou mayest understand it, and with wisdom give a true answer. If thou hast understanding, answer thy neighbour; if not, lay thy hand upon thy mouth, lest thou be caught in a word of folly, and be confounded. Honour and glory are in the talk of the intelligent man; the tongue of the unwise is his fall. Be not called a whisperer, and be not caught in thy tongue, and confounded. For confusion and penitence are upon the the thief, and the worst condemnation upon the double-tongued. Moreover, for the whisperer there is hatred, and enmity, and shame. Justify the small and the great alike." [1] Instead of a friend, become not an enemy to thy neighbour. For the evil man shall inherit reproach and shame, and every sinner in like manner that is envious and double-tongued. Extol not thyself in the counsel of thine own heart as a bull, lest perchance thy virtue be shattered in folly, and it consume thy leaves, and destroy thy fruits, and thou be left as a dry tree in the desert. For a wicked soul shall destroy him that hath it, and makes him to be laughed to scorn by his enemies, and shall bring him down to the lot of the impious." [2] Most dearly beloved, study to lift up the oppressed, and always help the necessitous; for if a man relieves an afflicted brother, delivers a captive, or consoles a mourner, let him have no doubt that that will be recompensed to him by Him on whom he bestows it all, and who says: "Inasmuch as ye have done it unto one of the least of my brethren, ye have done it unto me." [3] Strive, then, unceasingly to do what is good in such wise that ye may both obtain the fruit of good works here, and enjoy the favour of God in the future, to the intent that hereafter ye may be worthy to enter the court of the heavenly kingdom.—Given on the fourth day before the kalends of May (the 28th of April), in the consulship of the most illustrious Severus and Quintianus.

[1] Ecclus. v. 7–18.

[2] Ecclus. vi. 1–4.
[3] Matt. xxv. 40.

NOTE BY THE AMERICAN EDITOR.

In Bower's *History of the Popes* (ed. Philadelphia, 1847), vol. i. p. 22, may be seen an interesting note on the "Pontifical" of Bucherius, under the name of Pontianus. It was this bishop who is said to have condemned Origen. He probably shared the fate of Hippolytus in exile, and was martyred under Maximin the Thracian.

POPE ANTERUS[1]

THE EPISTLE.

To the brethren, most dearly beloved, constituted to be bishops in the provinces of Bœtica and Toletana, Bishop Anterus sends greeting in the Lord.

I should wish, my dearest brethren, always to receive the glad account of your sincere love and peace, so that the signs of your welfare might be promoted in turn by the dissemination of our letters among you, if our ancient enemy should give us quiet and deliverance from his attacks; who was a liar from the beginning,[2] the enemy of the truth, the rival of man — in order to deceive whom he first deceived himself, — the adversary of modesty, the master of luxury. He feeds on cruelties; he is punished by abstinence; he hates fasts, and his ministers preach to that effect, as he declares them to be superfluous, having no hope of the future, and echoing that sentence of the apostle, in which he says, "Let us eat and drink, for to-morrow we shall die."[3] O miserable boldness! O subtlety of a desperate mind! For he exhorts to hatred, and puts concord to flight. And because the mind of man is easily drawn over to the worse part, and chooses rather to walk by the broad way than laboriously to take its course by the narrow way, for this reason, brethren most dearly beloved, follow ye the better, and always leave the worse behind you. Do good, avoid evil, in order that ye may be found to be the disciples of the Lord in truth.

Now, of the transference of bishops, on which subject it has been your wish to consult the holy seat of the apostles, know ye that that may lawfully be done for the sake of the common good, or when it is absolutely necessary, but not at the mere will or bidding of any individual. Peter, our holy master, and the prince of the apostles, was translated for the sake of the common good from Antioch to Rome, in order that he might be in a position there of doing more service. Eusebius also was transferred from a certain minor city to Alexandria by apostolic authority. In like manner Felix, on account of the doctrine and the good life which he maintained, was translated by the common consent of the bishops and the other priests, and the people from the city in which, on the election of the citizens, he had been ordained, to Ephesus. For that man is not chargeable with shifting from city to city who does not do that of his own inclination or by the force of ambition, but who is transferred for the general good, or in virtue of some necessity, by the counsel and with the consent of the chief parties. Nor can he be said to transfer himself from a smaller city to a larger, who is placed in that position not by his own self-seeking or his own choice, but either as being driven out of his own proper seat by force, or as being compelled by some necessity, and who without pride and in humility has been translated and installed there by others for the good of the place or the people: for man looketh on the countenance, but the Lord seeth the heart. And the Lord, speaking by the prophet, says, "The Lord knows the thoughts of men, that they are vanity."[4] That man, therefore, does not change his seat who does not change his mind. Nor does he change his city who is changed not of his own will, but by the decision and election of others. And accordingly he does not shift from city to city who does not leave his own city for the sake of gain to himself, or of his own choice, but who, as has already been said, has been translated to another city either in consequence of being driven out of his own seat, or compelled by some necessity, or in virtue of the election and injunction of the priests and people. For as the bishops have power regularly to ordain bishops and other orders of priests, so, as often as any matter of advantage or necessity constrains them, they have power in the above-mentioned manner

---

[1] Anterus succeeded Pontianus in the bishopric of the Roman church (232-236 A.D.). The letter ascribed to him is one of the pseudo-Isidorian forgeries.
[2] John viii. 44.
[3] 1 Cor. xv. 32.
[4] Ps. xciv. 11.

both to transfer and to install. As ye have asked our opinion in these matters, though they are not subjects unknown to you, we give you these things in charge to hold them, lest, through the ignorance of some, that which is better and more profitable be avoided, and what is more profitless be taken up, even as we read in the holy Gospel: "Woe unto you, hypocrites! for ye pay tithe of mint, and anise, and cummin, and have omitted the weightier matters of the law, judgment, mercy, and faith: these ought ye to have done, and not to leave the other undone. Ye blind guides, which strain out a gnat and swallow a camel." [1] What is lawful is *with them* not lawful, and what is not lawful is lawful. Even as Jannes and Mambres [2] resisted the truth, so do they, being reprobate in mind, and lovers of pleasure rather than of God, teach that that is unlawful which is lawful, to wit, that bishops should shift from city to city in the manner already noted; and what is unlawful they teach as lawful, to wit, to omit to show mercy to those who endure straits: that is to say, they deny that a bishop belonging to another city should be bestowed for good, or for necessity's sake, upon those who have no bishop, and who want the sacred episcopal ministry; and that another episcopal seat should be assigned to bishops who endure persecution or straits. They contradict the sacred Scripture also, which testifies that God desireth mercy rather than judgment. [3]

What greater charity, I pray you, can there be, or what more profitable service of piety, on the part of any one to another, than to deliver him from the darkness of ignorance and the thick darkness of inexperience, and restore him, in fine, by the nutriment of the doctrine of the true faith, not for gain indeed, or ambition, but for instruction and edification? [For he becomes, so to speak, the hand for the maimed, the foot for the lame, the eye for the blind, [4] who unlocks the treasure of wisdom and knowledge to one wrapped in the darkness of ignorance, and opens up to such an one the brightness of the light and the ways of the Lord.] [5]

Now for both parties — namely, for those who endure a famine of the word of God, and for bishops who endure straits, when they are installed in other cities for the common good — no small degree of mercy is shown. And they who deny this, although they have the form of godliness, do yet deny the power thereof. [6] For in such a matter I make no recognition of race (*prosapiam*). If, however, any one of the wise,

whom the stress of this storm (or season) has allied with other leaders among the unwise, is stained with a participation in their deeds, yet the excellence of the wise man, although he may chance to be privy to their offences, makes him incapable of giving himself as a leader to sinners. The cause of public good and necessity is one thing, and the cause of self-seeking, and presumption, or private inclination, is another thing. On account of self-seeking, or presumption, or private inclination, bishops are not to be transferred from one city to another, but only on account of public good and necessity. And this is a matter which no one denies, except those of whom it is said, "They have erred through wine; they have not known the seer; they have been ignorant of judgment." [7] For if I were constrained to open up in narration things that have been brought to end, I would show you that no comfort comes from the comparison of such deeds. But, most dearly beloved, "stand ye in the ways, and see, and ask for the old paths of the Lord, and see what is the good way and the right, and walk therein, and ye shall find rest for your souls." [8] And, to speak according to the word of Wisdom: "Love righteousness, ye that be judges of the earth. Think of the Lord in goodness, and in simplicity of heart seek Him. For He is found of them that tempt Him not, and showeth Himself unto such as do not distrust Him. For froward thoughts separate from God; and His power, when it is tried, reproveth the unwise. For into a malicious soul wisdom shall not enter, nor dwell in the body that is subject unto sin. For the holy spirit of discipline will flee deceit, and remove from thoughts that are without understanding, and will not abide when unrighteousness cometh in. For wisdom is a benign spirit, and will not acquit a blasphemer of His words. For God is witness of his reins, and a true beholder of his heart, and a hearer of his tongue. For the Spirit of the Lord hath filled the world, and that which containeth all things hath knowledge of the voice. Therefore he that speaketh unrighteous things cannot be hid; neither shall vengeance, when it punisheth, pass by him. For inquisition shall be made into the counsels of the ungodly. And the sound of his words shall come unto the Lord, and unto the manifestation of his wicked deeds; for the ear of jealousy heareth all things, and the noise of murmurings shall not be hid. Therefore beware of murmuring, which is unprofitable; and refrain your tongue from backbiting, for there is no word so secret that it shall go for nought. The mouth that belieth slayeth the soul. Seek not death in the error of your life, and pull not upon your-

---

[1] Matt. xxiii. 23, 24.
[2] 2 Tim. iii. 8.
[3] Hos. vi. 6; *judicium*.
[4] Job xxix. 15.
[5] The bracketed passage is wanting in one manuscript.
[6] 2 Tim. iii. 5.
[7] Isa. xxviii. 7.
[8] Jer. vi. 16.

self destruction with the works of your hands; for God made not death, neither hath He pleasure in the destruction of the living. For He created all things that they might have their being, and He wished the nations of the world to be healthful. There is no poison of destruction in them, nor the kingdom of death upon the earth of the living. Righteousness is perpetual and immortal, but unrighteousness is the acquisition of death. And ungodly men with their hands and words called it to them; and when they thought to have it their friend, they consumed to nought, and made a covenant with it; because they are worthy of death who take part with it." [1] "For they said, reasoning with themselves, but not aright, The time of our life is short and tedious; and in the death of a man there is no remedy, neither was there any man known to have returned from the grave. For we are born of nothing, and we shall be hereafter as though we had never been. For the breath in our nostrils is as smoke, and speech is a little spark for the moving of our heart; which being extinguished, our body shall be turned into ashes, and our spirit shall vanish as the soft air. And our life shall pass as the trace of a cloud, and shall be dispersed as a mist that is driven away with the beams of the sun, and overcome with the heat thereof. And our name shall be forgotten in time, and no man shall have our works in remembrance. For our time is a very shadow that passeth away, and after our end there is no returning; for it is fast sealed, and no man shall come again." [2] And for this reason every one must see to it that he keep himself with all care, and watch himself for his own good, so that when his last day and the end of his life come upon him, he may not pass over to everlasting death, but to eternal life. For the deeds of those put under us are judged by us, but our own doth God judge. Sometimes, moreover, bishops are perverted through the fault of the people, to the end that those fall more precipitately who follow them. When the head languisheth, the other members of the body are affected thereby. And viler are those who corrupt the life and morals of the good, than those who spoil the property and goods of others. Let each one take care that he have neither an itching tongue nor itching ears; that is to say, that he neither be a detractor of others himself, nor listen to others in their detractions. "Thou sattest," saith he, "and spakest against thy brother; and thou didst slander thine own mother's son." [3] Let every individual abstain from a detracting tongue, and keep a guard upon his own words, and understand that all that they say

of others shall enter into the judgment wherewith they themselves shall be judged. No one readily refers to an unwilling auditor. Let it be the care of all of you, most dearly beloved, to keep not only your eyes, but also your tongue, pure. And let not another house ever know by your means what is done in any man's house. Let all have the simplicity of the dove, that they devise not guile against any one; and the subtlety of the serpent, that they be not everthrown by the crafty designs of others. It does not belong to my humble station and measure to judge others, and to say anything unfavourable of the ministers of the churches. Far be it from me that I should say anything unfavourable of those who are the successors to the apostolic status, and make the body of Christ with their sacred mouth; by whose instrumentality we too are Christians, and who have the keys of the kingdom of heaven, and exercise judgment before the day of judgment. Moreover, it is contained in the ancient law, that whoever has not given obedience to the priests should either be stoned outside the camp by the people, or with his neck beneath the sword should expiate his presumption by his blood. [4] Now, however, the disobedient is cut off by spiritual chastisement; and being cast out of the church, is torn by the rabid mouth of demons. [5] For it becomes those who have God in their heritage, to serve God free from all the hindrances of the world, so that they may be able to say, "The Lord is the portion of mine inheritance." [6] "O how good and pleasant is Thy Spirit, O Lord, in all things!" [7] And Thou sparest all because they are Thine, O Lord, who lovest souls. *Therefore chastenest Thou them* by little and little that offend, and warnest them of those things wherein they offend, and dost address them, that leaving their wickedness, they may believe on Thee, O. Lord." [8] "But Thou, our God, art gracious and true, long-suffering, and in mercy ordering all things. For if we sin, we are Thine, knowing Thy power. And if we sin not, we know that we are counted Thine." [9] "The spirit of those that fear the Lord shall be required of him; and in His regard they shall be blessed." [10] Wherefore, most beloved brethren, "let no corrupt communication proceed out of your mouth, but that which is good to the use of edifying, that it may minister grace to the hearers. And grieve not the Holy Spirit of God, whereby ye are sealed unto the day of redemption. Let all bitterness, and wrath, and anger, and clamour, and evil-speaking, be put away from you, with all malice.

[1] Wisd. i.
[2] Wisd. ii. 1-5.
[3] Ps. i. 20.

[4] Deut. xvii.
[5] Thus far Jerome.
[6] Ps. xvi. 5.
[7] Wisd. xii. 1.
[8] Wisd. xii. 2.
[9] Wisd. xv. 1, 2.
[10] Ecclus. xxxiv. 13, 14.

And be ye kind one to another, tender-hearted, forgiving one another, even as God in Christ hath forgiven you." [1] " Be ye therefore followers of God, as dear children ; and walk in love, as Christ also hath loved us, and hath given Himself for us an offering and a sacrifice to God for a sweet-smelling savour. But fornication, and all uncleanness, or covetousness, let it not be once named among you, as becometh saints ; neither filthiness, nor foolish talking, nor jesting, which are not convenient ; but rather giving of thanks. For this know ye, understanding that no whoremonger, nor unclean person, nor covetous man, who is an idolater, hath any inheritance in the kingdom of Christ and of God. Let no man deceive you with vain words : for because of these things cometh the wrath of God upon the children of disobedience. Be not ye therefore partakers with them. For ye were sometimes darkness, but now are ye light in the Lord : walk as children of light (for the fruit of the Spirit is in all goodness, and righteousness, and truth), proving what is acceptable unto the Lord. And have no fellowship with the unfruitful works of darkness, but rather reprove them. For it is a shame even to speak of those things which are done of them in secret. But all things that are reproved are made manifest by the light : for whatsoever is made manifest (*manifestatur*) is light. Wherefore He saith, Awake, thou that sleepest, and arise from the dead, and Christ shall give thee light. See then that ye walk circumspectly, brethren, not as fools, but as wise, redeeming the time, because the days are evil. Wherefore be ye not unwise, but understanding what the will of the Lord is. And be not drunk with wine, wherein is excess ; but be filled with the Holy Spirit ; speaking to yourselves in psalms, and hymns, and spiritual songs, singing and making melody in your hearts to the Lord ; giving thanks always for all things unto God and the Father in the name of our Lord Jesus Christ, submitting yourselves one to another in the fear of Christ." [2] Therefore, brethren, stand fast and hold the tradition of the apostles and the apostolic seat, " that our Lord Jesus Christ and our Father, which hath loved us, and hath given us everlasting consolation and good hope through grace, may comfort your hearts, and stablish you in every good work and word." [3] " Finally, brethren, pray for us, that the word of the Lord may have free course, and be glorified, even as it is with you, and that we may be delivered from unreasonable and wicked men : for all men have not faith. But the Lord is faithful, who shall stablish you, and keep you from evil." [4] Wherefore set your hearts continually in the strength (*virtute*) of God, and always resist the wicked, and tell these things, according to the word of the prophet, " to the generations following ; for this God is our God unto eternity, and He will rule us for ever and ever." [5] Hence ye who are set for examples (*in specula*) by the Lord, ought by all means to check and keep back those who devise crafty counsels against the brethren, or excite against them seditions and slanders. For it is an easy thing to deceive man with a word, but it is not so with the Lord. Wherefore ye ought to reprehend such persons, and turn away from them, to the end that, all darkness of this manner being completely done away, the Morning Star may shine upon them, and gladness arise in their hearts. " *And we have* confidence in the Lord touching you, brethren, that ye both do and will do the things which we command you." [6] For the more ye show forth your kindnesses to them, the greater a return have ye to look for from the omnipotent God whom they serve. May the omnipotent God keep you in His protection, and grant you to maintain honour and precept ; and may glory and honour be to God the Father Almighty, and to His only-begotten Son our Saviour, with the Holy Spirit, for ever and ever. Amen.

Given on the 12th day before the kalends of April (the 21st of March), in the consulship of the most illustrious Maximianus and Africanus.

---

[1] Eph. iv. 29-32.
[2] Eph. v. 1-21.
[3] 2 Thess. ii. 15-17.
[4] 2 Thess. iii. 1-3.
[5] Ps. xlviii. 13, 14.
[6] 2 Thess. iii. 4.

THE EPISTLES OF POPE FABIAN[1]

THE FIRST EPISTLE.

TO ALL THE MINISTERS OF THE CHURCH CATHOLIC.

OF THOSE WHO OUGHT NOT TO BE ADMITTED TO CLEAR THEMSELVES, AND OF THE DUTY OF HAVING NO FELLOWSHIP WITH THE EXCOMMUNICATED.

To the dearly-beloved brethren in the ministry of the Church Catholic in all regions, Fabian sends greeting in the Lord.

By the divine precepts and the apostolic institutes, we are admonished to watch in behoof of the position of all the churches with unwearied interest. Whence it follows that you ought to know what is being done in things sacred in the church of Rome, in order that, by following her example, ye may be found to be true children of her who is called your mother. Accordingly, as we have received the institution from our fathers, we maintain seven deacons in the city of Rome distributed over seven districts of the state, who attend to the services enjoined on them week by week, and on the Lord's days and the solemn festivals, in concert with the subdeacons, and acolytes, and servants of the succeeding orders, and hold themselves in readiness every hour for religious duty, and for the discharge of all that is enjoined upon them. In like manner ought ye also to do throughout your different cities, as may be convenient, that religious duty may be discharged zealously and regularly, without any delay or negligence. Furthermore, we have ordained in like manner seven subdeacons who shall stand by (*imminerent*) the seven notaries, and bring into one full and accurate account the histories of the martyrs, and lay them before us for our examination. And this, too, we urge you all to do, so that no doubt or questioning of these things may arise in later times; "for whatsoever things were written, were written for our learning."[2] And whatsoever things are written in truth in our times, are directed to the learning of future times. And therefore we enjoin these duties to be put in charge of the most faithful, that nothing false may be found in them, from which an offence (which may God forbid) may arise to the faithful. For this reason also we beg it of your love in paternal benignity, that the holy Church may now find the good-will of your love in all things, and obtain the comforts of your favour whenever there is necessity. And as the goodness of your zeal affords us the assurance that we ought to distrust it in nothing, but rather commit these things in all confidence to you as to wise sons of our church; so, small importance being attached to opportune occasions, your virtue ought to exert itself the more strenuously in labours, and keep off reproaches by all possible means, and with all zeal. We exhort you also, according to the word of the apostle, to be "stedfast and immoveable, always abounding in the work of the Lord; forasmuch as ye know that your labour is not vain in the Lord."[3] And in another place: "Watch ye, and pray, and stand fast in the faith. Quit you like men, and be strong. Let all things be done with charity."[4] Furthermore, we desire you to know this, that in our times, as our sins embarrassed us, and that ancient enemy who always goeth about like a roaring lion, seeking whom he may devour,[5] instigated him, Novatus came up out of Africa, and separated Novatianus and certain other confessors of Christ from the Church of Christ, and persuaded them into the acceptance of evil doctrine. From such persons, brethren, keep yourselves aloof, and beware of all who hold a faith and doctrine different from that which the apostles and their successors have held and taught, lest (which may God forbid) going after him ye fall into the toils of Satan, and be bound with his fetters. Wherefore with most earnest prayers we beg it of your brotherly love, that ye may deem it fit to remember our insignificance in your holy prayers, beseeching and entreating the Lord of

---

[1] Fabian was bishop of Rome from 236 to 250 A.D. The letters ascribed to him are rejected by all as spurious.
[2] Rom. xv. 4.
[3] 1 Cor. xv. 58.
[4] 1 Cor. xvi. 13, 14.
[5] 1 Pet. v. 8.

heaven that we, as well as our holy mother the Church of Christ, redeemed with His precious blood, may be delivered from the toils of Satan, who lieth in wait for us, and from troublesome and wicked men, and that the Word of God may have free course and be glorified, and that the evil doctrine of them, and of all who teach things contrary to the truth, may be overthrown and perish. We beseech you also to be zealous in praying in your pious supplications, that our God and Lord Jesus Christ, who will have all men to be saved, and no one to perish,[1] may, by His vast omnipotence, cause their hearts to turn again to sound doctrine and to the Catholic faith, in order that they may be recovered from the toils of the devil who are held captive by him, and be united with the children of our mother the Church. Be mindful also of your brethren, and have pity upon them, and labour for them by all means in your power, that they be not lost, but be saved unto the Lord by your prayers, and other efforts of your goodness. So act therefore in these matters that ye may approve yourselves as obedient and faithful children of the holy Church of God, and that ye may obtain the recompense of reward. These men, and all else who do not teach the true doctrine, and hold not the true faith, cannot act as accusers of any true believer, because they are branded with infamy, and are cut off from the bosom of our holy mother the Church by the sword of the apostles, until their return to correct conversation and belief. Hence by apostolic authority, and in agreement with all the sons of the same apostolic and universal Church, we resolve that all who come under suspicion with respect to the Catholic faith cannot be admitted as accusers of those who hold the true creed; for suspicions are always to be set aside. Rightly therefore are charges which are preferred by those who are objects of suspicion in the matter of the true faith, rejected. Neither are they at all to be credited who are unacquainted with the faith of the Trinity. In like manner we set aside and withdraw from all part in the accusing of the faithful, all those whom the decrees of the holy fathers in times past and times future alike anathematize. Accordingly, the believing ought always to be kept distinct from the unbelieving, and the righteous from the unrighteous; since the unbelieving and evil-minded, by every means in their power, are always troubling the believing, and striving to undo them; and consequently they are not to be received, but rejected and kept entirely at a distance, lest they may undo or defame the believing. For this reason, dearly beloved, beware of the pit of such persons, into which we know many have fallen. Beware of the snares (or darts) of such persons, and of the efforts of the ancient enemy, by which we have seen even those closely connected with us fall wounded before us. ·Watch the nooses of the liers in wait, by which they are wont to strangle associates and comrades. Follow not such, but keep them far off from you. Be ye, according to the voice of Truth, wise as serpents and harmless as doves.[2] See to it that ye neither run nor labour in vain; but, sustained by each other's prayers and supplications, strive ye to do the will of God; and from those persons whom I have mentioned, if they show themselves incorrigible, keep yourselves separate in all things. In like manner keep yourselves separate from all those of whom the apostle makes mention when he says, "with such persons, no, not to eat;"[3] since these latter, as well as the former, are to be rejected, and are not to be admitted before they have given satisfaction to the Church. For those with whom it is not lawful to eat are manifestly separated from all intercourse with the rest of the brethren until such satisfaction is given. Wherefore they ought not and cannot be admitted to the preferring of charges against the faithful, but they ought to be debarred from their society until the satisfaction already mentioned is given, lest these too should be made like them, or underlie their excommunication; for to this effect have the apostles decreed, saying, With the excommunicated no fellowship is to be held. And if any one, setting aside the rules wittingly, sings with the excommunicated in his house, or speaks or prays in company with them, that man is to be deprived of the privilege of communion. Such persons, therefore, are in all things to be guarded against, and are not to be received, because, according to the apostle, not only those who commit such things are condemned, but also those who consent with those who do them.[4] Whence also the blessed chief of the apostles, Peter, addressing the people at the ordination of Clement, says this among other things:[5] If this Clement is hostile to any one on account of his deeds, wait not ye for his saying directly to you, Be not on terms of friendship with this man. But mark ye carefully his will as ye ought, and second it without need of direct injunction; and separate yourselves·from that man to whom ye perceive him to be inimical, and speak not with those with whom he speaks not, in order that every one who may be in fault, as he desires to possess the friendship of all of you, may be zealous in effecting a reconciliation all the more quickly with him who presides over all, so that he may return to spiritual well-being (*redeat et salutem*) hereby, when

---

[1] 1 Tim. ii. 4.
[2] Matt. x. 16.
[3] 1 Cor. v. 11.
[4] Rom. i. 32.
[5] *Clementines*: Ep. of Clem. to James, xviii. [P. 221, *supra*.]

he begins to yield obedience to the charges of the president. If, however, any one is not friendly, and speaks with those with whom he (his chief) speaks not, such an one belongs to those who seek to exterminate the Church of God ; and though he seems to be with you in body, he is against you in mind and heart. And such an one is a much more dangerous enemy than those who are without, and who are openly hostile. For this man under the guise of friendship acts the part of an enemy, and scatters and ruins the church. And therefore, dearly beloved, in these apostolic institutes we warn and teach you, that your charity, being instructed therein (*effecta certior*), may hereafter study to act with greater care and prudence, so that perverse and unbelieving men may not have the power of injuring the faithful and well-disposed ; for the hope of such, and of all the ungodly, is like dust that is blown away with the wind ; and like a thin froth that is driven away with the storm ; and like as the smoke which is dispersed here and there with a tempest, and as the remembrance of a guest of a single day that passeth away.[1] With the utmost care, dearly beloved, are such persons to be guarded against, and avoided, and rejected, if they show themselves injurious. For the laws of the world, no less than those of the Church, do not admit the injurious, but reject them. Whence it is written, " The mouth of the wicked devoureth iniquity."[2] And the Lord,

speaking by the prophet, saith, "With the holy thou wilt show thyself holy ; and with the froward thou wilt show thyself froward ; and with the excellent thou wilt show thyself excellent (*electus*) ; and with the innocent man thou wilt show thyself innocent."[3] And the apostle says, " Evil communications corrupt good manners."[4] Wherefore, as has already been indicated, the wicked are always to be avoided and shunned, and the good and rightly-disposed are to be stedfastly followed, in order that, as far as possible, we may avoid the peril of sloth. And lest this pest may be spread abroad more widely, let us cut it off from us with all possible severity ; for the temerity of presumption does not intervene where there is the diligence of piety. Let every one of you, sustained by this apostolic representation, act according to his strength, and study in brotherly love and in godly piety to keep his own manners correct, and to help each other, and to abide in charity, and to keep himself in the will of God unceasingly, in order that we may praise the Lord together, and give Him thanks always without wearying. Fare ye well in the Lord, dearly beloved, and with the Lord's help strive to fulfil to the best of your ability the things before mentioned. — Given on the first day of July, in the consulship of the most illustrious Maximinus (or, Maximus) and Africanus.[5]

---

[1] Wisd. v. 14.
[2] Prov. xix. 28.

[3] Ps. xviii. 25, 26.
[4] 1 Cor. xv. 33.
[5] In the year 236.

THE SECOND EPISTLE.

TO ALL THE BISHOPS OF THE EAST.

THAT THE CHRISM [1] SHOULD BE RENEWED WITH CONSECRATION EVERY YEAR, AND THAT THE OLD SUPPLY SHOULD BE SET ASIDE TO BE BURNT IN THE CHURCHES ; ALSO CONCERNING THE ACCUSING OF PRIESTS, AND ON THE DUTY OF THE SHEEP NOT TO DARE TO BLAME THEIR SHEPHERD UNLESS HE ERRS IN THE FAITH.

FABIAN, bishop of the city of Rome, to all the bishops of the East, and to the whole body of the faithful, greeting in the Lord.

Your love for the seat of the apostles requires counsels which we neither can nor ought to deny you. It is clear, moreover, that our predecessors did this for the bishops of many districts ; and brotherly charity and the debt of obedience im-

pose the duty of so doing also upon us who, by the bountiful goodness of God, are placed in the same seat. Care, therefore, is to be had by your solicitude, that neither remissness may avail to neglect, nor presumption be able to disturb, those things which have been ordained by the apostles and their successors, and established under the inspiration of the Holy Spirit. But as it was proper that that should be defined which the use of right order required, so what has been so defined ought not to be violated.

I.

That new chrism should be made every year, and the old be burnt.

Now, among other matters, in your letter we find it stated that certain bishops of your dis-

---

[1] The unguent of oil and balsam used in the so-called sacrament of confirmation. [See p. 604, *supra*.]

trict adopt a different practice from yours and ours, and do not prepare the chrism at the Lord's supper every year, but keep it in use for two or three, making such a supply of the holy chrism once for all. For they say, as we find in the letter referred to, that balsam cannot be got every year; and besides that, even though it were got, there would be no necessity for preparing chrism every year, but that, so long as the one preparation of chrism is sufficiently large, they have no need to make another. They are in error, however, who think so; and in making such statements they speak like madmen rather than men in their right senses. For on that day the Lord Jesus, after supping with His disciples, and washing their feet, according to the tradition which our predecessors received from the holy apostles and left to us, taught them to prepare the chrism. That washing of their feet signifies our baptism, as it is completed and confirmed by the unction of the holy chrism. For as the solemn observance of that day is to be kept every year, so the preparing of that holy chrism is to be attended to every year, and it is to be renewed from year to year and given to the faithful. For *the material of* this new sacrament is to be made anew every year, and on the day already named; and the old supply is to be burned in the holy churches. These things we have received from the holy apostles and their successors, and we commit them to your keeping. The holy church of Rome and that of Antioch have been guardians of these things from the times of the apostles: these things also the churches of Jerusalem and Ephesus maintain. Presiding over these churches, the apostles taught these things, and ordained that the old chrism should be burnt, and permitted them to use it no longer than one year, and commanded them thereafter to use the new, and not the old material. If any one, therefore, ventures to go against these things, let him understand that the door of indulgence is barred against him on your part and on that of all right-minded men: for the perverse doctrine of most depraved minds, while it uses the reins too indulgently, slips into the sin of presumption; and it can by no means be cast out, unless it is cleared of all support and correction on the part of the intelligent. And those usages which the holy Church throughout the whole world uniformly observes with respect to the divine mysteries, and towards the subjects of baptism, are not to be regarded with indifferent concern, lest we make way for purposeless efforts and superstitions. We ought not, therefore, to bring over the untaught minds of the faithful to such practices as we have named, because they should be instructed rather than played upon. For good deeds make for our happiness, and evil deeds

prick us with the stings of sorrow. But here, however we are situated, we are among the hands of robbers and the teeth of raging wolves, and the contumacious are put in the place of the true sheep. And it is by the barking of the dogs and the staff of the shepherd that the fury of the wolves is checked. Those wounds, moreover, which cannot be healed by remedies, must be cut out with the knife. Neither can we keep silence, for, in seeking here to call back some from things unlawful, we are impelled by the instinct of our office, having been set on the watch-towers by the Lord with this object, that we should prove the diligence of our watchfulness by checking things that should be prohibited, and deciding for things that should be observed.

II.

Of the right of bishops not to be accused or hurt by detraction.

You desired also to consult us, as we find in the above-mentioned letter of yours, on the subject of the accusing of priests, — a thing which, as we learn also from the same epistle, is exceedingly frequent among you. You have intimated, besides, that very many notice that not a few in places of ecclesiastical dignity do not live in a manner conformable to the discourses and sacraments with which the people are served by their means. O miserable men, who in looking at these forget Christ, who long since indeed told us how that the law of God should be obeyed, rather than that those should be looked to for imitation who do not the things which they say; and bearing with the traitor himself even to the end, He sent him also along with the rest to preach the Gospel. For the apostles had no such custom, neither did they teach that it was one fit to be had. And to like effect their successors also, foreseeing by the Spirit of God things to come, have determined largely on such subjects. Besides, as you read in the Acts of the Apostles, " There was at that time among them that believed one heart and one soul; neither said any of them that ought of the things which he possessed was his own; but they had all things common." [1] For there was no laying of accusations against each other among them, except what was friendly; neither ought there ever to be such among their followers or among believers: for the Lord says, " Do not that to another which thou wouldst not have done to thyself." [2] And He says also, " Thou shalt love thy neighbour as thyself;" [3] and, " Love worketh no ill to his neighbour." [4] In accordance herewith, the apostles themselves and their successors de-

[1] Acts iv. 32.
[2] Matt. vii. 12; Luke vi.
[3] Matt. xxii. 39; Mark xii. 31.
[4] Rom. xiii. 10.

creed of old time that those persons should not be admitted to lay accusations who were under suspicion, or who but yesterday, or the day before, or a little time ago, were at enmity, as they come thus under suspicion, or who are not of good conversation, or whose life is reprehensible, or who are doubtful in the matter of the true faith. In like manner is it decided to be with those whose faith and life and liberty are unknown, or who are marked with the stains of infamy, or entangled in the snares of offences. Again, those have neither the right nor the power to accuse the priests or the clergy, who are incapable themselves of being made priests legitimately, and are not of their order; for just as the priests and the other members of the clerical order are debarred from laying accusations against the secular laity, so these latter, too, should be debarred and excluded from the right of bringing charges against the former. And as the former should not be admitted by the latter, so the latter should not be admitted by the former: for as the conversation of the priests of the Lord ought to be something separate from the conversation of these others, so should they be separate from them also in the matter of litigation; " for the servant of the Lord ought not to strive." [1] To the utmost of your power, dearly beloved brethren, do ye prohibit such accusations, and all unrighteous and injurious emulations, because contention is to be avoided by all means. " For a just man will fall seven times in a day, and will rise again; but the wicked shall fall into mischief. Rejoice not when thine enemy falleth," saith Solomon, " and let not thine heart be glad when he stumbleth; lest the Lord see it, and it displease Him, and He turn away His wrath from him. Fret not thyself because of evil-doers, neither be thou envious at the wicked: for the evil have not the hope of the future, and the candle of the wicked shall be put out. Envy not evil men, neither be thou desirous to be with them; for their mind meditates rapine, and their lips speak deceits." [2] Dearly beloved, beware of these things. Ponder these things, and minister comfort to the brethren in all things; for, as the Truth says in His own person, " By this shall all men know that ye are my disciples, if ye have love one to another." [3] For if in things secular each man's right and his proper position are kept for him, how much more ought there to be no confusion induced in matters of ecclesiastical order! And this is a right which will be duly observed if no deference is paid to mere power, but all to equity. Whence it is an established duty, that the bishops of each several district should exercise a watchful care over all those who live under their rule, and in the fear of God should dispose of all cases in which they are concerned, and of all matters in which they are interested. It is therefore extremely inequitable that any *bishops* should neglect their own cases, and mix themselves up with those of others. But those whose part it is to ordain such persons to the priesthood, and by whom they have been already ordained, ought to order the life and judgment of such by the exercise of a competent and regular administration; for, as the law says, " Cursed is every one that removeth his neighbour's landmarks. And all the people said Amen." [2] To this therefore, brethren, has God foreordained you, and all who hold the highest office of the priesthood, that ye should put all injustice out of the way, and cut off presumption, and help those who labour in the priesthood, and give no occasion for their reproach and trouble, but bring assistance to him who endures calumny and reproach, and cut off him who works calumny and reproach, and act for the help of the Lord in His priests. The Lord, moreover, has chosen the priests for Himself, that they should sacrifice to Him, and offer oblations to their Lord. He commanded the Levites also to be under them in their ministries. Whence He speaks to Moses in these terms: " And Eleazar the son of Aaron the priest shall be chief over the chief of the Levites, and have the oversight of them that keep the charge of the sanctuary." [5] For of these the Lord spake to Moses in this wise: " Take the Levites instead of the first-born among the children of Israel, and the cattle of the Levites instead of their cattle; and the Levites shall be mine: I am the Lord." [6] If the Lord willed the Levites to be His own, how much more has He taken the priests for Himself! And of these He says: " If any stranger cometh nigh, he shall be put to death." [7] All objects, moreover, that are the Lord's are to be handled carefully, and are not lightly to be injured; for even among men, those are reckoned faithful who attend to the interests of their masters rightly, and deal with them faithfully, and rightly observe the commands of their masters, and transgress them not. And those, on the other hand, are reputed unfaithful who deal with the interests of their masters carelessly and negligently, and despise their commands, and do not observe them as they ought. Accordingly we have set these matters before you, in order that those who now know it not may know this; viz., that the priests, too, whom the Lord has taken to Himself from among all men, and has willed to be His own,

---

[1] 1 Tim. ii. 24.
[2] Prov. xxiv. 17, etc.
[3] John xiii. 35.

[4] Deut. xxvii. 17.
[5] Num. iii. 32.
[6] Num. iii. 45.
[7] Num. i. 51.

are not to be dealt with lightly, nor injured, nor rashly accused or reprehended, save by their masters, seeing that the Lord has chosen to reserve their causes to Himself, and ministers vengeance according to His own judgment. For in these and other precepts of the Lord the faithful are distinguished, and the unfaithful at the same time disapproved. For these are rather to be borne with by the faithful than made subjects of reproach (*exprobrandi*) ; just as there is chaff with the wheat even to the last winnowing, and as there are bad fish with good even on to their separation, which is yet to be on the shore, — that is to say, at the end of the world. By no means, then, can that man be condemned by a human examination, whom God has reserved for His own judgment, that the purpose of God, according to which He has decreed to save what had perished, may be unalterable. And consequently, as His will suffers no change, let no man presume on matters which are not conceded to him. And herein is the meaning of that word which the apostle speaks : "Now therefore there is utterly a fault among you, because ye go to law one with another. Why do ye not rather take wrong? why do ye not rather suffer yourselves to be defrauded?"[1] To this, too, our Lord's word may refer : "And if any man will take away thy coat, and sue thee at the law, let him have thy cloak also."[2] And in another place : "Of him that taketh away thy goods, ask them not again."[3] Moreover, there are certain things which might be thought most trivial were they not shown in the Scriptures to be of more serious import. Who would ever consider the man who says to his brother "Thou fool" worthy of hell-fire, were it not that the Truth Himself told us so?[4] Those, furthermore, who commit those sins whereof the apostle says, "They who do such things shall not inherit the kingdom of God,"[5] are by all means to be guarded against, and are to be compelled to seek amendment if they do not choose it voluntarily, because they are marked with the stains of infamy, and go down into the pit, unless assistance is brought them by sacerdotal authority. Those also are to be dealt with in like manner of whom he says, "With such persons, no, not to eat ; "[6] because such persons are branded with infamy until they are restored by sacerdotal authority, and reinstated in the bosom of our holy mother the Church ; since those who are outside us cannot communicate with us. And it is manifest that these are outside us, and ought to be separated from us, with whom it is not lawful for us to eat

or to take food. In like manner also, all persons who underlie the charge of any manner of turpitude and dishonour, are rendered infamous ; and all who arm themselves against fathers are rendered infamous. "Sand, and salt, and a mass of iron, is easier to bear than a man without understanding, and foolish and impious."[7] "He that wanteth understanding thinks upon vain things ; and a foolish and erring man imagineth follies."[8] For their suspicion has overthrown many, and their opinion hath held them in vanity. "A stubborn heart shall fare evil at the last ; and he that loveth danger shall perish therein. A heart that entereth two ways shall not have rest ; and the evil heart in them shall be made to stumble. A wicked heart shall be laden with sorrows ; and the sinner shall heap sin upon sin."[9] The holy apostles and their successors, having such things in mind, and foreseeing, as being filled with the Holy Spirit, the course of wicked men, and having regard to the simple, determined that the accusing of priests should be a matter undertaken with difficulty, or never undertaken, that they might not be ruined or displaced by wicked men. For if this were made an easy matter to secular and wicked men, there would remain no one, or but the scantiest few ; seeing that it ever has been and still is the case — and (which is yet worse) that too in growing measure — that the wicked persecute the good, and that the carnal are hostile to the spiritual. For this reason, then, as has been already said, they decreed that such should not be accused at all ; or if that could not be avoided, that the accusing of such should be made a matter of great difficulty. And they determined also, as has been stated above, by what persons that function should not be assumed ; and they resolved further, that bishops should not be cast out from their own proper seats and churches. But if in any way the matter *of accusation* should be taken in hand before their rightful seat and all their property are restored by those laws, they should by no means be accused or criminated by any one, and should not answer any one on such charges, unless they choose to do so of their own accord. But after they have been reinstated, as has been before noted, and have had all their effects restored to them by those laws, when their affairs are arranged and set in order, they should then have a long period allowed them for the disposing of their case ; and thereafter, if need be, they should be regularly summoned, aud so come to the suit ; and if the matter seem just, they should answer the propositions of their accusers with the help of their brethren. For so long as their effects, or their churches

---

[1] 1 Cor. vi. 7.
[2] Matt. v. 40.
[3] Luke vi. 30.
[4] Matt. v. 22.
[5] Gal. v. 21.
[6] 1 Cor. v. 11.

[7] Ecclus. xxii. 15.
[8] Ecclus. xvi. 23.
[9] Ecclus. iii. 24, etc.

and property, are held by their adversaries, or by any person, no manner of reason allows that any charge ought to be preferred against them. And no one is at liberty by any means to bring any charge against them, whether superior or inferior, so long as they are dispossessed of their churches, effects, or powers. In like manner also it was decreed, and we too confirm the same statutes and hereby decree, that if any one among the clergy proves an enemy or traducer of his bishops, and seeks to criminate them, or conspires against them, at once, before the consideration of judicial investigation, he should be removed from the clerical order, and given over to the court (*curiæ*), to whicn he shall devote himself zealously all the days of his life, and shall remain infamous without any hope of restoration. And let no one ever presume to be at once accuser, and judge, or witness; for in every judicial investigation there must always be four persons present: that is, the judges elected, and the accusers, and the defenders, and the witnesses. In like manner we decree and ordain by apostolic authority, that the flock should not dare to bring a charge against their pastor, to whose care they had been consigned, unless he falls into error in the faith; for the deeds of superiors are not to be smitten with the sword of the mouth; neither can the disciple be above the master, as the voice of Truth saith, "The disciple is not above his master, nor the servant above his lord."[1] And pride is hateful before God and men, and all iniquity is execrable. "The Lord hath destroyed the memory of the proud, and hath left the memory of the humble in mind. The seed of men shall be honoured, this *seed* that feareth God. But that seed shall be dishonoured that transgresseth the commandments of the Lord. Among brethren, he that is chief is honourable; and they that fear the Lord shall be in His eyes. My son, saith Solomon, preserve thy soul in meekness, and give honour to him whom honour beseemeth."[2] "Blame not any one before thou examinest him; and when thou hast examined him, reprove him justly. Answer not a word before thou hearest the cause; neither interrupt with talk in the midst of thy seniors."[3] After the example of Ham the son of Noah, they are condemned who bring the faults of their fathers into public view, or presume to accuse or calumniate them; even as was the case with Ham, who did not cover the shame of his father Noah, but exhibited it for mockery. And in like manner those are justified by the example of Shem and Japhet, who reverently cover and seek not to display those matters in which they find their fathers to have erred. For if a bishop should happen to err from the faith, he should in the first place be corrected privately by those placed under him (*a subditis suis*). And if he show himself incorrigible (which may God forbid), then an accusation should be laid against him before his primates, or before the seat of the apostles. For his other actings, however, he is rather to be borne with by his flock and those put under him, than accused or made the subject of public detraction; because when any offence is committed in these matters by those put under them, His ordinance is withstood who set them before him, as the apostle says, "Whosoever resisteth the power, resisteth the ordinance of God."[4] But he who fears Almighty God, agrees in no way to do anything contrary to the Gospel, or contrary to the apostles, or contrary to the prophets or the institutions of the holy fathers. The priests therefore are to be honoured, and not to be injured or reproached. Thus read we in Ecclesiasticus: "Fear the Lord with all thy soul, and reverence His priests. Love Him that made thee with all thy strength, and forsake not His ministers. Honour God with thy whole soul, and honour the priest, and cleanse thyself beforehand with the shoulders (*propurga te cum brachiis*). Give him his portion, as it is commanded thee, of the first-fruits; and purge thyself concerning negligence with a few things. Thou shalt offer the gift of thy shoulders, and the sacrifice of sanctification, and the first-fruits of the holy things to the Lord. And stretch thine hand unto the poor, that thine atonement and blessing may be perfected."[5] We desire these things to become known not to you only, but through you to all the brethren, that we may abide in Christ of one accord and one mind, making no claim for ourselves through strife or vainglory, and being pleasers not of men, but of God our Saviour. To Him belongeth honour and glory, for ever and ever. Amen.

---

[1] Matt. x. 24.
[2] Ecclus. x. 7, etc.
[3] Ecclus. xi. 7, 8.

[4] Rom. xiii. 2.
[5] Ecclus. vii. 29-32.

THE THIRD EPISTLE

TO BISHOP HILARY.

THAT EXTRANEOUS JUDGMENTS SHOULD BE RE-JECTED, AND THAT THE ACCUSED PERSON SHOULD CARRY OUT HIS CAUSE IN HIS OWN LOCALITY ; AND THAT EVERY ONE WHO BRINGS FORWARD A CHARGE SHOULD INTIMATE IN WRITING HIS ABILI-TY TO PROVE IT, AND THAT IF HE FAILS TO PROVE WHAT HE ALLEGES, HE SHOULD BEAR THE PEN-ALTY WHICH HE ADVANCED.

FABIAN, to my dearly beloved brother Bishop Hilary.

We ought to be mindful of the grace of God to us, who, in the compassion of His own regard, hath raised us for this reason to the summit of sacerdotal dignity, that by cleaving to His com-mandments, and by being set in a certain emi-nence as overseers of His priests, we may restrain things unlawful, and inculcate things that are to be followed. For we have heard that in those western parts in which you dwell, the craft of the devil rageth so violently against the people of Christ, and breaketh forth in delusions so manifold, that it oppresseth and troubleth not only the secular laity, but the priests of the Lord themselves also. Wherefore, involved as we are in deep grief, we cannot conceal what we ought severely to correct. Accordingly a sufficient rem-edy must be employed for such wounds, lest a hasty facility in the cure may prove of no ser-vice for the deadly disease of the head ; and lest the trouble, by being too easily dealt with, may involve, through the defect of an illegitimate mode of cure, the hurt and the healers together in its evil.

I.

Of those who ought not to be admitted to the right of accusa-tion.

On this account, therefore, we decree and re-solve, that those who are not of good conversa-tion, or whose life is impeachable, or whose faith and life and liberty are unknown, should not have the power of accusing the priests of the Lord, lest vile persons should thus be admitted to the liberty of accusing them. In like manner, those who are involved in any matters of accusa-tion, or who are under suspicion, should not have a voice in laying charges against their seniors ; for the voice of the suspected and the inimical is wont to oppress the truth.

II.

Of extraneous judgments.

Moreover, by a general ordinance, and without prejudice to the authority of the apostles in all things, we prohibit extraneous judgments, be-cause it is not fit that he should be judged by strangers, who ought to have those of his own province and those elected by himself as his judges, unless an appeal has been made. Where-fore, if any one of the bishops is accused on pre-cise charges, he ought to be heard by all the bishops who are in the province ; for it is not right that an accused person should be heard elsewhere than in his own circuit. Again, if any one is of opinion that he has a judge adverse to him, he should claim the right of appeal ; and an appellant ought to be injured by no kind of oppression and detention ; but an appellant ought to have the liberty of righting his case, when wronged, by the remedy of appeal. There ought also to be liberty of appeal in criminal cases. And the right of appealing ought to be denied to no one whom judgment has destined for pun-ishment.

III.

Of the arraigned.

A person arraigned ought to plead his cause before his judge ; and an arraigned person may refuse to speak, if he choose so, before one who is not his own proper judge ; and indulgence (in-duciæ) should be granted to the arraigned as often as they appeal.

IV.

Of the case of any one bringing forward a charge in passion, or failing to prove his allegations.

If, then, any one in passion brings a charge rashly against any one, mere abuse is not to be taken for an accusation. But a certain time being allowed for dealing with the matter, the person should profess his ability in writing to prove what he has alleged in passion ; so that, if he should happen to think better of the things he uttered in passion, and decline to repeat or write them, the person may not be held as charged with the crime. Every one, therefore, who adduces a charge, ought to state in writing his ability to prove it. And, indeed, a cause should always be dealt with in the place where the charge is admitted ; and the man who fails to substantiate his allegation, should himself bear the penalty which he advanced.

V.

On the question of an accused bishop appealing to the seat of the apostles.

It is determined, moreover, that, in the case of an accused bishop appealing to the seat of the apostles, that should be held to be a settlement which is the decision of the pontiff of that same seat. On all occasions, however, in cases concerning priests, let this form be maintained, that no one be bound by a decision pronounced by another than his own proper judge. It is the duty also of all the faithful to be ready to help the oppressed and the miserable in their distress, in order that by the manifestation of another manner of recompense (*vindictæ*) they may be able to keep the recompense (*vengeance*) of God from themselves. For he offers (*libat*) things prosperous to the Lord who keeps off things adverse from the afflicted. Whence it is written, "A brother aiding a brother shall be exalted."[1] For the Church of God ought to be without spot or wrinkle, and therefore it ought not to be trodden and defiled by certain persons; for it is written, "My dove, my undefiled, is but one."[2] Hence, again, the Lord says to Moses, "There is a place with me (*penes me*), and thou shalt stand upon a rock."[3] What place is there that belongs not to the Lord, seeing that all things consist in Him by whom they were created? There is a place, however, with God — to wit, the unity of the holy Church — in which there is a standing upon a rock, while the perfection of the confession (*confessionis soliditas*) is held in lowliness. We admonish thee, our brother, and all our brethren who are rulers in the Church of Christ, which He hath purchased with His blood, to keep back, by whatever checks ye possess, all men from that abyss into which some brethren are slipping, in reviling the Lord's pastors, and persecuting them both by word and deed; and we counsel you not to suffer them to be wounded with the hook of passion : for it is written, "For the wrath of man worketh not the righteousness of God."[4] Hence it is said again, "Let every man be swift to hear, but slow to speak, and slow to wrath."[5] Now I doubt not that with God's help you observe all these things; but as an occasion for counsel has arisen, I also secretly attach my word to your good desires and deeds, so that what you are doing of yourselves and independently of admonition you may do presently not by yourselves alone, now that the counsellor himself is added to you. Wherefore, brethren, it becomes you and all the faithful to love each other, and not to calumniate or accuse one another : for it is written, "Love thy neighbour, and be faithful unto him. But if thou bewrayest his secrets, thou shalt follow no more after him. For as a man who destroyeth his friend, so is he that loseth the love of his neighbour. And as one that letteth a bird go out of his hand, so art thou who hast let thy neighbour go, and shalt

not get him again. Follow after him no more, for he is far off. For he is as a roe escaped out of the snare, since his soul is wounded. Further thou wilt not be able to bind him up, and after reviling there may be reconcilement; but to bewray the secrets of a friend is the despair of an unhappy mind. He that winketh with the eye worketh evil, and every one will cast him off. When thou art present, he will speak sweetly, and will admire thy words. But at last he will writhe his mouth, and slander thy sayings. I have hated many things, but nothing like him; and the Lord will hate him. Whoso casteth a stone on high, it will fall upon his own head; and a deceitful stroke shall make wounds in the deceiver. Whoso diggeth a pit shall fall therein; and he that placeth a stone in his neighbour's way shall stumble thereon; and he that setteth a trap for another shall perish in it. He that worketh mischief, it shall fall upon him; and he shall not know whence it cometh on him. Mockery and reproach are from the proud; and vengeance, as a lion, shall lie in wait for them. They that rejoice at the fall of the righteous shall be taken in the snare; and anguish shall consume them before they die. Wrath and fury are both abominations, and the sinful man shall have them both."[6] "He that desireth to be avenged shall find vengeance from the Lord, and He will surely keep his sins *in remembrance*. Forgive thy neighbour the hurt that he hath done thee; so shall thy sins also be forgiven thee when thou prayest. One man beareth hatred against another, and doth he seek pardon from the Lord? He showeth no mercy to a man which is like himself, and doth he ask forgiveness of his own sins from the Most High? He, though he is but flesh, nourishes hatred; and does he implore mercy from God? Who will entreat for pardon of his sins? Remember thy end, and let enmity cease. For corruption and death impend on His commandments. Remember the fear of God, and bear no malice to thy neighbour. Remember the covenant of the Highest, and wink at the ignorance of thy neighbour. Abstain from strife, and thou shalt diminish thy sins. For a furious man will kindle strife, and a sinful man will disquiet friends, and will make debate among them that be at peace. For according to the trees of the wood, so will the fire burn; and according as a man's strength is, so will his wrath be; and according to his riches, his anger will rise. An hasty contention will kindle a fire; and an hasty fighting will shed blood; and a tale-bearing (*testificans*) tongue will cause death. If thou blow the spark, it shall burn like a fire; and if thou spit upon it, it shall be quenched; and both these come out of thy mouth. The whisperer and double-

---

[1] Prov. xviii. 19.
[2] Cant. vi. 9.
[3] Ex. xxxiii. 21.
[4] Jas. i. 20.
[5] Jas. i. 19.

[6] Ecclus. xxvii. 17-30.

tongued is cursed; for he has destroyed many that were at peace. A backbiting (*tertia*) tongue hath disquieted many, and driven them from nation to nation. Strong cities of the rich hath it pulled down, and overthrown the houses of great men. It has destroyed the strength of peoples, and has scattered strong nations. A backbiting tongue hath cast out virtuous women (*viratas*, spirited), and deprived them of their labours. Whoso hearkeneth unto it shall never find rest, and shall never have a friend on whom he may repose. The stroke of the whip maketh marks; but the stroke of the tongue will break the bones. Many have fallen by the edge of the sword, but not so many as have fallen by the tongue. Well is he that is defended from the evil tongue, and hath not passed through the venom thereof; who hath not drawn the yoke thereof, nor hath been bound in her bands. For the yoke thereof is a yoke of iron, and the bands thereof are bands of brass. The death thereof is an evil death, and the grave were better than it. Its endurance shall not abide, but it shall possess the ways of the unrighteous. In its flame it shall not burn the righteous. Such as forsake the Lord shall fall into it; and it shall burn in them, and not be quenched; and it shall be sent upon them as a lion, and devour them as a leopard. Hedge thine ears (*sæpi aures*) about with thorns, and refuse to listen to the evil tongue, and make a door for thy mouth and bars for thine ears. Smelt (*confla*) thy gold and thy silver, and make a balance for thy words, and a right bridle for thy mouth. And beware lest thou slide perchance in thy tongue, and fall in the sight of thine enemies that be in wait for thee, and thy fall be irremediable unto death." [1] Let all beware of these things, and "keep thy tongue from evil, and thy lips from speaking guile." [2] " Finally, dearly beloved, be strong in the Lord, and in the power of His might. Put on the armour of God, that ye may be able to stand against the wiles of the devil; for we wrestle not against flesh and blood, but against principalities and powers, against the rulers of the darkness of this world, against spiritual wickedness in heavenly places (*cœlestibus*). Wherefore take unto you the armour of God, that ye may be able to withstand in the evil day, and to stand perfect in all (*omnibus perfecti*). Stand therefore, having your loins girt about with truth, and having on the breastplate of righteousness, and your feet shod with the preparation of the Gospel of peace; in all (*in omnibus*) taking the shield of faith, wherewith ye shall be able to quench all the fiery darts of the wicked one. And take the helmet of salvation, and the sword of the Spirit, which is the word of God." [3] It is our wish, brother, that those things which we have written to you should be made known generally to all, in order that things which touch the others should be made known to all. May Almighty God protect you, brother, and all our brethren everywhere situate, even to the end, — even He who has thought good to redeem the whole world, our Lord Jesus Christ, who is blessed for ever. Amen. — Given on the 16th day of October, in the consulship of the most illustrious Africanus and Decius.

---

[1] Ecclus. xxviii.
[2] Ps. xxxiv. 13.
[3] Eph. vi. 10–17.

NOTE BY THE AMERICAN EDITOR.

It should be borne in mind by the reader that the holy martyr Fabian must not be less esteemed because this forgery was put upon him long after his decease. The forger puts many good things into his work, to make it accord with the character to which he attributes good and bad together. So with all the Decretals : they are made specious by piety and texts of Scripture.

DECREES OF FABIAN

TAKEN FROM THE DECRETAL OF GRATIAN

I.

That the man who refuses to be reconciled to his brother should be reduced by the severest fastings.[1]

If any injured person refuses to be reconciled to his brother, when he who has injured him offers satisfaction, he should be reduced by the severest fastings, even until he accepts the satisfaction offered him with thankful mind.

II.

The man is rendered infamous who knowingly presumes to forswear himself.[2]

Whosoever has knowingly forsworn himself, should be put for forty days on bread and water, and do penance also for the seven following years ; and he should never be without penance ; and he should never be admitted to bear witness. After this, however, he may enjoy communion.

III.

A man and a woman subject to madness cannot enter into marriage.[3]

Neither can a mad man nor a mad woman enter into the marriage relation. But if it has been entered, then they shall not be separated.

IV.

Marriage relations in the fifth generation may unite with each other ; and in the fourth generation, if they are found, they should not be separated.[4]

Concerning relations who enter affinity by the connection of husband and wife, these, on the decease of wife or husband, may form a union in the fifth generation ; and in the fourth, if they are found, they should not be separated. In the third degree of relationship, however, it is not lawful for one to take the wife of another on his death. In an equable manner, a man may be united in marriage after his wife's death with those who are his own kinswomen, and with the kinswomen of his wife.

To the immediately preceding notice.[5]

Those who marry a wife allied by blood, and are separated, shall not be at liberty, as long as both parties are alive, to unite other wives with them in marriage, unless they can plead the excuse of ignorance.

V.

Blood connections alone, or, if offspring entirely fails, the old and trustworthy, should reckon the matter of propinquity in the synod.[6]

No alien should accuse blood connections, or reckon the matter of consanguinity in the synod, but relations to whose knowledge it pertains, — that is, father and mother, sister and brother, paternal uncle, maternal uncle, paternal aunt, maternal aunt, and their children. If, however, offspring entirely fails, the bishop shall make inquiry canonically of the older and more trustworthy persons to whom the same relationship may be known ; and if such relationship is found, the parties should be separated.

VI.

Every one of the faithful should communicate three times a year.[7]

Although they may not do it more frequently, yet at least three times in the year should the laity communicate, unless one happen to be hindered by any more serious offences, — to wit, at Easter, and Pentecost, and the Lord's Nativity.

VII.

A presbyter should not be ordained younger than thirty years of age.[8]

If one has not completed thirty years of age, he should in no way be ordained as presbyter, even although he may be extremely worthy ; for even the Lord Himself was baptized only when He was thirty years of age, and at that period He began to teach. It is not right, therefore, that one who is to be ordained should be consecrated until he has reached this legitimate age.

---

[1] Dist. 90, *Si quis contristatus.* Basil, *in Reg.*, c. 74.
[2] 6, Q. 1, *Quicunque sciens.* Regino in the *Book of Penance.*
[3] 32, Q. 7, *Neque furiosus.* And in the *Decret. Ivo.*, book vi., Regino adduces it from the law of Rome.
[4] 35, Q. 2 and 3, *De propinquis.* From the *Pænitentiale* of Theodorus.
[5] From the same.
[6] 35, Q. 6, *Consanguineos extraneorum.* And in the *Decret. Ivo.*, vii.
[7] *De Consecr.*, dist. 2, *Etsi non.* And in the *Decret. Ivo.*, i.
[8] Dist. 78, *Si quis*, 30; and in the *Decret. Ivo.*, iii.; from Martin Bracar, ch. 20.

THE DECREES OF THE SAME, FROM THE CODEX OF DECREES IN SIXTEEN BOOKS, FROM THE FIFTH BOOK, AND THE SEVENTH AND NINTH CHAPTERS.

I.	II.
That the oblation of the altar should be made each Lord's day.	That an illiterate presbyter may not venture to celebrate mass.
WE decree that on each Lord's day the oblation of the altar should be made by men and women in bread and wine, in order that by means of these sacrifices they may be released from the burden of their sins.	The sacrifice is not to be accepted from the hand of a priest who is not competent to discharge the prayers or actions (*actiones*) and other observances in the mass according to religious usage.

ELUCIDATIONS

I.

(From Clement to Melchiades, p. 607.)

THE early Bishops of Rome, who till the time of Sylvester (A.D. 325) were, with few exceptions, like him pure and faithful shepherds, and not lords over God's heritage, shall here be enumerated. But first let us settle in few words the historic facts as to the See.

St. Paul was, clearly, the Apostolic founder of the Roman church, as appears from Holy Scripture. St. Peter seems to have come to Rome not long before his martyrdom. Linus and Cletus could not have been Bishops of Rome, for they were merely coadjutors of the Apostles *during their lifetime.* Clement was the first who succeeded to their work *after their death;* and thus he should unquestionably be made the first of the Roman bishops, — a position of which he was eminently worthy, for his was the spirit of St. Peter himself,[1] as set forth in that incomparable passage of his first Epistle,[2] in which the Apostle bids all his brethren to be shepherds indeed, and " ensamples to the flock." We may therefore give the outline of this history as follows : —

1. St. Paul was the "Apostle of the Gentiles," and St. Peter of " the Circumcision."

2. St. Paul came first to Rome, and organized the Christians he found there after the pattern " ordained in all the churches."

3. He had Linus for his coadjutor, being himself a prisoner, until he went into Spain.

4. St. Peter came to Rome (*circa* A.D. 64), and laboured with the Jewish Christians there, St. Paul recognising his mission among them.

5. This Apostle (soon thrown into prison) had Cletus for his coadjutor.

6. In the Neronian persecution Linus seem to have suffered with St. Paul, and probably Cletus as well. The latter died before St. Peter.

7. St. Peter, therefore, about to suffer himself, ordains Clement to succeed him.

8. As he was the first "successor of the Apostles," therefore, in the See of Rome, and the first who had jurisdiction there (for the Apostles certainly never surrendered their mission to their coadjutors), it follows that Clement was the first Bishop of Rome.

9. This is confirmed by the earliest testimony, — that of Ignatius.

10. It agrees with Tertullian's testimony, and he speaks (as a lawyer and expert) from " the registers." Irenæus, speaking less precisely, may be harmonized with these testimonies without violence to what he reports.

---

[1] See his genuine Epistle, vol. i. p. 1, this series. Compare vol. i. pp. 69, 416, with vii. p. 478.

[2] 1 Pet. v. 1-4. The Bishops of Rome have only to restore themselves to the spirit of St. Peter as here set forth, and the schisms of the churches will be at an end. For Tertullian's testimony, see vol. iii. p. 258, note 9.

BISHOPS OF ROME.

1. Clement	A.D.	68 to A.D.	71.	16. Anterus	A.D. 235 to A.D.	236.
2. Evaristus . . .	"	72 " "	108.	17. Fabianus	" 236 " "	249.
3. Alexander . . .	"	109 " "	117.	18. Cornelius . . .	" 251 " "	251.
4. Xystus I. . . .	"	117 " "	127.	19. Lucius	" 252 " "	252.
5. Telesphorus. . .	"	127 " "	138.	20. Stephen	" 253 " † "	256.
6. Hyginus	"	139 " "	142.	21. Xystus II. . . .	" 257 " "	258.
7. Pius	"	142 " "	156.	22. Dionysius . . .	" 259 " "	269.
8. Anicetus	"	156 " "	168.	23. Felix	" 269 " "	274.
9. Soter	"	168 " "	176.	24. Eutychianus . .	" 275 " "	282.
10. Eleutherus . . .	"	176 " "	189.	25. Caius	" 283 " "	295.
11. Victor	"	190 " "	201.	26. Marcellinus . . .	" 296 " "	304.
12. Zephyrinus . . .	"	201 " "	218.	27. Marcellus . . .	" 308 " "	309.
13. Callistus	"	218 " "	222.	28. Eusebius	" 310 " "	310.
14. Urban	"	223 " "	230.	29. Melchiades . . .	" 311 " "	314.
15. Pontianus . . .	"	230 " "	234.	30. Sylvester	" 314 " "	335.

N.B. — After A.D. 325 the Bishops of *Rome* are canonical primates; the Bishops of *New Rome* primates equally, but second on the list; then Alexandria, Antioch, Ephesus. The Councils of Constantinople and Chalcedon state that these primacies were awarded because *Rome* and *New Rome* were the capitals of the *œcumene*, or empire. The primacy conferred no authority over the sister Sees of Apostolic foundation, and recognised no inequality among bishops, save those of such honorary distinction.

THE PATRIARCHATE.

1. From (A.D. 325) Sylvester to Gregory the Great, and his successor, who lived but one year, the Bishops of Rome were canonical primates.

2. Boniface III. accepted the court title of "Universal Bishop" (A.D. 606) from the Emperor Phocas, but it was not recognised by the Church.

3. From this time to Adrian I. many Bishops of Rome vied with those of Constantinople to augment their honour and power. The establishment of the Western Empire (A.D. 800) made their ambitious claims acceptable to the Latins; and they became primates of all Christendom in Western estimation, with extra-canonical and indefinite claims as "successors of St. Peter."

4. Nicholas I. (A.D. 863), by means of the False Decretals, gave shape to these extra-canonical claims, abrogated the Nicene Constitutions in the West by making these Decretals canon-law, and asserted a supremacy over the old patriarchates, which they never allowed: hence the schism of the West from the Apostolic Sees of the East, and from the primitive discipline which established the Papacy, as now understood.

5. From Nicholas I. (who died A.D. 867) the Latin churches recognised this Papacy more or less; the Gallicans resisting, though feebly, by asserting their "liberties," according to Nicene Constitutions.

6. Gregory VII., honestly persuaded that the Decretals were authentic, enforced these spurious canons without reference to antiquity, and pronounced the title of "Pope" the sole and peculiar dignity of the Bishops of Rome A.D. 1073. He reigned from A.D. 1061 to 1085.

7. The churches of England and France, which claimed to be outside of the "holy Roman Empire," under kings whose own crowns were "imperial," maintained a perpetual contest with the Papacy, admitted the extra-canonical "primacy," but resisted all claims to "supremacy."

8. School-doctrines were framed and enforced, but were extra-symbolic, and of no Catholic authority. They abased the episcopate to exalt the Papacy.

9. The Council of Trent, after the Northern revolt from the Papacy and School-doctrine, sat seventeen years (from A.D. 1545 to A.D. 1563) framing the " Roman-Catholic Church " out of the remainder of national churches, depriving them of their nationalities, and making out of them all, with the missions in America, one *mixed confederation*, to which it gave a new creed and new organic laws; debasing the entire episcopate (which it denied to be an order distinct from that of presbyters), and making the Pope the "Universal Bishop," with other bishops reduced to presbyters, acting as his local vicars.

10. The Gallicans feebly withstood these changes, and strove to maintain the primitive Constitutions by accommodations with their theory of the "Gallican liberties," as founded by St. Louis.

11. Gallicanism was extinguished by Pope Pius IX., who proclaimed the Pope "infallible," and thus raised his "supremacy" into an article of the Roman-Catholic faith.

12. The following is the modern creed of "Roman Catholics," which, with the latest additions, embodies a library of dogmas in the *eleventh* article, and now, since the decree of *Infallibility* makes the entire *Bullary* (a vast library of decrees and definitions), equally part of the Creed.[1]

THE TRENTINE CREED, OR THE CREED OF PIUS IV., A.D. 1564.

1. I most stedfastly admit and embrace Apostolical and ecclesiastical traditions, and all other observances and constitutions of the Church.

2. I also admit the Holy Scripture according to that sense which our holy mother the Church has held, and does hold, to which it belongs to judge of the true sense and interpretations of the Scriptures. Neither will I ever take and interpret them otherwise than according to the unanimous consent of the Fathers.

3. I also profess that there are truly and properly seven sacraments of the New Law, instituted by Jesus Christ our Lord, and necessary for the salvation of mankind, though not all for every one; to wit, Baptism, Confirmation, Eucharist, Penance, Extreme Unction, Order, and Matrimony; and that they confer grace; and that of these, Baptism, Confirmation, and Order cannot be reiterated without sacrilege. I also receive and admit the received and approved ceremonies of the Catholic Church in the solemn administration of the aforesaid sacraments.

4. I embrace and receive all and every one of the things which have been defined and declared in the holy Council of Trent concerning original sin and justification.

5. I profess, likewise, that in the Mass there is offered to God a true, proper, and propitiatory sacrifice for the living and the dead; and that in the most holy sacrament of the Eucharist there is truly, really, and substantially, the body and blood, together with the soul and divinity, of our Lord Jesus Christ; and that there is made a conversion of the whole substance of the bread into the body, and of the whole substance of the wine into the blood, which conversion the Catholic Church calls Transubstantiation. I also confess that under either kind alone Christ is received whole and entire, and a true sacrament.

6. I constantly hold that there is a Purgatory, and that the souls therein detained are helped by the suffrages of the faithful.

7. Likewise, that the saints, reigning together with Christ, are to be honoured and invocated, and that they offer prayers to God for us, and that their relics are to be respected.

8. I most firmly assert that the images of Christ, of the mother of God, ever virgin, and also of the saints, ought to be had and retained, and that due honour and veneration is to be given them.

9. I also affirm that the power of indulgences was left by Christ in the Church, and that the use of them is most wholesome to Christian people.

10. I acknowledge the Holy Catholic Apostolic Roman Church for the mother and mistress of all churches; and I promise true obedience to the Bishop of Rome, successor to St. Peter, Prince of the Apostles, and Vicar of Jesus Christ.

11. I likewise undoubtedly receive and profess all other things delivered, defined, and declared by the sacred Canons, and general Councils, and particularly by the holy Council of Trent.

---

[1] De Maistre, thinking to overthrow the Anglicans, and imagining the Thirty-nine Articles to be " terms of communion " in the Anglican Church, which they never were, commits himself rashly to the following position: " If a people possesses one of these *Codes of Belief*, we may be sure of this: that *the religion of such a people is false*." No people on earth has such an enormous *Code of Belief* as those who profess the creed of Pius the Fourth, and who accept the decrees of Pius the Ninth. See De Maistre, *Le Principe Générateur*, etc., p. 20, Paris, 1852. This Trent Creed is the fruit of the Decretals.

12. And I condemn, reject, and anathematize all things contrary thereto, and all heresies whatsoever, condemned, rejected, and anathematized by the Church.

This true Catholic faith, without which no one can be saved, I N.N. do at this present freely confess and sincerely hold; and I promise most constantly to retain, and confess the same entire and unviolated, with God's assistance, to the end of my life. *Amen.*

N. B. — (1) To this was added, Dec. 8, 1854, the new article of the Immaculate Conception of the Virgin Mary, to be believed as necessary to salvation.

N. B. — (2) To which was added (December, 1864) the whole *Syllabus.*

N. B. — (3) To which was added (July 18, 1870) the new dogma of Infallibility.

Observe, this " Creed " is imposed on all in the Roman Obedience, and especially on those who enter it from other communions, as that without which *no one can be saved.* The Catholic Creed of Nicæa is not sufficient. But the Seventh Canon of Ephesus not only forbids the composition of any other creed, but especially adds : " Those who *shall presume to compose another creed,* or to produce or offer it to persons desiring to return to the acknowledgment of the truth . . . from any heresy whatever, shall be deposed . . . if bishops or *other* clergy, and if they be laymen they shall be anathematized."

II.

(Donation of Constantine, p. 607.)

On this stupendous fraud I quote from Dupin, as follows : —

" Among the number of Constantine's edicts I do not place the Donation which goes under his name. Some have attributed this false monument to the author of the collection (Decretals) ascribed to Isidore, he being a notorious forger of such kind of writings ; and this conjecture is more probable than some others.

" By this Donation, Constantine is supposed to give to the Bishops of Rome the sovereignty of the city, and of the provinces of the Western Empire. I note some of the reasons which clearly prove this instrument to be a forgery : —

" (1) Not one of the ancients mentions this pretended liberality of the emperor. How could Eusebius, and all the other historians who wrote about Constantine, have passed over in silence, had it been a reality, the gift of a Western Empire to the Bishop of Rome ?

" (2) Not one of the Bishops of Rome ever refers to such a donation, though it would have been much to their advantage so to do.

" (3) It is dated falsely, and under consuls who flourished when Constantine was unbaptized ; yet his baptism is referred to in this instrument. Again, the city of Constantinople is mentioned in it, although it was called Byzantium for ten years subsequent to its date.

" (4) Not only is the style very different from the genuine edicts of the emperor, but it is full of terms and phrases that came into use much after the time of Constantine.

" (5) How comes it that he should have given one-half of his empire to the Bishop of Rome, including the city of Rome itself, without any one ever hearing of it for hundreds of years after?

" (6) The falsities and absurdities of this edict demonstrate that it was composed by an ignorant impostor. Thus by it, for example, the Pope is permitted to wear a crown of gold, and a fabulous history is given of the emperor's baptism by Sylvester : also, it contains a history of the emperor's miraculous cure of leprosy by Sylvester, all which do plainly prove the forgery. It is certain that the city of Rome was governed by the emperor, and that the Bishops of Rome were subject to him, and obeyed him, as all his other subjects.

" All that we have said plainly shows that the edict of Donation that bears the name of Constantine is wholly supposititious ; but it is not so easy to find out who was the author. However it be, this document has neither any use nor authority." [1]

---

[1] Dupin, *ut supra*, p. 17. See also Bryce's *Holy Roman Empire*, pp. 43 and 100. He pronounces " the Donation of Constantine ' to be " the *most stupendous* of all the mediæval forgeries. The Decretals certainly surpass it in their nature and their effects; but Mr. Bryce's reference to these is very feeble and unsatisfactory, after Dupin. See p. 156 of his work, ed. Macmillan, 1880.

MEMOIRS OF EDESSA

AND OTHER ANCIENT SYRIAC DOCUMENTS

[TRANSLATED BY THE REV. B. P. PRATTEN, B.A.]

INTRODUCTORY NOTICE

TO

MEMOIRS OF EDESSA AND OTHER SYRIAC DOCUMENTS

THE *Syriac Documents* here subjoined are to be regarded as interesting relics of the primitive ages, but neither wholly genuine nor in details authentic. They have been interpolated and corrupted so as to reflect, in some particulars, ideas wholly repugnant to those of Christian antiquity, and which first received currency in the period of the Iconoclastic controversy.[1] Yet the pages of Eusebius bear witness to the Edessene legends as of very early origin, and it is reasonable to suppose that they rest on some inquiries made by the contemporary Abgar concerning the great Prophet who had appeared in Galilee. The visit of the Wise Men from the East, and the history of Naaman the Syrian, lend antecedent probability to the idea that such inquiries may have been made. The mission of Thaddæus seems a historical fact; and if he found Abgar predisposed to believe, and familiar with the story of the Christ, the growth of the whole fable is sufficiently accounted for. Let me quote Wake in the Preliminary Discourse to his *Apostolic Fathers.* He says:[2] "That both the intercourse reported by Eusebius between our Saviour and this prince (Abgarus), and the report of the picture being brought to him, have been received as a matter of unquestionable truth in those parts, the authority of Gregorius Abulpharagius[3] will not suffer us to doubt. . . . But Gelasius[4] pronounced the epistle of our Saviour to be apocryphal. . . . Natalis Alexander judges both it and the reply of Abgar *supposititious;* and Dupin, after him, yet more solidly convicts it of such manifest errors as may satisfy all considering persons that Eusebius and Ephraem were too easy of belief in this particular, and did not sufficiently examine into it."[5]

But I cannot do better than refer the inquirer to Jones' work *On the Canon,*[6] where, even in early youth, I found the whole matter, and the story of the portrait of our Saviour, attractive reading. I owe to that work my initiation into the study of what I am now endeavouring to elucidate, in some degree, for others. I subjoin the words of Lardner,[7] in concluding his candid examination of the matter, as follows: "The whole history is the fiction of some Christian at Edessa, in the time of Eusebius or not long before. The people of Edessa were then generally Christians; and they valued themselves upon it, and were willing to do themselves the honour of a very early conversion to the Christian faith. By some one of them, or more united together, this history was formed, *and was so far* received by Eusebius as to be thought by him *not improper* to be inserted in his *Ecclesiastical History.*"

I conclude that Eusebius was led to put some confidence in it by the *antecedent probability* to

---

[1] Had the early Christians used *icons,* — i.e., pictures in their churches, — the churches themselves would everywhere have been visible proof against the Council of Frankfort and all who condemned *icons.* *Sculptured* images are not *icons,* technically.

[2] Abridged.

[3] Jacobite primate, died 1286.

[4] Bishop of Rome A.D. 492-496.

[5] Wake, *Apostolic Fathers,* p. 4.

[6] Vol. ii. pp. 1-31.

[7] *Credib.,* vi. 605.

which I have referred, favouring the idea that some knowledge of Christ had penetrated the mind and heart of Abgar even in our Saviour's lifetime. This idea receives some countenance from the fact recorded by St. Matthew:[1] "His fame went *throughout all Syria;* and they brought unto Him all sick people that were taken with divers diseases," etc.

The remarks I have quoted from the learned will sufficiently prepare the reader for the other *Syriac Documents* which follow these *Edessene Memoirs*, as I find it convenient to call them.

Here follows the INTRODUCTORY NOTICE by the translator : —

THESE Documents were selected by the late Dr. Cureton, from manuscripts acquired by the British Museum from the Nitrian Monastery in Lower Egypt, of which the first portion arrived in 1841, the second in 1843, and a third in 1847. The preparation of them for publication occupied the closing days of his life. It is to be regretted that his death occurred before he was able to write a preface : the more so because, to use the words of Dr. W. Wright, the editor of the posthumous work, "he had studied the questions connected with this volume for years and from every point of view." In a note occurring in the preface to his *Festal Letters of Athanasius*,[2] he says : "I have found among the Syriac MSS. in the British Museum a considerable portion of the original Aramaic document which Eusebius cites as preserved in the archives of Edessa, and various passages from it quoted by several authors, with other testimonies which seem to be sufficient to establish the fact of the early conversion of the inhabitants of that city, and among them of the king himself, although his successors afterwards relapsed into paganism. These, together with accounts of the martyrdom of some of the first bishops of that city, forming a most interesting accession to our knowledge of the early propagation of Christianity in the East down to about A.D. 300, I have already transcribed, and hope to publish." "He was himself firmly persuaded," adds Dr. Wright, "of the genuineness of the Epistles attributed to Abgar, king of Edessa, and our Lord : an opinion which he shared with such illustrious scholars as Baronius, Tillemont, Cave, R. Mountague (Bishop of Norwich), and Grabe."

Without attempting here to decide what degree of historical value belongs to these Documents, it may be proper to observe that the several matters contained in them are so far distinct from one another that they do not necessarily stand or fall together. Such matters are : the celebrated Epistles, the conversion of King Abgar Uchomo, the visit of Thaddæus, and the early prevalence of Christianity at Edessa. With regard to the letters said to have passed between Abgar and our Lord, it seems sufficient, without referring to the internal evidence, to remark, with Lardner and Neander, that it is inconceivable how anything written by Christ should have remained down to the time of Eusebius unknown to the rest of the world.[3] The conversion of Abgar is a distinct matter of inquiry. But on this again, doubt, to say the least, is cast by the statement that Abgar Bar Manu, who reigned between the years 160 and 170 A.D., is the first king of Edessa on whose coins the usual symbols of the Baal-worship of the country are wanting, these being replaced in his case by the sign of the Cross.[4] If this refers to a complete series of the coins of Edessa, the evidence afforded must be considered very strong. For although, to take a parallel instance, "we seek in vain for Christian emblems on the coinage of Constantine, the first Christian emperor,"[5] this may readily be accounted for by his preference of military distinction to the humbler honours conferred by his new faith, whilst it does not appear that *anti*-Christian emblems are found, and on the coins of his son and successor Christian emblems do make their appearance. The other two subjects referred to do not lie under the same suspicion. There is nothing in the nature of the case to disprove the visit of Thaddæus (or Addæus) — nothing improbable in the fact itself, whatever judgment may be formed of the details of it presented to us here. If, however, the visit of Thaddæus also should have to be ranked among apocryphal stories, this would not affect the

---

[1] Cap. iv. 24.
[2] P. xxiii.
[3] *Hist. of the Church*, vol. i. p. 109 (Foreign Theol. Lib.).
[4] Bayer, *Historia Edessena e nummis illustrata*, l. iii. p. 173.
[5] Humphreys' *Coin-Collector's Manual*, p. 364.

remaining point — that with which we are chiefly concerned in these Documents. "It is certain," says Neander, "that Christianity was early diffused in this country." How early, is not so certain. But the evidence furnished by the later portions of these Documents, which there is nothing to contradict and much to confirm, proves that early in the second century Christianity had already made many converts there. The martyrdoms of Sharbil and Barsamya are said to have occurred A.D. 113,[1] the year in which Trajan conquered the Parthian kingdom, of which Edessa was a part; and, whilst the pagan element was plainly predominant, we find the Christians sufficiently numerous to have a bishop and presbyters and deacons. This sufficiently falls in with the proof already adduced of the conversion of even a king of Edessa about fifty years later.

To the Documents which are presumably of the ante-Nicene age, Dr. Cureton added two Metrical Homilies by Jacob of Serug, who lived in the next century. But, as they are so closely connected with the most interesting portions of the rest, the martyrdoms, and are besides of considerable merit as compositions, the decision of the editors to insert them will, it is presumed, be approved by most readers. The two supplemental portions, one from the Latin of Simeon Metaphrastes, and the other from Le Vaillant de Florival's French translation of Moses of Chorene, have also been inserted.

The translation of the Syriac portions, although made with Dr. Cureton's version constantly in sight, may fairly be considered as independent. The only matter in which his authority has been relied on is — in the case of proper names, the supply of the necessary vowels, — for the text is vowelless. And even to this, one exception occurs, in the *Martyrdom of Barsamya*, where "Evaristus" has been adopted instead of his "Erastus." In regard to the sense, it has been frequently found necessary to differ from him, while a style somewhat freer, though, it is hoped, not less faithful, has been employed. The Metrical Homilies also have been arranged so as to present the appearance of poetry. The results of Dr. Wright's collation of the text with the MSS. have also contributed to the greater correctness of the work.

The translator desires very thankfully to acknowledge his obligations to Dr. R. Payne Smith, Regius Professor of Divinity in the University of Oxford,[2] the progress of whose *Thesaurus Syriacus* is regarded with so much satisfaction and hope, for his kindness in furnishing much valuable information respecting matters on which the lexicons are silent.

The notes marked TR. are by the translator. The others, where the contrary is not indicated, are, at least in substance, Dr. Cureton's: though their citation does not always imply approval.[3]

---

[1] It should have been 115.

[2] Now Dean of Canterbury.

[3] The translator takes the opportunity of correcting the error by which the preparation of Tatian's work in vol. iii. of the Edinburgh Series was ascribed to him. The credit of it is due in the first instance to his lamented friend Mr. J. E. Ryland, at whose request, and subsequently by that of the editors, he undertook to correct the manuscript, but was soon obliged by other engagements to relinquish the task. [The correction was duly made in this series. See vol. ii. pp. 59, 61.]

ANCIENT SYRIAC DOCUMENTS

RELATING TO THE EARLIEST ESTABLISHMENT OF CHRISTIANITY IN EDESSA AND THE NEIGHBOURING COUNTRIES.

FROM THE HISTORY OF THE CHURCH.[1]

THE STORY[2] CONCERNING THE KING OF EDESSA.[3]

Now the story relating to Thaddæus was on this wise : —

While the Godhead of our Saviour and Lord Jesus Christ was proclaimed among all men by reason of the astonishing mighty-works which He wrought, and myriads, even from countries remote from the land of Judæa, who were afflicted with sicknesses and diseases of every kind, were coming to Him in the hope of being healed, King Abgar[4] also, who was renowned among the nations on the east of the Euphrates for his valour, had his body wasting away with a grievous disease, such as there is no cure for among men. And when he heard and was informed of the name of Jesus, and about the mighty works which He did, — for every one alike bore witness concerning Him, — he sent a letter of request by a man belonging to him,[5] and besought Him to come and heal him of his disease.

But our Saviour at the time that he asked Him did not comply with his request. Yet He deigned to give him[6] a letter *in reply :* for He promised him that He would send one of His disciples, and heal his sicknesses, and give salvation[7] to him and to all who were connected with him.[8] Nor did He delay to fulfil His promise to him : but after He was risen from the place of the dead, and was received into heaven, Thomas[9] the apostle, one of the twelve, as by an impulse from God, sent Thaddæus,[10] who was himself also numbered among the seventy[11] disciples of Christ, to Edessa, to be a preacher and proclaimer of the teaching of Christ ; and the promise of Christ was through him fulfilled.

Thou hast in writing the evidence of these things, which is taken from the Book of Records[12] which was at Edessa : for at that time the kingdom was still standing.[13] In the documents, then, which were there, in which was contained whatever was done by those of old down to the time of Abgar, these things also are found preserved down to the present hour. There is, however, nothing to prevent our hearing the very letters themselves, which have been taken by us[14] from the archives, and are in words to this effect, translated from Aramaic into Greek.

Copy of the letter which was written by King [1] Abgar to Jesus, and sent to Him by the hand of Hananias,[2] the Tabularius,[3] to Jerusalem : —

"Abgar the Black,[4] sovereign [5] of the country, to Jesus, the good Saviour, who has appeared in the country of Jerusalem : Peace. I have heard about Thee,[6] and about the healing which is wrought by Thy hands without drugs and roots. For, as it is reported, Thou makest the blind to see, and the lame to walk ; and Thou cleansest the lepers, and Thou castest out unclean spirits and demons, and Thou healest those who are tormented with lingering diseases, and Thou raisest the dead. And when I heard all these things about Thee, I settled in my mind one of two things : either that Thou art God, who hast come down from heaven, and doest these things ; or that Thou art the Son of God, and doest these things. On this account, therefore, I have written to beg of Thee that Thou wouldest weary Thyself to come to me, and heal this disease which I have. For I have also heard that the Jews murmur against Thee, and wish to do Thee harm. But I have a city, small and beautiful, which is sufficient for two."

Copy of those things which were written [7] by Jesus by the hand of Hananias, the Tabularius, to Abgar, sovereign of the country : —

"Blessed is he that hath believed in me, not having seen me. For it is written [8] concerning me, that those who see me will not believe in me, and that those will believe who have not seen me, and will be saved. But touching that which thou hast written to me, that I should come to thee — it is meet that I should finish here all that for the sake of which I have been sent ; and, after I have finished it, then I shall be taken up to Him that sent me ; and, when I have been taken up, I will send to thee one of my disciples, that he may heal thy disease, and give salvation to thee and to those who are with thee."

To these letters, moreover, is appended the following also in the Aramaic tongue : —

"After Jesus was ascended, Judas Thomas sent to him Thaddæus the apostle, one of the Seventy.

And, when he was come, he lodged with Tobias, son of Tobias. And, when the news about him was heard, they made it known to Abgar : "The apostle of Jesus is come hither, as He sent thee word." Thaddæus, moreover, began to heal every disease and sickness by the power of God, so that all men were amazed. And, when Abgar heard the great and marvellous cures which he wrought, he bethought himself that he was the person about whom Jesus had sent him word and said to him : When I have been taken up, I will send to thee one of my disciples, that he may heal thy disease. So he sent and called Tobias, with whom he was lodging, and said to him : I have heard that a mighty man has come, and has entered in and taken up his lodging in thy house : bring him up, therefore, to me. And when Tobias came to Thaddæus he said to him : Abgar the king has sent and called me, and commanded me to bring thee up to him, that thou mayest heal him. And Thaddæus said : I will go up, because to him have I been sent with power. Tobias therefore rose up early the next day, and took Thaddæus, and came to Abgar.

"Now, when they were come up, his princes happened to be standing [9] there. And immediately, as he was entering in, a great vision appeared to Abgar on the countenance of Thaddæus the apostle. And, when Abgar saw Thaddæus, he prostrated himself before him.[10] And astonishment seized upon all who were standing there : for they had not themselves seen that vision, which appeared to Abgar alone. And he proceeded to ask Thaddæus : Art thou in truth the disciple of Jesus the Son of God, who said to me, I will send to thee one of my disciples, that he may heal thee and give thee salvation? And Thaddæus answered and said : Because thou hast mightily [11] believed on Him that sent me, therefore have I been sent to thee ; and again, if thou shalt believe on Him, thou shalt have the requests of thy heart. And Abgar said to him : In such wise have I believed on Him, that I have even desired to take an army and extirpate those Jews who crucified Him ; were it not that I was restrained by reason of the dominion of the Romans.[12] And Thaddæus said : Our Lord has fulfilled the will of His Father ; and, having fulfilled it, has been taken up to His Father. Abgar said to him : I too have believed

---

[1] Gr. τόπαρχος.

[2] Called Hanan in the original Syriac document ; and so in Moses Chor.: Eusebius has 'Ανανίας, which is copied here.

[3] Gr. ταχυδρόμου. But the post held by Hananias must have been one of more dignity than that of a *courier*. He was probably a Secretary of State. In *The Acts of Addæus* (*infra*) he is called, in connection with the name Tabularius, a *sharir*, or confidential servant.

It would seem that Tabularius has been confounded with Tabellarius, a letter-carrier. — TR.

[4] Or "Abgar Uchomo." The epithet was peculiar to this King Abgar. He was the fourteenth king : the eleventh was called Abgar Sumoco, or "the Red."

The occasion of the name "Black" is doubtful : it can hardly have arisen from the fact that Abgar was suffering, as Cedrenus asserts, from the black leprosy. — TR.

[5] "Head," or "chief." — TR.

[6] Comp. Matt. iv. 24 : "And His fame went throughout all Syria," etc. See also Moses Chor. B. ii. c. 30.

[7] Gr. ἀντιγραφέντα, "written in reply."

[8] [John ix. 39, and xx. 29, 31 ; Hab. i. 5 ; with Isa. lii. 15, liii. 1.]

[9] Cureton, "were assembled and standing ;" nearly as Euseb.: παρόντων καὶ ἑστώτων. But in 2 Sam. xx. 1, the only reference given by Castel for the word ܐܬ݂ܟ݁ܢܫܘ is used for the Heb. נִקְרָא, "he chanced." — TR.

[10] ܣܓܕ, like the προσεκύνησε of Eusebius, may be rendered "worshipped." — TR.

[11] ܪܘܪܒܐܝܬ ; Gr. μεγάλως, lit. "greatly ;" C. "nobly." But nothing more than *intensity* is necessarily denoted by either word. Compare, for the Syriac, Ps. cxix. 107, 167 ; Dan. ii. 12. — TR.

[12] Compare the letters of Abgar and Tiberius, *infra*.

in Him and in His Father. And [1] Thaddæus said : Therefore do I lay my hand upon thee in His name. And when he had done this, immediately he was healed of his sickness and of the disease which he had. And Abgar marvelled, because, like as he had heard concerning Jesus, so he saw in deeds by the hand of Thaddæus His disciple : since without drugs and roots he healed him ; and not him only, but also Abdu,[2] son of Abdu, who had the gout : for he too went in, and fell at his feet,[3] and when he prayed over him he was healed. And many other people of their city did he heal, and he did great works, and preached the word of God.

"After these things Abgar said to him : Thou, Thaddæus, doest these things by the power of God ; we also marvel at them. But in addition to all these things I beg of thee to relate to me the story about the coming of Christ, and in what manner it was ; and about His power, and by what power He wrought those things of which I have heard.

"And Thaddæus said : For the present I will be silent ;[4] but, because I have been sent to preach the word of God, assemble me to-morrow all the people of thy city, and I will preach before them, and sow amongst them the word of life ; and *will tell them* about the coming of Christ, how it took place ; and about His mission,[5] for what purpose he was sent by His Father ; and about His power and His deeds, and about the mysteries which He spake in the world, and by what power He wrought these things, and about His new preaching,[6] and about His abasement and His humiliation, and how He humbled and emptied and abased Himself, and was crucified, and descended to Hades,[7] and broke through the enclosure [8] which had never been broken through *before*, and raised up the dead, and descended alone, and ascended with a great multitude to His Father.[9]

"Abgar, therefore, commanded that in the morning all the people of his city should assemble, and hear the preaching of Thaddæus. And afterwards he commanded gold and silver to be given to him ; but he received it not, and said : If we have forsaken that which was our own, how shall we accept that of others?"

These things were done in the year 340.[10]

In order, moreover, that these things may not have been translated to no purpose word for word from the Aramaic into Greek, they are placed in their order of time here.

Here endeth the first book.

---

[1] In another piece, *The Teaching of Addæus*, i.e., Thaddæus, we have a portion of the original Syriac from which Eusebius' translation was made. The only portions that correspond are: in the present piece, from this place to " — accept that of others," near the end; and, in the following one, from the beginning to " — that which is not ours." Some of the variations are worthy of notice.

[2] See note 9, p. 657, *infra*.

[3] This answers sufficiently well to the Greek: ὃς καὶ αὐτὸς προσελθὼν ὑπὸ τοὺς πόδας αὐτοῦ ἔπεσεν; but, as the original Syriac, p. 12, reads " he too brought his feet to him, and he laid his hands upon them and healed him," the Greek translation must have been at fault.

For *brought* read *presented*. — Tr.

[4] The original Syriac has " I will not hold my peace from declaring this."

[5] So Euseb. The orig. Syr. has " His sender."

[6] The orig. Syr. has " the certitude of His preaching." The error seems to have arisen from the Greek translator confounding ܟܪܘܙܘܬܐ with ܩܘܫܬܐ.

More probably with ܚܘܕܬܐ, "newness (of his preaching)," which was freely translated by him (περὶ τῆς καινῆς αὐτοῦ κηρύξεως; and this, again, was by the Syrian re-translator rendered literally, as in the text. The word *certitude* (above) may be rendered *unerring truth*. — Tr.

[7] Or "Sheol," as in Hebrew. The orig. Syr. gives "the place of the dead."

[8] Eph. ii. 14.

[9] Comp. Matt. xxvii. 52.

[10] Valesius says that the Edessenes commenced their era with the 117th Olympiad, the first year of the reign of Seleucus. The year 340 corresponds, therefore, with the fifteenth year of Tiberius. It should be the *beginning* of the 117th Olympiad. — Tr.

ANCIENT SYRIAC DOCUMENTS

A CANTICLE OF MAR [1] JACOB THE TEACHER ON EDESSA. [2]

EDESSA sent to Christ by an epistle to come to her and enlighten her. On behalf of all the peoples did she make intercession to Him that He would leave Zion, which hated Him, and come to the peoples, who loved Him.

She despatched a messenger to Him, and begged of Him to enter into friendship with her. By the righteous king she made intercession to Him, that He would depart from the *Jewish* people, and towards the *other* peoples direct His burden.

From among all kings one wise king did the daughter of the peoples find. Ambassador she made him. To her Lord she sent by him: Come Thou unto me; I will forget in Thee all idols and carved images.

The harlot heard the report of Him from afar, as she was standing in the street, going astray with idols, playing the wench with carved images. She loved, she much desired Him, when He was far away, and begged Him to admit her into His chamber.

Let the much-desired Bridegroom kiss me: with the kisses of His mouth let me be blessed. I have heard of Him from afar: may I see Him near; and may I place my lips upon His, and be delighted by seeing Him with mine eyes.

Thy breasts are better to me than wine: for the fragrance of Thy sweetness is life for evermore. With Thy milk shall I be nourished; with Thy fragrance shall I grow sweet from the smoke of idols, which with its rank odour did make me fetid.

Draw me after Thee into Thy fold: for I am a sheep gone astray in the world. After Thee do I run, and Thy converse do I seek: that in me may be completed that number of a hundred, by means of a lost one which is found. [3]

Let Gabriel rejoice and be exceeding glad, with the company of all the angels, in Thee, the Good Shepherd, who on Thy shoulders didst carry the maimed sheep, that that number of a hundred might be preserved.

Thy love is better than wine; than the face of the upright Thy affection. By wine let us be reminded of Thee, how by the cup of Thy blood Thou didst grant us to obtain new life, and the upright did celebrate Thy love.

A church am I from among the peoples, and I have loved the Only-begotten who was sent *by God:* whereas His betrothed hated Him, I have loved Him; and by the hands of Abgar the Black [4] do I beseech Him to come to me and visit me.

Black am I, yet comely. Ye daughters of Zion, blameless is your envy, seeing that the Son of the Glorious One hath espoused me, to bring me into His chamber. Even when I was hateful, He loved me, for He is able to make me fairer than water.

Black was I in sins, but I am comely: for I have repented and turned me. I have put away in baptism that hateful hue, for He hath washed me in His innocent blood who is the Saviour of all creatures.

Here end the Extracts from the Canticle on Edessa. [5]

---

[1] Or " My Lord," or " Mr."—TR.
[2] This is taken from Cod. Add. 17, 158, fol. 56, where is added: " when she sent to our Lord to come to her."

[3] [Luke xv. 6.]
[4] See note on p. 652
[5] [This ancient imitation of the Canticles shows how that book was understood, as of Christ and His Church.]

ANCIENT SYRIAC DOCUMENTS

EXTRACTS FROM VARIOUS BOOKS CONCERNING ABGAR THE KING AND ADDÆUS THE APOSTLE.

I.

OF THE BLESSED ADDÆUS THE APOSTLE. FROM HIS TEACHING WHICH HE GAVE IN EDESSA BEFORE ABGAR THE KING AND THE ASSEMBLY OF THE CITY.[1]

AND, when he had entered the sepulchre, he was raised to life again, and came forth from the sepulchre with many. And those who were guarding the sepulchre saw not how He came forth from the sepulchre; but the watchers from on high — they were the proclaimers and announcers of His resurrection. For, had He not willed, He had not died, because He is Lord of death, the exit from *this life;* nor, had it not pleased Him, would He have put on a body, inasmuch as He is Himself the framer of the body. For that will which led Him to stoop to be born of the Virgin, likewise caused Him further to descend to the suffering of death. — *And a little after* (*we read*) : For, although His appearance was that of men, yet His power, and His knowledge, and his authority, were those of God.

II.

FROM THE TEACHING OF ADDÆUS THE APOSTLE, WHICH WAS SPOKEN IN THE CITY OF EDESSA.[2]

Ye know that I said unto you, that none of the souls which go forth out of the bodies of men are under *the power of* death, but that they all live and continue to exist, and that there are for them mansions and an abode of rest. For the reasoning *power* of the soul does not cease, nor the knowledge, because it is the image of the immortal God. For it is not without perceptions, after the manner of the bodily frame, which has no perception of that corruption which has acquired dominion over it. Recompense, however, and reward it will not receive apart from its bodily form, because what it experiences belongs not to itself alone, but to the bodily form also in which it dwelt for a time. But the disobedient, who have not known God, will then repent without avail.

III.

FROM THE EPISTLE OF ADDÆUS THE APOSTLE, WHICH HE SPAKE IN THE CITY OF EDESSA.[3]

Give heed to this ministry which ye hold, and with fear and trembling continue ye in it, and minister every day. Minister ye not in it with neglectful habits, but with the discreetness of faith. And let not the praises of Christ cease out of your mouth, and let not any sense of weariness come over you at the season of prayers. Give heed to the verity which ye hold, and to the teaching of the truth which ye have received, and to the teaching of salvation which I commit to you. Because before the tribunal of Christ will it be required of you, when He maketh reckoning with the pastors and overseers, and when He shall take His money from the traders with the usury of what they have taught.[4] For He is the Son of a King, and goeth to receive a kingdom, and He will return and come and make a resuscitation to life of all men.

IV.

Addæus[5] preached at Edessa and in Mesopotamia (he was from Paneus[6]) in the days of Abgar the king. And, when he was among the Zophenians, Severus the son of Abgar sent and slew him at Agel Hasna, as also a young man his disciple.

V.

71. and Narcissus.[5] For they did not suffer that selection of the Seventy-two to be wanting, as likewise neither that of the Twelve. This *man* was of the Seventy-two : perhaps he was a disciple of Addæus the apostle.

---

[1] Taken from Cod. Add. 14,535, fol. i.
[2] From Cod. Add. 12,155, fol. 53 vers.

[3] From Cod. Add. 17,193, fol. 36. See *Teaching of Addæus,* p. 657, *infra.*
[4] Or " of the doctrines." — TR.
[5] Extracts IV. and V. are from Cod. Add. 14,601, fol. 164, written apparently in the eighth century.
[6] i.e., Paneas. — TR.

VI.

FROM THE DEPARTURE [1] OF MARATH [2] MARY FROM THE WORLD, AND THE BIRTH AND CHILDHOOD OF OUR LORD JESUS CHRIST. BOOK THE SECOND.

In the year three hundred and forty-five, in the month of the latter Tishrin,[3] Marath Mary went out from her house, and went to the sepulchre of Christ: because every day she used to go and weep there. But the Jews immediately after the death of Christ seized the sepulchre, and heaped great stones at the door of it. And over the sepulchre and Golgotha they set guards, and commanded them that, if any one should go and pray at the sepulchre or at Golgotha, he should immediately be put to death. And the Jews took away the cross of our Lord, and those two other crosses, and that spear with which our Saviour was struck, and those nails which they drove into His hands and into His feet, and those robes of mockery in which He had been clad; and they hid them : lest, as they said, any one of the kings or of the chief persons should come and inquire concerning the putting to death of Christ.

And the guards went in and said to the priests : Mary cometh in the evening and in the morning, and prayeth there. And there was a commotion in Jerusalem on account of Marath Mary. And the priests went to the judge, and said to him : My lord, send and command Mary that she go not to pray at the sepulchre and at Golgotha. And while they were deliberating, lo ! letters came from Abgar, the king of the city of Edessa, to Sabina the procurator [4] who had been appointed by Tiberius the emperor, and as far as the river Euphrates the procurator Sabina had authority. And, because Addæus the apostle, one of the seventy-two apostles, had gone down and built a church at Edessa, and had cured the disease with which Abgar the king was afflicted — for Abgar the king loved Jesus Christ, and was constantly inquiring about Him ; and, when Christ was put to death and Abgar the king heard that the Jews had slain Him on the cross, he was much displeased ; and Abgar arose and rode and came as far as the river Euphrates, because he wished to go up against Jerusalem and lay it waste ; and, when Abgar came and was arrived at the river Euphrates, he deliberated in his mind : If I pass over, there will be enmity between me and Tiberius the emperor. And Abgar wrote letters and sent them to Sabina the procurator, and Sabina sent them to Tiberius the emperor. In this manner did Abgar write to Tiberius the emperor : —

" From Abgar, the king of the city of Edessa. Much peace to thy Majesty, our lord Tiberius ! In order that thy Majesty may not be offended with me, I have not passed over the river Euphrates : for I have been wishing to go up against Jerusalem and lay her waste, forasmuch as she has slain Christ, a skilful healer. But do thou, as a great sovereign who hast authority over all the earth and over us, send and do me judgment on the people of Jerusalem. For be it known to thy Majesty that I desire that thou wilt do me judgment on the crucifiers."

And Sabina received the letters, and sent them to Tiberius the emperor. And, when he had read them, Tiberius the emperor was greatly incensed, and he desired to destroy and slay all the Jews. And the people of Jerusalem heard it and were alarmed. And the priests went to the governor, and said to him : My lord, send and command Mary that she go not to pray at the sepulchre and Golgotha. The judge said to the priests : Go ye yourselves, and give her what command and what caution ye please.

VII.

FROM THE HOMILY COMPOSED BY THE HOLY MAR JACOB, THE TEACHER, ON THE FALL OF IDOLS.[5]

To Edessa he made his journey, and found in it a great work :
For the king was become a labourer for the church, and was building it.
The apostle Addæus stood in it like a builder,
And King Abgar laid aside his diadem and builded with him.
When apostle and king concurred the one with the other,
What idol must not fall before them ?
Satan fled to the land of Babylon from the disciples,
And the tale of the crucifixion had got before him to the country of the Chaldeans.
He said, when they were making sport of the signs of the Zodiac, that he was nothing.

VIII.

FROM THE HOMILY ABOUT THE TOWN OF ANTIOCH.[6]

To Simon was allotted Rome,[7] and to John Ephesus ; to Thomas India, and to Addæus the country of the Assyrians.[8] And, when they were sent each one of them to the district which had been allotted to him, they devoted themselves [9] to bring the *several* countries to discipleship.

---

[1] From Cod. Add. 16,484, fol. 19. It consists of an apocryphal work on the Virgin, of the fifth or sixth century.
[2] i.e., " My Lady" or " Madam" (= mea domina): it is the feminine form of " Mar."— TR.
[3] Beginning with the new moon of October. The *former Tishrin* was the month immediately preceding. — TR.
[4] The Greek ἐπίτροπος is used. — TR.

[5] From Cod. Add. 14,624, apparently written in the ninth century.
[6] From Cod. Add. 14,500, of the eighth or ninth century.
[7] [A note of the Middle Age. The reverse is taught in the Scriptures, but even Hebrew Christians slurred the name of Paul.]
[8] This is probably the correct reading: the printed text means " among the Assyrians." — TR.
[9] Lit. " set their faces." — TR.

ANCIENT SYRIAC DOCUMENTS

THE TEACHING OF ADDÆUS THE APOSTLE.[1]

. . . .

ADDÆUS[2] said to him : Because thou hast thus believed, I lay my hand upon thee in the name of Him in whom thou hast thus believed. And at the very moment that he laid his hand upon him he was healed of the plague of the disease which he had for a long time.[3] And Abgar was astonished and marvelled, because, like as he had heard about Jesus, how He wrought and healed, so Addæus also, without any medicine whatever, was healing in the name of Jesus. And Abdu also, son of Abdu, had the gout in his feet ; and he also presented his feet to him, and he laid his hand upon them, and healed him, and he had the gout no more. And in all the city also he wrought great cures, and showed forth wonderful mighty-works in it.

Abgar said to him : Now that every man knoweth that by the power of Jesus Christ thou doest these miracles, and lo ! we are astonished at thy deeds, I therefore entreat of thee to relate to us the story about the coming of Christ, in what manner it was, and about His glorious power, and about the miracles which we have heard that He did, which thou hast thyself seen, together with thy fellow-disciples.

Addæus said : I will not hold my peace from declaring this ; since for this very purpose was I sent hither, that I might speak to and teach every one who is willing to believe, even as thou. Assemble me to-morrow all the city, and I will sow in it the word of life by the preaching which I will address to you — about the coming of Christ, in what manner it was ; and about Him that sent Him, why and how He sent Him ; and about His power and His wonderful works ; and about the glorious mysteries of His coming, which He spake of in the world ; and about the unerring truth[4] of His preaching ; and how and for what cause He abased Himself, and humbled

His exalted Godhead by the manhood which He took, and was crucified, and descended to the place of the dead, and broke through the enclosure[5] which had never been broken through *before*, and gave life to the dead by being slain Himself, and descended alone, and ascended with many to His glorious Father, with whom He had been from eternity in one exalted Godhead.

And Abgar commanded them to give to Addæus silver and gold. Addæus said to him : How can we receive that which is not ours. For, lo ! that which was ours have we forsaken, as we were commanded by our Lord ; because without purses and without scrips, bearing the cross upon our shoulders, were we commanded to preach His Gospel in the whole creation, of whose crucifixion, which was for our sakes, for the redemption of all men, the whole creation was sensible and suffered pain.

And he related before Abgar the king, and before his princes and his nobles, and before Augustin, Abgar's mother, and before Shalmath,[6] the daughter of Meherdath,[7] Abgar's wife,[8] the signs of our Lord, and His wonders, and the glorious mighty-works which He did, and His divine exploits, and His ascension to His Father ; and how they had received power and authority at the same time that He was received up — by which same power it was that he had healed Abgar, and Abdu son of Abdu, the second person[9] of his kingdom ; and how He informed them that He would reveal Himself at the end of the ages[10] and at the consummation of all created things ; also *of* the resuscitation and resurrection which is to come for all men, and

---

[1] This fragment, extending to the lacuna on p. 658, is contained in the MS. No. 14,654, at fol. 33. It consists of one leaf only, and is part of a volume of fragments, of which the age is certainly not later than the beginning of the fifth century. — TR.
[2] See note 1 on p. 653. — TR.
[3] Moses Chor says that he had been suffering seven years from a disease caught in Persia.
[4] "The certitude." — C. [See p. 653, *supra*, note 6.]

[5] Eph. ii. 14.
[6] The vowels supplied in this word are conjectural, as is the case with most of the proper names in these Documents. Perhaps the name of this person is to be read Shalamtho, as there is a Σαλαμψιώ, the wife of Phasaëlus, mentioned in Jos., *Antiq.*, b. xviii. c. v.
[7] Who this was, does not appear. He may have been some connection of Meherdates king of the Parthians, of whom Tacitus, *Ann.*, xii. 12, speaks as having been entertained at Edessa by Abgar.
[8] According to Moses Chor. b. ii. ch. xxxv., the first, or chief, wife of Abgar was Helena.
[9] Probably one of the second *rank*. Tacitus, *Ann.*, vi. 31, 32, mentions a man named Abdus, perhaps the same as this one, as possessing great authority in the Parthian kingdom. [Note 2, p. 653 *supra*]
[10] Or " times." — TR.

657

the separation which will be made between the sheep and the goats, and between the faithful and those who believe not.

And he said to them : Because the gate of life is strait and the way of truth narrow, therefore are the believers of the truth few, and through unbelief is Satan's gratification. Therefore are the liars many who lead astray those that see. For, were it not that there is a good end awaiting believing men, our Lord would not have descended from heaven, and come to be born, and to *endure* the suffering of death. Yet He did come, and us did He send[1] . . . of the faith which we preach, that God was crucified for[2] all men.

And, if there be those who are not willing[2] to agree with these our words, let them draw near to us and disclose to us what is in their mind, that, like as in the case of a disease, we may apply to their thoughts healing medicine for the cure of their ailments. For, though ye were not present at the time of Christ's suffering, yet from the sun which was darkened, and which ye saw, learn ye and understand concerning the great convulsion[3] which took place at that time, when He was crucified whose Gospel has winged its way through all the earth by the signs which His disciples *my* fellows do in all the earth : yea, those who were Hebrews, and knew only the language of the Hebrews, in which they were born, lo ! at this day are speaking in all languages, in order that those who are afar off may hear and believe, even as those who are near. For He it is that confounded the tongues of the presumptuous in this region who were before us ; and He it is that teaches at this day the faith of truth and verity by us, humble and despicable[4] men from Galilee of Palestine. For I also whom ye see am from Paneas,[5] from the place where the river Jordan issues forth, and I was chosen, together with my fellows, to be a preacher.

. . . .

For, according as my Lord commanded me, lo ! I preach and publish the Gospel, and lo ! His money do I cast upon the table before you, and the seed of His word do I sow in the ears of all men ; and such as are willing to receive it, theirs is the good recompense of the confession *of Christ;* but those who are not persuaded, the dust of my feet do I shake off against them, as He commanded me.

Repent therefore, my beloved, of evil ways and of abominable deeds, and turn yourselves towards Him with a good and honest will, as He hath turned Himself towards you with the favour of His rich mercies ; and be ye not as the generations of former times that have passed away, which, because they hardened their heart against the fear of God, received punishment openly, that they themselves might be chastised, and that those who come after them may tremble and be afraid. For the purpose of our Lord's coming into the world assuredly was,[6] that He might teach us and show us that at the consummation of the creation there will be a resuscitation of all men, and that at that time their course of conduct will be portrayed in their persons, and their bodies will be volumes for the writings of justice ; nor will any one be there who is unacquainted with books, because every one will read that which is written in His own book.[7]

. . . .

Ye that have eyes, forasmuch as ye do not perceive, are yourselves also become like those who see not and hear not ; and in vain do your ineffectual voices strain themselves to deaf[8] ears. Whilst *they* are not to be blamed for not hearing, because they are by[9] nature deaf and dumb, yet the blame which is justly incurred falls upon you,[10] because ye are not willing to perceive — not even that which ye see. For the dark cloud of error which overspreads your minds suffers you not to obtain the heavenly light, which is the understanding of knowledge.[11]

Flee, then, from things made and created, as I said to you, which are only called gods in name, whilst they are not gods in their nature ; and draw near to this *Being*, who in His nature is God from everlasting and from eternity, and is not something made, like your idols, nor is He a creature and a work of art, like those images in which ye glory. Because, although this[12] *Being* put on a body, *yet* is He God with His Father. For the works of creation, which trembled when He was slain and were dismayed at His suffering of death, — these bear witness that He is Himself God the Creator. For it was not on account of a man that the earth trembled,[13] but on ac-

[1] The remainder of "*The Teaching of Addæus*" is taken from another MS. of the Nitrian collection in the Brit. Mus., Cod. Add. 14,644. It is one of those which were procured in the year of the Greeks 1243 (A.D. 931) by the abbot Moses during his visit to Bagdad. It appears to be of the sixth century.

[2] Both "for" and "willing" are conjectural, the MS. being damaged. — WRIGHT.

[3] Possibly "earthquake," for which sense see Mich., p. 161; and so on p. 659, *infra.* — TR.

[4] Properly "miserabie." Compare Rom. vii. 24; 1 Cor. xv. 19. — TR

[5] Otherwise Cæsarea Paneas, or C. Philippi: now Banias. — TR.

[6] Cureton: "the whole object of our Lord's coming into the world was." But ܘܠܚܘ is = *omnino.* — TR.

[7] A few lines are wanting here in the MS.

[8] The greater part of the word rendered "deaf" is conjectural. — WRIGHT.
The "your" looks as if it were impersonal: "it is useless for *any one* to talk to the deaf." — TR.

[9] "By" (ܒ) is not in the printed text. — TR.

[10] Lit. "the blame in which justice is involved (prop., buried) is yours." — TR.

[11] Comp. Prov. xix. 25. — TR.

[12] "This" is doubtful. — WRIGHT.

[13] I have very little doubt that we should substitute ܐܪܥܐ ܙܥܬ — *the earth trembled* — for ܡܢܗ ܕܐܪܥܐ — *who is from the earth.*
— WRIGHT. [Words in italics are by the translator.]

count of Him who established the earth upon the waters ; nor was it on account of a man that the sun grew dark in the heavens, but on account of Him who made the great lights ; nor was it for a man that the just and righteous were restored to life again, but for Him who had granted power over death from the beginning ; nor was it for a man that the veil of the temple of the Jews was rent from the top to the bottom, but for Him who said to them, "Lo, your house is left desolate." For, lo ! unless those who crucified Him had known that He was the Son of God, they would not have had to proclaim [1] the desolation [2] of their city, nor would they have brought down Woe ! upon themselves.[3] For, even if they had wished to make light of this confession,[4] the fearful convulsions which took place at that time would not have suffered them to do so. For lo ! some even of the children of the crucifiers are become at this day preachers and evangelists, along with my fellow-apostles, in all the land of Palestine, and among the Samaritans, and in all the country of the Philistines. The idols also of paganism are despised, and the cross of Christ is honoured, and *all* nations and creatures confess God who became man.

If, therefore, while Jesus our Lord was on earth ye would have believed in Him that He is the Son of God, and before ye had heard the word of His preaching would have confessed Him that He is God ; now that He is ascended to His Father, and ye have seen the signs and the wonders which are done in His name, and have heard with your own ears the word of His Gospel, let no one of you doubt in his mind — so that the promise of His blessing which He sent to you may be fulfilled [5] towards you : Blessed are ye that have believed in me, not having seen me ; and, because ye have so believed in me, the town [6] in which ye dwell shall be blessed, and the enemy shall not prevail against it for ever.[7]

Turn not away, therefore, from his faith : for, lo ! ye have heard and seen what things bear witness to His faith — *showing* that He is the adorable Son, and is the glorious God, and is the victorious King, and is the mighty Power ; and through faith in Him a man is able to acquire the eyes of a true mind,[8] and to understand that, whosoever worshippeth creatures, the wrath of justice will overtake him.

For *in* everything which we speak before you, according as we have received of the gift of our Lord, *so* speak we and teach and declare *it*, that ye may secure [9] your salvation and not destroy [10] your spirits through the error of paganism : because the heavenly light has arisen on the creation, and He it is who chose the fathers of former times, and the righteous men, and the prophets, and spake with them in the revelation of the Holy Spirit.[11] For He is Himself the God of the Jews who crucified Him ; and to Him it is that the erring pagans offer worship, even while they know it not : because there is no other God in heaven and on earth ; and lo ! confession ascendeth up to Him from the four quarters of the creation. Lo ! therefore, your ears have heard that which was not heard by you ; and lo ! further, your eyes have seen that which was never seen by you.[12]

Be not, therefore, gainsayers of that which ye have seen and heard. Put away from you the rebellious mind of your fathers, and free yourselves from the yoke of sin, which hath dominion over you in libations and in sacrifices *offered* before carved images ; and be ye concerned for your endangered [13] salvation, and for the unavailing support on which ye lean ; [14] and get you a new mind, that worships the Maker and not the

---

[1] Lit. "have proclaimed."—Tr.

[2] Cureton renders: "They would not have proclaimed the *desolation* of their city, nor would they have divulged the *affliction* of their soul in crying Woe !" Dr. Wright pronounces the two words whose equivalents are given in italics to be very doubtful. Dr. Payne Smith, instead of the latter of the two (ܐܠܝܐ), conjectures (ܐܦ ܐܠܕܚܡܐ). This conjecture has been adopted. "Brought down" (ܡܕܚܒ) is lit "caused to drop."—Tr.

[3] The ancient Syriac Gospel, Luke xxiii. 48, gives: "And all those who were assembled there, and saw that which was done, were smiting on their breast, and saying, Woe to us ! what is this? Woe to us for our sins !"

[4] i.e., Christianity.—Tr.

[5] Or "confirmed."—Tr.

[6] Perhaps "town" will not seem too insignificant a word if it be taken in its original sense of a fortified place, which the Syriac term also denotes. It seemed desirable to distinguish, if possible, the two words which have been rendered respectively "city" and "town" in these pages. The only exception made is in a single passage where *Rome* is spoken of.—Tr.

[7] These words are not in the letter of Christ to Abgar. They must therefore be, either a message brought by Addæus himself, or, much more probably, a later interpolation : earlier, however, than Ephraem Syrus, who alludes to them in his *Testament*. This notion of the immunity of the city of Edessa is referred to by several Syriac writers. Nor was it confined to the East : it obtained in very early

times in our own country, where the letter of our Lord to Abgar was regarded as a charm. In a very ancient service-book of the Saxon times, preserved in the British Museum, the letter follows the Lord's Prayer and the Apostles' Creed ; and an appended description of the virtues of the epistle closes with these words, according to the Latin version of Rufinus : "*Si quis hanc epistolam secum habuerit, securus ambulet in pace*." Jeremiah Jones, writing of the last century, says: "The common people in England have had it in their houses in many places in a frame with a picture before it ; and they generally, with much honesty and devotion, regard it as the word of God and the genuine epistle of Christ." Even now a similar practice is believed to linger in some districts. The story of Abgar is told in an Anglo-Saxon poem, published in *Abgarus-Legenden paa Old-Engelsk* by G. Stephens, Copenhagen, 1853. It consists of 204 lines, is a tolerably close rendering of Eusebius, and is ascribed by Stephens to Aelfric, archbishop of York from 1023 to 1052. Note that *ambulet* (above) is for *ambulabit*, apparently.—Tr.

[8] See Eph. i. 18.

[9] Lit. "obtain."—Tr.

[10] Or "lose."—Tr.

[11] Lit. "Spirit of holiness."—Tr.

[12] [Isa. lii. 15.]

[13] Prop. "lost," or "being lost," "perishing."—Tr.

[14] Lit. "support of your head."—Tr. The word rendered "support" is not in the dictionaries, but its derivation and form are known. Mar Jacob, *infra*, has a similar expression: "A resting-place for the head, etc." Where, however, his word is derived from a root meaning to "prop up" (ܣܡܟ), whereas the root of our word denotes to "bend itself," "bow down" (ܟܦ), and is often used of the declining day (as Luke xxiv. 29). It is used of the bending of the head in John xix. 30. The actual *leaning* of the head for support is not expressed in the verb, but would naturally be inferred from it.—Tr.

things which are made — *a mind* in which is portrayed the image of verity and of truth, of the Father, and of the Son, and of the Holy Spirit ; believing and being baptized in the triple and glorious names. For this is our teaching and our preaching. For the belief of the truth of Christ does not consist of many things.[1] And those of you as are willing to be obedient to Christ are aware that I have many times repeated my words before you, in order that ye might learn and understand what ye hear.

And we ourselves shall rejoice in this, like the husbandman who rejoices in the field which is blessed ; God also will be glorified by your repentance towards Him. While ye are saved hereby, we also, who give you this counsel, shall not be despoiled of the blessed reward of this *work*. And, because I am assured that ye are a land blessed according to the will of the Lord Christ, therefore, instead of the dust of our feet which we were commanded to shake off against the town that would not receive our words, lo ! I have shaken off to-day at the door of your ears the sayings of my lips, in which are portrayed the coming of Christ which has *already* been, and also that which is *yet* to be ; and the resurrection, and the resuscitation of all men, and the separation which is to be made between the faithful and the unbelieving ; and the sore punishment which is reserved for those who know not God, and the blessed promise of future joy which they shall receive who have believed in Christ and worshipped Him and His exalted Father, and have confessed Him and His divine Spirit.[2]

And now it is meet for us that I conclude my present discourse ; and let those who have accepted the word of Christ remain with us, and those also who are willing to join with us in prayer ; and afterwards let them go to their homes.

And Addæus the apostle was rejoiced to see that a great number of the population of the city stayed with him ; and they were *but* few who did not remain at that time, while even those few not many days after accepted his words and believed in the Gospel set forth in[3] the preaching of Christ.

And when Addæus the apostle had spoken these things before all the town of Edessa, and King Abgar saw that all the city rejoiced in his teaching, men and women alike, and *heard them* saying to him, " True and faithful is Christ who sent thee to us " — he himself also rejoiced greatly at this, giving praise to God ; because, like as he had heard from Hanan,[4] his Tabularius, about Christ, so had he seen the wonder-

ful mighty-works which Addæus the apostle did in the name of Christ.

And Abgar the king also said to him : According as I sent to Christ in my letter to Him, and according as He also sent to me, *so* have I also received from thine own self this day ; so will I believe all the days of my life, and in the selfsame things will I continue and make my boast, because I know also that there is no other power in whose name these signs and wonders are done but the power of Christ whom thou preachest in verity and in truth. And henceforth Him will I worship — I and my son Maanu,[5] and Augustin,[6] and Shalmath the queen. And now, wherever thou desirest, build a church, a place of meeting for those who have believed and shall believe in thy words ; and, according to the command given thee by thy Lord, minister thou at the seasons with confidence ; to those also who shall be with thee as teachers of this Gospel I am prepared to give large donations, in order that they may not have any other work beside the ministry ; and whatsoever is required by thee for the expenses of the building I myself will give thee without any restriction,[7] whilst thy word shall be authoritative and sovereign in this town ; moreover, without *the intervention of* any other person do thou come into my presence as one in authority, into the palace of my royal majesty.

And when Abgar was gone down to his royal palace he rejoiced, he and his princes with him, Abdu son of Abdu, and Garmai, and Shemashgram,[8] and Abubai, and Meherdath,[9] together with the others their companions, at all that their eyes had seen and their ears also had heard ; and in the gladness of their heart they too began to praise God for having turned their mind towards Him, renouncing the paganism in which they had lived,[10] and confessing the Gospel of Christ. And when Addæus had built a church they proceeded to offer in it vows and oblations, they and the people of the city ; and there they continued to present their praises all the days of their life.

And Avida and Barcalba,[11] who were chief men and rulers, and wore the royal headband,[12] drew

[5] Abgar had two sons of this name. This is probably the elder, who succeeded his father at Edessa, and reigned seven years. Bayer makes him the fifteenth king of Edessa.
[6] Abgar's mother: see p. 657.
[7] Lit. " reckoning." — Tr.
[8] The vowels in this name are supplied from the treatise of Bardesan. Whiston, from the Armenian form, writes the name Samsagram. He was sent, together with Hanan and Maryhab, as envoy to Marinus. See Mos. Chor. B. ii. c. 30.
[9] See Tac., *Ann.*, xii. 12.
[10] Lit. " stood." — Tr.
[11] The son of Zati (see p. 663, note 7, *supra*).
[12] Or " the headbands of the kings." Nothing appears to be known of the derivation of the word ‏ܩܘܡܪܐ‎, which does not occur in the ordinary lexicons. Dr. Payne Smith has favoured the translator with the following note: " ‏ܩܘܡܪܐ‎ is evidently some kind of ornament. In Ephs. ii. 379 (in the form ‏ܩܘܡܪܐ‎) it is an ornament worn by young people. B.A. (Bar Alii *Lex. Syro-Arab.*)

[1] Lit. " the truth of Christ is not believed in many things." — Tr.
[2] Lit. " the Spirit of His Godhead " = His Spirit of Godhead = His divine Spirit." — Tr.
[3] Lit. " the Gospel of." — Tr.
[4] See p. 652, note 3, *supra*.

near to Addæus, and asked him about the matter of Christ, *requesting* that he would tell' them how He, though He was God, appeared to them as a man : And how, said they, were ye able to look upon Him? And he proceeded to satisfy them all about this, about all that their eyes had seen and about whatsoever their ears had heard from him. Moreover, everything that the prophets had spoken concerning Him he repeated before them, and they received his words gladly and with faith, and there was not a man that withstood him; for the glorious deeds which he did suffered not any man to withstand him.

Shavida, moreover, and Ebednebu, chiefs of the priests of this town, together with Piroz[1] and Dilsu their companions, when they had seen the signs which he did, ran and threw down the altars on which they were accustomed to sacrifice before Nebu and Bel,[2] their gods, except the great altar which was in the middle of the town; and they cried out and said : Verily this is the disciple of that eminent and glorious Master, concerning whom we have heard all that He did in the country of Palestine. And all those who believed in Christ did Addæus receive, and baptized them in the name of the Father, and of the Son, and of the Holy Spirit. And those who used to worship stones and stocks sat at his feet, recovered from the madness[3] of paganism wherewith they had been afflicted. Jews also, traders in fine raiment,[4] who were familiar with the law and the prophets — they too were persuaded, and became disciples, and confessed Christ that He is the Son of the living God.

But neither did King Abgar nor yet the Apostle Addæus compel any man by force to believe in Christ, because without the force of man the force of the signs compelled many to believe in Him. And with affection did they receive His doctrine — all this country of Mesopotamia, and all the regions round about it.

Aggæus, moreover, who[5] made the silks[6] and headbands of the king, and Palut, and Barshelama, and Barsamya, together with the others their companions, clave to Addæus the apostle; and he received them, and associated them with him in the ministry, their business being to read in the Old Testament and the New,[7] and in the prophets, and in the Acts of the Apostles, *and* to meditate upon them daily; strictly charging them to let their bodies be pure and their persons holy, as is becoming in men who stand before the altar of God. "And be ye," said he, "far removed from false swearing and from wicked homicide, and from dishonest testimony, which is connected with adultery; and from magic arts, for which there is no mercy, and from soothsaying, and divination, and fortune-tellers; and from fate and nativities, of which the deluded Chaldeans make their boast; and from the stars, and the signs of the Zodiac, in which the foolish put their trust. And put not far from you unjust partiality, and bribes, and presents, through which the innocent are pronounced guilty. And along with this ministry, to which ye have been called, see that ye have no other work besides : for the Lord is the work of your ministry all the days of your life. And be ye diligent to give the seal of baptism. And be not fond of the gains of this world. And hear ye a cause with justice and with truth. And be ye not a stumbling-block to the blind, lest through you should be blasphemed the name of Him who opened *the eyes of* the blind, according as we have seen. Let all, therefore, who see you perceive that ye yourselves are in harmony with whatsoever ye preach and teach."

And they ministered with him in the church which Addæus had built at the word and command of Abgar the king, being furnished with supplies by the king and his nobles, partly for the house of God, and partly for the supply of the poor. Moreover, much people day by day assembled and came to the prayers of the service, and to *the reading of* the Old Testament,

---

and K. (Georgii Karmsedinoyo *Lex.*) render it (in the form مَلدُور جَازة (شَدَة), which may mean 'a circlet of jewels.'"

Cureton says: "These headbands of the king, or diadems, seem to have been made of silk or muslin scarves, like the turbans of orientals at the present day, interwoven with gold, and with figures and devices upon them, as was the case with that worn by Sharbil. See *Acts of Sharbil, sub init.*" The art. *Diadema* in Dr. W. Smith's *Antiqq.* seems to furnish a good idea of what is intended. The ornament was probably *white ;* and this has caused our expression to be sometimes confounded with the similar ܝܣܡ ܚܘܪܐ. See *Teaching of Simon Cephas,* init. — TR.

[1] The same name as Berosus, who is so called in the modern Persiah.
[2] These were the chief gods of Edessa, the former representing the sun, and the latter the moon.
[3] The reference seems to be to Mark v. 15. — TR.
[4] The "soft *clothing*" of Matt. xi. 8, where *the Peshito* and the "Ancient Recension" have the same word as appears here. Cureton renders it "silk," but remarks: "It would appear to be cotton or muslin, *lana xylina,* not *bombycina.*" [The word *clothing*, with *the Peshito and*, should be credited to the translator.]

[5] The text has not ?, but it is best to supply it. — TR.
[6] Cureton gives "chains," which in his notes he changes to "silks," or "muslins," adopting, with C., the reading ܡܚܝܠܐ instead of the ܡܚܠܐ of the printed text. Mos. Chor. calls Aggæus "un fabricant de coiffures de *soie*," according to the translation of Florival; or "quendam *serici* opificem," according to Whiston. It may be added that the word ܡܚܝܠܐ is doubtless the same as our "silk," which is only a form of *Sericum,* an adjective from *Seres,* the people whose country was the native home of the silk-worm. — TR.
[7] These terms could only have been used here in the sense of the Law of Moses and the Gospel. If by the Acts of the Apostles is meant the work of Luke, this passage seems to show that the compiler of this account of Addæus wrote some years subsequently to the events which he relates, or that it has been added by a later interpolator. For at the earlier period of Addæus's ministry no other part of the New Testament was written than the Hebrew Gospel of Matthew, which is probably the Gospel here meant.

and the New of the Diatessaron.[1] They also believed in the restoration of the dead, and buried their departed in the hope of resuscitation. The festivals of the Church they also observed in their seasons, and were assiduous every day in the vigils of the Church. And they made visits of almsgiving, to the sick and to those that were whole, according to the instruction of Addæus to them. In the environs, too, of the city churches were built, and many received from him ordination to the priesthood.[2] So that even people of the East, in the guise of merchants, passed over into the territory of the Romans, that they might see the signs which Addæus did. And such as became disciples received from him ordination to the priesthood, and in their own country of the Assyrians they instructed the people of their nation, and erected houses of prayer there in secret, by reason of the danger from those who worshipped fire and paid reverence to water.[3]

Moreover, Narses, the king of the Assyrians, when he heard of those same things which Addæus the apostle had done, sent *a message* to Abgar the king: Either despatch to me the man who doeth these signs before thee, that I may see him and hear his word, or send me *an account of* all that thou hast seen him do in thy own town. And Abgar wrote to Narses,[4] and related to him the whole story of the deeds of Addæus from the beginning to the end; and he left nothing which he did not write to him. And, when Narses heard those things which were written to him, he was astonished and amazed.

Abgar the king, moreover, because he was not able to pass over into the territory of the Romans,[5] and go to Palestine and slay the Jews for having crucified Christ, wrote a letter and sent it to Tiberius Cæsar,[6] writing in it thus: —

King Abgar to our Lord Tiberius Cæsar: Although I know that nothing is hidden from thy Majesty, I write to inform thy dread and mighty Sovereignty that the Jews who are under thy dominion and dwell in the country of Palestine have assembled themselves together and crucified Christ, without any fault *worthy* of death, after He had done before them signs and wonders, and had shown them powerful mighty-works, so that He even raised the dead to life for them; and at the time that they crucified

Him the sun became darkened and the earth also quaked, and all created things trembled and quaked, and, as if of themselves, at this deed the whole creation and the inhabitants of the creation shrank away. And now thy Majesty knoweth what it is meet for thee to command concerning the people of the Jews who have done these things.

And Tiberius Cæsar wrote and sent to King Abgar; and thus did he write to him: —

The letter of thy Fidelity towards me I have received, and it hath been read before me. Concerning what the Jews have dared to do in the matter of the cross, Pilate[7] the governor also has written and informed Aulbinus[8] my proconsul concerning these selfsame things of which thou hast written to me. But, because a war with the people of Spain,[9] who have rebelled against me, is on foot at this time, on this account I have not been able to avenge this matter; but I am prepared, when I shall have leisure, to issue a command according to law against the Jews, who act not according to law. And on this account, as regards Pilate also, who was appointed by me governor there — I have sent another in his stead, and dismissed him in disgrace, because he departed from the law,[10] and did the will of the Jews, and for the gratification of the Jews crucified Christ, who, according to what I hear concerning Him, instead of *suffering* the cross of death, deserved to be honoured and worshipped[11] by them: and more especially because with their own eyes they saw everything that He did. Yet thou, in accordance with thy fidelity towards me, and the faithful covenant *entered into by* thyself and by thy fathers, hast done well in writing to me thus.

And Abgar the king received Aristides, who had been sent by Tiberius Cæsar to him; and in reply he sent him *back* with presents of honour suitable for him who had sent him to him.

---

[1] Or "Ditornon." The reading of the MS. is not clear. It seems that it ought to be *Diatessaron*, which Tatian the Syrian compiled from the four Gospels about the middle of the second century. This was in general use at Edessa up to the fourth century, and Ephraem Syrus wrote a commentary on it. If this be so, we have here a later interpolation. [The translator says (of *Ditornon* and *Diatess.*): "The two words would differ but slightly in the mode of writing." He also corrects Cureton, who calls Tatian "the Syrian:" it should be "the *Assyrian*."]

[2] Lit. "the hand of priesthood:" and so *passim*. — TR.

[3] Strabo, *de Persis*, b. xv. (ch. iii.): "They sacrifice to fire and to water."

[4] See his letter in Mos. Chor., *infra*.

[5] Dio Cassius, liv. 8: "Augustus fixed as the boundaries of the empire of the Romans the Tigris and Euphrates."

[6] See it also, with some variations, in Mos. Chor., *infra*.

[7] It was Pilate's duty, as governor of Judea, to send an account to the Roman Government of what had occurred in respect to Jesus; and his having done so is mentioned by Justin Martyr, Tertullian, and several other writers.

[8] The word is evidently misspelt. The name intended may have been confounded with that of the Albinus who was made governor of Judea at a later period by Nero, A.D. 62. The same person is referred to, in the *Exit of Mary, infra*: "Sabinus, the governor who had been appointed by the Emperor Tiberius; and even as far as the river Euphrates the governor Sabinus had authority." The person meant can only be Vitellius, who was then governor of Syria, who removed Pilate from the administration of Judea, sending Marcellus in his stead, and ordered him to appear before Tiberius at Rome. The emperor died before he reached Rome.

[9] No mention is made by historians of any war with Spain. But about this time Vitellius, mentioned in the preceding note, was mixed up with the wars of the Parthians and Hiberians; and, as Hiberi is a name common to Spaniards as well as Hiberians, the apparent error may have arisen in translating the letter out of Latin into Syriac.

[10] Baronius says Pilate violated the law by crucifying our Lord so soon after sentence had been passed, whereas a delay of ten days was required by a law passed in the reign of Tiberius.

[11] Tiberius is said by Tertullian (*Apol.*, 5) to have referred to the senate the question of admitting Christ among the gods. This has been interpolated into the epistle of Tiberius to Abgar as given in Moses Chor., B. ii. c. 33. He also adds another letter from Abgar in reply to this.

And from Edessa he went to Thicuntha,[1] where Claudius, the second from the emperor, was; and from thence, again, he went to Artica,[2] where Tiberius Cæsar was: Caius, moreover, was guarding the regions round about Cæsar. And Aristides himself also related before Tiberius concerning the mighty-works which Addæus had done before Abgar the king. And when he had leisure from the war he sent and put to death some of the chief men of the Jews who were in Palestine. And, when Abgar the king heard of this, he rejoiced greatly that the Jews had received punishment, as it was right.

And some years after Addæus the apostle had built the church in Edessa, and had furnished it with everything that was suitable for it, and had made disciples of a great number of the population of the city, he further built churches in the villages[3] also — *both* those which were at a distance and those which were near, and finished and adorned them, and appointed in them deacons and elders, and instructed in them those who should read the Scriptures, and taught the ordinances and[4] the ministry without and within.

After all these things he fell ill of the sickness of which he departed from this world. And he called for Aggæus before the whole assembly of the church, and bade him draw near, and made him Guide and Ruler[5] in his stead. And Palut,[6] who was a deacon, he made elder; and Abshelama, who was a scribe, he made deacon. And, the nobles and chief men being assembled, and standing near him — Barcalba son of Zati,[7] and Maryhab[8] son of Barshemash, and Senac[9] son of Avida, and Piroz son of Patric,[10] together with the rest of their companions — Addæus the apostle said to them: —

"Ye know and are witness, all of you who hear me, that, *according to* all that I have preached to you and taught you and ye have heard from me, even so have I behaved myself in the midst of you, and ye have seen *it* in deeds also: because our Lord thus charged us, that, whatsoever we preach in words before the people, we should practise it in deeds before all men. And, according to the ordinances and laws which were appointed by the disciples in Jerusalem,[11] and by which my fellow-apostles also guided their conduct, so also *do* ye — turn not aside from them, nor diminish aught from them: even as I also am guided by them amongst you, and have not turned aside from them to the right hand or to the left, lest I should become estranged from the promised salvation which is reserved for such as are guided by them.

"Give[12] heed, therefore, to this ministry which ye hold, and with fear and trembling continue in it, and minister every day. Minister not in it with neglectful habits, but with the discreetness of faith; and let not the praises of Christ cease out of your mouth, nor let weariness of prayer at the *stated* times come upon you. Give heed to the verity which ye hold, and to the teaching of the truth which ye have received, and to the inheritance of salvation which I commit to you: because before the tribunal of Christ will ye have to give an account of it, when He maketh reckoning with the shepherds and overseers, and when He taketh His money from the traders with the addition of the gains. For He is the Son of a King, and goeth to receive a kingdom and return; and He will come and make a resuscitation *to life* for all men, and then will He sit upon the throne of His righteousness, and judge the dead and the living, as He said to us.

"Let not the secret eye of your minds be closed by pride, lest your stumbling-blocks be many in the way in which there are no stumbling-blocks, but a hateful[13] wandering in its paths. Seek ye those that are lost, and direct those that go astray, and rejoice in those that are found; bind up the bruised, and watch over the fatlings: because at your hands will the sheep of Christ be required. Look ye not for the honour that passeth away: for the shepherd that looketh to receive honour from his flock — sadly, sadly stands his flock with respect to him. Let your concern be great for the young lambs, whose angels behold the face of the Father who is unseen. And be ye not stones of stumbling before the blind, but clearers of the way and the paths

---

[1] This word has been so much distorted and disfigured by the transcribers, that I am unable to recognise what is the place intended. — CURETON.

[2] This word may be read *Ortyka*, and may be intended for *Ortygia* near Syracuse, which was not far from the island of Capreæ, where Tiberius then resided, seldom leaving it to go farther than to the neighbouring coast of Campania.

[3] Lit. "the *other* villages." So, in several passages of these Documents, "the rest of the other——." The habit of including two or more distinguished nations under a class to which only one of them belongs was not unknown among classical writers also: as when, e.g., Thucydides speaks of the Peloponnesian war as the most remarkable of all the wars that *preceded* it. Milton's imitation, "The fairest of her daughters, Eve" [*Paradise Lost*, iv. 324], is well known. — TR.

[4] The ◦ (and) seems to have been altered into ? (of). — WRIGHT. Perhaps "of " is the better reading. — TR.

[5] It is plain from the context here, as well as wherever it occurs in these early Syriac Documents, that this title (or that of Guide alone) is precisely the same as that of Bishop, although the Greek word ἐπίσκοπος had not yet obtained in the East. The first mention we find of the title *Bishop* (in these pages) is in the *Acts of Sharbil* about A.D. 105–112, where Barsamya is called "the Bishop of the Christians," although he is more generally designated as here. It is also found in the *Teaching of Simon Cephas, sub fin.*, which seems to have been written early in the second century or at the end of the first. The passage in the *Teaching of Addæus*, p. 665, *infra*, where it occurs, was interpolated at a much later period. [The parenthetic words of this note are supplied by the translator.]

[6] Perhaps Φιλώτας.

[7] Perhaps the same as Izates: see Jos., *Antiq.*, xx. ii. 1, 4; Tac., *Ann.*, xii. 14.

[8] This seems to be the person spoken of by Moses Chor., B. ii. c. 30, under the name "Mar-Ihap, prince d'Aghtznik," as one of the envoys sent by Abgar to Marinus.

[9] Tacitus writes this name Sinnaces: see *Ann.*, vi. 31, 32.

[10] Patricius.

[11] These are given at pp. 673 sqq., *infra*.

[12] Quoted in the *Epistle of Addæus, infra.*

[13] Probably "wicked," the meaning being that all such wandering is wilful. Cureton makes "hateful" the *predicate*: "error is abominable in its paths." — TR.

in a rugged country, among the Jews the crucifiers, and the deluded pagans : for with these two parties have ye to fight, in order that ye may show the truth of the faith which ye hold ; and, though ye be silent, your modest and decorous appearance will fight for you against those who hate truth and love falsehood.

"Buffet not the poor in the presence of the rich : for scourge grievous enough for them is their poverty.

"Be not beguiled by the hateful devices of Satan, lest ye be stripped naked of the faith which ye have put on." [1] . . . "And with the Jews, the crucifiers, we will have no fellowship. And this inheritance which we have received from thee we will not let go, but in that will we depart out of this world ; and on the day of our Lord, before the judgment-seat of His righteousness, there will He restore to us this inheritance, even as thou hast told us."

And, when these things had been spoken, Abgar the king rose up, he and his chief men and his nobles, and he went to his palace, all of them being distressed for him because he was dying. And he sent to him noble and excellent apparel, that he might be buried in it. And, when Addæus saw it, he sent to him, *saying :* In my lifetime I have not taken anything from thee, nor will I now at my death take anything from thee, nor will I frustrate the word of Christ which He spake to us : Accept not anything from any man, and possess not anything in this world.[2]

And three days more after these things had been spoken by Addæus the apostle, and he had heard and received the testimony concerning the teaching set forth in their preaching from those engaged with him in the ministry, in the presence of all the nobles he departed out of this world. And that day was the fifth of the week, and the fourteenth of the month Iyar,[3] *nearly answering to May.* And the whole city was in great mourning and bitter anguish for him. Nor was it the Christians only that were distressed for him, but the Jews also, and the pagans, who were in this same town. But Abgar the king was distressed for him more than any one, he and the princes of his kingdom. And in the sadness of his soul he despised and laid aside the magnificence of his kingly state on that day, and with tears mingled with moans he bewailed him with all men. And all the people of the city that saw him were amazed *to see* how greatly he suffered on his account. And with great and

surpassing pomp he bore *him*, and buried him like one of the princes when he dies ; and he laid him in a grand sepulchre adorned with sculpture wrought by the fingers — that in which were laid those of the house of Ariu, the ancestors of Abgar the king : there he laid him sorrowfully, with sadness and great distress. And all the people of the church went there from time to time and prayed fervently ; and they kept up the remembrance of his departure from year to year, according to the command and direction which had been received by them from Addæus the apostle,[4] and according to the word of Aggæus, who himself became Guide and Ruler, and the successor of his seat after him, by the ordination to the priesthood which he had received from him in the presence of all men.

He too, with the same ordination which he had received from him, made Priests and Guides in the whole of this country of Mesopotamia. For they also, in like manner as Addæus the apostle, held fast his word, and listened to and received *it*, as good and faithful successors of the apostle of the adorable Christ. But silver and gold he took not from any man, nor did the gifts of the princes come near him : for, instead of *receiving* gold and silver, he *himself* enriched the Church of Christ with the souls of believers.

Moreover, *as regards* the entire state [5] of the men and the women, they were chaste and circumspect, and holy and pure : for they lived like anchorites [6] and chastely, without spot — in circumspect watchfulness touching the ministry, in their sympathy [7] toward the poor, in their visitations to the sick : for their footsteps were fraught with praise from those who saw *them*, and their conduct was arrayed in commendation from strangers — so that even the priests of the house of [8] Nebu and Bel divided the honour with them at all times, by reason of their dignified aspect, their truthful words, their frankness of speech arising from their noble nature, which was neither subservient through covetousness nor in bondage under *the fear of* blame. For there was no one who saw them that did not run to meet them, that he might salute them respectfully, because the very sight of them shed peace upon the beholders : for just like a net [9] were their words of gentleness spread over the contumacious, and they entered within the fold of truth and verity. For there was no man who saw them that was

---

[1] One leaf apparently is lost from the MS. in this place.
What follows appears to be part of the reply of those addressed — their " testimony concerning the teaching set forth in their preaching." — TR.
[2] The reference seems to be to Matt. x. 7-10.
[3] May. The death of Addæus occurred before that of Abgar, which took place A.D. 45. It would appear, therefore, that his ministry at Edessa lasted about ten or eleven years.

[4] Compare the *Teaching of the Apostles*, Ord. xviii. p. 669, *infra*.
[5] This seems to apply to those who especially belonged to the ministry of the Church.
This is the only passage in the Documents in which women are spoken of as connected with the ministry. — TR. [The estate of deaconesses was of Apostolic foundation. Rom. xvi. 1.]
[6] The reference is only to their purity of life. It is not implied that they lived in seclusion. — TR.
[7] Lit. " their burden-bearing." — TR.
[8] Or " belonging to." — TR.
[9] An allusion to Matt. iv. 19: " I will make you fishers of men."

ashamed of them, because they did nothing that was not accordant with rectitude and propriety. And in consequence of these things their bearing was fearless as they published their teaching to all men. For, whatsoever they said to others and enjoined on them, they themselves exhibited in practice in their own persons ; and the hearers, who saw that their actions went along with their words, without much persuasion became their disciples, and confessed the King Christ, praising God for having turned them towards Him.

And some years after the death of Abgar the king, there arose one of his contumacious [1] sons, who was not favourable to peace ; and he sent *word* to Aggæus, as he was sitting in the church : Make me a headband of gold, such as thou usedst to make for my fathers in former times. Aggæus sent to him : I will not give up the ministry of Christ, which was committed to me by the disciple of Christ, and make a headband of wickedness. And, when he saw that he did not comply, he sent and brake his legs [2] as he was sitting in the church expounding. And as he was dying he adjured Palut and Abshelama : In this house, for whose truth's sake, lo ! I am dying, lay me and bury me. And, even as he had adjured *them*, so did they lay him — inside the middle door of the church, between the men and the women. And there was great and bitter mourning in all the church, and in all the city — over and above the anguish and the mourning which there had been within *the church*, such as had been the mourning when Addæus the apostle himself died.

And,[3] in consequence of his dying suddenly and quickly at the breaking of his legs, he was not able to lay *his* hand upon Palut. Palut went to Antioch, and received ordination to the priesthood from Serapion bishop of Antioch ; by which Serapion himself also ordination had been received from Zephyrinus bishop of the city of Rome, in the succession of the ordination to the priesthood from Simon Cephas, who had received *it* from our Lord, and was bishop there in Rome twenty-five years in the days of the Cæsar who reigned there thirteen years.

And, according to the custom which exists in the kingdom of Abgar the king, and in all kingdoms, that whatsoever the king commands and whatsoever is spoken in his presence is committed to writing and deposited among the records, so also did Labubna,[4] son of Senac, son of Ebedshaddai, the king's scribe, write these things also relating to Addæus the apostle from the beginning to the end, whilst Hanan also the Tabularius, a sharir of the kings, set-to his hand in witness, and deposited *the writing* among the records of the kings, where the ordinances and laws are deposited, and where *the contracts of* the buyers and sellers are kept with care, without any negligence whatever.

Here endeth the teaching of Addæus the apostle, which he proclaimed in Edessa, the faithful city of Abgar, the faithful king.

---

[1] i.e., refusing to accept Christianity: as a few lines before. — Tʀ. The person referred to would seem to be the second of the two sons of Abgar called Maanu, who succeeded his brother Maanu, and reigned fourteen years — from A.D. 52 to A.D. 65, according to Dionysius as cited by Assemani.

[2] This ignominious mode of execution, which was employed in the case of the two thieves at Calvary, seems to have been of Roman origin. The object of the king in putting Aggæus to this kind of death was, probably, to degrade and disgrace him.

[3] This paragraph is a barefaced interpolation made by some ignorant person much later, who is also responsible for the additions to the *Martyrdom of Sharbil*, and to that of Barsamya. For this Palut was made *Elder* by Addæus himself, at the time that Aggæus was appointed *Bishop*, or *Guide and Ruler*. This took place even before the death of Abgar, who died A.D. 45; whereas Serapion did not become bishop of Antioch till the beginning of the third century, if, as is here stated, he was consecrated by Zephyrinus, who did not become Bishop of Rome till A.D. 201.

[4] Moses Chor., ii. 36, calls him, in the translation of Le Vaillant de Florival, "Ghéroupna, fils de l'écrivain Apchatar;" in that of Whiston, "Lerubnas, Apsadari scribæ filius." Apchatar of the first, and Apsadar of the second, translator are evidently corruptions in the Armenian from the Adbshaddai (= Ebedshaddai) of the Syriac. Dr. Alishan, in a letter to Dr. Cureton from the Armenian Convent of St. Lazarus, Venice, says he has found an Armenian ms., of probably the twelfth century, which he believes to be a translation of the present Syriac original. It is a history of Abgar and Thaddæus, written by Ghérubnia with the assistance of Ananias (= Hanan), confidant (= sharir) of King Abgar.

SYRIAC CALENDAR.

A NOTE BY THE TRANSLATOR. — The following list of the Syrian names of months, in use in the empire and during the era of the Seleucidæ, several of which have been mentioned in these Documents, is taken from *Caswinii Calendarium Syriacum*, edited in Arabic and Latin by Volck, 1859. The later Hebrew names also are here added for comparison. It must, however, be noticed that " the years employed *in the Syrian Calendar*, were, at least after the incarnation, Julian years, composed of Roman months." (See *L'Art de vérifier les dates:* Paris, 1818, tom. i. p. 45.) The correspondence with the Hebrew months, therefore, is not so close as the names would indicate, since these commenced with the new moons, and an intercalary month, Veadar, following their twelfth month Adar, was added.

	SYRIAN.	HEBREW.
October	Tishri prior.	Tishri, or Ethanim.
November	Tishri posterior.	Bull, or Marcheshvan.
December	Canun prior.	Chisleu.
January	Canun posterior.	Tebeth.
February	Shubat.	Shebat.
March	Adar.	Adar.
April	Nisan.	Nisan.
May	Ajar.	Zif, or Iyar.
June	Chaziran.	Sivan.
July	Tamuz.	Tammuz.
August	Ab.	Ab.
September	Elul.	Elul.

ANCIENT SYRIAC DOCUMENTS

THE TEACHING OF THE APOSTLES.[1]

AT that time Christ was taken up to His Father; and how the apostles received the gift of the Spirit; and the Ordinances and Laws of the Church; and whither each one of the apostles went; and from whence the countries in the territory of the Romans received the ordination to the priesthood.

In the year three hundred and[2] thirty-nine of the kingdom of the Greeks, in the month Heziran,[3] on the fourth[4] day of the same, which is the first day of the week, and the end of Pentecost[5] — on the selfsame day came the disciples from Nazareth of Galilee, where the conception of our Lord was announced, to the mount which is called that of the Place of Olives,[6] our Lord being with them, but not being visible to them. And at the time of early dawn our Lord lifted up His hands, and laid them upon the heads of the eleven disciples, and gave to them the gift of the priesthood. And suddenly a bright cloud received Him. And they saw Him as He was going up to heaven. And He sat down on the right hand of[4] His Father. And they praised God because they saw His ascension according as He had told them; and they rejoiced because they had received the Right Hand conferring on them the priesthood of the house of Moses and Aaron.

And from thence they went up *to the city*, and[7] proceeded to an upper room — that in which our Lord had observed the passover with them, and the place where the inquiries had been made: Who it was that should betray our Lord to the crucifiers? There also were *made* the inquiries:[8] How they should preach His Gospel in the world? And, as within the upper room the mystery of the body and of the blood of our Lord began to prevail in the world, so also from thence did the teaching of His preaching begin to have authority in the world.

And, when the disciples were cast into this perplexity, how they should preach His Gospel to *men of* strange tongues[8] which were unknown to them, and were speaking thus to one another: Although we are confident that Christ will perform by our hands mighty works and miracles in the presence of strange peoples whose tongues we know not, and who themselves also are unversed in our tongue, *yet* who shall teach them and make them understand that it is by the name of Christ who was crucified that these mighty works and miracles are done? — while, I say, the disciples were occupied with these thoughts, Simon Cephas rose up, and said to them: My brethren, this matter, how we shall preach His Gospel, pertaineth not to us, but to our Lord; for *He* knoweth how it is possible for us to preach His Gospel in the world; and we rely on His care for us, which He promised us, saying: "When I am ascended to my Father I will send you the Spirit, the Paraclete, that *He* may teach you everything which it is meet for you to know, and to make known."

And, whilst Simon Cephas was saying these things to his fellow-apostles, and putting them in remembrance, a mysterious voice was heard by them, and a sweet odour, which was strange to the world, breathed upon them;[9] and tongues of fire, between the voice and the odour, came down from heaven[10] towards them, and alighted and sat on every one of them; and, according to the tongue which every one of them had severally received, so did he prepare himself to go

[1] This work is taken, and printed verbatim, from the same MS. as the preceding, Cod. Add. 14,644, fol. 10. That MS., however, has been carefully compared with another in the Brit. Mus. in which it is found, Cod. Add. 14,531, fol. 109; and with a third, in which the piece is quoted as *Canons of the Apostles*, Cod. Add. 14,173, fol. 37. In using the second, a comparison has also been made of De Lagarde's edition of it (Vienna, 1856). This treatise had also been published before in *Ebediesu Metropolitæ Sobæ et Armeniæ collectio canonum Synodicorum* by Cardinal Mai. It is also cited by Bar Hebræus in his *Nomocanon*, printed by Mai in the same volume. These three texts are referred to in the notes, as A. B. C. respectively. [It seems to me that this and the Bryennios fragment are alike relics of some original older than both. To that of vol. vii. (p. 377) and the *Apostolic Constitutions*, so called, this is a natural preface.]

[2] A. omits " three hundred and." They are supplied from B. The reading of C. is 342.

[3] This month answers to Sivan, which began with the new moon of June. — TR.

[4] C. reads " fourteenth."

[5] The day of Pentecost seems to be put for that of the Ascension.

[6] Syr. " Baith Zaithe." Comp. Luke xxiv. 50 sqq.

[7] Comp. Acts i. 12 sqq.

[8] [It is evident that the apostles had no such ideas until after the vision of St. Peter, Acts x. 9-35.]

[9] The reading of B. and C.; A. reads " answered them."

[10] B. reads " suddenly." [The translator interpolates *upon him*.]

to the country in which that tongue was spoken and heard.

And, by the same gift of the Spirit which was given to them on that day, they appointed Ordinances and Laws — such as were in accordance with the Gospel of their preaching, and with the true and faithful doctrine of their teaching : —

1. The apostles therefore appointed : Pray ye towards the east : [1] because, "as the lightning which lighteneth from the east and is seen even to the west, so shall the coming of the Son of man be : " [2] that by this we might know and understand that He will appear from the east suddenly.[3]

2. The apostles further appointed : On the first *day* of the week let there be service, and the reading of the Holy Scriptures, and the oblation : [4] because on the first day of the week our Lord rose from the place of the dead, and on the first day of the week He arose upon the world, and on the first day of the week He ascended up to heaven, and on the first day of the week He will appear at last with the angels of heaven.[5]

3. The apostles further appointed : On the fourth [6] day of the week let there be service : because on that *day* our Lord made the disclosure to them about His trial,[7] and His suffering, and His crucifixion, and His death, and His resurrection ; and the disciples were on account of this in sorrow.[8]

4. The apostles further appointed : On the eve *of the Sabbath*,[9] at the ninth hour, let there be service : because that which had been spoken on the fourth day of the week about the suffering of the Saviour was brought to pass on the *same* eve ; the worlds and creatures trembling, and the luminaries in the heavens being darkened.

5. The apostles further appointed : Let there be elders and deacons, like the Levites ; [10] and subdeacons,[11] like those who carried the vessels of the court of the sanctuary of the Lord ; and

an overseer,[12] who shall likewise be the Guide of all the people,[13] like Aaron, the head and chief of all the priests and Levites of the whole city.[14]

6. The apostles further appointed : Celebrate the day of the Epiphany [15] of our Saviour, which is the chief of the festivals of the Church, on the sixth day of the latter Canun,[16] in the long number of the Greeks.[17]

7. The apostles further appointed : Forty [18] days before the day of the passion of our Saviour fast ye, and then celebrate the day of the passion, and the day of the resurrection : because our Lord Himself also, the Lord of the festival, fasted forty days ; and Moses and Elijah, who were endued with this mystery, likewise each fasted forty days, and then were glorified.

8. The apostles further appointed : At the conclusion of all the Scriptures *other* let the Gospel be read, as being the seal [19] of all the Scriptures ; and let the people listen to it standing upon their feet : because it is the Gospel of the redemption of all men.

9. The apostles further appointed : At the completion of fifty [20] days after His resurrection make ye a commemoration of His ascension to His glorious Father.

10. The apostles appointed : That, beside the Old Testament, and the Prophets, and the Gospel, and the Acts (of their exploits), nothing should be read on the pulpit in the church.[21]

11. The apostles further appointed : Whosoever is unacquainted with the faith of the Church and the ordinances and laws which are appointed in it, let him not be a guide and ruler ; and whosoever is acquainted with them and departs from them, let him not minister again : because, not being true in his ministry, he has lied.

12. The apostles further appointed : Whosoever sweareth, or [22] lieth, or beareth false witness, or hath recourse to magicians and soothsayers and Chaldeans, and putteth confidence in fates and nativities, which they hold fast who know not God, — let him also, as a man that knoweth not God, be dismissed from the ministry, and not minister *again*.

---

[1] On praying toward the east, comp. *Apost. Constitutions*, ii. 57, vii. 44 ; and Tertullian, *Apol.*, 16.
A. C., ii. 57, contains an interesting account of the conduct of public worship. It may be consulted in connection with Ordinances 2, 8, and 10, also. — TR.
[2] Matt. xxiv. 27.
[3] B. and C. read "at the last." Ebediesu has "from heaven."
[4] i.e., the Eucharist. — TR.
[5] C. reads "His holy angels."
[6] For Ords. 3 and 4, see *Ap. Const.*, v. 13-15.
[7] B. reads "His manifestation."
[8] The reading of C.
This reading is preferable to that of A.: "were in this sorrow." — TR.
[9] Lit. "the evening," but used in particular of the evening of the sixth day of the week, the eve of the seventh: the evening being regarded, as in Gen. i. 5, as the first part of the day. Similarly, παρασκευή, which the Peshito translates by our word, is used in the Gospels for the sixth day, with a prospective reference to the seventh. — TR.
[10] See *Ap. Const.*, ii. 25.
[11] Comp. *Eccl. Canons*, No. 43. The Gr. ὑποδιάκονοι is here used, though for "deacon" the usual Syriac word is employed, meaning "minister" or "servant." From Riddle, *Christian Antiqq.*, p. 301, with whom Neander agrees, it would seem that subdeacons were first appointed at the end of the third century or the beginning of the fourth. — TR. [See vol. v. p. 417.]

[12] ‎ܠܕܘ‎, equivalent, not to ἐπίσκοπος, but to σκοπός = *watchman*, as in Ezek. xxxiii. 7.
[13] For this B. reads "world."
[14] B. has "camp."
[15] See *Ap. Const.*, v. 13.
Christmas, of which no mention is made in these Ordinances, is called "the first of all," the Epiphany being ranked next to it in the *Constitutions*. — TR. [See vol. vii. p. 492.]
[16] January: the Jewish Tebeth. "The former Canun" is December, i.e., Chisleu. — TR.
[17] The era of the Seleucidæ, 311 A.C., appears to be referred to. In this new names were given to certain months, and Canun was one of them. See p. 666, *supra*.
[18] *Eccl. Can.*, No. 69. — TR. See *Ap. Const.*, v. 13-15.
[19] Properly "the sealer:" for, although the word is not found in the lexicons, its formation shows that it denotes an agent. The meaning seems to be, that the Gospel gives completeness and validity to the Scriptures. — TR.
[20] C. reads "forty."
[21] See *Ap. Const.*, ii. 57; *Teaching of Simon Cephas, ad fin ; Eccl. Can.*, Nos. 60, 85. — TR.
[22] B. and C., as well as Ebediesu, read "and."

13. The apostles further appointed: If there be any man that is divided *in mind* touching the ministry, and who follows it not with a stedfast will,[1] let not this man minister again: because the Lord of the ministry is not served by him with a stedfast will; and he deceiveth man *only*, and not God, "before whom crafty devices avail not."[2]

14. The apostles further appointed: Whosoever lendeth and receiveth usury,[3] and is occupied in merchandise and covetousness, let not this man minister again, nor continue in the ministry.

15. The apostles further appointed: That whosoever loveth the Jews,[4] like Iscariot, who was their friend, or the pagans, who worship creatures instead of the Creator, — should not enter in amongst them and minister; and moreover, that if he be *already* amongst them, they should not suffer him *to remain*, but that he should be separated from amongst them, and not minister with them again.

16. The apostles further appointed: That, if any one from the Jews or from the pagans come and join himself with them, and if after he has joined himself with them he turn and go back again to the side on which he stood *before*, and if he again return and come to them a second time, — he should not be received again; but that, according to the side on which he was before, so those who know him should look upon him.

17. The apostles further appointed: That it should not be permitted to the Guide to transact the matters which pertain to the Church apart from those who minister with him; but that he should issue commands with the counsel of them all, and that that *only* should be done which all of them should concur in and not disapprove.[5]

18. The apostles further appointed: Whenever any shall depart out of this world with a good testimony to the faith of Christ, and with affliction *borne* for His name's sake, make ye a commemoration of them on the day on which they were put to death.[6]

19. The apostles further appointed: In the service of the Church repeat ye the praises of David day by day: because of this *saying:* "I will bless the Lord at all times, and at all times His praises *shall be* in my mouth;"[7] and *this:* "By day and by night will I meditate and speak, and cause my voice to be heard before Thee."

20. The apostles further appointed: If any divest themselves of mammon and run not after the gain of money, let these men be chosen and admitted to the ministry of the altar.

21. The apostles further appointed: Let any priest who accidentally puts *another* in bonds[8] contrary to justice receive the punishment that is right; and let him that has been bound receive the bonds as if he had been equitably bound.

22. The apostles further appointed: If it be seen that those who are accustomed to hear causes show partiality, and pronounce the innocent guilty and the guilty innocent, let them never again hear another cause: *thus* receiving the rebuke of their partiality, as it is fit.[9]

23. The apostles further ordained: Let not those that are high-minded and lifted up with the arrogance of boasting be admitted to the ministry: because of this *text:* "That which is exalted among men is abominable before God;" and because concerning them it is said: "I will return a recompense upon those that vaunt themselves."

24. The apostles further appointed: Let there be a Ruler over the elders who are in the villages, and let him be recognised as head of them all, at whose hand all of them shall be required: for Samuel also thus made visits from place to place and ruled.[10]

25. The apostles further appointed: That those kings who shall hereafter believe in Christ should be permitted to go up and stand before the altar along with the Guides of the Church: because David also, and those who were like him, went up and stood before the altar.[11]

26. The apostles further appointed: Let no man dare to do anything by the authority of the priesthood which is not in accordance with justice and equity, but in accordance with justice, and free from the blame of partiality, *let all things be done.*

27. The apostles further appointed: Let the bread of the Oblation be placed upon the altar on the day on which it is baked, and not some days after — a thing which is not permitted.

All these things did the apostles appoint, not

---

[1] Lit. "it is not certain (or firm) to him." — TR.

[2] The exact words of the Peshito of 1 Sam. ii. 3. The E. V., following the K'ri ולו, instead of the ולא of the text, renders "and by Him actions are weighed."

The Peshito translator may have confounded the Heb. verb תכן, which appears not to exist in Aramæan, with its own verb תקן (܏ܩܢ), through the similarity in sound of the gutturals כ and ק. — TR.

[3] See *Eccl. Canons*, No. 44. — TR.

[4] Comp. *Eccl. Canons*, Nos. 65, 70, 71. — TR.

[5] See *Eccl. Canons*, No. 35. — TR.

[6] See the letter of the Church of Smyrna on the martyrdom of Polycarp, and Euseb., *Hist. Eccl.*, iv. 15; [also p. 664, note 4, *supra*].

[7] Ps. xxxiv. 1.

[8] The particip. ܡܫܪܐ, though usually pass., may, like some other participles Peil, be taken actively, as appears from a passage quoted by Dr. R. Payne Smith, *Thes. Syr.*, s.v. This would seem to be the only possible way of taking it here. — TR.

[9] Comp. *Ap. Const.*, ii. 45 sqq.

[10] [Note the Institutions of Samuel, vol. vii. p. 531, and observe the prominence here assigned to that prophet. Comp. Acts iii. 24.]

[11] [But note the case of Ambrose and Theodosius; Sozomen, *Eccl. Hist.*, book vii. cap. 25.]

for themselves, but for those who should come after them — for they were apprehensive that in time to come wolves would put on sheep's clothing : since for themselves the Spirit, the Paraclete, which was in them, was sufficient : that, even as He had appointed these laws by their hands, *so* He would guide them lawfully. For they, who had received from our Lord power and authority, had no need that laws should be appointed for them by others. For Paul also, and Timothy,[1] while they were going from place to place in the country of Syria and Cilicia, committed these same Commands and Laws of the apostles and elders to those who were under the hand of the apostles, for the churches of the countries in which they were preaching and publishing the Gospel.

The disciples, moreover, after they had appointed these Ordinances and Laws, ceased not from the preaching of the Gospel, or from the wonderful mighty-works which our Lord did by their hands. For much people was gathered about them every day, who believed in Christ ; and they came to them from other cities, and heard their words and received them. Nicodemus also, and Gamaliel, chiefs of the synagogue of the Jews, used to come to the apostles in secret, agreeing with their teaching. Judas, moreover, and Levi, and Peri, and Joseph, and Justus, sons of Hananias, and Caïaphas[2] and Alexander the priests — they too used to come to the apostles by night, confessing Christ that He is the Son of God ; but they were afraid of the people of their own nation, so that they did not disclose their mind toward the disciples.

And the apostles received them affectionately, saying to them : Do not, by reason of the shame and fear of men, forfeit your salvation before God, nor have the blood of Christ required of you ; even as your fathers, who took it upon them : for it is not acceptable before God, that, while ye are, *in secret*, with His worshippers, ye should go and associate with the murderers of His adorable Son. How do ye expect that your faith should be accepted with those that are true, whilst ye are with those that are false ? But it becomes you, as men who believe in Christ, to confess openly this faith which we preach.[3]

And, when they heard these things from the Disciples, those sons of the priests, all of them alike, cried out before the whole company of the apostles : We confess and believe in Christ who was crucified, and we confess that He is from everlasting the Son of God ; and those who dared to crucify Him do we renounce. For

even the priests of the people in secret confess Christ ; but, for the sake of the headship among the people which they love, they are not willing to confess openly ; and they have forgotten that which is written : [4] " Of knowledge is He the Lord, and before Him avail not crafty devices."

And, when their fathers heard these things from their sons, they became exceedingly hostile to them : not indeed because they had believed in Christ, but because they had declared and spoken openly of the mind of their fathers before the sons of their people.

But those who believed clave to the disciples, and departed not from them, because they saw that, whatsoever they taught the multitude, they themselves carried into practice before all men ; and, when affliction and persecution arose against the disciples, they rejoiced to be afflicted with them, and received with gladness stripes and imprisonment for the confession of their faith in Christ ; and all the days of their life they preached Christ before the Jews and the Samaritans.

And after the death of the apostles there were Guides and Rulers[5] in the churches ; and, whatsoever the apostles had committed to them and they had received from them, they continued to teach to the multitude through the whole space of their lives. They too, again, at their deaths committed and delivered to their disciples after them whatsoever they had received from the apostles ; also what James had written from Jerusalem, and Simon from the city of Rome, and John from Ephesus, and Mark from Alexandria the Great, and Andrew from Phrygia, and Luke from Macedonia, and Judas Thomas from India : [6] that the epistles of an apostle[7] might be received and read in the churches that were in every place, just as the achievements of their Acts, which Luke wrote, are read ; that hereby the apostles might be known, and the prophets, and the Old Testament and the New ; [8] that *so might be seen* one truth was proclaimed in them all : that one Spirit spake in them all, from one God whom they had all worshipped and had all preached. And the *divers* countries received their teaching. Everything, therefore, which had been spoken by our Lord by means of the apos-

---

[1] Acts xvi. 4; comp. ch. xv.

[2] The belief was common among the Jacobites that Caïaphas, whose full name was Joseph Caïaphas, was the same person as the historian Josephus, and that he was converted to Christianity. See Assem., *Bibl. Orient.*, vol. ii. p. 165.

[3] [The visible Church and sacraments are necessary, on this principle, to the conversion of the world.]

[4] [Perhaps a metaphrase of Job v. 12, 13.]

[5] This would seem to have been written anterior to the time when the title of Bishop, as specially appropriated to those who succeeded to the apostolic office, had generally obtained in the East. [Previously named as in the Greek of 2 Cor. viii. 23.]

[6] For writings ascribed to Andrew and Thomas, see *Apocryphal Scriptures*, this volume, *infra.* Comp. *Eccl. Canons*, No. 85. — TR. There is no mention here of the Epistles of Paul. They may not at this early period have been collected and become generally known in the East. The Epistle of Jude is also omitted here, but it was never received into the Syriac canon: see De Wette, *Einl.*, 6th ed. p. 342.

[7] So the printed text. But " the apostles " seems to be meant. — TR.

[8] See note 10 on p. 668. — TR. It is plain from this that the Epistles were not at that time considered part of what was called the New Testament, nor the prophets of the Old.

tles, and which the apostles had delivered to their disciples, was believed and received in every country, by the operation[1] of our Lord, who said to them: "I am with you, even until the world shall end;" the Guides disputing with the Jews from the books of the prophets, and contending also against the deluded pagans with the terrible mighty-works which they did in the name of Christ. For all the peoples, even those that dwell in other countries, quietly and silently received[2] the Gospel of Christ; and those who became confessors cried out under their persecution: This our persecution to-day shall plead[3] on our behalf, *lest we be punished*, for having been formerly persecutors *ourselves*. For there were some of them against whom death by the sword was ordered; and there were some of them from whom they took away whatsoever they possessed, and let them go.[4] And the more affliction arose against them, the richer and larger did their congregations become; and with gladness in their hearts did they receive death of every kind. And by ordination to the priesthood, which the apostles themselves had received from our Lord, did their Gospel wing its way rapidly into the four quarters of the world. And by mutual visitation they ministered to one another.

1. Jerusalem received the ordination to the priesthood, as did all the country of Palestine, and the parts occupied by the Samaritans, and the parts occupied by the Philistines, and the country of the Arabians, and of Phœnicia, and the people of Cæsarea, from James, who was ruler and guide in the church of the apostles which was built in Zion.

2. Alexandria the Great, and Thebais, and the whole of Inner Egypt, and all the country of Pelusium,[5] and *extending* as far as the borders of the Indians, received the apostles' ordination to the priesthood from Mark the evangelist, who was ruler and guide there in the church which he had built, *in which* he also ministered.

3. India,[6] and all the countries belonging to it and round about it, even to the farthest sea, received the apostles' ordination to the priesthood from Judas Thomas, who was guide and ruler in the church which he had built there, *in which* he also ministered there.

4. Antioch, and Syria, and Cilicia, and Galatia, even to Pontus, received the apostles' ordination to the priesthood from Simon Cephas, who himself laid the foundation of the church there,[7] and was priest and ministered there up

to the time when he went up from thence to Rome on account of Simon the sorcerer, who was deluding the people of Rome with his sorceries.[8]

5. The city of Rome, and all Italy, and Spain, and Britain, and Gaul, together with all the rest of the countries round about them, received the apostles' ordination to the priesthood from Simon Cephas, who went up from Antioch; and he was ruler and guide there, in the church which he had built there, and in the places round about it.[9]

6. Ephesus, and Thessalonica, and all Asia, and all the country of the Corinthians, and of all Achaia and the parts round about it, received the apostles' ordination to the priesthood from John the evangelist, who had leaned upon the bosom of our Lord; who himself built a church there, and ministered in his office of Guide which *he held* there.

7. Nicæa, and Nicomedia, and all the country of Bithynia, and of Inner Galatia,[10] and of the regions round about it, received the apostles' ordination to the priesthood from Andrew, the brother of Simon Cephas, who was himself Guide and Ruler in the church which he had built there, and was priest and ministered there.

8. Byzantium, and all the country of Thrace, and of the parts about it as far as the great river,[11] the boundary which separates from the barbarians, received the apostles' ordination to the priesthood from Luke the apostle, who himself built a church there, and ministered there in his office of Ruler and Guide which *he held* there.

9. Edessa, and all the countries round about it which were on all sides of it, and Zoba,[12] and Arabia, and all the north, and the regions round about it, and the south, and all the regions on the borders of Mesopotamia, received the apostles' ordination to the priesthood from Addæus the apostle, one of the seventy-two apostles,[13] who himself made disciples there, and built a church there, and was priest and ministered there in his office of Guide which *he held* there.

10. The whole of Persia, of the Assyrians, and of the Armenians, and of the Medians, and of the countries round about Babylon, the Huzites and the Gelæ, as far as the borders of the Indians, and as far as the land[14] of Gog and Magog,

---

[1] Lit. "nod," or "bidding," or "impulse." — Tr. [See Tertull., vol iii. p. 252.]
[2] Lit. "were quiet and silent at." — Tr.
[3] Lit. "be an advocate." — Tr.
[4] [Heb. x. 33, 34.]
[5] C. reads "Pentapolis."
[6] A. has "the Indians;" C. "the Ethiopians."
[7] C. adds, "and built a church at Antioch."

[8] See note 3, p. 673, *infra*.
[9] [The omission of reference to St. Paul is a token of a corrupt and mediæval text here.]
[10] The reading of C. The ms. A. gives what Cureton transcribes as Gothia, which is almost the same as the word rendered "Inner." Possibly this explains the origin of the reading of A. "Galatia" was perhaps accidentally omitted. — Tr.
[11] C. has "the Danube."
[12] Or "Soba," the same as Nisïbis.
[13] The number seventy-two may have arisen from the supposition, mentioned in the *Recognitions* and in the *Apostolical Constitutions*, that our Lord chose them in imitation of the seventy-two elders appointed by Moses.
[14] Or "place." — Tr.

and moreover all the countries on all sides, received the apostles' ordination to the priesthood from Aggæus, a maker of silks,[1] the disciple of Addæus the apostle.

The other remaining companions of the apostles, moreover, went to the distant countries of the barbarians; and they made disciples from place to place and passed on ; and there they ministered by their preaching ; and there occurred their departure out of this world, their disciples after them going on *with the work* down to the present day, nor was any change or addition made by them in their preaching.

Luke, moreover, the evangelist had such diligence that he wrote the exploits of the Acts of the Apostles, and the ordinances and laws of the ministry of their priesthood, and whither each one of them went. By his diligence, I say, did Luke write these things, and more than these ; and he placed them in the hand of Priscus[2] and Aquilus, his disciples ; and they accompanied him up to the day of his death, just as Timothy and Erastus of Lystra, and Menaus,[3] the first disciples of the apostles, accompanied Paul until he was taken up to the city of Rome because he had withstood Tertullus the orator.[4]

And Nero Cæsar despatched with the sword Simon Cephas in the city of Rome.[5]

---

[1] See note 6 on p. 661,

[2] B. reads " Priscilla," C. " Priscillas." Prisca and Priscilla are the forms in which the name occurs in the New Testament.

[3] Probably the same as Manaen, mentioned in Acts xiii. 1, as associated with Paul at Antioch.

[4] [The failure to praise the work of him who "laboured more abundantly than all " others, is noteworthy, and can only be accounted for by Middle-Age corruptions of the text.]

[5] C. adds, " crucifying him on a cross." C. also adds, " Here endeth the treatise of Addæus the apostle."

[Possibly the *Duæ Viæ*, etc., followed here, as a second book; vol. vii. p. 377.]

ANCIENT SYRIAC DOCUMENTS

¹ THE TEACHING OF SIMON CEPHAS ² IN THE CITY OF ROME.³

IN the third ⁴ year of Claudius Cæsar, Simon Cephas departed from Antioch to go to Rome. And as he passed on he preached in the *divers* countries the word of our Lord. And, when he had nearly arrived there,⁵ many had heard *of it*, and went out to meet him, and the whole church received him with great joy. And some of the princes of the city, wearers of the imperial head-bands,⁶ came to him, that they might see him and hear his word. And, when the whole city was gathered together about him, he stood up to speak to them, and to show them the preaching of his doctrine, of what sort it was. And he began to speak to them thus : —

Men, people of Rome, saints of all Italy, hear ye that which I say to you. This day I preach and proclaim Jesus the Son of God, who came down from heaven, and became man, and was with us as *one of* ourselves, and wrought marvellous mighty-works and signs and wonders before us, and before all the Jews that are in the land of Palestine. And you yourselves also heard of those things which He did : because they came to Him from other countries also, on account of the fame of His healing and the report of the marvellous help He gave ; ⁷ and whosoever drew near to Him was healed by His word. And, inasmuch as He was God, at the same time that He healed He also forgave sins : for His healing, which was open to view, bore witness of His hidden forgiveness, that it was real and trustworthy. For this Jesus did the prophets announce in their mysterious sayings, as they were looking forward to see Him and to hear His word : Him who was with His Father from eternity and from everlasting ; God, who was hidden in the height, and appeared in the depth ;

the glorious Son, who was from His Progenitor, and is to be glorified, together with His Father, and His divine Spirit, and the terrible power of His dominion. And He was crucified of His own will by the hands of sinners, and was taken up to His Father, even as I and my companions saw. And He is about to come again, in His own glory and that of His holy angels, even as we heard Him say to us. For we cannot say anything which was not heard by us from Him, neither do we write in the book of His Gospel anything which He Himself did not say to us : because this word is spoken in order that ʾ the mouth of liars may be shut, in the day when men shall give an account of idle words at the place of judgment.

Moreover, because we were catchers of ˌfish,⁸ and not skilled in books, therefore did He also say to us : " I will send you the Spirit, the Para-cleťc, that He may teach you that which ye know not ; " for it is by *His* gift that we speak those things which ye hear. And, further, by it we bring aid to the sick, and healing to the diseased : that by the hearing of His word and by the aid of His power ye may believe in Christ, that He is God, the Son of God ; and may be delivered from the service of bondage, and may worship Him and His Father, and glorify His divine Spirit. For when we glorifȳ the Father, we glorify the Son also with Him ; and when we worship the Son, we worship the Father also with Him ; and when we confess the Spirit, we confess the Father also and the Son : because in the name of the Father, and of the Son, and of the Spirit, were we commanded to baptize those who believe, that they may live for ever.

Flee therefore from the words of the wisdom of this world, in which there is no profit, and draw near to those which are true and faithful, and acceptable before God ; whose reward also is laid up in store, and whose recompense standeth *sure*. Now, too,⁹ the light has arisen on the

---

¹ This is found in the same MS. as the preceding, quoted as A. There is also another copy of it in Cod. Add. 14,609, referred to here as B. [It looks like an afterthought of a later age, when the teaching of Peter was elevated into a specialty.]
² B. reads " the Apostle Peter."
³ [This apocryphal history proceeds on the theory that St. Peter *preceded* St. Paul at Rome, which cannot be reconciled with Scripture and chronology. Gal. ii. 9; Rom. i. 5-15.]
⁴ The reading of the MS. is " thirtieth."
⁵ From this place to " the light " (last line of text on this page), A. is lost, and the text has been supplied from B.
⁶ The MS. gives, " clad in the white."
⁷ Lit. " His marvellous helps." — TR. [See p. 652, *supra*.]

⁸ [Mark i. 16-17. Compare Jer xvi. 16.]
⁹ The text A. is resumed after this word. The reading " and now that the light," etc., seems faulty. The ʾ (that) might easily have been occasioned by the ʾ of the word which it precedes. — TR.

creation, and the world has obtained the eyes of the mind, that every man may see and understand that it is not fit that creatures should be worshipped instead of the Creator, nor together with the Creator: because everything which is a creature is *made to be* a worshipper of its Maker, and is not to be worshipped like its Creator. But this *One* who came to us is God, the Son of God, in His own nature, notwithstanding that He mingled [1] His Godhead with our manhood, in order that He might renew our manhood by the aid of His Godhead. And on this account it is right that we should worship Him, because He is to be worshipped together with His Father, and that we should not worship creatures, who were created for the worship of the Creator. For He is Himself the God of truth and verity; He is Himself from before *all* worlds and creatures; He is Himself the veritable Son, and the glorious fruit [2] which is from the exalted Father.

But ye see the wonderful works which accompany and follow these words. One would not credit it: the time lo! is short since He ascended to His Father, and see how His Gospel has winged its flight through the whole creation — that thereby it may be known and believed that He Himself is the Creator of creatures, and that by His bidding creatures subsist. And, whereas ye saw the sun become darkened at His death, ye yourselves also are witnesses. The earth, moreover, quaked when He was slain, and the veil was rent at His death. And concerning these things the governor Pilate also was witness: for he himself sent and made them known to Cæsar, [3] and these things, and more than these, were read before him, and before the princes of your city. And on this account Cæsar was angry against Pilate, because he had unjustly listened to the persuasion of the Jews; and for this reason he sent and took away from him the authority which he had given to him. And this same thing was published and known in all the dominion of the Romans. That, therefore, which Pilate saw and made known to Cæsar and to your honourable senate, the same do I preach and declare, as do also my fellow-apostles. And ye know that Pilate could not have written to the imperial government of that which did not take place and which he had

not seen with his own eyes; but that which did take place and was actually done — this it was that he wrote and made known. Moreover, the watchers of the sepulchre also were witnesses of those things which took place there: they became as dead men; and, when those watchers were questioned before Pilate, they confessed before him how large a bribe the chief-priests of the Jews had given them, so that they might say that we His disciples had stolen the corpse of Christ. Lo! then, ye have heard many things; and moreover, if ye be not willing to be persuaded by those things which ye have heard, be at least persuaded by the mighty-works which ye see, which are done by His name.

Let not Simon the sorcerer delude you by semblances which are not realities, which he exhibits to you, as to men who have no understanding, who know not how to discern that which they see and hear. Send, therefore, and fetch him to where all your city is assembled together, and choose you some sign for us to do before you; and, whichever ye see do that same sign, it will be your part to believe in it.

And immediately they sent and fetched Simon the sorcerer; [4] and the men who were adherents of his opinion said to him: As a man concerning whom we have confidence that there is power in thee to do anything whatsoever, [5] do thou some sign before us all, and let this Simon the Galilæan, who preaches Christ, see *it*. And, whilst they were thus speaking to him, there happened to be passing along a dead person, a son of one of those who were chiefs and men of note and renown among them. And all of them, as they were assembled together, said to him: Whichever of you shall restore to life this dead person, he is true, and to be believed in and received, and we will all follow him in whatsoever he saith to us. And they said to Simon the sorcerer: Because thou wast here before Simon the Galilæan, and we knew thee before him, exhibit thou first the power which accompanieth thee. [6]

Then Simon reluctantly drew near to the dead person; and they set down the bier before him; and he looked to the right hand and to the left, and gazed up into heaven, saying many words: some of them he uttered aloud, and some of them secretly and not aloud. And he delayed a long while, and nothing took place, and nothing was done, and the dead person was lying upon his bier.

And forthwith Simon Cephas drew near boldly towards the dead man, and cried aloud before

---

[1] The word so rendered is much effaced in B., but it seems to be ﺧﻤﺺ, " humbled."

This, however, might require a further change of the text, such as Cureton suggests, so as to give the sense, " He humbled His Godhead *on account of* our manhood," unless we translate " *in* our manhood" — neither of which renderings seems to give so good a sense as that in the text of A. — TR.

Respecting the word "mingled" (ﻣﺰﺝ), which was supposed to countenance the Eutychian heresy, see Assemani, *Bibl. Orient.*, vol. i. p. 81. — TR.

[2] Or "offspring." — TR.

[3] [On the *Acts of Pilate* see Lardner, *Credib.*, vi. p. 605, and Jones, *On the Canon*, vol. ii. p. 342. If Leucius Charinus forged what goes by the name, it does not prove that genuine records of the kind never existed. The reverse is probable. See vol. i. p. 179.]

[4] [Vol vii. p. 453. Compare vol. vi. p. 438, note 15; also vol. i. p. 171. On Justin's simple narrative all the rest was embroidered by a later hand.]

[5] From this place to "a gathering-place," p. 675, line 20, col. 2, the text of A. is lost.

[6] [St. Peter's visit could not have been previous to St. Paul's, and up to that time Simon had certainly not *corrupted* the Romans (Rom. i. 8). The subject may be elucidated by what follows, *infra*.]

all the assembly which was standing there : In the name of Jesus Christ, whom the Jews crucified at Jerusalem, and whom we preach, rise up thence. And as soon as the word of Simon was spoken the dead man came to life and rose up from the bier.

And all the people saw and marvelled ; and they said to Simon : Christ, whom thou preachest, is true. And many cried out, and said : Let Simon the sorcerer and the deceiver of us all be stoned. But Simon, by reason that every one was running to see the dead man that was come to life, escaped from them from one street to another and from house to house, and fell not into their hands on that day.

But the whole city took hold of Simon Cephas, and they received him gladly and affectionately ; and he ceased not from doing signs and wonders in the name of Christ ; and many believed in him. Cuprinus,[1] moreover, the father of him that was restored to life, took Simon with him to his house, and entertained him in a suitable manner, while he and all his household believed in Christ, that He is the Son of the living God. And many of the Jews and of the pagans became disciples there. And, when there was great rejoicing at his teaching, he built churches there, in Rome and in the cities round about, and in all the villages of the people of Italy ; and he served there *in* the rank of the Superintendence of Rulers twenty-five years.[2]

And after these years Nero Cæsar seized him and shut him up in prison. And he knew that he would crucify him ; so he called Ansus,[3] the deacon, and made him bishop in his stead in Rome. And these things did Simon himself speak ; and moreover also the rest, the other things which he had *in charge*, he commanded Ansus to teach before the people, saying to him : Beside the New Testament and the Old let there not be read before the people[4] anything else :[5] which is not right.

And, when Cæsar had commanded that Simon should be crucified with his head downwards, as he himself had requested of Cæsar, and that Paul's head should be taken off, there was great commotion among the people, and bitter distress in all the church, seeing that they were deprived of the sight of the apostles. And Isus the guide arose and took up their bodies by night, and buried them with great honour, and there came tò be a gathering-place there for many.

And at that very time, as if by a righteous judgment, Nero abandoned his empire and fled, and there was a cessation for a little while from the persecution which Nero Cæsar had raised against them. And many years after the great coronation[6] of the apostles, who had departed out of the world, while ordination to the priesthood was proceeding both in all Rome and in all Italy, it happened then that there was a great famine in the city of Rome.[7]

Here endeth the teaching of Simon Cephas.

---

[1] Perhaps Cyprianus, which is found written in Syriac in the same manner as the word here.

[2] This is the time often allotted to Peter's episcopate at Rome, although it is certain that he did not constantly reside there during that period : we find him the year after at Jerusalem. [The chronological incredibility of this residence in Rome has been fully demonstrated ; but it is so entirely inconsistent with the scriptural history, and with that of St. Paul in particular, that no other argument is necessary. On the other hand, it appears to me conclusively established, that St. Peter closed his life in Rome, under Nero. And I think this apostle's visit fully explained by the fact that the Roman Christians were so largely "of the circumcision," that St. Paul himself might naturally have invited him to share his own labours in Rome, on the well-known rule of his conduct (Rom. xv. 20 ; 2 Cor. x. 13-16). See vol. vi. elucid. p. 47.]

[3] B. has Lainus = *Linus*, the person undoubtedly meant. The error arose chiefly from the ⟍ [L] being taken as the sign of the accusative case. Below, the name appears as Isus, and in the *Acts of Barsamya* we have Anus.

This sign of the accusative may be omitted. — TR.

[4] In canon x. (see next note) it is said "in the pulpit of the church ; " and in the *Teaching of Addæus* it is said that "a large multitude of the people assembled for the reading of the Old Testament and the New." The inhibition seems, therefore, to refer only to public reading. [See p. 661, *supra*.]

[5] This agrees with the tenth canon in the *Teaching of the Apostles*. [See p. 668, *supra*.]

[6] That is, their martyrdom. But B. reads "labour."

[7] This abrupt termination seems to indicate that there was something more which followed. The famine referred to seems to be the same as that mentioned in the interpolated passage at the end of the *Acts of Sharbil*.

ANCIENT SYRIAC DOCUMENTS

ACTS OF SHARBIL,[1] WHO WAS A PRIEST OF IDOLS, AND WAS CONVERTED TO THE CONFESSION OF CHRISTIANITY IN CHRIST.[2]

In the fifteenth year of the Sovereign Ruler[3] Trajan Cæsar,[4] and in the third year of King Abgar the Seventh,[5] which is the year 416 of the kingdom of Alexander king of the Greeks, and in the priesthood of Sharbil and Barsamya,[6] Trajan Cæsar commanded the governors of the countries under his dominion that sacrifices and libations should be increased in all the cities of their administration, and that those who did not sacrifice should be seized and delivered over to stripes, and to *the tearing of* combs, and to bitter inflictions of all *kinds of* tortures, and should afterwards receive the punishment of the sword.

Now, when the command arrived at the town of Edessa of the Parthians, there was a great festival, on the eighth of Nisan, on the third *day* of the week: the whole city was gathered together by the great altar[7] which was in the middle of the town, opposite the Record office,[8] all the gods having been brought together, and decorated, and sitting in honour, both Nebu and Bel together with their fellows. And all the priests were offering incense of spices and libations,[9] and an odour of sweetness was diffusing itself around, and sheep and oxen were being slaughtered, and the sound of the harp and the drum was heard in the whole town. And Sharbil was chief and ruler of all the priests; and he was honoured above all his fellows, and was clad in splendid and magnificent vestments; and a headband embossed with figures of gold was set upon his head; and at the bidding of his word everything that he ordered was done. And Abgar the king, son of the gods, was standing at the head of the people. And they obeyed Sharbil, because he drew nearer to all the gods than any of his fellows, and as being the one who *according to* that which he had heard from the gods returned an answer to every man.

And, while these things were being done by the command of the king, Barsamya, the bishop of the Christians, went up to Sharbil, he and Tiridath the elder and Shalula the deacon; and he said to Sharbil, the high priest: The King Christ, to whom belong heaven and earth, will demand an account at thy hands of all these souls against whom thou art sinning, and whom thou art misleading, and turning away from the God of verity and of truth to idols *that are* made and deceitful, which are not able to do anything with their hands — moreover also thou hast no pity on thine own soul, which is destitute of the true life of God; and thou declarest to this people that the dumb idols talk with thee; and, as if thou wert listening to something from them, thou puttest thine ear near to one and another of them, and sayest to this people: The god Nebu bade me say to you, " On account of your sacrifices and oblations I cause peace in this your country;" and: Bel saith, " I cause great plenty in your land;" and those who hear *this* from thee do not discern that thou art greatly deceiving them — because "they have a mouth and speak not, and they have eyes and see not with them;" it is ye who bear up them, and not they who bear up [10] you, as ye suppose; and it is ye who set tables before them, and not

---

[1] There are two MSS. from which this piece is taken. The first is Cod. Add 14,644, fol. 72 vers. This, which is referred to as A., has been copied exactly, except that a few manifest errors have been corrected and some deficiencies supplied from the other. This latter, quoted as B., is Cod. Add. 14,645. It is some three or four centuries later than the first. They were first taken down by shorthand-writers, called *notarii* (notaries), or *exceptores*, by which name they are mentioned towards the end of this extract; the Greeks called them ταχυγράφοι. They were then arranged in proper order by persons called by the Greeks ὑπομνηματογράφοι, and by the Romans *Ab Actis.* — The use of ὑπομνήματα and other Greek words seems to show that these Acts were originally written in that language.

Notaries, i.e., *actuarii*, or at a later day *exceptores.* — Tr.

[2] The Latin *Acta*, to which the Greek ὑπομνήματα here employed corresponds, was used to denote the authorized records of judicial proceedings. — Tr.

[3] Αὐτοκράτωρ. — Tr.

[4] That is, A.D. 112. But the Greek era commences 311 or 312 B.C., and therefore A.G. 416 would answer to A.D. 105. There appears to be some error in the date.

[5] The king reigning in the fifteenth year of Trajan was Maanu Bar Ajazath, the seventh king of Edessa after Abgar the Black.

[6] It would thus appear that Paganism and Christianity were tolerated together in Edessa at this time, equal honour being attributed to the head of each religious party. Cf. *Teaching of Addæus*, p. 661: "Neither did King Abgar compel any man by force to believe in Christ."

[7] A little before the passage quoted in the last note it is said that this altar was left standing when the altars to Bel and Nebu were thrown down.

[8] Perhaps this is the same as the "Archives" mentioned p. 007, note 14.

[9] B. adds, "before the god Zeus."

[10] B. adds here: "And in all these things thou hast forgotten God, the Maker of all men, and because of His long-suffering hast exalted thyself against His mercy, and hast not been willing to turn to Him, so that He might turn to thee and deliver thee from this error, in which thou standest."

they who feed you. And now be persuaded by me touching that which I say to thee and advise thee. If thou be willing to hearken to me, abandon idols made, and worship God the Maker *of all things*, and His Son Jesus Christ. Do not, because He put on a body and became man and was stretched out on the cross of death, be ashamed of Him and refuse to worship Him: for, all these things which He endured — it was for the salvation of men and for their deliverance. For this *One* who put on a body is God, the Son of God, Son of the essence of His Father, and Son of the nature of Him who begat Him : for He is the adorable brightness of His Godhead, and is the glorious manifestation of His majesty, and together with His Father He existed from eternity and from everlasting, His arm, and His right hand, and His power, and His wisdom, and His strength, and the living Spirit which is from Him, the Expiator and Sanctifier of all His worshippers. These *are the* things which Palut taught us, with whom thy venerable self [1] was· acquainted ; and thou knowest that Palut was the disciple of Addæus the apostle. Abgar the king also, who was older than this Abgar, who himself worshippeth idols as well as thou, he too believed in the King Christ, the Son of Him whom thou callest Lord of all the gods.[2] For it is forbidden to Christians to worship anything that is made, and is a creature, and in its nature is not God : even as *ye* worship idols made by men,[3] who themselves also are made and created. Be persuaded, therefore, by these things which I have said to thee, which things are the belief of the Church : for I know that all this population are looking to thee, and I am well assured that, if thou be persuaded, many also will be persuaded with thee.[4]

Sharbil said to him : Very acceptable to me are these thy words which thou hast spoken before me ; yea, exceedingly acceptable are they to me. But, as for me, I know that I am outcast from[5] all these things, and there is no longer any remedy for me. And, now that hope is cut off from me, why weariest thou thyself about a man dead and buried,[6] for whose death there is no hope of resuscitation? For I am slain by paganism, and am become a dead man, *the property* of the Evil One : in sacrifices and libations of imposture have I consumed all the days of my life.

And, when Barsamya the bishop heard these things,[7] he fell down before his feet, and said to him : There *is* hope for those who turn, and healing for those that are wounded. I myself will be surety to thee for the abundant mercies of the Son Christ : that He will pardon thee all the sins which thou hast committed against Him, in that thou hast worshipped and honoured His creatures instead of Himself. For that Gracious One, who extended Himself on the cross of death, will not withhold His grace from the souls that comply *with His precepts* and take refuge in His kindness which has been *displayed* towards us. Like as He did towards the robber, *so* is He able to do to thee, and also to those who are like thee.

Sharbil said to him : Thou, like a skilful physician, who suffers pain from the pain of the afflicted, hast done well in that thou hast been concerned about me. But at present, because it is the festival to-day of this people, of every one *of them*, I cannot go down with thee to-day to the church. Depart thou, and go down with honour ; and to-morrow at night I will come down to thee : I too have henceforth renounced for myself the gods made *with hands*, and I will confess the Lord Christ, the Maker of all men.

And the next day Sharbil arose and went down to Barsamya by night, he and Babai his sister ; and he was received by the whole church. And he said to them : Offer for me prayer and supplication, that Christ may forgive me all the sins that I have committed against Him in all this long course of years. And, because they were in dread of the persecutors, they arose and gave him the seal of salvation,[8] whilst he confessed the Father, and the Son, and the Holy Spirit.[9]

And, when all the city had heard that he was gone down to the church, there began to be a consternation among the multitude ; and they arose and went down to him, and saw him clad in the fashion of the Christians.[10] And he said to them : May the Son Christ forgive me all the sins that I have committed against you, and all *in* which I made you think that the gods talked with me, whereas they did not talk ; and, forasmuch as I have been to you a cause of abomination, may I now be to you a cause of good : instead of worshipping, as formerly, idols made *with hands*, may ye henceforth worship God the Maker. And, when they had heard these things, there remained with him a great congregation

---

[1] Lit. " thy old age." — Tr.
[2] The Peshito, for Ζεύς in Acts xiv. 12, has " Lord of the gods."
[3] B. has " the work of men's hands." [Jer. xvi. 20.]
[4] B. makes a considerable addition here, which it is hardly necessary to quote, the words being in all probability only an interpolation. Cureton elsewhere remarks: " I have almost invariably found in these Syriac MSS. that the older are the shorter, and that subsequent editors or transcribers felt themselves at liberty to add occasionally, or paraphrase the earlier copies which they used " — a remark unhappily of very wide application in regard to early Christian literature. — Tr. [But Cureton is speaking for his pet idea.]
[5] Or " destitute of." — Tr.
[6] Lit. " a hidden dead man." — Tr.

[7] B. adds, " from Sharbil, his tears flowed and he wept."
[8] B. adds, " of baptism, baptizing him."
The " seal " (σφραγίς) is probably explained by such passages as Eph. iv. 30, that which bore the seal being regarded as the property of him whose seal it was. Thus Gregory Naz. (Orat. 40) speaks of baptism. See Riddle's *Christian Antiqq.*, p. 484. — Tr.
[9] [This identifies the " seal " with baptism.]
[10] B. adds, " and he sat and listened to the Scriptures of the Church, and the testimonies which are spoken in them, touching the birth and the passion and the resurrection and the ascension of Christ; and, when he saw those that came down to him — "

of men and of women; and Labu also, and Hafsai, and Barcalba, and Avida, chief persons of the city. They all said to Sharbil: Henceforth we also renounce that which thou hast renounced, and we confess the King Christ, whom thou hast confessed.

But Lysanias,[1] the judge of the country, when he heard[2] that Sharbil had done this,[3] sent by night[4] and carried him off from the church. And there went up with him many Christians. And he sat down, to hear him and to judge him, before the altar which is in the middle of the town, where he used to sacrifice to the gods. And he said to him: Wherefore hast thou renounced the gods, whom thou didst worship, and to whom thou didst sacrifice, and to whom thou wast made chief of the priests, and lo! dost to-day confess Christ, whom thou didst formerly deny? For see how those Christians, to whom thou art gone, renounce not that which they have held,[5] like as thou hast renounced that in which thou wast born. If thou art assured of the gods, how is it that thou hast renounced them this day? But, if on the contrary thou art not assured, as thou declarest concerning them, how is it that thou didst *once* sacrifice to them and worship them?

Sharbil said: When I was blinded in my mind, I worshipped that which I knew not; but to-day, inasmuch as I have obtained the clear eyes of the mind, it is henceforth impossible that I should stumble at carved stones, or that I should any longer be the cause of stumbling to others. For it is a great disgrace to him whose eyes are open, if he goes and falls into the pit of destruction.

The judge said: Because thou hast been priest of the venerable gods, and hast been partaker of the mystery of those whom the mighty emperors[6] worship, I will have patience with thee, in order that thou mayest be persuaded by me, and not turn away from the service of the gods; but, if on the contrary thou shalt not be persuaded by me, by those same gods whom thou hast renounced I swear that, even as on a man that is a murderer, so will I inflict tortures on thee, and will avenge on thee the wrong done to the gods, whom thou hast rebelled against and renounced, and also the insult which thou hast poured upon them; nor will I leave *untried* any kind of tortures which I will not inflict on thee; and, like as thine honour formerly was great, so will I make thine ignominy great this day.

Sharbil said: I too, on my part, am not content that thou shouldest look upon me as formerly, when I worshipped gods made *with hands;* but look thou upon me to-day and question me as a Christian man renouncing idols and confessing the King Christ.

The judge said: How is it that thou art not afraid of the emperors, nor moved to shame by those who are listening to thy trial, that thou sayest, "I am a Christian"? But promise that thou wilt sacrifice to the gods, according to thy former custom, so that thy honour may be great, as formerly — lest I make to tremble at thee all those who have believed like thyself.

Sharbil said: Of the King of kings I am afraid, but at *any* king of earth I tremble not, nor yet at thy threats towards me, which lo! thou utterest against the worshippers of Christ: whom I confessed yesterday, and lo! I am brought to trial for His sake to-day, like as He Himself was brought to trial for the sake of sinners like me.

The judge said: Although thou have no pity on thyself, still I will have pity on thee, and refrain from cutting off those hands of thine with which thou hast placed incense before the gods, and from stopping with thy blood those ears of thine which have heard their mysteries, and thy tongue which has interpreted and explained to us their secret things. Of those *gods* lo! I am afraid, and I have pity on thee. But, if thou continue thus, those gods be my witnesses that I will have no pity on thee!

Sharbil said: As a man who art afraid of the emperors and tremblest at idols, have thou no pity on me. For, as for me, I know not what thou sayest: therefore also is my mind not shaken or terrified by those things which thou sayest. For by thy judgments shall all they escape from the judgment to come who do not worship that which is not God in its own nature.

The judge said: Let him be scourged with thongs,[7] because he has dared to answer me thus, and has resisted the command of the emperors, and has not appreciated the honour which the gods conferred on him: inasmuch as, lo! he has renounced them.

And he was scourged by ten *men,* who laid hold on him, according to the command of the judge.

Sharbil said: Thou art not aware of the scourging of justice in that world which is to come. For thou wilt cease, and thy judgments also will pass away; but justice will not pass away, nor will its retributions come to an end.

---

[1] In B., in a passage added further on, he is styled "Lysinas," and in the *Martyrdom of Barsamya, infra,* "Lysinus" or "Lucinus." In the *Martyrologium Romanum* he is called "Lysias præses." Tillemont supposes him to be Lusius Quietus. But the time does not agree. The capture of Edessa under this man was in the nineteenth year of Trajan, four years later than the martyrdom.
[2] B. adds, "from the Sharirs of the city."
[3] B. has added several lines here.
[4] B. adds, "the Sharirs of the city."
[5] Lit. "in which they stand." — TR.
[6] Lit. "kings:" and so throughout. — TR.

[7] The Syriac is ܛܘܪܝܣ (*toris*), and is a foreign word, probably the Latin *loris,* which the Syriac translator, not understanding it or not having an equivalent, may have written *loris,* and a subsequent transcriber have written *toris.* It is plain that the later copyist to whom the text B. is due did not know what is meant: for he has omitted the word, and substituted "Sharbil."

The judge[1] said : Thou art so intoxicated with this same Christianity, that thou dost not even know[2] before whom thou art judged, and by whom it is that thou art scourged — *even* by those who formerly held thee in honour, and paid adoration to thy priesthood in the gods. Why dost thou hate honour, and love this ignominy? For, although thou speakest contrary to the law, yet I myself cannot turn aside from the laws of the emperors.

Sharbil said : As *thou* takest heed not to depart from the laws of the emperors, and if moreover thou depart *from them* thou knowest what command they will give concerning thee, so do I also take heed not to decline from the law of Him who said, "Thou shalt not worship any image, nor any likeness ; " and therefore will I not sacrifice to idols made *with hands :* for long enough was the time in which I sacrificed to them, when I was in ignorance.

The judge said : Bring not upon thee punishment[3] in addition to the punishment which thou hast *already* brought upon thee. Enough is it for thee to have said, " I will not sacrifice : " do not dare to insult the gods, by calling them *manufactured* idols whom even the emperors honour.

Sharbil said : But, if on behalf of the emperors, who are far away and not near at hand and not conscious of those who treat their commands with contempt, thou biddest me sacrifice, how is it that on behalf of idols, who lo ! are present and are seen, but see not, thou biddest me sacrifice? Why, hereby thou hast declared before all thy attendants[4] that, because they have a mouth and speak not, lo ! thou art become a pleader for them : *dumb idols* " to whom their makers shall be like," and " every one that trusteth upon them " *shall be* like thee.

The judge said : It was not for this that thou wast called before me — that, instead of *paying* the honour which is due, thou shouldst despise the emperors. But draw near to the gods and sacrifice, and have pity on thyself, thou self-despiser !

Sharbil said : Why should it be requisite for thee to ask me many questions, after that which I have said to thee : " I will not sacrifice "? Thou hast called me a self-despiser? But would that from my childhood I had had this mind, and had thus despised myself,[5] which was perishing !

The judge said : Hang him up, and tear him with combs on his sides. — And while he was

thus torn he cried aloud and said : *It is* for the sake of Christ, who has secretly caused His light to arise upon the darkness of my mind. And, when he had thus spoken, the judge commanded again that he should be torn with combs on his face.

Sharbil said : It is better that *thou* shouldest inflict tortures upon me for not sacrificing, than that I should be judged *there* for having sacrificed to the work of men's hands.

The judge said : Let his body be bent backwards, and let straps be tied to his hands and his feet ; and, when he has been bent backwards, let him be scourged on his belly.

And they scourged him in this manner, according to the command of the judge.

Then he commanded that he should go up to the prison, and that he should be cast into a dark dungeon. And the executioners,[6] and the Christians who had come up with him from the church, carried him, because he was not able to walk upon his feet in consequence of his having been bent backwards. And he was in the gaol many days.

But on the second of Ilul,[7] on the third day of the week, the judge arose and went down to his judgment-hall by night ; and the whole body of his attendants was with him ; and he commanded the keeper of the prison, and they brought him before him. And the judge said to him : This long while hast thou been in prison : what has been thy determination concerning those things on which thou wast questioned before me? Dost thou consent to minister to the gods according to thy former custom, agreeably to the command of the emperors?

Sharbil said : This has been my determination in the prison, that that with which I began before thee, I will finish even to the last ; nor will I play false with my word. For I will not again confess idols, which I have renounced ; nor will I renounce the King Christ, whom I have confessed.

The judge said : Hang him up by his right hand, because he has withdrawn it from the gods that he may not again offer incense with it, until his hand with which he ministered to the gods be dislocated, because he persists in this saying of his.

And, while he was suspended by his hand, they asked him and said to him : Dost thou consent to sacrifice to the gods? But he was not able to return them an answer, on account of the dislocation of his arm. And the judge commanded, and they loosed him and took him down. But he was not able to bring his arm up to his side,

---

[1] B. reads " governor " ($\dot\eta\gamma\epsilon\mu\dot\omega\nu$), and so generally in the corresponding places below.
[2] B. reads " discern."
[3] Or " judgment." — Tr.
[4] The word used is the Latin " officium " (= officiales, or corpus officialium — Tr.), which denoted the officers that attended upon presidents and chief magistrates. The equivalent Gk. $\tau\dot\alpha\xi\iota\varsigma$ is used below [in the *Martyrdom of Habib*, " attendants "].
[5] Or " soul." — Tr.

[6] Those who officiated at a " quæstio," or examination by torture. — Tr. The Latin " quæstionarii."
[7] i.e., Heb. אֱלוּל, from the new moon of September to that of October. [See p. 666, *supra.*]

until the executioners pressed it and brought it up to his side.

The judge said: Put on incense, and go whithersoever thou wilt, and no one shall compel thee to be a priest again. But, if thou wilt not, I will show thee *tortures* bitterer than these.

Sharbil said: *As for* gods that made not the heavens and the earth, may they perish from under these heavens! But thou, menace me not with words of threatening; but, instead of words, show upon me the deeds of threatening, that I hear thee not again making mention of the detestable name of gods!

The judge said: Let him be branded with the brand of bitter fire between his eyes and upon his cheeks.

And the executioners did so, until the smell of the branding reeked forth in the midst of the judgment-hall: but he refused to sacrifice.

Sharbil said: Thou hast heard for thyself from me, when I said to thee "Thou art not aware of the smoke of the roasting of the fire which is prepared for those who, like thee, confess idols made *by hands*, and deny the living God, after thy fashion."

The judge said: Who taught thee all these things, that thou shouldest speak before me thus — a man who was a friend of the gods and an enemy of Christ, whereas, lo! thou art become his advocate.

Sharbil said: Christ whom I have confessed, He it is that hath taught me to speak thus. But there needeth not that I should be His advocate, for His own mercies are eloquent advocates for guilty ones like me, and these will avail to plead [1] on my behalf in the day when the sentences shall be eternal.

The judge said: Let him be hanged up, and let him be torn with combs upon his former wounds; also let salt and vinegar be rubbed into the wounds upon his sides. Then he said to him: Renounce not the gods whom thou didst *formerly* confess.

Sharbil said: Have pity on me *and spare me* again from saying that there be gods, and powers, and fates, and nativities. On the contrary, I confess one God, who made the heavens, and the earth, and the seas, and all that is therein; and the Son who is from Him, the King Christ.

The judge said: It is not about this that thou art questioned before me — *viz.*: what is the belief of the Christians which thou hast confessed; but this *is what* I said to thee, "Renounce not those gods to whom thou wast made priest."

Sharbil said: Where is that wisdom of thine and of the emperors of whom thou makest thy boast, that ye worship the work of the hands of the artificers and confess them, whilst the artificers themselves, who made the idols, ye insult by the burdens and imposts which ye lay upon them? The artificer standeth up at thy presence, to do honour to *thee;* and thou standest up in the presence of the work of the artificer, and dost honour it and worship it.

The judge said: Thou art not the man to call *others* to account for [2] these things; but from thyself a strict account is demanded, as to the cause for which thou hast renounced the gods, and refusest to offer them incense like thy fellow-priests.

Sharbil said: Death on account of this is true life: those who confess the King Christ, He also will confess before His glorious Father.

The judge said: Let lighted candles [3] be brought, and let them be passed round about his face and about the sides of his wounds. And they did so a long while.

Sharbil said: It is well that thou burnest me with this fire, that *so* I may be delivered from "that fire which is not quenched, and the worm that dieth not," which is threatened to those [4] who worship things made instead of the Maker: for it is forbidden to the Christians to honour or worship anything except the nature of Him who is God Most High. For that which is made and is created is *designed to be* a worshipper of its Maker, and is not to be worshipped along with its Creator, as thou supposest.

The governor said: It is not this for which the emperors have ordered me to demand an account at thy hands, whether there be judgment and the rendering of an account after the death of men; nor yet about *this* do I care, whether that which is made is to be honoured or not to be honoured. What the emperors have commanded *me* is this: that, whosoever will not sacrifice to the gods and offer incense to them, I should employ against him stripes, and combs, and sharp swords.

Sharbil said: The kings of this world are conscious of this world only; but the King of all kings, He hath revealed and shown to us that there is another world, and a judgment in reserve, in which a recompense will be made, on the one hand to those who have served God, and on the other to those who have not served Him nor confessed Him. Therefore do I cry aloud, that I will not again sacrifice to idols, nor will I offer oblations to devils, nor will I do honour to demons!

The judge said: Let nails of iron be driven in between the eyes of the insolent *fellow*, and let

---

[1] Lit. "to be a plea." — Tr.

[2] Or "thou art not the avenger of." — Tr.
[3] Lit. "candles of fire." — Tr.
[4] The passage from this place to "in the eyes," below, is lost in A., and supplied from B.

him go to that world which he is looking forward to, like a fanatic.[1]

And the executioners did so, the sound of the driving in of the nails being heard as they were being driven in sharply.

Sharbil said: Thou hast driven in nails between my eyes, even as nails were driven into the hands of the glorious Architect of the creation, and by reason of this did all orders of the creation tremble and quake at that season. For these tortures which lo! thou art inflicting on me are nothing in view of that judgment which is to come. For those "whose ways are always firm," because "they have not the judgment of God before their eyes,"[2] and *who* on this account do not even confess that God exists — neither will He confess them.

The judge said: *Thou* sayest in words that there is a judgment; but I will show thee in deeds: so that, instead of that judgment which is to come, thou mayest tremble and be afraid of this one which is before thine eyes, in which lo! thou art involved, and not multiply thy speech before me.

Sharbil said: Whosoever is resolved to set God before his eyes in secret, God will also be at his right hand; and I too am not afraid of thy threats of tortures, with which thou dost menace me and seek to make me afraid.

The judge said: Let Christ, whom thou hast confessed, deliver thee from all the tortures which I have inflicted on thee, and am about further to inflict on thee; and let Him show His deliverance towards thee openly, and save thee out of my hands.

Sharbil said: This is the true deliverance of Christ *imparted* to me — this secret power which He has given me to endure all the tortures thou art inflicting on me, and whatsoever it is settled in thy mind still further to inflict upon me; and, although thou hast plainly seen *it to be* so, thou hast refused to credit my word.

The judge said: Take him away from before me, and let him be hanged upon a beam the contrary way, head downwards; and let him be beaten with whips while he is hanging.

And the executioners did so to him, at the door of the judgment-hall.

Then the governor commanded, and they brought him in before him. And he said to him: Sacrifice to the gods, and do the will of the emperors, thou priest that hatest honour and lovest ignominy instead!

Sharbil said: Why dost thou again repeat thy words, and command me to sacrifice, after the many *times* that thou hast heard from me that I will not sacrifice again? For it is not any *compulsion* on the part of the Christians that has kept me back from sacrifices, but the truth they hold: this it is that has delivered me from the error of paganism.

The judge said: Let him be put into a chest[3] of iron like a murderer, and let him be scourged with thongs like a malefactor.

And the executioners did so, until there remained not a sound place on him.

Sharbil said: *As for* these tortures, which thou supposest to be bitter, out of the midst of their bitterness will spring up for me fountains of deliverance and mercy in the day of the eternal sentences.

The governor said: Let small round pieces of wood be placed between the fingers of his hands,[4] and let these be squeezed upon them vehemently.[5]

And they did so to him, until the blood came out from under the nails of his fingers.

Sharbil said: If thine eye be not satisfied with the tortures of the body, add still further to its tortures whatsoever thou wilt.

The judge said: Let the fingers of his hands be loosed, and make him sit upon the ground; and bind his hands upon his knees, and thrust a piece of wood under his knees, and let it pass over the bands of his hands, and hang him up by his feet, *thus* bent, head downwards; and let him be scourged with thongs.

And they did so to him.

Sharbil said: They cannot conquer who fight against God, nor may they be overcome whose confidence is God; and therefore do I say, that "neither fire nor sword, nor death nor life, nor height nor depth, can separate my heart from the love of God, which is in our Lord Jesus Christ."

The judge said: Make hot a ball of lead and of brass, and place it under his armpits.

And they did so, until his ribs began to be seen.

Sharbil said: The tortures thou dost inflict upon me are too little for thy rage against me — unless thy rage were little and thy tortures were great.

The judge said: Thou wilt not hurry me on by these things which thou sayest; for I have room in my mind[6] to bear long *with thee*, and to behold every evil and shocking and bitter thing

---

[1] Or "dealer in fables," if the word employed here, which is a foreign one, be the Latin "fabularius," which is not certain.

[2] Ps. x. 5.— Tr.

[3] So Cureton. Dr. Payne Smith remarks: "Cureton's 'chest' is a guess from ‎ܟܐܣܐ‎.. The only sense of ‎ܟܣ‎ with which I am acquainted is *cadus*, a cask." The word occurs again in the *Martyrdom of Habib*. In both places it seems to refer to some contrivance for *holding fast* the person to be scourged. The root appears to be ‎ܟܣ‎, *custodivit, retinuit* (Castel). — Tr.

[4] The martyr Minias, about A.D. 240, had the same torture inflicted on him: "ligneis verubus præacutis sub ungues ejus infixis, omnes digitos ejus præcepit pertundi." See Surius, *Sanct. Vit.* Not "the same," perhaps. — Tr.

[5] Or "bitterly." — Tr.

[6] Here a few lines have been torn out of A., and are supplied from B.

which [1] I shall exhibit in the torment of thy body, because thou wilt not consent to sacrifice to the gods whom thou didst *formerly* worship.

Sharbil said: Those things which I have said and repeated before thee, thou in thine unbelief knowest not how to hear: now, supposest thou that thou knowest those things which are in my mind?

The judge said: The answers which thou givest will not help thee, but will multiply upon thee inflictions manifold.

Sharbil said: If the several stories of thy several gods are by thee accepted as true, *yet* is it matter of shame to us to tell of what sort they are. For one had intercourse with boys, which is not right; and another fell in love with a maiden, who fled for refuge into a tree, as your shameful stories tell.

The judge said: This *fellow*, who was formerly a respecter of the gods, but has now turned to insult them and has not been afraid, and has also despised the command of the emperors and has not trembled — set him to stand upon a gridiron [2] heated with fire.

And the executioners did so, until the under part of his feet was burnt off.

Sharbil said: If thy rage is excited at *my mention of* the abominable and obscene tales of thy gods, how much more does it become thee to be ashamed of their acts! For lo! if a person were to do what one of thy gods did, and they were to bring him before thee, thou wouldest pass sentence of death upon him.

The judge said: This day will I bring thee to account for thy blasphemy against the gods, and thine audacity in insulting also the emperors; nor will I leave thee alone until thou offer incense to them, according to thy former custom.

Sharbil said: Stand by thy threats, then, and speak not falsely; and show towards me in deeds the authority of the emperors which they have given thee; and do not thyself bring reproach on the emperors with thy falsehood, and be thyself also despised in the eyes of thine attendants!

The judge said: Thy blasphemy against the gods and thine audacity towards the emperors have brought upon thee these tortures which thou art undergoing; and, if thou add further to thine audacity, there shall be further added to thee inflictions bitterer than these.

Sharbil said: Thou hast authority, as judge: do whatsoever thou wilt, and show no pity.

The judge said: How can he that hath had no pity on his own body, so as to avoid suffering in it these tortures, be afraid or ashamed of not obeying the command of the emperors?

Sharbil said: Thou hast well said that I am not ashamed: because near at hand is He that justifieth me, and my soul is caught up in rapture towards him. For, whereas I *once* provoked Him to anger by the sacrifices of idols, I am this day pacifying Him by the inflictions *I endure* in my person: for my soul is a captive to God who became man.

The judge said: It is a captive, then, that I am questioning, and a madman without sense; and with a dead man who is burnt, lo! am I talking.

Sharbil said: If thou art assured that I am mad, question me no further: for it is a madman that is being questioned; nay, rather, I am a dead man who is burnt, as thou hast said.

The judge said: How shall I count thee a dead man, when lo! thou hast cried aloud, "I will not sacrifice?"

Sharbil said: I myself, too, know not how to return thee an answer, since thou hast called me a dead man and *yet* turnest to question me again as if alive.

The judge said: Well have I called thee a dead man, because thy feet are burnt and thou carest not, and thy face is scorched and thou holdest thy peace, and nails are driven in between thine eyes and thou takest no account of it, and thy ribs are seen between the *furrows of the* combs and thou insultest the emperors, and thy whole body is mangled and maimed with stripes and thou blasphemest against the gods; and, because thou hatest thy body, lo! thou sayest whatsoever pleaseth thee.

Sharbil said: If thou callest *me* audacious because I have endured these things, it is fit that thou, who hast inflicted them upon me, shouldest be called a murderer in thy acts and a blasphemer in thy words.

The judge said: Lo! thou hast insulted the emperors, and likewise the gods; and lo! thou insultest me also, in order that I may pronounce sentence of death upon thee quickly. But instead of this, which thou lookest for, I am prepared yet further to inflict upon thee bitter and severe tortures.

Sharbil said: Thou knowest what I have said to thee many times: instead of denunciations of threatening, proceed to show upon me the performance of the threat, that thou mayest be known to do the will of the emperors.

The judge said: Let him be torn with combs upon his legs and upon the sides of his thighs.

And the executioners did so, until his blood flowed and ran down upon the ground.

Sharbil said: Thou hast well done in treating me thus: because I have heard that one of the

---

[1] "Which" is not in the printed text. — Tr.
[2] The word used looks like a corruption of the Latin *craticula*. Eusebius, *Hist. Eccl.* v. 1, uses the Gk. word for this (τήγανον) in describing the martyrdom of Attalus, who "was set in the τήγανον, and scorched all over, till the savour of his burnt flesh ascended from his body."

teachers of the Church hath said,[1] "Scars *are* on my body, that I may come to the resurrection from the place of the dead." Me too, who was a dead man out of sight, lo! thine inflictions bring to life again.

The judge said: Let him be torn with combs on his face, since he is not ashamed of the nails which are driven in between his eyes.

And they tore him with combs upon his cheeks, and between the nails which were driven into them.

Sharbil said: I will not obey the emperors, who command that to be worshipped and honoured which is not of the nature of God, and is not God in its nature, but is the work of him that made it.

The judge said: Like as the emperors worship, so also worship thou; and that honour which the judges render, do thou render also.

Sharbil said: Even though *I* insult that which is the work of men and has no perception and no feeling of anything, *yet* do not *thou* insult God, the Maker of all, nor worship along with Him that which is not of Him, and is foreign to His nature.

The judge said: Does this your doctrine so teach you, that you should insult the very luminaries which give light to all the regions of the earth?

Sharbil said: Although it is not enjoined upon us to insult them, yet it is enjoined upon us not to worship them nor honour them, seeing that they are things made: for this were an insufferable [2] wrong, that a thing made should be worshipped along with its Maker; and it is an insult to the Maker that His creatures should be honoured along with Himself.

The judge said: Christ whom thou confessest was hanged on a tree; and on a tree will I hang thee, like thy Master.

And they hanged him on a tree [3] a long while.

Sharbil said: *As for* Christ, whom lo! thou mockest — see how thy many gods were unable to stand before Him: for lo! they are despised and rejected, and are made a laughing-stock and a jest by those who used formerly to worship them.

The judge said: How is it that thou renouncest the gods, and confessest Christ, who was hanged on a tree?

Sharbil said: This cross of Christ is the great boast of the Christians, since it is by this that the deliverance of salvation has come to all His worshippers, and by this that they have had their eyes enlightened, so as not to worship creatures along with the Creator.

The governor said: Let thy boasting of the cross be kept within thy own mind, and let incense be offered by thy hands to the gods.

Sharbil said: Those who have been delivered by the cross cannot any longer worship and serve the idols of error made *with hands:* for creature cannot worship creature, because it is itself also *designed to be* a worshipper of Him who made it; and that it should be worshipped along with its Maker is an insult to its Maker, as I have said before.

The governor said: Leave alone thy books which have taught thee *to speak* thus, and perform the command of the emperors, that thou die not by the emperors' law.

But Sharbil said: Is this, then, the justice of the emperors, in whom thou takest such pride, that we should leave alone the law of God and keep their laws?

The governor said: The citation of the books in which thou believest, and from which thou hast quoted — it is this which has brought upon thee these afflictions: for, if thou hadst offered incense to the gods, great would have been thine honour, like as it was formerly, as priest of gods.

Sharbil said: To thine unbelieving heart these things seem as if they were afflictions; but to the true heart "affliction imparts patience, and from it *comes* also experience, and from experience likewise the hope" [4] of the confessor.[5]

The governor said: Hang him up and tear him with combs upon his former wounds.

And, from the fury with which the judge urged on the executioners, his very bowels were almost seen. And, lest he should die under the combs and escape from still further tortures, he gave orders and they took him down.

And, when the judge saw that he was become silent and was not able to return him any further answer, he refrained from him a little while, until he began to revive.

Sharbil said: Why hast thou had pity upon me for even this little time, and kept me back from the gain of a confessor's death? [5]

The governor said: I have not had pity on thee at all in refraining for a little while: thy silence it was that made me pause a little; and, if I had power beyond the law of the emperors, I should like to lay *other* tortures upon thee, so as to be more fully avenged on thee for thine insult toward the gods: for in despising me thou hast despised the gods; and I, on my part, have borne with thee and tortured thee thus, as a man who so deserves.

And the judge gave orders, and suddenly the curtain [6] fell before him for a short time; and

---

1 [St. Paul's *Stigmata*. Gal. vi. 17; Phil. iii. 11.]
2 Or "bitter." — Tr.
3 Or "beam." — Tr.

4 Rom. v. 4. — Tr.
5 Lit. "of confessorship." — Tr.
6 The Latin "velum," or rather its plur. "vela."

he settled and drew up the sentence [1] which he should pronounce against him publicly.

And suddenly the curtain was drawn back again; and the judge cried aloud and said: As regards this Sharbil, who was formerly priest of the gods, but has turned this day and renounced the gods, and has cried aloud "I am a Christian," and has not trembled at the gods, but has insulted them; and, further, has not been afraid of the emperors *and* their command; and, though I have bidden him sacrifice to the gods according to his former custom, has not sacrificed, but has treated them with the greatest insult: I have looked *into the matter*, and decided, that towards a man who doeth these things, even though he were *now* to sacrifice, it is not fit that any mercy should be shown; and that it is not fit that he should *any longer* behold the sun of his lords, because he has scorned their laws. I give sentence that, according to the law of the emperors, a strap [2] be thrust into the mouth of the insulter, as into the mouth of a murderer, and that he depart outside of the city of the emperors with haste, as one who has insulted the lords of the city and the gods who hold authority over it. I give sentence that he be sawn with a saw of wood, and that, when he is near to die, then his head be taken off with the sword of the headsmen.

And forthwith a strap was thrust into his mouth with all speed, and the executioners hurried him off, and made him run quickly upon his burnt feet, and took him away outside of the city, a crowd of people running after him. For they had been standing looking on at his trial all day, and wondering that he did not suffer under his afflictions: for his countenance, which was cheerful, testified to the joy of his heart. And, when the executioners arrived at the place where he was to receive the punishment of death, the people of the city were with them, that they might see whether they did according as the judge had commanded, and hear what Sharbil might say at that season, so that they might inform the judge of the country.

And they offered him some wine to drink, according to the custom of murderers to drink. But he said to them: I will not drink, because I wish to feel the saw with which ye saw me, and the sword which ye pass over my neck; but instead of this wine, which will not be of any use to me, give me a little time to pray, while ye stand. And he stood up, and looked toward the east,[3] and lifted up his voice and said: Forgive me, Christ, all the sins I have committed against Thee, and all *the times in* which I have

provoked Thee to anger by the polluted sacrifices of dead idols; and have pity on me and save me,[4] and deliver me from the judgment to come; and be merciful to me, as Thou wast merciful to the robber; and receive me like the penitents who have been converted and have turned to Thee, as Thou also hast turned to them; and, whereas I have entered into Thy vineyard, at the eleventh hour, instead of judgment, deliver me from justice: let Thy death, which was for the sake of sinners, restore to life again my slain body in the day of Thy coming.

And, when the Sharirs of the city heard these things, they were very angry with the executioners for having given him leave to pray.

And, while the nails were remaining which had been driven in between his eyes, and his ribs were seen between the *wounds of the* combs, and while from the burning on his sides and the soles of his feet, which were scorched and burnt, and from the *gashes of the* combs on his face, and on his sides, and on his thighs, and on his legs, the blood was flowing and running down, they brought carpenters' instruments, and thrust him into a wooden vice, and tightened it upon him until the bones of his joints creaked with the pressure; then they put upon him a saw of iron, and began sawing him asunder; and, when he was just about to die, because the saw had reached to his mouth, they smote him with the sword and took off his head, while he was still squeezed down in the vice.

And Babai his sister drew near and spread out her skirt and caught his blood; and she said to him: May my spirit be united with thy spirit in the presence of Christ, whom thou hast known and believed.

And the Sharirs of the city ran and came and informed the judge of the things which Sharbil had uttered in his prayer, and how his sister had caught his blood. And the judge commanded them to return and give orders to the executioners that, on the spot where she had caught the blood of her brother, she also should receive the punishment of death. And the executioners laid hold on her, and each one of them severally put her to torture; and, with her brother's blood upon her, her soul took its flight from her, and they mingled her blood with his. And, when the executioners were entered into the city, the brethren and young men [5] ran and stole away their two corpses; and they laid them in the burial-place of the father of Abshelama the bishop, on the fifth of Ilul, the eve *of the Sabbath*.

I wrote these Acts on paper — I, Marinus, and Anatolus, the notaries; and we placed them

---

[1] The Gk. ἀπόφασις.
[2] This expression χαλινὸν ἐμβαλεῖν is used similarly in the life of Euthymus in *Eccl. Grœc. Monumenta*, vol. ii. p. 240.
[3] See *Teaching of the Apostles*, Ord. 1, p. 668, note 1. — Tr.

[4] Lit. "have pity on my salvation." — Tr.
[5] By a transposition of letters, B. reads "laics."

in the archives of the city, where the papers of the kings are placed.[1]

This Barsamya,[2] the bishop, made a disciple of Sharbil the priest. And he lived in the days of Binus,[3] bishop of Rome ; in whose days the whole population of Rome assembled together, and cried out to the prætor[4] of their city, and said to him : There are too many strangers in this our city, and these cause famine and dearness of everything : but we beseech thee to command them to depart out of the city. And, when he had commanded them to depart out of the city, these strangers assembled themselves together, and said to the prætor : We beseech thee, my lord, command also that the bones of our dead may depart with us. And he commanded them to take the bones of their dead, and to depart. And all the strangers assembled themselves together to take the bones of Simon Cephas and of Paul, the apostles ; but the people of Rome said to them : We will not give you the bones of

the apostles. And the strangers said to them : Learn ye and understand that Simon, who is called Cephas, is of Bethsaida of Galilee, and Paul the apostle is of Tarsus, a city of Cilicia. And, when the people of Rome knew that this matter was so, then they let them alone. And, when they had taken them up and were removing them from their places, immediately there was a great earthquake ; and the buildings of the city were on the point of falling down, and *the city* was near being overthrown. And, when the people of Rome saw it, they turned and besought the strangers to remain in their city, and that the bones might be laid in their places *again*. And, when the bones of the apostles were returned to their places, there was quietness, and the earthquakes ceased, and the winds became still, and the air became bright, and the whole city became cheerful. And, when the Jews and pagans saw it, they also ran and fell at the feet of Fabianus, the bishop of their city, the Jews crying out : We confess Christ, whom we crucified : He is the Son of the living God, of whom the prophets spoke in their mysteries. And the pagans also cried out and said to him : We renounce idols and carved images, which are of no use, and we believe in Jesus the King, the Son of God, who has come and is to come again. And, whatever other doctrines there were in Rome and in all Italy, *the followers of* these also renounced their doctrines, like as the pagans had renounced theirs, and confessed the Gospel of the apostles, which was preached in the church.

Here end the Acts of Sharbil the confessor.

---

[1] B. has several lines here in addition.
[2] The passage hence to the end is evidently a later addition by a person unacquainted with chronology : for it is stated at the beginning of these Acts that the transactions took place in the fifteenth year of Trajan, A.D. 112 ; but Fabianus (see next note) was not made bishop of Rome till the reign of Maximinus Thrax, about the year 236. [An index of the history of this postscript.]
[3] B. reads "Fabianus:" in A. the first syllable, or rather letter, has been dropped. — The mention of Fabianus probably arose from the fact of his having instituted notaries for the express purpose of searching for and collecting the Acts of Martyrs.
[4] The Greek ἔπαρχος. — TR.

FURTHER, THE MARTYRDOM OF BARSAMYA,[1] THE BISHOP OF THE BLESSED CITY EDESSA.

In the year four hundred and sixteen of the kingdom of the Greeks, that is the fifteenth year of the reign of the sovereign ruler, our lord, Trajan Cæsar, in the consulship of Commodus and Cyrillus,[2] in the month Ilul, on the fifth day of the month, the day after Lysinus,[3] the judge of the country, had heard *the case of* Sharbil the priest ; as the judge was sitting in his judgment-hall, the Sharirs of the city came before him and said to him : We give information before thine Excellency concerning Barsamya, the leader of the Christians, that he went up to Sharbil, the priest, as he was standing and ministering before the venerable gods, and sent and called him to him secretly, and spoke to him, *quoting* from the books in which he reads in the church where their congregation meets, and recited to him the belief of the Christians, and said to him, " It is not right for thee to worship many gods, but *only* one God, and His Son Jesus Christ " — until he made him a disciple,

and induced him to renounce the gods whom he had formerly worshipped ; and by means of Sharbil himself also many have become disciples, and are gone down to the church, and lo ! this day they confess Christ ; and even Avida, and Nebo,[4] and Barcalba, and Hafsai, honourable and chief persons of the city, have yielded to Sharbil in this. We, accordingly, as Sharirs of the city, make *this* known before thine Excellency, in order that we may not receive punishment as offenders for not having declared before thine Excellency the things which were spoken in secret to Sharbil by Barsamya the guide of the church. Thine Excellency now knoweth what it is right to command in respect of this said matter.

And, immediately that the judge heard these things, he sent the Sharirs of the city, and some of his attendants with them, to go down to the church and bring up Barsamya from the church. And they led him and brought him up to the judgment-hall of the judge ; and there went up many Christians with him, saying : We also will die with Barsamya, because we too are of one mind with him in respect to the doctrine of

---

[1] This is taken from the MS. cited as B. in the *Acts of Sharbil.* There is an Armenian version or extract of this still in existence: see Dr. Alishan's letter referred to on p. 665. [See elucidation, p. 689, *infra.*]
[2] This is a mistake for Cerealis, and the consulate meant must be that of Commodus Verus and Tutilius Cerealis, which was in the ninth (not fifteenth) year of Trajan, which agrees with the 416th year of the Greeks, or A.D. 105.
[3] See note on p. 678.
[4] Called Labu at p. 678.

which he made Sharbil a disciple, and in all that he spoke to him, and in all *the instruction* that Sharbil received from him, so that he was persuaded by him, and died for the sake of that which he heard from him.

And the Sharirs of the city came, and said to the judge : Barsamya, as thine Excellency commanded, lo ! is standing at the door of the judgment-hall of thy Lordship ;[1] and honourable chief-persons of the city, who became disciples along with Sharbil, lo ! are standing by Barsamya, and crying out, "We will all die with Barsamya, who is our teacher and guide."

And, when the judge heard those things which the Sharirs of the city had told him, he commanded them to go out and write down the names of the persons who were crying out, "We will die with Barsamya." And, when they went out to write down *the names of* these persons, those who so cried out were too many for them, and they were not able to write down their names, because they were so many : for the cry kept coming to them from all sides, that they "would die for Christ's sake along with Barsamya."

And, when the tumult of the crowd became great, the Sharirs of the city turned back, and came in to the judge, and said to him : We are not able to write down the names of the persons who are crying aloud outside, because they are too many to be numbered. And the judge commanded that Barsamya should be taken up to the prison, so that the crowd might be dispersed which was collected together about him, lest through the tumult of the multitude there should be some mischief in the city. And, when he went up the gaol, those who had become disciples along with Sharbil continued with him.

And after many days were passed the judge rose up in the morning and went down to his judgment-hall, in order that he might hear *the case of* Barsamya. And the judge commanded, and they brought him from the prison ; and he came in and stood before him. The officers said : Lo, he standeth before thine Excellency.

The judge said : Art thou Barsamya, who hast been made ruler and guide of the people of the Christians, and didst make a disciple of Sharbil, who was chief-priest of the gods, and used to worship them ?

Barsamya said : It is I who have done this, and I do not deny it ; and I am prepared to die for the truth of this.

The judge said : How is it that thou wast not afraid of the command of the emperors, *so* that, when the emperors commanded that every one should sacrifice, thou didst induce Sharbil, when he was standing and sacrificing to the gods and offering incense to them, to deny that which he had confessed, and confess Christ whom he had denied ?

Barsamya said : I was assuredly[2] made a shepherd of men, not for the sake of those only who are found, but also for the sake of those who have strayed from the fold of truth, and become food for the wolves of paganism ; and, had I not sought to make Sharbil a disciple, at my hands would his blood have been required ; and, if he had not listened to me, I should have been innocent of his blood.

The judge said : Now, therefore, since thou hast confessed that it was thou that madest Sharbil a disciple, at thy hands will I require his death ; and on this account it is right that thou rather than he shouldest be condemned before me, because by thy hands he has died the horrible deaths of grievous tortures for having abandoned the command of the emperors and obeyed thy words.

Barsamya said : Not to my words did Sharbil become a disciple, but to the word of God which He spoke : "Thou shalt not worship images and the likenesses of men." And it is not I alone that am content to die the death of Sharbil for his confession of Christ, but also all the Christians, members of the Church, are likewise eager for this, because they know that they will secure their salvation before God thereby.

The judge said : Answer me not in this manner, like Sharbil thy disciple, lest thine own torments be worse than his ; but promise that thou wilt sacrifice before the gods on his behalf.

Barsamya said : Sharbil, who knew not God, I taught to know *Him :* and dost thou bid *me*, who have known God from my youth, to renounce God ? God forbid that I should do this thing !

The judge said : Ye have made the whole creation disciples of the teaching of Christ ; and lo ! they renounce the many gods whom the many worshipped. Give up this way of thinking,[3] lest I make those who are near tremble at thee as they behold thee to-day, and those also that are afar off as they hear of the torments to which thou art condemned.

Barsamya said : If God is the help of those who pray to Him, who is he that can resist them ? Or what is the power that can prevail against them ? Or thine own threats—what can they do to them : to men who, before thou give commandment concerning them that they shall die, have their death *already* set before their eyes, and are expecting it every day ?

The judge said : Bring not the subject of Christ before my judgment-seat ; but, instead of this, obey the command of the emperors, who command to sacrifice to the gods.

---

[1] Lit. "authority."—Tr.

[2] See note 6 on p. 658.—Tr.　[The Syriac for "assuredly."]
[3] Lit. "this mind."—Tr.

Barsamya said: Even though we should not lay the subject of Christ before thee, *yet* the sufferings of Christ are portrayed indelibly [1] in the worshippers of Christ; and, even more than thou hearkenest to the commands of the emperors, do we Christians hearken to the commands of Christ the King of kings.

The judge said: Lo! thou hast obeyed Christ and worshipped him up to his day: henceforth obey the emperors, and worship the gods whom the emperors worship.

Barsamya said: How canst thou bid me renounce that in which I was born? when lo! thou didst exact *punishment* for this at the hand of Sharbil, and saidst to him: Why hast thou renounced the paganism in which thou wast born, and confessed Christianity to which thou wast a stranger? Lo! even before I came into thy presence thou didst thyself give testimony *on the matter* beforehand, and saidst to Sharbil: The Christians, to whom thou art gone *over*, do not renounce that in which they were born, but continue in it. Abide, therefore, by the word, which thou hast spoken.

The judge said: Let Barsamya be scourged, because he has rebelled against the command of the emperors, and has caused those also who were obedient to the emperors to rebel with him.

And, when he had been scourged by five *men*, he said to him: Reject not the command of the emperors, nor insult the emperors' gods.

Barsamya said: Thy mind is greatly blinded, O judge, and so also is that of the emperors who gave thee authority; nor are the things that are manifest seen by you; nor do ye perceive that lo! the whole creation worships Christ; and thou sayest to me, Do not worship Him, as if I alone worshipped Him — Him whom the watchers [2] above worship on high.

The judge said: But if *ye* have taught *men* to worship Christ, who·is it that has persuaded those above to worship Christ?

Barsamya said: Those above have themselves preached, and have taught those below concerning the living worship of the King Christ, seeing that they worship Him, and His Father, together with His divine Spirit. [3]

The judge said: Give up these things which your writings teach you, and which ye teach also to others, and obey those things which the emperors have commanded, and spurn not their laws — lest ye be spurned by means of the sword from the light of this venerable sun.

Barsamya said: The light which passeth away and abideth not is not the true light, but is *only* the similitude of that true light, to whose beams

darkness cometh not near, which is reserved and standeth fast for the true worshippers of Christ.

The judge said: Speak not before me of anything *else* instead of that about which I have asked thee, lest I dismiss thee from life to death, for denying this light which is seen and confessing that which is not seen.

Barsamya said: I cannot leave alone that about which thou askest me, and speak of that about which thou dost not ask me. It was thou that spakest to me about the light of the sun, and I said before thee that there is a light on high which surpasses in its brightness that of the sun which thou dost worship and honour. For an account will be required of thee for worshipping thy fellow-*creature* instead of God thy Creator.

The judge said: Do not insult the very sun, the light of creatures, nor set thou at nought the command of the emperors, nor contentiously resist the lords of the country, who have authority in it.

Barsamya said: Of what avail is the light of the sun to a blind man that cannot see it? For without the eyes of the body, it is not possible for its beams to be seen. *So* that by this thou mayest know that it is the work of God, forasmuch as it has no power *of its own* to show its light to the sightless.

The judge said: When I have tortured thee as thou deservest, then will I write word about thee to the Imperial government, *reporting* what insult thou hast offered to the gods, in that thou madest a disciple of Sharbil the priest, one who honoured the gods, and that ye despise the laws of the emperors, and that ye make no account of the judges of the countries, and live like barbarians, *though* under the authority of the Romans.

Barsamya said: Thou dost not terrify me by these things which thou sayest. It is true, I am not in the presence of the emperors to-day; yet lo! before the authority which the emperors have given thee I am now standing, and I am brought to trial, because I said, I will not renounce God, to whom the heavens and the earth belong, nor His Son Jesus Christ, the King of all the earth.

The judge said: If thou art indeed assured of this, that thou art standing and being tried before the authority of the emperors, obey their commands, and rebel not against their laws, lest like a rebel thou receive the punishment of death.

Barsamya said: But if those who rebel against the emperors, *even* when they justly rebel, are deserving of death, as thou sayest; for those who rebel against God, the King of kings, even the punishment of death by the sword is too little.

The judge said: It was not that thou shouldest

---

[1] Lit. "portrayed and fixed." — TR.
[2] [Guardian angels.] Comp. Dan. iv. 13. This designation was given to angels after the captivity, in which the Jews had become familiar with the doctrine of tutelary deities. — TR.
[3] Lit. "the Spirit of His Godhead." — TR.

expound in my judgment-hall that thou wast brought in before me, because the trial on which thou standest has but little concern with expounding, but much concern with the punishment of death, for those who insult the emperors and comply not with their laws.

Barsamya said: Because God is not before your eyes, and ye refuse to hear the word of God; and graven images that are of no use, "which have a mouth and speak not," are accounted by you as though they spake, because your understanding is blinded by the darkness of paganism in which ye stand —

The judge *interrupting* said: Leave off those things thou art saying, for they will not help thee at all, and worship the gods, before the bitter *tearings of* combs and harsh tortures come upon thee.

Barsamya said: Do thou *too* leave off the many questions which lo! thou askest me, and give command for the stripes and the combs with which thou dost menace me: for thy words will not help thee so much as thy inflictions will help me.

The judge said: Let Barsamya be hanged up and torn with combs.

And at that very moment there came to him letters from Alusis[1] the chief proconsul, father of emperors.[2] And he commanded, and they took down Barsamya, and he was not torn with combs; and they took him outside of the hall of judgment.

And the judge commanded that the nobles, and the chief persons, and the princes, and the honourable persons of the city, should come before him, that they might hear what was the order that was issued by the emperors, by the hand of the proconsuls, the rulers of the countries under the authority of the Romans. And it was found that the emperors had written by the hand of the proconsuls to the judges of the countries:[3] "Since our Majesty commanded that there should be a persecution against the people of the Christians, we have heard and learned, from the Sharirs whom we have in the countries under the dominion of our Majesty, that the people of the Christians are persons who eschew murder, and sorcery, and adultery, and theft, and bribery and fraud, and those things for which the laws of our Majesty also exact punishment from those who commit them. We, therefore, in our impartial justice, have commanded that on account of these things the persecution of the sword shall cease from them, and that there shall be rest and quietness in all our dominions, they continuing

to minister according to their custom and no man hindering them. It is not, however, towards them that we show clemency, but towards their laws, agreeing as they do with the laws of our Majesty. And, if any man hinder them after this our command, that sword which is ordered by us to descend upon those who despise our command, the same do we command to descend upon those who despise this decree of our clemency."

And, when this command of the emperor's clemency was read, the whole city rejoiced that there was quietness and rest for every man. And the judge commanded, and they released Barsamya, that he might go down to his church. And the Christians went up in great numbers to the judgment-hall, together with a great multitude of the population of the city, and they received Barsamya with great and exceeding honour, repeating psalms before him, according to their custom; *there went* also the wives of the chief of the wise men. And they thronged *about him*, and saluted him, and called him "the persecuted confessor," "the companion of Sharbil the martyr." And he said to them: Persecuted I am, like yourselves; but from the tortures and combs of Sharbil and his companions I am clean escaped.[4] And they said to him: We have heard from thee that a teacher of the Church has said, "The will, according to what it is, so is it accepted."[5] And, when he was entered into the church, he and all the people that were with him, he stood up and prayed, and blessed them and sent them away to their homes rejoicing and praising God for the deliverance which He had wrought for them and for the Church.

And the day after Lysinas[6] the judge of the country had set his hand to these Acts, he was dismissed from his authority.

I Zenophilus and Patrophilus are the notaries who wrote these Acts, Diodorus and Euterpes,[7] Sharirs of the city, bearing witness with us by setting-to their hand, as the ancient laws of the ancient kings command.

This[8] Barsamya, bishop of Edessa, who made a disciple of Sharbil, the priest of the same city, lived in the days of Fabianus, bishop of the city of Rome. And ordination to the priesthood was received by Barsamya from Abshelama, who was bishop in Edessa; and by Abshelama ordination was received from Palut the First; and by Palut ordination was received from Serapion, bishop of Antioch; and by Serapion ordination was received from Zephyrinus, bishop of Rome; and Zephyrinus of Rome received ordination from Victor of the

---

[1] This seems to be *Lusius* Quietus, Trajan's general in the East at this time.

[2] Or "kings." — TR.

[3] We have here probably the most authentic copy of the edict of Trajan commanding the stopping of the persecution of the Christians, as it was taken down at the time by the reporters who heard it read.

[4] Lit. "am far removed." — TR.

[5] 2 Cor. viii. 12. Both the Peshito and the Greek (if τίς be rejected) have "what it *hath*:" not "what it *is*." — TR.

[6] See note on p 678. — TR.

[7] Perhaps "Eutropius."

[8] What follows, down to the end, is a much later addition, evidently made by the same ignorant person as that at p. 685, above: see note 2 there.

same place, *viz.*, Rome; and Victor received ordination from Eleutherius; and Eleutherius received it from Soter; and Soter received it from Anicetus; and Anicetus received it from Dapius;[1] and Dapius received it from Telesphorus; and Telesphorus received it from Xystus;[2] and Xystus received it from Alexander; and Alexander received it from Evartis;[3] and Evartis received it from Cletus; and Cletus received it from Anus;[4] and Anus received it from Simon Cephas; and Simon Cephas received it from our Lord, together with his fellow-apostles, on the first day of the week, *the day* of the ascension of our Lord to His glorious Father,

which was the fourth day of Heziran,[5] which was *in* the nineteenth[6] year of the reign of Tiberius Cæsar, in the consulship of Rufus and Rubelinus, which year was the year 341; for in the year 309 occurred the advent[7] of our Saviour in the world, according to the testimony which we ourselves have found in a correct register[8] among the archives, which errs not at all in whatever it sets forth.

Here endeth the martyrdom of Barsamya, bishop of Edessa.

---

[1] That is "Pius." The blunder arose from taking the prefix D (?) as a part of the name.
[2] i.e., "Sixtus." — Tr.
[3] Or "Eortis." The person referred to is "Evaristus." Cureton reads "Erastus:" it does not appear why. — Tr.
[4] i.e., "Linus:" see p. 675, note 3. — Tr.

[5] See note 3 on p. 667. — Tr. [Also see p. 666, *supra*.]
[6] Put by mistake for "sixteenth," which agrees with the statement of Julius Africanus as to the date of our Lord's death; also with the year of the consulate of Rubellius Geminus and Fufius Geminus (the persons intended below), and with the year of the Greeks 341, which was A.D. 29 or 30.
[7] Prop. "rising," as of the sun. — Tr.
[8] The Greek εἰλητάριον: see Du Fresne, *Glossarium*.

ELUCIDATION

(See p. 665, note 4. Also, p. 685, note 1, of Barsamya.)

I FOUND at the Armenian Convent of St. Lazarus, near Venice, a version of the *Letter of Abgar*, translated into French "from the Armenian version of the fifth century," and published in 1868, which is now before me. It ascribes the original to *Laboubnia*, and adds: "The name *Léroubna*, mentioned only by *Moses of Chorène*, was not repeated after him by any one else, save, perhaps, *Mekhitar d'Aïrivank* (one of our chroniclers of the thirteenth century), who puts him among our historians, between *Tatien* and *Mar Ibas Gadina*, but without affirming whether he knew him only by name or also by his writings." The editor goes on to speak of his correspondence with Dr. Cureton (A.D. 1864) which is referred to in note 4, p. 665, *supra*. He notes the incomplete and mutilated character of the Syriac copies used by Cureton, and congratulates himself on the entire and integral condition of the Armenian, which he found in 1852 in the Imperial Library at Paris, as *Codex No. 88, MSS. Armen.* Here the name of the author is given as *Laboubnia*, and agrees with the Syriac. The interpolations he regards as made after the fourth century.

ANCIENT SYRIAC DOCUMENTS

MARTYRDOM OF HABIB THE DEACON.[1]

In the month Ab,[2] of the year six hundred and twenty of the kingdom of Alexander the Macedonian, in the consulate of Licinius and Constantine,[3] which is the year in which he[4] was born, in the magistracy[5] of Julius and Barak, in the days of Cona[6] bishop of Edessa, Licinius made a persecution against the Church and all the people of the Christians, after that first persecution which Diocletian the emperor had made. And Licinius the emperor commanded that there should be sacrifices and libations, and that the altars in every place should be restored, that they might burn sweet spices and frankincense before Zeus.

And, when many were persecuted, they cried out of their own accord: We are Christians; and they were not afraid of the persecution, because these who were persecuted were more numerous than those who persecuted *them*.

Now Habib, who was of the village of Telzeha[7] and had been made a deacon, went secretly into the churches which were in the villages, and ministered and read the Scriptures, and encouraged and strengthened many by his words, and admonished them to stand fast in the truth of their belief, and not to be afraid of the persecutors; and gave them directions.

And, when many were strengthened by his words, and received his addresses affectionately, being careful not to renounce the covenant they had made, and when the Sharirs of the city, the men who had been appointed with reference to this particular matter, heard of it, they went in and informed Lysanias, the governor who was in the town of Edessa, and said to him: Habib, who is a deacon in the village of Telzeha, goes about and ministers secretly in every place, and resists the command of the emperors, and is not afraid.

And, when the governor heard these things, he was filled with rage against Habib; and he made a report, and sent and informed Licinius the emperor of all those things which Habib was doing; *he wished* also to ascertain[8] what command would be issued respecting him and *the rest of* those who would not sacrifice. *For* although a command had been issued that every one should sacrifice, yet it had not been commanded what should be done to those who did not sacrifice: because they had heard that Constantine, the commander[9] in Gaul and Spain, was become a Christian and did not sacrifice. And Licinius the emperor *thus* command Lysanias the governor: Whoever it is that has been so daring as to transgress our command, our Majesty has commanded that he shall be burned[10] with fire; and that all others who do not consent to sacrifice shall be put to death by the sword.

Now, when this command came to the town of Edessa, Habib, in reference to whom the report had been made, was gone across *the river* to the country of the people of Zeugma,[11] to minister there also secretly. And, when the governor sent and inquired for him in his village, and in all the country round about, and he was not to be found, he commanded that all his family should be arrested, and also the inhabitants of his village; and they arrested them and put them in irons, his mother and the rest of his family, and also some of the people of his village; and they brought them to the city, and shut them up in prison.

And, when Habib heard what had taken place, he considered in his mind and pondered anxiously in his thoughts: It is expedient for me, *said he*, that I should go and appear before the judge of the country, rather than that I should remain in secret and others should be brought in *to him* and be crowned *with martyrdom* be-

[1] This is found in the same MS. as the preceding: Cod. Add. 14,-645, fol. 238, vers.
[2] August. — TR.
[3] They were consuls together in A.D. 312, 313, 315.
[4] It does not appear who is meant. — TR.
[5] The Greek στρατηγία, with a Syriac termination. Στρατηγοί was used for the Latin *Magistratus* or *Duumviri*
[6] He laid the foundation of the church at Edessa A.D. 313: see Assem., *Bibl. Orient.*, vol. i. p. 394.
[7] Called "Thelsæa" by Metaphrastes, p. 700, *infra*.

[8] Lit. "learn and see." — TR.
[9] The word used is probably ἐντολικός = *præfectus*: see Dr. Payne Smith, *Thes. Syr.* — TR.
[10] Dr. Wright's reading, by the change of a letter, for "shall perish." — TR.
[11] This place was on the right bank of the Euphrates, and derived its name from a bridge of boats laid across the river there. It was about forty miles from Edessa. — TR.

cause of me, and that I should find myself in great shame. For in what respect will the name of Christianity help him who flees from the confession of Christianity? Lo! if he flee from this, the death of nature is before him whithersoever he goes, and escape from it he cannot, because this is decreed against all the children of Adam.

And Habib arose and went to Edessa secretly, having prepared his back for the stripes and his sides for the combs, and his person for the burning of fire. And he went immediately [1] to Theotecna,[2] a veteran [3] who was chief of the band of attendants [4] on the governor; and he said to him: I am Habib of Telzeha, whom ye are inquiring for. And Theotecna said to him: If so be that no one saw thee coming to me, hearken to me in what I say to thee, and depart and go away to the place where thou hast been, and remain there in this time *of persecution;* and of this, that thou camest to me and spakest with me and that I advised thee thus, let no one know or be aware. And about thy family and the inhabitants of thy village, be not at all anxious: for no one will at all hurt them; but they will be in prison a few days only, and *then* the governor will let them go: because against them the emperors have not commanded anything serious or alarming. But, if on the contrary thou wilt not be persuaded by me in regard to these things which I have said to thee, I am clear of thy blood: because, if so be that thou appear before the judge of the country, thou wilt not escape from death by fire, according to the command of the emperors which they have issued concerning thee.

Habib said to Theotecna: It is not about my family and the inhabitants of my village that I am concerned, but for my own salvation, lest it should be forfeited. About this too I am much distressed, that I did not happen to be in my village on the day that the governor inquired for me, and that on my account lo! many are put in irons, and I have been looked upon by him as a fugitive. Therefore, if so be that thou wilt not consent to my request and take me in before the governor, I will go alone and appear before him.

And, when Theotecna heard him speak thus to him, he laid hold of him firmly, and handed him over to his assistants,[5] and they went together to conduct him to the judgment-hall of the governor. And Theotecna went in and informed the governor, and said to him: Habib of Telzeha, whom thine Excellency was inquir-

ing for, is come. And the governor said: Who is it that has brought him? and where did they find him? and what did he do where he was? Theotecna said to him: He came hither himself, of his own accord, and without the compulsion of any one, since no one knew anything about him.

And when the governor heard *this*, he was greatly exasperated against him; and thus he spake: This *fellow*, who has so acted, has shown great contempt towards me and has despised me, and has accounted me as no judge; and, because he has so acted, it is not meet that any mercy should be shown towards him; nor yet either that I should hasten to pass sentence of death against him, according to the command of the emperors concerning him; but it is meet for me to have patience with him, so that the bitter torments and punishments *inflicted on him* may be the more abundant, and that through him I may terrify many *others* from daring again to flee.

And, many persons being collected together and standing by him at the door of the judgment-hall, some of whom were members of the body of attendants, and some people of the city, there were some of them that said to him: Thou hast done badly in coming and showing thyself to those who were inquiring for thee, without the compulsion of the judge; and there were *others*, again, who said to him: Thou hast done well in coming and showing thyself of thine own accord, rather than that the compulsion of the judge should bring thee: for now is thy confession of Christ known to be of thine own will, and not from the compulsion of men.

And those things which the Sharirs of the city had heard from those who were speaking to him as they stood at the door of the judgment-hall — and this circumstance also in particular, that he had gone secretly to Theotecna and that he had not been willing to denounce him, had been heard by the Sharirs of the city — everything that they had heard they made known to the judge.

And the judge was enraged against those who had been saying to Habib: Wherefore didst thou come and show thyself to the judge, without the compulsion of the judge himself? And to Theotecna he said: It is not seemly for a man who has been made chief over his fellows to act deceitfully in this manner towards his superior, and to set at nought the command of the emperors, which they issued against Habib the rebel, that he should be burned with fire.

Theotecna said: I have not acted deceitfully against my fellows, neither was it my purpose to set at nought the command which the emperors have issued: for what am I before thine Excellency, that I should have dared to do this? But I strictly questioned him as to that for which

---

[1] Cureton has ܐܝܟ, which he renders "alone." Dr. Payne Smith considers this a mistake for ܝܢ ܒܪ.—TR.

[2] In Latin, "Theotecnus."
[3] Or "an old man."—TR.
[4] The Gk. τάξις here used corresponds to the Latin *officium.* See note 4 on p. 679.
[5] Or "domestics."—TR.

thine Excellency also has demanded an account at my hands, that I might know and see whether it was of his own free will that he came hither, or whether the compulsion of thine Excellency brought him by the hand of others ; and, when I heard from him that he came of his own accord, I carefully brought him to the honourable door of the judgment-hall of thy Worship.[1]

And the governor hastily commanded, and they brought in Habib before him. The officers said : Lo ! he standeth before thine Excellency.

And he began to question him thus, and said to him : What is thy name? And whence art thou? And what art thou?

He said to him : My name is Habib, and I am from the village of Telzeha, and I have been made a deacon.

The governor said : Wherefore hast thou transgressed the command of the emperors, and dost minister in thine office of deacon, which thou art forbidden by the emperors to do, and refusest to sacrifice to Zeus, whom the emperors worship?

Habib said : We are Christians : we do not worship the works of men, who are nothing, whose works also are nothing ; but we worship God, who made the men.

The governor said : Persist not in that daring mind with which thou art come into my presence, and insult not Zeus, the great boast of the emperors.

Habib said : But this Zeus is an idol, the work of men. It is very well for thee to say that I insult him. But, if the carving of him out of wood and the fixing of him with nails proclaim aloud concerning him that he is made, how sayest thou to me that I insult him? since lo ! his insult is from himself, and against himself.

The governor said : By this very thing, that thou refusest to worship him, thou insultest him.

Habib said : But, if because I do not worship him I insult him, how great an insult, then, did the carpenter inflict on him, who carved him with an axe of iron ; and the smith, who smote him and fixed him with nails !

And, when the governor heard him speak thus, he commanded him to be scourged without pity. And, when he had been scourged by five *men*, he said to him : Wilt thou now obey the emperors? For, if thou wilt not obey *them*, I will tear thee severely with combs, and I will torture thee with all *kinds of* tortures, and then at last I will give command concerning thee that thou be burned with fire.

Habib said : These threats with which lo ! thou art seeking to terrify me, are much meaner and paltrier than those which I had already set-

tled it in my mind to endure : therefore[2] came I and made my appearance before thee.

The governor said : Put him into the iron cask[3] for murderers, and let him be scourged as he deserves. And, when he had been scourged, they said to him : Sacrifice to the gods. But he cried aloud, and said : Accursed are your idols, and so are they who join with you in worshipping them like you.

And the governor commanded, and they took him up to the prison ; but they refused him permission to speak with his family, or with the inhabitants of his village, according to the command of the judge. On that day was the festival of the emperors.

And on the second of Ilul the governor commanded, and they brought him from the prison. And he said to him : Wilt thou renounce the profession thou hast made[4] and obey the command which the emperors issue? For, if thou wilt not obey, with the bitter tearings of combs will I make thee obey them.

Habib said : I have not obeyed them, and morever it is settled in my mind that I will not obey them — no, not even if thou lay upon me punishments still worse than those which the emperors have commanded.

The governor said : By the gods I swear, that, if thou do not sacrifice, I will leave no harsh and bitter *sufferings untried* with which I will not torture thee : and we shall see whether Christ, whom thou worshippest, will deliver thee.

Habib said : All those who worship Christ are delivered through Christ, because they worship not creatures along with the Creator of creatures.

The governor said : Let him be stretched out and be scourged with whips, until there remain not a place in his body on which he has not been scourged.

Habib said : *As for* these inflictions, which thou supposest to be *so* bitter with their lacerations,[5] out of them are plaited crowns of victory for those who endure them.

The governor said : How call ye afflictions ease, and account the torments of your bodies a crown of victory?

Habib said : It is not for thee to ask me concerning these things, because thine unbelief is not worthy to hear the reasons of them. That I will not sacrifice I have said *already*, and I say *so still*.

The governor said : Thou art subjected to these punishments because thou deservest them : I will put out thine eyes, which look upon this Zeus and are not afraid of him ; and I will stop thine ears, which hear the laws of the emperors and tremble not.

---

[1] Lit. " rectitude."—Tr.

[2] Lit. " then."—Tr.
[3] See note 3 on p. 681.—Tr.
[4] Lit. " Wilt thou renounce that in which thou standest?"—Tr.
[5] Lit. " scourgings."—Tr.

Habib said: To the God whom thou deniest here belongs that other world; and there wilt thou *be made to* confess Him with scourgings, though thou hast again denied Him.

The governor said: Leave alone that world of which thou hast spoken, and consider anxiously now, that from this punishment to which lo! thou art being subjected there is no one that can deliver thee; unless indeed the gods deliver thee, on thy sacrificing to them.

Habib said: Those who die for the sake of the name of Christ, and worship not those objects that are made and created, will find their life in the presence of God;[1] but those who love the life of time more than that — their torment will be for ever.

And the governor commanded, and they hanged him up and tore him with combs; and, while they were tearing him with the combs, they knocked him about. And he was hanging a long while, until the shoulderblades of his arms creaked.

The governor said to him: Wilt thou comply even now, and put on incense before Zeus there?[2]

Habib said: Previously to these sufferings I did not comply with thy demands: *and* now that lo! I have undergone them, how thinkest thou that I shall comply, and thereby lose that which I have gained by them?

The governor said: By punishments fiercer and bitterer than these I am prepared to make thee obey, according to the command of the emperors, until thou do their will.

Habib said: Thou art punishing me for not obeying the command of the emperors, when lo! thou thyself also, whom the emperors have raised to greatness and made a judge, hast transgressed their command, in that thou hast not done to me that which the emperors have commanded thee.

The governor said: Because I have had patience with thee, *therefore* hast thou spoken thus, like a man that brings an accusation.

Habib said: Hadst thou not scourged me, and bound me, and torn me with combs, and put my feet in fetters,[3] there *would* have been room to think that thou hadst had patience with me. But, if these things take place in the meanwhile, where is the patience towards me of which thou hast spoken?

The governor said: These things which thou hast said will not help thee, because they all go against thee, and they will bring upon thee inflictions bitterer even than those which the emperors have commanded.

Habib said: Had I not been sensible that they would help me, I should not have spoken a single word about them before thee.

The governor said: *I* will silence thy speeches, and at the same time as regards thee pacify the gods, whom thou has not worshipped; and I will satisfy the emperors in respect to thee, as regards thy rebellion against their commands.

Habib said: I am not afraid of the death with which thou seekest to terrify me; for, had I been afraid of it, I should not have gone about from house to house and ministered: on which account I did so minister.[4]

The governor said: How is it that thou worshippest and honourest a man, but refusest to worship and honour Zeus there?

Habib said: I worship not a man, because the Scripture[5] teaches me,[6] "Cursed is every one that putteth his trust in man;" but God, who took upon Him a body and became a man, *Him* do I worship, and glorify.

The governor said: Do thou that which the emperors have commanded; and, as for that which is in thy own mind, if thou art willing to give it up, *well;* but, if thou art not willing, *then* do not abandon it.

Habib said: To do both these things is impossible: because falsehood is contrary to truth, and it is impossible that that should be banished from my thoughts which is firmly fixed in my mind.

The governor said: By inflictions bitter and severe will I make thee dismiss from thy thoughts that of which thou hast said, It is firmly fixed in my mind.

Habib said: *As for* these inflictions by which thou thinkest that it will be rooted out of my thoughts, by means of these it is that it grows within my thoughts, like a tree which bears fruit.

The governor said: What help will stripes and combs give to that tree of thine? and more especially at the time when I shall command fire against it, to burn it up without pity.

Habib said: It is not on those things at which thou lookest that I look, because I contemplate the things which are out of sight; and therefore I do the will of God, the Maker *of all things,* and not that of an idol made *with hands,* which is not sensible of anything whatever.

The governor said: Because he thus denies the gods whom the emperors worship, let him be torn with combs in addition to his former tearings: for, amidst the many questions which I have had the patience to ask him, he has forgotten his former tearings.

---

[1] [Seems to be a reference to Rev. xx. 4.]
[2] Pointing to the image. -- Tr.
[3] Or "the stocks." The word is of the most indefinite kind, answering to ξυλον and *lignum.* -- Tr.
[4] For this sense, which appears to be the one intended, it is necessary to change ⳉⳝⳗⳐ into ⳉⳝⳗⳐ. -- Tr.
[5] [Jer. xvii. 5.]
[6] Lit. "it is written for me." -- Tr.

And, while they were tearing him, he cried aloud and said: "The sufferings of this time are not equal to that glory which shall be revealed in"[1] those who love Christ.

And, when the governor saw that even under these inflictions he refused to sacrifice, he said to him: Does your doctrine so teach you, that you should hate your own bodies?

Habib said: Nay, we do not hate our bodies: the Scripture distinctly teaches us, "Whosoever shall lose his life shall find it."[2] But another thing too it teaches us: that we should "not cast that which is holy to dogs, nor cast pearls before swine."[3]

The governor said: I know that in speaking thus thy sole object is that my rage and the wrath of my mind may be excited, and that I may pronounce sentence of death against thee speedily. I am not going, then, to be hurried on to that which thou desirest; but I will have patience: not, indeed, for thy relief, but so that the tortures inflicted on thee may be increased, and that thou mayest see thy flesh falling off before thy face by means of the combs that are passing over thy sides.

Habib said: I myself also am looking for this, that thou shouldst multiply thy tortures upon me, even as thou hast said.

The governor said: Submit to the emperors, who have power to do whatsoever they choose.

Habib said: It is not of men to do whatsoever they choose, but of God, whose power is in the heavens, and over all the dwellers upon earth; "nor is there any that may rebuke His hands[4] and say to Him, 'What doest Thou?'"

The governor said: For this insolence of thine, death by the sword is too small. I, however, am prepared to command *the infliction* upon thee of a death more bitter than that of the sword.

Habib said: And I, too, am looking for a death which is more lingering than that of the sword, which thou mayest pronounce upon me at any time thou choosest.

And thereupon the governor proceeded to pass sentence of death upon him. And he called out aloud before his attendants, and said, whilst they were listening to him, as were also the nobles of the city: This Habib, who has denied the gods, as ye have also heard from him, and furthermore has reviled the emperors, deserves that his life should be blotted out from beneath this glorious Sun, and that he should not *any longer* behold this luminary, associate of gods; and, had it not been commanded by former emperors that the corpses of murderers should be buried, it would not be right that the corpse of this *fellow* either should be buried, because he has been so insolent. I command, that a strap be put into his mouth, as into the mouth of a murderer, and that he be burned by a slow lingering fire, so that the torment of his death may be increased.

And he went out from the presence of the governor, with the strap thrust into his mouth; and a multitude of the people of the city ran after him. And the Christians were rejoicing, forasmuch as he had not turned aside nor quitted his post;[5] but the pagans were threatening him, for refusing to sacrifice. And they led him forth by the western archway, over against the cemetery,[6] which was built by[7] Abshelama,[8] the son of Abgar. And his mother was clad in white, and she went out with him.

And, when he was arrived at the place where they were going to burn him, he stood up and prayed, as did all those who came out with him; and he said: "O King Christ, since Thine is this world, and Thine the world to come, behold and see, that, while I might have fled from these afflictions, I did not flee, in order that I might not fall into the hands of Thy justice: may this fire, in which I am to be burned, serve me for a recompense before Thee, so that I may be delivered from that fire which is not quenched; and receive Thou my spirit into Thy presence, through Thy Divine Spirit, O glorious Son of the adorable Father!" And, when he had prayed, he turned and blessed them; and they weeping gave him the salutation, both men and women; and they said to him: Pray for us in the presence of thy Lord, that He would cause peace among His people, and restoration to His churches which are overthrown.

And, while Habib was standing, they dug a place, and brought him and set him within it; and they fixed up by him a stake. And they came to bind him to the stake; but he said to them: I will not stir from this place in which ye are going to burn me. And they brought fagots, and set them in order, and placed them on all sides of him. And, when the fire blazed up and the flame of it rose fiercely, they called out to him: Open thy mouth. And the moment he opened his mouth his soul mounted up. And they cried aloud, both men and women, with the voice of weeping.

And they pulled and drew him out of the fire, throwing over him fine linen cloths and choice ointments and spices. And they snatched away

---

[1] Rom. viii. 18. — Tr.
[2] Matt. x. 39. — Tr.
[3] Matt. vii. 6. — Tr.
[4] Chaldee, "restrain (literally, *smite*) His hand." See Dan. iv. 35. — Tr.

[5] Or "departed from his covenant." — Tr.
[6] The Gk. κοιμητήριον. — Tr.
[7] Cureton's "for" seems not so good, the reference not being to a single tomb. — Tr.
[8] Probably that in which Sharbil and Babai were buried: see p. 684, above.

some of the pieces of wood *which had been put* for his burning, and the brethren and some persons of the laity [1] bore him away. And they prepared him for interment, and buried him by Guria and Shamuna the martyrs, in the same grave ·in which they were laid, on the hill which is called Baith Allah Cucla,[2] repeating over him psalms and hymns, and conveying his burnt body affectionately and honourably *to the grave.* And even some of the Jews and pagans took part with the Christian brethren in winding up and burying his body. At the time, too, when he was burned, and also at the time when he was buried, there was one spectacle of grief overspreading those within and those without ; tears, too, were running down from all eyes : while every one gave glory to God, because for His name's sake he had given his body to the burning of fire.

The day on which he was burned was the eve *of the Sabbath,*[3] the second of the month Ilul — the day on which the news came that Constantine the Great had set out from the interior of Spain, to proceed to Rome, the city of Italy, that he might carry on war with Licinius, that *emperor* who at this day rules over the eastern portion of the territories of the Romans ; and lo ! the countries on all sides are in commotion, because no man knows which of them will conquer and continue in his imperial power. And through this report the persecution slackened for a little while from the Church.

And the notaries wrote down everything which they had heard from the judge ; and the Sharirs of the city wrote down all the other things which were spoken outside the door of the judgment-hall, and, according to the custom that existed, they reported to the judge all that they had seen and all that they had heard, and the decisions of the judge were written down in their Acts.

I, Theophilus, who have renounced the evil inheritance of my fathers, and confessed Christ, carefully wrote out a copy of these Acts of Habib, even as I had formerly written out *those* of Guria and Shamuna,[4] his fellow-martyrs. And, whereas he had felicitated them upon their death by the sword, he himself also was made like them by the fire in which he was burnt, and received his crown. And, whereas I have written down the year, and the month, and the day, of the coronation of these martyrs, it is not for the sake of those who, like me, were spectators of the deed, but with the view that those who come after us may learn at what time these martyrs suffered, and what manner of men they were ; *as they may learn* also from the Acts of the former martyrs, who *suffered* in the days of Domitianus and of all the other emperors who likewise also raised a persecution against the Church, and put a great many to death, by stripes and by *tearing with* combs, and by bitter inflictions, and by sharp swords, and by burning fire, and by the terrible sea, and by the merciless mines. And all these things, and things like them, *they suffered* for the hope of the recompense to come.

Moreover, the afflictions of these martyrs, and of those of whom I had heard, opened the eyes of me, Theophilus, and enlightened my mind, and I confessed Christ, that He is the Son of God, and is God. And may the dust of the feet of these martyrs, which I received as I was running after them at the time when they were departing to be crowned, procure me pardon for having denied Him, and may He confess me before His worshippers, seeing that I have confessed Him now !

And at the twenty-seventh question which the judge put to Habib, he gave sentence against him of death by the burning of fire.

Here endeth the martyrdom of Habib the deacon.

---

[1] Lit. "secular persons," or "men of the world." — Tr.

[2] In Simeon Metaphrastes, whose copy would seem to have had a slightly different reading, it is written *Bethelabicla,* and is said to lie on the north side of the city.

[3] i.e., the sixth day of the week. See note 9 on p. 668. — Tr.

[4] As Simeon Metaphrastes, *infra,* evidently made use of these *Acts of Habib* in his account of that martyr, it is probable that his narrative of the martyrdom of Guria and Shamuna also was founded on the copy of their *Acts* to which Theophilus here refers.

ANCIENT SYRIAC DOCUMENTS

MARTYRDOM[1] OF THE HOLY CONFESSORS SHAMUNA, GURIA, AND HABIB, FROM SIMEON METAPHRASTES.[2]

In the six hundredth year from the empire of Alexander the Macedonian, when Diocletian had been nine years sovereign of the Romans, and Maximian was consul for the sixth time, and Augar son of Zoaras was prætor, and Cognatus was bishop of the Edessenes, a great persecution was raised against the churches in all the countries which were under the sway of the Romans. The name of Christian was looked upon as execrable, and was assailed and harassed with abuse ; while the priests and the monks,[3] on account of their staunch and unconquerable stedfastness, were subjected to shocking punishments, and the pious were at their wits' end with sadness and fear. For, desiring as they did to proclaim the truth because of their yearning affection for Christ, they yet shrunk back from doing so for fear of punishment. For those who took up arms against true religion were bent on making the Christians renounce Christianity and embrace the cause of Saturn and Rhea, whilst the faithful on their part laboured to prove that the objects of heathen worship had no real existence.

At this period it was that an accusation was preferred before the judge against Guria and Shamuna. The former was a native of Sarcigitua, and the latter of the village of Ganas ; they were, however, both brought up at Edessa — which they call Mesopotamia, because it is situated between the Euphrates and the Tigris : a city previously to this but little known to fame, but which after the struggles of its martyrs obtained universal notoriety. These holy men would not by any means spend their lives in the city, but removing to a distance from it, as those who wished to be remote from its turmoils, they made it their aim to be manifest to God only.

Guria's purity and lovingness were to him a precious and honourable possession, and from his cultivation of the former the surname of *the pure* was given him : so that from his name you would not have known who he was, but only when you called him by his surname. Shamuna devoted his body and his youthful and active mind to the service of God, and rivalled Guria in excellence of character. Against these men an indictment was laid before the judge, to the effect that they not only pervaded all the country round about Edessa with their teaching and encouraged the people to hold fast their faith, but also led them to look with contempt on their persecutors, and, in order to induce them to set wholly at nought their impiety, taught them agreeably to that which is written : "Trust not in princes — in the sons of men, in whom is no safety."[4] By these representations the judge was wrought up to a high pitch of madness, and gave orders that all those who held the Christian religion in honour and followed the teaching of Shamuna and Guria, together with those who persuaded them to this, should be apprehended, and shut up in safe keeping. The order was carried into effect ; and, seizing the opportunity, he had some of them flogged, and others tortured in various ways, and induced them to obey the emperor's command, and then, as if he were behaving kindly and mercifully, he allowed others to go to their homes ; but *our two* saints, as being the ringleaders and those who had communicated their piety to others, he ordered to be still further maltreated in prison. They, however, rejoiced in the fellowship of martyrdom. For they heard of many in other provinces who had had to pass through the same conflict as themselves : among them Epiphanius and Petrus and the most holy Pamphilus, with many others, at Cæsarea in Palestine ; Timotheus at Gaza ; at Alexandria, Timotheus the Great ; Agapetus at Thessalonica ; Hesychius at Nicomedia ; Philippus at Adrianopolis ; at Melitina Petrus ; Hermes and his

---

[1] Cureton gives it in Latin. — Tr.

[2] This piece is taken from the well-known work of Surius, *De probatis Sanctorum vitis.* It does not appear who made this Latin translation.

Metaphrastes is a celebrated Byzantine writer, who lived in the ninth and tenth centuries. He derives his name from having written paraphrases, or metaphrases, of the lives of the saints. Fabricius gives a list of 539 lives commonly attributed to him. — Dr. W. Plate, in Smith's *Dict. Biog. and Myth.* — Tr.

[3] [A token of mediæval origin.]

[4] Ps. cxlvi. 3. — Tr.

companions in the confines of Martyropolis : all of whom were also encircled with the crown of martyrdom by Duke [1] Heraclianus, along with other confessors too numerous for us to become acquainted with. But we must return to the matters of which we were before speaking.

Antonius, then, the governor of Edessa, having permitted others to return to their homes, had a lofty judgment-seat erected, and ordered the martyrs to be brought before him. The attendants having done as they were bidden, the governor said to the saints : Our most divine emperor commands you to renounce Christianity, of which you are followers, and to pay divine honour to Jupiter by offering incense on the altar. To this Shamuna replied : Far be it from us to abandon the true faith, whereby we hope to obtain immortality, and worship the work of men's hands and an image ! The governor said : The emperor's orders must by all means be obeyed. Guria answered : Our pure and divine faith will we never disown, by following the will of men, who are subject to dissolution. For we have a Father in heaven whose will we follow, and He says : " He that shall confess Me before men, him will I also confess before My Father who is in heaven ; but he that shall deny Me before men, him will I also deny before My Father and His angels." [2] The judge said : You refuse, then, to obey the will of the emperor ? But can you for a moment think, that the purposes of ordinary men and such as have no more power than yourselves are to be really carried into execution, while the commands of those who possess supreme power fall to the ground ? They, said the saints, who do the will of the King of kings spurn and reject the will of the flesh. Then, on the governor's threatening them with death unless they obeyed, Shamuna said : We shall not die, O tyrant, if we follow the will of the Creator : nay rather, on the contrary, we shall live ; but, if we follow the commands of your emperor, know thou that, even though thou shouldest *not* put us to death, we shall perish miserably all the same.

On hearing this, the governor gave orders to Anovitus the jailor to put them in very safe keeping. For the mind which is naturally inclined to evil cannot bear the truth, any more than diseased eyes the bright beams of the sun. And, when he had done as he was commanded, and the martyrs were in prison, where many other saints also had been previously shut by the soldiers, the Emperor Diocletian sent for Musonius the governor of Antioch and ordered him to go to Edessa and see the Christians who were confined there, whether they were of the common or of the sacred class, and question them

about their religion, and deal with them as he should see fit. So he came to Edessa ; and he had Shamuna and Guria first of all placed before the tribunal of judgment, and said to them : This, and no less, is the command of the lord of the world, that you make a libation of wine and place incense on the altar of Jupiter. If you refuse to do so, I will destroy you with manifold punishments : for I will tear your bodies to pieces with whips, till I get to your very entrails ; and I will not cease pouring boiling lead into your armpits until it reaches even to your bowels ; after that, I will hang you up, now by your hands, now by your feet, and I will loosen the fastenings of your joints ; and I will invent new and unheard of punishments which you will be utterly unable to endure.

Shamuna answered : We dread " the worm," the threat of which is denounced against those who deny the Lord, and " the fire which is not quenched," more than those tortures which thou hast set before us. For *God* Himself, to whom we offer rational worship, will, first of all, strengthen us to bear these manifold tortures, and will deliver us out of thy hands ; and, after that, will also give us to rest in a place of safety, where is the abode of all those who rejoice. Besides, it is against nothing whatever but the body that thou takest up arms : for what possible harm couldst thou do to the soul ? since, as long as it resides in the body, it proves superior to torture ; and, when it takes its departure, the body has no feeling whatever left. For, " the more our outward man is destroyed, the more is our inward man renewed day by day ; " [3] for by means of patience we go through with this contest which is set before us. The governor, however, again, with a kind of protestation, in order that, in case they did not obey, he might with the more justice punish them, said : Give up your error, I beg you, and yield to the command of the emperor : ye will not be able to endure the tortures. The holy Guria answered : We are neither the slaves of error, as thou sayest, nor will we ever obey the command of the emperor : God forbid that we should be so weak-minded and so senseless ! For we are His disciples who laid down His life for us, so manifesting the riches of His goodness and His love towards us. We will, therefore, resist sin even to death, nor, come what may, will we be foiled by the stratagems of the adversary, by which the first man was ensnared and plucked death from the tree through his disobedience ; [4] and Cain was persuaded, and, after staining his hands with his brother's blood, found the rewards

---

[1] Dux.
[2] Matt. x 33. — Tr.

[3] 2 Cor. iv. 16. — Tr.
[4] Or " through his disobedience in the matter of the tree," if *per ligni inobedientiam* are the real words of the *Latin* translator, who is not, generally speaking, to be complimented for elegance or even correctness, but seems to have made a servile copy of the mere words of the Greek. — Tr.

of sin to be wailing and fear. But we, listening to the words of Christ, will "not be afraid of those that kill the body but are not able to kill the soul:" Him rather will we fear "who is able to destroy our soul and body."[1] The tyrant said: It is not to give you an opportunity of disproving my allegations by snatches of your own writings that I refrain from anger and show myself forbearing; but that you may perform the command of the emperor and return in peace to your homes.

These words did not at all shake the resolution of the martyrs; but, approaching nearer: What, said they, does it matter to us, if thou *art* angry, and nursest thine anger, and rainest tortures upon us like snow-flakes? For then wouldst thou be favouring us all the more, by rendering the proof of our fortitude more conspicuous, and winning for us a greater recompense. For this is the crowning point of our hope, that we shall leave behind our present dwelling, which is but for a time, and depart to one that will last forever. For we have "a tabernacle not made with hands"[2] in heaven, which the Scripture is accustomed also to call "Abraham's bosom," because of the familiar intercourse with God with which he was blessed. The governor, seeing that their firmness underwent no change, forthwith left off speaking and proceeded with the threatened punishments, giving orders to the jailor Anuinus that they should be severally hung up by one hand, and that, when their hands were dislocated by having to bear the entire weight of the body, he should further suspend a heavy stone to their feet, that the sense of pain might be the sharper. This was done, and from the third hour to the eighth they bore this severe torture with fortitude, uttering not a word, nor a groan, nor giving any other indication of a weak or abject mind. You would have said that they were suffering in a body which was not theirs, or that others were suffering and they themselves were nothing more than spectators of what was going on.

In the meantime, whilst they were hanging by their hands, the governor was engaged in trying other cases. Having done with these, he ordered the jailor to inquire of the saints whether or not they would obey the emperor and be released from their torture; and on his putting the question to them, when it was found that they either could not or would not return an answer, he ordered that they should be confined in the inner part of the prison, in a dark dungeon, dark both in name and in reality, and that their feet should be made fast in the stocks. At dawn of day, their feet were loosened from the confinement of the stocks; but their prison was close shut up, so that not a single ray even of sunlight could

make its way in; and the jailors were ordered not to give them a bit of bread or a single drop of water for three whole days. So that, in addition to all the rest, the martyrs were condemned to a dark prison and a long privation of food. When the third day arrived, about the beginning of the month of August, the prison was opened to admit light, but they were detained in it still up to the 10th of November. Then the judge had them brought up before his tribunal: Has not all this time, said he, sufficed to induce you to change your minds and come to some wholesome decision? They answered: We have already several times told thee our mind: do, therefore, what thou hast been commanded. The governor forthwith ordered that Shamuna should be made to kneel down on one side[3] and that an iron chain should be fastened on his knee. This having been done, he hung him up head downwards by the foot with which he had made him kneel; the other he pulled downwards with a heavy piece of iron, which cannot be described in words: thus endeavouring to rend the champion in twain. By this means the socket of the hip-bone was wrenched out of its place and Shamuna became lame. Guria, however, because he was weak and somewhat pale, he left unpunished: not that he regarded him with friendly eyes — not that he had any compassion on his weakness; but rather by way of sparing for another opportunity one whom he was anxious to punish: lest perchance, as he said, through inadvertence on my part he should be worn out before he has undergone the torments in reserve for him.

By this time two hours of the day had passed since Shamuna had been hung up; and the fifth hour had now arrived, and he was still suspended on high — when the soldiers who stood around, taking pity upon him, urged him to obey the emperor's command. But the compassion of sinners had no effect upon the saint. For, although he suffered bitterly from the torture, he vouchsafed them no answer whatever, leaving them to lament at their leisure, and to deem themselves rather, and not him, deserving of pity. But, lifting his eyes to heaven, he prayed to God from the depth of his heart, reminding Him of the wonders done in old time: Lord God, he said, without whom not even a poor little sparrow falls into the snare; who didst cheer the heart of David amid his afflictions; who gavest power to Daniel even against the lions; who madest the children of Abraham victorious over the tyrant and the flame: do Thou now also, O Lord, look on the war which is being waged against us, acquainted as Thou art with the weakness of our nature. For the enemy is trying to turn away

---

[1] Matt. x. 28. — Tr.
[2] 2 Cor. v. 1. — Tr.

[3] Lit. "with one foot." — Tr.

the workmanship of Thy right hand from the glory which is with Thee. But regard Thou us with looks of compassion, and maintain within us, against all attempts to extinguish it, the lamp of Thy commandments ; and by Thy light guide our paths, and vouchsafe us the enjoyment of that happiness which is in Thee : for Thou art blessed for ever, world without end. Thus did he utter the praise of the Umpire of the strife ; and a scribe who was present took down in writing what was said.

At length the governor ordered the jailor to release him from his punishment. He did so, and carried him away all faint and exhausted with the pain he suffered, and they bore him back to his former prison and laid him down by the side of the holy Guria. On the 15th of November, however, in the night, about the time of cock-crowing, the judge got up. He was preceded by torches and attendants ; and, on arriving at the Basilica, as it is called, where the court was held, he took his seat with great ceremony on the tribunal, and sent to fetch the champions Guria and Shamuna. The latter came in walking between two *of the jailors* and supported by the hands of both : for he was worn out with hunger and weighed down with age : nothing but his good hope sustained him. Guria, too, had also to be carried in : for he could not walk at all, because his foot had been severely galled by the chain on it. Addressing them both, the advocate of impiety said : In pursuance of the permission which was granted, you have, *doubtless*, consulted together about what it is expedient for you to do. Tell me, then, whether any fresh resolution has been come to by you, and whether you have in any respect changed your mind in regard to your former purpose ; and obey the command of the most divine *emperor*. For thus will you be restored to the enjoyment of your property and possessions, yea of this most cheering light also. To this the martyrs reply : No one who is wise would make any great account of continuing for a little while in the enjoyment of things which are but transient. Sufficient for us is the time already past for the use and the sight of them ; nor do we feel the want of any of them. That death, on the contrary, with which thou art threatening us will convey us to imperishable habitations and give us a participation in the happiness which is yonder.

The governor replied : What you have said has filled my ears with great sadness. However, I will explain to you what is determined on : if you place incense on the altar and sacrifice to the image of Jupiter, all will be well, and each of you will go away to his home ; but, if you still persist in disobeying the command of the emperor, you will most certainly lose your heads : for this is what the great emperor wills and determines. To this the most noble-minded Shamuna replied : If thou shalt confer upon us so great a favour as to grant us deliverance from the miseries of this life and dismissal to the happiness of the life yonder, so far as in us lies thou shalt be rewarded by Him who lays out our possessions on what is for our good. The governor replied to this somewhat kindly, as it seemed, saying : I have patiently endured hitherto, putting up with those long speeches of yours, in order that by delay you may change your purpose and betake yourselves to what is for your good, and not have to undergo the punishment of death. Those who submit, said he, to death which is only for a time, for the sake of Christ, will manifestly be delivered from eternal death. For those who die to the world live in Christ. For Peter also, who shines so brightly among the band of apostles, was condemned to the cross and to death ; and James, the son of thunder, was slain by Herod Agrippa with the sword. Moreover, Stephen also was stoned, who was the first to run the course of martyrdom. What, too, wilt thou say of John *the Baptist?* Thou wilt surely acknowledge his distinguished fortitude and boldness of speech, when he preferred death rather than keep silence about conjugal infidelity, and the adulteress received his head as a reward for her dancing?

Again the governor said : It is not that you may reckon up your saints, as you call them, that I bear so patiently with you, but that, by changing your resolution and yielding to the emperor's commands, you may be rescued from a very bitter death. For, if you behave with such excessive daring and arrogance, what can you expect but that severer punishments are in store for you, under the pressure of which you will be ready even against your will to do what I demand of you : by which time, however, it will be altogether too late to take refuge in compassion? For the cry which is wrung from you by force has no power to challenge pity ; whilst, on the other hand, that which is made of your own accord is deserving of compassion. The confessors and martyrs of Christ said : There needs not many words. For lo ! we are ready to undergo all the punishments thou mayest lay upon us. What, therefore, has been commanded thee, delay not to perform. For we are the worshippers of Christ the true God, and (again we say it) of Him of whose kingdom there shall be no end ; who also is alone able to glorify those in return who glorify His name. In the meantime, whilst these things were being said by the saints, the governor pronounced sentence against them that they should suffer death by the sword. But they, filled with a joy beyond the power of words to express, exclaimed : To Thee of right belongeth glory and praise, who art God of all, because it hath pleased Thee that we should carry on to its close the conflict we have entered upon, and that we should also receive at Thy hands the brightness that shall never fade away.

When, therefore, the governor saw their unyielding firmness, and how they had heard the final sentence with exultation of soul, he said to the saints: May God search into what is being done, *and be witness* that so far as I was concerned it was no wish of mine that you should lose your lives; but the inflexible command of the emperor to me compels me to this. He then ordered a halberdier to take charge of the martyrs, and, putting them in a carriage, to convey them to a distance from the city with some soldiers, and there to end them with the sword. So he, taking the saints out at night by the Roman gate, when the citizens were buried in profound slumber, conveyed them to Mount Bethelabicla on the north of the city. On their arrival at that place, having alighted from the carriage with joy of heart and great firmness of mind, they requested the halberdier and those who were under his orders to give them time to pray; and it was granted. For, just as if their tortures and their blood were not enough to plead for them, they still by reason of their humility deemed it necessary to pray. So they raised their eyes to heaven and prayed earnestly, concluding with the words: God and Father of our Lord Jesus Christ, receive in peace our spirits to Thyself. Then Shamuna, turning to the halberdier, said: Perform that which thou hast been commanded. So he kneeled down along with Guria, and they were beheaded, on the 15th of November. This is the account of what happened to the martyrs.

But forasmuch as the number sought for a third in order that in them the Trinity might be glorified, it found, oh admirable providence! Habib — at a subsequent time indeed: but he also, along with those who had preceded him, had determined to enter on the journey, and on the very day[1] of their martyrdom reached his consummation. Habib, then, great among martyrs, was a native of the same place as they, namely of the village of Thelsæa;[2] and he had the honour of being invested with the sacred office of the diaconate. But, when Licinius swayed the sceptre of the Roman empire and Lysanias had been appointed governor of Edessa, a persecution was again raised against the Christians, and the general danger threatened Habib. For he would go about the city, teaching the divine Scriptures to all he met with, and courageously seeking to strengthen them in piety. When this came to the ears of Lysanias, he gave information of it to the Emperor Licinius. For

he was anxious to be himself entrusted with the business of bringing the Christians to trial, and especially Habib: for he had never been entrusted with it before. The emperor, then, sent him a letter and commanded him to put Habib to death. So, when Lysanias had received the letter, search was made everywhere for Habib, who on account of his office in the Church lived in some part of the city, his mother and some of his relations residing with him. When he got intelligence of the matter, fearing lest he should incur punishment for quitting the ranks of martyrdom, he went of his own accord and presented himself to a man who was among the chief of the body-guard, named Theotecnus, and presently he said: I am Habib for whom ye are seeking. But he, looking kindly at him, said: No one, my good man, is as yet aware of thy coming to me: so go away, and look to thy safety; and be not concerned about thy mother, nor about thy relations: for they cannot possibly get into any trouble. Thus far Theotecnus.

But Habib, because the occasion was one that called for martyrdom, refused to yield to a weak and cowardly spirit and secure his safety in any underhand way. He replied, therefore: It is not for the sake of my dear mother, nor for the sake of my kinsfolk, that I denounce myself; but I have come for the sake of the confession of Christ. For lo! whether thou consent or no, I will make my appearance before the governor, and I will proclaim my *Master* Christ before princes and kings. Theotecnus, accordingly, apprehensive that he might go of his own accord to the governor, and that in this way he might himself be in jeopardy for not having denounced him, took Habib and conducted him to the governor: Here, said he, is Habib, for whom search has been made. When Lysanias learned that Habib had come of his own accord to the contest, he concluded that this was a mark of contempt and overweening boldness, as if he set light by the solemn dignity of the judicial seat; and he had him at once put on his trial. He inquired of him his condition of life, his name, and his country. On his answering that he was a native of the village of Thelsæa, and intimating that he was a minister of Christ, the governor immediately charged the martyr with not obeying the emperor's commands. He insisted that a plain proof of this was his refusal to offer incense to Jupiter. To this Habib kept replying that he was a Christian, and could not forsake the true God, or sacrifice to the lifeless works of *men's* hands which had no sensation. The governor hereupon ordered, that his arms should be bound with ropes, and that he should be raised up high on a beam and torn with iron claws.[3]

---

[1] i e., the anniversary. — Tr.
[2] In the Syriac account " Telzeha: " see p. 690, *supra*. — Tr.

[3] Compare the " combs " of the Syriac, p. 684, *supra*. — Tr.

The hanging up was far more difficult to bear than the tearing : for he was in danger of being pulled asunder, through the forcible strain with which his arms were stretched out.

In the meantime, as he was hanging up in the air, the governor had recourse to smooth words, and assumed the guise of patience. He, however, continued to threaten him with severer punishments unless he should change his resolution. But he said : No man shall induce me to forsake the faith, nor persuade me to worship demons, even though he should inflict tortures more and greater. On the governor's asking him what advantage he expected to gain from tortures which destroyed his whole [1] body, Habib, Christ's martyr, replied : The objects of our regard do not last merely for the present, nor do we pursue the things that are seen ; and, if thou too art minded to turn thy look towards our hope and promised recompense, possibly thou wilt even say with Paul : " The sufferings of this time are not worthy to be compared with the glory which is to be revealed in us." [2] The governor pronounced his words to be the language of imbecility ; and, when he saw that, notwithstanding all the efforts he made, by turns using smooth words and assuming the part of patience, and then again threatening him and menacing him with a shocking [3] death, he could not in either way prevail with him, he said, as he pronounced sentence upon him : I will not in-flict on thee a sudden and speedy death ; I will bring on thy dissolution gradually by means of a slow fire, and in this way make thee lay aside thy fierce and intractable spirit. Thereupon, some wood was collected together at a place outside the city on the northward, and he was led to the pile, followed by his mother, and also by those who were otherwise by blood related to him. He then prayed, and pronounced a blessing on all, and gave them the kiss in the Lord ; and after that the wood was kindled by them, and he was cast into the fire ; and, when he had opened his mouth to receive the flame, he yielded up his spirit to Him who had given it. Then, when the fire had subsided, his relatives wrapped him in a costly piece of linen and anointed him with unguents ; and, having suitably sung psalms and hymns, they laid him by the side of Shamuna and Guria, to the glory of the Father, and of the Son, and of the Holy Spirit, who constitute a Divine Trinity, which cannot be divided : to whom is due honour and worship now and always, and for evermore, Amen. Such was the close of the life of the martyr Habib in the time of Licinius, and thus did he obtain the privilege of being laid with the saints, and thus did he bring to the pious rest from their persecutions. For shortly afterwards the power of Licinius waned, and the rule of Constantine prospered, and the sovereignty of the Romans became his ; and he was the first of the emperors who openly professed piety, and allowed the Christians to live as Christians.

---

[1] Reading " totum " for " solum." — TR.
[2] Rom. viii. 18. — TR.
[3] Lit. " bitter." — TR.

ANCIENT SYRIAC DOCUMENTS.

MOSES OF CHORENE.[1]

HISTORY OF ARMENIA.

I.[2]

REIGN OF ABGAR ; ARMENIA BECOMES COMPLETELY
TRIBUTARY TO THE ROMANS ; WAR WITH HEROD'S
TROOPS ; HIS BROTHER'S SON, JOSEPH, IS KILLED.

ABGAR, son of Archam, ascends the throne in
the twentieth year of Archavir, king of the Persians. This Abgar was called Avak-air (great
man), on account of his great gentleness and
wisdom, and also on account of his size. Not
being able to pronounce well, the Greeks and the
Syrians called him Abgar. In the second year of
his reign, all the districts of Armenia become
tributary to the Romans. A command is given
by the Emperor Augustus, as we are told in the
Gospel of St. Luke, to number all the people in
every part. Roman commissioners, sent for that
purpose into Armenia, carried thither the statue
of the Emperor Augustus, and set it up in all
the temples. At this very time, our Saviour
Jesus Christ, the Son of God, came into the
world.

At the same period there was trouble between
Abgar and Herod : for Herod wished that his
statue should be erected near to that of Cæsar
in the temples of Armenia. Abgar withstood
this claim. Moreover, Herod was but seeking a
pretext to attack Abgar : he sent an army of
Thracians and Germans to make an incursion
into the country of the Persians, with orders to
pass through the territories of Abgar. But Abgar, far from submitting to this, resisted, saying
that the emperor's command was to march the
troops into Persia through the desert. Herod,
indignant, and unable to act by himself, overwhelmed with troubles, as a punishment for his
wicked conduct towards Christ, as Josephus relates, sent his nephew to whom he had given
his daughter, who had been married in the first

instance to Pheror, his brother. Herod's lieu-
tenant, at the head of a considerable army, hastened to reach Mesopotamia, met Abgar at the
camp in the province of Pouknan, fell in the
combat, and his troops were put to flight. Soon
afterwards, Herod died : Archelaus, his son, was
appointed by Augustus ethnarch of Judæa.

II.[3]

FOUNDING OF THE TOWN OF EDESSA ; BRIEF AC-
COUNT OF THE RACE OF OUR ILLUMINATOR.

A little while afterwards, Augustus dies, and
Tiberius becomes emperor of the Romans in
his stead. Germanicus, having become Cæsar,
dragging in his train the princes of the kingdom
of Archavir and of Abgar, celebrates a triumph
in respect of the war waged with them, in which
these princes had killed Herod's nephew. Abgar, indignant, forms plans of revolt and prepares himself for combat. He builds a town on
the ground occupied by the Armenian army of
observation, where previously the Euphrates had
been defended against the attempts of Cassius :
this new town is called Edessa. Abgar removed
to it his court, which was at Medzpine, all his
gods, Naboc, Bel, Patnicagh, and Tarata, the
books of the schools attached to the temples,
and even the royal archives.

After this, Archavir being dead, Ardachès, his
son, reigns over the Persians. Though it is not
in the order of the history with respect to time,
nor even the order according to which we have
begun these annals, yet, as we are treating of
the descendants of the king Archavir, even of
the blood of Ardachès his son, we will, to do
honour to these princes, place them, by anticipating the time, near to Ardachès, in order that
the reader may know that they are of the same
race, of the race of the brave Archag ; then we
will indicate the time of the arrival of their
fathers in Armenia, the Garenians and the Sou-
renians, from whom St. Gregory and the Gamsa-

[1] This extract is taken from the edition, in two volumes, printed
at Paris, of which the following is the title: MOÏSE DE KHO-
RÈNE, auteur du Ve Siècle : HISTOIRE D'ARMÉNIE, TEXTE
ARMÉNIEN ET TRADUCTION FRANCAISE, avec notes explicatives et
précis historiques sur l'Arménie, par P. E. LE VAILLANT DE
FLORIVAL.
[2] Book ii. chapter xxvi.

[3] Chapter xxvii.

rians are descended, when, following the order of events, we come to the reign of the king under whom they appeared.

Abgar did not succeed in his plans of revolt; for, troubles having arisen amongst his relatives in the Persian kingdom, he set out at the head of an army to allay and bring to an end the dissension.

III.[1]

ABGAR COMES INTO THE EAST, MAINTAINS ARDACHÈS UPON THE THRONE OF PERSIA; RECONCILES HIS BROTHERS FROM WHOM OUR ILLUMINATOR AND HIS RELATIONS ARE DESCENDED.

Abgar, having gone to the East, finds on the throne of Persia Ardachès, son of Archavir, and the brothers of Ardachès contending against him: for this prince thought to reign over them in his posterity, and they would not consent to it. Ardachès therefore hems them in on all sides, hangs the sword of death over their heads; distractions and dissension were between their troops and their other relations and allies: for King Archavir had three sons and one daughter; the first of these sons was King Ardachès himself, the second Garene, the third Sourene; their sister, named Gochm, was wife of the general of all the Ariks, a general chosen by their father Archavir.

Abgar prevails on the sons of Archavir to make peace; he arranges between them the conditions and stipulations: Ardachès is to reign with his posterity as he proposed, and his brothers are to be called Bahlav, from the name of their town and their vast and fertile country, so that their satrapies shall be the first, higher in rank than all the satrapies of Persia, as being truly a race of kings. Treaties and oaths stipulated that in case of the extinction of male children of Ardachès, his brothers should come to the throne; after the reigning race of Ardachès, his brothers are divided into three races named thus: the race of Garene Bahlav, the race of Sourene Bahlav, and the race of their sister, the race of Asbahabied Bahlav, a race thus called from the name of the domain of her husband.

St. Gregory is said to have sprung from the race Sourene Bahlav, and the Gamsarians from the race Garene Bahlav. We will relate in the sequel the circumstances of the coming of these personages, only mentioning their names here in connection with Ardachès, in order that you may know that these great races are indeed the blood of Vagharchag, that is to say, the posterity of the great Archag, brother of Vagharchag.

Everything being thus arranged, Abgar takes with him the letter of the treaties, and returns to his dominions, not in perfect health, but a prey to severe suffering.

IV.[2]

ABGAR RETURNS FROM THE EAST; HE GIVES HELP TO ARETAS IN A WAR AGAINST HEROD THE TETRARCH.

When Abgar had returned from the East, he learnt that the Romans suspected him of having gone there to raise troops. He therefore made the Roman commissioners acquainted with the reasons of his journey to Persia, as well as the treaty concluded between Ardachès and his brothers; but no credence was given to his statement: for he was accused by his enemies Pilate, Herod the tetrarch, Lysanias and Philip. Abgar having returned to his city Edessa leagued himself with Aretas, king of Petra, and gave him some auxiliary troops under the command of Khosran Ardzrouni, to make war upon Herod. Herod had in the first instance married the daughter of Aretas, then had repudiated her, and thereupon taken Herodias, even in her husband's lifetime, a circumstance in connection with which he had had John the Baptist put to death. Consequently there was war between Herod and Aretas on account of the wrong done to the daughter of Aretas. Being sharply attacked, Herod's troops were defeated, thanks to the help of the brave Armenians; as if, by divine providence, vengeance was taken for the death of John the Baptist.

V.[3]

ABGAR SENDS PRINCES TO MARINUS; THESE DEPUTIES SEE OUR SAVIOUR CHRIST; BEGINNING OF THE CONVERSION OF ABGAR.

At this period Marinus, son of Storoge, was raised by the emperor to the government of Phœnicia, Palestine, Syria, and Mesopotamia. Abgar sent to him two of his principal officers, Mar-Ihap prince of Aghtznik, and Chamchacram chief of the house of the Abahouni, as well as Anan his confidant. The envoys proceed to the town of Petkoupine to make known to Marinus the reasons of Abgar's journey to the East, showing him the treaty concluded between Ardachès and his brothers, and at the same time to call upon Marinus for his support. The deputies found the Roman governor at Eleutheropolis; he received them with friendship and distinction, and gave this answer to Abgar: "Fear nothing from the emperor on that account, provided you take good care to pay the tribute regularly."

On their return, the Armenian deputies went to Jerusalem to see our Saviour the Christ, being attracted by the report of His miracles. Having themselves become eye-witnesses of these wonders, they related them to Abgar. This prince, seized with admiration, believed truly that Jesus was indeed the Son of God, and said: "These wonders are not those of a man, but of a God. No, there is no one amongst men who can raise the dead: God alone has this power." Abgar felt in his whole body certain acute pains which he had got in Persia, more than seven years before; from men he had received no remedy for his sufferings; Abgar sent a letter of entreaty to Jesus: he prayed Him to come and cure him of his pains. Here is this letter:—

VI.[1]

ABGAR'S LETTER TO THE SAVIOUR JESUS CHRIST.

"Abgar, son of Archam, prince of the land, to Jesus, Saviour and Benefactor of men, who has appeared in the country of Jerusalem, greeting:—

"I have heard of Thee, and of the cures wrought by Thy hands, without remedies, without herbs: for, as it is said, Thou makest the blind to see, the lame to walk, the lepers to be healed; Thou drivest out unclean spirits, Thou curest unhappy beings afflicted with prolonged and inveterate diseases; Thou dost even raise the dead. As I have heard of all these wonders wrought by Thee, I have concluded from them either that Thou art God, come down from heaven to do such great things, or that Thou art the Son of God, working as Thou dost these miracles. Therefore have I written to Thee, praying Thee to condescend to come to me and cure me of the complaints with which I am afflicted. I have heard also that the Jews murmur against Thee and wish to deliver Thee up to torments: I have a city small but pleasant, it would be sufficient for us both."

The messengers, the bearers of this letter, met Jesus at Jerusalem, a fact confirmed by these words of the Gospel: "Some from amongst the heathen came to find Jesus, but those who heard them, not daring to tell Jesus what they had heard, told it to Philip and Andrew, who repeated it all to their Master."

The Saviour did not then accept the invitation given to Him, but He thought fit to honour Abgar with an answer in these words:—

VII.[2]

ANSWER TO ABGAR'S LETTER, WHICH THE APOSTLE THOMAS WROTE TO THIS PRINCE BY COMMAND OF THE SAVIOUR.

"Blessed is he who believes in me without having seen me! For it is written of me: 'Those who see me will not believe in me, and those who do not see me will believe and live.'

As to what thou hast written asking me to come to thee, I must accomplish here all that for which I have been sent; and, when I shall have accomplished it all, I shall ascend to Him who sent me; and when I shall go away I will send one of my disciples, who will cure thy diseases, and give life to thee and to all those who are with thee." Anan, Abgar's courier, brought him this letter, as well as the portrait of the Saviour, a picture which is still to be found at this day in the city of Edessa.

VIII.[3]

PREACHING OF THE APOSTLE THADDÆUS AT EDESSA; COPY OF FIVE LETTERS.

After the ascension of our Saviour, the Apostle Thomas, one of the twelve, sent one of the seventy-six disciples, Thaddæus, to the city of Edessa to heal Abgar and to preach the Gospel, according to the word of the Lord. Thaddæus came to the house of Tobias, a Jewish prince, who is said to have been of the race of the Pacradouni. Tobias, having left Archam, did not abjure Judaism with the rest of his relatives, but followed its laws up to the moment when he believed in Christ. Soon the name of Thaddæus spreads through the whole town. Abgar, on learning of his arrival, said: "This is indeed he concerning whom Jesus wrote to me;" and immediately Abgar sent for the apostle. When Thaddæus entered, a marvellous appearance presented itself to the eyes of Abgar in the countenance of the apostle; the king having risen from his throne, fell on his face to the earth, and prostrated himself before Thaddæus. This spectacle greatly surprised all the princes who were present, for they were ignorant of the fact of the vision. "Art thou really," said Abgar to Thaddæus, "art thou the disciple of the ever-blessed Jesus? Art thou he whom He promised to send to me, and canst thou heal my maladies?" "Yes," answered Thaddæus; "if thou believest in Jesus Christ, the Son of God, the desires of thy heart shall be granted." "I have believed in Jesus," said Abgar, "I have believed in His Father; therefore I wished to go at the head of my troops to destroy the Jews who have crucified Jesus, had I not been prevented by reason of the power of the Romans."

Thenceforth Thaddæus began to preach the Gospel to the king and his town; laying his hands upon Abgar, he cured him; he cured also a man with gout, Abdu, a prince of the town, much honoured in all the king's house. He also healed all the sick and infirm people in the town, and all believed in Jesus Christ. Abgar was baptized, and all the town with him, and the temples of the false gods were closed, and

---

[1] Chapter xxxi.
[2] Chapter xxxii.
[3] Chapter xxxiii.

all the statues of idols that were placed on the altars and columns were hidden by being covered with reeds. Abgar did not compel any one to embrace the faith, yet from day to day the number of the believers was multiplied.

The Apostle Thaddæus baptizes a manufacturer of silk head-dresses, called Attæus, consecrates him, appoints him *to minister* at Edessa, and leaves him with the king instead of himself. Thaddæus, after having received letters patent from Abgar, who wished that all should listen to the Gospel of Christ, went to find Sanadroug, son of Abgar's sister, whom this prince had appointed over the country and over the army. Abgar was pleased to write to the Emperor Tiberius a letter in these words : —

Abgar's letter to Tiberius.

"Abgar, king of Armenia, to my Lord Tiberius, emperor of the Romans, greeting : —

"I know that nothing is unknown to your Majesty, but, as your friend, I would make you better acquainted with the facts by writing. The Jews who dwell in the cantons of Palestine have crucified Jesus : Jesus without sin, Jesus after so many acts of kindness, so many wonders and miracles wrought for their good, even to the raising of the dead. Be assured that these are not the effects of the power of a simple mortal, but of God. During the time that they were crucifying Him, the sun was darkened, the earth was moved, shaken ; Jesus Himself, three days afterwards, rose from the dead and appeared to many. Now, everywhere, His name alone, invoked by His disciples, produces the greatest miracles : what has happened to myself is the most evident proof of it. Your august Majesty knows henceforth what ought to be done in future with respect to the Jewish nation, which has committed this crime ; your Majesty knows whether a command should not be published through the whole universe to worship Christ as the true God. Safety and health."

Answer from Tiberius to Abgar's letter.

"Tiberius, emperor of the Romans, to Abgar, king of the Armenians, greeting : —

"Your kind letter has been read to me, and I wish that thanks should be given to you from me. Though we had already heard several persons relate these facts, Pilate has officially informed us of the miracles of Jesus. He has certified to us that after His resurrection from the dead He was acknowledged by many to be God. Therefore I myself also wished to do what you propose ; but, as it is the custom of the Romans not to admit a god merely by the command of the sovereign, but only when the admission has been discussed and examined in full senate, I proposed the affair to the senate, and they rejected it with contempt, doubtless because it had not been considered by them first. But we have commanded all those whom Jesus suits, to receive him amongst the gods. We have threatened with death any one who shall speak evil of the Christians. As to the Jewish nation which has dared to crucify Jesus, who, as I hear, far from deserving the cross and death, was worthy of honour, worthy of the adoration of men — when I am free from the war with rebellious Spain, I will examine into the matter, and will treat the Jews as they deserve."

Abgar writes another letter to Tiberius.

"Abgar, king of the Armenians, to my lord Tiberius, emperor of the Romans, greeting : —

"I have received the letter written from your august Majesty, and I have applauded the commands which have emanated from your wisdom. If you will not be angry with me, I will say that the conduct of the senate is extremely ridiculous and absurd : for, according to the senators, it is after the examination and by the suffrages of men that divinity may be ascribed. Thus, then, if God does not suit man, He cannot be God, since God is to be judged and justified by man. It will no doubt seem just to my lord and master to send another governor to Jerusalem in the place of Pilate, who ought to be ignominiously driven from the powerful post in which you placed him ; for he has done the will of the Jews : he has crucified Christ unjustly, without your order. That you may enjoy health is my desire."

Abgar, having written this letter, placed a copy of it, with copies of the other letters, in his archives. He wrote also to the young Nerseh, king of Assyria, at Babylon : —

Abgar's letter to Nerseh.

"Abgar, king of the Armenians, to my son Nerseh, greeting : —

"I have received your letter and acknowledgments. I have released Beroze from his chains, and have pardoned his offences : if this pleases you, give him the government of Nineveh. But as to what you write to me about sending you the physician who works miracles and preaches another God superior to fire and water, that you may see and hear him, I say to you : he was not a physician according to the art of men ; he was a disciple of the Son of God, Creator of fire and water : he has been appointed and sent to the countries of Armenia. But one of his principal companions, named Simon, is sent into the countries of Persia. Seek for him, and you will hear him, you as well as your father Ardachès.

He will heal all your diseases and will show you the way of life."

Abgar wrote also to Ardachès, king of the Persians, the following letter : —

Abgar's letter to Ardachès.

"Abgar, king of the Armenians, to Ardachès my brother, king of the Persians, greeting : —

"I know that you have heard of Jesus Christ, the Son of God, whom the Jews have crucified, Jesus who was raised from the dead, and has sent His disciples through all the world to instruct men. One of His chief disciples, named Simon, is in your Majesty's territories. Seek for him, and you will find him, and he will cure you of all your maladies, and will show you the way of life, and you will believe in his words, you, and your brothers, and all those who willingly obey you. It is very pleasant to me to think that my relations in the flesh will be also my relations, my friends, in the spirit."

Abgar had not yet received answers to these letters when he died, having reigned thirty-eight years.

IX.[1]

MARTYRDOM OF OUR APOSTLES.

After the death of Abgar, the kingdom of Armenia was divided between two : Ananoun, Abgar's son, reigned at Edessa, and his sister's son, Sanadroug, in Armenia. What took place in their time has been previously told by others : the apostle's arrival in Armenia, the conversion of Sanadroug and his apostasy for fear of the Armenian satraps, and the martyrdom of the apostle and his companions in the canton of Chavarchan, now called Ardaz, and the stone opening to receive the body of the apostle, and the removal of this body by his disciples, his burial in the plain, and the martyrdom of the king's daughter, Santoukhd, near the road, and the apparition of the remains of the two saints, and their removal to the rocks — all circumstances related by others, as we have said, a long time before us : we have not thought it important to repeat them here. In the same way also what is related of the martyrdom at Edessa of Attæus, a disciple of the apostle, a martyrdom ordered by Abgar's son, has been told by others before us.

The prince who reigned after the death of his father, did not inherit his father's virtues : he opened the temples of the idols, and embraced the religion of the heathen. He sent word to Attæus : "Make me a head-dress of cloth interwoven with gold, like those you formerly used to make for my father." He received this answer from Attæus : "My hands shall not make a head-dress for an unworthy prince, who does not worship Christ the living God."

Immediately the king ordered one of his armed men to cut off Attæus' feet. The soldier went, and, seeing the holy man seated in the chair of the teacher, cut off his legs with his sword, and immediately the saint gave up the ghost. We mention this cursorily, as a fact related by others a long while ago. There came then into Armenia the Apostle Bartholomew, who suffered martyrdom among us in the town of Arepan. As to Simon, who was sent unto Persia, I cannot relate with certainty what he did, nor where he suffered martyrdom. It is said that one Simon, an apostle, was martyred at Veriospore. Is this true, or why did the saint come to this place ? I do not know ; I have only mentioned this circumstance that you may know I spare no pains to tell you all that is necessary.

X.[2]

REIGN OF SANADROUG ; MURDER OF ABGAR'S CHILDREN ; THE PRINCESS HELENA.

Sanadroug, being on the throne, raises troops with the help of the brave Pacradouni and Ardzrouni, who had exalted him, and goes to wage war upon the children of Abgar, to make himself master of the whole kingdom. Whilst Sanadroug was occupied with these affairs, as if by an effect of divine providence vengeance was taken for the death of Attæus ; for a marble column which the son of Abgar was having erected at Edessa, on the summit of his palace, while he was underneath to direct the work, escaped from the hands of the workmen, fell upon him and crushed his feet.

Immediately there came a message from the inhabitants of the town, asking Sanadroug for a treaty by which he should engage not to disturb them in the exercise of the Christian religion, in consideration of which, they would give up the town and the king's treasures. Sanadroug promised, but in the end violated his oath. Sanadroug put all the children of the house of Abgar to the edge of the sword, with the exception of the daughters, whom he withdrew from the town to place them in the canton of Hachdiank. As to the first of Abgar's wives, named Helena, he sent her to his town at Kharan, and left to her the sovereignty of the whole of Mesopotamia, in remembrance of the benefits he had received from Abgar by Helena's means.

Helena, pious like her husband Abgar, did not wish to live in the midst of idolaters ; she went away to Jerusalem in the time of Claudius, during the famine which Agabus had predicted ; with all her treasures she bought in Egypt an immense quantity of corn, which she distributed

---

[1] Chapter xxxiv.

[2] Chapter xxxv.

amongst the poor, a fact to which Josephus testifies. Helena's tomb, a truly remarkable one, is still to be seen before the gate of Jerusalem.

XI.[1]

RESTORATION OF THE TOWN OF MEDZPINE; NAME OF SANADROUG; HIS DEATH.

Of all Sanadroug's doings and actions, we judge none worthy of remembrance except the building of the town of Medzpine; for, this town having been shaken by an earthquake, Sanadroug pulled it down, rebuilt it more magnificently, and surrounded it with double walls and ramparts. Sanadroug caused to be erected in the middle of the town his statue holding in his hand a single piece of money, which signifies: "All my treasures have been used in building the town, and no more than this single piece of money is left to me."

But why was this prince called Sanadroug? We will tell you: Because Abgar's sister, Otæa, while travelling in Armenia in the winter, was assailed by a whirlwind of snow in the Gortouk mountains; the tempest separated them all, so that none of them knew where his companion had been driven. The prince's nurse, Sanod, sister of Piourad Pacradouni, wife of Khosran Ardzrouni, having taken the royal infant, for Sanadroug was still in the cradle, laid him upon her bosom, and remained with him under the snow three days and three nights. Legend has taken possession of this circumstance: it relates that an animal, a new species, wonderful, of great whiteness, sent by the gods, guarded the child. But so far as we have been informed, this is the fact: a white dog, which was amongst the men sent in search, found the child and his nurse; the prince was therefore called Sanadroug, a name taken from his nurse's name (and from the Armenian name, *dourk*, a gift), as if to signify the gift of Sanod.

Sanadroug, having ascended the throne in the twelfth year of Ardachès, king of the Persians, and having lived thirty years, died as he was hunting, from an arrow which pierced his bowels, as if in punishment of the torments which he had made his holy daughter suffer. Gheroupna, son of the scribe Apchatar, collected all these facts, happening in the time of Abgar and Sanadroug, and placed them in the archives of Edessa.

[1] Chapter xxxvi.

ANCIENT SYRIAC DOCUMENTS

HOMILY ON HABIB THE MARTYR, COMPOSED BY MAR JACOB.[1]

HABIB the martyr, clad in flame, hath called to
 me out of the fire,
That for him likewise I should fashion an
 image of beauty among the glorious.
Comrade of conquerors, lo ! he beckoneth to me
 out of the burning,
That, as for the glory of his Lord, I should
 sing concerning him.
In the midst of live coals stands the *heroic* man,
 and lo ! he calleth to me,
That I should fashion his image : but the blazing fire permits me not.

His love is fervid, glowing is his faith ;
 His fire also burneth, and who is adequate to
 recount his love ?
Nay, by reason of that love which led the mar-
 tyr into the fire,
 No man is able to recount his beauties divine.
For who shall dare enter and see in the blazing
 fire
 To whom he is like, and after what pattern he
 is to be fashioned among the glorious ?

Shall I fashion his image by the side of the
 youths, the children of the furnace ?
 With Hananiah shall I reckon Habib ? I know
 not.
Lo ! these were not burned there : how, then,
 is he like ?
He, *I say*, like them, when he was burned,
 and the youths not ?
Which, I ask, *the more* beautiful — Habib the
 martyr, or Azariah ?

Difficult for me is the image : how I am to
 look upon it, I know not.
Lo ! Michael was not burned by the flame ;
 But Habib was burned : which, then, *the more*
 beautiful to him that looketh upon him ?
Who shall dare say that this is repulsive, or
 that ;
 Or not so comely this as that, to him that beholdeth him ?

Three *there are* in the fire, and the flame cometh
 not near them ;
 But one was burned : and how shall I suffice
 to tell
That the Fourth *form* is that of Him who went
 down into the midst of the furnace,
 That He might fashion an image for Habib
 there along with *those of* the three ?
He giveth a place in the fire to him who was
 burned,
 That he may be, instead of Him the Fourth,
 by the side of the conquerors.

And, if of the three the beauties be glorious,
 though they were not burned,
 How shall not this one, who *was* burned, be
 mingled with the glorious ?
If a man have the power either to be burned or
 not to be burned,
 Of this man, who was burned, more exalted
 was the beauty than that of the three.
But, inasmuch as the Lord is the control *of all
 things*,
 He is to be praised, *both* where He rescues
 and where He delivers up.

Moreover, too, the will of the three who were
 not burned,
 And of him who was burned, is one and the
 same, in this case and in that ;[2]
And, had its Lord commanded the fire to burn
 them,
 Even those three on their part, burned they
 would have been ;

[1] The MS. from which this is taken is Cod. Add. 17,158, fol. 30
vers. Mar Jacob, bishop of Sarug, or Batnæ, was one of the most
learned and celebrated among all the Syriac writers. He was born
A D. 452, made bishop of Sarug A.D. 519, and died A.D. 521. He was
the author of several liturgical works, epistles, and sermons, and,
amongst these, of numerous metrical homilies, of which two are given
here. Assemani enumerates no less than 231. Ephraem Syrus also
wrote a similar homily on Habib, Shamuna, and Guria.
  The metre of the original in this and the following homily consists of
twelve sylables, and six dissyllabic feet ; but whether they were read as
iambs ortroches, or as both, appears to depend on the nature of the
Syriac accentuation, which is still an unsettled question. Hoffmann,
in his slight notice of the subject (*Gram. Syr.*, § 13), merely says :
" Scimus, poësin Syriacam non quantitatis sed *accentus* tantum
rationem habere, versusque suos *syllabarum numero* metiri. Quâ
tamen poëseos Syriacæ conditione *varietas morarum in pronun-
tiandis vocalibus observandarum* non tollitur." — Tr.

[2] Lit. " here and there." — Tr.

And, if He had signified to it that it should not burn that one man also,
He would not have been burned; nor had it been of himself that he was rescued.
To go into the fire was of their own will, when they went in;
But that they were not burned — *because* the Lord of the fire willed and commanded it.
Therefore one equal beauty is that of him who was burned,
And that of him who was not burned, because the will also was equal.

Beloved martyr! exalted is thy beauty; exalted is thy rank:
Graceful too thy crown, and mingled thy story with *that of* the glorious.
Choice gold art thou, and the fire hath tried thee, and resplendent is thy beauty.
And lo! into the King's crown art thou wrought, along with the victorious.
Good workman! who, in the doctrine of the Son of God,
Pursueth his course like a valiant [1] man, because of the beauty of his faith.

Habib the martyr was a teacher of that which is true;
A preacher also, whose mouth was full of faith.
Watchful was he, and prompt *for service;* and he encouraged with his teaching
The household of the house of God, through his faith.
Of light was he full, and he wrestled with the darkness
Which overspread the country from the paganism which had darkened it.
With the Gospel of the Son was his mouth filled in the congregations;
And as it were a leader of the way did he become to the villages when he arrived in them.

Zealous he was, because he was concerned for the doctrine
Divine, that he might establish the adherents [2] of the faith.
At the time when the winds of the pagans blew, a lamp was he,
And flamed forth whilst they blew upon him, and went not out.
All on fire was he, and filled with the love of his Lord, and was concerned
For this — that he might speak of Him without hindrance.[3]

The thorns of errour sprang up in the land from paganism;
And, as much as in him lay, he rooted them out by his diligence.
He taught, admonished, and confirmed in the faith,
The friends of Christ,[4] who were harassed by persecutors.
Against sword and against fire did he wrestle,
With love hot as the flame, and was not afraid.
Like a two-edged brand,[5] keen was
His faith, and against error did he contend.
Leaven did he prove to be in this land which had become exhausted [6]
Through fondness for the idols of vanity which error had brought in.
He was like salt by reason of his savoury doctrine
To this region, which had become insipid through unbelief.

A deacon was he, and filled the place of a high-priest
By the preaching and teaching of that which is true.
He was to the flock a good shepherd whilst he was *its* overseer;
And his life laid he down for the flock while he tended it.
He chased away the wolf, and drove off from it the beast of prey.
And he repaired the breaches, and gathered the lambs into their folds.
He went out secretly *and* encouraged the congregations:
He strengthened them, and exhorted them, and held them up.
And he forged armour of faith, and put it on them,
That they might not be ignominiously overthrown [7] by the paganism which abounded.

The flocks of the fold of the Son of God were being laid waste
By persecutors: and he encouraged the lambs and the ewes.

---

[1] Cureton has "prosperous," which Dr. Payne Smith condemns, remarking: "ܐ I find generally used for the Gk. ἄριστος, and once or twice for κράτιστος. It answers more frequently to *strenuus* = courageous, heroic." — TR.

[2] Lit. "the party" or "side." — TR.

[3] As in Gal. v. 7, answering to the Gk. ἐγκόπτω. The verb ܩܦ (Pa.) properly means to *disquiet* (as in John xiv. 1), then to *hinder*. — TR.

[4] The ordinary word for "Christians" in these documents is the borrowed Χριστιανοί: here a native word is used, formed from the one which we read as "Messiah." — TR.

[5] A corruption of the word σαμψηρά is used here. It is said by Josephus, *Antiq.*, xx. 2. 3, to have been the name given by the Assyrians to some kind of sword. Suidas mentions it as a barbarian word for σπάθη, a *broadsword.* Cureton's "scimetar" would be preferable, as being somewhat more distinctive, if it appeared that a scimetar could have two edges. — TR.

[6] The temptation was strong to render ܚܡܥ, "became unleavened" (or "tasteless"), a sense apparently required by the decided figure employed and by the language of the next couplet, where "insipid" corresponds to "salt." The word ܦܛܝܪܐ (= ἄζυμον), moreover, if not the Arabic ܦܛܝܪ (to which Schaaf, though it does not appear on what authority, assigns the meaning "*sine fermento massam subegit*"), seems to point in the same direction. Dr. Payne Smith, however, is not aware of any instance of the proposed meaning: he says, "My examples make ܚܡܥ = ἐκλείπω, to fail." — TR.

[7] Or "brought to contempt." — TR.

And he was an advocate to the household of
faith ;
And he taught them not to be daunted by
persecutors.
He taught them to run to meet death,
Without being afraid either of sword or of
fire.
In the teaching of the Son of God he prospered,
So that his faith pursued its course without
dread.

Then errour grew envious, became furious, and
was maddened, because of him ;
And she pursued after him, that she might
shed upon the earth innocent blood.
The Defamer, who hates the race of men,
Laid snares for him, that he might rid the
place of his presence.[1]
He who hateth the truth pursued after him to
put him to death,
That he might make his voice to cease[2] from
the teaching of the house of God.
And errour raised an outcry *demanding* that Habib should die, because she hated him ;
Vexation goaded her on, and she sought to
take away his life.

His story was talked about[3] before the pagan
judge of the country,
And the dear fame of him reached the king :
who in great rage,
And because the diadem was interwoven with
paganism, decreed[4] death
Against Habib, because he was full of faith.
And, when the command reached the judge, he
armed himself
With rage and fury ; and, with a mind thirst-
ing for blood,
And like hunters who lay nets for the young stag,
After Habib did they go out to catch *him*.

But this man was a preacher of the faith,
Who in the highway of the crucifixion was
prospering ;
And, that he might benefit by his teaching the
children of his people,
His work embraced the countries round about
him.
So, when error went out after him, she found
him not :
Not that he was fled, but that he had gone
out to preach the Gospel.
Then, because of the fury of the pagans, which
was great beyond all that was meet,
His kindred and his mother did they seize for
his sake.

---

[1] Lit. " society." — TR.
[2] Or " that his voice might cease." — TR.
[3] Lit. " mooted." — TR.
[4] Lit. " reached the king in great rage (i.e., *so as to cause* great
rage, ‿ being often = εἰς denoting result), and, because . . ., he decreed." — DR. PAYNE SMITH.

Blessed art thou, O woman ! mother since thou
art of the martyr.
For wherefore was it that they seized thee *and*
bound thee, iniquitously ?
What do they require of thee, O thou full of
beauty ? What, *I ask*, have they required
of thee ?
Lo ! they require of thee that thou bring the
martyr, that he may be a sacrifice.
Bring, oh bring thy sweet fruit to the place of
the oblation —
The fruit whose smell is fragrant, that it may
be incense to the Godhead.
Fair shoot, thy cluster bring from where it is,
That its wine may be for a libation whose
taste is sweet.

The lamb heard that they were seeking him,
that he might be a sacrifice ;
And he set out and came to the sacrificers
rejoicing.
He heard that others also were being afflicted
for his sake,
And he came that he might bear the suffering
which was his, in the stead of many.
The lot fell on him, to be himself alone a sacrifice ;
And the fire that was to offer him up was
looking out *for him* until he came.
Of the many who were bound for his sake
Not one single person was seized to die, but
only he.
He it was that was worthy, and for him was martyrdom reserved ;
And to snatch the martyr's place no man was
able.
And therefore of his own will did he present
himself
To the judge, that he might be seized, and die
for Jesus' sake.
He heard that they sought him, and he came
that he might be seized, even as they
sought him :
And he went in of himself before the judge,
and dauntless was his look.
He hid not himself, nor did he wish to flee from
the judge :
For with light was he imbued, and from the
darkness he would not flee.

No robber *was he*, no murderer, no thief,
No child of night : but all his course was run
in open day.
Wherefore from his flock should the good shep-
herd flee,
And leave his fold to be devoured by robbers ?
Wherefore should the physician flee, who goeth
forth to heal diseases,
And to cure souls by the blood of the Son of
God ?

A fearless countenance [1] did the *brave* man carry
with him, and a great heart;
And to meet death he ran, rejoicing, for Jesus'
sake.

He went in, he stood before the judge, saying to
him:
I am Habib, whom ye sought: lo! *here* I
stand.
And the pagan trembled, and amazement seized
him, and he marvelled at him —
At the man who was not afraid, either of sword
or of fire.
While he thought that he was fleeing apace, he
entered in and mocked him;
And the judge shook, for he saw him courageous in the *very* face of death.

A disciple he of that Son of God who said:
"Rise, come, let us go: for he that betrayeth
me lo! is here."
And to the crucifiers, again, He said: "Whom
seek ye?"
They say: "Jesus." And He said to them:
"I am He."
The Son of God of His own will came to the
cross;
And on Him the martyr looked, and presented
himself *uncompelled* before the judge.

And the pagan beheld him, and was smitten with
fear, and was exasperated *against him.*
His rage was excited, and he began in his fury
to put to him questions.[2]
And, as if he had been one who had shed on the
ground the blood of the slain,
He proceeded to question the saintly man, but
he was not ashamed:
Menacing him, and trying to terrify him, and to
frighten him,
And recounting the sufferings which were being prepared by him on his account.

But Habib, when questioned, was not afraid,
Was not ashamed, and was not frightened by
the menaces *he heard.*
Lifting up his voice, he confessed Jesus, the Son
of God —
That he was His servant, and was His priest,
and His minister.[3]
At the fury of the pagans, roaring at him like
lions,
He trembled not, nor ceased [4] from the confession of the Son of God.

He was scourged, and the scourgings were very
dear to him,
Seeing that he bore a little of the stripes of
the Son of God.
He was put into bonds,[5] and he looked on his
Lord, whom also they had bound;
And his heart rejoiced that in the path of His
sufferings he had begun to walk.
He ascended the block,[6] and they tore him with
combs, but his soul was radiant with light,
Because he was *deemed* worthy that on him
should come the agony of the sufferings
of crucifixion.

In the pathway of death had he set his face to
walk,
And what could he desire to find in it but sufferings?
The fire of sacrifice [7] was betrothed to him, and
for her did he look;
And she *on her part* sent him combs, and
stripes, and pains, to taste.
All the while that she was coming, she sent him
sufferings, that by means of them
He might be prepared, so that when she met
him she might not dismay him.
Sufferings purged him, so that, when the blazing
fire should put him to the proof,
There might not be any dross *found* in his
choice gold.
And he endured the whole of the pains that
came upon him,
That he might have experience *of suffering,*
and in the burning stand like a brave man.

And he accepted rejoicing the sufferings which
he had to bear:
For he knew that at their termination he
should find death.
And he was not afraid, either of death or of sufferings:
For with that wine of the crucifixion his heart
was drunk.
He despised his body, while it was being dragged
along by the persecutors;
And his limbs, while they were being torn
asunder in bitter agony.[8]
Scourges on his back, combs on his sides, stocks
on his feet,
And fire in front of him: still was he brave
and full of faith.

They taunted him: Lo! thou worshippest a
man;
But he said: A man I worship not,
But God, who took a body and became man:

---

[1] Lit. "openness of countenance." — TR.
[2] Prop. "agitate questions." — TR.
[3] Or "deacon." — TR.
[4] Or "so as to cease." — TR.

[5] Lit. "he entered into bondage." — TR.
[6] The *equuleus* is meant. — TR.
[7] Or "of the sacrifices." — TR.
[8] Lit. "bitterly." — TR.

Him do I worship, because He is God with Him that begat Him.

The faith of Habib, the martyr, was full of light ;
And by it was enlightened Edessa, the faithful *city*.

The daughter of Abgar, whom Addæus betrothed to the crucifixion —
Through it is her light, through it her truth and her faith.

Her king is from it, her martyrs from it, her truth from it ;
The teachers also of *her* faith are from it.

Abgar believed that Thou art God, the Son of God ;
And he received a blessing because of the beauty of his faith.

Sharbil the martyr, son of the Edessæans, more-ever said :
My heart is led captive by God, who became man.

And Habib the martyr, who also was crowned at Edessa,
Confessed these things : that He took a body and became man ;

That He is the Son of God, and also is God, and became man.
Edessa learned from teachers the things that are true :

Her king taught her, her martyrs taught her, the faith ;
But to others, who were fraudulent teachers, she would not hearken.

Habib the martyr, in the ear of Edessa, thus cried aloud
Out of the midst of the fire : A man I worship not,

But God, who took a body and became man —
Him do I worship. *Thus* confessed the martyr with uplifted voice.

From confessors torn with combs, burnt, raised up *on the block*, slain,
And *from* a righteous king, did Edessa learn the faith,

And she knows our Lord — that He is even God, the Son of God ;
She also learned and firmly believed that He took a body and became man.

Not from common scribes did she learn the faith :
Her king taught her, her martyrs taught her ; and she firmly believed them :

And, if she be calumniated as having ever worshipped a man,
She points to her martyrs, who died for Him as being God.

A man I worship not, said Habib,
Because it is written : "Cursed is he that putteth his trust in a man." [1]

---

[1] Jer. xvii. 5. — Tr.

Forasmuch as He is God, I worship Him, yea submit to be burned
For His sake, nor will I renounce His faith.

This truth has Edessa held fast from her youth,
And in her old age she will not barter it away as a daughter of the poor.

Her righteous king became to her a scribe, and from him she learned
Concerning our Lord — that He is the Son of God, yea God.

Addæus, who brought the bridegroom's ring and put it on her hand,
Betrothed her thus to the Son of God, who is the Only-*begotten*.

Sharbil the priest, who made trial and proof of all gods,
Died, even as he said, "for God who became man."

Shamuna and Guria, for the sake of the Only-*begotten*,
Stretched out their necks *to receive the stroke*, and for Him died, forasmuch as He is God.

And Habib the martyr, who was teacher of congregations,
Preached of Him, that He took a body and became man.

For a man the martyr would not have *submitted to be* burned in the fire ;
But he was burned "for the sake of God who became man."

And Edessa is witness that thus he confessed while he was being burned :
And from the confession of a martyr that has been burned who is he that can escape ?

All minds does faith reduce to silence and despise —
She that is full of light and stoopeth not to shadows.

She despiseth him that maligns the Son by denying that He is God ;
Him too that saith "He took not a body and became man."

In faith which was full of truth he stood upon the fire ;
And he became incense, and propitiated with his fragrance the Son of God.

In all *his* afflictions, and in all *his* tortures, and in all *his* sufferings,
Thus did he confess, and thus did he teach the blessed *city*.

And this truth did Edessa hold fast touching our Lord —
Even that He is God, and of Mary became a man.

And the bride hates him that denies His Godhead,
And despises and contemns him that maligns His corporeal nature.

And she recognises Him *as* One in Godhead and in manhood —

The Only-*begotten*, whose body is inseparable from Him.
And thus did the daughter of the Parthians learn to believe,
And thus did she firmly hold, and thus does she teach him that listens to her.

The judge, therefore, full of *zeal for* paganism, commanded
That the martyr should be led forth and burned in the fire which was reserved for him.
And forthwith a strap was thrust into his mouth, as *though he had been* a murderer,
His confession being kept within his heart towards God.
And they hurried him away, and he went out from the judgment-hall, rejoicing
That the hour was come when the crown should be given to his faith.
And there went out with him crowds of people, that they might bear him company,
Looking upon him, not as a dead man accompanied *to his burial*,
But as a man who was going away that by means of fire he might become a bridegroom,
And that there might be bestowed the crown which was by righteousness reserved for him.
They looked upon him as upon a man entering into battle,
And around him were spears, and lances, and swords, but he vanquished them.
They beheld him going up like a champion from the contest,
And in his triumph chaplets were brought to him by those who beheld.
They looked upon him as he vanquished principalities and powers,
Which all made war with him, and he put them to shame.
The whole congregation of the followers of Christ exulted over him,
Because he raised up the friends [1] of the faith by the sufferings which he bore.
There went forth with him the Church, a bride full of light;
And her face was beaming on the beloved martyr who was united to her.

Then did his mother, because it was the marriage-feast for her son,
Deck herself in garments nobler than her wont.
Since sordid raiment suited not the banquet-hall,
In magnificent *attire* all white she clad herself right tastefully.
Hither to the battle came down love to fight
In the mother's soul — *the love* of nature, and *the love* of God.

[1] Lit. " side," or " party." — Tr.

She looked upon her son as he went forth to be put into the flame;
And, forasmuch as there was in her the love of the Lord, she suffered not.
The yearnings of her mother's womb cried out on behalf of its fruit;
But faith silenced them, so that their tumult ceased.
Nature shrieked over the limb which was severed from her;
But the love of the Lord intoxicated the soul, that she should not perceive it.
Nature loved, but the love of the Lord did conquer in the strife
Within the soul of the mother, that she should not grieve for her beloved.
And instead of suffering, her heart was filled with all emotions of joy;
And, instead of mourning, she went forth in splendid apparel.
And she accompanied him as he went out to be burned, and was elate,
Because the love of the Lord vanquished that of nature.
And *clad* in white, as for a bridegroom, she made a marriage-feast —
She the mother of the martyr, and was blithe because of him.
" Shamuna the Second " may we call this blessed *one :*
Since, had seven been burned instead of one, she had been well content.
One she had, and she gave him to be food for the fire ;
And, even as that one, if she had had seven, she had given *them all*.
He was cast into the fire, and the blaze kindled around him ;
And his mother looked on, and grieved not at his burning.
Another eye, which gazeth upon the things unseen,
Was in her soul, and by reason of this she exulted when he was being burned.
On the gems of light which are in martyrs' crowns she looked,
And on the glory which is laid up for them after their sufferings ;
And *on* the promised blessings which they inherit yonder through their afflictions,
And *on* the Son of God who clothes their limbs with light ;
And *on* the manifold beauties of that kingdom which shall not be dissolved,
And *on* the ample door which is opened for them to enter in to God.
On these did the martyr's mother look when he was being burned,
And she rejoiced, she exalted, and in white did she go forth with him.

She looked upon him while the fire consumed his frame,
And, forasmuch as his crown was very noble, she grieved not.

The sweet root was thrown into the fire, upon the coals ;
And it turned to incense, and cleansed the air from pollution.
With the fumes of sacrifice had the air been polluted,
And by the burning of this martyr was it cleansed.
The firmament was fetid with the exhalations from [1] the altars ;
And there rose up the sweet perfume of the martyr, and it grew sweet thereby.
And the sacrifices ceased, and there was peace in the assemblies ;·
And the sword was blunted, that it should no more lay waste the friends of Christ.

With Sharbil it began, with Habib it ended, in our land ;
And from that time [2] even until now not one has it slain, since he was burned.
Constantine, chief of conquerors, took the empire,
And the cross has trampled on the diadem of the emperor, and is set upon his head.
Broken is the lofty horn of idolatry,
And from the burning of the martyr even until now not one has it pierced.
His smoke arose, and it became incense to the Godhead ;
And by it was the air purged which was tainted by paganism,
And by his burning was the whole land cleansed :
Blessed be he that gave him a crown, and glory, and a good name !

Here endeth the Homily on Habib the martyr, composed by Mar Jacob.

---

[1] Lit. " the sacrifices of." — TR.

[2] Lit. " from him." — TR.

A HOMILY ON GURIA AND SHAMUNA, COMPOSED BY MAR JACOB.

SHAMUNA and Guria, martyrs who made themselves illustrious in their afflictions,
Have in love required of me to tell of their illustrious deeds.
To champions of the faith the doctrine calleth me,
That I should go and behold their contests and their crowns.
Children of the right hand, who have done battle against the left,
Have called me this day to recite the marvellous tale of their conflicts : —

Simple old men, who entered into the fight like heroes,
And nobly distinguished themselves in the strife of blood :
Those who were the salt of our land, and it was sweetened thereby,
And its savour was restored, which had become insipid through unbelief :
Candlesticks of gold, which were full of the oil of the crucifixion,
By which was lighted up all our region, which had turned to darkness :
Two lamps, of which, when all the winds were blowing
Of every *kind of* error, the lights were not put out :

Good labourers, who from the spring of day laboured
In the blessed vineyard of the house of God right duteously :
Bulwarks of our land, who became to us as it were a defence
Against all spoilers in all the wars that surrounded us :
Havens of peace, a place also of retreat for all that were distressed,
And a resting-place for the head of every one that was in need of succour :
Two precious pearls, which were
An ornament for the bride of my lord Abgar, the Aramæan's son.

Teachers they were who practised their teaching in blood,
And whose faith was known by their sufferings.
On their bodies they wrote the story of the Son of God
With *the marks of* combs and scourges which thickly covered them.
They showed their love, not by words of the mouth alone,
But by tortures and by the rending of their limbs asunder.
For the love of the Son of God they gave up their bodies :

Since it beseemeth the lover that for his love
 he should give up himself.
Fire and sword proved their love, how true *it was;*
 And more beautiful than silver tried in *a fur-*
  nace of earth were their necks.

They looked on God, and, because they saw His
 exalted beauties,
 Therefore did they look with contempt upon
  their sufferings for His sake.
The Sun of righteousness had arisen in their
 hearts;
 And they were enlightened by it, and with *His*
  light chased they away the darkness.
At the idols of vanity, which error had brought
 in, they laughed,
 Instinct with the faith of the Son of God
  which is full of light.
The love of the Lord was as a fire in their hearts;
 Nor could all the brambles of idolatry stand
  before it.
Fixed was their love on God unchangeably: [1]
 And therefore did they look with scorn upon
  the sword,[2] all athirst as it was for blood.

With guilelessness and *yet with* wisdom stood
 they in the judgment-hall,
 As they had been commanded by the Teacher
  of that which is true.
Despising as they did kindred and family, guile-
 less were they;
 Forasmuch, also, as possessions and wealth
  were held in no account by them.
Nor guileless only: for in the judgment-hall with
 the wisdom of serpents *too*
 They were heedful of the faith of the house of
  God.

When a serpent is seized and struck, he guards
 his head,
 But gives up and leaves exposed all his body
  to his captors:
And, so long as his head is kept *from harm,* his
 life abideth in him;
 But, if the head be struck, his life is left *a*
  prey to destruction.
The head of the soul is men's faith;
 And, if this be preserved *unharmed,* by it is
  also preserved their life: [3]
Even though the whole body be lacerated with
 blows,
 Yet, so long as faith is preserved, the soul is
  alive;
But, if faith is struck *down* by unbelief,
 Lost is the soul, and life has perished from
  the man.

Shamuna and Guria of the faith as men [4]
 Were heedful, that it should not be struck
  down by persecutors:
For they knew that, if faith is preserved,
 Both soul and body are preserved from de-
  struction.
And, because of this, touching their faith were
 they solicitous,
 That that should not be struck *down* in which
  their very life was hidden.

They gave up their bodies both to blows and to
 dislocation,[5]
 Yea to every *kind of* torture, that their faith
  should not be stricken *down;*
And, even as the serpent also hides his head
 from blows,
 So hid they their faith within their hearts;
And the body was smitten, and endured stripes,
 and bore sufferings:
 But overthrown was not their faith which was
  within their hearts.

The mouth betrayeth the soul to death when it
 speaks,
 And with the tongue, as with a sword, work-
  eth slaughter.
And from it spring up both life and death to men:
 Denying *a man* dies, confessing he lives, and
  the mouth hath power over it.
Denial is death, and in confession is the soul's
 life;
 And power hath the mouth over them both,
  like a judge.
The word of the mouth openeth the door for
 death to enter in;
 This, too, calleth for life, and it beameth forth
  upon the man.
Even the robber by one word of faith
 Won him the kingdom, and became heir of
  paradise,[6] all fraught with blessings.
The wicked judges too, from the martyrs, the
 sons of the right hand,
 Demanded that by word of mouth only they
  should blaspheme;
But, like true men holding fast the faith,
 They uttered not a word by which unbelief
  might be served.

Shamuna, beauty of our faith, who is adequate to
 tell of thee?
 All too narrow is my mouth for thy praise,
  too mean for thee to be spoken of by it.
Thy truth is thy beauty, thy crown thy suffering,
 thy wealth thy stripes,
 And by reason of thy blows magnificent is the
  beauty of thy championship.

---

[1] Or "who changes not." — Tr.
[2] Σαμψηρά. — Tr.
[3] Or "salvation:" a different word from that used in speaking of
the serpent. — Tr.

[4] Lit. "as a man." — Tr.
[5] Or "rending asunder." — Tr.
[6] Lit. "the garden." — Tr.

Proud of thee is our country, as of a treasury
which is full of gold :
Since wealth art thou to us, and a coveted
store which cannot be stolen *from us*.

Guria, martyr, staunch hero of our faith,
Who shall suffice thee, to recount thy beauties
divine?
Lo! tortures on thy body are set like gems of
beryl,
And the sword on thy neck like a chain of
choice gold.
Thy blood upon thy form is a robe of glory full
of beauty,
And the scourging of thy back a vesture with
which the sun may not compare.
Radiant thou art and comely by virtue of these
thy sufferings, so abounding ;
And resplendent are thy beauties, because of
the pains which are *so* severe upon thee.

Shamuna, our riches, richer art thou than the
rich :
For lo! the rich stand at thy door, that thou
mayest relieve them.
Small thy village, poor thy country : who, then,
gave thee
That lords of villages and cities should court
thy favour?
Lo! judges in their robes and vestments
Take dust from thy threshold, as *though it
were* the medicine of life.
The cross is rich, and to its worshippers in-
creaseth riches ;
And its poverty despiseth all the riches of the
world.

Shamuna and Guria, sons of the poor, lo! at
your doors
Bow down the rich, that they may receive
from you *supplies for* their wants.
The Son of God in poverty and want
Showed to the world that all its riches are as
nothing.
His disciples, all fishermen, all poor, all weak,
All men of little note, became illustrious
through His faith.
One fisherman, whose " village " too was a home
of fishermen,[1]
He made chief over the twelve, yea head of
the house.[2]
One a tentmaker, who aforetime was a persecutor,
He seized upon, and made him a chosen
vessel for the faith.

Shamuna and Guria came from villages that were
not wealthy,
And lo! in a great city became they lords ;

And its chief men, its judges also, stand before
their doors,
And they solicit their charity to satisfy their
wants.
From their confession of the faith of the Son of
God
These blessed men acquired riches beyond
compute.
Poor did He Himself become, and the poor
made He rich ;
And lo! enriched is the whole creation through
His poverty.

The chosen martyrs did battle against error,
And in the confession of the Son of God stood
they firm like valiant men.
They went in and confessed Him before the
judge with look undaunted,[3]
That He too might confess them, even as
they confessed Him, before His Father.
There arose against them the war of pagans like
a tempest ;
But the cross was their helmsman, and steered
them on.
They were required to sacrifice to lifeless images,
But they departed not from their confession
of the Son of God.
The wind of idolatry blew in their faces,
But they themselves were as rocks piled up
against the hurricane.
Like a swift whirlwind, error snatched at them ;
But, forasmuch as they were sheltered by the
crucifixion, it hurt them not.
The Evil One set on all his dogs to bark, that
they might bite them ;
But, forasmuch as they had the cross for a
staff, they put them all to flight.

But who is sufficient to tell of their contests,
Or their sufferings, or the rending asunder of
their limbs?
Or who can paint the picture of their coronation,[4]
How they went up from the contest covered
with glory?

To judgment they went in, but of the judge they
took no account ;
Nor were they anxious what they should say
when questioned.
The judge menaced *them*, and multiplied his
words of threatening ;
And recounted tortures and all *kinds of* inflictions, that he might terrify them.
He spake great words,[5] that by fright and intimi-
dation,
By menaces too, he might incline them to
sacrifice.

---

[1] i.e., " Bethsaida." — Tr.
[2] Or " steward." — Tr.

[3] Lit. " with openness of countenance." — Tr.
[4] Lit. " portray the image of their crowns." — Tr.
[5] Lit. " magnified his words." — Tr.

Yet the combatants despised the menaces, and
the intimidations,
And the sentence of judgment, and all bodily
deaths ;
And they prepared themselves for insult and
stripes, and for blows,
And for provocation, and to be dragged along,
and to be burnt ;
For imprisonment also, and for bonds, and for
all evil things,
And for all tortures, and for all sufferings, rejoicing all the while.
They were not alarmed nor affrighted, nor dismayed,
Nor did the sharpness of the tortures bend
them to sacrifice.
Their body they despised, and as dung upon the
ground accounted they it :
For they knew that, the more it was beaten,
the more would its beauty increase ;
And, the more the judge increased his menaces
to alarm them,
The more did they show their contempt of
him, having no fear of his threats.
He kept telling them what tortures he had prepared for them ;
And they continued telling him about Gehenna,
which was reserved for him.

By those things which he told *them* he tried to
frighten them to sacrifice ;
And they spoke to him about the fearful judg-
ment yonder.
Truth is wiser than wise words,
And very hateful, however much it may be
adorned, is falsehood.
Shamuna and Guria went on speaking truth,
While the judge continued to utter falsehood.
And therefore were they not afraid of his threat-
ening,
Because all his menaces against the truth were
accounted *by them* as empty sound.[1]

The intercourse of the world they despised, they
contemned and scorned, *yea* they abandoned ;
And to return to it they had no wish, or to
enter it *again*.
From the place of judgment they set their faces
to depart
To that meeting-place for them all, the life of
the new world.
They cared neither for possessions nor for houses,
Nor for the advantages of this world, so full
of evil.
In the world of light was their heart bound captive with God,
And to "that" country did they set their face
to depart ;

And they looked to the sword, to come and be
a bridge
To let them pass over to God, for whom they
were longing.
This world they accounted as a little tent,
But that yonder as a city full of beauties ;
And they were in haste by the sword to depart
hence
To the land of light, which is full of blessing
for those who are worthy of it.

The judge commanded to hang them up by their
arms,
And without mercy did they stretch them out
in bitter agony.
A demon's fury breathed rage into the heart of
the judge,
And embittered him against the stedfast ones,
inciting him to crush them ;
And between the height and the depth he stretched
them out to afflict them :
And they were a marvel to both sides, *when
they saw* how much they endured.
At the old men's frame heaven and earth marvelled,
To see how much suffering it bore nor cried
out for help under *their* affliction.
Hung up and dragged along are their feeble
bodies by their arms,
Yet is there deep silence, nor is there one that
cries out for help or that murmurs.

Amazed were all who beheld their contests,
To see how *calmly* the outstretched forms bore
the inflictions *laid upon them*.[2]
Amazed too was Satan at their spotless frames,
To see what weight of affliction they sustained
without a groan.
Yea, and gladdened too were the angels by that
fortitude *of theirs*,
To see how patiently it bore that contest *so*
terrible that was.
But, as combatants who were awaiting their
crowns,
There entered no sense of weariness into their
minds.
Nay, it was the judge that grew weary ; yea, he
was astonished :
But the noble men *before him* felt no weariness
in their afflictions.

He asked them whether they would consent to
sacrifice ;
But the mouth was unable to speak from
pain.
Thus did the persecutors increase their inflictions,
Until they gave no place for the word to be
spoken.

[1] Lit. " as breath." — TR.

[2] Lit. " how much the outstretched forms bore in consequence of
the inflictions." — TR.

Silent was the mouth from the inflictions laid on
their limbs;
But the will, like that of a hero, was nerved
with fortitude from itself.
Alas for the persecutors! how destitute were they
of righteousness!
But the children of light — how were they clad
in faith!
They demand speech, when there is no place for
speaking,
Since the word of the mouth was forbidden
them by pain.
Fast bound was the body, and silent the mouth,
and it was unable
To utter the word when unrighteously questioned.

And what should the martyr do, who had no
power to say,
When he was questioned, that he would not
sacrifice?
All silent were the old men full of faith,
And from pain they were incapable of speak-
ing.
Yet questioned they were: and in what way, if
a man is silent
When he is questioned, shall he assent to that
which is said?
But the old men, that they might not be thought
to assent,
Expressed clearly by signs the word which it
behoved them to speak.
Their heads they shook, and, instead of speech,
by a dumb sign they showed
The resolve of the new man that was within.
Their heads hung down, signifying amidst their
pains
That they were not going to sacrifice, and
every one understood their meaning.
As long as there was in them place for speech,
with speech did they confess;
But, when it was forbidden them by pain, they
spake with a dumb sign.
Of faith they spoke both with the voice and
without the voice:
So that, when speaking and also when silent,
they were *alike* stedfast.

Who but must be amazed at the path of life,
how narrow it is,
And how straight to him that desires to walk
in it?
Who but must marvel *to see* that, when the will
is watchful and ready,
It is very broad and full of light to him that
goeth therein?
About the path are ditches; full also is it of
pitfalls;
And, if one turn but a little aside from it, a
ditch receives him.

That dumb sign only is there between the right
and the left,
And on "Yea" and "Nay" stand[1] sin and
righteousness.
By a dumb sign only did the blessed men plainly signify that they would not sacrifice,
And in virtue of a single dumb sign did the
path lead them to Eden;
And, if this same dumb sign had inclined and
turned down but a little
Toward the depth, the path of the old men
would have been to Gehenna.
Upwards they made a sign, *to signify* that upwards were they prepared to ascend;
And in consequence of that sign they ascended and mingled with the heavenly ones.
Between sign and sign were Paradise and Gehenna:
They made a sign that they would not sacrifice, and they inherited the place of the
kingdom.

Even while they were silent they were advocates
for the Son of God:
For not in multitude of words doth faith consist.
That fortitude of theirs was a full-voiced confession,
And as though with open mouth declared they
their faith by signs;
And every one knew what they were saying,
though silent,
And enriched and increased was the faith of
the house of God;
And error was put to shame by reason of two
old men, who, though they spake not,
Vanquished it; and they kept silence, and
their faith stood fast.
And, though tempestuous accents were heard
from the judge,
And the commands of the emperor were
dreadful, yea violent,
And paganism had a bold face and an open
mouth,
And its voice was raised, and silent were the
old men with pain,
Yet null and void became the command and
drowned was the voice of the judge,
And without speech the mute sign of the martyrs bore off the palm.
Talking and clamour, and the sound of stripes,
on the left;
And deep silence and suffering standing on
the right;
And, by one mute sign with which the old men
pointed above their heads,
The head of faith was lifted up, and error was
put to shame.

---

[1] Or "depend." — Tr.

Worsted in the encounter were they who spoke,
and the victory was to the silent:
For, voiceless they uttered by signs the discourse of faith.

They took them down, because they had van-
quished while silent;
And they put them in bonds, threatening *yet*
to vanquish them.
Bonds and a dungeon void of light were by the
martyrs
Held of no account — yea *rather* as the light
which has no end.
To be without bread, and without water, and
without light,
Pleased them well, because of the love of the
Son of God.

The judge commanded by their feet to hang
them up
With their heads downwards, by a sentence
all unrighteous:
Hanged up was Shamuna with his head down-
wards; and he prayed
In prayer pure and strained clear by pain.
Sweet fruit was hanging on the tree in that judg-
ment-hall,
And its taste and smell made the very deni-
zens of heaven to marvel.
Afflicted was his body, but sound was his faith;
Bound fast was his person, but unfettered was
his prayer over his deed.
For, prayer nothing whatsoever turneth aside,
And *nothing* hindereth it — not even sword,
not even fire.
His form was turned upside down, but *his* prayer
was unrestrained,
And straight was its path on high to the abode
of the angels.
The more the affliction of the chosen martyr
was increased,
The more from his lips was all confession
heard.
The martyrs longed for the whetted sword affec-
tionately,
And sought it as a treasure full of riches.

A new work has the Son of God wrought in the
world —
That dreadful death should be yearned for [1]
by many.
That men should run to meet the sword is a
thing unheard of,
Except they were those whom Jesus has en-
listed in His service by His crucifixion.
That death is bitter, every one knoweth lo! from
earliest time:
To martyrs alone is it not bitter to be slain.

They laughed at the whetted sword when they
saw it,
And greeted it with smiles: for it was that
which was the occasion of their crowns.
As though it had been something hated, they
left the body to be beaten:
Even though loving it, they held it not back
from pains.
For the sword they waited, and the sword went
forth and crowned them:
Because for it they looked; and it came to
meet them, even as they desired.
The Son of God slew death by His crucifixion;
And, inasmuch as death is slain, it caused no
suffering to the martyrs.

With a wounded serpent one playeth without
fear;
A slain lion even a coward will drag along:
The great serpent our Lord crushed by His
crucifixion;
The dread lion did the Son of God slay by His
sufferings.
Death bound He fast, and laid him prostrate and
trampled on him at the gate of Hades;
And *now* whosoever will draweth near and
mocketh at him, because he is slain.
These old men, Shamuna and Guria, mocked at
death,
As at that lion which by the Son of God was
slain.
The great serpent, which slew Adam among the
trees,
Who could seize, so long as he drank not of
the blood of the cross?
The Son of God crushed the dragon by His
crucifixion,
And lo! boys and old men mock at the
wounded serpent.
Pierced is the lion with the spear which *pierced*
the side of the Son of God;
And whosoever will trampleth on him, and
despiseth him, yea mocketh at him.

The Son of God — He is the cause of all good
things,
And Him doth it behove every mouth to cele-
brate.
He did Himself espouse [2] the bride with the
blood which flowed from His wounds,
And of His wedding-friends He demanded as
a nuptial gift [3] the blood of their necks.
The Lord of the wedding-feast hung on the
cross in nakedness,
And whosoever came to be a guest, He let fall
His blood upon him.

---

[1] Or " beloved." — TR.

[2] Lit. " purchase." — TR.

[3] ܦܘܪܢܣܐ, though not in the lexicons, is the same word that
appears in Castel as ܦܘܪܢܣܐ.

Shamuna and Guria gave up their bodies for His
sake
    To sufferings and tortures and to all the various
forms of woe.[1]
At Him they looked as He was mocked by
wicked men,
    And thus did they themselves endure mockery
without a groan.

Edessa was enriched by your slaughter, O blessed
ones :
    For ye adorned her with your crowns and with
your sufferings.
Her beauty are ye, her bulwark ye, her salt
ye,
    Her riches and her store, yea her boast and
all her treasure.
Faithful stewards are ye :[2]
    Since by your sufferings ye did array the bride
in beauty.
The daughter of the Parthians, who was espoused
to the cross,[3]
    Of *you* maketh her boast : since by your teach-
ing lo ! she was enlightened.
Her advocates are ye ; scribes who, though silent,
vanquished
    All error, whilst its voice was uplifted high in
unbelief.

Those old men [4] of the daughter of the Hebrews
were sons of Belial,[5]
    False witnesses, who killed Naboth, feigning
themselves *to be true.*

Her did Edessa outdo by her two old men full
of beauty,
    Who were witnesses to the Son of God, and
died like Naboth.
Two were there, and two here, old men ;
    And these were called witnesses, and witnesses
those.
Let us now see which of them were witnesses
chosen of God,
    And which city is beloved by reason of her old
men and of her honourable ones.
Lo ! the sons of Belial who slew Naboth are
witnesses ;
    And here Shamuna and Guria, again, are wit-
nesses.
Let us now see which witnesses, and which old
men,
    And which city can stand with confidence [6]
before God.
Sons of Belial were those witnesses of that adulterous woman,
    And lo ! their shame is all portrayed in their
names.
Edessa's just and righteous old men, her witnesses,
    Were like Naboth, who himself also was slain
for righteousness' sake.
They were not like the two lying sons of Belial,
    Nor is Edessa like Zion, which also crucified
the Lord.
Like herself her old men were false, yea dared
    To shed on the ground innocent blood wick-
edly.
But by these witnesses here lo ! the truth is
spoken. —
    Blessed be He who gave us the treasure-store
of their crowns !

Here endeth the Homily on Guria and Shamuna.

---

[1] Lit. " to the forms (σχήματα) of all afflictions." — Tʀ.
[2] This seems preferable to Cureton's " Ye are the stewards of
(her) faith." The expression exactly corresponds in form to that in
Luke xvi. 8 (Peshito): " the steward of injustice " = " the unjust
steward."
[3] Lit. " crucifixion." — Tʀ.
[4] Or " elders." — Tʀ.
[5] By this name the men referred to (not, however, the elders, but
the two false witnesses suborned by them) are called in 1 Kings xxi.
10, 13. The expression in the text is literally " sons of iniquity,"
and is that used by the Peshito. — Tʀ.

[6] Or " have an open countenance." — Tʀ.

INTRODUCTION TO ANCIENT SYRIAC DOCUMENTS

1. THE preceding *Memoirs of Edessa* and Syriac Documents were inserted in vol. 20 of the Edinburgh series, quite out of place as it seems to me; and the more so, as other Syriac fragments were to follow.

2. In vol. 22, equally out of place, and mixed up with incongruous material, followed the very interesting work of Bardesanes, to which I now assign a natural collocation with the Edessene Memoirs.

3. In vol. 24, with the *Liturgies* and other mixed material, comes the third Syriac fagot, another valuable and very interesting contribution severed from its due connections.

The reader of this volume will rejoice to find Mr. Pratten's scattered but most instructive translations here brought together, and arranged in less confused sequence and relations one with another. The several announcements prefixed to each have, in like manner, been here gathered and set in order.

It may be worth while, just here, to direct attention to the latest views of scholarship upon Syria, its language and its antiquities. A learned critic, who often supplies one of our weekly newspapers with articles on the Oriental languages worthy of the best reviews, has directed attention [1] to a searching *critique* of Mommsen's recent addition to his *Roman History*, of a chapter which " deals with Bible-lands in New-Testament times." Professor Nöldke of Strasburg, a leading Semitic scholar, in the *Zeitschrift* of the German Oriental Society, thus takes him to task : —

" Syria enjoyed a higher prosperity under the Romans *than Mommsen concedes*, and this continued into the Christian period. The Hellenization made rapid strides, but not in such a manner that the Greek language or Greek culture spread to a considerable degree; but rather, in such a way that European arts and manners of life were established, and that a number of elements of Occidental culture became powerful in the thinking and language of the educated. Mommsen, according to my conviction, considers the Hellenization of Syria *to have advanced much farther than it actually had*. That the language of the country had been entirely banished from the circles of the educated, and that it had assumed the position in reference to the Greek which the Celtic in full had assumed over against the Latin, is certainly an exaggerated view. The Aramaic was an old developed language (*Cultursprache*), which was already written before a single letter was seen in Latium. In the days of the Achæmenidian rulers this was the official language of Egypt, and even of Asia Minor, *and was accordingly spread far beyond the original territory*. Again we find this language in the days of the Roman emperors not only in Palmyra, but spread also in the whole country of the Nabatheans, and down to almost Medina; here again beyond its native limits, as the official written language. And that this was not merely a remnant of the former political supremacy is evident from the fact that the documents of Palmyra and those of the Nabatheans, in an equal manner, show a younger stage of development of language than that of the Achæmenidian period; this stage being virtually the same as is seen in the various Jewish literary works of that time."

As Mommsen is continuing his irreligious elaborations of history, it may be well to bear in mind his superficial ideas on such subjects, especially when he is reaching the affairs of early Christianity.

1. Our translator (Mr. Pratten) makes the following announcements : —

" The translation of the Syriac pieces which follow [2] is based on a careful examination of that made by Dr. Cureton, the merits of which are cordially acknowledged. It will, however, be seen that it differs from that in many and important particulars.

" Many thanks are due to the Dean of Canterbury for his kindness in giving much valuable help."

---

[1] *New-York Independent*, June 24, 1886.　　　　[2] That is, in vol. xxii. of the Edinburgh edition.

2. He thus introduces the treatise of Bardesanes :—

" Bardesan, or Bardesanes, according to one account, was born at Edessa in 154 A.D., and it is supposed that he died sometime between 224 and 230. Eusebius says that he flourished in the time of Marcus Aurelius. He was for some time resident at the court of Abgar VI., King of Edessa, with whom he was on intimate terms. He at first belonged to the Gnostic sect of the Valentinians; but abandoning it, he seemed to come nearer the orthodox beliefs. In reality, it is said, he devised errours of his own. He wrote many works. Eusebius attributes the work now translated, *The Book of Laws*, or *On Fate*, to Bardesanes. Many modern critics have come to the conclusion that it was written by a scholar of Bardesanes, but that it gives us the genuine opinions and reasonings of Bardesanes. The question is of interest in connection with the Clementine *Recognitions*, which contain a large portion of the work. The Syriac was first published by Cureton in his *Spicilegium*."

3. In introducing the *Mara bar Serapion* and the *Ambrose*,[1] he thus refers to his friend Dr. Payne Smith : —

The text of the two following short pieces[2] is found in the *Spicilegium Syriacum* of the late Dr. Cureton. This careful scholar speaks of the second of these compositions as containing "some very obscure passages." The same remark holds good also of the first. Dr. Payne Smith describes them both as "full of difficulties." So far as these arise from errors in the text, they might have been removed, had I been able to avail myself of the opportunity kindly offered me by Dr. Rieu, Keeper of the Oriental MSS. at the British Museum, of inspecting the original MS. As it is, several have, it is hoped, been successfully met by conjecture.

To Dr. R. Payne Smith, Dean of Canterbury, who, as on two previous occasions, has most kindly and patiently afforded me his valuable assistance, I beg to offer my very grateful acknowledgments.

B. P. PRATTEN.

---

[1] Vol. xxiv., ed. Edinburgh. The latter was formerly ascribed to Justin Martyr.
[2] The *Ambrose* and the *Serapion*.

ANCIENT SYRIAC DOCUMENTS

BARDESAN.[1]

THE BOOK OF THE LAWS OF DIVERS COUNTRIES.[2]

Some days since we were calling[3] to pay a visit to our brother Shemashgram, and Bardesan came and found us there. And when he had made inquiries after his health,[4] and ascertained that he was well, he asked us, "What were you talking about? for I heard your voice outside as I was coming in." For it was his habit, whenever he found us talking about anything before he came,[5] to ask us, "What were you saying?" that he might talk with us about it.

"Avida here," said we to him," was saying to us, 'If God is one, as ye say, and if He is the creator of men, and if it is His will that you should do that which you are commanded, why did He not so create men that they should not be able to do wrong, but should constantly be doing that which is right? for in this way His will would have been accomplished.'"

"Tell me, my son Avida," said Bardesan to him, "why it has come into thy mind that the God of all is not One; or that He is One, but doth not will that men should behave themselves justly and uprightly?"

"I, sir," said Avida, "have asked these *brethren*, persons of my own age, in order that 'they' may return me an answer."

"If," said Bardesan to him, "thou wishest to learn, it were for thy advantage to learn from some one who is older than they; but if to teach, it is not requisite for 'thee' to ask 'them,' but *rather* that thou shouldst induce 'them' to ask 'thee' what they wish. For teachers are 'asked' questions, and do not themselves ask them; or, if they ever do ask a question, it is to direct the mind of the questioner, so that he may ask

properly, and they may know what his desire is. For it is a good thing that a man should know how to ask questions."

"For my part," said Avida, "I wish to learn; but I began first of all to question my brethren here, because I was too bashful to ask thee."

"Thou speakest becomingly,"[6] said Bardesan. "But know, nevertheless, that he who asks questions properly, and wishes to be convinced, and approaches the way of truth without contentiousness, has no need to be bashful; because he is sure by means of the things I have mentioned to please him to whom his questions are addressed. If so be, therefore, my son, thou hast any opinion of thy own[7] respecting this matter about which thou hast asked, tell it to us all; and, if we too approve of it, we shall express our agreement with thee; and, if we do not approve of it, we shall be under obligation to show thee why we do not approve of it. But if thou wast simply desirous of becoming acquainted with this subject, and hast no opinion of thy own about it, as a man who has but lately joined the disciples and is a recent inquirer, I will tell thee *respecting it;* so that thou mayest not go from us empty away. If, moreover, thou art pleased with those things which I shall say to thee, we have other things besides to tell thee[8] concerning this matter; but, if thou art not pleased, we on our part shall have stated our views without any personal feeling."

"I too," said Avida, "shall be much gratified[9] to hear and to be convinced: because it is not from another that I have heard of this subject, but I have spoken of it to my brethren here out of my own mind; and they have not cared to convince me; but they say, 'Only believe,

[1] Lit. "Son of Daisan," from a river so called near Edessa. — Hahn. [Elucidation I. "The Laws of Countries" is the title. For "Various Countries" I have used "*Divers.*"]

[2] Called by Eusebius, *Hist. Eccl.*, iv. 30, *The Discourse on Fate* (Ὁ περὶ εἱμαρμένης διάλογος). This is more correct than the title above given: the "Laws" are adduced only as illustrations of the argument of the piece. The subject would, however, be more properly given as "The Freedom of the Will."

[3] Lit. "going in." Cureton renders, "we went up."

[4] Lit. "felt him."

[5] Lit. "before him." Merx: "ehe er kam."

[5] The word used is formed from the Greek εὐσχημόνως. [Here observe what is said (in Elucidation I.) by Nöldke on the Hellenization theory of Mommsen, with reference to this very work; p. 742, *infra*.]

[7] Lit. "hast anything in thy mind."

[8] Lit. "there are for thee other things also."

[9] ܢܒܣܡ is here substituted for the ܐܘܢ of the text, which yields no sense.

and thou wilt *then* be able to know everything.' But for my part, I cannot believe unless I be convinced."

" Not only," said Bardesan, " is Avida unwilling to believe, but there are many *others* also who, because there is no faith in them, are not even capable of being convinced ; but they are always pulling down and building up, and *so* are found destitute of all knowledge of the truth. But notwithstanding, since Avida is not willing to believe, lo ! I will speak to you who do believe, concerning this matter about which he asks ; and *thus* he too will hear something further *about it*."

He began accordingly to address us *as follows :* " Many men are there who have not faith, and have not received knowledge from the True Wisdom.[1] In consequence of this, they are not competent to speak and give instruction *to others,* nor are they readily inclined themselves to hear. For they have not the foundation of faith to build upon, nor have they any confidence on which to rest their hope. Moreover, because they are accustomed to doubt even concerning God, they likewise have not in them the fear of Him, which would of itself deliver them from all *other* fears : for he in whom there is no fear of God is the slave of all *sorts of* fears. For, even with regard to those things of various kinds which they disbelieve, they are not certain that they disbelieve them rightly, but they are unsettled in their opinions, and have no fixed belief,[2] and the taste of their thoughts is insipid in their *own* mouth ; and they are always haunted with fear, and flushed with excitement, and reckless.

" But with regard to what Avida has said : ' How is it that God did not so make us that we should not sin and incur condemnation ? ' — if man had been made so, he would not have belonged to himself, but would have been the instrument of him that moved him ; and it is evident also, that he who moves *an instrument* as he pleases, moves it either for good or for evil. And how, in that case, would a man differ from a harp, on which another plays ; or from a ship, which another guides : where the praise and the blame reside in the hand of the performer or the steersman,[3] and the harp itself knows not what is played on it, nor the ship itself whether it be well steered and guided *or ill,* they being only instruments made for the use of him in whom is the *requisite* skill ? But God in His benignity chose not so to make man ; but by freedom He exalted him above many *of His* creatures, and *even* made him equal with the angels. For look at the sun, and the moon, and

the signs of the zodiac,[4] and all the other creatures which are greater than we in some points, *and see* how individual freedom has been denied them, and how they are all fixed *in their course* by decree, so that they may do that only which is decreed for them, and nothing else. For the sun never says, I will not rise at my appointed time ; nor the moon, I will not change, nor wane, nor wax ; nor does any one of the stars say, I will not rise nor set ; nor the sea, I will not bear up the ships, nor stay within my boundaries ; nor the mountains, We will not continue in the places in which we are set ; nor do the winds say, We will not blow ; nor the earth, I will not bear up and sustain whatsoever is upon me. But all these things are servants, and are subject to one decree : for they are the instruments of the wisdom of God, which erreth not.

" *Not so, however, with man :* for, if everything ministered, who would be he that is ministered to ? And, if everything were ministered to, who would be he that ministered ? *In that case,* too, there would not be one thing diverse from another : yet that which is one, and in which there is no diversity *of parts,* is a being[5] which up to this time has not been fashioned. But those things which are destined[6] for ministering have been fixed in the power of man : because in the image of Elohim[7] was he made. Therefore have these things, in the benignity *of God,* been given to him, that they may minister to him for a season. It has also been given to him to be guided by his own will ; so that whatever he is able to do, if he will he may do it, and if he do not will he may not do it, and *that so* he may justify himself or condemn. For, had he been made so as not to be able to do evil and thereby incur condemnation, in like manner also the good which he did would not have been his own, and he could not have been justified by it. For, if any one should not of his own will do that which is good or that which is evil, his justification and his condemnation would rest simply with that Fortune to which he is subjected.[8]

" It will therefore be manifest to you, that the goodness of God is great toward man, and that

---

[1] Lit. " the wisdom of the truth."
[2] Lit. " are not able to stand."
[3] Or, " in the hand of the operator : " but it is better to employ two words.

[4] Or, " and the sphere."

[5] The word ܐܝܬܝܐ, here used, occurs subsequently as a designation of the Gnostic Æons. Here, as Merx observes, it can hardly go beyond its original meaning of *ens, entia, Wesen, that which is.* It evidently refers, however, in this passage to a *system* of things, a world.

[6] Lit. " required." [It is a *phenomenon* to find this early specimen of " anthropology " emanating from the far East, and anticipating the Augustinian controversies on " fixed fate, free-will, foreknowledge absolute." Yet the West did not originate the discussion. See vol. iv. p. 320. See the ethical or metaphysical side of free-will discussed in Eaton's *Bampton Lectures* for 1872, p. 79, ed. Pott, Young, & Co., New York, 1873. On St. Augustine, see Wordsworth's valuable remarks in his *Bampton Lectures* for 1881.]

[7] Gen. i. 27. The Hebrew itself, בצלם אלהים, is given in Syriac characters, without translation.

[8] Cureton renders, " for which he is created." Merx has, " das ihn gemacht hat."

freedom has been given to him in greater measure than to any of those elemental bodies [1] of which we have spoken, in order that by this freedom he may justify himself, and order his conduct in a godlike manner, and be copartner with angels, who are likewise possessed of personal freedom. For we are sure that, if the angels likewise had not been possessed of personal freedom, they would not have consorted with the daughters of men, and sinned, and fallen from their places. In like manner, too, those other *angels*, who did the will of their Lord, were, by reason of their self-control, raised to higher rank, and sanctified, and received noble gifts. For every being in existence is in need of the Lord of all; of His gifts also there is no end.

Know ye, however, notwithstanding *what I have said*, that even those things of which I have spoken as subsisting by decree are not absolutely destitute of all freedom; and on this account, at the last day, they will all be made subject to judgment."

"But how," said I to him, "should those things which are fixed *and regulated by decree* be judged?"

"Not inasmuch as they are fixed, O Philip," said he, "will the elements be judged, but inasmuch as they are endowed with power. For beings [2] are not deprived of their natural properties [3] when they come to be fashioned, but *only* of the full exercise of their strength,[4] suffering a decrease [5] *of power* through their intermingling one with another, and being kept in subjection by the power of their Maker; and in so far as they are in subjection they will not be judged, but in respect of that *only* which is *under* their own *control*."

"Those things," said Avida to him, "which thou hast said, are very good; but, lo! the commands which have been given to men are severe, and they cannot perform them."

"This," said Bardesan, "is the saying of one who has not the will to do that which is right; nay, more, of him who has *already* yielded obedience and submission to his foe. For men have not been commanded to do anything but that which they are able to do. For the commandments set before us are *only two, and they are* such as are compatible with freedom and consistent with equity: one, that we refrain from everything which is wrong, and which we should not like to have done to ourselves; and the

other, that we should do that which is right, and which we love and are pleased to have done to us likewise. Who, then, is the man that is too weak to avoid stealing, or to avoid lying, or to avoid acts of profligacy, or to avoid hatred and deception? For, lo! all these things are under *the control of* the mind of man; and are not dependent on [6] the strength of the body, but on the will of the soul. For even if a man be poor, and sick, and old, and disabled in his limbs, he is able to avoid doing all these things. And, as he is able to avoid doing these things, so is he able to love, and to bless, and to speak the truth, and to pray for what is good for every one with whom he is acquainted; and if he be in health, and capable *of working*,[7] he is able also to give of that which he has; moreover, to support with strength of body him that is sick and enfeebled — this also he can do.

"Who, then, is it that is not capable of doing that which men destitute of faith complain of, I know not. For my part, I think that it is precisely in respect to these commandments that man has more power than in anything *else*. For they are easy, and there are no circumstances that can hinder their performance. For we are not commanded to carry heavy loads of stones, or of timber, or of anything else, which those only who have *great* bodily strength can do; nor to build fortresses [8] and found cities, which kings only can do; nor to steer a ship, which mariners only have the skill to steer; nor to measure and divide land, which *land*-measurers only know how to do; nor *to practise* any one of those arts which are possessed by some, while the rest are destitute of them. But there have been given to us, in accordance with the benignity of God, commandments having no harshness in them [9] — such as any living man whatsoever [10] may rejoice to do.[11] For there is no man that does not rejoice when he does that which is right, nor any one that is not gladdened within himself if he abstains from things that are bad — except those who were not created for this good thing, and are called tares.[12] For would not the judge be unjust who should censure a man with regard to any such thing as he has not the ability to do?"

"Sayest thou of these deeds, O Bardesan," said Avida to him, "that they are easy to do?"

"To him that hath the will," said Bardesan, "I have said, and do *still* say, that they are easy. For this *obedience I contend for* is the proper behaviour of a free mind,[13] and of the soul which has

---

[1] The Greek στοιχεῖα.

[2] ‎ܡܐ‎, that which exists, especially that which has an independent existence, is used here of the Gnostic Æons. They were so called in respect of their pre-existence, their existence independent of time or creation. When they came to be "created," or more properly "fashioned," they were called "emanations."

[3] Lit. "of their nature."

[4] Lit. "the strength of their exactness," i.e., their exact (or complete) strength. Cureton has, "their force of *energy*."

[5] "being lessened," or "lowered."

[6] Lit. "do not take place by."

[7] Cureton renders, "have the use of his hands:" Merx gives "etwas erwirbt."

[8] Or "towns."

[9] Lit. "without ill-will."

[10] Lit. "every man in whom there is a soul."

[11] Lit. "can do rejoicing."

[12] The Greek ζιζάνια.

[13] Lit. "a mind the son of the free."

not revolted against its governors. As for the action of the body, there are many things which hinder it : especially old age, and sickness, and poverty."

" Possibly," said **Avida,** " a man may be able to abstain from the things that are bad ; but as for doing the things that are good, what man is capable *of this ?* "

" It is easier," said Bardesan, " to do good than to abstain from evil. For the good comes from the man himself,[1] and therefore he rejoices whenever he does good ; but the evil is the work of the Enemy, and therefore *it is that, only* when a man is excited *by some evil passion,* and is not in his sound natural condition,[2] he does the things that are bad. For know, my son, that for a man to praise and bless his friend is an easy thing ; but for a man to refrain from taunting and reviling one whom he hates is not easy : nevertheless, it is possible. When, too, a man does that which is right, his mind is gladdened, and his conscience at ease, and he is pleased for every one to see what he does. But, when a man behaves amiss and commits wrong, he is troubled and excited, and full of anger and rage, and distressed in his soul and in his body ; and, when he is in this *state of* mind, he does not like to be seen by any one ; and even those things in which he rejoices, and which are accompanied with praise and blessing *from others,* are spurned from his thoughts, while those things by which he is agitated and disturbed are *rendered more distressing to him because* accompanied by the curse of *conscious* guilt.

" Perhaps, however, some one will say that fools also are pleased when they do abominable things. *Undoubtedly :* but not because they do them *as such,* nor because they receive any commendation *for them,* nor because *they do them* with a good hope ;[3] nor does the pleasure itself stay long with them. For the pleasure which is *experienced* in a healthy state *of the soul,* with a good hope, is one thing ; and the pleasure of a diseased state *of the soul,* with a bad hope, is another. For lust is one thing, and love is another ; and friendship is one thing, and good-fellowship another ; and we ought without any difficulty to understand that the false counterfeit of affection which is called lust, even though there be in it the enjoyment of the moment, is nevertheless widely different from true affection, whose enjoyment is for ever, incorruptible and indestructible."

" Avida here," said I to him, " has also been speaking thus : ' It is from his nature that man does wrong ; for, were he not naturally formed to do wrong, he would not do it.' "

" If all men," said Bardesan, " acted alike,[4] and followed one bias,[5] it would *then* be manifest that it was their nature that guided them, and that they had not that freedom of which I have been speaking to you. That you may understand, however, what is nature and what is freedom, I will proceed to inform you.

" The nature of man is, that he should be born, and grow up, and rise to his full stature, and produce children, and grow old, eating and drinking, and sleeping and waking, and that *then* he should die. These things, because they are of nature, belong to all men ; and not to all men only, but also to all animals whatsoever,[6] and some of them also to trees. For this is the work of physical nature,[7] which makes and produces and regulates everything just as it has been commanded. Nature, I say, is found to be maintained among animals also in their actions. For the lion eats flesh, in accordance with his nature ; and therefore all lions are eaters of flesh. The sheep eats grass ; and therefore all sheep are eaters of grass. The bee makes honey, by which it is sustained ; therefore all bees are makers of honey. The ant collects for herself a store in summer, from which to sustain herself in winter ; and therefore do all ants act likewise. The scorpion strikes with its sting him who has not hurt it ; and thus do all scorpions strike. Thus all animals preserve their nature : the eaters of flesh do not eat herbage ; nor do the eaters of herbage eat flesh.

" Men, on the contrary, are not governed thus ; but, whilst in the matters pertaining to their bodies they preserve their nature like animals, in the matters pertaining to their minds they do that which they choose, as those who are free,[8] and endowed with power, and as *made in* the likeness of God. For there are some of them that eat flesh, and do not touch bread ; and there are some of them that make a distinction between the *several* kinds of flesh-food ; and there are some of them that do not eat the flesh of any animal whatever.[9] There are some of them that become the husbands of their mothers, and of their sisters, and of their daughters ; and there are some who do not consort with women at all. There are those who take it upon *themselves* to inflict vengeance, like lions and leopards ; and there are those who strike him that has not done them any wrong, like scorpions ; and there are those that are led like sheep, and do not harm their conductors. There are some that behave themselves with kindness,

---

[1] Lit. " is the man's own."
[2] Lit. " is not sound in his nature."
[3] Cureton, " for good hope." But ܣܒܪܐ ܥܠ is a common expression for " in hope," as in Rom. viii. 20.

[4] Lit. " did one deed."
[5] Lit. " used one mind."
[6] Lit. " in whom there is a soul."
[7] Φύσις.
[8] Lit. " as children of the free."
[9] Lit. " in which there is a soul."

and some with justice, and some with wickedness.

" If any one should say that each one of them has a nature so to do, let him be assured [1] that it is not so. For there are those who *once* were profligates and drunkards ; and, when the admonition of good counsels reached them, they became pure and sober,[2] and spurned their bodily appetites. And there are those who *once* behaved with purity and sobriety ; and when they turned away from right admonition, and dared to set themselves against the commands of Deity and of their teachers, they fell from the way of truth, and became profligates and revellers. And there are those who after their fall repented again, and fear *came and abode* upon them, and they turned themselves *afresh* towards the truth which they had *before* held.[3]

" What, therefore, is the nature of man ? For, lo ! all men differ one from another in their conduct and in their aims,[4] and such *only* as are of [5] one mind and of one purpose resemble one another. But those men who, up to the present moment, have been enticed by their appetites and governed by their anger, are resolved to ascribe any wrong they do to their Maker, that they themselves may be found faultless, and that He who made them may, in the idle talk *of men*,[6] bear the blame. They do not consider that nature is amenable to no law. For a man is not found fault with for being tall or short in his stature, or white or black, or because his eyes are large or small, or for any bodily defect whatsoever ; but he is found fault with if he steal, or lie, or practise deceit, or poison *another*, or be abusive, or do *any other* such-like things.

" From hence, lo ! it will be evident, that for those things which are not in our own hands, but which we have from nature, we are in no wise condemned, nor are we in any wise justified ; but by those things which we do in *the exercise of* our personal freedom, if they be right we are justified and entitled to praise, and if they be wrong we are condemned and subjected to blame."

Again we questioned him, and said to him : " There are others who say that men are governed by the decree of Fate, *so as to act* at one time wickedly, and at another time well."

" I too am aware, O Philip and Baryama," said he to us, " that there are *such* men : those who are called Chaldæans, and also others who are fond of this subtle knowledge,[7] as I myself

also once was. For it has been said by me in another place,[8] that the soul of man longs [9] to know that which the many are ignorant of, and those men make it their aim to do *this ;* [10] and *that* all the wrong which *men* commit, and all that they do aright, and all those things which happen to them, as regards riches and poverty, and sickness and health, and blemishes of the body, come to them through the governance of those stars which are called the Seven ; [11] and that they are, *in fact*, governed by them. But there are others who affirm the opposite of these things, — how that this art is a lying invention of the astrologers ; [12] or that Fate has no existence whatever, but is an empty name ; that, *on the contrary*, all things, great and small, are placed in the hands of man ; and that bodily blemishes and faults simply befall and happen to him by chance. But others, *again*, say that whatsoever a man does he does of his own will, in *the exercise of* the freedom which has been given to him, and that the faults and blemishes and *other* untoward things which befall him he receives as punishment from God.

" For myself, however according to my weak judgment,[13] the matter appears to stand *thus :* that these three opinions [14] are partly to be accepted as true, and partly to be rejected as false ; — accepted as true, because men speak after the appearances which they see, and also because these men see how things come upon them *as if* accidentally ; to be set aside as fallacious, because the wisdom of God is too profound [15] for them — that *wisdom* which founded the world, and created man, and ordained Governors, and gave to all things the *degree of* pre-eminence which is suited to every one of them. What I mean is, that this power is possessed by God, and the Angels, and the Potentates,[16] and the Governors,[17] and the Elements, and men, and animals ; but that *this* power has not been given to all these orders *of beings* of which I have spoken in respect to everything (for He that has power over everything is One) ; but over some things they have power, and over some things they have not power, as I have been saying : in order that in those things over which they have power the

---

[1] Lit. " let him see."
[2] Lit. " patient," i.e., tolerant of the craving which seeks gratification.
[3] Lit. " in which they had stood."
[4] Or " volitions."
[5] Lit. " have stood in."
[6] So Merx, " in either Rede." Cureton, " by a vain plea."
[7] Lit. " this knowledge of art (or skill)."

[8] To what other work of his he refers is not known.
[9] Cureton, " is capable." Dr. Payne Smith (*Thes. Syr., s. v.*) says, referring to ܐ as used in this passage: " *eget, cupit*, significare videtur."
[10] So Dr. Payne Smith. Merx renders, " Even that *which* men desire to do." Cureton has, " and the same men meditate to do."
[11] Lit. " the sevenths."
[12] Lit. " Chaldæans."
[13] Lit. " my weakness."
[14] Or ' sects " (αἱρέσεις).
[15] Lit. " rich."

[16] ܫܠܝܼܛܵܢܹܐ, Shlitâne. [Of Angels, see vol. i. p.269.]

[17] ܡܕܲܒ݁ܪ̈ܵܢܹܐ, Medabhrâne. Merx, p. 74, referring to the Peshito of Gen. i. 16, thinks that by the Potentates are meant the sun and moon, and by the Governors the five planets.

goodness of God may be seen, and in those over which they have no power they may know that they have a Superior.

"There is, then, *such a thing as* Fate, as the astrologers say. That everything, moreover, is not under the control of our will, is apparent from this — that the majority of men have had the will to be rich, and to exercise dominion over their fellows, and to be healthy in their bodies, and to have things in subjection to them as they please ; but that wealth is not found except with a few, nor dominion except with one here and another there, nor health of body with all men ; and that *even* those who are rich do not have complete possession of their riches, nor do those who are in power have things in subjection to them as they wish, but that sometimes things are disobedient *to them* as they do not wish ; and that at one time the rich are rich as they desire, and at another time they become poor as they do not desire ; and that those who are thoroughly poor have dwellings such as they do not wish, and pass their lives in the world as they do not like, and covet *many* things which *only* flee from them. Many have children, and do not rear them ; others rear them, and do not retain possession of them ; others retain possession of them, and they become a disgrace and a sorrow *to their parents*. Some are rich, as they wish, and are afflicted with ill-health, as they do not wish ; others are blessed with good health, as they wish, and afflicted with poverty, as they do not wish. There are those who have in abundance the things they wish for, and but few of those things for which they do not wish ; and there are others who have in abundance the things they do not wish for, and but few of those for which they do wish.[1]

"And so the matter is found *to stand* thus : that wealth, and honours, and health, and sickness, and children, and *all the other* various objects of desire, are placed under *the control of* Fate, and are not in our own power ; but *that, on the contrary*, while we are pleased and delighted with such things as are in accordance with our wishes, towards such as we do not wish for we are drawn by force ; and, from those things which happen to us when we are not pleased, it is evident that those things also with which we are pleased do not happen to us because we desire them ; but that things happen as they do happen, and with some of them we are pleased, and with others not.

"And *thus* we men are found to be governed by Nature all alike, and by Fate variously, and by our freedom each as he chooses.

"But let us now proceed to show with respect to Fate that it has not power over everything. *Clearly not :* because that which is called Fate is itself *nothing more than* a *certain* order of procession,[2] which has been given to the Potentates and Elements by God ; and, in conformity with this said procession and order, intelligences[3] undergo change when they descend[4] to *be with* the soul, and souls undergo change when they descend[4] to *be with* bodies ; and this *order*, under the name of Fate and γένεσις,[5] is the agent of the changes[6] that take place in this assemblage *of parts of which man consists*,[7] which is being sifted and purified for the benefit of whatsoever by the grace of God and by goodness has been benefited, and is being *and will continue to be* benefited until the close of all *things*.

"The body, then, is governed by Nature, the soul also sharing in its experiences and sensations ; and the body is neither hindered nor helped by Fate in the several acts it performs. For a man does not become a father before the age of fifteen, nor does a woman become a mother before the age of thirteen. In like manner, too, there is a law for old age : for women *then* become incapable of bearing, and men cease to possess the natural power of begetting children ; while other animals, which are likewise governed by their nature, do, *even* before those ages I have mentioned, not only produce offspring, but also become too old to do so, just as the bodies of men also, when they are grown old, cease to propagate : nor is Fate able to give them offspring at a time when the body has not the natural power to give them. Neither, again, is Fate able to preserve the body of man in life without meat and drink ; nor yet, even when it has meat and drink, to grant it exemption from death : for these and many other things belong exclusively to Nature.[8]

"But, when the times and methods of Nature

---

[1] [The Book of Job and the Book of Ecclesiastes, with the eloquent and pathetic remonstrance (chap. iii. 18–22) "concerning the estate of the sons of men," are proofs that God foresaw the struggles of faith against the *apparently* unequal ways and rulings of Providence. For popular answers see Parnell's *Hermit*, and Addison, *Spectator*, No. 237. But a valuable comment may be found in Wordsworth's *Bampton Lectures* (for 1881) *on the one Religion*, p. 5, Oxford, Parker, 1881.]

[2] Merx renders ܡܟܬܪ݁ܕ݁ by "emanation," quoting two passages from Eph. Syr. where the root ܪ݁ܕ݁ is used of the issuing of water from a fountain. Dr. Payne Smith says : "The word seems to mean no more than *cursus*: cf. Euseb., *Theoph.*, i. 31. 5, 55. 1, 83. 22, where it is used of the stars ; and i. 74. 13, where it means the course of nature."

[3] Read ܡܬܝܕܠ݁ for ܡܬܝܕܠ݁.

[4] Lit. "in their descents."

[5] Or "nativity," "natal hour" (ܡܟܢ ܒܝܬ = place of birth, "Geburtshaus :" Merx).

[6] Lit. "this agent of change." Cureton, "this alternation." "Das diese Veränderung bewirkende Agens" is the rendering of Merx.

[7] Dr. Payne Smith thinks the reference to be to the Gnostic νοῦς, ψυχή, and σῶμα, which seem to be spoken of just before. This difficult passage is rendered by Cureton : "And this alternation itself is called the Fortune, and the Nativity of this assemblage, which is being sifted and purified for the assistance of that which," etc. Merx has, " . . . zur Unterstützung des Dinges, welches . . . unterstützt worden ist und unterstützt bleibt bis zur Vernichtung des Weltalls."

[8] Lit. "are Nature's own."

have had their full scope, then does Fate come and make its appearance among them, and produce effects of various kinds : at one time helping Nature and augmenting *its power*, and at another crippling and baffling it. Thus, from Nature comes the growth and perfecting of the body ; but apart from Nature, that is by Fate, come diseases and blemishes in the body. From Nature comes the union of male and female, and the unalloyed happiness of them both ; but from Fate comes hatred and the dissolution of the union, and, *moreover,* all that impurity and lasciviousness which by reason of *the natural propensity to* intercourse men practise in their lust. From Nature comes birth and children ; and from Fate, that sometimes the children are deformed, and sometimes are cast away, and sometimes die before their time. From Nature comes a supply *of nourishment* sufficient for the bodies of all *creatures ;* [1] and from Fate comes the want of sustenance, and *consequent* suffering in those bodies ; and so, again, from the same Fate comes gluttony and unnecessary luxury. Nature ordains that the aged shall be judges for the young, and the wise for the foolish, and that the strong shall be set over [2] the weak, and the brave over the timid ; but Fate brings it to pass that striplings are set over the aged, and the foolish over the wise, and that in time of war the weak command the strong, and the timid the brave.

"You must distinctly understand [3] that, in all cases in which Nature is disturbed from its direct course, its disturbance comes by reason of Fate ; *and this happens* because the Chiefs [4] and Governors, with whom rests that agency of change [5] which is called Nativity, are opposed to one another. Some of them, which are called Dexter, are those which help Nature, and add to its predominance, [6] whenever the procession is favourable to them, and they stand in those regions of the zodiac which are in the ascendant, in their own portions. [7] Those, on the contrary, which are called Sinister are evil, and whenever they in their turn are in possession of the ascendant they act in opposition to Nature ; and not on men only do they inflict harm, but at times on animals also, and trees, and fruits, and the produce of the year, and fountains of water, and, *in short,* on everything that is comprised within Nature, which is under their government.

"And in consequence of this, — *namely,* the divisions and parties which exist among the Potentates, — some men have thought that the world is governed *by these contending powers* without any superintendence *from above. But that is* because they do not understand that this very thing — *I mean* the parties and divisions *subsisting among them,* — and the justification and condemnation *consequent on their behaviour,* belong to that constitution of things founded in freedom which has been given by God, to the end that these agents likewise, by reason of their self-determining power, [8] may be either justified or condemned. Just as we see that Fate crushes Nature, so can we also see the freedom of man defeating and crushing Fate itself, — not, however, in everything, — just as also Fate itself does not in everything defeat Nature. For it is proper that the three things, Nature, and Fate, and Freedom, should be continued in existence until the procession *of which I before spoke* be completed, and the *appointed* measure and number *of its evolutions* be accomplished, even as it seemed good to Him who ordains of what kind shall be the mode of life and the end of all creatures, and the condition of all beings and natures."

"I am convinced," said Avida, " by the arguments thou hast brought forward, that it is not from his nature that a man does wrong, and also that all men are not governed alike. If thou canst further prove also that it is not from Fate and Destiny that those who do wrong so act, then will it be incumbent on us to believe that man possesses personal freedom, and by his nature has the power both to follow that which is right and to avoid that which is wrong, and will therefore also justly be judged at the last day."

"Art thou," said Bardesan, " by the fact that all men are not governed alike, convinced that it is not from their nature that they do wrong? Why, then, thou canst not possibly escape the conviction [9] that neither also from Fate exclusively do they do wrong, if we are able to show thee that the sentence of the Fates and Potentates does not influence all men alike, but that we have freedom in our own selves, so that we can avoid serving physical nature and being influenced by the control of the Potentates."

"Prove me this," said Avida, " and I will be convinced by thee, and whatsover thou shalt enjoin upon me I will do."

"Hast thou," said Bardesan, " read the books of the astrologers [10] who are in Babylon, in which is described what effects the stars have in their *various* combinations at the Nativities of men ; and the books of the Egyptians, in which are described all the *various* characters which men happen to have ? "

---

[1] Lit. " a sufficiency in measure for all bodies."
[2] Lit. " be heads to."
[3] Lit. " know ye distinctly."
[4] Or " heads."
[5] Lit. " agent of change," as above. Merx: " das Veränderungsprincip."
[6] Lit. " excellence."
[7] i.e., zones of the earth. See p. 732, note 2, *infra.*

[8] Or, " power as to themselves."
[9] Lit. " the matter compels thee to be convinced."
[10] Lit. " Chaldæans."

"I have read books of astrology," [1] said Avida, " but I do not know which are those of the Babylonians and which those of the Egyptians."

"The teaching of both countries," said Bardesan, "is the same."

"It is well known to be so," said Avida.

"Listen, then," said Bardesan, "and observe, that that which the stars decree by their Fate and their portions is not practised by all men alike who are in all *parts of* the earth. For men have made laws *for themselves* in various countries, in *the exercise of* that freedom which was given them by God: forasmuch as this gift is in its very nature opposed to that Fate emanating from the Potentates, who assume to themselves that which was not given them. I will begin my enumeration *of these laws*, so far as I can remember *them*, from the East, the beginning of the whole world: —

"*Laws of the Seres.* — The Seres have laws forbidding to kill, or to commit impurity, or to worship idols; and in the whole of Serica there are no idols, and no harlots, nor any one that kills a man, nor any that is killed: although they, like other men, are born at all hours and on all days. Thus the fierce Mars, whensoever he is 'posited' in the zenith, does not overpower the freedom of the Seres, and compel a man to shed the blood of his fellow with an iron weapon; nor does Venus, when posited with Mars, compel any man whatever among the Seres to consort with his neighbour's wife, or with any *other* woman. Rich and poor, however, and sick people and healthy, and rulers and subjects, are there: because such matters are given into the power of the Governors.

"*Laws of the Brahmans who are in India.* — Again, among the Hindoos, the Brahmans, of whom there are many thousands and tens of thousands, have a law forbidding to kill at all, or to pay reverence to idols, or to commit impurity, or to eat flesh, or to drink wine; and among these people not one of these things *ever* takes place. Thousands of years, too, have elapsed, during which these men, lo! have been governed by this law which they made for themselves.

"*Another Law which is in India.* — There is also another law in India, and in the same zone, [2] prevailing among those who are not of the caste [3] of the Brahmans, and do not embrace their teaching, bidding them serve idols, and commit impurity, and kill, and do other bad things, which by the Brahmans are disapproved. In the same zone of India, too, there are men who are in the habit of eating the flesh of men, just as all other nations eat the flesh of animals. Thus the evil stars have not compelled the Brahmans to do evil and impure things; nor have the good stars prevailed on the rest of the Hindoos to abstain from doing evil things; nor have those stars which are well 'located' in the regions which properly belong to them,[4] and in the signs of the zodiac favourable to a humane disposition,[5] prevailed on those who eat the flesh of men to abstain from using this foul and abominable food.

"*Laws of the Persians.* — The Persians, again, have made themselves laws permitting them to take as wives their sisters, and their daughters, and their daughters' daughters; and there are some who go yet further, and take even their mothers. Some of these said Persians are scattered abroad, *away from their country*, and are *found* in Media, and in the country of the Parthians,[6] and in Egypt, and in Phrygia (they are called Magi); and in all the countries and zones in which they are *found*, they are governed by this law which was made for their fathers. Yet we cannot say that for all the Magi, and for the rest of the Persians, Venus was posited with the Moon and with Saturn in the house of Saturn in her portions, while the aspect of Mars was toward them.[7] There are many places, too, in the kingdom of the Parthians, where men kill their wives, and their brothers, and their children, and incur no penalty; while among the Romans and the Greeks, he that kills one of these incurs capital punishment, the severest of penalties.

"*Laws of the Geli.* — Among the Geli the women sow and reap, and build, and perform all the tasks of labourers, and wear no raiment of colours, and put on no shoes, and use no pleasant ointments; nor does any one find fault with them when they consort with strangers, or cultivate intimacies with their household slaves. But the husbands of these Gelæ are dressed in garments of colours, and ornamented with gold and jewels, and anoint themselves with pleasant ointments. Nor is it on account of any effeminacy on their part that they act in this manner, but on account of the law which has been made for them: in fact, all the men are fond of hunting and addicted to war. But we cannot say that for all the women of the Geli Venus was posited in Capricorn or in Aquarius, in a position of ill luck; nor can we possibly say that for all the Geli Mars and Venus were posited in

---

[1] Lit. "Chaldaism."

[2] The Greek κλίμα, denoting one of the seven belts (see p. 732, below) into which the earth's latitude was said to be divided. The Arabs also borrowed the word.

[3] Or "family."

[4] That is, their own "houses," as below. Each house had one of the heavenly bodies as its "lord," who was stronger, or better "located" in his own house than in any other. Also, of two planets equally strong in other respects, that which was in the strongest house was the stronger. The strength of the houses was determined by the order in which they rose, the strongest being that about to rise, which was called the ascendant.

[5] Lit. "the signs of humanity."

[6] The text adds ܘ̈ܠܝ̈ܐܣܘ.

[7] Lit. "while Mars was witness to them."

Aries, where it is written that brave and wanton [1] men are born.

"*Laws of the Bactrians.* — Among the Bactrians, who are called Cashani, the women adorn themselves with the goodly raiment of men, and with much gold, and with costly jewels; and the slaves and handmaids minister to them more than to their husbands; and they ride on horses decked out with trappings of gold and with precious stones.[2] These women, moreover, do not practise continency, but have intimacies with their slaves, and with strangers who go to that country; and their husbands do not find fault with them, nor have the women themselves any fear *of punishment*, because the Cashani look upon[3] their wives *only* as mistresses. Yet we cannot say that for all the Bactrian women Venus and Mars and Jupiter are posited in the house of Mars in the middle of the heavens,[4] the place where women are born that are rich and adulterous, and that make their husbands subservient to them in everything.

"*Laws of the Racami, and of the Edessæans, and of the Arabians.* — Among the Racami, and the Edessæans, and the Arabians, not only is she that commits adultery put to death, but she also upon whom rests the suspicion[5] of adultery suffers capital punishment.

"*Laws in Hatra.* — There is a law in force[6] in Hatra, that whosoever steals any little thing, even though it were worthless as water, shall be stoned. Among the Cashani, *on the contrary*, if any one commits such a theft as this, they *merely* spit in his face. Among the Romans, *too*, he that commits a small theft is scourged and sent about his business. On the other side of the Euphrates, and *as you go* eastward, he that is stigmatized as either a thief or a murderer does not much resent it;[7] but, if a man be stigmatized as an arsenocœte, he will avenge himself even to the extent of killing *his accuser.*

---

[1] The difficult word ⌊ܩܠܬ⌋ is not found in the lexicons. Dr. Payne Smith remarks that it could only come from ⌊ܩܠ⌋, which verb, however, throws away its ܠ, so that the form would be ⌊ܩܠܬ⌋. He suggests, doubtfully, that the right reading is ⌊ܩܠܬ⌋, from ⌊ܩܠ⌋, which is used occasionally for *appetite*, and forms such an adjective in the sense of *animosus, animâ præditus;* and that if so, it may, like ⌊ܢܦܫܢܝ⌋ in Jude 19 and 1 Cor. xv. 44, 46, be = ψυχικοί, *having an animal nature, sensual.* Eusebius and Cæsarius have σπατάλους, a word of similar force.

[2] Cureton's rendering, ("*and some* adorn themselves," etc., is not so good, as being a repetition of what has already been said. It is also doubtful whether the words can be so construed. The Greek of Eusebius gives the sense as in the text: κοσμοῦσαι πολλῷ χρυσῷ καὶ λίθοις βαρυτίμοις τοὺς ἵππους. If ⌊ܣܘܣܐ⌋, *horses*, be masc., or masc. only, as Bernstein gives it, the participle should be altered to the same gender. But Dr. Payne Smith remarks that Amira in his Grammar makes it fem. Possibly the word takes both genders; possibly, too, the women of Bactria rode on mares.

[3] Lit. "possess."
[4] The zenith.
[5] Lit. "name," or "report."
[6] Lit. "made."
[7] Lit. "is not very angry."

"*Laws*. . . . — Among[8] . . . boys . . . to us, and are not . . . Again, in all the region of the East, if any persons are *thus* stigmatized, and are known *to be guilty*, their *own* fathers and brothers put them to death; and very often[9] they do not even make known the graves *where they are buried.*

"*Such are* the laws of the people of the East. But *in the North, and in the country of the Gauls*[10] and their neighbours, such youths among them as are handsome the men take as wives, and they even have feasts *on the occasion;* and it is not considered by them as a disgrace, nor as a reproach, because of the law which prevails among them. But it is a thing impossible that all those in Gaul who are branded with this disgrace should at their Nativities have had Mercury posited with Venus in the house of Saturn, and within the limits of Mars, and in the signs of the zodiac to the west. For, concerning such men as are born under these conditions, it is written that they are branded with infamy, *as being* like women.

"*Laws of the Britons.* — Among the Britons many men take one *and the same* wife.

"*Laws of the Parthians.* — Among the Parthians, *on the other hand*, one man takes many wives, and all of them keep to him only, because of the law which has been made there in that country.

"*Laws of the Amazons.* — As regards the Amazons, they, all of them, the entire nation, have no husbands; but like animals, once a year, in the spring-time, they issue forth from their territories and cross the river; and, having crossed it, they hold a great festival on a mountain, and the men from those parts come and stay with them fourteen days, and associate with them, and they become pregnant by them, and pass over again to their own country; and, when they are delivered, such *of the children* as are males they cast away, and the females they bring up. Now it is evident that, according to the ordinance of Nature, since they all became pregnant in one month, they also in one month are *all* delivered, a little sooner or a little later; and, as we have heard, all of them are robust and warlike; but not one of the stars is able to help any of those males who are born so as to prevent their being cast away.

"*The Book of the Astrologers.* — It is written in the book of the astrologers, that, when Mercury is posited with Venus in the house of Mercury, he produces painters, sculptors, and bankers; but that, when they are in the house of Venus, they produce perfumers, and dancers,

---

[8] Eusebius has, Παρ' Ἕλλησι δὲ καὶ οἱ σοφοὶ ἐρωμένους ἔχοντες οὐ ψέγονται.
[9] Lit. "how many times."
[10] The text of Eusebius and the *Recognitions* is followed, which agrees better with the context. The Syriac reads "Germans."

and singers, and poets. And *yet*, in all the country of the Tayites and of the Saracens, and in Upper Libya and among the Mauritanians, and in the country of the Nomades, which is at the mouth of the Ocean, and in outer Germany, and in Upper Sarmatia, and in Spain, and in all the countries to the north of Pontus, and in all the country of the Alanians, and among the Albanians, and among the Zazi, and in Brusa, which is beyond the Douro, one sees neither sculptors, nor painters, nor perfumers, nor bankers, nor poets; but, *on the contrary*, this decree of Mercury and Venus is prevented from *influencing* the entire circumference of the world. In the whole of Media, all men when they die, *and even* while life is still remaining in them, are cast to the dogs, and the dogs eat the dead of the whole of Media. Yet we cannot say that all the Medians are born having the Moon posited with Mars in Cancer in the day-time beneath the earth: for it is written that those whom dogs eat are so born. The Hindoos, when they die, are all of them burnt with fire, and many of their wives are burnt along with them alive. But we cannot say that all those women of the Hindoos who are burnt had at their Nativity Mars and the Sun posited in Leo in the night-time beneath the earth, as those persons are born who are burnt with fire. All the Germans die by strangulation,[1] except those who are killed in battle. But it is a thing impossible, that, at the Nativity of all the Germans, the Moon and Hora should have been posited between Mars and Saturn. The truth is, that in all countries, every day, and at all hours, men are born under Nativities diverse from one another, and the laws of men prevail over the decree *of the stars*, and they are governed by their customs. Fate does not compel the Seres to commit murder against their wish, nor the Brahmans to eat flesh; nor does it hinder the Persians from taking *as wives* their daughters and their sisters, nor the Hindoos from being burnt, nor the Medes from being devoured by dogs, nor the Parthians from taking many wives, nor among the Britons many men from taking one *and the same* wife, nor the Edessæans from cultivating chastity, nor the Greeks from practising gymnastics, . . ., nor the Romans from perpetually seizing upon *other* countries, nor the *men of the* Gauls from marrying one another; nor *does it compel* the Amazons to rear the males; nor does his Nativity compel any man within the circumference of the *whole* world to cultivate the art of the ·Muses; but, as I have *already* said, in every country and in every nation all men avail themselves of the freedom of their nature in any way they choose, and, by reason

of the body with which they are clothed, do service to Fate and to Nature, sometimes as they wish, and at other times as they do not wish. For in every country and in every nation there are rich and poor, and rulers and subjects, and people in health and those who are sick — each one according as Fate and *his* Nativity have affected him."

"Of these things, Father Bardesan," said I to him, "thou hast convinced us, and we know that they are true. But knowest thou that the astrologers say that the earth is divided into seven portions, which are called Zones; and that over the said portions those seven *stars* have authority, each of them *over one;* and that in each one of the said portions the will of its own Potentate prevails; and that this is called *its* law?"

"First of all, know thou, my son Philip," said he to me, "that the astrologers have invented this statement as a device *for the promotion* of error. For, although the earth be divided into seven portions, yet in every one of the seven portions many laws are to be found differing from one another. For there are not seven *kinds of* laws *only* found in the world, according to the number of the seven stars; nor yet twelve, according to the number of the signs of the zodiac; nor yet thirty-six, according to the number of the Decani.[2] But there are many *kinds of* laws *to be seen as you go* from kingdom to kingdom, from country to country, from district to district, and in every abode *of man*, differing one from another. For ye remember what I said to you — that in one zone, *that* of the Hindoos, there are many men that do not eat the flesh of animals, and there are others that *even* eat the flesh of men. And again, I told you, *in speaking* of the Persians and the Magi, that it is not in the zone of Persia only that they have taken *for wives* their daughters and their sisters, but that in every country to which they have gone they have followed the law of their fathers, and have preserved the mystic arts contained in that *teaching* which they delivered to them. And again, remember that I told you of many nations spread abroad over the entire circuit of the world,[3] who have not been confined to any one zone, but have dwelt in every quarter from which the wind blows,[4] and in all the zones, and who have not the arts which Mercury and Venus *are said to* have given when in conjunction with each other. Yet, if laws were regulated by zones, this could not be; but they clearly are not: because those men *I have spoken of* are at a wide remove from having anything in common with many *other* men in their habits of life.

---

[1] So Eusebius: ἀγχονιμαίῳ μόρῳ. Otherwise "suffocation."

[2] So called from containing each ten of the parts or degrees into which the zodiacal circle is divided. Cf. Hahn, *Bardesanes Gnosticus*, p. 72.
[3] Lit. "who surround the whole world."
[4] Lit. "have been in all the winds."

" *Then, again*, how many wise men, think ye, have abolished from their countries laws which appeared to them not well made? How many laws, also, are there which have been set aside through necessity? And how many kings are there who, when they have got possession of countries which did not belong to them, have abolished their established laws, and made such *other* laws as they chose? And, whenever these things occurred, no one of the stars was able to preserve the law. Here is an instance at hand for you to see *for yourselves :* it is but as yesterday since the Romans took possession of Arabia, and they abolished all the laws previously existing *there*, and especially the circumcision which they practised. The truth is,[1] that he who is his own master is *sometimes* compelled to obey the law imposed on him by another, who himself *in turn* becomes possessed of the power to do as he pleases.

" But let me mention to you a fact which more than anything *else* is likely[2] to convince the foolish, and such as are wanting in faith. All the Jews, who received the law through Moses, circumcise their male children on the eighth day, without waiting for the coming of the *proper* stars, or standing in fear of the law of the country *where they are living*. Nor does the star which has authority over the zone govern them by force; but, whether they be in Edom, or in Arabia, or in Greece, or in Persia, or in the north, or in the south, they carry out this law which was made for them by their fathers. It is evident that what they do is not from Nativity : for it is impossible that for all the Jews, on the eighth day, on which they are circumcised, Mars should ' be in the ascendant,' so that steel should pass upon them, and their blood be shed. Moreover, all of them, wherever they are, abstain from paying reverence to idols. One day in seven, also, they and their children cease from all work, — from all building, and from all travelling, and from all buying and selling; nor do they kill an animal on the Sabbath-day, nor kindle a fire, nor administer justice; and there is not found among them any one whom Fate compels,[3] either to go to law on the Sabbath-day and gain his cause, or to go to law and lose it, or to pull down, or to build up, or to do any one of those things which are done by all those men who have not received this law. They have also other things in respect to which they do not *on the Sabbath* conduct themselves like the rest of mankind, though on this same day they both bring forth and are born, and fall sick and die : for these things do not pertain to the power of man.

" In Syria and in Edessa men used to part with their manhood in honour of Tharatha ; but, when King Abgar[4] became a believer he commanded that every one that did so should have his hand cut off, and from that day until now no one does so in the country of Edessa.

" And what shall we say of the new race of us Christians, whom Christ at His advent planted in every country and in every region? for, lo ! wherever we are, we are all called after the one name of Christ — Christians. On one day, the first of the week, we assemble ourselves together, and on the days of the readings[5] we abstain from *taking* sustenance. The brethren who are in Gaul do not take males *for wives*, nor those who are in Parthia two wives ; nor do those who are in Judæa circumcise themselves ; nor do our sisters who are among the Geli consort with strangers ; nor do those *brethren* who are in Persia take their daughters *for wives ;* nor do those who are in Media abandon their dead, or bury them alive, or give them as food to the dogs ; nor do those who are in Edessa kill their wives or their sisters when they commit impurity, but they withdraw from them, and give them over to the judgment of God ; nor do those who are in Hatra[6] stone thieves *to death ;* but, wherever they are, and in whatever place they are *found*, the laws of the *several* countries do not hinder them from obeying the law of their *Sovereign*, Christ ; nor does the Fate of the *celestial* Governors compel them to make use of things which they regard as impure.

" On the other hand, sickness and health, and riches and poverty, things which are not within the scope of their freedom, befall them wherever they are. For although the freedom of man is not influenced by the compulsion of the Seven, or, if at any time it is influenced, it is able to withstand the influences exerted upon it, yet, *on the other hand*, this *same* man, externally regarded,[7] cannot on the instant liberate himself from the command of his Governors : for he is a slave and in subjection. For, if we were able to do everything, we should ourselves be everything ; and, if we had not the power to do anything, we should be the tools of others.

" But, when God wills *them*, all things are possible, *and they may take place* without hindrance : for there is nothing that can stay that Great and Holy Will. For even those who think that they *successfully* withstand it, do not with-

---

[4] According to Neander, *General Church History*, i. 109, this was the Abgar Bar Manu with whom Bardesan is said to have stood very high. His conversion is placed between 160 and 170 A.D.

[5] For ﻢﻟ, Merx, by omitting one ﻮ, gives ﻢﻟ, " readings." But what is meant is not clear. Ephraem Syrus ascribes certain compositions of this name to Bardesanes. Cf. Hahn, *Bard. Gnost.*, p. 28.

[6] Or " Hutra."

[7] Lit. " this man who is seen."

---

[1] Lit. " for."
[2] Lit. " able."
[3] Lit. " commands."

stand it by strength, but by wickedness and error. And this may go on for a little while, because He is kind and forbearing towards all beings that exist,[1] so as to let them remain as they are, and be governed by their own will, whilst notwithstanding they are held in check by the works which have been done and by the arrangements which have been made for their help. For this well-ordered constitution of things[2] and *this* government which have been instituted, and the intermingling of one with another, serve to repress the violence of *these* beings,[3] so that they should not inflict harm *on one another* to the full, nor yet to the full suffer harm, as was the case with them before the creation of the world. A time is also coming when this *propensity to inflict* harm which still remains in them shall be brought to an end, through the teaching which shall be *given them* amidst intercourse of another kind. And at the establishment of that new world all evil commotions shall cease, and all rebellions terminate, and the foolish shall be convinced, and all deficiencies shall be filled up, and there shall be quietness and peace, through the gift of the Lord of all existing beings."

Here endeth the Book of the Laws of Countries.

———

Bardesan, therefore, an aged man, and one celebrated for *his* knowledge of events, wrote, in a certain work which was composed by him, concerning the synchronisms[4] with one another of the luminaries of heaven, speaking as follows : —

Two revolutions of Saturn,[5] 60 years ;
5 revolutions of Jupiter, 60 years ;
40 revolutions of Mars, 60 years ;
60 revolutions of the Sun, 60 years ;
72 revolutions of Venus, 60 years ;
150 revolutions of Mercury, 60 years ;
720 revolutions of the Moon, 60 years.

And this," says he, "is one synchronism of them all ; that is, the time of one *such* synchronism of them. So that from hence *it appears that* to *complete* 100 such synchronisms there will be *required* six thousands of years. Thus : —

200 revolutions of Saturn, six thousands of years ;
500 revolutions of Jupiter, 6 thousands of years ;
4 thousand revolutions of Mars, 6 thousands of years ;
Six thousand revolutions of the Sun, 6 thousands of years ;
7 thousand and 200 revolutions of Venus, 6 thousands of years ;
12 thousand revolutions of Mercury, 6 thousands of years ;
72 thousand revolutions of the Moon, 6 thousands of years."

These things did Bardesan thus compute when desiring to show that this world would stand only six thousands of years.

---

[1] Lit. " all natures."
[2] Lit. " this order."
[3] Lit. " natures."
[4] The Greek σύνοδοι.

[5] The five planets are called by their Greek names, Κρόνος, κ.τ.λ.

ANCIENT SYRIAC DOCUMENTS

A LETTER OF MARA, SON OF SERAPION.[1]

MARA, son of Serapion, to Serapion, my son: peace.

When thy master and guardian wrote me a letter, and informed me that thou wast very diligent in study, *though so* young in years, I blessed God that thou, a little boy, *and* without a guide *to direct thee*, hadst begun in good earnest ; and to myself *also* this was a comfort — that I heard of thee, little boy *as thou art, as displaying* such greatness of mind and conscientiousness :[2] *a character* which, in the case of many *who have begun well*, has shown no eagerness to continue.

On this account, lo, I have written for thee this record, *touching* that which I have by careful observation discovered in the world. For the kind of life men lead has been carefully observed by me. I tread the path of learning,[3] and from the study of Greek philosophy[4] have I found out all these things, although they suffered shipwreck when the birth of life took place.[5]

Be diligent, then, my son, in *attention to* those things which are becoming for the free,[6] *so as* to devote thyself to learning, and to follow after wisdom ; and endeavour thus to become confirmed in those *habits* with which thou hast begun. Call to mind also my precepts, as a quiet person who is fond of the pursuit of learning. And, even though *such a life* should seem to thee very irksome, *yet* when thou hast made experience of it for a little while, it will become very pleasant to thee : for to me also it so happened. When, moreover, a person has left his home, and is able *still* to preserve his *previous* character, and properly does that which it be-hoves him to do, he is that chosen man who is called "the blessing of God," and one who does not find aught else to compare with his freedom.[7] For, as for those persons who are called to the pursuit of learning, they are seeking to extricate themselves from the turmoils of time ; and those who take hold upon wisdom, they are clinging to the hope of righteousness ; and those who take their stand on truth, they are displaying the banner of their virtue ; and those who cultivate philosophy, they are looking to escape from the vexations of the world. And do thou too, my son, thus wisely behave thyself in *regard to* these things, as a wise person who seeks to spend a pure life ; and *beware* lest the gain which many hunger after enervate thee, and thy mind turn to covet riches, which have no stability. For, when they are acquired by fraud, they do not continue ; nor, even when justly *obtained*, do they last ; and all those things which are seen by thee in the world, as belonging to that which is *only* for a little time, *are destined* to depart like a dream : for they are *but as* the risings and settings of the seasons.

About the *objects of that* vainglory, too, of which the life of men is full, be not thou solicitous : seeing that from those things which give us joy there quickly comes to us harm. Most especially *is this the case with* the birth of beloved children. For in two respects it plainly brings us harm : in the case of the virtuous, *our very* affection for them torments us, and from their *very excellence of* character we suffer torture ; and, in the case of the vicious, we are worried with their correction, and afflicted with their misconduct.

Thou hast heard,[8] moreover, concerning our companions, that, when they were leaving Samosata, they were distressed *about it*, and, as if complaining of the time *in which their lot was cast*, said thus : "We are now far removed from our home, and we cannot return *again* to our

---

[1] [Elucidation I. p. 742, *infra*. See p. 722, *supra*.]
[2] Lit. "good conscience."
[3] Or, "my daily converse is with learning." So Dr. Payne Smith is inclined to take these difficult words, supplying, as Cureton evidently does, the pronoun ܗ݀ܝ. The construction would be easier if we could take the participle ܡܬܗܦܟ as a passive, and render: "It (the kind of life men lead) has been *explored* by me by means of study."
[4] Lit. "Græcism."
[5] The meaning probably is, that the maxims referred to lost their importance for him when he entered upon the new life of a Christian (so Cureton), or their importance to mankind when Christianity itself was born into the world. But why he did not substitute more distinctive Christian teaching is not clear. Perhaps the fear of persecution influenced him.
[6] That is, the matters constituting "a *liberal* education."

[7] Cureton's less literal rendering probably gives the true sense: "with whose liberty nothing else can be compared."
[8] Cureton: "I have heard." The unpointed text is here ambiguous.

735

city, or behold our people, or offer to our gods the greeting of praise." Meet was it that that day should be called *a day* of lamentation, because one heavy grief possessed them all alike. For they wept as they remembered their fathers, and *they thought of* their mothers [1] with sobs, and they were distressed for their brethren, *and* grieved for their betrothed whom they had left behind. And, although we had heard that their [2] former companions were proceeding to Seleucia, we clandestinely *set out, and* proceeded on the way towards them, and united our own misery with theirs. Then was our grief exceedingly violent, and fitly did our weeping abound, by reason of our desperate plight, and our wailing gathered *itself into* a dense cloud,[3] and our misery grew vaster than a mountain : for not one of us had the power to ward off the disasters that assailed him. For affection for the living was intense, as well as sorrow for the dead, and our miseries were driving us on without any way *of escape.* For we saw our brethren and our children captives, and we remembered our deceased companions, who were laid *to rest* in a foreign [4] land. Each one of us, too, was anxious for himself, lest he should have disaster added to disaster, or *lest* another calamity should overtake that which went before it. What enjoyment could men have that were prisoners, *and* who experienced *things like* these?

But as for thee, my beloved, be not distressed because in thy loneliness thou hast [5] been driven from place to place. For to these things men are born, since they *are destined* to meet with the accidents of time. But *rather* let thy thought be this, that to wise men every place is alike, and *that* in every city the good have many fathers and mothers. Else, *if thou doubt it,* take thee a proof from *what thou hast seen* thyself. How many people who know thee not love thee as *one of* their own children; and *what* a host of women receive thee as *they would* their own beloved ones ! Verily, as a stranger thou hast been fortunate ; verily, for thy small love many people have conceived an ardent affection for thee.

What, again, are we to say concerning the delusion [6] which has taken up its abode in the world? Both by reason of toil [7] painful is the journey through it, and by its agitations are we, like a reed by the force of the wind, bent now in this direction, now in that. For I have been amazed at many who cast away their children, and I have been astonished at others who bring up those that are not theirs. There are persons who acquire riches in the world, and I have also been astonished at others who inherit that which is not *of* their own *acquisition.* Thus *mayest thou* understand and see that we are walking under the guidance of delusion.

Begin and tell us, O wisest of men,[8] on which of *his* possessions a man can place reliance, or concerning what things he can say that they are such as abide. *Wilt thou say so* of abundance of riches? they are snatched away. Of fortresses? they are spoiled. Of cities? they are laid waste. Of greatness? it is brought down. Of magnificence? it is overthrown. Of beauty? it withers. Or of laws? they pass away. Or of poverty? it is despised. Or of children? they die. Or of friends? they prove false. Or of the praises *of men?* jealousy goes before them.

Let a man, therefore, rejoice in his empire, like Darius ; or in his good fortune, like Polycrates ; or in his bravery, like Achilles ; or in his wife, like Agamemnon ; or in his offspring, like Priam ; or in his skill, like Archimedes ; or in his wisdom, like Socrates ; or in his learning, like Pythagoras ; or in his ingenuity, like Palamedes ; — the life of men, my son, departs from the world, but their praises and their virtues abide for ever.

Do thou, then, my little son, choose thee that which fadeth not away. For those who occupy themselves with these things are called modest, and *are* beloved, and lovers of a good name.

When, moreover, anything untoward befalls thee, do not lay the blame on man, nor be angry against God, nor fulminate against the time thou livest in.

If thou shalt continue in this mind, thy gift is not small which thou hast received from God, which has no need of riches, and is never reduced to poverty. For without fear shalt thou pass thy life,[9] and with rejoicing. For fear and apologies for *one's* nature belong not to the wise, but to such as walk contrary to law. For no man has even been deprived of his wisdom, as of his property.

Follow diligently learning rather than riches. For the greater are *one's* possessions, the greater is the evil *attendant upon them.* For I have myself observed that, where *a man's* goods are many, so also are the tribulations which happen *to him;* and, where luxuries are accumulated, there also do sorrows congregate ; and, where riches are abundant, there is *stored up* the bitterness of many a year.

---

[1] Read ܐܘܼܟ݂ܠ̈ܬܗܘܢ, instead of ܐܘܼܟ݂ܠ̈ܬܗܘܢ, "peoples."

[2] Perhaps "our" is meant.

[3] Cureton: "and the dark cloud collected our sighs." But the words immediately following, as well as the fact that in each of the clauses the nominative is placed last, favours the rendering given.

[4] Lit., "borrowed."

[5] Lit., "because thy loneliness has."

[6] Or "error." He may refer either to the delusion of those who pursue supposed earthly good, or to the false appearances by which men are deceived in such pursuit.

[7] For ܡܬܚܫܒ read ܚܫܒܐ.

[8] Cureton: "A sage among men once began to say to us." This would require ܫܪܝ, not ܫܪܐ.

[9] ܚܝܝܟ

If, therefore, thou shalt behave with understanding, and shalt diligently watch over *thy conduct*, God will not refrain from helping thee, nor men from loving thee.

Let that which thou art able to acquire suffice thee ; and if, moreover, thou art able to do without property, thou shalt be called blessed, and no man whatsover shall be jealous of thee.

And remember also this, that nothing will disturb thy life very greatly, except *it be the love of* gain ; *and* that no man after his death is called an owner of property : because it is by the desire of this that weak men are led captive, and they know not that a man dwells among his possessions *only* in the manner of a chance-comer, and they are haunted with fear because these *possessions* are not secured to them : for they have abandoned that which is their own, and seek that which is not theirs.

What are we to say, when the wise are dragged by force by the hands of tyrants, and their wisdom is deprived of its freedom [1] by slander, and they are plundered for their *superior* intelligence, without *the opportunity of making* a defence ? *They are not wholly to be pitied.* For what benefit did the Athenians obtain by putting Socrates to death, seeing that they received *as* retribution for it famine and pestilence ? Or the people of Samos by the burning of Pythagoras, seeing that in one hour the whole [2] of their country was covered with sand ? Or the Jews *by the murder* of their Wise King, seeing that from that very time their kingdom was driven away *from them ?* For with justice did God grant a recompense to the wisdom of *all* three of them. For the Athenians died by famine ; and the people of Samos were covered by the sea without remedy ; and the Jews, brought to desolation and expelled from their kingdom, are driven away into every land. *Nay*, Socrates did " not " die, because of Plato ; nor yet Pythagoras, because of the statue of Hera ; nor yet the Wise King, because of the new laws which he enacted.

Moreover I, my son, have attentively observed mankind, in what a dismal state of ruin they are. And I have been amazed that they are not utterly prostrated [3] by the calamities which surround them, and *that* even *their* wars [4] are not enough for them, nor the pains *they endure*, nor the diseases, nor the death, nor the poverty ; but *that*, like savage beasts, they must needs rush upon one another in *their* enmity, *trying* which of them

shall inflict the greater mischief on his fellow. For they have broken away from the bounds of truth, and transgress all honest laws, because they are bent on fulfilling their selfish desires ; for, whensoever a man is eagerly set on *obtaining* that which he desires, how is it possible that he should fitly do that which it behoves him *to do* ? and they acknowledge no restraint,[5] and but seldom stretch out their hands towards truth and goodness, but in their manner of life behave like the deaf[6] and the blind. Moreover, the wicked rejoice, and the righteous are disquieted. He that has, denies *that he has;* and he that has not, struggles to acquire. The poor seek *help*, and the rich hide *their wealth*, and every man laughs at his fellow. Those that are drunken are stupefied, and those that have recovered themselves are ashamed.[7] Some weep, and some sing ; and some laugh, and others are a prey to care. They rejoice in things evil, and a man that speaks the truth they despise.

Should a man, then, be surprised when the world is seeking to wither him with *its* scorn, seeing that they *and he* have not one *and the same* manner of life ? "These" are the things for which they care. One of them is looking *forward to the time* when in battle he shall obtain the renown of victory ; yet the valiant perceive not by how many foolish objects of desire a man is led captive in the world. But would that for a little while self-repentance visited them ! For, while victorious by their bravery, they are overcome by the power of covetousness. For I have made trial of men, and with this result : that the one thing on which they are intent, is abundance of riches. Therefore also it is that they have no settled purpose ; but, through the instability of their minds, a man is of a sudden cast down *from his elation of spirit* to be swallowed up with sadness. They look not at the vast wealth of eternity, *nor consider* that every visitation of trouble is conducting us all alike to the same *final* period. For they are devoted to the majesty of the belly, *that* huge blot *on the character* of the vicious.

Moreover, *as regards* this *letter* which it has come into my mind to write to thee, it is not enough to read it, but the best thing is that it be put in practice.[8] For I know for myself, that when thou shalt have made experiment of

---

[1] Lit., " made captive."

[2] For ܣܿܟܗ read ܟܠܗ.

[3] No verb is found in the lexicons to which ܐܬܒܠܥܘ can be referred. It may perhaps be Eshtaphel of a verb ܠܥܐ, cognate with ܥܩܐ, " to be bent."

[4] For ܩܪ̈ܒܐ read ܡܪ̈ܥܐ.

[5] Or " moderation."

[6] Cureton : " dumb." The word ܚܪܫܐ has both senses.

[7] Or " penitent."

[8] So Dr. Payne Smith, who is inclined to take ܩܕܡ ܛܒܐܝܬ in the sense, " it goes before, it is best, with respect to it." Cureton translates, " it should also proceed to practice," joining ܘܗܘ with the participle just mentioned; whereas Dr. Smith connects it with ܘܢܬܚܡ, thus: " but that it should be *put* in practice is best with respect to it."

this mode of life, it will be very pleasant to thee, and thou wilt be free from sore vexation; because it is *only* on account of children that we tolerate riches.[1]

Put, therefore, sadness away from thee, O *most* beloved of mankind, — a thing which never in anywise benefits *a man;* and drive care away from thee, which brings with it no advantage whatsoever. For we have no resource or skill *that can avail us — nothing* but a great mind *able* to cope with the disasters and to endure the tribulations which we are always receiving at the hands of the times. For at these things does it behove us to look, and not *only* at those which are fraught with rejoicing and good repute.

Devote thyself to wisdom, the fount of all things good, the treasure that faileth not. There shalt thou lay thy head, and be at ease. For this shall be to thee father and mother, and a good companion for thy life.

Enter into closest intimacy with fortitude and patience, those *virtues* which are able *successfully* to encounter the tribulations that befall feeble men. For so great is their strength, that they are adequate to sustain hunger, and *can* endure thirst, and mitigate every trouble. With toil, moreover, yea even with dissolution, they make right merry.

To these things give diligent attention, and thou shalt lead an untroubled life, and I also shall have comfort,[2] and thou shalt be called "the delight of his parents."

For in that time of yore, when our city was standing in her greatness, thou mayest be aware that against many persons *among us* abominable words were uttered; but for ourselves,[3] we acknowledged long ago that we received love, no less than honour, to the fullest extent from the multitude of her people: it was the state of the times *only* that forbade *our* completing those things which we had resolved on doing.[4] And here also in the prison-house we give thanks to God that we have received the love of many: for we are striving to our utmost to maintain a life of sobriety and cheerfulness;[5] and, if any

one drive us by force, he will *but* be bearing public testimony against himself, that he is estranged from all things good, and he will receive disgrace and shame from the foul mark of shame *that is upon him.* For we have shown our truth — *that truth* which in our *now* ruined kingdom we possessed not.[6] But, if the Romans shall permit us to go *back* to our own country, *as called upon* by justice and righteousness *to do,* they will be acting like humane men, and will earn the name of good and righteous, and at the same time *will have* a peaceful country in which to dwell: for they will exhibit their greatness when they shall leave us free men, *and* we shall be obedient to the sovereign power which the time has allotted to us. But let them not, like tyrants, drive us as *though we were* slaves. Yet, if it has been *already* determined what shall be done, we shall receive nothing more *dreadful* than the peaceful death which is in store for us.

But thou, my little son, if thou resolve diligently to acquaint thyself with these things, first of all put a check on appetite, and set limits to that in which thou art *indulging.* Seek the power to refrain from being angry; and, instead of *yielding to* outbursts of passion, listen to *the promptings of* kindness.

For myself, what I am henceforth solicitous about is this — *that,* so far as I have recollections *of the past,* I may leave behind me a book *containing them,* and with a prudent mind finish the journey which I am appointed *to take,* and depart without suffering out of the sad afflictions of the world. For my prayer is, that I may receive *my* dismissal; and *by* what kind of death concerns me not. But, if any one should be troubled or anxious *about this,* I have no counsel to give him: for yonder, in the dwelling-place of all the world, will he find us before him.

One of his friends asked Mara, son of Serapion, when in bonds at his side: "Nay, by thy life, Mara, tell me what *cause* of laughter thou hast seen, that thou laughest." "I am laughing," said Mara, "at Time:[7] inasmuch as, although he has not borrowed any evil from me, he is paying me back."

Here endeth the letter of Mara, son of Serapion.

---

[1] This appears to show that the life of learned seclusion which he has been recommending is one of celibacy — monasticism.

[2] Or, "and thou shalt be to me a comfort," as Cureton.

[3] That is, "myself."

[4] Such appears to be the sense of this obscure passage. The literal rendering is, "We acknowledged of old that we received equal love and honour to the fullest extent from her multitude" (or, from her greatness); "but the time forbade *our* completing those things which were *already* accomplished in our mind." What things he refers to (for his words seem to have a particular reference) is not clear. The word rendered "greatness," or "multitude," is in reality two words in pointed MSS. Here it does not appear, except from the sense, which is intended.

[5] Lit., "We are putting ourself to the proof to *see how far we can* stand in wisdom," etc.

[6] "This is a very hopeless passage. . . . Perhaps the codex has ܠܡܘܪܒܢ, 'the kingdom of *our* ruin,' i.e., the ruined country in which we used to dwell. For possibly it refers to what he has said before about the ruined greatness of his city, captured by the Romans. I suppose Mara was a Persian." — DR. PAYNE SMITH.

[7] Or, "the time."

ANCIENT SYRIAC DOCUMENTS

AMBROSE.[1]

A MEMORIAL[2] which Ambrose, a chief man of Greece, wrote: who became a Christian, and all his fellow-senators raised an outcry against him; and he fled from them, and wrote and pointed out to them all their foolishness.

Beginning his discourse,[3] he answered and said:—

Think not, men of Greece, that my separation from your customs has been made without a just and proper reason. For I acquainted myself with all your wisdom, *consisting* of poetry, of oratory, of philosophy; and when I found not *there* anything *agreeable to what is* right, or that is worthy of the divine nature, I resolved to make myself acquainted with the wisdom of the Christians also, and to learn and see who *they are*, and when *they took their rise*, and what is *the nature of* this new and strange wisdom *of theirs*,[4] or on what good *hopes* those who are imbued with it rely, that they speak *only* that which is true.

Men of Greece, when I came to examine *the Christian writings*, I found not any folly [5] *in them*, as I had found in the celebrated Homer, who has said concerning the wars of the two trials:[6] "Because of Helen, many of the Greeks perished at Troy, away from their beloved home."[7] For, first of all, we are told[8] concerning Agamemnon their king, that by reason of the foolishness of his brother Menelaus, and the violence of his madness, and the uncontrollable nature of his passion, he resolved to go and rescue Helen from *the hands of* a certain leprous [9] shepherd; and *afterwards*, when the Greeks had become victorious in the war, and burnt cities, and taken women and children captive, and the land was filled with blood, and the rivers with corpses, Agamemnon himself also was found to be taken captive by *his* passion for Briseis. Patroclus, again, we are told, was slain, and Achilles, the son of the goddess Thetis, mourned over him; Hector was dragged *along the ground*, and Priam and Hecuba together were weeping over the loss of their children; Astyanax, the son of Hector, was thrown down from the walls of Ilion, and his mother Andromache the mighty Ajax bore away *into captivity;* and that which was taken as booty was after a little while, *all* squandered in sensual indulgence.

Of the wiles of Odysseus the son of Laertes, and of his murders, who shall tell the tale? For of a hundred and ten suitors did his house in one day become the grave, and it was filled with corpses and blood. He, too, *it was* that by his wickedness gained the praises *of men*, because through *his* pre-eminence in craft he escaped detection; he, too, *it was* who, you say, sailed upon the sea, and heard *not* the voice of the Sirens *only* because he stopped his ears with wax.[10]

The famous Achilles, again, the son of Peleus, who bounded across the river, and routed [11] the Trojans, and slew Hector,—this said hero of yours became the slave of Philoxena, and was overcome by an Amazon *as she lay* dead and stretched *upon her bier;* and he put off his armour, and arrayed himself in nuptial garments, and finally fell a sacrifice to love.

---

[1] This piece has much in common with the *Discourse to the Greeks* (Λόγος πρὸς Ἕλληνας), ascribed by many to Justin, which is contained in vol. i. pp. 271-272 of this series. Two things seem to be evident: (1) That neither of the two pieces is the original composition: for each contains something not found in the other; (2) That the original was in Greek: for the Syriac has in some instances evidently mistranslated the Greek.

[2] The Greek ὑπομνήματα.

[3] Lit., " and in the beginning of his words."

[4] Lit. " what is the newness and strangeness of it."

[5] The word also means " sin; " and this notion is the more prominent of the two in what follows.

[6] It is difficult to assign any satisfactory meaning to the word ܕܫܘܡ̈ܠܐ, which appears, however, to be the reading of the MS., since Cureton endeavours to justify the rendering given. " Calamities," a sense the word will also bear, seems no easier of explanation. If we could assume the meaning to be " nations " (*nationes*), a word similar in sound to that found in the text, explaining it of *heathen* peoples, Gentiles (comp. Tertullian, *De Idol.*, 22, " per deos nationum"), this might seem to meet the difficulty. But there is no trace in this composition of a *Latin* influence: if a foreign word *must* be used, we should rather have expected the Greek ἔθνη.

[7] *Il.*, ii. 177 sq.

[8] Lit., " they say."

[9] It has been proposed to substitute in the Greek copy λιπαροῦ, " dainty," for λεπροῦ. But the Syriac confirms the MS. reading. The term is thought to be expressive of the contempt in which shepherds were held. See vol. i. p. 271, note 1.

[10] In the Greek this is adduced as an evidence of his weakness: " because he was unable to stop his ears by *his* self-control (φρονήσει)."

[11] ܥܪܩ, the reading of the text, which can only mean " fled," is manifestly incorrect. The Aphel of this verb, ܐܥܪܩ, " caused to flee," is suggested by Dr. Payne Smith, who also proposes ܥܩܪ, " exstirpavit."

Thus much concerning *your* great "men;"[1] and thou, Homer, hadst deserved forgiveness, if thy silly story-telling had gone so far *only* as to prate about men, and not about the gods. As for what *he says* about the gods, I am ashamed even to speak of it: for the stories that have been invented about them are very wicked and shocking; passing strange,[2] too, and not to be believed; and, if the truth must be told,[3] fit only to be laughed at. For a person will *be compelled to* laugh when he meets with them, and will not believe them when he hears them. For *think of* gods who did not one of them observe the laws of rectitude, or of purity, or of modesty, but *were* adulterers, and spent their time in debauchery, and *yet* were not condemned to death, as they ought to have been!

Why, the sovereign of the gods, the very "father of gods and men," not only, as ye say, was an adulterer (this was but a light thing), but even slew his own father, and was a pæderast. I will first of all speak of *his* adultery, though I blush *to do so:* for he appeared to Antiope as a satyr, and descended upon Danaë as a shower of gold, and became a bull for Europa, and a swan for Leda; whilst the love of Semele, the mother of Dionysus, exposed both his own ardency *of passion* and the jealousy of the chaste Hera. Ganymede the Phrygian, too, he carried off *disguised* as an eagle, that the fair and comely boy, forsooth, might serve as cup-bearer to him. This said sovereign of the gods, moreover, killed his father Kronos, that he might seize upon his kingdom.

Oh! to how many charges is the sovereign of the gods amenable,[4] and how many deaths does he deserve *to die,* as an adulterer, and as a sorcerer,[5] and as a pæderast! Read to the sovereign of the gods, O men of Greece, the law concerning parricide, and the condemnation pronounced on adultery, and *about* the shame that attaches to the vile sin of pæderasty. How many adulterers has the sovereign of the gods indoctrinated *in sin!* Nay, how many pæderasts, and sorcerers, and murderers! So that, if a man be found indulging his passions, he must not be put to death: because he has done this that he may become like the sovereign of the gods; and, if he be found a murderer, he has an excuse *in* the sovereign of the gods; and, if a man be a sorcerer, he has learned it from the sovereign of the gods; and, if he be a pæderast, the sovereign of the gods is his apologist. Then, again,

if one should speak of courage, Achilles was more valiant that this said sovereign of the gods: for he slew the man that slew his friend; but the sovereign of the gods wept over Sarpedon his son when he was dying, being distressed *for him.*

Pluto, again, who is a god, carried off Kora,[6] and the mother of Kora was hurrying hither and thither searching for her daughter in all desert places; and, *although* Alexander Paris, when he had carried off Helen, paid the penalty of vengeance, as *having made himself* her lover by force, yet Pluto, who is a god, when he carried off Kora, remained without rebuke; and, *although* Menelaus, who is a man, knew how to search for Helen his wife, yet Demeter, who is a goddess, knew not where to search for Kora her daughter.

Let Hephæstus put away jealousy from him, and not indulge resentment.[7] For he was hated,[8] because he was old and lame; while Ares was loved, because he was a youth and beautiful in form. There was, however, a reproof *administered in respect* of the adultery. Hephæstus was not, indeed, *at first* aware of the love existing between Venus[9] his wife and Ares; but, when he did become acquainted with it, Hephæstus said: "Come, see a ridiculous and senseless piece of behaviour — how to me, who am her own, Venus, the daughter of the sovereign of the gods, is offering insult — to me, *I say,* who am her own, and is paying honour to Ares, who is a stranger to her." But to the sovereign of the gods it was not displeasing: for he loved such as were like these. Penelope, moreover, remained a widow twenty years, because she was expecting *the return of* her husband Odysseus, and busied herself with cunning tasks,[10] and persevered in works of skill, while all those suitors kept pressing her *to marry them;* but Venus, who is a goddess, when Hephæstus her husband was close to her, deserted him, because she was overcome by love for Ares. Hearken, men of Greece: which of you would have dared to do this, or would even have endured to see it? And, if any one "should" dare *to act so,* what torture would be in store for him, or what scourgings!

Kronos, again, who is a god, who devoured all those children *of his,* was not even brought before a court of justice. They further tell *us* that the sovereign of the gods, his son, was the only

---

[1] Or, "*your* heroes."

[2] This is not intended as a translation of ﺧ, which is literally "conquered." Dr. Payne Smith thinks it just possible that there was in the Greek some derivative of ὑπερβάλλω = " to surpass belief," which the Syrian translator misunderstood.

[3] This is conjectured to be the meaning of what would be literally rendered, "*et id quod coactum est.*"

[4] Lit., "of how many censures is . . . full."

[5] Since he could change his form to suit his purpose.

[6] That is, "the Daughter" (namely, of Demeter), the name under which Proserpine was worshipped in Attica.

[7] Because the behaviour of which he had to complain was sanctioned by the highest of the gods.

[8] For ﺍﻣﺰﺍ, "was tried," read ﺍﻣﻞﺍ. The Greek has μεμίσητο. Cureton: "forgotten."

[9] The word is "Balthi."

[10] Dr. Payne Smith reads ﻣﻴ ﺑﻠﺪﺍ instead of ﻣﻴ ﺑﺤﺪﺍ, word which, as Cureton says, is not in the lexicons.

one that escaped from him; and that the madness of Kronos his father was cheated *of its purpose* because Rhea his wife, the mother of the sovereign of the gods, offered him a stone in the place of the said sovereign of the gods, his son, to prevent him from devouring him. Hearken, men of Greece, and reflect upon this madness! Why, *even* the dumb animal that grazes in the field knows its *proper* food, and does not touch strange food; the wild beast, too, and the reptile, and the bird, know their food. As for men, I need not say anything about them: ye yourselves are acquainted with their food, and understand it *well*. But Kronos, who is a god, not knowing his *proper* food, ate up a stone!

Therefore, O men of Greece, if ye will have such gods as these, do not find fault with one another when ye do such-like things. Be not angry with thy son when he forms the design to kill thee: because he *thus* resembles the sovereign of the gods. And, if a man commit adultery with thy wife, why dost thou think of him as an enemy, and yet to the sovereign of the gods, who is like him, doest worship and service? Why, too, dost thou find fault with thy wife when she has committed adultery and leads a dissolute life,[1] and *yet* payest honour to Venus, and placest her *images* in shrines? Persuade *your* Solon to repeal his laws; Lycurgus, also, to make no laws; let the Areopagus repeal[2] theirs, and judge no more; and let the Athenians have councils no longer. Let the Athenians discharge Socrates *from his office:* for no one like Kronos has *ever* come before him. Let them not put to death Orestes, who killed his mother: for, lo! the sovereign of the gods did worse things than these to his father. Œdipus also *too* hastily inflicted mischief on himself, in depriving his eyes of sight, because he had killed his mother unwittingly: for he did not think about[3] the sovereign of the gods, who killed his father and *yet* remained without punishment. Medea, again, who killed her children, the Corinthians banish *from their country;* and *yet* they do service and honour to Kronos, who devoured his children. Then, too, as regards Alexander Paris — he was right in carrying off Helen: *for he did it* that he might become like Pluto, who carried off Kora. Let *your* men be set free from law, and let *your* cities be *the abode* of wanton women, and a dwelling-place for sorcerers.

Wherefore, O men of Greece, seeing that your gods are grovelling like yourselves, and your heroes destitute of courage,[4] as your dramas tell and your stories declare — then, again, *what shall be said* of the tribulations of Orestes; and the couch of Thyestes; and the foul taint *in the family* of Pelops; and concerning Danaus, who through jealousy killed his sons-*in-law*, and deprived them of offspring; the banquet of Thyestes, too, *feeding upon* the corpse *set before him by way* of vengeance for her *whom he had wronged; about* Procne also, to this hour screaming as she flies; her sister too, warbling, with her tongue cut out?[5] What, moreover, is it fitting to say about the murder committed by Œdipus, who took his own mother *to wife*, and whose brothers killed one another, they being *at the same time* his sons?

Your festivals, too, I hate; for there is no moderation where they are; the sweet flutes also, dispellers of care, which play as an incitement to dancing;[6] and the preparation of ointments, wherewith ye anoint yourselves; and the chaplets which ye put on. In the abundance of your wickedness, too, ye have forgotten shame, and your understandings have become blinded, and ye have been infuriated[7] by the heat *of passion*, and have loved the adulterous bed.[8]

Had these things been said by another, perhaps *our adversaries* would have brought an accusation against him, *on the plea* that they were untrue. But your own poets say them, and your own hymns and dramas declare them.

Come, therefore, and be instructed in the word of God, and in the wisdom which is fraught with comfort. Rejoice, and become partakers of it. Acquaint yourselves with the King Immortal, and acknowledge His servants. For not in arms do they make their boast, nor do they commit murders: because our Commander has no delight in abundance of strength, nor yet in horsemen and their gallant array, nor yet in illustrious descent; but He delights in the pure soul, fenced round by a rampart of righteousness. The word of God, moreover, and the promises of our good King, and the works of God, are ever teaching us. Oh *the blessedness of* the soul that is redeemed by the power of the word! Oh *the blessedness of* the trumpet of peace without war! Oh *the blessedness of* the teaching which quenches the fire of appetite! which, *though it* makes not poets, nor fits *men* to be philosophers, nor has *among its votaries* the orators of the crowd; yet instructs *men*, and makes the dead not to die, and lifts men from the earth *as* gods up to the region which is above the firmament. Come, be instructed, and be like me: for I too was *once* as ye are.

---

[1] The reading of the Greek copy, ἀκολάστως ζώσαν, is here given. The Syrian adapter, misunderstanding ἀκολάστως, renders: "and is without punishment."

[2] Cureton, "break."

[3] Lit. "look at."

[4] So in the Greek copy. The Syriac, which has "valiant," appears to have mistaken ἄνανδροι for ἀνδρεῖοι.

[5] The tradition seems to be followed which makes Procne to have been changed into a swallow, and her sister (Philomela) into a nightingale.

[6] Cureton: "play with a tremulous motion." But the Syriac very well answers to the Greek ἐκκαλούμενοι πρὸς οἰστρώδεις κινήσεις, if we take ◌ to denote *result:* q.d., "so as to produce *movement*."

[7] Greek, ἐκβακχευόμενοι.

[8] Lit. "bed of falsity." [Compare notes on vol. i. pp. 271 272.]

ELUCIDATIONS

I.

(Mara, son of Serapion, p. 735.)

I CANNOT withhold from the student the valuable hints concerning "the dialect of Edessa" by which Professor Nöldke [1] corrects the loose ideas of Mommsen, more especially because the fresh work of Mommsen will soon be in our hands, and general credit will be attached to specious representations which are sure to have a bearing on his ulterior treatment of Christianity and the Roman Empire.

Of the Syriac language Professor Nöldke says : —

"It was the living language of Syria which here appears as the *language of writing*. In Syria it had long ago been compelled to yield to the Greek as the *official language*, but private writings were certainly yet to a great extent written in Aramaic. We cannot lay much stress upon the fact that the respectable citizen in the Orient would have the schoolmaster of the village compose a Greek inscription for his tomb, of which he undoubtedly understood but little himself. And what a Greek this often was! That no books written by Aramaic Gentiles have been preserved for us, does not decide against the existence of the Aramaic as the language of literature in that day ; for how could such Gentile works have been preserved for us ? To this must be added, that *that particular dialect which afterward became the common literary language of Aramaic Christendom — namely, that of Edessa —* certainly had in the Gentile period already been used for literary purposes. The official report of the great flood in the year 201, which is prefixed to the Edessa Chronicles, is written by a Gentile. To the same time must be ascribed the letter, written in good Edessan language by the finely educated Marâ bar Serapion, from the neighbouring Samosata, who, notwithstanding his good-will toward youthful Christianity, was no Christian, but represented rather the ethical stand-point of the Stoicism so popular at that time. The fixed settling of Syriac orthography must have taken place at a much earlier period than the hymns of Bardesanes and his school, which are for us very old specimens of that language, since these hymns represent a versification much younger than the stage of development which is presupposed in this orthography. In general, it must be granted that *the dialect of Edessa had been thoroughly developed already in pre-Christian times ;* otherwise, it could not have been so fixed and firm in writing and forms of expression. And the Syriac *Dialogue on Fate*, which presupposes throughout the third century, treats of scientific questions, according to Greek models, with such precision that we again see that this was not the beginning, but rather the close, of a scientific Syriac literature, which flourished already when there were but few or possibly no Christians there. Of course I recognise, with Mommsen, that Edessa offered a better protection to the national language and literature than did the cities of Syria proper ; but circumstances were not altogether of a different nature in this regard in Haleb, Hems, and Damascus than they were in Edessa and Jerusalem. If, as is known, the common mass spoke Aramaic in the metropolitan city of Antiochia, it cannot safely be accepted that in the inland districts the Greek was not the language of the 'educated,' but only of those who had specially learned it. The Macedonian and Greek colonists have certainly only in a very small part retained this language in those districts down to the Roman period. In most cases they have been in a minority from the beginning over against the natives. Further, as the descendants of old soldiers, they can scarcely be regarded as the called watchmen of Greek customs and language."

II.

(No verb is found in the lexicons, etc., note 3, p. 737.)

The study of Syriac is just beginning to be regarded as only less important to the theologian than that of the Hebrew. The twain will be found a help, each to the other, if one pursues the study of the cognate languages together. In fact, the Book of Daniel demands such a preparation for its enjoyment and adequate comprehension.[2] Let me commend to every reader the

---

[1] For previous quotations refer to p. 721, *supra*.

[2] It must not be inferred that I speak as a Syriac scholar. I have laboured unsuccessfully, and late in life, to repair my sad neglect at an earlier period; and I can speak only as a penitent.

admirable example of Beveridge, who at eighteen years of age produced a grammar of the Syriac language, and also a Latin essay on the importance of cultivating this study, as that of the ver-nacular of our Lord Himself. This little treatise is worthy of careful reading; and right worthy of note is the motto which he prefixed to it, — "Estote imitatores mei, *sicut et ego sum Christi*" (1 Cor. xi. 1).

When one thinks of the difficulties even yet to be overcome in mastering the language, — the want of a complete lexicon, etc.,[1] — it is surprising to think of Beveridge's pioneer labours in extreme youth. Gutbir's *Lexicon Syriacum* had not yet appeared, nor his edition of the Peshito, which preceded it, though Brian Walton's great name and labours were his noble stimulants. Nobody can read the touching account which Gutbir[2] gives of his own enthusiastic and self-sacrificing work, without feeling ashamed of the slow progress of Oriental studies in the course of two cen-turies since the illustrious Pocock gave his grand example to English scholarship. All honour to our countryman Dr. Murdock, who late in life entered upon this charming pursuit, and called on others to follow him.[3] May I not venture to hope that even these specimens of what may be reaped from the field of Aramaic literature may inspire my young countrymen to take the lead in elucidating the Holy Scriptures from this almost unopened storehouse of "treasures new and old"?

---

[1] Dean Payne Smith has assumed the unfinished task of Bernstein.

[2] See his Preface to the Testament, published at Hamburg A.D. 1664. He had the type cut at his personal expense, and set up the press and lodged the printers in his own house.

[3] See his translation of the Peshito Syriac version, Stanford & Swords (Bishop Hobart's publishers), New York, 1855.

REMAINS OF THE SECOND AND THIRD CENTURIES

[TRANSLATED BY THE REV. B. P. PRATTEN.]

INTRODUCTORY NOTICE

TO

REMAINS OF THE SECOND AND THIRD CENTURIES

UNDER the title of *Fragments of the Second and Third Centuries* are grouped together, in the Edinburgh series, a mass of valuable illustrative material, which might have been distributed with great advantage through the former volumes, in strict order of chronology. Something is due, however, to the unity of authorship, and to the marked design of the editors of the original edition to let these Fragments stand together, as the work of their accomplished collaborator, the Rev. B. P. Pratten, with whose skill and erudition our readers are already familiar.[1]

I have contented myself, therefore, with giving approximate order and continuity, on chronological grounds, to the series of names subjoined. Bardesanes has been eliminated here, and placed more appropriately with the Syriac authors. The reader will find references which may aid him in seeking further information. Some of these names are of lasting value and interest in the Church. I prefer to call these " Fragments " their " Remains."

To each of the following names I have prefixed some details of information, with such dates as the learned supply.

The following is the

TRANSLATOR'S INTRODUCTORY NOTICE.

THE fragments that follow are the productions of writers who lived during the second century or the beginning of the third. Little is known of the writers, and the statements made in regard to them are often very indefinite, and the result of mere conjecture.

1. Quadratus was one of the first of the Christian apologists. He is said to have presented his apology to Hadrian while the emperor was in Athens attending the celebration of the Eleusinian mysteries.

2. Aristo of Pella, a Jew, was the author of a work called *The Disputation of Jason and Papiscus.* Nothing further is known of him. He flourished in the first half of the second century.

3. Melito was bishop of Sardis, and flourished in the reign of Marcus Aurelius. He wrote many works, but all of them have perished except a few fragments. The genuineness of the Syriac fragments is open to question.

4. Hegesippus also flourished in the time of Antoninus Pius and Marcus Aurelius. He is the first ecclesiastical historian ; but his book was rather notes for an ecclesiastical history, than a history.

5. Dionysius was bishop of Corinth in the reign of Marcus Aurelius. He wrote letters to various churches.

---

6. Rhodon went from Asia to Rome, and became a pupil of Tatian. After the lapse of his master into heresy he remained true to the faith, and wrote against heretics.

7. Maximus flourished about the same time as Rhodon, under the emperors Commodus and Severus.

8. Claudius Apollinaris was bishop of Hierapolis, and presented a defence of the Christians to Marcus Aurelius. He wrote many important works, of which we have only a few fragments.

9. Polycrates was bishop of Ephesus. He took part in the controversy on the Passover question. He died about 200 A.D.

10. Theophilus was bishop of Cæsarea. He was a contemporary of Polycrates, and, like him, engaged in the Passover controversy.

11. Serapion was ordained bishop of Antioch A.D. 190, but almost no other fact of his life is known. He wrote several works.

12. Apollonius wrote a work against the Montanists, probably in the year A.D. 210. This is all that is known of him.

13. Pantænus, probably a Sicilian by birth, passed from Stoicism to Christianity, and went to Judæa to proclaim the truth. He returned to Alexandria, and became president of the catechetical school there, in which post he remained till his death, which took place about the year 212 A.D.

14. *The Letter of the Churches in Vienne and Lyons* was written shortly after the persecution in Gaul, which took place in A.D. 177. It is not known who is the author. Some have supposed that Irenæus wrote it, but there is no historical testimony to this effect.

REMAINS OF THE SECOND AND THIRD CENTURIES

QUADRATUS, BISHOP OF ATHENS.[1]

[A.D. 126.] Quadratus[2] is spoken of by Eusebius as a " man of understanding and of Apostolic faith." And he celebrates Aristides as a man of similar character. These were the earliest apologists ; both addressed their writings to Hadrian, and they were extant and valued in the churches in the time of Eusebius.

FROM THE APOLOGY FOR THE CHRISTIAN RELIGION.[3]

OUR Saviour's works, moreover, were always present : for they were real, *consisting of* those who had been healed of their diseases, those who had been raised from the dead ; who were not only seen whilst they were being healed and raised up, but were *afterwards* constantly present. Nor did they remain only during the sojourn of the Saviour *on earth*, but also a considerable time after His departure ; and, indeed, some of them have survived even down to our own times.[4]

ARISTO OF PELLA.

[A.D. 140.] Aristo of Pella[5] is supposed to have been a Jew, whose work was designed to help the failing Judaism of his country. Though his work is lost, alike the original and the Latin translation of one " Celsus," it seems to have been a popular tract among Christians of Cyprian's time, and the Latin preface is often suffixed to editions of that Father.

The work of Aristo is known as the *Disputation of Papiscus and Jason*, and Celsus tells us that Jason was a Hebrew Christian, while his opponent was a Jew of Alexandria. Now, Papiscus owns himself convinced by the arguments of Jason, and concludes by a request to be baptized. Celsus, who seems to have been a heathen or an Epicurean, derides the work with scornful commiseration ; but Origen rebukes this, and affirms his respect for the work. All this considered, one must think Aristo was " almost persuaded to be a Christian," and deserves a place among Christian writers.

FROM THE DISPUTATION OF JASON AND PAPISCUS.

" I REMEMBER," says Jerome (*Comm. ad Gal.*, cap. iii. comm. 13), " in the *Dispute between Jason and Papiscus*, which is composed in Greek,, to have found it written : ' The execration of God is he that is hanged.' "

FROM THE SAME WORK.

Jerome likewise, in his *Hebrew Questions on Genesis*, says : " *In the beginning God made the heaven and the earth*. The majority believe, as it is affirmed also in the *Dispute between Jason and Papiscus*, and as Tertullian in his book

---

[1] But see Lightfoot, *A. F.*, part ii. vol. i. p. 524.
[2] On Quadratus and Aristides, consult Routh, *R. S.*, p. 71; also Westcott, *On the Canon*, p. 92.
[3] In Eusebius, *Hist. Eccl.*, iv. 3.

[4] [Westcott supposes the *Diognetus* of Mathetes (vol. i. p. 23) may be the work of Quadratus; *Canon*, p. 96.]
[5] Routh, *R. S.*, vol. i. p. 93. Westcott, *Canon*, p. 106. Grabe's mention. Routh's discussion, in annotations, is most learned and exhaustive.

Against Praxeas contends, and as Hilarius too, in his exposition of one of the Psalms, declares, that in the Hebrew it is : ' In the Son, God made the heaven and the earth.' But that this is false, the nature of the case itself proves."

PERHAPS FROM THE SAME WORK.

. . . And when the man himself[1] who had instigated them[2] to this folly had paid the just penalty (says Eusebius, *Hist.*, iv. 6), " the whole nation from that time was strictly forbidden to set foot on the region about Jerusalem, by the formal decree and enactment of Adrian, who commanded that they should not even from a distance look on their native soil ! " So writes Aristo of Pella.

FROM THE SAME WORK.

I have found this expression *Seven heavens* (says Maximus, in *Scholia on the work concerning the Mystical Theology*, ascribed to Dionysius the Areopagite, cap. i.) also in the *Dispute between Papiscus and Jason*, written by Aristo of Pella, which Clement of Alexandria, in the sixth book of the *Outlines*,[3] says was composed by Saint Luke.

CONCERNING THE SAME WORK.

Thus writes Origen :[4] . . . in which *book* a Christian is represented disputing with a Jew from the Jewish Scriptures, and showing that the prophecies concerning the Christ apply to Jesus : although his opponent addresses himself to the argument with no common ability,[5] and in a manner not unbefitting his Jewish character.

MELITO, THE PHILOSOPHER.

[A.D. 160–170–177.] Melito[6] may have been the immediate successor of the " angel " (or " apostle ") of the church of Sardis, to whom our Great High Priest addressed one of the apocalyptic messages. He was an " Apostolic Father " in point of fact ; he very probably knew the blessed Polycarp and his disciple Irenæus. He is justly revered for the diligence with which he sought out the evidence which, in his day, established the Canon of the Old Testament, then just complete.

In the following fragments we find him called Bishop of Sardis, Bishop of Attica, and Bishop of Ittica. He is also introduced to us as " the Philosopher," and we shall find him styled " the Eunuch " by Polycrates. It is supposed that he had made himself a cœlebs " for the kingdom of heaven's sake," without mistaking our Lord's intent, as did Origen. He was not a monk, but accepted a single estate to be the more free and single-eyed in the Master's service. From the encyclopedic erudition of Lightfoot we glean some particulars, as follows : —

1. I have adopted his date, as Lightfoot gives it, — that is, the period of his writings, — under the Antonines. The improbability of seventy years in the episcopate is reason enough for rejecting the idea that he was himself the " angel of the church of Sardis," to whom our Lord sent the terrible rebuke.

2. His silence concerning persecutions under Vespasian, Trajan, and Antoninus Pius cannot be pleaded to exempt them from this stain, against positive evidence to the contrary.

3. A coincidence with Ignatius to the Ephesians[7] will be noted hereafter.

4. Melito, with Claudius Apollinaris and even Polycrates, may have been personally acquainted with Ignatius ;[8] of course, one with another. These lived not far from Smyrna ; Asia Minor was, in the first century, the focus of Christian activity.

5. We know of his visit to the East from his own account, preserved by Eusebius. The Christians of proconsular Asia were accustomed to such journeys. Even Clement of Alexandria may have met him, as he seems to have met Tatian and Theodotus.[9]

6. Melito vouches for the rescript of Hadrian,[10] but his supposed reference to the edict of Antoninus does not bear close scrutiny as warrant for its authenticity.[11]

---

1 Barchochebas.
2 The Jews.
3 Ὑποτυπώσως.
4 *Contra Celsum*, iv. 52.
5 Οὐκ ἀγεννῶς.
6 Routh, *R. S.*, vol. i. p. 113. And see Westcott, *Canon*, p. 245.

7 Lightfoot, *A. F.*, vol. ii. p. 48.
8 *Ib.*, vol. i. p. 428.
9 Vol. ii. (*Stromata*) p. 301, this series.
10 Vol. i. p. 186, this series.
11 Lightfoot, *A. F.*, vol. i. p. 468.

7. The Apology of our author was addressed to Aurelius in his mid-career as a sovereign, about A.D. 170. Justin, Melito, Athenagoras, and Theophilus all tell the same sad story of imperial cruelty. Even when Justin wrote to Antoninus, Marcus was supreme in the councils of the elder emperor.[1]

8. He became a martyr, probably under Marcus Aurelius, *circa* A.D. 177;[2] some eminent critics have even dated his Apology as late as this.

I.

A DISCOURSE WHICH WAS IN THE PRESENCE OF ANTONINUS CÆSAR, AND HE EXHORTED[3] THE SAID CÆSAR TO ACQUAINT HIMSELF WITH GOD, AND SHOWED TO HIM THE WAY OF TRUTH.

HE began to speak as follows : —

"It is not easy," said Melito, "speedily to bring into the right way the man who has a long time previously been held fast by error. It may, however, be effected : for, when a man turns away ever so little from error, the mention of the truth is acceptable to him. For, just as when the cloud breaks ever so little there comes fair weather, even so, when a man turns toward God, the thick cloud of error which deprived him of true vision is quickly withdrawn from before him. For error, like disease[4] and sleep, long holds fast those who come under its influence ;[5] but truth uses the word as a goad, and smites the slumberers, and awakens them; and when they are awake they look at the truth, and also understand it : they hear, and distinguish that which is from that which is not. For there are men who call iniquity righteousness : they think, for example, that it is righteousness for a man to err with the many. But I, for my part, affirm that it is not a good excuse *for error* that a man errs with the many. For, if one man only sin,[6] his sin is great : how much greater will be the sin when many sin *together!*

"Now, the sin of which I speak is this : when a man abandons that which really exists, and serves that which does not really exist. There 'is' that which really exists, and it is called GOD. He, *I say*, really exists, and by His power doth everything subsist. This being is in no sense made, nor did He ever come into being; but He has existed from eternity, and will *continue to* exist for ever and ever. He changeth not, while everything *else* changes. No eye[7] can see Him, nor thought apprehend Him, nor language describe Him ; and those who love Him speak of Him thus : 'Father, and God of Truth.'

"If, therefore, a man forsake the light, and say that there is another God, it is plain from what he himself says that it is some created thing which he calls God. For, if a man call fire God, it is not God, because it is fire ; and, if a man call water God, it is not God, because it is water ; and, if *he so call* this earth on which we tread, or these heavens which are seen by us, or the sun, or the moon, or some one of these stars which run their course without ceasing by *Divine* command, and do not speed along by their own will, *neither are these gods;* and, if a man call gold and silver gods, are not these objects things which we use as we please? and, if *he so call* those pieces of wood which we burn, or those stones which we break, how can these things be gods? For, lo ! they are *for* the use of man. How can 'they' escape the commission of great sin, who in their speech change the great God into those things which, so long as they continue, continue by *Divine* command?

"But, notwithstanding this, I say that so long as a man does not hear, and *so* does not discern or understand that there is a Lord over these creatures, he is not perhaps to be blamed : because no one finds fault with a blind man though he walk ever so badly. For, in the same manner *as the blind, so* men also, when they were seeking after God, stumbled upon stones and blocks of wood ; and such of them as were rich stumbled upon gold and silver, and were prevented by their stumblings from *finding* that which they were seeking after. But, now that a voice has been heard through all the earth,[8] *declaring* that there is a God of truth, and there has been given to every man an eye wherewith to see, those persons are without excuse who are ashamed of *incurring the censure of* their former companions in error, and yet desire to walk in the right way. For those who are ashamed to be saved must of necessity perish. I therefore counsel them to open their eyes and see : for, lo ! light is given abundantly[9] to us all to see thereby ; and if, when light has arisen upon us,

---

[1] Lightfoot, *A. F.*, vol. ii.
[2] *Ibid.*, pp. 446, 494.
[3] "Which was *delivered* in the presence . . . and *in which* etc." This appears to be the sense intended, and is that given by M. Renan: "Sermo qui factus est." Cureton renders, " *Who* was in the presence, etc.," and supposes that Melito first saw and conversed with the emperor, and afterwards wrote this discourse. Melito speaks of it more than once as written. This view, however, does not dispose of the fact that Melito is here affirmed to have "exhorted (lit., *said to*) Cæsar, etc." It was clearly meant to be understood that

the discourse, or *speech*, was spoken: the references to writing merely show that it was written, either before or after the delivery.

[4] Cureton: "passion." The word ⎩⎰⎰ takes both meanings.

[5] Lit. "sojourn beneath it."
[6] Cureton: "act foolishly."
[7] Lit. "sight."
[8] Comp. Rom. x. 18.
[9] Cureton: "light without envy." But the expression resembles the Gk. ἀφθόνως, ungrudgingly, without stint.

any one close his eyes so as not to see, into the ditch he must go.[1] But why is a man ashamed of *the censure of* those who have been in error along with himself? Rather does it behove him to persuade them to follow in his steps; and, if they should not be persuaded by him, *then* to disengage himself from their society. For there are some men who are unable to rise from their mother earth, and therefore also do they make them gods from the earth their mother; and they are condemned by the judgments of truth, forasmuch as they apply the name *of Him* who is unchangeable to those objects which are subject to change, and shrink not from calling those things gods which have been made by the hands of man, and dare to make an image of God whom they have not seen.

"But I *have to* remark further, that the Sibyl[2] also has said concerning them that it is the images of deceased kings that they worship. And this is easy to understand: for, lo! even now they worship and honour the images of those of Cæsarean rank[3] more than their former *gods;* for from those their former gods both *pecuniary* tribute and produce accrue to Cæsar, as to one who is greater than they. On this account, those who despise them, and *so* cause Cæsar's revenue to fall short, are put to death. But to the treasury of other kings also it is appointed how much the worshippers in various places shall pay, and how many vesselfuls[4] of water from the sea they shall supply. Such is the wickedness of the world — of those who worship and fear that which has no sensation. Many of them, too, who are crafty, either for the sake of gain, or for vainglory, or for dominion over the multitude, both themselves worship, and incite those who are destitute of understanding to worship, that which has no sensation.

"I will further write and show, as far as my ability goes, how and for what causes images were made to kings and tyrants, and *how* they came to be regarded[5] as gods. The people of Argos made images to Hercules, because he belonged to their city, and was strong, and by his valour slew noxious beasts, and more especially because they were afraid of him. For he was subject to no control, and carried off the wives of many: for his lust was great, like that of Zuradi the Persian, his friend. Again, the people of Acte worshipped Dionysus,[6] a king,

because he had recently[7] planted the vine in their country. The Egyptians worshipped Joseph the Hebrew, who was called Serapis, because he supplied them with corn during the years of famine. The Athenians worshipped Athene, the daughter of Zeus, king of the island of Crete, because she built the town of Athens, and made Ericthippus her son king there, whom she had by adultery with Hephæstus, a blacksmith, son of a wife of her father. She was, too, always courting the society of Hercules, because he was her brother on her father's side. For Zeus the king became enamoured of Alcmene, the wife of Electryon, who was from Argos, and committed adultery with her, and she gave birth to Hercules. The people of Phœnicia worshipped Balthi,[8] queen of Cyprus, because she fell in love with Tamuz, son of Cuthar king of the Phœnicians, and left her own kingdom and came and dwelt in Gebal, a fortress of the Phœnicians, and at the same time made all the Cyprians subject to King Cuthar. Also, before Tamuz she had fallen in love with Ares, and committed adultery with him; and Hephæstus, her husband, caught her, and his jealousy was roused against her, and he came and killed Tamuz in Mount Lebanon, as he was hunting[9] wild boars; and from that time Balthi remained in Gebal, and she died in the city of Aphiki,[10] where Tamuz was buried. The Elamites worshipped Nuh, daughter of the king of Elam: when the enemy had carried her captive, her father made for her an image and a temple in Shushan, a royal residence which is in Elam. The Syrians worshipped Athi, a Hadibite, who sent the daughter of Belat, a person skilled in medicine, and she healed Simi, the daughter of Hadad king of Syria; and some time afterwards, when Hadad himself had the leprosy upon him, Athi entreated Elisha the Hebrew, and he came and healed him of his leprosy. The people of Mesopotamia also worshipped Cuthbi, a Hebrew woman, because she delivered Bakru, the paternal *king*[11] of Edessa, from his enemies. With respect to Nebo, who is *worshipped* in Mabug, why should I write to you? For, lo! all the priests who are in Mabug know that it is the image of Orpheus, a Thracian

---

[1] Lit. "to the ditch is his way." Comp. Matt. xv. 14.
[2] See vol. i. p. 280, this series, where the following lines are quoted by Justin Martyr from the *Sibylline Oracles:* —

"But we have strayed from the Immortal's ways,
And worship with a dull and senseless mind
Idols, the workmanship of our own hands,
And images and figures of dead men."

[3] Cureton: "those belonging to the Cæsars." But the Cæsars themselves are clearly meant.
[4] Cureton: "sacks full." The first word is used of a leathern pouch or wallet, as in Luke x. 4 (Peshito) for πήρα.
[5] Lit., "they became."
[6] Cureton, without necessity, reads the word "Dionysius."

[7] Cureton renders "originally." But comp. Judith iv. 3, where the same word answers to προσφάτως.
[8] Venus.
[9] Cureton's conjecture of [Syriac] or [Syriac] for [Syriac] has been adopted.
[10] Some have identified it with Aphek, Josh. xix. 30. The rites observed here were specially abominable.
[11] Cureton: "the patrician." Dr. Payne Smith, *Thes. Syr. s.v.*, regards the word as equivalent to πατηρ τῆς πολεως, *pater civitatis*, "a title of honour found in the Byzantine writers," and is inclined to think it a term belonging to the dialect of Edessa. A similar use of the same adjective is quoted from Buxtorf, *Lex. Chald. Talm.*, p. 12: "[Hebrew] cognomen R. Nachmanis, qui a celebritate familiæ sic cognominatus est, quasi *Patritius*." This view appears to be supported by the similar use of an adjective for a substantive above: "*persons* of Cæsarean rank," for "Cæsars."

Magus. Hadran, again, is the image of Zaradusht, a Persian Magus. For both of these Magi practised magic at a well which was in a wood in Mabug, in which was an unclean spirit, and it assaulted and disputed the passage of every one who passed by in all that country in which the town of Mabug is situated; and these Magi, in accordance with what was a mystery in their Magian system, bade Simi, the daughter of Hadad, to draw water from the sea and pour it into the well, so that the spirit should not come up and commit assault. In like manner, the rest of mankind made images to their kings and worshipped them; of which matter I will not write further.

"But thou, a *person of* liberal mind, and familiar with the truth, if thou wilt *properly* consider these matters, commune with thine own self;[1] and, though they should clothe thee in the garb of a woman, remember that thou art a man. Believe in Him who is in reality God, and to Him lay open thy mind, and to Him commit thy soul, and He is able to give thee immortal life for ever, for everything is possible to Him;[2] and let all other things be esteemed by thee just as they are — images as images, and sculptures as sculptures; and let not that which is only made be put by thee in the place of Him who is not made, but let Him, the ever-living God, be constantly present to thy mind.[3] For thy mind itself is His likeness: for it too is invisible and impalpable,[4] and not to be represented by any form, yet by its will is the whole bodily frame moved. Know, therefore, that, if thou constantly serve Him who is immoveable, even He exists for ever, so thou also, when thou shalt have put off this *body*, which is visible and corruptible, shalt stand before Him for ever, endowed with life and knowledge, and thy works shall be to thee wealth inexhaustible and possessions unfailing. And know that the chief of thy good works is this: that thou know God, and serve Him. Know, too, that He asketh not anything of thee: He needeth not anything.

"Who is this God? He who is Himself truth, and His word truth. And what is truth? That which is not fashioned, nor made, nor represented by art: that is, which has never been brought in-

to existence, and is *on that account* called truth.[5] If, therefore, a man worship that which is made with hands, it is not the truth that he worships, nor yet the word of truth.

"I have very much to say on this subject; but I feel ashamed for those who do not understand that they are superior to the work of their own hands, nor perceive how they give gold to the artists that they may make for them gods, and give them silver for their adornment and honour, and move their riches about from place to place, and *then* worship them. And what infamy can be greater than this, that a man should worship his riches, and forsake Him who bestowed those riches upon him? and that he should revile man, yet worship the image of man; and slay a beast, yet worship the likeness of a beast? This also is evident, that it is the workmanship of their fellow-men that they worship: for they do not worship the treasures[6] while they are laid by in the bag, but when the artists have fashioned images out of them they worship them; neither do they worship the gold or the silver considered as property,[7] but when the gravers have sculptured them then they worship them. Senseless man! what addition has been made to thy gold, that now thou worshippest it? If it is because it has been made to resemble a winged animal, why dost thou not worship the winged animal *itself?* And if because it has been made like a beast of prey, lo! the beast of prey itself is before thee. And if it is the workmanship itself that pleases thee, let the workmanship of God please thee, who made all things, and in His own likeness made the workmen, who strive to do like Him, but resemble Him not.

"But perhaps thou wilt say: How is it that God did not so make me that I should serve Him, and not images? In speaking thus, thou art seeking to become an idle instrument, and not a living man. For God made thee as perfect as it seemed good to Him. He has given thee a mind endowed with freedom; He has set

---

[1] Lit., "be (or, get to be) with thyself." Cureton: "enter into thyself." The meaning appears to be, "think for thyself."

[2] Cureton: "Everything cometh through His hands." It should rather be, "*into* His hands," i.e., "He has power to do everything." See note 7, p. 725.

[3] Lit., "be running in thy mind."

[4] The text has ܡܬܬܙܝܥ, which M. Renan derives from the root ܙܘܥ and translates "*commovetur*." This, although correct in grammar, does not suit the sense. The grammars recognise the form as a possible Eshtaphel of ܢܓܥ, "*tangere*," but it is not found in actual use. Dr. Payne Smith thinks the right reading to be ܡܬܬܙܝܥ, which gives the required sense.

[5] Or, "that which is fixed and invariable." There seems to be a reference to the derivation of ܩܘܫܬܐ (truth) from ܩܡ, *firmus (stabilis) fuit.* Cureton has strangely mistranslated ܗܘ ܠܐܝܬܘܗܝ ܗܘ ܕܠܐ, by "that which, without having been brought into existence, does exist." The first ܗܘ is nothing but the sign of emphatic denial which is frequently appended to ܠܐ, and ܠܐܝܬܘܗܝ is the infinitive of emphasis belonging to the second ܗܘ.

[6] Cureton: "materials." The printed text has ܣܡܡܢܐ "drugs." The correct reading, there can hardly be a doubt, is ܣܝܡܬܐ.

[7] Lit., "the property of the gold or silver," if the word ܩܢܝܢܐ is rightly taken. Although no such derivative of ܩܢܐ is found in the lexicons, the form is possible from the Palel of that verb: e.g. ܩܢܝܢܐ from ܩܢܐ. See Hoffmann, *Gram. Syr.*, sec. 87, 19.

before thee objects in great number, that thou on thy part mayest distinguish *the nature of* each thing and choose for thyself that which is good; He has set before thee the heavens, and placed in them the stars; He has set before thee the sun and the moon, and they too every day run their course therein; He has set before thee the multitude of waters, and restrained them by His word; He has set before thee the wide earth, which remains at rest, and continues before thee without variation:[1] yet, lest thou shouldst suppose that of its own nature it *so* continues, He makes it also to quake when He pleaseth; He has set before thee the clouds, which by *His* command bring water from above and satisfy the earth — that from hence thou mayest understand that He who puts these things in motion is superior to them all, and mayest accept *thankfully* the goodness of Him who has given thee a mind whereby to distinguish these things from one another.

"Wherefore I counsel thee to know thyself, and to know God. For understand how that there is within thee that which is called the soul — by it the eye seeth, by it the ear heareth, by it the mouth speaketh; and how it makes use of the whole body; and *how*, whenever He pleaseth to remove the soul from the body, this falleth *to decay* and perisheth. From this, therefore, which exists within thyself and is invisible, understand how God also moveth the whole by His power, like the body; *and* that, whenever it pleases Him to withdraw His power, the whole world also, like the body, will fall *to decay* and perish.

"But why this world was made, and why it passes away, and why the body exists, and why it falls *to decay*, and why it continues, thou canst not know until thou hast raised thy head from this sleep in which thou art sunk, and hast opened thine eyes and seen that God is One, the Lord of all, and hast come to serve Him with all thy heart. Then will He grant thee to know His will: for every one that is severed from the knowledge of the living God is dead and buried *even while* in his body. Therefore *is it that* thou dost wallow on the ground before demons and shadows, and askest vain petitions from that which has not anything to give. But thou, stand thou up from among those who are lying on the earth and caressing stones, and giving their substance as food for the fire, and offering their raiment to idols, and, while *themselves* possessed of senses, are bent on serving that which has no sensation; and offer thou for thy imperishable soul petitions *for that* which decayeth not, to God who suffers no decay — and thy freedom will be at once apparent; and be thou careful of

it,[2] and give thanks to God who made thee, and gave thee the mind of the free, that thou mightest shape thy conduct even as thou wilt. He hath set before thee all these things, and showeth thee that, if thou follow after evil, thou shalt be condemned for thy evil deeds; but that, if after goodness, thou shalt receive from Him abundant good,[3] together with immortal life for ever.

"There is, therefore, nothing to hinder thee from changing thy evil manner of life, because thou art a free man; or from seeking and finding out who is the Lord of all; or from serving Him with all thy heart: because with Him there is no reluctance to give the knowledge of Himself to those that seek it, according to the measure of their capacity to know Him.

"Let it be thy first care not to deceive thyself. For, if thou sayest of that which is not God: This is God, thou deceivest thyself, and sinnest before the God of truth. Thou fool! is that God which is *bought and* sold? Is that God which is in want? Is that God which must be watched over? How buyest thou him as a slave, and servest him as a master? How askest thou of him, as of one that is rich, to give to thee, and thyself givest to him as to one that is poor? How dost thou expect of him that he will make thee victorious in battle? for, lo! when thy enemies have conquered thee, they strip him likewise.

"Perhaps one who is a king may say: I cannot behave myself aright, because I am a king; it becomes me to do the will of the many. He who speaks thus really deserves to be laughed at: for why should not the king himself lead the way[4] to all good things, and persuade the people under his rule to behave with purity, and to know God in truth, and in his own person set before them the patterns of all things excellent — since thus it becomes him to do? For it is a shameful thing that a king, however badly he may conduct himself, should *yet* judge and condemn those who do amiss.

"My opinion is this: that in 'this' way a kingdom may be governed in peace — when the sovereign is acquainted with the God of truth, and is withheld by fear of Him from doing wrong[5] to those who are his subjects, and judges everything with equity, as one who knows that he himself also will be judged before God; while, at the same time, those who are under his rule[6] are withheld by the fear of God from doing wrong to their sovereign, and are restrained by *the same* fear from doing wrong to one another.

---

[1] Lit. "in one fashion."

[2] Or, "of what pertains to it."
[3] Lit. "many good things."
[4] Lit. "be the beginner."
[5] Cureton is probably right in so taking the words, although the construction is not quite the same as in the similar sentence a little below. If so, for ܐܠܨ we must read ܐܠܨ.
[6] Lit. "hand."

By this knowledge of God and fear of Him all evil may be removed from the realm. For, if the sovereign abstain from doing wrong to those who are under his rule, and they abstain from doing wrong to him and to each other, it is evident that the whole country will dwell in peace. Many blessings, too, will be *enjoyed* there, because amongst them all the name of God will be glorified. For what blessing is greater than this, that a sovereign should deliver the people that are under his rule from error, and by this good deed render himself pleasing to God? For from error arise all those evils *from which kingdoms suffer;* but the greatest of all errors is this: when a man is ignorant of God, and in God's stead worships that which is not God.

"There are, however, persons who say: It is for the honour of God that we make the image: in order, that is, that we may worship the God who is concealed from our view. But they are unaware that God is in every country, and in every place, and is never absent, and that there is not anything done and He knoweth it not. Yet thou, despicable man! within whom He is, and without whom He is, and above whom He is, hast nevertheless gone and bought thee wood from the carpenter's, and it is carved and made into an image insulting to God.[1] To this thou offerest sacrifice, and knowest not that the all-seeing eye seeth thee, and that the word of truth reproves thee, and says to thee: How can the unseen God be sculptured? Nay, it is the likeness of thyself that thou makest and worshippest. Because the wood has been sculptured, hast thou not the insight to perceive that it is *still* wood, or *that the stone* is *still* stone? The gold also the workman[2] taketh according to its weight in the balance. And when thou hast had it made[3] *into an image*, why dost thou weigh it? Therefore thou art a lover of gold, and not a lover of God. And art thou not ashamed, perchance it be deficient, to demand of the maker of it why he has stolen some of it? Though thou hast eyes, dost thou not see? And though thou hast intelligence,[4] dost thou not understand? Why dost thou wallow on the ground, and offer supplication to things which are without sense? Fear Him who shaketh the earth, and maketh the heavens to revolve, and smiteth the sea, and removeth the mountain from its place — Him who can make Himself like a fire, and consume all things; and, if thou be not able to clear thy-

self of guilt, yet add not to thy sins; and, if thou be not able to know God, yet doubt not[5] that He exists.

"Again, there are persons who say: Whatsoever our fathers have bequeathed to us, *that* we reverence. Therefore, of course, it is, that those whose fathers have bequeathed them poverty strive to become rich! and those whose fathers did not instruct them, desire to be instructed, and to learn that which their fathers knew not! And why, forsooth, do the children of the blind see, and the children of the lame walk? Nay, it is not well for a man to follow *his* predecessors, *if they be* those whose course was evil; but *rather* that we should turn from that path of theirs, lest that which befell *our* predecessors should bring disaster upon us also. Wherefore, inquire whether thy father's course was good: and, *if so*, do thou also follow in his steps; but, if thy father's course was very evil, let thine be good, and so let it be with thy children after thee.[6] Be grieved also for thy father because his course is evil, so long as thy grief may avail to help him. But, as for thy children, speak to them thus: There is a God, the Father of all, who never came into being, neither was ever made, and by whose will all things subsist. He also made the luminaries, that His works may see one another; and He conceals Himself in His power from all His works: for it is not permitted to any being subject to change to see Him who changes not. But such as are mindful *of His words*, and are admitted into that covenant which is unchangeable, 'they' see God — so far as it is possible for them to see Him. These also will have power to escape destruction, when the flood of fire comes upon all the world. For there was once a flood and a wind,[7] and the great[8] men were swept away by a violent blast from the north, but the just were left, for a demonstration of the truth. Again, at another time there was a flood of water, and all men and animals perished in the multitude of waters, but the just were preserved in an ark of wood by the command of God. So also will it be at the last time: there shall be a flood of fire, and the earth shall be burnt up, together with its moun-

---

[1] Lit. "into an insult of God." So M. Renan, "in opprobrium Dei." Cureton, admitting that this *may* be the sense, renders, "an abomination of God," and refers to the circumstance that in Scripture an idol is frequently so spoken of. But ܦܬܟܪܐ is not used in such passages (it is either ܨܠܡܐ, or, less frequently, ܓܠܝܦܐ), nor does it appear ever to have the meaning which Cureton assigns to it.

[2] Lit. "he."

[3] Lit. "hast made it."

[4] Lit. "heart."

[5] Lit. "be of opinion."

[6] This seems preferable to Cureton's, "and let thy children also follow after thee." Had this been the meaning, probably the verb ܢܐܙܠ would have been used, as in the preceding sentence, not ܢܗܘܐ.

[7] So the Sibylline oracle, as quoted by Cureton in the Greek: —

"And, when he would the starry steep of heaven
Ascend, the Sire Immortal did his works
With mighty blasts assail: forthwith the winds
Hurled prostrate from its height the towering pile,
And bitter strife among the builders roused."

[8] Lit. "chosen." The same expression, except that the similar ܓܢܒܪܐ is used for ܓܒܪܐ, occurs Sap. Sol. xiv. 6, as a translation of ὑπερηφάνων γιγάντων, *gigantes superbi*. See *Thes. Syr.*, *s. v.* ܓܒܪ.

tains; and mankind shall be burnt up, along with the idols which they have made, and the carved images which they have worshipped; and the sea shall be burnt up, together with its islands; but the just shall be preserved from wrath, like as *were* their fellows of the ark from the waters of the deluge. And then shall those who have not known God, and those who have made them idols, bemoan themselves, when they shall see those idols of theirs being burnt up, together with themselves, and nothing shall be found to help them.

"When thou, Antoninus [1] Cæsar, shalt become acquainted with these things, and thy children also with thee, *then* wilt thou bequeath to them an inheritance for ever which fadeth not away, and thou wilt deliver thy soul, and the souls of thy children also, from that which shall come upon the whole· earth in the judgment of truth *and* of righteousness. For, according as thou hast acknowledged Him here, *so* will He acknowledge thee there; and, if thou account Him here superfluous, He will not account thee one of those who have known Him and confessed Him.

"These *may* suffice thy Majesty; and, if they be *too* many, yet deign to accept them." [2]

Here endeth Melito.

II.

FROM THE DISCOURSE ON SOUL AND BODY.[3]

For this reason did the Father send His Son from heaven without a bodily form, that, when He should put on a body by means of the Virgin's womb, and be born man, He might save man, and gather together those members of His which death had scattered when he divided man.

And further on: — The earth shook, and its foundations trembled; the sun fled away, and the elements turned back, and the day was changed *into night:* for they could not endure *the sight of* their Lord hanging on a tree. The *whole* creation was amazed, marvelling and saying, "What new mystery, then, is this? The Judge is judged, and holds his peace; the Invisible One is seen, and is not ashamed; the Incomprehensible is laid hold upon, and is not indignant; the Illimitable is circumscribed, and doth not resist; the Impassible suffereth, and doth not avenge; the Immortal dieth, and answereth not a word; the Celestial is laid in the grave, and endureth! What new mystery is this?" The *whole* creation, *I say*, was aston-

ished; but, when our Lord arose from the place of the dead, and trampled death under foot, and bound the strong one, and set man free, then did the whole creation see clearly that for man's sake the Judge was condemned, and the Invisible was seen, and the Illimitable was circumscribed, and the Impassible suffered, and the Immortal died, and the Celestial was laid in the grave. For our Lord, when He was born man, was condemned in order that He might show mercy, was bound in order that He might loose, was seized in order that He might release, suffered in order that He might feel compassion,[4] died in order that He might give life, was laid in the grave that He might raise *from the dead.*[5]

III.

FROM THE DISCOURSE ON THE CROSS.[6]

On these accounts He came to us; on these accounts, though He was incorporeal, He formed for Himself a body after our fashion,[7] — appearing as a sheep, yet still remaining the Shepherd; being esteemed a servant, yet not renouncing the Sonship; being carried *in the womb* of Mary, yet arrayed in *the nature of* His Father; treading upon the earth, yet filling heaven; appearing as an infant, yet not discarding the eternity of His nature; being invested with a body, yet not circumscribing the unmixed simplicity of His Godhead; being esteemed poor, yet not divested of His riches; needing sustenance inasmuch as He was man, yet not ceasing to feed the entire world inasmuch as He is God; putting on the likeness of a servant, yet not impairing[8] the likeness of His Father. He sustained every character[9] *belonging to Him* in an immutable nature: He was standing before Pilate, and *at the same time* was sitting with His Father; He was nailed upon the tree, and *yet* was the Lord of all things.

IV.

ON FAITH.[10]

We have collected together *extracts* from the Law and the Prophets relating to those things which have been declared concerning our Lord Jesus Christ, that we may prove to your love that this *Being* is perfect reason, the Word of God; He who was begotten before the light; He who is Creator together with the Father; He who is the Fashioner of man; He who is all in all; He who among the patriarchs is Patriarch; He who in the law is the Law; among the

---

[1] The MS. has "Antonius."
[2] Cureton, for the last clause, gives "as thou wilt," remarking that the sense is obscure. The literal rendering is, "if thou wilt," the consequent clause being unexpressed. "If you please, *accept them*," seems what is meant.
[3] By Melito, bishop of Sardis.

[4] ﻢﺣﺭ seems to be the true reading, not the ﺪﺣﺍ of the printed MS.
[5] [Such passages sustain the testimony of Jerome and others, that this venerable and learned Father was an eloquent preacher.]
[6] By the same.
[7] Or "wove — a body from our material."
[8] Lit. "changing."
[9] Lit. "He was everything."
[10] Of Melito the bishop.

priests, Chief Priest; among kings, the Ruler; among prophets, the Prophet; among the angels, Archangel; in the voice *of the preacher*, the Word; among spirits, the Spirit; in the Father, the Son; in God, God; King for ever and ever. For this is He who was pilot to Noah; He who was guide to Abraham; He who was bound with Isaac; He who was in exile with Jacob; He who was sold with Joseph; He who was captain of the host with Moses; He who was the divider of the inheritance with Jesus the son of Nun; He who in David and the prophets announced His own sufferings; He who put on a bodily form in the Virgin; He who was born in Bethlehem; He who was wrapped in swaddling-clothes in the manger; He who was seen by the shepherds; He who was glorified by the angels; He who was worshipped by the Magi; He who was pointed out by John; He who gathered together the apostles; He who preached the kingdom; He who cured the lame; He who gave light to the blind; He who raised the dead; He who appeared in the temple; He who was not believed on by the people; He who was betrayed by Judas; He who was apprehended by the priests; He who was condemned by Pilate; He who was pierced in the flesh; He who was hanged on the tree; He who was buried in the earth; He who rose from the place of the dead; He who appeared to the apostles; He who was carried up to heaven; He who is seated at the right hand of the Father; He who is the repose of those that are departed; the recoverer of those that are lost; the light of those that are in darkness; the deliverer of those that are captive; the guide of those that go astray; the asylum of the afflicted; the bridegroom of the Church; the charioteer of the cherubim; the captain of the angels; God who is from God; the Son who is from the Father; Jesus Christ the King for evermore. Amen.

V.[1]

This is He who took a bodily form in the Virgin, and was hanged upon the tree, and was buried within the earth, and suffered not dissolution; He who rose from the place of the dead, and raised up men from the earth — from the grave below to the height of heaven. This is the Lamb that was slain; this is the Lamb that opened not His mouth.[2] This is He who was born of Mary, fair sheep *of the fold*. This is He that was taken from the flock, and was led to the slaughter, and was slain in the evening, and was buried at night; He who had no bone of Him broken on the tree; He who suffered not dissolution within the earth; He who rose from

the place of the dead, and raised up the race of Adam from the grave below. This is He who was put to death. And where was He put to death? In the midst of Jerusalem. By whom? By Israel: because He cured their lame, and cleansed their lepers, and gave light to their blind, and raised their dead! This was the cause of His death. Thou, *O Israel*, wast giving commands, and He was being crucified; thou wast rejoicing, and He was being buried; thou wast reclining on a soft couch, and He was watching in the grave and the shroud.[3] O Israel, transgressor of the law, why hast thou committed this new iniquity, subjecting the Lord to new sufferings — thine own Lord, Him who fashioned thee, Him who made thee, Him who honoured thee, who called thee Israel? But thou hast not been found to be Israel: for thou hast not seen God, nor understood the Lord. Thou hast not known, O Israel, that this was the first-born of God, who was begotten before the sun, who made the light to shine forth, who lighted up the day, who separated the darkness, who fixed the first foundations, who poised the earth, who collected the ocean, who stretched out the firmament, who adorned the world. Bitter *were* thy nails, and sharp; bitter thy tongue, which thou didst whet; bitter *was* Judas, to whom thou gavest hire; bitter thy false witnesses, whom thou stirredst up; bitter thy gall, which thou preparedst; bitter thy vinegar, which thou madest; bitter thy hands, filled with blood. Thou slewest thy Lord, and He was lifted up upon the tree; and an inscription was fixed *above*, to show who He was that was slain. And who was this? (that which we shall not say is *too* shocking *to hear*, and that which we shall say is very dreadful: nevertheless hearken, and tremble.) *It was* He because of whom the earth quaked. He that hung up the earth *in space* was *Himself* hanged up; He that fixed the heavens was fixed *with nails*; He that bore up the earth was borne up on a tree; the Lord *of all* was subjected to ignominy in a naked body — God put to death! the King of Israel slain with Israel's right hand! Alas for the new wickedness of the new murder! The Lord was exposed with naked body: He was not deemed worthy even of covering; and, in order that He might not be seen, the luminaries turned away, and the day became darkened,[4] because they slew God, who hung naked on the tree. It was not the body of our Lord that the luminaries covered with darkness when they set,[5] but the eyes of men.

---

[3] The Greek γλωσσόκομον.
[4] [For Phlegon's testimony, see references, vol. vii. p. 257. But note Lightfoot, *Ap. F.*, part ii. vol. i. p. 512; his remark on Origen, *Celsus*, vol. iv. p. 437, this series.]
[5] This is the rendering of ܐܥܪܒ; but Cureton has "fled," as though he read ܥܪܩ.

---

[1] By Melito, bishop of Attica. [Of this epigraph, which becomes Ittica below, I have never seen a sufficient explanation.]
[2] Lit. "the Lamb without voice."

For, because the people quaked not, the earth quaked; because they were not affrighted, the earth was affrighted. Thou smotest thy Lord: thou also hast been smitten upon the earth. And thou indeed liest dead; but He is risen from the place of the dead, and ascended to the height of heaven, having suffered for the sake of those who suffer, and having been bound for the sake of Adam's race which was imprisoned, and having been judged for the sake of him who was condemned, and having been buried for the sake of him who was buried.

And further on : — This is He who made the heaven and the earth, and in the beginning, together with the Father, fashioned man; who was announced by means of the law and the prophets; who put on a bodily form in the Virgin; who was hanged upon the tree; who was buried in the earth; who rose from the place of the dead, and ascended to the height of heaven, and sitteth on the right hand of the Father.

VI.[1]

He that bore up the earth was borne up on a tree. The Lord was subjected to ignominy with naked body — God put to death, the King of Israel slain !

FRAGMENTS.[2]

I.

FROM THE WORK ON THE PASSOVER.[3]

When Servilius Paulus was proconsul of Asia, at the time that Sagaris[4] suffered martyrdom, there arose a great controversy at Laodicea concerning *the time of the celebration of* the Passover, which on that occasion had happened to fall at the proper season;[5] and this *treatise* was *then* written.[6]

II.

FROM THE APOLOGY ADDRESSED TO MARCUS AURELIUS ANTONINUS.[7]

For the race of the pious is now persecuted in a way contrary to all precedent, being har-

assed by a new kind of edicts[8] everywhere in Asia. For unblushing informers, and such as are greedy of other men's goods, taking occasion from the orders *issued*, carry on their robbery without any disguise, plundering of their property night and day those who are guilty of no wrong.

. . . .

If these proceedings take place at thy bidding,[9] well and good.[10] For a just sovereign will never take unjust measures; and we, on our part, gladly accept the honour of such a death. This request only we present to thee, that thou wouldst first of all examine for thyself into the behaviour of these *reputed* agents of so much strife, and then come to a just decision as to whether they merit death and punishment, or deserve to live in safety and quiet. But if, on the contrary, it shall turn out that this measure, and this new sort of command, which it would be unbecoming to employ even against barbarian foemen, do not proceed from thee, then all the more do we entreat thee not to leave us thus exposed to the spoliation of the populace.

. . . .

For the philosophy current with us flourished in the first instance among barbarians;[11] and, when it afterwards sprang up among the nations under thy rule, during the distinguished reign of thy ancestor Augustus, it proved to be a blessing of most happy omen to thy empire. For from that time the Roman power has risen to greatness and splendour. To this power thou hast succeeded as the much desired[12] possessor; and such shalt thou continue, together with thy son,[13] if thou protect that philosophy which has grown up with thy empire, and which took its rise with Augustus; to which also thy *more recent* ancestors paid honour, along with the other religions *prevailing in the empire.* A very strong proof, moreover, that it was for good that the system we profess came to prevail at the same time that the empire of such happy commencement was established, is this — that ever since the reign of Augustus nothing untoward has happened; but, on the contrary, everything has contributed to the splendour and renown *of the empire,* in accordance with the devout wishes[14] of all. Nero and Domitian alone of all *the emperors,* imposed

---

[1] By the holy Melito, bishop of the city of Ittica. [For Melito, in Lightfoot's *Apost. Fathers,* consult part ii. vol. i. pp. 133, 328, 428, 443-446, 468-469, 494. See Lardner, *Credib.,* vol. ii. 157, etc.; Westcott, *Canon,* p. 246. See Polycrates, *infra;* on which consult Schaff, *History,* etc., vol. ii. p. 736. Above all, see Routh, *R. S.,* tom. i. pp. 113-153.]

[2] The following Fragments of Melito are translated from the Greek, except No. IX., which is taken from the Latin.

[3] In Eusebius, *Hist. Eccl.,* iv. 26. [Melito wrote two books on the Paschal and one *On the Lord's Day* (ὁ περὶ κυριακῆς λόγος), according to Eusebius. But is this *On the Lord's Day* other than one of the books on the Paschal? It may be doubted. Routh refers us to Barnabas. See vol. i, cap. 15, note 7, p. 147, this series. See also Dionysius of Corinth, *infra.*]

[4] He was bishop of Laodicea, and suffered martyrdom during the persecution under M. Aurelius Antoninus. — MIGNE.

[5] The churches of Asia Minor kept Easter on the fourteenth day from the new moon, whatever day of the week that might be; and hence were called *Quartodecimans.* Other churches, chiefly those of the West, kept it on the Sunday following the day of the Jewish passover. In the case here referred to, the 14th of the month occurred on the Sunday in question.

[6] Migne, not so naturally, punctuates otherwise, and renders, "which had happened *then* to fall at the proper season, and on that occasion this *treatise* was written."

[7] In Eusebius, *Hist. Eccl., l. c.*

---

[8] Migne thinks that by these are meant the orders given by magistrates of cities on their own authority, in distinction from those which issued from emperors or governors of provinces.

[9] The reference must be to private letters: for in any of the leading cities of Asia a mandate of the emperor would have been made public before the proconsul proceeded to execute it. — MIGNE.

[10] Ἔστω καλῶς γενόμενον seems to be here used in the sense of καλῶς alone. The correctness of Migne's translation, *recte atque ordine facta sunto,* is open to doubt.

[11] The Jews. Porphyry calls the doctrines of the Christians βάρβαρον τόλμημα. See Euseb., *Hist. Eccl.,* vi. 19. — MIGNE.

[12] Εὐκταῖος.

[13] Commodus, who hence appears to have been not yet associated with his father in the empire. — MIGNE.

[14] Εὐχάς.

upon by certain calumniators, have cared to bring any impeachment against our doctrines. They, too, are the source from which it has happened that the lying slanders on those who profess them have, in consequence of the senseless habit which prevails *of taking things on hearsay*, flowed down to our own times.[1] But the course which they in their ignorance pursued was set aside by thy pious progenitors, who frequently and in many instances rebuked by their rescripts[2] those who dared to set on foot any hostilities against them. It appears, for example, that thy grandfather Adrian wrote, among others, to Fundanus, the proconsul then in charge of the government of Asia. Thy father, too, when thou thyself wast associated with him[3] in the administration of the empire, wrote to the cities, forbidding them to take any measures adverse to us: among the rest to the people of Larissa, and of Thessalonica, and of Athens, and, *in short*, to all the Greeks. And as regards thyself, seeing that thy sentiments respecting the Christians[4] are not only the same as theirs, but even much more generous and wise, we are the more persuaded that thou wilt do all that we ask of thee.

III.

FROM THE SAME APOLOGY.[5]

We are not those who pay homage to stones, that are without sensation; but of the only God, who is before all and over all, and, moreover, we are worshippers of His Christ, who is veritably God the Word[6] *existing* before all time.

IV.

FROM THE BOOK OF EXTRACTS.[7]

Melito to his brother Onesimus, greeting:—

As you have often, prompted by your regard for the word *of God*, expressed a wish to have some extracts made from the Law and the Prophets concerning the Saviour, and concerning our faith in general, and have desired, moreover, to obtain an accurate account of the Ancient Books, as regards their number and their arrangement, I have striven to the best of my ability to perform this task: well knowing your zeal for the faith, and your eagerness to become acquainted with the Word, and especially because *I am assured that*, through your yearning after God, you esteem these things beyond all things else, engaged as you are in a struggle for eternal salvation.

I accordingly proceeded to the East, and went to the very spot where *the things in question* were preached and took place; and, having made myself accurately acquainted with the books of the Old Testament, I have set them down below, and herewith send you *the list*. Their names are as follows:—

The five *books* of Moses — Genesis, Exodus, Leviticus, Numbers, Deuteronomy; Joshua,[8] Judges, Ruth, the four *books* of Kings, the two of Chronicles, the *book of the* Psalms of David, the Proverbs of Solomon, also called *the Book of Wisdom*, Ecclesiastes, the Song of Songs, Job, *the books of* the prophets Isaiah, Jeremiah, of the twelve contained in a single book, Ɖaniel, Ezekiel, Esdras. From these I have made my extracts, dividing them into six books.

V.

FROM THE CATENA ON GENESIS.[9]

In place of Isaac the just, a ram appeared for slaughter, in order that Isaac might be liberated from *his* bonds. The slaughter of this *animal* redeemed Isaac *from death*. In like manner, the Lord, being slain, saved us; being bound, He loosed us; being sacrificed, He redeemed us. . . .

For the Lord was a lamb, like the ram which Abraham saw caught in the bush Sabec.[10] But this bush represented the cross, and that place Jerusalem, and the lamb the Lord bound for slaughter.

.   .   .   .

For as a ram was He bound, says he concerning our Lord Jesus Christ, and as a lamb was He shorn, and as a sheep was He led to the slaughter, and as a lamb was He crucified; and He carried the cross[11] on His shoulders when He was led up *to the hill* to be slain, as was Isaac by his father. But Christ suffered, and Isaac did not suffer: for he was *but* a type of Him who should suffer. Yet, even when serving *only* for a type of Christ, he smote men with astonishment and fear.

For a new mystery was presented to view, — a son led by his father to a mountain to be slain, whose feet he bound together, and laid him on the wood of the sacrifice, preparing with care[12] whatever was necessary to his immolation. Isaac on his part is silent, bound like a ram, not opening his mouth, nor uttering a sound with his voice. For, not fearing the knife, nor quailing before the fire, nor troubled by *the prospect of* suffering, he sustained bravely *the character of* the type of the Lord. Accordingly there lies

---

1 'Ἀφ' ὧν καὶ τὸ τῆς συκοφαντίας ἀλόγῳ συνηθείᾳ περὶ τοὺς τοιούτους ῥυῆναι συμβέβηκε ψεῦδος.
2 'Εγγράφως.
3 The reading of Valesius, σοῦ τὰ πάντα συνδιοικοῦντος αὐτῷ, is here adopted.
4 Περὶ τούτων.
5 In the *Chronicon Alexandrinum*.
6 'Οντως Θεοῦ Λόγου.
7 In Eusebius, *l. c.*

8 'Ιησοῦς Ναυῆ.
9 From Melito of Sardis.
10 The Hebrew word סבך, thicket, is not found as a proper name.
11 Τὸ ξύλον.
12 Μετὰ σπουδῆς. Migne: *Cum festinatione*.

Isaac before us, with his feet bound like a ram, his father standing by, with the knife all bare in his hand, not shrinking from shedding the blood of his son.

VI.

TWO SCHOLIA ON GEN. XXII. 13.[1]

The Syriac and the Hebrew use the word "suspended,"[2] as more clearly typifying the cross.

The word Sabek[3] some have rendered *remission*,[4] others *upright*,[5] as if the meaning, agreeing with the popular belief, were — a goat walking erect up to a bush, and there standing erect caught by his horns, so as to be a plain type of the cross. For this reason it is not translated, because the single Hebrew word signifies in other languages[6] many things. To those, however, who ask it is proper to give an answer, and to say that Sabek denotes *lifted up*.[7]

VII.

ON THE NATURE OF CHRIST.[8]

For there is no need, to persons of intelligence, to attempt to prove, from the deeds of Christ subsequent to His baptism, that His soul and His body, His human nature[9] like ours, were real, and no phantom of the imagination. For the deeds done by Christ after His baptism, and especially His miracles, gave indication and assurance to the world of the Deity hidden in His flesh. For, being at once both God and perfect man likewise, He gave us sure indications of His two natures : [10] of His Deity, by His miracles during the three years that elapsed after His baptism ; of His humanity, during the thirty *similar* periods which preceded His baptism, in which, by reason of His low estate[11] as regards the flesh, He concealed the signs of His Deity, although He was the true God existing before all ages.

VIII.

FROM THE ORATION ON OUR LORD'S PASSION.[12]

God has suffered from the right hand of Israel.[13]

---

[1] In the edition of the LXX. published by Card. Caraffe, 1581.
[2] κρεμάμενος. The Hebrew is נֶאֱחַז, the Syriac ‎, both meaning simply "caught."
[3] See note on the fragment just before.
[4] ἄφεσις..
[5] ὄρθιος.
[6] Lit. "when translated."
[7] ἐπηρμένος.
[8] In Anastasius of Sinai, *The Guide*, ch. 13.
[9] Or, according to Migne's punctuation, "His soul, and the body of His human nature." The words are, τὸ ἀληθὲς καὶ ἀφάνταστον τῆς ψυχῆς αὐτοῦ καὶ τοῦ σώματος τῆς καθ' ἡμᾶς ἀνθρωπίνης φύσεως.
[10] Οὐσίας. [Comp. note 13, *infra*.]
[11] Τὸ ἀτελές.
[12] Anastasius, *Guide*, ch. 12.
[13] ['Ο Θεὸς πέπονθεν ὑπὸ δεξίας 'Ισραηλίτιδος. Compare Tatian, vol ii. p. 71, note 2; also Origen, vol. iv. p. 480, note 4, this series. And see Routh, *R. S.*, i. p. 148. So "God put to death," p. 757, *supra*.]

Head of the Lord — His simple Divinity ; because He is the Beginning and Creator of all things : in Daniel.[15]

The white hair of the Lord, because He is "the Ancient of Days : " as above.

The eyes of the Lord—the Divine inspection : because He sees all things. Like that in the apostle : For all things are naked and open in His eyes."[16]

The eyelids of the Lord—hidden spiritual mysteries in the Divine precepts. In the Psalm : " His eyelids question, that is prove, the children of men."[17]

The smelling of the Lord—His delight in the prayers or works of the saints. In Genesis : " And the Lord smelled an odour of sweetness."[18]

The mouth of the Lord — His Son, or word *addressed* to men. In the prophet, " The mouth of the Lord hath spoken ; "[19] and elsewhere, " They provoked His mouth to anger."[20]

The tongue of the Lord—His Holy Spirit. In the Psalm : " My tongue is a pen."[21]

The face of the Lord—His manifestation. In Exodus, " My face shall go before thee ; "[22] and in the prophet, " The face of the Lord divided them."[23]

The word of the Lord — His Son. In the Psalm : " My heart hath uttered a good word."[21]

The arm of the Lord—His Son, by whom He hath wrought all His works. In the prophet Isaiah : "And to whom is the arm of the Lord revealed ? "[24]

The right hand of the Lord — that is, *His* Son ; as also above in the Psalm : " The right hand of the Lord hath done valiantly."[25]

The right hand of the Lord—*electio omnis.* As in Deuteronomy : " In His right hand *is* a fiery law."[26]

The wings of the Lord — Divine protection. In the Psalm : " In the shadow of Thy wings will I hope."[27]

The shoulder of the Lord — the Divine power, by which He condescends to carry the feeble. In Deuteronomy : " He took them up, and put them on His shoulders."[28]

The hand of the Lord — Divine operation.

---

[14] From *The Key.*
[15] Dan. vii. 9, 13, 22.
[16] Heb. iv. 13.
[17] Ps. xi. 4.
[18] Gen. viii. 21.
[19] Isa. i. 20.
[20] Lam. i. 18.
[21] Ps. xlv. 1.
[22] Ex. xxxiii. 14.
[23] Lam. iv. 16.
[24] Isa. liii. 1.
[25] Ps. cxviii. 16.
[26] Deut. xxxiii. 2.
[27] Ps. lvii. 1.
[28] Deut. xxxiii. 12.

In the prophet : " Have not my hands made all these things ? " [1]

The finger of the Lord — the Holy Spirit, by whose operation the tables of the law in Exodus are said to have been written ; [2] and in the Gospel : " If I by the finger of God cast out demons." [3]

The fingers of the Lord — The lawgiver Moses, or the prophets. In the Psalm : " I will regard the heavens," that is, the books of the Law and the Prophets, " the works of Thy fingers." [4]

The wisdom of the Lord — *His* Son. In the apostle : " Christ the power of God, and the wisdom of God ; " [5] and in Solomon : "The wisdom of the Lord reacheth from one end to the other mightily." [6]

The womb of the Lord — the hidden recess of Deity out of which He brought forth His Son. In the Psalm : " Out of the womb, before Lucifer, have I borne Thee.[7]

The feet of the Lord — *His* immoveableness and eternity. In the Psalm : " And thick darkness *was* under His feet." [8]

The throne of the Lord — angels, or saints, or simply sovereign dominion.[9] In the Psalm : " Thy throne, O God, is for ever and ever." [10]

Seat — the same as above, angels or saints, because the Lord sits upon these. In the Psalm : " The Lord sat upon His holy seat." [11]

The descent of the Lord — His visitation of men. As in Micah : " Behold, the Lord shall come forth from His place ; He shall come down trampling under foot the ends of the earth." [12] Likewise in a bad sense. In Genesis : " The Lord came down to see the tower." [13]

The ascent of the Lord — the raising up of man, who is taken from earth to heaven. In the Psalm : " Who ascendeth above the heaven of heavens to the east." [14]

The standing of the Lord — the patience of the Deity, by which He bears with sinners that they may come to repentance. As in Habakkuk : " He stood and measured the earth ; " [15] and in the Gospel : " Jesus stood, and bade him be called," [16] that is, the blind man.

The transition of the Lord — *His* assumption of *our* flesh, through which by His birth, His death, His resurrection, His ascent into heaven, He made transitions, so to say. In the Song of Songs : " Behold, He cometh, leaping upon the mountains, bounding over the hills." [17]

The going [18] *of the Lord* — His coming or visitation. In the Psalm.

The way of the Lord — the operation of the Deity. As in Job, in speaking of the devil : " He is the beginning of the ways of the Lord." [19]

Again : *The ways of the Lord* — His precepts. In Hosea : " For the ways of the Lord are straight, and the just shall walk in them." [20]

The footsteps of the Lord — the signs of *His* secret operations. As in the Psalm : " And Thy footsteps shall not be known." [21]

The knowledge of the Lord — that which makes *men* to know Him. To Abraham *He says :* " Now I know that thou fearest the Lord ; " [22] that is, I have made thee to know.

The ignorance of God [23] is *His* disapproval. In the Gospel : " I know you not." [24]

The remembrance of God — His mercy, by which He rejects and has mercy on whom He will. So in Genesis : " The Lord remembered Noah ; " [25] and in another passage : " The Lord hath remembered His people." [26]

The repentance of the Lord — *His* change of procedure. [27] As in the book of Kings : " It repented me that I have made Saul king." [28]

The anger and wrath of the Lord — the vengeance of the Deity upon sinners, when He bears with them with a view to punishment, does not *at once* judge them according to *strict* equity. As in the Psalm : " In His anger and in His wrath will He trouble them." [29]

The sleeping of the Lord — when, in the thoughts of some, His faithfulness is not sufficiently wakeful. In the Psalm : " Awake, why sleepest Thou, O Lord ? " [30]

The watches of the Lord — in the guardianship of His elect He is always at hand by the presence of *His* Deity. In the Psalm : " Lo ! He will not slumber nor sleep." [31]

The sitting of the Lord — *His* ruling. In the Psalm : " The Lord sitteth upon His holy seat." [11]

The footstool of the Lord — man assumed by the Word ; or His saints, as some think. In the Psalm : " Worship ye His footstool, for it is holy."

The walking of the Lord — the delight of

[1] Isa. lxvi. 2.
[2] Ex. xxxiv. 1.
[3] Luke xi. 20.
[4] Ps. viii. 3.
[5] 1 Cor. i. 24.
[6] Sap. viii. 1.
[7] Ps. cx. 3.
[8] Ps. xviii. 9.
[9] Ipsa regnandi potestas.
[10] Ps. xlv. 6; comp. Ps. v., xxix.
[11] Ps. xlvii. 8.
[12] Mic. i. 3.
[13] Gen. xi. 3.
[14] Ps. lxviii. 33.
[15] Hab. iii. 6.
[16] Mark x. 49.

[17] Cant. Cant. ii. 8.
[18] Gressus.
[19] Job xl. 19.
[20] Hos. xiv. 10.
[21] Ps. lxxvii. 19.
[22] Gen. xxii. 12.
[23] Nescire Dei.
[24] Luke xiii. 25.
[25] Gen. viii. 1.
[26] Esther x. 12.
[27] Rerum mutatio.
[28] 1 Sam. xv. 11.
[29] Ps. ii. 5.
[30] Ps. xliv. 23.
[31] Ps. cxxi. 4.

the Deity in the walks of His elect. In the prophet : " I will walk in them, and will be their Lord."[1]
The trumpet of the Lord — His mighty voice.

In the apostle : " At the command, and at the
voice of the archangel, and at the trumpet of
God, shall He descend from heaven." [2]

HEGESIPPUS.[3]

[A.D. 170.] One of the sub-Apostolic age, a contemporary of Justin and of the martyrs of
" the good Aurelius," we must yet distinguish Hegesippus [4] from the apologists. He is the
earliest of the Church's chroniclers — we can hardly call him a historian. His aims were noble
and his character was pure ; nor can we refuse him the credit due to a foresight of the Church's
ultimate want of historical material, which he endeavoured to supply.

What is commonly regarded as his defect is in reality one of his greatest merits as a witness :
he was a Hebrew, and looks at the Church from the stand-point of " James the Lord's brother."
When we observe his Catholic spirit, therefore, as well as his Catholic orthodoxy ; his sympathy
with the Gentile Church and Pauline faith of the Corinthians ; his abhorrence of " the Circumcision " so far as it bred sects and heresies against Christ ; and when we find him confirming the
testimony of the Apostolic Fathers, and sustaining the traditions of Antioch by those of Jerusalem,
— we have double reason to cherish his name, and to treasure up " the fragments that remain " of his
works. That touching episode of the kindred of Christ, as they appeared before Domitian, has
always impressed my imagination as worthy to be classed with the story of St. John and the robber, as one of the most suggestive incidents of early Christian history. We must lament the loss
of other portions of the *Memoirs* which were known to exist in the seventeenth century. He
was a traveller, and must have seen much of the Apostolic churches in the East and West ; and
the mere scraps we have of his narrative concerning Corinth and Rome excite a natural curiosity
as to the rest, which may lead to gratifying discoveries.

FRAGMENTS FROM HIS FIVE BOOKS OF COMMENTARIES ON THE ACTS OF THE CHURCH.

I.

CONCERNING THE MARTYRDOM OF JAMES, THE BROTHER OF THE LORD, FROM BOOK V.[5]

JAMES, the Lord's brother, succeeds to the
government of the Church, in conjunction with
the apostles. He has been universally called *the
Just*, from the days of the Lord down to the
present time. For many bore the name of
James ; but this one was holy from his mother's
womb. He drank no wine or *other* intoxicating
liquor,[6] nor did he eat flesh ; no razor came upon
his head ; he did not anoint himself with oil,
nor make use of the bath. He alone was permitted to enter the holy place :[7] for he did not
wear any woollen garment, but fine linen *only*.

He alone, *I say*, was wont to go into the temple : and he used to be found kneeling on his
knees, begging forgiveness for the people — so
that the skin of his knees became horny like
that of a camel's, by reason of his constantly
bending the knee in adoration to God, and begging forgiveness for the people. Therefore, in
consequence of his pre-eminent justice, he was
called *the Just*, and *Oblias*,[8] which signifies in
Greek *Defence of the People*, and *Justice*, in accordance with what the prophets declare concerning him.

Now some persons belonging to the seven
sects existing among the people, which have
been before described by me in the Notes,
asked him : " What is the door of Jesus?"

---

[1] Ezek. xxxvii. 27.
[2] 1 Thess. iv. 15. [The above has been shown to have no claim
to be the work of Melito. It is a compilation of the sixth century,
in all probability.]
[3] Westcott, *Canon*, p. 228.
[4] Routh, *Rel. Sac.*, vol. i. pp. 205-219. Lightfoot is culpably lax
in calling Rome " the Papal throne" (*temp. Anicet.*), and mistaking alike the testimony of Irenæus and of our author. *Ap. F.*, part
ii. vol. i. p. 435.
[5] In Eusebius, *Hist. Eccl.*, ii. 23. [Comp. Isa. iii. 10, *Sept.*]
[6] Σίκερα.

[7] Τὰ ἅγια.
[8] The reference appears to be to the Hebrew word עֹפֶל, *a rising
ground*, which was applied as a proper name to a fortified ridge of
Mount Zion. See 2 Chron. xxvii. 3. It has been proposed to read
ἐκαλεῖτο Σαδδὶκ καὶ Ὠζλιάμ, ὅ ἐστιν δίκαιος καὶ περιοχὴ τοῦ λαοῦ.
The text, in which not only a Hebrew word but also a Greek
(Δίκαιος) is explained *in Greek*, can hardly give the correct reading. [The translator suggests Ὠβλίας as the probable reading of
the LXX., though it is corrupted as above.]

And he replied that He was the Saviour. In consequence of this answer, some believed that Jesus is the Christ. But the sects before mentioned did not believe, either in a resurrection or in the coming of One to requite every man according to his works; but those who did believe, believed because of James. So, when many even of the ruling class believed, there was a commotion among the Jews, and scribes, and Pharisees, who said: "A little more, and we shall have all the people looking for Jesus as the Christ.

They came, therefore, in a body to James, and said: "We entreat thee, restrain the people: for they are gone astray in their opinions about Jesus, as if he were the Christ. We entreat thee to persuade all who have come hither for the day of the passover, concerning Jesus. For we all listen to thy persuasion; since we, as well as all the people, bear thee testimony that thou art just, and showest partiality to none. Do thou, therefore, persuade the people not to entertain erroneous opinions concerning Jesus: for all the people, and we also, listen to thy persuasion. Take thy stand, then, upon the summit[1] of the temple, that from that elevated spot thou mayest be clearly seen, and thy words may be plainly audible to all the people. For, in order to attend the passover, all the tribes have congregated *hither*, and some of the Gentiles also."

The aforesaid scribes and Pharisees accordingly set James on the summit of the temple, and cried aloud to him, and said: "O just one, whom we are all bound to obey, forasmuch as the people is in error, and follows Jesus the crucified, do thou tell us what is the door of Jesus, the crucified." And he answered with a loud voice: "Why ask ye me concerning Jesus the Son of man? He Himself sitteth in heaven, at the right hand of the Great Power, and shall come on the clouds of heaven."

And, when many were fully convinced *by these words*, and offered praise for the testimony of James, and said, "Hosanna to the son of David," then again the said Pharisees and scribes said to one another, "We have not done well in procuring this testimony to Jesus. But let us go up and throw him down, that they may be afraid, and not believe him." And they cried aloud, and said: "Oh! oh! the just man himself is in error." Thus they fulfilled the Scripture written in Isaiah: "Let us away with the just man, because he is troublesome to us: therefore shall they eat the fruit of their doings." So they went up and threw down the just man, and said to one another: "Let us stone James the Just." And they began to stone him: for he was not killed by the fall; but he turned, and kneeled down, and said: "I beseech Thee, Lord God *our* Father, forgive them; for they know not what they do."

And, while they were thus stoning him to death, one of the priests, the sons of Rechab, the son of Rechabim, to whom testimony is borne by Jeremiah the prophet, began to cry aloud, saying: "Cease, what do ye? The just man is praying for us." But one among them, one of the fullers, took the staff with which he was accustomed to wring out the garments *he dyed*, and hurled it at the head of the just man.

And so he suffered martyrdom; and they buried him on the spot, and the pillar erected to his memory still remains, close by the temple. This man was a true witness to both Jews and Greeks that Jesus is the Christ.

And shortly after Vespasian besieged Judæa, taking them captive.

CONCERNING THE RELATIVES OF OUR SAVIOUR.[2]

There still survived of the kindred of the Lord the grandsons of Judas, who according to the flesh was called his brother. These were informed against, as belonging to the family of David, and Evocatus brought them before Domitian Cæsar: for *that emperor* dreaded the advent of Christ, as Herod had done.

So he asked them whether they were of *the family of* David; and they confessed they were. Next he asked them what property they had, or how much money they possessed. They both replied that they had only 9000 *denaria between them*, each of them owning half that sum; but even this they said they did not possess in cash, but as the estimated value of some land, consisting of thirty-nine *plethra* only, out of which they had to pay the dues, and that they supported themselves by their own labour. And then they began to hold out their hands, exhibiting, as proof of their manual labour, the roughness of their skin, and the corns raised on their hands by constant work.

Being then asked concerning Christ and His kingdom, what was its nature, and when and where it was to appear, they returned answer that it was not of this world, nor of the earth, but belonging to the sphere of heaven and angels, and would make its appearance at the end of time, when He shall come in glory, and judge living and dead, and render to every one according to the course of his life.[3]

Thereupon Domitian passed no condemnation upon them, but treated them with contempt, as too mean for notice, and let them go free. At the same time he issued a command, and put a stop to the persecution against the Church.

---

[1] Πτερύγιον. [Matt. iv. 5.]

[2] Also in Eusebius, *Hist. Eccl.*, iii. 20.
[3] Τὰ ἐπιτηδεύματα αὐτοῦ.

When they were released they became leaders[1] of the churches, as was natural in the case of those who were at once martyrs and of the kindred of the Lord. And, after the establishment of peace *to the Church*, their lives were prolonged to *the reign of* Trajan.

CONCERNING THE MARTYRDOM OF SYMEON THE SON OF CLOPAS, BISHOP OF JERUSALEM.[2]

Some of these heretics, forsooth, laid an information against Symeon the son of Clopas, as being of *the family of* David, and a Christian. And on these charges he suffered martyrdom when he was 120 years old, in the reign of Trajan Cæsar, when Atticus was consular legate[3] *in Syria*. And it so happened, says the same writer, that, while inquiry was then being made for those belonging to the royal tribe of the Jews, the accusers themselves were convicted of belonging to it. With show of reason could it be said that Symeon was one of those who actually saw and heard the Lord, on the ground of his great age, and also because the Scripture of the Gospels makes mention of Mary the *daughter* of Clopas, who, as our narrative has shown already, was his father.

The same historian mentions others also, of the family of one of the reputed brothers of the Saviour, named Judas, as having survived until this same reign, after the testimony they bore for the faith of Christ in the time of Domitian, as already recorded.

He writes as follows: They came, then, and took the presidency of every church, as witnesses *for Christ*, and as being of the kindred of the Lord. And, after profound peace had been established in every church, they remained down to the reign of Trajan Cæsar: *that is*, until the time when he who was sprung from an uncle of the Lord, the afore-mentioned Symeon son of Clopas, was informed against by the *various* heresies, and subjected to an accusation like the rest, and for the same cause, before the legate Atticus; and, while suffering outrage during many days, he bore testimony *for Christ:* so that all, including the legate himself, were astonished above measure that a man 120 years old should have been able to endure *such torments*. He was finally condemned to be crucified.

. . . Up to that period the Church had remained like a virgin pure and uncorrupted: for, if there were any persons who were disposed to tamper with the wholesome rule of the preaching of salvation,[4] they still lurked in some dark place of concealment or other. But, when the sacred band of apostles had in various ways closed their lives, and that generation of men to whom it had been vouchsafed to listen to the Godlike Wisdom with their own ears had passed away, then did the confederacy of godless error take its rise through the treachery of false teachers, who, seeing that none of the apostles any longer survived, at length attempted with bare *and uplifted* head to oppose the preaching of the truth by preaching " knowledge falsely so called."

CONCERNING HIS JOURNEY TO ROME, AND THE JEWISH SECTS.[5]

And the church of the Corinthians continued in the orthodox faith[6] up to the time when Primus was bishop in Corinth. I had some intercourse with these *brethren* on my voyage to Rome, when I spent several days with the Corinthians, during which we were mutually refreshed by the orthodox faith.

On my arrival at Rome, I drew up a list of the succession *of bishops* down to Anicetus, whose deacon was Eleutherus. To Anicetus succeeded Soter, and after him *came* Eleutherus. But in the case of every succession,[7] and in every city, the state of affairs is in accordance with the teaching of the Law and of the Prophets and of the Lord. . . .

And after James the Just had suffered martyrdom, as had the Lord also *and* on the same account, again Symeon the son of Clopas, descended from *the Lord's* uncle, is made bishop, his election being promoted by all as being a kinsman of the Lord.

Therefore was the Church called a virgin, for she was not as yet corrupted by worthless teaching.[8] Thebulis it was who, *displeased* because he was not made bishop, first began to corrupt her by stealth. He too was connected with the seven sects which existed among the people, like Simon, from whom come the Simoniani ; and Cleobius, from whom come the Cleobiani ; and Doritheus, from whom come the Dorithiani ; and Gorthæus, from whom come the Gortheani ; Masbothæus, from whom come the Masbothæi. From these *men* also come the Menandrianists, and the Marcionists, and the Carpocratians, and the Valentinians, and the Basilidians, and the Saturnilians. Each *of these leaders* in his own private and distinct capacity brought in his own private opinion. From these have come false Christs, false prophets, false apostles — men who have split up the one Church into parts[9] through their corrupting doctrines, *uttered* in disparagement of God and of His Christ. . . .

There were, moreover, various opinions in the

---

1 Ἡγήσασθαι.
2 Also in Eusebius, *Hist. Eccl.*, iii. 32.
3 Ὑπατικοῦ. [St. John died a few years before.]
4 Τοῦ σωτηρίου κηρύγματος.

5 Also in Eusebius, *Hist. Eccl.*, iv. 22.
6 Ἐν τῷ ὀρθῷ λόγῳ.
7 [Elucidation, p. 785.]
8 Ἀκοαῖς ματαίαις.
9 Ἐμέρισαν τὴν ἕνωσιν τῆς ἐκκλησίας. [Acts xx. 29-31.]

matter of circumcision among the children of Israel, held by those who were opposed to the tribe of Judah and to Christ : such as the Es-senes, the Galileans, the Hemerobaptists, the Masbothæi, the Samaritans, the Sadducees, the Pharisees.

DIONYSIUS, BISHOP OF CORINTH.

[A.D. 170.] Eusebius is almost diffuse in what he tells us of this Dionysius,[1] " who was appointed over the church at Corinth, and imparted freely, not only to his own people, but to others, and those abroad also, the blessings of his divine labours." He wrote " Catholic Epistles ; " he addressed an epistle to the Spartans and the Athenians ; and, as Eusebius says, Dionysius the Areopagite, the convert of St. Paul, was the first bishop of Athens.[2] He wrote to the Nicomedians, refuting Marcion, and closely adhering to " the rule of faith." In an epistle to the Gortynians and others in Crete, he praises Philip for his courageous ministry, and warns them against the heretics. He seems to recognise Palmas as bishop of Amastris and Pontus, and adds expositions of Scripture, and rules regarding marriage, its purity and sanctity. He also inculcates tenderness to penitent lapsers and backsliders. With Pinytus, bishop of the Gnossians, he corresponds on similar sub-jects ; but Pinytus, while he thanks him and commends his clemency, evidently regards him as too much inclined to furnish " food for babes," and counsels him to add " strong meat for those of full age." He also writes to Chrysophora, his most faithful sister, imparting spiritual instruction.

FRAGMENTS FROM A LETTER TO THE ROMAN CHURCH.

I.

For this has been your custom from the be-ginning, to do good to all the brethren in vari-ous ways, and to send resources to many churches which are in every city, thus refreshing the poverty of the needy, and granting subsidies to the brethren who are in the mines.[3] Through the resources which ye have sent from the begin-ning, ye Romans, keep up the custom of the Romans handed down by the fathers, which your blessed Bishop Soter has not only preserved, but added to, sending a splendid gift to the saints, and exhorting with blessed words those brethren who go up to Rome, as an affectionate father his children.

II.

FROM THE SAME EPISTLE.[4]

We passed this holy Lord's day, in which we read your letter, from the constant reading of which we shall be able to draw admonition, even as from the reading of the former one you sent us written through Clement.

III.

FROM THE SAME.

Therefore you also have by such admonition joined in close union *the churches* that were planted by Peter and Paul, that of the Romans and that of the Corinthians : for both of them went [5] to our Corinth, and taught us in the same way as they taught you when they went to Italy ; and having taught you, they suffered martyrdom at the same time.[6]

IV.

FROM THE SAME.[7]

For I wrote letters when the brethren re-quested me to write. And these letters the apostles of the devil have filled with tares, tak-ing away some things and adding others, for whom a woe is in store. It is not wonderful, then, if some have attempted to adulterate the Lord's writings, when they have formed designs against those which are not such.[8]

---

[1] Book iv. cap. 24, from which these Fragments are collected. See Westcott, *On the Canon*, p. 206.
[2] See Lightfoot, *Ap. Fathers*, part ii. vol. i. p. 555, where he corrects the reading καὶ Πολύκαρπος.
[3] [Routh (also on Pinytus and Soter), *R. S.*, p. 177. This series, vol. vi. p. 102, note 3. Note also Lightfoot, *A. F.*, part ii. vol. ii. p. 192, note 1; and Westcott, *Canon*, p. 206.]

[4] [Comp. p. 758, note 8, *supra*. Also Ignatius, vol. i. p. 63, at note 2, this series.]
[5] MSS. " planted."
[6] The text is evidently corrupt.
[7] [For the reply of Pinytus, and what is said by Eusebius of seven other epistles, see Routh, *R. S.*, vol. i. pp. 181–184.]
[8] i.e., of such importance or of such a character.

RHODON.[1]

[A.D. 180.] This Rhodon[2] was supposed by St. Jerome to have been the author of the work against the Cataphrygians, ascribed to Asterius Urbanus more probably.[3] Eusebius[4] gives us the fragment from his work against Marcion, addressed to Callistion, which is here translated. He tells us that he was a pupil of Tatian, and expresses an intention of furnishing original solutions of Scriptural problems stated by Tatian,[5] and by that author explained in a manner apparently unsatisfactory. He also appears to have written against the blasphemous Apelles,[6] whose *Hexaëmeron* was an attempt to refute Moses; but whether he also fulfilled his promise concerning an Ἐπίλυσις of Tatian's Problems (or Questions), seems doubtful. Routh has devoted to the fragment here translated six pages of notes,[7] which he subjoins to the Greek text (of Eusebius) and a Latin version of the same.

WHEREFORE also they[8] disagree among themselves, maintaining as they do an opinion which has no consistency with itself. For one of their herd, Apelles, who prides himself on the strictness of his life,[9] and on his age, admits that there is *only* one first principle,[10] yet says that the prophecies *have come* from an opposing spirit, in which opinion he is influenced by the responses of a soothsaying[11] maid named Philumene. But others, among whom are Potitus and Basilicus, like Marcion[12] himself, introduce two first principles. These men, following the Pontic wolf, and not being able to discover any more than he the division of things, have had to recourse to rash assertion, and declared the existence of two first principles simply and without proof. Others of them, again, drifting *from bad* to worse, assume not two only, but even three natures. Of these men the leader and champion is Syneros, as those who adopt his teaching say. . . .

For the old man Apelles entered into conversation with us, and was convicted of uttering many false opinions. For example, he asserted that men should on no account examine into their creed,[13] but that every one ought to continue to the last in the belief he has once adopted.

For he declared that those who had rested their hope on the Crucified One would be saved, provided only they were found living in the practice of good works. But the most perplexing of all the doctrines laid down by him was, as we have remarked before, what he said concerning God: for he affirmed that there was *only* one first principle, precisely as our own faith teaches. . . .

On asking him, "Where do you get proof of this? or how are you able to assert that there is *only* one first principle? tell us," — he said that the prophecies refuted themselves, because they had uttered nothing at all that was true: for that they were discordant and false, and self-contradictory. As to the question, "How does it appear that there is *only* one first principle?" he said he could not tell, only he was impelled to that belief. On my thereupon conjuring him to speak the truth, he solemnly declared that he was expressing his real sentiments; and that he did not know "how" there could be one uncreated God, but that he believed the fact. Here I burst into laughter and rebuked him, because he professed to be a teacher, and yet was unable to confirm *by arguments* what he taught.

MAXIMUS, BISHOP OF JERUSALEM.

[A.D. 185–196.] He was a noted character among Christians, according to Eusebius; living, according to Jerome, under Commodus and Severus. He wrote on the inveterate question concerning the *Origin of Evil;* and the fragment here translated, as given by Eusebius, is also textually cited by Origen against the Marcionites,[14] if that Dialogue be his. The reader will not fail

---

[1] In Eusebius, *Hist. Eccl.*, v. 13.
[2] Or Rhodo.
[3] Vol. vii. pp. 333–338, this series, where I neglected to insert a reference to Routh, *Rel. Sac.*, vol. ii. pp. 183–217.
[4] *H. E.*, book v. cap. 13.
[5] Vol. ii. p 62, this series.
[6] See Origen, vol. iv. p. 567, this series.
[7] *Rel. Sac.*, vol. i. pp. 437–446.
[8] The Marcionites.

[9] Πολιτεία. See Migne's note.
[10] Ἀρχήν. [See vol. vii. p. 365, this series.]
[11] Δαιμονώσης.
[12] Some copies have "Marcion *the sailor*," and so Tertullian (*de Præscriptionibus*) speaks of him. [Vol. iii. cap. 30, p. 257, this series.]
[13] Τὸν λόγον.
[14] A fact which gave rise to a controversy, on which consult Routh, *Rel. Sac.*, vol. ii. p. 78.

to recollect that liberal citations out of this work are also to be found in Methodius, *On Free-Will.*[1] But all who desire fuller information on the subject will be gratified by the learned *prolegomena* and notes of Routh, to which I refer them.[2] Whether Maximus was the bishop of Jerusalem (A.D. 185) mentioned by Eusebius as presiding in that See in the sixth year of Commodus, seems to be uncertain.

FROM THE BOOK CONCERNING MATTER, OR IN DE-
FENCE OF THE PROPOSITION THAT MATTER IS
CREATED, AND IS NOT THE CAUSE OF EVIL.[3]

"THAT there cannot exist two uncreated *substances* at one and the same time, I presume that you hold equally *with myself.* You appear, however, very decidedly to have assumed, and to have introduced into the argument, this *principle*, that we must of unavoidable necessity maintain one of two things: either that God is separate from matter; or else, on the contrary, that He is indissolubly connected with it.

"If, then, any one should choose to assert that He exists in union *with matter*, that would be saying that there is *only* one uncreated *substance.* For either of the two must constitute a part of the other; and, since they form parts of each other, they cannot be two uncreated *substances.* Just as, in speaking of man, we do not describe him as subdivided into a number of distinct parts, each forming a separate created *substance*, but, as reason requires us to do, assert that he was made by God a single created *substance* consisting of many parts, — so, in like manner, if God is not separate from matter, we are driven to the conclusion that there is *only* one uncreated *substance.*

"If, on the other hand, it be affirmed that He is separate *from matter*, it necessarily follows that there is some *other substance* intermediate between the two, by which their separation is made apparent. For it is impossible that one thing should be shown to be severed by an interval from another, unless there be something else by which the interval between the two is produced. This *principle*, too, holds good not only with regard to this or any other single case, but in any number of cases you please. For the same argument which we have employed in dealing with the two uncreated *substances* must in like manner be valid if the substances *in question* be given as three. For in regard to these also I should *have to* inquire whether they are separate from one another, or whether, on the contrary, each of them is united to its fellow. For, if you should say that they are united, you would hear from me the same argument as before; but if, on the contrary, you should say that they are separate, you could not escape the unavoidable assumption of a separating *medium.*

"If, again, perchance any one should think that there is a third view which may be consistently maintained with regard to uncreated *substances*, — namely, that God is not separate from matter, nor yet, on the other hand, united to it as a part, but that God exists in matter as in a place, or possibly matter exists in God, — let such a person observe the consequence: —

"That, if we make matter God's place, we must of necessity admit that He can be contained,[4] and that He is circumscribed by matter. Nay, further, he must grant that He is, in the same way as matter, driven about hither and thither, unable to maintain His place and to stay where He is, since that in which He exists is perpetually being driven about in one direction or another. Beside this, he must also admit that God has had His place among the worst *kind of elements.* For if matter was once in disorder, and if he reduced it to order for the purpose of rendering it better, there was a time when God existed among *the* disordered *elements of matter.*

"I might also fairly put this question: whether God filled the whole of matter, or was in some part of it. If any one should choose to say that God was in some part of matter, he would be making Him indefinitely smaller than matter, inasmuch as a part of it contained the whole of Him;[5] but, if he maintained that He pervaded the whole of matter, I need to be informed how He became the Fashioner of this *matter.* For we must necessarily assume, either that there was on the part of God a contraction,[6] so to speak, of Himself, *and a withdrawal from matter*, whereupon He proceeded to fashion that from which He had retired; or else that He fashioned Himself in conjunction with matter, in consequence of having no place to retire to.

"But suppose it to be maintained, on the other hand, that matter is in God, it will behove us similarly to inquire, whether we are to understand by this that He is sundered from Himself, and that, just like the air, which contains *various* kinds of animals, so is He sundered and divided into parts for the reception of those *creatures*

---

[1] See vol. vi. p. 358, etc., this series, where I have spoken of Maximus as the original of the Dialogue ascribed to Methodius.
[2] Routh, *Rel. Sac.*, vol. ii. p. 85. See pp. 77-121, devoted to this author.
[3] In Eusebius, *Præp. Evang.*, vii. 22.

[4] Χωρητὸν, the reading of one MS., instead of χωρητικόν.
[5] For εἰ δὲ μέρος αὐτῆς, ὅλον ἐχώρησεν αὐτόν, Migne reads, εἰ γε (or εἰ δὴ) μέρος αὐτῆς ὅλον, κ.τ.λ.
[6] Συστολήν τινα.

which from time to time exist in [1] Him; or whether *matter is in God* as in a place, — for instance, as water is contained in earth. For should we say 'as in air,' we should perforce be speaking of God as divisible into parts; but if 'as water in earth,' and if matter was, *as is admitted*, in confusion and disorder, and moreover also contained what was evil, we should have to admit that God is the place of disorder and evil. But this it does not seem to me consistent with reverence to say, but hazardous rather. For you contend that matter is uncreated,[2] that you may not have to admit that God is the author of evil; and yet, while aiming to escape this *difficulty*, you make Him the receptacle of evil.

"If you had stated that your suspicion that matter was uncreated arose from the nature of created things as we find them,[3] I should have employed abundant argument in proof that it cannot be so. But, since you have spoken of the existence of evil as the cause of such suspicion, I am disposed to enter upon a *separate* examination of this point. For, when once it has been made clear how it is that evil exists, and when it is seen to be impossible to deny that God is the author of evil, in consequence of His having had recourse to matter for His materials,[4] it seems to me that a suspicion of this kind disappears.

"You assert, then, that matter, destitute of all qualities *good or bad*, co-existed at the outset with God, and that out of it He fashioned the world as we now find it."

"Such is my opinion."

"Well, then, if matter was without any qualities, and the world has come into existence from God, and if the world possesses qualities, the author of those qualities must be God."

"Exactly so."

"Since, too, I heard you say yourself just now that out of nothing [5] nothing can possibly come, give me an answer to the question I am about to ask you. You seem to me to think that the qualities of the world have not sprung from pre-existing [6] qualities, and moreover that they are something different from the substances *themselves*."

"I do."

"If, therefore, God did not produce the qualities *in question* from qualities already existing, nor yet from substances, by reason that they are not substances, the conclusion is inevitable, that they were made by God out of nothing. So that you seemed to me to affirm more than you were warranted to do, *when you said* that it had been

proved impossible to hold the opinion [7] that anything was made by God out of nothing.

"But let us put the matter thus. We see persons among ourselves making certain things out of nothing, however true it may be that they make them by means of something.[8] Let us take our illustration, say, from builders. These men do not make cities out of cities; nor, similarly, temples out of temples. Nay, if you suppose that, because the substances *necessary* for these *constructions* are already provided, therefore they make them out of that which already exists, your reasoning is fallacious. For it is not the substance that makes the city or the temples, but the art which is employed about the substance. Neither, *again*, does the art proceed from any art inhering in the substances, but it arises independently of any such art in them.

"But I fancy you will meet the argument by saying that the artist produces the art which is *manifest* in the substance *he has fashioned* out of the art which he *himself already* has. In reply to this, however, I think it may be fairly said, that neither in man does art spring from any already existing art. For we cannot possibly allow that art exists by itself, since it belongs to the class of things which are accidentals, and which receive their existence only when they appear in *connection with* substance. For man will exist though there should be no architecture, but the latter will have no existence unless there be first of all man. Thus we cannot avoid the conclusion, that it is the nature of art to spring up in man out of nothing. If, then, we have shown that this is the case with man, we surely must allow that God can make not only the qualities *of substances* out of nothing, but also the substances *themselves*. For, if it appears possible that anything *whatever* can be made out of nothing, it is proved that this may be the case with substances also.

"But, since you are specially desirous of inquiring about the origin of evil, I will proceed to the discussion of this topic. And I should like to ask you a few questions. Is it your opinion that things evil are substances, or that they are qualities of substances?"

"Qualities of substances, I am disposed to say."

"But matter was destitute of qualities and of form: this I assumed at the outset of the discussion. Therefore, if things evil are qualities of substances, and matter was destitute of qualities, and you have called God the author of qualities, God will also be the former of that which is evil. Since, then, it is not possible, on

---

[1] Τῶν γινομένων (ἐν) αὐτῷ, Migne.

[2] This word, ἀγένητον, is added from Migne's conjecture.

[3] Ἐκ τῶν ὑποστάντων γενητῶν.

[4] Ἐκ τοῦ ὕλην αὐτὸν ὑποτιθέναι.

[5] Ἐξ οὐκ ὄντων. [Note this phrase. Comp. vol. vi. p. 292, n. 3.]

[6] Ὑποκειμένων.

[7] For συλλελόγισται ὡς οὐκ ἀδύνατον εἶναι δοξάζειν, Migne reads, ὡς συλλελόγισται ἀδύνατον εἶναι δοξάζειν.

[8] Lit. "in something." Whether the materials or the art is meant is not very clear. Possibly there is a play of words in the use of the two prepositions, ἐκ and ἐν.

this supposition any more than on the other, to speak of God as not the cause of evil, it seems to me superfluous to add matter to Him, *as if that were the cause of evil*. If you have any reply to make to this, begin your argument."

" If, indeed, our discussion had arisen from a love of contention, I should not be willing to have the inquiry raised a second time about *the origin of* evil ; but, since we are prompted rather by friendship and the good of our neighbour to engage in controversy, I readily consent to have the question raised afresh on this subject. You have no doubt long been aware of the character of my mind, and of the object at which I aim in dispute : that I have no wish to vanquish falsehood by plausible reasoning, but rather that truth should be established in connection with thorough investigation. You yourself, too, are of the same mind, I am well assured. Whatever method, therefore, you deem successful for the discovery of truth, do not shrink from using it. For, by following a better course of argument, you will not only confer a benefit on yourself, but most assuredly on me also, *instructing me* concerning matters of which I am ignorant."

"You seem clearly to agree with[1] me, that things evil are in some sort substances :[2] for, apart from substances, I do not see them to have any existence. Since, then, my good friend, you say that things evil are substances, it is necessary to inquire into the nature of substance. Is it your opinion that substance is a kind of bodily structure?"[3]

" It is."

" And does that bodily structure exist by itself, without the need of any one to come and give it existence?"

"Yes."

And does it seem to you that things evil are connected with certain *courses of* action?"

" That is my belief."

" And do actions come into existence only when an actor is there?"

" Yes."

" And, when there is no actor, neither will his action ever take place?"

" It will not."

" If, therefore, substance is a kind of bodily structure, and this does not stand in need of some one in and through whom it may receive its existence, and if things evil are actions of some one, and actions require some one in and through whom they receive their existence, — things evil will 'not' be substances. And if things evil are not substances, and murder is an evil, *and* is the action of some one, it follows that murder is not a substance. But, if you insist that agents are substance, then I myself agree with you. A man, for instance, who is a murderer, is, in so far as he is a man, a substance ; but the murder which he commits is not a substance, but a work of the substance. Moreover, we speak of a man sometimes as bad because he commits murder ; and sometimes, again, because he performs acts of beneficence, as good : and these names adhere to the substance, in consequence of the things which are accidents of it, which, *however*, are not *the substance* itself. For neither is the substance murder, nor, again, is it adultery, nor is it any *other* similar evil. But, just as the grammarian derives his name from grammar, and the orator from oratory, and the physician from physic, though the substance is not physic, nor yet oratory, nor grammar, but receives its appellation from the things which are accidents of it, from which it popularly receives its name, though it is not any one of them, — so in like manner it appears to me that the substance receives name from things regarded as evil, though it is not *itself* any one of them.

" I must beg you also to consider that, if you represent some other being as the cause of evil to men, he also, in so far as he acts in them, and incites them to do evil, is himself evil, by reason of the things he does. For he too is said to be evil, for the simple reason that he is the doer of evil things ; but the things which a being does are not the being himself, but his actions, from which he receives his appellation, and is called evil. For if we should say that the things he does are himself, and these consist in murder, and adultery, and theft, and such-like, these things will be himself. And if these things are himself, and if when they take place they get to have a substantial existence,[4] but by not taking place they also cease to exist, and if these things are done by men, — men will be the doers of these things, and the causes of existing and of no longer existing. But, if you affirm that these things are his actions, he gets to be evil from the things he does, not from those things of which the substance *of him* consists.

" Moreover, we have said that he is called evil from those things which are accidents of the substance, which are not *themselves* the substance : as a physician from the art of physic. But, if he receives the beginning of his existence from the actions he performs, he too began to be evil, and these evil things likewise began to exist. And, if so, an evil being will not be without a beginning, nor will evil things be unoriginated, since we have said that they are originated by him."

---

[1] Migne, instead of παραστῆναι, conjectures παραστῆσαι, which, however, would not suit what appears to be the meaning.
[2] Οὐσίας τινάς.
[3] Σωματικήν τινα σύστασιν.
[4] Τὴν σύστασιν ἔχει.

"The argument relating to the opinion I before expressed, you seem to me, my friend, to have handled satisfactorily: for, from the premises you assumed in the discussion, I think you have drawn a fair conclusion. For, beyond doubt, if matter was *at first* destitute of qualities, and if God is the fashioner of the qualities *it now has*, and if evil things are qualities, God is the author of those evil things. The argument, then, relating to that *opinion* we may consider as well discussed, and to me it *now* seems false to speak of matter as destitute of qualities. For it is not possible to say of any substance[1] whatsoever that it is without qualities. For, in the very act of saying that it is destitute of qualities, you do *in fact* indicate its quality, representing of what kind matter is, which of course is *ascribing to it* a species of quality. Wherefore, if it is agreeable to you, rehearse the argument to me from the beginning: for, to me, matter seems to have had qualities from all eternity.[2] For in this way I *can* affirm that evil things also come from it in the way of emanation, so that the cause of evil things may not be ascribed to God, but that matter may be *regarded as* the cause of all such things."

"I approve your desire, my friend, and praise the zeal you manifest in the discussion of opinions. For it assuredly becomes every one who is desirous of knowledge, not simply and out of hand to agree with what is said, but to make a careful examination of the arguments *adduced*. For, though a disputant, by laying down false premises, may make his opponent draw the conclusion he wishes, yet he will not convince a hearer of this; but only when he says that which[3] it seems possible to say with fairness. So that one of two things will happen: either he will, as he listens, be decisively helped to reach that *conclusion* towards which he *already* feels himself impelled, or he will convict his adversary of not speaking the truth.

"Now, it seems to me that you have not sufficiently discussed the statement that matter has qualities from the first. For, if this is the case, what will God be the maker of? For, if we speak of substances, we affirm these to exist beforehand; or if again of qualities, we declare these also to exist already. Since, therefore, both substance and qualities exist, it seems to me unreasonable to call God a creator.

"But, lest I should seem to be constructing an argument *to suit my purpose*, be so good as to answer the question: In what way do you assert God to be a creator? Is He such because He changed the substances, so that they should no longer be the same as they had once been, but become different from what they were; or because, while He kept the substances the same as they were before that period, He changed their qualities?"

"I do not at all think that any alteration took place in substances: for it appears to me absurd to say this. But I affirm that a certain change was made in their qualities; and it is in respect of these that I speak of God as a creator. Just as we might happen to speak of a house as made out of stones, in which case we could not say that the stones no longer continue to be stones as regards their substance, now that they are made into a house (for I affirm that the house owes its existence to the quality of its construction, forasmuch as the previous quality of the stones has been changed), — so does it seem to me that God, while the substance remains *the same*, has made a certain change in its qualities; and it is in respect of such change that I speak of the origin of this world as having come from God."

"Since, then, you maintain that a certain change — namely, of qualities — has been produced by God, answer me briefly what I am desirous to ask you."

"Proceed, pray, with your question."

"Do you agree in the opinion that evil things are qualities of substances?"

"I do."

"Were these qualities in matter from the first, or did they begin to be?"

"I hold that these qualities existed in combination with matter, without being originated."

"But do you not affirm that God has made a certain change in the qualities?"

"That is what I affirm."

"For the better, or for the worse?"

"For the better, I should say."

"Well, then, if evil things are qualities of matter, and if the Lord *of all* changed its qualities for the better, whence, it behoves us to ask, come evil things? For either the qualities remained the same in their nature as they previously were, or, if they were not evil before, but you assert that, in consequence of a change wrought on them by God, the first qualities of this kind came into existence in connection with matter, — God will be the author of evil, inasmuch as He changed the qualities which were not evil, so as to make them evil.

"Possibly, however, it is not your view that God changed evil qualities for the better; but you mean that all those other qualities which happened to be neither good nor bad,[4] were changed by God with a view to the adornment *of the creation*."

"That has been my opinion from the outset."

---

[1] Migne reads οὐσίας for αἰτίας.
[2] Ἀνάρχως.
[3] Reading, with Migne, εἰ ὅ τι for εἰ τι.

[4] Or "indifferent:" ἀδιάφοροι.

"How, then, can you say that He has left the qualities of bad things just as they were? Is it that, although He was able to destroy those qualities as well as the others, He was not willing; or *did He refrain* because He had not the power? For, if you say He had the power, but not the will, you must admit Him to be the cause of these *qualities:* since, when He could have put a stop to the existence of evil, He chose to let it remain as it was, and that, too, at the very time when He began to fashion matter. For, if He had not concerned Himself at all with matter, He would not have been the cause of those things which He allowed to remain. But, seeing that He fashioned a certain part of it, and left a certain part as we have described it, although He could have changed that also for the better, it seems to me that He deserves to have the blame cast on Him, for having permitted a part of matter to be evil, to the ruin of that *other* part which He fashioned.

"Nay, more, it seems to me that the most serious wrong has been committed as regards this part, in that He constituted this part of matter so as to be now affected by evil. For, if we were to examine carefully into things, we should find that the condition of matter is worse now than in its former state, before it was reduced to order. For, before it was separated into parts, it had no sense of evil; but now every one of its parts is afflicted with a sense of evil.

"Take an illustration from man. Before he was fashioned, and became a living being through the art of the Creator, he was by nature exempt from any contact whatever with evil; but, as soon as ever he was made by God a man, he became liable to the sense of even approaching evil : and thus that very thing which you say was brought about by God for the benefit of matter,[1] is found to have turned out rather to its detriment.

"But, if you say that evil has not been put a stop to, because God was unable to do away with it, you will be making God powerless. But, if He is powerless, it will be either because He is weak by nature, or because He is overcome by fear, and reduced to subjection by a stronger. If, then, you go so far as to say that God is weak by nature, it seems to me that you imperil your salvation itself; but, if *you say that He is weak* through being overcome by fear of a greater, things evil will be greater than God, since they frustrate the carrying out of His purpose. But this, as it seems to me, it would be absurd to say of God. For why should not 'they' rather be *considered* gods, since according to your account they are able to overcome God : if, that is to say, we mean by God that which has a controlling power over all things?

"But I wish to ask you a few questions concerning matter itself. Pray tell me, therefore, whether matter was something simple or compound. I am induced to adopt this method of investigating the subject before us by *considering* the diversity that obtains in existing things. For, if perchance matter was something simple and uniform, how comes it that the world is compound,[2] and consists of divers substances and combinations? For by 'compound' we denote a mixture of certain simple *elements*. But if, on the contrary, you prefer to call matter compound, you will, of course, be asserting that it is compounded of certain simple elements. And, if it was compounded of simple elements, these simple elements must have existed at some time or other separately by themselves, and when they were compounded together matter came into being : from which it of course follows that matter is created. For, if matter is compound, and compound things are constituted from simple, there was once a time when matter had no existence, — namely, before the simple elements came together. And, if there was once a time when matter was not, and there was never a time when the uncreated was not, matter cannot be uncreated. And hence there will be many uncreated *substances*. For, if God was uncreated, and the simple elements out of which matter was compounded *were also uncreated*, there will not be two uncreated things only, — not to discuss the question what it is which constitutes objects simple, whether matter or form.

"Is it, further, your opinion that nothing in existence is opposed to itself?"

"It is."

"Is water, then, opposed to fire?"

"So it appears to me."

"Similarly, is darkness opposed to light, and warm to cold, and moreover moist to dry?"

"It seems to me to be so."

"Well, then, if nothing in existence is opposed to itself, and these things are opposed to each other, they cannot be one and the same matter; no, nor yet be made out of one and the same matter.

"I wish further to ask your opinion on a matter kindred to that of which we have been speaking. Do you believe that the parts *of a thing* are not mutually destructive?"

"I do."

"And you believe that fire and water, and so on, are parts of matter?"

"Quite so."

"Do you not also believe that water is subversive of fire, and light of darkness, and so of all similar things?"

"Yes."

---

[1] Migne reads ἐπ' εὐεργεσίᾳ for ἐστιν εὐεργεσία.

[2] The text has, σύνθετος δὲ ὁ κόσμος; which Migne changes to, πῶς δὴ σύνθετός ἐστιν ὁ κόσμος;

"Well, then, if the parts *of a whole* are not mutually destructive, and yet the parts of matter are mutually destructive, they cannot be parts of one matter. And, if they are not parts of one another, they cannot be composed of one and the same matter; nay, they cannot be matter at all, since nothing in existence is destructive of itself, as we learn from the doctrine of opposites: for nothing is opposed to itself — an opposite being by nature opposed to something else. White, for example, is not opposed to itself, but is said to be the opposite of black; and, similarly, light is shown not to be opposed to itself, but is considered an opposite in relation to darkness; and so of a very great number of things besides. If, then, matter were some one thing, it could not be opposed to itself. This, then, being the nature of opposites, it is proved that matter has no existence."

CLAUDIUS APOLLINARIS,[1] BISHOP OF HIERAPOLIS, AND APOLOGIST.

[A.D. 160–180.] This author, an early apologist, is chiefly interesting as a competent witness, who tells the story of the *Thundering Legion*[2] in an artless manner, and gives it the simple character of an answer to prayer. This subject is treated by Lightfoot, in his recent work on the *Apostolic Fathers*,[3] in an exhaustive manner; and the story, reduced to the simple narrative as Apollinaris gives it, receives from him a just and discriminating approval.

Apollinaris, as well as Rhodon, has been imagined the author of the work (ascribed to Asterius Urbanus) against Montanism, dedicated to Abiricius Marcellus.[4] This is sufficiently refuted by Routh,[5] whose Greek text, with notes, must be consulted by the studious.[6]

Apollinaris was bishop of Hierapolis on the Mæander, and, Lightfoot thinks, was probably with Melito and Polycrates, known to Polycarp, and influenced by his example and doctrine.[7] He addressed his *Apology*, which is honourably mentioned by Jerome, to M. Antoninus, the emperor. He also wrote *Adversus Gentes* and *De Veritate;* also against the Jews. Serapion calls him[8] "most blessed."

FROM AN UNKNOWN BOOK.[9]

"THIS narration (says Eusebius, *Hist.*, v. 5) is given" (it relates to that storm of rain which was sent to the army of the Emperor M. Antoninus, to allay the thirst of the soldiers, whilst the enemy was discomfited by thunderbolts hurled upon them) "even by those historians who are at a wide remove from the doctrines that prevail among us, and who have been simply concerned to describe what related to *the emperors who are* the subjects of their history; and it has been recorded also by our own writers. But historians without *the pale of the Church*, as being unfriendly to the faith, while they have recorded the prodigy, have refrained from acknowledging that it was sent in answer to our prayers. On the other hand, our writers, as lovers of truth, have reported the matter in a simple and artless way. To this number Apollinaris must be considered as belonging. 'Thereupon,' he says, 'the legion which had by its prayer caused the prodigy received from the emperor a title suitable to the occurrence, and was called in the Roman language the Thunder-hurling *Legion.*'"

FROM THE BOOK CONCERNING THE PASSOVER.[10]

There are, then, some who through ignorance raise disputes about these things (though their conduct is pardonable: for ignorance is no subject for blame — it rather needs further instruction), and say that on the fourteenth day the Lord ate the lamb with the disciples, and that on the great day of the *feast of* unleavened bread He Himself suffered; and they quote Matthew as speaking in accordance with their view. Wherefore their opinion is contrary to the law, and the Gospels seem to be at variance with them.[11]

FROM THE SAME BOOK.

The fourteenth day, the true Passover of the Lord; the great sacrifice, the Son of God instead

---

1 Westcott, *Canon*, p. 248.
2 See vol. i. p. 187, this series, and references in my note (11.) on same page. The incident occurred during the war against the Quadi, A.D. 174.
3 Part ii. vol. i. pp. 469–476.
4 See p. 766, note 3, *supra;* also vol. vii., this series, p. 338.
5 *Rel. Sac.*, tom. ii. p. 196; and *Ibid.*, tom. i. pp. 157–174.
6 *Rel. Sac.*, tom. i. p. 173.
7 *Ap. Fathers*, part ii. vol. i. p. 428.
8 See p. 775, *infra*.
9 [See vol. i. p. 187, note 2.]
10 This extract and the following are taken from the preface to the *Chronicon Paschale*.
11 [Routh, *R. S.*, vol. i. p. 160.]

of the lamb, who was bound, who bound the strong, and who was judged, *though* Judge of living and dead, and who was delivered into the hands of sinners to be crucified, who was lifted up on the horns of the unicorn, and who was pierced in His holy side, who poured forth from His side the two purifying elements,[1] water and blood, word and spirit, and who was buried on the day of the passover, the stone being placed upon the tomb.

POLYCRATES,[2] BISHOP OF EPHESUS.

[A.D. 130–196.] This author[3] comes in as an appendix to the stories of Polycarp and Irenæus and good Anicetus, and his writings also bear upon the contrast presented by the less creditable history of Victor. If, as I suppose, the appearance of our Lord to St. John on "the Lord's day" was on the Paschal Sunday, it may at first seem surprising that this Apostle can be claimed by Polycrates in behalf of the Eastern custom to keep Easter, with the Jews, on the fourteenth day of the moon. But to the Jews the Apostles became "as Jews" in all things tolerable, so long as the Temple stood, and while the bishops of Jerusalem were labouring to identify the Paschal Lamb with their Passover. The long survival of St. John among Jewish Christians led them to prolong this usage, no doubt, as sanctioned by his example. He foreknew it would quietly pass away. The wise and truly Christian spirit of Irenæus prepared the way for the ultimate unanimity of the Church in a matter which lies at the base of "the Christian Sabbath," and of our own observance of the first day of the week as a weekly Easter. Those who in our own times have revived the observance of the Jewish Sabbath, show us how much may be said on their side,[4] and elucidate the tenacity of the Easterns in resisting the abolition of the Mosaic ordinance as to the Paschal, although they agreed to keep it "not with the old leaven."

Our author belonged to a family in which he was the eighth Christian bishop; and he presided over the church of Ephesus, in which the traditions of St. John were yet fresh in men's minds at the date of his birth. He had doubtless known Polycarp, and Irenæus also. He seems to have presided over a synod of Asiatic bishops (A.D. 196) which came together to consider this matter of the Paschal feast. It is surely noteworthy that nobody doubted that it was kept by a Christian and Apostolic ordinance. So St. Paul argues from its Christian observance, in his rebuke of the Corinthians.[5] They were keeping it "unleavened" ceremonially, and he urges a spiritual unleavening as more important. The Christian hallowing of Pentecost connects with the Paschal argument.[6] The Christian Sabbath hinges on these points.

FROM HIS EPISTLE TO VICTOR AND THE ROMAN CHURCH CONCERNING THE DAY OF KEEPING THE PASSOVER.[7]

As for us, then, we scrupulously observe the exact day,[8] neither adding nor taking away. For in Asia great luminaries[9] have gone to their rest, who shall rise again in the day of the coming of the Lord, when He cometh with glory from heaven and shall raise again all the saints. *I speak of* Philip, one of the twelve apostles,[10] who is laid to rest at Hierapolis; and his two daughters, who arrived at old age unmarried;[11] his other daughter also, who passed her life[12] under the influence of the Holy Spirit, and reposes at Ephesus; John, moreover, who reclined on the Lord's bosom, and who became a priest wearing the mitre,[13] and a witness and a teacher — he rests at Ephesus. Then there is Polycarp, both bishop and martyr at Smyrna; and Thraseas from Eumenia, both bishop and

---

[1] Πάλιν καθάρσια, qu. παλινκαθάρσια = "re-purifiers."
[2] Westcott, *Canon*, p. 432, note 1; Lightfoot, *Ap. Fathers*, pp. 379, etc., 494.
[3] See Lardner, *Credib.*, vol. ii. cap. 23, p. 259.
[4] They cannot be satisfactorily answered, it seems to me, save by the appeal to John xx. 19, 26, Acts xx. 7, 1 Cor. xvi. 2, and Rev. i. 10, for "the Lord's day," and to the Council of Jerusalem (Acts xv. 28; Col. ii. 16) for the repeal of Sabbatical ordinances; and to the great laws (Matt. xvi. 19; John xiv. 26; Matt. xxviii. 20) of plenary authority given by Christ Himself to His Apostles.
[5] 1 Cor. 7, 8, and margin of Revised Version; also Acts xii. 4 and 12.
[6] Acts ii. 1, xx. 16; 1 Cor. xvi. 8.
[7] In Eusebius, *Hist. Eccl.*, v. 24.
[8] Ἀρραδιούργητον ἄγομεν τὴν ἡμέραν.
[9] Στοιχεῖα.
[10] [See vol. vii. p. 500, n. 6. Great confusions adhere to this name.]
[11] Δυο θυγατέρες αὐτοῦ γεγηρακυῖαι παρθένοι.
[12] Πολιτευσαμένη. [Phil. iii. 20, *Greek*.]
[13] Πέταλον. [Probably the ornament of the high priest; Exod. xxviii. 35, 36.]

martyr, who rests at Smyrna. Why should I speak of Sagaris, bishop and martyr, who rests at Laodicea? of the blessed Papirius, moreover? and of Melito the eunuch,[1] who performed all his actions under the influence of the Holy Spirit, and lies at Sardis, awaiting the visitation[2] from heaven, when he shall rise again from the dead? These all kept the passover on the fourteenth day *of the month*, in accordance with the Gospel, without ever deviating from it, but keeping to the rule of faith.

Moreover I also, Polycrates, who am the least of you all, in accordance with the tradition of my relatives, some of whom I have succeeded — seven of my relatives were bishops, and I am the eighth, and my relatives always observed the day when the people put away[3] the leaven — I

myself, brethren, I say, who am sixty-five years old in the Lord, and have fallen in with the brethren in all parts of the world, and have read through all Holy Scripture, am not frightened at the things which are said to terrify us. For those who are greater than I have said, "We ought to obey God rather than men."[4] . . .

I might also have made mention of the bishops associated with me, whom it was your own desire to have called together by me, and I called them together: whose names, if I were to write them down, would amount to a great number. These *bishops*, on coming to see me, unworthy as I am,[5] signified their united approval of the letter, knowing that I wore *these* grey hairs not in vain, but have always regulated my conduct in *obedience* to the Lord Jesus.

THEOPHILUS, BISHOP OF CÆSAREA IN PALESTINE.

[A.D. 180.] When Eusebius says that the churches of "all Asia" concurred in the Ephesine use concerning the Paschal, he evidently means Asia Minor, as in the Scriptures and elsewhere.[6] Throughout "the rest of the world," he testifies, however, that such was not the use. The Pal estinian bishops, after the Jewish downfall, seem to have been the first to comprehend the propriety of adopting the more Catholic usage; and our author presided over a council in Cæsarea, of which he was bishop, assisted by Narcissus, bishop of Jerusalem, with Cassius of Tyre and Clarus of Ptolemais, which confirmed it. It is to be noted, that Alexandria is cited by Theophilus as authority for this custom; and it is not quite correct to say that the *Western* usage prevailed at Nicæa, for it was the general use, save only in Asia Minor and churches which were colonies of the same. This fact has been overlooked, and is very important, in history.

FROM HIS EPISTLE ON THE QUESTION OF THE PASSOVER, WRITTEN IN THE NAME OF THE SYNOD OF CÆSAREA.[7]

ENDEAVOUR also to send abroad copies of our epistle among all the churches, so that those who easily deceive their own souls may not be able to lay the blame on us. We would have you know, too, that in Alexandria[8] also they observe *the festival* on the same day as ourselves. For the *Paschal* letters are sent from us to them, and from them to us: so that we observe the holy day in unison and together.

SERAPION,[9] BISHOP OF ANTIOCH.

[A.D. *circa* 190–200–211.] He was the eighth bishop of Antioch, a diligent writer and exemplary pastor. Little as we have of his remains, Lardner shows how very useful is that little. (1) He testifies to the Apostles as delivering the words of Christ Himself; (2) to the jealousy of the early Christians in sifting inspired writings from those of no authority as Scriptures; (3) to their methods, as in the case of the pseudo-gospel of Peter; and (4) to the utterly apocryphal

---

[1] [i.e., spiritually; embracing a chaste celibacy in deference to Christ. Matt. xix. 12.]
[2] Ἐπισκοπην.
[3] Ἡρυυε. Some read ηρτυε.
[4] Acts v. 29.
[5] Τον μικρον.
[6] See (Polycrates) p. 773, *supra*, and Eusebius, *H. E.*, book v. cap. xxiii., etc, pp. 222-226
[7] In Eusebius, *Hist. Eccl.*, v. 25.
[8] [Note, the authority of Alexandria is quoted, not that of Rome.]
[9] Westcott, *Canon*, p. 444. Lardner, *Credib.*, ii. 264, 417.

character of that book, which Grabe and others suppose to be the work of Leucius, a noted forger and falsifier. It had never been heard of in the great See of Antioch, and this famous bishop could only get sight of it by fishing it out of the dirty pool of the Docetæ.

I.

FROM THE EPISTLE TO CARICUS AND PONTICUS.[1]

THAT ye may see also that the proceedings of this lying confederacy,[2] to which is given the name of New Prophecy, is abominated among the whole brotherhood throughout the world, I have sent you letters of the most blessed Claudius Apollinarius, who was made bishop of Hierapolis in Asia.

II.

FROM THE BOOK CONCERNING THE GOSPEL OF PETER.[3]

For we, brethren, receive both Peter and the rest of the apostles as Christ *Himself*. But those writings which are falsely inscribed with their name,[4] we as experienced persons reject, knowing that no such writings have been handed down to us.[5] When, indeed, I came to see you, I supposed that all were in accord with the orthodox faith; and, although I had not read through the Gospel inscribed with the name of Peter which was brought forward by them, I said: If this is the only thing which threatens[6] to produce ill-feeling among you, let it be read. But, now that I have learnt from what has been told me that their mind was secretly cherishing some heresy,[7] I will make all haste to come to you again. Expect me therefore, brethren, shortly. Moreover, brethren, we, having discovered to what kind of heresy Marcion adhered, and seen how he contradicted himself, not understanding of what he was speaking, as you will gather from what has been written to you[8] — for, having borrowed this said Gospel from those who were familiar with it from constant perusal, namely from the successors of those who were his leaders *in the heresy*, whom we call Docetæ (for most of the opinions held by him are derived from their teaching), we were able to read it through; and while we found most of its contents to agree with the orthodox account of the Saviour, we found some things inconsistent with that, and these we have set down below for your inspection.

APOLLONIUS.[9]

[A.D. 211.] He was a most eloquent man, according to St. Jerome; and his writings against Montanism were so forcible as to call forth Tertullian himself, to confute him, if possible. He flourished under Commodus and Severus, and probably until the times of Caracalla. He bears testimony to the existence of a canon of Scripture,[10] and to its inspired authority as the rule of faith and practice; and he witnesses, by citation, to the Gospel of St. Matthew. The Revelation of St. John also, according to Eusebius, was employed by him in his works; and he preserves a tradition that our Lord bade the Apostles continue in Jerusalem for the space of twelve years. We cannot affirm that he was invested with any office in the Church.

CONCERNING MONTANISM.[11]

I.

BUT who is this new teacher? His works and teaching inform *us*. This is he who taught the dissolution of marriage; who inculcated fasting; who called Peruga and Tymius, small towns of Phrygia, Jerusalem, because he wished to collect thither people from all parts; who set up exactors of money; who craftily contrives the taking of gifts under the name of voluntary offerings; who grants stipends to those who publish abroad his doctrine, that by means of gluttony the teaching of the doctrine may prevail.

II.

We declare to you, then, that these first prophetesses, as soon as they were filled with the spirit, left their husbands. Of what falsehood, then, were they guilty in calling Prisca a maiden!

---

1 In Eusebius, *Hist. Eccl.*, v. 19.
2 Ψευδοῦς τάξεως.
3 In Eusebius, *Hist. Eccl.*, v. 12.
4 The reading of Migne, ὀνόματι, is adopted instead of ὀνόματα.
5 Τὰ τοιαῦτα οὐ παρελάβομεν.
6 Δοκοῦν.
7 Αἱρέσει τινὶ ὁ νοῦς αὐτῶν ἐνεφώλευεν.
8 The construction is not again resumed.
9 Routh, *Rel. Sac.*, vol. i. pp. 465–485.
10 Westcott, *Canon*, p. 433.
11 In Eusebius, *Hist. Eccl.*, v. 18.

Do you not think that all Scripture forbids a prophet to receive gifts and money? When, therefore, I see that the prophetess has received gold and silver and expensive articles of dress, how can I avoid treating her with disapproval?

III.

Moreover, Themison also, who was clothed in a garb of plausible [1] covetousness, who declined to bear the sign of confessorship, but by a large sum of money put away from him the chains *of martyrdom*, although after such conduct it was his duty to conduct himself with humility, yet had the hardihood to boast that he was a martyr, and, in imitation of the apostle, to compose a general epistle, in which he attempted to in-struct [2] in the elements of the faith those who had believed to better purpose than he, and de-fended the doctrines of the new-fangled teach-ing,[3] and moreover uttered blasphemy against the Lord and the apostles and the holy Church.

IV.

But, not to dwell further on these matters, let the prophetess tell us concerning Alexander, who calls himself a martyr, with whom she joins in banqueting ; who himself also is worshipped by many ; [4] whose robberies and other deeds of daring, for which he has been punished, it is not necessary for us to speak of, since the treasury [5] has him in keeping. Which of them, then, con-dones the sins of the other? The prophet the robberies of the martyr, or the martyr the covet-ousness of the prophet? For whereas the Lord has said, " Provide not gold, nor silver, nor two coats *a-piece*," [6] these men have, on the flat con-trary, transgressed the command by the acquisi-tion of these forbidden things. For we shall show that those who are called among them prophets and martyrs obtain money not only from the rich, but also from the poor, from orphans

and widows. And if they are confident *that they are right* in so doing, let them stand *forward* and discuss *the point*, in order that, if they be refuted, they may cease for the future so to trans-gress. For the fruits of the prophet must needs be brought to the test : for " from its fruit is the tree known." [7] But that those that desire it may become acquainted with what relates to Alexan-der, he was condemned by Æmilius Frontinus, proconsul at Ephesus, not on account of the name *of Christ*, but for the daring robberies he committed when he was already a transgressor.[8] Afterwards, when he had spoken falsely of the name of the Lord, he was released, having de-ceived the faithful there ; [9] and *even the brethren of* his own district,[10] from which he came, did not receive him, because he was a robber. Thus, those who wish to learn what he is, have the public treasury of Asia to go to. And yet the prophet, although he spent many years with him, knows *forsooth* nothing about him ! By convict-ing " him," we by his means clearly convict of mis-representation [11] the prophet likewise. We are able to prove the like in the case of many *others* besides. And if they are confident *of their in-nocence*, let them abide the test.

V.

If they deny that their prophets have taken gifts, let them confess thus much, that if they be convicted of having taken them, they are not prophets ; and we will adduce ten thousand proofs *that they have*. It is proper, too, that all the fruits of a prophet should be examined. Tell me : does a prophet dye *his hair* ? Does a prophet use stibium *on his eyes* ? Is a prophet fond of dress? Does a prophet play at gaming-tables and dice? Does a prophet lend money on in-terest? [12] Let them confess whether these things are allowable or not. For my part, I will prove that these practices have occurred among them.

PANTÆNUS,[13] THE ALEXANDRIAN PHILOSOPHER.

[A.D. 182–192–212.] The world owes more to Pantænus than to all the other Stoics put together. His mind discovered that true philosophy is found, not in the Porch, but in Nazareth, in Gethsemane, in Gabbatha, in Golgotha ; and he set himself to make it known to the world. We are already acquainted with the great master of Clement,[14] " the Sicilian bee," that forsook

---

[1] ἀξιόπιστον.
[2] κατηχεῖν.
[3] συναγωνίζεσθαι τοῖς τῆς καινοφωνίας λόγοις.
[4] Or, " whom many of them (the Montanists — reading αὐτῶν for αὐτῷ, worship."
[5] ὀπισθόδομος, a chamber at the back of the temple of Minerva, in which public money was kept.
[6] Matt. x. 9.
[7] Matt. xii. 33.
[8] παραβάτης, here meaning *an apostate*.
[9] This is explained by Rufinus to mean: " When certain breth-

ren who had influence with the judge interceded for him, he pretended that he was suffering for the name of Christ, and by this means he was released."
[10] παροικία.
[11] ὑπόστασιν, from ὑφίστημι, probably in the sense of *substitut-ing one thing for another*.
[12] ταβλαις καὶ κυβοις.
[13] Vol. ii. p. 342; Westcott, *Canon*, pp. 90, 381; Routh, *R. S.*, vol. i. pp. 375-379.
[14] Vol. ii. pp. 165, etc., and p. 301, note 9; also p. 342, Elucid. II., this series.

the flowers of Enna, to enrich Alexandria with what is "sweeter than honey and the honey-comb;" and we remember that he became a zealous missionary to the Oriental Ethiopia, and found there the traces of St. Matthias' labours, and those also of St. Bartholomew. From this mission he seems to have returned about A.D. 192. Possibly he was master of the Alexandrian school before he went to India, and came back to his chair when that mission was finished. There he sat till about A.D. 212, and under him this Christian academy became famous. It had existed as a catechetical school from the Apostles' time, according to St. Jerome. I have elsewhere noted some reasons for supposing that its founder may have been Apollos.[1] All the learning of Christendom may be traced to this source; and blessed be the name of one of whom all we know is ennobling to the Church, and whose unselfish career was a track of light "shining more and more unto the perfect day."

I.[2]

"IN the sun hath He set His tent."[3] Some affirm that the reference is to the Lord's body, which He Himself places in the sun:[4] Hermogenes, for instance. As to His body, some say it is His tent, others the Church of the faithful. But our Pantænus said: "The language employed by prophecy is for the most part indefinite, the present tense being used for the future, and again the present for the past."

II.[5]

This mode of speaking Saint Dionysius the Areopagite declares to be used in Scripture to denote predeterminations and expressions of the divine will.[6] In like manner also the followers of Pantænus,[7] who became the preceptor of the great Clement the Stromatist, affirm that they are commonly used in Scripture for expressions of the divine will. Accordingly, when asked by some who prided themselves on the outside learning,[8] in what way the Christians supposed God to become acquainted with the universe,[9] their own opinion being that He obtains His knowledge of it *in different ways*, — of things falling within the province of the understanding by means of the understanding, and of those within the region of the senses by means of the senses, — they replied: "Neither *does He gain acquaintance with* sensible things by the senses, nor with things within the sphere of the understanding by the understanding: for it is not possible that He who is above all existing things should apprehend them by means of existing things. We assert, on the contrary, that He is acquainted with existing things as the products of His own volition."[10] They added, by way of showing the reasonableness of their view: "If He has made all things by an act of His will (and no argument will be adduced to gainsay this), and if it is ever a matter of piety and rectitude to say that God is acquainted with His own will, and if He has voluntarily made every several thing that has come into existence, then surely God must be acquainted with all existing things as the products of His own will, seeing that it was in the exercise of that will that He made them."

PSEUD–IRENÆUS.

[A.D. 177.] This letter should have been made a preface to the works of Irenæus, or at least an appendix. It is worthy of his great name; "the finest thing of the kind in all antiquity," says Lardner. Critics of no mean name have credited it to Irenæus; but, as this cannot be proved, I have accordingly marked it as a *pseudonym*. The same writer condenses the arguments of others, on which he decides to adhere to the later chronology of Eusebius, assigning its date to the seventeenth year of Marcus Aurelius.[11] Naturally humane and comparatively gentle in other respects he was; but Stoicism, as well as heathenism, showed what it could exact of such a character in maintenance of the popular and imperial superstitions. Terrible is the summary of

---

[1] Vol. vi. p. 236. St. Luke, in the company of Apollos, may have met a *catechumen* of his in that "excellent Theophilus" of his writings (St. Luke i. 4, Greek), whose history shows that catechetical teaching was already part of the Christian system.

[2] In *Extracts from the Prophets*, written probably by Theodotus, and collected by Clement of Alexandria or some other writer.

[3] Ps. xix. 4.

[4] Φασὶ τὸ σῶμα τοῦ Κυρίου ἐν τῷ ἡλίῳ αὐτὸν ἀποτίθεσθαι.

[5] In the Scholia of Maximus on St. Gregory the Divine.

[6] Θελήματα.

[7] Οἱ περὶ Πάνταινον. [Vol. ii. pp. 165-167, this series.]

[8] Τὴν ἔξω παίδευσιν.

[9] Τὰ ὄντα.

[10] 'Ως ἴδια θελήματα.

[11] Vol. iv. p. 125, this series. Compare Lightfoot, *Ap. Fathers*, part ii. vol. i. pp. 499, etc., 510, etc.

Lightfoot concerning the barbarities of this darling of the "philosophers:" "It is a plain fact, that Christian blood flowed more freely under M. Aurelius than at any time previously during the half century since the Bithynian martyrdoms under Trajan, or was yet to flow at any time during the decades which would elapse before the Severian persecution. These persecutions extend throughout his reign: they were fierce and deliberate; aggravated, at least in some cases, by cruel tortures. They had the emperor's direct personal sanction. They break out in all parts of the empire, — in Rome, in Asia Minor, in Gaul, in Africa, possibly also in Byzantium."

Bishop Lightfoot accounts for the fact, that, in spite of this sanguinary character of the period, little complaint is heard from the suffering Church, by a simple statement which is honourable to Aurelius as a Roman and an emperor. He was such a contrast to the Neros and Caligulas, that the wretched Romans loved him as a father; to reproach him was, therefore, poor policy for Christians. They would have been answered, practically: "If so good a sovereign finds it necessary to punish you, the fault is your own; you have only to be as we are, and he will treat you as well as he does us."

Of this awful outbreak in Lyons and Vienne, says Lightfoot:[1] "The persecution was wholesale, so that it was not safe for any Christian to appear out of doors. No difference of age or sex was made. The prisoners were put to the most cruel tortures. All the elements of power combined to crush the brethren."

To forbear threatenings, to revile not again, to conquer through patient suffering, to persevere, "looking unto Jesus," and to be silent, like Him, before their murderers, was therefore the world-wide conduct of the saints. This golden letter shows what they were called to endure, and how they glorified Christ by their deaths, from the utmost Orient to the extreme limits of the West.

THE LETTER OF THE CHURCHES OF VIENNA AND LUGDUNUM TO THE CHURCHES OF ASIA AND PHRYGIA.[2]

It began thus: — "The servants of Christ who sojourn in Vienna and Lugdunum of Gaul to the brethren throughout Asia and Phrygia, who have the same faith and hope of redemption as ourselves, peace, grace, and glory from God the Father, and from Christ Jesus our Lord."

After some further preliminary remarks the letter proceeds: — "The greatness of the tribulation in this region, and the exceeding anger of the heathen *nations* against the saints, and the sufferings which the blessed Witnesses[3] endured, neither are we competent to describe accurately, nor indeed is it possible to detail them in writing. For with all his strength did the adversary assail us, even then giving a foretaste of his activity among us which is to be without restraint; and he had recourse to every means, accustoming his own subjects and exercising them beforehand against the servants of God, so that not only were we excluded from houses,[4] baths, and the forum, but a universal prohibition was laid

against any one of us appearing in any place whatsoever. But the grace of God acted as our general against him. It rescued the weak; it arrayed against him men like firm pillars, who could through patience bear up against the whole force of the assaults of the wicked one. These came to close quarters with him, enduring every form of reproach and torture; and, making light of grievous trials, they hastened on to Christ, showing in reality that the 'sufferings of the present time are not worthy to be compared with the glory that is to be revealed in us.'[5] And first they nobly endured the evils which were heaped on them by the populace, — namely, hootings and blows, draggings, plunderings, stonings, and confinements,[6] and everything that an infuriated mob is wont to perpetrate against those whom they deem bitter enemies. And at length, being brought to the forum by the tribune of the soldiers, and the magistrates that had charge of the city, they were examined in presence of the whole multitude; and having

---

[1] *Ap. Fathers*, part ii. vol. i. p. 499.

[2] This letter has come down to us in fragments quoted by Eusebius. We have used the translation of Lord Hailes as the basis of ours. [Compare Vol. i. p. 309, this series, and note the adhesion of the primitive Gallican Church to the East, — to the land of Polycarp and Pothinus. Concerning Pothinus, see Routh, *Rel. Sac.*, i. p. 328, and the correction by Lightfoot, *Ap. F.*, part ii. vol i. p. 430, etc. The Gallican Church may yet arise from the dust, and restore the primitive primacy of Lyons. God grant it!]

[3] We have translated μάρτυρες "witnesses" and μαρτυρία "testimony" throughout.

[4] Houses of friends and relatives. Olshausen takes them to be public buildings.

[5] Rom. viii. 18. [On quotations from Scripture, etc., see Westcott, *Canon*, p. 378, ed. 1855.]

[6] By "confinements" in this passage evidently is meant that the populace prevented them from resorting to public places, and thus shut them up in their own houses.

confessed, they were shut up in prison until the arrival of the governor.

"After this, when they were brought before the governor, and when he displayed a spirit of savage hostility to us, Vettius Epagathus, one of the brethren, interposed. For he was a man who had contained the full measure of love towards God and his neighbours. His mode of life had been so strict, that though he was a young man, he deserved to be described in the words used in regard to the elderly Zacharias : 'He had walked therefore in all the commandments and ordinances of the Lord blameless.'[1] He was also eager to serve his neighbour in any way, he was very zealous for God, and he was fervent in spirit. Such being the character of the man, he could not bear that judgment should be thus unreasonably passed against us, but was moved with indignation, and requested that he himself should be heard in defence of his brethren, undertaking to prove that there is nothing ungodly or impious amongst us. On this, those who were round the judgment-seat cried out against him, for he was a man of distinction ; and the governor, not for a moment listening to the just request thus made to him, merely asked him if he himself were a Christian. And on his confessing in the clearest voice that he was, he also was taken up into the number of the Witnesses, receiving the appellation of the Advocate of the Christians,[2] and having himself the Advocate, the Spirit,[3] more abundantly than Zacharias ; which he showed in the fulness[4] of his love, in that he had of his own good-will offered to lay down his own life in defence of the brethren. For he was and is a genuine disciple of Christ, 'following the Lamb whithersoever He goeth.'[5]

"After this the rest began to be distinguished,[6] for the proto-martyrs were decided and ready, and accomplished the confession of their testimony with all alacrity. But there appeared also those who were unprepared and unpractised, and who were still feeble, and unable to bear the tension of a great contest. Of these about ten in number proved abortions ; causing great grief and immeasurable sorrow amongst us, and damping the ardour of the rest who had not yet been apprehended. For these, although they suffered every kind of cruelty, remained nevertheless in the company of the Witnesses, and did not forsake them. But then the whole of us were greatly alarmed on account of our uncertainty as to confession, not because we feared the tortures inflicted, but because we looked to the end, and dreaded lest any one should fall away. Those who were worthy, however, were daily apprehended, filling up the number of the others : so that out of the two churches all the excellent, and those to whom the churches owed most of all their establishment and prosperity, were collected together in prison. Some heathen household slaves belonging to our people were also apprehended, since the governor had given orders publicly that all of us should be sought out. These, through the instigation of Satan, and through fear of the tortures which they saw the saints enduring, urged on also by the soldiers, falsely accused us of Thyestean banquets and Œdipodean connections, and other crimes which it is lawful for us neither to mention nor think of ; and, indeed, we shrink from believing that any such crimes have ever taken place among men. When the rumour of these accusations was spread abroad, all raged against us like wild beasts ; so that if any formerly were temperate in their conduct to us on account of relationship, they then became exceedingly indignant and exasperated against us. And thus was fulfilled that which was spoken by our Lord : 'The time shall come when every one who slayeth you shall think that he offereth service to God.'[7]

"Then at last the holy Witnesses suffered tortures beyond all description, Satan striving eagerly that some of the evil reports might be acknowledged by them.[8] But in an exceeding degree did the whole wrath of mob, general, and soldiers fall on Sanctus, a deacon from Vienna, and on Maturus, a newly-enlightened but noble combatant, and on Attalus, a native of Pergamus, who had always been the Pillar[9] and foundation of the church there, and on Blandina, through whom Christ showed that the things that to men appear mean and deformed and contemptible, are with God deemed worthy of great glory, on account of love to Him, — a love which is not a mere boastful appearance, but shows itself in the power which it exercises over the life. For while we were all afraid, and especially her mistress in the flesh, who was herself one of the combatants among the Witnesses, that she would not be able to make a bold confession on account of the weakness of her body, Blandina was filled with such power, that those who tortured her one after the other in every way from morning till evening were wearied and tired, confessing that they had been baffled, for they had no other torture they could apply to her ; and they were

---

[1] Luke i. 6.
[2] From the heathen judge.
[3] Luke i. 67.
[4] The writer refers to St. John's Gospel (xv. 13): "Greater love hath no man than this, that a man lay down his life for his friends."
[5] Rev. xiv. 4.
[6] This expression seems to refer to what took place in athletic combats. The athletes were tested before fighting, and those in every way qualified were permitted to fight, while the others were rejected. This testing, Valesius supposes, was called διάκρισις.

[7] John xvi. 2.
[8] The words here admit of two meanings: that something blasphemous might be uttered by them — such as speaking against Christ and swearing by Cæsar; or that some accusation against the Christians might be uttered by them — confirming, for instance, the reports of infanticide and incest prevalent against the Christians. The latter in this passage seems unquestionably to be the meaning.
[9] 1 Tim. iii. 15.

astonished that she remained in life, when her whole body was torn and opened up, and they gave their testimony [1] that one only of the modes of torture employed was sufficient to have deprived her of life, not to speak of so many excruciating inflictions. But the blessed woman, like a noble athlete, recovered her strength in the midst of the confession; and her declaration, 'I am a Christian, and there is no evil done amongst us,' brought her refreshment, and rest, and insensibility to all the sufferings inflicted on her.

"Sanctus also nobly endured all the excessive and *superhuman* [2] tortures which man could possibly devise against him; for the wicked hoped, on account of the continuance and greatness of the tortures, to hear him confess some of the unlawful practices. But he opposed them with such firmness that he did not tell them even his own name, nor that of his nation or city, nor if he were slave or free; but in answer to all these questions, he said in Latin, 'I am a Christian.' This was the confession he made repeatedly, instead of giving his name, his city, his race, and indeed in reply to every question that was put to him; and other language the heathens heard not from him. Hence arose in the minds of the governor and the torturers a determined resolution to subdue him; so that, when every other means failed, they at last fixed red-hot plates of brass to the most delicate parts of his body. And these indeed were burned, but he himself remained inflexible and unyielding, firm in his confession, being bedewed and strengthened by the heavenly fountain of the water of life which issues from the belly of Christ. [3] But his body bore witness to what had happened: for it was all wounds and weals, shrunk and torn up, and had lost externally the human shape. In him Christ suffering wrought great wonders, destroying the adversary, and showing for an example to the rest that there is nothing fearful where there is the Father's love, and nothing painful where there is Christ's glory. For the wicked after some days again tortured the Witness, thinking that, since his body was swollen and inflamed, if they were to apply the same tortures they would gain the victory over him, especially since the parts of his body could not bear to be touched by the hand, or that he would die in consequence of the tortures, and

thus inspire the rest with fear. Yet not only did no such occurrence take place in regard to him, but even, contrary to every expectation of man, his body unbent itself and became erect in the midst of the subsequent tortures, and resumed its former appearance and the use of its limbs, so that the second torture turned out through the grace of Christ a cure, not an affliction.

"Among those who had denied was a woman of the name of Biblias. The devil, thinking that he had already swallowed her, and wishing to damn her still more by making her accuse falsely, brought her forth to punishment, and employed force to constrain her, already feeble and spiritless, to utter accusations of atheism against us. But she, in the midst of the tortures, came again to a sound state of mind, and awoke as it were out of a deep sleep; for the temporary suffering reminded her of the eternal punishment in Gehenna, and she contradicted the accusers of Christians, saying, 'How can children be eaten by those who do not think it lawful to partake of the blood of even brute beasts?' And after this she confessed herself a Christian, and was added to the number of Witnesses.

"But when the tyrannical tortures were rendered by Christ of no avail through the patience of the blessed, the devil devised other contrivances — confinement in the darkest and most noisome cells of the prison, the stretching of the feet on the stocks, [4] even up to the fifth hole, and the other indignities which attendants stirred up by wrath and full of the devil are wont to inflict on the imprisoned. The consequence was, that very many were suffocated in prison, as many at least as the Lord, showing His glory, wished to depart in this way. For there were others who were tortured so bitterly, that it seemed impossible for them to survive even though they were to obtain every kind of attention; and yet they remained alive in prison, destitute indeed of care from man, but strengthened by the Lord, and invigorated both in body and soul, and they animated and consoled the rest. But the new converts who had been recently apprehended, and whose bodies had not previously been tortured, could not indure the confinement, but died in the prison.

"Now the blessed Pothinus, who had been entrusted with the service of the bishopric in Lugdunum, was also dragged before the judgment-seat. He was now upwards of ninety years of age, and exceedingly weak in body. Though he breathed with difficulty on account of the feebleness of the body, yet he was strengthened

---

[1] Heinichen construes differently. He makes the "torturers astonished that Blandina gave her testimony that one kind of torture was sufficient to deprive her of life." Perhaps the right construction is to make ὅτι mean "because" or "for:" "They were astonished at Blandina bearing her testimony, for one kind of torture was sufficient to have killed her."

[2] The words ὑπερβεβλημένως καὶ ὑπὲρ πάντα ἄνθρωπον naturally go with ὑπομένων, and therefore intimate that Sanctus' endurance was greater than human; but we doubt if this is intended by the writer.

[3] John vii. 38: "He that believeth on me, as the Scripture hath said, out of his bosom shall flow rivers of living water."

[4] The holes were placed in a line, so that the further the hole in which one leg was put from the hole in which the other leg was put, the more nearly would the two legs form a straight line, and the greater would be the pain.

by the eagerness of his spirit, on account of his earnest desire to bear his testimony. His body, indeed, was already dissolved through old age and disease, yet the life was preserved in him, that Christ might triumph through him. When he was brought by the soldiers to the judgment-seat, under a convoy of the magistrates of the city, and amid exclamations of every kind from the whole population, as if he himself were the Christ, he gave the good testimony. Being asked by the governor who was the God of the Christians, he said, ' If thou art worthy, thou shalt know.' Thereupon he was unmercifully dragged about, and endured many blows; for those who were near maltreated him in every way with their hands and feet, showing no respect for his age, while those at a distance hurled against him each one whatever came to hand, all of them believing that they would sin greatly and act impiously if they in any respect fell short in their insulting treatment of him. For they thought that in this way they would avenge their gods. And Pothinus, breathing with difficulty, was cast into prison, and two days after he expired.

"Upon this a grand dispensation [1] of God's providence took place, and the immeasurable mercy of Jesus was made manifest, — such an occurrence as but rarely happens among the brotherhood, yet one that does not fall short of the art of Christ. For those who in the first apprehension had denied, were imprisoned along with the others, and shared their hardships. Their denial, in fact, turned out at this time to be of no advantage to them. For while those who confessed what they really were, were imprisoned simply as Christians, no other accusation being brought against them, those who denied were detained as murderers and profligates. They, moreover, were doubly punished. For the confessors were lightened by the joy of their testimony and their hope in the promises, and by their love to Christ, and by the Father's Spirit. But the deniers were tormented greatly by their own consciences, so that when they were led forth their countenances could be distinguished among all the rest. For the confessors went forth joyous, with a mingling of glory and abundant grace in their looks, so that their chains lay like becoming ornaments around them, as around a bride adorned with golden fringes wrought with divers colours.[2] And they breathed at the same time the fragrance of Christ,[3] so that some even thought that they were anointed with this world's perfume. But the deniers were downcast, humbled, sad-looking, and weighed

down with every kind of disgrace. They were, moreover, reproached even by the heathens with being base and cowardly, and charged with the crime of murder; they had lost the altogether honourable, glorious, and life-giving appellation.[4] When the rest saw this, they were strengthened, and those who were apprehended confessed unhesitatingly, not allowing the reasoning of the devil to have even a place in their thoughts."

Eusebius omits something, saying that after a little the letter proceeded as follows : —

"After these things, then, their testimonies took every shape through the different ways in which they departed.[5] For, plaiting a crown from different colours and flowers of every kind, they presented it to the Father. It was right therefore that the noble athletes, after having endured divers contests and gained grand victories, should receive the great crown of incorruption.

"Maturus, therefore, and Sanctus, and Blandina, and Attalus were publicly[6] exposed to the wild beasts — that common spectacle of heathen barbarity; for a day was expressly assigned to fights with wild beasts on account of our people. And Maturus and Sanctus again endured every form of torture in the amphitheatre, as if they had had no suffering at all before. Or rather, like athletes who had overthrown their adversary several times,[7] and were now contending for the crown itself, again they endured the lashes[8] which were usual there; and they were dragged about by the wild beasts, and suffered every indignity which the maddened populace demanded in cries and exhortations proceeding from various parts of the amphitheatre. And last of all they were placed in the iron chair, on which their bodies were roasted, and they themselves were filled with the fumes of their own flesh. But the heathens did not stop even here, but became still more frantic in their desire to overcome the endurance of the Christians. But not even thus did they hear anything else from Sanctus than the utterance of the confession which he had been accustomed to make from the beginning. These, then, after life had lasted a long time throughout the great contest, were at last sacrificed,[9] after they alone had

---

[1] The dispensation is, that those who denied were not set free, but confined with the others; and that this harsh treatment and sad state of mind confirmed the resolution of those not yet apprehended to confess Christ. Various other explanations have been given, but this seems the most reasonable.

[2] Ps. xlv. 13.

[3] 2 Cor. ii. 15.

[4] Of Christian.

[5] We have adopted here an emendation of Routh's. The literal version of the common text is: "The testimonies of their departure were divided into every form."

[6] The Greek is εἰς τὸ δημόσιον, was led " to the public *building*" to the wild beasts. The public *building* is taken to be the amphitheatre.

[7] The words "several times" are represented in Greek by διὰ πλειόνων κλήρων, lit. "through several lots." When there were several athletes to contend, the pairs were determined by lot. After the first contest the victors were again formed into pairs by lot, until finally there should be but one pair left. See the process at the Olympic games described in Lucian Hermotimus, c. xi. p. 782.

[8] The bestiarii, before fighting with wild beasts, had to run the gauntlet.

[9] Rufinus translates *jugulati sunt*. Probably, "killed with the sword." The term may have been a technical one, being applied to the gladiators or bestiarii, whose death may have been looked on as a sacrifice to a god or a dead hero.

formed a spectacle to the world, throughout that day, instead of all the diversity which usually takes place in gladiatorial shows.

"Blandina [1] was hung up fastened to a stake, and exposed, as food to the wild beasts that were let loose against her; and through her presenting the spectacle of one suspended on something like a cross, and through her earnest prayers, she inspired the combatants with great eagerness: for in the combat they saw, by means of their sister, with their bodily eyes, Him who was crucified for them, that He might persuade those who trust in Him that every one that has suffered for the glory of Christ has eternal communion with the living God. When none of the wild beasts at that time touched her, she was taken down from the stake and conveyed back to prison. She was thus reserved for another contest, in order that, gaining the victory in many preparative conflicts, she might make the condemnation of the Crooked Serpent [2] unquestionable, and that she might encourage the brethren. For though she was an insignificant, weak, and despised woman, yet she was clothed with the great and invincible athlete Christ. On many occasions she had overpowered the adversary, and in the course of the contest had woven for herself the crown of incorruption.

"Attalus also was vehemently demanded by the mob, for he was a man of mark. He entered the lists a ready combatant on account of his good conscience, since he had been truly practised in the Christian discipline, and had always been a Witness of the truth among us. He was led round the amphitheatre, a tablet going before him, on which was written in Latin, 'This is Attalus the Christian;' and the people swelled with indignation against him. But the governor, learning that he was a Roman, ordered him to be taken back to prison and kept with the rest who were there, with regard to whom he had written to the Cæsar, and was now awaiting his determination.

"The intervening time did not prove barren or unfruitful to the Witnesses, but through their patient endurance the immeasurable love of Christ was made manifest. For through the living the dead were made alive; and the Witnesses conferred favours on those who were not Witnesses, and the Virgin Mother had much joy in receiving back alive those whom she had given up as dead abortions. For through the Witnesses the greater number of those who had denied returned, as it were, into their mother's womb, and were conceived again and re-quickened; and they learned to confess. And being now restored to life, and having their spirits

braced, they went up to the judgment-seat to be again questioned by the governor, while that God who wishes not the death of the sinner,[3] but mercifully calls to repentance, put sweetness into their souls. This new examination took place because the Cæsar had given orders that the Witnesses should be punished, but that if any denied they should be set free. And as now was commencing here the fair, which is attended by vast numbers of men assembling from all nations, he brought the blessed up to the judgment-seat, exhibiting them as a theatrical show and spectacle to the mobs. Wherefore also he again questioned them, and whoever appeared to have had the rights of Roman citizenship he beheaded, and the rest he sent to the wild beasts.

"Now Christ was greatly glorified in those who formerly denied; for, contrary to every expectation of the heathen, they confessed. For these were examined separately, under the belief that they were to be set free; but confessing, they were added to the number of the Witnesses. But there were also some who remained without; namely, those who had no trace of faith, and no perception of the marriage garment,[4] nor notion of the fear of God, but through their conduct caused evil reports of our way of life, that is, sons of perdition. But all the rest were added to the Church.

"Present at the examination of these was one Alexander, a native of Phrygia, a physician by profession. He had lived for many years in Gaul, and had become well known to all for his love to God and his boldness in proclaiming the truth, for he was not without a share of apostolic grace. He stood near the judgment-seat, and, urging by signs those who had denied to confess, he looked to those who stood round the judgment-seat like one in travail. But the mobs, enraged that those who had formerly denied should now confess, cried out against Alexander as if he were the cause of this change. Then the governor summoned him before him, and inquired of him who he was; and when Alexander said he was a Christian, the governor burst into a passion, and condemned him to the wild beasts. And on the next day he entered the amphitheatre along with Attalus; for the governor, wishing to gratify the mob, again exposed Attalus to the wild beasts. These two, after being tortured in the amphitheatre with all the instruments devised for that purpose, and having undergone an exceedingly severe contest, at last were themselves sacrificed. Alexander uttered

---

[1] Blandina was a slave: hence the mode of punishment. On this matter see Lipsius, *De Cruce*. [And my note, p. 784.]
[2] Lord Hailes remarks that this alludes to Isa. xxvii. 1.

[3] Ezek. xxxiii. 11.
[4] Heinichen renders " the bride's garment," and explains in the following manner. The bride is the Church, the garment Christ; and the sons of perdition had no idea what garment the Church of Christ should wear, had no idea that they should be clothed with Christ, and be filled with His Spirit. It is generally taken to be the marriage garment of Matt. xxii. 12.

no groan or murmur of any kind, but conversed in his heart with God; but Attalus, when he was placed on the iron chair, and all the parts of his body were burning, and when the fumes from his body were borne aloft, said to the multitude in Latin, 'Lo! this which ye do is eating men. But as for us, we neither eat men nor practise any other wickedness.' And being asked what name God has, he answered, 'God has not a name as men have.'

"After all these, on the last day of the gladiatorial shows, Blandina was again brought in along with Ponticus, a boy of about fifteen years of age. These two had been taken daily to the amphitheatre to see the tortures which the rest endured, and force was used to compel them to swear by the idols of the heathen; but on account of their remaining stedfast, and setting all their devices at nought, the multitude were furious against them, so as neither to pity the tender years of the boy nor to respect the sex of the woman. Accordingly they exposed them to every terror, and inflicted on them every torture, repeatedly trying to compel them to swear. But they failed in effecting this; for Ponticus, encouraged by his sister,[1] so plainly indeed that even the heathens saw that it was she that encouraged and confirmed him, after enduring nobly every kind of torture, gave up the ghost; while the blessed Blandina, last of all, after having like a noble mother encouraged her children, and sent them on before her victorious to the King, trod the same path of conflict which her children had trod, hastening on to them with joy and exultation at her departure, not as one thrown to the wild beasts, but as one invited to a marriage supper. And after she had been scourged and exposed to the wild beasts, and roasted in the iron chair, she was at last enclosed in a net and cast before a bull. And after having been well tossed by the bull, though without having any feeling of what was happening to her, through her hope and firm hold of what had been entrusted to her and her converse with Christ, she also was sacrificed, the heathens themselves acknowledging that never among them did woman endure so many and such fearful tortures.

"Yet not even thus was their madness and their savage hatred to the saints satiated. For wild and barbarous tribes, when excited by the Wild Beast, with difficulty ceased from their rage, and their insulting conduct found another and peculiar subject in the bodies of the Witnesses. For they felt no shame that they had been overcome, for they were not possessed of human reason; but their defeat only the more inflamed their rage, and governor and people, like a wild beast, showed a like unjust hatred of us, that the Scripture might be fulfilled, 'He that is unjust, let him be unjust still; and he that is righteous, let him be righteous still.'[2] For they threw to the dogs those who had been suffocated in prison, carefully watching them day and night, lest any one should receive burial from us. They then laid out the mangled remains left by the wild beasts, and the scorched remains left by the fire, and the heads of the rest along with their trunks, and in like manner for many days watched them lying unburied with a military guard. There were some who raged and gnashed their teeth at them, seeking to get from them further vengeance. Others derided and insulted them, at the same time magnifying their own idols, and ascribing to them the punishment inflicted on the Christians. There were persons also of a milder disposition, who to some extent seemed to sympathize; yet they also frequently upbraided, saying, 'Where now is their God, and what good have they got from that religion which they chose in preference to their life?' Such was the diversity which characterized the conduct of the heathens. But our state was one of deep sorrow that we could not bury the bodies. For night aided us not in this matter; money failed to persuade, and entreaty did not shame them into compliance; but they kept up the watch in every way, as if they were to gain some great advantage from the bodies of the Christians not obtaining burial.

Something is omitted. The letter then goes on:—

"The bodies of the Witnesses, after having been maltreated in every way, and exposed in the open air for six days, were burned, reduced to ashes, and swept by the wicked into the river Rhone, which flows past, in order that not even a vestige of them might be visible on earth. And these things they did, as if they had been able to overcome God, and deprive them of their second birth,[3] in order, as they said, that 'they may not have hope in a resurrection, trusting to which they introduce some strange and new mode of worship, and despise dangers, and go readily and with joy to death. Now let us see if they will rise again, and if their God can help them, and rescue them out of our hands.'"

Eusebius here breaks off his series of continuous extracts, but he makes a few more for special purposes. The first is the account which the churches gave of the character of the Witnesses:—

"Who also were to such an extent zealous

---

[1] She may have been his sister by birth, as some have supposed, but the term "sister" would have been applied had she been connected by no other tie than that of a common faith.

[2] Rev. xxii. 11. Lardner thinks the passage is quoted from Dan. xii. 10. *Credib.*, part ii. c. 16.
[3] παλιγγενεσία. The term refers here to the new state of affairs at the end of the world.

followers and imitators of Christ, who, being in the shape of God, thought it not an object of desire to be treated like God ; [1] that though they were in such glory, and had borne their testimony not once, nor twice, but often, and had been again taken back to prison after exposure to the wild beasts, and bore about with them the marks of the burnings and bruises and wounds all over their bodies, yet did they neither proclaim themselves Witnesses, nor indeed did they permit us to address them by this name ; but if any one of us on any occasion, either by letter or in conversation, called them Witnesses, they rebuked him sharply. For they willingly gave the title of Witness to Christ, 'the faithful and true Witness,' [2] and first-born from the dead, and the leader to the divine life. And they reminded us of those Witnesses who had already departed, and said : 'These indeed are now Witnesses, whom Christ has vouchsafed to take up to Himself in the very act of confession, thus putting His seal upon their testimony through their departure. But we are mean and humble confessors.' And with tears they besought the brethren that earnest prayers might be made for their being perfected. They in reality did all that is implied in the term 'testimony,' acting with great boldness towards all the heathen ; and their nobleness they made manifest through their patience, and fearlessness, and intrepidity. But the title of Witness, as implying some superiority to their brethren, [3] they refused, being filled with the fear of God."

After a little they say : —

"They humbled themselves [4] under the powerful hand by which they are now highly exalted. Then they pleaded for all, [5] but accused none ;

they absolved all, they bound none ; and they prayed for those who inflicted the tortures, even as Stephen the perfect Witness, 'Lord, lay not this sin to their charge.' [6] But if he prayed for those who stoned him, how much more for the brethren ! "

After other things, again they say : —

" For they had this very great conflict with him, *the devil*, on account of their genuine love, in order that the Beast being choked, might vomit forth those whom he thought he had already swallowed. For they assumed no airs of superiority over the fallen, but with those things in which they themselves abounded they aided the needy, displaying towards them the compassion of a mother. And pouring out many tears for them to the Father, they begged life ; [7] and He gave it to them, and they shared it with their neighbours. And departing victorious over all to God, having always loved peace, and having recommended peace to us, in peace they went to God, leaving no sorrow to their Mother, nor division and dissension to their brethren, but joy and peace, and concord and love."

"The same writing of the fore-mentioned martyrs," says Eusebius, "contains a story worth remembrance.

" For there was one of them of the name of Alcibiades, who lived an exceedingly austere life, confining his diet to bread and water, and partaking of nothing else whatsoever. He tried to continue this mode of life in prison ; but it was revealed to Attalus after the first conflict which he underwent in the amphitheatre that Alcibiades was not pursuing the right course in refusing to use the creatures of God, and in leaving an example which might be a stumbling-block to others. And Alcibiades was persuaded, and partook freely of all kinds of food, and thanked God. For they were not without the oversight of the grace of God, but the Holy Spirit was their counsellor."

---

[1] Phil. ii. 6.
[2] Rev. i. 5 and iii. 14.
[3] The Greek is τὴν πρὸς τοὺς ἀδελφοὺς τῶν μαρτύρων προσηγορίαν, generally translated, "offered to them by their brethren."
[4] 1 Pet. v. 6.
[5] The Greek is, πᾶσι μὲν ἀπελογοῦντο. Rufinus translated, "Placabant omnes, neminem accusabant." Valesius thought that the words ought to be translated, "They rendered an account of their faith to all;" or, "They defended themselves before all." Heinichen has justified the translation in the text by an appeal to a passage in Eusebius, *Hist. Eccl.*, iv. 15.

[6] Acts vii. 60.
[7] Ps. xx. 4.

NOTE BY THE AMERICAN EDITOR.

A FRENCH writer has remarked, "Ce n'est pas Spartacus qui a supprimé l'esclavage ; c'est bien plutôt Blandine."

ELUCIDATION

(In every succession, p. 764.)

HERE our author mentions that he noted the succession of Bishops at Rome, but he gives his list with no remark about Rome in particular. He adds that "in every succession and in every city (i.e., in every See) a primitive accordance with the law and the Gospel is maintained." How can our excellent Lightfoot[1] give it a colour wholly gratuitous in these words: "He interested himself in the succession of the Roman See, *intent, like Irenæus* in the next generation, on showing the permanence of the orthodox tradition, through the continuity of the Roman episcopate." Irenæus, who, above all the Westerns, is identified with the Orient!

Where is the evidence of any such idea or "intent"? As for Irenæus, his testimony has been sufficiently illustrated before, with proof that his words have not the slightest reference to the continuity of the Roman more than any other See, save only as the influx of visitors from other Sees helped to give it orthodoxy by their concurrent testimony.[2]

NOTE.

IT may be worth while to state here, that I have uniformly (mistakes excepted) put my chronological statements, at the head of introductions, into brackets, so as to make the reader sure that the Edinburgh edition is not to be responsible for them. Some have inferred, therefore, that what follows is from the Edinburgh; but I think my modes of expression sufficient, generally, to guard against misconception. Notes (like this) are sometimes marked, "By the American Editor," when I have feared a misleading ambiguity. Otherwise, I have been unguarded. All the introductions in these "Remains" are mine, save the prefatory paragraphs of the translator on pp. 747, 748. Annotations on my own material are not bracketed. The very large amount of work bestowed upon this edition can only be known by comparison with the Edinburgh. In several instances of delicate criticism I have obtained valuable aid from my beloved friend, F. P. NASH, Esq., of Hobart College, especially in questions of the low Latin or ambiguous Greek.

A. C. C.

---

[1] *Ap. Fathers*, part ii. vol. i. p. 435; and the same laxity, p. 384, coincident with his theory as to a *virtual* post-Apostolic development of episcopacy.

[2] Compare vol. i. pp. 415, 460, and vol. v. Elucid. VI.; also Elucid. XI. pp. 157-159, this series.

INDEXES

TESTAMENTS OF THE TWELVE PATRIARCHS AND EXCERPTS OF THEODOTUS

INDEX OF SUBJECTS

TESTAMENTS OF THE TWELVE PATRIARCHS AND EXCERPTS OF THEODOTUS

INDEX OF TEXTS

INDEX OF SUBJECTS

correct views of God, 231; denied by Simon Magus, 234; asserted by Peter, 286.

Sound mind, a, in a sound body, 229.

Spies in the enemy's camp, 236.

Stans, Simon Magus so called, 96, 99, 100, 233.

Stars, the motions of, 171.

Study, diligence in, recommended, 122, 152.

Submission, 292.

Sufferings, sin the cause of, 137, 143; salutary, 137; different effects of, upon heathens and Christians, 159.

Suggestions of the old Serpent, 147–149.

Sun, moon, and stars, motions of, 177; ministers of good and evil, 177.

Supper, the, of the gods, 202, 203.

Susanna, conduct of, 64.

Susidæ, customs of the, 188.

Swine, casting pearls before, 117.

Sword, not peace, but a, 153, 288.

Syro-Phœnician woman, the story of, amplified, 232.

Tactics, the, of Peter against Simon Magus, 236.

Teaching, advice about, 58; of Christ, 247.

Temple to be destroyed, 94.

Temptation, the, of Christ, 142, 274.

Ten commandments, the, and the ten plagues of Egypt, 128.

Ten pairs, the, 130.

Thanks due to God, 150.

Thetis, 197; and Peleus, Prometheus, Achilles, and Polyxena, 265.

Things corruptible and temporary made by the incorruptible and eternal, 122.

Thomas, address of, 93.

Thorn, no rose without its, 174.

Thysbe, 199.

Time of making the world, 174.

Tow smeared with pitch, 185.

Tower of Babel, 141.

Traditions from our fathers, are they to be followed? 253.

Transformation, a strange, wrought by Simon Magus, 206, 343, 344.

Tree of life, oil from the, 89.

Trick, the, of Clement upon Appion, 257.

Tripolis, the disciples at, 156; departure from, 157; ordination at, 156; Peter at, 270.

Truth, the, being conquered by, 209; error cannot stand with, 107; not the property of all, 123; self-evidence of, 123; veiled with love, 129; cannot be found by man left to himself, 230; vain search of philosophers for, 230; taught by the prophets, 230; test of, 247; and custom, 253.

Tumult, raised against the apostles, 94; is stilled by Gamaliel, 94; raised again by Saul, 95.

Types and forms, 176.

Tyre, Peter at, 267; address to the people of, 268.

Uhlhorn referred to, 69, 70, 74.

Unbelief and faith, 143.

Unclean, the, separation from, 116; not to be eaten with, 163; spirits, 116.

Union and obedience enjoined, 65.

Unity of God, 108, 109; proved by Peter from the Old Testament, 313, 315.

Universe, the, the product of mind, 267.

Unrevealed God, the, of Simon Magus, 325.

Useless things, why made, 176.

Vengeance often taken by creatures on sinners, 149.

Venus, the origin of, 198; allegory of, 201.

Vile things, why made by God, 176.

Virgin, the true, 57.

Virginity, Two Epistles concerning, 55–66; introductory notice to, 53, 54; genuineness of, 53; authorship of, 53; original language of, 54; literature on, 54.

Virginity, true, to be accomplished by perfect virtue, 55; irksomeness and enemies of, 56; divinity of, 57.

Virgins, true, known by their self-denial, 55, 56; object and reward of, 56; mortify the deeds of the flesh, 57, 58.

Virtue, perfect, necessary for true virginity, 55; arrangements of the world to secure the exercise of, 184.

Visits, rules for, 59.

Voyage, the, of the Church, 221.

War and strife proclaimed by Christ, 105, 106.

Water, the power of illustrating divine providence, 172; born of, 155, 289; baptized with, 290; regeneration by, 155, 184.

Way of salvation, the, 270.

Ways, the, of God, opposed to man's ways, 231.

Wedding garment, baptism the, 142.

Wicked, the, the success of, in this life a proof of immortality, 124; and righteous, chastisement of, 178; actions to be avoided, 336; One, the, why appointed over the wicked by a righteous God, 342; why entrusted with power, 335.

Wiles of the devil, 240.

Will, of God, irresistible, 120; freedom of the, 119.

Wise, the, divine things justly hidden from, 335.

Woman, the, of sorrowful spirit, 294; her story, 295.

Womb, the, 173.

Workman, the old, discussions with, 165 seq.; turns out to be Clement's father, 191.

Works, good, the necessity of, 155.

World, the, governed by the providence of God, 167; compounded of four elements, 168; made out of nothing by a Creator, 169; time of the creation of, why not made long before, 174; arrangements of, to secure the exercise of virtue, 184; after the flood, 86.

Worship, of heroes, 141, 276; due to God only, 146.

Worshippers of God, who are, 151; of the gods, like the gods they worship, 202.

Zacchæus, writes to James, 96; welcomes Peter at Cæsarea, 96; appointed by Peter bishop of Cæsarea, 151, 250; rescued Aquila and Niceta from Simon Magus, 164, 232.

Zeus, Poseidon, and Metis, 264.

Zoroaster, or Mesraim, a son of Ham, regarded as the author of the magic art, 140, 275; adored, 141, 276.

TWO EPISTLES CONCERNING VIRGINITY, AND CLEMENTINE RECOGNITIONS AND HOMILIES

INDEX OF TEXTS

APOCRYPHA OF THE NEW TESTAMENT

INDEX OF SUBJECTS

Abbanes, a merchant, buys the Apostle Thomas from the Lord, to be a carpenter for Gundaphoros, an Indian king, 535; thrown into prison by Gundaphoros, 539; released, 540.

Abel, killed by Cain, 565; buried by angels, 570.

Abgarus, king of Edessa, suffering from a disease, sends a letter to Jesus, 558; Jesus sends him an image of Himself on a towel, which heals him, 558; Thaddæus visits, 558.

Abiathar, the high priest, wishes to obtain Mary as wife for his son, 371; proclaims that a protector should be sought for Mary, 372; gives to Mary and Joseph "the water of drinking of the Lord" to drink, 373, 374.

Abudem, 447.

Acherusian Lake, the, 578.

Acts of the Apostles, Apocryphal, 354.
    Andrew and Matthias, 356, 517 seq.
    Barnabas, 355, 493 seq.
    John, 357, 560 seq.
    Paul and Thecla, 355, 487 seq.
    Peter and Paul, 355, 477 seq.
    Peter and Andrew, 526 seq.
    Philip, 355, 497 seq.
    Pilate, 416-434, 439-447.
    Thaddæus, 357, 558 seq.
    Thomas, 535 seq.

Acts and Martyrdom of Andrew, 356, 511 seq.

Acts and Martyrdom of St. Matthew, 528 seq.

Adam, in Hades testifies to Jesus, 436; delivered from Hades, 437; brought into paradise, 437, 456; and Eve and the family of, 565; sickness of, 565; sends Seth and Eve for the "oil of mercy," 566; the death of, 569; the body of, seen by Eve lying on the face, and angels praying for, 569; raised into paradise, 569; funeral rites for, and burial of, performed by angels, 570.

Adas, Finees, and Egias, the testimony of, to the ascension of Jesus, 422, 425, 432, 445, 447; report the resurrection of Karinus and Leucius, 254.

Advent, the second, of Christ, 584.

Ægeates, or Ægeas, proconsul, and the Apostle Andrew, 511; threatens Andrew with crucifixion unless he sacrifices to the gods, 512; threatened with violence by the people for his harsh treatment of Andrew, 513; calls Andrew before his tribunal, and again threatens him, 513; tortures Andrew, and orders him to be crucified, 513; the people cry out against, 514; visits Andrew on the cross, and desires to release him, 515; the miserable death of, 516.

Affrodosius, an Egyptian governor, convinced that the child Jesus is a god, 377.

Alexander, the Syriarch, falls in love with Thecla, and brings her before the governor of Antioch, 489; his atrocious conduct towards her, 490.

Amis, the city of, 558.

Ananias, the high priest of the Jews, a letter to, from the philosophers of Hellas respecting Philip, 504; comes to Hellas to oppose Philip, 505; discussion of, with Philip, 505; has his hand dried up and his eyes blinded, 505; Jesus appears visibly before, yet he remains in unbelief, 505; receives his sight through Philip's prayer, yet is still impenitent, 506; the earth swallows him up to the knees, 506; swallowed up as far as the neck, 506; a demon cast out in the presence of, but he will not believe, 507; goes down into Hades, 507.

Ananias, a cousin of King Abgarus, sent to Jesus, 558; returns with the picture of Jesus to the king, 558.

Andrew, Acts and Martyrdom of, 356, 511 seq.; and Matthias, Acts of, 356, 517 seq.; and Peter, Acts of, 526 seq.; conversation between, and Ægeates, 511; threatened by Ægeates with crucifixion, 512; cited before the tribunal of Ægeates, 513; apostrophizes the cross, 513, 514; tortured and crucified, 514; discourses to the people from the cross, 514; addresses Ægeates from the cross, 514, 515; refuses to be released from the cross, 515; surrounded with splendour on the cross — his dead body taken down by Maximilla, 515; another account of — Jesus appears to, and sends him to Matthew, to the country of the man-eaters, 517; the Lord, in the disguise of a pilot, conducts him by sea to the place of his destination, 518; requested by the pilot, he relates the miracles of his Teacher, and the cause of the Jews' rejection of Him, 519; gives a curious narrative of the ministry of Jesus, and of the opposition of men to Him, 519, 520; carried by the angels from the boat to the city of the man-eaters, 520; vision of his disciples, 521; Jesus appears to, as a child, 521; enters the city of the man-eaters, and visits Matthew in prison, 521; lays his hands on the men deprived of sight in prison, and heals them, 521, 522; walks about the city, and beholds its abominations, 522; by prayer stays the hand of inhuman executioners, 523; rebukes the devil, 523; sought for by the man-eaters, he shows himself to them, 523; dragged repeatedly by ropes through the city, till his hair and flesh are torn off, 523; causes an alabaster statue to send forth water, and flood the city, and drown the inhabitants, 524; sends down certain bad men into the abyss, 525; brings to life the men that were drowned, 525; when he is leaving the city, Jesus appears to him as a child, and sends him back, 525; caught up in a luminous cloud, and conveyed to a mountain, where were Peter and others, 526; Jesus appears to, and sends him to a city of the barbarians, 526; what befell him there, 526 seq.

Anemurium, the city of, Barnabas preaches at, 494.

Angel, an, appears to Anna, 362, 369;

APOCRYPHA OF THE NEW TESTAMENT

INDEX OF TEXTS

THE DECRETALS

INDEX OF SUBJECTS

THE DECRETALS

INDEX OF TEXTS

813

ANCIENT SYRIAC DOCUMENTS

INDEX OF SUBJECTS

ANCIENT SYRIAC DOCUMENTS

INDEX OF TEXTS

816

REMAINS OF THE SECOND AND THIRD CENTURIES

INDEX OF SUBJECTS

REMAINS OF THE SECOND AND THIRD CENTURIES

INDEX OF TEXTS

THE CHRISTIAN LITERATURE COMPANY take this occasion to thank their patrons for the generous support that their undertaking has received. A comprehensive general index to this entire series will soon be published, at the low price of two dollars and fifty cents ($2.50). The value of this extra volume will be greatly increased by the addition of Professor Riddle's Bibliography of Ante-Nicene Literature, for which no extra charge will be made. And it should not be overlooked, that, though the original design of including this Bibliography in vol. viii. was frustrated, Professor Riddle has been enabled, by the delay, to enrich his work very considerably, though it was previously of the greatest utility to the student, and even to all intelligent readers.